N A D A

L. SUPERIOR

L. HURON

L. MICHIGAN

PIKE'S ROUTE

MISSISSIPPI R.

FOXES

HANDCART
MIGRATION OF
THE MORMONS

MORMON TRAIL

Nauvoo

Franklin

Independence

St. Louis

KANSAS R.

Ft. Smith

RED R.

MISSISSIPPI R.

CHICKASAWS

CHOCTAWS

JACKSON

New Orleans

BATTLE OF
NEW ORLEANS

GULF OF MEXICO

Ft. Detroit

Ft. Dearborn

LINCOLN-DOUGLAS
DEBATES

SHAWNEES

FLATBOAT

Ft. Vincennes

Kaskaskia

Boonesboro

CUMBERLAND
GAP

CUMBERLAND R.

FLATBOAT

TENNESSEE R.

INDIANS ENROUTE
TO OKLAHOMA

CHEROKEES

CREEKS

BATTLE
OF THE
THAMES

L. ERIE

Ft. Duquesne

OHIO R.

DANIEL
BOONE

APPALACHIAN MTS.

BATTLE OF
KING'S MT.

FRONTIER
FORTRESS

Savannah

SEMINOLES

WOLFE
CAPTURES
QUEBEC

ST. LAWRENCE R.

BLOCK-
HOUSE

Ft. Ticonderoga

IROQUOIS

L. ONTARIO

Ft. Niagara

New York

Boston

Philadelphia

FORBES
ROAD

Washington

Williamsburg

Charleston

ATLANTIC OCEAN

THOMAS D. CLARK

FRONTIER
AMERICA

SECOND EDITION

CHARLES SCRIBNER'S SONS *New York*

MAPS IN THE TEXT BY LILI MAUTNER

END PAPER MAP BY RAFAEL PALACIOS

PRINTED IN THE UNITED STATES OF AMERICA

Library of Congress Catalog Card Number 69-11124

PREFACE TO THE SECOND EDITION

EVEN though a certain statistical proportion of population distribution to landed area had occurred by 1890, it took more than the absorption of most of the public lands to bring a halt either to the westward movement or to the pioneering process. There are no hard and fast agreements as to when or where the westward movement began or when it ended. If the personal and folk qualities of the movement are used as critiques, it has not yet ceased to be a force in American life. As historians at all levels of attainment continue to publish articles and books on the subject, the act of pioneering and exploitation of the continent assumes broad if not new dimensions. Old concepts are subjected to constant scrutiny, and in some cases to severe revision, if not open refutation. In more recent years the westward movement has come to be considered as a conditioning force on the American mind itself.

As states once carved out of public land celebrate anniversaries of one hundred and one hundred and fifty years, the importance of natural culture and constitutional government spreading across the country comes in full focus. These anniversaries suggest that enough time has passed for us to appraise successes and failures in these areas, but such an appraisal must be seen against the background of the successes and failures of federalism itself. As the impact of the federal government becomes greater in later years, views on state and local governments must of necessity be changed. Democratic principles come to have more meaning in their spread and adaptations than any original contributions arising from the pioneering experience.

The westward movement beyond doubt influenced greatly the development and adaptations of political institutions and regional reactions. At the same time it created sectional and local problems which required their own peculiar solutions. It would be difficult in many areas to separate problems of distinct frontier origins from those which were common to every national experience.

The significance of the westward movement lies only partially in areas

v

44343

of politics and government. In the broader fields of economics, cultural maturity, and social growth the impact of the ever widening frontier was great. No single historian can appraise the full social forces of pioneering in their broader ramifications. A tremendous variety of national personal characteristics shaped and colored the great adventure of moving west. Maybe none was basically unique to the pioneering experience, but at the same time none escaped the impress of the West. Language, folkways, personal demeanor, patterns of thought, religious responses, group and individual behavior, solutions to community problems, racial and social reactions, and the acceptance of change were all conditioned by frontier demands.

Basically the act of pioneering had a ruggedly masculine overtone. This, as much as a pronounced individuality, gave the movement human color and robustness. Its heroes, sung and unsung, live on in many forms. They are subjects of biographies, they are perverted into fictional characters in all sorts of dramatic productions, and are central figures in the great American folk legend. Characters of lesser stature who endured the toil and hardships of the frontier to build commonplace homes, to clear farms, to break the virgin sod, to lay out towns, and to build roads and railroads appear in the faceless multitude labeled "the people." They planted their forms of civilization on the land, blazed tomahawk rights and squatted on the land, entered preempted claims, and took advantage of public land sales and the Homestead Law to create communities, counties, and states. Some of them were greedy speculators, some were rascals and swindlers, some were corporations, while most were simple yeoman farmers; all pushed along together.

On a broader pattern the westward movement either had a strong international implication, or it created international rivalries and problems. Two major wars, a continuing conflict with the Indians, and international border incidents gave a distinct military flavor to the roll of the frontier. Many individuals gained more glory from military service than from breaking trail and being subjected to the harsh forces of settling the frontier.

The westward movement is treated here in light of its varied aspects. Emphases are placed upon the social and economic phases as well as upon the spread of government and central institutions. Efforts have been made to view this important period of national history from the perspective of people exploiting a vast area of land which offered a startling variety of resources, and by the effects these resources had upon the conditioning of civilization itself. Remarkably there resulted a homogeneity in governmental forms, in public economy, and in the warp and woof of society itself. At no time or place is there lack of awareness of the great variety of experiences and of events which shaped frontier history. No effort has been made to pursue a thesis, or to search for an underlying mystique of the western movement. To subscribe to the latter would be to ascribe to the American pioneer a sophistication which he did not have.

As years pass, the literature on the frontier increases in both volume and quality. Publishers and authors contribute a continuing stream of fresh materials. Equally as important, archival collections are swelled by yearly additions of original papers of all sorts. The Archives of the United States, for instance, constantly make available new materials of basic importance to the writing of western history. State historical society collections have grown tremendously in the past half-century, as have university and central archival holdings. Thus an author who undertakes to produce a general history of the westward movement cuts his literary cloth by a broad pattern. At best he can deal only with the central facts and use his best judgment in the selection of these facts.

In the same way the bibliography designed to extend the discussions of a general history cannot possibly present more than a fraction of the available materials for the study of the frontier. Collected bibliographies of many states now exceed the volume of that of the nation in 1890. Every state historical society publishes a journal, and many specialized societies and interest groups publish materials. The volume of periodical literature alone is overwhelming. An attempt has been made to include in this volume sufficient bibliographical references to give some notion of the central body of published sources now available.

CONTENTS

LIST OF ILLUSTRATIONS

LIST OF MAPS

ON THE FRONTIER, 1793. FROM CAMPBELL'S *Travels*

THE AMERICAN FRONTIER

THE AMERICAN FRONTIER
A Perspective

Everything is extraordinary in America, the social condition of the inhabitants as well as the laws; but the soil upon which these institutions are founded is more extraordinary than all the rest. When man was first placed upon the earth by the Creator, that earth was inexhaustible in its youth; but man was weak and ignorant. When he had learned to explore the treasures which it contained, hosts of his fellow-creatures covered its surface, and he was obliged to earn an asylum for repose and for freedom by the sword. At that same period North America was discovered as if it had been kept in reserve by the Deity and had just risen from beneath the waters of the deluge.

That continent still presents, as it did in primeval time, rivers which rise from never-failing sources, green and moist solitudes, and fields which ploughshare of the husbandman has never turned. In this state, it is offered to man not in the barbarous and isolated condition of the early ages but to a being who is already in possession of the most potent secrets of the natural world, who is united to his fellow-men, and instructed by the experience of fifty centuries. At this very time thirteen millions of civilized Europeans are peaceably spreading over those fertile plains, with whose resources and whose extent they are not accurately acquainted. Three or four thousand soldiers drive the wandering races of the aborigines before them; these are followed by the pioneers, who pierce the woods, scare off the beasts of prey, explore the courses of the inland streams, and make ready the triumphal procession of civilization across the waste. . . .

Millions of men are marching at once towards the same horizon; their language, their religion, their manners differ, their object is the same. The gifts of fortune are promised in the West, and to the West they bend their course.

—DE TOCQUEVILLE, *Democracy in America*

CHAPTER I

The Frontier in Motion

FROM the moment the first Spanish explorer recorded notes of his activities in the strange new land of North America, and the Englishman John Smith began preparation of his exciting memoirs of experiences on the Atlantic Coast, historians of one sort or another have written about the frontier. More recent scholars have posed important questions, striving by their answers to gauge the significance of the frontier in the history of the United States.

Many of these questions are fundamental ones which look for the meaning of American history in that of civilization in general. Of a more localized nature, however, are these: What contributions did the frontier make which may be clearly differentiated from those transported to North America from the Old World? How did an English and European culture, and later, an Atlantic Coastal one, respond to the immediate inland advance of the American population? Did the new and powerful environmental conditions aid in the process of democratization of the United States? Did the process of western expansion create in the breast of the American settler an unusual sense of freedom and political orderliness, plus a sense of spiritual release, which were to bring into existence a new system of government and a new social order?

It would be a waste of time to attribute a magic quality to the contributions to national culture made by the pioneering process. Frontier expansion in America closely resembled the roll of the sea. It broke, billowed and eddied against the various physical and social barriers which it encountered. The pattern of expansion was never uniform over any considerable geographical area, nor within any large segmented part of the more localized social organization. The movement bore telltale marks of the traditional origins of peoples and institutions—the flavor and coloration of the peculiar traditions of continental Europe, England, and the eastern Atlantic Coast. The frontier path was strewn, like that of a vast glacier, with the remains of older cultures, easily identified by their peculiar natures and characteristics.

Frontiers

There was no one frontier in America, nor was there a single frontier condition. Settlers shuffling down the gangplanks of the first immigrant ships were frontiersmen whether they landed in the Spanish Southwest, French Canada, or along the Atlantic Coast. Pioneers moving inland from Pennsylvania, Maryland and Virginia were the first to approach the Appalachian wall. Subsequently the movement divided and some of the settlers crossed the ranges and went on westward while others followed the valleys southward. In New York and New England still another stream pushed inland toward the St. Lawrence and the Great Lakes. With each succeeding decade the frontier movement fanned out in different directions without varying radically the pioneering pattern.

When settlers came in contact with woods, prairies and plains, they started life anew at elementary levels. Social and economic advances were almost always achieved from the same simple beginnings. The frontier was the place of trail and ground breaking in new country, and of establishing afresh social and political institutions. Settlers coming into contact with the vast areas of virgin lands and mineral resources behaved much alike, whether in the pine lands cotton belt or the mountainous gold diggings.

Frontier social conditions frequently prevailed longer than did the raw physical conditions of virgin lands. Pioneering involved certain approaches to life which were revealed in the realm of personal adjustments, attitudes, and intellectual flexibilities. It was not unusual for the frontier to linger in spirit long after Indians, animals and free lands became a legend. An arrested social pattern gave frontier life its own peculiar characteristics.

The safest general observation to be made about American frontier history is that it is variegated, erratic, colorful and spacious. It combines the broad interpretations of both human and national history with the most fragmentary details of local history. In its broader meaning the history of the frontier is the account of the molding of people of diverse origins and motives into a fairly homogeneous national group. In its more localized implications, it is the story of thousands of individuals, tiny communities, counties, towns, and sections making primitive beginnings and growing into mature and permanent political, economic, and social institutions.

One of the first and most important factors which should be considered is that of space. The influence of space should be measured in the elementary terms of distance, expanse of view, availability of land and isolative forces. The sense of freedom developed by the American frontiersman was not always a classical freedom of individual relationships in an established society. On the frontier, however, there was freedom from noises of neighborhoods, from devitalizing community squabbles, from certain social forms, and an escape from conformity with the mores of older societies.

Often isolated and excluded from close human associations, backwoodsmen developed a close affinity for the forest and soil. Tall trees towered overhead as regal landmarks. Woods were mysterious natural screens which concealed the naked topography of the land, and streams ran on as beckoning ribbons leading outward in their flow. From the time the first white man broke the silence of the forest with rifle and ax there was love of the out-of-doors. Even today, although vast areas of the great American forests have been sheared away, and the once virginal condition of the land is no more than legendary, nostalgia for the forest lingers.

European Approaches

Never before European exploitation of this continent did civilized man undertake to bring so much virgin territory under his control in so short a time. To reduce his thinking about American geography into a workable formula was a complex undertaking for the European. This accounts in part for the different European approaches made to the American continent. Spaniards and Frenchmen commonly sought immediate returns from the land, breaking trail for unbelievable distances. Englishmen on the other hand approached the continent with some degree of hesitancy. They were reluctant to sever their lines of communication with home until they had gained a foothold along the coast.

Whatever the approach to the continent, it was necessary for Europeans arriving in America to discard most of their traditional concepts of distance and space and to adopt an entirely new geographical scale. The land itself revealed almost innumerable variations in natural environmental conditions. There were the climate belts and the differing soil types which would create future economic and political divisions. A diversified pattern of stream and drainage systems conditioned lands for agricultural use and for industrialization, facilitated transportation and also influenced the location of urban centers. Even in adjoining neighborhoods differences in human responses to land were possible.

Distances and contours of terrain were important in determining the distribution of population on the continent. At the same time, the great expanse of land isolated large segments of American society. Out of this grew a spirit of provincialism which had both domestic and international significance. The varied characteristics of the North American continent produced a basic, if not unique, political problem for Americans. This was sectionalism, with its special interests which made compromise necessary in every major political issue that involved making general laws for an expanding country.

Geographical factors were of cardinal importance, therefore, in American frontier history, and the availability of vast quantities of virgin land exerted a continuing influence upon American life. Again, the economic and political limitations of the Old World conditioned the desires of immigrants for less restricted patterns of human life. The landowner of Europe wanted to repeat and expand his economic experiences in America, and landless persons abroad wished to copy in America the pattern of their privileged Old World neighbors. Land appeared indispensable to the personal freedom which many immigrants to North America hoped to find. Without it the newcomers could hope only to serve landed masters in a new environment, or to subject themselves to the uncertain life of urban industrialism during its formative years. One of the greatest factors in making land in North America so important was that settlers along the Atlantic Coast failed to find sources of quick mineral riches; consequently they turned to the slower processes of agriculture to gain livelihoods. Farming, from the beginning, became the main way of American frontier life, and the more available and desirable lands were, the more affluent were the social and economic patterns of individual settlers, and the shorter the pioneering period. After the first trials of the Jamestown settlers, agriculture became the major economic pursuit of European immigrants everywhere along the coast. This was true regardless of the qualities of the land. The primary accounts of original settlement are colored by the conditions of agriculture during the first years, a condition which continued as the frontier rolled westward.

The desirability of land was a highly relative factor that depended upon both quality and location. Fertile lands along the navigable rivers east of the mountains were certainly the most desirable. Lands located in the swamps, however, offered a serious threat to health, and required greater labor resources to exploit them. Lands which permitted cultivation of specific staple crops enjoyed an advantage over those which were not so specialized in use. Lands for growing grain and for grazing were at a premium. Along the New England frontier, land of good quality for extensive expansion was limited, and choices were made under much more restrictive conditions than prevailed in areas south of Connecticut. But whatever the availability of land might have been in any given place, one fact was applicable generally to most of the American frontier—the early population was an agrarian one, its life patterns were governed by agricultural conditions and limitations.

The fact that western lands early became involved in a complex system of colonial speculation is of great importance. While it is true that the Indian traders, such as those from Pennsylvania, Virginia and the Carolinas, were active in thrusting the frontier forward, it was the land speculator and squatter who focused lasting attention upon the region. Land represented prospective wealth, and speculators saw in it opportunities to gain fortunes. Though many speculative companies never really gained possession of lands, they nevertheless maintained a feverish interest in them. It was the private speculator and landholder who figured most prominently in pushing settlement westward.

Obviously land was the most important economic factor in the westward movement, but its social meaning surpasses its economic importance. It played a role in the political and psychological reactions of settlers. Participation in politics in some instances was based upon landholding, and in others ownership of land gave a sense of permanence. It was much easier to exercise an effective voice in political affairs and to seek office if a man owned land. Psychologically, land ownership brought with it definite local prestige and a degree of stability and security. For many European immigrants moving on to the American frontier, the ownership of land meant the difference between the old life of uncertainty and penury and a new life of permanence and economic promise. In his provocative view, *A Description of Kentucky* (London, 1792), the discerning Englishman Harry Toulmin included in his addenda an account of the rise to social and economic stability of Andrew the Hebridean who came as an indentured servant to western Pennsylvania. Toulmin traced in a concise narrative the exciting psychological changes which came over this poverty-stricken immigrant.

Settlers and the Land

For the vast horde of settlers who moved westward, the ownership of the land was the most important object in their lives. Almost from the beginning, frontiersmen came to regard the huge virginal domain as a God-given heritage which was theirs for the taking. Legislation, from the early Crown Laws to that of state governments, reflected the significance of the land question in the processes of American government. It was not an accident that the county clerk or land registry official became a primary figure, and that his records have been given extraordinary protection. The course of litigation in local and state courts reflect the arduous history of land ownership and the jealousies and furies which accompany it. There were few issues on which politicians and demagogues alike could make themselves more readily heard by the people than the subject of liberalizing the land law. The course of partisan politics in the West was often governed by individual attitudes toward the public land issue. A vast number of frontiersmen built up the warmest sentimentalities over homesteads which had been wrested from the wilderness. They became birthplaces, places of deaths and burials, of struggles and accomplishments, family ties, and of frustrations and disappointments. For thousands of Americans, the homesteads which they built in the wilderness were the only tangible accomplishments of a long, hard lifetime of labor and hope. The frontier homestead itself was often a most temporary dwelling, unlike the solid brick and stone structures of England and Europe; the flimsy wooden houses of the backwoods disintegrated and disappeared almost within the lifetime of the original settlers. The only physical things, in fact, which survived many of the settlers were their cleared and eroded fields.

Frontier sentimentalities were never so intense, however, that old landmarks could not be sacrificed to progress. An old house was outmoded and dragged down to make way for a new one. The rise of a new structure was a sign of progress, and the average American was afraid of becoming static. This attitude toward change carried over to everything the frontiersman used. A tool or a farm implement might be perfectly good, but a newer one performed a greater part of the farming task more efficiently. In fact, no American regarded the machine in current use as permanent; he looked to the future when a new model would do an even better job. Production of goods and the reduction of heavy manual labor were his two prime objectives. No ancient ancestral forms, no staid family and community traditions, bound the American to the past. Those European immigrants who appeared in the West were forced to disrupt the ancient patterns of their tradition-bound lives and adopt new methods of earning a livelihood. For the frontiersman the future was a throbbing challenge of change, and change was a manifestation of progress. It was from this condition that he drew much of his optimism and faith in the land. This was also a source for his intense nationalism and for his unlimited confidence in both himself and his country. He never looked upon either his own or his country's condition as they were, but as they would be.

Land and land laws, then, were among the most important formal factors in frontier expansion in America. The history of the westward movement, as we have seen, is nothing less than an account of how people carried on a conquest of vast areas of virgin soil. The political history of the region is colored largely by the process by which this was done. One of the thorniest problems encountered was that of distributing lands to both individuals and land companies. The land lobby in the colonial governments, and later in state and national assemblies, was a powerful force in the shaping of legislation. Individual settlers eventually were in great part to win their crusade for distribution of small blocks of lands at moderate costs. This effort went through many stages. There were first the squatters with their indiscriminate claims in many areas, then the various state efforts to adopt effective laws. There was the Land Ordinance of 1785 with its series of modifications; the claim clubs protecting settler rights to improvements while keeping prices at a minimum; the Pre-emption Law of 1841; and finally the Homestead Act of 1862. It is significant that the frontiersman seldom if ever lived beyond some kind of law in his land dealings. Peaceful and secure ownership of land required a certain amount of respect for established government, and the validation of land claims was one of the most powerful factors in creating a keen desire for an orderly and law-abiding society in the western movement.

Society

Early Indian traders and trappers produced the first body of dependable information about the vast and virginal frontier. With a few exceptions, there was no class of pioneers devoted solely to trapping and trading as a permanent occupation. In many cases, especially among the English colonials, traders followed the woods as a calling supplementary to their domestic activities on backwoods farms. These traders came into close association with the Indians, learning from them much of woodlore and crafts, and sometimes adopting for a time the Indian way of life. So long as white men remained traders and trappers, they could ill afford to disturb the *status quo* of the forests. To have injured the Indian economy would have destroyed their own trade. However, these early traders were not oblivious to the attractions of the lands. Doubtless scores of them, as they tramped along the Indian trails gathering furs, dreamed of the future when the trees would disappear and the hills would be converted to rolling farm meadowlands. In this first brief phase of contact with the woods, men tended to submerge their old cultural habits and to bow to the demands of a simple forest life. Trials of the woods were easier for those who brought a background of simplicity, a fact known to both Indian and trader. This condition of life, however, aside from being perpetuated in the romantic legends of the frontier, had little if any actual effect on the frontier movement in its larger implications.

Among the early backwoodsmen who entered the hinterlands were many whose primary economic interests were centered in the white settlements. Their activities in the wilderness were elementary efforts to improve their conditions in white civilization. With the passage of time, more adventurers fell under the seductive spell of the woods. They ranged far and wide in their wanderings with little or no other purpose than a temporary oblivion in the anonymity of the sprawling woodlands. This was largely true of such men as Daniel Boone, Michael Holsteiner, John Colter, Jim Bridger, Kit Carson and scores of others who achieved less notoriety. Boone spent his life alternating between a dream of isolation and adventure, and the lure of domesticity and security.

Relations between frontiersman and Indian in the American backwoods were an important factor in western history. The Indian was a vital part of most frontier development. First of all, Indian and European cultures were in direct conflict. One depended upon the woods or plains; the other upon plowed fields and pastures. One exploited basic natural resources for livelihood; the other relied upon cultivated crops. The source of conflict between the two, however, was much more fundamental. Racial differences and prejudices played a major role in the relationships of the two peoples. European whites looked upon the Indian as savage and heathen. His intellectual capacity was often held in low esteem, and his occupation of the land was considered a barrier to white Christian occupation. From the beginning of North American settlement there were Indian wars —wars that were provoked by both sides. Third party provocations were also fertile sources of conflict in the backwoods. In the French and Indian War it was the French, and after 1776, the British. There is no doubt that animosities against the Indians grew hotter because of this intervention by outsiders. Indian conflicts dragged on much longer than was necessary because of the central government's failure to devise an administrative plan to settle the two races side by side with essential justice to both. The search for an answer to the aggravating Indian problem became one of the basic themes in frontier history.

On the heels of hunter and trapper came land speculator and settler. The speculator sought land in large blocks; the settler sought a cabin site and farmstead. The pattern of the settler's frontier varied even more than that of the trapper and hunter. It is all but impossible to classify specifically the motives which sent people westward. Desire for land has been mentioned, but there were other reasons. First, and possibly most important, was the desire of settlers to escape the competition of older communities. Although the land was not densely settled, except in some areas in New England, economic competition was less ardent in the backcountry. There men could select land and escape the feeling of having to take the less desirable leavings of earlier claimants.

From the moment cattle were landed from Europe, grazers began their advance westward, keeping in advance of the settlement line in order to avoid complications with farmers over growing crops. With the army of aggressive settlers moving westward, there also marched ne'er-do-wells who concealed their failure to keep up in an established society, and who promised themselves greater success in the new country. Here the land could do no more than carry the frail and profligate for a time toward success. In many instances younger sons went West to make their fortunes in lieu of inheriting patrimonies. Criminals took to the backwoods, some criminal only in the technical sense that they had fallen victim to the whimsicalities of local statutes. Aside from relatively innocent technical offenders, there were murderers, bigamists, gamblers, counterfeiters, horse thieves and swindlers who found the backwoods temporarily free of lawyers, magistrates' processes and alert sheriffs.

Attractions of easily gained political office and remunerations from the practice of law in the new country brought lawyer, surveyor, and petty politician in search of fame and fortune. Few periods in the history of civilization offered the politically ambitious little man so great an opportunity to advance as did that of frontier America. Along with lawyer and politician came zealous religious and social reformers who sought isolation in the woods, free of meddling neighbors and unsympathetic legislative bigots. The frontier offered leaders of such organizations a chance to group their forces and to integrate their ideas in a temporarily controlled environmental condition. When they were finally forced into competitive situations, they attempted at least to check invasions from the outside. Such groups as the traveling Baptist churches, the Shakers and their communal villages, the Rappites, Robert Owen's New Harmony Colony, the Mormons in Ohio, Missouri, Illinois, and Utah, and the Amana Colony in Iowa found the frontier inviting.

Religious bodies recognized the golden opportunities offered them on the frontier for obeying the New Testament admonition to go into the world and preach the gospel. The missionary became almost as active an agent of frontier expansion as the hunter and farmer. It was not unusual for the preacher to be in the vanguard of the adventurers and hunters. Catholic priests were among the first white men to see much of the American backcountry in the southwest, along the Great Lakes, and in the Mississippi Valley. In the path of the old frontier, Baptist preacher Squire Boone, Daniel's brother, joined the latter in his lonely wanderings in Kentucky. Hard-shell Baptist ministers accompanied immigrant parties, and hardly had a community begun settlement before missionaries and circuit riders found it. Methodist, Catholic, and Presbyterian clergy came riding westward with saddlebags crammed with Bibles, commentaries, and instructions for founding churches and schools.

The various social bodies were sometimes highly interspersed in the frontier movement, and it would be a mistake for historians either to classify them too definitely, or to try to separate them. Many individuals were actually members of more than one group of the population. Hunters became farmers, even such avid woodsmen and scouts as Boone, Kenton, Colter, Manuel Lisa, and Kit Carson settling themselves on the land and turning to farming or business. Hard-bitten fur trappers and traders remained behind to see the woods cleared away, and to substitute the furrow for the trap line, the family fireside for the lonely winter camp. Criminals with records of offenses even more severe than technical violations of the law often became highly respectable citizens; and in time, descendants of squatters published records of their forbears in local histories. Indian fighters became noble defenders of the American home; speculators became big planters and solid citizens, and Yankee peddlers turned entrepreneurs.

Among the honored trail-breakers were the miners. Frontier expansion was greatly accelerated by the various rushes in its history. Land rushers were ever active. They continued their interest until the last "Sooner" and "Boomer" crossed the line into the Indian Territory. The mineral rusher was the most important of all those who moved into the unlikely regions of the West. People throughout the history of civilization have moved frantically to scenes of great and easy wealth, but possibly few or no earlier folk movements had more color, or involved more territory and people than did the gold and silver rushes of the western American frontier. This folk movement had enormous influence on continental American history; for within a decade or two, territory was organized first into mining communities and then into states. Otherwise, those parts of the West might have remained wilderness for a long time to come.

Development of gold, cattle, and construction camp communities presented peculiar problems of social relationships and law enforcement. Rowdy towns grew overnight, and wickedness and debauchery struggled, often successfully, to overcome virtue. Vigilantes combined the functions of law and court until political bodies could be organized. The rope substituted for the statute book, and the pistol served for judicial appeal. Sometimes compassionate vigilantes exercised executive clemency, and the aroused mobster stood in for the sheriff. All this social groping left its indelible mark on frontier history and American culture.

Adventurers, schemers, intriguers, and rascals found both suckers and anonymity along the frontier. Some of the most colorful chapters of backwoods history portray the activities of people who existed by using their base wits. Conspirators thrived. There were the French and Spanish conspiracies, the Kemper brothers in West Florida, Burr and Wilkinson, the Texas adventurers, Fort Snelling liquor dealers, and the routine activities of those cutthroats and prostitutes who followed the camps. Western steamboats carried sharpers and schemers aboard. Confirmed scoundrels had two reasons for following the receding lines of law and order: they were always assured of a certain amount of escape from their past; and gullible frontiersmen were easily victimized by their skin games.

As has been said above, criminality assumed various forms. Among the worst of the frontier criminals were those who by their lies set Indian and white man in conflict for their own nefarious purposes. They spied and gossiped on both groups. Horse thieves and cattle rustlers found it relatively easy to raid both settler and Indian property, and then to lay the blame on the other group. Faro dealers were almost as common on steamboats and in mining and cattle towns as were paddle wheels, saloons, and crude hotels. Coney-catchers with their famous walnut hulls and peas, trick dice experts and bunco players garnered cash wherever people assembled. Bandits lay concealed along the trails to rob lone victims of horse and purse, and to murder. Paper money sharpers moved through the country distributing their worthless souvenirs of the illegal printing trade. Transient thieves made lonely cabins considerably less than castles of security.

Shrewd peddlers came by, selling legitimate and worthless merchandise at exorbitant prices. Among these were the famous Yankee peddlers who combined integrity and trickery to make sales. They brought clocks, laces, cloth, shoe pegs, tinware, shoes, mirrors, small tools, cutlery, and gadgets. If the peddlers sometimes made the name Jonathan synonymous with sharp practice, and the wooden nutmeg a symbol of rascality, they satisfied an urgent need for necessary goods on the frontier. Because of these elements in the early economic society, plus the indiscreet and rash acts of local sons, jails, courthouses, and courts were created at the beginning of settlement.

Despite the rowdiness of the gold camp, the railhead, and the cattle town, the frontier was usually a place of great domesticity. One historian of the West has wisely observed that the most effective combination to attack the woods was that of a young man and a sturdy bride. Rugged as life was, its central activity was that of establishing a home and a simple agrarian way of life. Cabins and cleared fields were more characteristic of the permanent phases of the westward movement than were fur trading, gold mining, and trail driving. When the domesticated family man arrived with wife, cattle, and land warrant, both woods and solitude disappeared. The process by which clearings were made and temporary cabins raised from the ground was as repetitive as the phases of the moon. When western population moved onto the plains beyond the timberline, it adapted itself to dugout and sod house and repeated the process of pioneering with few changes

Settlers combined admirably their efforts to achieve a common purpose. Not only did they bring land under plow, but they added materially to western population with their large families, as was reflected in population figures between 1790 and 1860. Pioneer homes were primitive. Transportation of household equipment across the mountains was almost impossible. Acquisition of luxury goods had to await the future. Women subjected themselves to austere conditions; they were removed beyond adequate medical services, and often beyond the assistance even of primitive midwives to help them through the agonizing hours of childbirth. Though subjected to hardships, the frontier woman could be relied on for increasing the population, for labor on the farm, as a manufacturer of clothing, and for supplying the necessary element of domestic stability to frontier society.

Two things were at once noticeable in beginnings of settlement. The first-comers shucked off (if there were those who had ever known them) the superficialities of an older and better established society. There was neither time nor place for the minor amenities of old and settled communities. Social conventions thrived only where there was leisure and maturity of human relationships. Backwoods life was lived at the elementary social level of the forest and the primitive cabin. Neighborliness was both humane and necessary on the frontier. It was hard to maintain artificial social stratification where one's human contacts were limited and where differences in economic conditions remained undefined. Because of this condition, frontier society more often than not found a common level where one man was socially as acceptable as another.

At no time in American history has the physical man counted for more. Neighbors and sound muscles were indispensable for making clearings, rolling logs, raising cabins, and doing countless other chores which were essential to the process of settlement. Neighborly and common social endeavors eased the monotony of work. While it is true that social classification appeared as soon as society reached an elementary degree of maturity, the region had undergone the baptism of frontier beginnings and never quite lost its folksy characteristics. This was to become a durable American trait. Frontier associations combined neighborliness, friendliness, hospitality, and a general decrying of form and superficialities. The average man strove to reveal himself to his fellows as an unostentatious human being. He did this even in his humorous boasting where he made himself the butt of his stories. Pioneering was not necessarily individualistic. Frequently people moved westward in groups, as was attested by the long covered wagon trains to Oregon, Utah, and California.

For the average frontiersman, fortune was earned by long and arduous labor. His successes were measured in terms of his long-range accomplishments. Although American pioneer successes are evaluated historically by many standards, there is one that seems more orthodox than others. A young man coming on to the frontier with a young wife dented the forest with his first cornpatch, and his hastily built cabin became a home. By years of hard work he cleared away the trees, fenced the fields, and opened the range. He built one and perhaps other more improved houses. In time these became his accomplishments and his fortune. There were, of course, men who profited greatly from their labors and activities. They built good homes, consolidated smaller farms into large landholdings, achieved political distinction, and re-established social patterns which had existed east of the Appalachians and in Europe. But even so, back of most of these new-made economic aristocrats was the significant fact that they had tasted the rugged life of the frontier, and both their manners and views were tempered in its cauldron of labor.

Hard labor was a pronounced characteristic of the frontier. Contemporary travel accounts might leave the impression that the average frontier settler was ague-ridden, lazy and indifferent. No doubt many of them were, but it is obvious that the woods were cleared, homes built, fields plowed and planted, and the western country soon produced thousands of tons of produce which was transported to market only by the most arduous labor. People who worked so close to nature in the woods and fields never had the appearance of social progress or sophistication. What early traveler-observers saw were sweaty human beings wrestling with tasks which exhausted one generation before they were finished. To fail to comprehend the place of grinding, sweaty, devitalizing labor is to fail to understand the most important source of economic success on the frontier. Work became a habit of the settler, and throughout American history it has remained a national virtue—whether in the field behind a plow, or in a store behind the counter. To this extent the frontier adopted the old Puritan trait of glorifying labor. To gain a stake on the frontier usually required an enormous expenditure of energy. For this reason, the oft-repeated account of settlers moving on after a few years needs re-examination. There was a constant movement against the receding lines of the backwoods; restless settlers moved on in the ebb tide of this flood; but more often than not they were second-generation sons and daughters who set out for the West to relive the experiences of their parents.

Possibly one of the major blind spots in the study of frontier history is the tendency to give the impression that the movement was purely agrarian. While it is true that the farm was the main economic base, the county town, the village, and in time, the city itself became vital parts of the frontier movement. Without Cincinnati, Louisville, and St. Louis on the earlier frontier, and Chicago, San Francisco, Milwaukee, Salt Lake City, Omaha, and Denver on the later one, the West would have lacked market centers. The differences which existed between people who lived in towns and on backwoods farms were practically the same as have always existed between town and country people. Frontier town dwellers pioneered in the same way, but with institutions that lent themselves somewhat less well to the folksy and earthy manner of the robust young agrarian community.

Without St. Louis, the great Rocky Mountain fur trade would have been baseless; and without both St. Louis and Santa Fe, the subsequent overland trade would have been without important terminals. Chicago, Omaha, Denver, Independence, Kansas City, Santa Fe, Salt Lake City, and San Francisco, for one reason and another, were all vital landmarks in westward expansion. Where countrymen struggled with the land, built their isolated churches, established pitiful little country schools, and joined efforts with neighbors to assault the wilderness, townsmen also struggled with their own problems. They established stores, banks, warehouses, courthouses, wharves, newspapers, schools, theatres, libraries, churches, and town governments. They were most active in seeking internal improvement and in persuading outside capitalists to make investments. Both groups combined to establish a frontier economy, and to give a certain cultural tone to the advance of civilization westward.

Political Interests

Despite the rowdy overtones of the frontier advance and the colorful but nefarious records of a relatively small band of scoundrels, the westward movement was on the whole a remarkably orderly thing. The average backwoodsman, ignorant though he was of many of the refined institutions and conventions of older societies, was never oblivious of the need for social and political order. Never was there a louder wail of protest than that sent up by a frontier people when it was necessary to shear off a piece of lightly settled and politically unorganized territory in order to define the boundaries of a new state. The drive to organize a new political territory, even in violation of the population formula prescribed in the Ordinance of 1787, was immediate. Indian conflicts necessitated maintenance of a local militia, and this could be accomplished most effectively by organized government. Marriage, legitimacy of birth, and descent of estates could be maintained more securely under established law.

Frontiersmen manifested a keen interest in local government. Usually they moved westward with pronounced state loyalties. They looked upon established government as a badge both of progress and social responsibility. It is significant that in community beginnings there were nearly always some persons who had acquired political experience elsewhere and who moved west endowed with a sacred charge to perpetuate organized government. Whether or not these men arrived with the first hunters and land scouts matters little. They were always on hand in time to begin the necessary political agitation for territorial organization, to become members of constitutional conventions, and then to get elected to offices. Patronage-hungry politicians saw numerous new offices for disposal in the organization of new counties and state territories.

American frontiersmen were not without vanity, and the holding of political office and the acquisition of titles were balm to their ego. Backwoodsmen who may have regarded British titles of nobility with disdain were happy to be called "judge," "squire," or "colonel." A lonely settler boasted to visitors that in time all the land before him would be taken into a new state. There would be growing fields, thriving towns, and new roads. Politically there would be almost enough offices to go around.

American pioneers enjoyed the amenities which came with being a part of a definable geopolitical area; they liked listening to campaign speeches, going to barbecues, strutting around in military musters, being seen on courtdays, expressing vivid opinions, and finally voting a political point of view. They often engaged in debates regarding political theory, but they were eminently more practical in political applications. Actually they concerned themselves little with specific variations of governmental forms so long as these forms observed the orthodox pattern of the older states and the Union and guaranteed personal rights. It is well-nigh fruitless to search for specific and original contributions of the frontier to basic patterns of local and state governments. Generally it may be said that the newer constitutions were rather monotonous because of their similarities. This is not to say that many original ideas were not presented in debates in the constitutional conventions; actual contributions of the frontier to American political development, however, are to be sought outside the pale of formal government. The individual's political reactions were far more significant than the philosophy contained in static documents or in debates which were forgotten by all but historians as soon as they were ended.

Ordinarily the frontiersman was fascinated by the processes of legislating. He filled statute books with staggering numbers of private and regulatory acts, with detailed laws governing the organization of towns and villages, the founding of numerous public institutions, and the regulation of social and economic affairs. Most often such laws were little more than statutory ornamentations because neither legislator nor constituent scrupulously observed them. But in the passage of this body of legislation, the unsophisticated legislator revealed the historical nature of the times, the character of the people and the whimsicalities of young and uncertain state governments. Application of the law to an individual was another matter. He usually saw little need for legislation which curbed his individual actions, and he violated the law when its restrictions inconvenienced him.

Frontier political reactions were important not only in the West, but to the nation. A major chapter of American political history originated on the frontier and has constantly exerted vast influence on the course of American development. Long before Washington retired to Mount Vernon, Thomas Jefferson appreciated the importance of American expansion and its potential influences upon political changes. His administration and the administrations of his immediate successors were aware of the influence of the frontier. By 1820 frontier influence in American politics was pronounced, and the immediate issues of the period focused major national attention upon the West. The campaign of 1824 was essentially a tug-of-war for western support. Even though John Quincy Adams of Massachusetts went to the White House, his legislative program reflected a vital concern with the issues of an expanding country.

Andrew Jackson was to personify an important political period, and his name still symbolizes frontier political reactions. Jackson personally was rugged, opinionated, and vociferous in proclaiming his views. He exhibited a positive individuality which appealed greatly to frontiersmen who themselves struggled daily with stubborn problems. Rank-and-file voters seldom if ever examined Jackson's actions. He was a hero who had won a frontiersman's fight, a buckskin patriot on horseback who fought Indians and Britishers with impartial relish. Jackson's attitude toward Indians was precisely that of the border warriors who had returned from raids with grisly strips of brown skin to use for razor straps. His fight with the British at New Orleans ended a conflict which had flared up at King's Mountain and along the Wabash. New Orleans, dramatic incident as it was in American military history, was more important as a maker of heroes and political candidates. Private and general rushed home to capitalize on their deeds before the voters. They proclaimed loudly the heroism of "Old Hickory" at Chalmette and emphasized that they were there to help him. They had stood with him at Horseshoe Bend, or they had fought Tecumseh and Proctor with Harrison in Canada. Hundreds of veterans controlled courthouse rings by 1820 and held offices ranging from constable to governor.

Jackson the hero won votes, but it was Jackson the outspoken critic and headstrong man who made political history. When he began his rise to political fame, the frontier combined intense sentimentalism with pulsating expansionism. Population west of the Appalachians was growing at a staggering rate. Sectionalism was already an active factor in politics. Western needs were so numerous and so poorly defined that the time was ripe for the emergence of some outspoken leader who could make vocal the people's feelings and fears, prejudices, ambitions, and sense of need. The kernel of "Jacksonian Democracy" in the West was largely the popular attitude of the people, although the influence of the courthouse ring on American political history must not be overlooked.

The frontier was not, of course, the birthplace of the common man, but in few regions in history has he thrived so well. Every man was a potential officeholder who could advance as far as the voters would let him. He was most tender on the subject of taxation, of legislation that discriminated against his section and of certain general national policies.

In purely domestic matters, individual blunders were ignored, but the blunders of the masses of people became virtues. For instance, the foolhardy speculations of the 1820's and 1830's, the indiscriminate chartering of wildcat banks, the involvement of individuals in ill-advised speculations, the setbacks of depressions, and the handicap of undeveloped resources all served to enlarge the plea of the common man for public assistance. There was no better subject for the demagogue to belabor than the needs of the people. Delegates to constitutional conventions and legislators expended enormous energies in efforts to curb banking and speculators. There was love of speculation on the frontier, but at the same time there was fear of monetary power. This fear of money on the frontier was a major factor in creating suspicion of the East, and it also made the East dubious of the West.

As the frontier movement advanced, relationships between East and West assumed new meaning in American history. Almost every major political incident in national history after 1780 magnified the importance of sectional aspects of the country's growth. The East had its apprehensive movements about the effects of frontier expansion on its economy. There were times when the westward movement of population seemed to threaten its labor supply. Politically, the expanding West occupied a central position in the field of national legislation. Both administration and legislature grew sensitive to frontier demands. Despite differing sectional interests of the East and West, there began, after 1820, an ardent wooing of the West by eastern economic interests. In time, highways, canals, and railways reached out to capture the trade of the frontier. The new western states supplied farm products in ever-mounting quantities. At the same time transportation lines wedded East and West and were to contribute materially to the future military struggle between the North and South.

Population

Census reports from 1790 to 1870 showed a large migration from East to West. So numerous was this migration at times that there was genuine fear that older sections would be ruinously depopulated. Recurring economic panic swelled this tide of western movement. Agricultural panics sent families westward to seek cheap lands and fresh opportunities. There is little doubt that the frontier did relieve some economic pressures on eastern industrial communities, and population shifts at times may have reduced the eastern labor supply. To what extent the East was affected is still largely an unanswered question; however, it is doubtful that any of the fundamental problems of American urban growth were reduced by westward migration.

If the frontier relieved pressure on urban America before 1880, its significance lay more in the fact that native sons and daughters moved on further westward instead of turning back to eastern cities. It was not until the occupation of most of the western lands, and the time at which production of farm commodities approached a point of saturation, that the course of American migration was reversed. When this occurred there was a desertion of the land for the cities, but already the great frontier of free land had all but vanished.

Possibly the American frontier more effectively helped to reduce the excessive populations of the British Isles and Europe. Abroad, politically and economically oppressed peoples faced social and economic frustration. Hundreds of thousands of foreigners migrated to the American West where they abandoned Old World habits and customs. America felt the impact of the European immigrants. From the arrival of the first immigrants on the Atlantic seaboard to the coming of wealthy British younger sons to the cattle country, the frontier had great attraction for foreigners. Still, a historian is almost unable to evaluate with certainty the importance of the frontier in relieving social pressures at home and abroad. The appearance of foreigners on the frontier presented an irregular pattern. Sometimes they were in the first wave of settlers, but most often they came in a secondary population movement. There were, however, immigrant communities which divided themselves into smaller settlements, and areas of considerable size were populated by foreign-born people.

No doubt the American social melting pot was most effective on the frontier. It was relatively easy for the immigrant to modify, and even to forget, his old national customs. Germans married Swedes in sparsely settled frontier communities in Iowa, Minnesota, and Kansas; Irishmen even learned to tolerate Britishers, and Scandinavians intermarried with Italian and French settlers. The strong nationalistic sentiment of the frontier tended to erase Old World loyalties and facilitated social absorption of various groups. Greatest of all influences, however, were those of economic and social necessity. Frontier chores ignored national origins in their demands, and common problems demanding common solutions were great homogenizers of peoples.

Orthodoxy vs. Individualism

Despite the fact that frontiersmen accepted new social groups and applied new methods of performing the arduous task of pioneering, there was a marked sense of orthodoxy and conformity about the westward movement. Except, as we have seen, where economic progress was concerned, there was a distinct tendency to retain established basic social patterns. Religious denominations flourished; in fact, there have been few times in history when there was so much denominational transmutation as there was on the American frontier. There were few fundamental doctrinal differences between most of the groups, and such as appeared were over narrow interpretations of the Scriptures and the use of rituals. There were, of course, situations where the more emotional types of religions supplanted those based on a restrained Calvinistic point of view. The only major radical departures from the adopted Old World pattern were those of the Shakers and Mormons, and the Shakers were of British origin. Thus when frontier expansion ceased, the church differed little from that of colonial America.

Orthodoxy was a basic note in almost every other aspect of human association on the frontier. The man who differed from the crowd became a marked man. There were colorful characters, of course, but frontiersmen were intolerant of the unusual. They were critical of originality, and it took a truly indifferent and courageous man to parade an eccentricity. Critical remarks and gossip wounded more deeply in the backwoods, and few individuals relished community disapproval.

The frontier press was a model of conformity. If an original and imaginative editor varied his offerings, he did so in the area of human whimsicalities. Editors aired their views, published commonplace news, printed human-interest stories which ranged from the unusual to the naughty and risqué, but they never overlooked the fundamental and ancient dignities of their profession. Except in temporarily rowdy frontier communities, there was always a profound desire to maintain a social *status quo*, an overweening respect for sober propriety.

Westward-moving pioneers adapted their institutions to changing conditions. Had there been radical revisions of established Old World and eastern social and institutional patterns, it is doubtful that a unified nation could have been created. But although frontiersmen were conformists within the limitations of a rugged environment, they were also protestors. Their protests constitute a vital chapter in American history. Resistance to the whisky tax, the Alien and Sedition Laws, tariffs, restrictions on free access to western lands, banking, Indian management, monetary ad-

ministration and resentment of legislative neglect of farmer interests give
frontier history a strong regional flavor.

Frontiersmen developed an orthodox institutional history, but they were
economically prodigal. With ax and torch they slashed through the forests.
Soils were dredged of their fertility, deep gullies gashed the face of the
earth, and impoverished homesteads were deserted when the owners moved
away. An old frontier adage said that many a man had buried three wives
and had worked the fourth down to skin and bones, that he had gutted
three farms, and that he was growing gullies on the fourth. To their lasting discredit, many frontiersmen prostituted nature's bounty. They developed profligate habits which were shameful in the eyes of frugal
foreigners. Many of the charges of prodigality made against Americans
have arisen from abuse of the continent's land resources.

Few frontiersmen, however, troubled their thoughts with self-recrimina-
tion over wasteful habits. They looked hopefully to future chroniclers
to appraise charitably their actions. In this they were not to be disappointed. Since the latter half of the eighteenth century the frontier has
been the theme of thousands of books. Yearly, new volumes add to the
story of the westward movement. Occasionally western novels are popular
enough to become best sellers and to win literary awards. Beginning with
Beadle and Monro's lusty dime novels, contract writers have ground out
paper-backed thrillers which compressed stories of pioneering, rascality,
virtue, and blood and thunder into chronicles of courage and accomplishment, and which never exhausted the reading public. Indian fighters,
savage painted braves, sneaking white traitors, beautiful virgins, and un-
principled seducers wore the fictional boards thin with their ceaseless activities. Old timers cudgeled their aging brains and turned their gnarled hands
to the task of writing their memoirs, publishing their works as diaries,
journals, autobiographies, and reminiscences. Scarcely a major woodsman
allowed his fame to go unchronicled. Even Daniel Boone left behind him
a flowery ghost-written autobiographical description of his exploits.

Individual frontiersmen were proud of their roles in the westward movement. With an eye to the future, they left for the unborn reader piles of
firsthand accounts of what it was like to be a pioneer. Many of those who
did not professedly turn historian innocently left informal accounts of
their experiences in yellowing bundles of letters written to homefolks.
In some instances their literary offerings in book or manuscript form have
become more valuable than the blocks of lands which the authors helped
to settle. Vast library and manuscript holdings contain these precious
literary remains as living monuments to the westward movement. A six-
teen-page pamphlet journal of an Oregon trail pioneer who went from

Napoleon, Indiana, to the Willamette Valley enjoys the distinction of being more valuable than a half-dozen covered wagons. Lyman C. Draper, Reuben T. Durret, William M. Darlington, and William R. Coe all made important collections of frontier books and manuscripts. Libraries such as the Wisconsin State Historical Society, the Filson Club, the University of Chicago, the University of Pittsburgh, the Library of Congress, the New York Public Library, and the Huntington Library all contain invaluable collections of frontier materials. Besides these, state historical libraries, societies, and universities own good collections. The major energies of most local historical societies have been devoted to the collection of pioneer materials. Vast numbers of articles which appear annually in state historical journals, and in national historical journals, like the *Mississippi Valley Historical Review*, treat of the frontier.

Scholarly historians have joined forces with old timers in writing of the westward movement. In 1893 Frederick Jackson Turner of the University of Wisconsin read his provocative essay, "The Significance of the Frontier in American History," before the American Historical Association in Chicago. This essay was by no means the first one on the subject, but it served forcefully to call the attention of scholars to the neglect of the frontier in the writing of American history. It likewise suggested the vast amount of materials which awaited exploitation. Professor Turner presented frontier history largely in an institutional sense. He outlined the pioneering process, and described briefly the environmental and isolative influences which transformed Old World ideas and institutions into American ideas and institutions. His discussion of the role of the frontier in the democratization of America was to provoke a continuing discussion of his point of view. Since that moment when he read his paper in Chicago, Professor Turner has had his ardent defenders and his zealous disputants. They have both amplified his point of view and questioned his contentions. Beyond the realm of academic argumentation over the Turner essay, other historians have examined frontier history in its complex phases and have contributed materially to an understanding of the American people.

Westward pioneering was one of the Americans' proudest achievements. Periodically, local chroniclers mine their local archives seeking materials from which to produce anniversary pageants, and male citizens are set to growing scraggly beards with the apparent belief that their pioneer ancestors lived without benefit of razors, soap, and water. Fur neckpieces are wound into loose imitations of coonskin caps, and long rifles are taken from dusty museums and attics to arm woodsmen without forests. Women garb themselves in smothering sunbonnets and linsey-woolsey, or waddle about in sagging hoopskirts to revive temporarily the memory of their

long-suffering great-grandmothers. When an organization wishes to prop-
agandize its members into supporting some campaign or other, it leaps to
the typecase to set puerile orations proclaiming the virtues of our American
forefathers who laid Indians and the woods low with unfailing hands.
Every Saturday afternoon from Brooklyn to San Diego, and from Albert
Lea, Minnesota, to Dry Prong, Louisiana, Hollywood delivers its full quota
of celluloid revivals of the frontier. Cowboys, cattle rustlers, stagecoach
robbers, prostitutes, virtuous daughters of simple-minded frontier bankers,
helpless ministers, miners, and covered wagon pilgrims meekly resettle
the continent. In endless double features the frontier lives dangerously again
in coonskin cap, buckskin britches, long smoking rifles, quick action pistols,
astride sweating horses, aboard smoking high-stacked steamboats, and
swaying atop careening stagecoaches. Whether or not the frontier was
truly a place where American history was democratized may remain an
open question for all time to come, but that it was a crucible in which
people were given a fiery test of sinew and courage is definitely beyond
academic dispute. The conquest of the continent was relatively short and
complete, and the story of that conquest is largely the early history of the
American people.

FROM
WILLIAM
SMITH's
Account
of the
Expedition
Against the
Ohio
Indians,
1765

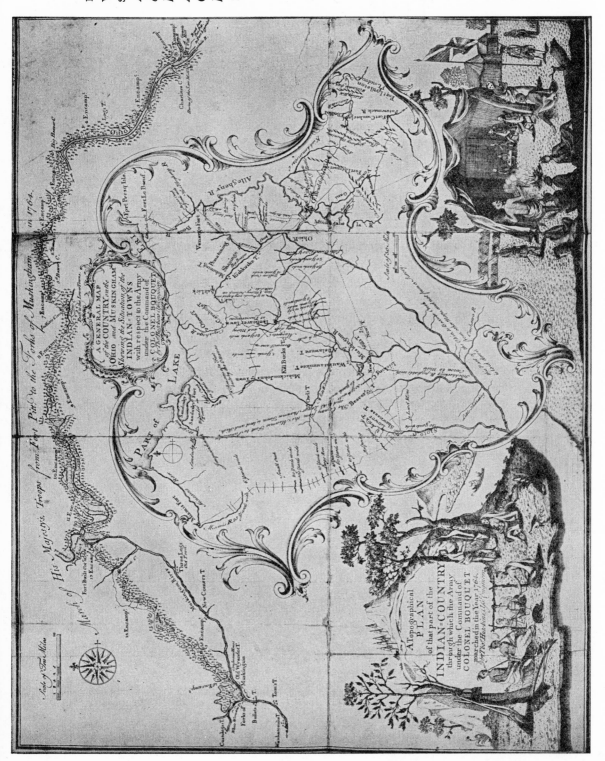

THE ALLEGHENY FRONTIER

THE

ALLEGHENY FRONTIER

There was once a time at which we also might have created a great French nation in the American wilds, to counterbalance the influence of the English upon the destinies of the New World. France formerly possessed a territory in North America, scarcely less extensive than the whole of Europe. The three greatest rivers of that continent then flowed within her dominions. The Indian tribes which dwelt between the mouth of the St. Lawrence and the delta of the Mississippi were unaccustomed to any other tongue but ours; and all the European settlements scattered over that immense region recalled the traditions of our country. Louisburg, Montgomery, Duquesne, Saint-Louis, Vincennes, New Orleans, (for such names they bore,) are words dear to France and familiar to our ears.

—DE TOCQUEVILLE, *Democracy in America*

CHAPTER II

T HE beginning of the folk movement across the great American frontier no doubt resulted largely from social and economic conditions of Western Europe and Britain in the sixteenth and seventeenth centuries. The settlement of the eastern part of the North American continent was an initial step in opening the wider frontier. Immigrants to Jamestown, Quebec and Plymouth were as much frontiersmen as those who drifted downstream or climbed through mountain passes in later years. The colonial frontier was a conditioning ground on which prospective western settlers were seasoned for their subsequent moves.

Because of the complex background of American beginnings neither time nor place can be designated for the opening of the westward movement. There is a distinct geographical break which separated what may be termed the old colonial empire from the frontier. The tidewater and immediate hinterland were bound to the eastern shoreline by both economic and political interests. Beyond the first tier of western ridges, however, the focus reflected internal changes and new introspections on the conditions of American life. Economically it can be said that the promise of profits from the Indian trade plus the availability of endless stretches of relatively free lands radically revised attitudes towards the bounties of the continent.

In the broader fields of international trade and politics, the rivalry of British colonial and French traders in the Indian country plus the larger forces of power politics spurred the opening of the West. The broader world-wide political implications between Britain and France brought the western American frontier into greater prominence than it might otherwise have had. The internal trade rivalry of the decade 1740–1750, climaxed by the French and Indian War, gave great impetus to British-American frontier expansion prior to the American Revolution. This period of the mid-eighteenth century opens this study. Picking up the story of the American frontier at this particular moment may be making little more than an arbitrary beginning, but it is no more so than were the marks on the historic lead lines used on river steamboats. A prominent mark indicated that it was safe to proceed, and mid-eighteenth century seems to be that mark for a beginning of the study of frontier history. At least this is the time when one set of major national actors quit the stage, and a powerful new group, the American frontiersmen, rushed forward to take their places.

Following the French and Indian War the westward movement opened a major chapter in American history. Many complex British colonial administrative problems stemmed from the greatly enlarged western territory. Perplexing economic and military questions were intimately involved in the management of the vast backwoods. Land became at once a vital issue which required more astute administration than the British were prepared to give it. Indian trade and relations involved complexities which neither the British colonial official nor the American backwoodsman was patient enough to understand and control. This was the setting and the problem which opened the great westward movement which within a century and a half rolled across the whole North American continent.

Frenchmen, Backwoodsmen and Traders

In 1755, the cartographer and surveyor Lewis Evans wrote that "between 4 and 10 degrees longitude west from Philadelphia there is a spacious country which we call Alleghaney from the name of a river which runs thro' it and is the main branch of the Mississippi . . . In this country all our Indian trade centers . . . the most of our return is Deer Skins. The Indian traders have had great credit with the merchants." Evans perceived that English expansion had reached the threshold of one of its great frontier landmarks—the immediate trans-Allegheny region. The year 1750 was in some respects one of fairly well-defined demarcations; it marked the beginning of a new phase of western expansion and the approaching end of international rivalries for peltry and land in the Ohio, St. Lawrence and Great Lakes area.

Certainly the great triangle of land outlined by the Ohio-Mississippi-Great Lakes-St. Lawrence was not unfamiliar to white men. Since 1606 the French had been moving either towards or across this area. Between 1668 and 1682 Robert Sieur de LaSalle had intermittently explored the Ohio Valley and traveled down the Mississippi to the Gulf Coast. Subsequently other traders, explorers, priests and military officials were abroad in the rich lake-shore and river-valley country to promote private and French governmental interests. Many of them came to save souls; others dreamed of making personal fortunes.

The early decades of the eighteenth century saw the French begin a pincers movement across the western country. Working down the Great Lakes chain from Quebec and Montreal, French explorers and traders made their line of invasion along lakes Ontario and Erie to Detroit, down the Maumee River, the Wabash, and then down the Ohio and Mississippi to Natchez and New Orleans. French outposts along this route became landmarks in frontier history; along the lakes were forts Frontenac, Niagara, Detroit, Michillimakinac; down the Maumee-Wabash passage were Miami, Ouiatenon and Vincennes; westward, on the Mississippi, were Kaskaskia and Cahokia.

From our perspective of American history it is now evident that the French made one of their most serious tactical blunders in their plan for fortifying the frontier against English intrusion. Although it was doubtless good strategy for them to develop a strong backwoods cordon around the slowly expanding English colonies, such a restraining wall had to be tight and strong to check the push of settlement from the east. Backwoods geography offered the French three natural lines of traffic and defense. The first might have been the Lake Erie-French Creek-Allegheny-Ohio-Mississippi passage; the second lay along the Lake Erie-Miami-Ohio-Mississippi route; and, the third and more distant one was the Lake Erie-Maumee-Wabash connection to the Ohio and Mississippi rivers. The first, or Ohio passage, was direct and in closest proximity to British activity. It would have brought the French line hard against the colonial boundaries of England and would have checked the eastern competitor at his own back door. Travel down the Ohio was both direct and relatively fast and safe. There were disadvantages, however, in making the long portages from the site of the future Presque Isle by way of French Creek to the Allegheny River and into the Ohio. Transportation would have to be greatly facilitated for the route to become efficient. Garrisoning and protecting this tight frontier would involve considerable manpower and eternal vigilance, with a constant threat of border warfare hanging over the French. Added to this would be the tedious job of maintaining a dependable alliance with the Indians.

In 1701, Detroit was founded on the Detroit River between lakes Erie and Huron, and nineteen years later forts Miami and Ouiatenon were planted on the Miami and the Wabash. About 1731, Vincennes was located on the east bank of the Wabash in what is now southern Indiana. Choosing the Maumee-Wabash line placed the French between 350 and 500 miles west of the immediate point of contact with the westward-moving English. This decision left a large area of highly fertile Indian country open to hostile Indian traders and land speculators. It also left an important segment of Indian population exposed to the seduction of traders and their goods, from Pennsylvania and Virginia. The wide margin of territory also gave the British an opportunity to gain a foothold across the mountains without immediately facing armed conflict with the French. British adventurers and traders quickly used this geographical advantage to promote their commercial interests. Proof of their success were the major Indian trading posts of Logstown, the Shawnee towns, Pickawillany and its associated Twightwees posts; and there were by 1750 well-worn trading paths into the interior. Journals of Christopher Gist, Conrad Weiser and Frederick Christian Post give good first-hand views of this area in the 1750's. Activities even west of these posts showed how far the trading frontier was in advance of the colonial settlement line. It was, in fact, so far in advance that it was already threatening to breach the French frontier line along the Maumee and Wabash Rivers.

The French moved rapidly across the trans-Allegheny frontier, whereas the British colonials moved slowly. The French did not delay their advance by establishing a front of agricultural and commercial settlements. The British, on the other hand, hesitated to leave the coast and the eastward flowing rivers. Their economic philosophy was conditioned to a combined land and maritime commerce. Although not as demonstrably sentimental about the homeland as the French colonials, the British-Americans were reluctant to give up even a tenuous contact with home and its supply of traditional culture, capital and manufactured goods. Periodic samplings of the settlement lines throughout the seventeenth and early eighteenth centuries show a slowly spreading movement inland along the Atlantic coastal shelf. This was no surging tide of settlers pushing forward feverishly to exploit new lands and to engage in rich Indian trade for the sake of taking quick profits and getting out. Rather it was a leisurely spreading but highly absorbent roll forward which penetrated and colored all beneath it. Whereas Frenchmen could boast of daring and far-reaching exploits in the seventeenth century by Radisson, Groseilliers, Frontenac, Nicolas Perrot, Marquette and Joliet, Father Hennepin, Tonty and LaSalle, there were few English adventurers who had been far inland. Among the English was Abram Woods, who ventured up the James above Petersburg and, as some historians contend, even reached the Ohio. In 1671, Thomas Batts and Robert Fallam had crossed the ridges to spy upon "the ebbing and flowing of the waters on the other side of the mountains in order to the discovery of the South Sea. . . ." A year earlier the fabulous John Lederer had reached the summit of the Blue Ridges and wrote in his fantastic journal that he saw the Atlantic Ocean on the east, and by some geographical aberration he believed "that the Indian Ocean does stretch an arm or bay from California as far as the Appalatean Mountains answer-

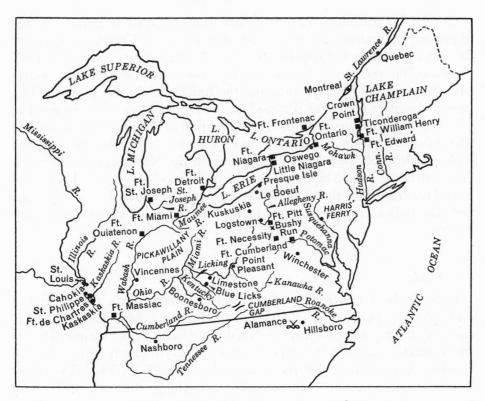

FRONTIER POSTS AND FORTS, 1750–1781

able the Gulfs of Florida and Mexico on this side from the opposite direction."

French explorers had already visited the shores of most of the Great Lakes and could prove Lederer wrong. Already Robert LaSalle had found that the Indian Ocean was not so errant as the German had thought. In 1673, James Needham and Gabriel Arthur crossed the Carolina Blue Ridges and saw the land beyond, but no rush of adventurers followed after them. In 1716, Governor Alexander Spotswood led a highly convivial party of gentlemen up to the crest of the Virginia Blue Ridges and looked into the great valley. Elsewhere along the American frontier there was gradual movement westward. Along the Mohawk in New York the Albany traders and settlers were venturing inland, and so it was along the Susquehanna, the Potomac, and the Connecticut. By 1750 the colonial Indian trader had become a prominent personality on the Allegheny-Monongahela-Ohio frontier, and his influence extended to all the major coastal towns, especially Philadelphia, Boston and Charleston.

During this period, two international treaties played an important part in pushing the Indian trade westward—the Treaty of Utrecht in 1713 and the Treaty of Aix-la-Chapelle in 1748. A third treaty of considerable domestic importance was that drawn between commissioners from Maryland, Virginia and Pennsylvania, and the Indians of the Six Nations. This treaty, signed at Lancaster, Pennsylvania, in June, 1744, was supposed to have clarified once again the confused question of Indian claims to land in Maryland and Virginia, and it was to have reviewed certain territorial and trade problems between Pennsylvania and the Six Nations. Actually it was hoped that the friendship between the British colonials and the Indians would reach further: that it would insure not only amicable trade relations but also Indian friendship, even in the face of a backwoods war with France.

Fur Trade

In the rivalry between France and England after 1730 the fur and Indian trade played a major role. Old World fur-trading centers had shifted because of an increasing supply of North American pelts. Vienna, Danzig and Lübeck, once the fur capitals of Europe, had been superseded by London, Amsterdam and Paris. Traders could reach far and wide in the American wilderness for their prizes by maintaining close association with Indians and the trappers who ventured into the vast area of the West. The trader who came with bales of goods, strings of wampum, casks of rum, glib tongue, whimsical humor, and keen observant eyes shaped a pattern which was to prevail throughout a major portion of American frontier exploration and exploitation. He was the first in most cases to see the new country, to form friendship with its natives, to solve the riddle of its maze of streams, and to convey vast geographical and economic knowledge and experience to subsequent settlers and speculators.

Several types of traders visited the American frontier throughout its restless history. There were those who left behind them reputations of tasks brilliantly performed both in terms of profits and of assistance to their governments; there were other malicious individuals who sought profits at any costs and cared little for future consequences; and finally, there were those nameless men who quietly facilitated the exchange of goods for furs, and whose casual conversations often became sources of information for expansion. These traders made little profit, had limited ambition, and often came to be more like Indians than white men.

By the middle of the eighteenth century four sectional groups of traders had become famous. These were the Albany, Pennsylvania, Virginia and Carolina traders. Pennsylvanians were quick to take advantage of the opportunities which lay beyond the mountains in the rich Ohio Valley. Virginia traders were somewhat less active largely because of their interest in the southwestern valley area. In the Ohio country the Virginians never became so effective beyond the mountains as their northern rivals. Albany traders reached out to the Mohawk-Great Lakes country, and the Carolina traders trafficked as far westward as the Mississippi.

From Pennsylvania came many traders who were key men both in the western commerce and in Indian and French affairs. Perhaps the most famous of these was George Croghan, an Irish Protestant who arrived in eastern Pennsylvania from Dublin in 1741. He settled in the Conodoguinet Valley near Carlisle. Croghan's new home was strategically located on the trail westward. He began trading almost immediately upon his arrival in Pennsylvania. Ten years later his way stations were located at the mouth of the Pine Creek on the Allegheny, at Oswegle Bottom within five miles of the forks of the Allegheny and Monongahela, and at Logstown eighteen miles below the forks of the rivers forming the Ohio. Further down stream he had a post at the mouth of Beaver Creek. Croghan's traders, however, traveled as far as the Wabash and Lake Erie to the west and northwest; to the south they traded at the mouth of the Scioto and across Kentucky to Eskippikithiki and along the Kentucky River. Some of them may have even doubled back to compete with the Carolinas for the southern Indian trade by crossing Kentucky to reach the Cherokees in the Tennessee country.

George Croghan had certain personal attributes which made him an excellent trader. He was more highly adaptable to primitive social conditions than were most white men. He regarded the Indian not only as a factor in a profitable trade but also as a human being who conformed to definite economic and social patterns, and who reacted to conditions in the light of his experience. Croghan had patience enough to go through the long and tedious process required by his primitive neighbors for reaching agreements. How patient he was is illustrated by a brief excerpt from a letter which he wrote Richard Peters, secretary of the Pennsylvania Council in 1758. He asked Peters to "Excuse boath Writing and peper, and gues at my Maining, fer I have this minitt 20 drunken Indians about me . . ." Having an Indian wife was of further advantage in claiming kinship with his neighbors and in bringing himself down to their level of simple understanding.

Some of the other traders important enough to be noted by name were Andrew Montour, William Trent, Michael Teaffe, John Fraser, Lewis Evans and Robert Callendar. Competing with the English were Frenchmen who operated from the semimilitary posts scattered along the frontier from Vincennes on the Wabash to Quebec. In some respects they had the advantage of their British neighbors because they had military establishments at their backs whose administrators made it a matter of policy to help French woodsmen to succeed. British traders operated as individuals and often had to overcome by personal ingenuity obstacles which a vigilant political policy or active military backing would have cleared away. On the other hand, if the French had a military and governmental advantage, the Pennsylvania and Virginia traders enjoyed greater advantage in having ready supplies of cheap goods of fair quality. British manufacturers turned out materials in greater quantity and variety than did their French competitors; moreover, the backwoods traders could deliver them with more facility, a thing of major importance in the Indian trade. Equally as important an advantage as cheap trade goods was the English ability to pay good prices for skins and furs—especially for deer and elk skins.

British colonial traders had a further monopolistic advantage in the sale of the two important commodities of rum and strouds (coarse cloth blankets named after the town of Stroud). During King George's War, the St. Lawrence waterway was virtually closed to the French trade by fleet action, and what the British fleet failed to do, the long icy winter season of nine months' duration completed. Coupled with these handicaps, the distance from the western woods to the trading centers in Montreal and Quebec was great and hazardous as compared with that from Pickawillany to Philadelphia. Because of the treacherous rapids in the St. Lawrence it required twenty to thirty days to go from Montreal to the Niagara Falls.

The whole matter of manufacturing and financing was far removed from the highly competitive backwoods scene. Traders seldom began operation on their own; they were financed by merchants and banks as far away as London. When George Croghan was bankrupted by the raids of the French and Indian War, his list of creditors indicated a complex system of financing not unlike that of a modern business man. Names such as Gratz, Miranda, Franks, Hanley and many others became associated with the backwoods trade as financiers and merchants. Behind these men were the banks and organized trading groups of the Empire. Behind all of these was the official English desire for national prestige and outlets for English manufactured goods. For the British manufacturer the Indian trade was a significant outlet for his product. Although an enormous amount of goods found its way to the trading posts, the real importance of the trade was actually a hope for future monopoly by British traders.

Two important factors, other than international rivalry, entered into the conditions of trade: transportation to the frontier, and the continuing availability of skins and furs. Transportation costs usually ran from twenty to fifty per cent of the total investment in goods. If a trader lost his supplies in the western woods he reckoned his loss in both the purchase price and the heavy cost of delivery. Usually traders traveled in pairs or in small groups. Possibly the most efficient small land trading unit was composed of two men and twenty horses. Each horse bore a load of approximately 150 pounds strapped to a special type of pack saddle. The horse train was strung out in single file along narrow paths, and great care had to be exercised to keep the animals from swaying and bumping into trees and overhanging rocks, or from sliding off inclines and destroying the packs. Horses were hobbled and belled and turned out at night to forage for their food. Apparently the Virginia and Pennsylvania traders preferred moving goods over land. Nevertheless the long deep-bellied Indian canoe was constantly in use. When canoes were used, however, larger crews were needed, and the responsibility for safety of the boats and reliability of the crews became much greater.

Traders' packs contained a large variety of goods. There were guns, lead, gunpowder, rum, flints, strouds, vermilion, tomahawks, blanketing, linens, calicoes, wampum, lace, thread, gartering, ribbons, stockings, knives, brass kettles and pots, traps, brass wire, files, awls, needles, buttons, combs, jews' harps, bells, whistles, looking glasses, rings, and assorted jewelry. These goods were traded at what approximated a scale of standard prices, with the English trying to undersell the French, and the Virginia and Pennsylvania traders trying to undersell each other. Occasionally a trader undertook a little "chiseling" in isolated places, and a few of them wound up in trouble with their customers. Little or no money of any sort passed back and forth; payment for goods was made in skins and furs. The most acceptable peltries were deer, elk, buffalo, bear, beaver, racoon, fox, cat, muskrat, mink, otter, fisher, and a miscellaneous assortment of less prized skins such as squirrel, rabbit, woodchuck and others.

An Advancing Line of Settlement

Led by the British colonial fur traders, the frontier settlements were spreading slowly but methodically westward. Three layers of folk movement were in evidence in most of the region. In New York there were the old settlements around the coastal sounds and the Hudson estuary which spread out along the river itself. A second layer deflected up the Mohawk. A third was thrust in behind this spreading movement, beginning the exploitation of the primitive hinterlands of the Scoharie and German flats. Along the St. Lawrence the ubiquitous Scotch-Irish or Albany trader had made his appearance. In Pennsylvania by 1750, the three definite layers of population could be identified as the Old Quaker element in the Phila-delphia-Delaware Bay area, the Palatinate Germans who moved into the Susquehanna Valley, and the later Scotch-Irish and Germans who moved hard against the mountain range and were poised for a crossing of the ridges at the first propitious moment. To the south, Virginians were distributed in successive stages of socio-economic development from the tidewater to the Piedmont and across the Blue Ridges into the great valley. North Carolina, South Carolina and Georgia had not gone so far in developing successive layers of population expansion. In these colonies the population was largely coast- and river-bound and had made no phenomenal move inland. In New England a somewhat precise land survey system had been the source of a more even and methodical inland movement than elsewhere in the colonies. Nevertheless the colonial population increase, though relatively small in 1750, was sufficiently dynamic to make the frontier a vital aspect of British expansion.

By 1750 there were more than a million and a half people in the British colonies. The growth of population was not great in comparison with the amount of land to be absorbed within the area of the established colonies, but it exerted pressure on frontier expansion out of proportion to that of most intensively integrated societies. Already a stirring restlessness was characteristic of much of the backwoods population; it was on the move. Immigrants coming into the colonies found it most often to their economic and social advantage to move to the western fringe of the older settlements and to begin building their homes in unbroken country. Such was the case of the Scotch, Irish and Germans who moved to the Susquehanna in Pennsylvania and then turned southward into the valley of Virginia where an abundance of cheap fertile land was available to them.

Just as the Virginia, Pennsylvania and Carolina traders had done, the backwoods settler would establish a pattern of economic behavior of his own. Many of those along the raw edge of the frontier were cattlemen who gained a livelihood by grazing scrawny woods cattle. The cowpen was about as characteristic of much of the broad Allegheny frontier as was the heavily stockaded fortress. A seaman who accompanied Braddock's expedition into western Virginia and Pennsylvania in 1755 has left a vivid description of this type of primitive economy.

> From the heart of the Settlements we now got into the Cow-pens, the Keepers of these are very extraordinary Kind of Fellows, they drive up their Herds on Horseback, and they need to do so, for their Cattle are near as wild as Deer; a Cow-pen generally consists of a very large Cottage or House in the Woods, with about fore-score or one hundred Acres, inclosed with high Rails and divided; a small Inclosure they keep for Corn, for the family, and the rest is the Pasture in which they keep their Calves; but the Manner is far different from anything you ever saw; they may perhaps have a stock of four or five hundred to a thou-

sand Head of Cattle belonging to a Cow Pen, these run as they please in
the Great Woods, where there are no Inclosures to stop them.

Back of the cowpen area the observant seaman had seen yeoman farmers struggling with the forest, cultivating their small patches of tobacco
and corn, and tending young orchards of apples, peaches and pears. These
backwoodsmen were also struggling with another realm just as important
—their society. In Pennsylvania, in the Susquehanna Valley, the farmer
was more thrifty and prosperous than his contemporary to the south. Land
was important to him, and his interest was ever focused on its availability.
It is safe to say that at mid-eighteenth century, land was becoming a more
powerful magnet in attracting settlers than it had been during most of
the past century.

French Anxiety

It was clearly evident by 1750 that British expansion would soon force
its way through the eastern tier of mountain ranges and that the advanced
focal point was at the forks of the Allegheny and Monongahela rivers,
at the head of the Ohio. It was also clear that if British expansion were to
take place in this region the French barrier would have to be forced back.
Conversely the French realized that if they were to hold the western country they would have to check British expansion at the watershed of the
Appalachians.

Friction increased daily in the field of Indian trade. It was easy enough
to sow seeds of suspicion in the minds of the Indians for they could view
the settlements already creeping up to their hunting grounds. Not even
all the favorable conditions of trade with the English could overcome this
fear and suspicion that Indian lands were in jeopardy. France claimed the
western country by right of discovery by LaSalle and the subsequent activities of French traders and explorers, including Baron de Longeuil who
in 1739 had placed metal shields on trees, laying claim to the Ohio country
in the name of "His Most Christian Majesty." England dated its claim
to the western country from the ambiguous London Company charter
of 1606 which granted land from sea to sea, if such a boundary existed.
In 1713 the English had asserted a claim to the area under the terms of the
Treaty of Utrecht; more properly, the land was asserted to belong to the
Iroquois, who in turn were claimed as British subjects. As early as 1744
it was reasonably clear that someone would have to forfeit his claim in
the Ohio Valley and that such a surrender could only be accomplished
at the end of a bitter armed conflict. At Montreal the governor general,
La Galissoniere, was thoroughly aware that his government would have

to take some immediate step to head off English exploitation of the region. A strong and tangible French claim had to be reasserted on the Ohio Valley.

An expedition was organized to go along French Creek from Lake Erie to the Allegheny, and then to the Ohio and down that stream to a point beyond the line of immediate dispute. Céleron de Blainville, a former commandant at Detroit, was chosen for the task. His entourage was organized at Montreal, and it left that city on June 15, 1749. Céleron went out to accomplish a multiple purpose—to try to bluff English traders out of the country, to make friends with the Indians and to reassert in fact a claim to the country. Although he took with him a fairly substantial company, his journey proved hazardous because of the antagonism of the British traders and their Indian friends. At more than one place he faced possibility of harm if not annihilation. He found as he went along that the British were firmly entrenched in the Indian trade. Their goods were more attractive, and they paid better prices for skins and furs; especially were their prices better for deer skins which were in greater demand in England than on the continent. At the mouths of six streams Céleron, amidst much pomp and ceremony, buried leaden plates with inscriptions stating ownership of the land. He likewise attached metallic shields to the trees, hoping to leave behind him tangible evidence of his journey.

In five months he had covered a distance of approximately 1200 leagues, returning to Montreal on November 9, 1749. His report was certainly not heartening to his superiors. It revealed that the English had made strong headway in the Indian country and would be most difficult to check; and that three hundred British traders, approximately, would stop at nothing short of war to dispossess the French. It was also a discouraging fact that the Indians were likewise hostile. Furthermore, Céleron's expedition did much to excite the British and to make them conscious of the impending crisis in the Ohio Valley.

On the British side, colonial officials were faced with the blunt proposition that British expansion would be checked at the watershed of the Appalachians, and that the great area of rich lands and Indian trade would be barred to them if France were allowed to proceed on its revealed course. To the frontier settler inching his way westward, it was made plain that not only would he lose the prospect of further rich lands, but his very door would face a hostile Indian frontier under French domination. In London the banker, the merchant, and the manufacturer realized that this vital outlet for capital and goods would be blocked. Also, the Crown would suffer an unpleasant loss of prestige if it let the Ohio country slip from its grasp.

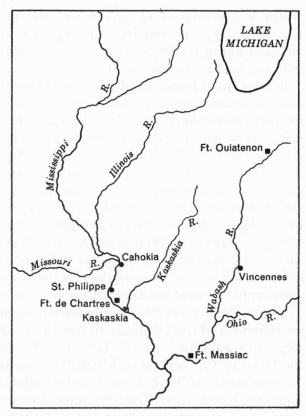

FRENCH POSTS
IN THE
WESTERN COUNTRY

Land Companies

In the face of the strong rivalry for the Ohio frontier, the British from 1746 to 1749 tried an old approach with a new twist. Three or four major land companies were created to act as spearheads for speculators who could facilitate land claims and thrust forward the settlement line. The existence of such companies in British expansion in America was as old as the London Company, but the new organizations combined colonial investment with well-defined purposes capable of immediate accomplishment in the special situation. On July 13, 1749, Sir William Gooch, lieutenant governor of Virginia, concluded a long period of negotiation with a grant of 200,000 acres of land to the Ohio Land Company, provided that a hundred families would settle on it within seven years. Actually the origin of this land company project went back to 1743 when James Patton made some explorations in the upper Ohio Valley; in 1744 at the making of the Treaty of Lancaster the project was given new impetus by the discussions with the Six Nations. Thomas Lee, one of the Virginia commissioners who helped to make the treaty, organized the Ohio company, which was composed of prominent men in Virginia, Maryland and London, in 1747. It came into existence as an organization speculating in land and Indian trading and promised to wield a considerable amount of influence both in America and England.

In 1745, John Robinson of King and Queen County, Virginia, secured 100,000 acres of land on the Greenbrier River, and in 1749 a company of speculators calling themselves the Loyal Land Company sought 800,-000 acres of land in southwestern Virginia. The latter body likewise included prominent Virginians, among them John Lewis, Peter Jefferson, Joshua Fry, and Edmund Pendleton. In contrast with the other companies they secured their grant of land without the hobbling provision of settling families on it. Yet the Loyal Company was the first to make a move toward laying physical claim to its grant. On March 12, 1749, Dr. Thomas Walker, a graduate of William and Mary College with considerable frontier surveying experience, was employed to locate the Loyal Company's western lands. He was to travel southwestward and to cross over the mountain ridges until he found suitable territory for settlement.

Doctor Walker and five companions left his house in Albemarle County on March 6, and from that date to April 13 he traveled down the Virginia ridges to Cave Gap, which he later named Cumberland Gap in honor of the Duke of Cumberland, celebrated for his bloody suppression of the Jacobite revolt of 1745. From Cumberland Gap, Doctor Walker went down the Cumberland River for some distance and returned northeastward across the rugged mountains of present-day Kentucky and West Virginia. Passing over the mountains from the Greenbrier country, the surveyors reached Albemarle County on July 13. Doctor Walker's journal is an interesting document describing primitive travel. He records the number of animals killed and the bountiful supply of meat to be had on the frontier; however, with regard to land prospects, the journey must have been discouraging, despite the fact that the party had unknowingly crossed one of the richest bituminous coal beds in North America. Behind him, Walker left the name of the corrupt Duke of Cumberland on a gap, a mountain, and a river; but for all practical purposes his journey was a failure even to the extent that it created animosity among the rivals of the Loyal Land Company and helped to confuse the land policies of Virginia.

While the Loyal Land Company was attempting to survey its block of western lands in the wild mountains of Kentucky, the Ohio Company was engaging in Indian trade and preparing to locate its grant of lands. An initial depot was established at the mouth of Wills Creek across the Potomac in Maryland, and from this base, efforts were made between 1750 and 1754 to open a road directly to the head of the Ohio and to facilitate traffic with the Indians. Following the precedent of the Loyal Land Company, the Ohio directors employed the North Carolina surveyor Christopher Gist to make in their interest an exploratory visit through the Ohio Valley. In some respects Gist's journey into the back country was the most interesting made by an Englishman up to 1760. He was instructed by his employers to "particularly observe the ways and passes through all the mountains you cross, and take an exact account of the soil, quality, and product of the land; the width and depth of the rivers, and several falls belonging to them; together with the courses and bearings of the rivers and mountains as near as you conveniently can; You are also to observe what nations of Indians inhabit there, their strength and number, who they trade with, and in what commodities they deal." Most important in the instructions was the admonition to locate fertile land on which prospective settlements might be made. Except for the latter instruction, Céleron de Blainville might have substituted Gist's orders for his own. Also, Gist carried an invitation for the Indians to meet at Logstown in 1752 to receive gifts and to make a treaty with the Virginians.

Gist began his journey at that famous early frontier landmark, Colonel Thomas Cresap's house at Old Town, Maryland. He started westward on October 31, 1751, and traveled up the Susquehanna, then westward along the Juniata to the mountain trail which led to Shannopin's Town at the forks of the Monongahela and the Allegheny. Thence he journeyed eighteen miles down the Ohio to Logstown, to the two Shawnee towns, and across the country to Pickawillany and back to the Ohio by way of the Miami River. Gist was actually an unwelcome guest of both Indians and traders, though he claimed a friendship and association with George Croghan. He was, however, given information which prevented his stumbling into a band of French allied Indians in Kentucky. When he reached the area of the mouth of the Kentucky River he was told that he could not go on to the Falls of the Ohio because of the presence of the enemy. Turning eastward toward North Carolina, Gist, like Walker, had to cross the deeply serrated Appalachians. His account of struggling through the entanglements of mountain laurel and up and down steep slopes anticipates the hard experience of hundreds of pioneer families moving westward in subsequent years.

Since one of Gist's main purposes was to locate fertile land, his account of the journey is highly descriptive of the country. He had to be careful not to reveal his purpose to the Indians, even to the extent of taking compass readings in secret at one or two points. Though he was good at description, Gist's journal does not indicate any full appreciation of the true quality of the land he crossed. In many stretches along his route the surveyor saw some of what was to become the most productive farm land in the western country.

Organization of the Ohio Company had brought together in a common enterprise a considerable number of influential men. With Thomas Lee as president, they constituted a pressure group which until 1763 influenced many decisions about the area around the head of the Ohio. No doubt the French became the more apprehensive lest this organization get a foothold across the mountains. Céleron's expedition certainly resulted from the Company's securing a charter.

Although Gist brought home a fascinating and informative journal, and the Indian trade promised extensive profits when properly exploited, the provision that one hundred families be settled within seven years placed a serious obstacle in the Company's way. Before settlement could take place, Indian titles had to be quieted. Virginia and the Indians of the Six Nations had not made entirely clear to each other in the Lancaster agreement the conditions by which Iroquois warriors were to pass and be fed on their way through Virginia territory to war against their bitter enemies the Catawbas. Also, Virginians under the leadership of Thomas Lee were said to have complicated matters by laying strings of wampum along the crest of imaginary ridges, indicating that they would stay east of the mountains and the Indians would remain west of them. As early as 1722 Governor Spotswood had negotiated a similar agreement with the Six Nations. A treaty council was called to meet in Logstown in 1752 to deal with some of the ambiguities which had arisen. The principal hope, however, was the securing of permission to lay claims to land west of the mountains. Before the Ohio Company or any other land claimants could make headway in the Ohio Valley, the Indians would have to surrender their rights to land immediately about the headwaters of the Ohio.

The Logstown conference was unpromising from the start. To begin with, it involved bitter jealousy between New York and Virginia about which colony had the right to hold treaty conferences with the Six Nations. Not only was it doubtful that any important group of Indians could be brought to terms binding enough to permit transfer of land and the peaceful possession of it, but there was certain proof that the Pennsylvania traders were sure to try and block Virginia expansion. Pennsylvania was not officially represented at Logstown, but both George Croghan and Andrew Montour were present, the latter acting as interpreter for Governor Robert Dinwiddie.

Reaching an agreement with the Indians of the Six Nations was complicated by several factors. Pennsylvania traders were opposed to the Ohio Company's plan and actively propagandized against it among the Indians.

Failure of the detailed administration by the British of their North American colonial affairs was revealed in the whole complex dispute over the undetermined western boundaries of Virginia and Pennsylvania. Likewise, the failure to develop a centralized Indian agency made Indian negotiations at best a piecemeal affair. Whatever may have been the selfish corporate interests of the Ohio Company in 1752, one thing seemed clearly only a matter of time, and that was war with France over the possession of the western country. If British colonials were to hold the frontier, forts must be erected at once at strategic points, and the head of the Ohio was possibly the most important point of all. Perhaps the most tangible result of the conference, and subsequent Winchester conferences, was the securing of permission from some of the Ohio Indians to fortify Logstown. But the loss of two precious years, 1750–1751, had kept the Ohio Company from getting a tenable hold in the Ohio Valley.

Building log forts was not a new idea in colonial defense, but these log strongholds more and more came to be identified with expansion on the raw outer edges of the American frontier. Before 1763 the western landscape from northern New York to Georgia was to be dotted with a cordon of semimilitary posts which varied all the way from strong blockhouses to heavily fortified posts like Fort William Henry in New York. The first step of the Ohio Company toward the West was the building of Fort Cumberland on the Potomac. Its next important move was the location of a trail as direct as possible to the Monongahela in the neighborhood of the Ohio. During 1751–1752 Christopher Gist, Thomas Cresap and the famous Delaware chief, Nemacolin, were engaged in exploring and blazing this new route. In 1752, a storehouse was located near the mouth of Red Stone Creek, and plans were underway to begin construction of the fort at the forks of the rivers. Final agreement for the building of this important central post was given by a committee of the Company in July, 1753. Immediate arrangements were to be made by Gist, William Trent and Thomas Cresap. This was to be no orthodox trading post. George Mason ordered twenty swivel guns and other arms from John Hanbury, a Company partner in London. Indecision about the precise location of the fort delayed the work of building it. Several people, including Washington, took a hand at locating this post, but it was not until the fall of Fort Duquesne five years later that a satisfactory location was made. Before William Trent could get underway with construction, pressure from the French became so great that building the fort had become a matter of emergency.

The French themselves, experienced hands at frontier defense, had already erected a series of posts across the westernmost part of their backwoods domain. In order to prepare further for an impending crisis they

tightened their pincers by building a series of forts from Lake Erie southward. The moving spirit in this renewed French attempt to stabilize their
claim to the west was the Marquis Ange de Duquesne. Under the direction of Michel Péan and Pierre Paul Marin, forts were begun south of Lake
Erie at Presque Isle, Le Boeuf and Venango along the French Creek-
Allegheny approach to the Ohio. The latter fort was placed on the site
of the displaced John Fraser's trading post.

Signs of War

Tension had developed so rapidly along the line of French-British contact that it seemed impossible to complete the Ohio Company fort before
hostilities would break out. For the Virginians, peace and speed were
absolutely necessary if they were to establish a foothold. If the French
should strike before the fort could be finished and garrisoned, then the
Ohio Valley would be closed to further British activity. One means short
of war was left to Governor Dinwiddie, and that was a positive and authoritarian one involving little or no diplomacy. He sent twenty-one-year-old
George Washington with a party of guides, interpreters and hunters to
visit Logstown and the New French forts of Venango and Le Boeuf.

Washington left Will's Creek about mid-November, 1753. He had as
his guide Christopher Gist, who by that time had moved into the lower
Monongahela Valley. The party went to the forks of the Ohio, then to
Logstown to meet Half King, the Seneca sachem, and northward to
Venango. Arriving at Venango on December 4, Washington became acquainted with the famous Frenchman, Captain Phillipe Thomas Joncaire,
and the commissary, LaForce. He was to capture LaForce six months later
at the skirmish of the Great Meadows. From Venango he moved upstream
to deliver Governor Dinwiddie's message to Legardeur de St. Pierre, commandant at Le Boeuf. At the latter place he was received with great courtesy, but St. Pierre answered the governor's message only by saying that
he was under military orders from the Marquis Duquesne and that obviously both of them would have to consider Dinwiddie's charges of encroachment on British territory as a political matter which the two home
governments must solve between them. Washington was placed in a situation almost comical. Not only was he anxious about the reply to the note
which he bore, but he was concerned likewise about possible French conversations with his Indian companions, especially the fickle chief Half
King. Half King went at liquor with more zest than Washington thought
good, and as long as the French supply held out he seemed to be willing
to forget his grievances against both Joncaire and St. Pierre. It was with
the greatest difficulty that he was persuaded to leave and so permit the
young Virginian to be on his way.

Washington's visit to the French was of no value except to give the young officer a harassing experience in the woods and the waters where on at least two occasions he almost lost his life. Officially the visit to the French meant that Governor Dinwiddie was playing one last desperate card in a game of bluff.

Washington's attitude toward the western problem was one of the utmost urgency. Following his visit, the British colonials had not long to wait for a decision from the French. On April 17, 1754, a French force of approximately one thousand men marched on the unfinished Fort William Trent and forced its acting commander, Ensign Edward Ward, to surrender it. Delays caused by rivalry between Virginia and Pennsylvania, muddling by the Privy Council and the Board of Trade, the indifference of colonial councils and of the assemblies of Maryland and the Carolinas, plus the ambitions of selfish landed interests and the stumbling block of Indian refusal to permit settlement west of the watershed of the Appalachians—all had been disastrously time-consuming. The fort at the head of the Ohio was captured by the French before it was completed, and its fall marked the collapse of British influence for a considerable space of time in the rich Ohio Valley.

The focal point of French-English rivalry was along the Ohio-Allegheny-Lake Erie front, the pin point of contact being the forks of the Monongahela and Allegheny rivers. Whoever controlled that strategic position had a direct approach to the Indians and their rich trade from three directions. Elsewhere the points of contact, away from the Great Lakes, reached from Lydius (Fort Edward, fifteen miles above Saratoga, New York) to the Susquehanna, to the Upper James and Valley settlements in Virginia, to the Yadkin and Catawba valleys in North Carolina, and the Santee, Saluda and Wateree settlements in middle South Carolina, and southward to Augusta, Georgia, on the Savannah River.

In the southwest the Indian trade had flourished over a long period of years. Since the latter half of the seventeenth century, skin and fur traders had penetrated the Indian country as far inland as the Tennessee and Alabama rivers; and each year they had shipped considerable quantities of peltry abroad from the port of Charleston. All along this line there was possibility of a French-inspired Indian attack. From Mobile, New Orleans and Natchez the French could reach the southern Choctaws, Chickasaws, Creeks, Cherokees and Catawbas. Along the northeastern frontier from the mouth of the St. Lawrence to the Ohio, the French could readily make a penetration at several strategic points, and then entrench themselves in the back country whence they could threaten English settlements all along the colonial line.

Washington had in a limited way borne home with him from Le Boeuf and Venango a sense of this advantageous enemy strategy. He was passionately alert to the need for immediate action, and he found in the irascible but energetic Dinwiddie the force necessary to begin an aggressive movement. Neither the frontier traders nor the chief administrative officials of Pennsylvania, Maryland and Virginia had difficulty in appraising the French threat, but the colonial assemblies and the people were indifferent to the predicament in the West.

Before any intelligent analysis of the outbreak of the French and Indian War on the frontier can be made, it is necessary to restate a few premises. English settlement on the frontier was moving westward rather rapidly once it was begun, and there was a definite division between the types of population which inhabited the coastal areas and that which poured into the hinterland. This difference was to be measured in conflicting points of view, local political interest, and experience in the colonies. The last three decades of colonial expansion westward had involved a strong element of speculation, and many of the colonial governors even had interested themselves in these ventures. Dinwiddie, for instance, had a strong personal concern in the Ohio Company. Between the governors and the general assemblies there was conflict over matters of taxation, control, and almost all other colonial policies. In Pennsylvania and Maryland, this conflict was greatest between the people as represented in the assemblies and the tax-free proprietary interests. Religious differences appeared, especially where there were concentrations of Quakers who had particular notions about dealing with the Indians, and, certainly in the early stages of international friction, who objected to war with the French and Indians no matter how seriously the frontier was threatened. There was no strong unity among the colonies, and all of them lacked fiscal systems which would permit proper support of militia, and, most important of all, militia action beyond the boundaries of the colonies themselves. In the case of Maryland, Virginia and Pennsylvania there was a vagueness about western boundary lines which brought conflict when there should have been co-operation in the construction of western forts. There were no trained military officers and no local militia units which could be thrown into immediate action. Because the people were uninformed, they were selfish and indifferent to the frontier struggle except where it affected them directly.

Washington Assumes Command

All these problems faced Governor Dinwiddie in January, 1754, when Major Washington made his report on his journey to the French forts. It was clear to both Dinwiddie and Washington that Virginia had to take positive action. The colonial assembly had been in recess since December

19 and would not meet again until April. In the month of the spring thaw the French would surely take the posts on the Ohio, closing the frontier. Washington was commissioned in late January, 1754, to raise a militia company of a hundred men and begin conditioning them for campaigning against the French. In the meantime, Governor Dinwiddie made appeals to the governors of the Carolinas, Maryland, Pennsylvania and New York.

Washington found that recruiting a hundred men was a herculean task, and those who volunteered were usually undesirable soldiers. In Williamsburg the assembly was as lackadaisical as were Washington's troops at Alexandria; in the end the governor received no assistance worthy of consideration. Dinwiddie was forced to use such resources and authority as he already possessed to raise an army and to commission its officers. Joshua Fry was made colonel and twenty-two-year-old George Washington was lieutenant colonel.

Washington's task as field officer was to reach the Ohio fort as quickly as possible. In another race with time he was delayed first by recruiting, but once he reached Winchester, Virginia, and began seeking supplies and transportation he faced the almost insuperable task of commandeering wagons and teams from indifferent and selfish owners. Because of these delays Washington lost the race to the Ohio, and his predictions of an early spring move by the French came true. His task now became one of trying to recapture the fort. He moved his army over the Little Crossing-Youghiogheny-Great Meadows-Red Stone trail, making a road as he went, and never being too sure that it would not wind up at a dead end on a cliff top. Added to the problems of recruiting, transportation, and supply was the more haunting one of how well would the Virginia troops fight, and how well would Washington himself behave under fire.

On the morning of May 28, 1754, this little army faced a small contingent of French at Great Meadows. The French leader Jumonville was killed, and LaForce (Washington's erstwhile host at Venango) was taken prisoner. Although the skirmish was a victory for the militia, it was at the same time an alarm to the French, and Washington's army could reasonably expect immediate retaliation. A strategic retreat was made to the site of the emergency Fort Necessity, where trenches were opened. The Virginians had not long to remain in suspense. On the drab rainy day and night of July 3–4, Washington was forced to withstand an assault, to surrender his fort and to move his men back to Winchester. His defeat bore all the marks of colonial befuddlement and mismanagement, and it seemed as if the French could overrun the English settlements at will.

By 1754 the struggle against the French and their Indian allies had ceased to be a thing of regional or local concern. Every colony that had a hinterland frontier was to be involved. On June 19, 1754, a conference of colonial delegates met in the City Hall at Albany to discuss common problems of union and to seek common support of the action against the French menace. Frontier problems had at least forced the colonies to recognize their lack of unity and had magnified the dangers which each of them might experience in the face of a powerful enemy. Recognition of this fact seems to have been common among the delegates. There were questions of how a union might be facilitated and how costs should be apportioned, an ever-present problem. Little tangible good came from the Albany Congress of 1754, however, other than bringing to the surface the tremendous number of crosscurrents which were hindering an effective unity of sections and the development of adequate frontier defense. Possibly the only specific accomplishment was the action taken to secure the appointment of regional Indian agents. The varied reactions of the colonial delegations were eloquent testimonies to the high degree of vulnerability of the British Empire in North America at the middle of the eighteenth century.

Because of the failures of the Albany Congress and its proposed plan of united action, there was but one stern reality for settlers and traders along the frontier. They had been driven from their hinterland cabins and their customers; they would know the meaning of hair-raising screams and uplifted tomahawks, and their family scalps would serve as tokens in an undeclared war with the French and Indians. In Pennsylvania and Virginia, settlers along the raw outer edge of the frontier were forced back to the safety of older Piedmont settlements behind the mountains. Along the mountain ridges a bloody chapter of frontier horror and destruction was being written. In the safety of the colonial seats of government, assemblies and governors disputed over taxation of proprietary grants while refusing to see the frontier conflict in its proper perspective. Possibly nothing could have been done by the French to check their savage allies in their excesses, even if less bloodthirsty men than Duquesne and the Marquis Vaudreuil had been in command. In inciting the Indians to attack the British, the French had no doubt overemphasized the idea of robbery and carnage.

The inborn bitterness which infected the Indian over the rivalry for possession of the western country was both deep and intense. From the standpoint of Indian psychology, their hatred was not necessarily partisan. They had no more to gain from the French than from the British. There were, however, two serious drawbacks connected with the British trade: first, the British colonials did not accompany their trade with a protective armed force; second, the expanding American colonial settlements promised eventual extinction of the skin- and fur-bearing animals by destroying the woods. Thus it was that the Indian, fundamentally, was faced with making one of two fortuitous choices between sides in a white man's struggle for domination along the Great Lakes and in the Ohio Valley. He wanted neither, except on his own economic and social terms.

When George Washington was forced out of the Pennsylvania woods in 1754, he left the Ohio Valley to the control of the French. There was little reason at the moment to believe that the colonies alone could rally their forces and embark upon a plan of concerted action. There would come a time of dire emergency and fright when the various colonial governments would be frightened into striking back, but that moment was not in 1754–1755. Impetus for a second invasion of the frontier had to come from England itself. No doubt the failure to develop a colonial militia was taking its toll, but military leadership was a responsibility of the home government.

Braddock

On March 12, 1755, two regiments of troops started for Virginia under the command of General Edward Braddock. Two additional regiments were to be raised in New England, and Pennsylvania and the southern colonies were to supply as many more. Braddock, who had seen service in the Jacobite rebellion and under the Prince of Orange on the Continent, was sent to America to give experienced leadership to the English and colonial troops. In the early weeks of his arrival in America he exhibited some capacity to bluff the several colonial governors attending the Alexandria, Virginia, conference into something like a plan of concerted action. Among the many aspects of his plan, he proposed an offensive campaign that would take the war to the French at three vital points. William Johnson of New York was made a major general and was instructed to organize a militia troop and the Indians of the Six Nations for an attack on Crown Point. Governor William Shirley and William Pepperrell of Massachusetts were to go by way of Fort Oswego to take Niagara. Braddock himself would strike at Fort Duquesne.

Fundamentally General Braddock lacked the tact and energy necessary for execution of his plans. He refused to understand the complexities of colonial politics and economics and depended upon the young and subservient men around him to agree with him and do his work. He failed to effect any real unity of effort among the colonies or to gain from them any competent amount of material support. In Pennsylvania, it was Benjamin Franklin and Governor Robert Morris who secured for him the use of 150 wagons and a quantity of wheat, and who were able to get work begun on the road west of Shippensburg. In Virginia, Governor Dinwiddie was able to secure a limited appropriation of paper money, to supply some militiamen, and to assist in the impressment of some inefficient wagon transportation.

Problems ahead of General Braddock were typical of the raw frontier. The first, and most unmanageable one, was that of inert distance. Uncertain information about the mileage to Fort Duquesne, and the inability of the unimaginative general thoroughly to grasp its meaning, made this factor a basic problem. There had been a remarkable amount of traveling to and from the neighborhood of the forks of the Ohio between 1748 and 1755, but there was still no definite dependable trail which avoided the more serious mountain barriers. From May to July, General Braddock was to struggle with precisely the same road and wilderness aggravations which had thwarted Washington only a year before. Some idea of traveling conditions can be gained from Braddock's statement:

> I wait now for the last convoy and shall, if I do not meet with further Disappointments, begin my march over the Alleghaney Mountains in about five days. The difficulties we have to meet with by the best Accounts are very great; the Distance from hence to the forts is an hundred and ten miles, a Road to be cut and made the whole way with infinite Toil and Labor, over rocky Mountains of an excessive Height and Steepness, and many stoney Creeks and Rivers to cross.

Braddock's worries were so similar to Washington's that the younger officer, eager to learn the military art, could check his experience against that of his superior officer as they crawled toward the Ohio. There was the same need for wagons and pack horses, the same failure of commissary officials and contractors to supply adequate materials. There were the same disciplinary problems with raw colonial troops who walked off in the night when they became dissatisfied. Woods and mountain barriers were unchanged, and it was no easier to build a road than before. Braddock lacked one support which Washington had, and that was an Indian ally as reliable as Half King who could serve as ears and eyes for his expedition. It was one hundred and ten miles to Duquesne from Fort Cumberland, and the army in much of the journey averaged little over two miles a day. Dragging heavy-draft Virginia and Pennsylvania wagons loaded with food supplies, ammunition and cannon over the new cut road was an exhausting task.

By July 8, however, the front ranks of the army of 1,500 men were within eight miles of Fort Duquesne. By predawn of July 9 it had looped around the mouth of Little Turtle Creek and crossed the ford of the Monongahela, and was pressing forward on the right-hand side of the stream. The terrain was more favorable to movement now, and there was space between the trees for passage of the wagons. Engineers were in front, marking trees which had to be removed. Amid the somewhat incautious group of officers, Washington was again riding over familiar ground.

Nearby was Fraser's Cabin which he and Gist had reached in a half-frozen state on their return from Venango and Le Boeuf. This time, it seemed the British would be able to drag their cannon into advantageous positions to pound the French fort at Duquesne into submission. Again the British flag would fly at the head of the Ohio.

This moment in early morning, July 9, 1755, is one of some dispute in frontier history. It would appear that General Braddock used no common sense at all. Once he had come so close to the French and Indian stronghold, it was inevitable that they would know of his position, and that they would use every element of surprise to stop him. From what happened, it would seem that no scouts were ahead of the army's advance to check on possible enemy activity. It was audacious indeed to cross an army over the Monongahela and to allow it to become bunched in a ravine with sheltered ridges rising on either side. The first warning that 300 French and Indians were upon the British troops came when engineer Harry Gordon in the forefront saw them break from cover. Almost at once there came a blood-curdling warwhoop, and the British troops were caught in a murderous cross fire which seemed to pour out of the mountainsides.

Braddock's command was startled; the ungodly savage screams unnerved both officers and soldiers. Carelessly, the wagon train was badly dispersed. The part under Colonel Thomas Gage was too close on the advance column for Braddock to straighten out his line without becoming entangled with his advancing transportation. Before the troops could be deployed, they had been forced to recoil on Gage's command, and the whole army was now in stunned, staggering confusion. Dunbar's unit, too far in the rear to support the surprised advance, proved not only worthless but in its flight for safety was downright demoralizing.

General Braddock and an unreasonably large number of his officers were either badly wounded or killed. Before midafternoon the British troops were in retreat. The invisible enemy kept to cover except when an occasional warrior rushed out to snatch a British scalp. Nightfall came with intense darkness, and the groans and screams of wounded men added to the eerie atmosphere of the withdrawal. Occasionally a horse stepped over a fallen soldier, or there came a cry for help from darkness as the army felt its way back to safety. Supplies were destroyed. Powder kegs were burst and their contents thrown in water, guns were spiked, barrels of precious flour were destroyed, and wagons wrecked. Colonial teamsters, including Daniel Boone and John Finley, cut their horses' traces and departed in wild flight.

What had been a fairly orderly army of 1,500 men now straggled back across the Youghiogheny in sore defeat. General Braddock was wounded, and four days later Washington buried his body in the middle of the road which he had so laboriously opened from Fort Cumberland to the Monongahela. The crusty British officer left behind him a gruesome story of disaster. Actually engaged in battle were 1,459 men, and of this number sixty-three officers and 914 men were either killed or wounded. Braddock's military defeat was complete. The loss of men and supplies was ruinous, but of perhaps greater importance was the loss of official papers which revealed the plans for the three-headed British attack on the French.

For Braddock's march on Duquesne was, as already noted, only one part of a general campaign. It had been planned that, 200 miles to the east, Governor William Shirley and William Pepperrell would attack Fort Niagara from Fort Oswego. Correctly, it was assumed that should Niagara fall into English hands the narrow girth of the French supply line to the Indian country would be cut, and the whole Ohio Valley could be reopened to the English trade; but nothing came of the plan. William Johnson's campaign against Crown Point was not successful, although he did defeat and capture the French commander Dieskau at Fort Frederic on September 8, 1755. The French who escaped this battle fell back to Lake Champlain, and Johnson built Fort William Henry at the head of Lake George and restored and staffed Fort Edward south of that vicinity.

It is hardly the purpose here to make a study of frontier military tactics, but it is necessary to emphasize some of the factors in Braddock's defeat. He was stubborn and dictatorial. He failed to utilize the experience of men like Washington and others who knew firsthand of frontier conditions. His opinions of the Americans were influenced largely by his unfortunate experience in extracting assistance from them. Braddock was deprived of necessary Indian aid, and as a result he failed to establish an effective scouting service. His movements to the Ohio were too slow and too cumbersome to permit his advance on Fort Duquesne to have the slightest element of surprise. His knowledge of the route he traveled seems never to have projected more than five or ten miles ahead. In battle the English troops were not deployed properly to defend themselves against a wilderness attack. Part of this was faulty tactics, and part of it was due to inexcusable surprise so near the enemy's post of defense. But the devitalizing failure of transport and supply was clearly the responsibility and fault of the colonial governments and people.

In July, 1755, the French menace on the colonial frontier grew more intense. Frontier settlement could no longer go forward. Most of that which had reached the raw frontier had to be withdrawn. It was unsafe for Virginians to go far beyond Fort Cumberland; Pennsylvanians were stopped on the Juniata; settlers and traders north of that point were halted on the lower Mohawk and in the internal areas of New England. The

Ontario and St. Lawrence front was aflame with French resistance. The report of the Marquis de Vaudreuil to the French minister on August 8, 1756, illustrates how the frontier was besieged. The first half of this report is filled with accounts of murder and scalping of colonial troops and settlers. "A Party commanded by M. de Céléron had a fight near Cresap's fort in the rear of Cumberland," wrote Vaudreuil. "They killed eight Englishmen, whose scalps the Indians were unable to take, as they found themselves, in the dusk of evening, within musketfire of the fort. We had two savages killed and one wounded." Again, he wrote, "Finally, Mr. Dumas writes me that for more than a week he had done nothing but take in scalps; that no English party comes out without losing men, and that it was impossible for him to report exactly all the raids made by our savages."

War with France might be only imminent so far as the American colonies were concerned, but for the backwoodsmen it was already a reality. Immediate steps had to be taken, following Braddock's defeat, to provide protection for a long exposed line from the upper St. Lawrence Valley to the Altamaha in Georgia. The only possible defense under such dire circumstances was resort to the small frontier log fort. Therefore, a string of posts was established all the way across the exposed area. Some of the more famous of these were forts Edward, Stanwix, Bull, Cumberland, Cresap's, Will's Valley, Loudon, Ligonier, Chiswell, Byrd and Long Island. The Virginia chain of forts was perhaps the most concentrated line of defense in the colonies. In the summer of 1756 the general assembly was sufficiently aroused to support this plan, and the task of building and protecting them was up to Washington and his backwoods army, as we shall see. It was in the construction and defense of these frontier posts that most American colonials got their first taste of military defense under their own direction and by methods of warfare proper for the terrain. Washington's highly irregular army was staffed by men from the ranks; their clothes were those of the furrow and the trail; and their weapons were their own trusty rifles and knives. Their mode of attack was based firmly upon the frontier admonition of "Every man to his own tree, and the devil take the hindermost."

THE FRONTIER AT WAR

*The three most powerful of Spain's rivals waged many a long war
with one another to decide which should grasp the sceptre that
had slipped from Spanish hands. The fleets of Holland fought with
a stubborn obstinacy to wrest from England her naval supremacy;
but they failed, and in the end the greater portion of the Dutch
domains fell to their foes. The French likewise began a course of
conquest and colonization at the same time the English did, and
after a couple of centuries of rivalry, ending in prolonged warfare,
they also succumbed. The close of the most important colonial
contest ever waged left the French without a foot of soil on the
North American mainland; while their victorious foes had not only
obtained the lead in the race for supremacy on that continent, but
had also won the command of the ocean. They thenceforth found
themselves free to work their will in all seagirt lands, unchecked
by hostile European influence.*

—THEODORE ROOSEVELT, *The Winning of the West*

CHAPTER III

IN the struggle for dominance in North America it was said whimsically that the "French were cowards and the British fools." Whether or not either contention was remotely true is open to question. The French had been victorious, but their future at Fort Duquesne depended upon exceptionally good luck, continued British muddling, and continuing strong Indian support. Johnson, Shirley and Pepperrell had not suffered defeat at Crown Point and Niagara in the same sense that Braddock did at Duquesne, but their campaigns were almost futile.

Summing up the situation, at the end of 1755 the credits in the undeclared French and Indian War in America definitely favored the French. The Indian trade was largely closed to the English, and all the major frontier forts with the exception of Oswego were under French control. A majority of the western Indians were allied with France and were ready to do its bidding. The American settlers on the extended settlement line deep in the western country were in an exposed and defenseless position. Since

55

transportation facilities into the hinterland were undeveloped, military supplies in adequate amounts could not be transported without great effort. Settlers who had pushed inland with Christopher Gist to the upper Monongahela were forced back. The three western Virginia counties of Augusta, Hampshire and Frederick had gangling settlement frontiers which were exposed throughout. Gaps through the mountains west of Staunton and the James River valley were dangerous entry ways. During the embattled months of 1755 and up to the fall of 1756, hostile Indians sneaked up to Virginia cabin doors, bringing war in its bloodiest form to women and children.

Southward from Virginia, the Carolina and Georgia frontiers were exposed to possible French and Indian attack from bases as far away as Mobile, Natchez and New Orleans. Although the actual forward settlements in these colonies were not so widely extended as in Virginia, they were just as vulnerable. Above the Potomac, the entire Pennsylvania frontier from the Susquehanna westward was exposed to the bloody raids from the west. New Yorkers as far east as Albany could take little comfort in the dependability of their frontier defenses, and even settlers in the Connecticut River valley were exposed to molestation.

Before discussing further the colonial crisis of 1756 to 1763, some facts should be reviewed. Perhaps at no time did the French have a force of sufficient size to overpower the American colonials—if the latter could be properly mobilized and directed. The fear of the French, and more especially of the Indians, which prevailed up and down the frontier after 1755 must be regarded from a general colonial point of view as largely psychological. There were adequate supplies in existence to feed an army during an extended campaign, and much equipment could be made available by effective organization. There was even a good leadership potential in the colonies which needed only some sensible legislation to bring it to the surface.

Balanced against these colonial advantages were almost as many drawbacks, notably the lack of unity and the absence of a centralized and clearly defined Indian policy. Not until 1756 and 1757 were the northern and southern Indian agencies organized under the administrations of William Johnson and Edmund Atkins. In 1754 the Albany Congress had revealed the first of these fundamental weaknesses when it indicated that Parliament should enact unification legislation to reduce the possibilities of secession and nullification, if nothing more. There was woeful lack of common purpose and effort in all colonial projects. Paper money proved a handicap not only to intercolonial relationships but within the colonies themselves as well. Conflict between the people and the proprietors in Maryland and Pennsylvania was a stumbling block; so were differences in religious and social points of view, especially the friction between the Pennsylvania Quakers and their neighbors. Sectional influences and the effects of distance between tidewater and frontier helped to create within nearly all the colonies a lack of concern with border affairs. Rivalry between northern and southern colonies and constant bickering between colonial governors and general assemblies blocked intelligent support of a forthright border military campaign. The failure of the British government to develop a colonial army, officered by men holding rank equal to those of home troops, was now being realized by the Empire. Absence of a clear-cut military policy between colonies and the home government had caused Americans to leave almost the entire responsibility for frontier defense up to London. Colonial militia laws obviously were inadequate for mounting a campaign against an enemy who had to be dealt with beyond boundaries of both county and colony. Short-term enlistments and the slipshod practice of hiring substitutes made impossible any continuity in military organization. There was lack of experienced colonial officers who had demonstrated enough leadership to prepare and lead an army in an international war. The lack of both propaganda and news created and spread a sense of fear of the impending crisis. Finally, the age-old combination of apathy, rascality, selfishness and ignorance played their parts.

In Search of a Leader

These were some of the disheartening facts which faced the British in North America after Colonel Thomas Dunbar withdrew the shattered army from the western Pennsylvania woods in the summer of 1755. This chapter of Pennsylvania and Virginia frontier history might have been entirely different if Dunbar had reorganized Braddock's forces and then shown enough courage and leadership capacity to make a stand against the enemy; instead he went into winter quarters within the safety of Philadelphia with still four months of fighting weather ahead of him. The woods along the Monongahela and the Youghiogheny were littered with the valuable supplies, which were destroyed, but even more disturbing was the fact that the colonials were left to shift for themselves.

William Shirley of Massachusetts succeeded Braddock as commander of British troops in America. This was a fortunate choice because the new commander could at least unify the New England colonies, and he had the energy and courage for the task. Shirley, unlike his predecessor, had some humility and considerable American military experience. In King George's War he had proved himself an able strategist. Tact, patience and knowledge of primitive warfare were qualities needed above all others in 1755.

To the south, chief military responsibilities fell largely upon the shoulders of local colonial authorities. Twenty-three-year-old George Washington was made commander of the Virginia troops on September 6, 1755, and entrusted with the task of defending the frontier. Washington's problems were again those which had beset his military career to date: poor personal health, desertions, short-term enlistments, refusal of militiamen to go beyond their counties to fight, quibbling between legislature and governor, and the inferior quality of men inveigled into the Virginia militiamen. The common need for an efficient frontier patrol in Virginia, Maryland, Pennsylvania and New York was actually a common one, and was purely one of defense until a better coordinated plan of attack could be organized. There was, as noted in Chapter 2, an imminent need for defense posts placed at easily communicable intervals all the way from the Savannah and Tennessee rivers to the southern tip of Lake Champlain. In Virginia alone, approximately eighty-one of these forts or stations were erected. Fortunately for the backwoodsmen the legislature had become frightened enough, following Braddock's defeat, to grant £40,000 for support of Washington. Governor Morris of Pennsylvania was just as concerned with the exposure of the Pennsylvania frontier beyond the Susquehanna, but in persuading his Quaker-dominated assembly to make the necessary appropriations he was not so successful as Governor Dinwiddie.

Despite failures of the governors to secure colonial aid for forthright campaigning according to an overall plan of strategy, the building of forts progressed. This mode of frontier defense was to become common throughout American backwoods history. The term "fort" as used here, however, is a general one which does not properly connote the wide variations in the designs of the frontier strongholds. Important posts like forts Cumberland, Oswego, William Henry, Edward, Niagara, Frontenac, and Crown Point were designed after Old World fortifications. They were located at highly strategic points and were intended to be semipermanent. There were living quarters for a garrison, commissary facilities and ammunition chambers. Outlying walls were sometimes made of brick or stone, the ramparts and batteries were of earth and log, and the approaches were barricaded with pointed stakes. The second, and perhaps more common, type of fortification was the backwoods log fort. They varied in size and shape but were much alike in organization and purpose. Their puncheon or picket walls made of upright logs were imbedded deeply enough in the ground to prevent their being pried out of place. The tops of these were sharpened so as to impale anyone attempting to scale them. At the corners were heavy log block houses with overhanging second stories from which to guard the walls. The courtyard served as stock pen, and cabins arranged around the walls provided living quarters. The small stations or blockhouses were less formal in their structure. These primary strongholds were nothing more than loghouses with somewhat thicker walls which enabled the occupants effectively to resist light gunfire. Their heavily barred doors and second-story vantage points made them efficient barriers against lightly armed and small war parties. Perhaps the simplest and most effective weapon that could be used against these stations was fire. On the whole the frontier fort was adequately protective except where artillery was used. In the wagon trains of the British forces were the heavy guns necessary to destroy the French forts, but it was not until the later years of the war that they were used with any marked degree of success.

A Costly Year

From the Tennessee River to Louisburg the fighting months of 1756 began with sharp conflict with French military power again in the ascendant. Along the Allegheny frontier, the old story of bloodshed and pillage was being written in new and more hideous chapters. Struggling with interminable administrative details, young Colonel Washington wrote Governor Dinwiddie that if dying by inches would relieve the suffering of the people along the valley frontier he would make the sacrifice. With first-hand knowledge of the struggle, he wrote the governor: "I see their situation, know their danger, and participate in their sufferings . . . In short, I see inevitable destruction in so clear a light, that, unless vigorous measures are taken by the assembly, and speedy assistance sent from below, the poor inhabitants that are now in forts, must unavoidably fall, while the remainder of the country are flying before the foe." From the settlers came stories of horror. Families were murdered and kidnapped. Infants had their brains smashed out against trees and posts, sickly children were put to the knife, women and girls were abused, the bodies of fallen men were mutilated and their scalps taken, houses and barns were left in flames. No one in any of the outlying settlements knew when an innocent child going to a spring for water, or to drive up a milk cow, would come screaming to the fort with a trail of Indians in hot pursuit. One example of Indian hostility and bloodthirstiness was the manner in which the inhabitants of Silvert's Fort in Virginia were treated. Forty of its fifty occupants were lined up in two rows about ten feet apart and were cut down with tomahawks. For the Virginia and Pennsylvania frontier, 1756 was a year of blood.

Along the coast and across the sea the war had become enmeshed in political snarls. Colonial assemblies still argued with royal governors about taxation and neglected the urgent military problems of recruiting and supply. Since political control and influence were predominantly coastal, the new settlements of the backwoods were all but helpless to impress their desperate needs upon the lawmakers. It might have been more to the frontier's advantage had a less militant and aggressive governor than Dinwiddie been in Williamsburg, and this might also be said of Governors Dobbs of North Carolina, Sharpe of Maryland, and Morris of Pennsylvania.

In New York and the New England states the administration of military affairs had hit an unfortunate snag. There was enmity between William Johnson and Governor William Shirley. Shirley enjoyed the confidence of the New Englanders; he had given his colony possibly the most common-sense administration in the history of the royal governorship. In military affairs he demonstrated the same intelligence, even though he and William Pepperrell had failed to achieve their specific objective in the Niagara campaign of 1755. Possibly if he had been given time and support, Shirley could have brought the war along the St. Lawrence and Lake Ontario to a fairly early climax. This, however, was not to be. He had powerful enemies in high places, including William Johnson, Lieutenant-Governor De Lancey, Peter Wraxall, Goldbrowes Banyar, Thomas Pownall, Daniel Claus, and Benjamin Franklin. In the face of this opposition, Shirley was relieved of his command of colonial troops on March 17, 1756, when John Campbell, Earl of Loudoun, assumed responsibility for colonial military affairs. The Earl of Loudoun was poorly equipped from the standpoint of both temperament and experience to undertake the vast organizational task necessary to defeat the French.

But before describing the campaign further from the colonial point of view, we must examine what was happening among the French, in Britain's domestic politics, and in the field of eighteenth-century international relations. The French were in a strong position in North America at the beginning of 1756, having even overcome the defeat suffered in the battle of Lake George, which 1,700 French soldiers had lost to William Johnson's 3,500 recruits. From the strategic center of Fort Duquesne they exercised an enormous influence over the Ohio Valley Indians. So well placed were they that they could actually order at will Indian attacks on the thin faltering line of English frontier settlements. Perhaps even more important was the ultimate threat—that they would strike at the stronghold of the old and established settlements beyond the Blue Ridges and the Susquehanna. Niagara, Crown Point, Frontenac, Montreal, Quebec, and Louisburg stood as bastions of French power. On September 1, 1755, the English force was strung out between Fort Edward, just south of the big bend of the Hudson and the southernmost tip of Lake George. On September 8, battle was joined on the future site of Fort William Henry. After hard fighting the British were able to stand off the French and to capture Baron Dieskau, commander of all the French forces in North America. The threat to Crown Point had been deterred, but at considerable cost in men and the loss of the commanding general. This setback, however, was soon overcome by the appointment of the Marquis de Montcalm, who brought to America as his associates in command the capable officers Francois de Lévis-Leran and Bourlamaque. In the landing of large numbers of French regulars along the St. Lawrence, the French officers could take real satisfaction; their ships had successfully dodged the British navy to deliver men and matériel without mishap.

There were to be other reasons for rejoicing by the French. On August 14, 1756, Montcalm's forces captured Fort Oswego and shipped their British prisoners away to Montreal. The French troops who had come to America with their young commander proved to be good fighters, and they tightened the French hold along the St. Lawrence-Great Lakes-Ohio frontier. Montcalm's victory also helped to complete consolidation of the Indian allies.

A British colonial pessimist at this point might easily have decided that French conquest of all America was only a matter of time. From the colonial standpoint the picture was indeed gloomy. It was impossible for the Earl of Loudoun to plan an overall campaign which would require free movement of troops from one section to another. Except for North Carolina, the southern colonies were unwilling to assist in a concerted campaign up the Mohawk to deliver a blow against the French at some vulnerable spot near the source of their military activity.

For the British officers, the French and Indian War presented an interesting problem in military tactics. The colonial frontier had a wide perimeter which was vulnerable at almost every point. By pushing hard, the French could have placed themselves astride the British line of supply and defense and could have divided the colonies. At the same time the French had to keep their line well protected to prevent the British from breaking their defense and completely destroying *their* line of communication and supply. Tactically, all colonial campaigns had to be planned from inside a difficult convex land area so that they would strike outward. Complete success required simultaneous blows at a series of points. Any attempt to deliver one overwhelming blow was out of the question so long as dependence had to be put on colonial troops. Necessarily this situation produced hot arguments among officials who attempted to plan a mode of attack. Loudoun, with considerable wisdom, wished to check the French activities as near the eastern head of the perimeter as possible by taking Quebec.

A Faltering Ministry

At home, in England, our gloomy critic could have found little in the government's action to encourage him. The Newcastle ministry in power represented about all the faults that were then troubling the colonial system. If neglect, corruption and indifference in the handling of the colonies were not the precise reasons for failure, at least a badly defective understanding and administration of colonial affairs must be charged against the ministry. Possibly the most damaging criticism that can be leveled at the home government was its failure to pursue a policy which would unify the colonies for their own protection. In 1756, disunity was still one of the most threatening problems in North America.

Fortunately the Newcastle ministry was not without able critics. William Pitt, an eloquent young man with demagogic tendencies, raised many unpleasant issues, among them the military and naval failures against the French. In 1756 Pitt was to have a brief opportunity to help plan British colonial and foreign policy, but his initial services in the ministry were of short duration. However, after repeated blundering efforts by George II and Newcastle to solve Britain's political and military problems, William Pitt was again taken into the ministry and in 1757 was entrusted with power to plan and conduct an aggressive war.

England faced a great national emergency not only in North America but on the continent of Europe as well. At sea Boscawen and Hawke had failed to halt French naval passage to and from Canada. Typhoid fever breeding in filthy water casks had played havoc with the striking power of the fleet, and delay caused by the ravaging disease allowed the French an opportunity to reinforce Canada without serious interruption. Admiral Sir George Byng had disgraced the navy at Minorca and was to be shot for cowardice. On land, in North America, things had gone from bad to worse. The French had captured Oswego and had control of Lake Ontario, and the cordon was about to be drawn tighter about the British all along their frontier. The Lake Champlain–Lake George passageway pointing toward the heart of New York was open except for Fort William Henry and Fort Edward, and there was even a question how well they might resist a strong assault from Frontenac and Crown Point.

Pitt saw that positive administration and planning were perhaps even more badly needed than were troops and arms. Pitt had listened to the mutterings of the common people; he knew the troubles of the colonials, and he was one Englishman who could see over the wall of the Alleghenies. Mistakes of a century had to be corrected immediately. He proposed that the colonies be divided into two military districts: the southernmost one was to consist of Pennsylvania, Maryland, Virginia, the Carolinas, and

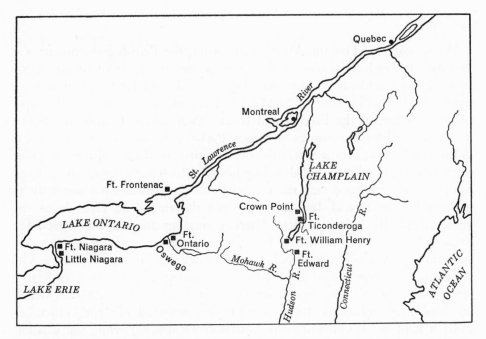

MILITARY POSTS ON THE ST. LAWRENCE–LAKE CHAMPLAIN FRONTIER, 1754–1763

Georgia; the other colonies made up the northern district. English troops were to be sent to North America, and the British fleet was to be placed in position to render effective blows against France. Loudoun was left in command for the time being, but soon even this arrangement was to be changed. The new policy of dealing with the Indians through agents was to be speeded up in order to lessen resentment from the tribes along the border.

A study of Pitt's ascendancy in British politics is a story of political success. He came to office at a time when an old political party was too senile to be effective, and its successor was yet unborn. The old Whig party had already caved in atop the ruins of the old Tory organization, and there was no new and decisive body to point a new political direction. But the British Empire was engaged in a world war, and there was desperate need for a man of action. How much intimate understanding Pitt had of the American frontier situation, or how sincere he was in his utterances is beside the point. Leaving political patronage to the old borough-monger, Newcastle, Pitt seized power in the ministry of war and used it to good advantage. He showed himself a master of strategy on a world scale; he knew the art of picking the right men for the right places; he was eloquent enough to capture the support of the masses; and he was a good enough administrator to back his political success with good planning and support.

World War

While war raged on the American frontier, the British government was heavily involved elsewhere. What had begun at the head of the Ohio in 1754 as an undeclared war over Indian trade and land was in time to spread as far afield as India, the West Indies and the continent of Europe. On the continent, the French and Indian War was known as the Seven Years' War. It had a complex of causes. Perhaps the most direct one, so far as England was concerned, was the need to protect the Electorate of Hanover, fatherland of the English ruling house, which brought about an English alliance with Frederick the Great. France was interested not only in striking Britain abroad, but by 1756 even threatened an invasion of the home island. In Austria, Maria Theresa, nursing an undying hatred for Frederick the Great because of his seizure of Silesia, was willing to make any concession which would help her win back her imperial holdings. The Austrian court was busily engaged in swallowing its pride and forgetting past animosities and forming an alliance with France. This alliance, which involved a reshuffling of claims, was a highly desirable one for France because it kept her traditional rival Austria from striking while she was engaged in war with Britain. Thus it was that the balance of power in Europe was both threatened and realigned.

In May, 1756, Britain formally declared war against France. Three months later the army of Frederick the Great was ready to march against Austria. Thus the Versailles agreement, so far as it involved England and its imperial holdings, was disrupted and a world war began.

In America the opening of so great an international struggle had twofold significance. First, France had an excellent army, and if French troops and supplies could be transported to Canada there was real danger of decisive consequences. Second, the international aspects of the war assured for the colonies the use in America of both British naval and military forces, equipped with British materials. Although this latter decision was a genuine encouragement to the colonials, a declared war was sure to intensify the struggle on the frontier.

This changed world political situation placed a new emphasis upon American participation in the war. Even in Pennsylvania where Quakers had so doggedly opposed war, there was a slackening of their resistance. By 1757, with the arrival of news of a serious colonial reverse at Fort William Henry, the Quaker experiment started so gloriously by William Penn was rapidly coming to an end. In three eastern counties there were twenty-six Quaker representatives in the assembly, while five western counties sent only ten. In the face of the crisis on the frontier and abroad, the Quakers could hardly expect to hold out against war. Because of this, the Friends in England prevailed upon their American brethren to step down and permit control of the government to fall into the hands of representatives who had no religious scruples against participation in war. Elsewhere, changes in colonial attitudes were brought about somewhat by the emergencies of the moment, but more so no doubt by the promise that the home government would bear the expenses of the war.

Early in 1757 little immediate hope was offered for the British colonials. The decisions made abroad were scarcely felt along the frontier. There was no evidence that the French were being thwarted at any point. They had on the North American continent 6,600 trained troops, to say nothing of the uncounted Indian allies who greatly extended France's striking power. The French, however, had the responsibility of holding tight the line which they had established across the British frontier. The threatening barrier of Fort William Henry had to be removed. So long as that fort remained effective, there was grave danger that a British thrust would be made against Crown Point and Ticonderoga. In fact, on January 17, 1758, Roger's Rangers had captured several Frenchmen on the shore line of Lake Champlain as high up as the vicinity between Crown Point and Ticonderoga.

Almost precisely a month later, a thrust was made against William Henry by Pierre Rigaud. Although this assault seriously battered Captain William Eyre's men, it failed to reduce the fort. Eyre's command, however, had won little more than a moral victory and had to fall back to recoup its strength.

During the spring and summer months, the British re-manned Fort William Henry and deposited a new store of supplies. The French knew well that until this important enemy defense position could be taken their whole chain of posts along the St. Lawrence-Champlain system was seriously exposed. On August 3, 1758, three thousand French troops and two thousand Indians were led against the British stronghold by the Marquis de Montcalm, and for six days the fight raged with heavy losses on both sides. The artillery in the fort failed, and the British and colonial troops were exhausted from lack of sleep and physical exertion. On August 9, the fort was surrendered with the honors of war which included an assurance against Indian retaliation. However, Montcalm failed to take proper precautions and the British wounded and captured were murdered in the most horrible manner. Packs were snatched from the backs of retreating soldiers. Prisoners were taken at will, and when the French undertook to recover them the prisoners were killed by their Indian captors.

Perhaps the American people along the frontier have never been more frustrated. News of the fall of Fort William Henry had a highly demoralizing effect. It seemed on the surface that nothing could stop the French.

The western waterways were now under their domination, and from a tactical viewpoint they could choose the places at which they would strike. So long as French naval forces could hold on to the strong point at Louisburg they were in a position to bring enormous pressure to bear on the hinterlands of the British colonies.

Some notion of the dismal prospect of building up a striking power in the southern colonies can be gained from the following facts. In September, 1757, Washington had only 700 troops from a population of approximately 200,000 people. Maryland, with 180,000 population, furnished only 200 men. Pennsylvanians were retreating from their frontier, with Fort Augusta the pivotal point of defense and Reading becoming virtually a place of refuge for retreating settlers. Southward, in the Carolinas, the spearhead of settlement was pushing up the Cape Fear and Yadkin Rivers, and westward toward Ninety-Six in the Congaree and Broad river valleys, but had not fanned out as yet against the western mountain ranges. In the Mohawk Valley the forward movement of population was badly blunted, and there was grave danger of devastating attack from the north and west.

The disorganization in the British colonies was to a great extent an important element of French success during the first years of conflict, and brought comfort no doubt to Governor Vaudreuil and Montcalm, even though 1757 was not entirely a year of rejoicing. To keep an army in the field and the Canadian civilian population happy, it was necessary to have food. It was impossible to support an army of almost seven thousand men on the then available supplies in Canada. Before a campaign could be launched, the supply ships had to come from France, and they could not arrive until June and July. Not only was there uncertainty about when ships might penetrate the northeastern fogs and reach port, but there was constant dread of attack from the British navy. Food shortages resulted quickly in the disaffection of the Indians and the growing unrest of the civilian population. So desperate was the need for bread that the Canadians even consumed their seed wheat. In the closing months of 1757 the bright French hopes in America were becoming clouded with doubt.

New Leadership

William Pitt's aggressive administration began to make its influence felt at last. The new economic policy of military supply lessened the old handicap of equipping and maintaining an army at the whim of an apathetic public. A more co-operative spirit among the colonial assemblies made it easier to secure recruits, and the hysterical fear of the frontiersman was beginning to penetrate other sections of the colonies. Quaker surrender in Pennsylvania opened the way for more effective resistance in the strategic center of the war.

Possibly the most important changes which occurred in this period were the replacing of the Earl of Loudoun with James Abercromby and the appointment of James Wolfe, Jeffrey Amherst and John Forbes to strategic commands. France, kept busy in Europe in 1758, was not prepared to engage in war on so wide a stage, especially when so much of the basic food supply for the far-extended armed services had to come from the mother country and be transported through waters patrolled by enemy ships. And yet it had become clear that the war would determine, once and for all, whether France or Britain would exercise an imperial power.

In the spring of 1758 John Forbes moved into Pennsylvania to take command of the troops supplied by the crown and the colonies. Forbes was a hardheaded man who exhibited real military leadership. It may be that his obstinate attitude kept him from securing more effective support from the colonial governments, but he at least demonstrated that he could cling to an objective. To recite his problems of manpower would be a boring repetition of Washington's, Braddock's, and Loudoun's experiences. No assembly was able to deliver more than half its promised quota. Maryland delivered none, while North Carolina could send only two hundred Crown troops. In his correspondence with William Pitt, John Forbes described his colonial troops as inferior. He believed "that a few of their (colonial forces) principle officers excepted, all the rest are an extream bad collection of broken innkeepers, Horse jockeys, & Indian traders, nor can it well be otherwise, as they are a gathering from the scum of the worst people in every country, who have wrought themselves up into a panick at the very name Indians."

Forbes' mission was to take Fort Duquesne. On top of the old arguments between governors and assemblies over the control of troops and the taxation of proprietary estates, Forbes had to contend with the new jealousy between Pennsylvania and Virginia over the route to be followed by the expedition to the Ohio. He could follow the Braddock route which only needed some patching and clearing of brush; or he could follow a direct route westward from Carlisle to Raystown and thence through the wilderness to Loyalhanna and the Ohio, a distance of 197 miles from Carlisle to present-day Pittsburgh.

Possibly there is no single reason why Forbes chose the unbroken wilderness route. It was more direct, and it led away from a heavily settled area which, up to the Susquehanna, was capable of supplying large quantities of necessary materials. Also, Forbes would have a good harbor behind him at Philadelphia. At least one historian has speculated that Forbes might have been superstitious about the old road from Fort Cumberland. Already the Virginia and Maryland farmers were antagonized by the two former campaigns, and to follow Braddock's road would reopen these old sores.

Two military roads into the frontier would be highly useful. The fact that the new road would have to cross the steep Laurel and Chestnut ridges but would avoid the hazardous crossings of the Youghiogheny and the Monongahela was perhaps one of the most important considerations.

From the Virginia point of view, the Forbes decision to cut a new road had been brought about by the undue influence of Pennsylvania. One of the bitterest opponents to Forbes' decision was Washington, who had just recovered from an extended illness and was ready to take the field again, but perhaps was not temperamentally in a condition to suffer such a blow. Aside from his Virginian partisanship, Washington was convinced in 1758, as he had been in 1754, that speed and proper timing were the important factors in attacking the French successfully. His thinking was conditioned by both his own notions of what was the best season for frontier warfare and the knowledge that colonial troops could hardly be kept in the field after the middle of November. No one knew how long it would take Forbes to cut his road and move his troops to Duquesne, but it was likely he could not succeed before the end of 1758, and the Virginia assembly had provided for the release of its troops on December first.

On August 1, the troops began to cut a road and move westward from Raystown. For the next four months they were to hack their way through the woods and construct a clumsy roadbed over a mountainous terrain. It is doubtful that Forbes himself believed he would reach his objective before spring, or that he had the slightest idea of the psychological effect his long approach had upon his waiting enemy. The French knew, of course, that he was coming in force, and that he was doing a creditable job of consolidating his defenses behind him. Moving slowly up the new road were thirteen companies of regular Highlanders, four companies of Royal Americans, a force of Carolinians, 2,000 Virginians, and 2,700 Pennsylvanians. Along with the white forces were bands of Catawba and Cherokee Indians.

By September 3, Colonel James Burd and his command had reached Loyalhanna, forty miles east of Duquesne, and had begun the construction of Fort Ligonier. Eleven days later, Major James Grant, Captain James Byrd (of Virginia) and Andrew Lewis moved forward and made the first and only important contact with the French and Indians, a short but disastrous encounter which forced the English back to Fort Ligonier.

But at Fort Duquesne itself the Indian allies had either already deserted the French or were leaving in force. The Indians were again listening to English entreaties. The fabulous Moravian missionary Christian Frederick Post had gone in July, and again in October, to confer with the chiefs of the upper Ohio. Although he was not an official agent, he represented a semiofficial interest and was most influential in persuading the Indians to

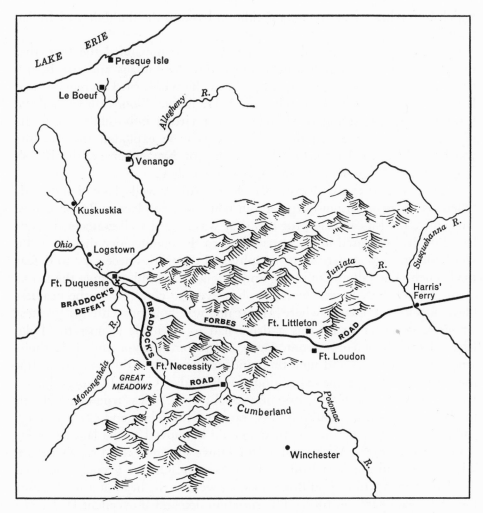

THE CAMPAIGN AGAINST THE FRENCH ON THE UPPER OHIO

desert the French. Post actually held council with the Indians just across the river from Fort Duquesne.

In addition to Post's work, an Indian council was held in October, 1758, at Easton, Pennsylvania, at which assurances were given of a reopening of the Pennsylvania trade. Further promises were made that Indian rights to lands west of the Allegheny Mountains were to be carefully observed. The signing of the Easton treaty on October 24 with the Six Nations and representatives of nine other tribes did vast harm to the French-Indian alliance. When a French representative came before the chiefs in Post's presence they spurned him and kicked his wampum belt from one to the other with disdain. There were no more Indian goods at Duquesne with which to further attract them, a condition basic to the durability of Indian friendship.

It was clear to Marchand de Ligneris, who commanded the fort, that the French could not hold out against both the Indians and the British troops. The food shortage which had beset the whole St. Lawrence-Great Lakes campaign was perhaps felt most at Duquesne. Floods threatened the fortresses; transportation of supplies was a virtual impossibility. On the night of November 23–24 the powder kegs were exploded and the fort was left a blackened ruin. On the morning of November 25, the British moved in to take control of the upper Ohio Valley.

Elsewhere in 1758 the British were successful. A well-planned and well-timed assault against Louisburg had put that strategic place in British hands. The entire British campaign for this year was indeed well-conceived. William Pitt demonstrated in his instructions to the commander that he had a workable grasp of American geography and the tactics necessary to defeat the French. The fall of Louisburg and Duquesne would crumple the flanks of the French line. It was necessary, however, to concentrate the heaviest blow against the center where Montcalm was holding with his greatest strength. In order to do this a drive had to be made against the Lake Champlain–Lake George front. James Abercromby commanded six thousand British regulars and nine thousand provincials on this campaign, but the spiritual leader of the expedition was Brigadier General George Howe who made and executed the organizational plans. As was true of nearly all the British expeditions, this one was fraught with delays and exasperations, and it was summer before the forces could be moved to the lake frontier.

On July 6, 1758, Abercromby and Howe engaged the French before Ticonderoga on the west bank of Lake George. On the French side, two excellent officers, Lévis and Bourlamaque, were at the head of a smaller but more seasoned garrison force. The situation demanded excellent leadership of the English and quick decision to capitalize on any French mistakes or weaknesses. Howe was capable of doing this, but Abercromby was definitely not. When a French bullet felled General Howe, the British forces were left virtually leaderless.

On the night of July 8, the army of superior numbers withdrew from the field after suffering almost sixteen hundred battle casualties. Even so heavy a loss of life and wounded was not nearly so serious to the British-Colonial cause as was a failure at the center of the overall attack. Abercromby had been misinformed as to the number of French troops present, and he had allowed his artillery to be left behind the lines in the attack of July 8. Had he ordered up his heavy guns the French no doubt would have been forced to retire to Lake Champlain. Abercromby withdrew to the head of Lake George, and this strategic campaign was bogged down until the next year, despite talk of undertaking a new assault against Ticonderoga. It was amply demonstrated that this central area was no place for a politically appointed officer. Here the services of a Wolfe, a Forbes or an Amherst were imperative.

Perhaps one of the most rugged campaigns in the New York area was that of Lieutenant Colonel John Bradstreet. Bradstreet was an erratic man of great energy and determination. He prepared his expedition on the lower Mohawk and then moved it westward to the scene of action. He too was beset by transportation and manpower problems. It is easy to imagine how little a frontier army liked pulling boats against a stiff current and passing them over treacherous rapids. In his reports, Bradstreet calls attention to desertions and the illnesses of his men. About three thousand bateaux men, provincial soldiers, bushrangers and regulars made up his force, and his objective was the important *entrepôt* of the Great Lakes–Ohio region—Cadaraqui, or Fort Frontenac. He proposed to reduce the fort and place the British astride the French life line at the head of the St. Lawrence.

Vaudreuil, the Canadian governor-general, knew of the approach of the British, but he was completely offguard and believed that they only intended refortifying Lake Oneida. Consequently Frontenac and the important Cadaraqui warehouses were left in an almost defenseless condition. By August 30 the French position was untenable, and the commandant de Noyan was forced to strike his colors. The British, although they had failed at Ticonderoga, had bottled up the entire St. Lawrence Valley by taking Louisburg at the mouth and Fort Frontenac at the head.

There remained the two important posts of Niagara and Quebec to be reduced. On July 25, 1759, after a heavy assault, Niagara was surrendered by the French commandant Captain Pouchot, and this last major stronghold on Lake Ontario and the Niagara River was in British hands. In the stinging siege of the fort the British suffered the loss of the brilliant John Prideaux, who had planned and executed the attack. In September, Jeffrey Amherst led the fight against the center of the French line of defense in what was little more than a mopping-up campaign against the old strongholds of Ticonderoga and Crown Point. By the time snow fell in the area, the British were in undisputed control of the Lake George–Lake Champlain area.

From February 17 to September 17, 1759, British forces under the command of James Wolfe pushed the war against France to the walls of Quebec in what was one of the most dramatic sieges on the North American continent. By bulldog determination, naval superiority, and good military tactics, Wolfe was able to assault the French from the river, drawing them out from their walls to fight on the Plains of Abraham. In his dying moments he saw his forces rushing headlong to victory. The heart of New France was pierced, and the remainder of the war was a matter of removing the broken French forces from other strongholds, the most important of which was Montreal.

Victory

With the end of approximately a decade of French-English conflict in North America, the British were victorious. There were, however, in victory certain significant factors which related immediately to the frontier. In the rapid advancement of the Indian trade and the frequent counciling with representatives of the tribes, a definite pattern of future frontier advancement was developed. A line of forts was established which pushed the frontier safety-belt forward more rapidly perhaps than would otherwise have been possible. The opening of military roads such as those of Braddock and Forbes and the use of the stream and portage connections across New York from the Mohawk to the Oswego Valley stepped up interest in several frontier areas.

In five years of fighting and frontier defense the colonials had gained considerable experience in the military art which would serve them in the future. It is, however, difficult to assess the real value of colonial troops in the conduct of the war. No doubt the truth lies somewhere between the caustic appraisal of John Forbes who regarded them as ex-innkeepers and horse jockeys and the purely subjective appraisal of a colonial dame who looks upon her prerevolutionary forebear as a powdered and bewigged hero, a highly individualistic daredevil who was daunted by nothing. The preponderance of evidence coming from many contemporary sources is frankly less than exultant about the general run of colonial soldiers. They were individualistic, but more often than not they allowed their individualism to be directed solely toward the protection of themselves and what they regarded as their rights. When their short terms of enlistment expired they went home—come what might in any impending attack against the enemy. They disliked cold weather and would not expose themselves to a hard winter siege even when their decision threatened so hard-won a victory as that of Duquesne.

The colonial militiamen followed the individualistic pattern of their general assemblies. This was especially true in Pennsylvania, Maryland, Virginia and the Carolinas. Many of the failures of the war were directly attributable to the stubborn conflicts between legislators and governors. There is no doubt whatsoever that the French and Indian War would have been of short duration had the resources of manpower and matériel been properly directed. But the English home government also contributed to dilatoriness in the pursuit of war. Corruption in both political and military affairs in England up to 1757 was enough to defeat a nation. Selection of officers was made on the feeble basis of favoritism rather than ability. Consciousness of incompetence made for stubbornness in accepting intelligent suggestions. The haughty manner of royal officials provoked a timidity in the approach to solutions of difficulties on the part of the colonials. Few British regular officers prior to the Pitt regime were willing to take advice from better-informed colonials. In dealing with American assemblies and civil officials they lacked patience, and so they were never able to consolidate the colonies into a unit. While it is true that British colonial troops performed enormous feats of campaigning against the enemy, one of the main factors in victory was the weight of British naval and military organization which could be concerted against the enemy.

While British colonial militiamen were muddling through long haphazard campaigns, the French were not without their worries. Corruption, double-dealing, personal jealousies among officers in high places, and the lack of economic support free of dependence upon an uncertain supply line from home all contributed to their failure. France had made the fatal mistake of becoming involved in a world war in which she was forced to gamble her full strength and resources with no possibility of concentrating an overwhelming amount of power at any one place.

Indian Relations

The Indians on the frontier had watched the two great powers fight it out in the backwoods without clearly comprehending the ramifications of the white man's dispute. Indians were of necessity opportunists. They never forgot that their own interest dictated that they keep the white man away from their lands while they maintained friendly enough relations with the victor to permit future trade. The end of the war settled nothing for the Indians; it did not even give them a clear-cut notion of who had won.

The end of fighting in the French and Indian War in America actually brought about an anomalous situation for the Indians. Britain was victor, and there was the prospect that a vast extent of land would be transferred to British possession. In time, white men at a far distant treaty council and well away from the wampum strings of the Indians would trade in western lands without the aboriginal owners being aware of the transaction. If Britain now owned the territory by conquest, she might make whatever disposition of it she pleased. This exchange of international landlords, so far as the Indians could comprehend it, meant an end of their own possession of their country. Obviously the simple Indian in the western woods had no more knowledge of the international treaty involving American territory than he had of the true power of England. His only means of understanding the new power was his observation of the limited units of the frontier army which were stationed in the frontier forts. If the English had used strong and impressive forces in taking over the surrendered French posts, they would have delayed, if not prevented, the Indian uprising of 1764.

England's first duty in her new role on the American frontier was that of garrisoning certain of the existing forts and building others. In the Detroit area were Detroit, St. Joseph, Michilimackinac, Miami, and Ouiatenon. On the Mississippi there were forts at the mouth of the Iberville, the Ohio, and the Yazoo rivers. Eastward, the old posts of Le Boeuf, Venango, Niagara, Stanwix, Oswego, William Henry, Louisburg, Crown Point and Ticonderoga had to be occupied. Plans were made for two commanders, one for the southern and the other for the northern district.

Peace in the western woods was only a relative matter. France's military force had withdrawn, but the French trader and straggler remained. They still had the willing ear of some of the Indians, and the manner in which British military occupation of the western country took place invited trouble. Pressures for both Indian trade and lands by overzealous traders and speculators were quickly felt by the already suspicious Indians, and their animosity was easily aroused. It was easy for French die-hards to fight a rear guard action by spreading false rumors that there had been no actual defeat of the French—merely a temporary withdrawal which would permit them to come back and join forces with the Indians and drive the English out of the western woods. Much of the Indian attitude could be summed up in a Chippewa's statement. He said, "Although you have conquered the French you have not conquered us! We are not your slaves. These lakes, these woods, these mountains were left to us by our ancestors. They are our inheritance; and we will part with them to none."

British officials were aware of the bitterness which confronted them in the Ohio and Great Lakes region. As early as September, 1760, Major Robert Rogers and George Croghan were sent to occupy Detroit. On November 29, 1760, Major Rogers halted the advance of his green-clad forest rangers and waited for the surrender of Detroit by Captain François de Bellestre. From Detroit, plans were made to occupy the other French forts in the area. Rangers were sent to Miami and Ouiatenon, and an effort was made to garrison Michilimackinac.

While Major Rogers dealt with the military affairs of the surrender, George Croghan was engaged in discussion with the Indians. He sought to recover prisoners of war and return them to the east, to reopen trade channels, to oblige the Indians by offering the services of a gunsmith, and to make plans for a great council to be held in the spring to settle the major differences growing out of the war. Croghan and his fellows labored under one serious handicap. They did not have sufficient supplies to promote an even flow of trade, and the end of the war found the English thrust so far onto the frontier that transportation facilities necessary to carry goods to the troubled spots were merely projected. With the French gone and the English unprepared to deliver goods, it was difficult to put down any dissatisfaction which might arise among the four or five tribal groups on the far outskirts of the new British empire. At the same time the British showed little inclination to continue their recent practice of supplying gifts to the Indians in exchange for their friendship and opposition to the French.

On top of these difficulties, the ever-present issue of stabilized prices arose. With French competition wiped out, the English traders were less willing to pay the highly competitive prices which had prevailed for the last fifteen years; also, the matter of distance of transportation greatly altered the price structure. Rum, which had been a treacherous commodity in the Indian trade, now caused some rather serious trouble. It had been used freely by the British during their intense competition with the French. When, in time of peace, the English realized the great liability of encouraging drunkenness among the Indians (and they had created a desire for drink) they found it extremely difficult to dry up the trade. Some of the temperance lectures delivered in the name of George III were among the most coy speeches in American history.

Finally, English policy as enunciated by Lord Jeffrey Amherst curbed the power of William Johnson to promise any changes for the future. Indian friendship now had to rest upon good intentions rather than expectation of lavish gifts. This policy might have been a sound one on the part of a frugal military commander burdened with all kinds of supply difficulties, but for Indians who were already suspicious it came as conclusive proof that the English really did mean to take all from the land they could possibly get and give as little in return as possible. Frugality might have paid in other circumstances, but at this time it did little to brighten the links in the chain of friendship which were so frequently emphasized in conversations with the Indians.

Lord Jeffrey little understood the Indian problem. Worse still, he had little or no respect for the Indian himself. At best his information came through secondary sources. He neither knew by firsthand information nor was he capable of understanding the complexities of relationships on the frontier. It must not be forgotten that although the French in Canada had capitulated, the Indian war itself had not actually ended. The evil bird of border discontent could still fly from Indian tribe to Indian tribe, and from French community to French community. Although Sir William Johnson, George Croghan and others had done a fine job of placating the Indians in the fall of 1760, they did not tell the tribes the whole truth about future dealings. Inevitably the truth would come out in day-to-day trading, and inevitably there would be discontent if not open conflict.

In the fall of 1762 the command at Detroit was changed. Pleasure-loving Captain Donald Campbell was sent westward to the Sault, and Major George Gladwyn, a veteran of Braddock's march, was placed in command at Detroit. On the surface the situation around the fort was quiet. Gladwyn had no intimation of the widespread dissatisfaction which was only awaiting a leader to band the malcontents together and direct their wrath at the British posts. Never could the Indians have found a more propitious moment to strike. The top military officers ignored rumors of trouble, and the curtailment of the Indian agents' activities partially closed many of the sources of information. Possibly a more astute policy would have uncovered the discontent and unmasked its leader, the Ottawa Pontiac.

Before discussing further the oncoming conflict with the Indians it seems wise to review briefly some important facts of Indian civilization and economy. Recurring with great frequency was the question of trading. Prices paid for British trade goods were scaled in terms of stated numbers of skins of animals of the various marketable types. There could be no fractional measurement of prices because any rise or decrease was not reflected in terms of fractions of skins. As trade expanded, there was naturally a decrease in the number of animals available. Just as British goods were worth more at Detroit than at Fort William Henry, so furs for the Indians were often worth more at the place of exchange than they were at the scene of their capture because of the ever-increasing distance involved. Hunting grounds in much of the area were not capable of maintaining a heavy crop of fur-bearing animals year after year, and so the Indians had to follow a practice of rotation from one ground to another after a given pattern of migration. Therefore, it was necessary for them not only to have full possession of their lands, but to have lands in abundance. So, when the bales of fur to be transported abroad mounted at port cities, the possibility of conflict between Indian and land speculator and settlers in the western country became just that much greater. The white man could not have furs in increasing amounts and the land too; nor could he assume simply because a particular hunting range was not being actively utilized that it was available for settlement.

Passing the War Belts

During the winter of 1762–1763, war belts were being handed around, especially among the Senecas, Hurons, Chippewas, Pottawattomies, Delawares, Shawnees, and Miamis. In the spring definite plans were being formulated to attack the British posts. By this time Pontiac had apparently gained leadership and was able to bring together a considerable number of the associated tribes. He first led a small Indian company into Detroit on May 1. Ten of his warriors were able to spy on the fortress and to secure definite information about its personnel, arrangements and strength. A plot was formulated by which Pontiac would again appear and would be admitted to the fort by Major Gladwyn; this time the Indians would be armed and ready for action.

But Pontiac, Indian-like, had failed in several fundamental parts of his plan. First, he did not have the full support of the assembled Indians at the River Ecorse council; second, he did not really comprehend so extensive and continuing an action in full detail. He did not really think through the possible alternative outcomes, since his plan extended no further than the making of the initial attack. Finally, the lapse of two days was entirely too much time for Pontiac's planned secret attack on Detroit to be kept quiet. Major Gladwyn was informed of the impending attack and was prepared for it when the Indians arrived. For a night and part of a day Gladwyn had to decide how he would receive his hostile visitors. He finally decided to display strength in such a way as to bluff them and reveal to them that their plot was known.

Exactly who Gladwyn's informant was is disputed. Romantics say that a young Indian maiden, Catherine, in love with the commandant, disclosed the secret. This matter of Gladwyn's informant is an example of the romantic turn of mind which has obscured facts of American history at many periods. In the first edition of Francis Parkman's *History of the Conspiracy of Pontiac*, the story is told of the beautiful Objiwa girl with whom Major Gladwyn had some romantic attachment and who informed the commandant. This account seems to rest upon the testimony of Jonathan Carver and was followed by others, including Lewis Cass, who repeated it for fact. The beautiful Indian maiden was in fact a haggard old woman, and there is no reliable information that she was the informant. Someone did inform Major Gladwyn, and he saw fit not to disclose who it was. With all the rumors and close observation of Indian temper and gossip among the French, it stands to reason that much of the secret would at least have suggested itself.

On May 7, 1763, the attack came. About three hundred Indians sauntered into the post, but they were surprised by a show of force and after some discussion withdrew. Two days later a desultory fight began in which some whites were killed and three or four captured. Gladwyn was left in a trying situation. His force was small, and his supplies severely limited. If he held out against the Indians, it would be almost by sheer will power. Perhaps the most damaging incident in the siege was the ill-timed and headstrong assault against the Indians before Detroit led by the ambitious Captain James Dalyell. With 247 men and against Major Gladwyn's judgment, Captain Dalyell attempted a surprise attack on July 31, 1763. The resulting defeat of "Bloody Run" was disastrous and only served to prolong the siege.

Outside Detroit, Indian victories came without too much struggle. Using fantastic ruses the Indians gained admission to several of the posts. At Sandusky a small band of Indians seized the commandant in council and captured his fort. A group of five boats and their crews were seized by Indians on the shore of Lake Erie not far from Detroit. Another boat party was captured at Sault Ste. Marie, and then Fort Joseph fell into savage hands. Miami fell on May 27, and on June 1 Ouiatenon was taken. The most dramatic capture of all was Michilimackinac by the Chippewas on June 2. Later that month Fort Edward Augustus was abandoned. To the east, attacks were made along the Monongahela River in May and June. A siege was laid against Fort Pitt, and skirmishes were made against the old French posts of Venango, Le Boeuf and Presque Isle.

The siege of Fort Pitt lacked the vigor of the one at Detroit, but the woods about the head of the Ohio were infested with warriors. Twenty-six miles east of Pittsburgh on August 5, 1763, Colonel Henry Bouquet's troops were surrounded by Delawares, Shawnees, Mingoes and Hurons. The story of white troops encircled by Indians was repeated for the third time in this vicinity. This time, however, an experienced hard-hitting officer had control. When Bouquet saw that he was in jeopardy, with Indians on all sides and under cover, he ordered his men to make a quick retreat, hold their fire until the Indians broke cover, and then open on them. This was a successful maneuver, and the battle of Bushy Run became one of the most famous in western Pennsylvania history. To all intents and purposes this victory cleared western Pennsylvania of Indians up to Fort Pitt. Supplies and personnel were brought up, and this section entered upon a new phase of expansion.

West of Fort Pitt, the siege of the frontier continued into the fall, but Pontiac's losses from his own ranks and the failure of the French assistance to arrive brought this longest of all Indian sieges to a halt. Indian losses were uncounted but heavy. Because they lost both a crop and a hunting season, there was marked dissatisfaction among the tribes.

More important, though, was the fact that the Indians had failed to stop white expansion into the west. Misunderstanding the white man's potential power, they brought to a climax for a time the inevitable struggle between the two civilizations. No doubt this Indian war did a great deal to relieve the white man's conscience of much of its guilt in taking lands and furs in the northwestern country. It mattered little in the long run that all forts except Pittsburgh, Detroit and Niagara had capitulated. This meant only a consolidation of power for the future, and possibly a tighter control on the Indian trade by the proscription of authorized trading posts.

As for Pontiac himself, he moved westward and finally reached St. Louis and Kaskaskia. He was killed under mysterious circumstances, and his career ended on a note of failure. However, he had the satisfaction, for whatever it was worth, of having made the most successful fight to date in Indian conflict with the white man.

In order to cement the British claim on the west, General Thomas Gage dispatched forces under Colonel Bouquet and the erratic John Bradstreet to restore some of the western posts and to bring peace to the Ohio–Great Lakes country. George Croghan went west in 1765 as a civilian agent among the Indians, with the tedious job of restoring commercial relation-ships with a people who had been highly wrought up for ten years. At Ouiatenon he negotiated successfully with Pontiac and apparently made peace with the great chieftain. The next summer Croghan went out to Fort Chartres on the Mississippi and there met the Indians of the region in a conference. At that time the British flag was raised over Chartres and Kaskaskia, and the British claim to the west was again given an element of tangibility. Of more practical importance, Croghan's mission helped to extend British trade to and even beyond the Mississippi.

A COLONIAL INTERLUDE

Thus we behold Kentucke, lately an howling wilderness, the habitation of savages and wild beasts, become a fruitful field; this region, so favourably distinguished by nature, now become the habitation of civilization, at a period unparalleled in history, in the midst of a raging war, and under all the disadvantages of emigration to a country so remote from the inhabited parts of the continent. Here, where the hand of violence shed the blood of the innocent; where the horrid yells of savages, and the groans of the distressed, founded in our ears, we now hear the praises and adorations of our Creator; where wretched wigwams stood, the miserable abodes of savages, we behold the foundations of cities laid, that, in all probability, will rival the glory of the greatest upon earth. And we view Kentucke situated on the fertile banks of the great Ohio, rising from obscurity to shine with splendor, equal to any other of the stars of the American hemisphere.

—Daniel Boone, *with a generous bit of help from* John Filson,
The Discovery, Settlement and Present State of Kentucke

FROM THE
*Pennsylvania Journal
and Weekly
Advertiser,* 1765

March 14.

PUBLIC NOTICE *is hereby given,*

THAT the subscriber, in consequence of repeated solicitations, hath been induced to lay out a town on the east side of Susquehannah, about four miles above Mr. John Harris's ferry, in Paxtang township, Lancaster county; the situation whereof has as many good qualities to recommend it (if not more) than any town hitherto erected in the back parts of Pennsylvania; being remarkably healthy, and on a high level bank, which commands a most delightful prospect for several miles along the river. Nor is it exceeded by many in respect of its convenience for trade, as the inhabitants along Susquehannah for a considerable distance above Wioming, and those upon Juniata, as far as Bedford, Franks town, &c. may with the greatest ease, at almost any season of the year, convey their produce to the place by water; and timber fit for building, &c. may be floated down the river at a very trifling expence. The town may be constantly supplied with a great variety of fish, among which are Salmon, Trout, Rock, and Perch, excellent of their kind, and with which the river thereabout is known to abound. The plan of the town is regular and beautiful; the lots and squares are very large, and the streets and alleys wide and commodious. The soil in and about the intended town is rich and fertile, fit for gardens and every kind of husbandry: in short, as to the situation in general, it is in every respect advantageous and inviting.

The subscriber will attend upon the spot on the second day of April next, at which time the lots will be disposed of by way of ballot, on the most reasonable terms. Sufficient time will be allowed for building, and due encouragement given by
JOHN COX, Junior.

N.B. A convenient lot for a brick yard, back of the town, will be granted to the settlers for 25 years. Also four lots, proper for erecting places of public worship, clear of ground rent forever, the 1 m.

CHAPTER IV

A Royal Blunder

THE fighting in the Seven Years' War was over in America by 1760, but peace could not be made until the struggle ended elsewhere in the world. In India, on the high seas and on the continent, Great Britain was generally successful and in an excellent position, therefore, to write into the Treaty of Paris (February 10, 1763) geographical provisions that brought into existence a far-flung British empire. In Section VII of the Paris treaty the new boundaries of Britain in America were stipulated as being "fixed irrevocably by a line drawn along the middle of the river, and the lakes Maurepas and Pontchartrain to the sea . . . and everything which he (the French monarch) possesses or ought to possess on the left bank of the Mississippi, except the town of New Orleans and the island on which it is situated, which shall remain to France. . . ." Provisions were made for the use of the Mississippi River, and freedom of that stream was guaranteed to British subjects. Section IV assured the transfer of Canada to Britain, and the French sugar islands were covered in an additional section. However, of greatest importance to the frontier movement in America was the huge block of territory added by the cession of Canada and in the Ohio and Mississippi valleys.

Possibly a hazy thought existed in the minds of certain Englishmen that there should be a restraining force west of the British colonies, for fear that the colonies might revolt; but after the experience of war it was not hard to prove that unity among the several colonies was indeed remote. Britain was without a rival westward to the Mississippi, and trader, speculator and settler were poised ready to cross the mountains at the earliest moment.

Away in London there was much talk around the coffee-house tables of the effects of the treaty with France. Some thought the sugar-producing islands of the West Indies would be more profitable than the fur trading territory of the West and Northwest. However, the arguments that made sense in the light of frontier history were those which contended that a greater demand for English goods would be assured by a growing white population in North America and a monopoly in Indian trade. The availability of so large an expanse of cheap lands would tend to keep the colonies agricultural and industrially noncompetitive. There would be no imaginary international boundaries drawn arbitrarily through the forest for ignorant frontiersmen to disobey and so cause border wars. Westward expansion would absorb an enormous amount of energy which might otherwise go into jealous fights against the Crown's administration and would check any crusading for independence.

Acceptance of the terms of the treaty placed England in the situation of having to recognize the forces of western expansion. As early as 1754, this principle had been enunciated by some of the colonial governors when they promised lands beyond the mountains to reluctant volunteers as payment for their military services in the colonial army. Approval of the charters of the Ohio and Loyal land companies a dozen years before was a similar admission that such expansion would occur.

Whatever the formal recognition of the forces of expansion might have been, the Crown revoked them abruptly in the "Royal Proclamation Concerning America," October 7, 1763. News had reached London on August 5 of Pontiac's conspiracy, and in September news of the fall of the forts arrived. This information hastened issuance of the proclamation on October 7 to reassure the Indians that the British did not expect to encroach upon their lands. Reviewing the territorial gains of the British government on the North American continent, the proclamation described the area involved in the treaty agreement with France and acknowledged the legitimate claims of men who fought in the colonial army to amounts of land varying from fifty acres for privates to five thousand acres for field officers. Reviewing briefly the question of British-Indian relations, the proclamation then clearly recognized Indian rights to lands west of the mountains, "As also," read the royal order, "all land and territories lying to the westward of the sources of the rivers which fall into the sea from the west and northwest aforesaid . . ."

Perhaps no other royal proclamation to date caused such consternation in America. Yet the policy enunciated by it in 1763 was one founded over a long period of American colonial history. In 1744 at the Treaty of Lancaster council, this question of encroachment on Indian lands west of the mountains had arisen, and the Indians were given assurance that such would not be the case. Again, in 1752 the question arose at the council of Logstown, and it was later revived at Winchester. When the Pennsylvania authorities met the Indians at Easton on October 8, 1758, on the eve of the fall of Fort Duquesne, the promise was repeated that no settlement would be made in the Ohio Valley. This was one of the major factors in weaning the Indians at the fork of the river away from the French. Frederick Post, though he skillfully parried the issue of future settlement policy, sensed what it would take to win the friendship of the Indians. On September 1, 1758, Post had assured the chiefs that the English did not intend to take their land from them; they wished only to drive the French away. In a meaningless speech, Post said further that he personally had not one foot of land and when he died he would not even take up the space on which he walked. Two months later the chief Ketinshund told Post, "That all the nations had jointly agreed to defend their hunting place at Allegheny, and suffer nobody to settle there; and as these Indians are very much inclined to the English interest, so he begged us very much to tell the Governor General, and all other people not to settle there. And if the English would draw back over the mountain, then they would get all the other nations into their interest; but if they staid and settled down there, all the nations would be against them; and he was afraid it would be a great war, and never come to peace again."

Repeatedly, the "Easton Principle" was restated to the Indians. In 1758, Colonel Henry Bouquet had assured the Indians at Fort Pitt that the English came to trade with them—not to take their lands. Subsequently George Croghan gave assurances that Indian lands would be left inviolate. A year later, General John Stanwix, commander of the forces of the southern division, repeated the promise. Later at Pittsburgh, General Monckton endorsed his predecessor's assurances. On his own authority in 1761 Colonel Bouquet refused to allow holders of grants from the Ohio Company to settle in the disputed area along the Ohio, and in December of that year the Board of Trade issued instructions to the colonial governors forbidding them or other officers "to pass any grant or grants to any person whatever of any lands within or adjacent to the territories occupied by the said Indians or the property possessions of which at any time has been reserved to or claimed by them." Although this order has one or two ambiguous phrases, it was clear in its intent.

Several major points of contention were involved in carrying out the terms of the royal proclamation. The colonies—especially Virginia, the Carolinas, Pennsylvania and Connecticut—had charters which granted them lands west of the mountains, and the proclamation ignored these. Failure of the Crown to develop an overall Indian policy and the leaving of this responsibility to the individual colonies prior to 1756 resulted at this time in overlapping agreements and a confusion which aroused suspicion of the Englishman's real intentions in his Indian dealings. The old boundary and trade rivalry between Virginia and Pennsylvania was a factor.

In London, the people who helped to formulate the policy expressed in the proclamation had failed to see the actual situation in America because of the moribund state of the Board of Trade and the narrow interest in the fur and Indian trade. One memorialist pretty well typified much of the uninformed thinking when he wrote, "The British colonies are to be regarded in no other light, but as subservient to the commerce of their mother country; the colonists are merely factors for the purpose of trade, and in all considerations concerning the colonies, this must be always the leading idea." Lord Egremont, Secretary of State, in a letter to Lord Shelburne, president of the Board of Trade, set forth almost identical ideas. He was afraid that the vastness of Canada and the West would permit people to escape into the backwoods beyond the control of the government. Of even greater importance was the possibility that the aggressive settler would outrun the reach of commerce and would set up factories and trading industries of his own.

The proclamation of 1763 was a complex document. It obviously reflected many strands of interests, but its general principle certainly rested upon a policy which had been established by colonial officials after a somewhat extensive period of dealing with the Indians. Long before, the Indian had seen that his economic system and that of the white man could not be harmonized. Clearing the forests, planting farms and building homesteads brought quick and permanent destruction to the primitive life of the woods. Wisely, the Indian councils in the 1740's saw that unless some miracle occurred it was only a matter of time until settlers from the East would follow in the footsteps of the trader down the Ohio and westward to destroy their hunting grounds. With a simple blind hope, they had re-

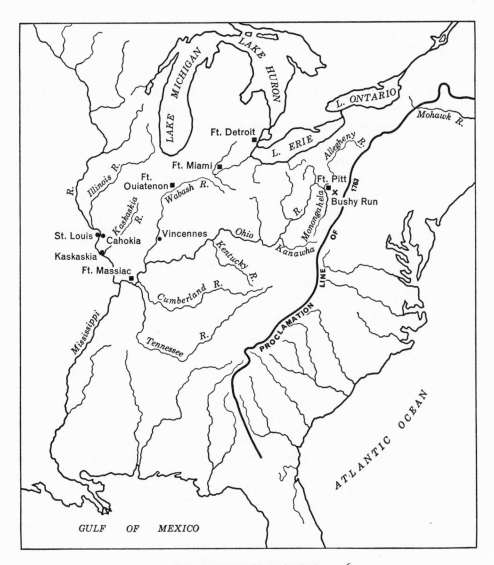

THE OHIO-MISSISSIPPI FRONTIER, 1763

peated at numerous councils with the whites their verbose and vague request that this would not happen. The Indian little understood that the voracious roll of white settlement westward was as nearly inevitable as any act of man could be. British and colonial officers entrusted with the problem of frontier consolidation and defense realized that peace was indeed uncertain in the western woods and that almost any gesture on the part of the white man toward the Indian's hunting ground would touch off a costly Indian war.

Western Policies

Admitting all the complexities of the Treaty of Paris and the emergency-inspired Royal Proclamation of October 7, 1763, there were some questions more confusing than all the others. What was the ultimate intention of the government in the matter of administering this western territory? Where was the boundary line precisely to be drawn? There was a consciousness that the pressure of population would be exerted against the western line. To lessen such pressure, Quebec province was created in the north, and provisions were made to form the two new southern provinces of East and West Florida. This organization of the new provinces was based on the fallacious assumption that the western movement could be diverted from its course.

Any plans regarding the western lands which might have been matured in connection with the proclamation were certainly never put in force. The issues involved in the administration of western lands were in fact the problems of controlling an expanding population and land frontier. At the outset it is necessary to remember that land and furs were important in colonial economics. Both were to be had in abundance west of the mountains. No one could hold the backwoods trader in check without an elaborate inspection and police system, or by simply destroying him; for he lived by the simple rule of going where the furs were to be had and paying little attention to formal rules. The same was true of the land scouts. The difficulty of making a little land claimant, who moved from one backwoods cabin and cornpatch to another, respect an intangible line on the ground was insuperable. The big land hunter and corporate speculator was favored by political manipulation and influence.

Again, it must be understood that at no place in the eastern coastal colonies was there an actual absorption of the land which remotely approached a system of intensive farming or urbanization. In time, Baltimore was to have a greater population than all the colonies had in 1750. But the lodestone of wealth was land. To think of the boom in western lands in the eighteenth century in modern monetary terms would be fallacious. Actually the pressure being exerted by individual settlers against the western frontier line was that of a relatively poor people who were seeking good land clear of the competition of the older communities; however, their ability to pay any considerable price for their holdings was virtually nonexistent. Speculation, however, wise or unwise, was characteristic of the eighteenth century. Elderly men in England could remember the exciting days of the South Sea Bubble. Some men possibly had invested in earlier flamboyant schemes and lost their fortunes, but not their insatiable desires for easy gain which might well be satisfied through western land. Expansion of British trade and sea power only added fuel to the wild flame of speculation. And the eighteenth century was not notable for moral scruples in gaining riches. The availability of so much unclaimed land on the America frontier, therefore, was an open sesame to both colonial and English adventurers. The hopeful land speculator was to play an important part in the administration of the frontier until the outbreak of the American Revolution, and even afterwards.

It is not the purpose of this study to enter upon a discussion of the many fiscal policies which were involved in colonial issues with the home government, even though financial responsibility for the frontier French and Indian War was a basic factor. In order to present anything like a clear picture of what occurred in frontier policy from 1760 to 1775, it is necessary to remember that development took place on at least three separate levels. First, there were Indian traders who plied their business from northern New York to Georgia and who of necessity penetrated the frontier wherever Indians, furs, and skins were to be found. Actually the proclamation of 1763 had little bearing on their movements. A large number of these individuals had lost heavily in the war, and those in Pennsylvania, Virginia and New York now called themselves the "Suffering Traders" in their efforts to secure government indemnity for their losses. Long and generous lists of goods destroyed were drawn up and application was made for land to compensate for these losses. Leaders in this effort were George Croghan, Robert Callendar, Joseph Galloway, William Johnson, William Trent, Baynton, Wharton, Morgan and Company, and others. These individuals exercised an enormous amount of influence on the frontier, and they could reach out into wider fields of political favoritism to help their cause along. William Franklin, governor of New Jersey, was interested, as was his father, Benjamin Franklin, and Thomas Lee of Virginia. The injured traders likewise found high-placed friends abroad in England.

"Suffering Traders" and Speculators

A second group of interested people were those who constituted an intricate association of land speculators represented in the Ohio, Loyal and numerous other speculative companies. These people had ready access to political influence but seem not to have been as able as their trader competitors in presenting their claims.

On a third level were the sixteen families who had followed Joist Hite into Virginia in 1732, those who came on the heels of Moravian missionaries, the hordes of Scotch and Irish, and others who crossed the Blue Ridges and the first tier of the Alleghenies in search of land. In the decades 1750–1770 the valleys all across the frontier filled up with these westward-moving people. An imaginary political boundary meant next to nothing to them, nor could any befuddled administrative policy stem the tide. To have curbed this movement would have required an active military force functioning from well-established posts all the way across the western country. Besides, a strict and orderly policy of land distribution would have been needed to force an absorption of available lands east of the mountains.

Speculators and "suffering traders" threatened to breach the policy of the proclamation by dealing directly with the Indians. William Johnson arranged a meeting with the Indians of the Six Nations at Fort Stanwix on Oneida Lake for October, 1768. At this conference, compensation for traders' goods was sought by securing from the Indians a grant of land on the east bank of the Ohio. On November 5, such a grant was made. It lay east of the Ohio, north of the Little Kanawha, west of the Laurel Mountains and the Monongahela River, and south of the established Pennsylvania line. Furthermore, William Johnson purchased in behalf of the Crown for a small sum the Six Nations' claim to land south of Kittanning, east of the Alleghenies, and north of the Tennessee River. This latter boundary was indeed a far-fetched one, and the Six Nations' claim to it was ephemeral at best. Johnson pretended to base his belief in the validity of the claim on the fact that he had heard an Indian say that the Six Nations owned land south to the Tennessee. Although Johnson's primary speculative interest was the grant which might be given the Indiana Company which he represented, he cleverly embraced the larger area so that the Crown in ratifying the larger purchase would automatically recognize the Indian grant to the Indiana Company to satisfy damages to the "suffering traders."

While Johnson was negotiating the northern Indian agreement, by which he was actually overstepping his administrative authority and making an agreement with the Indians for land which lay in the southern area, John Stuart, southern Indian agent, was negotiating the treaty of Hard Labor on October 14, 1768. At this latter treaty council in South Carolina, the Cherokee Indians agreed to give up the lands north of a line drawn from Mount Tryon to New River, and from that point along a straight line to the confluence of the Kanawha River with the Ohio. This line was not surveyed until 1769 because the treaty itself was not drafted until November—too late for surveying in the mountainous country. Thus in two treaties the English had quieted Indian claims to a block of land lying in present-day Virginia, West Virginia and western Pennsylvania.

From an administrative point of view, the fact that the western boundaries of the Carolinas, Georgia, Virginia and Pennsylvania had not been definitely determined was most confusing in protecting the lands of the Indians. In all of the negotiations the question of white intrusion was raised,

and efforts were made to protect the illegal outlying settlements by except-
ing them in the Indian treaties. In 1769 Lord Camden and Charles Yorke
added more confusion to the issue of Indian grants of territory by the unofficial opinion that lands bought of native tribes in India carried with them
valid titles. Attempts were made in America to apply this principle to the
purchase of western Indian lands, but when given a test in court the principle was declared inapplicable. Sovereignty rested with the colonies, and
it was they who had final jurisdiction over land grants.

The land company, as has been said before, offered a major approach
to the frontier. To begin with, the companies offered a unified front of
influential men who could manipulate politics in a manner that promised
favor. Also, they proposed to deal in areas of from 100,000 acres up to
the vast spread of new and independent colonies.

Possibly the most important land company in the period that followed
the Treaty of Paris was the Indiana Company, which in its original con-
ception was to be used to pay trader losses and to open the way for land
speculation in the upper Ohio Valley. William Trent and Samuel Wharton
were sent to London on behalf of the Indian traders to facilitate the granting of a charter. So long as Lord Shelburne remained secretary of state for
the southern department there was a chance that the Indian grant would
be officially recognized; but when a shuffle in secretaries brought Lord
Hillsborough to office, the company had an active and crafty opponent.
At a time when discouragement was greatest and it was necessary to get
around the various objections raised by Lord Hillsborough in the Board of
Trade and in the Privy Council, Trent and Wharton were able to enlist
the aid of the London banker, Thomas Walpole. For five years efforts were
made to secure the royal approval of a new proposition which included not
only the original grant proposed for the traders and colonial speculators,
but an added area which would interest English speculators of vast political influence. Both Trent and Wharton remained abroad for a considerable
time working with the problem, but opposition from rival companies and
individuals, as well as the confused state of colonial affairs, prevented actual
approval of the grant.

The new colony of Vandalia, projected by the Walpole group and
named in honor of Queen Charlotte, was to include the lands in the so-
called Cherokee grant which, according to Evans' map of 1773, included
the area east of an arbitrary line drawn from the mouth of the Scioto River
southward to Cumberland Gap, and then northeastward in an elliptical
line to the course of the Greenbrier River, thence to a point below Fort
Pitt on the Monongahela River and along the Ohio to the mouth of the
Kanawha. This latter boundary included most of the territory contained
in a second treaty with the Cherokees called the Lochaber Treaty. Meeting

at Lochaber, in western South Carolina, October 18, 1770, the treaty makers rearranged the western Virginia boundary so as to preserve Long Island in the Holston River for the Cherokees. In compensation for this concession the line across the southwestward boundary of the western grant was allowed to take a deeper slice from the western territory between the Holston and the mouth of the Kanawha.

As we have seen, considerable political manipulation was back of all the negotiation for land. In London, Trent, Wharton, Franklin, Walpole and many others strove mightily with the government for favors. High officials were willing to lend their influence for speculative opportunities in western lands. There is evidence that Lord Shelburne was influenced by "scare" information that there was danger of another expensive Indian war. Sir William Johnson had cleverly made it appear that the Indians had voluntarily negotiated the agreement to give up the lands claimed by the Vandalia company—and that it would endanger border peace to do otherwise. It was true that peace in the South with the Cherokees was endangered from time to time, but it was hardly true that the Indians' feelings would have been in any way hurt by failure of the Crown to accept their western lands.

Briefly, the importance of the long period of maneuver for favored positions in securing western lands lay, not in the actual accomplishments of the companies, but in the fact that the Indian claims east of the Ohio were being gradually challenged and absorbed. The proclamation line of 1763 was almost completely ignored in the end as settlement moved westward. Samuel Wharton estimated in 1768 that five thousand families had moved over the line, and that if they were not protected a general Indian war would result.

Surveyors

The land speculator was influential in erasing the old territorial lines and in undoing the work of the Indian agents. In the South, Stuart had reached an amicable agreement with respect to the territory northeast of a line from Chiswell's lead mine to the mouth of the Kanawha. Two years later this boundary was shifted southwestward in such a way as to give the Virginians a large slice of territory from below Long Island to the Kanawha; but when the Donelson line was run in 1771 by John Donelson between Virginia and the Cherokees, the speculators pushed it deeper into Indian territory and included the area southwestward to the Kentucky River. Thomas Walker and Andrew Lewis were foremost among the speculators who were determined to take as big a bite as possible out of the western area for Virginia. Stuart accepted the Donelson line, no doubt believing that since it was not opposed by the Cherokees, it would open that much more territory to settlement and would save energy in future controversies.

In all the negotiations during this period five things stand out: the almost insatiable desire for western lands; inaccuracy of specific geographical details; lack of a true sense of western boundary problems by the British home government; a tremendous amount of jealous controversy; and a continuous jockeying for advantage by special interest groups.

Before actually discussing the process of crossing the mountains by white surveyors, adventurers, and settlers, the place of this territory in Indian economy must be stressed. The area which is modern Kentucky, for instance, never had a permanent Indian population in most of the region. It was to a large extent "no man's" land which was hunted over by both northern and southern tribes, but none lingered behind to establish homes. Eskippakithiki, at the foot of one of the Appalachian ridges where the bluegrass area begins, was the only important Indian trading post in the region.

Expansion of white settlement was to take place up and down the entire frontier from Maine to Georgia, but the most intense pressure was to be exerted in the middle area—from Fort Pitt and Winchester, Virginia, to the Cumberland River. In this region, geography was a decisive influence. The great valley which stretched across western Virginia was to feed the flow of settlement in the direction of Cumberland Gap. At the same time a second arm of settlement was moving up the Cape Fear to the Catawba and Yadkin and into the western valley streams by way of the French Broad from North and South Carolina.

Officials of the Loyal Land Company gave able assistance to topography by trying to hasten settlers into this area, even encouraging them to cross the Holston Valley, and to move beyond the Clinch Mountain range into the Powell Valley.

Watauga Settlements

Moving southwestward, the population followed two lines of advance. One came from the settled areas of Virginia and remained close to Virginia territory. This group created demands for established political institutions as they moved westward. Obviously such a population movement was slower than that which ran ahead of both the Virginia and North Carolina frontiers and established settlements on the Watauga in 1768.

Four settlements appeared in the upper Holston Valley between 1768 and 1772—Watauga, North Holston, Nolichucky, and Carter's Valley. Development of this new western area was the result of unusual activity on the part of traders and land hunters, coupled with a dissatisfaction with administrative affairs in North Carolina. Watauga lay within colonial North Carolina, although the upper western North Carolina and Virginia boundary had not been determined. When the treaties of Hard Labor and

Fort Stanwix were made, frontier settlers assumed that they were at liberty to make claims beyond the mountains and proceeded to do so. Back of this long distance move to the Watauga were all the disputes and handicaps which grew out of the Granville proprietary control of the piedmont area of North Carolina in the neighborhood of Orange County, and also the dissatisfaction with Governor William Tryon's highhanded actions. Rather than tolerate poor and discriminatory administration of political affairs, it was easier for the disgruntled populace to move away to a new settlement.

Perhaps no more important island of settlement was ever made on the American frontier than that along the upper Holston. William Bean, the Russell brothers, William Stone, John Chisholm and George Grey were among the first to begin settlement; James Robertson and John Honeycut built a cabin on Roane's Creek near the Watauga a few miles above William Bean's settlement. Robertson, a Scotch-Irishman, went out from Wake County, North Carolina, to investigate the possibilities of western settlement and later in the same year moved his own and ten neighboring families across the mountains. Almost immediately a party of Virginians, including John Carter, Valentine and John Sevier, and others appeared on the Holston and settled in Carter's Valley. Then came the Welsh Indian trader, Evan Shelby, who by now was shifting his commercial interest from the Great Lakes country to the upper Tennessee. By 1771, an established island of settlement was in existence. When the Battle of Alamance occurred in North Carolina in May, 1771, there followed a considerable migration to the Holston beyond the zone of confusion and dissatisfaction. Not only did the establishment of settlement as far west as the upper Holston Valley constitute a phenomenal, and, to date, the most distant movement of English colonial population, but here was established an excellent base of operation for future expansion into much of the lower frontier. Equally as significant as the planting of settlements in the upper Tennessee Valley was the emergence of the three famous frontier leaders, James Robertson, John Sevier and Isaac Shelby, who were among the first arrivals in the new country.

Long Hunters

Doubling back a bit on the strict chronology of settlement of the old Virginia–North Carolina–Tennessee frontier, it is necessary to define some of the trader-hunter activities. By the time the lower Appalachian frontier was opened to trade after 1750, a new generation of American frontiersmen had grown up. Conditioned to the woods, they had spent their lives so close to the raw frontier that it was difficult for them to separate their farming activities from their hunting and woodsmen interests. As backwoods farmers they grazed cattle in the woods and supplemented meager incomes by trapping and trading in furs and skins. Hunting, for the average backwoods boy, came as natural as hoeing corn or building log cabins. Some of the hunters went into the western woods as members of organized parties, while others traveled alone. So active were the organized parties that the years 1760–1770 may well be called the "long hunting" decade. Immediately following the Grant campaign of Virginia against the Cherokees in 1761, the so-called Virginia and Carolina traders were everywhere. South of the Ohio some of the more famous ones came from the Yadkin Valley in North Carolina. Their plan was to secure pelts, dried buffalo tongues and tallow, and to ship them down the Mississippi by canoe, then to return by sea to coastal North Carolina.

Among the first hunting parties of this period was one of eighteen men among whom were Elisha Walden, Henry Scaggs, William and John Blevin, Charles Cox, William Pittman, William Harrelson and a man named Newman. These men hunted in the upper Tennessee and Cumberland River country. In 1766, another party composed of John Stewart, John Baker, Benjamin Cutbird and James Stewart crossed the mountains,

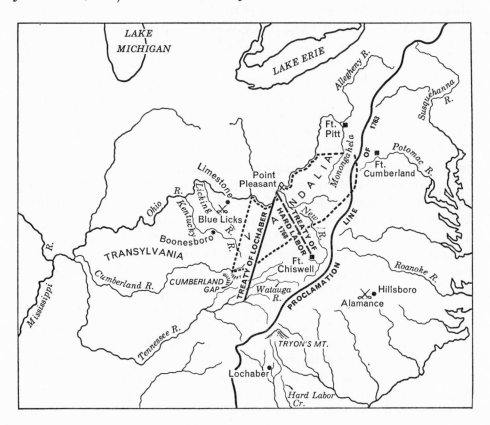

THE TRANS-APPALACHIAN FRONTIER

worked their way down the maze of headstreams of the Tennessee, crossed the Clinch ridges and found themselves in the Cumberland Valley. They went from the headwaters of the Tennessee to the Cumberland, to the Ohio and down the Mississippi to Natchez. In the middle of this decade a party of South Carolina hunters saw Michael Holsteiner and James Harrod on the bank of the Cumberland near present-day Nashville.

The Cumberland Valley between Cumberland Gap and Nashville was wild country. Perhaps there are few streams south of the Ohio which present such hazards as does the upper Cumberland. In the lower Appalachians there are the falls, and frequent narrows lined with treacherous boulders and "sucks," or whorls, which must have made the navigation of canoes exceedingly treacherous. Rocky cliffs towered overhead at these narrows, creating traps in which white men were occasionally caught by the Cherokees.

At French Lick (now Nashville) Timothe Demunbreun established a trading post. In the year 1766–1767, Uriah Stone's party of long hunters visited the French Lick country. Three years later the famous Knox-Mansker-Bledsoe-Drake party was in the big bend country, and described the scene at the French Lick. They wandered through woods cluttered with a thick undergrowth of cane before they reached the lick. Not only did they see game in fabulous numbers, but they claimed that "one could walk for several hundred yeards around the lick and in the lick on Buffelow Skuls and bones, and they found out the cause of the Canes growing up so suddenly . . . which was in consequence of many Buffelows being Killed." In 1777 James Smith, Joshua Horton, Uriah Stone and William Baker explored further along the Cumberland, and middle Tennessee came more and more into focus among the far-ranging hunters.

Mention in the above paragraph of the French Lick introduces the subject of the lick in early frontier history. A lick was a spot of earth where a fissure had occurred between the surface of the ground and the Ordovician strata, from which a chemical ooze containing salt, sulphuric acid and other minerals had been forced upward. Because of the rather high saline content of the water and earth, herbivorous animals, including buffalo, deer and elk came to lick the salt. For a space of a hundred yards or so the earth atop the fissure was licked and tramped bare. All a hunter had to do was take his stand at a lick and wait for game to appear. On one occasion, Bledsoe's Lick in Tennessee was so thickly crowded with animals that Isaac Bledsoe was afraid to dismount his horse for fear of being trampled to death. There were scores of licks and stamping grounds across the frontier. Some of the more famous were Mansker's, Bledsoe's, French, Blue, Big Bone, Bullitt's, Flat, Grassy, Salt and others.

The same hunters who traveled along the Tennessee streams crossed the mountains and explored Kentucky. In the latter part of the decade Daniel Boone had crossed through Cumberland Gap and, becoming confused by the maze of valleys that opened out toward the Pine Mountain Range, had spent a somewhat miserable time in the rough mountain laurel country. In 1769–1771 Boone was back in the Kentucky country, this time with John Finley as a trusted guide and companion.

The West was not unknown to Finley, for he had traveled through it as an Indian trader. In fact, he was well enough acquainted with it at an early date to describe his adventures beyond the mountains to Daniel Boone while the two were serving as wagoners in Braddock's march. The peddler Finley appeared in the winter of 1769 at the Boone cabin on the Yadkin where the two plotted a hunting trip to Kentucky. Boone already had a casual arrangement with Judge Richard Henderson by which he served as a land scout. On May 1, 1769, John Finley, Daniel Boone, Squire Boone, John Stuart, Joseph Holden, James Mooney and William Cooley set out for the Kentucky country. This was a characteristic Yadkin Valley long hunting party. The group rode horses and was equipped with salt, blankets, traps, a camp kettle and two or three days' rations. It was the practice of the long hunting parties to carry only enough food supplies to enable them to reach hunting territory beyond the settlement line.

From the Yadkin, the Finley-Boone party followed the beaten path southwestward to Cumberland Gap. Once at this important spot, it was necessary for the party to decide either to cross over to the Cumberland River and follow this Kentucky drainage system (following approximately along the old Warrior's Path, into the central, or so-called prairie section), or to go directly north to the Kentucky River. Boone's party moved up the South Fork of the Kentucky River to Station Camp Creek near the present town of Irvine, then down the Kentucky and Red rivers to the famous Indian Old Fields or Eskippikithiki area.

This hunting party tramped over much of central Kentucky. At Station Camp Creek they were still on the edge of the mountains, but Eskippikithiki was on the tableland between mountain and Bluegrass plain. Boone and Stuart were once captured by the Indians, but they escaped, recaptured some of their horses and returned to camp. While on the edge of the Bluegrass the party amused itself by reading *Gulliver's Travels*. When attacked by Indians the men went into action; and as Alexander Neeley, who had lately come from North Carolina with Squire Boone, said, "they had driven the Lullbegruds away." Today the small creek beside which they were located is called Lullbegrud.

In the fall, when Boone's companions returned to North Carolina, he was left with Stuart, Neeley and his brother Squire. Stuart and Neeley were lost, and twice during the next eighteen months Squire returned to

North Carolina. Daniel remained alone in the great forest, exploring the Kentucky and Green river valleys, as well as the Cumberland country of north-central Tennessee. It is difficult to say what his ideas were. Certainly he sought furs and skins, and no doubt he was spying out the land; but possibly most important of all to Boone himself, he was enjoying the freedom of the woods. On one amusing occasion Boone was singing to his dogs when he was stalked by a party of long hunters under the leadership of the famous Casper Mansker. That particular party, incidentally, had accumulated a rather large cache of furs in southern Kentucky, which in time was lost to the Indians. One of the Bledsoes, a member of the party, carved his sentiments on a tree, "1300 deerskins lost, ruination by God."

Daniel and Squire Boone were unable to return to North Carolina with their packs of furs and skins. Cherokee Indians relieved them of their catch before they could cross the mountains, and Daniel Boone went home financially as distressed as he was two years before when he had gone out to Kentucky. But Boone's influence on the early Kentucky frontier was not to be measured in terms of material returns from the woods, but rather by his information of the western country and his ability to dramatize his knowledge in a quiet way. Boone is a rather difficult person to characterize briefly. He was taciturn, yet he left behind him a host of adventure stories. He spent two years in the western country without doing anything tangible toward establishing a personal land claim, yet it is clearly evident that he was a man of ambition and great pride of accomplishment. Perhaps his most pronounced personal characteristics were his great courage and leadership and the fact that he inspired his associates with confidence. He also seems to have held a great fascination for the Indians.

By the year 1771, when Daniel and Squire Boone returned to North Carolina, the desire to settle western lands was approaching a mild fever stage. Where hunters and traders had tramped along stream beds and land hunters had made general exploratory journeys, the surveyor laying out specific tracts now appeared as far west as the Ohio. Settlement was moving closer on the road to the Ohio from the valley country of Tennessee and Virginia. In 1769 a project for settlement was planned for the area as far west as Powell's Valley under the leadership of Joseph Martin of Albemarle County, Virginia. Although this venture failed for the moment, it was indicative of the ambitions of the period.

County-making

Our discussion so far has centered about the Indian trader, the white hunter, the land company, the military forces ensconced in log forts, the Indian agents, and the frontier-treaty approaches to the backwoods. The organized county which established a pattern of civil government over large unexploited areas provided a more mature approach. Out of Virginia's vast Augusta County were formed Botetourt County in 1769 and Fincastle in 1772. Governor Dunmore doubtless violated his authority in this action, but he justified it by explaining that force of population and land speculating activity necessitated more intensified civil government than was possible in the unwieldy county of Augusta. Among the early Botetourt and Fincastle county officials were men who became famous westward to the Ohio and southward to the Gulf of Mexico. William Christian became county surveyor, and his deputies were William Russell, Daniel Smith, Robert and William Preston, Robert Doak and James Douglas. The practice of forming counties to keep abreast of the settlement line became an important frontier political device. Counties came into existence ahead of towns and states; the pattern of future state governments and the traditions of local politics were to reflect the powerful county influence.

Captain Thomas Bullitt advertised in 1772 that he was on his way to the Ohio country to survey soldiers' lands which were freed of the restrictions of 1763 and that he would oblige possible clients by surveying their private claims. He was accompanied by Hancock Taylor, James Harrod, James Douglas and James Hite. This expedition was not altogether successful because of Indian attacks along the way and because, in the end, the influential Fincastle County surveyor, William Preston, refused to validate surveys made by this rival in his county. A second party of surveyors, the McAfee brothers, James, Robert and George, came from William Preston's headquarters by way of the Kanawha Valley to Kentucky and surveyed land along the Salt River. Not only did they survey soldiers' claims but likewise nonmilitary homestead plots of four hundred acres each. These early surveyors demonstrated their ability to pick out good land.

There was the same activity at the upper end of the Ohio Valley; possibly the pressure of population moving westward was even more intense. Land along the Allegheny and Monongahela rivers was being claimed, and speculators in almost unlimited numbers, including Colonel George Washington, John Connolly and George Rogers Clark, were eyeing the fertile Ohio Valley with designs of settlement and land sales. By 1767 the Mason and Dixon line had been extended beyond the Maryland boundary, and the entire Virginia-Pennsylvania boundary was in a faltering process of negotiation. An additional step was taken two years later when Pennsylvania disposed of land in the Pittsburgh area and when Bedford County was created in 1771—an action which threatened to weaken the claims of the Vandalia Company and George Croghan's own personal claims. Thomas and Michael Cresap had moved to the Redstone section, and Arthur St. Clair was claimant of a large block of land in the neighborhood.

Thus the western country was involved in a complicated quarrel between the two colonies and among numerous individuals who were sensitive on the subject of specific colonial jurisdiction. Possibly those claimants having the least tenable claims preferred that Virginia assume jurisdiction over the areas. George Croghan became so aroused over the race for land claims that he resigned his commission as deputy Indian agent in favor of Alexander McKee, and devoted his full time to fur-trading and land surveying. Lingering disputes arose when he encroached on lands claimed by Washington and others. In the meantime, Pennsylvania hastened to obstruct any attempt Virginia might make to extend her jurisdiction by creating Westmoreland County, which absorbed the area at the head of the Ohio on which the fort was located. For the next two years, 1772–1774, there was a tug of war between Virginia and Pennsylvania over possession of the lands east of the Monongahela. Stirring the pot of contention no doubt were Governor Dunmore of Virginia, Dr. John Connolly and George Croghan on one side; Pennsylvania settlers and Lt. Governor Penn's agents on the other. Before the upper Ohio Valley could be opened to orderly settlement, the boundary dispute between the two colonies had to be adjudicated, and Indian affairs had to assume a quieter aspect.

Along the Ohio and Kentucky

To insure a clear picture of the various crosscurrents on the American frontier from 1773–1775, it is necessary to summarize conditions as they existed. On two fronts the Indian trade was being carried on with ever-expanding activity: in the south, the traders were penetrating deeply into Indian country; and in the north traders were enjoying a restoration of their peaceful relations with the Indians. Although activity in this area had been confined to only three or four fortified centers, the trade was perhaps greater than ever. The old rivalry between Virginia and Pennsylvania had become more and more pronounced as Virginians emphasized their desire for land. Surveys were either underway or impending all the way from Pittsburgh to the Falls of the Ohio. Not only were Virginia surveyors setting out from the head of the Ohio, but they were cutting likewise across the Greenbrier and Kanawha country from the Virginia Valley and Holston settlements. Pennsylvania traders looked upon Virginia land hunters as undesirable competitors. Already it was almost a foregone conclusion that the land south of the Ohio would fall into the hands of Virginia speculators and settlers. Men like George Croghan, however, were caught between the upper and nether millstones of desire to continue the trade, loyalty to Pennsylvania, and a strong wish to participate in land speculation. So long as there was hope that the Vandalia Company might succeed, it was to Croghan's interest to hold on. The Shawnee, Delaware and Cherokee Indians had especial reason to regard the advancing white surveyors and land claimers as poachers on their domain. Daniel Boone and his party had been informed that the game in the woods was essentially Indian cattle, and the white man had no right to slaughter it and to make off with furs, skins and meat. Such acts in the opinion of the Indians constituted the most brazen kind of thievery. Also, the white man failed to respect the treaty boundaries. The Hard Labor treaty had established a line from the Holston to the Kanawha. Subsequently the Treaty of Lochaber had greatly expanded this area; and when the Donelson line was run in 1771, it had taken an additional thick slice to the Kentucky River. In 1773–1774, Virginia surveyors were blithely disregarding the treaty lines and were surveying about the Falls of the Ohio, thirty-five miles south of the already generous bite of the Donelson survey.

Some adventures of the first major wave of surveying parties in Kentucky have already been described. By rights, the first settler in the Kentucky country should have been Daniel Boone, and, had he been able to carry out his plans, he would have been. But hunting and surveying, as he was to find, differed radically from making settlement. In the first two, a man could slip away from antagonized Indians, make friends of them, or die as a single individual resisting them; but bringing a family onto the frontier to plant a settlement involved much greater responsibilities. To begin with, it was necessary to make a permanent location which took a period of time relatively longer than making a hunting camp. Settlements so deep on the frontier as Kentucky were subjected to quick and devastating assaults unless they were protected by blockhouses and log forts.

In 1773, Boone with his own family and six other families began the cumbersome move from North Carolina. Bringing women, children, household goods and livestock over the trail was a slow and tedious process. In Powell's Valley, the Boone party was joined by the Bryan families. As the settlers advanced toward Cumberland Gap they constituted a rather self-sufficient band. In the Gap, however, young James Boone and James Russell were murdered by the Cherokees. When news of the Indian attack got out, the party became hysterical and retreated, against Daniel Boone's wishes, to the security of the Clinch Valley.

Boone had begun the movement toward Kentucky, but others were striving for the same goal. Breaking way to this part of the frontier was a highly variegated activity, and not all the attempts to reach this country were in the line of historical vision at the same moment. While Boone, the long hunters and surveyors were entering Kentucky from the east, a dramatic young adventurer, Simon Kenton, was seeking entry from the Ohio. Kenton was born in Fauquier County, Virginia, in the year of General Braddock's defeat; like Boone, he became a natural woodsman. At sixteen years of age he fought with a rival in love and believed he had killed him. He escaped bare-handed to the western woods, going eventually to Fort Pitt where he formed a friendship with various persons traveling up and down the Ohio. From 1770 to 1775 the young woodsman was to make at least three visits to Kentucky, where he was instrumental in opening the path to white settlers from the north by way of Limestone Creek into central Kentucky. Many general studies tend to overlook this rugged hunter, but he became one of the best woodsmen in the history of the Ohio-Kentucky frontier. From 1774–1812, Kenton was present at the occurrence of more major events in frontier history than any other frontiersman. He made many land claims, but he either learned little about the laws governing them or was too indifferent to register his property properly, and he lost it; but without his fine sense of woodcraft and his services the Ohio Valley pioneers would have found settlement more difficult.

Frontier exploitation in this latter part of the eighteenth century was to be colored by the adventures of hundreds of individuals. It was they who made the real advance. While the complex intercolonial snarl was being untangled at the head of the Ohio, surveyors representing the powerful southwestern Virginia interests under the domination of William Preston were in Kentucky making surveys. Hancock Taylor and John Floyd were back at the Falls where Bullitt had surveyed. Floyd was laying claims to lands in both the Licking Valley and about the Ohio Falls, actually duplicating the work of Bullitt which Preston had refused to recognize. Taylor was staking out claims on the rich Elkhorn plateau. A third party under the leadership of James Harrod, and numbering such prominent pioneers as Abram Hite, and Jacob and James Sandusky, surveyed claims over a rather large scope of territory south of the Kentucky River and below the Donelson survey. They began building cabins on the present site of Harrodsburg.

Dunmore's War

All of the surveyors, and especially those who had crossed the Donelson line south of the Kentucky River, were conscious of the Indian menace. Few if any of the surveyors seemed to have appreciated the real extent of the trouble. On June 27, 1774, Daniel Boone and Michael Holsteiner (or Stoner) appeared at Harrod's camp bearing news of the impending Dunmore's War. These two had come to warn the Virginia surveyors to return to the settlements, but Floyd had already left the Falls, Douglas was on his way home, and Hancock Taylor was to lose his life just south of the Kentucky River in present-day Madison County. Boone, anxious to help make the first settlement, even in the face of emergency, lingered at Harrodsburg long enough to assist in the building of a cabin; but the news of the war caused Harrod's men to give up when the first attacks were made on them, and settlement of Kentucky was delayed another year.

Dunmore's War was a natural consequence of the tremendous activity of speculators and surveyors on the frontier. Its causes were numerous and involved. Rivalry between Virginians and Pennsylvanians was one important factor, for each had propagandized against the other in their Indian dealings. The push for lands along the south bank of the Ohio disturbed the Indian peace of mind. Lack of gumption (or perhaps dishonesty) on the part of Dr. John Connolly as Lord Dunmore's representative at Fort Pitt led to overt acts which threatened the peace. The scars of Pontiac's conspiracy were still tender, and the atmosphere of Indian villages gave evidence on occasions of a surly spirit. Use of the Ohio River as a channel of passage for hunters and surveyors inspired jealousies, and rivalries over hunting grounds provoked anger. For at least two decades, the displaced Shawnees had been increasing in numbers, and their attitude toward the whites grew continually more petulant. On top of these fundamental causes there was animosity on the part of the Wyandottes, Delawares and Miamis. There were also numerous personal incidents which provoked trouble. One of these at Pittsburgh was the firing on the Shawnee chiefs, whom George Croghan, deputy Indian agent, was holding as hostages. Another incident was the so-called Greathouse atrocity which resulted in the murder and horrible mutilation of members of Chief Logan's family at Baker's Bottom by Daniel Greathouse. Following this incident, there were bushwhackings and murders on both sides.

Along the settlement frontier, the murder of young Boone and Russell, the Greathouse atrocity, and the firing on traders' boats on the Ohio created a state of near hysteria. As in the years when French and Indians were raiding, settlers fell back to the safety of forts and older communities. To all intents and purposes the Powell and Clinch River valleys were deserted, and a state of warfare prevailed. Certainly Dr. Connolly's note of April 16, 1774, to people along the Ohio, did nothing to allay the popular anxiety. In this note he virtually declared a state of war to exist.

On June 10, Governor Dunmore issued instructions for the militia of the western counties to assemble for war against the Indians. County lieutenants in Fincastle, Botetourt and Augusta counties were called on for men and supplies. Dunmore prepared to lead a militia force into the Indian country by way of Pittsburgh; the frontiersmen from western and southwestern Virginia and the Holston Valley were to go overland to the mouth of the Kanawha under the command of Colonel Andrew Lewis. Lewis' task was somewhat reminiscent of that which had faced Washington in the west some twenty years before. However, he had relatively little trouble organizing an army of 1,100 men from the Holston, the Virginia valley, and the Powell River country, which, in some respects, was the best frontier army ever assembled. It was a purely native product composed of hunters, surveyors, Indian traders and backwoods farmers. Electing its officers, arranging to a large extent for its own supplies, and fighting according to frontier tactics, it was potentially a hard-fighting force. At daybreak on October 10, 1774, Colonel Lewis' army was attacked by the Shawnees under the command of the famous Chief Cornstalk. Fighting was hard and losses were heavy. Fortunately for the whites, Chief Cornstalk misinterpreted a flanking movement by George Matthews, John Stewart and Isaac Shelby as the arrival of additional troops and directed his braves to retire.

With the end of this pitched battle, Dunmore's War was over. Governor Dunmore himself had marched out to the Hockhocking and Scioto country and opened negotiations which sought peace for the Virginians both along the Ohio and to the south of it. Dunmore was possibly overzealous in his attack upon the Indians; historically his reputation has been clouded by the strong insinuation that he had a selfish interest in land speculation and had stirred up the war to facilitate his acquisitions. This was assuredly not true, for the Treaty of Charlotte made no suggestion that territory north of the Ohio was involved. Before the treaty could be completed in a subsequent meeting at Pittsburgh, however, the colonies became engaged in the dispute which resulted in the American Revolution.

ENGRAVING BY LONGACRE AFTER THE PORTRAIT BY CHESTER HARDING, 1835. FROM THE *National Portrait Gallery*.

THE
REVOLUTIONARY FRONTIER

There prevails an opinion, I find, which is industriously cultivated by Henderson, the famous invader mentioned in my last letter to your lordship, that people may take up lands of the Indians by lease although they can not purchase of them without militating against the King's Proclamation of 7th of October, 1763, and accordingly I understand his bargain with the Cherokee Indians that at first I understood to be a purchase is now reported to be a lease of 999 years of a tract of country four hundred miles square to which I am informed many of the wretched and desperate people of this Province talk of resorting upon the invitation given out by Henderson whose doctrine is clearly in my opinion contrary to the express words as well as the meaning and design of the Royal proclamation referred to.

—GOVERNOR JOSIAH MARTIN of North Carolina to
LORD DARTMOUTH, 1775

CHAPTER V

Kentucky

THE end of Dunmore's War saw a renewal of land-hunting activities and the establishment of new settlements along the Ohio, in the Holston Valley, and beyond Cumberland Gap in Kentucky. On March 15, 1775, James Harrod and members of his original party returned to the country south of the Kentucky River and began anew to plant a permanent settlement. A fort was built, and cabins were made ready for occupation.

While these adventuresome surveyors and land hunters were busy in Kentucky, a second party was ironing out the preliminaries to developing a colony west of the Appalachians. Judge Richard Henderson, like scores of Virginians and other North Carolinians, coveted a large block of western lands. Using the same device that had been employed repeatedly by promoters to secure title to virgin territory, he organized a land company, known first as the Richard Henderson, then the Louisa, and finally as the Transylvania Land Company. The latter organization came into existence during the winter of 1774-1775. In the early spring months it had gone so far as to open negotiation with the Cherokee Indians for millions of acres lying generally south and west of the Kentucky, north of the Cumberland River, east of the Ohio and west of the Cumberland Mountains.

Members of the Transylvania Company were Judge Henderson, a Virginia-born North Carolina jurist who had been involved indirectly in the Battle of Alamance of 1771 in Orange County, North Carolina, Thomas and Nathaniel Hart, James Hogg, Alexander Roxborough, Jesse Benton, John Williams, Lancelot Johnston, John Luttrell, J. Bacon and William Johnston. Their first objective was to secure claim to the lands south of the Ohio to which the various recent Indian treaties with Virginia did not convey title. The lands in Kentucky would fall below the so-called Donelson line, which, without reasonable doubt, recognized the Kentucky River as the southern boundary of lands involved in the Lochaber Treaty. The guiding spirit of this undertaking was Richard Henderson, who apparently nurtured a dream of founding a new colony. Lands in the projected Transylvania were to be distributed by the proprietors with the agreement that purchasers would pay an annual quitrent in perpetuity.

East of the mountains a basic settlement on Transylvania lands was made by Joseph Martin in Powell's Valley. This settlement, begun in 1775, was to serve as a way station for immigrants moving toward Cumberland Gap. A clever advertising campaign created a fever for moving west in North Carolina and throughout the Holston Country. Prospective settlers were anxious to secure land claims in the highly touted new country. While land-hungry settlers in the Hillsborough area of North Carolina were getting poised to move westward, William Johnston was busy during December, 1774, purchasing trade goods from Scotch merchants at Fayetteville. Such goods were to be traded to Cherokee Indians for Kentucky lands. In all, the Transylvania Company planned to spend £10,000 in goods and sterling. From Fayetteville, Johnston's wares were hauled to Hillsborough where they were inspected by the ancient Cherokee chieftain Atta Kullakulla. He was accompanied by a squaw and a buck, and all were present to determine if the goods were of a satisfactory quality and quantity. They were then shipped to the Sycamore Shoals in the Holston to await the making of a treaty.

On the south bank of that river, near present Elizabethton, Tennessee, Cherokees began to assemble in January, 1775; and by the time the council met in March, between five hundred and twelve hundred braves were on hand to help negotiate the treaty and to receive presents. When negotiations for the transfer of Indian territory began on March 14, a distinguished group of white frontiersmen was also present, including Richard Henderson, the Harts, John Sevier, James Robertson, Isaac Shelby, John Williams and Daniel Boone.

Trade goods prominently displayed on the treaty grounds were attractive and highly conducive in effecting the transfer of Indian lands beyond the mountains to the Transylvania Company. Most important among the chiefs were Atta Kullakulla, or Little Carpenter, Oconostota, the Raven, and Dragging Canoe. Two distinct attitudes prevailed. The older chiefs were willing to sell lands to which they had at best the most tenuous claims—and even less notion of their true value. The young and surly chief Dragging Canoe, however, was dissatisfied. He and his followers saw the wide disparity between the value of the goods and the land. It was he who told Henderson he had bought a noble bargain but that it would be a dark and bloody ground—a prophecy which was to come true in a remarkably short time in the Transylvania country.

On March 17 the Sycamore Shoals purchase was completed. A trail right was then obtained across Cherokee lands to Cumberland Gap. So sure were the managers of the Transylvania Company that they would obtain title to Indian lands that Daniel Boone and twenty-eight companions were hustled off to Kentucky on the opening day of the council to blaze a trail to the south bank of the Kentucky River. Going considerably west of the ancient Warrior's Path, which led from the Gap northward to the Ohio opposite the mouth of the Scioto, the Boone party crossed from the Cumberland River to the Rockcastle and thence to the Kentucky. This trail followed generally the route of the Wilderness Road. In Boone's party was the young and highly literate Virginian, Felix Walker, who described the glories of penetrating the primeval Kentucky country. For this romantic young journalist it was somewhat akin to entering paradise. The tall trees of the Kentucky ridges, the bright green waters of the Cumberland and the Rockcastle, and finally the rich cane-grown plains of the limestone lands appealed mightily to him. On March 24, after fourteen days of trail hacking, he wrote: "On entering the plain (the bluegrass) we were permitted to view a very interesting and romantic sight. A number of buffaloes of all sizes, supposed to be between two and three hundred, made off from the lick in every direction; some running, some walking, others loping slowly and carelessly, with young calves playing, skipping and bounding through the plain." That day young Walker was to stand with his party and look down on the Kentucky River flowing northward through its deep limestone gorge.

His paradise, however, was to reveal its true colors on the morning of March 25. An Indian attack came fast and fatal for the little party of trailbreakers. Captain William Twetty and his Negro slave were left dead, and Felix Walker was seriously wounded. For Boone the attack was sobering, if not frightening. Dragging Canoe's prophecy was being fulfilled.

Behind Boone's party came Henderson with about forty companions. By the first week in April work was begun on a fortress on the south side of the Kentucky. Preparations were made to plant a corn crop, and Transylvania Colony was on its way to realization in the new settlement of Boonesboro.

By May there were three Kentucky settlements—Boonesboro, Harrod's Town, and Benjamin Logan's or St. Asaph's. All three were south of the river in Indian territory, constituting definite encroachments upon lands reserved by the Proclamation of 1763 as well as those restricted by the subsequent agreements of Hard Labor and Lochaber. Considerable space could be devoted to discussing the legality of the Transylvania Company claim. To begin with, the western country was technically closed to settlement by the Crown. Virginia claimed the area by Charter right, but there was extreme doubt whether the colony of North Carolina might even claim much of it. If North Carolina did own some of the Kentucky lands, there was a colonial law which prohibited their sale in large blocks to speculators. Likewise the Treaty of Lochaber contained a clause which restricted further sale of Cherokee lands except by permission of the superintendent of southern Indian affairs. Henderson took a long gamble by moving onto the Kentucky frontier. A contention is made that he based his claim on the famous extralegal and informal Yorke-Camden decision which maintained that East Indians could give legal possession to their lands. Clearly this decision could not hold up when applied in North America, and it is also doubtful that Henderson had seen its contents before making the Sycamore Shoals treaty. Some historians now doubt that the so-called Lord Mansfield interpretation of the Yorke-Camden decision was ever given to Henderson. The shrewd Henderson was gambling on being able to make settlement and grant numerous tracts of land to settlers without interference from either Virginia or North Carolina. Other facts on the debit side of the Transylvania ledger need examination. The Cherokees did not own the land which they "sold." This land was a common hunting ground. Judge Henderson, though an able man, was far from being an empire builder as has been claimed. It seems nearer the truth to speak of him as a fast-moving opportunist who, like scores of other people, hoped to get his land venture so well consolidated that he would be able to fend off his competitors. At all events, Henderson's rivals came to Kentucky in numbers too large and created too much opposition for him to silence them.

Richard Henderson made an immediate move to establish an independent colony. He outlined a land policy at once, and plans were made to distribute town lots to the inhabitants at Boonesboro. In May he took the second step when he called a meeting of legislative delegates from the other settlements at Boonesboro. When this assembly came to order under the spreading sycamores on the bank of the Kentucky, it constituted one of the most interesting meetings of its kind in American history. No constitution or charter was in existence and none was contemplated. The proprietors exercised the powers of initiative and veto. Henderson, playing the combined parts of a John Locke and a Demosthenes, outlined the problems of government and in eloquent phrases told his hearers that they were men of destiny. Nine laws, ranging from a provision for courts to one for improving the breed of horses, were passed. Transylvania had now given statutory substance to its existence.

Virginia vs. North Carolina

Hardly had the rapping of the legislative gavel died away at Boonesboro before a new personal factor appeared in Kentucky. Since 1772 the youthful red-headed George Rogers Clark had been on the Ohio surveying lands for various claimants. He was present during the troubles in Baker's Bottom when members of Chief Logan's family were killed, and during Dunmore's War he served as scout with Simon Kenton and Simon Girty.

Since that time he had resumed surveying along the Ohio. Following the Ohio River southward in late spring, 1775, he searched for lands for the Ohio Company. He first appeared in Kentucky at Harrodsburg (Harrod's Town), and from that base he scouted lands about Boiling Springs and St. Asaph's. Almost immediately he saw that Virginia's interest in the western country could hardly survive the aggressiveness of the Transylvania Company.

At this juncture, let us take notice of the sharp personal conflict which was brewing. Pro-Henderson historians of the frontier regard Clark as thoroughly unscrupulous, while those with a pro-Virginia bias regard him as a positive and enlightened factor in western settlement. While it is hardly necessary to pass judgment on the character of either Henderson or Clark, their intentions were important keys to the future. Both were seeking land and possibly fame. One wished to achieve his ends by establishing an independent colony, the other desired the glory and protection of Virginia. They were joined in a fantastic struggle in which both the rewards and the risks were great.

Clark proposed to check Henderson's activities by taking his argument directly to Williamsburg. A meeting of citizens was called to assemble at Harrod's Town on June 8, 1776, and at that time Clark and John Gabriel Jones were elected delegates to represent the Kentuckians' interest before the Virginia Assembly. Clark was by no means alone in opposing the Transylvania scheme. Perhaps had each little settler been left to his own devices he would have accepted the terms of Transylvania grants with little more than private grumbling; but the land speculators feared Henderson, and it is not without significance that one of the most influential of them, Isaac Hite, was at Harrod's Town in 1776.

Before the Kentucky delegates could reach the capital, however, the Assembly had adjourned until fall. In the meantime Clark had had opportunities to discuss the Kentucky situation with many people, of whom the most important were Thomas Jefferson and Patrick Henry. The latter was much interested in western lands, and since he was then governor of the new state of Virginia, he was in a position to meet the challenge of the Transylvanians with genuine authority. Back in Kentucky Judge Henderson was attempting, through James Hogg, to get the newly organized Continental Congress to recognize Transylvania as a fourteenth colony; but however willing many delegates in Philadelphia might have been, they were unwilling to act without Virginia's consent. Already Clark had accomplished his purpose, and Henderson's cause was fading.

On December 7, 1776, Kentucky County was created out of Fincastle County. The new division consisted of the territory west of the mountains and had its seat at Harrod's Town. At the same time the assembly appropriated funds with which to buy a supply of lead and powder for the new county. Henderson's disappointment was poulticed with a 200,000 acre grant of land along the Ohio north of the Green River. With the creation of the Kentucky County the prospective Transylvania Colony of 2,000,000 acres passed into oblivion.

Tomahawk and Firebrand

While Virginia and North Carolina rivals maneuvered politically to gain possession of the western country, the greater struggle of the Revolutionary War was in its first disturbing phases. For the western country this was important. Along the entire fringe of the Indian frontier, conditions underwent a significant change. To Indians who had been dealt hard blows by American colonials and British regulars alike, this change of sentiment must have been past their understanding. Indian agents like John Stuart in the south, who had been working for peace and protection of the border settlers, were provoking raids against them. In the upper Ohio Valley, Dr. John Connolly remained a vigorous agent of the British cause, and he had ready access to some of the Ohio chiefs in the last conference which was planned to conclude the Treaty of Charlotte. However, Connolly was not to operate without competition; six commissioners were appointed by Virginia to maintain peace with the border tribes.

Deeper on the frontier and at Detroit the British propaganda machine worked with more efficiency. Already the Indians were anxious to believe charges against the backwoods settlers, and it was easy for British agents to convince them that the American backwoodsmen were robbing them of their lands and game. Also, it was relatively simple for the British to pay the prices in trade goods necessary to purchase Indian alliances. At Detroit, Colonel Henry Hamilton was a diligent Indian diplomat. He knew that Indian allegiance was for sale, and he was willing to buy it. Successfully he traded and propagandized for Indian support, and by 1776 he had made much headway in inflaming the frontier from Pittsburgh to Cumberland Gap.

Indian attacks on Kentucky had sent George Rogers Clark and John Gabriel Jones scurrying to Williamsburg for gunpowder and lead, and Virginia support. Before these men could return with their supplies the bloody year of the "Three 7's" had begun. Settlers who had moved from the stockade into the open country now hustled back to their protective walls, and by July only the three stations of Boonesboro, Harrod's Town, and St. Asaph's remained. Indian raiders from across the Ohio came both in war parties numerous enough to sustain a siege and in bands of half-dozens. The trail back to Cumberland Gap saw timid pioneers fleeing to the safety of the settlements. Every tree hid a potential enemy; every low-ing of a nervous milk cow heralded a possible attack.

There was an awareness that the savage attacks were being inspired from the British posts beyond the Ohio, and, with much justice, the propaganda machine in Kentucky worked overtime. Hamilton, it was said with some degree of truth, was paying bounties for scalps, and it was he, the old "ha'r buyer," who had turned the red devils loose to murder and pillage the vulnerable settlements. Almost as destructive as the loss of life was the fact that livestock had to be driven in from the ranges, and that settlers were kept from their corn patches. A long and fearsome chapter of border warfare was written about the settlements in this uncertain time.

While Kentuckians were being harassed by the first bloody raids from across the Ohio, the Cherokees of Tennessee, prodded by John Stuart and the British War Office, were in a warring mood. There were individual murders of traders at first, and rumors were brought back of dissatisfaction among the tribes. Traders who ventured into the Cherokee villages at once detected signs of impending trouble. The big attack was planned against the Watauga settlements. A war party of 700 braves, a part of which was led by Dragging Canoe, was to make a surprise attack at Watauga, while another band was to rush on to Virginia. Before the trap could be sprung, the Indian maiden Nancy Ward divulged the plan and the white settlements were saved. There were 170 settlers capable of bearing arms at Watauga, and this little band fought and defeated a far superior party of Indians in the battle of Island Flats. The story of Nancy Ward is as romantic as Parkman's account of Catherine at Detroit, and perhaps more authentic.

The British had planned a coordinate frontier attack with their sea raid against Charleston. Stuart and Cameron were to push their Indian warriors forward at the moment Sir Peter Parker approached the coast, but the latter was defeated at Sullivan's Island and the backwoods attack was dissipated. British Indian agents had overplayed their hands and militiamen in Virginia, the Carolinas and Georgia were thoroughly aroused. The fight was taken to the Cherokee villages. Troops from four states were led by a combination of officers consisting of General Griffith Rutherford of North Carolina, Colonel Andrew Williamson of South Carolina, Colonels Mc-Bury and Samuel Jack of Georgia, and Colonels Martin Armstrong and William Christian of Virginia. These forces smashed at the Cherokee villages, and shortly the Indians were on the run. The Cherokee Overhill villages were reduced to ruins, and the tribes were left to face starvation without the comforting assurances of their trouble-making friends Stuart and Cameron. By July, 1777, except for sporadic raiding by malcontents, the Indian war in the southwest was over for the time being and a peace treaty was signed. Tactically, the British failed miserably in this aspect of their southwestern border plans. Not only were the Indians defeated, but settlers were attracted to the region from the ranks of the militiamen. Thus a stronghold of resistance was built against an invasion from the East Coast, and a growing bulwark faced any attempt that might come from the west to break through to the east. For the Kentucky settlements it was indeed fortunate that the border war of the Watauga and Holston settlements was over before that along the Ohio became so oppressive.

The names of James Robertson, John Sevier, Isaac Shelby and scores of other frontiersmen who acquitted themselves with ability and a bravery approaching recklessness were written indelibly upon the annals of this old border area. John Sevier was a dashing hero of the Tennessee settlements. A handsome, athletic, blond fellow with a full sense of the dramatic, he became almost a legend. One of the stories tells how this young backwoodsman was standing guard at the Watauga fort when he heard a scream and saw a graceful young woman running for the gate like a gazelle, followed by a train of warriors in hot pursuit. A shot from Sevier's gun dropped the nearest brave, and a quick thrust over the wall with his strong arms snatched Bonnie Kate Sherrill upward to safety and future matrimony.

Clark of the Ohio

Inside Cumberland Gap and along the Ohio the struggle which had been proving so bothersome early in 1777 did not abate during the summer and fall months. White resistance from Kentucky to Pittsburgh faltered, and the Delawares, Shawnees, Wyandottes and Mingoes dominated the Ohio Valley. Had all of these Indians been fully united and well-directed, no white settlement could have resisted them. Fortunately the British were never able to accomplish this objective. Henry Hamilton remained in the position of power at Detroit, and prisoners taken from Kentucky cabins were subjected to the horrors of being "stretched out" on crossed poles, made to run the gauntlet, or burned at the stake. Warriors returning from raids against the settlements proudly dangled blond scalps from their belts. Inventories of British trade goods more and more included unusually large numbers of scalping knives and tomahawks which were made readily available to the warriors. Even if there is serious doubt that specific bounties were paid for scalp locks, Indians could not be prevented from making war after their own methods.

Feeble efforts were made in Kentucky County to organize and maintain a militia. The rising Indian fighters, Daniel Boone, James Harrod, John Todd, Jr. and Benjamin and George Rogers Clark were captains.

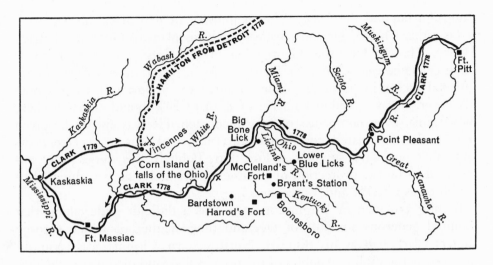

THE OHIO VALLEY IN THE REVOLUTIONARY CAMPAIGN

Spying out enemy activities along the trails were such seasoned scouts as Simon Kenton and Michael Holsteiner. But there were not more than 150 men in all to defend the Kentucky forts in the early years of the strife. Relief from the settlements east of the mountains was on the way under the command of the county lieutenant John Bowman, and a band of Yadkin men were to arrive in the fall, but at the moment in 1777 the future for Kentucky was most unpromising.

At Harrod's Town, however, Clark was developing a plan of action to check the raids against the forts and to sweep the British from the Northwest. Not until the fight could be taken to the centers of British and Indian activity would the settlements be spared from attacks.

To facilitate his plan, Clark had to know first-hand of the situation at the British-held posts of Kaskaskia and Vincennes. Two young woodsmen, Samuel More and Benjamin Linn, were chosen by lot to visit beyond the Ohio and to bring back information needed to secure favor for such an audacious plan as an attack against these posts. More and Linn were gone two months. Disguised as Indian traders, they were able to visit Vincennes and Kaskaskia and brought away much information of conditions at these places. There seemed to be no anxiety at either place about an attack from Kentucky, and the French inhabitants were only mildly friendly to the British. On the other hand, the British had been thorough enough in their propaganda to build up a genuine fear of the American Long Knives.

With the report of his western scouts in hand, Clark again set out for Virginia in the fall of 1777 to secure permission and support for a bold campaign beyond the Ohio. After a journey of 620 miles, he was back at his father's home. He soon made known his plans to Governor Patrick Henry, Thomas Jefferson, George Mason and George Wythe. There is some evidence that Governor Henry's love of western lands was an influential factor in persuading him to agree to support Clark's proposal. However, it was agreed in January, 1778, that Clark should raise anywhere in Virginia seven companies of fifty men each. He was also to be given £1,200 in depreciated continental currency, and was to receive boats and other necessary supplies at Fort Pitt. Publicly, his duties were announced to be the protection of Kentucky; privately, he was directed to march on Kaskaskia and Vincennes.

Raising 350 men in Virginia in 1778 was a difficult undertaking that required generous amounts of tact and time, neither of which George Rogers Clark had at his disposal. Northwestern Virginia was seriously involved in the raiding troubles of the upper Ohio, and men were reluctant to leave their homes. After recruiting only 150 men, Clark departed for the Falls of the Ohio hoping that additional troops could be raised in the Holston Country. When he arrived at his destination, he found only part of a company of volunteers awaiting him. Instead of 350 men, he had only 175 dependable troops for the expedition.

Shifting his base of operations from the interior settlement at Harrod's Town, Clark chose the strategic Corn Island opposite the mouth of Bear Grass Creek and just above the Falls of the Ohio. At this place he had an easily defended spot on which to erect his station, and, since all traffic up and down the river had to stop and prepare to negotiate the rapids, it would be relatively easy to control the stream. Once at the Falls, the men were informed of the full purpose of the expedition, and preparations were quickly made for the departure. On June 23, 1778, the river was at a satisfactory level to pass the boats over the rocky falls, and Clark with 175 men rowed out into the swirling waters of the upper Ohio just as the sun went into total eclipse. Clothed in the garments of the frontier—leather trousers, a fringed leather coat, shot-bag, game pouch, with a hunting knife strapped to his waist, and a skin cap—the average militiaman in this company looked like the fiend from hell which the French had been led to expect.

Clark's venture depended for success upon speed and secrecy. If the approach of his miniature army was discovered, there was almost no chance that it could capture a single post. Double-manning the oars, the party rowed swiftly down to the abandoned Fort Massiac. Here Clark first showed his command of strategy. He realized that by going up the Mississippi against an excessively stiff current he would lose time, wear his men down, and almost certainly be discovered. At Fort Massiac, therefore, the boats were beached and the men set forth on foot across 120 miles of river-bottom forest land to the Kaskaskia River. Fortunately Clark's forces were supplemented by a boat load of American traders, among whom was John Saunders, a fairly able guide.

Traveling single file across the rough, heavily-wooded bottoms of southern Illinois, the party made rather fast but tremendously fatiguing headway. The only unfortunate incident on the journey was a temporary loss of the way by John Saunders. On the evening of July 4 the little army reached its first objective—the south bank of the Kaskaskia. A captured farm family was able to give Clark valuable information. He learned that for the moment at least there was no suspicion of the enemy's approach at the fort.

After dark the army passed over the river, and in a short time the British commandant Rocheblave was a prisoner of war. Within a fraction of an hour after Clark's men had reached the wall, the fort and the town were in American hands without bloodshed.

The capture of Kaskaskia put Virginia forces far out of reach of their base of operation, so it was necessary for Clark not only to seek the friendship of the French, but to impress the Indians as well. He was equipped to perform this latter task. By bluster and some tact he was able to win over the tribes to friendship for the Americans. At the same time he quickly allayed the anxiety of the French. He permitted the inhabitants to worship undisturbed in their church, and he conveyed to them the news which he had received just before leaving the Falls, that France was supporting the colonies in their struggle with Britain. Quickly, a small company under the command of Joseph Bowman was sent northward toward St. Louis to take St. Philippe, Prairie du Rocher and Cahokia. From Cahokia the Americans visited the Spanish across the river, and Clark and Governor de Leyba became close friends—so close in fact that the young Virginian fell in love with the governor's beautiful sister Teresa.

Fighting forces involved in this western campaign were indeed limited, and the actual combat potential was almost negligible. More important than either guns or ammunition were the major personalities. Clark's northwestern campaign was to succeed largely because of the work of several individuals; perhaps none was more important than Father Pierre Gibault, priest of the Kaskaskia church. It was he who carried the first news of Clark's presence in the western country to the inhabitants of Vincennes. Although he refused to act as a political emissary, he did in his conversations prepare the way for the political commission under the direction of Captain Leonard Helm. When Helm arrived at Vincennes in late August, 1778, he immediately took command of Fort Sackville and waited for future British developments.

Vincennes was one of the early French chain of posts guarding the frontier. North of it were the stations of Ouiatenon and Detroit, connected directly by the Wabash and Maumee rivers. At Detroit, Lieutenant-Governor Hamilton was in almost as precarious a position as were Clark's Americans. He could not afford to allow the Americans to hold on to Kaskaskia and Vincennes without their becoming a serious threat to the whole British frontier. In August and September he was busy organizing his British and Indian forces and preparing supplies for the long land-and-river journey to Vincennes. Hamilton faced many problems akin to those of the French and Indian War. He lacked seasoned men, supplies were hard to secure, and he could not be too sure he would leave a secure situation behind him at Detroit.

Traveling up the Maumee River, Hamilton's command made its way to the headwaters of the Wabash and then started downstream to Vincennes. Moving down the shallow Wabash with heavily laden bateaux was an enormous task. Beaver dams had helped to raise the water to a navigable depth at some places; at others shallows had to be deepened by use of temporary dams. By the time Hamilton's force reached Vincennes in late December it numbered more than five hundred British, Canadians and Indians, with Canadians and Indians overwhelmingly in the majority. Hamilton had possibly no more than thirty-three regulars. Leonard Helm was forced to surrender as quickly as he had taken possession of the fort, enabling Hamilton to settle down in winter quarters and await the arrival of spring. Many of the Canadians returned to Detroit, and the Indians wandered back to their villages.

Once situated in Fort Sackville, Hamilton followed the long established frontier practice of waiting out the winter. To campaign in the bad weather of the lower Ohio Valley, even if he had the men and supplies, seemed out of the question, and the high waters of the Embarras and the Big and Little Wabash, he believed, offered a perfect wall of safety. It must also be pointed out that Hamilton was not altogether master of his situation regardless of the season. Although he had recaptured Vincennes, his victory was purely a token matter. He had only a handful of regular troops. No one could say what passive resistance the French would offer, or what comfort and aid they were capable of giving the Americans. Although he had just crossed the Indian territory and had received much aid from them, there was great uncertainty that Hamilton could depend upon them in the face of French opposition. Too many of the old injuries and blunders of Pontiac's Conspiracy were still fresh in mind, and some of the Indians still believed that the French would win and that the old trading alliances would be restored.

From Clark's viewpoint, he had either to go against the long established military practice of fighting in winter or perish. There was only one road of promise open and that was to strike the British in Vincennes at the most unexpected moment. Surprise had been his greatest element of victory at Kaskaskia. An inventory of Clark's striking force reveals that he had just slightly over one hundred frontier militiamen, and he could count in addition on a limited number of French volunteers. The most important of the volunteers was the rugged, black-haired Italian, Francis Vigo. Vigo, who was a business partner of Governor de Leyba, and who was familiar with the Indian trails in the area, was a courageous man and was willing to act as guide.

On the morning of February 5, 1779, the *Willing*, a rowed galley carrying two 4-pounders and four swivel guns, set off down the Mississippi River to Vincennes under the command of John Rogers. The crew's principal duty, it has been said, was to patrol the Ohio and so make sure the British did not escape downstream. At the same time Clark set out overland at the head of a tiny army of 172 men for a goal 180 miles eastward across three rivers and through heavy forest much of the way. Clark used all the psychology known to him to keep his men in good spirits and moving forward under the most discouraging conditions. Within twenty miles the going became exceedingly tedious. High water and cold weather, coupled with a lack of food, taxed the energy and spirit of every man. By indomitable determination the men passed over the Embarras and the Wabash, and then over the flooded plain east of the river to the fort.

By the bold strategy of informing the French inhabitants that the Long Knives were before the town, Clark was able to secure their support, to frighten away the Indians who had come to town, and to approach Fort Sackville in secrecy. The actual assault on the fort was a matter of keen marksmanship rather than force. Had the English been able to use their heavier guns (and the number of these available is a matter of some conjecture) to good advantage, an army several times the strength of Clark's might not have rushed the fort. But wounding the gunners by fire directed at the loopholes made Hamilton's artillery ineffective. After two exchanges of requests for surrender, Clark and Colonel Hamilton met in the town church on February 25 and the fort was surrendered. Hamilton and twenty-five of his men were sent back to Williamsburg as prisoners of war under the guardianship of Major John Williams and Lieutenant John Rogers.

Victory at Vincennes for George Rogers Clark was still a questionable advantage. He still believed he needed to capture Detroit to check completely the British activities in the region, but that course was not open to him because he lacked support. Sitting at Vincennes with almost as

many prisoners of war as he had men in his command, he was in no position to plan a further campaign, and in the face of a determined attack
down the Maumee and Wabash he was hardly in a position to hold on to
his gains. Vincennes was too far removed from Virginia to secure either
attention or support adequate for the moment's needs.

An appraisal of Clark's northwest campaign has long involved heroic
and nationalistic emotions. Historians have presented it from many viewpoints, ranging all the way from outright idolatry to one approaching
ridicule. Clark won, without a doubt, an important victory, but it was
something less when evaluated in terms of a major military accomplishment. Factually his small forces were never really engaged in even a light
test of battle strength. Clark himself would have been the first to admit
this. Had he really thought in terms of heavy campaigning he would have
been foolhardy to have left the Falls of the Ohio, but More and Linn had
brought him the important news that perhaps he could succeed along the
Wabash without having to fight too hard for victory. The French and
Indians would not stand by the British, and the British armed forces were
weak anyway. Hamilton was a victim possibly of his own personal shortcomings, but certainly more so of the muddled British western policy. It
is only necessary to re-examine British mismanagement in the French and
Indian War and Pontiac's Conspiracy to realize Hamilton's position. The
British were never able to give Detroit the support in men and supplies
so necessary to make it a bastion of imperial expansion. Clark's victory,
therefore, is to be evaluated as an effect of further administrative and political befuddlement in the management of British armed forces and Indian relations rather than as a triumph of arms.

Furthermore, from the administrative point of view, Clark's victory
was the work of economic as well as armed forces. An interesting chapter
in the northwest campaign is that pertaining to the aid given by Oliver
Pollock of New Orleans. Pollock, successful in gaining French friendship,
was able to negotiate for supplies and credit. Clark drew on him to the
extent of $25,000, and the government of Virginia for a smaller amount,
making his entire financial obligation $33,000. In 1779 he was faced with
an additional draft of $10,000. This money was spent for powder, lead,
food supplies, Indian trade goods, rum and sugar, and the services of boatmen to row upstream. Possibly of greater importance was the fact that
New Orleans was kept open to the Americans. Besides his services as
agent, Pollock redeemed paper continental money in New Orleans in
silver and at face value. No recognition of this assistance had been made
by the Virginia government up to 1779, and Pollock was faced with
bankruptcy.

At Vincennes, meanwhile, Clark was unable to move on his Detroit objective. Troop reinforcements which reached him were too few to undertake a campaign through Indian country, and Colonel John Bowman had dissipated his resources in an abortive attack on the Shawnees and Delawares in the neighborhood of Chillicothe. The summer of 1779 was the right moment to strike at Detroit. There were approximately 100 men at the fort, and supplies were almost exhausted. A quick surprise assault would have landed the fort in American hands, but such a force would have gone through Indian territory, an undertaking fraught with more uncertainty than attacking the British.

Success of the Americans from this point on, in the so-called Illinois country, has to be measured more in terms of a propaganda victory than as a military accomplishment. The British were perturbed by Clark's brash letters, by the rapidly growing French-American friendship even at Detroit, and the winning over of important segments of Indian support. Back in Kentucky, news of Clark's victories was taking momentous effect on the large number of settlers who were streaming across the mountains to make settlement. The time was rapidly approaching when Kentucky would be strong enough to withstand even a considerable attack from across the river without serious threat to its very existence. In the summer of 1779 when Clark returned to the Falls of the Ohio, the population had grown so fast that already plans were under way for the founding of the town of Louisville.

Daniel Boone's War

While George Rogers Clark had been recruiting troops in the Redstone settlements in Pennsylvania for his Kaskaskia expedition, tragedy had befallen Boonesboro. On January 8, 1778, Daniel Boone and a group of salt-making companions were captured at the Lower Blue Licks by Indians who no doubt were inspired to attack by the British at Detroit. The prisoners were taken beyond the Ohio to be dealt with by the British. At Detroit, Boone was claimed by the famous Shawnee Chief Blackfish and was returned to the Miami villages. Adopted as a son and held in great affection by the Indians, he no doubt enjoyed life there, but his mind was troubled by the knowledge that the British-Canadian DeQuindre and others were prodding the Indians to attack Boonesboro.

On June 16, 1778, Sheltowee, as Boone was called, made his escape on horseback. In four days he traveled the 160 miles on horseback and afoot to Boonesboro and was able to warn settlers that an attack was on its way. His arrival in Boonesboro brought excitement and renewed courage. The fort was in no condition for a siege, and he hastened its preparation. His escape from the Indians, however, threw the enemy's timing out of order—Blackfish and DeQuindre did not arrive before Boonesboro until the night of September 6—and in the meantime some of the suspicious settlers began to believe that Boone had misinformed them about the attack.

For ten days British and Indians laid siege to the frontier fort, trying repeatedly and unsuccessfully to open its gates by clumsy diplomacy, to rush it, to set it on fire, and finally to tunnel underneath it from the Kentucky River, but all these efforts failed. DeQuindre was unable to keep the braves pitted against the fort, and on the rainy night of September 16, 1778, the enemy withdrew and Boonesboro was saved.

Although this was a minor military skirmish in its actual proportions, the fact that Boonesboro survived the siege was one of the momentous incidents in the western struggle. Had this fort fallen to the British and Indians the other two Kentucky strongholds would doubtless have capitulated, and Clark would have been left surrounded in the Illinois country with no possible hope of supplies and only the Mississippi and lower Ohio rivers left open for escape.

The Upper Ohio

On the upper Ohio, Fort Pitt was again to be the center of struggle. For the Indians in the Ohio country the war promised trouble if not possible destruction, since any excuse that brought white men into the Indian territory meant a possible encroachment on their lands and interruption of their trade. Again the Indian had everything to lose and little to gain in the white man's struggle. Knowing this, in the fall of 1776, 640 members of the Ohio tribes pledged their neutrality. Their neutral attitude, however, did little actually to settle the frontier problems.

Congress was afraid of Indian support, and it failed also to appreciate the importance of Fort Pitt. In brief, the upper Ohio was involved in local quarrels, ineffective support and administration, and British propaganda. General Edward Hand had been given the task of using Fort Pitt to advantage, but not even he could quiet the old quarrels, although he tried to promote friendship. Through David Zeisberger and his Moravian Indians active steps were also taken. Six forts, of which Fort Henry at Wheeling and Fort Randolph at the mouth of the Kanawha were the most important, were built to protect the frontier.

Patrols along the frontier became involved in constant skirmishes with the Indians. On one occasion Hand led militiamen against the Shawnees but succeeded only in disgracing himself by killing four squaws. So embarrassing was the "Squaw Campaign" that Hand resigned in 1778, and Washington appointed Lachlan McIntosh to take his place. McIntosh's problems of administration at Fort Pitt were not essentially different from those of his predecessors. He was able neither to silence the old border rivalries between Virginia and Pennsylvania, nor to control all the bickering among individuals struggling for position in the Indian trade. Congress remained indifferent to the needs of this vital frontier post and let it fall almost into a state of disrepair.

The two major objectives at Fort Pitt were to mount attacks on Detroit and to keep peace with the Indians. Neither objective was realized, but the British were also unable to achieve their purposes. Meanwhile, under the leadership of Colonel Daniel Brodhead, Fort Henry, down the river from Fort Pitt, became a focal center of frontier troubles. A man of direct action, Brodhead proposed a bold thrust against the British and Indians. His raid against the Delawares was of some vital consequence, and had it been managed properly this campaign might have caught Governor General Haldimand off guard at Detroit. But Brodhead and Clark were at cross purposes, and the former's impulsiveness almost brought failure to both campaigns.

Settlers moving onto the Ohio frontier complicated the protection of the area. It was almost impossible to prevent encroachment in areas where trouble with the Indians was certain, and to prevent the settlers from taking direct action against the enemy. They complicated Indian diplomacy and defense. Possibly the most notable incident of this kind was the brutal destruction of the friendly Moravian Indians in the missionary village of Gnaddenhütten in March, 1782. This heartless raid stirred the Indians to fiercer attacks. In June of that year the Americans were engaged in the fierce battle of Sandusky, in which the frontiersmen were forced back with the loss of several prisoners including Colonel William H. Crawford. The bloody fate of these prisoners, especially the sadistic burning of Colonel Crawford at the stake, has become a classic story of Indian brutality. Campaigning beyond the Ohio from the upper forts brought little or nothing in the way of victory, but both sides were kept somewhat impotent by local conditions and failure of support from their respective political bodies.

New York–Pennsylvania

North of Fort Pitt, the New York frontier campaigns were to play key roles in the war. Since British forces were concentrated in New York, it was obvious that much activity would take place in its frontier areas. The localities of these new attacks were virtually the same ones involved in the French and Indian War. The Six Nations were allies of the British as they had been twenty years before. The only difference was the substitution of American patriots for the French.

As a part of General Howe's coastal campaign, one branch of the British Army under General John Burgoyne was to move down Lakes Champlain and George to the Hudson and then join forces on the lower river with General Howe. In June, 1777, he reached Lake Champlain, and during that summer he moved southward to Freeman's Farm and Saratoga where on October 17 he was defeated by the Americans.

At that time, and after, the New York–Pennsylvania frontiers underwent practically the same experience as did the Kentucky settlements. Raids were made against the settlements along the Mohawk and southward to the Susquehanna. In June, 1777, the Andrustown and Wyoming massacres occurred. General Horatio Gates was encouraged to check these bloody attacks by raiding the Six Nations, and plans were formulated not only to protect these frontier areas, but to take the Americans to Detroit. Before they could be matured, Indian attacks were made against German Flats and Cherry Valley along the Mohawk, and by the end of 1778 it was clearly evident that immediate action was imperative.

The answer to the frontier demand for defense was the Sullivan-Clinton campaign which was organized to take the fight directly to the troubled spots on the frontiers of the two states. Washington planned the campaign himself and placed General John Sullivan and General James Clinton in charge. After careful preparation the expedition got started in 1779, and the two commands came together at Tioga, Pennsylvania. Fortunately, the British had failed to reinforce Joseph Brant and John Butler, who were directing the savage raids, and the drive of Sullivan and Clinton from the east and Brodhead up the Allegheny River from Fort Pitt caught them unprepared for a heavy attack. In the battle of Newtown, August 29, approximately four thousand American troops engaged one thousand troops under Brant and Butler and won a major victory. Not only were the Americans successful in formal battle, but a massive destruction of Indian and Tory property along the frontiers of the two states brought some degree of peace for the next year or two. This expedition was also important because it destroyed vast food resources which were being drawn upon by the British, and because much specific geographical knowledge was gained by militiamen who later became settlers in the region.

King's Mountain

While Washington was struggling with the British around New York and Philadelphia, and the Sullivan-Clinton campaign was underway in the north, the southern mountain frontier along the Holston and the Tennessee was in a continuous state of alarm. Indeed, the region immediately east of the mountains became the scene of the bitterest border

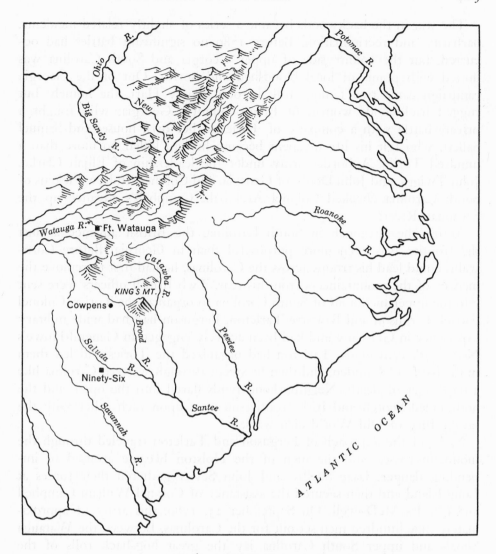

KING'S MOUNTAIN CAMPAIGN

struggle of the war. From Savannah, Georgia, to Guilford Courthouse in North Carolina, there raged from 1778 to 1781 an intensely bitter fight between British-led American Tories and fierce backwoods patriots. Like all border wars engaging neighbor against neighbor, this one was a constant repetition of brutality. Among the Tory leaders in the Carolinas and Georgia were James and Daniel McGirth, Thomas Brown, and Colonel Grierson. All of them incurred the wrath of the backwoodsmen by murdering and pillaging the settlers.

The war in the backwoods became a series of slightly related incidents, barbarity and recrimination. Before 1780 no significant battles had occurred, but the countryside of upper Georgia and South Carolina was dotted with points of local bloodshed and horror. Out of the Georgia campaign came two famous folk heroes: Nancy Hart, the homely but rugged backwoods woman of Elbert County, Georgia, who fought a private battle with a company of Tories in her own house; and Samuel Sallett, who felt his life misspent because he had killed no more than a hundred Tories. A border army under the leadership of Elijah Clarke, John Twiggs, and John Dooly of Georgia, and Colonel Andrew Pickens of South Carolina checked Colonel Archibald Campbell's advance up the Savannah River.

Across the Savannah in South Carolina, the British advance against the frontier was even more purposeful than in Georgia. Before Cornwallis could lead his troops across the Carolinas, he had first to remove the menace of the mountaineers from his rear. Two British officers were sent into the upper piedmont of South Carolina to organize the Tories, Colonel Patrick Ferguson and Banastre Tarleton. Ferguson had had wide military experience in Germany and had been actively engaged in General Howe's New York campaigns. Tarleton had organized the Tories and led them in the battle of Camden, and then he swept through western Carolina like a messenger of death. Neighborhood feuds flared into the open, and the hotblooded Scotch and Irish frontiersmen set upon each other with the savage fury of Old World clan wars.

News of the approach of Ferguson and Tarleton traveled through the mountain passes, and the men of the Holston became aroused to impending danger. Isaac Shelby and John Sevier gathered their forces at Long Island and then secured the assistance of Colonel William Campbell and Charles McDowell. On September 25, 1780, this army of approximately nine hundred men set out for the Carolinas. Between the Watauga Shoals and upper South Carolina lay the great hog-back rolls of the Smokies and the Blue-Ridges. Under skillful guidance the troops followed the gorges of the upper Holston to the divide, and then by Paddy's Creek, a branch of the Catawba, down the eastern slopes. Hastening eastward, the mountain men gathered volunteers as they went. On the headwaters of the Catawba they were joined by the fierce North Carolinian, Colonel Benjamin Cleveland, and 350 militiamen. Colonel William Campbell was elevated to top command with Shelby and Sevier in the important secondary positions. Colonel McDowell, an officer of doubtful capacity, was judiciously removed from a position of jealous rivalry by being sent away to General Gates with the request that a general officer be sent to direct the frontier army.

Speed was urgent if Ferguson were to be taken by surprise, or if he were to be confronted at all in the upcountry, for already he was moving eastward to more suitable fighting ground than he found among the steep hills. He had gathered his troops on the border between North and South Carolina in the neighborhood of King's Creek and Mountain. In hot pursuit was an army of approximately fifteen hundred selected backwoodsmen who had been twice screened for endurance to do battle on the rugged advance. In the last organization of the militiamen, their forces had been pared down to approximately nine hundred men in top condition. Ahead of them Ferguson had taken refuge atop King's Mountain, where he believed "all rebels outside of hell" could not attack successfully. However, he was not in so strong a position to withstand a determined rebel army as he might have placed himself if he had been given more warning. His Tory forces were somewhat depleted by leaves from duty, and he was too far removed from Colonel Cruger's base of operation at Ninety-Six to secure immediate reinforcement.

Pushing forward at a phenomenal rate of speed, the mountain men counted on some degree of surprise and a favorable geographic situation. The way the enemy was grouped and the lay of the ground were most favorable for an encirclement. After the frontier colonels conferred on a plan of battle, each command was informed which position it was to occupy. Men were instructed specifically in the ticklish strategy of rushing up to the crest of the hill and then falling back to regroup if the pressure became too great. Also, they were instructed to take cover behind trees if need be, and to push the attack "Indian" or "man-to-man" style. When the mountaineers had advanced to within a quarter of a mile of the crest, their presence was discovered and they were forced to ride hard to gain the shoulder of the ridge, tie their horses and rush headlong into the fight. Ferguson had armed his men with hunting knives attached to rifle barrels and ordered a bayonet attack. The first rush of the defenders forced the backwoodsmen down the ridge, but while one group retreated, that from the opposite side rushed up, and for an hour the battle surged back and forth. Patrick Ferguson was urging his men on to battle with the incessant shrill notes of a silver whistle, but near the middle of the fight the notes of the whistle died with its owner. His body, riddled by a volley of rifle fire, fell from the saddle. In an hour the engagement was ended and the men of Patrick Ferguson's army were either dead, badly wounded or captured. Fighting had been ferocious. At first the officers had difficulty getting their individualistic militiamen to respect the flags of truce or to regard the traditional rights of prisoners of war. The whole conduct of this undisciplined frontier army constitutes one of the most mixed stories of triumph and unmilitary-like conduct in American history. Officers had no legal control over their men and found it impossible to check many of their evil tendencies. The army was without technical legal status. No government had created or supported it. It had no means of paying for services, no sustained system of supplies, and its officers had no power of court martial.

Nolichucky, Clark's Station and Blue Licks

Turning homeward from King's Mountain, the mountain men carried prisoners of war, loot of battle, and the grim satisfaction that their home-land was free of threat from the British invader. But many of the re-turning heroes hardly had time to dismount and greet their families before they were called away to clear the Tennessee border of another threat from the Cherokees. Such British agents as John McDonald worked among the Indians in an effort to incite them against the whites, despite the fact that many of the Indians wished for peace. Two unrelenting chiefs, Dragging Canoe and Oconostota, wanted war. Major Joseph Martin was given by Virginia the delicate task of keeping the Cherokees and Chicka-maugas quiet by diplomacy, but by December, 1780, this seemed to be an impossibility. Upon Sevier's return from King's Mountain the Indian situation was so threatening that for the second time he and his men found themselves riding against the enemy. At Long Creek, a branch of the Nolichucky River, the Indians were engaged in battle, and on December 16, 1780, they were defeated in a cleverly fought action. This expedition took the rifle and torch to the ancient valley towns of Chota, Tellico and Little Tuskegee. It then penetrated deep into the eastern Tennessee moun-tains up the Tellico River. Sevier led his troops against the Cherokees and Chickamaugas again in the spring of 1781. This campaign, along with the subsequent one the next year, broke the Indian hold on much of the Tennessee Valley land. By 1782 the southwestern Indians were in a pitiful plight. As Old Tassel, an important Cherokee chief, said in a letter to the Governor of North Carolina, they faced starvation.

It is true, of course, that British agents kept the border Indians from southwest Virginia to Georgia in a state of unrest, but the real core of trouble was the encroachment of white settlers. This was the theme of Old Tassel's letter. White settlers were building cabins on the Indians' hunting lands. He said he hoped the Governor of North Carolina and Virginia would "take pity on your younger brother, and send Col. Sevier, who is a good man, to have your people moved off our land." Agreements made at Hard Labor and Lochaber were quickly forgotten. Old Tassel saw the real point at issue. It was not Sevier and Shelby leading frontier troops into the Indians' country that was most disturbing; it was the forward-creeping line of smoking cabin chimneys that symbolized the true meaning of white frontier expansion for the Indians. Nowhere on the frontier did white and Indian economy come more readily into conflict than in east Tennessee.

While John Sevier and his Tennesseans were putting down the Indian uprisings in the Tennessee Valley, their Kentucky neighbors to the north were having similar difficulty. As we have seen, the Kentucky frontier had little or no peace after 1775; the expeditions of George Rogers Clark and John Bowman left little room for border quietude. While Clark and Bowman were beyond the river striking at the anchor points of British control of the Northwest, the British at Detroit during the last months of the Revolution were encouraging frequent raids across the river to Kentucky. Two of these numerous attacks stand out as major incidents in border warfare. In the spring of 1780 British officials at Detroit hoped to revive their war effort by undertaking a rather far-flung strategic move to attack all the way across the western American frontier and to press the settlements to surrender. One major objective was Clark's Station at the Falls of the Ohio. If an attack could be effected before Clark could return from Vincennes, so much the better.

In May, 1780, Major Arent de Peyster ordered Captain Henry Bird to attack the Kentucky settlement with a force of 150 whites and as large a band of Indians as he could muster. Captain Bird finally assembled his army at the mouth of the Miami River, and by June 9 they were encamped on the present site of the city of Cincinnati. Conflict arose between the white officers and the Indian chiefs. The latter refused to attack Fort Nelson out of fear of George Rogers Clark, and consequently the expedition followed the Licking River southward to the white stations at Hinkston's and Ruddell's forts. On June 24 the British and Indians surprised the Kentuckians and, aided by the use of two small field pieces which were directed against the log blockhouses, took the two forts by assault. This attack was a military success, but because the excessive brutality of the Indians toward their victims sickened their British companions the raid further into Kentucky was called off.

Because these sporadic attacks caused great anxiety, George Rogers Clark learned what it was like to be a victim of public dissatisfaction. He proposed to fortify the Ohio River below Louisville to head off an Indian and British attack from the south, but people living along the upper Ohio felt that they were much more apt to be attacked from Detroit. Possibly as a consequence of this public pressure, Clark was provoked into leading an expedition against the Indians in the Miami Valley in 1782. Although he was unsuccessful in engaging the foe in pitched battle, he did them considerable damage by destroying their villages and crops.

The concluding major British and Indian thrust against Kentucky came in 1782, under the leadership of Captain William Caldwell. The first attack of this campaign took place against Little Mount. An obstreperous band of Wyandottes had refused to wait for the English to move and started the attack on their own. They defeated the small band of whites and captured their station, but their act put the settlements on guard.

In August of 1782, Caldwell led a combined army of approximately two hundred Canadians and Indians against the settlements in central Kentucky. Following roughly the route taken two years before by Captain Bird, he attacked Bryan's Station near Lexington on August 14. This attack and the half-hearted siege that followed had every earmark of immaturity. Failure to take the fort and the impending danger of attack from a stronger Kentucky defense forced Caldwell to withdraw his troops and begin a retreat out of Kentucky. The Kentuckians followed him to the Licking River, where in an impulsive moment hotheads provoked an attack which led the frontiersmen into a trap. This battle of the Blue Licks on August 19, 1782 resulted in a bloody defeat marked only by a needless loss of pioneer lives. The invaders withdrew from the country, however, and so ended British assaults against the Kentucky settlements.

The backwoods played an important role in the American Revolution, although except for King's Mountain and Saratoga there were no major battles. Clark's victories at Kaskaskia and Vincennes, Boone's at Boonesboro, and the Clinton-Sullivan successes were more nearly timely moves on the periphery of the international chessboard than important actions of arms. Hand, McIntosh and Irvine at Fort Pitt had no major military accomplishments to their credit, nor did John Bowman and the other Kentuckians. On the opposing side, the British had been unable to organize and carry out large scale attacks on the American settlements. The omnipresent lack of trade goods, dependable militiamen, unified Indian policy, transportation facilities, and the deterrent influence of inert distance paralyzed them. Uncertain commanders, a plague on the British effort twenty years before in the same territory, again exhausted them in the Revolution. Had the British been able to unify the Ohio country Indians and to consolidate their warriors, numbering almost ten thousand, into a single fighting unit, they no doubt could have wiped out the frontier settlements. The fact that American Indian diplomacy, however deficient it was in general, did prevent such a unification and did deflate British influence was possibly the most significant achievement in the West during the Revolution. The Indians themselves were divided by intertribal rivalries and fears of the advancing frontiersmen, a situation very fortunate for the frontiersmen.

The British depended upon a combination of regulars, militiamen and

Indian warriors. The warriors, however, seldom if ever adjusted themselves to disciplined and planned strategy, and were liabilities in the execution of any attack that required sustained effort. The Indians were suited
neither by temperament nor by tradition to follow a semicontinental mode
of warfare. Their supply facilities were so highly individualized and
fortuitous that they were usually unequipped to campaign where food
was not readily available in the countryside. They responded to no set
discipline, and conferences between British and Indian commanders must
have been delaying and frustrating. Also, there were so many British misgivings over Indian brutalities to prisoners and noncombatants that there
was often a lack of spirited push for fear of the horrible consequences.

From the border point of view, the expansion and success of the white
settlements during the Revolution is one of the truly phenomenal aspects
of American expansion. Had the British struck hard and concerted blows
at forts Pitt, Randolph, and McIntosh and the Kentucky settlements in
either 1778 or 1779, the West might have been lost. While it is true that
the Americans could never get organized sufficiently to capture Detroit,
they were growing stronger with each succeeding year. Month by month
a greater reservoir of manpower was concentrating on the frontier. This
shifting of population to the outer fringes of settlement built up an important stabilizing resource which eventually made attack from both
Indians and British appear foolhardy. The Indians came to respect this
fact, even though they were somewhat successful in the attack on Bryan's
Station and in the defeat of the frontiersmen at Blue Licks in 1782.

Although the frontier attitudes toward extended enlistments in the
militia and the necessity for discipline were serious barriers in the conduct
of effective campaigns against the enemy, the frontiersmen were effective
fighting men when their homes and families were threatened. A curious
transition had occurred in their attitudes between 1756 and 1780. There
were, of course, no fundamental differences in personality and environment between those colonial troops who were with Washington in the
defense of the Virginia frontier and those who rode with Sevier and
Shelby, or those who marched with Clark and Bowman. Yet the latter
were far more responsive to border needs for defense. Possibly the American frontiersmen never showed greater determination than at King's
Mountain or Boonesboro. The fact that Fort Pitt withstood attack, and that
the New York, Pennsylvania, Tennessee, and Kentucky outposts repelled
British Indian assaults is evidence of the determination of the advancing
settlers to take and to hold the western country. In the twenty years between 1763 and 1783, the superficialities of political restrictions on frontier expansion were virtually swept away. Administrative controls were
placed largely in that effective frontier political instrument, the county.

THE FRONTIER ON THE OHIO AND MISSISSIPPI

And here we must regret the unfortunate death of young Mr. Payne, on board Capt. Blackemore's boat, who was mortally wounded by reason of the boat running too near the northern shore opposite the town, where some of the enemy lay concealed, and the more tragical misfortune of poor Stuart, his family and friends to the number of twenty-eight persons. This man had embarked with us for the Western country, but his family being diseased with the small pox, it was agreed upon between him and the company that he should keep at some distance in the rear, for fear of the infection spreading, and he was warned each night when the encampment should take place by the sound of a horn. After we had passed the town, the Indians having now collected to a considerable number, observing his helpless situation, singled off from the rest of the fleet, intercepted him and killed and took prisoners the whole crew, to the great grief of the whole company, uncertain how soon they might share the same fate; their cries were distinctly heard by those boats in the rear.

—JOHN DONELSON, *Journal of a Voyage from Fort Patrick Henry to the French Salt Springs on the Cumberland*

Sketch of Cleveland under the hill in 1800

A CONTEMPORARY SKETCH BY CAPTAIN ALLEN GAYLORD OF NEWBURG

CHAPTER VI

THE end of the Revolutionary War in the East brought no clean-cut cessation of hostilities on the frontier. The conflict between settlers and Indians and British stragglers could neither be concluded on the field of battle nor around the council table. Still, although there were periodic outbreaks east of the Ohio after Cornwallis surrendered in Virginia, these were nothing more than indecisive raids and skirmishes such as those of Bird and Caldwell against the Kentucky forts, or the Chickamauga and Cherokee outbreaks in Tennessee.

The captivating pursuits of settlement and land speculation once more occupied the frontier. The frontier battles were no longer of basic importance. Militiamen who accompanied the Clinton-Sullivan raid were attracted to the new country through which they had traveled in western New York and Pennsylvania. Those frontiersmen who dashed into the Cherokee and Chickamauga Indian valleys behind Sevier and Shelby had seen land there which was to their liking.

131

We have already noted that interest in land hunting and speculation had been continuous since the days of the 1730's and '40's. Some of the individuals who had first participated in land hunting and in the organization of land companies were still actively promoting their interests. Members of the Ohio, Loyal, Vandalia, Indiana, and all the other companies were still anxious to secure land. Added to the list of the older speculative organizations were many new ones which had come into existence to seek wealth and fame for their stockholders.

In all this rush for land and the making of settlements in the West, there were three distinct kinds of individuals who carried on the labors. We have already described them in an earlier chapter, but they will bear repetition here—and for that matter, they are perennial. First, there was the speculator, who, if he lived today, would be an enterprising businessman overseeing industrial and commercial investments. Land represented future wealth to the Colonial and Revolutionary entrepreneur; land not only excited his economic interests, but land speculation also carried with it a certain amount of political influence as well as an aura of romance. Even as early as this period there was the individual who had such a mania for the ownership of land that he gave substance to the backwoods expression "land pore." The second type was the footman of western expansion, the land scout, or hunter, who prowled the wild country for settlement sites, desirable blocks of land, and other advantages which would promote the personal fortunes of his employers as well as their prospective new settlements. Finally there was the little settler who came looking for cheap lands and new opportunity; sometimes for a chance to escape the wrath of patriots, debts, a faulty monetary system, tenantry, or to seek religious freedom. Not infrequently a settler came westward to avoid a court summons and a sheriff's shackles because of some crime he had committed. Simon Kenton, for instance, escaped to the frontier because he believed he had killed a rival in love. But whatever the cause, land was the magic attraction; its availability and distribution are basic to an understanding of the westward movement at this point in its history.

As a prelude to the gigantic population shift westward, the signing of the Treaty of Paris in 1783, by which the Revolutionary War came to an official close, had an important influence on expansion. The broad area east of the Mississippi River which had been in dispute since 1740 was now placed under American control. Characteristic of private land grants, the descriptions of the new territorial boundaries were found to be vague indeed when attempts were made to apply them specifically. Of importance were the general boundaries—the river on the west, the thirty-first parallel on the south, and the fact that the Mississippi was open to free use by frontier navigation at least as far as this point. The secret agreement in the treaty concerning the southern boundary was to cause considerable dispute before it was finally settled to the satisfaction of Spain. The territorial boundaries outlined in the Treaty of Paris generally followed clearly defined natural lines, and decisions on this particular point should have been obvious ones, but the fact that the great fur trading and military posts were in the new American area either reflects British lack of knowledge and appreciation of this fact or some highly competent and shrewd management on the part of the American commissioners. Actual British surrender of the Northwest fur trading lands and posts took place only after much further diplomatic negotiation, however, and even then not until a second war between America and Britain had loomed as a distinct possibility.

The area opened for immediate frontier expansion, so far as European claims were concerned, was greatly extended. There still remained the tedious question of Indian ownership. Again the Chippewa Indians could say, as one of their number did on an earlier occasion: "These lakes, these woods, these mountains were left to us by our ancestors. They are our inheritance; and we will part with them to none." The Indian, however, was not in so solid a position to declare his wrath as he was in 1763. For the white settler, land seemed at that moment to be an inexhaustible resource. Rash prophets might have predicted, as some did, that it would take centuries to consolidate these new gains.

Ceding new territory was only one aspect of the Treaty of Paris of 1783. Behind it was the complex story of diplomatic negotiation among Franklin, Jay and John Adams for the states, Vergennes for France, and Lord Shelburne and Richard Oswald for Britain. Possibly the Shelburne ministry in restricting British claims gave serious thought to administrative costs. No doubt there was the fresh memory of all the difficulties England had experienced in the region. There was knowledge of, if not profound respect for, the feverish determination of the American frontiersmen for expansion; Spain was becoming a strong rival west of the river; and finally some Englishmen wished to hold on to and develop Canada instead of the territory south of the lakes.

From the standpoint of the frontier, the Treaty of 1783 had many meanings. It is difficult, if not almost impossible, for example, to ferret out of the great mass of materials relating to the crosscurrents of diplomatic conversations and pressures any conclusive notions of the influences of the Clark campaigns. Possibly the political meaning of such an undertaking was great as a background factor, but it is doubtful that it was a direct factor. It would be hard, however, to overemphasize the meaning to American expansion of the great block of available northwestern territory. Old trade and border rivalries multiplied where the Indian trade was concerned. The lack of respect for territorial agreements among rival traders, and even the British frontier military forces, lingered on to cause friction. Within a remarkably short time the interruption of free navigation down the Mississippi River was to play havoc with public opinion. During the next two decades the indefiniteness of parts of the boundary in the neighborhood from the Lake of the Woods to the headwaters of the Mississippi and also eastward from the Mississippi along the thirty-first parallel would prove to be stubborn international issues.

The fur and Indian trade was wholly involved in the inefficient border administration, but the most important of the frontier speculative issues was the status of land companies. Not one of the companies seeking grants immediately preceding the war was able to get its requests honored. The end of the war and the signing of the treaty either forced the companies into liquidation or caused them to have to make new approaches all over again to Congress instead of the Crown. The manipulations of the land companies during the Revolution tell a badly tangled story of American patriotism and rank opportunism. Many American names intimately associated with the Revolution were likewise associated with land speculations, such as Benjamin Franklin, Arthur Lee and Patrick Henry.

The frontier land question was important also because of its significance to the small settler and as a general political issue. No state government before 1776 was technically in a position to enact adequate land laws to protect itself against chaos in the individual land claims. Three factors figured prominently in the occupation of the small land claims: first, the squatter (as has been said) took land where it pleased him to do so; second, land companies claimed vaguely bounded and conflicting blocks; and third, no orderly system had been devised for making surveys of claims. This last condition held true even though land surveying was a popular profession.

Through Cumberland Gap

Beginning with the Watauga settlement, new communities began to appear west of the mountains. One of the important individuals who helped to break the barriers of the western mountain ranges and to plant a new settlement on the head of the Holston River was James Robertson. Born in Brunswick County, Virginia, Robertson had moved westward at an early age. He went from Brunswick to Wake County, North Carolina and in 1770 reached the Holston, where he planted his first crop of corn in the backwoods. In the late fall of 1779 he again plunged deep into the frontier, this time leading an overland party of settlers through Cumberland Gap to Dick's River in central Kentucky and then southward to the bend of the Cumberland at the French Lick. A second company of this expedition went by boat from Long Island in the Holston to the Little Tennessee, down the Big Tennessee to the Ohio, up the Ohio to the Cumberland, and then to Robertson's new settlement at the present site of Nashville.

This was perhaps one of the most adventurous folk movements in the history of the frontier region east of the Mississippi. Leading the party of some forty craft was John Donelson's flatboat, the *Adventure*. This well-known surveyor and Indian scout set forth down the Holston with a company of men, women and children. It was his hope that he could run by the villages of the hostile Chickamaugas without molestation, but this was not to be. The Indians beset the flotilla, and misfortune dogged its steps for many miles. Boats were grounded or impaled on rocks, some members of the party allowed their canoes to get too near the bank and were wounded or killed by the Indians. Where the Cumberland Mountains towered above the narrow throat of the stream, the angry attackers poured damaging pot shots on to the boats; and to add to the confusion and anxiety, one of the women gave birth to a baby. One boat laden with smallpox victims lagged considerably behind so that the whole party would not be infected. It was overhauled and captured by the Indians and its passengers were tortured and put to death. But in death the whites were to have fierce retribution. Their disease spread fatally through the Indian villages.

At Muscle Shoals, Robertson and Henderson were to leave a signal that the boats could be beached and the settlers moved overland to the Cumberland. When Donelson reached the upper end of the rapids, he could find no indication that they had kept their promise, and so it was necessary for him to continue the voyage on the river. Anchored above the rapids of the rocky shoals the fateful decision was made to take women, children and inexperienced boatmen over an unknown and awesome stretch of water. This water hazard was almost as treacherous as the Indians concealed above the Cumberland narrows, but Donelson's frontier Tennesseans were able to keep their craft upright through the rapids and negotiated the Tennessee to the Ohio. They then pushed their clumsy boats against the heavy winter current of the Cumberland to the pioneer settlement at the French Licks.

The tiny settlement of Nashboro was a direct offspring of Boonesboro. In 1776, when Virginia's General Assembly nullified the claim of the Transylvania Company, Richard Henderson turned, not to the 200,000 acre grant north of the Green River, but to the fertile plateau area in the bend of the Cumberland. The Walker and, subsequently, the Henderson surveys made it clearly evident that Nashboro was well within the boundary of North Carolina.

If we substitute James Robertson and John Donelson for Daniel Boone and Captain William Twetty, the Cumberland River for the Kentucky, and the bitterly cold winter of 1779-1780 for the mild spring and summer of 1775, the histories of Henderson's two frontier settlements are not too different. Henderson repeated his earlier promotional attempts to set up a government on the banks of the Cumberland. It was to have a formal existence and be somewhat reminiscent of the beginnings of the Plymouth Colony. Henderson's backwoods settlers drafted the "Cumberland Compact" of government and repeated the plan followed at Boonesboro. A more liberal land policy permitted settlers to register claims for 400 acres upon the payment of a ten dollar fee. In 1779 corn was bought at Boonesboro and moved downstream aboard a flatboat to the infant Nashboro early in 1780. Thus it was that the settlers were sustained in bread until they grew a crop of corn of their own.

Nashboro was a product of the desire of both speculator and settler to acquire land. The fact that many separate stations or settlements sprang up so rapidly along the Cumberland before the conclusion of the Revolutionary War indicates once more how impelling was this westward population movement. To the north, successive population figures for Kentucky prove the volume of this westward-moving tide. In 1775 there was an estimated population of 100 persons; eight years later there were 12,000; and by 1784, 30,000 settlers had crossed the mountains to Kentucky. Although Tennessee's population increase was not so impressive for the first years, it was not to be ignored.

A vigorous population movement brought all sorts of political and social problems. Perhaps no political issue was more urgent than the need for a clear-cut policy of land survey and distribution. At least three classes of land claims were recognized, and all three were in sharp conflict. Companies and land syndicates claimed large blocks of land; individual squatters sought title to definite small plots; and soldiers who had fought in the Revolutionary War were given warrants in payment for their services. As early as 1776 Virginia had to concern itself with its western land problems.

Land Problems

By 1783 there were in existence at least two distinct systems of land survey and dispersal. The New England plan had followed the policy of granting new claims after a survey had laid out townships. Land was deeded to the individual in such a way that settlement was a continuous and orderly progress; this insured against conflicting claims and avoided the troublesome remnants of waste lands lying among the settled claims. Landholding in New England was on a much smaller scale than in the southern colonies where the plantation system of vast acreage prevailed. Also, the New England community was more dependent upon close co-operation among neighbors in their daily activities, especially during the long cold winters. Neighbors lived closer together and in more intimate association than was usually true of other sections. In the larger southern colonies, especially in Virginia, land was a highly desired source of wealth even though it was most plentiful. The rule prevailed that a man could select plots of land which appealed to him, and by 1776 the practice of hit-or-miss surveys governed only by personal whims and fancies was firmly implanted on the frontier. All along the border line of settlement people were pushing in and claiming blocks of land which suited them most, giving little or no thought to the woeful issues of conflicting claims which were to arise in the future courtrooms of the area.

Although the New England land system followed orderly methods of survey and the Virginia practice ignored this principle, the more important difference between the two plans was the fact that one prescribed survey before grant and the other allowed grant in advance of survey. It is readily seen that the latter practice contained many liabilities. Private land companies had made both claims and surveys. Reservations were made for veterans who served in the Virginia line for prescribed periods, and individual warrants were issued to numerous individual claimants. Recognizing its land policy to be a most urgent problem, the Virginia assembly on June 24, 1776, provided that each individual claimant should be allowed four hundred acres of land whether or not he held prior title from Henderson's Transylvania Company or from the Crown. Four days later the assembly adopted a state constitution which nullified all land claims made by the Crown, assumed ownership of lands granted by France in the Treaty of 1763, and forbade private individuals from purchasing tracts from the Indians. This final provision was in fact a supplementary revenue act and may hardly be considered a well-reasoned plan for dispersing Virginia's large public domain. By January 24, 1778, the state's land affairs were in such a chaotic state that the issuance of new grants was halted from that date until a new law could be drafted.

George Mason prepared the new law, the famous act of 1779, and on June 22 provisions were made for the granting of a basic plat of four hundred acres, and the registering of an option for an additional thousand acres. It was the prevailing popular belief that four hundred acres was all the land an individual holder could bring under cultivation. The additional thousand acres was for speculative purposes, or to provide for the needs of numerous prospective heirs. There was no limitation, however, on the number of claims which an individual might make, nor could a man be prevented from registering a claim in the name of another. By the same law, prospective claimants were required to purchase warrants, to employ registered surveyors and chain carriers, to register surveyed plats within six months, and to secure warranty deeds from the land clerks. On the other hand clerks were required to register all plats in durable books, to ascertain that they did not duplicate registered claims, and to issue deeds of warranty. It can be seen at once that this law required a considerable amount of administrative organization to make it effective, and when deeds were required in large numbers as in the years from 1779 to 1785 the system tended to break down.

The land warrant was an interesting legal instrument. It was a printed and officially sealed form which, aside from some necessary formal phraseology, contained a date, the name of the purchaser, and the amount of land which he was entitled to register. In no way was the holder of the warrant guaranteed lands. The warrant was not a deed, but it was to be filed with an authorized surveyor's certificate describing a specific plot of land as evidence of payment of the necessary legal purchase price.

Perhaps no more clumsy system of land distribution could have been devised. With the rush of settlers westward after 1779 the land clerks' offices were swamped, and there was such a demand for the services of surveyors that it was almost impossible for many people to make any kind of a clear sustainable record. Plats sometimes overlapped one another, sometimes two to six times. Great blocks of good lands were left unclaimed, and these were left on the state's hands in large crazy-quilt blocks of so-called waste or undesirable plats which could not be sold but which complicated the platting of salable lands. The courts were never able to work out an entirely equitable system of determining the soundest and earliest claims to lands.

Following the wild confusion of 1776 and the restatement of the law in 1779, the Virginia General Assembly settled on an informal but basic test by which a prior claimant could be sustained. The new law declared "that no family shall be entitled to the allowance granted to settlers by this act, unless they had made a crop of corn in that country, or resided there at least one year since the time of their settlement." A second part of the same provision stipulated that all those who before January 1, 1778, "had marked out or chosen for themselves, any wasted or unappropriated lands, and built any house or hut, or made other improvements thereon, shall also be entitled to the pre-emption the like terms, of any quantity of land, to include such improvements, not exceeding one thousand acres. . . ." This was the first time the famous "corn patch and cabin" law had been written into the statutes, but since the beginning of English settlement on this continent it was looked upon as a valid testament of settlement intentions. The practice became famous in the older areas where the system of metes and bounds prevailed.

In disputes involving land claims, one or the other side tried to prove prior ownership by citing initials cut on a tree, the outlines of a cabin foundation, or proof of a patch of corn. In 1780 James Berry undertook to establish in court the validity of his land title. His proof was to the effect that the prior claimant had planted corn on the land in 1776, and he submitted the following affidavit: "William Henderson by Nathaniel Henderson this day claimed a settlement and preemption to a tract of land in the District of Kentucky on account of raising a crop of corn in the county in the year 1776."

The most distinctive characteristic of much of the early frontier movement south of the Ohio was this chaos of land titles. It led to some of the famous frontier lawsuits, among which were Kenton *vs.* McConnell, Green *vs.* Biddle, Beard *vs.* Smith, and Marshall et al. *vs.* George Rogers Clark. This furious litigation among conflicting claimants advertised the prosperous possibilities of the law to the young men of Virginia with law training. Large numbers of able lawyers came west not only to protect the interests of clients, but to devote themselves to other fundamental political matters. Among these were Henry Clay, John Breckinridge, Caleb Wallace, George Nicholas, and Humphrey Marshall. For some of the frontier states the indefiniteness of the land system provoked some fascinating legal history and involved varying theories of ownership of real property in the realm of the common law. In view of the confusion which resulted from granting land prior to survey with the limited surveying staff available, it is little wonder that many famous pioneers, among them Daniel Boone and Simon Kenton, lost their lands because of the technicalities in the registry laws.

Descriptions of lands located by the metes and bounds formula were nothing short of statements of faith. To begin with, the claimant backed his best judgment and selected land which he believed to be of the most desirable quality. He established his lines so as to avoid sinks, swampy places, mountainsides and rock outcroppings, leaving these unproductive plots to the state. Provisions were made in the Virginia law of 1779 for a proportional length to width survey, except where mountains crowded in upon small stream valleys. When a settler located land he wanted to claim, he cut his initials on a tree. He then stepped off measurements in terms of poles or rods, establishing landmarks of his choice until he had bounded his property. When he had cut his initials, he blackened the letters by burning gunpowder in them. Where a man was unable to cut letters, he hacked three ax marks or tomahawk wounds on a tree, and

seared them with gunpowder. A characteristic description for land boundaries outside the so-called public land areas is the following Kentucky
survey of May 1, 1781, for 500 acres of land: "Beginning on David Vance's
west line of his pre-emption at two sugar trees and an ash, thence north 30°
155 poles to three sugar trees then north 60° west 330 poles crossing two
small branches to two ashes and sugar trees thence south 30° west 377
poles to a buckeye, hoop ash, and sugar tree, thence 60° east 130 poles to
the beginning." Not a single permanent landmark was established in this
description, and what is more confusing is the fact that possibly no
two persons could agree thoroughly upon the specific identification of
all the trees mentioned. What, for instance, was a "hoop ash"? To qualify
as an early surveyor it was necessary to be well-versed in both geometry
and botany. Failure to establish some scientific common agreement on
names of trees alone in land line controversies cost lives and thousands
of dollars.

It is true, of course, that not all lands surveyed within the states outside
New England followed an indiscriminate pattern born of haste and expediency, but this pattern predominated. The Virginia system caused
landholders so much grief that every member of that state's land-centered
economy was conscious of it. Every deed transfer involved a certain
amount of boundary confusion, and anxiety over the validity of a survey
was a normal annoyance in land purchase. Thomas Jefferson, as governor
of Virginia, had seen the havoc which haphazard survey was causing. He
at least was amenable to the adoption of a more orderly survey plan when
time came to arrange distribution of public lands in the Northwest
Territory.

With the signing of the Treaty of 1783, Congress assumed the administrative problems of the Crown, with the important addition of increasing pressure from a westward moving population. The states in
1783 faced numerous immediate problems: adjusting the Indian conflict;
paying of state debts incurred in war; proportioning of governmental
responsibilities among the states; disposing of public lands, permitting a
free but governable flow of settlers westward; providing for the organization of new states; and adjusting international border disputes. Before Congress could tackle so intricate a task, the various state land claims
on the frontier had to be reconciled. The problem was by no means concentrated in the Northwest and Kentucky; Tennessee and Alabama lands
were likewise involved.

In Tennessee and the shoals area of northern Alabama the vigorous issue
of land speculation involved the question of state jurisdiction. First on the
list was the problem of how to deal with the semidetached Watauga
territory of North Carolina. As early as 1772 the Wataugans had made

plans for independent self-government in the Articles of the Watauga Association. These preceded the Boonesboro laws by three years and were six years older than the Cumberland Compact of Nashboro. The detached settlements had proved that they were able to defend themselves against border British and Indian raids, and even after the war they were still called upon to defend themselves against Indian hostilities. Coupled with these factors were the highly personal ones of leadership. Colonel Arthur Campbell, John Sevier, General William Russell, William Tipton, William Cocke and a score of others were active in urging separation from the parent state. None of them, however, was more persistent than Arthur Campbell, who was the combined Patrick Henry and Tom Paine of the Holston backwoods. It was he who first voiced the reasons and desire for separation, and it was he who provided the movement with a real spiritual leadership.

Grievances of the Wataugans were those common to most western communities far removed from the site of government. There was likewise a strong element of uncertainty in the matter of a cession of the western territory of North Carolina, owing to wishy-washy legislation which had first provided for separation of the western settlement and had then repealed the act of cession in 1784. The North Carolina legislature was under the domination of low country conservatives who would have been glad to have their state relieved of the western settlements, largely because of the expensive Indian raids and also because they were indifferent to frontier problems in general. On the other hand, some of the western land speculators actually preferred to remain under North Carolina's jurisdiction because they believed it would be easier to claim large blocks of land with governmental blessings. If the territory should fall under the control of a legislature nearer the scene of action and composed of members who were alert to the importance of the rich unexploited territory, speculators could expect little favor.

State of Franklin

In August, 1784, a convention assembled at Jonesboro to discuss the organization of a new state. A vote strongly favoring such a move was taken, and a constitutional convention was called for December 14 of that year. The list of delegates who appeared at this convention was almost a roll call of influential men in the Tennessee country. A vote taken on forming an independent state showed a substantial majority in favor. The convention drafted a constitution and paved the way for the establishment of a representative assembly to govern the new state of Franklin.

Creation of this state of Franklin was actually an act of rebellion in the face of North Carolina. Land speculators, chief of whom was John Sevier, saw to it that the new constitution contained no radicalism. The framers had no intention of veering sharply away from the North Carolina plan of government. Perhaps more damaging than any radicalism which might have appeared in this initial effort at state-making on the frontier was the conflict in which the new state found itself with the Indians and the land speculators. Cherokee and Chickamauga Indians were made unhappy by a failure to carry out a proposed treaty negotiation by which they were to be paid for their lands; the speculators were thrown into a panic by the North Carolina cession laws and the creation of a new state.

Unfortunately this frontier state-making effort degenerated into a hot battle between the local leaders, John Sevier and John Tipton—the latter, a militant opponent of the Franklin scheme. Although the state of Franklin failed to endure, the movement in east Tennessee for future independent statehood had several important and portentous aspects. The constitution as originally proposed was almost entirely democratic in its provisions. White men twenty-one years of age were given the right to vote. The people could vote directly for the governor, and important legislation was to be submitted to the people for their appraisal. As it turned out, however, the document as adopted was, as has been said, almost a copy of the conservative North Carolina constitution. Land speculation was a basic factor on both sides in the movement for independent statehood, but this pressure also underwent some material changes before 1789 when the state of Franklin had passed into oblivion. Even though the new state died aborning, the idea of statehood on a broader scale and a congressional distribution of public lands rapidly became fundamental issues.

Three Indian Treaties

While movements for separate statehood were being agitated in both Tennessee and Kentucky, Congress had to deal with a much larger question—the administration of the lands of the Northwest Territory. Almost immediately, the small states with fixed boundaries and the larger states which had access to great areas of western lands locked horns. States like Rhode Island, New Jersey and Delaware felt that the states which had western lands would be at a greater advantage in relieving themselves of the cost of the Revolutionary War. The point was made, with sound reason, that since all the states were equally involved in the common revolt, war costs were a common responsibility. For the central government the sale of public lands was a necessity because it needed money urgently. Land was a painless source from which money might be obtained.

After considerable political maneuvering, the distribution of western lands was made a fundamental issue in Maryland when that state refused to ratify the Articles of Confederation. A solution for this problem had been sought by the Congressional Committee on Finance in September, 1778, when it proposed to withhold the granting of public lands until the end of the war. The most equitable solution was outright cession of western lands to Congress. Maryland ratified the Articles of Confederation when Virginia consented, in 1781, to cede its public lands, except for Kentucky and its military grant north of the Ohio between the Scioto and the Little Miami rivers. The western lands were eventually all placed in congressional hands by 1802, although the states had agreed to give up their land claims before the Articles of Confederation went into effect in 1781.

With vast tracts of northwestern lands in its possession, Congress had to plan immediately for their administration and dispersal. It was necessary to make two approaches to the task. The western lands were also Indian lands, and the signing of the Treaty of Paris had not quieted Indian title claims. Some Indians maintained, rightly, that the white diplomats had traded their lands without their consent. As at the end of the French and Indian War, the victorious government once again had to make readjustments in the management of its Indian affairs.

On March 4, 1784, a commission of five members was appointed by the Congress of the Confederation to confer with the Six Nations and with some of the Ohio Indians in an attempt to establish a new Indian boundary. This council got underway on October 3, 1784, when three of the five commissioners met with representatives from the Six Nations, the Delawares and Shawnees at Fort Stanwix in New York. By the ensuing Treaty of Fort Stanwix, the Indian claim to the lands represented generally in the Lake Erie-Allegheny-West Branch river triangle and the area north of the Ohio was granted to the states. This treaty, however, settled only a part of the Indian issue. It was necessary for Congress to enter into a second round of negotiations directly with the Ohio tribes who claimed they had been cheated in the Fort Stanwix agreement. In January, 1785, representative Wyandotte, Delaware, Chippewa and Ottawa chiefs made the Treaty of Fort McIntosh which set aside the areas that were to be regarded as belonging to the Wyandottes, Delawares and some of the Ottawas, and quieted Indian title claims to lands lying outside the specified areas. These two treaties left the troublesome Shawnees still without a fixed agreement with the government of the Confederation. On October 22, 1785, a third conference was held, this time at the mouth of the Big

Miami, to deal with the Shawnees. This meeting was slow in getting underway, for though the weather was intensely cold the sullen Shawnees chose
to take their time in coming to the council site. When they did arrive it was
clear they were being advised by English traders to be wary. At long
last, the Treaty of Fort Finney, signed February 1, 1786, established
a boundary line between the Shawnees and the American settlers.

Although agreements had been reached with the Indians in three important treaties, actually little had been accomplished in securing the peace.
Again it should be pointed out that Indian economy in the Ohio region
demanded large areas of land which would permit a rotation of hunting
and trapping activities. Now that such large areas were turned over to the
Confederation, the system of rotation could no longer prevail. Likewise,
these treaties did not include any known device to check the pressure of
westward-moving white settlement. Much time might be spent in a
discussion of difference between white and Indian culture patterns, but
in fact the press of westward settlement appears at this point to have been
well-nigh inevitable, and lasting peace could not be obtained until the
Indian and his claim to the land were both submerged.

Northwest Territory

Pressure from white speculators, veterans and independent settlers
forced a final congressional decision on the administrative procedure and
disposition of the western lands. When the Virginia cession was accepted in 1784, it was provided that the area should be formed into states,
and that the so-called Virginia military lands between the Scioto and the
Little Miami rivers should be retained to pay off the state's Revolutionary
War veterans. Although there were other cessions in prospect, the granting of the important Virginia claim opened the way for the formulation of
a congressional plan of management. On March 1, 1784, Virginia ceded
her lands, and on that day a committee of five, composed of Thomas Jefferson, David Howell, Elbridge Gerry, Hugh Williamson of North Carolina,
and Jacob Reed of South Carolina was appointed to deal with the question
of temporary territorial government until a permanent plan could be
established. The report which this committee submitted reflects Jefferson's love of performing such a task.

Several of the principles laid down in the committee's report were of
fundamental importance. They reflected a fixed sense of colonial philosophy on the part of Congress. A provision was made that the free male
population should meet at a specified place to establish a temporary government, to endure until the population of a given area should equal
twenty thousand free inhabitants. Then the territory was forever to re-

main a part of the United States; it was to be subject to the Articles of the Confederation and to the Congress of the United States; and it was to bear its proportionate share of the federal debt. All future states carved from the area should be republican in form. A fifth provision incorporated in the original report, but which was for the time stricken out, provided that after 1800, slavery should not exist in the territory. Perhaps the most unusual aspect of the committee report was the recommendation (which bore the strong Jeffersonian stamp) that seven states bearing the classical names of *Michigania, Cherronesus, Sylvania, Assenisipia, Metropotamia,* and *Polisipia* plus eight or nine unnamed states should be carved out of the Northwest Territory according to prescribed surveys which followed along the various parallels.

When the committee report was finally adopted in the form of the Ordinance of 1784, the slavery clause was missing, but new provisions were included. There was to be no taxing of government property, non-resident proprietors should be taxed no higher than others, and it was guaranteed that the government should have full authority to dispose of public lands. Also, the provision about population in the original report was changed to read that a new state could be admitted to the union when the number of inhabitants of the area equaled that of the least populated state then existing. Provisions were made for the steps by which a territory might be formed and finally created into a state. This so-called Jeffersonian Ordinance was designed as a basis for territorial government, and despite arguments to the contrary it did constitute a summary plan of government for all future public territory under Congressional jurisdiction.

On March 16, 1785, a proposal was made by Rufus King of Massachusetts to amend the Ordinance to return the antislavery clause. This issue appeared in the Congressional minutes from time to time for the next two years, but it was not until a full new committee report was made and again amended that the slavery clause was actually on its way to adoption. This new report was made on April 26, 1787, by a committee of five composed of William Samuel Johnson, Charles Pinckney, Melancton Smith, Nathan Dane, and John Henry. The committee had drafted a plan of territorial government but had failed to include many of the fundamental clauses which were finally incorporated in the Ordinance. Among these features were guarantees of civil and religious liberty, rights of conscience and education, and the right of compact which was forever to remain unaltered except by common consent.

As finally adopted, the Ordinance of 1787 became one of the important but highly controversial documents in American history. It was within itself a bill of rights, presaging those which were later to be incorporated in the first eight amendments of the Constitution of the United States. It recognized the validity of education in an organized society and acknowledged the fact that religion and morality were necessary to good government. In the same article a moral plan was outlined for dealing with the Indians, and if it had been observed in the future, much of the disgrace described so effectively by Helen Hunt Jackson in her *Century of Dishonor* might have been avoided.

The second section of the Ordinance of 1787 is possibly of the greatest importance from the standpoint of property holding in the United States. It destroyed, as had the thirteen states, the feudalism which had persisted in America in the form of limited land titles, and placed the descent of property in either the individual testator's hand or put in the reach of chancery, decisions which could be made on the basis of equitable distribution of estates. This was a vitally needed piece of legislation and it clarified the whole involved issue of property descent in the United States. Another important aspect of the Ordinance was a repetition of the provision for the admission of new states, which were to be limited in the Northwest Territory to no fewer than three and no more than five, thus further destroying the recommendation of the first report that there be many states. Finally, the slavery clause found its way into the Bill of Rights of the document and it ordained that instead of waiting until 1800 to abolish the institution, "There shall be neither slavery nor involuntary servitude in the said territory. . . ." Significantly this section did recognize the legality of slavery elsewhere by providing that fugitives should be returned to their rightful owners if they escaped into an area under the jurisdiction of the Ordinance. The slavery section, or Article VI, however, was not submitted until the other sections had been voted upon. It is significant that the word "free" as applied to qualified voters was not removed from the sections first approved. Nathan Dane did not submit the slavery clause until he believed that Congress was ready to adopt it.

At least one student of the Ordinance of 1787 and the one re-enacted in 1789 says the document was nothing more than a legislative act. Its immediate creation was provoked by a necessity for efficient management in the Northwest Territory. However, some of its cardinal points go far beyond the problems of the frontier. Descent of property, a fuller restatement of fundamental human and political rights, and a discussion of slavery extension are of great importance. From the perspective of history the document in scope must be considered to be national rather than sectional. For the frontier it was important. If there were no other reasons, the clearly defined restrictions placed by it on the business of state-making guaranteed that there would be no radical departures from the earlier pattern of state government. There can be little doubt that conservative federalism received its biggest guarantee in the Northwest Ordinance. The federal government became more important in westward expansion than ever before, and the influence of the individual states was wiped away. Concisely, the central government stepped into the position of the Crown with a practical colonial system that was to work. Whatever independent spirit western state-makers might have had, they did little to demonstrate it because they lived safely within the prescribed fundamental structure of governmental planning. The Ordinance guaranteed that there would be a looking back to the seat of the national government in the future. The plan of administrative organization of territorial government established a system of federal patronage that was to have vital political influences upon the future.

A historian, of course, cannot say what might have happened had no such plan been adopted, or had the true Jeffersonian plan succeeded, but he can say what did happen. A fundamental plan of state-making prevailed which exhibited in broad general outline little or no variance from the fundamental structure of the original thirteen states. The broad general effect of the Ordinance itself, however, is to be evaluated in American history in terms of complex court interpretations and general development of state governments where specific provisions were either observed or ignored. One student of the Ordinance declares that it was irreconcilable to the principles of Anglo-American doctrine and was repugnant to the political doctrines of the Revolutionary era. One further fact has to be kept in mind and that is the relationship between the Ordinance and its contemporaneous document, the Constitution of the United States.

Since the distribution of land had been almost the basic issue in the discussion of the whole problem of the Northwest Territory, it became imperative that Congress agree on some system by which surveys and sales of the public domain could be made. As has been said earlier, there were two systems of land survey in effect: the New England township plan and the indiscriminate one used elsewhere. Congress now had a golden opportunity to pass legislation pertaining to the Northwest by starting with a virgin, unsurveyed territory. There were no legitimate settlements in the area except for Detroit and the French villages of Kaskaskia, Cahokia and Vincennes. Troops patrolled the fringe along the Ohio to keep squatters out of the region; hostile Indians also made crossing the river hazardous.

Land Ordinance of 1785

On May 20, Congress passed the Land Ordinance of 1785 which established a rectangular system of survey. This plan recognized the square mile of 640 acres instead of the geographical mile of 850.4 acres as a basic unit of measurement. Lands were to be blocked out in ranges six miles in width instead of the original "hundred" plan of ten square miles, and these in turn were to be marked off into townships of six mile squares. Each township was then to be surveyed in thirty-six square-mile sections containing 640 acres each—the sections to be numbered from one to thirty-six. A portion of the mineral resources was to be reserved to the government, and each sixteenth section was reserved for the maintenance of schools in the area. Other provisions were made regarding methods of distributing the land and the location of the first seven ranges. This law is an interesting study in both compromise and mathematics. A semblance of the New England township system prevailed, but in this case the township became a precise standard unit of land measurement instead of local government. The indiscriminate system of land location was ignored as well as the old and entangling practice of location before survey. No doubt the greatest compromise was on the issue of sale only by townships containing the large amount of 23,040 acres. This question was finally resolved by selling alternate townships in the smaller parcels of 640 acres. The provision for support of religion by sale of public lands was struck out by the peculiar method of counting majority votes against the number in the Congress rather than by actual vote on the issue, and the ordinance was ready for final adoption.

With the passage of the land ordinance, the first surveys along the Ohio were begun. Thomas Hutchins was employed for three additional years as official geographer. Already he had considerable knowledge of the western country because of his twenty-two years of frontier service to the British army. Deputy surveyors were selected from the various states, and the geographer's line running east and west from the Ohio to the Tuscarawas River was begun on October 22, 1785.

Beginning in May, 1785, Hutchins began to lay out the seven original ranges which extended from the Ohio River northward to the basic geographer's line. By April, 1787, four of the original ranges were surveyed, but it was not until 1789 that the entire lot of seven ranges was completed. This long delay in surveying and making lands ready for sale provoked considerable pressure from Congressmen who wished to collect money from the sales as rapidly as possible. Those members of Congress who favored the indiscriminate location of land and its immediate sale offered some threat to the slower and more orderly plan. By July, 1787, land in the first four ranges was ready for sale, and between September 21 and October 9 of that year, 72,794 acres were actually disposed of by public auction in New York. The original disposal plan was revised so as to remove the sales from the states to the seat of national government. It was a matter of grave disappointment to Congress that so small an amount of land was disposed of in the first sales, and possibly it was a greater disappointment that no entire township was sold.

New Land Companies

There was great pressure for land by veterans of the Revolutionary War. Virginia had satisfied this pressure somewhat by its military grant, and some other states had reduced their obligations by granting state lands. However, the many veterans living in states which had no immediate access to public territory had to look to the great block of territory beyond the Ohio. Congress was particularly sensitive to this pressure. The process of public land sale was not simply finding a buyer and making an immediate disposal of sections and townships. Again the long-standing private land company and its desire for large blocks of the public domain figured heavily with the private buyer. There was no official restriction on secondary sales as to the amount, great or small, which an individual might purchase, nor were the terms of payment specified. The only rule which the seller and buyer had to observe was the official plan of survey. A further deterrent to the purchase of land beyond the Ohio following 1787 was the uncertainty of Indian relationships. Even though the government had gone to considerable trouble and expense to negotiate a series of treaties with the various tribes, there was still much unrest among them.

Actively engaged in the survey of the seven original ranges were Benjamin Tupper and his associate General Rufus Putnam, a framer and signer of the Newburgh or Soldier's Petition of 1783. Both men were veterans of the war and were active in soldiers' affairs. They understood the prevailing attitude in the East as well as the great possibilities for land speculation and settlement along the Ohio. A call was sent out for the various Massachusetts counties to send delegates to a public meeting on March 1, 1786, at the Bunch of Grapes Tavern in Boston. There the Ohio Company Associates (unrelated to the old colonial company of the same name) opened subscription books for $1,000,000 to be paid in specie certificates. In many respects this was one of the most momentous organizations of a land company. Its original management might not have been too imaginative, but before the committee approached Congress with a proposition to extend the privilege of purchase, the ingenious and tenacious Reverend Manasseh Cutler had become an important figure in promoting the interest of the new organization. Momentarily Congress was disappointed by the sales of public lands, and at the same time much of its attention was diverted from land sales to the governmental problems of both the Confederation and the Northwest Territory. The generous offer of a million dollars with additional future payments for a private purchase was attractive, even though it necessitated violating an important principle laid down in the Land Ordinance of 1785. One of the great worries of land dispersal had been the private sale, and to alleviate accusation of corporate favoritism, the public auction device was created. Fortunately for the Ohio Company committee, the official conscience was pliable on the subject of land speculation, and the Reverend Cutler understood the workings of the contemporary official mind. Thus playing a "cloak and dagger" game, threatening to withdraw his company's rich offer unless certain terms were granted in the contract, he was able to secure his own terms. By shrewd management Congress was brought to approve the sale, and on October 27, two contracts granting land to the Ohio and Scioto companies were signed by Cutler for the Ohio Company, and Winthrop Sargent, Benjamin Tupper's son-in-law, for the government. A large tract of land—1,500,000 acres for the Ohio Company and 5,000,000 for the Scioto Company—was involved in the contract. This land was to be located along the Ohio between the seven ranges and the Scioto. A payment of $500,000 was agreed to at the signing of the contract; another $500,000 was to be paid upon completion of the survey; and the remainder was to be paid in terms to be specified later. Deeds were to pass the property on in proportion to payments made from time to time.

Land companies flowered bountifully in the 1780's and early 1790's. Perhaps the most famous, next to the Ohio Company, was the John Cleves Symmes Company which procured a grant between the two Miami rivers. The Royal Flint–Joseph Parker Associates wanted 2,000,000 acres along the Ohio and an additional million acres on the Mississippi. George Morgan and Associates sought a tract on the Mississippi before title had been negotiated with the Indians. The Symmes grant went into effect on October 15, 1788, but the others failed for one reason or another. Aside from the techniques of land disposal employed and the extreme interest of this phase of American land speculation, the many complex details of these enterprises have little bearing at the moment on the more important aspects of settlements along the frontier.

The new Ohio Company was on the verge of accomplishing the objective set by the old organizations as far back as 1748. At high noon on April 7, 1788, General Rufus Putnam led his forty-eight companions from Massachusetts ashore below the mouth of the Muskingum to establish the village of Adelphia beyond the Ohio. Traveling overland to Pittsburgh and drifting southward down the Ohio aboard the famous flatboat *Mayflower*, Putnam's company re-enacted under reasonably predictable conditions the landing of the Pilgrims on the New England Coast 160 years before. A meeting was held in the open, and a series of laws reminiscent of those made at Boonesboro in 1775 were enacted. Copies were tacked to trees for settlers to read and obey. Return Jonathan Meigs was made legal administrator, and the settlement was ready to form both a county and a territorial government. On July 2, 1788, the town's name was changed to Marietta in honor of Marie Antoinette, and seven days later General Arthur St. Clair arrived on the Ohio to begin his duties as territorial governor. George Washington observed that "No colony in America was ever settled under such favorable auspices as that which has just commenced at the Muskingum. Information, property and strength will be its characteristics. I know many of the settlers personally, and there never were men better calculated to promote the welfare of such a community." Marietta was an important beginning of settlement on the frontier. Until 1788 penetration of the Ohio Valley had been made largely by men who had extensive border experience before they actually reached the outer fringes of the West, but at Marietta a new channel of migration was opened by which New Englanders came directly to the area. This was one of the significant influences which in time was to make itself felt in westward expansion. The New England farmers brought to the frontier a new sense of agricultural economy, and their preachers and teachers gave impetus to the provisions of the Northwest Ordinance for schools. The street names and local nomenclature of Marietta reflected a classical interest which was hardly a social manifestation of pioneers elsewhere in the great American backwoods.

Below Marietta the Ohio settlement was begun less happily. A composite part of the Ohio Associates' venture was the more speculative Scioto Company. It is difficult to say precisely what the association between the two was, except that many of the officials of one were associated with the other. Among these were Winthrop Sargent, Manasseh Cutler, Joel Barlow, William Duer, Rufus Putnam and Flint. This speculative company pre-empted five thousand acres of land, hoping to improve their financial resources by the time the land could be officially surveyed. The promotors believed they could sell enough land abroad to pay the initial costs, and on the eve of the French Revolution, 1789, Joel Barlow went to France to turn the tide of French emigrants toward the Ohio country. Acting with the power of attorney for William Duer, he tramped the streets of Paris trying unsuccessfully to find purchasers for his wild lands.

In his moment of disappointment Barlow became acquainted with a trifling Englishman, William Playfair, who understood both the French language and temperament. Playfair was convinced that to succeed it was necessary to organize a French company, which he did under the title of the *Compagnie de Scioto*. With extravagant descriptions of the Ohio paradise (which he had never seen) he set out to trap his victims.

William Sibley, a historian of the French "Five Hundred" said years later that the highly colored prospectus promises: "A delightful little boat ride from Havre de Grace, with refreshing ocean zephyrs as a tonic incident, would bring one to the lovely plain between the Muskingum and the Scioto Rivers, where would be found a salubrious climate in which frost, even in winter, was almost unknown. The great river skirting it, destined in a few years to become the leading channel of territorial commerce, was called 'The Beautiful,' and was so crowded by large and delicately edible fish that they struggled in piscine rivalry first to swallow the baited hook or achieve entanglement in the fatal meshes of the net. The native trees produced spontaneously great quantities of delicately flavored sugar, a peculiar plant yielded ready-made candles (cat-tails), coal, iron, lead, silver and gold were jutting out of every stony ledge, and a single boar and sow in the course of three years would produce three hundred pigs without the least care being taken of them."

It was an irony of fate indeed that Frenchmen could be so deluded about a land which their fellow countrymen had so recently surveyed and fought so vigorously to retain. Their ignorance reflected an indifference to North America which was general in Europe. No doubt Playfair's seductive description of an established community with all the civilized institutions which delighted the Parisian heart was important in persuading people to invest both their money and their lives in the venture. The common people were left untouched by Playfair's campaign. "Scarcely a dozen common laborers were included in their number," says Sibley. "The remainder were carvers and gilders to His Majesty, peruke and coach makers, friseurs, doctors, artists, lawyers, jewelers, dancing masters, bootmakers, confectioners, waiters, bar-tenders, milliners, shop keepers, clerks, ladies and gentlemen, and one penniless stowaway, Monsieur Valodin, who cast his lot with the others without a sou in his pocket or change of linen in his possession. They were a miniature Paris in diversity of occupation, ebullient spirits and aesthetic tastes, all but a very few of them being accustomed to luxury either by position, property, or association with people of independent means. There were no thieves, or dissolute persons among them, and the majority, both male and female, were possessed of fine education and courtly manners. Their intention was to found an ideal little French city on their continental utopia, to be called Gallipolis, as soon as their disembarkation was effected."

Early in 1790, when the French investors arrived in Alexandria, Virginia, the Scioto Company had no disposable lands, and no plans had been made by Colonel Duer to establish such settlers anywhere on the Ohio. An agreement was reached by which 200,000 acres of Ohio Company lands were transferred to the French immigrants, and arrangements were made to transport them to the Ohio. Major John Burnham of Essex, Massachusetts, was directed to recruit fifty volunteers to go out to the Ohio to work for six months at building blockhouses and cabins. A town was located on high ground four miles below the mouth of the Great Kanawha on the north bank of the Ohio, and the French survivors of the Playfair-Barlow swindle moved in to establish Gallipolis. Later on, Congress gave these settlers approximately 25,000 acres of land to compensate for their misfortunes. Certainly all was not lost by these Frenchmen, even if they were cheated out of their funds and were unprepared for settlement in the raw American wilderness. They did escape the rigors of the French Revolution, and their troubles in Gallipolis can hardly be said to match the upheaval in France.

In the same year that the Ohio Associates were planting their settlement upstream at Marietta, John Cleves Symmes, a New Jersey speculator, was preparing to take up a large grant of land in the great northern bend of the Ohio just above the mouth of the Big Miami. Symmes had drawn together New Jersey Revolutionary War veterans in a grandiose scheme which he had advertised in a glowing circular from Trenton. Somewhat in the manner of William Playfair, Symmes had described his tract early in 1788 as a Garden of Eden where vegetables, crops and livestock could be produced in great abundance. To make the initial payment on the lands he collected $88,333.30 from investors who wished to share in the great benefits.

Symmes had little realistic understanding of the hardships of frontier outposts. He did not reach the Miami settlement until late summer of 1788, and the story of settling along the Ohio was begun in the face of Indian resistance and approaching winter. Associated with Symmes were such men as John Filson, the frontier's first notable literary figure; Robert Patterson, founder of Lexington, Kentucky; Mathias Denman and John Ludlow. For the next six years the Miami settlements were fraught with hardship and uncertainty, but settlement did take place. Near the mouth of the Little Miami, Benjamin Stites and a party of settlers founded Columbia; a few miles downstream Denman, Ludlow and Patterson founded a settlement on their tract opposite the mouth of the Licking which they called Losantisville, and early in 1789 John Cleves Symmes himself planted the settlement of North Bend. These three village sites have long been swallowed up by Cincinnati and extending settlements along the river.

While Judge Symmes's settlements made a beginning, his casual management of his land grant led to much conflict because of overlapping and conflicting claims and the sale of lands outside his legal boundaries. Eventually, this nucleus of settlement was to absorb the area between the two Miami Rivers, which was soon to become an important military and commercial center. White settlement by 1790 was extended along the north bank of the Ohio to the mouth of the Big Miami, and it was being turned northward toward the headwaters of the two streams.

WIDENING THE ARC
OF SETTLEMENT

August 21, 1794. *We are now lying within half a mile of a British garrison. A flag came to the commander-in-chief, the purport of which was that he, the commanding officer of the British fort, was surprised to see an American army so far advanced in this country; and why they had the assurance to encamp under the mouths of His Majesty's cannons! The commander-in-chief answered, that the affair of yesterday (Fallen Timbers) might well inform him why this army was encamped in its present position, and had the flying savages taken shelter under the walls of his fort, his Majesty's cannons should not have protected them.*

—B. Van Cleve, "Daily Journal of Wayne's Campaign,"
The American Pioneer

CHAPTER VII

THE period of struggle which engaged the American frontier for two decades after the Treaty of Paris had three distinct component parts. The first part, as has been already described, was for land along and beyond the Ohio and in the great virginal southwest; the second was with the Indians; and the third was with the governments of England and Spain.

Beyond the Ohio in the Wabash-Maumee-Great Lakes frontier, the British were most obstinate about relinquishing their posts on American soil. Detroit, Niagara and other strategic trading stations remained centers of rivalry for Indian trade and the fomenting of border disturbances. The Indians themselves had just reason for apprehension over the spread of American settlement. After 1788 there was a determined beginning of white exploitation at Marietta; down the river at the great North Bend there was the beginning of another ominous white foothold. Everywhere scouts and surveyors continued their feverish search for fertile western lands. Although troops were stationed along the Ohio to drive poaching whites back across the river, the pressure became too great for such a limited patrol. Every year an increasing number of flatboats drifted away from Pittsburgh bearing settlers, farm implements, and household goods on their way to wedge the settlement line deeper into Indian territory.

Harmar and St. Clair

While the Ohio Valley was the scene of one restless horde of settlers drifting to new homes, a second horde moved down the rivers and over trails in the Tennessee and Georgia backwoods. Henderson's Cumberland settlement became a major focal center, and the great valley trough opening from Virginia and the Carolinas was disgorging through the mountain gaps a yearly crop of migrants from the east. The banks of the Mississippi were like a magnet drawing these surging adventurers onward. To the Indian in the woods it was clear that either the hungry land seekers had to be checked or the hunting grounds would soon be lost. No Indian treaty negotiated after 1763 had brought anything more than temporary peace of mind to tribes who hunted where major land exchanges were executed. Some of the agreements, like that at Fort McIntosh, bred deep suspicion and bitter dissatisfaction. British, Spanish and Indian agitators understood these impending changes, and they used their knowledge to their own selfish advantage. There were many displeased Indian leaders and equally as many disgruntled traders.

The situation in the Northwest was almost precisely as it was during Pontiac's War except that dispossessed English instead of French traders lingered in the great woods to create dissension. In Pontiac's place was Joseph Brant, a Mohawk chief with much natural ability in leadership, who was adept at agitation. In the Detroit River Council of 1786 it was he who held out for equal and universal recognition of the northwestern Indian confederacy. He sought the same diplomatic regard for the Indian nation as that which organized white nations had for each other. Among the British partisans were, aside from Colonel John Graves Simcoe and Sir Frederick Haldimand (old hands at making border trouble), Alexander McKee, British Indian agent, Matthews Elliott and Simon Girty.

Possibly there could have been no more unfortunate time for the Congress of the Confederation to attempt to work out a stable Indian policy. There were too many pressing domestic problems to solve, including the method of distributing western lands. No change was made from the British procedure of administering the Indian affairs. Superintendents of the northern and southern Indian departments were retained, and traders were allowed to go and come and trade at will. Failure to control the traders was one of the most serious flaws in Indian regulations. Cheating, overcharging, sale of liquor, robbery and nearly every other disreputable practice was tolerated. By 1792 these nefarious dealings became so bad that Congress made half-hearted efforts to regulate the traders by legislation passed in 1792 and 1793.

Before 1792, however, relations between the Americans and western Indians had become so strained that a major effort had to be made to secure peace. In July, 1788, Governor Arthur St. Clair and Richard Butler, northern Indian agent, called a meeting of the tribes to take place on the upper Muskingum for the purpose of talking peace. Governor St. Clair was able to renegotiate terms of the Fort Stanwix treaty with the Iroquois. With the other tribes he renewed the antagonizing Fort McIntosh boundaries which covered the heart of the Ohio country from Lake Erie along the Cuyahoga to the great portage, and then westward to the Maumee, to the head of the Big Miami, and southward to the mouth of the Kentucky. The meeting failed to achieve continuing peace because of Indian indecision and animosity, and it was clear that new border troubles, largely the fruit of British and Canadian agitation, would become even worse before adjustments could be made. Failure to reach an agreement with the irreconcilable Shawnees and Miamis, who in truth offered the greatest immediate threat to the expanding white borderland, made all the other treaties worthless. Kentucky settlements below the river were haunted by the fear of horse-thieving raids which often led to bloodshed. In turn, unauthorized white forays in the Indian country reciprocated the ferocity and the thievery. As the river became a more active channel for transporting settlers westward, nests of marauders planted themselves on the northern banks and harrassed settlement parties. Attempts to destroy these bands were not successful, and western safety reached a disastrously low point.

By spring, 1790, border friction threatened open warfare. General Josiah Harmar organized troops to protect the river frontier, but his initial efforts were unsuccessful. He led a force of approximately fifteen hundred men to the heads of the Wabash and Maumee streams, where he failed to do more than destroy some villages and further antagonize the Indians. His difficulty arose not so much from Indian resistance as from failure of the militia to function satisfactorily. Harmar's ill-starred expedition reflected the ineffectiveness of American arms generally during the first decade following the American Revolution. Before the last straggler of Harmar's disintegrating army stumbled back to the Ohio, Governor Arthur St. Clair was organizing an armed force to reopen the attack against the villages at the headwaters of the Miami and Wabash. Pennsylvanians, Virginians, Kentuckians and a small number of regular troops were formed into an undisciplined and inexperienced army and sent into the woods without proper scouting and intelligence information. By October, 1790,

Harmar advanced again as far as the headwaters of the Maumee where his willful and badly led army was defeated and scattered by a heavy Indian assault. Harmar retreated to Fort Washington, and conditions along the northwestern border were left in a more threatening state than ever.

With the failure of the Harmar expedition it was necessary for the Americans to make a second and more vigorous effort to avoid being driven back across the Ohio. Governor St. Clair set to work to rebuild the frontier forces, this time giving more attention to strategy. General Charles Scott was to lead his three thousand mounted Kentuckians against the ancient post at Ouiatenon, and Governor St. Clair was to direct an attack against the villages at the heads of the Wabash and Maumee rivers. James Wilkinson was sent against the Indians at Eel River, but he failed to do more than slight punitive damage. For the next three years the Ohio frontier was in a state of intermittent warfare. The Americans had accomplished nothing more than further irritation of the enemy and had left their situations open to vigorous counterirritation by the British and Canadians. Poor administration and the problem of finances contributed to the lack of American military order and leadership.

The spring and summer of 1791 were spent in preparation for a raid into the northwest. On November 4 along the upper Wabash, St. Clair's motley band of fourteen hundred men was put to rout. The American troops were fortunate in breaching the encircling Indian lines so they could retreat. An analysis of St. Clair's defeat would reveal all of the failures of the inferior United States military organization, plus the personal failures of General St. Clair himself. He had rushed into the campaign without proper conditioning of his men, the commissary department had failed to deliver supplies, militiamen were obstreperous about obeying orders, St. Clair himself failed to take the precaution of intensive scouting which was so necessary in the advance of a frontier army, and, finally, Congress itself was to blame for its failure to pass and facilitate effective legislation for the creation of an adequate national army.

St. Clair's defeat left the Indians and their British friends victorious but irritated in the western woods. If the enemy were to be dislodged, the army of the United States had to be stronger and better led than at any time since 1783. In Philadelphia, President Washington faced a vital responsibility to the West in his selection of a frontier general. Possibly never had frontier military fortunes been at such a low ebb. Alert leadership would not be enough; it was necessary to secure more adequate support for the army, to mold the western militia into a tighter fighting organization, and to prepare the frontier forts for support of a sustained raid into the interior. At the same time, every effort had to be made to negotiate a peace with the Indians and to remove the British from the northwest posts by diplomacy if possible. Behind these border troubles was British failure to observe the terms of the Treaty of Paris. Already a considerable amount of negotiation and diplomatic correspondence had passed, and between 1791 and 1795 the issue was to be a major one in the preservation of peace between this country and England. The whole question of the Indian trade was of primary importance. The treaty of 1783 had made little or no difference in the activities of the British traders. They continued their trade in much the same way as they had done following the French and Indian War. The British military had held on to their important northwest posts in the same way, and many Indian tribes had come to look upon them as allies who would support them in their war with the Americans.

Between 1785 and 1796 northwestern problems were further complicated by the indefiniteness of the boundary line between the head of the Mississippi River and the Lake of the Woods, the collection of debts owed to Britons by Americans, the creation of an Indian buffer state, and the ambition of several individuals including Governor Haldimand, John Graves Simcoe, and Guy Carleton (then Lord Dorchester) and Lord Grenville. On the American side of the issue there were also many factors —the American position in the disturbing and turbulent affairs of Europe, our foreign trade, the partisan conflict in the new government, and, in fact, the very uncertainties of getting the government itself organized. Many American personalities were also to be important in securing diplomatic clarification of the border dispute. Among these were George Washington, John Jay, Thomas Jefferson and Edmund Randolph.

It is against this background that we must study the strictly military problem. In 1792 the American position on the northwest frontier was precarious because of the failures of Harmar and St. Clair. Although military posts had been established along the Ohio River frontier from Pittsburgh to Fort Washington, there were still wide gaps between the settlements and forts through which warring parties could slip across the river or cut communications. The Indians had grown bolder after their successes against the American arms, and a greater effort appeared necessary to defeat them. In Canada, Lord Dorchester and his colleague John Graves Simcoe suspected an American drive against the British-held posts below the Great Lakes, and they made preparations to resist even in the face of danger of causing another war between Britain and America.

Congress itself had to preserve American territorial integrity by seeing to it that the British lived up to treaty agreements. When George Hammond was sent as British minister to the United States in 1791 he brought instructions to negotiate the northwest issue, provided the United States would carry out the terms of the treaty applying to the collection of debts. This still left the Indian problem which was being aggravated by Canadian officials regardless of what the British foreign office had to say.

Washington moved effectively to strengthen the military forces west of the mountains. Leadership had been the weakest link in frontier protection, and after the failures of Harmar and St. Clair the government could no longer temporize with the problem. The young republic's prestige as well as its territorial integrity were at stake. On March 5, 1793, Congress passed an act to enlarge the army, and President Washington selected Anthony Wayne as its commander. It has been said that Washington believed Wayne had courage and little else, but the Pennsylvanian had certainly proved himself an excellent soldier at Philadelphia, Brandywine, Germantown, Stony Point and Yorktown. Though somewhat a braggart in manner, he was a good disciplinarian and a meticulous soldier.

From Fort Washington to Fallen Timbers

Wayne set out for the Ohio to prepare his army. He had one distinct advantage over his unfortunate predecessors in that the recent military act made possible the organization of a more effective army. Advancing on the Indian frontier with the new army was a slow process. Delay was caused partly by the American peace commissioners who were seeking again to strengthen the old agreements contained in the Stanwix and Fort McIntosh treaties.

Wayne's experience in organizing his army was a revealing commentary on frontier military attitudes. Raw undisciplined troops were highly unreliable. Paying strict attention to the conditioning and disciplining of his army, the General found that desertion and failure to perform duties at assigned posts was a threat to national safety. Although his forces were small, he had the greatest difficulty in training troops. His men, demoralized by past failures, were frightened from the start; yet in the view of republican opinion the severe disciplining of troops was almost out of the question. A failure to observe the general tenor of the American mind toward military affairs might have resulted in injury to the army, if not the refusal of a great body of militiamen to serve.

Wayne first began drilling his troops at Legionville in Pennsylvania, then moved down the Ohio by stages until he reached Fort Washington, within the present day Cincinnati, in May, 1793. At no time could the Americans afford to appear as aggressors. Their resistance to the Indians and the British had to be made clearly in the area of defense and protection of American soil. To protect international peace, they had to exhaust every possible resource to secure agreement short of war. By late 1793,

Wayne's new army had begun to shape up. Soon it would be ready for the drive into the northwest woods to recoup the prestige of arms lost by Harmar and St. Clair; but at the same time the Indian force was growing.

Wayne's soldiers came from St. Clair's frustrated army. There were Kentuckians, Virginians, Ohioans, Pennsylvanians, soldiers of fortune, young officers seeking adventure—among whom were William Henry Harrison, William Clark and Meriwether Lewis—and traders and Indian scouts. Besides the troops directly under Wayne's command there were nearly a thousand mounted Kentuckians who fought under the direction of General Charles Scott. Marching against the Indians was no new adventure for either Scott or his wild semidisciplined men. They had made a thrust toward Ouiatenon just two years before, and under the new commander in chief they were out to recapture some of their lost honor in battle.

Wayne moved cautiously from one post to another as he advanced toward the enemy. He went from Fort Washington eighty miles up the Big Miami to Fort Greenville where he spent the winter of 1793. A detachment was sent ahead to construct Fort Recovery at that place where St. Clair had been surrounded and defeated in 1791. In August, Wayne moved his troops up to the Au Glaize River and there built the log Fort Defiance. While the army moved forward, constant efforts were made to secure peace without fighting. At the same time, however, Indian attacks on moving supply trains, troops, and even on Fort Recovery itself were taking place.

Since the beginning of 1793, British encouragement of Indian resistance to the Americans had been growing. But nothing the British did had quite such rousing results as the speech which Lord Dorchester delivered to an assembly of Indian chiefs on February 10, 1794. He told his hearers that he would not be surprised if Britain were not at war with the Americans by the end of that year. As a follow-up to this highly incendiary speech by a Canadian governor, the lieutenant-governor constructed a fort at the Miami Rapids. So far as the Indians could see, their British friends were ready at a moment to begin war with the Americans. By distributing arms and other supplies to the Indians, it was clearly revealed to them that they were expected to resist every peace move. William McKee asked that the best guns available be sent to him for trade with the Indians, and he asked for long rifles to match those used by American troops.

Dorchester's speech was tremendously influential in its immediate effect on both Indian and backwoods opinion. To the extent that it removed all possibility of any effective peace move or of a division in Indian resistance, it was successful; but from the more durable point of view of governmental policy it was wholly irresponsible. Whatever the attitude of the British government toward the weak American republic, there is little or no evidence that the British Foreign Office wished to pursue so aggressive a policy. That the Dorchester speech was made has been proved beyond any reasonable doubt. At Philadelphia the British minister George Hammond admitted that it had been delivered but he repudiated its authority.

While the western woods were aflame with the war spirit and Wayne's troops waited out the winter in Fort Greenville, the Department of State in Philadelphia was trying to secure peace and understanding short of war. John Jay, a former secretary of foreign affairs under the Confederation, and since 1790, Chief Justice of the United States Supreme Court, was the man best-equipped by experience to treat diplomatically with the British. He spent the summer of 1794 in England discussing with Lord Grenville, British Foreign Minister, the various points at issue between the United States and England. His mission no doubt came at a propitious moment because of the highly explosive situation in Europe, and England could hardly afford to chance war with the United States or to lose its profitable trade. Britain's interest was turned toward France and possible war on the Continent. To go to war in North America would have necessitated dividing British naval and military resources at a time when the nation could ill afford to take a chance. Lord Grenville assured Jay that he had just learned of the tense relations along the United States-Canadian frontier, and among the early concessions made to the American minister was a promise to remove the British from Northwest posts. Despite this promise, Grenville raised the old question of collecting British debts in America without interference from either national or state governments. Lord Dorchester was given a reprimand for his intemperate speech and was finally recalled as a further palliative to the Americans. British soldiers were to be kept out of the conflict between Wayne's legionnaires and the Indians, even though the temptation to join in the struggle was great.

While diplomats in London continued their conversations during the summer, Anthony Wayne's responsibilities on the frontier had not decreased. He was preparing to fight Indians, not the British, though he did have to keep in mind the possibility that some incident might cause conflict between the two rival groups. His task was made extremely ticklish by the presence of British forces at posts in the Indian country. He had to pursue his enemy to the doors of the forts, but at the same time prevent any act of violence against their occupants. In the destruction of Indian property he was forced at the same time to take chances of opening the bigger conflict by destroying houses and crops belonging to British subjects.

Since early in 1793 the American forces had been getting a taste of

Indian hostility. Supply trains and isolated companies of soldiers were attacked and a comparatively large number of Americans killed and wounded in these sporadic skirmishes. Scouts like William Wells and William Miller who had lived for years with the Indians kept a close check on the location and activities of the enemy. Occasionally Indians harassed Wayne with impulsive spite raids, but in all the activity around the advancing army, there was little or no chance that it would be subjected to a disastrous assault as were Harmar's and St. Clair's troops. No American frontier army to date had been so well protected by good spying and scouting, and it is fairly certain that no other was so well-drilled and disciplined as were Wayne's troops.

Early in August, 1794, Wayne had advanced to Fort Defiance and was now confronted by the Indian forces. Before the Americans were between fifteen hundred and two thousand braves of the combined forces of all the northwestern tribes. A proffer of peace from Wayne's camp was little more than an empty gesture to placate the United States government and public opinion. There in the western woods, hovering under the very shadows of the British forts, the Indians hoped to repeat the routs of Harmar and St. Clair, and they banked heavily on the support of their white allies. This was possibly the largest and best-organized Indian army that had ever been brought together, and never before had so strong an attacking white force been brought to the line of battle.

Wayne wore Indian patience and resistance down with three days' delay before finally meeting the Indians in battle. During this period the braves were kept in battle lines with only one meal a day, and their hunger rapidly destroyed their morale. Perhaps even more demoralizing was the nervous strain of anxiety and expectation of a momentary attack.

On the morning of August 20, Wayne's patience and careful preparation were to be tested. The Indians, concealed in the fallen timbers of a tornado path, were in an unusually difficult position to attack, but the American troops came up to the battle line ready to absorb and return enemy fire. For possibly the first time in a major battle, troops were prepared to rush an Indian ambuscade with the bayonet. For forty minutes that hot summer morning the American front line scrambled over the tangled tree trunks and debris, flushing the Indians from hiding and driving them back. The braves fell back and left the field before all the army had entered the battle. In the assault only thirty-three Americans were killed and approximately a hundred were wounded. Indian losses were unknown, but they were appraised as much higher. Among the enemy dead were those who had belonged to Caldwell's Canadians. There were even British subjects among the prisoners.

Because the Indians were attacked under the very shadow of the British post, there was, of course, grave danger that a bullet from the gun of a heedless soldier would go astray and strike the neutral British stronghold. Fortunately no such accident occurred. The only conflict between the British and Americans was a hot exchange of letters between the British commandant, Major William Campbell, and General Wayne. Campbell's letters in which he emphasized his military duties were petulant and threatening. Wayne deflated his ego by asking him to withdraw from the post which he held illegally.

The Battle of Fallen Timbers was decisive. Not only were the Indians routed in battle, but the infidelity of their British friends was exposed. They were denied the haven of the British forts in their flight, and even worse, they were denied further supplies of ammunition and guns. Because the Americans had destroyed cornfields, villages and other property, the Indians were faced with starvation and destruction by approaching winter. Fallen Timbers demonstrated the value of careful preparation and discipline before initiating a campaign. On the larger front the American success quickly cleared the border atmosphere so far as Canadian and British officials were concerned, and it opened the way for a permanent adjustment of Indian and trade misunderstandings. Once and for all in this area the old scare of an Indian buffer state was cast into oblivion. At the same time the way was opened for permanent settlement of boundary questions, which to date no treaty had specifically defined.

Throwing the Hatchet into Deep Water

Back at Fort Greenville, General Wayne was faced with all the problems generated by an idle army: disease, desertion, mutiny and dissension. Before him in the woods was the great unsettled issue of coming to terms with the Indians. A treacherous winter on short rations and emergency shelter, however, did its work. By January, 1795, Wayne began the laborious task of assembling enough representatives from the tribes to insure the making of a durable treaty.

The treaty makers took their time—six months—in coming to Fort Greenville, but by July there were enough representatives on hand to begin the task of making a peace agreement. When at last the treaty council was opened, almost a year after the defeat of the Indians, Wayne was able to give assurance on two points: the Americans and British were going to remain at peace for the time being; and the British were going to remove themselves from the frontier posts.

He approached the Indians with a certain knowledge of the contents of Jay's Treaty; in fact, Wayne's advance into the Northwest was geared to the peace negotiations so far as his attitude toward the British was concerned. He was able to meet his fellow councilors with the assurance that the Americans and Indians were going to sign a treaty of peace and that he was going to dictate its terms.

As an Indian diplomat, Wayne proved just as good as he was a frontier soldier. He engaged himself in almost endless stilted conversation with the chiefs. When they spoke in their highly figurative way Wayne was able to reply in kind. He referred to the fifteen states as so many fires, and to peace as burying the hatchet. Since they were so near the Great Lakes, the bloody hatchet was to be thrown into deep water where the sands of the currents would obscure it forever. Young men of the future would be unable to dive deep enough to recover it as young men of the past had done. Typical of the hatchet-hiding talk was the speech of Masass, a Chippewa chief, who stood in council holding a small wampum belt and said, "Notwithstanding I am so small a man, I do now, in the name of the three nations (Ottawas, Chippewas, and Pottawattomies) throw the hatchet into the middle of the great lake, where it will be so covered, as never to be found, as long as white people and Indians live."

The Treaty of Greenville, signed August 3, 1795, was the most widely representative agreement made to date with the western Indians. Present were thirteen hundred braves representing the Wyandottes, Shawnees, Delawares, Ottawas, Chippewas, Miamis, Eel River, Pottawattomies, Weas, Piankeshaws, and Kickapoos. Distribution of representation was in proportion to the relative importance of the various tribes. The treaty provided for the cession of the territory covered by the earlier agreements made at Fort Stanwix, McIntosh, Muskingum and Fort Finney, plus sixteen strategic spots which controlled possible military points of vantage, river carrying paths, and important trading posts. On the map of Ohio and Indiana it ceded the lands west of the Cuyahoga, and south of a negotiated line running westward from the great portage on the Cuyahoga across the headwaters of the Muskingum to the headwaters of the Maumee and Wabash and then southward to a negotiated point on the Ohio opposite the mouth of the Kentucky River.

It would be difficult to assess the importance of this major Indian treaty to westward expansion. Most of modern Ohio and a sizable strip of eastern Indiana was opened to white settlement. For the first time since the beginning of intense activity on the part of English speaking people along the Ohio River, the region was virtually free of future Indian menace. Just as important was the fact that a precedent for making treaties with the Indians was established and was to last for almost a century, and that the pattern for advancing white American civilization was set with some rigidity.

Western Commerce and Diplomacy

While General Wayne was waiting patiently at his headquarters at Fort Greenville from August, 1794 to August, 1795, for the Indian tribes to assemble, diplomats in London were threshing out broader issues of frontier expansion. John Jay labored under the handicaps created by Alexander Hamilton in his too frank conversations with the British minister George Hammond. Because of Hamilton's garrulity, Lord Grenville was well-informed as to American conditions and aspirations and Jay was left with little or no opportunity for diplomatic finesse. Hamilton went so far in fact in making American ideas known to Hammond that he virtually outlined the treaty. Jay in London was left to accept the best terms procurable.

Jay was able, however, to secure three vital concessions important to the American frontier: removal of British troops from American soil, British alliance in case of future Indian wars, and settlement of the Northwest boundary between the head of the Mississippi and the Lake of the Woods. There were, of course, other major issues discussed in the treaty, but these pertained mostly to the broader international issues of collecting Tory debts and the conditions of conducting a free maritime commerce. The issues of impressment and illegal search and seizure were left unsettled.

On November 14, 1794, John Jay affixed his signature to the treaty. This new agreement between England and the United States provided for the removal of the British from the Northwest posts by June, 1796. Traders, however, were permitted free access to the American woods, fur trade, portages, steam passages and trails. The Lake of the Woods boundary was to be settled by survey and negotiation sometime in the future. Jay resisted the proposed cutting of a deep slice into the American woods which would have removed approximately 35,000 square miles of territory. This area in the future was to become the richest mineral deposit in the United States. Likewise he was successful in turning aside the question of free admission of British goods to the Northwest by way of Canada. Had he succumbed to this proposal it is possible that the very heart land of American commerce would have been stifled by the competition of British goods within the next century.

Compared with other treaties made by the United States the Jay Treaty was perhaps of second-rate importance. It did settle some pressing frontier problems, and delayed war over others until 1812 when the United States was in a much more secure position to wage war. In the arguments which preceded the ratification, partisan politics expressed themselves in attitudes toward the treaty's adoption. John Jay was none too popular with those senators who represented western constituencies because of the prejudices existing against him over the Jay-Gardoqui Treaty of 1784 which proposed closing the Mississippi River to American use for twenty-five years. Outside the Senate the American press devoted considerable space to a discussion of the agreement with Britain, and in some areas there was noisy denunciation of the treaty as well as some ridiculous demonstrations against it in the form of abuse of Jay personally.

On the frontier of 1795 it was clear to the observant that furs and skins were becoming scarcer in the old hunting grounds, and prospects were that the focal center of this ancient trade would be shifted farther west. Already the hour was ripe, and a wave of settlers was poised to break over the Ohio country cleared by the Treaty of Greenville. Behind this push of settlement was the momentum of the frontier movement across the American hinterland. Nothing short of a great natural disaster could have checked it. Already the seed of statehood was planted in the soil of the great Northwest. Before real adjustment could be made to the new territorial gains beyond the Ohio, the "fifteen fires" to which General Wayne referred so frequently before his Indian hearers at Greenville promised to be nineteen, with three of these being carved out of the great hunting grounds of Ohio, Kentucky, and Tennessee.

Parallel with the British struggle in the Northwest Territory was that with Spain in the Southwest. In 1783 when the second Treaty of Paris was made, the thirty-first parallel was established as the boundary between the United States and Spain. The Mississippi River was to be opened to free navigation by Spain, the United States and England. All three parties failed to appreciate the fact that within a phenomenally short time the free use of the river was to have a much broader implication than the mere transportation of furs, Indian trade goods and frontier military supplies. For more than a century, traders and explorers had been moving along the western rivers, and since 1768 and the appearance of the long hunters, river traffic had become important to American frontiersmen.

The settlement of Kentucky and Tennessee made use of the Mississippi an economic necessity. As farms were brought into production, trade goods changed from the relatively light and highly portable skins and furs to the heavy and cumbersome products of the field. Indian canoes gave way to flatboats, and Indian traders and pioneers became combination farmers and boatmen. The continuous stream of settlers moving into the area increased the importance of the Mississippi River to a degree that was too little appreciated along the eastern coast, especially in New England.

Another factor has to be given some attention if we would comprehend the course of events in domestic and foreign relations during the last two decades of the eighteenth century. Once frontiersmen had crossed the mountains they formed a highly possessive mental set, not only toward western lands but western rivers too. At the same time backwoodsmen developed a remarkably self-pitying attitude toward themselves because of their treatment by the remainder of the country. Isolation blinded them to general national conditions; they had only limited intercourse with people of other sections, and they were dependent upon their own slender intellectual and political resources in the solution of their everyday problems. This condition of mind, plus the intrigue and trickery employed by such self-seeking opportunists as James Wilkinson and others in dealing with the Spanish downriver, served to create a considerable amount of justified suspicion and dissatisfaction. When American boatmen were relieved of their crafts and cargoes at Natchez on the border, relations between the two nationalities became strained. Added to the friction over use of the river was perhaps the larger conflict over the precise location of the international boundary. Spain claimed northward to 32° 28', and the Americans to 31°.

This was the stage setting as early as 1784, when John Jay had entered into negotiations on behalf of the American Confederation with the suave Don Diego Gardoqui, minister of Spain to the United States. The immediate cause of this flare-up over the southeastern boundary with Spain was that country's sudden closing of the Mississippi to free navigation from Natchez to the Gulf. While Spain had a perfect right to close the river, it was hardly acting the part of a good neighbor by doing so, and certainly it was not looking to a happy future in North America by incurring frontier wrath. Already Spain was showing signs of panic over American expansion.

To the government of the Confederation, the impulsive act came at a most crucial moment in American history. The nation was all but bankrupt, the army was almost nonexistent, the tax and monetary systems were chaotic, and the central government was without either national traditions or experience in foreign affairs. Yet the new republic did have something to offer Spain in trade, and possibly it might form an alliance against Britain. The American trade was important to both nations, and Spain showed signs of being willing to make adjustments.

Gardoqui in Philadelphia was most patronizing in his behavior toward Jay and his family. Even Washington was a recipient of Spanish generosity in the form of a fine Castilian jackass—the famous "Royal Gift," progenitor of much of the American mule industry. Gardoqui's generosity, however, did not extend to the point of an unconditional re-opening of the Mississippi River to American trade. On the other hand the Americans, Jay, Washington and many members of the Confederation Congress, were willing to concede Spanish demands for closure of the river. Apparently, with the greatest honesty and sincere well-meaning, Jay and his associates in government were willing to surrender use of the river for another quarter of a century in exchange for larger concessions in foreign trade. Little did the eastern politicians appreciate the phenomenal growth of the Ohio and Mississippi Valley settlements, nor did they realize that the American frontiersman could be so vigorous in arousing public opinion in his favor when his best economic interests were threatened.

When terms of the proposed Jay-Gardoqui Treaty were publicized, violent public reaction throughout the western country blasted all possibility of drafting a treaty acceptable either to Spain or to the Confederation. With the failure of this diplomatic gesture at re-establishing harmonious relationships, Spain allowed her restrictive policy to prevail for the next decade. This static condition threatened to bankrupt as well as check the spread of Americans living near the western rivers. Each succeeding year caused the cry against Spanish policy to grow louder and the criticism of the national government more intense. By 1787 Spain, accepting this frontier grumbling at near face value, began to feel that new settlers could be won away from the American nation. Some Americans like James Wilkinson gave the Spanish ample reason to believe this could be done.

In 1784 Wilkinson had arrived in Lexington, Kentucky, from a farm in Bucks County, Pennsylvania. Back of his farming activity was a variegated career in the American Revolutionary Army in which he had less than a shining record of bravery and accomplishment though he had achieved the rank of brigadier general. Wilkinson was a handsome man who was forward in manner, and who was possessed of good power of expression in both his speech and his writings. Landing in Kentucky in the midst of agitation for separate statehood, he entered the political field with marked success in local elections of delegates to the various separation conventions. His lack of stability of character has long been a subject of discussion in the pages of American history. For more than thirty years his name was to be intimately linked with the more disturbing aspects of the history of the American frontier.

In 1787 Wilkinson loaded a flatboat on the Kentucky River at present day Frankfort and set out for New Orleans. At Natchez the intendant halted his boat, but the persuasive General was finally permitted to proceed to New Orleans. Once in the Spanish city he entered into conversation with Don Esteban Miró, governor of Louisiana. Wilkinson asked for a monopoly to trade through the Spanish blockade; Miró sought help in clinging to Spain's foothold in the Mississippi Valley partly by bringing about the disaffection of disgruntled Kentuckians. In order to secure his aims the shifty American swore allegiance to the Spanish king and entered into a conspiracy to work for the Spanish cause in Kentucky. That Wilkinson's venture was successful was reflected in the $7.00 differential in tobacco prices between New Orleans and Kentucky.

Back in Kentucky in 1788 the oily general attempted to carry out a half-hearted and unsuccessful plan to promote Spanish interests in one of the numerous separation conventions. Two years later he again visited New Orleans where he renewed his intrigues and reaped a harvest of Spanish dollars. His young assistant Philip Nolan brought back to Frankfort on muleback $6,000 which had been received for a shipment of cured meats, butter, grain and hides.

French and Indian Intrigue

For ten years, 1785–1795, the foreign offices of Spain and the United States allowed nature to take its course in their diplomatic relationships, while economic pressure on the frontier grew exceedingly heavy, and there was a rising demand that the river be opened to free traffic. Confronting Spain was the difficult task of protecting its widely extended boundary from the mouth of the Saint Mary's River to the Mississippi, and from Natchez to St. Louis, a well-nigh impossible undertaking. Already American settlers were threatening to breach this line in several places. At the same time the political alignments in Europe were being reshuffled and world peace was again in jeopardy. England had long since regained its dominion over world trade as well as a decisive influence in affairs on the Continent. France was in the midst of her revolutionary era, and Spain was sinking to a position of a second-rate power. Because of the growing strength of the American West and the ever weakening position of Spain, control of the Mississippi and the gulf coastal fringe of Spanish territory was most precarious.

When provisions of the Jay Treaty became public knowledge, Spain's security in North America became even less certain. Manuel Godoy, Spanish foreign minister, was willing in 1795 to bring to fruition the long-pending diplomatic discussions of the previous decade. Thomas Pinckney, a former governor of South Carolina then minister to Great Britain, was dispatched from London to Madrid to reopen treaty negotiations which had become stalemated in 1784. After some diplomatic sparring in which Pinckney forced Godoy's hand by requesting his passport, the two diplomats were able to reach an agreement and to draft the Pinckney or San Lorenzo Treaty, October 27, 1795. The new Spanish agreement recognized the obvious on the American frontier. The Mississippi was to be opened to American use with the all-important privilege of transshipment of goods from New Orleans. This latter "right of deposit" was vital to American shippers because free use of the river meant little without access to port facilities in the Spanish city. The Florida-Louisiana border was to be established along the thirty-first degree parallel between the Chattahoochee and the Mississippi Rivers; a line from Flint River, a branch of the Apalachicola, was to run east to the head of the St. Mary's and thence down the middle of that stream to the sea; citizens of each government were to be removed inside their respective borders, and a survey of the boundary was to be made within a short time.

However, execution of the treaty was strung out piece-meal fashion until almost 1800. Instead of bringing peace and order to the southern borderland it brought only chaos and suspicion of the proposed solutions of many issues. Despite the agreement that Americans might enjoy a right of deposit in New Orleans for three years, consular agents were denied residence in Spanish territory. This restriction led to subterfuge which placed unofficial representatives in the port until after the turn of the century.

Two years after the San Lorenzo Treaty was signed, the United States government dispatched Captain Isaac Guion from Fort Washington (Cincinnati) to occupy the Chickasaw Bluffs, Walnut Hills, and Natchez. Andrew Ellicott, Surveyor General for the United States, was directed to co-operate with the Spanish in establishing the boundary between the United States and Spanish territory south of the thirty-first parallel. Ellicott's experience was a rugged one, partly because he was better with compass and chain than at diplomacy. The Spanish officials at New Orleans, including Carondelet and Gayoso, used obstructionist tactics to delay the survey. For almost three years there was bickering over the conditions under which the boundary would be established. Also, Spanish posts, one of which was Fort Stephens in Alabama, were maintained as long as possible before they were turned over to the Americans. In 1800 the line was completed from the Mississippi eastward to the Chattahoochee. In the meantime Congress had created the Mississippi Territory (1798), and President Adams had appointed Winthrop Sargent, a fellow New Englander, to be governor.

Settlement of most of the southwestern frontier was still some years in the future. Whites moved up and down the river; Natchez, Walnut Hills at the mouth of the Yazoo, and Chickasaw Bluffs began to accumulate handfuls of settlers, but strife between white frontiersmen and Indians in that great, rolling, sand-strewn and pine-studded country was still to run a bitter course. It was not until the force of a new and expanding economic order exerted itself fully that the Indians and the woods gave way.

After nearly fifteen years of frontier uncertainty and strife, the Jay and Pinckney treaties clarified many border problems. Wayne's army had broken the back of Indian resistance in the Ohio country, and the Treaty of Greenville threw a canopy of protection against Indian attack over the major portion of the new frontier lands in Ohio. Clearly the end of the first lingering phase of border history in that country was ended. An orderly system of public land dispersal was functioning, and the land itself was already being diverted to cultivation and the production of goods which would force an even more decisive American policy of free access to the western river system and the sea.

Details of the confused and intricate diplomatic history of the Mississippi Valley are many. But most of the more dramatic events consist of intrigue, manipulation, opportunism, frontier boasts and panic. Several incidents which occurred in this early growing period were important enough to trouble the political waters, one of which was the French conspiracy. From 1789 to 1795, Kentuckians were much aroused over two political issues: opening the Mississippi River to free navigation and giving aid and comfort to the French revolutionists. These westerners were either unable or unwilling to distinguish between the French government which had aided the American revolutionary cause, and the revolutionary forces in France which were destroying that government. Over a period of five years the columns of the *Kentucky Gazette* were laden with arguments and news about France. Most of this material was of a decidedly emotional nature and not in any sense an objective appraisal of the French struggle.

Intermixed with warm discussions of the French Revolution was equally heated argument favoring unrestricted use of the Mississippi River, and criticism of the East and its attitude. The sting of the proposed Jay-Gardoqui Treaty was still fresh, and westerners were ever suspicious of their fellow Americans along the Atlantic seaboard. Out of the extended discussion of such issues, these points are clear: Kentucky frontiersmen were ready to support strong republican assaults on federalism, on the Spanish down the river, and on Congress to make that body acutely aware of western needs. In several Kentucky towns democratic or republican clubs came into existence, and after the landing of the French minister, Edmond Charles Genet, in Charleston, South Carolina, in April, 1793, they took on a decided pro-French flavor. Genet wished to encourage attack against Spain from the north, apparently by elaborate plans which involved the organization of a frontier army under the leadership of George Rogers Clark. There was definite reason for believing that other prominent frontiersmen would lend assistance.

Had Thomas Jefferson given Genet the enthusiastic support he hoped for, possibly such an attack would have occurred. Jefferson, however, could not support any such plan, and by the time Genet reached Philadelphia the West was without sufficient French encouragement to attack Spain. Nevertheless such prominent Kentuckians as George Rogers Clark, Benjamin Sebastian, George Muter, John Brown, and John Breckinridge had become implicated in the so-called "French Conspiracy." The French agents André Michaux, Auguste du Chaise, and Depauw visited the West bearing political felicitations to the area and supposedly in avid search of botanical knowledge. Washington and Jefferson had dispatched letters of warning ahead of the visiting "botanists," and Isaac Shelby, governor of Kentucky, was spared any embarrassment he might have incurred from supporting the French.

From 1783 to 1803 the Southwest was almost as important in frontier expansion as was the Northwest. In 1789 North Carolina ceded its western lands, and in 1790 the Southwest Territory was created by an act of Congress. It is rather difficult to be geographically specific about the area of this new political division. Politically it included only the Tennessee Territory, yet its territorial governor as Superintendent of Southern Indian Affairs exercised a far broader administrative authority. From 1790 to 1796, when Tennessee was admitted to statehood, this political division prevailed. It will be recalled that an ever-increasing population had been moving into this area since 1768, and in years subsequent to 1783 the arrival of migrating parties was a regular occurrence.

Almost precisely the same pattern prevailed in the Southwest as in the Northwest from 1763 to 1783. Indian traders were abroad seeking customers and profits from the Cumberland River to the Gulf. The loyalist trading house of Panton, Leslie and Company, operating out of East Florida and Georgia, enjoyed a thriving trade. Its virtual control over the Indians' lives by regulation of the flow of goods and credits became a target for more than one filibusterer who wanted to share in the trade. William Panton was an important political power over the Indians, and his influence became significant enough in the early 1790's to be a factor in both American politics and border diplomacy.

The Southwest spawned fabulous characters and intriguers. Perhaps none was more interesting than Alexander McGillivray, a Creek chieftain born of a French-Indian halfbreed mother and a Scottish father. Educated in Charleston, South Carolina, and subjected to strong Loyalist influences as a youth, he remained pro-British throughout his life. At the outbreak of the American Revolution his father Lachlan McGillivray returned to Scotland, and he rejoined the Creek Indians in the Alabama woods. During the war he served as a British agent, and later he became a trader and planter. As the Spanish-American struggle along the border developed,

McGillivray played one power against the other. In 1784 he accepted a fairly substantial bribe from the Spanish government to act as its agent. Six years later he was called to New York, where he was given a handsome annual gratuity plus a gaudy uniform and a commission in the United States Army. In 1792 General McGillivray forgot his allegiance to the Americans and repudiated the New York treaty to accept an even larger allowance from Spain for his influence and to reinstate the Spanish-Creek treaty of 1784.

While McGillivray was collecting gratuities and uniforms, another fabulous frontier adventurer was making filibuster history. William Augustus Bowles, a twenty-seven-year-old Maryland loyalist, was in the Creek country first as an agent of Lord Dunmore and John Miller, challenging the monopoly of Panton, Leslie and Company. Not only did he seek to capture the famous company's trade, but he possibly dreamed of taking the Florida territory away from the Spanish. Twice Bowles was in the prison custody of the Spanish government, and twice he returned to Florida to disturb the peace of mind of the officials of Spain and Panton, Leslie and Company. His influence with the Creek Indians reflected itself in the anxiety of the United States Government and of the backwoodsmen who were subjected to attacks.

Pressure of white advance, and the rivalries and land-speculating activity of American adventurers, brought on a virtual state of Indian warfare and raiding all the way from South Georgia to Kentucky. This border war was one of numerous local skirmishes which tended to grow in intensity as Spanish arms and ammunition were supplied to the braves. Like the older border war in the valley of Virginia thirty years earlier, this one consisted of murders, burnings, robbery and kidnaping. Indians stole settlers' property, captured women and children, slew white men and played havoc in general. On the other hand the whites retaliated in kind until the final defeat of the Creek Indians in 1814 in the famous border campaign in the Horseshoe Bend country.

Strong Indian resistance was to have a marked effect on the spread of white civilization. Because of the pressure of Indian resistance the settlements became more populous and land was exploited in a more orderly fashion. It is possible that had there been no Indian barrier across the restless settlers' paths, the Tennessee and Georgia backwoodsmen would have developed a widely scattered and disconnected pattern of settlement which would have delayed the organization of new counties and states.

Two rather important incidents figure in the confused and complex picture of southeastern border expansion. The first of these was the unfortunate Blount conspiracy. William Blount, a North Carolina Federalist, moved to Tennessee after the adoption of the United States Constitution. A man of considerable public acumen, he had supported the conservative point of view in the Constitutional Convention and was influential in trying to get North Carolinians to ratify the Constitution. In 1790 President Washington appointed him governor of the Southwest Territory and also superintendent of the southern Indian department. Both offices gave Blount considerable power in the new country and placed him in an excellent position to carry on his speculative activities in western lands. Like Andrew Jackson, the young frontier lawyer, Blount suffered financial loss in 1796 by the failure of the speculator merchant David Allison of Philadelphia. Allison had helped both Jackson and Blount to secure credit in the purchase of goods and had issued them notes for the purchase of western lands. Blount weathered the financial storm caused by Allison's failure, but the value of his large holdings of western lands had shrunk disastrously.

Blount was sent to the United States Senate in 1796 by the first Tennessee legislature, and while a member of that body he became involved back home in an ill-defined scheme to aid the British in attacking the Spanish in Florida. This was a characteristic frontier attempt to secure the favor of a foreign government in an effort to protect local interests. In this case land prices, the right to trade in Indian territory, and free use of the Mississippi River were all involved. In a letter addressed to James Carey, a Cherokee interpreter, Blount proposed in a more or less veiled manner a fantastic plan of filibustering against the Spanish border in order to aid Britain. Armed forces from Kentucky and the East would be combined with those of Tennessee and frontier Georgia. Possibly Blount thought of a triple-headed attack on the Spanish which would drive them out of Pensacola, Mobile and the other centers, and would then converge on New Orleans and the river. Carey got drunk and exposed the contents of Blount's letter to some of his opponents, who published them. Blount was expelled from the Senate, but officers sent to Tennessee to arrest him failed to secure the co-operation of local officials and returned empty-handed. In their reaction to this unpleasant affair, the frontiersmen of Tennessee established a pattern of behavior which was to prevail often in future reactions toward political virtue. Blount, in their view, was indiscreet, but not guilty of a crime. The interest of frontier Tennessee had not suffered and respect for the Union was not an overwhelming force with them. As a reward for his past services and as an expression of confidence for his future dependability the displaced senator was elected to the presidency of the Tennessee Senate.

The Yazoo Companies

An integral part of the border disturbances was land speculation. Both private claimants and organized land companies were ready to secure possession of blocks of virgin territory. John Sevier of Watauga fame had a longstanding interest in the land surrounding the Muscle Shoals, and he expended prodigious energy to secure it. The South Carolina Company secured claim to lands about the famous Walnut Hills overlooking the wide sweeping bend of the Mississippi at the mouth of the Yazoo River. Virginia speculators, including Patrick Henry, claimed lands upstream at the Chickasaw Bluffs at the mouth of Wolf River, and Tennesseans had widely dispersed interests in lands from Muscle Shoals to the Mississippi River.

These combined speculative groups were known as the Yazoo companies, largely because their claims included the great Mississippi delta country. In all, approximately twenty million acres of land, located in present day Tennessee, Alabama and Mississippi, were involved. The Georgia legislature first proposed in 1789 to sell these lands for $207,000, but there was disagreement over the type of currency which would be acceptable as payment. In 1795 the second sale took place, in which a much larger area of between thirty-five and fifty million acres was sold for $5,000,000. Sale of the Yazoo lands quickly became a scandal in which speculator and legislator alike were subjected to bitter public scorn. Bribery and rascality abounded in securing the passage of the act permitting sale of the land. In an attempt to undo the corrupt act of the previous legislature, the Georgia assembly of 1796 paved the way for the famous case, *Fletcher* vs. *Peck* (1810), in which the Supreme Court of the United States upheld the Yazoo land sales on technical legal grounds, and in doing so forced the federal government to pay in 1814 to the Yazoo land claimants the fabulous sum of $4,282,151.12½ to compensate them for their property.

Both William Blount and the Yazoo land speculators failed to accomplish their immediate purposes. Blount was humiliated, if not disgraced, for his part in the western intrigue; the companies were well paid for their fraudulent but ingenious activities. Tennessee was admitted to the Union in 1796, but much of the southwestern borderland was still the scene of white and Indian conflict and of border intrigue between Americans and Spaniards. Other dramatic incidents in both local and international history were to occur before the region was finally settled by American frontiersmen. Nevertheless the future of the Southwest was assured.

In two decades the great western frontier arc of the late eighteenth century had been much extended. The frontier of this date was a restless place. It was this spirit of unrest and tension which hastened both the British and Spanish treaties, and it was western suspicion of eastern intents along with Old South planter interests that to some extent helped place in the United States Constitution a clause requiring a two-thirds vote of the Senate for treaty ratification. By the time the international problems of foreign expansion were cleared away, a tide of settlers approaching runaway proportions was converting old Indian hunting grounds into homesteads and cornfields. Where deer, elk, buffalo, beaver and mink had once flourished, the domestic cow, pig and sheep of white civilization grazed in circumscribed pastures and ranges. Where squaws once tended corn patches and kept house in flimsy Indian villages, whole families of whites pulled down the trees and planted spreading acres in corn, cotton and small grains. Smoke that billowed from stick and dirt chimneys of permanent log and stone houses was even more symbolic of the white man's certain conquest of the land.

FORMATIVE
POLITICAL YEARS

It is true our population is small, but among us there are some aspiring men who wished to display their talents in civil and political life, as well as in hunting, horse-racing and fighting: and as they could not get into office, without having a new county, they applied for and obtained one. This was the only motive for so doing, and not as some suppose, a disrelish for our former practices and modes of life.

Now sir, I assert it boldly, that ten men cannot be found among my constituents, who upon an impartial trial, would not be either sentenced to the penitentiary, sold out as vagrants, or imprisoned for debt. But as long as trials are carried on in our own county, the administration of justice is perfectly harmless; for being all nearly in the same situation, and having the whole management of it among ourselves, we so mould it as to suit our peculiar circumstances.

—WILLIAM LITTELL, *The Festoons of Fancy*

A VIEW FROM THE *New York Magazine* FOR JULY, 1796

CHAPTER VIII

POLITICAL organization was of major importance in the process of western expansion. Government at all levels kept up fairly well with the movement of population, and, in the case of the important local unit, the county, it often outran the settlement line. Before an intelligent approach can be made to frontier politics and governmental organization, it is necessary to develop some understanding of the county and its role on the frontier. Too little attention has been given to this division of local government. By the very nature of the westward movement, the local community was isolated, and the more immediately influential branches of government were those which served the people in a limited and isolated geographical region. While it is true that the larger national and international issues filtered down to localities and generated much heat, it was the local political system that actually facilitated expressions of opinions.

Counties

In the older states east of the mountains, counties were created both as local governing units and as extensions of state authority. Pennsylvania, for instance, created the great western county of Westmoreland in order to extend its authority to the Ohio and to head off Virginia in the bitter frontier rivalry for the western river outlet. Virginia was possibly more active in expanding its claims by use of the county than were any of the other states. Blanket authority was thrown over vast areas of land both below and beyond the Ohio. Illinois County was created in the Northwest Territory before George Rogers Clark returned from his Kaskaskia and Vincennes expedition. Earlier in the state's frontier history, Augusta County had blanketed the vast western country. Such counties as Botetourt, Fincastle and Kentucky were created not only to extend state jurisdiction, but to intensify it as sufficient settlers moved into the western country.

Several important factors in American political history are represented in the role played by the county in frontier expansion. Where large counties were created as blanket claims over vast stretches of virgin territory, they often existed primarily to hold the land for the state, or to insure its exploitation by certain chosen speculators. County surveyors, sheriffs, lieutenants and other officials found themselves in good positions to better their economic situations when they were permitted to operate in sparsely settled areas. Even a cursory examination of land deeds will reveal this fact. As population increased, the county became the most effective branch of government for serving the most people with the least inconvenience to them. Great masses of backwoods people were seldom conscious of the functioning of government above the county level. County offices became the highly desirable local positions, for reasons of social prestige as well as economic gain, and counties were created in relatively generous numbers to satisfy the clamor for offices. As towns and centers of business expanded, economic pressure often became almost as important as politics in forcing the multiplication of counties. Every promising village dreamed of itself as a county seat, with periodic meetings of courts and their attendant crowds to boom trade and to give importance to the town. Obviously there was nothing original about either the township or the county on the frontier. This system of local government was older than the American colonies themselves—possibly as old as the beginning of the modern history of England. It was, however, ideally suited to the needs of an extraordinarily small geographical pattern. Possibly no other system of local government could have succeeded so well.

Frontier counties had a multiplicity of offices. Most important of these were sheriff, county and circuit or probate clerks, lieutenant, surveyor, judge, overseer, magistrate, coroner, supervisor, and constable. Men often made the offices, and the extent of their influence was governed largely by their own ambitions; but generally the more influential were sheriffs, county surveyors and lieutenants, who controlled tax collections, land surveys, and local militia affairs. Strong-willed men like County Lieutenant William Preston of Fincastle County, Virginia, assumed enormous powers, and even shaped the pattern of land grants over an area as large as the future state of Kentucky.

When a county seat was established, there was quickly developed about it a tight politically-minded group known as the "courthouse ring." As composite political bodies, these rings were basically the most important local political influences in American history. The local ring was close to the people, and it kept its collective finger on the grass roots political pulse at all times. Men and political issues were translated through these rings to a decisive mass of voters. Advice, admonitions, and instructions which came from the courthouses often influenced elections on a much broader scale than either the county or the state. Sheriffs, magistrates and even judges knew the importance of keeping their political fences in good order if they were to deny the old frontier slogan that rotation in office was the will of the people.

County government must be analyzed before it is possible to understand the organization and workings of new states. The county plan or organization, more than any other one institution, was responsible for the spread of a relatively uniform system of government across the frontier, but an analysis is a difficult task. There were no written constitutions or laws on a county level which document the development. It is true that state laws outlined the plans and functions of county government, but they were not specific as to broader implications. Except for land, trial and personality documents, there is no body of materials which explains the political philosophy of development or records practical milestones. Seldom if ever have reform crusades occurred to improve county governments on a broad scale. Few personalities in this local branch of government attracted widespread attention to themselves, and what influence they had was exerted in the most private fashion upon their constituents. County politicians and county government both tended to follow a rigidly conservative political routine which permitted few or no new ideas that departed from the established pattern to take hold. Yet, for the individual on the frontier, the county records are about the only sources which take cognizance of his ever having lived.

Every territory in its approach to statehood has first had organized counties, and much of the background of state-making must be viewed through the experiences of these local units of government. In 1774 Virginia reached far out into the west by the organization of Fincastle County which covered most of the present state of Kentucky. This political expansion took place only three years after John Donelson had surveyed his line across Kentucky, and a year before Richard Henderson negotiated the Treaty of Sycamore Shoals. Two years later, the Virginia assembly created Kentucky County, and in 1780 the lands west of the mountains were divided into three counties. Within the next twelve years, eleven more were created. Virginia tried further to stabilize her western district by creating a special land court in 1780 and a district court of appeals in 1782, but neither move satisfied the desire for frontier autonomy.

The territory itself was a new device, largely of frontier origin, which facilitated the creation of states from the vast western lands. Obviously new states were inevitable, if for no other reason than the inertia of distance and space, but population movements into a reasonably definable region were never great enough or sufficiently integrated in the beginning to permit the organization of a state. For this reason the territorial stage was a political chrysalis in which a geographical area awaited institutional maturity without foregoing the conveniences of necessary administrative organization.

Let us take Kentucky as a case in point. As late as 1784 Indian activity both north and south of Kentucky was disturbing. The Cherokees, especially the Chickamaugas, were threatening to invade the country from the south, and for ten years Shawnee raids from north of the Ohio had harassed the Kentucky country. Colonel Benjamin Logan, the famous Indian-fighting frontiersman, called a meeting of local representatives to assemble in Danville in December. There was no evidence at the moment that the Kentuckians were beginning a long and tedious process of separating the western district from Virginia; ten conventions were necessary before a constitution could be drafted.

Possibly no other prospective state had to cope with so many difficult problems. Sentimentality for Virginia was one of the foremost stumbling blocks, but there were at least a dozen other complicating factors. Conservative landowners and speculators were hesitant about separation for fear Virginia land laws would be altered; back in Virginia there was reluctance in high places to see Kentucky pull away from the mother state.

Within the next eight years other complications arose. By 1787 the preliminaries of the famous Spanish conspiracies were evident, and that same year James Wilkinson had returned from New Orleans with a handsome profit on his first cargo of western produce. Not only had Wilkinson learned of the profitable New Orleans market, but he likewise had reached an agreement with Miró, the Spanish governor there, that had far-reaching importance for the struggling district of Kentucky. We do not know specifically what agreement Wilkinson and Miró made, but tangible results were to be noted in trade advantages which the Kentuckian enjoyed. The Kentucky farmers were vitally interested in the development of markets for their produce, and there was perhaps no single issue between 1786 and 1792 on which public opinion could be aroused more effectively. Contemporaneously with the opening of the separation question, the whole diplomatic issue of the Mississippi Valley and the Northwest was being agitated, and the problems of the Confederation were making themselves felt in backwoods Kentucky. Among the many outside influences which disturbed the Kentuckians was the constant friction over issues, real or imagined, which grew up between the Kentucky District and Virginia. Scores of petitions begging relief from all sorts of oppressions were sent to the Virginia assembly. Administration of political affairs in the western country was difficult under the most favorable conditions, but the disjointed post-Revolutionary era brought an added amount of confusion and dissatisfaction.

Frontier State-making

In 1782 the Kentuckians were aroused by the academic argument of Tom Paine in his pamphlet *The Common Good.* He took up the broader question of Virginia's claim to the Northwest Territory which, in this instance, included Kentucky, contending that the Proclamation of 1763 had nullified the state's title to land west of the Allegheny Mountains. If this proved to be true then the whole system of land laws and claims was threatened with nullification. As early as August, 1782, a petition from the inhabitants of Kentucky asked that the Congress of the Confederation admit the Kentucky counties as a state. Two years later a pair of flagrant rascals named Galloway and Pomeroy appeared in Lexington and Louisville and spread the rumor that Congress would soon redistribute the lands of the western district. Both men were arrested, tried, fined, and forced to leave the western country. But their departure did not erase the fear which they had implanted in the minds of the people. To threaten land claims with invalidity was to destroy the foundation of the westward movement in areas where individual states had made grants.

Statehood for Kentucky was inevitable, but many questions had to be answered first. The rights of the people had to be guaranteed, and ownership of land under Virginia laws had to be assured. An outlet for trade down the river had to be opened permanently, the Indian menace removed, and all divergent elements of local political opinion satisfied. These were issues, complex within themselves, which were almost insoluble when considered collectively. Carried over to the Kentucky frontier was the ancient Vir-

ginia struggle between the landed cliques who exercised tremendous influence over the course of government and public affairs. Injected into all
these complexities was the fundamental question of what constituted a free
civil government for a state.

Possibly at no other time or place in the western movement were so
many able men assembled as in Kentucky. The great valley of Virginia
had fed into the backwoods many of its ablest sons, men who had come fresh
from the political struggles of the mother state in the post-Revolutionary
years. Many of them, like George Nicholas, Caleb Wallace, David Rice,
Benjamin Sebastian, Benjamin Logan, Robert Breckinridge and Samuel
McDowell, were endowed with knowledge of government, and some of
them were conversant with the higher realms of political theory embodied
in the writings of John Locke and others. Between 1786 and 1790 thirty men
organized themselves into the Danville Political Club in which they debated almost every conceivable issue related to the making of a constitution.
In fact, this club did draft a constitution which it believed would best suit
Kentucky. The ideas of the Political Club turned up in the numerous
separation conventions and later in the constitution itself.

Virginia gave its consent for separation of Kentucky in three enabling
acts which prescribed the necessary steps by which this could be done.
Kentucky was to secure the necessary guarantee of admission to the Confederation, it was not to revoke the Virginia land laws, and Virginia was
to retain certain undistributed military lands. The final act required Kentucky's admission to the Union under the Constitution of the United States.
After eight years of debate and nine conventions, Kentuckians finally consolidated their many political arguments and contentions into a will to
create a new state. The length of time and the multiplicity of meetings
reflected not so much the difficulty delegates had in formulating a constitution as the thoroughness with which the fundamental issues that confronted the western country were discussed and the endless conflict between social and economic groups as to who should make major political
decisions.

Unlike the extended process through which the ultimate call of a constitutional convention was effected, the final convention was of short duration, lasting less than the month of April, 1792. Delegates to this convention
were overwhelmingly Virginian in origin, and its leadership was definitely
divided between the conservative landowning gentry and the liberal religious group which wanted, if not abrupt abolition of slavery, at least to
leave the way open for its eventual destruction. This conflict was personified
in the leadership of George Nicholas, lawyer, and David Rice, Presbyterian
minister, with Nicholas winning support. By 1792 important changes had
occurred in Kentucky and the nation. The Indian menace was practically a

thing of the past for the immediate Kentucky frontier. Beyond the Ohio, it is true, the great conflict was in the making, but the old and nagging fear of death and destruction from this source was past for Kentuckians. A great degree of assurance was built up by the rapid increase of the population, which had reached approximately 73,000. Economically the western country was in the first stages of prosperity, and, although no general agreement had been made with Spain regarding use of the Mississippi River and its market facilities in Natchez and New Orleans, there was hope that this could be accomplished. It is unlikely that any considerable number of frontiersmen doubted that the river would not be opened. They did not conceive the diplomatic process by which this might be done, but they shared the view attributed to the defiant Benjamin Logan who, after being roughly treated by Spanish customs officials, said that the next time he came downriver he would bring enough men with him to eat his beef.

Before a Kentucky constitution was made, a national constitution had been drafted and ratified and a more stable central government brought into existence. By the time the Kentuckians answered all their own questions and reached the stage of setting pen to paper, well-defined decisions had been reached on at least five major issues. Delegates to the convention were to be carefully selected as representatives of the people; demagogues were to be discouraged. The right of the vote should be free without property qualifications, officeholders would be held to no religious oath, representation should be based on population and not on county units, and the primogeniture laws were to be nullified. Possibly the decision to grant the high court appellate jurisdiction only, except in specific land cases, should be included as fundamental. Arguments advanced for white manhood suffrage and popular representation were based on the distinct frontier contention that everybody helped to resist the Indians and conquer the western woods; therefore every male twenty-one years of age was entitled to a voice in the conduct of government.

Kentucky's first constitution was on the whole a conservative document with certain liberal aspects, reflecting to a great extent the personal views of its framers. George Nicholas, born in Williamsburg, a protégé of George Wythe and a friend of Jefferson, Madison, Henry, Marshall, and Washington, possibly had the greatest personal influence on the document. Unlike the United States Constitution, the Kentucky Bill of Rights was set out in a definite list of twenty-six numbered sections. The lower house of legislature was elected directly by the people, but the senators were to be selected by an electoral college or commission. The governor (there was no lieutenant governor) was to be elected in the same way and was to serve for four years. He was given the right of veto over laws, and provisions were made for him to call the assembly into special session. The conservative point of view of the convention showed itself in a restrictive article pertaining to slavery. Some slight provision was made for emancipation, but terms prescribed made it almost impossible to attain except upon the payment of full cost of the slaves to their owners. A wise provision specified that if within five years the constitution needed revision, a second convention should be called; the delegates had failed to devise a workable system of courts with a clear line of appeal established and specified jurisdiction for each branch. Endless popular discussion had centered about the questions of voting and the fundamental rights of individuals and representations, but the judicial problem seems to have been too technical for frontier statesmen to grasp fully. Even George Nicholas appeared not to have comprehended the broad administrative problems of the courts.

The Kentucky constitution, by reason of being the first devised for a frontier state, was of great precedental importance. What were its sources? The Bill of Rights is verbatim that of the Pennsylvania constitution of 1790. There is also some remote kinship with various other articles. Structurally the new constitution followed the pattern which had been used in several states. While the Bill of Rights is directly traceable to the Pennsylvania document, the fundamental principles appear in nearly all of the state documents which were in effect at that time, as well as in the classic sources of free men. Some sections, such as those pertaining to voting, the primogeniture law, and the basis of representation, reflected the democratizing influence of the frontier. Failure to make the governor and senators directly elective by the people, the safeguards for slavery, denial of membership in the legislature to ministers of the gospel, and the general administrative provision reflected a most conservative point of view, which was principally of Tidewater Virginia origin. By ignoring education, the Kentuckians failed to encourage a major democratizing force.

Kentucky was admitted to the Union as the first of the western frontier states on June 1, 1792. Its constitution reflected the thinking both of the Northwest Ordinance and the Constitution of the United States. Further, it acknowledged the strong impetus of local government which existed long before its adoption. The western district had survived Wilkinson and Miró's plotting and Virginia's desire to have it admitted safely to the Union according to the dictates of the enabling acts. The state government was organized in Lexington four days after the date of admission with the old frontier hero Isaac Shelby as governor.

The United States Constitution

While Kentuckians at Danville discussed the complex problems of separating the western district from Virginia, they were also sensitive to outside pressures. The first of these was the change in the nature of the Union.

The constitutional fathers in Philadelphia had completed their work in 1787 and had submitted it to the states for ratification.

There was opposition to ratification of the federal constitution on the part of frontiersmen in several sections, but nowhere was the issue more clearly defined than in the western Virginia district of Kentucky. Opposition here developed between western delegates who sided with Patrick Henry and George Mason, and the federalists such as George Nicholas and Humphrey Marshall. Three aspects of the constitutional question disturbed the Kentucky delegation: first, the vague but disturbing one of a strong central government in which the chief executive possessed certain fundamental powers; second, the uncertainty of Kentucky's own position in its struggle for independent statehood; and finally that ever-virile issue, free navigation of the Mississippi River. Since the new federal constitution contained a clause pertaining to treaty-making, it was easy enough for the opponents of ratification to question this in their arguments. Patrick Henry attempted to excite the western delegates by raising doubts, but Madison was able to answer his arguments and to clarify thinking on this point. Actually, Patrick Henry and George Mason were working on the western delegates in what was called a "scuffle for Kentucky votes" against Virginia's ratification.

Arguments such as those in the Virginia convention and those which appeared in the public press prejudiced the cause of the federal government in the West during its formative years. Much of the fear which existed on the frontier was the product of wilful dissemination of misinformation, academic arguments which were accepted by many as literal truth, and a genuine fear that the new government would be oppressive. Isaac Shelby professed to believe the President of the United States would use the army to inflict the executive will of the government upon the people. Newspaper columns were filled with varying points of view, most of them adverse in nature.

Whisky and Taxes

There was strong opposition to Hamilton's excise tax policy in Congress, and many of the arguments against it were reported in the press. For several decades excise taxes had been anathema to the people. Hamilton's proposal was reminiscent of the hated British levies. The whisky tax was not new—Pennsylvania had collected a gallonage tax in the past—but what was new was the plan for dividing the country into revenue districts which ignored state lines. Another disturbing feature was the fact that tax collection was levied directly against the little man; and payments were to be made in cash, which would exhaust his slender holdings in specie.

When the Hamiltonian fiscal policies were publicized, the frontier farmer perhaps saw only the tax laws which applied to his product. Whisky was an important commodity in western Pennsylvania and Kentucky. The fact that cargoes could be passed through the Spanish blockade by a little bribery indicated its high marketability. It could be transported to a rather stable market with little danger of loss except by leakage. Whisky was basic in the barter system which of necessity prevailed on the frontier. Distilling was as much a part of the domestic economy as making soap, lard and flour. To single out this commodity for taxation only intensified the frontiersman's sense of injury. He was denied free use of the river, he felt that by some failure of the government his roads were either non-existent or impassable much of the year, and instead of placing a tax on his product he believed that the government should help the western farmers by exerting all of its energies to remove the Spanish blockade from the river.

Before the government could collect the whisky tax, it was necessary for internal revenue agents to register stills in operation, to secure information about stocks on hand, and to mark barrels and other containers. However logical and necessary this procedure, it was new and foreign to anything the independent western farmer had experienced. He felt that this was an invasion of his private rights. Because of this irritation it was easy to plant in the mind of the average backwoodsman in a most impressive way the highly technical idea that he had certain prescribed rights which the government would invade. When a farmer ran afoul of the federal law in western Pennsylvania he had to stand trial in Philadelphia, far removed from his background and friends.

Opposition to the whisky tax had its initial stages in a meeting in Pittsburgh in 1791 which sought repeal of the levy. A resolution adopted at this meeting said that the western Pennsylvanians would deal harshly and inhospitably with revenue officers, and there is evidence that they carried out their threat prior to 1794. Resistance to collection of the tax grew in such proportions that the government could not further ignore the opposition. In August, 1794, President Washington took action by issuing a proclamation to recruit fifteen thousand militiamen from Virginia, Maryland and Pennsylvania. Slightly more than twelve thousand were actually assembled, and this army started its slow advance into western Pennsylvania. Its movement was somewhat reminiscent of Washington's own attempt to reach the head of the Ohio in 1754. Attempts by a special commission to effect a negotiated agreement with the rebellious western farmers failed, but when the army finally reached the scene of trouble, resistance melted away and order was restored without conflict. A similar reaction in Kentucky would have resulted in open resistance if the Pennsylvania farmers had succeeded. Farmers and distillers in that state were highly incensed at the collection of the whisky tax, and when Thomas Marshall, collector of internal revenue, published the names of tax delinquents, it was evident that both he and the tax would have vigorous opposition.

The disturbance over the whisky tax came at a moment when the frontier was agitated over many diverse issues. The Wayne campaign against the Indians perhaps prevented a more violent resistance to the government, and the organization of the new state of Kentucky absorbed much energy that might have been spent in such resistance. Anxiety over the opening of the Mississippi River was also a distraction, for western boatmen and farmers were hopeful that the United States government would give them relief from this oppression. Locally, the French and Spanish conspiracies had created suspicion of both men and governments. The growing friction between the United States and France excited westerners because of their sympathy for the latter. On top of this was the sectional antagonism between the West and the East.

The frontier, as has been said elsewhere, was hospitable to the eighteenth-century democratic societies, and there was a direct relationship between them and the frontier reactions to national issues. Between 1793 and 1798 these groups were ready to examine critically any issue which arose. Republican newspapers did much to arouse opinion. The Kentucky *Gazette* carried a disproportionate amount of news and comments on current national and international affairs. Pseudonymous writers made frequent and bitter comments on these same affairs. Elsewhere attacks upon the administration of John Adams, the second President, many of them coming from militant French immigrant editors, inflamed the public mind. In the summer of 1798, Congress responded to administrative pressure and enacted the body of legislation known as the Alien and Sedition Laws.

Federalist Curbs

Popular opposition to the Alien and Sedition Laws was not stimulated by a purely legalistic attitude. It is hardly possible to explain any incident of this period which bore upon frontier history without associating it with the keen desire to have unrestricted access to the Mississippi River. Virginian politicians even in 1788 knew this. Other issues, of course, had irritated and frustrated the people as we have seen. In national politics the Federalists held the whip hand momentarily, but the people were beginning to imbibe the heady wine of bi-partisan politics. An impending war with France, the selection of John Adams over Thomas Jefferson for president, the organization of new state governments plus the founding of the Northwest Territory, and the growing population of the frontier all helped to create an air of excitement and expectancy. Politics west of the mountains was anything but static.

John Adams was unpopular in the west because of the belief that he was pro-British and favored eastern over western interests. The opponents of the Federalist policies cultivated this view. In the midst of such shifting political sands came the passage of the Alien and Sedition Laws. The first protest against these Federalist-inspired laws was organized by the citizens of Clark County, Kentucky, on July 24, 1798. They adopted a set of resolutions saying, among other things, that all officers of the federal government were servants of the people, war with France was impolitic, an alliance with Britain was dangerous, and the Alien and Sedition Laws were unreasonable invasions of individual rights. Rapidly this sentiment spread. George Nicholas and young Henry Clay took an active part in open attacks on the acts of Congress and the administration. In November the Kentucky legislature adopted a set of resolutions which were largely the handiwork of Thomas Jefferson, but which were introduced by John Breckinridge. These resolutions, inviting action by other states, came pretty close to being an expression of the Republican party's faith, and were a protest against federal encroachments upon a state's rights. The states, they maintained, had the privilege of judging infractions of the Constitution by Congress and the administration, and they maintained the Constitution to be a compact. While it is true that the Kentucky Resolutions as such were not strictly of frontier origin, they received warm support in the newly organized state. What was more important was the fact that they were a tremendously important factor in implanting the Republican party securely in the West.

Tennessee

The conflicts which arose in the 1790's checked neither the vigorous flow of population westward nor the agitation for the creation of new states. Along the southern border of Kentucky, the Southwest or Tennessee Territory was in the process of expanding its settlements, and these would be shortly consolidated into a new state.

The pioneer history of Tennessee was not unlike that of Kentucky. In 1768 it had its beginning in the Watauga settlement, and by 1796 there were at least three communities which had either formed independent semiterritorial governments or had made local compacts. The state of Franklin had embraced the eastern communities, and the Cumberland and Clarksville compacts had served the Cumberland Valley settlers. Before 1796 eleven counties had been formed, but unfortunately these were not grouped in a contiguous area as were the counties of Kentucky; local problems were therefore of a somewhat peculiar nature, yet the county system had already established a tradition of government in the region. Some Tennessee historians have claimed that their local governmental form stemmed directly from England—that it was the southern tidewater county government transplanted west of the mountains. A peculiarity of the political organization in Tennessee was the subsequent creation by the legislature of the two judicial districts of Washington and Miro. Washington District included the eastern counties while Miro embraced the Cumberland or western area. Naming the western district for the Spanish governor Don Esteban Miró reflected the desire to trade down the Mississippi and possibly some thought of defection. These divisions prevailed until 1809, when the state was divided into five numbered judicial districts.

In 1789 North Carolina made a second cession of its western territory to Congress, and the next year the Southwest Territory was created. For the next five years people migrated to both the eastern and middle group of counties. The population showed a steady increase, and with this development sentiment for the creation of an independent state arose again. Also, local officials like William Blount had their eyes on national offices as prospective senators and congressmen, to say nothing of the numerous state offices. Blount set in motion the process by which a convention might be assembled, a constitution drafted and a state delegation sent to report the action in Philadelphia and to petition for the immediate admission of Tennessee to the Union. The first problem was that of ascertaining whether or not there resided in the territory the necessary 60,000 persons. Census-takers were sent among the people to determine this fact, and at the same time to ask for *yea* and *nay* votes on calling the convention and to give instructions for the election of five delegates to the convention from each of the eleven counties. It was revealed that there were 77,263 inhabitants, and of those voting, there were 6,504 *yeas* and 2,563 *nays*.

Governor Blount issued a call in November, 1795, for an election of delegates to a convention to be held in Knoxville in January, 1796. Unlike Kentucky, the Tennesseans were freed by one voluntary act from North Carolina, and when they came to consider independent statehood they had only to draft a constitution. For twenty days the convention labored at the task of reworking the North Carolina Constitution so as to adjust it to frontier needs and whims. When the convention was finished with its labors, copies of the new document were printed at the office of the Knoxville *Gazette* and Joseph McMinn delivered it to President Washington in Philadelphia.

The first Tennessee constitution reflected the strong economy-mindedness of the conventions. Salaries of public officials were prescribed, and tax rates on land and town lots were limited in such a manner that the holder of improved lands would not suffer an increased tax assessment because of that fact. Organization of state government followed the orthodox plan of three major divisions of legislative, executive and judicial branches. Property qualifications were required of legislators and the governor, and the voter had to be either a freeholder or a town lot taxpayer. A Declaration of Rights of thirty-two sections granted freedom of religion and forbade the use of a test oath as prerequisite to officeholding. In this area the frontier statesmen broke sharply with the North Carolina constitution which restricted officeholding to people who believed in God, the efficacy of the Protestant religion, and the authority of the Old and New Testaments. However, the Tennesseans did retain the clause which forbade ministers of the gospel to become members of the legislature, thus restricting the ministers with more grace and subtlety in Tennessee than in North Carolina. Ministers were told in the parent document that they should not dissipate their energies in such mundane tasks as politics.

The Tennesseans were forehanded. Not only did they create a state out of a federal territory, but they elected William Cocke and William Blount United States senators to go on to Philadelphia and be ready to enter the Senate immediately upon the admission of the state. Kentucky had been admitted without difficulty, and there was reason to believe Tennessee's admission would be little more than a perfunctory act.

In Philadelphia, however, a sectional and partisan issue was raised. Washington was preparing to retire from the Presidency, and political lines were beginning to be drawn between Federalists and Republicans. The admission of Tennessee was assumed to be advantageous to the Republicans. Washington submitted the new Tennessee constitution without comment, and immediately the Federalists raised objections to admission of the state. The adverse arguments centered about two major questions: whether or not Congress had the initiative in the formation of new states, and whether the Tennessee census count could be accepted as legal and valid. Long arguments were presented by both sides, with James Madison advocating admission. The Senate proposed to delay admission, but this decision was reversed by the lower house, and on June 1, 1796, Tennessee was admitted as the sixteenth state. Admission came so late that Cocke and Blount were forced to return home unseated and to seek re-election before the next session of Congress.

Tennessee's admission to the Union was a landmark in frontier history. It had come into existence within a federal territory, although it had existed in part as a settled area prior to the American Revolution. This was the first time the formula for the organization of a state as prescribed in the Northwest Ordinance was put to a test. The admission of Tennessee wiped away several scars of former attempts to organize an independent government from North Carolina territory beyond the mountains. However, North Carolina political traditions were not discarded in the new constitution. Present in the document were both the philosophy and conservatism of the North Carolina constitution, and despite their isolation and new-found independence the designers of the fundamental rules of government for the new state followed in the main the older plan of government.

Kentucky's Second Constitution

Two years after Tennessee was admitted to the Union its neighbors to the north in Kentucky re-examined their document. Provisions were made in 1792 for this reappraisal after a period of five years, and the people were instructed to make such adjustments as seemed necessary. In five years, however, the tenor of Kentucky sentiment and politics had undergone considerable change. The landed conservatives had become frightened over the fact that the institution of slavery might be injured if not destroyed in a second convention. But when it became clear that the people would call a second convention, the conservatives took over the leadership of the revisionary movement, and they were successful in sending an instructed delegation to the new convention.

Changes made in the new Kentucky document permitted direct election by the people of the governor and senators; provisions were made for a lieutenant-governor, and the complex court snarl was simplified. Actually the fundamental structure of the first constitution was left largely intact. The significance of the second document lies not so much in the fact that it made revolutionary advances in constitutional government as in the fact that this was the document used by so many of the other states as an example by which to formulate their own constitutions.

Ohio

Five years after the creation of Tennessee, the citizens of the Ohio District, chafing under the partisan political pressure of Governor Arthur St. Clair and the Federalists, sought to rid themselves of this handicap. Politically, the easterners who settled in the Marietta area and on the upper Ohio offered a sharp contrast to the southerners down the river. A sectional issue which first showed the difference between northern and southern points of view had reared itself in the arguments over the admission of Tennessee and was to continue throughout the movement for the organization of the state of Ohio.

The experience of Ohio in its progress toward statehood was somewhat different from that of its southern neighbors. Since July 25, 1788, there had been an organized government in the Northwest Territory, and provisions had been made in the Northwest Ordinance for the eventual organization of states. Because of this, members of the territorial assembly not only sought to set up an administrative system for the larger region, but specifically looked forward to the day when there would be five thousand eligible voters in the area along the Ohio and an independent territory could be formed there. Part of this sentiment was engendered by a genuine desire to form a state; part of it revolved around personalities. Governor Arthur St. Clair was hardly a man who inspired firm loyalties, nor did his program necessarily encourage enthusiastic support. Personally he was stubborn, haughty and often oblivious to the general trend of opinion about him. He had the distinct asset of being a good organizer, however, and was on the whole an efficient administrator. He had brought with him from Pennsylvania that state's legal code which was used as a source for organizing a body of laws for the territory. The first session of the territorial assembly was called in Marietta, and before it had organized itself the governor committed an act which revealed his philosophy of personal administration. He organized Washington County on his own volition. In the immediate future the organization of counties was to be one of the chief sources of irritation in Ohio's early history.

Between 1788 and 1801 many laws were enacted, and an even larger number borrowed from the older states and published in the famous Maxwell Code. This volume of laws reflected with great clarity both the problems of the new territory and its general progress. The decade and a half of political history in the Northwest Territory, 1788–1803, is colored largely by political disharmony. Governor St. Clair stirred up much dissension, and when he was away from the region the territorial secretary, Winthrop Sargent, all but provoked open revolt. The sources of these disputes were many. There was a fundamental conflict between differing points of view of the northern and southern factions, or between future Republicans and Federalists, and between Sargent and St. Clair on the one hand, and the land speculators, the people, the administrators of local government, and the local communities, on the other, especially Cincinnati, Chillicothe and Marietta. The rugged frontier question of creating new counties and the location of county seats kept many Ohio communities in turmoil among themselves. The courts were unsatisfactory because the people doubted both their efficiency and ability to render justice.

Before 1800 St. Clair found his administration faced with the inevitable issue of creating a state within the territory. It was apparent by 1798 that there were already five thousand males in the territory of voting age, and time had come to take a census. As in Tennessee the question arose as to who should initiate the count—the governor or the people. Constables were instructed by the leaders of the state territorial movement to take a census. When Governor St. Clair saw that such action was underway and that there could be little doubt of its outcome, he issued a proclamation opening the way for the creation of a territorial assembly. This body opened its first session on September 24, 1799, and from that point on the history of territorial government in Ohio was one of conflict among personalities. Thomas Worthington led the Republicans while St. Clair spoke for the Federalists. Associated with Worthington were such influential persons as Nathaniel Massie, Edward Tiffin and William Henry Harrison, territorial secretary since 1798. Supporting St. Clair were James Ross, Rufus Putnam and Paul Fearing. Land speculation, the shortcomings of the federal land law, unsatisfactory relationships with the government of the Northwest Territory, the creation of new counties, taxes, road building, the location of the new state capital, and the general laws—all were sources of friction.

Governor St. Clair's opposition to organization of the state territory had been a lost cause from the start. The press of population increased with each year, and only a foolish person indeed would have predicted an insufficient population by 1803 to permit the creation of the state of Ohio. Already in 1800 there were 45,356 persons, and the roads westward were swarming with new immigrants. Since the national election had brought Thomas Jefferson to the Presidency, the Republicans were assured a friendly reception in Washington. Early in 1802, agitation for independent statehood was strong, and on April 27 Congress passed an enabling act permitting the organization of a new state.

Up to this point the arguments in the Ohio Territory had revolved around personalities and political control. Few or no advanced political ideas such as those debated in the Danville Political Club in Kentucky had been set forth. In November, 1802, thirty-five delegates, a majority of whom were Republicans, met in Chillicothe and began the task of drafting a new constitution. Within twenty-nine days the document was finished. Contrary to the philosophy emphasized in it of the sovereignty of the people, the new constitution, like those of Kentucky and Tennessee, was sent directly to Washington for acceptance by Congress without having first been ratified by voters. Republicans under the leadership of the "Chillicothe Junto" dominated the convention, especially after Governor St. Clair destroyed any influence he might have had in an intemperate address to the delegates. The delegates were young men, most of them in their thirties. Not one could claim to be a seasoned statesman. They relied heavily upon the new Tennessee Constitution, sometimes adopting its precise wording, at other times using only its philosophy. The governor was made little more than an administrative figurehead without the right of veto. He was forced to submit to frequent election and could serve only six out of each eight years. The court system was cumbersome and poorly defined, but public education was provided for—a distinctly progressive innovation in constitution-making, as was the prohibition of a poll tax. Slavery was forbidden, but Negroes were denied the right to vote despite great emphasis upon the inalienable rights of man to determine the nature of his government. The right to vote was restricted to men twenty-one years of age who were taxpayers, or who worked on the roads in their counties and townships.

Again, the Ohio Bill of Rights was a compilation of the guarantees of the classic freedoms outlined so many times before in constitution-making. Innovations were to be found in the regard for education and the slightly different attitude toward religion. Fundamentally the Ohio Bill of Rights, like those of several other states, represented in a conservative manner all of the gains made by freedom-loving people over several centuries. On the whole the document was conservative in tone.

In the frontier movement, the admission of this new state was significant because it established the pattern by which the rest of the Northwest Territory was to be divided into states in keeping with the provisions of the Northwest Ordinance. The Republicans were triumphant in the admission of the new state, and Edward Tiffin of the "Chillicothe Junto" became the first governor.

A distinguished historian in later years was to look back on the admission of Ohio to the Union and to regard the act as a signal landmark in constitutional history. Although his judgment is not without its element of exaggeration, his enthusiasm is within reason. "The admission of Ohio into the Union as a state," he wrote, "was attended with no general demonstrations, and aroused very little interest beyond her own bounds. Yet every Republican observer of days and seasons, every Republican who on the fourth of each March and the fourth of each July, heard speeches and drank toasts in honor of the triumph of Jeffersonian principles and the rights of man, might well have marked the admission of Ohio. The adoption of her constitution was a political event. It was another triumph for the rights of man; another victory in that great struggle on the results of which are staked the dearest interests of the human race."

The movement for independent state government in Ohio paralleled attempts to revise the national land law in such a way as to give the average settler an opportunity to purchase a tract of land in a quantity and on terms which matched his economic condition. Governor St. Clair and other officials were becoming aware of the squatter problem. Earlier, squatters had crossed the Ohio from Kentucky before agreements had been made with the Indians, and they had to be forced back. By 1795 they were again moving across the river into the public domain, and unless some legal means could be devised to sell them land on easier terms, they would become most difficult to dispossess. The original Land Ordinance of 1785 contained three provisions which worked definite hardships on little buyers. Land could be purchased only in township quantities, payment had to be made shortly after purchase, and the buyer had to go to Philadelphia to make the transaction.

Inevitably the western land question was to become a live political issue in the tumultuous closing years of the eighteenth century. In 1796 a new land law was passed which remedied some of the defects of the Ordinance of 1785. The township of six square miles was preserved although there was pressure to reduce it to half that size. A surveyor general was provided for, and payments for lands, at the official price of $2.00 per acre, could be spread over twelve months. Half the townships offered for sale were to be divided into saleable tracts of 640 acres, and land offices were to be opened at Cincinnati and Pittsburgh.

While making slight progress, the new law did not solve the western land problems. Squatters continued to cross the Ohio and to settle on lands in the public domain. By 1800 the heavy population growth and the dissatisfaction with the federal land system evoked many complaints from settlers to which the ears of politicians were keenly attuned. William Henry Harrison, a Virginian who came out to the frontier with Wayne's army, had served one year as secretary to the Northwest Territory when he was elected a delegate to Congress in 1799. In 1800, he, with Albert Gallatin, promoted a further revision of the laws regulating land sales, and on May 10, 1800, Congress passed the new act which went far in liberalizing conditions of land sales. One fourth of the townships west of the Muskingum River were to be sold in half sections of 320 acres each, with a series of payments extending over a period of four years which would lighten the financial burden. Four land districts were created with offices in Chillicothe, Cincinnati, Steubenville and Marietta.

The land law of 1800 ended neither dissatisfaction nor the influx of squatters, but it did mark the beginning of a long series of laws which were to liberalize the terms by which the settler could procure land from the government.

The turn of the eighteenth century found the frontier movement well advanced. An important political precedent had been set in the formation of the new western states. The new constitutions established a rather conservative tradition of governmental expansion for the rest of the frontier. New states patterned their constitutions and governments on the older ones.

Frictions between state and federal governments had arisen and been adjusted. Unsuccessfully, the central government's authority had been challenged in the whisky rebellion and the Kentucky Resolutions, but the voice of protest was heard clearly in Philadelphia and later in Washington. In the election of 1800 the influence of the western voter was felt for the first time, and the rising tide of population made the frontier a new factor in American politics. A marked spirit of expansion prevailed all across the frontier. Only one significant barrier blocked the West and that, despite the Pinckney treaty, was Spanish control of the Mississippi, but each year saw increasing pressure for governmental action on this issue. As forests were felled, as western fields produced in rapidly increasing abundance, and as farm products piled up awaiting a free market, inevitably the river would be freed, and the administration which removed this barrier could count on strong frontier political support.

Log Tavern Indiana.

Published by I. Drury, 36 Lombard St. London

G. Harley Lithog.

Drawn by Henry W. Foster

A FRONTIER LOG HOUSE FROM WELBY'S *Visit to North America*, 1821

A PIONEER WAY OF LIFE

A PIONEER WAY OF LIFE

The peculiarities, or, to speak more properly, the developments of character, which may be said to distinguish the population of the West, may be readily enumerated; and they are all created by the peculiar circumstances in which the people have been placed in that new world. They are,

1. A spirit of adventurous enterprise: a willingness to go through hardship or danger to accomplish an object. . . . The Western people think nothing of making a long journey, of encountering fatigue, and of enduring every species of hardship. . . .

2. Independence of thought and action. They have felt the influence of this principle since their childhood. Men who can endure anything: they have lived almost without restraint, free as the mountain air, or as the deer and buffalo of their forests—and who know they are Americans all—will act out this principle during the whole of life. . . .

3. An apparent roughness, which some would deem rudeness of manners.

These traits characterize, especially, the agricultural portions of the country, and also in some degree the new towns and villages. They are not so much the offspring of ignorance and barbarism, (as some would suppose), as the results of the circumstances of a people thrown together in a new country, often for a long time in thin settlements; where, of course, acquaintances for many miles around are soon of necessity, made and valued from new adventitious causes. Where there is perfect equality in a neighborhood of people who know but little about each other's previous history or ancestry—but where each is lord of the soil which he cultivates. Where a log cabin is all that the best of families can expect to have for years, and of course can possess few of the external decorations which have so much influence in creating a diversity of rank in society. These circumstances, have laid the foundation for that equality of intercourse, simplicity of manners, want of deference, want of reserve, great readiness to make acquaintances, freedom of speech, indisposition to brook real or imaginary insults, which one witnesses among the people of the West.

—BAIRD, *Valley of the Mississippi*

CHAPTER IX

IN 1801 the census taker publicized an astounding population gain for the frontier areas of the United States. There were 887,331 persons in that part of the country classified as "western." Of these, 82,297 were slaves with every region reporting in this category except that designated as "Northwest of the Ohio River." The census classified the population in three age ranges: 297,737 children under ten years; 88,241 adults over forty-five; and the largest class, 419, 407, between ten and forty-five. Men outnumbered women 405,431 to 372,371.

It is almost impossible to present similar data for a comparable region in 1790. The Southwest had a population of 35,691, or 16,548 males and 15,365 females, 361 not classified, and 3,417 slaves. Possibly the best comparable figure can be had for Kentucky. In 1790 that district had 73,677 persons, or 32,211 males and 28,925 females, 12,430 slaves, and 114 not classified. Within the next ten years Kentucky had gained an additional 157,282 persons.

One might go to great lengths to interpret even these elementary population statistics at the turn of the eighteenth century. But for general observation two factors are pertinent: the frontier population was growing phenomenally, and no single general statement can be made valid enough to explain this increase. Males outnumbered females, and obviously early mortality took a heavy toll of children one to ten years of age.

Up to this point, we have discussed frontier history in the light of major domestic and international struggles and changes. Gaining control and insuring safe occupancy of the land was possibly the most important single aspect of frontier expansion before 1800; thus the larger phases of military and diplomatic affairs have of necessity been considered first. Spread of population has been discussed in the abstract, except where individuals stood out in military, speculative and political leadership. Back of the whole frontier movement were hordes of settlers who exhibited a strange mixture of courage, fear, individualism, indecision, determination, emotionalism, and direct motivation. One general statement about these frontiersmen which will withstand considerable challenge is that the folk movement westward was without uniformity in all of its parts. It did not follow a set geographical course, and "Westward" was more indicative of the nature of the movement than its true direction. This society was not classless. It developed neither a spirit of political radicalism nor even of social liberalism as it went along. Viewpoints often differed even within narrow sectional lines.

Some historians have used the term "individualism" to characterize much of the personal aspect of this westward movement. Possibly this personal attribute would be more accurately described in terms of ingenuity, forbearance, and resourcefulness. There were individualists on the frontier, just as there are individualists in all free societies. Modern urban civilization possibly produces as many individualists as did the frontier. At times frontier individualism amounted to little more than personal peculiarities and hard-headedness. The early fortress community which frequently initiated settlement along the outer fringes was anything but an individualistic one. On a broader scale all the settlements were dependent not only upon one another, but upon older communities east of the mountains. Rarely was a serious Indian attack without its story of mutual assistance of some sort; and the same was true of individual settlers and their families. There were tasks too difficult to be performed alone, and out of this condition grew the most highly developed practice of common, or co-operative, workings in American history.

Exploitation of the land was never a uniform process, nor was the establishment of communities. It can hardly be said that the beginning of Marietta was comparable with that of Boonesboro, nor was Vincennes similar to Watauga. It is this complexity which has caused many historians to by-pass a treatment of the region's social growth.

Frontiersmen generally developed a degree of self-reliance. The first people to reach the frontier were forced to reduce their mode of living to the barest essentials in order to maintain life. Food either had to be gathered from the country or produced quickly from half-cleared patches in the woods. At best it was unvaried and monotonous. Sustenance and not variety was the major objective; meat without bread, and often without salt, was the lot of many. Dr. Daniel Drake wrote that his people:

> From the time of their arrival in Kentucky 14 months before, they had suffered from want of bread, and now they found themselves doomed to the same deficiency another year. There was no fear of famine, but they cloyed on animal food, and sometimes almost loathed it, though of excellent quality. Deer were numerous and wild turkies numberless. The latter were often so fat that in falling from the tree when shot their skins would burst. There was no longing for the "*flesh* pots" of native land, but their hearts yearned for its neat and abounding *wheat-bread* trays.

Bread in the earliest years when available had to be made from poorly prepared grain, and it was difficult to keep either grain or bread fresh for any considerable length of time. Ingenuity and forbearance were the twin virtues of necessity when the white man placed himself in the arms of raw, untamed nature. There was no standard interval of time in which nature remained untamed. Sometimes it was exceedingly short; at others it was unreasonably long. Roughly it was considered that a newly cleared field could not be conditioned for peak production in less than three years, the time required to clear away the debris of falling trees and for smaller stumps to decay.

The first places where prospective settlers actually came into direct association with the new frontier were along the trails and rivers. Their first approach to the trans-Appalachian frontier was by packhorse and flatboat. Neither facility permitted transportation of more than the barest essentials for beginning domestic life anew. These were largely tools, needed to create new household and farming equipment, and seeds to produce fresh crops. Women and younger children swapped rides on weary packhorses, while men and boys struggled beside animals loaded with panniers strapped to pack saddles, or drove cows, sheep and hogs before them. Day after day and week after week these immigrant parties forced their way westward, not knowing what lay before them. The laborious crossing of the mountains and the hours spent at the poles of lumbering flatboats further conditioned them for their new homes.

An Ohio immigrant boy recalled in later life his family's journey from Carlisle, Pennsylvania, westward in 1784:

> We were provided with three horses, on one of which my mother rode carrying her infant, with all the table furniture and cooking utensils. On another were packed the stores of provisions, the plough irons, and other agricultural tools. The third horse was rigged out with a pack saddle, and two large creels (panniers), made of hiccory widths in the fashion of a crate, one over each side, in which were stowed the beds and bedding, and the wearing apparel of the family. In the centre of these creels, there was an aperture prepared for myself and sister, and the top was well secured by lacing, to keep us in our places, so that only our heads appeared above. Each family was supplied with one or more cows, which was an indispensable provision for the journey.

A Home in the Woods

For the great mass of the early immigrants to the frontier two things were generally true: First, they had already been conditioned by life in the backwoods for at least a decade prior to their arrival at the Appalachian divide, and were equipped to undertake a basic and primitive conquest of the new country. Much of this first wave of early frontier population was of valley origin in Pennsylvania, Virginia and the Carolinas, and the valley people had experienced few refinements whose loss they would have to forget or bemoan in their new homes. Second, the new western population moved along a heavily timbered and abundantly watered frontier where human life could be maintained with little more than elementary effort. Although soil qualities varied radically and there were vast stretches of swampy bogs, rock outcroppings and steep slopes with poor soil, all of it was in an undeveloped state. If a circle were drawn from a central point at the mouth of the Licking River opposite Cincinnati with its perimeter touching the Great Lakes, the Alleghenies at Pittsburgh, and the Upper Tennessee at Watauga, it would encompass some of the most fertile land and the most variable weather conditions in the eastern United States. The French botanist F. A. Michaux said there were only eighteen species of trees in France which attained a greater height than thirty feet, while in the early frontier area there were 140 species. It was said that in the Ohio Valley trees six or seven feet in diameter were to be found at every step, and that the ground was covered with rich mold which exceeded in depth that of fertile soil to be found anywhere else. Rainfall was generous, and such a thing as an extended or general drought was almost unknown.

Under these conditions the frontiersman established his new home and, if not a new, at least a fresh economy. Homes were quickly built from materials at hand. Simplest of all semipermanent structures was the log cabin which could be built from timbers cut on the site of the house. In an emergency it was possible for one man to construct a cabin. Describing the settler abodes along the Ohio, in 1802 F. A. Michaux said:

> Their homes are built on the banks of the river, and almost all in beautiful situations; but the way which they are constructed, bears no analogy to the charming spots on which they stand, as they are nothing but log-houses without windows, and so small, that two beds take up almost their whole internal space. Two men can with ease build one of these houses in less than three days, while their wretched appearance would seem to indicate an uncommon scarcity, though in country covered with forests.

A log cabin presented an insignificant appearance against a background of heavy timber because it had to be made of poles light enough to be lifted or rolled onto walls at heights up to ten or twelve feet. The log cabin was a highly flexible structure varying from fifteen to twenty-five feet in width, depending largely upon the taper of the poles. Crude chimneys could be built of mud and sticks or stone; roofs were either of brush or crudely riven boards; doors and even windows could be cut into the walls without too much difficulty. Frequently houses were faced east and west with doors on either side so that the sun would shine in most of the day. Walls could be built high enough to permit a crude second story under the apex of the roof. Wall cracks were filled with blocks of wood and daubed with mud and grass "cats" to seal out wind and rain. As demand increased for additional room, a lean-to was built across the back to serve as an extra bedroom and storage space.

A reminiscent pioneer writing in the *American Pioneer* in October, 1843, recalled that:

> Our cabin was twenty-four by eighteen. The west end was occupied by two beds, the centre of each side by a door, and here our symmetry had to stop, for on the side opposite the window, made of clapboards, supported on pins driven into the logs, were our shelves. Upon these shelves my sister displayed, in ample order, a host of pewter plates, basins, and dishes, and spoons, scoured and bright. It was none of your new-fangled pewter made of lead, but the best London pewter, which our father himself bought of Townsend, the manufacturer. These were the plates upon which you could hold your meat so as to cut it without slipping and without dulling your knife. But alas! the days of pewter plates and sharp dinner knives have passed away never to return. To return to our internal arrangements. A ladder of five rounds occupied the corner near the window. By this, when we got a floor above, we could ascend. Our chimney occupied most of the east end; pots and kettles opposite the window under the shelves, a gun on hooks over the north door, four split-bottom chairs, three three-legged stools, and a small eight by ten looking glass sloped from the wall over a large towell and combcase. These, with a clumsy shovel and a pair of tongs, made in Frederick, with one shank straight, as the best manufacture of pinches and blood blisters, completed our furniture, except a spinning wheel and such things were necessary to work with. It was absolutely necessary to have three-legged stools, as four legs of anything could not all touch the floor at the same time. . . . We got our chimney up breast high as soon as we could, and got our cabin daubed as high as the joists outside. It never was daubed on the inside, for my sister, who was very nice, could not consent to "live right next to the mud." My impression now is, that the window was not constructed till spring, for until the sticks and clay was put on the chimney we could possibly have no need of a window; for the flood light which always poured into the cabin from the fireplace would have extinguished our paper window, and rendered it as useless as the moon at noonday.

Inside cabin walls lent themselves to the support of crude beds; floors varied from tamped platings of dampened clay to smoothed long puncheons. Hearths were built of flagstones. Corners were fitted with cross-sticks for storage shelves and racks. Cross poles overhead often supported a rough second-story board floor, and a ladder of pegs driven into the wall served as a stairway.

Log cabins had virtues other than being quickly built and adaptable to crude housekeeping. Relatively speaking, they gave protection against Indian attack. They resisted gunfire effectively, except where chance shots penetrated vulnerable cracks, or doors were thrust open by surprise attacks. Fire was the greatest threat to the log cabins. Despite their isolation, however, early cabin homes were usually crude havens of peace and safety. De Tocqueville was impressed with this type of abode and left a splendid description of both the physical appearance and spirit of a backwoods homestead.

> Beyond this field, at present imperfectly traced out, we suddenly came upon the cabin of its owner, situated in the center of a plot of ground more carefully cultivated than the rest, but where man was still waging an unequal warfare with the forest: there the trees were cut down, but their roots were not removed, and the trunks still encumbered the ground which they so recently shaded. Around these dry blocks, wheat, suckers of trees, and plants of every kind grow and intertwine in all luxuriance of wild untutored nature. Amid this vigorous and various vegetation stands the house of the pioneer, or, as they call it, log-house. Like the ground about it, this rustic dwelling bore marks of recent and hasty labor; its length seemed not to exceed thirty feet, its height fifteen; the walls as well as the roof were formed of rough trunks of trees, between which a little moss and clay had been inserted to keep out the cold and rain.

The log fort was closely akin to the log cabin, but its function in western history is often misunderstood. To begin with, the pattern of frontier forts, as has been said earlier, varied with the whims of their builders. Sometimes they were elaborate places like Boonesboro, Harrodsburg, and Nashboro; at other times they were little more than stout one-room log houses fitted with loopholes and lookouts.

The chief purpose of the fort was obviously protection from the Indians. The social purposes, however, were even more important. For a small number of people they were semipermanent homes, but for the mass of frontiersmen they were merely resting places where newcomers could wait in safety while they gained their bearings in the new country. Almost everything about most of the forts, except the safety of their walls, was distasteful to most people. By force of fear and necessity large numbers of uncongenial people were often forced to live together in crowded conditions. Privacy, freedom of movement, and choice of associates were impossible. In many instances frontier families were relatively more secure in the open country trying to ward off minor Indian attacks than cooped up in filthy forts trying to resist disease and upset nerves. Colonel William Fleming of Botetourt County, a member of the Virginia Land Commission and a physician, visited Kentucky in 1780. He recorded in his journal a vivid description of conditions at Fort Harrod. The spring was inside the enclosure, and Fleming wrote, ". . . the whole dirt and filth of the fort, putrid flesh, dead dogs, horse excrements and human odour [ordure] . . . . the ashes and sweepings of filthy cabbins . . . . steeping skins to dress and washing every sort of dirty rags and clothes in the spring . . . . makes the most nauseous potation of the water . . . . and will certainly contribute to render the inhabitants of this place sickly." Despite its many drawbacks, however, the log fortress became the symbol of much of western expansion, and there were many moments in early frontier history when cabin settlers would have been lost outside fortress walls.

Once the land was safe for the permanent settler to locate a home and to think of his situation as one with some degree of permanency, the log house became popular. Log cabins were left off to one side to be used as outhouses or were destroyed altogether the moment the settler could build a more commodious home of square hewn logs. Log houses differed somewhat in design, but the nature of the building material tended to limit them to the standard "double" or "dog-trot" type—a structure of two large square rooms on either end with a hall or breezeway in between. The hall could be enclosed or left open as the owner chose. A long gallery or porch was usually built across the front, and a long shed room extended across the back. Log rooms, like those of pole cabins, could be just so large because of the weight and uniformity of logs. Cracks in these structures were securely sealed with thin wood fillers and clay, chimneys were most often of squared stone blocks, windows were cut in the sides, roofs were made of hand-riven boards, and floors were of log puncheons or whipsawed lumber.

Wherever the New England and Pennsylvania influence touched the frontier, and materials were available, there was a tendency to erect stone houses. Virginia and Carolina tastes ran more to use of bricks, and these were often burned near the site of the house. Of whatever materials the homes were built, their location was vitally important. Before the Indian menace was checked, safety was a primary matter of concern, but the ready availability of fresh water was always a decisive factor. In the older settlements where the "metes and bounds" system of land survey prevailed, homesteads were often located in a valley so that the land all around up to the ridgetops could be viewed from the house. Later under the rectangular system of survey, when ridgetops ceased to be natural landmarks, home locations tended toward the top of knolls and ridges.

Home units on the frontier multiplied at a phenomenal rate after 1785. There is perhaps no greater fallacy about the American frontier than that ancient whimsicality of the backwoodsman who, upon hearing a dog barking in the distance, informed his wife, 'We got to be gittin' on— country's too crowded." Some people did take this attitude, but the reverse was true of the great mass of settlers. So anxious were most people for an increased population that a native told an early visitor, "A numerous family is the most prosperous cattle we can raise in these woods, Mr. Johnson."

Almost without fail the early writings on the frontier emphasized the need for population, and the authors gloried in the progress shown by the census counts of 1800 and 1810. In 1781 there was an additional migration to Kentucky, and Humphrey Marshall, the historian, said:

> Until this period there had been a serious deficiency of females. Nor was it practicable to resort to the strategem of the Benjamites; nor that of Romulous, to supply the wanted numbers. The abundant emigration that year, silenced all complaints on that subject. And a license to marry, was the first process issued by the clerk, of either court.

Already the great portion of the frontier was in its most fecund years. Marriages usually took place early in life, and the growth of families was rapid. It was not unusual for fathers and mothers to have families of six or eight children before they were thirty years of age. A numerous family was helpful in the fields and about the house, it was company, it gave fathers and mothers great parental pride, and it was in keeping with frontier mania for population. Family responsibility for formal education, welfare, and future security of children was virtually unknown except for the handing down of land. The "planned" family worked in reverse of the modern understanding of the term; a family's size was more often governed by physiological rather than economic and sociological factors.

Marriage and the Household

Three moments in frontier life created excitement. These were birth, marriage, and death. The first of these was more momentous to the person being born than to his family and neighbors, except that his presence swelled the population. Not so the latter two. A marriage, unless it was a hasty affair, was most often a happy community occasion involving quiltings, house-raisings and warmings, a wedding party, a dance, an infare—all of them offering excuse for entertainment to the community. No set formula was followed in marriage since conditions varied with place and circumstance. Both the housewarming and the wedding dance were boisterous. Houses were "warmed" with *bran* dances in which corn siftings were spread over the floor so that the oily germ of the kernel was pressed into the wood, making it smoother and more tolerable as a living room. This frontier term has been thoroughly corrupted by the modern and synthetic hillbilly radio bumpkins who talk about "barn" dances. The frontiersman would have derided the idea of dancing in a barn, and historically the term "barn" is nothing short of an egregious typographical error. Weddings were accompanied by much drinking, some drunkenness, and much folksy joking and suggestive pranking. Infares were "day after" dinners served in the groom's home where young couples were set up on their own. New couples started life with only the basic utensils and tools; they had no furniture which could not be made with an ax and a drawing knife. As Humphrey Marshall, who was prodigal with punctuation marks, has written of social life:

> Then, the women did the offices of the household—milked the cows—cooked the mess—prepared the flaxspun, wove, and made, the garment, of linen, or linsey; the men hunted, and brought in the meat—they planted, ploughed, and gathered in the corn—grinding it into meal, at the hand mill, or pounded it into hominy, in the mortar, was occasionally the work of either; or the joint labor of both. The men exposed themselves alone to danger; they fought the Indians; they cleared the land; they reared the hut, or built the fort—in which the women were placed for safety. Much use was made of the skins of deer for dress—while buffalo, and bear, skins were consigned to the floor, for beds, and covering. There might incidentally, be a few articles, brought to the country for sale, in a private way; but there was no store, for supply. Wooden vessels, either *turned* or *coopered*, were in common use, as table furniture. A tin cup, was an article of delicate luxury; almost as rare as an iron fork. Every hunter carried his knife; it was no less, the implement of a warrior; not unfrequently, the rest of the family was left with but one, or two, for the use of all. A like workmanship, composed the table, and the stool—a slab, hewed with the ax—and sticks of a similar manufacture, set in, for legs, supported both. When the bed, was by chance, or refinement, elevated above the floor, and given a fixed place, it was often laid on slabs, placed across poles supported on forks, set in the earthen floor; or where the floor was puncheons—the bedstead, was hewn pieces, pinned on upright posts, or let into them by augur holes. Other utensils, and furniture, were of a corresponding description—applicable to the time.

The institution of marriage often presented a dilemma to frontiersmen. It was not unusual in some places for settlements to be far distant from communities where legal marriages could be performed. Often this problem was solved by common law matings, many of which were later regularized. Among the first laws considered by the early legislatures were those governing marriages. Designated persons were authorized to perform the ceremony, and provisions were made for keeping marriage records. As new counties were established, the recording of marriages was made mandatory by the granting of licenses. Legislatures assumed the right to establish marriageable ages and to grant divorces. Because there were fewer females than males, the marriageable age for females was generally lower. Girls were legally marriageable at fourteen and boys at sixteen or seventeen.

There was a certain spirit of gallantry about the laws granting divorces in which the woman's side of the case apparently received the more generous hearing. Almost constantly, early newspapers, and occasionally handbills, told stories of both men and women shirking the responsibilities of marriage. Unfortunate or hasty marriages commonly resulted in divorce, and sometimes cases of bigamy were exposed. Bigamy occasionally resulted from a belief that a husband or wife had died as a captive of the Indians. Such was the case of Rebecca Boone's marriage while Daniel was a captive of Chief Blackfish. Sexual irregularity prevailed, of course, but generally speaking, illicit love and illegitimacy of childbirth were scorned. A woman who gave birth to a child out of wedlock perhaps did not suffer entire social ostracism, but she did lose social caste. Again, bastardy was an early subject of legislation. The frontier was rather conservative when it came to preserving the ideals and integrity of the family unit as the central social force in frontier expansion.

Women were about as active as men in the conquest of the frontier. By 1775 the Boone women had reached the banks of the Kentucky, and at Fort Pitt there were white women at an early period. In Watauga, Marietta, Cincinnati and at Nashboro women figured in the making of initial settlement. Wherever a cabin was built, there was soon a woman to keep it in order. Women suffered from Indian attacks and were killed, captured and abused. They helped to clear away the forest, to build new homes, and experienced untold hardships from lack of comforts and conveniences. They cooked food, kept house, spun yarn, wove clothing materials, coverlets, and knitted socks by the scores. Not only did they do the chores of the household, but they also helped with work in the fields, acted as nurse to the sick, and often bore numerous children with no more aid than that of a frightened husband. It was the average woman's lot on the frontier to bear her burden of hardship and to surrender her youth before she was two score years of age.

Writing of the life of pioneer woman, J. L. McConnell described the homecoming of a bridal couple.

The "happy couple" ride up to the low rail-fence in front—the bride springs off without assistance, affectation, or delay. The husband leads away the horse or horses, and the wife enters the dominion, where, thenceforward, she is queen. There is no coyness, no blushing, no pretense or fright or nervousness—if you will, no romance—for which the husband has reason to be thankful! The wife knows what her duties are and resolutely goes about performing them. She never dreamed, nor twaddled, about "love in a cottage," or "the sweet communion of congenial souls" (who never eat anything): and she is, therefore, not disappointed on discovering that life is actually a serious thing. She never whines about "making her husband happy"—but sets firmly and sensibly about making him *comfortable*. She cooks his dinner, nurses his children, shares his hardships, and encourages his industry. She never complains of having too much work to do, she does not desert her home to make endless visits—she borrows no misfortunes, has no imaginary ailings—she is, in short, a faithful, honest wife: and "in due time" the husband must make *more* "three-legged" stools—for the "tow heads" have now covered them all.

Whether for a couple beginning life anew or for an established family, tools, utensils and pieces of furniture were limited. An ax, a broadax, an adz, a drawing-knife and at least one augur bit were the basic instruments of pioneering. The common "pole" ax was the most effective single tool in American history up to 1860. Rather than the more dramatic long rifle, it should have become the symbol of backwoods conquest. Like other workaday tools, it has often been overlooked by chroniclers of the frontier, but its usefulness was uppermost in the minds of those men who leveled the forest. It was remarkable what a man could do with an ax. De Tocqueville described a backwoods scene in which settlement was actually in progress:

> We soon afterward heard the stroke of the hatchet (axe), hewing down the trees of the forest. As we came nearer, the traces of destruction marked the presence of civilized man; the road was strewn with shattered boughs; trunks of trees, half consumed by fire, or cleft by wedges, were still standing in the track we followed. We continued to proceed till we reached a wood in which all the trees seemed to have been suddenly struck dead; in the height of summer their boughs were leafless as in winter; and upon closer examination, we found that a deep circle had been cut around the bark, which, by stopping the circulation of the sap, soon kills the tree. We were informed that this is commonly the first thing a pioneer does; as he cannot, in the first year, cut down all the trees which cover his new parcel of land, he sows Indian corn under their branches, and puts the trees to death in order to prevent them from injuring his crops.

Worldly Goods

Few historians, unfortunately, have examined the inventories of circuit clerks and probate courts to determine what property the frontiersmen actually accumulated. A list of these possessions constitutes a rather clear picture of the pattern of life. Early appraisers took their tasks seriously and listed everything in sight. In inventories of approximately a hundred estates prior to 1800 in a famous frontier county the following tools were listed: axes, broadaxes, frows, adzs, joiners, planes, chisels, gimlets, augurs, wedges, hand and crosscut saws, hammers, files, rasps, hinges, locks, vises, and cooper's tools. Added to these were the elementary cobbler's tools consisting of lasts, awls, knives, and coarse needles. Plow tools consisted of hoes, plow irons, grindstones, shares, scythes and cradles, reaping hooks, and wagon irons. Arms and gun equipment were standard entries. These were rifles, shot guns, pistols, locks, frizzens, wipers, pouches, molds, mountings, ladles, flints, bore irons, sulphur, and saltpetre. Household utensils were Dutch ovens, brass and iron kettles, frying pans, skillets, pots, cleavers, steelyards, sausage mills, mortars and pestles, sifters, funnels, knives, and measures. Dishes were most often wooden bowls, delft ware, china and pewter ware, porringers, bowls, canisters, knives, forks, spoons (wood, pewter, iron and silver), buckets, noggins and piggins, trenchers, bottles, candle molds, stands, snuffers, and tallow strainers. Furniture consisted of beds, chests, bed ticks, sheets, blankets, quilts, coverlids, feathers, tables, chairs, skin-covered trunks, cupboards, fire shovels and dogs, trammels, pokers, and spits.

No one family owned all or even any appreciable number of the items listed above. Some of these were owned only in small numbers in a single county. Plow tools, parts of tools, utensils, household furnishings, and even guns were locally manufactured in many frontier communities. Only two irons were necessary to make a plowstock, main- and heel-bolts. A spinning wheel required only two small metal spindles. Boxes, troughs, buckets, piggins and noggins, trays, and all other receptacles were made from wood. Hoppers were made of coarse staves and hollowed logs, as were scores of other devices.

Household furnishings were almost purely "homemade." Nowhere else in the country was so much fine furniture wood available as in the Ohio and Mississippi valleys. There were cherry, maple, tulip poplar, oak, chestnut, blue and white ash, pine, and basswood. Christopher Gist in 1751 described the Scioto country as "fine, rich land, with large meadows and fine clover bottoms, with spacious plains covered with rye; the woods chiefly large walnuts, and hiccories, here mixed with poplars, cherry trees, and sugar trees." An early Ohio law made it a public offense to chop down a walnut, ash, cherry, or white wood tree on another's land.

Before the eighteenth century ended, cabinetmakers had arrived on the frontier with drafts and catalogs illustrating the so-called period furniture which could be copied with fairly simple tools and from native woods. Designs of Thomas Chippendale, Robert and James Adams, and Thomas Shearer were copied at an early date, and later, Hepplewhite and Sheraton designs appeared. Sometimes ambitious cabinetmakers, with time and material, shaped Queen Anne pieces. Long slender spindles were turned out on clumsy foot-propelled lathes for backs of Windsor chairs. Corner cupboards of walnut and cherry replaced the shabby makeshift corner shelves of the pole cabins. Four-poster and stocky cord beds supplanted the staked beds in a short time, and bedroom space was conserved by the use of trundle beds which could be pushed out of sight in the daytime.

As early as 1793 Harry Toulmin wrote: "Among the manufactures from wood, *cabinet wares* make the most conspicuous figure. Joiners are to be met with in all parts of the state, and there are ten hands regularly employed in this department in (the) town of Lexington." Among these craftsmen were Joseph Putnam, Porter Clay (a brother of Henry), Daniel Weible, and John Spangler. They not only copied the pieces they saw in the form books, but there is evidence that they had seen examples of some of the pieces which they reproduced. Certainly this was true of the New England and Pennsylvania Queen Anne pieces. Except for improvisations which were often crude, frontier craftsmen did not introduce any new designs. They adapted and created, however, much of that nondescript category known today as "Early American."

Possibly in no phase of human life were the fleeting stages of frontier social metamorphoses more evident than in the home and its furnishings. Log cabins were deserted for permanent structures. Crude household furnishings were destroyed the moment new and permanent fixtures could be made available, and households grew in efficiency and refinements as rapidly as their occupants prospered from the land. A sure sign of a family's growing prosperity was the abandonment of crude straw and rush beds for feather ticks, and the discarding of skin robes and covers for handwoven coverlets. The great downriver trade soon supplied limited numbers of luxuries such as curtains, window shades, lamps, andirons and other knickknacks. Commercial intercourse with New England and Pennsylvania introduced other goods, so that within a decade there was a stratification in quality among homes which originally contained only the barest necessities.

The Farm

Basically, however, frontier culture was agrarian. Land and farming constituted the principal industry. Even manufacturing centered around the activities of the farm. A farmer turned surplus products into processed foods, whisky, and fabrics. Corn, wheat, rye, and fruit went into liquors. Meat was cured for an outside market, and hemp, flax, wool, and cotton were turned into rope, bagging, and coarse homespun cloth and clothing. County seat towns were essentially market and supply centers. Politics was based on agrarian attitudes and demands. So, in approaching an understanding of the backwoodsman, this strong agricultural background must be considered as of first importance. In many of the pioneer's distinctive characteristics he was no more than a primitive American farmer exhibiting the influence of the average isolated farm and its powerful environment.

Across the early frontier, crops varied somewhat with the wide sectional distribution of settlements. Settlers who plodded the long journey beside packhorses, or combined the use of packhorses and boats to reach the new country, brought with them the makings of a new regional economy. Panniers dangling clumsily at the horses' sides not only transported household goods, keepsakes, poultry, and children, but likewise precious packets of seeds.

Because of its versatility, corn was foremost of the frontier crops. It was an ideal plant for pioneering. Without it, the first white settlers would have been forced to endure a drab and debilitating diet. From tender roasting ear to flinty dry grain it was highly edible. As a tender milky grain it could be roasted in the shuck, piled under live coals and ashes and then gnawed from the cob; more mature grains were grated from the cob on coarse pieces of perforated iron and pounded into journey cakes or "gritted" bread. Dry grains were soaked in alkali leached from wood ashes until they shed their coats and were boiled as whole hominy, or they were pounded into grits and meal in crude mortars, or were parched and eaten whole. Early varieties of corn were inferior and inbred, but the plant was productive under the most slipshod methods of cultivation. As one observer said:

> The farmer or cultivator of the soil, in the first settlement of this region, had it not in his power to deviate from the common course pursued in the opening and improving of new countries; to clear the ground and prepare it for the plough, when time and circumstance enabled him to do so; but in most cases the Indian corn from which the staff of life was produced, was planted and cultivated with the hoe, without the logs being removed; and, for many years, the small grain was put in the ground in the most slovenly manner.

One of the grain's greatest virtues was the fact that it could be crushed into coarse meal by the clumsy grinding of slowly revolving water mills and hand mortars. Finally, there was almost no such thing as a complete failure of a corn crop from natural causes on any part of the American frontier prior to 1810.

Wheat, oats, barley and rye were other important grain crops. Wheat became a main source of flour for bread, and, like corn, it flourished on nearly all the frontier lands. Its only drawbacks were in harvesting from rough log and stump strewn ground, storing and grinding. Slow moving stones that would crush corn only pounded wheat into a gummy mass. A fast mill race and good "French" stones were necessary to produce a satisfactory grade of flour. When experienced millwrights arrived on the frontier, they channeled streams into long swirling races and cut and faced durable stones out of flinty limestone ledges. By 1800 flour production in many of the settled areas led other manufactured products. Within two decades, in fact, wheat was to become an economic catalyst which was to hasten frontier expansion and influence the course of improved transportation facilities.

Tobacco, hemp, flax, cotton and the lowly sorghum seed were carried aboard emigrant caravans. Tobacco and hemp thrived in Kentucky, Ohio and Tennessee, as tobacco had in tidewater Virginia and Maryland. Flax, a household plant, grew over a wide area, and cotton culture in time advanced southward with the settlers who moved down the great valley. In Kentucky, rolling bluegrass hills which once had been the grazing ground for great herds of buffalo and elk were now waving green fields of aromatic hemp, and along the Ohio this plant promised to be a profitable field crop. Early in the towns there were hemp breaks, looms and rope-walks which turned coarse fibers into cloth, bagging for grain, rope to rig flatboats on the western waters, and binding for the sails of ships which put out from New Orleans. Patches of flax yielded a more refined fiber, and when spun, flaxen and woolen yarns were mixed as warp and woof for the famous frontier cloth, linsey-woolsey. Often flax alone was spun and woven into a fine grade of native linen.

Garden and fruit seeds were enormously important. Though somewhat limited, the variety of garden seeds is significant. Beans, peas, potatoes, onions, turnips, beets, cabbage, pumpkin, cucumbers and melons were the common ones. Garden and truck patches yielded abundantly and gave families a welcomed variety of food in most seasons. Apples, peaches and grapes were the principal fruits. The apple was somewhat symbolical of the approach of settlement, especially where New Yorkers, New Englanders and Pennsylvanians settled across the mountains. This fruit was eaten raw, made into cider, cooked in pies and tarts, dried, packed in stone churns with sulphur, preserved in syrup and converted into vinegar and brandy. A list of the varieties of apples found on the early frontier is reminiscent of the places of origin of many immigrants. There were the

Roxbury Russet, Newtown Pippin, Habbardstown Nonsuch, Baldwin, Codling, Early Sweet Bough, Harvest, Pound Sweet, Henrick, Sproat and Yellow Bell Flower. Most of these varieties were of New England origin, but frontier soils produced wonderful variations of this fruit since seedling apple qualities are highly variable. Many of the new types of American apples had their beginning with these early frontier seedlings. Many rugged old trees became landmarks living for fifty to seventy-five years and were firmly entwined in family and community traditions.

Herbs and savories such as sage, marjoram, mint, thyme, sweet basil, garlic, catnip, and peppers were important. All of these gave zest to what might otherwise have been drab and unexciting food. Without sage and pepper at least three of the favorite frontier dishes—sausage, liver pudding and head cheese—would have lacked piquancy.

Much attention was given to improved methods of farming, especially in Kentucky and Ohio. In Kentucky in 1799, the dreamy-eyed Swiss immigrant John James Dufour organized the Kentucky Vineyard Society, hoping to make his fortune by selling fine Madeira and Burgundy wines from his vines. When this failed, he moved away to found Vevay in Indiana. Local societies were organized for the purpose of disseminating useful information and the improvement of agriculture. At both Marietta and Cincinnati there were groups who hoped to hasten agricultural progress by encouraging new methodology and plant selection.

Just as field crops were basic to frontier livelihood, so was livestock. Fundamentally, much of the frontier region settled prior to 1810 was grazing country. Characteristic of this was Christopher Gist's description of the Big Miami Valley as he saw it in February, 1751. He spoke of a "country well-watered with a great number of little streams and rivulets; full of beautiful natural meadows, covered with wild rye grass, bluegrass and clover; and abounds with turkeys, deer, elk, and most sorts of game, particularly buffaloes, thirty or forty are frequently seen feeding in one meadow; in short, it wants nothing but cultivation to make it a delightful country."

Twenty-five years after Gist viewed the western country and wrote so glowingly of much of it, settlers with milk cows in tow crossed the mountains. The cow, along with the ax and the rifle, was certain proof of domestic frontier advance. Descendants of the cattle graziers, described earlier by a sailor traveling with Braddock's army, moved on with the advancing fringe of the frontier. They were not exciting people with peculiar dress and fancy guns who went about shooting up towns and lusting after women. Little or none of the great pioneering legend today honors them; rather they were often regarded as dirty, shiftless and ignoble white trash. Nevertheless their moment in early American history is assured. Instead of performing exciting annual round-ups, calf-ropings, and long hours of range riding, these early western cowboys were rather placid individuals, lulled into a semiconscious state by the lazy cadence of a melodic bell ringing out the whereabouts of matronly bell cows. The cowpen was a common institution across the frontier, and the wild pea vines of the Carolinas and Virginia, the rye, buffalo grass and trim cane which covered the land from Pittsburgh to New Orleans, turned animals into prime meat and hides. In the northern Ohio Valley, graziers learned to cure meats and leather, while those south of the river drove their animals back to the older settlements for sale. André Michaux wrote in 1802,

> That the number of horned cattle is very considerable in Kentucky; those who deal in them purchase them lean, and drive them in droves of from two to three hundred to Virginia, along the river Potomack, where they sell them to graziers, who fatten them in order to supply markets of Baltimore and Philadelphia. The price of a good milch cow is, at Kentucky, from ten to twelve dollars.

About 1783 the first shorthorn cattle were imported into Virginia by Gough and Miller. Two years later James Gray and the Patton brothers brought grade cattle to central Kentucky from the famous Matthew Patton herd. Here they began breeding heavier beef types and established the blooded stock industry. In 1790 Matthew Patton himself left Virginia and moved his herd of cattle out to Kentucky, where two famous members of the herd, the bull Mars and the cow Venus, became the primogenitors of a much improved western cow.

The range cattle industry in the early West did have pennings in which new calves were marked and branded, cattle ready for market were cut out of the herd, and those of various owners were temporarily separated. Every owner had his individual earmark and brand which were registered in a brand book in the county courthouse. Earmarks were V-shaped bits, corner crops and slits. An example of a description of marks would be, "a bit in the lobe of the left ear, a crop off the right tip," or "Two bits in the right, and a middle slit." Brands were owners' initials, circles, squares and other easily identified markings.

The marking of cattle had two purposes, the checking of ownership in the natural process of grazing and the prevention of rustling. If a man killed a domestic animal in the woods—hog, sheep, or cow—he was supposed to be able to produce the head and hide for inspection. Cattle brought for sale were often checked, and the seller, if called upon, had to prove that his marks were registered brands. In this early phase of frontier history, cattle ran at large; but as fields and crops began to appear there was necessity either to fence crops or ranges. This latter condition caused an extended and bitter argument in many areas of the frontier. The professional grazier undertook to escape fence restriction by keeping abreast of settlement and grazing his herd on the public domain.

Just as the early cattlemen grazed forest lands far and wide, so did the hog drovers. Possibly the easiest animal to control in a herd is the common farm hog. Frontier drovers were able to drive their animals through the forests slowly enough for them to forage along the way, and once they passed beyond the great valley plateau, the eastern mountain and piedmont farmers were ready to supply grain at regular feeding stations. The early pioneer hog was a rugged animal ever bordering on savagery. With long nose, flaring nostrils, sharp ears, slender hams, arched mane and razor-keen tusks he was able to forage for himself, but it took two years to produce a marketable amount of meat on his rangy frame. This did not much matter, since it took drovers almost that long to reach a market. Hog droving as a way of life was even less exciting and dignified than cattle grazing. Hog drovers were also labeled ne'r-do-wells, but they have been memorialized in folk culture in the famous game song "Hog Drovers":

> Hog drovers, hog drovers, hog drovers we air,
> A-courtin your darter so sweet and so fair,
> Can we git lodgin' here, O here,
> Can we git lodgin' here?

Quickly the hog was to become big business in the Ohio Valley. Within two decades Cincinnati had acquired the nickname "Porkopolis," and newspapers and almanacs were full of material about swine culture. Between 1800 and 1840 the famous Poland China breed was developed in the Big Miami Valley by John Wallace of the Union Village Shakers, father of the western blooded hog industry. He combined woods hogs with the imported Russian and Byfield types and produced the more efficient Poland China.

Sheep were important to frontier economy. The first settlers brought these animals with them for the purposes of supplying wool and soft, pliable leather and fleece for clothing. This animal, however, was not highly adaptable to early frontier conditions where wolves and bears preyed upon them. Frequent contemporary notes indicate the difficulty farmers had in protecting their flocks. Community hunts were organized to destroy predatory animals so that sheep culture might prosper. By 1800 the danger in the older settlements had ceased to be wild animals and had become dogs. Nevertheless the demand for wool made sheep raising a necessity, and woolen clothing was the type most frequently produced by home spinners and weavers.

Horses, and later mules, were indispensable on the frontier. One of the favorite pawns in the white and Indian wars were horses. Both whites and Indians crossed and recrossed the Ohio repeatedly to raid each other's horse corrals. Daniel Boone and John Stuart were involved in combatting horse-thieving Indians in their first encounter in Kentucky. Droves of spare horses were mentioned repeatedly in frontier military orders. One of the big problems Virginia had in its western defense was securing enough horses to keep an expedition mounted. The horse was a sure means of transportation, a source of safety in case of hasty retreat, a draught animal for pulling plows and transporting materials. When a frontiersman lost his horse, he suffered a major calamity. Before 1810, breeding hardly kept abreast of the demand for animals.

Many frontiersmen not only used their horses for all their domestic needs, but they took great pride in their ownership and in their animals' speed and stamina. Often a frontiersman's personal honor was staked on the speed of his horse, and to lose a race was to lose prestige. The stocky animal known as the quarter horse was introduced early into Kentucky and it quickly became a part of the frontier's sporting legend. Whatever the breed of the horse, it was a lucky young husband whose bride brought, as a part of her dowry, a fertile brood mare.

The discussion of crops and livestock reveals fairly well the stable sources of the frontier diet. Among the various sectional and international groups who migrated westward, meat was universally favored. There was at first an abundance of game, but it hardly endured the initial process of settlement. Domestic meats were quickly substituted for the vanishing natural supply. Pioneers coming from areas south of New York had a pronounced fondness for salt pork, cooked alone or combined with vegetables and stews. Smokehouses and salting troughs were as important as log stables, plow tools, and household utensils. Vegetables in season, potatoes stored in freeze-proof banks, green and dried corn, wild berries, fresh and dried fruits, and maple and sorghum syrups lent some variety to diet. Fried foods, too much corn and wheat bread, lack of vegetables, and poor preparation of foods were often manifested in dietary disorders.

Health

Health was ever a problem on the American frontier. Not only did the frontiersman have physical ailments arising from dietary lacks, but he fell victim to lymphatic disorders and all of the communicable diseases, including the dreaded smallpox. Rheumatism, scurvy, tuberculosis, arthritis, and acute intestinal troubles took their toll. The vast category of seasonal frontier ailments, including the general one called "ague," all but defeated pioneers in certain ill-favored localities. Quite generally it was believed that miasma arising from decaying humus matter in the woods and newly cleared fields was threatening to health. Several early authors wrote at length about the deleterious effect of woods miasma—hence one explanation why frontiersmen destroyed trees at so furious a rate. Night air and swamp dampness were generally considered injurious to health. Some argued that effluvium from rotting logs and branches following the clearing of lands was a threat to health, and there was widespread belief that it took three to four years to condition a homestead and the land about it to healthful living. That a family would lose some members during this time was accepted stoically as the natural course of human affairs.

That diseases took a heavy toll of pioneer life is reflected in the differentials in the various age groups mentioned at the beginning of this chapter. In 1789 Dr. Samuel Brown of Lexington, Kentucky, introduced the anti-smallpox vaccine and began successfully to combat both the disease and the blind prejudice against inoculation. The Kentucky legislature in 1800 went so far as to restrict the use of the vaccine to almost impossible conditions.

Doctors of varied training and capabilities appeared on the frontier. Some of these were sincere men, some were cranks, and far too many were quacks. Dr. William Goforth, born in New York City, was possibly one of the first to vaccinate against smallpox. He landed on the Kentucky frontier in 1788, and in 1799 moved to Columbia, Ohio. He had as a pupil young Daniel Drake whose family had moved from Virginia to Kentucky. Later there were Drs. Ephraim McDowell, Benjamin Dudley, True and Farley.

Frontier medication was generally of the home-administered type. Handbooks of medicine were part of family equipment. Medicine was made from herbs and other folk concoctions. But whatever the brew, the home remedies were administered with a tremendous amount of superstition and misguided psychology. Snakebite, for example, was treated with a variety of remedies which ranged all the way from application to the wound of pieces of the offending snake to a freshly killed chicken. A contemporary observer wrote the following description of snakebite treatment,

> The method is to scarify the part, and rub salt, then put on a poultice of the touch-me-not plant, and to drink plantain juice and milk. The juice of the walnut bark likewise is serviceable as a blister, and the puccoon root (a red root used by the Indians for paint) upon being rubbed on the limb affected will prevent the extension of the poison.

Patent medicines in the form of cordials, bitters, cathartics and ointments made early appearances in the West. As soon as there were newspapers, the ubiquitous medicine men made their wares known to the public. Pretending to have recovered ancient Indian medical secrets, these early quacks and frauds no doubt reaped a bountiful harvest from a beleaguered people.

Amusements

Social life on the frontier was hardly as doleful as medical recipes and remedies made it seem. Generally the frontiersman was fond of sports. His amusements and games were not like those of the present in which so much emphasis is placed upon group participation; however, much hunting and many games and other forms of amusement were of a group nature. More often one frontiersman bragged of his personal prowess and found himself challenged by another to a test of strength or marksmanship. These contests involved footraces, wrestling, jumping, swimming, hunting, shooting at targets, casting knives or tomahawks (a game called long bullets), horseracing, and lifting logs with handsticks. Wherever men and boys assembled—at church, county court, muster drills, log-rollings and house-raisings—there were contests of some sort. The term "better man" on the frontier had neither moral nor intellectual implications. At log-rollings one man challenged another to a lift. "Grab a root and growl," was the old lifting cry. Both men maneuvered to get "the long end of the stick" and "to pull down" his opponent. To be defeated was humiliating if not slightly disgraceful, and many a self-conscious man went home from a log-rolling unhappy because he had been bested in a test of strength.

On May 17, 1796, hunters rendezvoused at Irvine's Lick in Kentucky and killed the astounding number of 7,941 squirrels in a single day. There was some considerable element of vengeance behind the big community squirrel hunts, for this animal was a common nuisance that ate up the hog mast and invaded corn fields. One early historian wrote that

> . . . in the autumn of certain years, they became itinerate, traveling simultaneously by the millions from the north to the south; destroying whole fields of corn in a few days, if not gathered, and eating everything in their way, like the locusts of Africa, while traveling forward without stopping long in any place; swimming large rivers; and perhaps before winter return again by the same route toward the north.

Being able to hit a mark so small as a moving squirrel was a manifestation of manliness. Sometimes it had political implications when candidates were called upon to demonstrate their capability for officeholding by shooting at targets. Horse races were informal affairs which most often took place when two owners met and began bragging about their mounts, or on muster days or about mills, courthouses—and even on Sundays about the churches. There was possibly nothing the average frontiersman disliked more than having his horse belittled. The horse represented an investment of money, and any weakness the animal had reduced its usefulness and future sale. Gander-pulling combined horsemanship with personal endurance and prowess. A gander's head was greased with lard, and the bird suspended upside down so that a man sitting in a saddle could just barely get a grip of the head and try to jerk it off as the horse, encouraged by a sharp rap of a board, bolted forward. On parts of the frontier more immediately under the influence of the Virginians and Carolinians, ring tournaments were of some importance as sources of amusement. Occasionally bearbaiting and cockfights captivated the vigorous interest of frontiersmen. Both of these were bloody sports, and their popularity indicated to some degree a harshness of spirit.

Men and women participated together in many forms of frontier amusement. Some of these were highly utilitarian while others had no excuse other than amusement. Woods-clearing days, house-raisings, log-rollings, corn-shuckings, syrup-making (often called stir-offs), apple-sulphurings, bean-stringings, hog-killings and even wakes brought people together in frolicsome moods. The common working, in which neighbors helped to perform tasks too difficult for single families, was a general custom. When a man had a new ground full of logs to roll, or a house to raise, he invited in his neighbors to help him; but he in turn was obligated to furnish an extraordinarily good dinner. Also, he held himself in readiness to return the work when there was a call for his services. If a man fell ill and was unable to plant or cultivate a crop he could depend on men in the community to assist him.

Quiltings brought men and women together in a holiday mood. One of the constant tasks of the frontier woman was that of providing warm bed clothing for her family. Handspun and woven coverlets were made from native materials, and quilts were fabricated from myriad scraps of material sewn in intricate patterns. No frontier home had a complete air of domesticity without its quilting frame suspended from the ceiling in such a manner that it could be raised and lowered at will.

Although frontier courtships were rapid affairs, the average youth found it difficult to make his first approach to a girl. Play-party games not only brought young people out to parties, but they also paired them off in couples, and since many of these games had kissing as a main objective, they were most efficient in helping courtship along. Frontiersmen created some new games, but they kept alive at least a score of those imported from the Old World. Such old favorites as "Frog in the Middle Pond,"

"Farmer in the Dell," "London Bridge," and "Marching Around the Levee" helped to while away many a tedious night.

No form of amusement was more popular than the dance, especially where religious views toward such relaxation were not too strict. There were many forms of the frontier dance, but perhaps the most common was the jigging Virginia reel with its hilarious running sets. Cabins were cleared of furniture and the dance went on as long as the callers and fiddlers were sober enough to keep the sets going.

Zithers, banjoes, guitars and fiddles were popular musical instruments. In order to amplify the sound of the fiddle, "strawbeaters" tapped heavy straws or slender wood reeds up and down on fiddle bridges in rhythm with the music. All of these instruments were portable. Importation of the heavier instruments such as the harpsichord, spinet and harp had to await the opening of roads and the coming of steamboats.

Just as the ancient play-party games survived, so did the dance tunes. Musicians everywhere knew by memory such old favorites as *Sugar in the Gourd, Barbara Allen, Fair Eleanor, Sour Wood Mountain, Old Joe Clark, Fisher's Hornpipe,* and *Froggy Went A' Courtin'.* Along with these, many English and Scotch folk tunes commemorating local personalities and incidents were added to the musicians' repertoire.

Mark of the Backwoods

Just as dancing and play-party games were forms of relaxation, so was bragging. Many frontiersmen engaged in harmless boasting and tall lying just for the fun of it. One of the most common forms of stretching the truth was by outlandish comparison. Seldom were things compared in their normal relationship; either they were made utterly ridiculous by understatement, or patently unbelievable by outrageous exaggeration. In a new country where achievements of a lasting nature were for the future, the extent of natural resources unknown, and individuals unhampered by lack of opportunity, imaginations ran wild. Bigness was generally considered a superlative virtue, and so frontiersmen colored their stories and boasts. Bragging and bantering were perhaps certain manifestations of social immaturity. Frontier humor was often expansive in nature. Much of it, because of obvious greenness, was self-incriminating; some of it was droll with a deep philosophical undertone; and some of it had no other merit than the gross perversion of word usage. Greenness on the frontier was a highly relative quality, depending largely upon whether it was the native or his more sophisticated visitor, who made the notes from which published contemporary accounts were written. But whatever form frontier humor took, the American frontiersman on the whole was good-natured. A failure to consider this sense of humor with a degree of seriousness would be a failure to comprehend one of the most human character traits of the pioneer.

Some frontiersmen took themselves most seriously—even to believing they were men of destiny—but on the whole the hardships were softened with good nature, and courage was kept high by outlandish banter and bragging. However, there was occasionally an undertone of self-pity in which the pioneer felt he had been either neglected or discriminated against by the rest of civilization. He sometimes felt his sacrifices and hardships were for the manifest and patriotic cause of national expansion. Examples of this were the interminable fervid orations and toasts of the Fourth of July celebrations which were little short of expressions of extravagant nationalistic dreams.

Many visitors to the frontier thought they found the people silent and discourteous, even surly. They were neither discourteous nor surly as a people, but they were momentarily shy and took their time in finding out who a stranger was and what he wanted. Too many frontiersmen had been exploited by both travelers and peddlers for those accusations of silence and inhospitality to have much validity. It was always necessary to exercise great care with strangers because rascals and even criminals were often at large, and a settler could not always be sure that one of these was the stranger at his gate. Once a stranger was taken into a house he was welcomed to bed and board and plied with endless questions about the world outside. People were often starved for news and new topics of conversation.

Because of peculiar conditions and disassociation from better educated and more refined people, frontier speech and manners were strongly modified. New words were added; old ones were given new implications, if not new meanings. Possibly the most important ways in which the language was changed were in accent, pronunciation and coloration. A contemporary said:

> The dialect is different. The enunciation is different. The peculiar and proverbial colloquy is different. The figures and illustrations, used in common parlance, are strikingly different. We regret, that fidelity to our picture, that frankness and truth compels us to admit, that the frequency of profanity and strange curses is ordinarily an unpleasant element in the conversation.

Frontiersmen in much of the West, for some reason not readily discernible, developed a coarse nasal tone of voice bordering on a whine, and this in turn produced phonetic changes apparently for no other reason than intellectual laziness. Southern immigrants tended to drawl, while New Englanders introduced a sharpness of tone and enunciations. *Sparrow* became *spar'*; *here*, *there*, and *their* became *h'yar*, *thar*, and *their'n*; *we*, *yours*, *his*, *against*, *figure*, and *horse* became *we'ns*, *your'n*, *his'n*, *agin'*, *figger*, and *hoss*. *It*, *get*, *cover*, *heard*, and *card* became *hit*, *git*, *kiver*, *heer'd*, and *cyard*. Old letters, public documents, and other contemporary papers reflect these corrupted spellings and pronunciations. Of greater importance was the number of metaphors and figures of speech which crept into the language, such as "claim jumping," "staked and ridered," "slick as elm bark," "caught with his britches down," "dull as a frow," "fastened his knuckles to the ground," "stumped," and "shooting shy of the mark."

A large portion of the frontier population increase, 1780–1810, was by native birth. Immigration was also an important source. People came westward from all the eastern states, with Pennsylvania, Maryland, New York, New England, Virginia and the Carolinas feeding the stream with the most people. Foreign countries, especially Scotland, Ireland, Germany, Switzerland, France and England sent the bulk of the newcomers. Many of the foreign immigrants came directly to the frontier without previous backwoods experience. They arrived with their strange speech, folk customs and outlooks, but the hardships of frontier life, rapidity of marriages, and the lack of strong national and racial prejudices tended to destroy old state and international ties. Some environmental, national and international customs were molded into a new culture pattern. Language was no doubt influenced by the new influx of foreign words, but basically frontier modifications of speech were of four origins: the cherished reminders of ancient English forms; a blending of several national languages by an isolated and literal-minded people who were without standards of form; a common usage which reduced the English language to a sloven and elementary vernacular; and everyday experiences in a brusque and rugged environment.

To assume that all frontier influences were purely rural would be erroneous. There were towns, although as has been said, they were often little more than country meeting places. However, there were as early as 1810 such important places as Pittsburgh, Wheeling, Marietta, Lexington, Louisville, Nashville, Harrodsburg, Knoxville, Abingdon, and St. Louis. Many of these were strategically located on rivers; others grew up in farming centers where considerable official business, manufacturing and trade were conducted. A third group of villages and towns came into existence largely by accident of accretion. A man of some natural leadership gathered around him a "settlement" of neighbors. A store and a mill were established, then a church, a cabinetmaker and blacksmith shop, and soon there was a town. Many of the more important places like Marietta, Cincinnati, Nashville and Lexington did some elementary town planning by regulating the survey and distribution of lots in order to keep down jealousy and to promote orderly growth of the boroughs. Town governments were nearly always the children of necessity, as their early minutes indicate. They concerned themselves almost altogether with limiting the liability of people living together. Muddy streets, livestock running at large, horse racing in the streets, fires, and sanitation were the major topics of concern.

As business centers, towns were of erratic growth. Most of them were primarily limited market centers for farm products and livestock. Because they lacked transportation facilities, inland towns had little opportunity to grow beyond a certain elementary stage. In most communities, county court days and militia musters attracted farmers to the towns, not to attend court alone, but to sell and trade in agricultural produce. During the earlier years, merchandising was done principally by itinerants who came with bales of textiles, iron and tinware, and notions. They rented storehouses and established temporary businesses where they exchanged goods for country produce and livestock. Early newspapers contained long lists of goods available. Assortments of textiles always headed the list, but there were also hardware, knives, razors, tools, tableware, soap, tinware, nails, chocolates, raisins, snuff and spices.

When stocks of goods were sold, the trader informed his customers he was ready to receive their produce, and he moved on to a down-river market where he could sell for cash. Frontier towns in many cases quickly outgrew their elementary beginnings and became in a minor way new metropolises, with schools, churches, taverns, theatres and newspapers. Seldom did the towns east of the Mississippi exhibit the spirit of rowdiness and lawlessness of the later Far West. On the contrary, except for some of the river ports, the old frontier towns and villages were relatively quiet and home-loving. There were few wild bordellos with lewd women and bloodthirsty men, saloons with their famous gambling rooms, or sheriffs and big posses. The picturesqueness of these early towns was to be seen more in their crude personalities, primitive streets, lack of sanitary facilities, homes, public buildings, crowded and dirty taverns, and the variety of goods for sale, than in the fortnightly occupants of the local jails. Because of limited transportation facilities most frontier towns had to be fairly well self-contained, and as a result often became extremely provincial.

Not all of the trade was carried on in towns. Almost before the Indians were driven away, the peddler took up his pack where the Indian trader left off. Yankee peddlers traveled up and down streams and over the primitive trails selling tinware, cutlery, textiles, clocks, medicines, spices and notions. Many of these were men who had spent long winter evenings in New England preparing goods for sale in the next summer. In time, the frontier peddler was to become as much a figure on the frontier as his predecessors of the Indian trails. Legends were to grow up about them, and before the middle of the nineteenth century they had carried both Yankee ingenuity and cantankerousness to almost every cabin door on the frontier.

Religion

While peddlers and itinerant merchants were bringing goods and progress to frontier doors, missionaries and itinerant preachers were fanning into flames the sparks of religion. Like every other aspect of frontier culture, religion had a vari-colored history. Certainly the backwoodsmen were not godless men, nor were they all without some church background prior to 1785. Because the earlier frontier movement had its beginning in the colonial period, its religious background reflects the conflicts which developed east of the mountains in the various "awakenings" or revolts against the established church. The so-called Great Awakening in Virginia and the Carolinas in the middle of the eighteenth century was a powerful influence in grouping and directing serious religious attention toward the frontier. It took some time for religious groups to become well enough organized, after they were freed of the authoritarian restrictions in the older states, to undertake an active missionary movement in the West.

The church on the frontier was developed largely by five major denominations—Presbyterian, Methodist, Baptist, Catholic, and Congregational. The Presbyterian Church had its background in Pennsylvania and Virginia, and, beyond this, largely in Scotland. In 1785 the famous Presbyterian missionary David Rice of Hanover County, Virginia, visited Kentucky, and in the neighborhood of Danville he established three congregations. The Methodist missionary efforts were begun as early as 1782 in the Holston Valley, and in 1784 at Redstone, Pennsylvania. Francis Asbury, that indefatigable man of God, rode over the mountains repeatedly to establish congregations and to supervise the Methodist circuits. Possibly the Methodist Society was best equipped of any of the organized bodies to spread the gospel. Its method of using circuit riders was almost ideally suited to sparse settlements where they worked with family and small community groups. Too, the Methodist doctrine of free election and grace with its extreme emotionalism, plus the utter poverty and democracy of the circuit riders, appealed to the average settler.

Baptist history on the frontier is rather vague. Certainly there were Baptists in the Holston River Valley, in western Pennsylvania and Virginia, and in the Carolinas. This faith was Calvinistic, literal-minded, fearful of centralized government, adamant in its belief in immersion, and willing to accept services of a volunteer and self-appointed unpaid clergy. Some branches required a vision as proof of conversion. Most congregations were so loosely united that they could scarcely be said to have had any real association among themselves, yet there are several significant landmarks in Baptist history.

In the fall and winter of 1781, those determined Baptist ministers, Lewis and Elijah Craig, led a congregation from Spottsylvania County, Virginia, to Gilbert's Creek in central Kentucky. Preaching from the books of Genesis and Exodus as they went, the Craigs, like Moses, led their flock forth across the great Appalachian wilderness, across the Clinch, the Powell, the Cumberland and the Rockcastle rivers to the edge of the Bluegrass. In the new church at Gilbert's Creek, Lewis Craig opened the old Bible from which he had read the Scripture for his last sermon back in Spottsylvania, and there he temporarily resettled his congregation west of the mountains. Elijah, like Aaron of old, soon made an idol in the new and fertile land. On the North Fork of the Elkhorn he and a partner named Parker discovered the process of making bourbon whisky.

There were Baptist preachers all through the frontier. The old church at Columbia, Ohio, was a foundation stone for the denomination. One of the early preachers, John Taylor of Woodford County, Kentucky, has left a worthy historical record of Baptist activities in his *Ten Baptist Churches*. Henry Clay's mother, Mrs. Watkins, and his brother Porter became ardent workers for the church.

There were Catholics, of course, among the early immigrants from Maryland, Virginia and Pennsylvania. These came either from the old colonial church or were recent immigrants, especially from Ireland. In 1787 the Reverend John Carroll, vicar-general of the London District, visited the Catholic settlers in Kentucky, and Father Whelan, a French-educated priest, was sent west in 1787 to serve the Catholic colony about Bardstown. Whelan had difficulty both with his parishioners and with their neighbors, and he finally left his post in 1790. Three years later Stephen Badin, the first priest ordained in the United States, became pastor to the Catholic mission in Kentucky. Elsewhere on the frontier there were Catholics at Vincennes and Kaskaskia, and at Detroit, but apparently there was little communication among the groups.

After 1787 a stream of Congregationalists moved from New England to the West. This group worked in close communication with the Presbyterians, and at times ministers and congregations were taken over by the presbyteries. Congregationalism remained within a closely defined line of migration and failed to make itself so influential in general frontier movement.

It would be a mistake to assume that the frontier church was either liberal or thoroughly democratic. Generally, congregations and individual church members in the earliest years were too preoccupied with problems of safety and economics and were too poor to establish church houses. Services were held about the neighborhoods in cabin homes and under the most informal conditions. Protestant ministers were not too concerned about what group their auditors belonged to, just so they were hospitable and attentive. Ministers themselves were not always affiliated with a denomination. In many instances independent preachers went forth to expound the gospel as they understood it, ignoring the organized faiths. As the frontier advanced and church houses with organized congregations and governing boards became more common, greater efforts were made to discipline members. It is not uncommon to find frequent entries in old church minutes of trials in which communicants were lectured for drunkenness, sexual irregularities, and other moral breaches. Frequently, such individuals were turned out of the church.

Literal interpretations of the Scriptures and narrow doctrinal tenets early became the shibboleths of militant bigots in and out of the pulpit. Modes of baptism were within themselves points of controversy, and the old issue of ritual and form often destroyed congregational harmony. Before the end of the eighteenth century, bigotry and intra-church disputing had practically smothered any spark of religious liberalism which might have been fanned into flame. One reason for this was the fact that the field for mission work on the frontier was most fertile. Yet the primitive conditions of religious pioneering often attracted only the self-sacrificing or zealous illiterate who had far more physical stamina than toleration and common sense. Many appeals from the pulpit were made to simple impressionable people who were easily persuaded by strong metaphorical arguments and heightened prejudices. There were, however, many ministers and missionaries, like Francis Asbury and David Rice, who gave able and informed leadership.

Much of the preaching was loud, picturesque and emotional. The Old Testament was a source for texts which emphasized the existence of a wrathful personal God, and fierce personal retribution was assured for sins committed. Backwoods preachers were marvelous orators; using a peculiar kind of reverential quaver of voice and repetitive pulpit refrain, they made resounding and intoxicating appeals to their unsophisticated listeners. A contemporary minister said:

> The hoary orator talks of God, of eternity, a judgment to come, and all that is impressive beyond. He speaks of his "experiences," his toils and travels, his persecutions and welcomes, and how many he has seen in hope, in peace, and triumph, gathered to their fathers; and when he speaks of the short space that remains to him, his only regret is, that he can no more proclaim, in the silence of death, the mercies of his crucified Redeemer.

Itinerant preachers traveling along through long stretches of melancholic woodlands had time to think out and organize oratorical extravaganzas that literally smelled of sulphur. As it was said:

> Hence the preaching was of a highly popular cast, and his first aim is to excite the feelings—Hence, too, excitements, or in religious parlance, "awakenings," are common in all this region. Living remote, and consigned the greater part of the time, to the musing loneliness of their condition in the forest, or the prairies; when they congregate on these exciting occasions, society itself is to them a novelty, and an excitement.

Religious music was in itself designed to excite both participants and hearers. Song services were largely without benefit of instrumental accompaniment. Hymns, some of ancient origins, others improvised, were often sung without key and pitch. Many congregations followed the practice of "lining out" songs; that is, a song leader read a sentence from the song and the congregation sang it in a chant that was without rhythm or color. There were the basic *Watts Hymns, Mercer's Cluster, Dover Selection, Methodist Hymn Book* and the *Baptist Harmony*. Later there were the *Southern Harmony*, prepared by Singing Billy Walker, and the *Columbian Harmony*.

Among the early preachers who made powerful appeals were Baptists Lewis Craig, Ambrose Dudley, John Taylor, Moses Bledsoe, and William Waller; Presbyterians James McGready, William McGee, James Balch, Robert Marshall and Barton W. Stone; Methodists Bishop Francis Asbury, William McKendree, John McGee and William Burke. Besides these, there were scores of lesser preachers who worked with isolated congregations, unnoticed even by their own denominational historians.

In 1800 the frontier was rocked by a storm of spiritual emotionalism, the like of which the country had never experienced. This revivalism started along the Muddy River in Logan County, Kentucky, in the summer of that year, and rapidly spread elsewhere. In the beginning this revival was largely inspired by Presbyterians, but before it reached a climax all the denominations but Catholic were involved. The great revival was held at Cane Ridge in Bourbon County, Kentucky. There all the Protestant denominations participated. Thousands of people came from great distances. All of the emotional manifestations prevalent in earlier communal meetings were to be observed—shouting, swooning, jerking, preaching, self-berating, hysterical screaming, crawling on the ground in imitation of lowly snakes, and passing into unconsciousness. Meetings were continuous, day and night, until the crowds were physically and emotionally exhausted. The result of this meeting, as nearly as it can be determined, was the institution of the annual camp and revival meeting where people came and camped in wagons, tents, and log cabins for weeks. This important communal religious activity became an American institution. A new denomination, the Disciples of Christ, was partly organized at Cane Ridge. Two Shaker colonies were planted in Kentucky and one in Ohio indirectly because of disaffections growing out of the Cane Ridge revival. The whole frontier saw a crusade of marked zeal in which church membership was materially increased.

Explanations of this strange religious phenomenon are many, aside from the purely spiritual ones. People on that part of the frontier were brought into a large crowd possibly for the first time in their lives, and they were highly excited by this fact. Many of those exhibiting the greatest emotions were youths. The oratorical powers of the ministers aroused both orators and auditors, and the fear engendered by horrendous descriptions of lost souls further disturbed the equilibrium of the assembly. Possibly another fact should be cited as an explanation. By 1800 much of the Ohio River frontier was relatively free of dread of Indian attack, and fields and businesses were productive of a sense of security which approached a state of hysterical thankfulness.

Home missions and special church groups continued to sow seed on the frontier with an ever-increasing return. After 1800 the church became as permanent an institution as the county courthouse, and denominationalism constituted a rallying point for increased activity. As for the frontiersman himself, he quickly changed from an objective to a highly partisan participant in the expansion of his chosen faith. Once this condition prevailed, there was little or no opportunity for any considerable amount of toleration in a country which under other circumstances might have been highly liberal in its religious attitudes.

View of the Rocky Mountains on the Platte 50 miles from their Base.

ONE OF THE VIEWS FROM THE CONTEMPORARY NARRATIVE OF MAJOR STEPHEN LONG'S EXPLORING EXPEDITION TO THE ROCKIES IN 1820

LOUISIANA

Mr. Monroe, still affected by the distrust of his colleagues, did not hear without surprise the first overtures that were frankly made by M. de Marbois. Instead of the cession of a town and its inconsiderable territory, a vast portion of America was in some sort offered to the United States. They only asked for the mere right of navigating the Mississippi and their sovereignty was about to be extended over the largest rivers of the world. They passed over an interior frontier to carry their limits to the great Pacific Ocean.

—Barbé-Marbois, *The History of Louisiana*

CHAPTER X

O N February 17, 1801, in the House of Representatives of the United States Congress, the tie between Thomas Jefferson and Aaron Burr for the Presidency of the United States was belatedly broken. In the preceding three months many political enemies as well as new alignments had been made. Thirty-six ballots were cast before a decision, which should have been obvious at the outset, was reached. Members from Vermont and Maryland cast blank ballots. South Carolinians refrained from voting, and so did James A. Bayard of Delaware, thus defeating Burr. Jefferson was now President-elect of the United States, and Republicanism, though somewhat battered by the extended political storm, was triumphant. From November to February the nation had been caught in a ground swell of political manipulation, chicanery, calumny and panic. The Gardoqui negotiations in the excise tax dispute and finally in the passage of the Alien and Sedition Laws were again plaguing the country. As far as most of the frontier vote in the election of 1800 was concerned, the division of sentiment was on a sectional basis. The West had certain well-defined problems which it could never hope to solve under Federalist domination.

Down the Great River

The three most fundamental issues, as we have seen, were protection of American privilege of trade down the Mississippi, the organization of territorial governments from the public domain, and sharp revision of public land laws. With the elevation of Jefferson to the Presidency on March 4, 1801, the frontier moved a step nearer solution of these issues. Jefferson himself little realized how far western demands would involve him within the next four years. On the frontier, public sentiment for unqualified use of the river was intense. Whatever the technical facts might have been in regard to diplomacy and treaty agreements with Spain, the western farmers asked only one pragmatic question: would the river remain free and open? If not, then they would take the necessary steps to guarantee such a condition. Farmers who have perishable products awaiting an outlet to market are seldom either diplomatic or academic in their reasoning. In this case their impatient demands required that the United States either buy the Isle of Orleans and open the river, or take it! It little

233

concerned the average uninformed man on the frontier which decision his government made.

Two powerful factors forced to the front this issue of the use of the river and Spanish port facilities. The annual increase in agricultural products reflected a phenomenal population increase. Terms of the Treaty of San Lorenzo (or Pinckney Treaty) permitted American goods awaiting transshipment to be deposited in warehouses in New Orleans. Produce from upriver might be stored in official warehouses or, as was the case in practice, in warehouses built or rented by the shipper. So long as these latter structures were subject to official inspection, they were approved. Goods moving through legitimate channels were passed duty free, the shipper paying normal storage charges. Practically, this meant that upriver flatboats could unload their cargo without waiting for seagoing vessels. Most of the goods sold actually went into the coastal trade to be consumed along the East Coast. The only serious drawbacks in the application of this section of the treaty were smuggling of both goods and money past the port authorities into channels of illegitimate trade and the whimsicalities of Spanish official policy.

Although the Treaty of San Lorenzo was formulated in 1795, it was not until 1798 that the deposit provisions were facilitated. This arrangement was to endure for three years. If at the end of that time the Spanish wished to remove the American trade from the Port of New Orleans, they were obligated to locate a new place of exchange somewhere in the vicinity of the harbor.

Superficially the behavior of the American boatmen was irritating to many people in New Orleans. Farmer-boatmen, away from home approximately three months and experiencing considerable hardship journeying downstream, let go their pent-up emotions in the French city. They caroused, played practical jokes, swarmed into bordellos, gawked in the churches, cluttered up the already filthy city with their rubbish, blustered through crowds shouting their lusty oaths, and in general, disrupted life.

Of more importance were the long-standing conflicts between border officials over the precise location of territory, and the rivalry for Indian friendship in the Choctaw and Creek country. As administrative costs of government in the Mississippi Valley increased for the Spanish, ever-increasing evidence of the prosperity of the republican American settlements aroused jealousy. The various so-called "conspiracies" in the western settlements—such as the French conspiracy in Kentucky, the activities of James Wilkinson, and the Blount affair in Tennessee—did nothing to soothe either the American or the Spanish public mind.

On the International Chessboard

Before the right-of-deposit agreement ran its course of three years, the Valley of the Mississippi was to become involved as a pawn on the international chessboard of western Europe. Rising out of the confusing period of revolution in France, Napoleon Bonaparte had extravagant dreams of a far-flung empire that would rival if not surpass that in the making for Britain. To the south of France, Spain and its empire were declining under the unimaginative and loosely managed administration of Charles IV. Expenses of government for the scattered possessions were heavy, while returns from some of them were meager if not nonexistent. Louisiana had never been a profitable economic venture for Spain. By 1800 it was clear to Foreign Minister Luis de Urquijo that it was an expensive liability. Its only real value at the moment was as a trading pawn. There was an opportunity to trade it back to France in exchange for the Kingdom of Etruria, where Charles hoped to enthrone the house of Parma in the person of his son-in-law.

On October 1, 1800, when Louisiana was once again placed in the hands of France by the secret Treaty of San Ildefonso, Spain not only relieved itself of the heavy drain of the colony, but also escaped anxiety over its possible conquest by the Americans. A year later the French and Spanish governments virtually completed the arrangements of transfer initiated in the Treaty of San Ildefonso by further negotiations in that of Aranjuez. The secret agreements between France and Spain were not effected without considerable emotion expended on both sides. Godoy, the Spanish minister, undertook to hold up the delivery of Louisiana until the Duke of Parma's son was given the reign of Tuscany or Etruria. Napoleon became furious and threatened conquest of Louisiana from Santo Domingo.

The fate of Louisiana was in the making on two far removed and unrelated fronts. Napoleon's impetuous attitudes toward Spain and his 1802 assault on Santo Domingo were of great concern to American diplomatic and administrative officials. It was not until May, 1801, that the first inkling of a secret treaty between France and Spain reached Washington, and not until the next year that Jefferson had a clear concept of what had taken place and what might be expected in the future. While this disturbing news on the diplomatic front was filtering through, pressure for security in the West was rising fast as trade increased. The Republican administration could ignore neither the disturbing diplomatic picture nor the demands of the frontiersmen.

One of the first movements in the direction of insuring security along the western rivers was a letter from Jefferson to E. I. Du Pont de Nemours (who was on his way to France in May, 1802) and also one to Robert

Livingston, the recently appointed minister to France. Removed as Jefferson was by three thousand miles of ocean and lacking intimate insight into the personalities of Napoleon and Talleyrand, it was impossible for him to interpret the mercurial natures and fickleness of this pair. For the moment, the more realistic fact was the attitude of frontiersmen along the western rivers. They hated foreign domination of American soil; they had no respect for the Spanish troops who supported their country's authority; and they felt that the ordinary morals and rules of law applying to international relations had little or no meaning where their outlets to the river mouths were concerned. There was no kinship, and there could be none, between the two nations and their peoples. The very natures of the two governments were in open conflict.

Jefferson focused attention immediately upon the commercial aspects of the Louisiana question by proposing the purchase of New Orleans rather than Louisiana. By May, 1802, he was fully aware of the delicate situation which would exist if France advanced into Louisiana. On April 18, he had written Livingston that "the day France takes possession of New Orleans fixes the sentence which is to restrain her forever within her low water mark. It seals the union of two nations, who in conjunction can maintain exclusive possession of the ocean. From that moment we must marry ourselves to the British fleet and nation." For a man "passionately devoted to peace," this was a strong threat and reflected the even stronger sentiment which prevailed along the western rivers.

Scarcely had the first shock of the transfer of Louisiana subsided and E. I. Du Pont de Nemours sailed for France before the westerners were again excited by the intentions of Spain. On October 18, 1802, Juan Ventura Morales, acting intendant of Louisiana, made public the Spanish intention to revoke the right of deposit at New Orleans. The meaning of this proclamation was shrouded in secrecy, but its immediate effects upon American public opinion were crystal clear. At first it was thought Morales' act was stimulated by France as an antagonistic act toward the Americans; later research, however, has established the fact that Morales acted upon private orders directly from the Spanish Crown. Perhaps the purpose of its publication was the desire of Godoy to create confusion and to provoke a threat from the Americans against France. So secret were the instructions to Morales that neither the governor of Louisiana nor the Spanish minister in Washington knew of their precise contents.

Morales' proclamation did not actually check trade through the harbor of New Orleans, but it did restrict American traffic to open river transfers of goods from flatboats to ships. This meant that the two groups of crafts had to make direct connections in the harbor, or else the loaded boats had to remain in the harbor where the cargoes were subject to thievery, deterioration from the weather, and possible loss by sinking. Probably the most distinct change that Morales' order brought about was the checking of illicit money exchanges which were being made through the deposit authority. The Spanish were being drained of their cash resources by illegal exchanges which had not passed through the official warehouses. Spanish traders as far away as Mexico were affected. The officials knew of this trade because the considerable sums of Spanish money offered for deposit indicated a flourishing smuggling business.

In 1801 peace prevailed in Europe for the moment. Napoleon could engage a large part of his army in taking possession of Haiti and Santo Domingo—a first step toward New Orleans. During October of 1801 he readied an expedition to the West Indies under the leadership of his brother-in-law General Leclerc, ostensibly for the purpose of subduing Negro rule on Santo Domingo and re-establishing slavery. The first expedition, of 10,000 men and a large amount of equipment, arrived at its destination in January, 1802. Within the next ten months Leclerc's forces were beset by disaster. In a dramatic defense, the Negroes under the leadership of the famous Toussaint L'Ouverture held the French forces at bay, and before fall, yellow fever had almost destroyed the white army. With bitter passion, Negro laborers resisted the possibility of re-enslavement, and yellow fever destroyed more than 24,000 French soldiers. In all, more than 40,000 Frenchmen lost their lives in Santo Domingo. Such losses were enough to stagger even so headstrong a dictator as Napoleon. By November, 1802, Louisiana was farther away from French domination than Napoleon and Talleyrand could have believed possible. To bring under control the re-acquired French possessions in North America would bleed France white of men and resources. Not only were there the threats of reaction by the American backwoodsmen and the diseases of the semitropical southern country, but there were few safe bases of supply. There was also the fearful task of transportation by sea through an unfriendly British fleet.

Robert Livingston of New York had been appointed minister to France in the fall of 1801. He had a good background of foreign affairs. Since 1776 he had been associated with the diplomacy of the nation and had been a considerable personal influence in domestic politics. His ministry to France was entrusted with two specific responsibilities: to endeavor to purchase West Florida and the Isle of Orleans, and to arrange payment of spoliation claims owed by France to American citizens.

His first task was to learn from authoritative sources whether France had secured possession of Louisiana from Spain. When Livingston approached Talleyrand with this question, the Frenchman denied its validity. Through manipulations of Godoy of Spain, however, Rufus King, the American minister in London, was supplied a copy of the agreement made at San Ildefonso. Livingston thus had full knowledge of the actual retrocession, but he was still trying to secure official confirmation from France when Du Pont de Nemours arrived in Paris with additional instructions.

During the first phase of Livingston's discussion of the Louisiana question, France had been moving toward occupation of the ceded territory, and Napoleon's government was in no mood to listen either to American complaints or proposals. Pichon, the French minister in Washington, sent fairly accurate appraisals of American sentiment back to his government, but he could hardly convey to Napoleon and Talleyrand the frame of mind or the strong threats and language of the frontiersmen. Too, Pichon did not enjoy the full confidence of his government, and because of this his communications were virtually ignored. Could Napoleon and Talleyrand have had full knowledge of future events, both Pichon's notes and Jefferson's threat that the United States would ally itself with the British Navy might have carried more import.

Louisiana Purchase

So aroused did the administration in Washington eventually become that Thomas Jefferson wrote James Monroe on January 10, 1803: "I have but a moment to inform you that the fever into which the western mind is thrown by the affairs at New Orleans stimulated by the mercantile, and generally, the federal, interest threatens to overbear our peace." He then told his Virginia neighbor that he wished him to go on a special mission to France. Selection of Monroe was based upon confidence in his diplomatic ability and on his popularity in the West. Because of his association with and interest in the frontier, there was no other man better prepared to represent its point of view on such a mission. Monroe's instructions were to the effect that if France would sell New Orleans and the Floridas, the United States would pay up to ten million dollars. If the purchase could not be made, then he was to negotiate for a small area to be used for warehousing and storing produce awaiting transshipment. If this proposal failed, he would be given further instructions.

While Monroe was en route to France, Livingston labored over the Louisiana problem. Dealing with Talleyrand was exceedingly difficult. Americans already had had long experience with this wily ex-Bishop of Autun, and the foreign minister himself had a bright memory of the XYZ incident which resulted in his removal from office. Although he had been in America, he had no love for the country. Also, before the opening months of 1803, there was no intention of disposing of Louisiana, and the American request might as well have been for a block of territory along the Seine.

Before Monroe's arrival in France, a sudden break came in Livingston's negotiations. In the first place, Barbé-Marbois, who had returned as Minister of Finance, was easier to deal with than Talleyrand. Barbé-Marbois had spent considerable time in the United States and had even married an American woman. In the second place, two additional developments tended to ease further the attitude of France toward Louisiana. First, Spain suddenly restored the American right of deposit in New Orleans and took from the French the advantage of decreeing that a new place of deposit which would restrict both American trade and smuggling should be located under terms of the Pinckney Treaty. At the same time a new threat of war in Europe and the shocking failure of the expedition to Santo Domingo convinced Napoleon that he would lose Louisiana in a struggle with Britain, and it might now be used as bait with which to keep the Americans out of such a war and perhaps ally them with him against Britain.

From January to March, Napoleon turned over in his mind the idea of selling Louisiana to the United States. Two dramatic moments preceded the actual negotiations in the Louisiana sale. On March 12 the diplomatic corps was present at a reception in Madame Bonaparte's drawing room when Bonaparte confronted the British minister Whitworth with the stern proposition that he would have either Malta or war. The second was his quick personal decision to sell Louisiana, which created consternation among some of his intimates. When his actions were known to his brothers Lucien and Joseph, they stood about his bath and protested his impulsive action so hotly that a valet fainted. The real break in the Louisiana question came on Easter Sunday, April 10, 1803, when, after religious services, Napoleon informed Marbois and another minister that he wished to open negotiations for the sale of the American possession.

Talleyrand actually approached Livingston first with the idea of selling all of Louisiana to the United States, but it was Barbé-Marbois who began official negotiations. In opening the way for the sale of the Louisiana Territory Napoleon announced: "I renounce Louisiana. It is not only New Orleans that I cede; it is the whole colony without reserve." He urged Marbois to lose no time in discussing the sale with Livingston. He was willing to dispose of the American possession for 50,000,000 francs, but his shrewd finance minister doubled this sum.

There followed a period of quibbling over price during which Livingston was anxious to complete the purchase without too much assistance from Monroe. Monroe's mission to France had piqued the minister because he felt that it might be criticism of his actions, and Livingston was human enough to want the sole credit for settling the Mississippi question. The Americans bid 20,000,000 francs; but Barbé-Marbois held out first for

100,000,000, and then 80,000,000 plus an additional settlement of American claims against France. The final purchase price was 60,000,000 for Louisiana, and 20,000,000 more to pay spoliation claims made against France by American citizens. The total purchase price therefore amounted to approximately $15,000,000 plus considerable expense in the future settlement of the American claims. The sale was concluded on April 30, 1803, and three days later its conditions were approved by the ministers. With justice Livingston wrote that he was "content to be charged with (it) to my latest posterity."

The sale of Louisiana to the United States involved several major questions. France had promised not to alienate the territory from its Latin owners. The transfer from Spain to France had not taken place publicly. When Spain learned of the sale, what its reaction might be was an open question; certainly there would be an outburst of anger, but since that government was incapable of forcing Napoleon's hand she would get nowhere by citing the antialienation agreement in the San Ildefonso Treaty. At no time in the negotiations, despite the fact that Livingston had made strong presentations on the Florida purchase issue, did France even hint at the inclusion of the Floridas in the Louisiana sale.

Jefferson and his colleagues had been so busily engaged in the purchase of Louisiana that they failed to give consideration to the constitutionality of such a move until it was virtually an accomplished fact. As soon as Monroe was dispatched to France, Jefferson began to turn over in his mind the constitutionality of purchasing additional territory, and for the next six months he contemplated the idea of proposing a constitutional amendment to cover such an act. An amendment was drawn in rough outline, in which territory north of the 32nd parallel would be reserved for the time being to the Indians. As Henry Adams said, Jefferson's proposal was "a strange shoot on the constitution." The President received no encouragement for his idea and finally it was dropped.

Finally there was the important question of the boundaries of the purchase. Perhaps nowhere did this question embarrass the American purchasers more than along the short Mississippi boundary to the Gulf of Mexico. Where did the Isle of Orleans cease? At Lake Borgne, the Pearl, or the Perdido? Talleyrand and Barbois had information concerning the boundary, though it is doubtful that the French themselves knew precisely where they were. Following Napoleon's maxim that it was well to create an obscurity, they left the Americans in the dark.

For one American at least, the Louisiana Purchase was a blow. News that the United States was to obligate itself to the extent of fifteen million dollars when Monroe's instructions presumed an expenditure of two million dollars tried the frugality of Albert Gallatin, Secretary of the Treasury, almost to the breaking point.

The word that the United States was well along toward ownership of Louisiana reached the frontier near the first of July, 1803. There was little quibbling among western farmers and boatmen as to whether or not Livingston and Monroe's act was constitutional. To them it was highly expedient, and for the moment expediency had more practical meaning than strict constitutionality. After considerable political skirmishing between Federalists and Republicans, with John Randolph of Roanoke bearing the brunt of the affirmative argument, the treaty was ratified by Congress and formal steps were taken to occupy the new territory.

Almost six months of anxious waiting concerning Louisiana followed because of the hostile attitude of the Spanish. Congress authorized the organization of an armed force on October 28, and General James Wilkinson and Governor W. C. C. Claiborne were authorized to prepare an army of six thousand men to protect American interest in the new territory. Not only was there danger from the Spanish, but also from the French Creole population which might find itself momentarily under the French flag.

On November 30, amidst considerable pomp and ceremony, with the protection of a small band of American volunteer militiamen, the Spanish commissioners Salcedo and Casa Calvo formally delivered Louisiana to Pierre Clement de Laussat of France. On December 20, Laussat transferred the territory to the United States commissioners Claiborne and Wilkinson. The United States had come into possession of a vast landed area, and what was more important, large portions of it were ideally suited to agricultural purposes. Some of the Louisiana Purchase contained fabulously fertile soils which in the near future were to add their piles of produce to that which came downstream to New Orleans from the eastern valley country.

Although the French had surrendered possession of Louisiana, the new landlord, the United States, was in doubt over the precise limits of the bargain. As has been indicated above, the boundaries were hazy indeed; and to the southeast, the "Florida Issue" of the immediate future was born with the Louisiana sale. Clarification of the Louisiana boundaries would come by exploration, national expansion and conflict.

Up the Missouri

Before James Monroe set sail for France, a second act of the great Louisiana drama was unfolding. While discussions were hottest in the

western country and in France, plans to explore the great western
country were already in an advanced preliminary stage. It is impossible to
say specifically what President Jefferson had in mind in the early stages
of planning for an expedition into the Northwest. When the idea first
came under discussion, he certainly did not know that Louisiana would
become American territory so quickly. Captain Gray discovered the
mouth of the Columbia River in 1792, and that same year Jefferson had
proposed that the American Philosophical Society subsidize an expedition to the headwaters of that stream. In 1801, the subject was again renewed and Meriwether Lewis was selected to go up the Missouri with the
French botanist, André Michaux; but before this party could start, the
French government directed Michaux to withdraw.

There were several reasons why Jefferson was interested in such an
undertaking. Early exploration would give the United States some advantage. There was dissatisfaction with the restrictive factorage system
which attempted to regulate the Indian trade east of the Mississippi River
after 1795, and already there were signs of the pressure of population
which was to increase with each succeeding year. Possibly the factor which
excited Jefferson personally was that of satisfying his scientific curiosity
about the nature of the land. Finally, the rising British fur trade in the
upper Mississippi and Missouri valleys invited immediate American competition.

British encroachment in the western territory aroused a genuine concern. Jay's treaty only clarified the northern boundary as far as the Lake of
the Woods. Beyond that point it was open to exploitation. Since the latter
years of the eighteenth century, traders had been active as far north as the
Mandan villages on the Missouri, and the Scotch fur traders were in the
Minnesota lake country about the headwaters of the Mississippi.

Jefferson sought passports of Spain, France, and Britain for his private
secretary Meriwether Lewis and a party of soldiers and laborers in the
spring of 1803. The President drafted instructions for the explorers. They
were to observe the courses of the rivers, take frequent readings with the
astrolabe to establish their precise locations, chart all islands, and outline the
terrain of the country. Human and animal life was to be observed carefully; any unusual landmarks were to be recorded; Indian tribes, their locations and customs were to be described; and soil fertility, weather conditions and seasonal changes were to be noted. The expedition was not to be
without its commercial importance. The explorers were to keep their eyes
open for fur trading possibilities. Jefferson presupposed that the expedition would meet with Indians, and after giving considerable detailed instructions on what knowledge the party should secure, he suggested that

Lewis "carry with you some matter of kine pox; inform those of them with whom you may be of its efficacy as a preservative from smallpox."

Meriwether Lewis selected as his companion officer, William Clark, a younger brother of George Rogers Clark, who had already seen service with Anthony Wayne. He was young, vigorous, and intelligent. Lewis was to select the other men for the expedition from the frontier army and from citizen volunteers. In the organization of his command he had to make certain that he secured men of good health, good humor, and physical adaptability. That the going would be rough was a certainty, and since Jefferson realized that the journey up the Missouri might be exhausting, he instructed Lewis to return by boat from the Pacific if this seemed expeditious. Emphasis on the condition of the fur trade was significant.

Detailed plans for the Lewis and Clark Expedition were already formed in Jefferson's mind as early as January, 1803, and by April of that year he showed the previously described instructions to Meriwether Lewis. At that moment he could only acknowledge that the United States was proposing to encroach both upon Spanish territory and a British trading area. To insure the government's securing the information it wanted from the proposed expedition, its literate members were instructed to keep journals. Jefferson thought it important that one of the diaries be kept on damp-resistant birch bark.

Before Lewis began actual organization of the expedition, the Louisiana Purchase was completed, and a new motive was added to the search for knowledge in the vast western territory. Immediately after celebrating the Fourth of July, 1803, Lewis left Washington for Pittsburgh where he meant to assemble supplies and collect men from military posts along the river. From Pittsburgh he moved down the Ohio to meet William Clark. From Louisville, Clark took the boats down the Ohio to the Mississippi and then upstream to establish camp on the east bank at the mouth of the Rivière du Bois directly opposite the mouth of the Missouri. Lewis went overland by Vincennes. At the Rivière du Bois camp, supplies were assembled and organized, boats were made ready, and a company of men brought together. Outstanding among them were John Ordway, Patrick Gass, George Drouillard, John Colter, the Fields brothers, young George Shannon, and the good-natured Negro slave, York. In all, the party contained forty-three men, among whom were fourteen soldiers, nine civilian Kentuckians, and two Frenchmen who were to propel the three craft— one keelboat and two pirogues. Packed aboard the boats was a heavy cargo consisting of twenty-one bales of Indian trade goods, fourteen barrels of "parchmeal," twenty barrels of flour, seven barrels of salt, fifty kegs of pork, fifty bushels of meal, guns, ammunition, and tools. Late in the afternoon of May 4, 1804, the famous exploration party broke camp and entered the Missouri. Before beginning their journey upstream the men attended the transfer ceremonies in St. Louis, when upper Louisiana Territory was formally ceded to the United States.

The course of the Missouri was fairly well known from its mouth to the Mandan villages, fifty or sixty miles north of present-day Bismarck, North Dakota. Late in October Lewis and Clark had covered the first leg of the journey to the Mandan villages in time to go into winter quarters. At Fort Mandan they built huts, took their goods ashore, beached their boats and settled down to spend an intensely cold winter. Their wait, however, was one neither of boredom nor of idleness. Indian activities, many of them so voluptuous that they were described in Latin in one of the journals, proved entertaining. The white men, with the exception of Lewis and Clark, entered into even the most intimate social life of the Indians, and for years to come, physical characteristics of native people in the upper Missouri Valley reflected the activities of that winter. The natives engaged in their highly emotional buffalo and medicine dances for the entertainment of their visitors. Not all of the party's time, however, was spent in celebrating with the Indians. Relics and specimens of all sorts, among which were the horns of a Rocky Mountain sheep, were collected and packed in boxes to be shipped downstream in spring to St. Louis and then forwarded to Washington for the President's inspection.

When the ice broke in the spring of 1805 and the river was again opened, a small party of boatmen turned back to St. Louis, while an exploring group of thirty-two men moved upstream, leaving the Mandan winter quarters on April 7. Added to the company were the three Charbonneaus. Toussaint Charbonneau, a French fur trader, was married to the captive Shoshone squaw Sacajawea, who had been brought downstream as a captive of the Minnetarees and sold as a slave to the trapper. They had with them an infant which was a great care for Sacajawea. For the next seven months the party advanced up the Missouri, crossed the Rockies through the Lemhi and Lolo passes to the Clearwater and down the Snake and the Columbia rivers to the Pacific Ocean.

On their way to the Pacific the exploring party observed at least two or three changes in topography and animal life, and witnessed a most touching human scene when Sacajawea again saw her people. Saturday, August 17, near the headwaters of the Missouri, William Clark, Charbonneau and Sacajawea were making their way on foot along the river,

> but they had not gone more than a mile before Captain Clark saw Sacajawea, who was with her husband one hundred yards ahead, begin to dance and show every mark of the most extravagant joy, turning round him and pointing to several Indians, whom he saw advancing on

horseback, sucking her fingers at the same time to indicate that they were of her native tribe . . . and just as we approached it a woman made her way through the crowd towards Sacajawea, and recognizing each other, they embraced with the most tender affection. The meeting of these two young women had in it something peculiarly touching, not only in the ardent manner in which their feelings were expressed, but from the real interest of their situation. They had been companions in childhood, in the war with the Minnetarees they had both been taken prisoners in the same battle, they had shared and softened the rigors of their captivity, till one of them had escaped from the Minnetarees, with scarce a hope of ever seeing her friend relieved from the hands of her enemies.

Between April 7 and November 7 the explorers moved up the Missouri, crossed the Rockies, and then reached the Pacific on the other side. On the latter date they struggled through the fog which bound the mouth of the Columbia River. The tide ran high, and the water was salty. In the afternoon the haze lifted and they saw "the delightful prospect of the ocean, the object of all our labors, the reward of all our anxieties. This cheering view exhilarated the spirits of all the party, who were still more delighted on hearing the distant roar of the breakers." Rather than endure the rigors of winter in the mountain passes Lewis and Clark went into winter quarters at Fort Clatsop. The second winter proved to be a trying experience with its cold, dampness, and lack of food. Living on fish, poor game fowl, and an occasional animal, the party found life much more tedious than at Fort Mandan. When spring broke, the expedition chose to retrace its steps overland rather than wait for a ship. Leaving the Pacific coast winter quarters on March 23, 1806, it recrossed the Rockies, explored much of the Yellowstone, and hastened back to St. Louis, arriving there at noon on September 23, after an absence of two years and four months.

As exciting as was the Lewis and Clark adventure, its meaning for future frontier expansion was even more thrilling. For the first time Americans had actual knowledge of the extent of the vast northwest country— a region that had been shrouded in mystery ever since the first decade of the seventeenth century and the searches for the fabulous northwest passage. Both the Missouri and the Columbia valleys were partially explored. East of the mountains, Lewis and Clark not only charted the main stream of the Missouri, but also explored several of its forks including the Yellowstone. The party performed an excellent job of reporting their findings. The American fur trade was given a new impetus, a route to the Northwest was opened, and the extent of the great Missouri Valley was fairly well revealed. The location and mode of life of many of the Indians were described, and it was not without foreknowledge of them that future adventurers approached the western territory. Finally the Lewis and Clark expedition ushered in an era of far-flung trail breaking which sought to discover courses of rivers and to push claims to a generous national boundary westward.

Zeb Pike

On a clear Friday morning, September 9, 1805, as the Lewis and Clark expedition struggled in the maze of headstreams on the upper Missouri well on their way to the Rocky Mountain wall, a second party of exploration was setting forth to hunt for the headwaters of the Mississippi. At 4 P.M. of that day, Zebulon Montgomery Pike, acting under orders from General James Wilkinson, began the ascent of the Mississippi. The expedition consisted of a sergeant, two corporals, and seventeen privates transported in a seventy-foot keelboat loaded with supplies for four months. Six months later Pike reached what he hoped to be the head of the Mississippi River. On February 1, 1806, he described his arrival at Leech Lake. Pike himself was not too certain that Leech Lake was the head of the Mississippi, and his journal indicates that he did not know of the other and longer branch of the river which went on beyond to Lake Itasca. Pike's journal is highly descriptive and gives some notion of British trading activity in that region.

Cold weather wrought considerable hardship to the upper Mississippi expedition. It was delayed, and deterred from exploring the country as it might have done under more favorable conditions. Possibly Pike's principal objective was the gathering of geographical knowledge to facilitate the terms of Jay's Treaty and to thwart the British invaders. Since 1763 this particular area of the northwest country had been in a state of confusion. When Pike arrived back in St. Louis on April 30, after an absence of eight months and twenty-two days, he brought with him a description of the river; data on the Indians, the white traders and their posts; and a fairly good geographical description of soils and fauna which were to prove useful in future explorations of this area.

Pike's claim to a place in American frontier history rests on more than his journey up the Mississippi. Two and a half months later he was again at the head of an exploring expedition. This time he traveled westward up the Missouri and Osage and then overland across the great plains of Kansas and Colorado in search of the headwaters of the Arkansas. Leaving Bellefontaine on July 6 in two boats with a party of twenty-four white men (including Dr. J. H. Robinson and Lieutenant James Biddle Wilkinson, a son of the General) and fifty-one Osage and Pawnee refugees who were being returned to their friends, Pike was off on a bitter and weird adventure. Once again he was carrying out the instructions of General James

Wilkinson and not Congress. Precisely four months to the hour after leaving Bellefontaine he first glimpsed the famous mountain peak which was to bear his name. At two o'clock on the afternoon of November 15 he saw what he first thought was a "small blue cloud." Climbing the first foothills of the Rocky Mountain chain, his cotton-clad men shivered in the increasing cold. Their horses were weakened by the journey and wearied by a heavy load of buffalo meat which they were transporting.

During a bitter November and December, the explorers wandered about the headwaters of the Republican and Smoky Hill forks of the Kansas, explored the upper Arkansas almost to its head, then turned southward to the headwaters of the Red. Thereafter, they crossed through the Sangre de Cristo Mountains to the upper reaches of the Rio Grande. So extreme was the cold that most of the horses gave out, and the men suffered from severe frostbite. Not only was their thin clothing a poor defense against the cold, but their shoes were worn out from travel. Two of the men suffered so severely that they lost their feet.

On February 24 the badly depleted American party was met by a company of Spanish troops under Malgares who took them to Santa Fe as prisoners. All the way across the plains Pike had followed in the wake of the Spaniard and his six hundred mounted men. This officer had been sent out from Santa Fe to drive back any poachers who might invade Spanish territory. All along the trail the Americans had checked the size of his forces by counting his camp fires. Just before Pike and his companions were started southward to Santa Fe, the unfortunate men left stranded along the trail sent bones from their feet as tokens of their suffering and begged that they not be left behind to die. From Santa Fe the Americans were taken on to Albuquerque and then to Chihuahua. At the latter place, Salcedo, former governor of Louisiana, relieved Pike of his papers and returned him to the United States by way of San Antonio and Nacogdoches to Natchitoches in Louisiana. After a year's absence, the explorers arrived on home soil on July 1, 1807.

Pike might well look back with misgivings on the unpleasantness of his journey to the headwaters of the Arkansas, but his sojourn as a prisoner of the Spanish government had its pleasant moments. Wherever he went the American officer was treated with warm hospitality, and he made many friends. Malgares, who had him in charge, became a warm friend of the Captain. As a prisoner of the Spanish government Pike gained a vast fund of knowledge of both the geography of the Southwest and the nature and location of the white settlements in that area. While it is true that he was relieved of his notes, he was able to make some records and stuff them into the gun barrels, but more importantly, he preserved a remarkably accurate record of his observations in his memory.

It is almost impossible to say even now what the true purpose of Pike's expedition really was. Possibly he was doing nothing more than carrying out the military orders of a highly untrustworthy superior officer who never saw fit to reveal the true import of his acts. If Pike was on a spying expedition, he was indeed poorly equipped for such an undertaking. If he was carrying out a treasonable mission, the surrender of his notes would have served as evidence against him in the future. His expression of surprise at being in Spanish territory no doubt was faked. He did not resist capture by the Spanish; in fact some historians think he invited it. He was bound to have known that his crude barricade on the Rio Grande was in Spanish territory, yet he pretended to be wholly surprised when informed that he was on the Rio Grande instead of the Red River.

Whatever might have been the true motives of this expedition, Pike and his men paid an inhuman price for their part in it by such exposure to cold when they were all but naked. It must have been with considerable surprise that Pike found himself under a cloud of suspicion because of his association with Wilkinson when he arrived in Natchitoches. He promptly refuted any connection with his commanding officer's schemes and continued to serve in the United States Army, dying a hero's death in the attack on Toronto in April, 1813. In 1907, Pike's original notes and journals were discovered by Professor Herbert E. Bolton in the National Archives in Mexico City and were returned to the United States in 1910. Recovery and study of these papers has thrown little light on the purpose of the expedition other than the one mentioned. One significant contribution of the Pike expedition was the concept that west of the ninety-eighth meridian lay a vast desert country.

A third and minor expedition was led by Thomas Freeman into the Red River country. This famous southwestern surveyor had gone south with Samuel Ellicott, but the two had become involved in a dispute over a woman whom Ellicott had in his company, and Freeman was discharged from the surveying party. In 1804 he was commissioned by President Jefferson to explore the Red River. Not until 1806 did he go at the head of a small but able party of surveyors to trace the course of the river and to make other observations. This party reached the present-day border of Oklahoma, Texas and Arkansas, where it was forced to turn back because of Spanish resistance. Freeman's adventure was successful in exploring the lower part of the Red River and in establishing unusually successful astronomical landmarks.

Burr and Wilkinson

Contemporary with the Lewis and Clark and the Pike expeditions, there occurred a political and military incident of some importance to the frontier. Since the Presidential campaign of 1800, Aaron Burr of New York had been an alien factor in the Jefferson administration. He was, in fact, a political enigma who several times was frustrated in his career by realistic politics. A man of considerable ability, both as lawyer and politician, he was also handsome in appearance, genteel of manner, and charming to women. Intellectually he was rather precise, and had he chosen he might have become as important an intellectual or theological figure as were his immediate forbears.

After attending Princeton University, Burr had studied law in a private office, but from the outbreak of the Revolutionary War until 1799, he saw considerable service as a soldier. He lacked two personal characteristics which might have enabled him to reach great heights in his career: as an orator he was not vigorous enough to sway crowds; and he seems to have been devoid of the necessary traits of character and practical sense to keep his interest focused on a single purpose. Many men as well as women were fascinated by his personality, and unfortunately in the furtherance of his ambitions he collected about him an army of rascals, schemers, self-seekers and stupid opportunists. His absorbent rather than analytical mind created fantastic dreams and anticipations on the basis of gossip, rumor, wishful thinking and flattery. Morally he was unpredictable, and the political revolution at the turn of the eighteenth century was a treacherous period for an impressionable and unstable man. Burr's name had not been entirely free of association with intrigue prior to 1801, and after that date he became more and more a prophet for the dissatisfied political elements in the country, and particularly in the disturbed West.

By 1804 Burr's political future was badly clouded. He could no longer expect to continue as a part of the Jefferson administration, and his only hope of success was to re-establish himself in New York. If he lacked talent to electrify an audience with his oratory, he possessed ability to organize and manipulate a machine. As a candidate for governor of that state he found political intrigue aplenty, but in all fairness, the evidence seems to favor the opinion that he was willing to let democratic forces decide the issues. Burr was not a rabble rouser, no matter what his other moral discrepancies were.

In the New York gubernatorial campaign, Burr's name became associated with a shadowy New England movement for separation from the Union, despite his strong opposition to Federalist principles. Opposed to him in New York were Alexander Hamilton and his fellow Federalists, and a strong Republican faction whose candidate was Morgan Lewis. Lewis's defeat of Burr left him politically stranded.

During the campaign, old wounds of the 1790's were reopened and new ones inflicted. In the press post mortems on the election, Hamilton continued a persecution of at least fifteen years duration, in which he gave a gratuitous appraisal of Burr's morals and integrity. This led quickly to an open conflict between the two men. Burr invoked the code of the duel to seek satisfaction of his defamer, and the two men agreed to meet on the New Jersey bank of the Hudson to finish with pistols a dispute started long before in private correspondence, in Congress, and in the newspapers. Early in the morning of July 11, 1804, at Weehawken, Hamilton received Burr's fatal shot, and a chain of events began which bore directly upon frontier history.

Ten days after the duel, Burr slipped away from New York City to escape the clutches of the law in both New York and New Jersey. He visited friends in Georgia ostensibly to avoid public exposure, but more specifically to explore possibilities of filibustering in East Florida and Mexico. He then returned to Washington at the opening session of Congress to complete his obligations as presiding officer of the United States Senate. On March 4, 1805, this phase of Burr's political career closed. He was free to make a new start wherever he chose. Certainly he could not return to New York. The West beckoned with its unlimited economic and political possibilities. Had he been willing to make a modest and solid new start he might have built a brilliant political career that would have sent him back to Washington an honored citizen; but before Burr could decide on such a course, an opportunity to fish in troubled waters in the West and to achieve quick and grandiose glory suggested itself.

The West was a land of adventure as well as dissatisfaction; many Americans and the French and Spanish Creoles, whose political situation had been arbitrarily changed because of the Louisiana Purchase, were amenable to intrigue. Louisiana, West Florida, Mexico, and even the states west of the mountains offered opportunities under proper leadership. Out of office, the expatriated New Yorker became a central figure in nebulous western adventures. He was sought out by schemers who had plans for exploiting both frontier and international uncertainties. Even before the expiration of his term of office he had discussed the West with his old friend General James Wilkinson. If fate had wilfully intended that Burr should meet further disaster it could have done no better than send him Wilkinson with a fresh and heady proposal for vast action. The General, fresh from accepting Louisiana as one of the American commissioners, was well informed about the situation along the lower Mississippi. More significantly, he had a long-time experience in both frontier and Spanish intrigue.

Within a few weeks after Burr had left the Vice-Presidency, other names appeared on the growing list of his well-wishers. Among these were Jonathan Dayton, a former congressman from New Jersey and a heavy speculator in Ohio lands, United States Senators John Smith of Ohio, and John Adair and John Brown of Kentucky, Congressman Matthew Lyon of Kentucky, and Andrew Jackson of Tennessee. Many others would have their names associated with Burr's activities. One of them was Daniel Clark of New Orleans, an Irish immigrant who had come to New Orleans in 1786. From long experience in dealing with the Spanish, French and Americans he was perhaps the best-informed man on the commerce of the Mississippi Valley.

By early summer, 1805, Burr's plans probably involved no more than a scheme to join Dayton in land speculation in the Miami Valley and the building of a badly needed canal around the rocky shoals of the Ohio Falls. But being of an expansive turn of mind and willing to listen to all sorts of proposals and suggestions, Burr began to encompass more and more ground in his scheme. American smugglers who had traded through the Spanish deposit system at New Orleans already knew the value of the Mexican trade, and some of them saw in this Spanish possession a golden opportunity for filibustering. There was also a possibility that the states and territories west of the mountains could be alienated from the Union if the right approach were made at this opportune period of unrest. Burr had not given up some Mexican plans which he had developed immediately after the Hamilton duel. A vainglorious man who saw himself playing the central role in such an adventure as the future sovereign of an empire, he seems to have let his dreams far exceed realities.

Before Burr could undertake any scheme, he needed a large sum of money—possibly more than any individual or group of individuals could supply. Beyond the need for funds was the more important one of naval and military support if he were to move against the Spanish empire. He sent Charles Williamson to approach the English Minister Anthony Merry for assistance. Again fate dealt Burr a hard blow. Merry was a blundering social snob of no ability whose dislike of the informal social attitude of Jefferson and hatred of the American Union led him along a highly unrealistic line of thought. He believed that in some way he could help bring about the nation's dissolution. It was not difficult to get him to communicate favorably to his government upon the Burr scheme. The Englishman's foolish enthusiasm no doubt gave Burr undue hope of international assistance. Relying upon Wilkinson for help on the frontier was another weakness in his hope for success.

Against this background of misguided expectations Burr set out for the West in April, 1805, going by Pittsburgh and then downriver to Cincinnati. On the way he stopped at Blennerhassett's Island where he became acquainted with Mrs. Harman Blennerhassett. She and her impractical Irish husband were later to figure prominently in Burr's plans.

In Cincinnati he met Jonathan Dayton, John Smith and others. He then crossed the river to visit in Lexington, Frankfort, Louisville, Nashville, Natchez, and New Orleans. In all these towns he received a cordial welcome. His net gathered in opportunists as he went. Some of them, like Andrew Jackson and Daniel Clark, fortunately became involved no deeper than as hosts at royal social entertainment for the ambitious New Yorker, while others offered themselves as ready aides for any plan he might wish to execute.

This new western conspiracy was almost like an old-time melodrama with two villains playing vigorously independent parts. While Burr moved from town to town in the Mississippi Valley enjoying a gay social whirl and talking in veiled terms of the future, the second villain, General James Wilkinson, was in St. Louis resorting to his standard trick of playing both ends against the middle, and fraying both of them in the process. He sought to remain in the good graces of his former Spanish friends, yet to avail himself of any advantage which the Burr scheme might yield. Burr's visits to the western towns were marked by two features: he was able to travel prodigious distances over uncertain roads in remarkably short time; and he interviewed and visited with hordes of people great and small. Everywhere he turned he was lionized by his hosts, some of whom were interested in his future venture. In New Orleans he worked with the informal group called the "Mexican Association," and he seems to have received support from merchants and churchmen who were ambitious to overcome conditions imposed by Spain. Yet, despite all this, Burr had far to go before he could bring his western scheme to a point of execution.

Before Burr could make an overt move, he had to be certain that Wilkinson was ready to act with him. That Machiavellian scoundrel was still in St. Louis sounding out his fellow army officers as to their possible support of a filibuster. Before Burr could reach that city, it was fairly well revealed to General Wilkinson that his colleagues were loyal to their government. It was during this visit of Burr's in the spring of 1806 that Wilkinson began to show signs of coolness. Burr no doubt was disgusted when he found that his colleague was trying to have Burr appointed to Congress from the Indiana Territory, a thing that Burr had no notion of accepting.

In early fall Burr was back in Washington seeking to hasten British assistance. Williamson had not reported from his mission, and it was time to put pressure on Anthony Merry. At the same time Burr and Dayton engaged in a fantastic scheme to raise money from the Spanish government through its minister Casa Yrujo. They proposed to reveal the details of Burr's plans against Spain for a sum of money. Merry and Williamson, however, had failed to interest their government. The Spanish minister was already starting a backfire in the press which in time was to be fanned into the devastating flames of exposure, for the Spaniard's queries in the newspapers caused other people to ask questions. The winter in Washington was unproductive of funds. Burr became entangled with several notorious opportunists, among whom was General William Eaton, a tiresome lobbyist who had marched across Tripoli at the head of a ragged company of troops in the nation's service, and who was now seeking a hero's reward from an indifferent government. Another disgruntled hero with whom Burr had long-time association was Commodore Thomas Truxtun. Truxtun had shielded his friend following the Hamilton duel, but in 1806 he was shrewdly able to draw the line between bitter dissatisfaction and treason, and he kept clear of Burr's plans.

Before Burr could organize his affairs to return to the West, a genuine war scare developed in 1806, and part of the frontier readied itself to strike at Spain. In Tennessee and Kentucky, militiamen were being drilled. Jefferson had given Wilkinson instructions to act to protect the nation's interests along the Spanish borders. Wilkinson was then in a happy position to adjust his relationships with Spain almost as he chose. In the meantime he had cooled off toward Burr.

On July 29, 1806, Burr made the fatal mistake of writing Wilkinson in cipher revealing his plans to leave for the Ohio. He sent this letter by Peter V. Ogden and Samuel Swartwout. Wilkinson spent months deciphering and rephrasing this communication in such a manner as to clear himself and to convict Burr in the public mind. When the contents of the Burr cipher letter were revealed in Washington, President Jefferson took immediate notice of Burr's activities. From that time on Burr's activities in the West became a series of failures. When he sought to organize forces on the Ohio at Blennerhassett's Island, he was frustrated by militiamen acting almost altogether on their own initiative. They attacked Blennerhassett's famous estate destroying household furnishings, boats and supplies. In Frankfort, Kentucky, the Federalist district attorney, Joseph Hamilton Daviess, arraigned him before the federal court on a treason charge, and the newspaper editors Street and Wood kept up a vigorous attack on him in their subsidized *Western World*. Twice Burr was before the court, and both times he won acquittal of treason and conspiracy. Later he made his way down the Mississippi. Possibly most of the members of the Burr flotilla had no other idea than that they were colonists on their way to settle the Bastrop grant on the Washita River in Louisiana. Burr had bought that 400,000 acre tract from a Colonel Lynch, and it was a scheme to claim this land that comprised the major body of Burr's correspondence and conversation in the later phases of his activities in the West. Upon being released from arrest in Mississippi, Burr bid his companions a touching goodbye and set off across the country toward Florida. On the way, he was again recognized, arrested and taken to Fort Stoddart, and then started on a long overland horseback ride through Georgia and the Carolinas to Richmond to stand trial for a fourth time in the federal court. Under the jurisdiction of Judge Caesar Rodney, Burr's case was a classic example of the miscarriage of justice. Rodney's methods were a greater threat to American liberty than several frustrated Burr expeditions. Although Burr won acquittal in Mississippi, his followers were hauled into court and abused. It was clear that he would probably be rearrested on trumped-up charges, and after taking a sorrowful farewell of his river companions he set out from the Mississippi across country toward East Florida. Burr was brought to trial in the United States Circuit Court in Richmond, Virginia, in what became a celebrated case. Chief Justice John Marshall presided and, in his restricted definition of treason, made it difficult to convict the defendant. He was indicted, but was not convicted. Many prominent persons were brought into the case as witnesses, chief of whom was James Wilkinson. Dressed in full military garb, General Wilkinson made an impressive figure, but the Burr trial came near being his downfall. In the greater court of history Wilkinson stands convicted of gross duplicity, if not treason.

Up and down the Mississippi many people, some of them completely innocent, became involved in the Burr expedition, though the expeditionary force was never large or well armed. Both frontier and political propaganda made the army seem large and dangerous when in fact it never got beyond being a modest flotilla of nine flat boats bearing a negligible amount of military supplies. In fact, the force was hardly sufficient to take and hold momentarily a remote flatboat landing. Any party of western farmers floating their produce down the river were better equipped to defend themselves than Burr's expedition.

While Burr was moving on his famous expedition, Wilkinson advanced to the Sabine where his coming hastened the Spaniard Cordero's retreat across that stream. Wilkinson proposed a neutral ground between the two forces to await a more formal decision of the two governments as to the western boundary. This agreement was made more official in the "Neutral Ground Treaty" of November 5, 1806. Thus the border issue between Spain and the United States was left suspended at the Sabine for the time being. In this field-made treaty Wilkinson actually did more to confuse American-Spanish relations in this area of the Southwest than did a dozen Burr debacles.

Later Wilkinson moved into New Orleans where he placed the city under military law, and frightened the territorial officials out of their wits by reading to them Burr's secret letter and then picturing an attack by a large force. The New Orleans affair was a disturbing one in which illegal excesses by General Wilkinson, not Burr, were the real threat to personal safety and liberty.

Burr's expedition into the West was of no importance when measured in terms of tangible accomplishments, but it did serve to reveal the unrest of the frontier and to draw together many border malcontents. It also revealed to both England and Spain a deeper unity of interest among the states than they possibly had anticipated. For the West itself the "conspiracy" had its semiromantic aspects. The Burr story became a part of a frontier saga and gathered a certain patina of romance as bitter memories faded. A few individuals were ruined politically, but others succeeded in using the incident as a springboard to success. The archfiend of the whole scheme, James Wilkinson, went unpunished. His act of turning evidence against Burr was perhaps one of the greatest bits of treachery up to that date in American history. Unfortunately western military affairs were to remain under his domination for several years to come.

Florida

Since the beginning of the eighteenth century, the Florida country adjoining the Mississippi was a factor in the white conquest of the North American continent. In 1763 this territory had been given to Britain by "Article Seven" of the Treaty of Paris; in 1782 it was given back to Spain when the northern boundary was fixed at the 31st parallel. When France negotiated the secret treaty of San Ildefonso in 1801, the West Florida country was specifically excepted from the Louisiana Territory. Subsequently when France sold Louisiana, it was definite that West Florida was not included, despite the fact that it was of primary interest in the initial negotiations of the United States with France.

When American officials and diplomats contended that Florida was a part of the purchase, they were expressing a future annexation policy rather than a fact of contractual agreement. Several things contributed to American interest in this region. First, since it bordered on the Mississippi River, that stream was threatened so long as it remained in foreign hands. Second, it was a thin swampy borderland which contained the mouths of the Pearl, Pascagoula and Mobile Rivers and formed an artificial barrier between the Mississippi Territory and the Gulf of Mexico. By controlling the mouth of the Mobile River and the Bay, Spain still had possession of a strategic spot in the port of Mobile where vessels unfriendly to the United States could be docked, sheltered and refitted. Finally, ever since the beginning of the westward movement, the lower Mississippi country had experienced an infiltration of English-speaking immigrants. In the 1790's Governor Quesada had extended an invitation to the American

settler to move to Florida. Even that early, Jefferson had had his eye on
Florida and had written Washington that he wished a hundred thousand
Americans would accept the governor's invitation in order that they could
accomplish peacefully what would have to be done later by war.

The nature of the migration to the West Florida Territory was not
without its fascinating aspects. In the vanguard of this movement were
Tories, land speculators, Indian traders, fugitives from justice, private
filibusterers, soldiers of fortune, and backwoods settlers. The name of
Kemper became intimately associated with the history of the swamp and
pine country. In 1804 Reuben Kemper and his brothers Samuel and
Nathan, with a small party of followers, touched off a premature revolt
in which they hoped to capture Baton Rouge and to bring West Florida
under American control. Six years later they struck another blow at
Spanish authority in an unsuccessful assault on Mobile.

The West Florida country could be considered by Spain as no more
than a foothold from which the southwestern American frontier could be
harassed; otherwise no one could possibly have believed that it was any
more than a liability to the mother country. No realist could have thought
Spain would stand up against the pan-Americanism of the Jefferson administration and the overweening power of American backwoodsmen
in the area. Had there been no other factors, the contention that the
territory of the United States should comprise all the land east of the
Mississippi River was enough to force its absorption into the Union.
Also, Jefferson and Madison, in the face of impending war with Britain,
had become aware of the naval importance of the Gulf Coast and the
Florida peninsula.

American diplomats in Paris and Madrid undertook to clarify the
Florida issue with no success. Livingston, Monroe, and John Armstrong
had all labored at the task. For six years the latter sought the good office
of Napoleon to secure West Florida for the United States, but again the
inscrutable nature of Talleyrand resisted all approaches. Personally, Armstrong advocated taking the territory without aid from Napoleon, and this
sentiment coincided with the thinking of Jefferson. As early as 1804
Congress and the President showed an inclination to seize the territory
without further efforts at negotiation. The Mobile Act was passed in
February of that year, whereby Congress legalized the extension of
American authority over all the territory in which streams arising on
American soil emptied into the Gulf. This early act, in fact, outlined the
West Florida Territory to the Perdido River without specifying boundary
lines. The Mobile Act had little tangible results beyond revealing for a
second time what Americans conceived to be the eastern boundary of the
Louisiana Purchase. It was not until the European conflict developed more

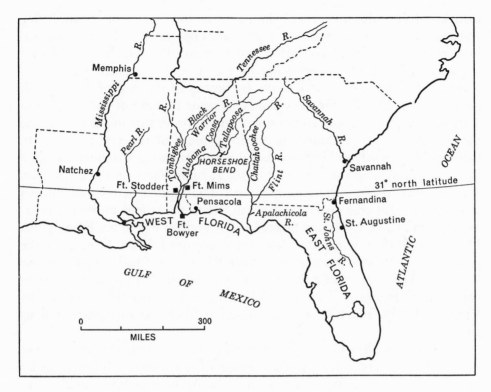

THE GULF FRONTIER

clearly, and England and Spain were forced into an alliance against Napoleon, that a pronounced policy of American occupation was formulated.

Out of the whole complicated story of activities in the West Florida country, only one clear-cut fact emerged: it was only a matter of time until the United States would possess the territory. Conflict developed rapidly between the American settlers who had moved over the 31st parallel to settle in Spanish country. This push of frontiersmen created a nationalistic surge which neither Spanish authority nor force of arms could forestall. If for no other reason, the backwoodsmen who had moved in were bound to win by the sheer weight of numbers. This conflict was brought to a dramatic end by the Baton Rouge revolt of September 23, 1810.

The insurgents, no doubt encouraged by American officials, were led against the fortress at Baton Rouge by Philemon Thomas and John Ballinger, a Kentuckian. The fort was under the command of Carlos Dehault de Lassus, Spanish commandant at Baton Rouge, and the youthful Luis de Grandpré. Early in the morning of September 23, the rebels attacked the fort, killed Grandpré, captured the garrison, tore down the Spanish flag and ran up their banner with its single star. This revolt had been preceded by a period of political confusion and maneuvering which resulted in a formal declaration of independence by the American expatriates.

The Baton Rouge revolt was the beginning of the end of the Spanish hold on West Florida. Six days later Governor Holmes of the Mississippi Territory had instructions to put down any disorder that might arise along the border, and this included the territory south of the 31st parallel. On October 27, President Madison issued a proclamation extending United States authority over the area west of the Perdido River on the contention that this was legally American territory. The United States took formal possession of this area on December 7th, when the troops under the command of W. C. C. Claiborne hoisted the American flag at St. Francisville. In 1810 and 1811 when the Americans occupied West Florida to the Perdido, the parishes west of the Pearl River were made a part of the Louisiana Territory, while the counties east of the Perdido were made a part of the Mississippi Territory. The Spaniards, under the command of Vincente Folch, and later Governor Zuñiga, held on to Mobile and its port.

As the war of 1812 became a certainty, it was more important than ever that the United States have full possession of the port of Mobile in order to prevent the succoring of enemy vessels. As long as Spain held on to Mobile there was also the danger of British occupation of the Floridas. In March, 1813, James Wilkinson was ordered from New Orleans to Mobile to take the city. He arrived there in April, and almost without a struggle from its weakened garrison he accomplished the capitulation of the last important Spanish foothold immediately west of the Perdido.

A WAR OF EXPANSION

A WAR OF EXPANSION

Could a country boundless in extent, with numerous lines of forts and garrisons, liable to invasions and predatory incursions at every point, be defended, and at the same time a war carried on, by a less number of regulars than twenty-five thousand? If the legislative councils err in such a case, they ought to err on the side of safety and vigor. The question is—will you embark in a war which shall be feeble and protracted to a great length of time, or will you make a vigorous stroke to put an end to this territorial war at once. Canada is the avowed object. Suppose you conquer Upper Canada, you must leave men behind to hold it, when you march to Quebec. Your rear must be protected; it would be a new mode of warfare to leave it unprotected! Gentlemen will be deceived if they calculate upon the treason of the Canadian people. Well, sir, you lay siege to Quebec, garrisoned, I am informed by seven or eight thousand British forces; you must have at least double that number to take possession of the place. . . .

—HENRY CLAY,
before the House of Representatives, December 31, 1811

CHAPTER XI

THE forces of western expansion, which had wrought phenomenal changes along the American frontier by 1800, gained even more momentum in the next two decades. Population increases had reached 1,000,000 in 1810. In 1800 the famous Division Act, which had separated the Ohio Territory from that of the Northwest, established the Indiana Territory west of an arbitrary line drawn from a point on the Ohio opposite the mouth of the Kentucky River northward by way of Fort Recovery to the Canadian border. William Henry Harrison became governor of the new territory, and the process of pioneering was rapidly extended to it. To the south, the population and political development of the Territory of Louisiana advanced sufficiently to bring about its admission as a state in 1812. Inland, east of the Mississippi, a restless population movement was crowding into western and southern Georgia, Alabama and Mississippi Territories, and the Floridas. Whether population and economic expansion moved westward or southwestward it carried with it the same germs of intense nationalism, speculation and agrarian interest.

By 1810 the old Spanish barriers east of the Mississippi were either removed or were in an advanced process of being permanently breached. Annexation of East Florida was almost a certainty. The two great barriers to frontier geographical and economic expansion were the Indians and the unsettled conditions of maritime commerce on the high seas. Actually the basic conditions of expansion in 1810 differed only slightly from those of 1750 and 1780, except for the intensity of nationalism and the expansion of agricultural production in the Ohio Valley. Absent from the latter phase of frontier advance was that ancient and emotional argument over opening the Mississippi River to western commerce. The river was then open, and commerce could move freely; yet that ghost of international interference with river traffic had not moved so far into the background that it could not rattle its chains menacingly on occasions.

This period, 1805–1815, introduced a confused picture in American history. Historians have written at length on the occurrences of this decade. Some of them have interpreted events in the light of international affairs as they bore upon American use of the high seas, while others have dealt fully with conditions on the frontier as they affected settlers moving against the Indian barrier and the activities of the British in Canada. Others have viewed conditions in the West in the light of a growing agrarian unrest, which demanded open access to the sea lanes of international trade. All of these things were important, and no one was entirely disassociated from the others.

Naturally attitudes in the West were shaped largely by the inertia of isolation. Possibly no force in the whole complex situation was more pronounced than that of sectionalism. Since the opening of the trans-Allegheny frontier during the latter quarter of the eighteenth century, sectionalism was a rising force in shaping both political and economic attitudes. At no time was this fact more pronounced than in the antagonisms against the proposed Jay-Gardoqui Treaty, or in the rebellion against the whisky tax. As early as the election of 1800, this attitude had been exerted in national politics with the result that, as population and voters increased, the frontier vote became more consequential in national elections. It was not too difficult to convince the Virginia dynasty in the White House of this.

There was an insatiable demand for land. Land was available on all sides, but the omnivorous desire for more was little short of a mania. Advertisements in local papers along the frontier offered acreage for sale in the unexploited sections. Individual settler, land speculator, western army officer and congressman, all were victims of this overweening desire. A wasteful system of using land by most farmers made it desirable for many of them to plan to move on periodically as they exhausted the soils of their farms. Land and timber were wasted with the same reckless abandon. The ax, plow and firebrand slashed through the country with devastating results in many areas. These were the real instruments behind the desire for greater blocks of free lands. Some of the more thoughtful frontier leaders may have believed that the western prairie lands which Zebulon Pike and others described in their journals were unfit for habitation and cultivation; they may have believed that within a short time the western population would have to redirect its courses north through Canada and southward through the Floridas. Already the idea of the American Desert was becoming a fixed part of the frontier attitude toward the semiarid lands to the west. But this was not too serious a barrier to the thinking of the average settler who yearned only for fresh lands.

The Eagle Flies High

While territorial and economic expansion was taking place, a new set of political leaders developed on the frontier. In the prevailing national spirit, these individuals were men of dominant personalities. In Kentucky, young and aggressive Henry Clay, recently arrived from Virginia, and his neighbor, Richard Mentor Johnson, inherited the mantles of George Nicholas and John Breckinridge. To the south, Andrew Jackson and Felix Grundy were assuming the leadership relinquished by John Sevier and William Blount. Beyond the mountains, John C. Calhoun and Langdon Cheves gave South Carolina a strong political position in the first decades of the new century. Peter B. Porter of New York was an important force, and on the extreme western frontier William Henry Harrison's experienced leadership epitomized western expansion. Besides these individuals there were dozens of others ranging from United States senators to courthouse ring bosses who held to the same expansionist points of view.

Nearly all the discussions of this period by historians stick closely to the great issues at stake. Few of them go beyond the attitudes of the national leaders in analyzing the personal elements of the struggle. Before it is possible to understand the spirit of frontier growth and attitudes, we must consider the fact that in many western communities the average man was either illiterate or not literate enough to read dispassionately on national issues. He did not always have available to him the resources which would thoroughly inform him on any broad question. Never has there been a time in American history when flamboyant oratory has had more effect on public opinion. An early and highly discerning scholar in the Ohio Valley advised a group of young students to cultivate the art of oratory as the most important form of expression for that day. The influence of the press itself had an oratorical flavor, for great numbers of people secured both news and their impressions of contemporary events from public readings of the papers at taverns and other public places.

At no time has the American mind been more receptive to picturesque and heroic figures of expression. Toasts drunk on patriotic occasions were vigorous in their nationalistic sentiments, nearly always heroic, and many times openly militant. In oratory and toasts, the American eagle became highly predatory, American manhood primitively sacrificial, and American expansion across the continent as inevitable as the spreading of the sun's rays. In these early oratorical outpourings was born the spirit of Manifest Destiny, which by 1811 had become a sectional passion along the frontier. Wherever in the Western Hemisphere there was air in which the great eagle could flap his wings, there was a place for American interests to expand.

Tangibly, American difficulties and issues between 1800 and 1812 were dual. There were international problems such as impressment of American seamen, the rights of American merchants to trade on the high seas, boundary disputes, and the general turmoil of world conditions. Some of these, except for their hurt to national pride and dignity, had little bearing on frontier opinion. However, it would be an error to assume that conditions of international trade were not without profound interest to western farmers. Napoleon's Decrees and the British Orders in Council, plus the American responses in the nonintercourse acts of 1806 through Macon's Bill Number Two of 1810, were significant; for any interference with free trade ultimately affected the West. Frontier farmers depended upon an open and flourishing sea-going trade to market the products of their fields. Between 1800 and 1806, western farmers were fairly prosperous, but for the next five years they faced a depression because of the uncertainties of their world market. The great struggle to open the Mississippi River has obscured this equally important matter of sea-borne trade.

Two radical changes in point of view occurred in the West after 1806. Fully ninety per cent of its products reached market in either raw or semi-processed condition, and the plea then was for factories to correct this situation. Western hemp, tobacco, wool, meat, grain and cotton could be turned into finished goods. A western Fourth of July toast in 1809 reminded a public audience that "The plough, the spindle, and the loom— what the sword of the Revolution achieved, it remains for them to perpetuate—national independence!" In Kentucky and Ohio there was relatively heavy production of hemp, flax and wool. Under the impulsive leadership of Henry Clay, the Kentucky assembly adopted a resolution in 1809 which proposed to dress its members in new garments of homespun; and at the same time lawyers and judges were restrained from referring to British laws adopted after July 4, 1776. There was much unadorned demagoguery in all of this emotionalism, but it reflects the spirit of the age. So aroused did Clay, the Republican, and Humphrey Marshall, the cantankerous old Federalist die-hard, become over such matters, that they took their argument to the dueling ground. Clay received a painful flesh wound in the leg.

Henry Clay had served two piecemeal terms in the United States Senate before he was elected to the House of Representatives in 1811. Upon his arrival in the House he was elected to the Speakership, a position which gave him excellent opportunities for leadership over his "War Hawk" colleagues, as the rabid expansionists were called. By then the public mind in the West had become highly inflamed. Clay and other war-minded individuals advocated taking Canada and Florida. In fact the taking of Canada became a sort of monotonous refrain of the "War Hawks." John Randolph of Virginia said, "Ever since the report of the Committee on Foreign Relations came into the House, we have heard but one word like the Whippoorwill, but one monotonous tone, Canada, Canada, Canada." One of the outbursts which had provoked the eccentric Randolph was

Clay's famous statement, "The conquest of Canada is in your power. I trust that I shall not be deemed presumptuous when I state that I verily believe that the militia of Kentucky are alone competent to place Montreal and Upper Canada at your feet." His colleague Felix Grundy of Tennessee believed that the British could be driven off the continent and that the Canadian people could be made brethren of the people of the United States. Peter B. Porter saw in the impending war with Britain an opportunity to secure adequate compensation for earlier spoliation of the Americans.

Tippecanoe

In the West, aside from economic factors already mentioned, there was the age-old Indian menace. The Treaty of Greenville had forced the Indian barrier deep into the western country and had reduced those British posts which had earlier stimulated strife between the onrushing white men and their red neighbors. So long, however, as an Indian or a British trader remained in the land, there was suspicion of British encouragement of border warfare and danger of Indians blocking expansion. William Henry Harrison, with the encouragement of President Jefferson, engaged in a series of land purchases in Indiana Territory which threatened the Indians in the Wabash Valley with eventual removal from their homeland. No one was more certain of this than the Shawnees and their highly intelligent chief Tecumseh.

Harrison's first major activities in the West covered a period of eleven years in which he carried out to the letter the instructions of the administration in Washington. The fifteen Indian treaties which he negotiated were thinly veiled acts of white aggression which operated on a divide-and-conquer principle. Separate treaties signed with the tribes brought closer the inevitable explosion which would renew border warfare between the two races. Up to 1811 it was only astute diplomacy that stayed open conflict. Pressure from land-hungry settlers was almost irresistible, but fear of war with Britain allied with the western Indians had a restraining influence.

Realizing that their fate in the Wabash country was at stake, the Shawnee brothers, Tecumseh and the Prophet, kept their people aware of their danger. These two notable Indians, said to have been twin brothers, were born in Ohio, and back of them was a long history of resistance to white expansion. Their father, Pucksinwa, had been killed in the battle of Point Pleasant. The Prophet was of a fanatically religious turn of mind, and he used his mystical evangelistic abilities to stir his people to action. Spending long hours in prayer and preaching a primitive doctrine of race destiny, he was able to make a considerable impression on the more emotional members of his tribe.

Tecumseh was a man of genuine statesmanlike qualities. He possessed real ability in leadership, and he approached resistance to white expansion in a realistic manner. Alone, a tribe could do nothing; nor could the Indians of a single section resist encroachment of settlers. Indians north and south would have to be consolidated into a confederation. Tecumseh's eyes turned southward where Cherokees, Choctaws, Chickasaws and Creeks struggled against the same odds. Visiting the council fires of the southern Indians, the Shawnee chieftain had a great effect upon the harassed Creeks. Speaking in threatening terms of omens in the sky and a thunderous stamping of his angry foot that would set off a mighty roar, he converted many of his hearers. He knew very well that a comet would soon sweep the sky with its fiery tail, but he hardly predicted the famous earthquake of 1811 which bore out his second threat.

While Tecumseh visited the southern tribes, the Prophet continued his revivalism. In some respects the two brothers worked against each other. Depending upon emotionalism altogether, the Prophet was oblivious to the importance of organization and timing. His notion was that an attack against the whites should come at any feverish moment that presented itself, and not necessarily at a time most advantageous to the warriors.

In 1809 Harrison negotiated a treaty for the Indian claim to the last significant block of territory along the Wabash. Attempts to survey this area led to the famous battle of Tippecanoe. In November, 1811, a frontier army under Harrison's command pushed up the Wabash to disperse the concentration of Indians at Prophet's Town. This army, if such it could be called, was a loosely organized band of individualistic militiamen from Indiana, Ohio and Kentucky. One of the officers was the famous Joseph Hamilton Daviess who had prosecuted Aaron Burr at Frankfort.

The straggling frontier force was characteristic of national defense in this era, when government touched the taxpayer's pocket as lightly as possible. Militiamen were organized by local companies under command of elective officers, whose rank was designated by plumes in their hats and high-flown military titles. Seldom were these organizations governed by established military rules; they preferred to make and break their own as they pleased. Muster days on the frontier were social occasions where officers strutted, and privates caught up with their drilling, drinking and fighting. Like the federal government, state legislatures that had a tender feeling for the taxpayer entrusted all military responsibilities to the local companies. They were especially sensitive as to duration of service, which ranged from thirty days to six months. It was not unusual for recruits to offer service for one or two months, and then prepare to go home before they had worn away the first throes of homesickness. It was well-nigh impossible to give a militiaman formal training because of his personality and the brevity of his enlistment. Not only was he untrained, but he was often bold enough to say when and where he would fight, no matter what the odds of victory would be under a more flexible plan of movement.

On November 6, Harrison crossed the brushy bottom lands of the Wabash and arrived at the mouth of the small Tippecanoe Creek which trickled down beside a rising tongue of land that marked its confluence with the wider main stream. Atop this ridge was a wooded strip which ran back in a narrow well-situated tableland, apparently an ideal camping spot. Here weary men unloaded their baggage, dropped their arms and went into camp for the night.

Beyond the Wabash, in a sweeping expanse of bottom land, the braves of the Prophet gathered about him as he went through the mystical ritual in which he prophesied annihilation of the whites and restitution of the proud Indian nations. The warriors were worked up to high fervor, and while the Prophet was still under his religious spell, they filed across the Wabash and clambered up the brushy ridge during the pre-dawn hours of the brisk morning of November 7. The white camp was thrown into maddening confusion. Riflemen knew not whether it was foe or comrade at whom they emptied their guns. When the storm of battle lulled, 188 whites were downed and a large number of Indians killed and wounded. Joseph Hamilton Daviess, who had rushed from a Kentucky courtroom to take command of militiamen, was killed.

William Henry Harrison, the enterprising young Virginian who had enjoyed abundant opportunities on the frontier, found himself elevated in those fierce morning hours to future military and political glory. In years to come, voters who could not tell within five hundred miles the location of Tippecanoe Creek knew the political appeal of its euphonious name.

As at Point Pleasant on the Ohio in 1774, the Indians might have been highly pestiferous if not victorious had they only held to the field. Their failure to overrun the whites was frustrating, but their desertion of the Prophet's town was even more disastrous. British arms were discovered among the Shawnee stores, and a new wave of anti-British sentiment added piquancy to the vigorous frontier outpourings of oratory.

Canada, Canada!

Tippecanoe was of course a side issue in the greater intersectional and international dispute. In its broader implications it included the fields of diplomacy, rivalry at sea, sectional conflict, as well as oratorical crowing by young nationalistic cocks who shook the halls of Congress with their effusions, and the old frontier doubts and fears. Yet the Indian fighting on the Wabash frontier was part of a well-known pattern. The walls of Fort Necessity were as much a part of it as the wooded crown of Tippecanoe Ridge. Coming as it did, the fight was a godsend to the embattled orators.

Plans were made to increase the national army to 35,000 men and to activate 100,000 militiamen. Naval vessels and seamen were readied for the tussle at sea. And the Twelfth Congress was loud with cries of sectional interests. "War Hawks" who had aroused the homefolks now turned their attack upon the sluggish and penurious pacifists who hoped diplomacy would yet win the battle of interests abroad. On June 18, 1812, the pacifists' walls were breached, and the United States Senate voted for war by the somewhat slender margin of nineteen to thirteen.

The narrow majority in the Senate, and the vote of seventy-nine to forty-nine in the House, reflected the fact that not all the country wanted war. New Englanders were opposed to the struggle, though the British acts on the high seas had been most injurious to their commerce. From the viewpoint of easterners, provocation for war lay in the area of violation of neutral rights rather than interest in American expansion. In fact there was a strong opposition to expansion on the part of many people.

That same day a reluctant President Madison signed the bill, and the nation was at last embarked upon a war of baffling proportions and complexities which neither the War Hawks nor their opponents seemed to have comprehended. Now the whippoorwill cry of "Canada! Canada!" had to be made good.

So far as the frontier was concerned, the important issues of arms were to be settled along the Great Lakes–St. Lawrence line, and on the frost-covered stubblefield of a sugar cane plantation below New Orleans. The primary points of land contact with the British and Indians were to be those places which already were stained with the blood of historic struggles of white conquest. Political orator-expansionists had looked at the map in the shade of the legislative hall and not in the light of military realities. Henry Clay's boasts of a quick victory in Canada were the vaporings of the debater's platform, but now they had to be tested with military leadership, government appropriations, good administration, brave men under fire in battle with infuriated Indians fighting for their last foothold in the great hunting grounds east of the Mississippi, and British troops led by shrewd imaginative officers who themselves fought to keep a foothold on the continent.

The Lake Erie-Detroit River isthmus was selected as one of the first major points of contact. On a broader scale campaigning was to follow a three-point approach. At that time fewer than four hundred men stood guard beyond the Wabash and Maumee rivers. At the tip of Lake Michigan a struggling band of fifty-three men held on to Fort Dearborn—an insufficient force to stem even a mild Indian attack. To carry out the necessary widely dispersed campaign required the services of trained tacticians who could co-ordinate the movements of the army with precision. This was precisely what the country lacked. The army was without dependable officers and soldiers. The penurious years of the Virginia dynasty had allowed the armed forces to dwindle away to less than a skeleton force. The infant military academy up the Hudson had graduated its first classes, but most of its alumni were still callow young lieutenants learning the hard lessons of the field. Its capable warriors were to await another generation to distinguish themselves.

Politicians who talked boldly of war had not troubled themselves to look behind the scenes at the antiquated leadership available. Foremost among the relics of the patriots' war who were still able to take the field was General Henry Dearborn, who had been rusting away in the safe service of the Custom House and whose past experience had never been more valorous than that acquired by a deputy quartermaster-generalship. Thomas Pinckney of Spanish treaty fame was promoted to a major general in the South, and James Wilkinson, Wade Hampton, James Bloomfield, James Winchester and William Hull were made brigadiers. Wilkinson had been in the field all the time, but there were times when it was legitimate to question which army he served.

Not all the spavined leadership wore the stars of generals. The hopelessly senile Dr. William Eustis, of Revolutionary war surgical fame, was Secretary of War. With this panel of military and civilian leadership it was plain from the outset that the United States command was inadequate to make or execute plans for a war of many fronts. Dr. Eustis' office only added confusion to a muddled organization. Before the declaration of war an effort was made to raise an army of fifty thousand men.

William Hull, governor of Michigan Territory, urged Madison and Eustis to make every effort to hold the western Indians in check. Possibly it was he who suggested that a three-prong attack by way of Detroit, Niagara and Sackett's Harbor be directed against Canada.

Hull had been sent away as early as April to guard Detroit. His command consisted of three Ohio regiments of militia and one of regulars—in all about sixteen hundred men. Leaving Urbana, Ohio, with women and children, including the leader's own daughter and grandchild, this frontier army set out to cut its way through more than two hundred miles of heavy Ohio and Michigan forest lands. For twenty-five days in the heat of June and July it struggled through forest and bog, floundered across streams, and battled clouds of mosquitoes and maddening black flies to reach its destination. At the Falls of the Maumee the fagged army found the schooner *Cuyahoga* at anchor, a welcome sight to trail-weary men who saw in the boat a blessed means of transportation for their burdensome packs and equipment. The decks of the boat were loaded with the supplies of the army, including a small trunk that contained the precious official papers of the commanding general. With the heavy dunnage safely aboard the schooner, the lightly equipped army put off into the woods again to battle its way to Detroit.

Threshing his way through the matted forest, General Hull was unaware that war had been declared two days after he had left Urbana. A stupid War Department had enlisted the further services of a blundering postal service to inform the General of this important fact. Ahead of him, the British, behind the ramparts of Fort Malden on the Canadian side of the river, waited for ship and army to appear. Fortress guns commanded the narrow river approach, and any American vessel sailing into this trap was fair game. When the *Cuyahoga* with its precious cargo of supplies, equipment, and official instructions hove into sight, it was taken as the first prize of the Detroit campaign.

While General Hull moved towards Detroit, General Henry Dearborn, commanding the eastern end of the Great Lakes campaign, floundered in the political mire of Boston and Albany, unaware that he was entrusted with anything so vital as the protection of the Erie-Niagara approach to Canada. He was supposed to cut British communications and to cover Hull's eventual attack. Instead, this strategic spot remained uncovered, and Hull's unhappy army was left to the undivided attention of the British.

Not only did General Dearborn leave Niagara unguarded, but he further complicated conduct of the war by entering into an unauthorized armistice with the unduly optimistic British ambassador Sir George Prevost. Sir George had heard of the repeal of the Orders in Council and assumed that the basic cause of war had been removed and peace would be regained. Following the great patriotic celebration on the Fourth of July, and while General Dearborn remained in a blissful state of inaction, General Hull reached Detroit. He found the fortress tenable, but unequipped to stand an extended seige.

Eustis, knowing nothing of that end of Canada beyond a cursory map exploration, had instructed Hull to cross the Detroit River at once and to advance as far as possible into Canada. However, he had forgotten to instruct Dearborn, until it was too late, to be in position to support such a move. It was to General Hull's credit that he lost little time in passing his army over the river. Unfortunately there crossed the river with the bewhiskered general an overwhelming burden of doubt and fear. The thought that Indians behind him might be attacking his daughter and grandchildren was paralyzing.

Advantage of prior information was with the British at Fort Malden, but the power of aggressive attack was still with the Americans. The population in the sparsely settled neck of upper Canada was friendly to General Hull, but it was nearly impossible for an army to live off such sterile country. A clever and deceptive fast-moving drive would have cut the British off from their supplies and severed their communications. But such a move required quick action, decisive direction, and unlimited courage. To execute such a move denied the commanding officer time to stop and worry about Indians pouring down in the rear, the approach of British gunboats on the river, or failure of his own supply lines. Late in July, a rear-guard Indian attack frightened General Hull, and between that date and August 8 the last of his courage ran out. Several times in American history, armed forces have failed to achieve victory because of their leader's panic. The retreat from Malden and recrossing the river to the safety of the walls of Detroit was a classic example of this sort of defeat.

The British forces, not so numerous at the outset as General Hull's, were well led by General Isaac Brock, Governor of Upper Canada, and young Henry Proctor, who sought promotion and fame in this far-flung command post of His Majesty's army. These officers were decisive, daring and alert in contrast to the American commander. Crossing the Detroit River in their turn, the British moved up to within shelling distance of the American fort.

Locked up in solitude, General Hull had lost the respect of his officers. His command was threatened with mutiny. Between August 8 and 16 the British swarmed across the river, and the audacious young Brock demanded Detroit's surrender. He marched his men with impunity under the yawning mouths of the two heavy 24-pound fortress guns. A quick-witted artillerist could have inflicted murderous blows on the invaders, but no such officer stood behind the ramparts of Detroit. While British troops paraded past the silent guns, General Hull sat sprawled on a pile of dunnage, chewing tobacco in such profusion that his whole bosom front was besmeared with amber. Old age, indecision, incapacity and near cowardice had overtaken him in this tragic moment. He surrendered the American army without trying its striking power. Again the British were in possession of the strategic post at Detroit where many times before they had struggled to decide the fate of the Northwest.

Britain's allies, Tecumseh and his braves, could take heart at this new move to boot the Americans from their homeland. To the west, Fort

Dearborn had been reduced by fire and its occupants captured and murdered. The carpet of white civilization was being rolled up from its outer edge. News of Hull's surrender came like the mournful tolling of a great national funeral bell, for the Americans had been repulsed in their first attempt to invade Canada, American soil had been seized, and the frontier was again open to Indian raids.

General Hull, guilty of gross personal faults, became a scapegoat for all the numerous failures of the war. He had to answer in substance for the blunders of both the War Department and General Dearborn. So busy were the scapegoat hunters that few took time to realize there was still opportunity in 1813 to cut the British forces in two by a quick thrust across the narrow waistline on the Niagara front. The old strategic posts of Niagara, Queenstown, Lake George, Lake Champlain and Oswego were again objectives of war, as in the French and Indian War of fifty-seven years before. But strategic advantage and war objectives never realize themselves; leadership is required to turn them into victories.

Possibly no greater comedy of tactical errors was ever to occur in American military history than along this front. Since May, 1812, Henry Dearborn had fought the war by leisurely correspondence with the be-fogged penmen of Washington. He had made almost no discernible plans; certainly he had not prepared to take the offensive. While Hull was sur-rendering in tobacco-smeared disgrace at Detroit, Dearborn was clocking his own progress with false armistices and a frustrating visit to New England. General Stephen Van Rensselaer, in command of New York militia, gathered his forces at Lewiston in midsummer. General Dearborn was supposed to concentrate his efforts on Lake Champlain. The blunders of Van Rensselaer along the Niagara River almost defy belief. By Octo-ber there were approximately six thousand men on his front, while on the Canadian side the British could marshal only about fifteen hundred. The Niagara troops, under the command of local political officers selected for reasons of popularity (with the exception of the fabulous Irish-born Virginian, General Alexander Smythe), lacked the capacity to take the offensive.

Before a fair assessment of the situation along the Niagara can be made, we must remember that the War Department had failed hopelessly to furnish supplies and equipment. The congressmen who had blithely voted for war failed to support it on the grand scale of their estimate of its forthcoming glories. Men were inadequately clothed, fed, armed, housed, and mounted. Health conditions were fantastic; a mere recital of the numbers of men in camp tells nothing of their physical condition as a fighting force. Leadership was weak and inexperienced. Jealousy be-tween regulars and militiamen was ruinous. However, there were present

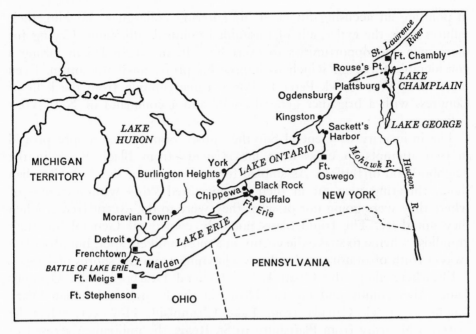

NORTHWESTERN CAMPAIGNS IN THE WAR OF 1812

several young officers who were to distinguish themselves in their country's service. Among these were Winfield Scott, Jesse D. Elliott and John Ellis Wool.

Elliott demonstrated what courage and forthright action could accomplish when on the night of October 9, 1812, he and 124 men captured the brig *Caledonia* and destroyed the *Detroit* at Fort Erie. The following night General Van Rensselaer attempted to cross the river from Lewiston to Queenstown, but in the darkness of early morning a careless blunder (allowing the lead boat to put off with all the oars) brought this attempt to a sudden halt. Three days later a second crossing was attempted. Across the river, Captain John Wool led the troops up the treacherous face of the cliffs to challenge the British in a stinging attack which brought death to Isaac Brock, who had bluffed Hull into surrender at Detroit. Relief troops were hastened out from Fort George to stem the American assault, and John Brant's Indians prowled the river ledges and ravines to threaten a rear-guard attack. General Van Rensselaer was unable to prod his New York militiamen into crossing the river to support their comrades, Wool and Scott. Scott was forced to surrender, and the Americans retired defeated within easy reach of victory.

At Buffalo, the pompous old Falstaffian General Smythe displayed a real genius for grinding out endless handbill tirades for his men. He excelled in pointing an accusing finger at his faltering colleagues. To him, their failures were the evil result of misguided political affiliations. Crying for more men and opportunities to exert himself, he succeeded in raising a considerable force on which to impose his professional patriotism. Even the famous War Hawk Peter B. Porter came running from the halls of Congress with a brigadier general's stars and a command of New York volunteers.

The insincerity of General Smythe's gusty oratory was amply proved in two attempts to cross over into Canada from Black Rock in the neighborhood of Buffalo. Assembled for an invasion of the dark Canadian shore, shivering men sat in their ice-encrusted skiffs with no sense of where they were going nor of what they were to do, except freeze, when they got there. The frigid blasts not only cooled off General Smythe's grandiose scheme to strike the enemy in a most unlikely spot, but also blew away a froth of oratory and military clowning from the shores of Erie.

Elsewhere along the Great Lakes, General Dearborn (like Generals James Abercromby and George Howe in the French and Indian War) sought to attack Canada from Lake Champlain. However, when he marched his army from Plattsburg to St. Regis, the militiamen refused to cross into Canada, and the attack failed. The war had bogged down on three fronts. Six months had elapsed, and the Americans not only were not in Canada, but the British flag waved from the staff above Detroit.

Before the end of 1812 the people of the West were aroused. Frontiersmen saw not only their national honor but even their homes threatened. News of Hull's surrender had reached the settlements like a chilling blast from the lake shore, and the people of Indiana, Ohio and Kentucky were ready to make war in earnest. Anthony Wayne's earlier victory at Fallen Timbers and the Treaty of Greenville were threatened with undoing. The Ohio and Indiana frontiers were opened to renewed Indian attacks. New forces from the border states and territory were recruited, and in command of these new troops General Harrison started quickly back upon the road to fame. Along the Michigan frontier Brigadier-General James Winchester of Tennessee was given Hull's old command, and his was the task of reopening the drive against Canada before the end of 1812.

In Kentucky, Isaac Shelby, Governor for the second time, called for fifteen hundred volunteers, and men came in droves. Farm boys dropped the hoe and grabbed the rifle; two thousand of them arrived at the muster grounds to become heroes and would not be denied the privilege of driving the British out of the Michigan woods. Six Kentucky congressmen, including the vociferous War Hawk Richard M. Johnson, deserted the legislative hall for the campaign tent. While men flocked into the rapidly filling militia companies, women struggled gallantly to supply them with clothing. The wheel, the loom and the needle worked overtime making clothing for the heroes on the long march.

Roads in northern Ohio and Indiana became virtually impassable in the heavy fall rains, but in spite of them Harrison hustled to make a winter attack. He wished to dislodge the enemy beyond Fort Wayne, and if possible to sit out the rest of the winter behind the sheltering walls of Detroit itself. Late in January, 1813, the frontier army was in position to strike at Frenchtown on the Raisin River. A cold wind blew down the river, and the militiamen shivered on the field, their fingers numbed. The officers were not yet alerted to the enemy before them. The Americans were successful at first, and then were numbed into a ragged reverse at arms.

Half frozen, the troops withdrew to a less active position. Then there followed a bloody assault against the American wounded and prisoners, and against the carelessly exposed men in camp. The tomahawk and knife, which slashed away the lives of defenseless men, stirred up a bitter resentment that gave the war in this quarter a fierce new impetus. When the British failed to control their bloodthirsty allies, a stirring cry went up from the people of the West to "Remember the Raisin!" Isaac Shelby heard the news of the Frenchtown debacle while in attendance at the theatre in Frankfort. Years before, such news had sent him scurrying across the Blue Ridges to become a hero at King's Mountain. Again he led a determined army to help rescue American honor from the slough of defeat.

Experience along the frontier taught the folly of making a headlong rush against the main objective. Harrison planned to creep back from the safety of one fortress to that of another, and to force with decision the enemy's retreat to Canadian soil. Between January and October, American officers gathered troops and whipped them into a semidisciplined fighting force. The old Indian fighters were there: Green Clay, William Whitley, Duncan McArthur and Lewis Cass; even the aging Simon Kenton had come along as a visitor to see the last great struggle in this area where he had suffered so many times in running the Indians' gauntlet. Month by month the raw militia companies grew stronger and better ordered. By early fall approximately ten thousand men were on hand. Leadership and spirit were good, and the officers had matured their plans.

"We Have Met the Enemy . . ."

While the army gathered its forces and poised for a thrust, Commodore Oliver Hazard Perry, natural fighting man of the sea, molded raw seamen and landlubbers into a naval force and completed construction of a wobbly fleet of homemade warships to challenge the power of the haughty Captain Barclay on Lake Erie. The only swift way to dislodge British land forces was to cut their water communications—a thing that was obvious in 1812. So long as Proctor's army could be supplied by British vessels, he could sit securely at Detroit and Malden and defy American assaults. Perry had been sent to Presque Isle to take command of ships still being built. Not only were there no ships, there were no supplies and no trained sailors. He arrived on Lake Erie in March, and it was not until August that he was able to relieve the ships pinned down by the British naval forces at Black Rock and to warp his newly constructed vessels out of the shallow harbor water into the lake.

The young commander was a man of great ambition and energy. Less courageous men such as Dearborn, Van Rensselaer and Alexander Smythe had faltered in this area. With three brigs, five schooners and the sloop *Trippe*, Perry set forth to stalk Captain Robert H. Barclay in command of three ships, a schooner, a brig and a sloop. Spreading sail and moving out on the bosom of the lake, the young Perry hoisted a blue flag on which bold white lettering spelled out the dying words of his old commander Lawrence: "Don't Give Up the Ship!"

Early in the morning of September 10, 1813, Captain Barclay's fleet turned about into battle line. Near noon a running fight was begun off Put-In-Bay, and there followed a thrilling naval duel. His flagship *Lawrence* hammered into wreckage, the American commander pitched over the reeling vessel's side into a skiff and rowed over to take command of the *Niagara* and re-enter the fight. With unrelenting determination and cool maneuvering Perry brought Barclay and his fleet finally to defeat. Failure of the British navy to break Perry's bulldog grip would radically change the situation for Proctor and his Indian braves around the western end of Lake Erie. The jubilant Perry penned his famous message to Harrison that he had "met the enemy and they are ours!"—the first cheering word in two years of war in this quarter.

Between Sandusky Bay and Port Clinton there were more than five thousand militiamen with their officers, Winchester, Harrison, Shelby, Clay, Cass, McArthur, and Johnson. For the first time in the war the Americans had control of the lake, and Perry's battered fleet was free to transport land forces across to Canada and to reconnoiter Fort Malden and other British points of concentration. Late in September a fleet of American and captured British vessels put out from Mid-Sister Island for Hartley's Point across the mouth of the river. Ahead of them on land, General Proctor began a retreat from Malden and Amherstburg. The guns that had brought to bay the *Cuyahoga* and Hull's precious trunk of official papers were now silent.

On October 5, the two armies joined battle along the winding banks of the Thames. The Americans shredded the thin British lines, but real resistance came from Tecumseh's army. Hidden securely in the underbrush where they could open fire with deadly effect at close range, the Indians were obscured from Harrison's forces. To draw their fire, twenty men volunteered in a forlorn hope to rush the line and to expose themselves to blistering attack from the Indians. Astride a white horse, Richard M. Johnson led the suicide band up to the muzzles of the Indian guns. A burst of fire dropped most of his companions and seriously wounded him. Bursting into the open, Tecumseh was downed by one of the most controversial shots in frontier history. Who did it? The brave and bleeding Johnson, reeling astride his white charger and waving his doubled-barreled fllintlock pistol, or his fellow-Kentuckian, William Whitley? No matter who shot him, when Tecumseh fell, his braves fled the field.

Like Perry, Harrison could shout triumphantly that he too had met the enemy beyond the Detroit and made them his. He had avenged the humiliation of the year before. So far as Indian destiny was concerned, he had concluded the fight started that gloomy November morning on the rising ground above the Tippecanoe. Painted warriors creeping through the brush after Tecumseh was downed suffered a defeat that was more lasting even than those experienced in Pontiac's War and under the stinging fire of Wayne's troops at Fallen Timbers. The door to Indian land was again flung wide—this time to be staked and chained open. A rushing horde of settlers would in a short time raise even Fort Dearborn from the ashes and obscure the site of the old trading post. Here would be built the foundations of a new town.

Victory on the Thames and on Lake Erie by no means broke the back of British resistance in Canada. To the zone of the old Van Rensselaer and Dearborn command, Secretary John Armstrong had transferred that sinister figure of frontier military perfidy, James Wilkinson. Wilkinson had seen service along the Gulf, but nowhere had he proved himself capable of directing an army in a campaign. Now he was entrusted with the responsibility of making a thrust against Montreal—a challenge that demanded nerve, imagination and ready decision. After a season of aimless maneuvering, the American troops were withdrawn to winter quarters, and the effect of Harrison's victory on the Thames was obliterated. So completely did Wilkinson fail that Harrison resigned his generalship in protest. Again the Erie-St. Lawrence-Champlain frontier was subjected to quick attack by the enemy. There was little indication that the Americans were going to deliver on Henry Clay's proud boast and take Canada.

Jackson to the Fore

As the focal centers of the war shifted around in the East, there was trouble in the Southwest. Not unlike the beginnings of the struggle in the Northwest, an angry prelude of Indian fighting was topped off with a victory against the British. Just as circumstances along the Wabash and failure at Detroit thrust William Henry Harrison to the front, so the war in the Southwest made Andrew Jackson a frontier hero of great proportions.

In the first flush of war Jackson had alerted the Tennessee militia and proposed to lead it against Canada. He had seriously accepted the congressional boasts and proposed to make them good. His appeal to arms, issued from his estate, the Hermitage, on March 7, 1812, was a choice piece of contemporary bombast.

By 1812 Jackson had become a political and military leader of his section. The red-headed, freckled-faced Carolinian had made rapid headway in his new home in Tennessee—but men, not law books, were Jackson's interest. Somewhat frail in stature, he was a man's man in demeanor and a natural orator. His picturesque language could envelop an ordinary situation in an aura of color and drama, which enabled him to lead extrovert men like himself to great heights of achievement. Since 1802 Jackson had been a major general of Tennessee militia, and as a prominent member of the Blount political faction he had served terms in Congress as both representative and senator. Privately he was a successful farmer and trader and had distinguished himself as an important sportsman on the race track. His temperament bespoke the nature of his environment and times.

Before 1812 Jackson had only limited military experience; hence his cocksureness of his ability to lead an army to quick victory. Jackson's offer of his own services and those of 2,500 militiamen was accepted in Washington with grace, but the befuddled War Department, looking more to politics than victory, never ordered him to take the field.

While Hull was failing at Detroit, Jackson waited out the preliminary months of the war in irritating idleness. In October, 1812, a call came for Governor Blount to send fifteen hundred men to New Orleans to assist Wilkinson in his West Florida campaign. During the freezing winter of 1812–1813, when the cold blue waters of the Cumberland were clogged with ice chunks, Jackson organized his forces, a part of which he sent away under the command of John Coffee. The other part floated down the freezing river with their impetuous leader. A little more than a month later, the Tennesseans were in Natchez where Jackson waited for further instructions. Jackson and his men had fallen victims of the War Department's blundering and the heartless manipulations of Wilkinson to keep the fiery Jackson away from the springs of military glory. He was ordered to disband his companies and to send the men home. To his ever-lasting credit, the master of the Hermitage assumed financial responsibility for leading his troops home through six hundred miles of wilderness to dismiss them above the Cumberland in front of the state capitol.

Though Wilkinson found an excuse not to accept the services of the Tennessee militia, it was not because of peace in the Gulf Coastal country. From the days of the first American-Spanish bickering over the West Florida country, there was little peace in the region. Wilkinson's capture of Mobile had not removed the cause of conflict. British vessels cruised menacingly along the coast, and a horde of adventurers from within the Floridas and Alabama Territory had sought aid of the enemy through the Spanish port of Pensacola.

North of Mobile in the Alabama River bottoms there was unrest among the Creek Indians. Along the headstreams of the Coosa and Tallapoosa, Tecumseh had excited many of the southern Indians in spite of the efforts of Colonel Benjamin Hawkins to preserve the peace. The Shawnee's eloquence and fanaticism had aroused the more militant Creeks to oppose the whites. As already noted, he used the approaching visibility of a comet in the sky as a heavenly omen which validated his words.

Along the coastal frontier, Indians in co-operation with the British and private filibusterers threatened white settlers. Leaders of these border rebels were William Weatherford and Peter McQueen, Scotch-Spanish-French-Creek mixed breeds who made common cause with the Creeks and Seminoles. They proposed to carry on a harassing campaign with the aid of the British at Pensacola. Equipped with enemy guns and supplies, these border brigands set up a paralyzing state of fright among the settlers, which drove them into the forts at Stoddert on the Alabama and Mims on Lake Tensaw.

Some effort was made to strengthen Fort Mims, then under the com-mand of Daniel Beasley. Late in August, 1813, the border raiders surprised the fort and butchered more than four hundred of its occupants in one of the bloodiest holocausts in American history. News of the Mims massacre was carried to Fort Stoddert and was speeded from there to the white settlements in Georgia, Mississippi, and Tennessee.

Here was another occasion when frontiersmen were shocked into vigorous action by a beastly assault against settlers on the raw edge of the settlement line. Unfortunately for the southern Indians as a whole, they stood more or less indicted for collaborating with the British. When word of the Fort Mims disaster reached Nashville, Jackson and his volunteers would not again be denied an opportunity to fight in the war. From a sickbed where he was recovering from a badly infected shoulder wound —the result of a fight with the Benton brothers a month before—the emaciated cock of the Tennessee militia, General Jackson, gave instructions for the invasion of the Creek country of Alabama. In phenomenal time he drove his troops into northeastern Alabama, plunged across the Tennessee River and invaded the hilly wilderness that barred his way southward to the Creek villages. From November to March the Tennessee army beat its way into the wilderness and skirmished with the warring Creeks as they went. On March 27, 1814, the Indians were cornered in the sweeping horseshoe bend of the Coosa River where the blistering battle of Tohopeka saw the Creeks beaten into submission. Weatherford's warriors were hemmed inside the big bend of the river and were slaughtered by bullets poured in from all sides. Fighting side by side, the 2,000 volunteers and a band of friendly Creeks littered the battlefield with the bodies of 557 Indians and permanently crushed their resistance in this area. Jackson had proved himself a grim fighter in this, his maiden battle.

The ailing hero, who battled short-term recruits almost as savagely as he fought Indians, could not rest on his laurels. He believed the source of the Alabama difficulties to be along the Spanish coast at Pensacola, and as soon as he could make known his terms to the cowed Creeks, he proposed to march against that troubled spot. Gathering both friend and foe from among the Indians about him, he read the rigorous terms of defeat to them. "By the eternal," Creeks, comrade and foe alike, were Indians and all of them were to surrender large slices of their lands, and to open the door for the white encroachment which marked the end of their old way of life.

Success in the Alabama woods had its reward. When Harrison surrendered his commission as a major general because of James Wilkinson's failure in the New York campaign, a vacancy was made for Jackson's appointment. He was now placed in command of the Seventh Military District, which brought Mobile and New Orleans within his territory. For the first time a man of positive action commanded the Florida frontier, and a spirit of determination prevailed among both officers and men.

The British fleet had operated from the tip of Mobile Bay to Pensacola. The three focal points were Fort Bowyer on the Bay, Mobile and Pensacola, and it was these three places which first received the new commander's attention. Brushes with the enemy at both Fort Bowyer and Pensacola, however, were only of minor importance. The real drive was sure to come at New Orleans. For Jackson, a strategist of genuine native ability, the big question was the route which the British would take to their objective. By land to the Walnut Hills or by water to the mouth of the Mississippi? By cutting across the short land bight to the Mississippi, they could forage on the country and entrench themselves as they approached New Orleans.

In Washington, the reassembled government was in no position to direct the movements of a frontier army. John Armstrong proved no more decisive as Secretary of War than Dr. Eustis. President Madison himself was battered into inaction by the conflicting forces within the nation, and had it not been for James Monroe's assumption of the duties of the War Department, the southwestern campaign might have been slowed down, if not defeated, by delays and confused instructions. The Seventh Military District was enlarged to include Georgia and Kentucky, giving Jackson access to a greater source of manpower.

In the field, the impulsive Jackson had three distinct assets. He could identify a major move of the enemy when he saw it; he could make tactical plans for movement over a treacherous terrain and among treacherous people; and he had good subordinate officers in men like John Coffee, John Adair, and William Carroll. The new major general was never a man to make a negative approach to an objective. His invasion of Pensacola had been practical, but quite without sanction of international law, and the social and political crosscurrents in New Orleans would have frustrated a less bold man. His movement of troops from Pensacola and Mobile to New Orleans in the fall of 1814 was a phenomenal accomplishment in itself. Fortunately Jackson and Coffee led men who were seasoned to wilderness travel, and the lower country was not entirely strange to many of them. As Tennessee and Kentucky farmer-flatboatmen they had often struggled home from market through the monotonous stretches of Mississippi wilderness.

In New Orleans, Governor W. C. C. Claiborne appeared relieved to turn over command of the city to the Tennessee general. As political aide, Edward Livingston, a former Congressional colleague and a skillful man at manipulating certain forces, gave Jackson material assistance while embarrassing him in other areas.

By December 1, the American contingent was in New Orleans, and their enemies were hovering about Cat and Ship islands in the Gulf of Mexico. No reliable map of the New Orleans countryside was available. Jackson and his subordinates had to reconnoiter both the lower river and the Lake Borgne-Chef Menteur approaches, as well as the intervening River Aux Chênes route. Not only was it necessary to scout the terrain, but a line of battle between the major approaches had to be organized in such a way that defenses could be concentrated at three or four points in quick order.

By mid-December Jackson was able to improve his established lines and to keep a vigilant watch on the movements of the enemy. In the latter activity he had at his disposal the eyes of many loyal persons who knew the bayou country, and especially the pirate Laffitte brothers and Dominique You, who could check every movement made on the water approaches to New Orleans. For the Barataria pirates, watching the enemy was an old game at which they were exceedingly adept. Aboard the British ships there was much cocksureness. The commanding officers disdained a tedious land maneuver. With their trained men they expected success from a co-ordinated headlong ground and naval push—a costly assumption as it turned out.

Actually there was no such thing as a single battle of New Orleans; each phase of the fighting was of campaign proportions. Hostilities opened on the morning of December 22 and lasted for the next seventeen days. One of the first moves was a surprise attack at Bonaventura in which Jackson was able to shift his defensive forces quickly enough to turn the British back. On January 8, 1815, the British made their final push across the stubble-lined plains of Chalmette. The Americans, safely ensconced behind the Rodriguez Canal barriers, inflicted a serious loss on the British. When the smoke of battle had lifted, 2,600 men were counted as killed, wounded and captured. North of the Rodriguez battle line, 8 Americans died and 13 were wounded.

Those poorly armed and fortified troops who had been stationed west of the Mississippi gave ground to the foe, and the battle, had it been prolonged, could have been disastrous. As it was, the only real harm was caused by Jackson's hot impulsive words of criticism, which resulted in a future letter-writing duel that grew almost as furious as the fighting at Chalmette.

Just before New Orleans was fought, American arms won a victory of heroic proportions on the northern front. While Jackson's riflemen were holding to the sand spit below Mobile at Fort Bowyer, General Alexander Macomb and Commander Thomas MacDonough fought to drive the British out of the country at the head of Lake Champlain. Regulars and militia under Macomb's command were inadequate to combat the fifteen hundred British regulars who poured down from Montreal to cut their way into the heart of New York. Sir George Provost, Governor-General of Canada, led these veterans; to the Americans digging their defenses into the ground on the lake side of the Saranac River it seemed that nothing short of a miracle would stop them.

On the lake between Crab Island and Cumberland Head, Commander MacDonough stationed his fleet, and on September 11, 1814, he fought it out with Commodore George Downie's command of lake boats. The fleets were almost equal in size and man power, but the Americans enjoyed the advantage of being stationed and ready for attack when the British moved into position. Early in the opening battle, Downie was killed by a rolling gun carriage. Thrice MacDonough was knocked unconscious but revived and continued the fight. At the end of two hours and twenty minutes, the British struck their colors. MacDonough, like Perry at Put-In-Bay, had maneuvered a homemade navy to a fine victory. Downie's defeat took the spirit out of Sir George Prevost's attack, and he withdrew his veteran land forces in the face of vastly inferior American opposition. The victory on Lake Champlain was important in establishing the American foothold in the upper Great Lakes country, and gave the commissioners, then bringing the Treaty of Ghent to a conclusion, a strong reason for holding out for a claim to the lakes. At the same time this defeat of a picked British army brought some sense of revenge for the burning of Washington.

From a diplomatic point of view the battle of New Orleans had been a useless effort, for it had been fought after the signing of the Treaty of Ghent which officially ended the state of war. From the broader point of view it was a major incident in frontier history. Within itself it was a purging action. Not only did it prevent the British from gaining control of the Louisiana city, but it swept away almost the last vestige of international intrigue and uncertainty from the mouth of the Mississippi River. After 1815 the great plug of uncertainty was removed, and the full Americanization of the southwest was set in full motion. Its greatest secondary influence was the immortalizing of Andrew Jackson as a great border hero and leader of the common man.

The land successes of the War of 1812 were proud frontier achievements. At the Thames, at Lake Erie, Horseshoe Bend, Lake Champlain, Mobile, New Orleans and at Fort Stephenson, buckskin-clad frontiersmen had fought with vigor, even if they had objected to terms of enlistment when there was no enemy in sight. Though the Americans had failed to fulfill the dream of the orators and storm Canada, many of them, in their own private opinions, at least had become heroes. On the frontier the military victories not only brought immediate sectional satisfaction, but it brought an end, except for a few peripheral skirmishes, to the long drawn out Indian warfare east of the Mississippi. Tecumseh's confederation died aborning, and his people were eventually to lose their hold in the old Northwest. In the South, sorrowing Creeks, Cherokees, Choctaws and Seminoles saw their homeland gobbled up by onrushing white hordes that drove their lowing herds before them into the piney woods pastures. Indeed, as Tecumseh predicted, an angry Indian god had stamped his foot in mighty displeasure, and in time the broken children of the forest were to be removed along a trail of tears and death to lands beyond the Mississippi to await a second assault by land-grabbers who were moving westward.

A war record, honorable or otherwise, became almost necessary for success at the polls. Whether a political aspirant sought at the hands of the voters to wear a constable's badge or to sit in the White House, a war record was indispensable. The number of heroes made by the war was unlimited. Even some of the administration in Washington, including President Madison, achieved heroic stature overnight. The war period had been one of revivalism in which an adolescent nation determined its capacity to protect itself. Its issues and victories became part of a holy national crusade. The blunderings and mismanagement of affairs in Washington and in the field were conveniently forgotten, and victory became the accomplishment of everybody except the obstructionists in the East.

No heroes were greater in self-estimation than those hundreds of common soldiers who had carried long rifles in battle. Tarrance Kirby of Bowling Green, Kentucky, half a century later dusted off his hero's laurels in a plea to President Abraham Lincoln to release two Confederate grandsons who had been imprisoned by the Union Army. The distressed Kentuckian wrote Lincoln:

> We the undersigned respectfully petition your honor that some 12 months ago my grandsons William Bradley & Van. Fulgium was captured by the Federal Soldiers—and are at this time in prison at Camp Morton Ind. at the time they wer captured they wer on there way home having served out there time in the Rebble armey—and was likely to be conscripted whech they wer vary much opposed to. he is vary desieras to take the Amnester Oath give bond and return home and live a quiet sitizen. They are the Grand children of the Old Hero that served his country in the War of 1812. Four companies to rescue the Bleeding Fruntiers of Michigan and Ohio— While Indians was yeling around my Ears like Ten Thousand Wild Panthers in the woods swearing in Indian Language that they would have my scelp or hear before day—or make ther Hatchets drunk in my Blood—but bore it with corage and fortitude I foute the First Battle at Tippecanoe and the Second Battle at the River Reasen then drove the Indians frum ther to detroit—then across the river to Canida, then drove Proctor & Elliott from Mauldin to Moraviantown—then I Shouted Triumph Victory over Proctor & Elliott and Tecumseh whole torso. I hope kill Tecumseh and *hope Skin him* and brot Two peices of his yellow hide home with me to my Mother & Sweet Harts after a few days rest—ther was a call for volunteers to defend N Orleans I volunteered at the first tap of the drum under the immortal Andrew Jackson—I fougth the Battle of 8th January & was wounded—throwed them Head and Heels cross and file, they covered 10 Acres with death Blood and Wounds, and sent them Home with a dabsend to Old England which made a Mash of Lord Wellington's Army and when they got there they could not tell the news—

A relatively small number of men in proportion to the population took part in the struggle. Not over fifty or sixty thousand men were ever engaged, and the bulk of the fighting was done by as few as five to eight thousand men. Of this number disease and accident injured more than the shellfire of battle. About five thousand men were killed and injured.

Economically the War of 1812 produced a spiraling inflation which sent prices of farm products soaring. Land was planted in vast crops, and towns and villages saw manufacturing plants spring up overnight. Speculation in land reached feverish proportions, and the immediate postwar years seemed to promise eternal prosperity. The war itself cost approximately $127,000,000, about half of which was paid out in subsequent years as pensions. Primitive and infant banking systems were organized before their managers knew how to manage them. They were unable to withstand the clamor for money, and the printing presses rolled out poorly printed bills in amounts that exceeded, in some cases, the property values of the states which chartered them. In Kentucky alone the legislature in 1818 sanctioned the issuance of $28,000,000 in new, and as it proved, wellnigh worthless bills.

Even though a spirit of sectionalism became more pronounced, nationalism which had budded so roundly in 1806 was ready to burst into full bloom. With the West becoming a more powerful factor in national politics, its webbing of pressures and political behavior promised to bear heavily in future national elections. Years immediately following 1815 saw a great flurry of frontier development in which the stream of expansion ran almost unbridled not only to the Mississippi, but leaping that stream poised itself to overflow broad stretches of country inside the great prairie ring.

The Treaty of Ghent

Formally, the Treaty of Ghent had ended the war. This agreement brought to an end an extended period of diplomatic negotiation which started almost with the first shots of the war. Diplomats had sparred and sought advantage in the major issues of impressment, the fishing banks, and establishment of territorial boundaries. The British had sought again to establish an Indian buffer zone which would have halted westward expansion in the Northwest and granted them control of the Great Lakes chain. Such a decision would have left the old festering sore of disgruntled Indians seeking to snatch their lands back from white occupation. Failure to establish such a zone was just as great a defeat for the Indians as the one they had suffered on the battlefield along the Thames. They not only lost their hold on the region immediately involved, but the

way was cleared in a remarkably short time for Indian removals from this
area to the land beyond the Mississippi. For the frontier as a whole the
end of the War of 1812 was a landmark period. A new era of westward expansion had begun.

In the southeastern part of the United States, the final settlement of the
Florida question was made possible by events in America and in Europe
following the war. Defeat of the British cleared West Florida of all foreign
threats and left Spain almost defenseless in its remaining Florida possession. Since the misguided expedition of George Mathews in 1812, this
latter area might well be considered a piece of unfinished business for the
Madison administration. Spain's hope of retaining Florida was indeed a
vain one; yet the United States had to tread lightly in its diplomatic negotiations because of uncertain conditions in Latin America, where revolutions were destroying Spain's hold in the Western Hemisphere.

Had the disposition of the East Florida issue depended upon diplomacy
alone, the transfer of that territory might have been made to the United
States through the quiet exchange of diplomatic notes and agreement to
terms of a treaty of cession. But the troubled borderland of this region
created police problems which left the United States little choice of
measures to keep peace along its boundaries. Escaping slaves, Indians,
border ruffians, and opportunists of every sort had populated the area since
1783. To bring peace in this wild country demanded the services of a
strong-willed man who would focus his attention on the trail of a fleeing
fugitive rather than on an imaginary international boundary.

Such a man was Andrew Jackson. There was no man in the country
capable of more direct action than the hero of New Orleans. In 1817 when
he was sent to patrol the Florida border, he not only chased his quarry
inland, but he also took the fort at St. Marks and the town of Pensacola.
In his dash to these places he captured the British subjects Alexander
Ambrister and Robert Arbuthnot, dumped the Spanish governor out of
bed at Pensacola, and frightened the inhabitants of that place half to
death. A court-martial trial found the British traders guilty of border in-
cendiarism, and Jackson ordered the death penalty. The aged Arbuthnot
was a patriarchal man in appearance and had a humane record as a trader.
Ambrister was a dashing young adventurer who had come to Florida at
the insistence of an uncle, and was no doubt harmless as a threat to American security. His death at the hands of American troops in Florida left
a prospective bride awaiting his return to England.

Jackson's actions were inexcusable, but he had the plea of emergency
on his side. Mistreatment of the Spanish governor, no doubt provoked,
was likewise censurable. It was Old Hickory's expressed regret that he
had not administered to him the same treatment which he gave the British

traders. In Washington there was serious question of Jackson's actions and a desire to recall him, but there was at the same time a distinct timidity as to who would undertake the task. In the ensuing argument with the General it was revealed that he claimed to be operating under a secondary set of orders which had been delivered to him directly from James Monroe by Congressman Rhea of Tennessee—a claim which ever since has intrigued Jacksonian biographers and historians of the period. Jackson's actions, while injurious to the cause of international peace, were popular at home, and he became more of a hero than ever to the common people. To them he was a man not afraid to act as he saw fit, and his actions, like the thinking of those who so heartily approved them, were glorious simplifications of the immediate situation with Spain.

Fortunately in 1817 Spain's government was so sorely beset by domestic troubles within her crumbling empire that it had no time for enlisting the aid of other European countries in undertaking a fresh war against the United States. Revolutions in the Latin American countries diverted major attention from the side issues of East Florida. Thus it was that the strong course of action taken by Secretary John Quincy Adams and Andrew Jackson brought the frustrated Spanish ambassador Don Luis de Onis to the point of ceding Florida in the Adams-de Onis Treaty of February 22, 1819. This agreement actually was more important than was the one made at Ghent. It defined for the first time the all-important western boundaries of the Louisiana Purchase as this area touched on Spanish territory to the west. Beginning at the mouth of the Sabine on the Gulf of Mexico, the boundary was to follow up the west bank of this stream to the 32nd parallel, thence northward to a junction with the Red River, thence along the Roxo or Red River to 100 degrees longitude, thence northward to the Arkansas to its source in latitude 42 degrees, then, curiously, by that parallel "to the South Sea." This included all of the islands in the rivers, and the boundaries were made subject to subsequent resurveys. This western boundary was based on the map included in John Melish's *Travels*, 1815, and reissued in 1818.

As conditions to the cession of Spain's remaining possession east of the Mississippi to the United States, the religious freedom of the Spanish Catholics was assured; Spanish vessels loaded with products of that nation were to be permitted freedom of the Florida harbors on the same terms as American vessels, a privilege which was to be granted to no other nation. Finally, the American government was to pay damage claims against Spain up to five million dollars. Thus Manifest Destiny east of the Florida River had asserted itself, even though parts of the Florida peninsula remained frontier country until after 1900.

The northern boundary of the United States was still undefined in wide areas, and the naval war on the Great Lakes had made this water boundary area an extremely precarious one. If the agitation to take Canada should again develop, a strong naval force would be necessary to turn an enemy back. Despite a treaty of peace between the United States and England, some British officials thought another war not unlikely; and certainly they favored an adequate naval force in the Great Lakes, which was in fact advocating an arms race. This was the situation in 1817 when Charles Bagot, British ambassador, and Richard Rush, Acting Secretary of State, began an exchange of diplomatic notes on the subject. Their correspondence led to the administrative agreement that the Great Lakes would not be armed, except for the minimum force necessary to administer revenue laws. This decision, which in 1817 brought to an end more than a half a century of bickering, has prevailed ever since.

Just as important as the Rush-Bagot agreement were the boundary negotiations which cleared up some of the ambiguities of the Treaty of 1783 and made the 49th parallel a definable boundary from the Lake of the Woods to the watershed line of the Rockies. Straightening out this line did three significant things: it alleviated friction among the fur traders around the headwaters of the Mississippi; Britain recognized the purchase of Louisiana and the extension of its northern boundary; and, finally, by stopping at the crest of the Rockies, the whole troublesome Oregon question was left open to future negotiations.

Thus in 1820 the national boundaries were stabilized. It seemed that a long time must elapse before there would be further pressures on the border. John Quincy Adams could take genuine pride in his diplomatic accomplishments. He and President Monroe had done as well or better by the nation than had John Adams at Paris in 1783 and Thomas Jefferson with the Louisiana Purchase in 1803. Little did these statesmen appreciate the fermenting situation in the country. Victory at the treaty table had blinded them to the surging virility of a young and fecund nation that was rushing westward in search of new adventures and economic security.

CONTEMPORARY VIEW OF GRAND RAPIDS IN 1831 BY ELDER JOHN BOOTH

PEOPLING THE GREATER FRONTIER

PEOPLING
THE GREATER FRONTIER

I have often stood and viewed with wonder, whole caravans of emigrating families, having sometimes a dozen wagons in company, as they passed along the streets of Louisville, Cincinnati, Brownsville, Pittsburgh, or Wheeling. I have a thousand times met them on the summits of the Alleghenies; and, as they passed, wagon after wagon, the women and children sometimes riding, and often walking after in an irregular line, and the men driving the teams, or urging on the livestock, I have been reminded of the beautiful lines of Virgil, which represent the Trojan Prince supporting the drooping spirits of his followers amid the turmoils of a long and perilous voyage. With a verbal change, it might be used by many a father of a family, as he pursues his long and toilsome way across these lofty mountains, seeking a new residence, in an almost unknown land:

> *Per varios casus, per tot discrimina rerum*
> *Tendimus Hesperiam, sedes ubi fata quietas*
> *Ostendunt.*
>
> —BAIRD, *View of the Valley of the Miss.*

CHAPTER XII

EVEN as the last echo of rifle fire died away on the Plains of Chalmette, and long before the last disabled veteran of MacDonough's gallant fleet hobbled away from the hospital, the effects of the War of 1812 were being felt in the nation. Around a crescent whose points were anchored at Presque Isle on Lake Erie and at the mouth of St. Mary's River in Florida there was ceaseless activity. In a wide sweep population moved deep into the backwoods of Indiana, Illinois, Michigan, Missouri, Louisiana, Mississippi and Alabama. The valleys of Virginia and Tennessee emptied a never-ending stream of settler families to the southwest. The great frontier movement may also be compared to a vast forest fire, caught in a wild breeze that swept it beyond newly cleared fire trails, swirling onward out of hand. Wherever land was available there was no apparent force to restrain the advance of population which at times threatened to drain some older coastal settlements.

Three powerful technological instruments hastened this migration. While Tecumseh counciled with the Creeks squatting about their council fires in middle Alabama, Nicholas Roosevelt made ready his famous steamer *New Orleans* for its maiden journey southward on the western waters. While William Henry Harrison battled the Prophet's braves on Tippecanoe Creek, this famous boat was anchored above the falls at Louisville awaiting its first major test—the negotiation of a hazardous barrier of rock and wild water. Captain Roosevelt had left Pittsburgh on October 11, 1811, and four days later he was in Louisville. Apparently little or no advance notice reached that city of the boat's approach. When it arrived at the waterfront and released its steam, the startled inhabitants believed a comet which was visible at the moment had fallen into the river; and after the *New Orleans* was able to negotiate the falls and enter the lower river, came the mighty earth tremble which the Indians credited to the angry god's foot. It seemed as if the earth itself was aware of the revolution which the clumsy steamer would cause in river transportation within the next two decades. In January, 1812, the *New Orleans* nosed her way to a landing amidst the swarm of upriver flatboats in her namesake city. Captain Roosevelt's adventure downstream had been successful, and in a remarkably short time the steamboat was to prove itself a highly practical vehicle in empire building.

Less dramatic, but possibly more significant, was the simple little machine that the Yankee schoolteacher Eli Whitney invented in 1793 to strip the lint from cotton seeds. The cotton gin developed a limited domestic industry into an important factor in world trade. A clumsy box in the beginning, it quickly proved itself capable of rearranging the economy of the older southern agrarian sections and pushing their boundaries far beyond the normal schedule of frontier expansion.

Following in the path of the cattle grazers and border adventurers came slaveholders seeking large plantations, yeoman farmers abandoning exhausted soil, and all the competitive aspects of an older society. Nomadic herdsmen living off the largesse of free grazing ground on the public domain helped to destroy the advantages they enjoyed by telling friends and relations back home about the good quality of the lands. A dissatisfied farmer in South Carolina heard of the rich lands in Georgia, Alabama, or Mississippi and he packed up. With wife, children, slaves, utensils, implements, and driving a lowing herd in the wake of this party, he set out across country to the New Canaan. An eloquent legend of this movement is chiseled on country churchyard tombstones across the South where the settlers left their bodies as they went. Engraved on the stones are the proud lines, "Born in York District, South Carolina"; "Born at Flat Rock, North Carolina"; "Born in Old Virginia." Friends remembered, even in death, that the victims had come from Dublin, Londonderry, Cork and nearly all the other Old-Country counties which had hustled off shiploads of poverty-stricken immigrants to the new country.

What had been wild Indian country, unbroken in most cases except for the great trader and drover paths, now swarmed with new settlers. They came with sharpened axes to deaden the trees; they set the woods on fire to kill the snakes, mosquitoes, and undergrowth. Their crude cabin walls rose from the ground, and mud-daubed chimneys sent up their spirals of smoke, signs of civilization in its most elementary form. Corn and cotton fields grew like widening bald spots on the landscape, and before long, settler voices were raised in loud supplications for salvation in camp meetings and log churches. The people settled down for at least a year of physical adaptation to chills, fevers and other regional maladies which were sure to thin the ranks of newcomers.

Westward the People

For some people the venture westward served no other purpose than to fill an early grave, yet a remarkably large number of people escaped so gloomy a fate. The census-taker recorded an astounding fermentation in each of the three succeeding decades, 1810–1840. At the turn of the century Mississippi had a scattered population of 8,850 people, but the end of the decade, 1840, found the region to contain 375,651 souls who had withstood the chills, fevers and epidemic diseases. These people had come from almost all the older southern states and most of the countries of western Europe. Mother Virginia had fed into the great valley stream 40,777 persons, who had joined 27,439 Tennesseans on their way to the new cotton country. North Carolina had sent 17,000 and South Carolina 27,908 immigrants. This new country was a fecund land; 140,885 persons could claim it as their birthplace. Across the eastern border, Alabama's population had grown from 10,000 in 1810 to almost 600,000 in 1840, and the places of their origin were practically the same as those of the people who settled in Mississippi.

Sandy loam soil in the pine-studded country was easy to cultivate, and rich bottom lands that had widened their borders with long years of accretion and natural composting were answers to dreams of migrating farmers. Many a weary traveler from the sandy lands of the Carolinas dropped to his knees in a pleasant vale in Mississippi, scraped the heavy leaf mould aside and dug madly into the soil to determine the depth of its brown loam. Acres that rolled out before the eyes of wandering households were reckoned in terms of bales of cotton and bushels of bottom land corn. A grove of oaks billowing in the breeze on a knoll above a good spring of water which bubbled up clear and cold from a bed of white sand became a dream of a home site. Miles of pine forests interspersed with hardwoods, rolling hills, and freshwater streams looked just like the country back home to that vast throng of seaboard southerners who moved inland. There was the same fresh spring water, plentiful pine knots to start quick fires, sluggish creeks, aromatic pines, blackberry thickets, muscadine vines, hickory nuts, sassafras bushes, pounding rainstorms, sharp twisting gusts of coastal winds and blinding flashes of lightning with their deafening afterclaps of thunder, hot weather, mosquitoes, swarming black gnats—all those things which were a part of the southern countryman's natural environment.

While yeoman farmers pushed forward in search of lands, the more prosperous farmers and slaveholders went forth to search the river banks for suitable plantations and cotton landings. They, no less than their little farmer neighbors, asked of the country good land, ready access to water transportation, and a living environment to which they could make the easiest adjustment. It was not unusual for overseers and slaves to go ahead and establish farmsteads a year or two in advance of a family's appearance in the new country. Like the morning sun, they lifted the fog of the unbroken wilderness, built houses and barns, prepared garden plots, condi-

tioned the livestock, and even built mansion houses, so that the act of pioneering was made less strenuous for masters, and their women folk and children.

Rather generally, the Negro slave was a good frontiersman. He withstood the hardships of the country with less wear and tear than did his
master, and he had some natural affinity for the woods. There were not
enough slaves on the continent in the first half of the nineteenth century to
bring the billion-and-a-half acres of southern lands fully under the plow.
For this reason the southern frontier was a seller's market for slaves.
When the degree of practicality of slave labor came under serious question in Virginia and Kentucky, owners found it profitable to sell them
South. So prevalent did this practice become that in Kentucky the threat
of "behave or be sold South" kept wilful slaves in check. When Kentuckians who moved down the river to buy rich cotton lands in the Mississippi Delta went home to purchase the surplus and unprofitable slaves, they
told kinsmen and old neighbors of the fruitful opportunities in the fabulously rich down-river country. Within a remarkably short time, big
cotton planters had pushed up islands of plantation country in a sea of
forest and of modest farms. Side by side the two groups labored to develop a stratified society and to conquer the great backwoods.

Alert immigrants learned that the rich prairie lands spilling over into
Mississippi from Alabama's black belt could be brought into cultivation
with a minimum effort and that returns would be highly rewarding. Along
the Tombigbee, the Black Warrior, the Alabama, Tallapoosa, Pearl,
Noxubee and Coosa, bottom lands became a pattern of sprawling plantations which spread back from the stream banks with their slave economy.
In the Mississippi and Yazoo delta, and eastward in the big winding bend
of the Tennessee, other plantation owners founded a new economy. River
bottoms grew white with cotton and heavy with corn. The fall nights
were loud with the melancholy moaning of steamboats gliding up to
sandbank landings to receive the reward of the land. The bluffs at Natchez
and Walnut Hills, with the surrounding loess country, saw the same
economy develop. Steamboats that were only experimental machines
twenty years before now hastened downstream with rows of cotton bales
banked up to their pilot houses and smokestacks.

Although the history of slavery in the new Gulf States is a complete
story in itself, it has an important bearing on the frontier. Not only did the
institution aid in the conquest of the wilderness; it likewise affected the
general social structure of the region. After 1820 the interstate slave trade
became an important economic factor. Slaves were brought into the new
Gulf coastal states by the thousands. Soon the music of the period reflected this involuntary hegira in such nostalgic songs as "Carry Me Back
to Ol' Virginny," "My Darling Nellie Grey," and, subsequently, "My

Old Kentucky Home." All of these were essentially laments of the slaves in an expanding cotton belt.

The movement of slaves onto the frontier was reflected more tangibly in the increased slave population of the region. Characteristic of the region was the phenomenal increase in Alabama from 21,780 slaves in 1820 to 127,360 in 1840. Between these dates, slaves constituted 32 to 42.9 per cent of the population. Generally in the Gulf coastal region there was an annual increase of 18 per cent during these same decades. It was this aspect of southern frontier expansion and population increase that was to become so important in the creation of a regional consciousness and a particular economic pattern.

These frontiersmen who turned vast stretches of sand hills and river bottoms into communities, towns, counties and states shared common heritages and folk mores. Methodist, Baptist and Presbyterian ministers wandered through the forests to organize congregations and to found churches. Circuit-riding Methodists were as diligent in searching out the unsaved as they were vigorous in describing the wrath of God to come. Baptist ministers were often resident watchdogs who preached without pay and reached the pulpit after they had received from heaven a vision and a call to preach. As with the ministers who had earlier stormed the ramparts of sin at Cane Ridge, picturesqueness of description, a steadfastness to what was very often self-contrived doctrine, and a persistence of faith rather than education were their trustworthy weapons of attack. Presbyterians were faced with the same challenges as their more militant colleagues, but they were somewhat more disciplined in their approaches. The saga of the eccentric Lorenzo Dow, who raised his voice for the Lord and Methodism wherever there were hearers to listen, and whose other activities were fantastic, is characteristic of much of the religious history in the southern backwoods Mississippi Territory.

Concentric circles of kinship related virtually everybody in many areas of the southern frontier, if not by blood, then for "old time's sake." As was true on the older frontier to the north, neighbor helped neighbor in the burdensome tasks of house-raising, logrolling, and harvesting. Families worked together as units, and not infrequently children later married and settled down on the surplus lands about the homesites to help found a patriarchy. Fathers frequently became patriarchs, wise by the effortless accumulation of age if not in innate wisdom. Mothers became repositories of folk remedies, family sentimentalities, and the arts of cooking. Thus it was that the common heritage of the frontier fused into a vast regional consciousness—possibly the most pronounced blend of folk characteristics in American civilization.

The frontier influence lingered in many places in the South longer than in other regions that saw a tide of civilization flow over them. The vast land mass was so overwhelming and the isolative forces so impenetrable that the so-called "cutting edge" was not a wide bar that thrust forward with a definable swath; rather it was a vast stamping process which crushed the more rugged environmental conditions underfoot with such slowness and thoroughness that many decades were required to complete the task. Rowdiness, a hot temper, cocksureness in personal prowess and politics, self-consciousness of backwardness, and illiteracy were all elements of the southern viewpoint. A stern Protestant conscience was no bar to excesses when temptation came in the form of liquor, cards, cockfights, horse racing, and feminine wiles.

The great void of isolation tended to focus the individual's attention upon himself, and personal honor and dignity were matters of great moment. To besmirch a man's honor was an act which called for an accounting if the offended was to enjoy the full esteem of his friends. Thus it was that fighting was a natural element of every public gathering and the substance of a long docket in the magistrate's court. Hot-headedness no doubt was an hereditary characteristic of much of the southern population, but self-consciousness of one's dignity and importance was a factor that thrived on frontier conditions. The southern frontier was the only place in the whole westward movement where there existed a pronounced vertical society. Slaveholders, yeoman farmers and backwoodsmen alike approached the wilderness in their own particular manner. To a large extent historians have laid error upon error in treating most of the so-called "poor whites" as people inferior to their more materialistic planter neighbors. Unfortunately this large segment of frontiersmen have been judged quantitatively against a backdrop of slavery and cotton-belt aristocracy. What came to be considered a slovenly and backward development of the southern whites was the frontier process working normally within an overwhelming land mass, while the "big" plantation cotton economy tackled the job in the more accessible areas. This latter system developed an artificially stimulated culture and economy which in the long range of frontier history was far less significant than that of the plain people.

The Dynamic Frontier

In the Northwest the older process of pioneering was moving forward as a continuous story of American expansion. A restless flood of immigrants was crowding westward. From Kentucky and Tennessee, frontiersmen who had been on the road since the first migration beyond the mountains began were seasoned to backwoods conditions. The act of severance from an older and more permanently established society held for them little dread or danger of frustrating homesickness. They well knew the carefree art of pulling up stakes and setting out for new and strange country. Characteristic of this moving population was the story of Squire Ezekiel Hogan who had moved from Virginia to western North Carolina and then on to Tennessee. On the way he said he had thrown away a "sight of plunder" and still had enough left for a respectable sale when he was ready to move on to Missouri. He informed his neighbors that:

> THE SUBSCRIBER WILL repose for sail AT MY HOUSE, ALL HIS FURNITURE TO WITT: a two whele cart a yoke of stiers one cretur two bedstids a wonnut cubbered one crib of korn a flok of gooses two skillets and a oving with a broken leg seven cheers a yanky clock 4 emty barls 1 ches press one rifel two shot guns ditto the old oman's spinnin' whele and other truk to numerous to particularize.

Along the earlier frontier one generation had cleared away the trees. At least one generation had worn out the stumps on the frontier. Down the rivers pitched their clumsy flatboats loaded with families, household goods, farm implements and even animals. On the Kentucky, the Licking, the Tennessee, the Cumberland, the Green and the Barren they set out to search for new but ever-fleeting opportunities. Their packhorses and cumbersome covered wagons clattered overland through the forest in the search of new and magical settlements. From a meager cabin home nestled on a knoll beside a spring branch in Hardin County, Kentucky, the Lincolns crossed the Ohio to Gentryville, Indiana. Slightly to the south of them but almost on the same geological ridge, the Davis family heard the siren call of the fertile new cotton belt in Mississippi and moved away in an opposite direction, but to the frontier nonetheless.

Up the Ohio, the big migration was under way. The Indians had been driven back from the great river, and eager families could set forth down stream with only snags, currents, boatwreckers, landsharpers and malaria to disturb them. Some came in fancy arks with boxes secured amidship as living quarters and dry storage. Smoking fires built on mounds of dirt served as cooking places and temporary hearthstones and sources of heat to break the brisk chill of the damp river air.

Boatmakers, both honest craftsmen and rascals, plied a rich trade at the head of navigation. Immigrants, after struggling with the problems of bad roads to Pittsburgh, chose to take the easy route by river the rest of the way to that undesignated place in the West where they were to found new homes. For a small amount of money a leaky raft could be purchased. For a larger sum, and with more care and selection, a better ark or broadhorn could be had which would insure a dry journey. In some instances, its precious lumber could be used to build a new home. With an unruly steering oar in one hand and a copy of Zadoc Cramer's *The Navigator* or Cuming's *Western Pilot* in the other, immigrants set off on voyages of great national adventure. As they drifted along studying their elementary navigational guides, this new wave of pioneers could spot the landmarks of their pioneering predecessors. At Blennerhassett's Island the guidebooks described the part the island had played in the Burr conspiracy. At the mouth of the Kanawha the Logan-Cresap affair was reviewed, and downstream on the right was the mouth of the Scioto, just ninety miles below the capital city of Columbus in Ohio. At any of the numerous mouths of streams the traveler could change his course and go inland. Up the Scioto there were still rich farm lands which beckoned; up the Muskingum the traveler could join those settlers who had come westward by boat or overland around the lake. All the way downstream it was possible to join in that stream of newcomers who were crossing over from Kentucky and Tennessee to populate the Indiana, Illinois and Missouri territories south of the 38th parallel.

A technological factor less sensational than either the steamboat or the cotton gin was the common wagon. It had been in existence for a long period, but its period of most practical early use was contemporary with the two other new machines. As settlements increased, roads were opened and it became possible to use wheeled vehicles. The first settlement of Kentucky, Tennessee and Ohio was accomplished largely by use of the pack horse and the flatboat. There was almost no significant use of wagons, carts and carriages, and it was not until state governments were organized in these territories that effective public attention was given to roads. With the second phase of settlement, however, the wagon became a basic vehicle of westward expansion. In an earlier chapter there was a discussion of the use of wagons by Braddock and Forbes in western Virginia and Pennsylvania, but these wagons had come from the more densely populated farming communities of eastern Virginia and Pennsylvania, and the roads over which they were hauled were cut as a part of military expediency, not because of settlement and inland commerce.

Before the wagon could be used with any satisfaction, the numerous pioneer trails had to be widened, bridges and ferries established, and state legislatures created. In the middle of the eighteenth century the Conestoga wagon was introduced in the country around Lancaster, Pennsylvania. It was a heavy and clumsy vehicle with wide tires, massive running gears, and box bodies which sloped down from either end to prevent the loss of cargo on hilly roads. Traditionally the gears of these wagons were painted blue and the boxes red with scenic panels on the sides. Flexible wood staves were bowed across to support canvas coverings, which in turn were pulled tight with drawstrings front and rear. After 1800, settlers moved into new country with wagons and carts. The boats floating down stream were laden with these vehicles. In many instances it was possible to drive through the forest during dry seasons and to ford streams without benefit of roads and bridges.

The advent of the wagon was a necessity before the agricultural frontier could make any material advancement. Only a limited number of settlers at best could secure ready access to streamside farms and the easy transport of their products. Not only did the wagon speed up folk and crop movement, but the manufacture of these vehicles created a new frontier industry. Many towns had their wagon works, and it was not at all unusual for country blacksmiths to make wagons on the side.

Along with the wagon came the carriage and the stagecoach. The latter was a commercial carrier which transported paying passengers and at the same time created a demand for taverns. In time, wagon camps and stagecoach taverns grew into well-known landmarks. Travel accounts of the period devote considerable space to describing both stagecoach travel and life in the taverns. Slowmoving stagecoaches were great leveling instruments. Foreigners who came to see American democracy at work most often got monstrous doses of it in crowded carriages which almost jostled the passengers to death. Distinguished visitor and greenhorn backwoodsman alike shared a common board at mealtimes and battled the same cold and bedbugs on pallet beds on tavern floors. But the important thing was not the immediate comfort of the traveler nor the speed of the freight wagons, but rather the certain promise of improved transportation facilities in the future.

Steamboats plied all the western streams wherever there was water enough to float them. Some reckless pilots said they asked only for heavy dews to speed them on their way across country. Lower decks of these vessels were crammed with freight: animals, wagons, plowtools, furniture, and household plunder in general, millstones, stocks of peddlers' goods, clocks, gadgets, and even coffins. Settler, merchant, Yankee speculator, land hunter, preacher, European traveler and government official all were going westward. As Robert Baird wrote:

> Whilst above, in the deck cabin, there is everything that may be called human—all sorts of men and women, of all trades, from all parts of the world, of all possible manners and habits. There is the half-horse and half alligator Kentucky flatboatman, swaggering and boasting of his prowess, his rifle, and his wife. One is sawing away on his wretched old fiddle all day long; another is grinding a knife or razor; here is a party playing cards; and in yonder corner is a dance to the sound of a jew's harp; whilst few are trying to demean themselves soberly, by sitting in

silence or reading a book. But it is almost impossible—the wondrous tale and horrible Indian story they are telling; the bottle and the jug are freely circulating; and the boisterous and deafening laugh is incessantly raised, sufficient to banish every vestige of seriousness, thought and sense.

Amidst this confusion, and even in the minds of those lank and laconic men who sat astride piles of freight leaning their chins forward on long, bony, calloused hands, there worked the silent factor of the great American dream. Whether drifting down the wild current amidst snags and sand-bars, obeying the navigational instructions "to keep well over to the right shore, round the head bar of the island," or struggling overland in rickety carts and covered wagons, or rushing headlong aboard crowded and explosive steamboats, floating hells of gamblers and sharpers, everybody who claimed to be a settler dreamed of the rich lands of the West. Up the White, the Wabash, the Embarrass, the Miami, the Mississippi and hundreds of lesser streams they came. In that rich center band of Indiana Territory which stretched across from Illinois on the west to Ohio on the east, there were the outlines of almost forty counties by 1830. An exuberant contemporary author boasted that there was "not a finer district of country of the same extent in the United States. . . . Almost every part of it possessed a fine soil, covered in its natural state with heavy forest of oak, poplar, walnut, hicory, ash, sugar maple, beech, wild cherry, honey locust, coffee tree, hackberry, cucumber tree, linden, etc., etc., with dogwood, iron wood, spice bush, and other small underwood." This was the new Wabash Eden over which white men and Indians had fought on a November morn just two decades before. The land was black, rich and level, and as further proof of its desirability there were the towering forest trees. In keeping with an old frontier adage which prevailed across the timber belt, big trees meant good land.

Almost 275,000 square miles of fertile land, a staggering total of 175,000,000 acres, awaited the axe, torch and plow of the lonely settler pushing westward with herd, field and garden seeds, and family. Here in the great territory between the rivers and south of the lakes was an empire twice the size of the British Isles and almost twice as fertile. When the plow was dragged through much of the soil, it turned up black as coal dust. To eyes that had grown old staring into the red furrows of Virginia and the Carolinas this was too good to be real. After 1800, the census-takers recorded their fabulous stories of population increases in this vast northwest country. In thirty years Ohio had increased from 45,365 persons in 1800 to 937,903 in 1830, and ten years later there were 1,500,000. Where a straggling population of 5,000 held on to the fringes of Indiana in 1800, there was a comfortable backlog of 343,031 in 1830 and twice that many in 1840. In the three decades from 1810 to 1840 Illinois' population expanded from 12,282 to 476,183, and Michigan grew from 4,776 to 212,267 in the same period. Population poured into these new northwestern areas from the great feeder states of the eastern seaboard and all but prostrated the joyful contemporary statisticians by such phenomenal growth. In 1850 New York had sent 24,310 people to Indiana, 133,756 to Michigan, 83,975 to Ohio, and 67,180 to Illinois. In the same years Virginia fed over the mountains 24,756 to Illinois, 85,975 to Ohio, 1,504 to Michigan, and 41,819 to Indiana. The New England states emptied their towns into Michigan, Indiana and Illinois.

In this period older frontier states such as Kentucky and Tennessee were feeding immigrants both into the West and the South. The fatuous term "native son" actually had little meaning in most of the new states where more than two-thirds of the population was born elsewhere. That these new states were agrarian is attested to by the fact that in four of the northwestern states alone, approximately a quarter of a million individual farming units were in operation in 1840, and the income from farm produce formed a strong backbone of both regional and national economics.

Moving westward, people of various sectional and social backgrounds were fused into populations with distinctive personalities. Buckeyes, Hoosiers, Suckers, Wolverines, Half-horse-half-alligators, Red horses, Crackers, Sandhillers, and Yankees became familiar names to describe people undergoing certain environmental changes on the frontier.

Possibly no one knows the specific origin of the term Hoosier, but no one informed in frontier history is in any doubt as to its earlier implications. In the humorous folk literature, the Hoosier turned up in New Orleans aboard a flatboat loaded with corn and bacon, speaking in a high sharp nasal voice that at once bespoke social naivete, but no less sharpness in a trade. He had a wry and unpredictable sense of humor and a literalness of reaction that was constantly astonishing. Dressed in nondescript backwoods clothes of crude home manufacture, he was an agent of frontier advancement and trade. Somewhat indicative of the popular concept of the Hoosier and his backwoods condition was the Hoosier's reply when he first heard the Scripture's account of Lot's wife turning to a pillar of salt outside the wicked cities of Sodom and Gomorrah. "Had that happened to her in Indiana," said the greenhorn, "the cows would have licked her up before sundown."

The Suckers fared little better in contemporary literature which described the earlier citizens of Illinois as ignorant and naive. So it was with other people advancing in the vanguard of the frontier directly westward across the thick belt of the continent. In the social structure of these venturers there was little if any fundamental difference from that already described in a former chapter.

Characteristic of the comments on population expansion were the views of the Reverend Robert Baird. The fact that various streams of Europeans and of Americans from all sections flowed into the western country and created the new American settler, speaking the English language, adjusting Old World and eastern conditions, and in general increasing the population of the frontier, he found exciting. Baird wrote:

> In traveling over the West, I have been struck with a fact which is somewhat remarkable. It is the manner in which the country has been colonized. The emigration of the Valley of the Mississippi seems to have gone on in columns, moving from East almost due West, from the respective states from which they originated. From New England the emigrating column advanced through New York, peopling the middle and western parts of that state in its progress; but still continuing, it reached the northern part of Ohio, then Indiana, and finally Illinois.

He then described the advance of the middle and southern columns of population movement as they advanced from Pennsylvania, Virginia, and the Carolinas. Baird believed the pattern of migration was the best key to the diversities of customs of the frontier. If one knew an emigrant's social background east of the mountains, he could pretty well predict the type of society he would create west of the mountains.

In terms no doubt too general, the literary preacher undertook to identify definite characteristics of each sectional group. New Englanders were assumed to be intelligent, industrious, economical, enterprising, moral, and fond of institutions for the promotion of knowledge and religion. The Pennsylvania mixture of Germans, Scots–Irish partook of all the virtues and failings of their old and new world backgrounds, while southerners were distinguished for their highmindedness, generosity, liberality, hospitality, indolences, and "too often dissipation." He did add that "the southern character, however, is a noble one, when moulded by good influences."

Families that moved with the frontier made their own social patterns as they went. Backwoods towns, churches and schools gave some distinct cultural tones to the communities, while courthouses and jails, village groggeries (euphemistically called groceries), political speakings, militia musters, square dances, house-raisings and logrollings left a more indelible imprint on social life. Fundamentally there was little difference, North or South, in the actual social structures of the communities. Everywhere the problems were those of wresting cleared land from the towering forests, breaking the rough virgin soil, building county site towns, erecting water-mills and tiny factories, and opening seminavigable streams to flatboat and steamboat travel. Whether one planted corn, cotton, hemp, tobacco or wheat, the economic problems were much the same.

With great monotony contemporary literature of the frontier tells the doleful story of the uncertainty of health. Malaria, typhoid, smallpox, cholera, amoebic infections, and tuberculosis took their regular toll. The frontiersman was convinced that the rotting mold on the forest floor, the miasma from swampy bayous and bogs, and the presence of certain plants all caused sickness. Milk sickness was frightening across Ohio, Indiana and Illinois. One of the most famous victims of this illness was the illiterate backwoods woman Nancy Hanks, mother of Abraham Lincoln. Pioneers believed rightly that this disease, which manifested itself in sweating, clammy skin, intermittent temperatures, cramps, and other symptoms of poisoning, came from some plant. Not until this century was the true source of this frontier scourge scientifically determined. Two weeds, rayless goldenrod and snakeroot, are the principal sources for tremetol, a poisonous substance. With a half score of medical books, some of which resorted to botany, folklore and sorcery, such as the one by Dr. Peter Smith, *The Indian Doctor's Dispensary*, and that fantastic publication by Dr. Richard Carter, *Valuable Medical Prescriptions for the Cure of All Nervous and Putrid Disorders*, published in Versailles, Kentucky, 1815, the pioneers had to rely largely upon their own inadequate medical resources.

Steamboats coming upstream with hundreds of passengers from Europe, the West Indies and New Orleans always threatened the health of people inland. Because of the constant contact with a seagoing commerce, New Orleans was regarded not only as a great commercial city, but likewise as a source of the deadly scourges that swept upstream at regular intervals in the summer seasons. Yellow fever was a constant seasonal threat, but possibly the most dreaded disease of all was Asiatic cholera. The year 1833 became famous as a season of deadly plague. River towns from New Orleans to St. Louis and Pittsburgh were stricken with the disease. In Kentucky, especially, the epidemic all but depopulated some of the towns. A water-borne disease, it thrived in communities where the water supply was contaminated and other sanitary facilities were primitive. Elsewhere along the frontier hundreds of people fell victims to the cholera's deadly attack. Doctors, no matter what their training, were helpless to combat it. Other than the surface symptoms they knew nothing of its true nature, nothing of sanitation, and nothing of the proper methods of treatment. Most of them fell back on the two stock reliances of their profession, bleeding and heavy dosages of calomel.

Life, of course, was uncertain on the frontier. However, it was a timid soul indeed who held back because he was afraid to take his chances in the new land. A surprisingly large number did escape death from accidents and epidemic diseases. Everywhere the contemporary travelers turned in the Northwest, they found people either prospering or poised ready to enjoy the fruits of the land. Where the forests were largely unbroken by settlement, there was an astounding amount of game: passenger pigeons, turkeys, ducks, geese, bear, deer, elk, squirrels, and rabbits. Land produced corn in vast quantities and other field crops in like proportions. Proof of the fertility of the soil was to be seen in the river commerce. Timothy Flint described the procession to market of the farmers and manufacturers from the new states. Kentuckians, Ohioans, Indianians, Missourians and "Suckers" from Illinois were to be seen in the huge fleets of flatboats that rode the currents southward. At the famous New Madrid eddy, Flint saw flatboats from almost every settled point on the Ohio and Mississippi and their tributaries. There were Kentuckians with hemp, tobacco, grain, meats, whisky and cloth from their farms. Ohioans came with farm produce and manufactured Yankee notions, produce from Indiana, cattle, horses, grain and meat from Missouri and Illinois. "Some boats," wrote the minister-observer, "are loaded with corn in the ear and in bulk; others with barrels of apples and potatoes. Some have loads of cider and what they call cider royal, or cider that has been strengthened by boiling and freezing. There are dried fruits, every kind of spirits manufactured in these regions, and in short, the products of the ingenuity and agriculture of the whole upper country of the West. They have come from regions thousands of miles apart. They have floated to a common point of union. The surfaces of the boats cover some acres." Added to the hubbub of farmers' boats on their way to market were merchants' boats loaded with Yankee notions, and settlers drifting down to the Mississippi before they turned their faces northward to western Illinois and Missouri. The whole scene was one of ceaseless activity. Across the older settlements spread the news of the amount of corn and wheat produced on an acre, of the color and texture of the soil, of the availability of land, and of the freedom which was promised in the new country.

No population booms in this nation's history received more publicity than did this era of frontier expansion after 1815. Travelers from abroad and along the eastern seaboard came to view the process, the Yankees and seaboard travelers to do missionary work, to look for markets for their goods, and to find new homes; the foreigners to view the operation of American democracy in its greatest moment of flux, to see the natural sights, to ride the steamboats, to ask thousands of inane questions, to find land for prospective emigrants, and to compare the raw American frontier civilization unfavorably with that of Old England and Europe. These visitors have left behind a vast and variegated record of fact, gross mis-representation, exaggeration of what they saw, and overdrawn accounts of their experiences. Some wrote understandingly and truthfully of the scene before them, appreciating the fact that what they saw and ex-perienced was only a beginning, not the maturity, of a fresh spread of American society. Others were unable to see the promise of the land and the people because they blinded themselves with invidious comparisons. This might even be said of Mrs. Frances Trollope who established herself in business in Cincinnati, but her background of experience was hardly suited for a proper understanding in all cases of what she saw. Possibly the more objective were those visitors who, like Timothy Flint and Morris Birkbeck, spent considerable time in the new country. Guidebook editors presented much objective material in the form of statistics, but their textual matter was often too favorable to be wholly dependable.

The democratic process on this part of the frontier was to be seen in almost every aspect of human relationships. Noticeable was the fact that the deeper the Americans penetrated into the continent the less apt they were to tolerate any significant amount of immediate social stratification. Human relationships were gauged in terms of immediate personal needs, and a man was not only ready but obligated by community custom to assist his neighbor along no matter who he was. Poverty was a matter of the moment for many people; the land held out the same promise to every-body for the future. Competition for wealth would grow with the eco-nomic refinements of permanent settlement. False modesty was left be-hind with the discarded furniture and the property accumulations which came with sedentary life in older communities. More sophisticated and dis-criminating travelers often commented on men and women undressing be-fore each other in the same room, on strangers of mixed sexes conversing with each other while still abed, and on small bedrooms crowded with sleepers of both sexes. All of this occurred without any appreciable amount of promiscuity. The informalities of political campaigning, militia musters, and the holding of courts intrigued visitors who were used to the fancy-uniformed and bewigged dignity of foreign military men and judges. In fact the whole process of social organization was geared to the needs of the moment and place. All in all the most noticeable characteristic of this restless throng of people moving on with the receding frontier was the self-inspired sense of destiny. Most frontiersmen regarded the present moment as a necessary interval of time passage; certainly they looked little to the past. They were agents of the future who built houses, farms, towns, counties, states and personal fortunes.

Michigan and Missouri

One segment of the frontier population varied somewhat from the general pattern presented above. While emigrants from the older southern states predominated in the flow of population into the West and Southwest, the New England and Middle Atlantic states supplied immigrants to the Michigan Territory. Six New England states, with New York and Pennsylvania, sent 174,131 persons to this area out of a total population of 395,071 in 1850. In several ways Michigan proved a distinct innovation in westward expansion. Its pioneer population, except for the small portion of the old French element, was almost completely homogeneous, and there was little or no regional fusion as in Ohio, Indiana, Illinois and Missouri. The New England cultural pattern was now spread out to an area where it had more geographical freedom of expansion than ever before in its history.

Michigan lay at the western edge of the territory which was to feel the greatest effects of the Erie Canal. Commerce in the Ohio and Mississippi basins was directed southward by the natural force of river currents, but with the opening of the important New York canal in 1825, the commerce of the Great Lakes region was to be given an easterly direction—a fact that was to become of major importance in determining sectional differences within the next three decades. Because of this water access to market, in which both steamboats and horse-drawn barges overcame the handicap of single directional river currents, the marketing of produce from along the Great Lakes became a much more certain thing than it had been in many areas of the earlier frontier. Added to this was the influential fact that the Erie Canal could deliver farm produce into the eastern market, where prices were high and the market far more stable than in the lower Mississippi River markets. Opening of the Chicago Road across Michigan insured additional access to market and hastened the inland penetration of the Territory. A major portion of the Michigan country was heavily wooded, and for the first time the woods were to be exploited by the commercial lumbering business. After 1850 this became an important industry. One authority estimated that there were nine times as many varieties of trees in Michigan as in Britain, and the Michigan varieties were infinitely more productive of lumber.

This movement of New Englanders and New Yorkers into Michigan Territory was not composed of adventurers, hunters, and shiftless cattle grazers. Only in the early French and trader phases of early Michigan pioneer history were such folk sharers in the story of the Great Lakes frontier. The people who finally got down to the business of settling in this area were small, middle-class farmers and merchants, already steeped in a tradition of thriftiness and domestic order. They came looking for land for use in the immediate present, and for their future progeny. Wide stretches of forest were challenges to their industry rather than barriers against neighbors. They had a fondness for village life and the institutions which thrived in a more populous community. New Englanders imported the Congregational Church, while New Yorkers brought the Baptist faith with them.

The relatively young population was absorbed in a common mission of exploitation of well-distributed economic opportunities, and it developed a harmonious society. Generally this was the first time the traditionally and geographically limited New England society had an opportunity to expand in a region where resources were so abundant and where the natural restrictions were not so burdensome. While older communities elsewhere on the frontier struggled with even the most elementary problems of society, this wave of immigration brought with it an impetus to establish schools, colleges and newspapers. From the number of newspapers that began publication rather early after settlement, it would seem that the immigrant to this part of the frontier was not ready to sever himself from the rest of the world. In many other areas, sprawling counties characterized the spread of local government; but along the Lakes the tightly organized township system moulded communities into units in which a more intimate and concerned point of view towards government found ready means of expression. Likewise this device of local government promoted an orderly progress across the Territory. This was evident in 1848 when the great wave of immigration from overseas swept over the frontier. By that time Michigan was so well integrated that much of this influx was forced to jump over into Illinois, Iowa and Wisconsin.

One other region in the widely arcing crescent was to experience a surging tide of settlement in the postwar decade. Even before the outbreak of the war Missouri lands had become extremely popular in some quarters. Advertisements which appeared early in the century in many frontier newspapers made this area sound tremendously exciting. For the adventurous hunter and woodsman there was challenge in the virgin lands beyond the Mississippi where one could either follow the Missouri northwestward or the sprawling oak-forested lands westward. It was ideally suited for expansion of the kind of social and economic system which had conquered the woods of Kentucky and Tennessee and was then bringing to the plow the fields of Indiana. Virginia, the Carolinas, Kentucky and Tennessee drained many of their communities into the new country. Kentucky alone had sent approximately seventy thousand people across the river by 1850, including Daniel Boone, who found an opportunity to start all over in a sparsely settled country and to correct some of the mistakes he had made earlier by allowing the orderly processes of government and the wiles of landsharks to confuse and rob him. Kit Carson's family moved from Madison County to Boone's Lick. Virginia contributed many of her sons, among them William Clark and Moses Austin.

Austin went out to Missouri to develop lead mining. Since early boyhood he had been interested in the lead and pewter business, and during the American Revolution he was associated with the working of the famous Chiswell mines in western Virginia which had been promoted by a group of colonial tidewater gentlemen. In Missouri, Austin acquired possession of a league of land about the Mine à Burton near the town of Potosi. Here he labored for several years in developing the old French industry.

Missouri pioneers, aside from the original French settlers, followed the older patterns of the frontier. Some fathers, it was said, advised their sons to stay at least fifty miles ahead of courthouses and lawyers if they were to be completely happy. Families came, their worldly goods stowed aboard wagons which suited their fancies, and built cabins in scattering farms and clearings. This migrating population was definitely of the yeoman class, but it lacked the orderly institutional seasoning and background of those New England pioneers who settled Michigan. Most of the Missouri immigrants had little or no fear of severing themselves from the outside or of moving beyond the influence of established institutions. Churches were as informal as those of Kentucky and Tennessee. Speech was of the same sloven and backwoodsy character as in the older communities. Travelers among them found numerous colorful social curiosities to enliven their accounts.

Even lawyers who traveled the circuits found life primitive and exciting. An unnamed Missouri lawyer has left a revealing diary of his experiences on the early circuit. Coming from the East, he settled in Gasconade County, just south of the Missouri River in the central part of the state. He brought with him a toothbrush, and when he went to a public well to use it, the natives stood around and gazed on in awe. The judgment of the crowd, as expressed by one of the bolder spectators, was: "Well! Well! I've seed a power of strange things in this world, but I never before seed a man scrubbing his teeth." Certainly not all Missourians were so green, but they were in many instances isolated people who had moved through two layers of the great western wilderness! They had enjoyed no opportunity to form associations with the more sophisticated society of the eastern seaboard.

A Backwoods Pattern

By the time Indiana, Illinois, Missouri and Michigan were ready to be admitted into the Union, a clearcut type of western American backwoodsman had developed. His social habits were often those of an arrested civilization fully two generations removed. Except in more favorable situations, education had made little headway in refining the individual settler. Behavior oftentimes was uncouth and bold, and human differences, however slight, were resolved by the rule of bare knuckle and thumb in fights and brawls. Religion was as vigorous an expression as it had ever been on the frontier. Sin bore a powerful stamp of ministerial disapproval, but people were little deterred from its commission. This part of the frontier was to produce at least four colorful ministers in John M. Peck, J. A. Axley, Timothy Flint and Peter Cartwright. Peck and Flint were temperate missionaries, with Peck working tirelessly for his people. Axley and Cartwright were militant Methodist circuit riders who made the western woods ring with furious attacks on the devil, and Baptists and their work. Camp meetings, love feasts, quarterly meetings and associational meetings often turned into emotional frenzies.

Law enforcement was by rule of impulsive reason on the part of illiterate justices of the peace. Even the higher courts often ruled by what appeared to be the law rather than by the strict prescriptions of the statutes. Lawyers practicing before frontier courts had to be good psychologists. Not only did they have to appraise their opposing council, but judge and jury likewise. Many a favorable decision went to an attorney, not because he had law and justice on his side, but because he could explain his points in the clearest everyday terms. A lawyer who could reduce legal terminology and points of evidence to simple terminology had a tremendously valuable asset. Lacking this ability, he still had an important weapon in thunderous oratory with which he swept his hearers away from the case at issue and focused their attention on the great truths of God, home and country.

A classic case of the timidity with which judges sometimes approached the sentencing of criminals who had politically important family connections is one described by Governor Thomas Ford in his *History of Illinois*. A man named Green was before the court on trial for murder, and the jury found him guilty. The judge, wishing to tread gingerly on the toes of the Green family, called the prisoner before him and said: "Mr. Green, the jury in their verdict say you are guilty of murder, and the law says you are to be hung. Now I want you and all your people down on Indian Creek to know that it is not I who condemns you, but it is the jury and the law. Mr. Green, the law allows you time for preparation, and so the court wants to know what time you would like to be hung?" The prisoner nonchalantly replied: "May it please the court, I am ready at any time; those who kill the body have no power to kill the soul; my preparation is made, and I am ready to suffer any time the court may appoint." After searching the almanac to make sure he did not set a hanging date on Sunday, the judge gave the prisoner four weeks grace. The prosecuting attorney objected to the informality of the judge's approach to his duty, but the judge remonstrated, "O! Mr. Turney, Mr. Green understands the whole matter as well as if I had preached to him a month. He knows he has got to be hung this day four weeks. You understand it in that way, Mr. Green, don't you?" In laying the blame on the jury, the judge in this unusual case revealed one of the great weaknesses in law enforcement in sparse frontier communities. Men often were afraid to serve on juries because an adverse decision in a case might land them in trouble with their neighbors.

Although there was a rugged and uncouth side to the American backwoodsman as he moved over the vast landed area from the Great Lakes to the Gulf, he was actually childlike in his nature. Ruffians along the rivers and in the towns led many travelers to assume that all frontiersmen had a rough cast. Basically, the frontiersman was a hospitable individual who welcomed the arrival of a stranger and was as generous to him as conditions would permit. He would give up his place at the table, his side of the bed, and even turn his favorite horse out of the stable so that his guest might be hospitably treated. With childlike curiosity he asked endless questions, but he never intended to be impudent or offensive. His tone of voice, and his colorful language with its rich colloquialisms, was highly communicative at its best and hopelessly illiterate at its worst; but in an elementary way it added new elements to the national speech.

The frontiersman was not without a sharp native ability, but he was still so unsophisticated that peddlers and sharpers from afar could carry on a highly profitable trade with a remarkably small amount of capital goods. Peddlers of tinware, gadgets, clocks, dry goods and notions followed the restless American westward, sought out his new home, and sold him their wares at good profits. While the brethren of the Yankee peddler took to the sea and sailed to distant world harbors in search of trade, landbound Yankees in the backwoods ferreted out customers wherever they lingered long enough to build cabins. They were forerunners of the more formal salesmen of the commercial East and of future American industrial greatness.

After 1820, the "clacking" of Yankee wagons and their owners' lonesome whistling became an inseparable part of the civilization in the western woods. One observer said:

There is no part of the inhabited West that has not been visited by the Yankee clock peddler. He will find his way, with his wagon load of clocks, through a country that any one else would at once pronounce utterly impassable with a wheeled conveyance. If he finds a road already made, well and good; otherwise, he will make a road for himself. He will, without hesitation, drive into woods never before penetrated by civilized man and will find his way through without accident. He only asks whether any one is living in the country; if so, he will find him out and sell him a clock.

Jonathan Yankee drove through trackless woods, over muddy roads, or over no roads at all, and forded swollen streams as nonchalantly as his fellow New Englanders strolled the streets of Waterbury and Salem. If he were asked how he expected to get his wagon through such a country, he would reply that the road is not half as bad as some roads he had driven over. A contemporary author remarks that the Yankee peddler "was never taken by surprise—accidents never came unexpected, and strange events never disconcerted him. He would whistle *Yankee Doodle* while his horses were floundering in a quagmire and sing *Hail Columbia* while plunging into an unknown river!" His pack was loaded with calicoes, cotton checks, gingham, tin cups, iron spoons, coffee pots, spools of thread, papers of pins, cards of horn buttons, cakes of shaving soap, bolts of ribbon, pepper boxes, sausage stuffers, tablecloths, tin plates, knives and forks, "warranted pure steel" razors, neckcloths, hose, jew's harps, wax dolls, clocks and nutmeg. Packs were skillfully organized. One ingenious merchant came West with a valuable cargo of New England-made shoes compactly stowed in cast iron coffins so that he turned a neat profit on his entire shipment.

Towns

As towns and cities developed, local merchants claimed the trade which had once gone to itinerants. Along the Ohio River, Cincinnati and Louisville had grown into important trade centers. The story of business and growth in the former city was carefully recorded in periodic statistical directories. In 1812, the year that General Harrison assumed command of the western army, Cincinnati was a city of 4,000, and almost each succeeding four-year period saw that number more than doubled in each census count. In 1840, there were 46,381 people. The number and character of businesses and manufacturing plants which existed in the city sounded like a recitation of most of the needs of man in a civilized society. So important had the packing business become that in Cincinnati the new breeds of hogs were of almost as much importance as the latest styles of women's clothes. Almost the same thing was true of Louisville which grew from a riverside village of 1,300 in 1800 to a city of 21,000 in 1840, and its pattern of economic development was little different from that of its upriver neighbor.

Both Cincinnati and Louisville were to be influential in the expansion of the frontier. They were both market and supply centers. Each had full access to the rivers by steamboat, and both places were in a position to trade with the southern and western areas as they developed. Characteristic of the importance of Louisville was the removal thence of Benjamin Franklin Avery and his ten sons from Aurora, New York, in 1825, to be near the frontier market for their farm implements. They soon became prosperous manufacturers selling their plow tools wherever western and southern farmers existed. Their neighbor, the Scotch manufacturer E. C. Brinly, likewise contributed to Louisville's importance as a farm implements center.

Two other cities—New Orleans and St. Louis—were to have an immediate bearing upon westward expansion. Both were in the Louisiana Purchase, and both had an early French origin. New Orleans was blessed by being at the foot of the river system, so that nearly all river-borne trade of the Mississippi Valley either flowed into it or passed through its harbor. The city's history fell into two parts as we have seen—the French and Spanish periods up to 1803, and the American period after that date. Because each of these three national groups left indelible marks on its growth, plus the influence of the rich frontier trade that sent flatboats and steamboats down river, laden with the rich products of the upper valley country, there was an aura of romance about New Orleans which colored the history of no other city in North America in precisely the same way. By 1835 it had a population of 46,082 and had reached truly urban proportions, not only in size but also in spirit and tradition.

At the other extreme of the French settlement line on the Mississippi was St. Louis. This upriver city was in many respects like its downriver sister, but St. Louis was more isolated, less a depot for a flourishing river trade, and not in as good a position to communicate with the Old World as New Orleans. Yet this frontier city, more than its older rival Ste. Genevieve, possessed the germ of important urban growth. It became a trading center for settlers who swarmed into central Missouri, and it continued to grow as the fur capital of the West. St. Louis was the point of departure for an important segment of the American fur trade and for other types of traders who ventured up the Missouri or went directly overland to the Far West. The steamboat traffic which made New Orleans even more important as the years advanced was in time to make St. Louis a major upriver commercial center. It quickly became the most important port on the Mississippi above the confluence of the Ohio.

The significance of the town on the frontier, however, was not to lie solely with those big centers of trade which enjoyed peculiar geographical advantages. Villages which became county seats were the centers of influence in wide stretches of the country. Court and muster days, elections, speakings, patriotic celebrations and other events brought people to town to hear the news, talk politics, trade horses, buy land, attend to legal business and savor the rising impulse of expansion about them or learn the extent of the periodic economic depressions. None of these towns was large; many had less than a thousand population for the first fifty years of their existence. Like the settlers who cleared away the woods to plant settlements in the rural areas, town dwellers went through rugged preliminary stages of building log houses and cabins. Log stores, courthouses and taverns were commonplace. Travelers visiting these country towns often commented upon the poor and crowded tavern accommodations. Groceries, or doggeries, were built almost before the survey of the lots was completed, and rowdiness and drunkenness were common.

Town building was a characteristic activity of the frontier. It was the basic inspiration for many speculative ventures. The man who could secure a favorably located tract of land, lay out town lots, and manipulate the location of a courthouse and a row of log stores, was well on his way to making a modest fortune. Unfortunately for most speculators there were too many others trying to woo Lady Luck with the same intent, and it was not at all unusual for their failures to have significant bearing on the stability of frontier economic conditions. Ambitions to found towns and to speculate in real estate were the source of the unrestrained "puffing" which was so characteristic of the West.

Not all of the towns, of course, were the results of speculation. Many of them enjoyed a normal, healthy growth because the territory around them was being well-developed. However, even the most promising village got caught up in the feverish period of expansion during the years following the War of 1812. What was a settler's primitive village in 1806 had grown by 1818 into a town with numerous stores, a half-dozen manufacturing plants, schools, churches, newspapers and municipal debts. Merchants and manufacturers bet on a continuing growth for the years ahead. All the money they could find they sent east to buy goods and machinery to enrich the future. In this way much of the frontier, while enjoying a feverish speculative boom, was actually draining away so much of its negotiable capital that it was unable to stem even the most modest financial recession.

An institution that is frequently overlooked by the historian was the ragged, ill-kept, informal country store. This facility had one of its most flourishing periods on the early nineteenth-century frontier. When enough people moved into a community to justify the undertaking, an enterprising countryman bought a stock of goods and began business at a crossroads. One such famous store was Denton Offutt's, at New Salem, Illinois, in which Abraham Lincoln was once a clerk. The map of new states admitted after 1812 is dotted with places which were no more than country stores. Some of these crossroads grew into towns, many of them remained country store seats, and others disappeared. But one of the chief means through which goods were delivered into customers' hands was these stores. Once they appeared in the new communities there was little chance of trade for the Yankee peddlers and the store boats which drifted along the streams; consequently many peddlers and boat merchants themselves became country storekeepers.

The National Domain

While settlers rushed into the new country and Indian claims were silenced by one means or another, the Jeffersonian experiment with the great national domain was being given a thorough trial. The federal government had disposed of an astounding amount of land between 1789 and 1820. In terms of dollars, land sales amounted to $44,000,000. In the four years following 1815, settlers bargained for $17,000,000 worth of land, but this represented a vast credit business in which the Treasury had collected no more than half the amount of the purchase price. During this latter five-year period, land speculations were almost unbelievable. Not only did optimistic purchasers buy from the national government, but they also acquired large blocks of land from the states which offered their holdings at a fractional amount of the established federal price. States like Georgia, Alabama, Kentucky, Tennessee and Mississippi offered enormous bargains in public lands. In the sense that the Jeffersonian scheme of land sales as devised in 1800 was drawing large numbers of people onto the frontier, it was a success. Unfortunately it contained the bankrupting credit provision which stimulated both speculation and depression. The panic of 1819 badly undermined both speculator's and settler's ability to continue the purchase of lands.

Obviously the credit system was a failure so far as the yielding of revenue to the federal government was concerned. In April, 1820, Congress adopted the so-called Land Law of 1820. This act provided that the purchaser should pay $1.25 in cash instead of the old price of $2.00 per acre for land purchased at the public auctions, but he might buy as little as eighty acres. Abolition of the credit system hit the little buyer hard, even though the amount of land he had to buy was modest. The same depression that had so badly shaken the land dispersal system had likewise injured the frontier banks, and it was well-nigh impossible to obtain acceptable money. Men with money enjoyed the advantage of the new reduced prices for land. In time, settlers devised the scheme of pre-empting land claims, and neighbors banded together to protect this extralegal device. Before the last of the public domain was placed in private hands, the old pre-emption practice had become the claim club, an extralegal association of public land claimants, in the latter phases of disposing of public lands.

Utopias

Few virginal areas in the world's history have offered such an abundance of public lands and such ripeness for social experimentation as the American frontier of the first half of the nineteenth century. At least four social groups dreamed of the good life and struggled to establish it in idyllic western colonies—the Shakers, the Rappites, the Owenites and the English colonists in Illinois.

Ever since the Great Revival in 1801 the Shakers had been industriously building their "millennial" communities of solid buildings with twin doors. Organized around the teachings of Mother Ann Lee, this order embraced celibacy and resorted to a rapacious form of proselytism. They persuaded husbands and wives, most often beyond child-bearing age, orphans, immigrants, and the homeless to accept their board and shelter. When new members came into the order, their worldly possessions were turned over to the colony and their personal papers carefully filed away. Marriage vows were dissolved and parental relationships forgotten as converts became members of the common community. Shaker journals record a fabulous story of spiritual visitations. Everybody from the Hebrew fathers of old to Benjamin Franklin were said to have been present at their celebrations. Religious orgies, consisting of dances and other physical excesses, were interpreted by the outside world as lewd and lascivious, and in some instances Shakers were subjected to serious interference by their neighbors.

On the material level, Mother Lee's disciples followed a highly successful program of improved agriculture and advanced handicrafts. They produced fine, pure-bred livestock and improved field and garden seeds. They ground a superior quality meal and flour, and made good wine, furniture and iron work which were sold to the public. Although the Shakers never recruited a significant number of members, and their belief in the millenium gave them only a temporary lease on earthly hope, it was their practice of celibacy which proved their doom. In the Ohio Valley their Poland China hogs, their durable antique furniture and their sturdy buildings are the only tangible landmarks left behind. Long ago the faithful were laid to rest in unmarked graves beside their villages.

George Rapp, a Württemberg vinedresser, moved from Germany to America in 1803 and established a pietistic sect of celibates. From Pennsylvania, the Rappites moved west to the banks of the Wabash in present-day Posey County, Indiana. Beginning in 1815 this colony was successful in many of its undertakings. Its members were industrious, and, like the Shakers, they were able to extract a good return from the forest, field and workshop. One serious difficulty was the tug of adventure and independence from the land outside. Bolder members of the colony were drawn away. Another drawback was the fact that Indiana was too far removed from the main stream of arriving European immigrants to supply the necessary new recruits.

In 1824 Rapp sold his colony site to the Scotch millmaster, Robert Owen, and returned to Economy, Pennsylvania, to re-establish his organization. Robert Owen had succeeded in the textile business and had developed a marked social consciousness, an unusual trait in manufacturers of his day. He sought, in association with William Maclure, to activate a plan of social relationships that would help to effect the perfectibility of man. For two years, 1825–1827, Owen and members of the New Harmony Society attempted to organize a social community around the founder's ideas of human relationships. The colony was designed to carry on a highly diversified series of activities, which ranged from printing a newspaper, the *New Harmony Gazette*, and scientific experimentation to the performance of menial farming chores. By 1827 the project was a failure. Disappointment resulted partly from a lack of industry and common sense because of dissension within the ranks and from the seductive attractions of frontier lands. Owen's and Maclure's efforts did not go entirely for naught. New Harmony attracted to America such brilliant scientists and social philosophers as Gerard Troost, Thomas Say, Frances Wright and David Dale Owen.

West of the New Harmony Community in Illinois was the English colony organized by Morris Birkbeck and George Flower. These men were English landlords who sought to relieve the economic plight of their countrymen. In 1816 Birkbeck secured land in the prairies of southeastern Illinois and began the development of an English colony. By enthusiastic advertising, the promoters attracted many of their countrymen to the freedom of the Illinois frontier. For the newcomers, the land gave abundant promise, but the great amount of labor required to break the heavy soil of the prairies was discouraging. Unlike other communal groups this English settlement was purely economic in nature and attempted only to better the lot of Englishmen caught in the pinch of depression at home. William Cobbett, a self-exiled critic of English society and politics, attacked this western colony from the perspective of a New York farm in his famous book, *A Year's Residence in the United States of America*. His ill-founded criticism resulted in the publication of at least five other books of contemporary description. Both Flower and Birkbeck prepared extensive refutations of Cobbett's slander. Henry Bradshaw Fearon, who came to America to determine the truth for thirty-nine prospective immigrant families, published his first-hand observations in his *Sketches of America*. The Illinois colony failed as a cohesive organization, but, like New Harmony, it brought many valuable immigrants to Illinois, and the famous controversy with William Cobbett did much to publicize the prairie lands, which to date had not been attractive to woods-dwelling pioneers. Although the first half of the nineteenth century produced much social unrest in Europe, England and along the eastern seaboard in the United States, the expansive influences of the frontier were too powerful for communal societies to endure.

There have been few periods in American history so exciting as that from 1815 to 1840. No radically new social, political or economic patterns were originated, but old patterns were subjected to enormous changes and new applications. That part of the American frontier population which might be called residual took its second long step in its advance away from the eastern seaboard; its tendencies toward developing a distinctive regional character underwent a new phase in advancing maturity. Perhaps no advance was made in maturing the general condition of the common man in the frontier movement, but it was important that each year armies of yeoman settlers flocked to the region. At the same time, a strong sense of regionalism and of nationalism was being nurtured in the various geographic areas of the frontier. Not only did frontiersmen proudly proclaim themselves citizens of a new territory or state, but they also boasted with equal pride of being a part of the bigger nation. In their minds they were fulfilling their country's fundamental destiny. Evidence of this was apparent on many occasions when squatters on public lands contended that instead of violating the law they were performing a great patriotic service by making their communities more attractive to settlers.

After 1840 it is doubtful that a single fundamental change was made in the pioneering experience. This is not to say that much of the older pattern was not subjected frequently to many new and dramatic experiences and that there were not to be many mercurial thrusts in various parts of the frontier which momentarily outran the certain but plodding advance of stable settlement across the country. The steamboat and subsequently the canal and the railroad were to magnify the importance of economic intercourse among the sections. Competition of major field crops and the spread of slavery were to emphasize the lines of sectionalism and promote a superficial economic and social stratification in parts of the frontier. Involved also was the delicate question of personal morals in conflicting sectional attitudes within the expanding nation. Immediately, the admission of five new public land states between 1816 and 1820 was of the greatest political importance.

A SLAVE ON SALE AS
SKETCHED BY THE
VISITING FRENCH
ARTIST HERVIEU.
FROM FRANCES
TROLLOPE'S
*Domestic Manners
of the Americans,*
1832

ENLARGING THE POLITICAL PERIMETER

And provided also, That the further introduction of slavery or involuntary servitude be prohibited, except for the punishment of crimes, whereof the party shall be duly convicted; and that all children of slaves, born within the said state, after the admission thereof into the Union, shall be free, but may be held to service until the age of twenty-five years.

—JAMES TALLMADGE, JR., *The Tallmadge Amendment*

CHAPTER XIII

IMMEDIATELY following the War of 1812, it was clear that two new states would shortly petition Congress for admission. Indiana had defined its borders, its population was expanding rapidly, and time would quickly effect the change from Territory to statehood. Settlers entering the Territory between 1800 and 1816 boosted the population beyond the necessary sixty thousand required for admission. At the same time the Gulf coastal Mississippi Territory was undergoing a similar evolution. Much of the population in the two territories had migrated from the same areas, the marked exception being northern Indiana. Both territories were parts of the Ohio-Mississippi basin, both had been influenced by events of the war, and both were intensely agricultural. The only important difference in the latter field was the types of staple crops; Indiana's soils produced excellent grains, while Mississippi's was adaptable to cotton culture.

New States

When Indiana's petition arrived in Congress, it might have been accepted in the conventional manner and without delay had the Mississippi petition not been on the horizon as well. There was no question about the Territory's population count, and, most important of all, its boundaries were fairly regular and well-defined. Also, this Territory had benefited from being under the jurisdiction of both the laws of the Northwest Territory and of a fairly well-developed territorial political organization.

Mississippi presented a different picture. Its boundaries were most complex, and in one instance scarcely defined. Also, the Territory embraced approximately twice as much area as Indiana, which brought up locally the unhappy question of reasonable access of all the citizens to their government. Mississippi's boundaries extended from the Gulf of Mexico to the southern border of Tennessee, and from Georgia's western boundary to the Mississippi River, an area approximating 100,000 square miles.

Geographically this vast region contained several distinct sections. The Black Belt which lay diagonally across the southeastern portion was being developed as a plantation region; so was the rich Tennessee Valley in the north, and the Yazoo basin to the west. The loess country surrounding Natchez supported an old civilization which dated from the arrival of the French and Spanish in the lower Mississippi Valley. Interspersed among the fertile cotton belts were thousands of square miles of pine hills and plains.

Unfortunately, social and commercial intercourse among the various rich cotton areas, or among the hill country sections would be very difficult. Had there been close proximity and association, a division of the Territory might have been made on a purely economic basis, but no reasonable geographical pattern could be used to include an economically harmonious segment of the population. The Mississippi territorial representative, William Lattimore, proposed to Congress an east-west divisional line to run from the mouth of the Yazoo to the Georgia boundary. He spoke however, without first determining the views of his constituents. An east-to-west division proved unacceptable; so an equitable boundary running from the Gulf to the Tennessee River had to be established. In order to save Mobile for the Alabama Territory, the dividing line was begun some distance west of that city and was run northwestward to avoid serious alterations in the border counties already formed in the southern parts of both territories. About one-fourth the distance up the border between the two territories, the line turned northward to the Tennessee River.

Thus the boundary question in Mississippi delayed the organization of that State and also held up the admission of Indiana. Congress apparently wanted to consider the two petitions for statehood at approximately the same time. There is no indication, however, that conscious efforts were made to balance the sectional membership of the Union. There appears to have been far more competition and friction among the people in the different sections of the original Mississippi Territory than was manifested by congressmen and senators. Alabama settlers feared the predominance of leadership of the Mississippi River clique. At the same time there was rivalry between the Tennessee Valley population and that of the Gulf coastal area. Slavery was no more an issue at the moment in Mississippi than it had been in Kentucky and Tennessee a quarter of a century earlier.

Congress passed the Indiana enabling act on April 19, 1816, and on June 10, delegates met in a constitutional convention at Corydon. Nine days later, forty-three representatives assembled to consider the handiwork of the special drafting committee, and to sign the new constitution which was sent on to the President and Congress for final approval. In keeping with earlier frontier practices, the people of Indiana were denied the privilege of voting on the acceptance of the new constitution.

Little real glory can go to the small drafting committee which labored at Corydon. Its members gave small evidence of being gentlemen of marked imagination, or of burning zeal to devise a fundamental document filled with original and revolutionary ideas of democracy. With one exception, there was not a single fresh principle embodied in the constitution. A careful comparison of the Corydon document with other state constitutions reveals a close adherence to the clearly blazed legalistic path of former conventions, but this action differed little from what had happened in other state constitutional conventions. Essentially, the Indiana constitution followed the outline and details of the second Kentucky document. Except for changes in phraseology to serve the needs of purely local conditions, and the editing of the Kentucky sentence structure, the two documents, except for the bill of rights, were fundamentally the same. The bill of rights, for that matter, belonged to Ohio, and the essence of human rights and the avowal of general principles were distilled from the Declaration of Independence. Delegates to the convention were motivated, apparently, by two basic notions: that speedy admission of the new state was urgent; and that few or no embarrassing technicalities would be raised in Congress if two acceptable constitutions were used as patterns.

A year after the passage of the Indiana act, Congress enabled Mississippi to seek statehood. From July 7 to August 15, 1817, Mississippi delegates met in Lorenzo Dow's brick church in the village of Washington, and there with scissors, paste pot, and a copy of the current Kentucky constitution, they edited and pieced together their basic plan of government. In a state where the slave population and cotton economy were expanding phenomenally, the Mississippi delegates were satisfied to accept the Kentucky slavery clause—even to precise punctuation marks—and to insert it in their constitution with the addition of only one minor phrase. With the exception of the slavery and suffrage clauses, there was little or no fundamental difference between the Indiana and Mississippi constitutions, a fact which in itself reflected the absence of a sectional struggle over the formation of new states.

Two or three facts stand out in a comparison of these new constitutions with the earlier state documents. Kentuckians seemed to have had a marked fondness for fine phrases and pompous oratorical flights. The founding fathers of the newer states were more matter-of-fact in stating their general provisions, and they were definitely better editors. Both the Indiana and the Mississippi delegates organized their bills of rights better than the Pennsylvanians and Kentuckians. Also, the Indiana and Mississippi framers expressed more confidence in youth than did their elder neighbors.

In both of the new states, the age limits for representatives, senators, and governors were lowered to twenty-one, twenty-four, and thirty years respectively, whereas the older documents required these officials to be twenty-four, thirty, and thirty-five years of age. Hoosiers and Mississippians endeavored to give their handiwork some gloss of originality. Granted that they took provisions from the Kentucky constitution, they grounded its glorious oratorical flights, plucked the eagle feathers off its lofty sentiments, and went home to their people to enjoy the fame of statesmen.

Mississippians deviated from the popular constitutional pattern in one significant respect. In 1811, delegates to the constitutional convention in the neighboring state of Louisiana had seen fit to review their geographical limits in the light of the greater Louisiana area, and they undertook to stabilize their state's boundaries by inserting the Territory's physical description as a preamble to the constitution. Since the division of the Mississippi Territory from Alabama created a perplexing issue over the eastern boundary and there was grave danger of future misunderstandings, the constitutional delegates adopted the Louisiana idea. This practice was to be followed elsewhere, and in nearly all cases where plaguing boundary problems arose, precise geographical descriptions of boundary limitations were substituted for more idealistic preambles.

Within two years after the admission of Indiana and Mississippi, two more new states were carved out of the frontier. Illinois had accumulated sufficient population to justify a petition for statehood and admission to the Union. Like Mississippi Territory it had a disputed boundary along its northern border. Wisconsin Territory contended that its southern boundary extended to the tip of Lake Michigan, while Illinois claimed the dividing line, 42° 30'. After some maneuvering in Congress the more northerly line was established, and the Chicago area was saved for Illinois. The next year Alabama Territory was authorized to draft a constitution and to prepare for statehood. In both instances, peculiar local conditions influenced steps toward the creation of new states, but these made little real difference in the kinds of governments that were established.

The Alabama constitution contained a somewhat liberal provision for education which was absent in the Illinois document. Except for the Kentucky slavery clause which the southerners adopted verbatim, the Alabama constitution could have served the people of Illinois just as adequately as it did the southerners. There was no fundamental difference between the main structural features of the two documents; both owe a large amount of credit to their Kentucky neighbors.

In one fundamental respect, however, the four new constitutions discussed here differed from the parent Kentucky document; they made provisions for one-day elections and the secret ballot, instead of extended periods of elections and the *vive voce* method of casting votes. In making this innovation the framers of the new constitutions broke what had become a hallowed political tradition and upset both office seekers and voters.

Candidates, from the days of colonial Virginia, had found the voice voting device to their liking. Not only could they keep up with the progress of elections, but they could employ mild intimidation on wavering supporters, who, under the cover of secrecy, might have strayed away to the opposition. From some voters' points of view, doing away with the three-day election took much of the glamor and excitement out of the democratic process. Many a thirsty patriot came early to elections in the older states and stayed late during the three days of hot hustings. They came with insatiable appetites for free gingerbread and liquor, and were happy to engage in an occasional fight. They also savored strong out-pourings of oratory. These older election customs inspired George Bingham to make two of his best-known paintings.

Where Kentuckians continued both to enjoy and to regret their election day debaucheries, candidates in the newer states had to plan their campaign programs so that election results could be directed, if not controlled, in spite of the secret ballot. Election day activities had to be made intensely attractive in order to bring out the voters. Had the old-line, stump-speaking type of politician been in control of constitution-making, we may doubt that such radical reforms in the election process would have occurred.

Education had gained some attention by the 1830's, and this fact is reflected in the new constitutions. Indiana planned a full-scale educational system from the elementary grades through the university and wrote in tangible, constitutional provisions which were something more than a pious statement of high ideals. Alabama and Mississippi followed somewhat the same pattern, except that the Mississippians were more vague and idealistic in expressing their respect for learning. The Illinois founding fathers ignored the subject.

All four constitutions reflected contemporary economic needs by requiring state control of banks. Only state banks, and such branches as the general assemblies chose to create, were deemed legal in all the new states.

By 1819 the first great wave of postwar state-making ended with the admission of Alabama. Scarcely any significant differences were to be noted in the processes by which the four new states were created. Some local fears, problems, and manipulation of delegates were indicated in isolated phrases and sections, but in essence the new documents were monotonously alike. In their bills of rights, all four made identical professions of belief in the rights of man. Except for Negroes, mulattoes, and Indians, men were considered to be free. In Mississippi, the constitution made special provision for Choctaw and Chickasaw Indians to be given comparable rights with white men when they sought them. Otherwise there were no basic differences in racial attitudes.

It is not enough merely to examine the new state constitutions in order to understand the application of democracy on the frontier. The functioning of government is of even more importance than any simple statement of basic political principles. How well the constitutions were applied depended upon what bodies of statute laws were adopted and what was the quality of legislation enacted by the initial general assemblies. In Indiana and Illinois, the statute laws of the Northwest Territory, Ohio, Pennsylvania and Kentucky were adapted in whole or in part. Alabama and Mississippi adopted the old territorial laws, plus various collected state statutes. Alabama, for instance, was influenced by the work of Harry Toulmin who had made a compilation of the Kentucky statutes. Much early legislation of necessity dealt with the peculiar local needs of the various states; all of it pertained to the functioning of local government, the courts, and economic affairs. Much of it was necessary from the outset to implement the functional sections of the constitutions. Some of the early laws went beyond the specific letter of the constitutions and gave a peculiar sectional flavor to the local statutes.

Early state constitutions and their making have become important in the writing of much frontier local history. In nearly every instance, state historians have considered the drafting of the first constitutions to have been a relatively original process. Except for tracing back a few basic ideas to sources, most local writers have considered state-making independently of the general history of the frontier. Yet the whole process of forming new governments was closely interrelated despite any sectional diversities that might have existed.

State-making was fundamentally a manifestation of the expansion of the frontier population. West of the Mississippi, the flood of population continued rolling onward. Timothy Flint, busily implanting the word of God in the minds of the people, found time to describe the passing show of migration to Missouri. In that area, speculators were as greedy for land as ever. Every landgrabber appeared to believe that his day of great opportunity had arrived.

Next to yarns about Indian raiding and hunting, said Flint, the currently popular place of settlement was the subject most discussed. Between 1815 and 1820, Boone's Lick was a focal point. Two Kentucky families were represented as meeting on the St. Charles Road,

The one going to Boon's Lick and the other coming from it. They had formerly been neighbors in Kentucky. The person retreating from Missouri first questions the other, why he was leavin' Old Kentucky. The reply was, "The range is all eaten out and I am going to Boon's Lick." "Why," he asked in his turn, "are you coming away?" "Oh! the people die there,"—I used his very phrase—"like rotten sheep. They have filled one grave yard already, and have begun upon another. Turn about, and go back: after all there is nothing like old Kentuck." "I am determined however," said the immigrant, "to go on." "Well, go on, but I tell you, you will shake."

Flint had seen immigrants making their way across the ferry at St. Charles by the hundreds. "Between the second and third years of my residence in the country, the immigration from the western and southern states of this country poured in at flood stage, the power and strength of which could only be adequately conceived by persons on the spot." They came with six horse wagons, "the whole appearance of the train, the cattle with their hundred bells; the wagons, often carrying two or three tons, so loaded that the mistress and children are strolling carelessly along in a gait which enables them to keep up with the slow traveling carriage;— the whole group occupies three quarters of a mile." This milling throng of settlers, their Negro slaves moving in the vans of their trains, perhaps did not appreciate the political fermentation they were causing. They came, said Flint "with delight and expectancy in their faces." A sectional storm of which they knew nothing was soon to break over their heads, causing the aging Jefferson to say of the ensuing argument over slavery expansion, that "it came like a fire bell in the night." Since 1810, 45,741 persons had arrived in Missouri, and of this number 6,500 were slaves.

A Fire Bell in the Night

Missouri was soon ready to petition for statehood. On March 16, 1818, territorial representative John Scott presented a memorial asking that the Territory be permitted to frame a constitution. On the surface there was nothing unusual about this new petition. Alabama, a slave state, was in the process of being admitted; two years before, Mississippi had come into the Union. Missouri had every reason to believe that it would be admitted in the same way. At the same time Maine was ready to form an independent government under a constitution. Its admission seemed a certainty once it drafted a constitution because the precedent was fresh. Five new states had been admitted within the last decade.

It was not until December 18, 1818, that Congress began consideration of the Missouri Bill, presented to the House by Speaker Clay. This particular moment in American history was charged with considerable excitement. Credit was expanded and the first tremors of the great financial panic of that year were being felt.

There was some previous indication of a controversy over the Missouri Bill. The American Convention for Promoting the Abolition of Slavery had met the preceding December in Philadelphia where a petition to Congress was adopted seeking the abolition of slavery from territories which would seek statehood in the future. Hardly had the Missouri memorial arrived, when John Sergeant of Pennsylvania proposed a resolution seeking to secure a guarantee of religious liberty in future constitutions for new states.

The House went into executive session on February 18, 1819. James Tallmadge, Jr. of New York exploded a bombshell in the executive session when he proposed his famous amendment to prohibit further expansion of slavery in Missouri. He proposed freeing the children of slaves already there when they reached the age of twenty-five years. This proposal was unexpected. Except for the Philadelphia convention there had been no unusual slavery agitation at the time. The Quakers had continued their opposition to slavery and a few southerners had spoken of gradual emancipation. Tallmadge himself seems to have had nothing in his personal background that would suggest an antislavery crusade. He was of early New England extraction, but his people had migrated to New York several generations before. Tallmadge was elected to Congress from New York in 1817. He was a man of ability and marked social presence, gentle in his demeanor. He was most solicitous about political patronage, and his political activities were marked by a pronounced partisanism. Apparently his proposed amendment to the Missouri Bill was more academic than humanitarian in nature.

Possibly some politicians prior to 1819 had thought of the desirability of maintaining a balance between free and slave states, but this fact does not seem to have figured in their voting on the admission of new states. During the next two years, 1819–1821, however, the Congress was to see a sharp sectional conflict developed in the ensuing debates. The House, on the basis of a purely sectional vote, favored a part of the Tallmadge Amendment. The Senate by a less clearly defined sectional vote opposed the amendment. In February, 1820, Senator Jesse B. Thomas of Illinois proposed an amendment which would restrict the spread of slavery in the Louisiana Purchase above the boundary of 36° 30′ north latitude except in Missouri. Essentially this was the bill that was finally adopted, and the one by which Missouri was admitted to the Union. In conference it was agreed that the Maine-Missouri combination should be abandoned since

Maine had already been admitted to the Union. The state of Missouri should be admitted with the right to regulate slavery, but the Thomas amendment regarding the rest of the Louisiana Territory was to be accepted.

Missouri was admitted in 1821. Its constitution was a reasonable facsimile, if not a precise copy, of the older documents. Numerous sections and sentences were drawn directly from the great parent source, the second constitution of Kentucky, and much of the remainder came from the constitutions of Alabama, Ohio, Delaware, Pennsylvania and Illinois. Missouri had drafted its constitution the year before admission to the Union, and there seems to have been an intention on the part of the people of the Territory to operate as an independent political unit, even if statehood was denied them.

The conference agreement between the two Houses did not end the debates. Greater issues were involved: the restrictions which Congress might place on new states, and the equality of the states within the Union. In all, the actual debate on slavery was of less than three hours duration. But the ensuing public outburst reflected something more important at that time. Eli Whitney's cotton gin had converted cotton growing into a multimillion dollar industry. Slavery promised to be a profitable form of labor. In the course of debate in Congress, the southern mind revealed a changed attitude toward the antislavery charges, and the northern mind a ripening for a crusade against the institution. In assuming that slavery would eventually disappear, people in the free states had failed to appreciate its rising economic importance. The expansion of slavery into frontier areas had come so quickly and so vigorously that the country had failed to realize what was happening.

Much of the original thinking about slavery in the Louisiana Territory was as academic as that which had brought restrictions of the institution in the Northwest Territory; it had involved no vigorous crusading on the one hand, or determined defense of the institution on the other. While it is true Louisiana had been admitted as a slave state into the Union, no general policy had been established concerning slavery in the Louisiana Territory, despite the fact there were slaves in the area. The Tallmadge Amendment injected an entirely new point of view into the thinking about the creation of new states. Almost immediately the press, North and South, took up a discussion of both slavery extension and the Missouri controversy. State legislators and public speakers used it as a subject for their orations. Social reformers were attracted by the issue. Even diplomatic negotiations pending at the moment had a bearing on public opinion. This was especially true in regard to the territory involved in the newly made Adams-de Onis

Treaty. The eventual organization of Florida was discussed at some length. Northerners and southerners became clearly aware of their sectional differences, and the race to form an alliance with the expanding West was begun.

Possibly of greatest importance in the discussion of the Missouri controversy both in and out of Congress was the raising of the moral issue of slavery. Some of its opponents called it a violation of the Scriptures, a sin against humanity, and an injury to democracy. No other attack upon the institution could have generated more heat in the South than did this one. The moral attack upon slavery also involved the long-standing issue of New England opposition to the Three Fifths Compromise, an issue which had significant political implications since it had a direct bearing upon representation and taxation. One historian has said that the argument over the admission of Missouri ended an era of liberal social thought in the South. Whether or not this is true depends upon a definition of liberalism. Certainly political alignments in time were to be shaped by the issue. From 1819 on to the Civil War, frontier history was colored by this unsettled question. Out of it grew disputes over Texas, New Mexico and California. The Compromise of 1850 and the Kansas-Nebraska question were rooted in the Missouri question.

With the admission of Alabama, all the land east of the Mississippi River, except that of Michigan, Wisconsin and Florida had been organized into states. Creation of the three last states was only a matter of time. Already, Michigan and Wisconsin were feeling the pressure of an expanding population. A native American population was moving onto the frontier, and the impetus of immigration from abroad was becoming stronger. With the exception of Florida, these new territories, along with Arkansas, were in the direct line of the great westward movement.

Westward expansion and the period of war brought economic prosperity to the West. While the territories were getting themselves organized and admitted into the Union as states, the frontier was experiencing a major economic advance. Early settlers on the frontier often operated their farms and small businesses without much cash money. A system of barter enabled many of them to dispose of their farm products and to procure necessary materials. Collections of family papers of the first two decades of the nineteenth century contain a mass of promissory notes and other records of petty financial transactions which were necessary to conduct business when currency was lacking. Many of these promissory notes even served the purpose of currency, being passed from hand to hand until they matured.

Boom and Bust

With the end of the War of 1812, the frontier underwent four years of inflation. Banks were established in many towns to facilitate vastly expanded financial transactions. Land prices went to undreamed-of heights. For the first two years after the end of the war, farm prices remained at a fairly high level. Cotton production in the new southern states had risen from 35,000 bales in 1800 to 350,000 in 1820, and to 509,158 bales in 1824. During the same period grain production rose to a new high, and public lands were being disposed of at a rapid rate. The debt of public lands rose from $3,000,000 in 1815 to $17,000,000 in 1818, and $22,000,000 a year later. In the older states, prices of improved lands and town lots reached an unprecedented level.

During this period of inflation, banks became indispensable. In Kentucky, for instance, the legislature undertook to solve the state's monetary problems by creating more banks and permitting the new institutions to issue money in an ever-increasing volume. By 1818 the Kentucky State banks, capitalized at $7,000,000, had placed approximately $27,000,000 worth of paper money in circulation with almost no specie to support it. Naively, the legislators believed that all a bank had to do was to print its money and accept in exchange personal notes and mortgages, and all would be well. The rising spiral of economic conditions was believed to be permanent. Elsewhere, state banks attempted to follow the same pattern. Since Congress had failed to renew the charter of the United States Bank in 1811, financial responsibility fell upon the shoulders of local and state banks.

Local banks were already functioning in 1811 in Marietta, Lexington, Detroit and Chillicothe. Between 1811 and 1820 an unknown number of new state banks were organized in every trading center in the Ohio and Mississippi valleys. As in the case of the famous "forty thieves," or branches of the Bank of Kentucky (except that there were *forty-seven* of them!), all the state banks issued paper currency. By the peak of economic expansion in 1818 some of these banks issued paper bills so hurriedly that they were printed on one side only. There was paper currency for all, and so long as prices of farm products and manufactured goods remained high, this paper was popular and served a useful purpose. There was little gold and silver specie, and before 1816 there was no competition from the Second United States Bank which had begun operation under the new banking law of April 10 of that year. At the same time there were 246 state banks in existence.

Speculation reached a virtual frenzy by 1818. Blocks of western lands were turned into towns, and lots were offered for sale at inflated prices which promised enormous profits to the sellers. This was a period, however, in which large numbers of people accumulated heavy debts either because they were speculating or because they were extending their operations. There was vibrant hope of profit, and investors were anxious to see the sweeping spiral of inflation continue its upward swirl. Nor did speculators alone profit by the rising flood of bank notes—so did counterfeiters and sharpers. No one could be certain of the validity of even the legitimate notes; to spot a counterfeit among the varied and poorly printed bills which changed hands so often required genius. Banks manipulated their credits and made misleading statements about the validity of their credits and notes.

Counterfeiters and rascals produced notes bearing the names and endorsements of banks which either did not exist, or were in such isolated locations that few people could check their issues of currency. State legislators were quick to grant new bank charters, but they were totally ignorant of the economics of banking. They knew nothing of the importance of continuous bank inspections or of business cycles. In granting charters which gave state and wildcat banks powers to organize and operate, legislators seemed satisfied that they had set up safeguards sufficient to protect both depositors and investors. Once the Second United States Bank and its branches entered the field, the golden stream of currency soon showed many traces of contamination. When the branches of the United States Bank began late in 1817 to select the state banks whose currency they would accept, they cast more than customary suspicion upon the validity of a great bulk of the notes then in circulation.

By midsummer, 1818, the United States Bank changed its fiscal policy and instructed its branches to accept only its own paper on deposit. By this order, the branches were also instructed to cease receiving the notes of other branches. The United States Land Office entered on a similar policy. After this date, the discount on independent bank paper rose sharply, ranging at first from 10 per cent to 50 per cent. By December, 1819, many of the wildcat banks had ceased operation. As the deflation of bank currency increased, the western newspaper press raised a loud hue and cry. Almost every cliché in the enraged editors' vocabularies was put into print in pleas for the financial salvation of the people. A great part of the accompanying anger was directed at the specie policy of the Bank of the United States. The Bank came to be regarded as a devouring monster, out to consume its competition and the fruit of the common man's labors. Once the panic of 1819 swept over them, Kentucky, Indiana, Illinois, and Tennessee were left virtually without independent banking facilities. Ohio suffered heavily, but many of its local banks weathered the financial crisis.

Caught in the panic of 1819, many of the western states projected schemes to save the debtor from complete economic ruin. These were called variously stop laws, stay laws, replevin laws and relief legislation. In Kentucky in December, 1818, the legislature which had enacted the law permitting a disastrous expansion of branch banks, passed the so-called "replevin law" which permitted a stay of execution of notes for sixty days if the creditor refused to accept independent bank notes in payment. Thirty days later the same assembly increased the period of the moratorium to two years. This type of relief was attempted in most of the other western states. The fight for relief was not based on the need of the speculator who had contributed so heavily to conditions of disaster, but upon the hardships and ruin of the common man. Here was a major political issue for the self-seeking politicians, and they were quick to recognize the opportunity before them.

Failure of the independent banking system, dramatic though it was, was a manifestation rather than a cause of the panic of 1819. This economic reversal grew out of a multitude of causes. Inflation caused by the war at home and abroad had run its course, and the nation's economy was again settling down to a highly reduced condition. European economic conditions were unsettled. Purchases of American grain, cotton and other products dropped off. At the same time the expanding agricultural belt on the frontier was creating a much greater supply of farm products. Cotton farmers in the South suffered from the competition of the East Indian cotton grower. Hemp producers in Kentucky and Ohio fell victims to competition from Bengal jute. English manufacturers re-entered the American field, and local manufacturers were unable to compete with them either in price or quality of goods. American wages and prices were much higher, and the relatively young American manufacturing companies could not produce cheaper goods by the American standard of wages.

During the years 1812–1815, when British goods were off the market, American producers experienced a great expansion of their industries. For instance, domestic spinners used 10,000 bales of cotton in 1810, and 90,000 in 1815. Hezekiah Niles said in the latter year, "your profits at present are exceedingly great, your works are more productive than the mines of Mexico." Yet he warned them to keep up their quality and to preserve their market. Iron manufacturing and its associated industries showed a comparable rise in output with cotton. As the cotton belt expanded there was a corresponding increase in demand for hempen rope and bagging with which to wrap the annual crop. There was also a demand for meat, grain, and livestock.

Boatyards in the West, building first flatboats and then steamboats, did an inflated business. Traffic on the rivers showed a vast increase. Movement of freight and goods on the western rivers was heavy. Good crop years and an expanding number of farmers flooded the lower Mississippi

Valley markets with their products. Part of this resulted from the fact that much of the land which had been cleared during the past decade was now reaching a point of maximum productivity. Natural resources in the upper Ohio Valley were being exploited for the first time. Coal was being mined in the Pittsburgh area, and iron ore in various places in the West. Nationally, the income from manufacturing increased to almost $200,000,000.

The first year of peace after 1815 saw British wool threatening the market for that commodity in Ohio, Kentucky and Tennessee. Iron smelters in western Pennsylvania and Kentucky were faced with ruin by British competition. As a result the western states combined forces with eastern manufacturing states to secure the tariffs of 1816 and 1824. These pleas for protection against the competition of cheap foreign goods were not unlike those made by harassed debtors for relief legislation in 1819 and 1820.

Because of the panic of 1819, the westward movement underwent certain fundamental changes, one of which was a revision of the public land law. The act of 1820 reduced the price of land from $2.00 to $1.25, and the amount of land which could be purchased by an individual to eighty acres. Certain adjustments were made to enable persons who had already bought land on credit to reclaim their investment in the amount they had paid.

Dependable money available in 1820 was far less than it was in 1818. In some instances practically no safe currency was left in circulation. Prices toppled from high levels to less than cost of production. In 1821 corn was selling for ten cents a bushel in Cincinnati, wheat brought a quarter, and liquor went begging at fifteen cents a gallon. During the first six months of 1819, cotton prices dropped 50 per cent, falling from $.33 to $.165. Discontent in the East and in the older border settlements caused a faster flow of population to the frontier. So many people were forced into bankruptcy by the panic that it was necessary to liberalize debtor laws. Some of the new states followed the example of their eastern neighbors and abolished the practice of imprisonment for debt; a few included these restrictions in their constitutions.

Possibly one of the most important results of the panic was the development of an antibank attitude. Few people understood the functioning of a bank in economic society, nor did they take the trouble to learn. Banks came to be regarded as oppressive institutions that ironed the little man down by bringing on a depression and by deflating his wealth. Likewise, state legislators learned an important lesson about their relationships to the courts and the federal government when their relief and tax laws began to be reviewed by the state and federal courts. In Kentucky, Tennessee, Ohio, and Missouri relief laws were declared invalid by the local courts, while in Maryland the Supreme Court declared the local tax laws aimed at

the Bank of the United States to be invalid in McCullough *vs.* Maryland
(1819). Maryland had undertaken to tax the notes of the Second United
States Bank, but Justice Marshall held that a state could not interfere with
the federally chartered bank. Five years later the Court handed down a
similar ruling in Osborn *vs.* the United States Bank. In this latter case the
state of Ohio had undertaken to tax branches of the United States Bank.

Because of the panic, western farmers and little business men learned
the importance of politics and legislation in the course of their economic
affairs. Politicians also learned how potent could be the influence of the
little man in deciding the course of elections. "Relief" partisans made a
strong appeal to debt-ridden voters, and in most of the frontier states they
were elected to offices. In the immediate future "reliefers" would align
themselves for the most part with Jackson, while the antirelief people
would prefer the more conservative leadership of men like Henry Clay
and his colleagues. Issues growing out of the economic and political upheavals between 1819 and 1824 provoked Henry Clay to propose his
famous American system of internal economic relationships.

On March 30, 1824, Clay in one of his most famous speeches pleaded for
an American economic system. He did not wish to destroy the European
market for American products, but at the same time he wished to develop
within the country a self-sufficient plan of trade that would develop a
system of manufactures and a market for farm produce. He proposed a
wedding of the agrarian West to the staple-producing South and the industrial East. His speech is a classic document in protectionist doctrine and
also a ringing plea for a type of American economic isolationism. Clay in
1824 was bringing the Hamiltonian argument of American protection and
industrialism up to date. His plea to the West was for the creation of new
and rich markets for the sagging farm economy. To the East his argument
offered relief from the migration of labor to the free lands of the frontier.
To the cotton producers of the South he offered a stable market for their
staple.

Academically, Speaker Clay's eloquent argument of 1824 may have contained many sound elements. It had, however, a fundamental practical
weakness. As yet a system of transportation to facilitate prosperous trade
among the sections was lacking. In 1817 President Monroe had vetoed the
Bonus Bill which would have established a system of intersectional transportation over the Cumberland Road. Because of the availability and the
directional course of water transportation, the South was won away from
the American system of interdependence by the foreign spinners, who,
despite the competition of East Indian cotton, were able to offer an increasing demand for southern cotton.

During the decade 1818 to 1828, the frontier was caught up in the sectional issues which promised to breach the Union. A consciousness of peculiar sectional interests grew out of the War of 1812, the Missouri question, and the panic of 1819. Before the last vestiges of the acute panic had worn away, a pattern of sectional and partisan politics was created which was to color elections for all time to come. Especially important was the fact that future state-making on the frontier was placed in a new sectional perspective.

Exciting Trial of Speed between Mr. Peter Cooper's Locomotive, "Tom Thumb," and one of Stockton & Stokes' Horse-Cars.

The trial took place on the Baltimore and Ohio Rail-Road, on the 28th August, 1830. The sketch represents the moment the Engine overtook and passed the Horse-Car, the passengers filled with excitement.

A SKETCH FROM W. H. BROWN, *History of the First Locomotives in America,* 1871

BREAKING THE BONDS OF ISOLATION

BREAKING THE BONDS
OF ISOLATION

The first wagon load of merchandise that was brought over the mountains on the southern route or that now nearly traversed by the national road was in 1789. They were for Jacob Bowman, who had settled at Brownsville as a merchant in 1787, and is still residing at that place. The wagoner was John Hayden, who also resided in Fayette County, until his death a few years ago. He drove four horses, brought out about twenty hundred pounds, for which he received three dollars per hundred, and was nearly a month making the trip to and fro, from Hagerstown, Maryland, a distance of about one hundred and forty miles. By means of the great improvement in the road, six horses will now haul seventy or eighty hundred, between the same places in seven days, for one dollar per hundred.

—JAMES L. BOWMAN, *The American Pioneer*

CHAPTER XIV

FRONTIERSMEN burrowing deep into the western woods soon found themselves isolated from the towns in the coastal area. Because there was no adequately developed system of roads and trails, isolation slowed phases of the westward movement. Distance and conditions of travel often anchored people in the older settlements. Those who braved the uncertain journey westward found the going tedious and disheartening, and the distances great. It was impossible to cross the Appalachian barrier without traveling a great distance to get beyond its rugged western slope. Travel involved not only hazard to personal comfort but to life and limb as well. Both water and land travel presented peculiar kinds of handicaps and hazards. To go from Baltimore to Cincinnati in the late eighteenth century was to undertake a journey that became in fact a campaign against mud, low-hanging tree branches, rocky precipices, and wayward river currents. Along the way there were at best the most meager accommodations in dirty, insect-ridden taverns. No public agency had yet concerned itself with improving the lot of the traveler or of breaking the bonds of frontier isolation.

To aggravate further the condition of isolation, the western population in its decades of growth after 1780 did not concentrate itself within a compact community pattern. Settlements were so far apart that communication from one to another was just as difficult as with the older settlements east of the mountains. Trails and roads from one settled region to another were still in the future.

Roads

The land routes which penetrated most of the frontier before 1860 underwent a series of common developments. Most of the early roads originated as Indian and game trails—such as the route which began in western Maryland and crossed western Pennsylvania to the head of the Ohio, or the route southwestward down the valley of Virginia to Cumberland Gap and then northwestward across what would be Kentucky to the mouth of

339

the Scioto beyond the Ohio. These trails were fascinating landmarks in the wilderness. They usually led to salt licks and good grazing grounds, and they sought out mountain passes and easy fording places across the bigger streams. Seldom were they blazed or otherwise marked, never were they improved; and always they were obstructed by overhanging limbs, under-brush, and rock and earth slides. Animals and warriors alike went around obstacles as they developed. Indian packhorses were never so heavily laden as were those of white traders and settlers. Game trails, of course, followed the whimsical meanderings of animals. A legend persists that east of the Mississippi the buffalo always found the easiest grades and made the safest crossings of streams. Along with the drawbacks already mentioned, these trails could be completely obliterated by the growth of vegetation. Yet it was along such trails that white frontiersmen broke the way into the west-ern country.

Land travel on the frontier has at least two chapters in its early history. First there was the phase in which arterial roads were opened between the major places of settlement, and then there was the appearance of thousands of miles of "settlement" trails that began "nowhere" and connected with the main roads. One of the first of the main roads west was that cut by George Washington and General Braddock. This road followed an ancient Indian and trader path which was blazed to the Ohio in 1753 by Washing-ton, Thomas Cresap and the Delaware chieftain, Nemacolin, and was called Nemacolin's Trail. A year later Washington led his troops to Fort Neces-sity. Still a year later he was back on the road with General Braddock helping him cut and widen it to the place of his doom at the mouth of Little Turtle Creek. This road crossed rugged mountain country which con-tinued to baffle engineers and road builders until it was finally brought under control in the twentieth century by the builders of the famous Pennsylvania Turnpike with its high fills and tunnels.

Before fighting in the French and Indian War ceased, a second road west was opened across Pennsylvania to the head of the Ohio. This time the intrepid British officer John Forbes mapped the way and pushed his forces across the rugged terrain of western Pennsylvania to his objective at the confluence of the Allegheny and Monongahela rivers. In time, Forbes' Road was to hasten travel and trade in this region, and its importance was reflected in the increased frontier population in the Ohio Valley. Politically it no doubt helped give Pennsylvania a tighter claim to this western territory.

Southwestward across Virginia ran the famous Warrior's Path which followed the towering eastern wall of the rocky Appalachians to the deep defile at Cumberland Gap. Thomas Walker had gone this way on his famous land-scouting expedition in 1750, and it was he who recorded the existence of the famous gateway. This Warrior's Path connected the Valley of Virginia with that of the Ohio, and it helped clear up any geographical mystery about this part of the western country. The trail from Cumberland Gap to the south bank of the Kentucky was made famous in 1775 by Daniel Boone and his party of trail blazers who went forward in the pay of the Transylvania Company. From that date until after the founding of the state of Kentucky, this Wilderness Trail remained a hazardous path through the highlands where mud and uncertain fording places made travel treacherous at best, and where every storm blocked the trail with fallen timber.

United States mail service was opened on the Wilderness Trail in 1792, but within a short time post riders found that they could deliver the mail only with the greatest uncertainty and inconvenience. Maintenance of a dependable schedule was out of the question, and the postmaster general threatened to remove the service, but Governor Isaac Shelby persuaded him to give the state a chance to improve the trail. In 1797 a report was made that a wagon road had been opened from central Kentucky to Cumberland Gap, and that now the first wheeled vehicles could reach the settlements in the bluegrass country. Despite the optimism in this report that the Wilderness Road was now improved, actually the route did not become an improved road until after 1865.

While Kentuckians struggled none too successfully with their pioneer trail, the federal government was becoming concerned with a post road across southeastern Ohio from Wheeling, Virginia, to Maysville, Kentucky. Colonel Ebenezer Zane was given the contract to open a road over the most feasible route and to locate the safest crossings of the Muskingum and Scioto rivers, for which he would be given choice grants of public lands. His choice of river crossings was proved sound by the growth of the towns of Zanesville, Lancaster and Chillicothe. Zane's Trace formed an important loop through the earliest settled area of Ohio and speeded up the journey around the big bend of the Ohio from Wheeling to Maysville. Of equal importance was the fact that Colonel Zane's road connected directly with that branch of the Wilderness Trail which extended on to Maysville and the Ohio from central Kentucky. In a remarkably short time, emigrants from Pennsylvania and Virginia were crowding into the Ohio country and making settlements in the heavy wilderness which shaded its fertile soil.

In 1810, and before the National Road was built, twenty-year-old Margaret Van Horn Dwight went out from New Haven to Warren, Ohio. On the way she kept a diary for her cousin Elizabeth Woolsey. Her description of a wagon camp on Laurel Hill is a vivid one. She wrote, "We came but 9 or 10 miles to day, & are now near the 6th Mountain—in a

tavern fill'd with half drunken noisy waggoners— One of them lies singing directly before the fire; proposing just now to call for a song from the
young ladies—I can neither think nor write he makes so much noise
with his *love songs;* I am every moment expecting something dreadful &
dare not lay down my pen lest they should think me listening to them—
They are the very worst wretches that ever liv'd, I do believe,—I am out
of all patience with them— The whole world nor any thing in it, would
tempt me to stay in this State three months—I dislike everything belonging
to it—I am not so foolish as to suppose there are no better people in it
than those we have seen; but let them be ever so good, I never desire to
see any of them— We overtook an old waggoner whose waggon had
got set in the mud, & I never heard a creature swear so—& whipt his
horses till I thought they would die—I could not but wonder at the patience and forbearance of the Almighty, whose awful name was so blas-
phem'd—. . . ."

When Congress passed the enabling act in 1802 which permitted Ohio
Territory to seek statehood, provision was made for the retention of 5
per cent of the income from the sale of public lands to finance "the laying
out and making public roads leading from the navigable waters emptying
into the Atlantic, to the Ohio, to the said state, and through the same, such
roads to be laid out under the authority of Congress, with the consent of
the several roads of the several states through which the road shall pass."
The next year Congress appropriated 2 per cent of the so-called "5 per
cent fund" to finance location of a national road east of Ohio, and 3 per
cent to be used in the state. This act may be considered a landmark in
public internal improvements legislation. It was the beginning of federal
aid to highway construction, although the principle was to have a severe
test in the flame of political partisanism within the next three decades.

Discussion of the Ohio enabling act led to appointment by Jefferson of
a reviewing committee, which was to recommend a procedure for locating
the great road from the Atlantic to the Ohio. This committee proposed a
survey of the route from Cumberland, Maryland, to a point on the Ohio.
Again, the proposed route followed Washington's and Braddock's old way
westward, passing through parts of Maryland, Pennsylvania, and Virginia.
Pennsylvania imposed only the mild restriction that it go through Uniontown and Washington. By later political manipulation on the part of
Henry Clay, the immediate western terminus was to be Wheeling in
western Virginia.

Thomas Jefferson signed the important National, or Cumberland, Road
Bill on March 29, 1806, and the legal way was cleared for making the final
survey and beginning construction. Enactment of this legislation was
brought about by the pressure of a rising western population. Settlers be-

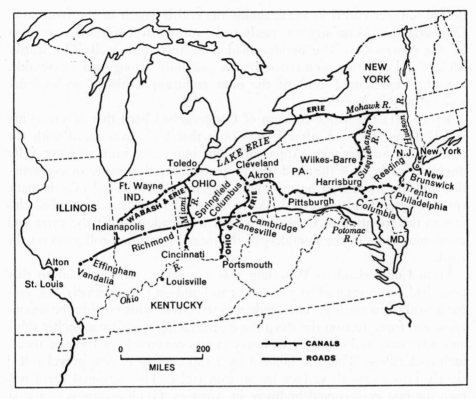

ROADS AND CANALS BEFORE 1850

yond the mountains were beginning to have political influence, and their purchasing potential for eastern merchandise was not forgotten.

The special survey committee observed modestly in its first report that "the face of the country within the limits prescribed is generally very uneven, and in many places broken by a succession of high mountains and deep hollows, too formidable to be reduced within five degrees of the horizon, but by crossing them obliquely, a mode which, although it imposes a heavy task of hillside digging, obviates generally the necessity of reducing hills and filling hollows, which, on these grounds, would be an attempt truly quixotic."

Preliminary arrangements for building the National Road were completed in April, 1811, and a contract was let to construct the first ten-mile stretch of the road west of Cumberland. By 1818 the pike was opened to Wheeling, and the endless stream of freight wagons that were dragged into that place by jangling four-horse teams more than justified its construction. The first year, more than a thousand wagons bearing an average of two tons each were unloaded in the warehouses of the western terminus, and there was promise all along the way of an increasing freight business.

Before summer ended in 1822, almost the entire length of the road from Cumberland to Wheeling was ready to be turned over to the government by the contractors. The builders had done their task well. The sturdy bridges and fills they constructed were not only strong and serviceable, but they represented some of the most enduring works of architecture and masonry in America.

Up to 1822 the major concern of Congress had been that of surveying and building the road; after it was built that body was faced with the problem of maintenance. Apparently this important issue was not fully discussed at the time the road was projected. Yet the nature of construction and the amount of heavy wheeled traffic which passed over it made constant attention a necessity. When the road superintendent called this fact to the attention of Congress, a plan was made to shift the extra and continuing costs to the shoulders of the users by erecting toll gates on the road.

From Cumberland to Wheeling was 130 miles, and the road to that point had cost a total of $1,718,846.35 to build—a phenomenally low cost for a road of its quality. The grade was sixty feet wide outside the mountains, and forty feet on the steep slopes. Surfacing was fifteen inches thick and was composed of a base of heavy stones covered by a layer of three-inch rock filling. This was bonded by a top coating of fine gravel rolled tightly into a smooth surface by an iron roller. The National Road was then the best constructed highway in America. Grades were as gentle as they could be made, and sharp curves and bends were kept to a minimum.

When the road was completed to Wheeling and formed a junction with Ohio steamboat traffic, its promoters were satisfied to take a breathing spell. President Monroe took administrative refuge behind the Constitution when he vetoed the Congressional proposal to erect toll gates to collect maintenance funds. His objection was sustained, and the question of federal aid to internal improvements was again confused. It was now up to Congress to appropriate money directly for repair and upkeep or let the road go to pieces. Extension of the route on to the Mississippi was also involved in this issue of funds.

Beyond the Ohio, the people had all but given up hope that the road which was so eloquently promised them in 1802 and 1805 would be constructed. In 1820, however, Congress appropriated an additional $10,000 to survey the route to the left bank of the Mississippi. Five years later, on July 4, 1825, Ohio orators standing in the courthouse yard at Circleville proclaimed the virtues and joys of American freedom, and predicted a rich economic future for their state—for on that day, opposite the courthouse, they turned the first earth which marked the beginning of construction of the National Road on westward from Wheeling. This extended route passed through Zanesville, Columbus, and Springfield and went on toward Indianapolis and St. Louis. On March 3, 1825, James Monroe signed an appropriation bill for $150,000 to finance extension of the National Road through Ohio and Indiana, and by 1829 had appropriated $750,000 more. Not until 1852, and the expenditure of considerable state funds, did the road finally reach Vandalia, Illinois, where it ended as a part of the original National Road. Not only had it to meet the competition of the canal age, but already the pressure of the railroad was upon it. In the meantime parts of it had been given over to the states through which it ran, and by the middle of the century federal ownership and control had been given up.

From Cumberland to Vandalia, the great road cut across the heartland of America east of the Mississippi. Long before it tumbled down the steep ridge to its terminus at the steamboat landing and warehouses in Wheeling, streams of Conestoga freight wagons made their restless way westward over it with groaning burdens of freight. Mail coaches drawn by spans of fancy coach horses, their swaggering jehus drawing the reins and making a loud clatter with their blaring horns as they passed, hastened over the road, for "The United States Mail must go through." Andrew Jackson, Henry Clay, and dozens of congressmen traveled over it by stage coach to the national capital to serve in its legislative and executive offices. Special stagecoaches were constructed to deliver the newly elected Presidents, Jackson, Harrison, and Taylor. Northerners and southerners alike traveled this way. Foreign visitors went by the road to view the country, to savor tavern life, to complain about American habits and peculiarities, and to appraise the success of the great democratic experiment from what they experienced aboard swaying stagecoaches and in the taverns. Theatrical and circus companies, the great Swedish singer Jenny Lind, and the fabulous Phineas Taylor Barnum were all travelers over the road.

Wagon drivers, a special breed of American, beat and thundered their way over the hills and out of mudholes. Their sweating teams strained to deliver towering loads of textiles, farm implements, salt, tools, furniture, sea foods, Yankee notions, and merchandise of all sorts to their western destinations. Private and public freight wagons bulged with the household goods of settlers on their way to the new country beyond the Ohio, and even later to that beyond the Mississippi. Piles of furs, skins, hemp, whisky, cured meats, potash, and tobacco went east. Thousands of bushels of corn and wheat and endless barrels of flour sought passage to market. From the hemp fields of Kentucky and Ohio came much of the nation's cordage and bagging. From the western still houses came hogsheads of cheap whisky, and from the local smokehouses came the great portion of the nation's bacon and pork. Wayside wagon yards were crowded with rowdy drivers spinning yarns of road adventures, and bragging of their romances along the way with tavern scullions and the female contingent of settler caravans.

National Road taverns were institutions in themselves. They catered to all sorts of people, and offered accommodations of varying degrees of quality. Like the modern motels and tourist courts, some of the frontier taverns were places where quiet families could find meals and lodging with a minimum amount of dirt and bedbugs. Others were dirty and bug-ridden, and their moral standards were to the taste of the more promiscuous travelers. Whatever their quality, the taverns were as much a part of the highway system as were the roadways, bridges, and ferries.

Crossing the numerous streams was a problem. One reason the construction costs of the National Road were kept at so reasonable a level was that the larger streams were not bridged until much later. At Wheeling, for instance, the bridge across the Ohio River was not constructed until long after the road was opened on into Ohio. Rivers and creeks were crossed by ferries. Ferrying places themselves became scenes of adventure, and many of them grew from night wagon camps into villages and towns. Operators of ferries were often men of circumstance and wealth in their communities, and they contributed materially to the movement of traffic along the way.

While trees and underbrush still overlapped Braddock's Road up from the Potomac to the Pennsylvania highlands, frontier flatboatmen were drifting southward down the Ohio with cargoes of farm produce to be sold in the New Orleans market. Coming home, they trudged the weary miles through the sandy pine country of the Choctaw and Chickasaw nations. The homeward trace led diagonally five hundred miles northeastward from Natchez to the Muscle Shoals on the Tennessee River, and then to Nashville. Possibly no one knows its date of origin; like most other hinterland routes, it evolved from prehistoric days of Indian and game travel. From Natchez, traffic followed the old Spanish road southward to New Orleans, and from Nashville two roads went northward to connect that place with Louisville, Lexington and Maysville. The roads to Nashville were in fact essentially extensions of Zane's Trace and the Wilderness Road. The easternmost road offered a direct route from Washington Courthouse to New Orleans by way of Maysville, Lexington, Nashville, Florence and Natchez. Permission to use the road was granted in treaties made with the Chickasaw and Choctaw Indians in 1801.

In the same year that Thomas Jefferson signed the bill creating the National Road, Congress provided for the expenditure of six thousand dollars to "construct" a road from Nashville to Natchez so that the mail could be carried between those points. Obviously the appropriation would pay little more than the cost of blazing the trail and locating fording places across the river. Part of the funds had to be used to secure Choctaw and Chickasaw permission to cross their lands. The Indians were jealous of the use of this trace and kept control of the ferries so they could regulate use of the road. The Natchez Trace never became an improved or heavily used road as did many other frontier highways; yet it was an important artery of travel before the coming of the steamboat. After 1787, the army of western boatmen who came south to New Orleans each market season to deliver the rich products of the frontier farms returned home over the trace afoot and on horseback. In time the story of this road was to be marred by bloodshed and plunder. While the highway bandits robbed only a small number of the travelers along the Natchez Trace, the accounts of their heartless banditry have survived even the road itself.

Internal improvements as a political issue established three important, though unsuccessful landmarks prior to 1820. Jefferson had proposed a system of public roads in 1806, and Albert Gallatin had made plans for such a program only to have them wrecked by war. In 1817 James Madison vetoed the Bonus Bill which further blocked federal aid to internal improvements.

Dozens of other roads were either developed from early settlers' trails, or were surveyed across the forest lands along aboriginal routes. One of the longest of these was the military post road which was authorized in 1807 to be extended from Athens, Georgia, in a crescent-like swing across the Lower South to New Orleans. Another public road was authorized to be built from Dayton, Ohio, to Vincennes, Indiana, and from Vincennes to St. Louis. A north to south road was planned in 1826 to bisect Indiana from Lake Michigan to Madison on the Ohio by way of Indianapolis. This so-called "Michigan Road" became an important feeder route to the north and was to figure in the increased population of Illinois and Wisconsin. In 1816 a public road was authorized to be built from Fort Meigs to the Western Reserve. In addition to these major intersectional roads, there came into existence during the first half of the nineteenth century a web of highways connecting communities, towns and cities. Provisions were made by state legislatures for the construction of these roads either by private toll companies, or by a system whereby every able-bodied male gave so many days work a year to cut and maintain local roads.

Rivers

Whether the trails or the streams were the more effective means of penetrating the western country is open to debate. Certainly both means of travel were used from the beginning. Fur traders and adventurers came in canoes and pirogues to trade and to spy out the land. Then came settlers drifting downstream in clumsy flatboats with their heavy burdens of farm and household goods. When the fields were cleared, mountains of farm produce were sent downstream to market. From 1787 to approximately 1820, the flatboat was the only means by which heavy freight could be moved cheaply on the frontier. Its history was to extend to 1860, but the fact that a flatboat could not return upstream limited its use. Not even the more maneuverable keelboat could overcome the powerful river current except by enormous human effort. Western streams did not permit use of sails. There were too many sharp bends, and not enough breeze to sustain a course against the heavy down-driving currents. Boats had to be moved upstream either by poling or paddling, or by the treacherous cordelling along the banks.

River navigation had long challenged American inventors, and after 1780 they explored the idea of applying steam to boat propulsion. At least five names stand out in this era: John Fitch, John Stevens, Oliver Evans, James Rumsey, and Robert Fulton. Rumsey and Fitch perhaps came closest to perfecting steamboats. Rumsey's model boat worked in a small stream at Lexington, Kentucky, but he was unable to secure backing to build a boat of cargo-carrying proportions. John Fitch came near the realization of his dream by actually operating a boat for a time between Philadelphia, Trenton, and Burlington, but he too lacked the necessary financial banking. Later historians have done much to reduce the importance of the original work of Robert Fulton, saying that he applied the practical ideas of Fitch, Rumsey, Evans and Stevens in the building of the *Clermont*.

All the steamboat inventors were somewhat handicapped by the peculiar idea that they should have a monopoly over streams and sole use of their inventions. This was one of Fitch's mistakes. Apparently he could not understand how he could operate boats profitably in the face of competition. All the inventors failed to comprehend how much freight would be available. They also failed to appreciate the frontier's potential productive capacity. Before the passing of the first decade of the nineteenth century it was obvious even to the most isolated settler that if the West were to prosper it had to reach a market where it could sell its products and make purchases of manufactured goods. In 1811 Nicholas Roosevelt, in association with Robert Fulton and Robert R. Livingston, undertook to further their fortunes by introducing a practical steamboat on the western streams. In that year the *New Orleans* journeyed downstream from Pittsburgh to open a new transportation era in American history. This boat continued in the New Orleans-Natchez trade, demonstrating the practicability of upstream traffic, until it was lost in 1814. In quick order other boats made their appearance: the *Vesuvius, Aetna, Comet, Enterprise, Washington,* and a second *New Orleans*.

Henry Shreve's *Enterprise* made important steamboat history. A 75-ton vessel, it was launched at Brownsville, Pennsylvania, in 1814, and entered the New Orleans trade immediately. Going south in 1815, this boat, loaded with cargo, returned to Louisville and went on to its home port up the Allegheny River. To it belongs the distinction of being the first boat to navigate upstream the full distance of the Mississippi and Ohio rivers. In a short time the *Washington* proved further that a prosperous traffic could be carried both ways by water.

Before the Shreve boats could fully enjoy the prosperity which awaited their owners on the rivers, their operation became involved in a series of legal arguments over the Fulton-Livingston-Roosevelt claim to monopolistic patent rights on the steamboat. Livingston and Fulton claimed in 1817 that Daniel French, Henry Shreve and others were not entitled to use patented knowledge of steamboat building and navigation because this right belonged exclusively to the original company. French and Shreve's boats *Washington, Oliver Evans,* and *Franklin* were the subjects of litigation.

These suits have little historical meaning, but they did much to popularize the use of the steamboat. Only one state along the Mississippi, Louisiana, ever consented to the monopoly, and the Livingston-Fulton contentions were not sustained in the high court of that state for lack of jurisdiction. Finally in 1824 the whole contention was brought to a close in the federal court case of Gibbons *vs.* Ogden. A correspondent of the Cincinnati *Gazette* gave expression to the public attitude toward a promise of faster navigation on the western waters. He wrote that "The invention of the steamboat was intended for us. The puny rivers of the East are only as creeks, or convenient waters on which experiments may be made for our advantage." It is doubtful if ever a more timely invention served the American people than the steamboat, and it benefited no part of the United States more than the frontier. Easterners had access to the sea by sail, but westerners had only the downstream river currents and their own muscular energy with which to create a two-way mode of transportation.

Once the steamboat demonstrated itself to be a practical vessel for river traffic, refinements became immediately necessary. Three urgent demands of the West were speed, diversity, and cheapness of freight rates. It took the *Enterprise* 25 days, 2 hours and 40 minutes to cover the 1,350 miles from New Orleans to Louisville. Ten years later the *Tuscarora* made the trip in 7 days and 16 hours, and in 1853, the famous *Eclipse* covered the distance in 4 days, 9 hours and 30 minutes. Throughout the period before 1860, designers and engineers worked to perfect boilers, engines, and machinery that would be safe and efficient. At the same time boats were designed to carry the maximum amount of freight and passengers at the greatest speed and at the cheapest possible cost. A brief note of freight charges will demonstrate how well they succeeded. In 1815 the *Aetna* accepted freight in New Orleans for Louisville at the rate of $0.045 per pound for heavy goods and $0.05 for light goods. Five years later goods were carried from New Orleans to Pittsburgh for $1.00 per hundredweight, and in 1842–1843 steamboat owners in a meeting in New Orleans established a rate of $0.25 for heavy goods and $0.333 for light goods. Within the next decade, prices had dropped to $0.15 per hundredweight.

Population statistics for the West advanced in proportion to the increased use of steamboats. The western population in 1815, the year the *Enterprise* came upstream, was approximately 1,000,000 persons. Within twenty-five years it had increased to 6,000,000; twenty years later there were approximately 15,000,000 persons west of the mountains. Statistics are given elsewhere for the growth of the western towns and cities. Pittsburgh, Cincinnati, Louisville, St. Louis, and New Orleans were to reflect the influence of river traffic in both their population growth and the expansion of their wealth.

Wherever there was water enough in streams to float a light draft hull, the steamboat became a factor in transportation. The Ohio and Mississippi rivers were more than navigable streams. Their lateral streams poured into them millions of tons of freight. The Wabash, Kentucky, Scioto, Miami, Cumberland, Tennessee, Red, and Illinois rivers offered almost as much freight at times as the main streams. Without these smaller streams, the development of many industries, such as iron, coal, and salt, might have been kept to a small scale. Agricultural production was hampered because of the availability of cheap river freight. The freeing of the West from its reliance upon the East for capital, and the fact that the West no longer had to send so much of its specie East to sustain its local economy, were important effects of improved transportation.

Socially, the steamboat made many changes in frontier life. The faster boats did not take immigrant families completely off the roads, but they did speed up the journey over long stretches of the route to hinterland places of settlement. Where families drifted formerly for days without end downstream on rafts and flatboats, or trudged over long muddy miles of roads and trails, they now crowded the decks of steamboats to western landing places nearer their destinations. Business and pleasure travel increased many times, and the boats became more and more luxurious. By 1840 the first-line packet boats were floating palaces. The plebian freight business was kept below decks, and the lacy upper quarters were available to thousands of passengers who traveled the rivers. No inland carriers ever hauled a more motley assortment of humanity in general association than did the steamboats. There were native and European immigrant families going to new and strange homes; rough flatboatmen lolling on the lower decks, playing cards, swearing, and boasting; planters strutting about displaying themselves and their womenfolk; Yankee peddlers sizing up customers and abhorring the presence of slave traders. There were land speculators, foreign visitors, flirtatious women, slick-talking gamblers wise in the ways of the naive traveler, soldiers, preachers, and politicians—all associated in a milling throng. Many a naive, unsophisticated passenger, away from home for the first time aboard a steamboat, was gulled by a sharpy who played innocent with him.

The western steamboat was more than timber formed into a graceful craft with bright markings and trappings. It was more than a set of high-pressure boilers, tall stacks, and long greasy engines driving their stroke arms in an elbow action to turn the paddle wheels. It was a personality and an institution all in one. To its owner and crew it was an object of personal love; to its passengers it was a place of adventure and travel. There was romance about its hard-swearing captain and mate, its structure, whistle, bell, schedule, and the mishaps with currents and snags. The average steamboat churned its way up and down stream for two to ten years, until boilers, engines and hulls were worn beyond use by the constant contact with river silt. The main rivers were lined with hulks—the victims of fires, explosions, snaggings and groundings. If a boat remained in service for three years, it possibly made its owners a profit, and its loss was not too lamentable from an investment standpoint.

Long after other individual machines of travel have been forgotten, the names of the *Kate Adams*, the *Henry Shreve*, the *Eclipse*, the *Natchez* and the *Robert E. Lee* will be remembered. Social life has never created a more pleasantly exciting atmosphere than that surrounding the cabins and salons of the western river boats. Their sumptuously supplied dining tables wrote a rich chapter in American gastronomy. Even the heartless and cheating gamblers and rascals have taken on a sort of romantic coloration with the passage of time. The hastily devised and irresponsible races between boats, which today would turn members of the Coast Guard and Department of Commerce inspection crews pale with fright, are part of a fascinating chapter in frontier history.

The solid facts of the importance of the steamboat are to be found in the rapidity with which the continent was settled after 1815, and the enormous economic impact which river commerce was to have upon the nation's economy. Even that intangible but powerful factor, sectionalism, was to be amplified by the steamboat. For almost half a century the rivers and their boats directed a tremendous amount of commerce southward and united the sections in a common economic interest.

Boat yards and builders studded the Ohio, and every year after 1811 numerous new vessels glided into the river. The new boats bore the labels of proud builders whose improvements in machinery and design gave their craft better claims to freight and passenger patronage. Some of them were wide-beamed boats with cumbersome wheelhouses amidships, while others had high fenders sheltering stern wheels. The argument went on interminably as to which was faster and more efficient—the side-wheeler or the stern-wheeler.

Making a more modest claim to a place in the sun of the steamboat era were the thousands of malaria-ridden woodcutters who lined the river banks with their towering ricks of heavy green timbers. A thousand miles of virgin forest on either side of the river was felled to raise steam on the Mississippi, Missouri and Ohio. At all hours of the night and day, an army of sweating, straining deckhands hauled this wood aboard to be fed to greedy boilers. In time the supply of wood was exhausted, and the boatmen had to look elsewhere for fuel. The mines of Pennsylvania began to pour into steamboat holds their burdens of coal, and the woodcutters became shanty boatmen or moved away from the river banks to become little farmers.

Canals

New Orleans enjoyed the trade which came her way because of the course of the western streams. Since 1787, western produce had met foreign shipping in this down-river port. Diplomatic negotiations in the 1790's had provided for the up-river trade to pass through the Spanish port into the hands of foreign merchants, but the city made little effort to insure the continuation of the trade. There were inadequate market facilities for the gradual sale of produce once the rush season was over. No elevators for the storage of vast quantities of grain were available. Proper refrigeration and storage facilities for meat were lacking. Northwestern farmers who reached the New Orleans market in the rush season had to sell at ruinously competitive prices because the market was glutted, and because their meats and grain would not keep in the hot, humid climate of the lower river. Failure of the New Orleans merchants to appreciate fully these basic facts and to reorganize their market facilities was an important factor in robbing the city of this rich trade before the end of the decades 1840–1860. In 1847, the editor of DeBow's *Review* said the cost of transporting a barrel of flour from Cincinnati to New York by the Ohio and Erie Canal systems was $1.35, while the cost by way of New Orleans might be as much as $1.75. Receipts of flour in New Orleans in 1844 were 502,507 barrels, while 717,466 went to New York by canal. Flour landed in New Orleans suffered weather damage of $0.25 to $0.50 a barrel. All shipments going through the port had to be transferred to seagoing vessels, which meant further costs and damage.

Locally, New Orleans business interest became centered around cotton. They saw a prosperous future for their port in handling the nonperishable staple. Local New Orleans capital was invested largely in those businesses which catered to the cotton plantation economy. While this was happening, northern canals and railroads were stealing away the great grain and meat trade of the rapidly expanding Northwest, and the steamboat industry began to suffer losses of freight and traffic.

During the first twenty years of steamboat operation on the Ohio, the rock-lined falls at Louisville created a serious barrier. Flatboatmen were not always able to run these treacherous shoals without special pilots, and steamboats were unable to pass without a skilled pilot and a good head of water. Many boats were unable to maintain an Ohio River schedule because of the uncertainty about when they might enter the upper river. Some even had to unload their cargo and haul it around the falls in order to cross the rocky barrier.

Early in the history of steamboat operation on the Ohio, a canal to by-pass this water hazard was discussed. In 1817, when the first steamboat crossed the falls and continued its journey on to Cincinnati, interest in a by-pass became greater. A special commission was appointed in 1820 to make a survey of the most desirable route. For the next eight years locating the canal became a battle fought by the rival interests of Kentucky and Indiana, and there was some reason to believe that jealousies between Louisville and Cincinnati delayed the beginning of the project. Finally the canal was located on the Kentucky bank of the river, and by 1828 it was ready to receive boats for passage. Although not a canal in the truest sense of the word, this short Portland by-pass facilitated the movement of freight and passengers in the western country. The river channel, except for the locks at Louisville, was open from New Orleans to Pittsburgh except in unusually dry seasons.

Discussion of the Portland Canal project in the West broadened interest in this means of inland transportation. Since 1784, Virginians and Marylanders had toyed with the idea of building a canal westward toward the Ohio. Part of this Chesapeake and Ohio Canal was built and is still used. The public mind in 1828 was largely conditioned to water travel, and the rivers and soils, especially in Ohio, were highly adaptable to the construction of canals comparable to those in France and Holland. Ohio's most pressing need in 1820 was conceived to be for transportation to a market where wheat, corn, and pork products could be sold for the highest prices and where merchandise could be bought cheaper. We have seen that when the western farmer reached the great flatboat market in semitropical New

Orleans he found it glutted and the price low. He could not wait with his boat and goods because of the expense and the damage which the goods suffered and so was often forced to sell his wares at less than transportation cost. Flour was worth $8.50 in New York, and $3.50 in Cincinnati, but it was impossible to reach the New York market from Ohio by a cheap means of transportation.

By 1820 several canal projects were either organized or revived. In Pennsylvania, a canal westward was contemplated; in New York, a waterway connecting the Hudson River with Lake Erie was being planned. The Erie Canal project had been made a reality in 1817 by legislative act. Governor De Witt Clinton's memorial contained much material and many arguments that were potent far beyond the borders of New York. By 1825 the Erie Canal was completed and its immediate success stimulated further canal building. Farmers in Ohio, Michigan, and even in Illinois could hear Clinton's plea for a shortened route to the New York market, and certainly they understood the financial advantages which he claimed for that port city.

Although Clinton appealed in vain to Ohio politicians to give financial support to the Erie Canal, the import of his message was not lost on Ohio's Governor Ethan Allen Brown. The latter saw the importance of internal waterways to his state, and in 1821 he appealed to the legislature to agree to the appointment of a special committee to survey the canal subject and to determine its possibilities for Ohio.

For three years the committee examined physiographical data, freight rates and commodity price differentials. Their findings were convincing. Three valleys in Ohio were suited to canalization—the Scioto, the Muskingum, and the Miami. After three years of surveying and reporting, the Ohio legislature was persuaded to pass a canal act in February, 1825. Passage of this bill involved all of the political hesitancy common in frontier assemblies because of the tax assessments involved. Those individuals living near the canal routes were enthusiastic, but those living at a distance were opposed to the state's spending tax money for waterways. This was a common pattern which was to prevail throughout in securing support for highways, canals and railroads. On July 4, 1825, at Licking Summit, at the top of the ridge between the Scioto and Muskingum rivers, the first spade of dirt was turned which resulted in connecting the Ohio with Lake Erie. By 1850 three arterial canals had been constructed across Ohio. These connected Cincinnati, Portsmouth, and Marietta with Lake Erie and gave internal water transportation to every major settled area of the state.

In addition to the Ohio canals, an important interstate channel was opened from Toledo to Lafayette, Indiana, by way of the Maumee and Wabash rivers. The building of this canal followed the orthodox pattern of construction, but a federal grant of land enabling its construction marked a significant beginning of this kind of aid to internal improvement projects. Congress granted the equivalent of one-half of every five sections in width on each side of the canal to be sold to finance its construction. Ohio alone received over 480,000 acres of public lands to be sold at auction under terms of the act. Later, this bill was amended and nearly 500,000 acres of land was given to the project.

Construction of a system of canals in Ohio and Indiana greatly facilitated the movement of produce to the eastern market by way of Lake Erie and the Erie Canal. At the same time, merchandise coming westward reached customers at a much cheaper rate than was possible by river.

Illinois talked more about a canal system than any of the western states, and accomplished less. The issue was before the public from 1822–1850. No legislature met during the period without argument over internal improvements. The issue was involved in a complex spirit of sectionalism, strong bipartisan politics, and lack of capital. The basic idea was to connect the Mississippi with the Wabash and Miami canals and with the eastern markets. In southern Illinois, there was a strong Mississippi River partisanship. At Chicago, there was agitation to connect Lake Michigan with the Mississippi River over the low water pass by way of the Des Plaines and Illinois rivers. Provision was made to support the building of canals with grants of public lands, but politics, sectional bickering, and the panic of 1837 delayed, if not defeated, the internal improvements project. By 1850 the inland canals had contributed heavily to increasing the population and industrialization of Ohio and Indiana, but the canal system, like that of the earlier turnpikes, was not to function long without the serious competition of railroads.

Neither the steamboat nor canal had reached even the first stages of full operation before there was a demand for a faster and more flexible system of transportation. Use of rivers and canals for the movement of heavy freight had the distinct disadvantage of restricting the markets for produce. This fact became more evident as the population increased in the more intensive farming regions of the west. The older Atlantic and Gulf coastal market centers became concerned about the expanding frontier, with its increasing mountains of produce and the large numbers of prospective customers in the region. Baltimore, for instance, had reached the Ohio market by 1818 over the National Road, and then almost immediately lost it to the steamboat and river. The steamboat was faster and cheaper than wagon freight. Merchandise went out from Baltimore in greater quantity than produce arrived from the west, which created an imbalance of trade. Philadelphia was also reaching out to the west by way of Pittsburgh for the trade of the Ohio Valley.

Railroads

By 1825 it was clear that the port of Baltimore was declining and that a more satisfactory means of transportation had to be developed. Also, the coal and iron industry of the western mountain slopes showed indications of expansion and would require additional facilities. On February 28, 1827, the Maryland legislature chartered the Baltimore and Ohio Railroad Company to build a railroad from the Chesapeake Bay to the Ohio. Construction was begun on July 4, 1828, with the aged Charles Carroll of Carrollton turning up the first spade of dirt.

From the beginning, the Baltimore and Ohio management experienced every difficulty that could be met in American railroad building. There were no trained engineers and operators available; originally, no one had any clear concept of the use of steam locomotives; there was little or no knowledge of what constituted an adequate grade and a satisfactory road-bed for ties and rails. In fact, no one really knew what type of rails would support heavy traffic. There was indecision, to begin with, as to whether the railroad would be operated as a superhighway with restricted use, or as a privately owned railroad. Introducing this new idea in transportation inevitably created jealousies, and almost immediate legal opposition was raised by the Chesapeake and Ohio Canal Company. For a time the project was halted.

By 1830 the railroad company had thirteen miles of track in operation, but not until the next year was steam power used to draw the "trains." Encouraging amounts of local freight became available almost from the start. Lateral roads were constructed to Washington and Winchester, and in 1842 the road was in operation to Cumberland, Maryland.

The great panic of 1837 halted railway and canal construction temporarily, and many companies failed. The Baltimore and Ohio Railroad was forced to do extraordinary financing and managing in order to pull itself through the crisis. By 1845, however, the Baltimore and Ohio was enjoying bright promise for the future. Eight years later, on Christmas Eve, the gap in the rails was closed at Rosby's Rock 18 miles east of Wheeling, and the trains reached the Ohio. Before the Baltimore and Ohio reached this point, it had been engaged in a wild race with the Pennsylvania and Erie railroads for the rich cargoes of the Ohio Valley. At the same time Virginians were planning a road to the Ohio, and it now became necessary for the Baltimore and Ohio to build on to Parkersburg and then to Cincinnati.

Like Baltimore and New York City, Philadelphia had an eye on western trade and was experimenting with various ideas for improved transportation. Pennsylvania was engaged in a rather extensive program of canal and highway expansion to compete with the New Yorkers. Within its own borders it had the tremendous task of uniting its various sections by improved means of communication. By 1846 a series of short lines had been built in the state, but no through connection to Pittsburgh was made. In this year the legislature chartered the Pennsylvania Railroad Company with permission to complete the railway connections between Harrisburg and Pittsburgh. Large financial resources were put at the disposal of the company, and builders and investors alike were anxious to reach Pittsburgh in time to capture the rich trade which Pennsylvanians considered theirs by right. By 1852 the Pennsylvania Railroad was in operation to Pittsburgh and was looking to a future when it could build its main line on to Indianapolis and Terre Haute. By this time local roads in Ohio were forming a network of iron north and south and creating important junction points for the expanding eastern arterial systems.

New York City had already gained first-hand knowledge of the luscious profits that were to be made in the western trade. The Erie Canal was piling New York's warehouses high with produce from frontier farms. Yet there was no reason to suppose that this condition must continue to prevail. Future prosperity rested heavily upon the city's western trade, and it was necessary to be ever alert to the developing competition. Since early colonial days New Yorkers had wanted a direct trail or road to Lake Erie on the state's western boundary. Now that the railroad had captivated the American mind, this ambition was revived. The New York Assembly chartered the Erie Railroad Company, April 24, 1832. Between that date and 1853, when a connecting line was completed to Lake Erie, the company made about all the mistakes possible for an early nineteenth century internal improvements organization. So anxious were its promoters to monopolize the trade of the Ohio Valley that a restriction was placed upon the width of the gauge which later handicapped it when it was necessary to receive freight from lateral lines.

One of the biggest drawbacks was lack of adequate funds. The legislature gave the company little more than the meager amount necessary to make survey fees; the larger requests for construction funds were refused. One of the first appeals for public lands to aid in the building of a railroad was made by the Erie Company. These appeals met with little or no success, except that one land company made a concession in its prices to purchasers, provided they in turn would make grants to the road. There was also the question of whether the road should be constructed in parts, or whether the entire line should be constructed at one time. In the twenty years that it was building, the Erie was the victim of bad management and foolish experimentation. One such experiment was the laying of track upon a series of short piles sunk into the ground. Before the company discovered that pilings had an uncanny way of sinking down at uneven heights, it had lost a considerable amount of money. Rivalry from canal patrons who could influence the course of local politics caused trouble, as did the great panic of 1837. In spite of its troubles, the Erie Railroad proved in this period to be a happy financial adventure. By 1860 it had penetrated the Great Lakes frontier and had all but supplanted its rival, the Erie Canal, as a transportation lifeline to the grain and meat producing West.

A second railroad which connected with Rochester and Buffalo was extended westward from New York City between 1832 and 1853. Its early history is that of a series of local roads being built from one town to another, handicapped most of the time by opposition from supporters of canals. Fortunately, the managements of the various short, central New York roads had the foresight to build their lines on a common gauge so that freight movement was facilitated from one line to another. In 1853 these local roads were consolidated by charter into a single system—the New York Central—and New York City had a second connection with Lake Erie. Before 1860 the New York Central had formed a connection through Cleveland with Cincinnati, and with Chicago over connecting lines.

In all sections of the seaboard the railroad craze found support. Much of the Old South in the 1820's was not only in close proximity to the frontier, but much of it was still a part of the frontier. If Atlantic seaboard cities to the southward were to expand and prosper, they had to reach out and claim a share of the stream of trade which was going to New Orleans by steamboat and to New York by canal. Charleston, South Carolina, though far removed from the Ohio Valley, had to form either a canal or a railway connection with that region. Merchants of this Carolina city saw that the business of their port and of their own houses was becoming static. There were dreamers among them who conceived the idea of building a canal to the Ohio. It would follow the tidewater and piedmont rivers to the mountains, cross the Appalachian barrier by a series of locks and tunnels, and then reach Cincinnati by river and canal on the other side. This fabulous idea was given encouragement by even so conservative a leader as Robert Y. Hayne. Characteristic of the coast country people, the Charlestonians had little knowledge of Appalachian and Ohio valley topography, and their project collapsed.

Of more immediate and practical concern to the Charleston merchants in 1827 was the fact that their neighbors to the south in Savannah were draining away the increasing trade of that river valley. Either a canal or a railroad to tap the Savannah River was a necessity for the immediate future. English experiments with the railroad were encouraging. A short line was under construction in Pennsylvania, and there was a possibility that a road could be made to pay in South Carolina. In December, 1827, the legislature of South Carolina chartered the Charleston and Hamburg Railroad, and three years later a six-mile stretch of road had been built. In 1831 the Charleston and Hamburg made American railroad history by using one of the early steam locomotives, appropriately named the "Best Friend of Charleston."

Although the early use of steam locomotives was of great importance to the frontier, the financial and engineering problems of the road were probably of equal importance. Some of these were peculiar to the southern swampy country; the major one, however, resulted from the necessity of building a long stretch of track through a sparsely populated country to reach a point where freight was available. This was true of the South generally and largely explains why the development of southern railroads lagged. There was a serious lack of local capital to finance even the short line to Hamburg, and there were no experienced railway managers or engineers. In Columbia, the legislators were prejudiced in their friendly attitude toward river and canal projects. If railway officials considered revenue from freight, they had to recognize the fact that their revenue would come from hauling a highly seasonal staple crop to market, and that during much of the year the freight business would be light. Strong competition from the steamboat lines and a woefully provincial attitude on the part of planters and merchants further limited the business that the railroad might expect from its territory. A diversity of economic interest in the various parts of the South was lacking, which further handicapped railway expansion.

The Charleston and Hamburg railroad was directed eventually toward a terminus on the Ohio, but many other projected lines within the South had no other purpose than that of connecting inland towns with points of river navigation. The railroads were to be maidservants to steamboats. One of the best examples of this sort was the Lexington and Ohio which was chartered January 27, 1830, with the primary purpose of rescuing the old frontier town of Lexington from its setback caused by the river trade at Louisville. In chartering this road, the legislature left the western terminus unspecified by saying "Ohio." This was done to give Lexington an opportunity to choose the place where it could best redirect river trade away from Louisville and Cincinnati. Also, the directors might be placed in a position to secure financial help in a pinch from the highest bidder for the western terminus of the road. Local promoters and capitalists were more optimistic in their oratory at the beginning than the engineers were efficient in grading and laying track. By 1845 the road had reached Frankfort, but its track was miserably built, and not until 1852 did it reach Louisville.

While Bluegrass farmers and bankers wrestled with the building of their uncertain little line to the Ohio, promoters in Nashville, Tennessee, looked to the bigger prize of regional freight. They conceived of connecting railroads that would place their city in a strategic position to trade in all directions. One of the first lines to be built out from Nashville was the Nashville and Chattanooga which connected with the Tennessee River and the Western and Atlantic Railroad into central Georgia. Not to be outdone by their rival on the Cumberland, Memphis promoters sought to meet the Nashville and Chattanooga at a junction point on the Tennessee River and then build on to connect with the Atlantic Coast trade at Charleston. The building of the Memphis and Charleston Railroad was started in 1846, and by 1857 it had formed a connection with the Georgia systems, and the Charleston and Hamburg.

The completion of the route from the Mississippi to the Atlantic Coast was one occasion when southern oratory recognized no bounds. Charlestonians came west over the new railroad, bringing along a barrel of salt water dipped from the Atlantic. On the Chickasaw Bluffs, frock-coated citizens marched out to the wedding of the ocean to the river. The clear ocean water was poured into the muddy flood of the Mississippi, and symbolically a good share of the river trade was diverted to Charleston.

Before the wedding of the Atlantic and the Mississippi occurred, other railway matchmakers were readying their homely brides for union at the altar of the Ohio River. Ambitious merchants, bankers and entrepreneurs in Mobile sought to span the wide wastes of the southern pine barrens of Alabama and Mississippi, and to connect their city with the Ohio at Cairo, and the Mississippi at St. Louis. For sixteen years prior to 1860 the Mobile and Ohio management struggled to push their road to completion. New Orleans and Mississippi citizens bestirred themselves to rescue their city and state from the ferocious competition that was being developed on all sides of them. Mississippians struggled to penetrate the forest barrier which blocked them from the rivers and markets for their cotton. They chartered and began a series of short-line railroads which were directed northward toward the Ohio and Mississippi. These roads, the New Orleans, Jackson and Great Northern, the Central of Mississippi and the Mississippi and Tennessee, like the Mobile and Ohio, did not connect with the northern rivers until the first guns of the Civil War had been fired.

Louisville reached a point in 1850 when it could no longer rely on the Ohio alone to guarantee it a place in the southern economic sun. In that year the Kentucky and Tennessee legislatures chartered a company to build 185 miles of track connecting Louisville and Nashville. This was to form a link of one of the most important railways in the South. Connecting with the Nashville and Chattanooga and the Central of Georgia systems, the Ohio Valley and the lower South were brought closely into association, as the volume of freight carried by the Louisville and Nashville line was to prove. By 1859 this road was completed to Nashville, and after 1861 it was to become a major objective in the tug of war between Confederate and Union forces.

Every one of the southern states had an elaborate network of local railroads under way, the history of which could be written in this brief statement: lack of experienced management and money. The long and unproductive spans of country through which the railroad companies had to build often defeated the builders. A sparse population, poverty-stricken state governments, panics, and a focal interest in cotton production all served to keep the region isolated. It was of major significance that neither the New Orleans road across Mississippi nor the Mobile and Ohio completed their intersectional connections before 1860.

While its neighbor to the south was chartering the Lexington and Ohio Railroad, Ohio was adopting a charter for the Ohio and Steubenville Railroad that was in fact a statement of general policy in the chartering of roads for the future. From the outset Ohio enjoyed a distinct advantage in the field of railway construction. The National Road, the Erie Canal, and the internal canal system had directed the interest of the East toward Ohio. The population had grown rapidly, and the amount of produce being offered for sale each year was growing in staggering proportions. Also, internal improvements in Ohio were already well developed. The biggest drawback to the railroads was the fact that so much capital and energy had gone into the building of the canal system.

Building railroads in Ohio was not quite as difficult as it was in the states where a mountainous region had to be crossed or where several hundred miles of barrens lay between sources of freight supply and markets. Generally the terrain was favorable for laying track without having to build heavy grades. By 1832, twelve Ohio railroads had been chartered, but the sale of stock was so difficult that many of these ambitious dreams died at birth. The panic of 1837 virtually halted railroad activity, and it was not until after 1840 that it was revived. By 1856, 4,687 miles of road were projected, and 2,593 miles were in operation. Connections had been formed over the Erie, Pennsylvania, Baltimore and Ohio, and the New York Central with the Atlantic Coast, and connections with St. Louis and Chicago were completed. Possibly no state in the Union in 1860 was more adequately served by rail than Ohio. Its roads ran both north and south between Lake Erie and the Ohio River, and east and west between sources of supply and the important eastern market centers.

North of Ohio, Michigan struggled with distances and financial panic between 1831 and 1854 to build connecting railroads to Chicago and to junctions with the Ohio system. Two important roads were developed in this period, the Michigan Central and the Michigan Southern. Both had histories of local operation before they were connected with Chicago. In 1849 the Central formed a connection with lake steamers going to Chicago, and by 1860 both the Southern and the Central were operating into the city. Connections with the railroads of Ohio gave the state an outlet as far south as Louisville; and to the east, direct junctions with the Erie and New York Central provided a railway connection to the Atlantic Coast.

Indiana showed the same enthusiasm for internal improvements as Ohio, but a lack of population, a major focal center, and unwillingness to concentrate on a few projects injured the state's development. Between 1830 and 1840 several internal projects were begun with much enthusiasm, but not one of them was near completion by 1840. A railroad was chartered to connect the principal cities from north to south, beginning at Madison on the Ohio. State finances were inadequate to support this project, and the panic of 1837 further weakened it. However, the Madison road reached Indianapolis by 1850, and in the succeeding decade, the state had projected a system of rails of almost 1,500 miles, but only a small part of it was in operation. The most important connections were from the Ohio to Chicago, and from Cincinnati westward toward St. Louis. Completion of the Michigan roads across the northern part of the state formed an important connection just prior to 1860.

Up to 1840 the states west of Ohio had developed no major focal centers. Towns were small, and the populations of Indiana and Illinois were distinctly agrarian. Possibly no people on the frontier were more isolated than those in Illinois. Farmers living on the rich lands of the central part of the state could produce almost unlimited amounts of corn, wheat and pork, but only those living near the rivers could deliver their produce to market. Farmers in the central counties were landlocked. The stream system of Illinois was not conducive to the creation of well-dispersed transportation facilities or the development of diversified markets. Attempts at solving transportation problems by the legislature involved dealing with the tightest sort of state sectionalism and jealousy. No section was willing to waive its immediate claims upon the state in favor of another section. As a result of this highly sensitive and provincial state of mind, legislators attempted to deal with the state's internal problems politically. An ambitious scheme of internal improvements was outlined by the legislative act of 1837 in which various projects were to be organized and developed simultaneously. This placed a heavy burden on a poverty-stricken state treasury, and the panic of 1837 with its accompanying panic failures and ruinous prices disrupted the Illinois scheme. Again in 1840 Illinois internal improvements were crippled by panic.

Between 1836 and 1860 numerous railroads were chartered in Illinois, and many of them made progress with construction. None of them, however, was more important than the Central, or Illinois Central Railroad Company. The history of this road embodies a considerable amount of nineteenth-century Illinois history. This company was chartered January 18, 1836, to build a railroad across central Illinois from Cairo, at the confluence of the Ohio and the Mississippi, to a point on the Illinois-Michigan Canal. As yet Chicago had not shown promise of becoming the focal center of the lake area, to say nothing of the whole national railway system. The route of this road was located so that it and a series of lateral branches would break the tight isolation of rural Illinois. Between 1836 and 1850, the Illinois Central Company went through a series of failures caused by a lack of capital, mismanagement of funds, lack of experience, failure of an English investment company, and the lack of security in Illinois bonds. Possibly the greatest single fact was that the state of Illinois had chosen to build more railroad than it could finance.

The Illinois Central project did not lack for supporters, chief of whom was Sidney Breese. Breese was elected to the United States Senate and, as a member of that body and later as chairman of the public lands committee, introduced a bill requesting Congress to grant the state of Illinois pre-emption rights to large blocks of public lands, with profits from their sale to be used to finance the building of the railroad. Breese's bill met with little success until his junior colleague Stephen A. Douglas, who had been elected to the Senate in 1847, joined him. Between that date and 1850 Douglas reworked the Breese bill. He proposed that alternate sections of public lands for six miles back from both sides of the right-of-way be granted to the state of Illinois to enable that state to finance the building of the Central railroad. Douglas argued that such a line would be of national rather than local importance. The first votes on this proposal showed both bipartisan and sectional reactions. Between 1848 and 1850, Senator Douglas was able to effect some charter changes in the Central Company in Illinois. Visiting Mississippi and Alabama, he developed support from promoters of the series of lines being built across eastern and central Mississippi toward the Ohio, and from backers of the Mobile and Ohio who were struggling toward the same goal. Back in the Senate in 1850 he persuaded the strict constructionists of the Gulf States to favor the

Illinois Central bill by exerting tremendous pressure upon them from their constituents in Alabama and Mississippi. On September 17, 1850, Congress passed the Douglas Bill, and three days later President Millard Fillmore signed it. Although this was not the first federal land grant for internal improvements, Douglas had pushed through Congress a major piece of legislation. Within the next twenty years large areas of the public domain would be used to encourage the expansion of railroads across the country.

Illinois received 2,595,000 acres of federal land, which it was required to sell at $2.50 or more per acre. The route of the railroad was to extend northward from a point near the confluence of the Ohio and Mississippi River to Centralia. From that point one branch was to go northeastward to Chicago and another northwestward by way of Galena to Dubuque, Iowa. This Iowa terminal was provided for by the Jones Amendment, introduced by Senator George W. Jones of Iowa. From Cairo north to the terminus was 750 miles, much of it through undeveloped territory, a fact which made financing the road more difficult.

The federal law allowed only six years in which to complete construction. As many as ten thousand men were employed at a time to push the Illinois Central forward. One historian of the road estimates that 100,000 men in all were employed on the vast construction jobs. These consisted of laborers from the Ohio Valley and foreign immigrants. Foreigners who came to work on the railroad either settled in Illinois, or went on westward to the new states where they exerted a significant social and political influence. Within five years, by September 27, 1856, the main line from Chicago to Cairo was finished. The Illinois Central Railroad itself, along with the roads from the East and the western lines projected from the city, made Chicago the center of the westward movement after 1850.

Improved transportation facilities, highway, river, canal and railroad, greatly facilitated the spread of westward population; furthermore, the process of pioneering was speeded up by three to ten years in places where transportation was adequate. Settlers might break ground one year, and in almost the next year enjoy the conditions of a settled community. The tide of population began to rise by 1820 in proportion to the increasing improvement of roads and the effectiveness of steamboats as common carriers. Coincident with the increasing importance of the steamboat were technical improvements in the plow and other farm implements.

The production of commodities increased. Between 1814 when Jethro Wood of New York introduced his cast iron plow and the 1840's when John Deere, in his Illinois blacksmith shop, used a steel plow to turn up the sun-baked soil of the prairies, a virtual revolution occurred in western agriculture. Whitney's cotton gin had undergone refinements, and new types of bagging with steel ties had been introduced to make the cotton bale more manageable and less apt to come apart under rough handling by freight carriers. Cyrus T. McCormick in 1847 deserted his pleasant Virginia valley for the greater challenge of the black prairie lands of the Northwest. McCormick's biggest problem was his choice of the right place to locate his factory so that he would be in the midst of the new agricultural boom. He took his reaping machine to Chicago, where he soon saw grain production reach a staggering number of bushels annually. In estimating the growth of the grain industry, it is significant to know that even McCormick had a host of competitors by 1860.

The National Road, the Erie Canal, and the Baltimore and Ohio, Pennsylvania, Erie, and New York Central railroads all reached the Ohio and Mississippi Valleys before 1860. Within the decade 1850–1860 western commerce was almost completely redirected by these lines of transportation. The struggle which developed between the North and South from 1830 on was greatly stimulated, first by the enormous increase in demand for goods by the Northwest, and then by the necessity for a diversified market for farm produce where a quick seasonal sale could be made without suffering from oversupply. The South failed to attract onto its frontier before 1860 a sufficient population to offset the waste in the long and profitless barren stretches between its railroad terminals. Southern roads were slow in building, they were inefficient in operation, and they were too disconnected to create a really significant and competitive market center anywhere in the South. At the same time, at least three eastern markets—New York, Philadelphia, and Baltimore—were reaping a rich harvest from the West.

FRONTIER ARTS AND SCIENCES

We of this generation are but pioneers; we have done much, but nothing in comparison with what the next generation will do. We are their "hewers of wood and drawers of water"; we came and saw and conquered, but the spoil is theirs; ours is emphatically the age of bile—theirs will be the golden. The State of Ohio has progressed with a rapidity that has far outstripped the most sanguine anticipations. We feel no disposition, however, in looking forward to her maturity, to indulge in castle building. Everything around us— improvement in building—the bustle of business in villages—the emigration of intelligent and enterprising men—the successful prosecution on the canals—the improvement in roads—the increased travel and facilities afforded travellers—the increased attention to education—public opinion chastened and operating more powerfully on society—a higher tone of moral feeling pervading the community—these and a variety of other facts show distinctly, that Ohio is rapidly progressing in all that renders a people happy and respectable.

—CALEB ATWATER, "Prospects of Ohio," *Ohio State Journal*

CHAPTER XV

MANY established cultural institutions were transferred to the frontier from east of the mountains and adapted to new conditions. Often they took on peculiar characteristics that gave them some regional distinction. None made a greater appeal to the backwoodsman than did the local newspaper. It brought him news, no matter how stale; often it confirmed his narrow political views, or antagonized him by expressing contrary opinions. It entertained him with a variety of matter. A predominant characteristic of westerners, as is said elsewhere, was a hunger for news. One reason for the popularity of backwoods tavern commonrooms was the presence of a newspaper, and someone to read it aloud to those who were illiterate.

Newspapers and Periodicals

John Scull's Pittsburgh *Gazette* was the first newspaper to be published in a purely frontier community. This journal appeared in July, 1786, and was the product of an amateur editor and printer. A year later, John and

367

Fielding Bradford of Lexington, Kentucky, published the Kentucky *Gazette*. Like Scull, the Bradfords learned something of newspaper operation in Philadelphia and Pittsburgh. Both publishers had bought their meager equipment in Philadelphia and learned to set type largely by self-taught methods. Equipment for the Kentucky *Gazette* was transported to Maysville by boat, and then by packhorse to Lexington. News appearing in the first issue came along with the equipment, and much of the type was set on the river journey from Pittsburgh. On August 11, 1787, after the type had been pied, Editor Bradford placed the first issue of his paper in the hands of his backswoods subscribers. For the next fifty years the Kentucky *Gazette* was a seminal frontier newspaper. Its office produced a vigorous journal, and also a small army of future editors and printers who moved on to other states to found papers of their own. Locally, the *Gazette* was an active forum where individuals freely expressed their views. It carried news, advertisements, reminiscent articles, and hot controversial writings which reflected rather brilliantly the processes of economic, political and social development.

Bradford did not monopolize the western newspaper field for long. In November, 1793, William Maxwell, compiler of the famous "Maxwell Code" of the Northwest Territory, published the first issue of the *Centinel of the North-Western Territory* in Cincinnati. Three years later this pioneer journal became the property of Edmund I. Freeman who changed its name to *Freeman's Journal*. In 1799 Joseph Carpenter began publication of the *Western Spy and Hamilton Gazette*, and in 1804 the first issue of the *Liberty Hall and Cincinnati Mercury* was published. Across the line in Indiana Territory, Elihu Stout began publication of the Indiana *Gazette*, and changed its name to the *Western Sun* in 1807. The appearance of the newspaper was a high point in the germination of the cultural phase of frontier expansion.

Soon after 1800 almost every newly established community had its printer and newspaper. The printing press followed on the heels of the first settlers, and by 1840 all of the new states and territories had rapidly growing lists of newspapers. Editors gave space to the activities of state and national organizations as well as to local political news. Legislative actions were adequately described, and favored political leaders were kept constantly before the people. Doubtless much of the success of the Jeffersonian party on the frontier was due to the good press support which it received. News columns were thrown open to controversies, political and hypothetical; to correspondents who aired their personal feelings; to groups who queried candidates on embarrassing issues; and to local organizations promoting ventures of social improvement. In fact, news was often so scarce and facilities for securing outside information so badly limited that peppery letters helped to fill gaps of white space.

Frontier editors performed lasting services to posterity in another way. Many of them, like John Bradford and William Maxwell, were actively engaged in the settlement of their communities. They experienced the struggle first-hand and were able to analyze many of the contemporary forces. In his latter years John Bradford of the Kentucky *Gazette* published a series of historical notes in which he reviewed many phases of the settlement of the Ohio Valley. Local historians also wrote of their experiences and published their work in the local papers. Thus at a remarkably early date the newspapers began to reflect a consciousness on the part of the first settlers of their historical roles.

By 1825 the western paper mills were able to supply more abundant printing stock, and mechanical equipment was easily available. A generation of trained printers had come into existence, and the newspaper became as necessary as the rifle and the axe in the westward movement. As trade increased along the Ohio, the number of papers multiplied. Current prices, advertising, and commercial news became necessary. Between 1826 and 1830 at least three daily papers began publication. The first of these was the Cincinnati *Commercial Register* which appeared in 1826. Soon thereafter the *Daily Cincinnati Gazette* and the *Commercial Advertiser* made their appearances. Downriver, Shadrach Penn of Louisville converted his weekly *Public Advertiser* into a daily paper; and almost before the ink dried on his first issue, he had a vigorous competitor in the New Englander George Dennison Prentice. Prentice went south in 1830 to glorify Henry Clay in a campaign biography. He remained to organize and edit the pro-Whig Louisville *Journal*, and to make a major editorial reputation for himself.

Western printshops produced a stream of handbills, pamphlets, almanacs and books. John Bradford printed the *Kentucke Almanac* in 1788—the first pamphlet in western history. Four years later he printed the *Acts* of the Kentucky General Assembly, and by the end of the decade he had published other official material. Before 1840, frontier printers had produced an appreciable volume of legislative, court and official proceedings, pamphlets, directories, and new editions of standard literary works which had originated elsewhere. Some of the early printers set an unusually high standard of graphic art which is not now equalled by most of the modern presses in the region.

Printing equipment was reasonably durable. Outmoded hand presses and other equipment were moved on to new offices out on the frontier to continue their mission of journalistic pioneering. The rate at which the number of newspapers on the frontier multiplied was almost unbeliev-able. Ralph Leslie Rusk says there was one paper for 75,000 people when Bradford began publication of the Kentucky *Gazette*, and fifty years later there was one newspaper for every 12,000 in the population. By 1840 al-most one-fourth of the papers in the United States were published in the West; that is, 354 of the 1,404 appeared in the western states.

The frontier was a newspaper editor's Eden. If he did not make a fortune, he at least found opportunities aplenty. Papers varied in popularity with the personalities and political points of view of the editors, but the press generally was a highly popular institution. Prospective editors chose to be-lieve that a literary periodical could share the same general popularity, but the Middle West a hundred and fifty years ago was not fertile ground for the nurturing of a literary magazine. The first purely literary periodical to make its appearance was the *Medley, or Monthly Miscellany*, printed in Daniel Bradford's shop. The first issue, consisting mostly of selected matter from other publications, appeared in December, 1803. For a year it struggled for existence and then gave up.

Following the failure of the *Medley*, the West was without a periodical until 1819 when William Gibbs Hunt's *Western Review and Miscellaneous Magazine* was published in Lexington, Kentucky. Like its predecessor, Hunt's publication contained a tremendous amount of borrowed material with some original pieces by such contributors as Constantine Rafinesque and Caleb Atwater. Again the editor was unable to prevent bankruptcy, and in July, 1821, his publication became only a memory and a dusty file. The eccentric Rafinesque, a wandering naturalist and universal genius, attempted to found a periodical with the ambitious title, *Western Minerva, or American Annals of Knowledge and Literature*. He had neither the business ability nor tact necessary to sustain a periodical, and soon the *Minerva* failed.

Perhaps the most successful of all the western magazines was Timothy Flint's *Western Magazine and Review* published in Cincinnati. Flint had a good background for his venture in the field of western publication. The *Review*'s pages were filled with somewhat more solid materials than those which had appeared in its Kentucky predecessors. There was more originality to it, and the critical articles were of solid worth. Three volumes of this periodical appeared before the author found himself in financial straits and stepped aside to permit James Hall to pre-empt the western literary field with his *Illinois Monthly Magazine*. Hall, like Flint, had an intimate knowledge of western life, but in 1830–1832, Vandalia, Illinois, was hardly a town where a literary magazine would flourish, and soon Hall's publication ceased.

Among the better periodicals before 1850 in the Ohio Valley was the monthly *American Pioneer*, edited by John S. Williams and published by the Logan Historical Society. This periodical, which was issued in Cincinnati during the years 1842–1843, contained many short articles on varied subjects relating to the frontier. Some of the most useful are the fascinating first-hand accounts of experiences in the backwoods, including flatboat journeys to New Orleans, incidents of immigration, and frontier warring. On the whole, however, the frontier was hardly the place to carry on a sustained literary publication. Either money was too scarce or a taste for the kind of material that the average magazine carried was lacking. On the other hand, some religious periodicals with institutional association enjoyed considerable popularity and were published for several years.

Books and Authors

Books were more to the liking of the westerners, and many volumes of native origin came from the frontier. Until recently both historians and literary scholars have tended to overlook this rather significant collection of writings. Authors were conscious of the meaning of the westward movement as it influenced the unrefined frontier society. Masses of backwoods people had either been out of touch with the more sophisticated patterns of society in the older settled regions, or they were born on the frontier and had developed their own peculiar social forms. In many instances it was not isolation alone which gave color to local literature, but rather the sharp contrasts which existed between the older and more refined society and that of the raw, surging, struggling, and unwashed border society. Generally, the frontiersman reduced his thought processes and communicative formula to a simple, colorful and direct figure of idiomatic speech which eloquently reflected environmental conditions.

Many imaginative authors who recorded this aspect of frontier social life were men who had observed first-hand the vicissitudes of the land and the people. Many of them had been lawyers, steamboat men, newspaper editors, or doctors; some had even served in the pulpit. More sophisticated literary critics may question whether or not the frontier local-colorists wrote worthy literature. It is not the purpose to undertake here a resolution of this contentious point. What the authors of the frontier wrote was the literature the frontier produced, and an objective analysis of it would fairly well establish the fact that it ranks among some of our most important local-color literature. What the frontiersmen did and said may have been stupid and in some cases barbaric and uncouth when measured by more polite standards, but it was never unimaginative or colorless.

One of the earliest frontier literary contributions was William Littell's *Festoons of Fancy* (1814). Littell, a native of New Jersey, arrived in

Kentucky near the turn of the century. He began the practice of law and quickly established himself before the Kentucky bar as an able but eccentric scholar. During his first decade in the West, he had abundant opportunity to observe the eddying course of human life. Politicians strove for picayunish advantages; pious frauds led double lives; bullies, fops, and mountebanks were active; plain people sought the benefits of the proximity of government and yearned for the multiplication of counties. A host of other characters of varying qualities and motives lumbered across the local scene. Adapting a Biblical style in his writings, Littell introduced the art of satire to the frontier. While men of conscious destiny like John Filson, William Maxwell, Humphrey Marshall and Caleb Atwater wrote in a high and serious vein, Littell punctured a regional bubble with his humorous pen. He was a forerunner of those other lawyers and journalists who would win a degree of immortality in books describing plain people.

Possibly the dean of these writers was Augustus Baldwin Longstreet, lawyer, editor, and university president. Judge Longstreet early devoted his literary talents to describing the bumptious life of frontier Georgia. His *Georgia Scenes* (1835), first published in newspapers, became a classic in book form. The observant judge was a keen student of the whimsicalities of an isolated society, and his characters, crude and unlettered, were impudent and audacious. Using the rich dialect speech forms of the day, Longstreet paraded across his pages an army of people who individually would not have left their marks in history except as cold statistical digits in census reports, or as parties to frequent suits in the courts of a justice of the peace. The witty Georgia lawyer not only dignified these people as human beings with loves, hates and national ambitions, but he gave them permanency in frontier literature. His accounts of Georgia theatricals in 1809, of fighting and horse-swapping are social documents which capture the mode of frontier life.

Across the line in Alabama, Johnson J. Hooper, a North Carolinian expatriate turned newspaperman, took up the study of frontier character where Judge Longstreet left off, and in 1845 he published his *Adventures of Simon Suggs*. Although Simon was a crude bumpkin with neither social nor literary pretensions, he gave to the frontier movement that great practical axiom: "It is good to be shifty in a new country." Captain Suggs of the Tallapoosa Volunteers, however, became more than an axiomatic figure in frontier literature. In his wanderings and sage outpourings he displayed a basic folk humor and called attention to materials on the American scene whose use in later years would make the frontier a central theme in a great body of literature.

In nearby Tennessee, George W. Harris created a blood brother to Captain Suggs in his frolicsome character, Sut Lovingood. Sut was an uninhibited greenhorn of the frontier who was not afraid to try anything once, "even if it throwed him." Brash, raw and bumptious, Harris' character personified an important segment of the unrefined population that eddied in the backwoods. He was as much a part of the contemporary scene as were General Jackson and General Harrison. As chief disturber of country dances, the culprit behind the breaking-up of lodge meetings, and the perpetrator and butt of practical jokes, he had his mission in life. Joseph Glover Baldwin, Virginia-born, moved to the Mississippi frontier early in the 1830's, and later to Alabama. He had a shrewd understanding of humanity and a keen eye for the changing scenes about him. Taking notes upon the life he observed as a frontier lawyer, he later compiled the popular book *Flush Times in Alabama and Mississippi*. In many respects this was one of the most solid works of its kind. Baldwin was able not only to use the local dialect to good effect, but he had sufficient social understanding to make a scholarly analysis of backwoods society.

David Crockett was a genuine flesh-and-blood character of rare nature of West Tennessee. He was as tangible as a drink of muddy branch water, and as rowdy as a backwoods legend. He appealed to his neighbors because he disdained learning and preferred politics and courting in nature's own raw and untutored style. His name early became synonymous with wild yarn-spinning and tall-talking. He was one of the earliest rip-roarers who amused themselves by "barking" squirrels with a rifle, turning pestiferous panthers wrongside out, "grinning" bark off gnarly trees, scratching their heads with forked streaks of lightning, and spitting a yellow stream of tobacco juice that plucked chickens' eyes at the distance of a long corn row.

In point of fact, this blood-and-thunder character was born in the backwoods village of Rogersville, Tennessee. Every breeze that blew in that region was waving people westward, and Davy went with the wind. After many misadventures he settled down on a farm, but being restless and shiftless he packed up his wife and two daughters and moved on nearer the Mississippi. He served briefly with General Jackson in the Creek campaign, but he did not become a hero worshipper of the Master of the Hermitage. On his less than triumphant march westward, the colonel served the grassroots apprenticeship to political success, rising through constable and justice of the peace to militia colonel. Later he served two terms in the United States Congress.

Davy Crockett was frank-spoken, boastful, unlettered—a rich backwoods character who gave the national legislative halls a ring of the "natural." How much of the writing attributed to him was his own is still a subject for dispute. By the time of his death, as one of the heroes of the Alamo, at least five books of an autobiographical nature had capitalized on his name and career, and the Crockett *Almanac* was an American institution. It is not the purpose here, however, to sort out the strands and set right the tangled skein of authorship of these books. It is enough to say that Crockett yarns were productive of a flood of "original" narratives about the frontier.

Across the Mississippi, Joseph M. Field and John S. Robb made St. Louis a home of humorous writings. Fields with his book *The Drama in Pokerville*, and Robb with his *Streaks of Squatter Life* raised themselves above the herd of commonplace printer-editors. Much of their material appeared first in the original newspaper and special feature journal, the St. Louis *Reveille*. Both authors were major contributors to William T. Porter's New York journal *The Spirit of the Times*, which began publication in 1831 as a sporting periodical. After 1836 it introduced an increasing number of original articles about the frontier, and during the years 1844 to 1854 it carried some of the best of the backwoods yarns. Porter's editorial desk became a clearing house for much of this type of material. In time he gathered together the best of the stories and published them under *The Big Bear of Arkansas, and Other Tales*, the *Drama of Pokerville*, and *A Quarter Race in Kentucky, and Other Sketches*.

Whether or not these humorous folk stories were in fact authentic narratives of life on the frontier matters little. They were not seriously challenged, if challenged at all, by contemporary readers. Storytelling was a man's art, and the tougher the author made conditions appear, the more mighty he appeared to his hearers and readers. On the other hand, many stories made the teller appear to be a greenhorn of the first water, but a proud and unselfconscious one at that. Travelers' accounts, contemporary letters, diaries and personal memoirs tend to document much of this huge body of original material. In recent years scholars have given serious attention to the writings of the first half of the nineteenth century. It may be true that many of the authors held themselves apart from the life which they described so picturesquely, but the scholarly *Dictionary of Americanisms* largely confirms their acquaintance with vernacular and dialect.

Just as the frontier grew its bumper crop of comic writers, so it became the theme of a vast list of travel accounts. Travelers of almost every nationality and from every section of the eastern seaboard came west to see the country, to view the natives with horror and to predict the doom of civilized man in the great slough of the backwoods. From the beginning of settlement in the Ohio Valley, travelers established a well-beaten path, or "grand tour," to the region. This route led from New York to Philadelphia, then westward to Pittsburgh, down the Ohio to Cincinnati, across the river to Kentucky, back across to Indiana, southward across Tennessee, and downriver to New Orleans. A later route led westward to St. Louis and backwoods Missouri and back across Illinois and Michigan to the East. One of the first major visitors was Dr. François André Michaux, following in 1802 in the footsteps of his father who had come west a decade earlier. He visited Ohio, Kentucky and Tennessee west of the mountains, and two years later he published a solid narrative of his journey in Paris under the title *Travels to the Westward of the Alleghany Mountains in the States of Ohio, Kentucky and Tennessee*. This French scientist compressed a good analysis of frontier society into a remarkably brief space.

Following Michaux came the disgruntled Englishman Thomas Ashe, who had the announced purpose of exploring the western rivers. He quickly gained the reputation of being a "bone stealer" because he was said to have robbed Dr. William Goforth of the collection of mastodon bones which he had gathered at the Big Bone Lick in Kentucky. Ashe published an account of his travels in three volumes, but his use of facts was reckless even by the most charitable appraisal. Christian Schultze, an American traveler, set out to determine the veracity of the British visitor. In his two volumes, *Travels on an Inland Voyage* (1810), he presented a fascinating and dependable picture of the river society. He was one of the first authors to quote the half-horse-half-alligator boasts which he said he had heard from the lips of two Kentucky flatboatmen near Natchez.

Few western travel accounts contain so much solid material as does that of the New England minister Timothy Flint, whose extended missionary journey took him from North Reading, Massachusetts, to Louisiana. This highly literate minister lived among the frontier people long enough to understand fully their nature, foibles, virtues and failures. His background was one of intimate association with the country, and there is missing from his writings the angularity and misinformation which mars other accounts. Flint's *Recollections of the Last Ten Years* is made up of letters which he wrote to his father James Flint, and of notes which he made as he moved about the Mississippi Valley. Because he made contemporary society live for his readers, his book lives today as the classic account of the life it describes.

Charles Fenno Hoffman, a one-legged New York poet-author, deserted the editorial offices of the *Knickerbocker Magazine* to ride across the frontier. He sent back accounts of his experiences to the *New-York American*, and later gathered these into two volumes which he published in 1835 under the title of *A Winter in the West*. He had a fondness for the frontier country, and his observations are far kinder than those of many foreign visitors.

Not all foreign travelers came to view the American scene as the home of democracy. Many were advance men for emigrant groups, like Henry Bradshaw Fearon, Morris Birkbeck, James Flower, and others who sought suitable places to make settlement. In these collective accounts the modern reader is given a more or less intimate picture of the domestic frontier. These emigrant authors were writing for people who wished to know about the everyday things of frontier American life; consequently their reports are not without significance as social documents.

No traveler, not even the irascible Charles Dickens, aroused the people of the Ohio Valley as did Mrs. Frances Trollope. This caustic English lady came to America in 1827 to found a department store in Cincinnati. After three years experience, her store was a failure, and so were her various attempts to reform the unsophisticated society of that city. She kept careful notes of what she saw in America, and when she returned to England she wrote and published her book *Domestic Manners of the Americans*. The text is caustic, satirical, witty and penetrating. Few books about America ever stirred up so much wrath, ridicule and revilement. There is no doubt that the great body of Mrs. Trollope's criticism was accurate, and that the storm of outrage which greeted her book was the defiance of a people who actually were hopeful of raising themselves to the polite level of society advocated by the prying English storekeeper. Because it was deserved, the sting of her lash was all the keener.

The stream of foreign travelers to the frontier remained flush, and with monotonous regularity visitors returned home to write and publish accounts of their experiences. Today some of these books are rare pieces of Americana. The traveler kept up with the advance of the frontier, and occasionally one even overreached it. John Bradbury, a Scotsman, who was one of the earliest visitors up the Missouri River, wrote of his experiences with the British immigrant in mind. His book, one of the most useful of the early descriptions of this region, gives an insight into the primitiveness of native life that is equalled only by the Lewis and Clark journals.

As the far West came into focus during the first decades of the nineteenth century, a score of travel narratives describe journeys on that frontier. Among these were Thomas Nuttall's *A Journal of Travels into the Arkansa Territory, during the Year 1819;* Samuel Parker's *Journal of An Exploring Tour Beyond the Rocky Mountains, Under the Direction of the A. B. C. M., Performed in the Years 1835, '36, and '37,* and Henry Schoolcraft's various journals of early exploration along the Upper Mississippi. James Ohio Pattie's narrative of his travels in the Southwest, and the voluminous account of Father De Smet's travels along the Upper Missouri and in Oregon are classics. Father De Smet had an opportunity to observe Indian life in that area at first hand for a long time, and his missionary reports and journals constitute a major source of information on this part of the West.

The list of travel accounts describing the West might be multiplied into many hundreds without doing more than reciting authors and titles, or piling up conflicting points of view and narrow observations. For the most part, travelers came looking for a mature society, and were unable to evaluate what they actually found because of their lack of experience in viewing a virginal country coming under the control of a civilization which was for the moment primitive. Essentially, the great mass of travelers came to see how well American democracy was working as it spread itself over the continent. Scores of them believed that it was failing, or that it had become completely submerged under the inert layer of uncouth informality and general rudeness which the traveler encountered. They disliked the frontiersman's food, his outspoken individuality, his lumpy beds, crowded tavern common rooms, muddy roads, the pallidness of the natives, the unattractive womenfolk, the frontiersman's loud boasting, his pugnaciousness, political attitudes, extreme nationalism, and narrow religious views. A great mass of this material is obviously worthless item for item, but it is collectively important as a literary mural of the trials and moods of the American as he made contact with the raw western country.

If travelers often viewed the Western American scene from the pedestal of outside superiority and from a condition where they were assured they could escape the next day or next month, there were native sons who took time to look about them and to record their observations. The volume of western books bearing early imprints is rather extensive, and it is surprising that native western authors and publishers were so successful in their labors. John Filson of Kentucky led the parade with his famous book, *The Discovery, Settlement, and Present State of Kentucke*, Wilmington, Delaware, 1784. Before the middle of the next century almost every frontier state had its own historian who had published at least one book. Humphrey Marshall of Kentucky published a one-volume history of his state in 1812, and in 1824 he enlarged it to two volumes. He presented local history from the warped point of view of a strong-willed and aroused Federalist. North of the Ohio, Salmon P. Chase published *A Sketch of the History of Ohio in 1833*, but it was Caleb Atwater who undertook a more ambitious work in his *History of the State of Ohio, Natural and Civil*, Cincinnati, 1838. Nine years before, George Washington Stipp of Xenia, Ohio, had gathered a number of the better sections of John Bradford's reminiscent notes about the conquest of the older frontier and published them in 1827 under the title of the *Western Miscellany, or, Accounts Historical, Biographical, and Amusing*.

James H. Lanman's *History of Michigan, Civil and Topographical* was published in 1839, almost before the fresh influx of American settlers had raised their axes; even by that date Michigan had a history. Illinois had two governors who turned historians, John Reynolds and Thomas Ford. Both these men knew most of the personalities of the period about which they wrote; both had intimate personal knowledge of state politics. Reynolds was a humorless eccentric who wrote a narrow and partisan volume, while Ford was more colorful. He not only recorded much factual material about his state's history, but he also analyzed frontier politics. He was unable to write with complete objectivity, but because he had a good sense of personal and social history, much of his material has lasting value. All of the other frontier states eventually produced historians whose contributions were of more than passing importance. In the 1840's several legislatures became mildly interested in subsidizing state histories. John B. Dillon of Indiana undertook such an authorized volume, but the legislature failed him before he got past the year 1816. Lewis Collins undertook a history of Kentucky at the instigation of the general assembly of that state.

Books that covered either larger areas than single states or were confined precisely to single topics were numerous. Two of the more important were Timothy Flint's two-volume *Condensed Geography and History of the Western States* (1828), and John W. Monette's *History of the Discovery and Settlement of the Valley of the Mississippi by the Three Great European Powers, Spain, France, and Great Britain* (1846). Both these studies are basic for an early understanding of the broader phases of frontier expansion. Of a monographic nature were Robert B. McAfee's *History of the Late War in the Western Country* (1816), and Samuel L. Metcalfe's *A Collection of Some of the Most Interesting Narratives of the Indian Warfare in the West* (1821). In 1832 John A. McClung's *Sketches of Western Adventure* came from the press. The War of 1812 stimulated a throng of historians, anxious either to interpret the late war with Britain, or to record their own heroic parts in the struggle. They were clearly convinced that they had flirted with destiny, and they did not want the fact forgotten.

Competing with the historians were the annalists, J. H. Perkins, James R. Albach, J. M. Peck and Charles Cist. The first three of these collaborated in the preparation and publication of Perkins' *Annals of the West* (1846). This statistical and factual volume went through several editions, the last one covering the history of the West up through 1857. Charles Cist, somewhat more modest in his project, confined his attention to Cincinnati. His work is important for its factual contents, and also because it documents the process of urbanization on the banks of the Ohio.

Not all the literary grist went to the mills of the historian and statistician; the creative writers were most active. James Hall used the western theme in *Harpe's Head: A Legend of Kentucky* (1833), and in his famous

Legends of the West (1832). Possibly Judge Hall's most important book was his *Notes on the Western States* (1836, 1838, 1842, and 1884). Not only was Judge Hall a prose writer and historian, but he also shared honors with his fellow Pennsylvanian, William Davis Gallagher, as one of the important poets of the West. Gallagher, like Hall, edited several literary magazines including the *Literary Gazette*, the *Cincinnati Mirror*, and the *Western Literary Journal and Monthly Review*. By profession he was a newspaperman with strong political leanings, but between fighting for the Whig party and magazine editing he produced a series of volumes of poetry entitled *Erato No. I, II,* and *III*. One of his best poems was *Miami Woods*. Frontier poets were indeed numerous, and their soulful outpourings consumed vast quantities of ink and paper.

Novelists found the western scene a good source for their art. Frederick W. Thomas wrote three or four novels, among them *Clinton Bradshaw, East and West,* and *Howard Pinckney: a Novel.* Caroline Kirkland attempted to fictionalize the westward movement in her book *A New Home —Who'll Follow?* Benjamin Drake, a brother of the famous Cincinnati physician Daniel, published a life of the Sauk Indian chief, Black Hawk, and tried his hand with some success in the fictionalized *Tales and Sketches from the Queen City*—a humorous publication which caricatures western life, but not without a strong element of truth in its satire.

The early West was to be distinguished not so much by the novels which were written contemporary with its development as by those which were written in a later period about pioneering. It is doubtful that any of the novels written before 1880 about the frontier measured up to the greatness of the movement. The Beadle Series of "dime novels" found the adventures of frontiersmen good picking, as did the Beadle, Adams, and Munro series. Emerson Bennett of Cincinnati used various western themes to good advantage in the novels which he prepared for the "yellow back" trade. From Mark Twain to Elizabeth Madox Roberts, at least three generations of modern writers have dredged the frontier theme in their books. The noble pioneer was to become as much a romantic bit of property as the noble red man.

Almost as romantic as the books of fiction are the prolific writings of the clergymen who labored along the outer fringes of westerly settlement. Among the earliest clerical authors was Father Stephen Badin of Kentucky who discussed the role of the church in *The Real Principles of Roman Catholics in reference to God and Country* (1805). Eighteen years later John Taylor recorded an extensive record of Baptist activities in his *History of Ten Baptist Churches*. The major books of religious biography were those of James B. Finley, Maxwell Pierson Gaddis, Peter Cartwright, and William Henry Milburn. Finley, a Cincinnati Methodist circuit rider, led an exciting life in the backwoods. He saw the country grow up about him, and his observations were mature and exact. In editing Finley's *Sketches of Western Methodism* (1855), W. P. Strickland added a number of biographical sketches of other ministers who had ridden through the backwoods on repeated spiritual missions. William Henry Milburn's *The Rifle, Axe and Saddle-Bags, and Other Lectures* (1857) and *The Pioneers, Preachers and People of the Mississippi Valley* (1860) cover many subjects as well as those usually discussed by preachers. In the final chapter of the latter work the author does much to validate the writings of Longstreet, Hooper, Harris and others.

Choicest of all frontier clerical memoirs is the *Autobiography of Peter Cartwright, the Backwoods Preacher* (1856). "Uncle Peter" was born in Virginia, moved to Kentucky and between that state and Tennessee he began his relentless half-century pursuit of the Devil. The Devil went west, and his vigorous adversary followed him to Illinois. Preacher Cartwright became a scarred veteran of more than fifty annual Methodist conferences and innumerable tussles with sin in every imaginable form. He attacked horse racing and card-playing sinners with the same vigor that he assaulted Baptists, Presbyterians and Shakers. Brother Cartwright was plain-spoken, ungrammatical, belligerent and roistering in his pulpit behavior. On the other hand, he had little patience with "jerkers" and "babblers" whom he considered emotionally unstable in their religious protestations.

In the spring of 1825, young Cartwright had taken stock of his situation and thought he saw in it the will of Providence that he desert the land of slavery and go to live in a free territory. On the Illinois frontier he knew cheap land would be available where he could raise a numerous family, and souls were as destitute there as any place in the land. His autobiography is a colorful volume of self-glorification, but any man who could turn a backwoods Saturday night dance into an experience meeting before the fiddler had nipped the bottle or drawn the bow was certainly an extrovert of strong powers. Scores of preachers of all faiths told their stories in much the same vein of self-glorification as did the Illinois circuit rider. Their books are now, except for long and tiresome scriptural disputations, valuable as chapters in social history.

Few authors discussing religious developments on the nineteenth century frontier were willing to do so objectively and with calmness. They engaged opponents in bitter controversies. Such men as David and Nathan Rice, Adam Rankin, Robert Owen, Barton W. Stone, Alexander Campbell, Richard McNemar and scores of others argued such questions as infant baptism, modes of church government, infallibility of the church, the cholera as a scourge of God, the divinity of Christ, the Roman Catholic

Church, the Mormons, the causes and cures of infidelity, and the nature of sin. No argument was complete until both contenders had put their words in print and scattered them far and wide. From a literary point of view this material has only an antiquarian interest. Some of it is bad-tempered, some is in bad taste, some stupid, and almost all of it intolerant. However, it documents rather eloquently the fact that much of the church leadership on the frontier was highly partisan and intolerant. A reader searches in vain for any realization that the frontier might have offered the greatest latitude for liberal religious practice or differing points of view. The first half of the nineteenth century saw the continuance of an almost rigid religious conservatism which placed great stress on denominationalism and narrow, literal interpretations of the Scriptures, and which sought to restrict the individual's private conduct.

Before 1830, Lexington and Cincinnati were the main publishing centers. An astonishing number of books found their way to print in shops located in these towns. Printers, however, did not wait for local authors to grind out manuscripts; they devoted much of the energy of their typesetters and presses to reproduction of books of all sorts. Copyrights seemed to have meant little to the frontier publisher who sought to turn a penny by supplying a book-starved region with the standard works of the moment. It is not at all unusual to discover a Lexington or Cincinnati imprint on a book that was written and originally published elsewhere.

The extensive list of pamphlets, periodicals, and books published make it evident that the westerner was neither altogether illiterate nor uninterested in literature. He was conscious of western expansion, and many contemporary works of native origin show that authors were concerned early with historical interpretation of the frontier movement. A consciousness of the importance of the frontier movement in the growing nation is revealed, and a fear that unless contemporary historians recorded the story the pioneers would be forgotten. Most of the writings that undertook to analyze the history of the frontier contain a strong flavor of both provincialism and nationalism. Authors proclaimed the joys of living in the new country, begged for an increase in population, and boasted of the future. Literate men found it impossible to put the pen aside; the vastness of the new country inspired them to make a permanent record of their times. Caleb Atwater boasted for Ohio that:

> Every river in the West is vexed with our oars, and every lake is whitened with our sails. The majesty of our forest is borning before us, and delightful villages, towns and cities rear their glittering spires in the forest's stead. Indeed our mild climate, our fertile soil, and numerous rivers, without falls in them, moving majestically along, as noiselessly

almost as the root of time; with the broad and beautiful Ohio washing
our whole southern border, and Lake Erie, with impulse almost resistless,
our citizens are invited to industry, activity, enterprise and wealth.

Artists and Actors

The frontier produced a creditable number of artists who have left behind a record of their artistic attainments and also tangible evidence of
the general appearance of individuals on the frontier. Most of the early art
was of a personal variety. Strangely enough, the vast stretches of virgin
country and the inspiring vistas which appeared at every hand seem not
to have inspired landscape painters of any appreciable importance. Among
the first of the frontier artists was William West who lived for a time in
Lexington, Kentucky. He had as a contemporary Asa Park who combined portraiture with painting still life. The first major western artist was
Matthew Harris Jouett, second son of the famous Captain Jack Jouett who
rode to Monticello before Cornwallis' troops to save the Virginia Assembly
from capture. Young Jouett was educated in Transylvania University and
went East in 1816 to study with Gilbert Stuart. Before his death in 1827
this industrious Kentuckian is known to have produced 334 portraits.
Other Kentucky painters were John Grimes and Joseph Bush. Both men
were influenced by Jouett and were reasonably good portrait artists.

Jouett had for neighbors the Ohio painters, Thomas Cole, William
Watkins, Frederick Eckstein, Lily Martin, Sala Bosworth, William Henry
Powell, and Charles Sullivan. Like the Kentuckians, these artists devoted
their skill largely to portraiture and found commissions enough to keep
themselves alive. Many of their paintings are still in existence. Possibly the
most outstanding of the Ohio artists prior to 1860 was Thomas Worthington Whittredge who received formal training in Europe. He departed from
the traditional personal art and produced nature paintings, some of which
are in the Corcoran Gallery. Powell painted the mural "DeSoto Discovering the Mississippi" for the rotunda of the Capitol at Washington. Christopher Harrison, George Winter, and James Otto Lewis were early Indiana artists. Winter and Lewis gained reputations for their Indian paintings. In 1833 Lewis published seventy-two of his paintings made at Detroit
in the *North American Aboriginal Portfolio*.

An influx of German immigrants into the Ohio Valley in the first half of
the nineteenth century brought to the frontier many wood carvers. Others
were endowed with similar talents in stone work but had to resort to
tombstone carving to gain a livelihood. A native son, Shobal Vail Clevenger, learned something of the art of sculpture from Frederick Eckstein
and David Guion. His particular talent was in making portrait busts. He had

for contemporaries Henry Kirke Brown and Hiram Powers of "Greek Slave" fame. In fact Brown, Powers and Clevenger were encouraged by Eckstein, and the three had worked together in Dorfeuille's Western Museum in Cincinnati. South of the river in Kentucky, another rural lad was serving a most unpromising apprenticeship to art, building stone fences and chimneys, and chiseling crude figures on tombstones. This was Joel Tanner Hart, who created some of the good political busts of his period.

Missouri contributed the able *genre* painter, George Caleb Bingham. Though born in Virginia, Bingham had spent nearly all of his life on the frontier. Beginning as a self-taught artist, he studied abroad and in the East. His paintings of frontiersmen in various moods became documentary of the frontier movement. Possibly his best paintings were "Raftsmen Playing Cards," "Emigration of Daniel Boone," "County Election," and "Verdict of the People." In these paintings Bingham captured much of the spirit of the swirl of life about him and preserved it in a graphic form that equalled contemporary humorous writings. In Louisiana, Thomas Bangs Thorpe combined humorous writings with descriptive painting to record his concepts of frontier life. While he was writing and publishing his "Big Bear of Arkansaw" stories, *Mysteries of the Backwoods* and *The Hive of the Bee-Hunter*, he was painting "The Prairies of Louisiana," "Wild Turkey Hunting," and "Watercraft of the Backwoods."

John Banvard of Louisville, Kentucky, set out in 1840 to portray the Mississippi River on a wide panoramic painting. He produced a canvas almost three miles long, which he claimed was the largest painting in existence. Banvard's work was photographically accurate, but it had little artistic merit. He exhibited his painting both in the United States and England. A less original type of art was produced by Basil Hall with a *camera lucida*. He was able to recreate scenes along the western rivers and in the clearings. He had an eye for clothing details, facial expressions, and social behavior. In publishing his selection of forty plates, he chose only the clearer impressions; fortunately, however, all of his prints are now owned by the Indiana University Library, and the unpublished collection indicates a much wider range of drawings.

The frontier underwent many architectural changes, but it produced few early architects. For the most part house designs were copied from plan books. In Kentucky young Gideon Shryock became interested in the field of architecture and went to Philadelphia in 1823 to study under William Strickland. When he returned to Kentucky, he was commissioned to design a new State house. In this building Shryock introduced Greek revival lines to the West and helped to break the tidewater Georgian tradition. During his career he was to have a profound influence on architecture west of the mountains. A claim is made for him that he designed the State house in Arkansas. The classic revival style was adopted everywhere. Private homes, state houses, and courthouses showed its influence. Introduction of the power-driven sawmill made enough lumber available to change the appearances of buildings, if not always to improve architectural lines.

Almost from the beginning of organized society in the West there were theatricals. Early amateur companies of thespians in Kentucky gave their plays in Transylvania University and in the courthouses at Lexington and Louisville. By 1811 Cincinnati had become a theatrical town, and soon other places across the frontier were taken into the circuits. Many of the early performances were given by amateur players who engaged in theatricals either for art's sake or as a part of benefit programs. In time, professional actors and managers such as Noble Luke Usher, Samuel Drake, N. M. Ludlow, Sol Smith and James Caldwell monopolized the field. While the theatre was popular on the frontier, it is doubtful that plays of western origin were favored. Following a standardized formula, the routine programs nearly always consisted of a tragedy and a comedy. Sometimes it was difficult for unsophisticated audiences to distinguish between the two, and not infrequently the only tragedy and comedy present were the disastrous reactions of the patrons.

By 1840 the towns of Cincinnati, Louisville, Lexington, Indianapolis, St. Louis, and Detroit had developed theatres of some permanence, and the drama became the most popular form of entertainment. The theatre, however, had to compete with circuses, itinerant performers, magic shows, animal trainers, and balloon ascensionists. Conservative religious groups were opposed to stage performances, and it was not unusual for a manager to be forced into debates with his attackers. City councils often handicapped managers by imposing ruinous taxes on their performances. But despite these drawbacks, an astonishingly large number of theatrical ventures were undertaken, and an enormous number of plays were performed. Shakespearean and Victorian dramas were given with moderate success on the western circuit, and many famous American actors were hardened to audience reactions by their boisterous receptions in backwoods theatres. For the enthusiastic patrons the plays took them away from the realities of life, and at the same time gave them a feeling of patronizing the arts.

Scientists

The sciences on the frontier had a highly practical application. One of the most important attractions which brought settlers westward was land. Land was important, however, for its surface wealth, and not for what lay beneath it. Mineral and other resources, unless they could be exploited by the most elementary processes, were either ignored or left to future development. There was, of course, an interest in salt, lead, potassium nitrate, and iron. Some coal beds were developed, but in Kentucky, Indiana, and Illinois rich coal beds lay untouched for years. The Missouri, Illinois, and Iowa lead mines were exploited early, and so were some of the iron ore banks, but there was little or no scientific knowledge available as to the extent or general availability of mineral resources. Not until farmers became concerned with the relationship between their lands and the annual production of field crops did western legislators concern themselves with the importance of having geological surveys made of their states.

Surveying was one of the earliest frontier professions, but surveyors were strictly surface workers. They were primarily interested in establishing landmarks and determining in a superficial way the general lie and qualities of lands. Few of them made serious attempts to describe topography on a broad pattern. Knowledge of the courses of streams and their interrelationships was often secondary to locating blocks of desirable land. Such matters as the general "dips" and rises of the topography were not fully determined until long after settlement had occurred. There were, however, various individuals who became interested in primitive archaeology because of the existence of numerous Indian mounds in the Ohio and Mississippi valleys. Occasionally, local archaeologists like Caleb Atwater, William Goforth, Ephriam Squier, Edward Hamilton Davis of Ohio, and John Clifford of Kentucky, dug into Indian mounds and made other preliminary archaeological discoveries, but no sustained geological exploration had taken place.

In December, 1831, Tennessee began what appears to have been the first orderly geological survey on the frontier. This state was fortunate in securing the services of Dr. Gerard Troost. A native of Amsterdam, Dr. Troost had a long and varied scientific career already behind him when he came to America. He was a member of the so-called "boatload of knowledge" which went out to New Harmony, Indiana, in 1825. In this adventure he was associated with William Maclure, Thomas Say, Robert Dale Owen and C. A. Lesueur. Two years later he left New Harmony and took his scientific collection to Nashville where he remained the rest of his life. There, a progressive legislature appointed him geologist, mineralogist, and assayist for that state. A diligent laborer, he prepared ten reports, including contour maps, which covered the various resources of Tennessee. To these he added pioneering studies in the archaeology and anthropology of the region.

While Dr. Troost was introducing scientific geology to Tennessee, David Dale Owen was in England studying chemistry and geology. Upon his return to America he studied medicine for a time and then began his professional career under the direction of the Dutch scientist at Nashville. Owen's first independent work was a preliminary survey of Indiana in 1837. The next year he was commissioned by the federal government to make a survey of Iowa and Wisconsin, and later of Minnesota and the Bad Lands of South Dakota. His report of 1839 was the result of close organization and good administration. After extensive work on the Upper Mississippi and Missouri, he was employed to survey Kentucky. His reports in this region are of genuine historical significance. Working furiously, he was able to produce a highly acceptable scientific survey that still has much merit. At the time of his death, Dr. Owen was working sixteen hours a day on the first geological survey of Arkansas.

Ohio was one of the most active states in the field of the sciences. For many years various individuals had demonstrated an intelligent amateur interest in geology and geography. W. W. Mather prepared the first geological report in 1838. This report, however, amounted to little more than a preliminary surface survey which established some information about rock formations, location of coal beds, and the general surface contour of Ohio. In the other frontier states, legislatures were becoming aware of the economic importance of mineral resources. Illinois employed Dr. J. C. Norwood to search out its hidden wealth, and in the South, Mississippi employed Dr. John Millington and B. L. C. Wailes to report on the resources of that state.

Scientific investigation of natural resources was only a part of the bigger picture in developing curiosity about the frontier. Botanists of every description found the virgin West an inexhaustible source of study. With its hundreds of plants and varied soil and climatic conditions, there was no end of fresh materials which could be added to collections, which brought enduring fame to their discoverers. The French botanists, André and François Michaux, began a long tradition of foreign botanical visitations to the frontier. None of these was more assiduous in his labors than the Scotsman John Bradbury. He was one of the first to visit the Missouri Valley and to leave a good elementary description of both plant and animal life. His *Travels in the Interior of America, in the Years 1809, 1810, and 1811,* is essentially a preliminary natural history of the Missouri River frontier.

In 1811 the eccentric Franco-German-Italian scientist Constantine Rafinesque arrived in Lexington, Kentucky, to accept a professorship in Transylvania University. He was prompted to come west by his English friend, John Clifford, who had settled in Lexington where he had engaged in considerable research into natural phenomena. When Rafinesque arrived in Kentucky, he showed an insatiable desire to gather specimens and knowledge in great haste. He spent eight years exploring the Ohio Valley and in bringing together a large collection of all sorts of data. Because of his personal peculiarities and eccentricities he sometimes fell victim to the jocular frontiersmen. No one seemed to enjoy joking the serious-minded Italian more than the French naturalist John J. Audubon.

Rafinesque proposed the organization of a botanical garden in Lexington, where he hoped to collect plants which would be both ornamental and of great use to farmers. He proposed to select the best stocks of "fruit trees and grape vines, mountain rice, madder, senna, opium, ginseng, rhubarb, castor oil, new kinds of grain and pulse, etc." During his eight years in Kentucky, he became not only a striking community figure, but he grew in scientific stature. When he was not in the woods gathering new specimens for his collection, he was busy writing many of his nine hundred published articles.

Other naturalists who interested themselves in western life were David B. Thomas, John L. Riddell, Allen Lapham, and Thomas Nuttall. Although all these men made important pioneering contributions, the work of none was of greater significance than that of Nuttall. His visits to the trans-Mississippi West between 1809 and 1835 took him over the vast area between Louisiana and Oregon; his journals and scientific materials are of importance both in the field of exploration and the natural sciences.

Early in the century Alexander Wilson, the famous Pennsylvania ornithologist, visited the Ohio Valley where he became acquainted (under none too favorable circumstances) with John J. Audubon. Although Wilson's paintings of western birds are of great importance, he could hardly be called a regional scientist. On the other hand Audubon belonged, scientifically at least, to the region. Few more romantic figures came to the frontier than this French emigrant who reached Kentucky by way of Philadelphia. Though the circumstances of his birth and background are now established beyond any reasonable doubt, some of the romantic legend that he was the Lost Dauphin of France still persists. He came West as a merchant, but he failed in business. Audubon's heart was in the woods and not at the counter and mill hopper. Largely a self-taught artist and ornithologist, he was able to produce almost photographic paintings of American birds. In spite of the various criticisms of his works, they still remain important. The large and colorful plates in his elephantine edition of *Birds of America* were made from specimens which he collected in the western country. In both his bird and animal studies he left significant records of frontier wild life. Important also are his observations of human life as recorded in his journals and voluminous notes, and the fact that he created a popular interest in ornithology.

Another young scientist was to know the joys of exploration in the unsettled West. He was Thomas Say, great-grandson of William Bartram, who became intensely interested in entomology. In 1819 Say accompanied Major Stephen Long on his two expeditions to the West. Much of the material which went into his monumental *American Entomology; or Descriptions of the Insects of North America* (1824–1825) was gathered on his two western visits.

Scientists looking for information about the mineral resources and natural life of the vast expanse of the West came in droves, and so did persons interested in Indian life. George Catlin, a Pennsylvania artist, traveled among the western tribes between 1832 and 1838. In his own words, he visited "the vast and pathless wilds which are familiarly denominated the great 'Far West' of the North American Continent." He had seen a delegation of "ten or fifteen noble and dignified-looking Indians from the 'Far West,' [who] suddenly arrived in that city [Philadelphia] arrayed and equipped in all their classic beauty, shield and helmet, with tunic and manteau,—tinted and tasselled off, exactly for the painter's palette." In 1832 he went up the Missouri on the second trip of the *Yellowstone*. During his eight years in the West, which seem to have been spent largely in the region east of the Rockies, he painted in the Mandan villages, and among the Apaches in the Southwest.

Catlin produced more than six hundred paintings and displayed them here and abroad in his Indian Gallery. In 1841 he published his *Letters and Notes on the Manners, Customs, and Condition of the North American Indians*. This book in its various colored and black and white editions is an important social document. Another Indian painter was Alfred Jacob Miller who went West in 1837 and doubtless influenced the popular concept of the western Indians.

Prince Maximilian of Wied-Neuwied went up the Missouri in 1833 aboard the *Yellowstone*. He was accompanied by Charles Bodmer, the Swedish portrait painter. Maximilian was essentially interested in ethnology, and his *Travels in the Interior of North America* (1839) is a good contemporary study in this field. It is doubtful, however, that this text is as important as the atlas prepared by Bodmer. The artist gave close attention to form, movement, spirit, and details of dress and arms. He made some of the most accurate documentary paintings in existence of the western Indians. From 1836 to 1884, T. L. McKinney, superintendent of Indian trade under James Madison, and James Hall produced their famous folio volumes *History of the Indian Tribes of North America, with Biographical Sketches and Anecdotes of Their Principal Chiefs*. The 120 illustrations in these volumes came from the War Department collection of Indian portraits. McKinney's *Memoirs, Official and Personal*, also contains ethnological material and constitutes a major scientific footnote.

Education

Basic to all frontier intellectual advance was the region's philosophy of education. Frontiersmen dreamed of bettering conditions for their children, but they hardly knew what they wanted. Education promised greater advantages but at the same time it offered certain liabilities. Education was expensive, and, too, there was fear of the changes it might make in individuals; yet the subject was a great challenge to the American pioneer. At least a semblance of training was required to provide professional men to perform necessary services in the region. Engineering of various elementary types was a necessity in exploiting the country's resources. Rising frontier commerce demanded a rudimentary knowledge of business practices. Legal practice required more than the elementary three R's, if the lawyer was to advance beyond the magistrate courts. Frontier doctors had to secure training despite the fact they could remain illiterate quacks in many areas without being found out. Even agriculture in time was to make a demand for better educational facilities. A practical education could yield practical results in everyday affairs.

Slightly derogatory terms applied to educated men such as "book larnin'," "letter larned," and "college dandies" were not always helpful. One of the most unfortunate traditions in American life (if not of frontier origin, then certainly a well-nurtured belief in that area) was the attitude that education was impractical and unsettled the individual for a productive life in the future. The cause of education suffered by invidious comparison. The following paragraph, of Indiana origin, illustrates this fact:

> . . . straight shooting are more important than philosophy; and a dead Indian is much more to the point than a dead language. Preachers are all right: we want them in our pulpits. But a lot of training is by no means essential to good preaching. And anyway we don't have to train them here. When we want trained ones we can send back East for them, where they have more time to think about John Calvin and John Wesley. And as for teachers—can't any young lawyer or preacher teach the boys and girls all they need to know? Give them a little spelling, a little ciphering, and a little handwriting, with a liberal sprinkling of the rod, and they'll have more than their fathers had before them. Did Tippecanoe Harrison graduate from a seminary? Did Old Hickory Jackson know any Latin or Greek when he swung the British agents in Florida higher than Haman?

There was a genuine respect for education on the one hand and uncertainty about it on the other. There was both suspicion and disdain of the person with a college education, especially if he persisted in speaking the English language correctly.

Another strong tradition which has persisted in America is the one which has caused educated men to level themselves with common illiterates in speech and manner. If an educated man sought office on the frontier, he kept the fact of his college background well concealed and spoke the sloven vernacular of his constitutents. Unlettered backswoodsmen did not necessarily lack respect for education, but they were self-conscious of their own limitations. They saw in the educated man a special capacity to outsmart and humiliate them. To them education took on some mysterious powers, and in trying to understand it they lost their sense of perspective. Persons who had traveled long distances, who came as peddlers, rascals, adventurers, and quacks of every type, persisted in swindling the country-men, and many backswoodsmen looked upon all superior mental development as a means to a nefarious end. Frontiersmen were proud in their own way in the face of snobbery, and many an imperfectly educated man in-curred the jealousy of his neighbors by parading his learning.

There was the utmost respect for the three R's. Most of the early settlers saw in this basic educational program an opportunity for their children to avoid the humiliation of total ignorance. Education to thousands of peo-ple meant simply the ability to write one's name, to cipher well enough to conduct a simple business, and to be able to spell out enough of a newspaper to keep track of the main local news and political trends. Early educational efforts on the frontier were of three types. There were the private acad-emies, the common public schools, and the colleges and seminaries. Private academies were the more important of the earliest schools. They were conducted by all sorts of people, from denominational missionaries to itinerant teachers who taught subscription schools. Literally hundreds of these academies came into being all over the western country. Preachers supplemented their meager incomes by keeping school during the week. Struggling lawyers combined teaching school with pleading at the bar. Surveyors, whose lines did not always fall in pleasant places, supplemented their incomes by holding school during bad weather. Yankee peddlers ran out of stock and stayed in one place long enough to impart learning to the young, as did roving Irishmen. Farmers dropped the pitchfork and plow handle for the hickory rod and the roll book. Foreign exiles of all sorts came to teach arts, which ranged from the study of languages to ballroom dancing, fencing and dueling. But the most satisfactory sources of teacher supply were the eastern colleges which sent numbers of their gradu-ates to the West.

Early public schools were little more than dame schools. They were most often located in isolated places in poor buildings and early acquired the name "old field." In some instances public support was sufficient to finance a meager term of three or four months. Teachers in these schools, like those in the private academies, came from every group in American and European society, except a trained teaching profession. The only requirements for prospective teachers were to be able to raise a goose-quill pen and a switch with equal vigor. Teaching was first of all a physical challenge. Not infrequently new teachers had to demonstrate that they could whip every boy in school in order to last out the first week. More prospective teachers were examined on their disciplinary powers than on their intellectual equipment.

For most itinerant teachers, life was precarious at best. They were handed about to board with one family after another. They had little privacy and enjoyed few comforts. The highly adaptable ones became members of families with whom they lived; others were eccentric and crotchety and became nuisances and butts of practical jokes. At best they all took family leavings, and the informalities of their lives were all but overwhelming. Many an enemy of public education pointed to the shortcomings of these ignorant "old field" teachers as evidence of its undesirability. In the Kentucky Constitutional Convention of 1849, Ben Hardin opposed a public school system on the grounds that the average school teacher was unable to answer correctly questions as to the number of days in the week, or weeks in the month.

By no means were all the frontier teachers ignorant drunkards, or birds of passage. There were many good teachers who succeeded both in the classroom and in subsequent professions. Scarcely a man in early public life escaped a brief experience of teaching school. Possibly one of the fundamental weaknesses of the primitive and disorganized system of education was the fact that the schoolroom was the training ground for bright young men who were conditioning themselves for more lucrative and respected callings.

Not until the 1820's did the public school movement on the frontier, along with the movement in the rest of the nation, have a mild awakening. Some western states resorted for support of schools to the painless use of "literary funds" which had been accumulated from various sources, while others sought means of public support that would place a minimum financial burden on the people. No politician could expect an extended future in office after he had advocated increased taxes for schools. Governors of the various states wrote splendid briefs for the public schools but gave little initiative and leadership to the movement to activate their pious words. Oratorically the public school idea was synonomous with democracy. The subject soared high on the wings of the American eagle. The virtues of good training were said to be necessary in a strong young democracy battling its way forward against the blind forces of men and nature. But the heat of taxpayer resistance evaporated this oratorical fog at the polls and in the legislative halls.

Across the frontier, educational needs were nearly always discussed in terms of the needs of the common man. Good schools, it was said repeatedly, would equalize American society, yet scarcely a single leader came from the masses to crusade for the cause. Although the public school movement had the support of thousands of common people at the local level, the bigger movement when it came was of national origin. Social fermentation in the late 1820's and 1830's included interest in many phases of cultural betterment, but in the West the educational phase was to receive the greatest emphasis. Some ardent supporters even argued that money spent in building schools would reduce the cost of jails because education would reduce the crime rate.

Between 1825 and 1850 all the frontier states became a part of the general crusade for state free-school systems. In 1829 the Western Academic Institute was founded in Cincinnati to advance the cause of public education in Ohio and its neighboring states. Handbills, pamphlets, and memorials were distributed, and speakers were sent around to encourage local leaders to seek support for schools. In all the states there were able men who saw the vision of general education in a democracy. Samuel Lewis, Caleb Atwater, and Calvin E. Stowe of Ohio, Caleb Mills of Indiana, Samuel Galloway of Illinois, and Benjamin O. Peers, Ryland T. Dillard, and Robert Jefferson Breckinridge of Kentucky were among the men who not only kept the cause of public schools alive, but were instrumental in helping to create state educational systems. In 1829 Nathan L. Guilford succeeded in getting the people of Cincinnati to establish public schools. That same year Benjamin O. Peers and Alva Woods, President of Transylvania University, prepared a report on the means by which a needed school system could be built in Kentucky, but the wise men of Frankfort were asleep. Seven years later, 1836, the Ohio legislature sent Professor Calvin E. Stowe of Lane Seminary abroad to study the continental European schools and to make his famous report of 1837.

While Professor Stowe was engaged in his European survey, the federal government was distributing to the states surplus funds accumulated in the national treasury. In several of the frontier states these funds were reserved for educational purposes. In some cases, the funds were given outright to the schools; in others the money was invested in internal improvement projects for roads, canals and railroads. The great depression of 1837 tended to slow up the crusade for schools and to prevent legislatures from levying the necessary taxes for their support. Provision for the donation of each sixteenth section of land for educational purposes by the Northwest Ordinance of 1787 had been a healthy gesture, but for all practical purposes it meant almost nothing in the establishment and maintenance of adequate schools. Even if each sixteenth section had been the most desirable land in the township, and even if it had been leased under the most favorable conditions, the income still would not have supported a school system. Population increases and changing concepts of educational needs made the eighteenth-century idea obsolete before it could be applied.

The educational awakening before 1850 resulted in the inclusion of educational clauses for the first time in some new state constitutions and a strengthening of those that were already in existence. In Indiana and Michigan, framers of the first state constitutions outlined a public school system from the elementary to college level. From 1830 on, a multiplicity of school laws appeared so that by 1860 it was almost necessary for legislatures to have elaborate codifications to keep track of their labors. Teaching became a more stable profession, and women began to invade the field which heretofore had been reserved to men. School terms were lengthened, facilities improved, and the common man's need for education became more clearly defined and fixed in the popular mind. Curricula were greatly expanded, and the reverence for the three R's was greatly reduced. But the favorable figures on illiteracy must be accepted as purely relative. It is possible that a more skillful qualitative check would have revealed a less happy condition than that which seemed to prevail when literacy meant only the ability to read and write one's name.

Higher education had a more extensive history on the frontier than the elementary schools. In 1780 the Virginia General Assembly chartered Transylvania Seminary. About the same date, Washington College was chartered in eastern Tennessee, and in 1792 Manasseh Cutler and his associates made plans for a seminary of higher learning at Marietta. The first forty years of the nineteenth century saw the organization of a large number of colleges and universities. Among these were Miami University (1809), Ohio University (1810), Vincennes University (1810), Indiana Seminary (University) (1820), University of Michigan (1817), Illinois College (1833), and Wisconsin University (1836).

Frontier colleges often resulted from missionary labors. Outside ministers brought intellectual light to the frontier. They sought to train laborers to work in the vineyard for their denominations. At Crawfordsville, Indiana, in 1832, James Thomson, a home missionary for the Presbyterian Church, called a meeting of eight or nine men to found Wabash College. Action of this kind was repeated many times across the frontier where the institutions of higher learning were to have an important impact. They prepared ministers, lawyers, doctors, teachers and other professional groups. Their enrollments were small, but their graduates became leaders in both politics and the professions. They not only fanned a spark of intellectual aspiration into a flame of learning, but they reduced the barriers of ignorance and intolerance about them. The frontier colleges were not always liberal institutions, however. There were frequent fights among faculties and between faculties and the churches which promoted the colleges. At Transylvania University disputes among faculty members destroyed the medical school. Narrow denominationalism and bigotry drove Horace Holley from the presidency and the last spark of liberalism from Kentucky.

Not all frontier educational development is to be evaluated in the light of teachers and schools, nor by laws passed, nor by constitutional provisions for school systems. Possibly, the basic factor in the early educational history was the kind of textbooks which were available to pioneer pupils. The first schoolmasters often had to supply their own texts in the form of manuscript copies of teaching materials, and these in turn were dictated to pupils as school exercises. By 1800 western printshops were supplying new printed texts which they pirated from the labors of authors and printers in other parts of the country. In 1812 the eclectic *Kentucky Preceptor* was published by Maccoun and Tilford in Lexington, Kentucky. The preface of this little gray-backed book said that it contained "The most fascinating and instructive historical accounts, dialogues and orations, with the different kind of reading in prose and verse."

Western printers and authors produced a steady stream of school books and texts after 1820. Among these were Murray's *English Reader*, Bate's *Western Preceptor*, James Hall's *Western Reader*, Ray's *Little Arithmetic*, Morse's *The American Universal Geography*, John Kilbourn's *Ohio Gazetteer*, and the Samuel Goodrich histories. Noah Webster's *American Spelling Book* (the Blueback Speller) had a ready sale on the frontier almost from its publication date. At least one edition of this famous book was pirated and printed in a Lexington, Kentucky printshop, which perhaps was the reason why Webster spent so much of his time agitating for an adequately protective copyright law.

The most famous of the textbooks of western origin were the McGuffey *Eclectic Readers*. The *First* and *Second Readers* appeared in 1836, and the next year the *Third* and *Fourth* were added to the list. It was the last that became the favorite of the series. These readers contained little or no material that was of frontier origin, but they pointed morals and adorned tales.

William Holmes McGuffey was himself of the frontier. He was born in Washington County, Pennsylvania, in 1800, and moved out to Ohio where he became active in college teaching in Cincinnati and Oxford, with a brief period in Paris, Kentucky. In Cincinnati he was located in one of the chief centers of western printing. He found a publisher willing to undertake the publication of his books, and soon after the appearance of the first two readers he saw his texts gain in popularity every year. In Louisville, J. P. Morton and Company offered serious competition with a list of readers and grammars, but they never quite captured the lucrative early market.

There was little originality of authorship in the early textbooks. Webster offered the most original matter in his new system of spelling and word selections. The early text writers were more concerned with offering moral lessons and aphorisms in pleasant selections than they were in presenting their own ideas. It would be well-nigh impossible to appraise precisely the influence of the large numbers of textbooks which appeared in the West prior to 1850, but one general fact may be stated: They contributed heavily to a spirit of nationalism in this period of American history. Also, they offered a sort of literary stabilization in the repetitive cultural process as American settlers moved on further westward and made still newer beginnings.

BEYOND THE SABINE

These discussions have resulted in the insertion of a clause in the general appropriation law passed by both houses providing for the outfit and salary of a diplomatic agent to be sent to the Republic of Texas whenever the President of the United States may receive satisfactory evidence that Texas is an independent power and shall deem it expedient to appoint such minister, and in the adoption of a resolution by the Senate, the constitutional advisers of the Executive on the diplomatic intercourse of the United States with foreign powers, expressing the opinion that, "the State of Texas having established and maintained an independent government capable of performing those duties, foreign and domestic, which appertain to independent governments, and it appearing that there is no longer any reasonable prospect of the successful prosecution of the war by Mexico against said State, it is expedient and proper and in conformity with the laws of nations and the practice of this government in like cases that the independent political existence of said State be acknowledged by the Government of the United States." Regarding these proceedings as a virtual decision of the question submitted by me to Congress, I think it my duty to acquiesce therein, and therefore I nominate Alcée La Branche, of Louisiana, to be chargé d'affaires to the Republic of Texas.

—Andrew Jackson, March 3, 1837

AN EPISODE IN THE FIGHT FOR TEXAS FROM GREEN'S *Journal of the Texian Expedition*

CHAPTER XVI

Spanish Visitors

THE vast wedge of territory lying between the Sabine and Rio Grande rivers has had a long and diversified history. Before white explorers began roaming over that part of the country it was a land of conflicting Indian claims. Pineda, rounding the Gulf Coast from Jamaica to Tampico in 1519, was possibly the first white explorer to see the coastal line of the country.

Nine years later a small group of refugees from Narvaez's ill-fated expedition landed on Mal Hado Island—or the Island of Misfortune. After most disheartening hardships in Florida, they had skirted the coast for thirty days in five horsehide boats. For the next six years these victims of shipwreck and ill fortune, with Cabeza de Vaca at their head, were in Texas and New Mexico, wandering among the natives. Suffering extreme privations, these lonely wanderers journeyed to Mexico City, following a sinuous trail back to white civilization. In the immense and arid country through which they passed de Vaca and his companions were never free of danger from the Indians, nor from starvation. Playing the roles of physician and merchant, the ingenious de Vaca had good luck with his patients and found a ready market for his meager wares. As he and his companions moved on from tribe to tribe, stories of their fame and powers grew; before they reached Mexico their long and frustrating journey had become almost a triumphant march. They saw buffalo on the way and picked up at first hand much information which was to be of use to white men struggling against the elements in that country.

Long after de Vaca and his weary companions had made their way back to a reunion with their countrymen in Mexico City, other Europeans had touched on the Texas coast. The land itself, however, continued to be undisturbed by white visitors for many decades to come. When Spain began its period of expansion up from Mexico, priests were sent out with the flag and the Cross to modern Coahuila, and even beyond the Rio Grande. One of the first of the religious expeditions was that led by Mendoza López in 1683–1684. But it was not until the early part of the eighteenth century that Jesuit, Dominican and Franciscan missionaries crossed the Rio Grande to plant permanent missions and to bring religion to the Indian tribes. With the missions came soldiers and Spanish political organization. The *presidio* of the Mexican-Texas frontier combined civil and religious authorities, and above the Rio Grande appeared the famous settlements of Bexar (San Antonio), La Bahia, and Nacogdoches.

Spain was not to monopolize a claim to the present territory of Texas. During the latter half of the seventeenth century some of La Salle's followers shared honors with the stranded followers of Narváez. Many of them reached the Texas coast and made records of their visit. It was not, however, until the French traders of the middle decades of the eighteenth century began their search far and wide for skins and furs that an international rivalry was begun. Wherever there were Indians on the vast Louisiana frontier, French traders found their way to their villages. Natchitoches on the Red River in the northwestern part of modern Louisiana became a major contact point for traders going and coming in the territory between the Sabine and Rio Grande. To the South, the Gulf Coast offered an inlet to Texas, and there were frequent white penetrations in this region.

Spain extended its outposts eastward to check French migration into Texas before it got started. Nacogdoches was founded in the eighteenth century as the extreme eastern outpost. This *presidio* became the eastern terminus of the Camino Real, the ancient trail from Laredo on the Rio Grande to Natchitoches on the Red River in Louisiana. It passed through the important pueblos of Bahia on the San Antonio River. To the north was the Camino Bexar on which were located the important Alamo and Bexar missions. In time, Nueve Jean and Salcedo were founded.

International rivalries in Texas were influenced largely by happenings on the European continent. When war was declared between France and Spain in 1718, there was skirmishing between the nationals of the two countries in the Southwest. Spaniards were driven back by the French from Nacogdoches to Bexar.

Spanish movement into Texas was extremely slow. At least four factors retarded spread of settlements. The area involved was vast, coupled with the mountain barrier of northern Mexico and the aridity of much of the intervening territory. The Indian menace made it most difficult to establish settlements without the support of considerable military force. Because of the arbitrariness of Spanish law, new settlements could be located only by strict governmental approval. Finally, the population of Mexico was too sparse to force expansion above the Rio Grande.

East of the Sabine, the situation was radically different from that in Mexico. Louisiana's population was expanding with some degree of rapidity, and it began early to exert pressure on the eastern Texas boundary. By the end of the eighteenth century the American frontier expansion also promised an invasion of the Spanish hinterlands from the mouth of the St. Mary's River on the Atlantic to the Sabine. Observant Spanish territorial officials had little difficulty interpreting the future course of American expansion. Already in the last quarter of the eighteenth century the fields of Ohio, Kentucky, and Tennessee were pouring a rich stream of farm products down the river. It was, however, the restless American traders and settlers who pushed their way to the banks of the great river. By the end of the century frontiersmen not only demanded control of the Mississippi, but they were even clamoring for the possession of Louisiana Territory. Again, prophetic Spaniards were able to see in this slackening of Spanish control over North American territory the beginning of Spain's retreat from the North American continent.

To the east, no natural barrier—no mountain range or broad expanse of water or desert lands—lay athwart the path of American expansion. Neither the Red nor the Sabine River was a barrier. The most arid lands faced Mexico. The mountain range barred Spaniards, not Americans. Rivers formed inroads up from the Gulf, and the task of opening trails and roads was a relatively easy one. Pack animals could be taken anywhere, and, except for certain stream crossings, there were few places on the American continent where pioneers could travel more easily with wheeled vehicles. There was everywhere an abundant supply of wood, water, grass, and game. Only one serious obstacle stood in the way—the lack of harbors along the Gulf Coast.

No doubt one of the greatest attractions in Texas for Americans was the availability of vast acreage of good lands. Except for the political barrier, Texas was a veritable bonanza of soil to the Americans. Soil in the eastern part of the territory was highly adaptable to the system of agriculture which the settlers had used all the way from Pennsylvania and Virginia to the Mississippi. This was especially true of those settlers who were crowding up to the Mississippi across the pine woods of the Lower South. Coming westward with families, slaves and herds, the backwoodsmen sought land in vast quantities. In the long range of border history there was actually little or no break in the expansion of the American frontier settlement from the Susquehanna to the Rio Grande.

The American Horde

Spanish authorities appreciated the ultimate meaning of this onrush of Americans, but they could not determine how it was to be stemmed. Uppermost in the administrative mind at an early date was the necessity of restricting American trade with both Indians and Mexicans. Just as the British had enjoyed an advantage in the trade with the Indians of the Upper Ohio, so the Americans had an advantage in Louisiana and Texas. Their supply of trade goods was near at hand; they offered a more lucrative market for the Indians' products; the Indians were not threatened with enslavement by the Americans. Immediately after the sale of Louisiana by France to the United States, Spanish officials attempted to create a buffer against American expansion. First it was difficult to distinguish between bona fide Spanish nationals and American frontiersmen. Even those settlers who were admitted were to be moved as far away from the Louisiana boundary as Bexar.

One of the major objectives of the Spanish border officials was the protection and promotion of the Catholic Church. Before a foreigner could be officially admitted to the region, he had to prove that he was of acceptable character, friendly to Spain, and a communicant of the Catholic Church. Finally he had to agree to be sent to a place which the officials believed was most desirable for planting a settlement. This usually meant that the immigrant was moved well back from the border.

The beginning of American invasion of Texas dates back to the decade 1790–1800. At the turn of the century at least thirteen Americans lived beyond the Sabine. Americans who had crossed the Mississippi into the wide Louisiana frontier could cross over into Texas by using their Spanish passports. For the first thirty years of the nineteenth century, American visitations and migrations into Texas rose and fell with the relaxing and tightening of border controls. Three territorial governors stood out in their struggle against the American menace. These were Manuel Marie de Salcedo, Antonio Cordero and Nemesio Salcedo.

Every year after 1790 saw its share of problems arise in connection with the admission of foreigners to Texas. There is no way of knowing how much manipulation, favoritism and bribery took place. On the face of the record, however, most border officials, though baffled, seem to have been honest and conscientious. After the sale of Louisiana by France to the United States, border intrigue became a threat to Spanish control of Texas. Beginning with the Burr episode in 1805–1806, one bit of intrigue followed another on to 1836.

James Wilkinson and his agents clearly had designs on the region. One of the most interesting traders who moved in and out of Texas between 1790 and 1801 (when he was killed at the Brazos River) was Philip Nolan. This adventurer had been closely associated with James Wilkinson and no doubt used his preceptor's business methods. In 1791 he made his first visit to Texas, where he engaged in the fur and horse trade. He returned to Louisiana on two or three occasions with horses, and at one time maintained corrals on the Trinity and Brazos rivers. In 1801 he was warned to stay out of Texas, and when he entered the region against instructions he was killed in an encounter with Don Nemesio Salcedo's Spanish militiamen. Wilkinson's name was prominent on the Spanish frontier, but it is difficult to say for what reason. When George Morgan of New Jersey sought permission to enter Texas, he found his way blocked by the famous General. Apparently Wilkinson even made some serious efforts to persuade Kentucky families to move into the Spanish territory. But whatever his political professions, Wilkinson's basic interest was trade with the region.

Almost from the beginning of foreign immigration to Texas, there was talk of bringing settlers to the country from Europe. French, Swiss, and Irish colonizers all sought to settle the Southwest at an early date, and all of them received official encouragement to do so. Bartholomew Tardiveau helped establish French royalists in Spanish Louisiana. Nor did individuals only seek admission to Texas; the governments of Britain and France exhibited more than passing interest in the vast Spanish hinterland.

Napoleon's influence upon Spain in the decade 1800–1810 was disastrous for Spanish policy in Texas. Certainly the sale of Louisiana placed the Americans in a much more strategic position to invade Texas. Antonio Cordero and Simon Herrera both had extensive experience on the border, and in 1808 they were involved in plans to keep Americans out. Herrera had agreed to the establishment of the neutral zone between the Arroyo Hondo and the Sabine River in 1806, and he saw in the subsequent assembly of the American militia on the Louisiana border a threat to the

Spanish territory. But rumors of American invasions were common. At one time the story was afloat that several thousand Kentuckians were being organized to force their way into Texas.

The War of 1812 had an important bearing upon the American attitude toward Texas. Some of the speeches of the expansionist orators knew neither geographical nor oratorical bounds. Many of them focused attention upon the Southwest. American occupation of West Florida and the threats to East Florida bolstered Spanish determination to keep American settlers east of the Sabine. In the course of the war, American armed forces came to the lower river country, and some of them were even directed to the Sabine boundary and elsewhere along the Louisiana frontier.

Between 1812 and the Mexican Revolution in 1821 which freed Mexico from Spanish control, both American officials in Washington and filibusterers in Texas encouraged the Mexicans to overthrow Spanish rule. Henry Clay espoused the revolutionary cause of the various Latin colonies, and the United States early adopted a policy of recognizing the new republics as they broke from Spain and came into separate existence.

On the border of Texas the Spanish officials warred against filibusterers who encouraged revolution and against the spread of anti-Royalist sentiment. By 1813 both Bahia and Bexar had passed temporarily out of Royalist control. During the next seven years Spain herself encouraged the settlement of Texas, and an effort was made to distribute huge blocks of public lands to Spanish nationals. As the crisis of Mexican revolution approached a final break and Spain faced the loss of the Southwest, Spain opened the Texas border even to foreigners if they would take an oath of allegiance to respect the monarchy and its laws. Possibly the fact that the Spanish king accepted the Adams-de Onis (Florida) Treaty was stimulated in part by the belief that this would divert the tide of American territorial expansion temporarily away from Texas.

Many Americans had entered Texas before 1813, as we have already noted. Some remained there; others only passed through, intent on little more than trade with the Mexicans and Indians; and some were driven out as undesirables by the Spanish officials. In 1813 Richard (Ricardo) Reynal Keene, the first of the American contractors, appeared in Texas, armed with the consent of the *Cortes* to make claim to a Texas grant of land. Entering Texas through upper Louisiana, he proposed to found a Catholic colony populated by Americans, Irishmen, Spaniards and other Europeans. Neither French Louisianans nor continental Frenchmen were to be permitted to enter the colony. Keene's proposed colonial scheme, however, seems never to have gone beyond the paper planning stage.

The Austins

On December 23, 1820, Moses Austin, a New Englander, who moved westward by way of Virginia, Kentucky, and to the lead mines of Missouri, came to Bexar with a proposition that he be allowed to form a settlement in Texas with Spanish citizens who had been transferred to American soil by Napoleon's sale of Louisiana. Austin was a highly interesting frontiersman. He knew what it meant to be successful and then to fail in business. The War of 1812 had injured his lead mining business in Missouri, and before he could recover his economic fortunes the panic of 1819 virtually bankrupted him. Between 1812 and 1820, Austin had been seeking new means by which he might recoup. One of his efforts took him to the Red River in Arkansas Territory, where he hoped to do some farming and possibly to speculate in lands. By 1819 he had conceived the idea of planting a colony in Texas.

In the summer of 1820 he set out upon his long horseback journey to Bexar, accompanied by a slave who jogged along on muleback. In Bexar, Austin had little or no difficulty in communicating with Antonio Martinez, commandant-general of the eastern Mexican provinces. Like Keene, this new caller had entered Spanish territory by way of Louisiana with a Spanish passport, and specifically as a Spanish citizen. He had an acceptable religious history, and his character reference was sound. He proposed bringing to Texas at least three hundred families who would accept membership in the Catholic Church, swear allegiance to Spain, and observe Spanish law. In a remarkably short time, January 17, 1821, the Spanish-Mexican commander General Joachim Arredondo approved Austin's request, and he was officially cleared to begin the organization of a colony between the Colorado of Texas and the Brazos rivers.

Moses Austin's journey back to Natchitoches was an arduous one. He suffered long exposure and exhaustion, and in May, 1821, he died of pneumonia. The responsibility of carrying out the Texas colonization scheme fell on the shoulders of his son Stephen. Stephen Austin was born in Virginia and was educated in the East and at Transylvania University in Kentucky. He had worked with Moses in the lead mining business and knew enough about his father's affairs to take immediate leadership in the colonization of Texas. His political and judicial background in Missouri had equipped him for his future career as *empresario,* or general manager, of the American colony in Texas. In late summer and fall of 1821 Stephen was in Texas scouting lands which he wished to claim. These were located between the Guadalupe and Colorado rivers, and six leagues above the Bexar-Nacogdoches Road, and down the Brazos-San Jacinto watershed to the Gulf.

Austin originally proposed a generous system of land grants. Men, single or married, were to be given 640 acres; married men were to receive 320 more, with an addition of 160 acres for each child and 80 for each slave they brought along. Thus a married man with four children and two slaves under Austin's proposed scheme would be entitled to 1800 acres. Settlers coming to the Austin colony were to embrace the Catholic religion and to swear allegiance to the laws of Mexico.

In addition to devising a scheme of land grants, Stephen Austin suggested to Governor Antonio Martinez the desirability of collecting a surveyor's fee, and a premium of $0.125 per acre for the *empresario* or promoter and manager of the settlements, to repay him for his expenses and efforts at making surveys and registering titles.

The prospect of so huge a land bounty was a great temptation to frontiersmen. Fifty families awaited Stephen Austin's return to Nacogdoches to be on their way to the new Texas Eden. Elsewhere in the Old West families were anxious to begin the march. From Kentucky, Missouri, and Tennessee letters poured in seeking an opportunity to move westward. It seems clear in this connection that a generous area of virgin land was the basic attraction for restless backwoodsmen who drifted toward the Southwest. This, rather than an opportunity to expand the slave system, put settlers on the road to Austin's colony, though slaves did accompany the early immigrants to their new homes.

Opening of Texas to settlement by foreigners in 1820 was one of the most timely incidents in American frontier history. The panic of 1819 had taken a heavy economic toll of settlers who had pushed out onto the fringe of civilization. Even people who lived in the older settlements felt the sharp sting of the depression. Money became both scarce and of uncertain value. Settlers who had involved themselves in debt for their lands were glad of an opportunity to move on to so vast a supply of practically free lands, despite the religious and political restrictions. The willingness to follow Austin to Texas was an example of the American psychosis to move away to the Elysian fields of lands free from present troubles. The Florida Treaty of 1819 presaged the slackening of Spain's hold on her North American empire, and large numbers of prospective Texas settlers no doubt foresaw a day in the immediate future when Spanish rule would end. The Mexican Revolution changed conditions under which the American immigrants held their claims. Now they were subjected to the laws of the new State of Mexico and its vacillating rules. In the usual turmoil which accompanied revolution in a Latin country there was little possibility for political stability in the Austin settlements.

By December, 1821, the rising tide of emigration from Louisiana had spilled over into Texas. The first families arrived on the Austin grant. In

January a ship, the *Lively*, carrying supplies for the Austin colony, came out from New Orleans, but missed the mouth of the Brazos River and was lost along with its precious freight and passengers.

In 1822 Stephen Austin was forced to return to Mexico City to adjust problems which had arisen in the settlement of his colony. It was also necessary for him to secure passage of legislation which would permit him to operate as an *empresario*. For a year he waited for the unpredictable Mexican congress to move. During that time he saw the ruthless Iturbide become emperor, and then he witnessed the waning of the new monarch's power. On April 14, 1823, the government finally approved the terms of Austin's grant and he was now free to proceed. Specifically, this official approval was for colonization between the Guadalupe and Colorado rivers. A revision of the terms of individual land grants was less generous than that originally proposed by Austin. Heads of families were to receive one *labor*, or 170 acres. Cattle grazers were to receive 4,428 acres. All immigrants were to improve their lands within six years. They were to be permitted to bring with them duty-free household goods and farming implements to the value of $2,000; the *empresario* was to receive a generous grant of premium lands when he had settled three hundred families. Other administrative details as to the location of grants and the means of their distribution were settled. Perhaps one of the most important sections pertained to the introduction of slaves. Under the original proposal slaves were not to be bought and sold in Texas, and slave children born there were to be freed at age fourteen.

Before Stephen Austin returned to his colony from Mexico City, the settlers began to protest. Rumors were set afloat that he was profiteering in the distribution of lands. His commission of a "bit" an acre was considered too much. The fact that he received a considerable grant of land for himself was regarded by some of his colonists as being sufficient reward for his services. The Texas pioneers still regarded themselves as American backwoodsmen squabbling with authority over the matter of public land distribution; they did not fully realize that they had moved into a new legal jurisdiction. In time these complaints reached Mexico City, and in 1824 Jose Antonio Saucedo, acting political chief of Texas, denied that Austin had the right to collect the acreage fee. Instead, settlers would be required to pay a smaller amount. This ruling was made despite the law passed in 1823 by the Mexican congress which permitted the collection of the higher fee. Austin was caught in the unhappy predicament of having to deal with obstreperous settlers on one hand, and with the perfidy of Mexican officials on the other. American settlers understood neither the Spanish language nor the temperament of the Mexican officials. They assumed that because they had traveled to Texas under bad conditions they had made a personal sacrifice that entitled them to rewards. Personal independence to them meant resistance and obstinacy toward oppressive authority. Among the early arrivals in Texas were some American volunteers who had participated in the Mexican revolutionary struggles, and there were also the perennial filibusterers who for the last three decades had eyed the main chance for fortune in Mexico. None of these tended to lighten the *empresario*'s problems in founding his colony.

Coahuila-Texas State

Stephen Austin had to give this venture an enormous amount of administrative attention. Few or no other frontier leaders possessed his common sense and tact. He informed himself on the problems of the Mexican government, he understood the mental processes of the Spanish-speaking peoples, and he knew precisely the pattern of behavior which the American colonists would have to follow to secure official sufferance. Making settlement in Texas, aside from the peculiar political problems, was little different from making settlement in frontier Tennessee or Indiana. There was need for a militia to guard against Indian attacks. Whatever the structure of Mexican laws, there was need for practical local legislation that fitted American needs. The *empresario* was largely responsible for the adoption of these local laws and for the interpretation of all Mexican statutes. In short, he had to obey the Mexican law, yet govern his colony within the general traditions of Anglo-American legal structure. Though they orally accepted Mexican law, the American frontiersmen never actually regarded it seriously when it was applied to them individually. Despite his multifarious difficulties, Austin soon succeeded in locating his first three hundred families on Texas lands.

In a short time Austin found that he had competition from other *empresarios* who sought the advantages of rather generous land grants. Competition, however, seems to have bothered Austin little if at all. Settlers from most of the southern states were anxious to move to Texas, and only the disturbing restrictions on slavery slowed down immigration from this source. There was grave danger that a planter crossing the border with a band of slaves would suffer serious property loss by their gaining freedom. The requirement of membership in the Catholic Church no doubt caused others to hesitate leaving the United States. After 1823, Texas existed as a part of the Mexican state of Coahuila-Texas. The settlers were further obligated, by the rather liberal colonization law of 1824, to observe the laws of this governmental division. One difference in the Coahuila-Texas state law from that of the federal government was the requirement that *empresario* contracts be fulfilled within six years.

Settlers who took up claims in the valleys of the Gulf coastal streams found themselves in possession of highly productive cotton lands. In time there was very little difference in the pattern of Texas agriculture and that of the black lands of Alabama, Mississippi and Louisiana. Immigrants pushed into the new lands with cotton-growing implements and with gins. Soon economic observers mentioned the location of gins, grain mills and saw mills. Texas was beginning a mild period of economic expansion, but more important was the near-phenomenal increase in population. Missouri, Louisiana, Arkansas, Tennessee, Mississippi, Alabama, Kentucky, and even the eastern states all contributed settlers to the Texas movement. Austin's settlements alone showed a growth of population of 2,021 in 1828 to 4,248 in 1830 and 5,665 in 1831. Five years later the Texas population was estimated to be between 25,000 and 30,000. Attempts by Mexico to introduce European immigrants to counteract American influence failed.

A Wayward Daughter

Such a strong tide of immigration between 1824 and 1831 made it inevitable that friction would result in several places. One of the first important uprisings occurred between December, 1826, and January, 1827. This incident was to outline the course of future events in Texas between the American settlers and the Mexican Government. Between 1823 and 1824, Hayden Edwards, a prospective *empresario*, went through the delicate and frustrating experience of securing a government permit to plant a colony in Texas. He took up his vigil first in Mexico City and later in Saltillo. His petition carried the conventional request for managerial privileges, but he had made a request for territory in the vicinity of Nacogdoches and along the Louisiana boundary, much of which had already at least two layers of claims upon it.

Like most international border regions on the North American continent, the land immediately west of the Sabine had filled up with a mixture of nationalities and races, motivated by a highly varied set of purposes. Some were smugglers, some were fugitives from justice, and many of them were innocent but drifting backwoodsmen who had crossed the Spanish border without being especially conscious of what they were doing. In granting lands in this area to Hayden Edwards, the Mexican government required him to respect all established titles, to maintain civil order, and, after he had located a hundred families, to appoint a commissioner who was to locate a town. To accomplish this end Edwards was allowed to organize a militia for police purposes.

From the outset there was need for infinite tact and judiciousness, neither of which Edwards seems to have possessed. Almost immediately there was bickering, gossiping, and misunderstandings among the settlers. Lack of experience and integrity on the part of Captain José Sepulveda, a Mexican adventurer and military figure, and a failure of Edwards to comprehend the arbitrary nature of the Mexican officialdom resulted in the virtual annulment of his authority. *Ex parte* charges were made that he had organized a militia company, that he had withheld grants from rightful claimants, that he had undertaken to form a town, and that he had done things which he believed himself authorized to do. Edwards himself had been victimized by the government; it had withdrawn its grant of authority without telling him it had done so.

In this moment of political crisis Hayden Edwards, with his brother Benjamin, organized a small company of armed men and seized Nacogdoches and the Spanish archives on December 16, 1826. In the meantime, Mexican military forces made up of native Mexicans and Austingrant colonials were on their way to Nacogdoches under the leadership of José Saucedo and Colonel Mateo Ahumada to stamp out this so-called Fredonian Rebellion. Troops under the command of Colonel Peter Ellis Bean and Laurence Richard Kenny were nearer Nacogdoches, and they quickly quelled the rebellion. The Edwards brothers and a handful of their followers escaped across the Sabine on the night of January 28, 1827, and the Fredonian revolt ended. At the same time there was a restlessness among the Cherokee Indians of the region. Partly stimulated by the white philanthropist Dr. John Dunn Hunter, they prepared for war, but actually their uprising was the beginning of the end of their occupancy of the Sabine country. Whatever suspicions the Mexican government had that the Fredonian incident was partly inspired by the United States to establish a political foothold in the region seem to have been groundless. At no time did Austin's tact and co-operation serve better to allay Mexican fears. Possibly no American official even knew of the Fredonian Revolt.

Though the first colonial revolt in Texas was repressed without difficulty, a situation was in the making after 1826 which in time would arouse an almost universal resistance to Mexican laws and administrative controls. To begin with, the government of Mexico had been torn by factional strife and disorganization since 1821. Not enough time had elapsed to permit the organization of a smoothly functioning republican government, and both political experience and the necessary integrity to carry out a consistent policy of any duration seem to have been missing. With typical Spanish delay and indifference, the governmental needs of the growing Texas population were almost ignored. The Mexican officials failed to realize that the swelling tide of American migration brought with it a strong Anglo-American tradition of legal and social organization which was necessary for the orderly functioning of their type of society. Few or none of the Americans understood the legal philosophy of the Spaniard. More evident was the absence of civil and criminal courts and law enforcement officers. Within a short time the need for courts was manifest. Criminals could escape justice because of technicalities and lack of means for bringing them to justice. At the same time innocent persons suffered loss of time and money and might be convicted under the law because of administrative failures.

West of the Sabine, the three issues of religion, slavery and education constantly entered official discussions of Texas. Slavery was one of the thorniest problems, and it was dealt with in the most indecisive manner until 1830 when the institution, already planted in Texas, was given official recognition. Recognition of existing conditions did not preclude a restriction on further expansion. In the case of religious toleration the problem was even more personal and vital than that of slavery expansion. One of the characteristics of the American frontier movement was the proliferation of the church groups. The Protestant churches had been most active since 1750, and there was scarcely a settler who got completely beyond the reach of his own church. As has been said, the settlers entering Texas in the 1820's had to subscribe, outwardly at least, to the tenets of the Catholic Church. Whether or not they did this in good faith is obviously open to question. Even assuming that the early settlers had embraced most sincerely the Catholic faith, the necessary priests and churches to serve their spiritual needs were lacking. In fact the Catholic Church was never able to solve this problem. Marriages were performed by civil officials, the couples promising to have religious ceremonies performed when opportunities presented themselves. Actually, private religious services were held among the Protestants, and it was not unusual for Protestant ministers to hold only slightly veiled meetings among the people. Technically, of course, there were not supposed to be any ministers of the Protestant churches in Texas, but they, like their parishioners, had followed the call of available cheap lands westward.

Aside from legal and social needs, the demand for a trade outlet for the rising Texas economy was imperative. In no other phase of their management of Texas affairs did the Mexican officials exhibit greater lack of administrative capacity and foresight than in economic affairs. The Texas cotton farmers, like those in lower southern states, were expanding their cotton acreage and increasing their annual production at a phenomenal rate. Unfortunately the Texans lacked access to either Mexican or foreign markets. There was no open shipping port where Texas products could be sent off to market. Under the prevailing conditions, Texas farmers were worse off than were Ohioans, Kentuckians, and Tennesseans in the eighteenth century when there was danger that Spanish officials in

New Orleans would remove the right of deposit in that port. It was impossible to accumulate wealth in Texas under these hard conditions of trade; yet on the other hand the time was ripe for smuggling and winking at the laws. It was not accidental that the Texas coast was a haven for pirates, and that the Laffittes and Dominique You enjoyed a thriving coastal trade in the region. It was no wonder that much dissatisfaction and resistance developed in regard to Mexican laws. The need for a separate state of Texas within the Republic of Mexico was great, and this became a topic of much discussion. Austin himself strongly favored such a division of territory and authority.

The Road to Independence

By 1830 the movement of American population across the border to Texas had reached sizable proportions. As has been said, neither Mexican laws nor administrative efficiency effected even a light control over Texan affairs. There was a sharp conflict in social and legal traditions, in industry and in economic hopes for the future. Actually the only thing the Mexicans could do, if they were to retain their authority, was to stop the flow of immigrants and goods across the Sabine from the United States. No doubt the talk of American expansion in such states as Missouri, Kentucky, Tennessee and Louisiana, and stories appearing in the American newspapers did nothing to allay Mexican fears. The diplomatic gestures of John Quincy Adams toward extension of the western boundaries of Louisiana and the outspoken sentiments of Andrew Jackson did much to create apprehension of American expansionism.

By 1830 General Manuel de Miery Teran had realized that Texas was lost to Mexico unless the central government took some quick and sane steps to reverse the trends of the moment. Realizing fully the import of American immigration and the establishment of American institutions in the region, he proposed military occupation of Texas, especially the eastern part, colonization by Europeans and Mexicans in Texas, and the nurturing of an economic bond between Texas and Mexico by stimulating coastal trade. Behind Teran's suggestions was a genuine fear of what the United States might do along the Louisiana boundary. Possibly the most decided effect of his recommendations was a tightening of contract and immigration laws as they applied to Americans.

On April 6, 1830, the famous law restricting American activity was passed by the Mexican congress and signed by the president of the Republic. It formalized General Teran's suggestions, opened the coastal trade to foreign vessels, and strengthened the existing religious provisions.

Sections 10 and 11 of the April law dealt a heavy blow to the further

Americanization of Texas. These forbade further introduction of slaves and closed the Texas border to American immigration. Actually this law closed the era of the *empresarios* and the contract immigrant. From 1830 on, Texas history was to be marked by three important features: the migration of intractable Americans who ignored the law, an increased animosity and anxiety over the increased militarization of the region, and louder pleas for a separation from Coahuila and the establishment of the state of Texas. Stephen Austin's conciliatory and cautious policies were coming to have less influence. "Incidents" became more frequent. George Fisher and John Davis Bradburn, for example, aroused opposition among the people in 1832 by their discriminatory activities. Fisher was collector of customs at the mouth of the Brazos, and Bradburn commanded the military post. In time the activities of these men all but provoked a revolution before they were removed from their posts.

By 1832 the crosscurrents of Texas politics and social unrest were so threatening that no amount of legislation, no amount of European and Mexican immigration could stem the tide. The great body of Texans possibly had no desire to do more than establish a state separate from Coahuila. Politically, they favored the rising new leader Santa Anna. Because of his liberal promises they regarded him as a progressive leader who would give Mexico the government it so desperately needed. Stephen Austin continued to pursue a temperate course in which he emphasized the necessity of loyalty to Mexico. He desired statehood, but a period of watchful waiting seemed to him the only course.

On October 1, 1832, a convention of fifty-eight delegates met at San Felipe to seek relief from the stringent law of 1830 and to procure certain economic concessions—a more liberal tariff policy and a continuing policy of permitting the generous importation of necessary domestic goods from the United States. A second convention met at San Felipe during the first two weeks of April, 1833, and produced a state constitution modeled on that of Massachusetts of 1780. This document was largely an American state constitution, embodying many republican ideas which at the moment were foreign to Mexican political concepts. Its most significant effect was to focus the demand for the formation of the state of Texas.

In July, 1833, Stephen Austin sailed from Matamoros for Vera Cruz on his way to present to the central government the Texas plea for statehood. When he arrived in Mexico City, Santa Anna was away with his army trying to crush his opponents and the last spark of republicanism in the northwestern Mexican states. He left behind him as acting president the milder Gomez Farias. Austin's usual tact and persuasiveness failed to gain the favor of Farias, even though the latter was reputed to be well educated and liberal in his thinking. There was delay over every question, and it was evident that Texas statehood would be withheld for a long time, if it really ever would be considered. This condition was highly disturbing to Austin because he knew the prevailing state of mind back in Texas, and he was afraid that some hasty act would lead to serious difficulty with Mexico. While in this impatient frame of mind he wrote the Ayuntamiento in October, 1833, suggesting that it take the necessary steps to establish an independent state—a letter which was to cause him much trouble.

Farias possibly interpreted Austin's anxious action as an attempt to separate the state from Mexico only to lead it into union with the United States. This idea was strengthened when the contents of Austin's letter to the Texas Ayuntamiento were made known. As a result, Austin was thrown into jail in January, 1834. For the next eighteen months, a part of the time in solitary confinement, Austin was a prisoner of the state while the mills of Mexican justice ground slowly. A procession of judges and lawyers was called into the case, but only delays occurred.

Austin was not released from prison and technical arrest until June, 1835, and he was unable to return to Texas before July. During his imprisonment many changes had occurred in Texas. Public sentiment was even stronger for separation than Austin had imagined. One reason for the existence of an active public opinion was the influence of William Wharton's newspaper, *The Advocate of People's Rights*, which had been in publication since 1833. By 1835 it was clear that President Santa Anna had abandoned all of his republican sentiments toward government. Instead he was striving to centralize political control in the presidency.

In Mexico City, Austin had studied Santa Anna's political methods at close range, and he was convinced that the president could not be trusted. For the next decade and a half, the course of Texas history was to be troubled by the antics of this militant gamecock. On two different occasions he was to invade the region with an army. Santa Anna was one of those strange enigmas of history. He was born in Jalapa in 1794, and through the next fifty years he was to be seasoned in the hard school of border warfare. He was shrewd, ruthless, vain, poorly educated, and tyrannical. He was easily swayed by flattery, and had the Latin's love of the colorful uniform and military glory without having the general's sense of leadership and strategy. Possibly his greatest defect of character was insincerity and treachery. Even his private social morals were open to serious criticism.

Remember The Alamo

By 1835, Santa Anna had practically crushed the last resistance to his rule in Mexico. With the deposition of Farias, he smothered the last spark of liberalism in the central government. Beyond the Rio Grande the Texas situation showed possibilities of getting out of hand. Not only were the Americans in Texas exhibiting a marked restiveness, but Santa Anna's old liberal comrade, Lorenzo de Zavala, was there uttering conscience-wounding challenges to the new dictator of Mexico. It was clearly evident that Texas was the weak spot in Santa Anna's control of the country.

He was justified in this belief, for on November 1, 1835, the Texans held a consultation in Washington-on-the-Brazos on the course of affairs and mapped plans for the future. They protested against the centralist activities of Santa Anna and viewed restrictions on American immigration as a serious thing. This protest received considerable publicity. Reminiscent of Jefferson's arraignment of George III, in the Declaration of Independence, the rebellious Texans charged General Santa Anna with many shortcomings, the most serious of which was the overthrow of the republican constitution of 1824.

In answer to the action of the Texans, Santa Anna ordered his brother-in-law, General Martin P. Cos, to invade Texas with an army of just under a thousand men. Operating from Saltillo, the army had a difficult time getting organized to make the long, hard journey across the wastelands between that place and the Texas coast. Even Santa Anna, when he arrived on the scene, had to use persuasion to secure supplies for his army. The march from Laredo to San Antonio was disastrous. Almost before the Mexican force had arrived at its destination, death and sickness had depleted its ranks. By February 23, 1836, however, Santa Anna had assembled some 5,000 to 7,000 men in Texas, and he was ready to attack a bold little band of 187 men who had taken refuge behind the walls of the ancient Alamo Mission.

On the morning of March 6, 1836, Santa Anna ordered his buglers to blow the blood-curdling Old-World *deguello* signifying that no quarter would be given the rebels. Behind the walls of the Alamo were at least three men who already had a claim to border fame. They were William B. Travis, born in the militant upcountry county of Edgefield in South Carolina. He had become one of the more aggressive Texas rebels and had established a reputation as a leader for independence. With Travis was Jim Bowie, who had behind him a rather long career of border activities, including a possible turn at smuggling. Bowie also had been active in the movement for independence. The third man of fame was David Crockett of Tennessee. When the Mexicans had breached the outer walls of the Alamo they fought from room to room until the last Texan was killed. Santa Anna could reckon his own loss at fifteen hundred men killed and wounded.

The Texans declared their independence on March 2, 1836. Invasion of the territory by the Mexican army had hastened the act of independence.

An interim government was established, and the resistance to Santa Anna became truly a war of independence, similar to that of the American colonies against England. The causes of separation of Texas from Mexico, as has been shown, were almost as numerous and complex as were those of the early American struggle. Certainly there was a wide gulf between the attitudes and points of view of the American settlers and Mexican officials in regard to human rights and the nature of democratic government. When Santa Anna threatened the already none-too-satisfactory constitution of 1824, he pulled the political temple down so far as Texans were concerned.

While Santa Anna was advancing through the settled region of East Texas, General José Urrea was engaging the rebels along the coast from Matamoros to the Brazos. On March 20, 1836, he was before Goliad, where he captured a force of approximately four hundred men under the command of J. W. Fannin. Just two years before, Fannin had emigrated to Texas from Georgia. Like Travis and Bowie, he had been active in the independence movement. His first contact with the Mexican army was in the opening revolutionary battle of Gonzales on October 2, 1835. He was assigned the responsibility of gathering supplies along the Trinity, and it was this task which he was performing when General Urrea appeared in that area.

The capture of Fannin and his men at Goliad led to one of the most cold-blooded and inhumane acts of war in America. Urrea had accepted the surrender of the Texans in an orthodox manner, and apparently they were to be treated in the customary manner as prisoners of war. However, on March 23 a hotly vindictive letter from General Santa Anna commanded that the prisoners be shot. Four days later they were led into the open and all but eight who were declared noncombatants and thirty-five escapees were killed and their bodies partly burned. In his mass execution General Urrea destroyed 330 prisoners, a horrible and bloody act.

Sam Houston, the famous Tennessee ex-governor who had been selected to command Texas troops in March, 1836, was faced with the tedious responsibility of drawing together all the scattered Texas troops to prevent a recurrence of the Alamo and Goliad disasters. Settlers were burning and destroying their property and flocking out of the path of the Mexican army. Houston steadily fell back. There was much criticism of his retreating tactics, but he had little choice. He had on hand neither enough men nor supplies to make a determined stand, and until these could be collected, retreat was the only way open. At least in retreat Houston had the advantage of selecting the time and battlefield on which to fight. His retreat took him across the Brazos, and almost at the same time Santa Anna also crossed that river.

The vainglorious Santa Anna was tired of tramping in the mud of Texas river bottoms, and both military glory and the society of his lady friends seemed to be fleeting pleasures under his present environmental conditions. He had 800 men, and General Cos joined him with 400 more. Before him, Sam Houston had a smaller force of 783 men. On April 20, the strutting Mexican general became aware that what he had believed to be a fleeing enemy was standing athwart his path at the confluence of the San Jacinto River and the Buffalo Bayou. When he received this news he lost his poise and ran shouting wildly to his men that the enemy was upon them. Houston grouped his command and moved it silently up to the enemy's position.

On the afternoon of April 21, a Texas fifer blew a falsetto battle march to the slightly salacious tune of "Will You Come to My Bower I Have Shaded for You." Thereafter for eighteen or twenty minutes firing was sharp, and then it died away to desultory individual shots. But that was long enough for the proud Mexican army that had played so much havoc at the Alamo and Goliad to be put to rout. Its gaily caparisoned commander fled the field, shedding his identifying uniform as he went. Taking shelter in the pines, he threw off the pursuit momentarily and clothed himself in a disreputable garb. He was taken prisoner as a common fugitive, however, and closer examination revealed a fine shirt and expensive studs which betrayed Santa Anna's identity. Behind him on the San Jacinto battlefield was the wreckage of an army. Houston said the Mexicans lost 630 killed, 208 wounded, and 730 more were taken prisoners. There is, however, some discrepancy in these figures.

In December, 1835, after having counseled patience and an alliance with the liberal party in opposition to Santa Anna, and two months before the Texas Declaration of Independence was issued, Stephen Austin had abandoned tact and patience in the face of Mexican aggression. He, William H. Wharton, and Branch T. Archer were sent off to the United States to enlist assistance in the form of cash and sympathy. This committee went to Washington, New York and elsewhere seeking aid. It also concerned itself with official and public opinion. To thousands of Americans the independence struggle in Texas was a repetition of American history. There was an abundance of sympathy for the Texas patriots, and many adventurous men and boys rushed there to take part in the revolution. The American press carried a tremendous amount of news and editorial comment on the subject. In Washington, President Jackson was said to have kept such a close watch on the turn of events beyond the Sabine that he even predicted the spot where Sam Houston would stand and fight Santa Anna.

On May 14, 1836, the Texas military revolution came to a formal end when the Treaty of Velasco was signed between President David G. Burnet and Antonio López de Santa Anna. In this document Santa Anna agreed, among others, not to take up arms again against Texas. All Mexican troops were to be withdrawn. Texans held as prisoners were to be released, private property taken in the campaign was to be restored to its owners, and the Mexican army was not to delay its evacuation of Texas. This treaty was an acknowledgement of Texan independence, but it had the distinct weakness of having been signed by General Santa Anna when he was under duress as a prisoner of war.

Final disposition of the captive Mexican general presented a problem. Santa Anna was rightfully looked upon as the instigator of the crime at Goliad and the major oppressor of the people. Many hotheads believed hanging was too good for him, while General Houston and others believed the famous prisoner was worth more alive than dead. He could prevent further conflict between Texas and Mexico if he could be trusted to keep the peace. As a result, the general was sent as a technical prisoner to Washington to be interviewed by officials of the United States Government, including President Jackson. He was finally released and returned to Vera Cruz aboard the United States frigate *Pioneer* in February, 1837. During the next decade this wily Mexican kept busy preparing for his return to politics and for war with Texas.

Independence

Six months of military activity in Texas had seen the dramatic and tragic defeat at the Alamo, the Goliad massacre, and finally the smashing victory of Houston's hastily organized army at San Jacinto. Politically the Texans had moved rather fast in bringing about their independence. Three years before, in 1833, the San Felipe convention had petitioned for separate statehood, and in 1835 many meetings of citizens were still involved in defining the rights of Texas citizens as interpreted under the constitution of 1824. After the famous consultation in Washington-on-the-Brazos took place in 1835, Texas moved rapidly toward its final declaration of independence in March, 1836. Out of these political meetings emerged several important Texas leaders, among them David G. Burnet. Burnet was born in New Jersey but had moved to the frontier where he had conducted a mercantile business. Later he studied law. When the Republic of Texas came into existence, he was made interim president to serve from the spring of 1836 until October, 1837, when he was succeeded by Sam Houston.

Four major problems faced the independent government of Texas. There was great uncertainty as to what action the Mexican Army might take. It was quite possible that some leader might reorganize the Mexican forces and lead them against the rebellious republic. The battle of San

Jacinto had defeated and destroyed only a part of Mexico's military potential. Secondly, from the very beginning, the Republic of Texas was short of funds. Characteristic of a frontier agrarian country, Texas had few developed resources which could be used to stabilize a fiscal system. Most important of all, there was no adequate program of taxation. The only hope for quickly available funds lay in the ability of Austin, Archer and Wharton to negotiate loans in the United States. Their mission, however, failed to accomplish this purpose. American investors were most reluctant to make investments in Texas securities before political and economic kinks were combed out of the new government.

The third problem was the somewhat curious one of disbanding the volunteer army. This organization was created largely under the guidance of Sam Houston. Hundreds of volunteers had come from the United States. They sought adventure, possibly military glory, but most likely they desired to become eligible for considerable grants of land. They were hardly motivated by strong patriotic feelings; consequently the volunteer soldiers were difficult either to discipline or disband. Conflict on the command level had resulted in a duel between General Felix Huston and Albert Sidney Johnston when President Houston had appointed Johnston to command the troops. Houston finally furloughed the troops on May 18, 1837, and ended the army controversy. Finally, there was the question of recognition by foreign governments.

Possibly the most important single theme in the history of the Texas Republic was its attempt either to secure recognition or to be annexed by the United States. The first attempts to gain recognition failed because a lack of technical organization made formal and orderly recognition impossible. Not until President Mirabeau B. Lamar and a new slate of officers were inaugurated in December, 1838, was it possible to set up the machinery for entering into diplomatic negotiations with other governments. Washington tended to go slow in the recognition of Texas because of the attitude which Mexico might take and because of the various internal political and sectional attitudes which prevailed. After lengthy debate, and considerable political sparring between President Andrew Jackson and Congress, Jackson, as one of his last official acts, granted Texas recognition just before midnight, March 3, 1837.

Recognition by the United States was an important step in the stabilization of Texas' political and economic affairs. The Republic functioned under a constitution which gave it the general political form of an American state. Administratively, the organization was almost precisely that of the United States Government, with a president, a cabinet, a small diplomatic corps, and the orthodox legislative bodies and courts. In July, 1838, Britain partially recognized Texan independence insofar as recognition applied to trade between the two countries; and on January 14, 1840, France recognized the Republic. In the same year Britain and the Netherlands received the diplomatic agents of Texas.

On both sides of the Texas border, political forces worked to bring about annexation by the United States. Since Texans were anxious for annexation, an enormous amount of manipulation and negotiation went on to bring this about. In Washington the Texas question involved first of all the major sectional issues, most important of which was the extension of slavery. There was scarcely a month after 1836 when the Texas question did not appear in the congressional discussions. In the Texas capital the issue was debated on many occasions. Possibly to encourage affirmative action in Washington, the Texas government carried on an increasing amount of negotiation with Britain and France—even creating the frightening idea that through the fundamental weaknesses of the Texas government these two nations might gain a powerful foothold on the North American continent.

During the feverish period, 1840–1845, the course of expansionism took decided directions. Congress passed a joint resolution early in 1844 to permit the President of the United States either to arrange for the annexation of Texas or to negotiate a new treaty with the Republic. In March, 1845, President Polk sent Andrew Jackson Donelson out to Texas to sound out sentiment toward the pending admission of Texas as a state. Between that date and December 29, 1845, when Texas was formally admitted to the Union, several necessary steps were taken; among them were ratification of the annexation agreement on July 4, and the drafting of a state constitution to conform with that of the United States. Texas entered the Union on these terms: all boundary issues would be adjusted by the United States; the state would retain its public lands, the income from them was to be applied to the Republic's debt; and as many as four new states might be created from the Texas Territory provided any potential state lying north of the 36° 30′ line barred slavery. With the annexation of Texas, the United States frontier was extended to the Rio Grande, and the gates were opened wide to expansion and settlement in that direction.

Between 1833 and 1845, expansion of American settlement had been rapid. United States newspapers had printed a tremendous amount of descriptive material about Texas. Foreign and American travelers had visited the region and prepared seductive accounts of the country and of their experiences. Newspaper reports of the long and hot debates in Congress on the Texas question served largely to stimulate immigration. By the date of annexation what might be called a Texan society had developed; however, it was no more than an extension of the kind of society which existed in the border states in the Ohio and Mississippi valleys. Life on the Texas frontier was most primitive, and when immigrants arrived at their destinations they seldom brought many of the accouterments of civilization. Homes were crude and uncomfortable, containing no more than the bare necessities for human life. Social life bore the marks of isolation, generous space, individual ruggedness, and human crudeness. Drinking, fighting, bragging, and carousing were almost characteristic of early Texas society. Even the chief officials of the Republic frequently exhibited these rugged traits of character.

A characteristic summary of Texas conditions was the remark that "Texas was hard on women and oxen." No doubt it was. Hundreds of letters written back to Mississippi, Alabama, Tennessee, Kentucky and other states told both of the extreme hardships and the wonderful opportunities in the new land. It is doubtful that many people read aright the hardship statements, preferring to hear instead of rich lands, good cotton crops, and fresh opportunities. "Gone to Texas" became a meaningful legend in the older states. Men went to escape debts or impending arrest for crimes, too many wives and children, soil exhaustion and their own frustrations. All the anxieties of man might be solved by rushing over the Sabine to the new Eden. Sheriffs ran away and left their badges and electorates behind, farmers abandoned their fields, ministers deserted their pulpits, and enterprisers of every sort rushed west to the rising new state. Viewing the Texas scene in 1840, the young British observer Francis Sheridan said,

> I certainly never was fully aware of the merits of the "go ahead" principle until I came here. 3 years ago—the population of Texas was 20,000 souls—Black and White, men women & children— They now amount to 200,000, increasing at the rate of 1000 per week. Galveston then was no bigger than Velasco, it has now 5,000 inhabitants. Austin the new seat of govt the site of which was only surveyed last October, is now a flourishing little town with 7 or 800 inhabitants.

No radical change took place in the social adjustments of most American immigrants to Texas. Many of them had already passed through the hard school of the frontier and regarded their crossing of the Sabine with no more feeling than a move beyond the Wabash or the Red. As has been said, there was remarkably little environmental difference between East Texas and the rest of the South. Yet few people on the frontier developed a more definite state of mind than did people in this region. It is hardly enough to say they had moved to a big country, and because of this regarded everything through the enlarged vision of a dweller in great open spaces. The whole country was large, and pioneers everywhere could lay claim to the same expansive vision. Neither hardships nor accomplishments were any greater here than elsewhere. The people of Texas, however, did undergo one extraordinary experience on a rather large scale that was not precisely duplicated in the other frontier regions. They expatriated themselves and fought to establish an independent republic. When they entered the Union in 1845 they did so largely on their own terms, and it was not without an enormous amount of pride that they proclaimed their achievements. Fundamentally, Texas frontiersmen were sentimentalists. On February 16, 1846, when Anson Jones struck the Lone Star flag, there was a show of genuine emotion. They were happy about annexation, but their troubled republic did not pass without a tear.

Annexation of Texas to the Union touched off a chain reaction of events which ran a full course between 1845 and 1861. Waiving any discussion of the validity of the points of view of the antislavery expansionists and the proslavery group, their arguments did much to trouble the national scene in this decade and a half. Texas was a fresh catalyst of sectional issues which became warmer with each agitation. The five years following the annexation of Texas saw the United States involved in an expansionist war which raised many issues and made the solutions of problems both old and new an urgent necessity. Out of annexation came many of the tensions which led to the Compromise of 1850 and an adjustment of controversies over the new territories which for a time allayed sectional passions.

No one doubted in 1845 that the annexation of Texas by the United States was almost certain to bring war with Mexico. Fears and jealousies beyond the Rio Grande were easily aroused, and there still lingered in Mexican breasts a desire to avenge the humiliation caused by the loss of so much valuable territory and the failures of their army in the campaign of 1836.

SANTA FE—END OF THE TRAIL

THE ROAD TO SANTA FE

THE ROAD TO SANTA FE

The arrival produced a great deal of bustle and excitement among the natives. "Los Americanos!"—"Los Carros!"—"La Entrada de la Caravana!" were to be heard in every direction; and crowds of women and boys flocked around to see the new-comers; while crowds of léperos hung about as usual to see what they could pilfer. The wagoners were by no means free from the excitement on this occasion. Informed of the 'ordeal' they had to pass, they had spent the previous morning in 'rubbing up;' and now they were prepared, with clean faces, sleek combed hair, and their choicest Sunday suit, to meet the 'fair eyes' of glistening black that were sure to stare at them as they passed. There was yet another preparation to be made in order to 'show off' to advantage. Each wagoner must tie a brand new 'cracker' to the lash of his whip; for, on driving through the streets and the plaza pública, every one strives to outvie his comrades in the dexterity with which he flourishes this favorite badge of authority.

—JOSIAH GREGG, *Commerce of the Prairies*

CHAPTER XVII

Every step westward beyond the Mississippi took American civilization nearer a junction with that of Imperial Spain. For three centuries Europeans had drifted northward toward the region beyond the Rio Grande. The trans-Mississippi plains beckoned to early American adventurers, and after 1807 the western mountains had drawn trappers and traders in increasing numbers. These advance men of the rising tide of settlement had gone into the upper Missouri Valley in search of adventure and profit, and many had followed the mountain ranges southward as far as the sign of fur-bearing animals led them—sometimes beyond the Spanish border.

One of the first Spaniards to work his way inland was Cabeza de Vaca. Across de Vaca's dimming trail came Coronado following the rumors of cities of gold at *Cibola*. On his northward venture toward *Quivira*, the legendary city, he no doubt touched on what was to be the Santa Fe Trail. These prospectors were the outriders from Spain; the movement of population itself was much slower. First to come to the region after Coronado's golden dreams had faded were those tenacious forerunners of settlement in the Southwest, the priest-missionaries, who moved deeper and deeper into the vast unexploited and Godless lands of the north. They, along with occasional adventurers, kept alive an interest in the great plains and wilderness. One of the latter was Don Juan de Oñate, who visited New Mexico in 1598.

For the next century the history of the country above the Rio Grande is the story of numerous penetrations by Spanish adventurers and traders. In 1609 Santa Fe was founded and survived Indian revolt, Comanche and Navaho raids, and the eighteenth-century rivalry between Frenchmen and Spaniards. By the beginning of the eighteenth century, Frenchmen from the Mississippi Valley were appearing in the Southwest. For the sixty-three years following, numerous foreign individuals or parties either wandered into Santa Fe or were brought in as prisoners by jealous Spanish officials who looked after their trade monopoly with sharp eyes.

Associations with the Indians of the northern plains led French traders deeper into the frontier. Most of these traders came from Vincennes, Kaskaskia, and, later, from St. Louis. Some were from the Illinois country;

possibly a few had wandered down from the Great Lakes, traveling with the Indian tribes or setting out alone to seek adventure. Unlike the first Spanish explorers, the French seemed to have no delusions about caches of treasure in the region. They did, however, learn of the profitable trading possibilities in the Spanish city.

Probing the Southwest

In 1739 the Mallet brothers reached Santa Fe from the Illinois country. Later, Governor Bienville of Louisiana sent out a party under the leadership of Fabry de la Bruyère which reached Santa Fe and spent considerable time dealing with the Indians. Within the next twenty years, numerous parties visited the Spanish settlements and the Comanche and Apache Indians. Had the French hold on the North American continent endured, there might have been serious rivalry between France and Spain for the trade of the Southwest.

Whether or not the Spanish and French traders looked upon the territory southwestward from the Mississippi and Missouri rivers as the great American desert failed to alter the fact that the hot sands along the route proved a serious barrier. Later American traders approached this area possibly somewhat handicapped by knowledge of Zebulon M. Pike's description of the region as incapable of sustaining human life in any degree of comfort. It is doubtful, of course, that many of the early traders even knew of Pike, but they learned first-hand the conditions of the land which had made such a deep impression upon this explorer.

Buffalo, Indian, Spaniard, Frenchman and American, all had tramped over the trail leading southwestward to Santa Fe before the end of the second decade of the nineteenth century. Already the general trail southwestward was known, though in many places an indefinable thing—no more than hoofprints in the blazing sands of the Arkansas and Cimarron valleys. In its extremity, it ran for 780 miles from what later became Westport Landing and Independence on the Missouri to the Little Arkansas River, to Walnut Creek, and then up the north bank of the Arkansas to Bent's Fort, where it turned southward through Raton Pass to San Miguel and Santa Fe. The cutoff ran from San Miguel across the Canadian River to the Cimarron and then crossed the high, dry, desert sands to the confluence of the Cimarron and the Arkansas. In time American traders were to establish more detailed landmarks. Among these were Council Grove, Walnut Creek, Fort Dodge, the Caches, Bent's Fort, Fort Lyon, Cimarron Crossing, Raton Pass, and the Canadian River.

From Independence to Council Grove was 145 miles; it was at this latter place that the caravans were organized. Until they reached Council Grove, individual wagoners were more or less upon their own responsibility.

Earlier, when travelers crossed the plains they followed little more than a general direction and their own judgment in reaching Santa Fe. At one time wagon tracks ranged over a wide belt of open country. Along the Arkansas and Cimarron rivers, and going southward down the slope of the mountains, vehicles were forced to follow a relatively narrow roadway.

By 1820 American civilization was prepared to make bold thrusts onto the Great Plains, and even to cross them. Zebulon Montgomery Pike made the most dramatic early crossing of the plains when he followed the upper reaches of the Arkansas to its mountain sources. He was the first of many Americans going westward who pretended ignorance when they were charged with invading Spanish territory. In Pike's footsteps came other parties of hunters and traders to arouse Spanish suspicions, or to get caught like him in the official nets. Three Americans, LaLande, Pursley and Ezekiel Williams preceded Pike to Santa Fe. Pursley, a Kentuckian, liked the country so much that he remained there; LaLande made off with his employer's goods and failed to return, and Captain Williams returned to write of his hardships. Coming immediately after Pike was a trader named Baudoin, sent out by Manuel Lisa and Jacques Clamorgan from St. Louis.

News of the profits in Santa Fe traveled fast, and a trading party composed of James McLanahan, James Patterson, Reuben Smith, and Emanuel Blanco traveled overland to that market. They went up the Red River from Louisiana in 1809, and were captured and thrown in jail for two years by the Spanish authorities. Disappearance of these men aroused some excitement along the Mississippi, and there was even a threat that a large and militant company would go to their rescue.

Three years after McLanahan's party went out from Louisiana, Robert McKnight led a band of hunters up the Missouri and then crossed the plains to Mexico. McKnight and his men were captured and jailed in Chihuahua where they remained until after Mexico won its independence in 1821. Their goods were confiscated and the proceeds used to feed them meagerly until they were freed. Others went overland with varying fortunes to capture the Santa Fe trade. Some of them, like Joseph Philibert and Auguste Pierre Chouteau from St. Louis, escaped serious trouble, while others like David Merriwether's company were subjected to great suffering and indignities. Merriwether and his companions, after being jailed and mistreated, were freed and ordered from the country, but not until they had knelt and kissed the document prescribing their fate.

One thing was clear. The Santa Fe trade promised to be a profitable one, and the Spaniards did not want American competition. But in 1821 Spain's administrative control of Mexico ended. The new republic now governed the country, and there was less jealousy of Americans than had been earlier. Hardly had news of Mexico's independence drifted north-ward than the first major trading expedition got under way to Santa Fe. In 1821 William Becknell and Colonel Benjamin Cooper set out with separate pack trains for the rich market to the southwest. Cooper was way-laid and robbed by the Indians, but Becknell went on to struggle with the hardships of the trail and to sell his goods at five times their worth in St. Louis. Five months later he was back at Franklin, Missouri, to tell his success story and to prepare for a second trip. Becknell, of course, was not the first trader to reach Santa Fe in the 1820's. There were hunting parties which visited the town, and a Mr. Glenn was returning from Santa Fe just as Becknell and Cooper were setting out. He discovered Indians on the trail before Cooper and predicted his failure to get beyond the Arkansas.

In 1822 Becknell was ready again to visit Santa Fe, this time with wagons. On May 12 he "crossed" his company of twenty-one men and three wagons over the Missouri from Arrow Rock and struck out across country to the Arkansas River. Straying horses and thieving Osages caused him trouble. Two members of his party went in search of missing horses and were stripped and whipped by the Indians. Had it not been for the presence of the St. Louis trader Pierre Chouteau, matters might have be-come much worse. Hauling wagons across the plains and over steep and treacherous cliffs, and ferrying them across the rivers was an arduous un-dertaking. But they knew that a seller's market awaited them in Santa Fe. A plodding wagoner could dream of the romance and excitement of the town and of the silver that he would bring home.

Coming home, Captain Becknell noted in his brief journal that he was able to shorten the journey to forty-eight days. At Santa Fe he had been hospitably received, and his trade had been good. Dragging his wagons northward he left tracks in the sands which pointed the way for the next thirty years.

Never before had the Mexicans had access to a market where they could purchase iron, cutlery, tools, Yankee notions and good grades of textiles. The demand was brisk for colored cloth of every kind—calicoes, drillings, shirting, velveteens, domestic ticking and chambrays. After 1837 there was a restriction on the coarser types of American cloth which made it unprofitable to transport them to the distant Mexican market.

Prairie schooners manufactured first in Pittsburgh, then in St. Louis and Independence, were packed carefully so that goods would remain dry and in place. Every vehicle was loaded in such a manner that it would carry the maximum cargo without being overloaded for the treacherous stretches on the road. Skilled packers learned by experience how to load a freight wagon so as to insure safe delivery of the goods. Each wagon, weigh-ing between five and seven thousand pounds, was drawn by six yoke of oxen or three to five pair of mules. Wagon boxes were wrapped with heavy osnaburg sheets to keep off sun and rain, and occasionally mackinaw sheets were placed next to goods to insure them against damage. There was distinct sensitivity in Santa Fe against faded goods, as purchasers feared they were being sold cast-off merchandise.

On the Trail

In the struggle across the plains, drivers became exhausted. The Indian menace kept men on edge from the time they entered the plains until they reached the mountains. Marauding parties threatened death at every turn. A mule skinner had to be as adept at handling a rifle as a whip, and in the years following Becknell's pioneering journey, caravans were organized with military precision. A captain was selected, and every driver had to submit to his orders. The captain determined the numbers of wagons and men and divided the company into groups in which it was to move the rest of the way. The captain had the responsibility of setting the length of the day's travel, choosing camp sites, arranging the wagons in a circle at night, and planning for any emergencies that might arise. Once the company got underway, the train of wagons strung out across the plains looked like an army on the march.

Some wagons were drawn by oxen, while others were pulled by horses and mules. The ox was an excellent draft animal, able to pull a heavy load a long distance under adverse circumstances, and to do a reasonably good job of foraging for his food. He had a serious drawback in his hoofs which were tender and difficult to shoe. No one had found an ox shoe that would endure the long journey, although so long as the weather remained dry, buffalo skin pouches that covered the feet could be used to a good advantage. Keeping the feet of horses and mules in condition was also a difficult task. Mules tended to stand the journey better than horses, and it was much more practical to shoe them than horses. Many mule teams went unshod but their hoofs tended to become worn and slick, making traction difficult. This meant that animals lost efficiency in their drawing power.

Mule skinners in the Santa Fe trade lived rugged lives. Each man was supplied with approximately 120 pounds of flour, 120 pounds of bacon, 10 pounds of coffee, 20 pounds of sugar and a handful of salt. Once on the plains, buffalo meat was made available by hunters. When caravans entered the Indian country, no one could ever be certain that he would get a full night's sleep. Horned frogs and rattlesnakes kept the trains tingling with excitement. When a snake or frog crawled into bed with a skinner, it was difficult to tell whether or not the Comanches were raiding the camp. All along through the prairies drivers fired their guns at rattlers. Gregg says in his *Commerce of the Prairies:*

> As we were toiling through the sandy hillocks which border the southern banks of the Arkansas, the day being exceedingly warm, we came upon a perfect den of these reptiles [rattlesnakes]. I will not say "thousands," though this perhaps was nearer the truth—but hundreds were coiled or crawling in every direction. They were no sooner discovered than we were upon them with guns and pistols, determined to let none escape.

Loaded caravans made approximately sixteen miles a day across the plains. At night, guards were posted to prevent the camps from being surprised. Early in the morning all was hustle and bustle. Animals that had been staked out to graze during the night were hurried up to the wagons, to be harnessed and hitched. The cry of "Catch up! Catch!" threw the morning camp into pandemonium. As Gregg wrote:

> . . . on such occasions, a scene of confusion ensues, which must be seen to be appreciated. The woods and dales resound with the gleeful yells of the lighthearted wagoners, who, weary of inaction, and filled with the joy at the prospect of getting underway, become clamorous in the extreme. Scarcely does the jockey on the race-course ply his whip more promptly at that magic word go than does these emulous wagoners fly to harness their mules at the spirit stirring sound of "Catch up!" Each teamster vies with his fellows who shall be soonest ready; and it is a matter of boastful pride to be first to cry out—"All's set!"

A swearing perspiring skinner dragged a balky mule into place, kicked him up to his position at the tongue or into the lead, threw collar and hames over his shoulders, jerked the belly band tight, kicked the mule in the belly to make him deflate his lungs and be ready to go on the signal "Stretch Out!" Wielding a long whip on a short heavy stock, drivers pushed their teams ahead with the diligence of stagecoach drivers hastening to keep a mail schedule.

Mrs. Susan Shelby Magoffin described realistically the breaking of camp. She and her husband arrived at Council Grove when the caravan was getting ready to move on.

> The teamsters were just "catching up," and the cracking of whips, lowing of cattle, braying of mules, whooping and hollowing of the men was a novel sight rather. It is disagreeable to hear so much swearing; the animals are unruly tis true and worries the patience of their drivers, but scarcely I think they need be so profane. And the mules I believe are worse, for they kick and run much faster. It is a common circum-

stance for a mule (when first brought into service) while they are hitching him in, to break away with chains and harness all on, and run for half hour or more with two horsemen at his heels endeavoring to stop him, or at least to keep him from running among the other stock.

On the trail the wagoners faced excessive heat and drouth, but occasionally rains came down on them and stirred the road to a loblolly. Stream crossings caused great difficulty. Wagons were always becoming stalled, and men whooped, holloed, and pushed their way out. Mrs. Magoffin described the scene when Owen and Aull's wagon train became stuck in a wet-weather creek bed.

> The last wagon did not get over till 9 o'clock. It stuck in the mud and when two drivers with eleven yoke of oxen failed to move it some more hands went down from the camp and they "whipped out," a teamster's term meaning they fell to work with their whip handles and beat the poor oxen, whooping and yelling all the time, till one is almost induced to believe their throats will split. They continue this till fear of their oppressors will compel the brutes to pull till they move it, and as a reward for their perseverance they come off with bloody necks from the yoke rubbing, and their heads and backs well whip-lashed.

Los Carros!

Thus it was that day after day, mudhole after mudhole, and one accident after another, the wagon trains ground on until they reached the mountain range, and then turned toward Santa Fe. There was new meaning to life now. Going down the slope toward the sleepy mountain Mexican town, men began to dream of profits, but perhaps more of them thought of the social life which awaited their arrival. The observant Gregg was on hand in 1831 to describe the scene before Santa Fe as the Missouri traders came into sight.

> It was truly a scene for the artist's pencil to revel in. Even the animals seemed to participate in the humor of their riders, who grew more and more merry and obstreperous as they descended toward the city. I doubt, in short, whether the first sight of the walls of Jerusalem were beheld by the crusaders with much more tumultuous and soul-enrapturing joy. The arrival produced a great deal of bustle and excitement among the natives. "*Los Americanos!*"—"*Los Carros*"—"*La Entrada de la Caravana!*" were to be heard in every direction; and crowds of women and boys flocked around to see the newcomers; while crowds of *leperos* hung about as usual to see what they could pilfer.

Once in Santa Fe the trader had constantly to be on guard against thieves. In addition to its legion of beggars, the town also sheltered a band of thieves who waited for the caravans to arrive so that they could pilfer their cargoes. It took almost as many men to guard against this petty thievery as it did to transport the goods from Missouri. And it took an exceedingly sharp bargainer to deal with the Mexicans, who lived by the economic philosophy of selling high and buying cheaply and who neither sold nor bought without haggling.

If there was excitement in the town, there was even more among the wagoners. Men "slicked" themselves up. They put on their best suits "to meet the 'fair eyes' of glistening black that were sure to stare at them as they passed." They tied new crackers to their whips which they popped loudly as they drove into the public square. Like the old caravans that sailed into European ports from the East, the Americans came with wares to enliven the tempo of life in Santa Fe for months to come.

Santa Fe was a characteristic back-country Spanish-American town. Located twelve or fifteen miles from the bank of the Rio del Norte, it nestled at the base of a mountain. In 1831 it had a population of three thousand people, with an additional three thousand in nearby villages. The town was laid out with little or no planning. Streets ran off somewhat like spokes in a wagon wheel. In the middle of the town was a public square enclosed by the governor's house, the barracks, the calaboose, the governmental offices, and the military chapel and the church of Our Lady of Guadalupe. Dwelling houses ranged in quality from miserable, dirty, mud hovels up to somewhat palatial family dwellings. All of them were of adobe construction. Walls were two or three feet thick; roofs were flat and made of hard-packed mud plates tamped onto heavy pine joists. Floors were mud-coated and glossed over by frequent wettings at the time of construction. Living in even the best of these houses was somewhat akin to living in a basement.

Viewed from a distance, Santa Fe was unimpressive. In fact, the traveler was upon it before he realized a town existed, except for foreknowledge that he was nearing his destination. Aside from the actual social life of the town, the American frontiersmen who went with the trading caravans looked upon conditions there with considerable disdain. Back in Missouri they had left a primitive social environment, but it had arisen out of an entirely different set of surroundings and customs. Log houses, lack of sanitation, dirt floors, crowded and bug-ridden bedrooms, and a mixing of the sexes was the rule rather than the exception in the American backwoods. But Spanish customs and mores, plus the adobe-type house gave a new flavor to the Southwest. Although this was not the first time or place where backwoods America met backwoods Spain and Mexico, it was one of the most exciting places.

At Santa Fe the American traders met an interesting collection of human beings. Aside from the women who were always on hand to savor the fruits of a thriving commerce, there was a society which was as far removed from the usual American social pattern as could be imagined. From top to bottom of the social scale, a philosophy prevailed that life should be lived with as little human exertion as possible. Society was stratified into a hierarchy reminiscent of a medieval city. Economic gain for the future, the acquisition of social and material prestige depended more upon fortuitous circumstances and the will of God than upon the push and energy of the individual. Politeness and gentility were more important than profits and ambitions. The personal behavior of the hospitable natives of Santa Fe was a gracious outgiving thing which baffled the Americans. Be it said this graciousness had a chastening effect upon many unsophisticated mule skinners, whose only sense of grace was the ability to crack a long whip.

Mexican clothing intrigued the American visitors. Where American men were accustomed to drab male dress, the Mexican dandy seemed a walking spectrum. His garb was a mixture of European and Mexican country style. Josiah Gregg recorded a description of one dashing Beau Brummel of the Rio del Norte. The *caballero's* riding costume consisted

> of a *sombrero*—a peculiarly-shaped low crowned hat with wide brim, covered with oil cloth and surmounted with a band of tinsel cloth gaudily embroidered with braid and fancy barrel-buttons: a curiously-shaped article called *calzoneras*, intended for pantaloons, with the outer part of the legs open from hip to ankle—the borders set with tinkling filigree buttons, and the whole fantastically trimmed with tinsel and lace cords of the same materials.

Trousers were held up by rich sashes wound tightly about the body. Leggings or *botas* held the trouser legs in place in the saddle, and the dandy was topped off by a colorful *serape saltillero* which was either draped about the shoulders, or the head was thrust through a hole so the *serape* rested on the shoulders. Horses were almost as gaudily caparisoned as were their riders.

The women of Santa Fe were black-eyed, black-haired, and of fair complexion. Like their men, whether of high or low estate, the young ones were unusually attractive in the eyes of the American traders. Details of their dress did not escape the observant Gregg.

> The ladies never wear either hat, cap or bonnet, except when they walk abroad, the *rebozo* (or scarf), or large shawl, is drawn over the head. The *rebozo* is by far the most fashionable: it is seven or eight feet in length by nearly a yard in width, and is made of divers stuffs—silk, linen

or cotton, and usually variegated and figured in the warp by symmetrically disposed threads waved in the dying. It is certainly a beautiful specimen of domestic manufacture.

In other respects the Mexican women dressed differently from their American sisters. They exposed their ankles and portions of their breasts to the delight of their visitors. There was an absence of the many petticoats which gave the American women of the 1830's an overstuffed appearance. Gregg wrote,

> The ordinary apparel of the female peasantry and the *rancheras*, is the *anaguas* or petticoat of homemade flannel; or, when they were able to procure it, of a coarse blue or scarlet cloth, connected to a wide list of some contrasting colored stuff, bound around the waist over a loose white chemise, which is the only covering for the body, except the *rebozo*. Uncouth as this costume may appear at first, it constitutes nevertheless a very graceful sort of undress—in which capacity it is used even by ladies of rank.

It was largely to satisfy the feminine desire for a variety of better textiles that the Americans blazed the trail to Santa Fe.

In other ways the Santa Fe women attracted attention to themselves. They smoked *cigarritos* openly and without apparent timidity. As Mrs. Magoffin said of a social party, "When all that were in were seated, out came the little cigarritos, and the general smoking commenced." Gregg saw cigarettes in the mouths of all; in the parlor, the ballroom and everywhere else they were presented to the ladies as regularly as any other type of refreshments. It was not uncommon to see a gay senorita being whirled around madly in a dance with a lighted cigarette in her mouth. These were made of finely ground tobacco rolled in corn shucks. Women were not modest in the American sense and did not blush at discussing with their menfolk everything that came to mind. Even the vulgar and repulsive became topics of mixed conversations. Above all, the girls wanted to keep their skin fair and rosy. They smeared their faces with a ghastly, thick, white paste that made them look like plaster mannequins, or they painted their faces with the blood-like *alegria* which made them appear to be bleeding to death. This was done to fend off the damaging rays of the sun. Older women attempted to retain their youthful appearances by wearing wigs and painting a bloom on their cheeks.

Santa Fe was inhabited by a normally stratified Mexican society. There were the beggars who prowled the streets begging alms, especially on Saturday mornings, giving the town the appearance of an oriental city. When confronted with outstretched bony hands, and obsequious weak voices reciting heart-rending tales of human misfortunes and tragedies, the visitor might well imagine himself in Jerusalem, Calcutta or Cairo. This was a part of the religious tradition, for the faithful gained grace and favor by giving alms. American travelers, unaccustomed to begging, were critical of so much human degradation, but the natives took this condition in their stride without giving much thought to social reform. Happiness came first, but human suffering was one of the natural attributes of life.

As for Spanish-speaking people everywhere, the joys of life in New Mexico were varied. Drinking of wines and liquors was a pleasant and relaxing pastime in the arid Southwest. The fruit of the vine came from Mexico and El Paso, and was dispensed in numerous saloons, which as one contemporary observer said competed actively with the churches. Sports were many. There were horse races, bull-baiting, dog and cock fighting, and gander pulling in American backwoods style in which a gander or cock was suspended from overhead and riders dashed around in a circle trying to snatch off its greased head. A variation of this was to bury the fowl's body in the ground with its greased head left sticking up so that riders could dash by, swinging from their saddles to snatch at it.

An enticing pastime was gambling. Everybody, men, women, and children, gambled. They flocked to the roulette wheels or placed their meager funds on the flip of a card at the monte tables. Possibly one of the most famous women in the early Southwest was Doña Gertrudes Barcelo, or Doña Tula as she was called. She came down from Taos, a good-looking, black-eyed lass, to work in a Santa Fe gambling house. Being a quick-witted girl, she placed side bets of her own, and soon was mistress of a gambling establishment. Time and nervous strain served her badly, as it did most Santa Fe belles; she lost her teeth, and her crowning black hair thinned out so that it was necessary for her to don a wig. In time the fading Doña Tula was called upon to lend Colonel David A. Mitchell of the United States Army one thousand dollars that he might carry out his orders to open communication with Chihuahua. Doña Tula was generous with her loan, exacting the promise of Colonel Mitchell that he would squire her to a formal ball.

To the strains of fiddles, *bandolies* and tombé, dances were nightly affairs in Santa Fe. The *bailes* and *fandangos* were occasions of much gayety, and Americans like James Ohio Pattie who came with puritanical inhibitions soon forgot them and found new joys in life. But the social pleasures at the end of the long journey over the Santa Fe Trail were of only superficial importance. A speedy disposition of the cargo was the main objective of the annual visits of the caravans.

The caravans brought a large variety of goods which were not readily available to the people of New Mexico, but there was a certain amount of official red tape and profiteering which had to be tolerated. Every wagon load of freight had to pass through customs, and a duty was paid on goods before they could be exposed for sale. The official rate of duty varied from year to year, and from governor to governor. As in Mexican law itself there were frequent changes, but the rates charged by customs collectors represented the whims and avarice of the governors themselves. Some of them, like Manuel Armijo, collected small fortunes while passing on to the central treasury a remarkably small portion of the total sum collected.

Once clear of customs, traders could offer their goods in either wholesale or retail lots. If they sold at wholesale the prices were cheaper. The mode of sale depended largely upon the amount of time the trader had to spend in New Mexico before his note matured at home. Some traders followed the market to other towns, going on as far as Chihuahua, El Paso, Durango, and Matamoros. Some even drifted southward to Mexico City. When cargoes were disposed of, and traders were ready to start home, they took with them droves of mules, jacks and jennets, furs, buffalo skins, Mexican silverware, silver dollars, and chinaware which had come up from Vera Cruz. The jacks which went up the trail sired the famous Missouri mules. The droves of Mexican mules which came up the trails pulled the freight wagons on their repeated trips back to Santa Fe.

A Trail of Expansion

The inflow of silver money into the western United States was to have an important influence upon border finances. Missouri banks, especially, showed the vitalizing effects of a healthy balance of trade with Mexico. Josiah Gregg's chart of this Santa Fe trade has been quoted many times. He estimated the monetary returns between 1822 and 1843 to have been $2,912,000, and from 1828 to 1843 the trade averaged more than $150,000 a year, with the latter year running to $450,000. Neither the number of proprietors of caravans nor the number of men engaged in the trade were large. The largest number of proprietors was ninety, and the smallest, five. In the year that $450,000 worth of goods went to market there were only thirty proprietors, but the largest number (350) of men were engaged in transporting the goods.

Unfortunately the trade on the Santa Fe Trail reached its heaviest proportions in those years when Jacksonian Democracy was at its height, and there was little or no chance to secure public aid in improving the road. Though Thomas Hart Benton made strong representations in its behalf in Congress, the road failed to receive public assistance. Congress was also dilatory in supplying necessary military assistance to guard travelers against injury from the Indians. Major Bennett Riley led four infantry companies out in 1829 to protect the caravan of that year. He waited on the northern bank of the Arkansas for the caravan to return and escorted it home in reasonable safety. For the most part, however, the men of the caravans served as drivers and guardsmen, and by competent management the traders were able to stave off the Indian attacks.

Merchants hauling goods over the Santa Fe Trail before 1848 were faced with many uncertainties. A stubborn team of mules might become excited and run away with a wagon, destroying both its contents and themselves. Storms on the prairies might do serious damage, and there was always danger of breakdowns, fording mishaps, and loss of teams by sickness. The greatest menace of all, however, was from jealous Indians, who lurked along the trail to drive off livestock, kill the traders, and destroy wagons and cargoes. The Indian menace in time became a problem too big for a wagon train company to handle. Another trail difficulty was the lack of a definitely marked route. Sometimes wagoners missed the route and failed to take advantage of the most advantageous roadway and stream crossings.

By 1841 the so-called "Missouri Traders" were threatened with competition. In that year the Texas-Santa Fe Expedition set out from Austin, Texas, to open a thousand-mile trade route to Santa Fe and, possibly, to snatch New Mexico away from the Mexicans. Accompanying this expedition was the American citizen, George Wilkins Kendall, editor of the New Orleans *Picayune*. Before the Texans could reach Santa Fe they were captured by Captain Damasio Salazar, and a tragic march to prison in Mexico City began which resulted in much brutality and suffering. When Kendall was finally released on orders from General Santa Anna, he returned to the United States and wrote his account of the bloody Santa Fe Expedition which served to stir up sentiment against Mexico both in Texas and Missouri. Within the next five years other unpleasant incidents, growing out of Texas wrath over the ill-fated Santa Fe fiasco, marred the history of the Santa Fe Trail. Trade came to a virtual standstill by 1845, and it was not until after 1848 that the trail was again safe from the ravages of war.

In the history of the Santa Fe Trail, from its opening by Captain Becknell in 1821 down to 1845, several famous people became associated with its history. One of these was the colorful scout and trader Christopher (Kit) Carson, who was born in Madison County, Kentucky. When he was a baby of two he was taken to Boone's Lick, Missouri. When he was seventeen he was apprenticed by his mother to a harness-maker near Franklin. Listening to the tales of the adventurers who had gone into the Southwest, young Carson became more interested in following the wagons along the Santa Fe Trail than in making saddles. In 1826 he ran away from home and went out with the caravan of that year. For the rest of his life he lived in the

Southwest, becoming in his brief fifty-nine years a legendary figure as frontier scout.

In 1828 James Magoffin of Kentucky started a trade to Santa Fe, and shortly he was joined in a partnership by his brother Samuel. The Magoffin brothers carried on the same kind of trade as the other wagoners who trudged over the long miles to New Mexico and Mexico where they carried on an established business throughout the years. In 1846 Samuel Magoffin took his wife, Susan Shelby, to Santa Fe. Like the imaginative Josiah Gregg, Mrs. Magoffin kept a careful journal of her experiences. She associated not only with American army officers who passed in and out of the town during the Mexican War, but she recorded a most human picture of life about her. As the first American woman in Santa Fe, her clothing, her housekeeping methods, and her position in the military society of the moment excited much curiosity.

Long commercial caravans stirring up great clouds of trail dust as they crawled over the plains were picturesque thrusts of American civilization into the deeper frontier of the Southwest. Income from this trade was not large, as American economic incomes have been measured in the past. The labor of delivering goods to this faraway market required superhuman endurance, and the suffering of the animals that drew the wagons was inconceivable. Those worn skeletons of oxen that stumbled into Santa Fe after having been whipped through many boggy stretches of ground, and the raw festered shoulders of mules and horses, were but the manifestations of a blustering young economic venture putting everything it had in the business of succeeding. But animal suffering and income were incidental to the fact that the Santa Fe Trail linked the old civilization of Spanish Mexico with that of the American frontier. Santa Fe was the fusing point. What had started out as a series of pack mule tracks became an established road.

Landmarks came into existence, one by one, as traders had memorable experiences along the way. One of these places was the Caches. Here, in the winter of 1822, a trader named Beard and his companions were forced by the heavy snows to bury their cargo, hole up in the ground, and wait the winter out. When suitable traveling weather came again, much of their livestock was dead or unable to continue the journey. It was not until members of the party went to Taos for new stock that they were able to deliver their goods in Santa Fe. These pits were located near the one hundredth meridian, approximately on the boundary between the United States and Mexico.

Some types of property were perfectly safe when left behind on the plains. The Bryant party ran into trouble on its return trip from Santa Fe in 1828 and was forced to abandon its wagons and stock and set forth afoot for Missouri. A part of the return cargo was silver money, and members of the party, though beset by Indians, were reluctant to leave their wealth behind. They set out with ten thousand Mexican silver dollars, but when they reached Chouteau's Island in the Arkansas, they buried the money. Suffering thirst and starvation to the point of exhaustion, they finally succeeded in reaching Missouri. The next spring William Y. Hitt, one of the stranded wagoners, went out with Major Riley's command, and in July he was back at the island where his party had buried their money. Rains had washed the earth off the coins, but they lay untouched though exposed to view.

Two forts were built along the Trail. In 1832 William Bent and a party of traders established a fort on the north bank of the Arkansas. In time this fort was moved down the river where it became a center of activity both for the mountain trade and trade which went on to New Mexico. Opposite the mouth of the Cimarron was located a series of army camps which in time grew into Fort Dodge. As time passed, this place was an important way station not only for the caravans but for the cattle trade and the expanding Santa Fe Railroad.

Following the Mexican War, the Santa Fe Trail became a part of a spreading network of western roads and trails. The great road connected the United States and northern Mexico, and it also connected with other roads which led across the Southwest to the Pacific Coast. When the modern system of transcontinental roads was developed, Highways 66 and 50 followed generally the direction which had led Pike, Becknell, and the Magoffins to Santa Fe. Political changes which took place after 1848 were greatly facilitated by the active intercourse between Missouri and the capital city of New Mexico.

MEN

AGAINST THE MOUNTAINS

*There is perhaps, no class of men on the face of the earth, says
Captain Bonneville, who lead a life of more continued exertion,
peril, and excitement, and who are more enamoured of their occupations, than the free trappers of the west. No toil, no danger, no
privation can turn the trapper from his pursuit. His passionate
excitement at times resembles a mania. In vain may the most vigilant and cruel savages beset his path; in vain may rocks, and precipices, and wintry torrents oppose his progress; let but a single
track of a beaver meet his eye, and he forgets all dangers and defies
all difficulties.*

—WASHINGTON IRVING, *Adventures of Captain Bonneville*

CHAPTER XVIII

FUR trading was one of the earliest and most important American frontier industries. By the middle of the eighteenth century, control of the fur trade figured prominently in the conflict of two empires in the Ohio Valley and along the Great Lakes.

Pennsylvania, Virginia and Carolina traders were the first English-speaking fur gatherers to penetrate the western country. Ever since the seventeenth century, French trappers and traders had been moving along the St. Lawrence, around the Great Lakes, and over the Ohio and Mississippi Valley trails. They bought furs, accumulated geographical knowledge, and established relationships with the Indians.

Furs and skins yielded a profit to both national groups, and so did the

439

sale of trade goods. Fur trading, however, never promised to be a long-range industry because of its highly fluctuating source of supply. It could stand only a limited amount of competition without resulting in serious friction among the traders. Like many natural resources, fur-bearing animals existed in limited numbers, but their capacity for reproduction was good if competitive destruction was not keen enough to kill off the breeding stock. So long as normal trapping took place and a certain amount of rotation occurred, the supply of pelts was adequate for a prosperous trade, but when groups of organized trappers developed intensive rivalry, the animal resources were quickly reduced or destroyed.

Types of pelts taken by trappers varied somewhat from one area to another. Mink, otter, civet, beaver, fox, raccoon, and badger were the most important. Farther west in the upper Missouri country, the major source of supply was beaver.

The American beaver is an animal of singular habits which lives along mountain streams where there is a constant flow of fresh water and an abundance of willow, aspen, and cottonwood for food and dam-building material. It averages thirty to fifty pounds in weight, with some animals weighing even more. Its fur is fine-textured and glossy and is ideally suited for making hats, coats, and heavy collars. Beaver hutches or houses are built behind dams which maintain the water level at an approximately even height. Runways and bedding quarters are under water so that the animals may move about without exposing themselves to dangers on the surface. The beaver is so constructed physically that it can propel itself through water with its webbed hind feet, and the thick bare paddle-like tail serves as rudder, trowel, and brace to balance the animal when it sits in an upright position. It cuts green timber for building dams and houses and as a source of food. It fells trees by slashing wedge-shaped cuts at the foot of the bole with its sharp front teeth. Persons fortunate enough to have observed beaver felling trees say that it is a co-operative affair in which the parents take turns at the cut. Contrary to tradition the beaver is unable to control the pitch of a tree. If it falls toward the site of the dam, then the animal is in luck; otherwise, he is forced to cut and roll the bolts of wood to the dam. Logs and limbs are cut into short blocks fitted into dams and the cracks are chinked with mud; the purpose of the obstruction is to check rather than stop the flow of water. Unfortunately for both beaver and trapper, the streams silt up and the dens have to be moved from time to time. Though colonies are well established, the beaver itself may travel long distances from its haunts during the summer months.

Fur trapping has ever had its romantic appeal to people on this continent. The solitude of the woods, the dangerous rivalry of white men for furs, association with the Indians, the exploration of new and strange country, and constant exposure to physical hardships and danger were all parts of the great adventure. The fur trader was a lusty trailbreaker who pushed his way into each succeeding strip of wild country ahead of the settler, and frequently he left his bones scattered along the way as gruesome landmarks of his failure to survive the rigors of his calling. Possibly he sought personal freedom as much as profit from his efforts, but his very diligence helped destroy the frontier which gave him a challenge and a reason for his existence.

Although the fur trade has endured in America since the seventeenth century, it has had two major phases of historic importance. These were the old border years when Englishmen competed with Frenchmen for pelts in the western woods, and the first forty years following Lewis and Clark's exploratory visit to the Pacific when American "mountain men" competed with British in the mountain area. Explorations in the Northwest by Lewis and Clark were the beginning of an exciting period of pioneering. Canadian traders were already in part of the upper Missouri Valley. By 1793 Alexander MacKenzie had struggled across Canada, and had crossed the headwaters of the Fraser River to the mountains and down the Bella Coola to the coast. Early in the nineteenth century the Hudson's Bay and the Northwest Fur companies were rapidly making their way westward across the continent. Lewis and Clark met fur traders at the Mandan village during their first winter on the Missouri. But as yet the Americans had not reached out beyond the area of the Great Lakes and the upper Mississippi. New York was still an important market place for western furs, and the demand for beaver hats and coats and stoles for feminine shoulders created a brisk market here and abroad.

The Lewis and Clark expedition awakened interest in trade and expansion in St. Louis. Adventurers of several nationalities were on hand to follow up the trails broken by the famous explorers. For some years under the Spanish rule of Louisiana a monopolistic company had existed which had for its purpose the exploration of the *Haut Missouri*, but it failed to accomplish its task. With the publicity given by the Lewis and Clark explorations, however, the Missouri River became a challenging theme. Jefferson's request that the surveyors gather information about animal life helped to hasten trappers upstream where beaver could be taken along the confusing maze of headstreams of both the Missouri and Columbia basins. Within a decade and a half, St. Louis was to rival New York and Montreal fur markets.

On the Track of the Beaver

Manuel Lisa, a young Spaniard, had moved upriver from New Orleans before the sale of Louisiana. At the turn of the nineteenth century he was engaged in fur trading and learning the ways of the West in the school of experience. In early spring, 1807, he led the first organized American trapping party up the far reaches of the Missouri. With forty-two boatmen and trappers he overcame the pressure of the stiff Missouri current and reached the mouth of the Big Horn. Near this place he established Fort Manuel, the earliest structure of this sort located in the region. This venture was successful enough to encourage the organization of a company, and in 1808 the first of the great Missouri fur companies was formed with Lisa, William Clark, Pierre Chouteau, and Andrew Henry as partners. This new organization was named the Missouri Fur Company, and immediately Lisa and Henry led a formidable trapping and hunting party of 350 men to the Rocky Mountains to take beaver. On this visit Andrew Henry went on to the Three Forks territory and across the Divide where he spent the next three years.

In time, a veritable fleet of bateaux, canoes, and keelboats were to negotiate the turbid Missouri. Boats were inched every mile upstream by oar, pole, cordelle, and sail. It was necessary to carry enough food and supplies on board to sustain the crews until they reached the buffalo range. Gaudy trade goods were loaded on the boats along with blankets, powder, lead, guns and traps to be exchanged for furs. Moving a trapping party inland was an arduous undertaking which required great human stamina and courage. The wild Missouri's current had tested the muscles of the sweating, swearing boatmen before the last pack of beaver was hustled downstream. Where banks were smooth enough and no entanglements of snags cluttered the shallows, boats could be eased along with cordelles. These were ropes fastened just enough off-center of the boats to pull their noses slightly out from shore, but not enough to retard their movement. Struggling forward, the *voyageurs* hauled the ropes across their shoulders, and to a rousing chorus of French boat songs stumbled through the shallows and clambered over the slimy, caving banks. Whatever the method used in going upstream prior to 1831 and the coming of the steamboat, manpower was necessary and had to be rugged enough to labor for days and weeks without extended rest.

In wait for the St. Louis boatmen were the implacable Mandan, Sioux, Arikara, Crow, and Blackfeet Indians, and in time this native gantlet was to become both tedious and threatening. Lisa's first party had at least two brushes with the Indians. Fortunately they were forewarned, and when an Arikara attempt was made to assault his boats Lisa lined up his two swivel guns and made ready to sweep their band. Later his party had a brief skirmish with the Mandans. News of the coming of the trappers spread through the Indian country like wildfire, but Lisa, like some of his earlier countrymen, knew the art of cultivating native good will. Chittenden said of him that he knew when to be friendly and when to be stern. Before he finished his journey up to the Big Horn his swivels had helped to convert other roistering bands as well as the Arikaras into fairly peaceful neighbors, all of them, in fact, but the irascible and treacherous Blackfeet.

Beyond the mouth of the Platte, Lisa's trading party was fortunate in having with them John Colter. Born near Staunton, Virginia, Colter had accompanied Lewis and Clark to the Pacific, but he had turned back to the mountains in 1806 at the Mandan villages to become one of the first mountain men to hunt in this rich country. During 1806–1810 he had experienced tremendous hardships, but he had explored widely in the wilderness country. Accounts of Colter's exploits read like an ancient Norwegian saga, and his experiences are a rich part of the American frontier legend. He crossed the Yellowstone Park area and visited in the hot springs and geysers area, known for a long time as "Colter's Hell," and was wounded several times in brushes with the Indians. Whether or not he saw the springs and geysers is open to question. In 1810 Colter left the mountains for the quietude of a Missouri farm, but not before he had been important to the Lisa party, and information gathered by him had led to the exploitation of a vast strip of country. He knew where to find beaver about the Three Forks, and he had an intimate and painful understanding of Indian behavior.

Upper Missouri

News of Lisa's success aroused much interest in beaver in St. Louis. During the winter of 1808–1809 Lisa made preparations to go again up the Missouri. For the next ten years he was to be the most important figure in the Missouri trade. Before he retired he was to run a fabulous boat race with Wilson Price Hunt of the American Fur Company, to help keep a fragile peace with the Indians and to make a modest profit for his partners. Lessons he learned during the early years subsequently became standard practice in the trapping industry. Lisa was a natural kind of man who fitted perfectly into the harsh life of the river and trapline. He could control rugged crews of excitable *voyageurs* and headstrong trappers, and he never had enough conscience to neglect his own best interest, no matter what it cost his rivals. He was master at handling a tiller oar, an auxiliary sail, a cordelle, and at bucking a boat against foaming rapids and the piles of driftwood. In a booming voice raised in song, he urged his reluctant crews forward and made them forget momentarily the pain of fatigue and rebellious muscles. His first companies were organized roughly into a hierarchy of trappers, skinners, and oarsmen, with the trappers enjoying the greatest prestige. Henry Brackenridge's description of Lisa's laborious journey upstream in pursuit of Wilson P. Hunt of the American Fur Company is a graphic account of the sweat and fatigue necessary for covering the staggering fifteen hundred to two thousand mile journey to the rich beaver streams of the Three Forks.

Once in trapping territory, a reasonably safe means of storing property had to be devised. To entrust it to the walls of a log cabin was to invite disaster. Because storage bins had to be concealed, the trappers used the underground cache. This subterranean storage bin was made by stripping back the sod from a well-drained plot of ground and then scooping out a hole so as to leave no tell-tale traces of fresh soil. Loose dirt was dumped in running water away from the place of its removal. When the hole was sufficiently deep, it was lined with leaves, boughs and buffalo skins to seal out the seepage of moisture. Goods and furs were packed tightly in these earthen bins, and the mouth was filled with dirt, tamped tightly, and then re-covered with sod. The spot was then drenched with water to destroy the scent of the goods and furs so that predatory animals were not attracted. Frequently campfires were burned over the mouths of cache holes for further concealment of their location. If steep banks were available, pits were dug in them and they were sealed in the same way as the underground depositories. Throughout the important years of the fur trade the cache was in common use.

Among the western trappers there were four distinct groups who gathered furs. There were Indians who sold pelts to white traders; there were free white traders who came upstream either alone or in parties and operated independently, selling their furs where they pleased; the fur companies had their own contract trappers who were obligated to deliver their catches to their creditors to pay for traps and supplies; and there were also company partners who also engaged in trapping. These groups constituted a loosely knit fraternity in the western woods. They adhered with remarkable fidelity to certain rules, and there was a definite recognition of company leadership by all groups. Joint action was important in the face of Indian attacks when small bands of whites would be confronted by hundreds of attackers. An unwritten rule of the woods was that every trapper extended hospitality to a visitor, even though he was a hated competitor.

Backing up the trappers were the company traders who spent most of their time shuttling back and forth between St. Louis and the mountain rendezvous. They had the responsibility of assembling supplies and of delivering them at the trading places upstream; at the end of the summer they returned to St. Louis with precious cargoes of furs. There was no time when a party was more vulnerable to Indian attack than when it was transporting heavy cargoes of goods and furs. Like the early Spanish galleons which plied between the mines of Mexico and Spain, the fur pack trains invited raids. They were rich in both cargo and pack horses, or in cargo and boats. Pack horse trains on narrow mountain trails or loaded boats tossing about in wild mountain currents were difficult to maneuver and were well-nigh defenseless against pillage when attacked. Because of this vulnerability there was an enormous difference in the measure of ultimate success between the loading of a season's catch in the mountains and the dumping of it into the safety of a St. Louis warehouse. When the fruits of a big season could run the gantlet of Indian attacks, eddies and snags, and reach the market, the profits were apt to be most encouraging. On the other hand, when too many misfortunes befell trappers and traders, bankruptcy was a certainty. Fortunately, profits were good enough to justify the faith of businessmen who operated supply houses dependent on the success of the fur industry.

Beaver skins were the most popular in the mountain trade, but many other pelts found their way into the packs. This was especially true where many fur-bearing animals remained active in the bitterly cold seasons. Trapping seasons, however, were closely regulated by the habits of the beaver and were divided into two parts. The first lasted from early fall and the thickening of fur until the streams were iced over; the second opened with the spring thaw. By the calendar, these seasons were from late August or early September to December 1, and from late March until June 1, when the spring moult began. Beaver were taken in heavy traps set in fairly shallow water. Green sticks of cottonwood or willow rolled in castoreum were suspended overhead for bait. Castoreum was a granular substance taken from the sex glands of beavers. Often this lure was almost as valuable as were the pelts, and trappers were careful to save all the glands that came to hand. Without the temptation of castoreum a trap line was almost a fruitless venture. Traps had to be staked in such a way that their victims were forced into water deep enough to drown them; otherwise, they crawled onto the ground, gnawed off the entrapped foot and escaped. Free trappers skinned, cleaned, and stretched their own pelts; but many contract men turned green pelts over to workers who scraped and stretched the skins, and when they were dry pressed them into packs of eighty pelts each.

Almost from the beginning, horses and mules were used to transport furs over the stretches of territory where boating was too hazardous for safe delivery. With the coming of William Ashley, pack trains were driven all the way across the plains to St. Louis by way of the North Platte trail. A fur pack was suspended from each side of a pack saddle, and a third was nestled down on top; thus each horse or mule carried at least 240 skins. Pack trains were forced to string themselves out on the mountain trails. Indians often planned to catch these elongated trains in narrow mountain passes and cause stampedes. If trail drivers had warning of impending attacks, they bunched their horses in a tight defensive huddle.

There was little glory or comfort in the mountain trade for the pack animals themselves. The mountain journeys were long and hard, grazing often was meager, and the packs rubbed painful sores wherever they touched. Thousands of horses and mules labored for days without end under swaying packs which sawed their backs and bellies raw. Larpenteur has left a vivid description of the condition of a mountain pack train: "To see the mules rolling and dusting is interesting and shocking at the same time," he wrote; "most of them, having carried their burdens of 200 pounds weight for about 2000 miles, return with scarcely any skin on their backs; they are peeled from withers to tail, raw underneath from use of the surcingle, and many are also lame." It would be impossible at this late date to convey with accuracy the enormous suffering of the pack animals that were driven back and forth between St. Louis and the Rocky Mountains in the fur trade.

The Life of the Mountain Man

Assembling the widely scattered trappers and Indians for the market of goods and the purchase of furs was difficult at times. Two methods were used: one, the fixed trading post, or fort; and the other, a central place agreed upon as a temporary meeting ground. William Ashley introduced the latter method into American fur trade, although the Hudson's Bay Company had followed this practice earlier in the Snake River Valley. Ashley organized the first general American rendezvous in 1825 on Henry's Fork after an experimental one had been held the year before by Thomas Fitzpatrick on the Sweetwater in Wyoming.

The annual rendezvous which followed this beginning were the trade fairs of the mountain region. They took place at centrally located spots such as Pierre's Hole, Ogden, Green River, and elsewhere; in all there were thirteen annual meetings. Usually they occurred in early July and lasted until all furs were sold and supplies bought. These meetings were more, however, than mere commercial events; they were social occasions. Trappers came together for a frolic. Indian trappers came with wives and daughters, and white trappers brought their native concubines, and for at least ten days they all engaged in the debaucheries of the camp. They drank whisky with the greatest abandon, gambled, consorted with the placid Indian women, played games, fought, swapped yarns and books, and equipped themselves for the next year's hunt. With childlike enthusiasm they purchased beads, vermilion, bright cloth, and gew-gaws from the traders; with even more childlike enthusiasm, perhaps, the Indian maidens accepted many of these things in exchange for favors past and promised. Of a more utilitarian nature were the purchases of saddles, guns, powder, lead, three-point blankets, knives, axes and cooking utensils. Occasionally overland traders brought with them small amounts of spices, coffee, tea, sugar, flour and meal; like the pack trains of medieval Europe they took these exciting gifts of civilization to the frontier.

Life for the mountain man was hard and exacting. At its worst it was all but unbearable, and at its best it was a life of constant vigilance and impending danger. Loneliness added materially to its monotony. Despite their isolation and carefree behavior at rendezvous time, most mountain men had varying degrees of education. During the freezing months of winter they had little more to do on the outside than gather firewood. The rest of the time they spent reading Shakespeare, the Bible, commentaries on the Scriptures, books of sermons, scientific treatises, and newspapers. Winter-bound trappers passed books around from camp to camp until they were soiled and worn beyond use. Jedediah Smith was an example of a fairly well-read trapper; he not only knew Shakespeare, but like an ancient Hebrew prophet sustained by faith among the barren peaks of the Sinai hills, this pious disciple found in his Bible a solace amid the most tortuous hardships.

Hostile Indian bands constantly threatened the peace and safety of the mountain men. Thieves broke up their trap lines, and their nights were made uneasy by raiders who ran off their horses or stole their property. Death was a frequent visitor. An arrow, a bullet, or a well-aimed tomahawk could cut short a trader's life. A misstep on the brink of a cliff and a mountain man was hurtled into eternity. Wild rapids in boulder-choked streams whirled his canoe or bull boat into a suck and disgorged his battered body in a quiet eddy downstream, or a towering grizzly bear gathered him in its arms and squeezed and bit him to death. In one famous case, a she-bear pulled out hunks of Hugh Glass's flesh and threw it to her cubs before his companions rescued him. Mortality in the field among these men was exceedingly high, running possibly to 75 or 80 per cent. Men endured unbelievable pain. Almost every Indian raid left maimed and dying victims. Rabid wolves attacked sleeping victims and doomed them to weeks of mental agony and dread before death. Diseases of all sorts took their toll where there was no access to medical care. Yet the wild mountain country with its breath-takingly beautiful valleys and "holes," its paradisiacal streams of cold green water, the lure of the chase, and the freedom of the woods gripped men's souls.

Men who came from Virginia, Kentucky, Missouri, New York and the New England states all but forgot their backgrounds. With their Indian common-law wives and concubines they begot half-breed children and became an inseparable part of the wilderness. The true mountain man adopted a realistic philosophy of self-preservation. A bosom friend might fall mortally wounded at his feet, and he would dash off to safety, leaving his companion's body behind to be mutilated. There were few opportunities in surprise attacks for gallant stands in the face of milling red men. Well out beyond the limits of civilization the mountain men developed rules by which they lived, but no laws with which to trammel themselves. Competition grew fierce, and more than once the sanctity of contract was trampled underfoot in this great wilderness which existed outside the pale of statute law and where expediency offered greater rewards than the integrity of one's word and bond.

Astorians

In April, 1808, while Manuel Lisa's men were running their trap lines in the midst of the second half of their first trapping season, John Jacob Astor was organizing the American Fur Company in New York. Astor, an immigrant boy from Waldorf, Baden, Germany, came to this country in 1783 to seek fame and fortune. On the way across the Atlantic he became friendly with a fellow passenger who had traded in furs with the Indians. When he landed in New York, Astor disposed of the flutes he had brought with him and went into the fur business. By the last decade of the eighteenth century he was well on his way to making a fortune.

In these early years he was a trading factor in furs rather than a trapper, and as the Great Lakes and Mississippi Valley were opened by war and treaty to full American exploitation, he extended his field of operation in their direction. In his earlier years he traded with both the Northwest and Mackinaw fur companies and had relied largely upon Canadian *voyageurs* and trappers to supply him with raw furs. Later he was to fight these same interests in the expansion of his own trapping empire.

Little did the members of the New York legislature who granted Astor his charter for the American Fur Company realize that they were helping to produce one of the great commercial struggles of the American continent. Astor's, in a sense, was the first corporate American fur trading organization. There were, of course, the colonial companies, and Lisa's organization in St. Louis, but Astor's firm was of more far-reaching implications. The German immigrant boy had set the stage for an exciting three decades of domestic and international rivalries.

His first competitive struggles were with the Hudson's Bay and Northwest companies which moved westward by way of the Canadian rivers. Within three years this expansive capitalist was looking beyond the Mississippi River and even the continent to new fields of trade. He planned to enter the great northwestern beaver country and to move into the Russian and Chinese trade in the same venture. To achieve this it was necessary to send parties of hunters and trappers to the Northwest to establish a base near the mouth of the Columbia River. Wilson Price Hunt, a New Jersey-born trader, was selected to lead the overland party of the Pacific Fur Company. This company was organized as a subsidiary of the American Fur Company to enable Astor to dominate the American fur trade and to carry on the fur trade with China. Hunt was a poor leader and ill-conditioned for the rigors of the rugged mountain trails. He associated with him Ramsay Crooks and Donald MacKenzie, both of whom were in time to become famous as traders in the Rocky Mountains. Following the well-established Astor pattern, Hunt began organizing his party in Montreal, and by September, 1810, he had paddled down the Great Lakes, the Fox and Wisconsin rivers, and then down the Mississippi to St. Louis.

In St. Louis, Hunt busied himself organizing a hunting party, but this was not easy for an outsider to accomplish. Quickly he was beset with irritations caused by tricky competitors; coupled with this were the demoralizing pleasures of a carefree and seductive frontier river town. Because of these worries, Hunt moved his camp out of the city as quickly as possible to a site near St. Joseph, where he spent the winter of 1810. On March 12, 1811, he began his journey upstream with a party which included the two British natural scientists, Thomas Nuttall and John Bradbury, and Pierre Dorion, the interpreter, with his wife and two children. Before Hunt's boats had pulled away from the Nadowa winter quarters, the preliminary skirmishes of the War of 1812 had already occurred. International friction, added to the normal competitive resistance of the British traders, offered the Americans an overwhelming challenge.

Not all the competition for Hunt's party, however, was to come from the British. When Hunt began his journey upstream, Manuel Lisa was completing preparations in St. Louis to go upstream to look for Andrew Henry, who had not been seen for two years, and to collect the year's catch of furs. Nineteen days and 240 miles behind, Lisa began a mad race to overtake Hunt before he reached the Sioux country. From its beginning, this race upriver was a test of human endurance. Lisa gained rapidly on his less experienced rival. Shouting and singing encouragement to his men, manning a pole or an oar, or jumping overboard to tug at the cordelle, the determined Spaniard drove his men ahead almost day and night. Hunt had no experience with the Missouri River Indians. He believed that Lisa only wanted to precede him in order to stir the Indians up against him and to delay his arrival in the beaver country long enough to insure the Missouri Fur Company's getting the season's catch. In fact, neither white party was strong enough to stave off a determined Indian attack, but combined they could pass the villages without serious threat.

The race itself had excellent chroniclers in the two Englishmen who were with Hunt, and the imaginative Brackenridge who accompanied Lisa. Brackenridge wrote graphically of their progress against the stream. On June 2, after both parties had experienced slight Indian resistance, Lisa overtook the Astorians and the two companies moved on for a short time together. But Hunt was weary in Lisa's company and decided to desert the river for the pack train in order to evade the Blackfeet. This necessitated the purchase of horses and the complete re-ordering of the expedition. After a month of costly delay the party was ready to go on horseback toward the grave uncertainties of the western mountains. On July 18, 1811, Hunt was again on the road to the Columbia Valley.

From July to February the overland Astorians suffered tremendous privations. This company of sixty-one men and Pierre Dorion's squaw and two children struggled overland against insuperable odds of mountains, whirling rapids and frigid weather. From the Arikara country they traveled through the Teton Pass to Henry's Fork, and from there on foot and in boats to the Snake and Umatilla rivers. The rigors of winter destroyed many of the men and brought all of them near the point of starvation. So short was the food supply that they sought to extract sustenance from the buckskin of their clothing and packs. Stumbling on, the first of the party reached Astoria on February 15, 1812, 340 days after they had left the Nadowa Camp on the Missouri. They had traveled approximately thirty-five hundred miles, a thousand of which had been spent wandering about aimlessly in search of food and the trail.

There was a reverse side to the Astorian plan. Astor had engaged briefly in the China trade, and he planned to develop this interest further. He conceived of a successful trading company as one which diversified its activities. Thus it was that he organized his entry into the Northwest as a double-barreled affair. While Hunt was pushing up the Missouri in his wild race with the Missourians, Captain Jonathan Thorne was setting out from New York with cargo and men aboard the ship *Tonquin*. On the coast, the *Tonquin's* company was to join forces with Hunt's party to exploit the beaver and China trade at the same time.

Captain Thorne was an unimaginative, stubborn seaman, conditioned to strict sea discipline, and his voyage to the Northwest Coast was fraught with almost as much hardship and bickering as was Hunt's overland expedition. After numerous misadventures, the *Tonquin* reached the mouth of the Columbia on March 22, 1811, to find the waters troubled both by storm and season. After several disastrous attempts to send small boats across the bar, the impulsive Thorne finally succeeded in taking his ship into the calmer waters of the river's mouth. On April 12, David Stuart and a party of sixteen men began work on what was to become Fort Astoria. Captain Thorne's actual destination beyond the Columbia was Nootka Sound and Vancouver Island. Quickly he unloaded the goods intended for the Columbia post and set off to visit the Indians at the latter place. He failed to follow the advice of his interpreter, and the treacherous Nootka Sound Indians murdered the entire crew except for the interpreter. The *Tonquin* herself was blown up by a critically injured crew member touching off the powder magazine, but not before it was crowded with Indians who had come to snatch up the spoils of their murderous raid.

At Astoria, Hunt showed no more administrative capacity than he had demonstrated on the trail. American attempts to establish trapping posts throughout the Pacific Northwest resulted in indifferent success. Soon after their arrival at the mouth of the Columbia they became aware of competitors—the Northwest Fur Company posts and their diligent Scots trappers. Two Indian messengers in search of the Canadians innocently conveyed this information to the Americans. Not only were the Northwest trappers settled in their posts on the Peace and Fraser rivers, but they were busily engaged in establishing others. To meet this competition the Americans felt called upon to build post for post with their rivals, but they were hampered in doing so by a lack of manpower. David Stuart of the Pacific Fur Company, a subsidiary of the American Company, was successful in establishing a winter post on the Columbia near the mouth of the Okanakan, and in the wild competitive race of locating new posts and seeking furs, the Astorians ranged over thousands of miles of virgin territory. Donald MacKenzie, for instance, explored southward to the present Willamette and its headwaters in the Umpqua country.

On the far western frontier, as everywhere else in the country, the War of 1812 disrupted British-American relationships. Unfortunately for the Americans the British on the Pacific Coast were the first to receive news of the declaration of war, and after 1813 the Canadians were emboldened to push the Americans out of the Northwest. They had at their command more men, and because of their trade relations with the natives they could direct fierce Indian attacks against their rivals. By threatening the American posts with attack from land and sea, the Northwest managers forced them to withdraw their men from most of the outlying posts. Making good use of "scare propaganda" that two British gunboats, the *Isaac Todd* and *Phoebe*, would appear at any moment, George McTavish did serious damage to the Astorians' nerve. To attempt to defend the American fort against fire from gunboats appeared foolhardy, so arrangements were made to surrender the fort by June 1, 1814, if no further assistance arrived. Long before the date set Hunt became discouraged, and Astoria was turned over to the Northwest Company officials in April. Immediately they changed the name to Fort George. This unfortunate incident brought to a close the activities of the Pacific branch of the American Fur Company.

Surrender of Astoria brought deep pain to John Jacob Astor, and he never really forgot the humiliation of his Pacific Coast debacle. The surrender of Astoria has resulted in an extended historical dispute. Various individuals in Astoria have been accused of duplicity. Possibly there were too many Scotsmen in the employ of the American company for its good at a time when it had to meet both successful economic competition and the challenge of patriotism. Also, Astor was unable to secure assistance from either the United States Army or Navy in protecting his interest in the Northwest. When Hunt returned to New York, he brought neither furs nor profits, but the Astorians had accumulated four years of rugged experience, a considerable amount of geographical information, and an even fuller knowledge of British and Indian trickery.

Missourians continued to trade up the great river with varying success while the Astor party was beyond the Rockies. The War of 1812 disrupted the demand for furs, and trapping activities were limited during the three years of its duration. Free trappers continued to run trap lines, and an occasional trader found his way upstream, but the major American company ventures were slowed down. It was not until 1822, when General William Ashley of St. Louis entered the trade, that the American fur companies again entered the field as major competitors.

Ashley

Ashley, perhaps the most successful of all the native traders, typified much of the personal element in the history of the frontier. He was a Virginian who, like Stephen Austin and others, had followed the promise of fortune westward to Missouri. In Missouri, Ashley engaged in the manufacture of gunpowder. Here he became associated with Andrew Henry, and during the early years of the 1800's these men heard much of the profits to be made in the fur trade. Like Virginians everywhere, Ashley became a militia officer and participated actively in local politics. Passing in and out of St. Louis he came to know many of the trappers and traders who came to its market. When Ashley entered the fur trade with Andrew Henry, there was already a distinguished group of experienced river and mountain men congregated in and about the western market. Among these were Milton, William, Andrew and Solomon Sublette, Kentuckians; James Bridger, a Virginian; Thomas Fitzpatrick, Etienne Provost, David E. Jackson, Jedediah Smith, and the famous mulatto James P. Beckwourth.

Ashley and Andrew Henry teamed up to trap in the mountain beaver streams. When they led their company out of St. Louis in 1822, it was the largest organization of American trappers to date to enter the field. This new band was to make some interesting innovations in trading practices. Ashley soon depended more upon the free white and contract trappers than the Indian hunters. He was not to establish himself, however, until he had undergone some harassing experiences with the Indians. On his first journey upstream some of his men were killed in Indian skirmishes. The company lost many horses and furs to marauding bands, which reduced its opportunities to make profits. Apparently the appearance of so many white men in Indian country stirred the Blackfeet and Arikaras to new efforts at resistance, and Ashley was to reap the harvest of their ill-will.

On his second journey up the Missouri, William Ashley got a full taste of Indian violence. When his keelboats, *Yellowstone* and *Rocky Mountain*, reached the Arikara villages, the Indians undertook to rob and kill his men. First making a show of friendliness, they sold him horses and engaged in trade generally; one of the chiefs even invited Ashley to visit his cabin. So well did the Indians conceal their real intentions that the sun set on a scene of peace and goodwill, but before morning those of the white party who had camped on the beach were caught in a heavy attack. The Indians created pandemonium among their visitors by outnumbering and outmaneuvering them. Before Ashley's company could effect a retreat, thirteen men had fallen and eleven more were badly wounded. General Ashley had made several tactical blunders, in addition to allowing himself to become over-confident in the face of so much pretended friendship. Leaving his men overnight on the beach next to the villages was an act of folly which cost dear, but nothing he did hurt more than presenting himself before his men as a reluctant warrior in battle. The fight with the Arikaras taught the white traders once again that the upper Missouri Indians were not to be trusted. Traders from St. Louis were to face situations comparable to that which had arisen with the Arikaras many times in the future, but because of Ashley's sad experience they knew that a show of friendship meant disaster in the end.

The battle with the Arikaras brought Colonel Henry Leavenworth and his Sixth Infantry command from Fort Atkinson into action. Colonel Leavenworth's march upriver started with news of the massacre of Immel and Jones, Missouri Fur Company partners, who were trapping on the Yellowstone. He was already on his way when news of Ashley's troubles reached him. In his subsequent encounter with the Arikaras he had Sioux as allies, and all the advantage lay with the soldiers, especially since they were equipped with two swivel guns. The skirmish which followed, however, was hardly a credit to the United States Army. Leavenworth's tactics made little sense, even at this late date, and certainly they made no sense at the time to his Sioux allies. The Arikaras went unscathed; Ashley was forced into a temporary retreat; and in a short time the Sioux were to give the trappers and traders trouble along the river.

Mountain Men

Ashley took out from St. Louis with his first two parties a group of young men who were to become the most famous of all the mountain men. Among these were William and Milton Sublette, David E. Jackson, Hugh Glass (of grizzly bear fame), the Irishman Thomas Fitzpatrick, Seth Grant, Jedediah Smith, and Jim Bridger. Smith and Bridger got their first taste of Missouri River navigation and Indian fighting on the second Ashley trip. Bridger was a callow youth of eighteen, and the Bible-reading and praying Smith was twenty-five years old.

During the winter of 1823–1824, the Ashley trappers ranged over a broad expanse of country along the Missouri, the Big Horn, the Platte, the Green, Wind and Sweetwater rivers. Beaver were plentiful and the catch was generally profitable. Thomas Fitzpatrick found South Pass and was able to take his band across the mountains to rich beaver streams at the head of the Snake River. However, the small band of Hunt's men led by Ramsay Crooks had preceded him through South Pass on their return to the East.

The St. Louis traders' activities were highly successful after 1823. Parties under the leadership of Henry, Fitzpatrick, the Sublettes, Smith and Provost returned to the first major rendezvous in 1825 with rich caches of fur. They had combed the mountain areas around the headwaters of the Missouri for new beaver grounds, had crossed the Great Divide and trapped at the headwaters of the Columbia, they had followed the Snake to its junction with that stream, and had explored numerous other stream courses which were to become well known in Rocky Mountain history. To carry on a successful trade Ashley was forced to seek a new route to the trapping grounds to avoid the drudgery of the upriver pull in boats and the treachery of the Indian villages. He introduced the pack train to bring trade goods to the rendezvous and to carry furs back to St. Louis. By following the overland route along the North Platte he bisected the great triangle of the Missouri and cut off at least five hundred miles of the journey. Following this route, he opened a new passage to the Rocky Mountains and the important fur-bearing streams, and outlined the great trail followed not only by traders and trappers going to the mountains, but also by settlers in subsequent years on their way to Oregon.

In three years William Ashley made a modest fortune out of the fur trade and retired to St. Louis to engage in merchandising and politics.

When he left the trade in 1826, he sold his Rocky Mountain Fur Company interests to three of his men, William Sublette, Jedediah Smith and David E. Jackson. Some of Ashley's traders, including Smith, secured large quantities of cheap furs from Indians and trappers obligated to the Hudson's Bay Company. When he returned to St. Louis after his last rendezvous, he was able to claim the greatest cash income made by any individual trader to date.

Mountain Prophet

None of Ashley's accomplishments was more important than that of having brought to the frontier an unusually able group of young associates. One of these, Jedediah Smith, had a great curiosity about western geography and was the epitome of the mountain man. Smith was a pious man who carried his Bible as constantly as he did his hunting knife, and in the long periods of solitude in the mountain fastnesses he became a keen student of the Scriptures. His face was frequently raised in prayer; he constituted a sort of missionary, working both the trap line and the cause of salvation. As a young New Yorker, Jedediah had clerked on a Lake Erie boat; from the Great Lakes he had drifted into St. Louis where he joined Ashley's second expedition.

For the next three years he engaged in trapping and exploration in the three basins of the mountain country. He made extended visits to the British posts in the Columbia Valley and gained a rather precise knowledge of what was taking place in this disputed territory. When he found himself a partner in the Rocky Mountain Fur Company he set out on one of his most exciting ventures. Entering the region about the Great Salt Lake, Smith passed southward through country as yet unvisited by Americans. Going by Utah Lake down the Sevier River, he crossed over to the Colorado Valley in late summer or early fall, 1826. Following the Colorado for some distance he turned westward and crossed the Mojave Desert to San Diego. In California, the mountain man had difficulty with the Spanish governor, but he secured the timely aid of Captain W. H. Cunningham of the Boston ship *Courier*. Attempting to go east again, he found it impossible to take his full party across the Sierra Nevada range; so he left all of his men but two west of the mountains and returned to the site of the 1827 rendezvous.

Late the next summer, Smith returned to California with an enlarged party and rejoined his company. His journey was filled with hardship. He lost ten of his eighteen men in battle with the Mojave Indians. Again he had difficulty with the Spanish authorities, and again he had to appeal to an American ship captain for help. He was instructed to leave California. Following the Sacramento River, he reached its American fork where he spent the winter of 1827. Turning northwestward in the spring the American party sought to reach the Columbia River; but a murderous Indian attack befell them on the Umpqua River, where all but three members of the party were killed.

Smith and two companions escaped and made their separate ways to the British post in Vancouver, where they spent the winter. Leaving Vancouver in March, Smith traveled up the Columbia, and in early August he met David E. Jackson searching for him. Through the hospitable aid of Dr. John McLoughlin, factor for the Hudson's Bay Company, he had been able to recover the furs taken from his party by the Indians. In exchange for them he received a London draft which was much easier to transport than the furs he might have brought with him. In the larger view, his journey had been successful in opening one of the major passageways to California, and he had gathered a tremendous amount of highly practical geographical information about the West Coast.

By the time Jedediah Smith returned to the field of his company's operation in 1828, he found an increasing amount of competition. The American Fur Company was again in the mountain trade and was rapidly crowding out the individual trader and trapper. The end of the War of 1812 had brought about several major adjustments in international affairs that bore upon the fur trade, one of the most important of which was the clarification and negotiation of border agreements which more or less separated the competitive forces of British and American trappers. By shrewd pressure, the Congress of the United States was led to pass the act of 1816 which excluded foreigners from operating on American soil. Political favoritism, however, was sought by several of the larger fur interests, and competition in Washington frequently became as vigorous as it was on the headwaters of the Missouri.

The American Fur Company's second advance westward was the beginning of a bitter fight for monopolistic control of the mountain trade. The St. Louis fur interests had never been friendly toward Astor's company, and it was not until 1822 that the famous New Yorker finally got his foot in the Missouri door. Fortunately for him, he was able to bring to his side the powerful political support of Lewis Cass of Michigan and Thomas H. Benton of Missouri. Through Senator Cass, Astor was able to get legislation passed through Congress which slackened government controls over the Indian trade and which gave his company distinct advantages. There are few stories of bare-knuckle business competition in American economic history to equal that of the fur trade after John Jacob Astor's revamped company took to the field in 1822.

The American Fur Company's new western branch went ruthlessly after control of the trappers' supply business as well as the crop. In competition along the western rivers, the little trader was crowded out of business by questionable means. Critics of Astor's company accused his agents of resorting to acts of violence in order to destroy competitors. Fur trapping and trading gradually became a highly specialized and well-organized drive for profits. Astor's war with the Hudson's Bay and Northwest companies was nothing short of high drama. Under the able direction of Dr. John McLoughlin, fur gathering became a fine art, and the well-regulated posts of "The Company" as the Hudson's Bay Company was called, were models of efficiency and administrative management. Dr. McLoughlin himself was a phenomenal character on the frontier, and his forceful personality was deeply imprinted upon the Pacific Northwest.

As rivalries developed among the fur companies, they destroyed the industry in many areas by trapping them dry. This was done in the Green River section by the British. The American Fur Company itself resorted to similar tricks to crowd out its more formidable competitors, but its favorite trick was to absorb serious competition into the company. This was done in the case of its most troublesome rival, the Columbia Fur Company.

By 1832 Astor's company had pretty well covered the Missouri and Rocky Mountain area. It had established posts and had filled the beaver country with both contract and free trappers. By strategically locating trading posts, its managers had brought the Indians to terms of peace, and the fur trade with them had become a stable business. In 1831 the company introduced steam navigation to the upper Missouri. The *Yellowstone* was taken to Fort Tecumseh opposite the mouth of the Teton River in the summer of 1831. The next year it went on to the confluence of the Yellowstone. The boat was built in Louisville, and it made navigational history in the upper Missouri trade. Quickly the steamboat proved that goods could pass up and down the river with speed and safety. The laborious hand propulsion of the keelboats upstream and their dangerous return voyages were things of the past. Manifests of the *Yellowstone* showed to what extent the Astor empire was exploiting the resources of the country. Not only did it bring a heavy shipment of fur pelts, but it carried a mountain of buffalo skins and ten thousand pounds of tongues. The introduction of steam to the upper river marked the passing of the first phase of the fur industry. After that it became a highly commercialized business which filled the mountains with agents well supplied with trade goods from safely fortified market centers. By 1840, the rich days of the fur trade were ended, and the frontier entered a new phase of expansion. Furs met with serious competition from silks and other materials, and profits declined. Astor disposed of his fur trading interest and engaged in real estate speculation in New York City.

Wyeth, Walker and Bonneville

Though marked changes came in the fur trade after 1830, many exciting chapters in its history were still to come. During these years many other interesting personalities entered the western trade, none more notable, perhaps, than the New England ice merchant, Nathaniel J. Wyeth of Cambridge, Massachusetts. Wyeth had fallen under the magic spell of Hall Jackson Kelley, a dreamy teacher who had become enamored of Oregon as early as 1815, and had conjured up from fact and fancy a fabulous story of its beauties and possibilities which he put in a book. He offered his readers free land, plentiful natural resources, and hope for eternal happiness. Wyeth organized a trading company and secured the backing of New England business men for a scheme which shows evidence of paralleling the earlier Astor venture in that Wyeth wished to combine sea and overland exploration. He hoped to ship his heavy freight by sea and to lead personally an overland expedition. On March 10, 1832, he started from Boston with twenty men dressed in fantastic frontier uniforms of cotton, wool and leather. His wagons were equipped with caulked bodies which would permit their being floated across streams. At the same time a Captain Lambert was sent around by sea to the mouth of the Columbia in the *Sultana*.

Once in St. Louis the Wyeth party seemed green and inexperienced in comparison with that of William Sublette and Donald MacKenzie, who were preparing to return to the mountains. Fortunately Wyeth, after several of his men deserted, was able to secure the protection of William Sublette's leadership. Sublette was on his way to the rendezvous at Pierre's Hole, and the New Englanders were given their first taste of plains travel under his guidance. At Pierre's Hole, the St. Louis trader turned back and left Wyeth to his own management beyond that point. On the last of August, Wyeth and a small band of trappers set out for the mouth of the Columbia to meet the *Sultana*. They made the passage by October, but news was waiting them of the wreck of their vessel in the Society Islands, and the expedition seemed headed for failure.

After spending the winter in a Hudson's Bay Company post, Wyeth traveled eastward in the spring, crossing through the high ranges of the Rockies near the Tetons. He finally reached the site of the rendezvous on the headwaters of the Green River. For a time he agreed to join forces with Captain Bonneville, but suddenly he decided to return home. Before leaving the mountains, however, he made an agreement with the Rocky Mountain Fur Company through Milton Sublette to bring out a large quantity of merchandise for use at the next rendezvous.

Back in New England, Wyeth again organized a company, secured additional support from his creditors, and in 1834 returned to the Mississippi to carry out his contract with the Rocky Mountain Fur Company. With merchandise, a good company of men, a band of missionaries under the guidance of Jason and Daniel Lee, and the scientists Thomas Nuttall and J. K. Townsend, Wyeth set out from Independence on the overland journey to the mountains. This time Sublette was his rival, hustling on to the rendezvous to corner the market. When Wyeth reached the rendezvous with his merchandise, the Rocky Mountain Fur Company refused to stand by its contract and left him stranded. Quickly, he had to make plans to dispose of his goods. In a vengeful spirit against his faithless contractors he moved on through South Pass to the Snake to establish a post. Northeast of Soda Springs, the New Englander located his station, and on August 6 he christened it Fort Hall in honor of an earlier member of his company. From Fort Hall, Wyeth went on to the Columbia where he established Fort William on the Sauvies Island at the mouth of the Willamette River.

He engaged in the trapping, timber and fishing business, but nothing he did succeeded. Hard luck pursued him. His ship the *May Dacre* was struck by lightning and was delayed. He lacked the equipment necessary for his enterprises and the market to make the salmon industry pay. His attempts at growing grain and tobacco likewise were disappointing. Wyeth was a good business man but the competition and natural obstacles were too great to be overcome. He sold Fort Hall to the Hudson's Bay Company, abandoned Fort William and returned to the ice business in Boston in 1836.

Although his years of adventure in the West were financial failures, Wyeth had helped to establish American claims to the Northwest, had planted Fort Hall in the midst of the American Fur Company empire, and had struck a hard lick at the people who betrayed him in 1834. To have carried out his original plans would have required years of work and a vast amount of capital, neither of which he had. But helping further to open the road to Oregon was a monumental accomplishment, and his famous way station at Fort Hall was to be important in subsequent years in the movement of settlers to that region. Stories of his adventures and of Oregon advertised the country, and in a remarkably short time settlers were on their way over the long and arduous route to claim land in the Northwest.

During the three years that Nathaniel Wyeth was struggling to make a fortune in the western trade, a second visionary adventurer went into the mountains to try his hand at trading and exploitation. This was the French-born Benjamin Louis Eulalie de Bonneville, Captain in the United States Army. Securing a leave from the army, this expansive opportunist got the backing of New York businessmen to finance his western ventures. In summer, 1832, Bonneville reached the mountains and selected a site for a fort on the high elevation near the headwaters of the Green River. Bonneville's men were pretty well distributed over the central Rocky Mountain range during that trapping season, and before the season ended he found himself involved in one of those famous dog-eat-dog mountain struggles for trapping grounds. His first years in the mountains ended with a remarkably slender catch of furs for the number of men engaged in trapping and the amount of money invested in the expedition.

During his second year in the mountains, Bonneville attempted to broaden his field of activities by a desperate search for profitable trapping grounds. One of his efforts was directed toward the Great Salt Lake Basin. The hunting party contained Joseph Reddeford Walker, Zenas Leonard and George Nidiver. Walker, like so many of his fellow trappers, was a Virginian who had moved westward by way of Tennessee, Missouri, and New Mexico. When he was directed to explore the territory about the Great Salt Lake, he no doubt had broader orders to find fresh beaver country. He left the Green River rendezvous in 1833 with fifty men, and by November he had crossed to Monterey in California. He had gone from the Great Salt Lake to the Humboldt, or Ogden's River, where he was beset by the Digger, or Crow, Indians. From the Humboldt the party crossed over to Walker's Lake, then over the Sierra Nevada range and on to Monterey. This journey was almost as hazardous as Wilson Price Hunt's adventures on the way to the mouth of the Columbia. Desert, drouth, dust, rocks, thirst and hunger beset the party during the first leg of the journey. Cold, hunger, and a difficult terrain, coupled with frustration, all but defeated them on the Sierra Nevada stretch. When Walker's men reached Monterey they enjoyed the honor of having been the first Americans to cross the present state of Nevada and the western mountain range in a direct route to California. Much of Walker's route subsequently was in use as the most direct route to the coast.

Young Zenas Leonard kept a vivid journal of the hardships which befell the party when it was lost in the virtually impenetrable mountains.

> Some of these precipices appeared to us to be more than a mile high. Some of the men thought that if we could succeed in descending one of these precipices to the bottom we might thus work our way into the valley below—but on making several attempts we found it utterly impossible for a man to descend, to say nothing of our horses. We were then obliged to keep along the dividing ridge between the two of these chasms which seemed to lead pretty near the direction we were going— which was west—in passing over the mountains, supposing to run north and south. In this manner we continued until the 25th without any particular occurrence except that of our horses dying daily, the flesh of

which we preserved for food. Our course was rough and tiresome, having to encounter one ledge of rocks after another. On the 25th [October] every man appeared to be more discouraged and downspirited than ever, and I thought that our situation would soon be beyond hope if no prospect of getting from the mountain would now be discovered.

Once on the western slope the going was much easier, and food was readily available. On the coast the trappers found a Captain Bradshaw and his ship the *Lagoda* of New England. After calling on Governor Echeandía, Walker began collecting supplies and horses to undertake the return trip eastward to the rendezvous.

On February 14, 1834, the Walker party began its long march eastward. This calvacade was made up of fifty-two mounted men, three hundred extra horses, fifty head of cattle and thirty dogs. The route of the party lay over the southern mountain passes, but much of it was through desert areas where it was next to impossible to find grass and water for so large a company of animals. After a bitter struggle against the desert, Walker came on his former path and followed it back to the Humboldt where again he had Indian troubles. Despite delays, he was back in the central Rocky Mountain area in time to begin a new trapping season when the furs thickened in September.

Possibly Walker's journey overland to California was the most concrete accomplishment of the Bonneville venture. Yet it went unappreciated by the Captain and by earlier historians writing of this part of the fur trade. Walker has been accused of insubordination for his failure to carry out vague instructions, and of horse-thievery. Evidence seems clearly to indicate that he was guilty of neither; on the horse-thievery charge his name has been confused with that of an Indian renegade of Mormon fame.

Captain Bonneville seems to have been adept at leading a party into the mountains, but a poor businessman after he got there. His fur trading attempts were failures, and his personal accumulation of geographical information was neither original nor adequate. Hiram Martin Chittenden, himself an army man, was most critical of the Frenchman for overstaying his leave by a year. Had it not been for the colorful three-volume account of Bonneville's adventures by Washington Irving, and the impulsive act of Andrew Jackson in restoring his commission in the army, Bonneville might have passed quietly from the pages of history.

To the Southwest, trappers and traders were active in the Santa Fe trade. Many of the men who worked in the upper reaches of the mountains, including Jim Bridger and Thomas Fitzpatrick, trapped in the south also. The two Patties, Sylvester and James Ohio, participated in the southwestern trade, and so did Christopher (Kit) Carson. Just as St. Louis was a primary base of operation for the traders who went up the Platte and the

Missouri, Santa Fe served the traders in its area. Much of the early American interest in the Spanish town of Santa Fe was generated by the possibilities in the fur trade.

For four colorful decades the fur trade in the West stimulated vigorous trailbreaking and pioneering. Trappers and traders paid a high price in men killed and maimed in this era of exploration, but they created a legend of hardy men struggling against nature and their fellow men. They broke trails throughout the West from the borders of Mexico to Canada, and from the Missouri to the Pacific. No stream capable of maintaining a colony of beavers was left unexplored. Mountain men suffered heavy casualties; sometimes as many as ninety out of a hundred gave up their lives in Indian skirmishes and by accidents. Zenas Leonard met some of his old friends at San Tepac in Spanish territory and was able to assemble some interesting information on what had happened to Bonneville's original party.

> Here I met again some of the companions who came with me in the first instance from the United States. I inquired about others, whom I held in kind remembrance. Some had died by lingering diseases, and others by the fatal ball or arrow, so that out of 116 men, who came from the United States in 1824, there were not more than sixteen alive.

A surprisingly large number of the mountain men kept diaries and journals. Among these were Larpenteur, Franchère, Ogden, Ashley, Wyeth, McLoughlin, Townsend, Leonard and Pattie. The travelers and scientists Nuttall, Maximilian, Bradbury, and Brackenridge have also left revealing accounts of life in the mountains as they saw it. Collectively these personal writings constitute a rich saga of the spreading of an elementary civilization across the continent.

The fur trade was not so important because of the civilization which it planted upon the country, however, but because it opened the trails which invited settlers. Forts and posts of the trappers and hunters became the way stations and town sites of the settlers. Knowledge of landmarks such as passes, valleys, trails and condition of stream courses made the movement of civilization much easier, and knowledge of the location and natures of the numerous Indians removed all elements of uncertainty as to what might be expected of them. International boundaries were defined in the Northwest partly on the basis of incidents in the fur trade. Because of the long standing rivalries in this region, there was more emotionalism in the arguments over location of the precise boundaries of the United States than would have been otherwise. Soon, where once the mountain men had trod, settlers would come with wagon train, women folk and lowing herd to take possession of the country with herd and plow, and with county, town and regional economy.

A MODERN RECONSTRUCTION OF A CHEROKEE VILLAGE, C. 1760–1810

ACROSS THE SETTLER'S PATH

ACROSS
THE SETTLER'S PATH

At the end of the year 1831, whilst I was on the left bank of the Mississippi at a place named by Europeans Memphis, there arrived a numerous band of Choctaws (or Chactas, as they are called by the French of Louisiana.) These savages had left their country, and were endeavouring to gain the right bank of the Mississippi, where they hoped to find an asylum which had been promised them by the American Government. It was then the middle of winter, and the cold was unusually severe; the snow had frozen hard upon the ground, and the river was drifting huge masses of ice. The Indians had their families with them; and they brought in their train the wounded and sick, with children newly born, and old men upon the verge of death. They possessed neither tents nor wagons, but only their arms and some provisions. I saw them embark to pass the mighty river, and never will that solemn spectacle fade my remembrance. No cry, no sob was heard amongst the assembled crowd: all were silent. Their calamities were of ancient date, and they knew them to be irremediable. The Indians had all stepped into the bark which was to carry them across, but their dogs remained upon the bank. As soon as these animals perceived that their masters were finally leaving the shore, they set up a dismal howl, and, plunging altogether into the icy waters of the Mississippi swam after the boat.

—DE TOCQUEVILLE, *Democracy in America*

464

CHAPTER XIX

Most of the history of the American frontier is colored by the white man's relationships—perhaps it would be nearer the truth to say his rivalry—with the Indians. The two were competitors for the greatest prize on the North American continent, land. There was scarcely an area in the path of the westward movement where the white man's culture did not conflict with that of the Indian's. No war in which Americans were engaged until the war with Spain was without its Indian phase, and few settled communities were without their local conflicts. Because of this important fact it is imperative to make some general observations before discussing in greater detail Indian history before 1849. Since the white man was the aggressor, and the eventual victor in the race for the continent, major emphasis must be given his attitudes and actions.

There is little doubt that the tangled web of eighteenth- and nineteenth-century Indian history involved a problem of social justice. It is difficult to deal with this subject without adverting to this fact. Yet moral appraisals based on a mere historical evaluation of an incomplete set of facts are not worth much. Socially, the inert Indian culture was unable to withstand the dynamic thrust of white population, and in giving way before it, the former inevitably suffered defeat, displacement and social tragedy. In the light of contemporary conditions, the fate of the Indian was one result of times in transition. President Andrew Jackson was conscious of the social element in the conflict which had arisen, and, with not a little guilt of conscience, he undertook to sweep away the cobwebs of restraint with the broom of apologetic oratory. In his second annual message, an important social document, he wrote:

> Doubtless it will be painful to leave the graves of their [Indian] fathers, but what do they more than our ancestors did or than our children are now doing? To better their condition in an unknown land our forefathers left all that was dear in earthly objects. Our children by thousands yearly leave the land of their birth to seek new homes in distant

465

regions. Does humanity weep at these painful separations from everything animate and inanimate, with which the young heart has become entwined? Far from it. It is rather a source of joy that our country affords scope where our young population may range unrestrained in body or mind, developing the power and faculties of man in their highest perfection. These remove hundreds and almost thousands of miles at their own expense, purchase the lands they occupy, and support themselves at their new homes from the moment of their arrival. Can it be cruel in this government when by events it cannot control, the Indian is made discontented in his ancient home to purchase his lands, to give him a new and extensive territory, to pay the expenses of his removal, and support him a year in his new home?

Elsewhere in this book conflict between the civilized white man and the red savage has been described. There can be little doubt that a strong racial bias existed in the white man's attitude toward the Indian. Such terms as "savage," "red devils," "dogs," "niggers," "friends," "bucks," and "squaws" indicated both fear and hatred. But the heart of the perpetual rivalry with the Indian on the frontier was the white man's insatiate desire to possess the land. The historian cannot justify the methods by which large areas of land were acquired from their Indian owners by all sorts of tricks of frontier diplomacy. From the unsophisticated settler's point of view there was never any need to go behind a land claim, to determine its history, or to validate its original ownership except in cases where two white claimants were in dispute.

The Indian Treaty as Policy

Bred in a tradition of political grants of the great American domain from absentee foreign powers and constant diplomatic exchanges of Indian possessions, the average white man considered the land to be the property of one or another white political body rather than that of any Indian tribe or nation. There was every reason for him to believe this. From the beginning of European settlement on the North American continent down to 1775, either the English or a European sovereign power controlled land grants to white settlers. After that date the states, and later the federal government, exercised political control over the western domain. This, of course, was not altogether true since the white man did resort to the use of Indian treaties to secure both quietus of Indian claims to the land, and removal of the tribes.

The Indian treaty was usually a temporary device used to reduce friction and conflict which resulted from immediate population pressures on the frontier line, or to extend the boundaries of a trading empire. The westward movement went forward by a patchwork of treaties which cleared the red occupants peaceably from slices of territory by negotiation, or which concluded wars which the Indians lost. This technique of placating the aborigines had its origin on the arrival of the first settlers, and it was used down to the last quarter of the nineteenth century. The treaty had serious limitations aside from a mere lack of foresight or good faith; probably few agreements were made with prior intent that they would be willfully violated. But treaties seldom involved an area large enough to provide for any appreciable span of time. In order to negotiate at all when territorial grants were involved, it was necessary in many instances to bite off only limited strips of territory which fell within boundaries understood by the Indian. In numerous instances it was necessary to review the terms of treaties at least once a year. The Indian regarded them more in the sense of leaseholds than as outright cessions.

Few Indians were sufficiently well educated or politically astute enough to comprehend fully the true meaning of a formal or paper agreement. The paper transfer of land, so sacred to the white man, often meant little or nothing to the Indian. Although a treaty may have been clear to the particular Indians sitting about the council fire, it was often unintelligible to their absent fellow tribesmen. Equally important was the fact that the great mass of white men on the frontier either had only limited understanding of the contents of a treaty or none at all. Historians often forget that many important treaties were minority agreements and that important factions within both tribes and nations were in disagreement with the actions of their representatives in the councils. The Indian's sense of democracy was radically different from that of the white man. Chiefs were selected for various reasons of leadership, and seldom did they have authority to speak for their tribes on policy matters. Because of a strong sense of individualism there was no such thing as a majority and minority rule among most Indian communities. The majority could not bind the minority, and in turn the minority group at the treaty council certainly could not bind the majority.

Settlers almost always followed the practical policy of pushing westward as far as possible and then waiting to see what happened. They understood clearly that the only course of appeal in cases of treaty violations was with arms. A vast number of treaty failures resulted from adventurers and settlers willfully exceeding the limitations set forth in Indian agreements. Knowledge of this fact often interfered with future treaty-making. Selfish frontier interests specialized in living outside of the law, and because of enforcement difficulties they could not always be brought to justice.

Another source of difficulty in negotiating the Indian treaty was the matter of annuities. This custom of passing gifts at the making of an agreement was of Indian origin. During the period of French and English rivalries the treaty gifts grew larger and larger, and Indian expectations increased in proportion. By the first quarter of the nineteenth century the annuity scheme was a corrupting influence in negotiating agreements on the one hand and a sop to the white man's conscience on the other. The annuity came to be regarded as payment in fee simple for Indian lands.

Just as serious as flagrant and willful violations of treaties were governmental shortsightedness, penury, and administrative failures in dealing with Indian affairs. Before the passage of the Dawes Act in 1887, the United States Government showed little originality in administering Indian affairs. This government adopted the British policy of relying upon treaties and using Indian agencies. The agency plan was patriarchal in nature and was largely a failure from the beginning for the obvious reason that it lacked funds, adequate personnel and, sometimes, honest administration. Also, the vast amount of territory and the scattering of the tribes involved in the district administered by the agency made close supervision an impossibility. Corruption of Indian agents was always a threat to sincere attempts to effect what was from the beginning an inadequate program.

Among other reasons for failures of Indian policies was the fact that contemporary politicians did not really understand the structure of frontier expansion. No one foresaw, for instance, the phenomenal increase of population that gave each succeeding decade of westward advance a tremendous momentum. Patriotic orators and compilers of local statistics made predictions that this would happen, but they seldom had any realistic understanding of what it would mean. Finally, it is not without significance that broad stretches of Indian territory were involved in major international agreements with the understood, but undeclared, intention that sooner or later they would fall into the hands of white settlers. Both the Confederation and the United States extended authority over lands which had not been formally acquired from the Indians in the Northwest Ordinance, the Louisiana Purchase, and subsequent boundary agreements with England and Spain.

Efforts were made early in the game to remove Indians from frontier areas by promising them vast land resources elsewhere and by agreeing that they would remain unmolested in their new homes. It was believed that the Indians would be removed so far in advance of the settlement line that they would be completely out of the path of the spread of settlement for the predictable future. The great mistake in this policy was the naïveté of the predictions for the future. Often the Indians were encouraged to move onto what was believed to be waste lands unfit for white settlement. All in all, in no area of eighteenth- and early nineteenth-century thinking was there a more confused condition than in this phase of administering Indian affairs, and so one acute conflict after another arose as expansive pressures exerted themselves against the back country.

The white man adopted an attitude toward the Indian's occupation of the land which would today bring forth a loud cry of protest from the press; the wave of adverse public opinion would be all but overwhelming. But in the nineteenth century the tide of public opinion was running the other way, and so ran the political mind. Few people in these earlier decades considered that pushing the Indians off the land constituted a moral breach, and certainly there was no important public outcry against prevailing practices. Instead, western politicians made good use of the white man's determination to claim the country for himself. To the average frontiersman the Indian made wasteful use of the land. He was not able to support a large population on it, and he little appreciated its potential productivity. It took hard, righteous work to convert the virgin country into fields for thrifty husbandmen, and the Indian had not accomplished this. In this respect the Indian was regarded as sinful not only because he was without the Christian religion but also because of his failure to improve the land. He was looked upon as the prodigal son who like his Biblical counterpart had wasted his birthright, or like the foolish man who buried his talent and allowed his fortune to remain dormant. Again referring to Jackson's second annual message, we find the President summarizing the attitude of his period in this bit of demagoguery.

> Philanthropy could not wish to see this continent restored to the condition in which it was found by our forefathers. What good man would prefer a country covered with forests and ranged by a few thousand savages to our extensive republic, studded with cities, towns, and prosperous farms, embellished with all the improvements which art can devise or industry execute, occupied by more than 12,000,000 happy people, and filled with all the blessings of liberty, civilization, and religion?

The Decline of Indian Power

In the earlier phases of Indian relations no one could possibly have foreseen the technological advances which became so vital in western expansion. Before the end of the American Revolution the improved long rifle became an accurate and deadly instrument against the Indian, who was equipped with the primitive bow, stone-tipped arrow, crude spear, and trade gun. When the passing years saw the introduction of the revolver, the Indian faced not only removal from his lands, but actual extinction. The cotton gin was to swell the flood of white expansion into the lower

South, and within three decades in that region Indian removal became a major social and political issue. Simultaneously, the steamboat propelled an increasing population westward at a greatly accelerated pace. Perfection of the plow and the invention of mechanical harvesting machinery helped change conditions from what they had been when many treaties were made. Within two score years after the introduction of the railroad, the revolution in transportation affected nearly every Indian tribe in the United States. It was then that the old promise of perpetuity contained in treaties began to have a strange immediacy.

The purchase of Louisiana was a milestone in Indian history; Lewis and Clark and Zebulon M. Pike began the invasion of the far western Indian territory. Later, such long-distance explorations came with greater frequency and had more important implications. The Rocky Mountain fur trade, the opening of the Santa Fe Trail, and the road to Oregon were all important wedges. Lumbering across the great plains, the Mormon wagons reached a new island of settlement in the Far West, and around it broke the violent waves of the gold rushes. Back of the constantly surging swell of native frontier population, a flood of European immigrants was flowing in.

The time was approaching when a new and definite policy of Indian relations would have to be developed. There was a prevailing idea that the red men would eventually have to be established upon reservations. Depletion of natural sources of food supply and the enforced invasion of eastern tribes threatened the plains and western Indians with severe hardships if not starvation. Solution of the problem by removal of the Indians from areas desired by the whites had been used almost from the beginning of English settlement on the continent. Likewise, the idea of an Indian state or reservation had prevailed at least since the making of the Lancaster Treaty in 1744. The British raised this issue of an Indian state repeatedly in dealing with the frontier, and even Thomas Jefferson believed it would be necessary to organize such a territory. Andrew Jackson had also expressed an opinion on the desirability of a permanent Indian territory.

The War of 1812 bore sharply on the condition of the Indians east of the Mississippi River. Failures at Tippecanoe, the Thames and Horseshoe Bend were the beginning of the end of Indian occupation of the region and marked the end of major Indian military activities east of the river. In the Northwest, the defeated tribes who had followed Tecumseh's leadership, like those who had followed Pontiac, were left badly shattered and had little choice other than to move beyond the Mississippi. In Alabama, the Creeks were hurt badly by their defeat and Jackson's harsh terms of surrender. Within a decade following the war the advancing frontier created an immediate Indian problem in Florida, Georgia, Alabama, Mississippi and Illinois.

In Florida the Indian upheavals were incidental to the greater international rivalries between the United States, England and Spain. In the first half of the year 1818 General Jackson brought a temporary decision at least on the Seminole problem in his famous Florida campaign and prepared the ground for one which would be final. The famous Tennessean was also to play an important political role in the last act in the drama of the Cherokees, Creeks, Choctaws and Chickasaws, who unhappily found themselves in the path of the expanding cotton belt. Between 1820 and 1840 both the federal government and the southern states faced the tedious task of removing the southern Indians to lands west of the Mississippi.

Cherokees and Creeks

Indian affairs in the South were complicated by many factors. There was the basic issue of Indian possession of lands which white settlers both wanted and were determined to have. In the mountain areas of North Carolina, eastern Tennessee and northern Georgia, the Cherokees owned rich valleys where cotton could be grown; but even more unfortunate for them was the discovery of gold in their Georgia hills about Dalonegha. This gave their territory a new popularity. Characteristic of gold mining "rushes," a rough and unsympathetic white population moved in and sought to dispossess the Indians. To the south along the Chattahoochee River, and in Alabama and central Mississippi, the Creeks, Choctaws and Chickasaws were also in possession of fertile lands. It made little difference that these tribes for the most part had developed a rather high degree of civilization. They had even established churches and had native ministers of the Christian faith. Among them were such leaders as Chief John Ross, Jesse Bushyhead, Major John Ridge, and George Guess (Sequoyah). The Cherokees were in fact becoming like their white neighbors, and no longer, if ever, could they be called savage. Their land, however, was their undoing. Indians and whites were unprepared to live as neighbors on fertile land. The settlers moving southwestward countenanced no exception to the rule.

The conflict which arose between the Georgians and the Cherokees and Creeks was not altogether the fault of the settlers. In April, 1802, the federal government had entered into what was known as the Georgia Compact in which it agreed with the state of Georgia that it would, among other things, extinguish Indian land titles within the state as part payment for the cession of Georgia's western lands. This meant in reality removal.

The extinction of Indian land titles and their removal were to take place as soon as this could be accomplished peacefully and on reasonable terms. Little had been done to carry out this promise, and Georgians began to exert pressure on the federal government. As the state's population expanded, rapid changes occurred in its internal political structure. New counties were created, public lands were disposed of by lottery, and the modest settler rather than the speculator was encouraged to buy homesteads. As this new policy took effect, the pressure of landseekers was felt along Georgia's western and mountain frontier. Failure to carry out the federal government's promises became increasingly serious for the Georgians. But some aspects of Georgia politics were just as important as the failure of the central government to tackle its southwestern Indian problem. George M. Troup, an impulsive politician and a friend to the cotton planters, became governor in 1823. An old Jeffersonian with a vigorous record in both the national House of Representatives and Senate, he came to the governorship with ripe experience. Among his many plans for improvement in Georgia was the removal of the Cherokee and Creek Indians from the state.

When the first boom of Troup's oral cannonade was heard in Washington, the Monroe administration bestirred itself and made a gesture toward securing a peaceful relinquishment of titles to Indian lands in Georgia. In fact some kind of negotiation had been in process in this region since the end of the War of 1812. Because of a conflict in views between the Upper and Lower Creeks along the western Georgia border, there was more than the usual resistance to the government's proposals. The Upper, or Alabama, Creeks were determined to make no further concessions, while the Lower Creeks under the leadership of the mixed-breed chieftain William McIntosh, Governor Troup's first cousin and a brigadier general in the United States Army, were more amenable to the government's terms. On February 12, 1825, after failing to come to terms with the Upper and Lower Creeks, the Indian agents signed the Treaty of Indian Springs in which they gave up approximately 4,700,000 acres of land between the Flint and Chattahoochee rivers. So bitter was resentment against Chief McIntosh that he was killed in April of that year. Likewise the more experienced Indian agents were opposed to the Indian Springs Treaty, and at the same time Governor Troup assailed President Monroe for his tardy action.

When John Quincy Adams came to office, he inherited this hot Georgia Indian row. Governor Troup had become even more embittered. The United States Senate did not ratify the Indian Springs agreement, and its revision in the Washington Treaty of 1826 restored to the Creeks nearly a million acres of their Georgia lands. During the next four years, the state of Georgia and the United States continued the argument. At times Troup and his fellow Georgians became so aroused that they all but threatened armed resistance against the Union.

By 1828 the United States Government was finally able to begin the removal of the Creeks to lands west of Arkansas. The Washington Treaty had granted the Creeks the same number of acres they had held in Georgia, and they were to be paid $400,000 in money. There still remained the Cherokees in the mountains. These Indians had adopted a constitution in 1827 and had established an Indian state within the boundaries of Georgia in an attempt to avoid the treatment accorded the Creeks. White Georgians were equally as determined, first under the leadership of Governor Troup, and then under that of George R. Gilmer, that the mountain Indians should be removed from the state. The Georgia assembly assisted by passing legislation extending the state laws over the Cherokees and permitting occupation of their territory by white settlers. The latter move involved Georgia and the United States at once in a ticklish States' rights issue.

Two famous Supreme Court cases resulted from this dispute. The first was the Cherokee Nation *vs.* Georgia, in which a Cherokee, George Corntassel, was tried and convicted for murder by the state court. An appeal was taken to the United States Supreme Court in 1830, seeking to restrain Georgia from enforcing its laws against the Cherokees. The Court followed the line of reasoning that, since the Cherokees were not citizens, they could not sue as a party to a suit before the court. Georgia quickly executed Corntassel and made further litigation on this point an academic matter.

Two years later, another suit, Worcester *vs.* Georgia, was filed before the Supreme Court. Samuel A. Worcester and ten New England missionaries were arrested on the charge that they had violated the Georgia law which prohibited white people from entering the Cherokee country unless they had first sought the permission of the governor and had taken an oath to support the laws of the state. Violation of this law carried a penalty of four years' imprisonment. This strange statute had found its way into the books after the political and social plight of the southern Indians had provoked what amounted to a racial crusade among New England missionaries. Worcester and his colleagues had come South primarily to try to prevent white encroachment upon Indian lands. This emotional situation had stirred the Georgians to a resistance that was anticipatory of the future abolition disputes. Worcester and Elizur Butler immortalized themselves in their famous suit against Georgia. Chief Justice John Marshall's decision, declaring the Cherokees an independent nation with boundaries defined by treaty agreement with the United States, reversed the decision of the Georgia Superior Court. President Jackson's refusal to enforce this decision became a milestone in executive-judiciary history.

Historians have treated this case repeatedly and have usually dismissed the matter with the President's statement that Marshall had made his decision—let him enforce it. There was more to Jackson's refusal to have the decision carried out than this. He reasoned, and it was virtually impossible for the courts to say him nay, that the Constitution prohibited the formation of one state within another, without the consent of the former. He also observed that, in admitting states with defined boundaries but containing Indian lands, it was presupposed that the Indian claims would be satisfied and the Indians removed. He believed that not one of the new states would have been formed otherwise.

Dancing Rabbit

West of Georgia, Indian problems in Alabama and Mississippi were also coming to the surface, largely because of the furor in Georgia. Between 1826 and 1835, the titles to lands of the Cherokees, Creeks, Choctaws and Chickasaws were surrendered. Possibly the most important of the four agreements with the Indians in this region was the Dancing Rabbit Treaty of September 27, 1830, which brought about the cession of 7,796,-000 acres of Choctaw lands in western Alabama and central eastern Mississippi. One of the principal figures in the negotiation of this treaty was Greenwood Leflore, son of a French-Canadian trader and innkeeper, and a half-breed mother.

Before the Choctaws and government agents met on the flat and trampled Noxubee Creek council ground in the swampy backwoods of Mississippi, President Jackson had already presented his views in his first inaugural address, and the important Indian Removal Act had been passed by Congress in May of that year. Long before these more publicized actions, the Indian agents had been trying to negotiate removal during both the Monroe and Adams administrations. Immediately preceding the Dancing Rabbit Council, a considerable amount of backstage manipulation had taken place to prepare the Indians for the meeting. Leflore had received material encouragement to lend his influence and power to bring about a successful negotiation of the treaty. Other chieftains and influential Indians had been swayed before the meeting by promises of public lands and annuity dollars. Government agents promised the Indians a happy and early removal to their new homes beyond the Mississippi and dwelt on the idea of large land grants in the West. Their soft words and liquid gifts made land cession a momentary pleasure for many Choctaws. For the more reluctant natives, the commissioners painted a disturbing picture of Alabama and Mississippi officials unable to control the flood of omnivorous white settlers who would push into the Indian country and lay forceful claim to their lands. Historically, the Dancing Rabbit Treaty cannot be regarded as one of the more benevolent and virtuous acts of the Jackson administration. The commissioners documented this fact by their haste in leaving the treaty grounds.

On its face, the Indian Removal Act of 1830 was a rather innocuous piece of legislation, but it gave President Jackson the desired authority to exchange large blocks of western lands with the eastern tribes for their holdings east of the Mississippi River. There is little doubt that Jackson's personal animus entered into his anxiety to remove the Indians from their homelands. In his annual message to Congress in December, 1835, he summarized much of the popular attitude toward the Indian and revealed his own thinking on the subject of removal.

> All previous experiments for the improvements of the Indians have failed. It seems now to be an established fact that they cannot live in contact with a civilized community and prosper. Ages of fruitless endeavor have at length brought us to a knowledge of this principle of communication with them. The past we cannot recall, but the future we can provide for.

A measure of Jackson's sense of providing for the Indians was to be found in the ninety or so treaties which he signed during his administration.

Public opinion in the communities bordering the Indian country east of the Mississippi not only favored Indian removal to the western lands, but there was no objection from people moving westward. The popular concept of the western plains country was still being conditioned by the "Great American Desert" idea expressed by Zebulon M. Pike, and perpetuated by Stephen H. Long and other travelers in the region. Frontiersmen were quite satisfied to remove the eastern Indians into this arid region with the belief that maybe never again would they block the path of expanding white settlements. Obviously there was either little concern for the ultimate fate of the Indians, or the belief prevailed that they could adjust themselves to the hard conditions of the barren region.

The decade 1830–1840 witnessed the removal of approximately sixty thousand Indians from the states east of the Mississippi. Those in the Great Lakes area were removed from reservation to reservation with a minimum amount of friction. There was little or no acute and dramatic suffering on their part. Remnants of the old warring tribes of Wyandots, Shawnees, Delawares and others were so badly defeated and frustrated that they had little or no resistance left. As President Andrew Jackson said in his first inaugural address, "By persuasion and force they have been made to retire from river to river and from mountain to mountain, until some of the tribes have become extinct and others have left but remnants to preserve for awhile their once terrible names."

Indian removal in the southern states was an altogether different story. Despite the serious defeat of the Creeks in Alabama by Jackson's forces, the southern Indians were far from being a defeated people. In Georgia, Tennessee and the Carolinas, the Cherokees were well entrenched and had developed a culture and economic system which promised them future security. West of them, the Mississippi Choctaws and Chickasaws were proud Indians even though they had not advanced so far toward adopting the white man's culture patterns as had their Cherokee neighbors. These Indians had a fairly stable social and political organization of their own. Because of this, their removal to the western territory challenged government officials to make major provisions for their welfare. To begin with, many of the Indians were either reluctant to leave their home country or refused outright to go. Under the most efficient handling, the transportation of the Southern Indians to the West would have required the most astute organization and management. In fact, political favoritism, corruption, mismanagement, defective organization, uncertain transportation facilities, and lack of good faith on the part of both state and federal governments, made the trip westward a fatal ordeal for many.

Death and privation were constant partners for many of the parties that set out for new homes. Steamboats, flatboats, wagons, packhorses and even footpaths were all called into use. Contractors were supposed to set up rest and supply depots ahead of the various parties; but characteristic of government contractors, many of them located their stations in the wrong places, stocked their storerooms with the wrong goods, and otherwise nullified their efforts. Another serious drawback for many Indians was the bad timing of the removals. Many of them failed to plant crops or otherwise to provide for themselves until they were ready to leave. In many instances idleness played havoc with morale, with many Indians turning to drink and mischief to stave off the boredom of waiting.

Once on the trail, all of these failures began to take their toll. The three major southern crossings on the Mississippi were Vicksburg, Arkansas Post and Memphis. Two upper routes from eastern Tennessee and northern Alabama and Georgia led up into Kentucky and across the Ohio at Paducah to Illinois and Missouri. Because of the long period of time involved in the removals, there was of course a great variation in conditions, but nearly every disaster that can plague mankind beset some of the parties —drouth, flood, food shortages, cold, heat and storm.

Nearly all the emigrant parties had grievous experiences, but none of them exceeded the woes of the Cherokees who followed the so-called "Trail of Tears" westward in 1838. To begin with, many of these Indians were forced from their homes like animals from holes and were forced to begin their journey out of Tennessee, Georgia and North Carolina without

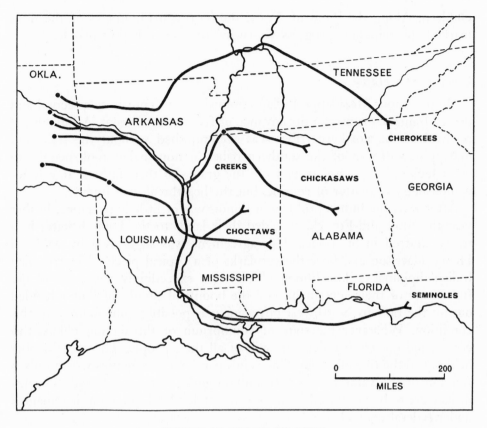

ROUTES OF INDIAN REMOVAL

suitable preparation for the move. So embittered were many of these people that they refused to accept the clothing offered by the government agents, and their conditions were made much more difficult because of their belligerence. Once assembled, the defenseless Indians were held in assembly camps until the forced marches were begun. The day-to-day journals of these forced marches record the deaths, births, desertions and hardships that occurred. The Cherokees dawdled along the way and could not be hurried on to their destination. Approximately 11,500 of them were moved in 1838, and approximately 4,000 died along the way. No more pathetic mass movement of people has occurred on this continent. Like the Hebrews of old who wandered in the desolate wilderness, these distraught people straggled along the trail westward. Dysentery, climatic diseases, old age, malnutrition, exposure and exhaustion all claimed their victims. Children died in every night encampment, old people gave up the ghost day and night, and expectant mothers died in bearing their trail children. Along the Trail of Tears, the hastily made graves of the dead marked the reluctant progress westward of a once happy people.

Chief Black Hawk

On the upper Mississippi, Indian removal was to constitute a second and just as dramatic chapter in the advance of frontier settlement. Although the removal of the northern tribes was accomplished without the stain and unhappiness of that of the southern tribes, it nonetheless took people, to use a Jacksonian phrase, away from the graves of their fathers. It was accomplished as a matter of routine, but the heartbreak was intense.

After 1804 the Indian problem in Illinois was of little importance. In that year the Sauk and Fox chiefs ceded their lands to the United States in a treaty drafted in St. Louis. This agreement was supervised by William Henry Harrison and bore the earmarks of a typical piece of Harrisonian Indian diplomacy. The Illinois chiefs were exceedingly vague about the full nature of their agreement, and the bountiful supply of liquor handed out by the famous Northwest governor was possibly contributory to this condition. Whatever the state of equilibrium of the signing chiefs, this cession did not truly reflect the will of all their people. The actual bribes held out to the five chiefs by Harrison's party were annuities worth only a fraction of the value of the fifty million acres of land involved. The Indians were to be permitted to occupy the ceded land so long as it remained under federal control.

In the intervening years between 1804 and 1825, the various groups of Sauks and Foxes accepted the terms of the St. Louis cession. Even so, there have been few cases in frontier history where the Indian mind failed more completely to grasp the meaning and comprehensiveness of a treaty than in northern Illinois. A major illustration was Chief Black Hawk's subsequent contention that he did not know his people had given away their ancient village when he touched the goose quill pen in making the treaty of 1816. Here on the Mississippi River frontier, the story of white and Indian conflict followed an established pattern. Squatters pushed westward with little regard for either federal law or treaty provisions. They encroached upon the Indian's grounds with no misgivings, and little or no apparent feeling of denying him his rights. They were convinced, as was usually the case, that the Indian had no property rights which the white man had to respect. There was, however, one mitigating circumstance in the white settlers' favor. They too were seldom if ever fully apprised of the terms of a treaty, and where they were not acting in violation of an agreement they had a right to expect protection from the army and militia.

Inevitably, conflict resulted as settlers pushed into the Indian country.

The Sauks and Foxes found themselves abused for trespassing on squatters' fields on the one hand, and they were corrupted by white traders on the other. Under the leadership of Chief Keokuk, the Indians were finally persuaded to move across the Mississippi River to Iowa. This move, however, was not accomplished without a tremendous amount of conflict within their tribal ranks. Again there was a misconception of what could be expected from their former allies and friends, the British and the neighboring tribes. Black Hawk, a seasoned old warrior who had supported the British in the War of 1812, childishly believed that both they and the Canadian Indians would assist him in rescuing his homeland. His jealousy of Keokuk was also a factor in his discontent.

Black Hawk and his unhappy situation are the materials out of which the "noble savage" legends are made. Any objective view of the subject at the time, it seems, would have revealed two important things. First, the chiefs had been exceedingly generous in giving up lands in the St. Louis treaty of 1804; and, second, they did not intend—as Black Hawk so stoutly maintained—to give up their village sites. Had General Lewis Cass been diligent, he might have helped the Indians establish the latter fact. In attempting to regain their property, Black Hawk and his followers pursued about the only course open to a confused and primitive people who felt the sting of shameful wrong. Suffering from hard conditions in their new home, they dreamed of the joys and abundance of the old one back across the river. In Illinois they had lived in their villages for many generations. The land had brought forth rich harvests there; streams, woodlands and meadows had supplied meat and bread in abundance. There above the Rock River were the graves of their ancestors and the sites of their century-old homes, places that were now being defiled by the settlers. This nostalgia brought about constant crossings back over the river in violation of the treaty signed on June 30, 1831, which forbade these periodic visitations. On an early expedition to gather their abandoned crops, the Fox braves settled an old score with a band of their ancient enemies, the Menominees, by slaying twenty-eight of their people. This stirred up fear and resentment among the whites.

In 1832, Chief Black Hawk determined to go home to the old Indian fields in the Rock River bottoms to grow a crop of corn in spite of the treaty restrictions. Since he went on a peaceful mission, he believed the whites would honor his intentions. But the sight of his band crossing the river in view of Fort Armstrong terrorized the settlers. General Henry Atkinson sent up the shrill and hysterical frontier cry of "Indians!" and echoing the General's frantic whoop, Governor John Reynolds delivered a frenzied speech in which he called for volunteers to repel the savage invasion. A frontier army of militiamen came galloping to camp to elect officers and take the field. Excitement and fame were to be sought on the banks of the Rock River! Among the officers elected were Samuel Whitesides and Major Isaiah Stillman. The latter was to prove in good time that he had far less moral and physical courage than Isaiah of old. Major Stillman, an inexperienced officer, led two mounted battalions in search of Black Hawk's highly domesticated band.

Settlers in the surrounding country were in panic. The floundering band of frustrated Fox and Sauk were multiplied by thousands in some of the settlers' tales, and there were dire predictions of bloody massacres and murders. While this commotion was at its height among the settlers, Black Hawk was in an equally disturbed state of mind. He had learned that none of his friends, not even the Winnebagos and Potawatomi, would support him. His only hope for safety lay in getting his people back across the Mississippi. No doubt he would have accomplished this with a little more time and a little less crowding, but before the Indians could escape, Major Stillman's mounted forces were on them.

Hoping to make the best of a precarious situation, Black Hawk sent three warriors under flag of truce to apprise his pursuers of his intention to recross the river. He made the mistake of sending along observers to see what happened to his messengers. When the bearers of the flag approached the militiamen, there was such a wild commotion that the observers broke and ran. A party of the undisciplined troops dashed off after them, a flag bearer was killed, and the whole command went out of hand. Before the onslaught of charging backwoodsmen, Black Hawk and his forty warriors had no choice but to make a death stand. At the first volley, however, the foolish militiamen were thrown into panic, and turned and fled. They ran past their camp and pushed onto Dixon, Illinois, before they stopped.

Writing twenty-three years later, Governor Thomas Ford explained away the so-called battle of "Stillman's Run" by saying in his *History of Illinois:*

> A retreat of undisciplined militia from the attack of a superior force, is apt to be a disorderly and inglorious flight; and so it was here, each man sought his own individual safety, and in the twinkling of an eye the whole detachment was in utter confusion. They were pursued in their flight by thirty or forty Indians, for ten or twelve miles, the fugitives in the rear keeping up a flying fire as they ran, until the Indians ceased pursuing.

News of Stillman's Run spread rapidly. As it went from mouth to mouth it gained in ferocity, and the number of Indians said to be involved became overwhelming. No account better illustrates the ridiculous exaggeration of Indian forces than that attributed by Governor Ford to an itinerant

Kentucky lawyer-colonel who rushed into battle to destroy the enemy with a long rifle and a copy of *Chitty on Pleading*. On the first burst of fire the visiting colonel ran off the field leaving behind his honor and his saddle-bags containing *Chitty*. He did not, however, become so frightened in the process that he lost a Kentuckian's art of description. He claimed that he saw:

> Black Hawk's army coming down upon us in solid column; they deployed in the form of a crescent upon the brow of the prairie, and such accuracy and precision of military movements were never witnessed by man; they were equal to the best troops of Wellington in Spain.

After outlining the organization of this vast Indian army, the highly imaginative barrister told his hearers:

> It was a terrible and glorious sight to see the tawny warriors as they rode along our flanks attempting to outflank us with the glittering moonbeams glistening from their polished blades and burnished spears. It was a sight well calculated to strike consternation into the stoutest and boldest heart, and accordingly our men began to break in small squads for tall timber.

This was a wonderfully contradictory account of what a few rifle shots in the twilight could do for a frightened settler's nerve and imagination.

Following this fiasco in the field, the upper Illinois settlements were again thrown into pandemonium. It was necessary for Governor Reynolds to call for a new crop of volunteers to take the field. The summer of 1832 was spent in forcing Black Hawk's straggling band out of Illinois. No doubt Black Hawk was heartened by his temporary victory at Stillman's Run and was emboldened to carry on a war when he should have been hustling back across the river to safety. He and his people went on a nightmarish march in the swampy lands of the Illinois river bottoms. Constantly they had to fight rear-guard skirmishes, and by August of that year they were exhausted and near the point of destitution. At the same time their presence greatly agitated the whites.

Four thousand regulars and militiamen under such officers as Major Henry Dodge, General Alexander Posey, Colonel Jacob Fry and General James D. Henry now took the field against Black Hawk. The same problems of discipline and order confronted them as had beset the militia officers who had first gone out against the Indians. To begin with, it was all but impossible to get Black Hawk's straggling band to stand and fight. For weeks the frontier forces wandered over difficult terrain in search of their quarry. Conditions were so unfavorable that desertions depleted ranks, and for a time it looked as if the whites would again be defeated.

But Black Hawk's people had virtually reached the end of their endurance. The trail of their retreat was lined with exhausted elderly tribesmen. In late July they reached the Wisconsin River and attempted a crossing when they were beset by militiamen. There occurred the battle of Wisconsin Heights which resulted in a draw because General Henry failed to follow up his advantages. On August 2, 1831, the Indians were finally cornered on the bank of the Mississippi at the mouth of Bad Axe River, and the bloody battle of Bad Axe occurred. Infantry fire from the bank and artillery aboard the steamboat *Warrior* raked the retreating Indian band. Men, women and children were cut down, or picked off as they attempted to cross the river. This battle closed the major Indian conflict in the eastern part of the upper Mississippi valley. Black Hawk had brought to an inglorious end a long and arduous history of resistance that was begun by Pontiac in the same general region.

The Seminoles

While Indians from Georgia, Alabama and Mississippi were being removed, and the Sauk and Fox war was in progress in the Northwest, the Seminoles of Florida were continuing what had become a virtually perpetual conflict. The Seminoles, so-called, were runaway Creeks who had retreated for one reason or another to the swampy country of Florida. Since 1810 they had known the bitterness of white attack. Jackson had fought them in 1812 and again in 1818. In 1832 they were faced with still another war. The Seminole situation, however, had one or two peculiar aspects. First, these Indians were pretty well buried in an inaccessible country into which they could melt away when hard-pressed without leaving traces of their going. Then, there were Negro fugitives among them who made the Indians suspect by their white neighbors. The runaway tribesmen, with something approaching a kindred feeling, had opened welcoming arms to escaping slaves from the adjoining plantation country. When the Seminoles were first confronted with the proposal of removal to the west, they had to think of their Negroes who would be caught in the government's net and returned to slavery.

Like all other Indians east of the Mississippi, the Seminoles had entered into a treaty agreement with the United States defining their boundaries. In 1823 they had agreed in the Moultrie Creek Treaty to move into the region south of Tampa Bay. Nine years later they were asked to enter into a second major agreement with the government. Meeting the chiefs at Payne's Landing, the government agents, led by Colonel James Gadsden, persuaded the Indians to send seven of their trusted chiefs to examine the western territory now proposed for them and report their impressions back to their people. This virtually obligated the Seminoles to agree to removal from Florida. In the western country the seven chiefs were maneuvered into implying, if not saying outright, in the Fort Gibson Treaty that they were pleased with the plains country. This piece of diplomatic finesse was designed to commit them to agree to leave Florida within the next three years. The whole negotiation was faithless, and this, plus fear of their prospective neighbors beyond the Mississippi, caused the chiefs to refuse agreement with the dishonest proposal of the government agents.

Outbreak of the Seminole War followed closely on the government's revelation of its faithless hand, and the next ten years were troubled ones for both whites and Indians. A few Seminoles submitted to removal and left Florida, but the majority of them withdrew into the swamps and began a bloody guerrilla war. Possibly the most important leader among them was Osceola, or Powell. Like many southern Indian leaders, Osceola was a mixed-breed Creek, born in the Tallapoosa country in Alabama. Participating in all the Seminole struggles since 1812, he had led the resistance movement in 1835 to both the Payne's Landing and Fort Gibson treaties, and was imprisoned because of his dramatic refusal to agree to removal. Osceola had a bitter hatred, and not without ample reason, for the white man.

In an attempt to suppress the Florida tribes both the United States Army and Navy were called into service and were consolidated into the Florida Squadron. But with shrewd leadership and a favorable natural terrain, the Indians were able to strike their oppressors quick and deadly blows and then escape into the impenetrable glades. Among the famous officers who saw service in the Seminole War were General Edmund Pendleton Gaines, Zachary Taylor, who gained his nickname of "Old Rough and Ready" there, George Gordon Meade, Thomas J. ("Stonewall") Jackson, William Selby Harney, and Alexander Macomb. Fighting was nearly always desultory and indecisive. The troops undertook to establish and maintain a cordon of forts which would check the Indian raids. From the army's point of view it was impossible to get the Seminoles sufficiently well concentrated to strike a telling blow against them.

In 1837 the Indians were robbed of their most important leader when Osceola was taken prisoner. This act was nothing short of treachery, for, when he was taken, Osceola was on his way under a flag of truce to confer with General Thomas S. Jesup at Fort Mellon. He had been influenced to do this by a delegation of Cherokees, including John Ross, Jesse Bushyhead, Major Polecat, Thomas Woodward, and Richard Fields, who had been brought to Florida to persuade the Seminoles to give up and go west. General Jesup's unseemly action touched off an explosion among the Cherokees and in the press, and brought humiliation to the Seminoles. One of their chiefs, Wildcat, made his escape and stirred his people anew in a wave of bitterness. But the odds were too great against the Indians. In 1840 Colonel Harney discovered the key to Seminole security when he went up the Miami River and penetrated the Everglades. He hanged the famous chief Chekika and another Indian and captured their people. Within two years the back of Indian resistance was broken, and on August 5, 1842, Colonel William J. Worth and Billy Bowlegs negotiated a treaty which allowed the rest of the Seminoles to remain in southwestern Florida.

During the ten years of war, large numbers of Seminoles had either given up voluntarily or submitted to removal to the west, or they were captured and forcibly removed. Their experiences on the trail differed little from those of their northern neighbors who had suffered privation and death by the wayside. There still remained in the Everglades a small band of Seminoles who have held on tenaciously to the present day. The same thing has been true of the Choctaws and Cherokees. Determined members of both groups retreated to the fastness of mountain and swamp and refused to leave their homeland. In some cases homesick Indians wandered back from the west. Today they still survive in the land of their ancestors. Nevertheless, the last of the Seminole removals brought a virtual end to Indian history east of the Mississippi River.

Indian Politics

Removal of the Indians, however, was not to bring peace for the government. Even before this program was begun, there was already friction and conflict on the great plains and the western mountains which prefaced a new chapter in Indian history. Subsequent organization of the new western territories and states was accompanied by Indian conflict. Opening the Santa Fe, Oregon, and California trails thrust long tentacles of white influence into the West, and it was only a matter of time until the pressure of settlement in places was almost as great as that which had forced removal of the eastern tribes. The Texas struggle was accompanied by its own bitter Indian resistance, and one of the most colorful phases of that state's history was the fight against the plains tribes. Discovery of gold and silver in California and the Rocky Mountains hastened a flow of white population into remote places which otherwise might have remained undisturbed Indian country for many decades.

From the beginning of British domination of the North American continent, the management of Indian affairs was basically political. Nearly every Indian treaty had back of it a tremendous amount of political pressure exerted by frontiersmen who sought to clear their path of stubborn Indian resistance. Yet removal was at best no more than a temporary expedient. It was obvious to both thoughtful Indian agents and politicians that the federal government would have to develop a more definite policy for solution of frontier rivalries for the land between white settlers and Indians.

In 1834 Congress passed the Indian Intercourse Act, which was largely a revised form of one of the earliest regulatory measures adopted by the government. The philosophy behind this new law was as old as the British agitation for a separate Indian buffer state which would guarantee a degree of permanence of Indian residence and the integrity of tribal land titles. Once the Indians had been removed to their western lands, it was still necessary for the national government to protect them against white invasion, although some congressmen voting for removal may have believed that they were solving permanently the western Indian problem. Those ancient troublemakers, the white traders, were prohibited by the Act from entering Indian territory except under license and regulation of the United States Government, but terrific enforcement difficulties limited the Act's effectiveness. Historically, the law proved to be only a slight deterrent in the spread of white settlement.

Indian removal in many instances, as has been said, was little short of being a tale of horrors, and if the responsible government officials viewed it at all objectively, they must have felt a sense of guilt and shame. However, a satisfactory administrative method for handling so delicate an internal problem was lacking. Under the War Department, the management of Indian affairs had a distinct military flavor, and the sale of licenses and trade goods, along with other privileges, involved a disturbing amount of graft and corruption. Not even the creation, in 1832, of the Office of Indian Affairs alleviated this unsatisfactory situation. Between 1832 and 1849, the Indian Commissioner remained responsible to the Secretary of War. There was much public agitation to have this changed. At the same time there was strong public pressure to remove the administration of public lands from the Treasury Department. Congress responded to these joint demands by creating the Department of the Interior, which was given supervision of both Indians and public lands.

This transfer of administrative authority, however, was not to end internal administrative rivalries. Almost to the end of the century the issue of transferring Indian affairs back to the War Department was a lively one. Nevertheless the passage of the Indian Affairs Act in 1849 ushered in a new era of government relationships with its Indian wards. It marked the period when attention shifted almost completely from the old Atlantic Indian country to that of the trans-Mississippi West.

SKETCH OF WHAT WAS LATER TO BE OREGON CITY ON THE WILLAMETTE BY CAPT. HENRY JAMES WARRE, 1846

THE FRONTIER IN OREGON

Oregon is a part of the North American continent, to which, it is confidently affirmed, the title of the United States is the best now in existence. For the grounds on which that title rests I refer you to the correspondence of the late and present Secretary of State with the British Plenipotentiary during the negotiation. The British proposition of compromise, which would make the Columbia the line south of 49°, with a trifling addition of detached territory to the United States north of that river, and would leave on the British side two-thirds of the whole Oregon Territory, including the free navigation of the Columbia and all the valuable harbors on the Pacific, can never for a moment be entertained by the United States without an abandonment of their just and clear territorial rights, their own self-respect, and the national honor.

—JAMES KNOX POLK, *First Annual Message*

CHAPTER XX

AMERICAN penetration of Oregon covered a long period of years, and involved many phases of American frontier expansion. The Northwest Coast had challenged the imagination of Americans since 1792. When the Lewis and Clark expedition returned, and when their journal was published, interest was further heightened.

Earliest knowledge of the present Oregon country dates back to 1788 and 1792 when Robert Gray and John Kendrick of Boston went trading in the Nootka Sound area. Gray discovered the mouth of the Columbia in 1792. While the fur trade pushed up the Missouri from the east, the American Fur Company sent the *Tonquin* out under Captain Thorne in 1811 to retrace the route of Robert Gray. Wilson Price Hunt's overland Astorians were driving toward the same goal. As has been said in another chapter, the Americans were checked by the conflict of 1812, and it was not until after the signing of the Treaty of Ghent that the American Fur Company was able to reclaim its northwestern base. By the time company traders were again on the Columbia, the territory west of the Rocky Mountains had become the subject of diplomatic agreement between the United States and Great Britain.

The Northwest in Transition

The western boundaries of Louisiana were defined in the Adams-Onis Treaty (1819), and Spain's claims north of the 42nd parallel were liquidated. Although Spain was thus removed from the Northwest, and the United States had acquired more than an exploratory claim to the region, international rivalries were far from ended. In 1821 the Russian Czar issued a *ukase* which proposed to keep foreign vessels back at least one hundred miles from the coast of Russian America north of the 51st parallel. By conventions made in 1824 and 1825, Russia retreated north of the 54° 40′ line, leaving the United States and Great Britain in joint occupation of the territory to the south.

An agreement of joint occupation had been formulated in 1818, two weeks after the return of Astoria to the Americans, by which nationals of both Britain and the United States might have access on an equal basis to rivers and hunting lands for ten years. Nine years later joint occupation was extended for an indefinite period. These agreements were made at a time when the United States was involved in rather extensive diplomatic negotiations on other subjects. During the 1820's, Secretary of State Adams was occupied in making agreements with both Spain and Britain, and in formulating the Monroe Doctrine. Matching wits with George Canning, Adams was wise enough not to agree to a final settlement of the Oregon question on a basis of division at the Columbia River. In 1827 the Joint Occupation Agreement was extended until one party gave a year's notice of a desire to terminate the arrangement. By waiting for a propitious moment to establish the boundary west of the Rocky Mountains, the United States was placed in a more favorable position to seek a deeper bite of territory.

In the intervening years between 1811 and 1842, commercial activities in the Northwest focused American minds upon the Oregon question. Diplomats of both countries were involved in long discussions and counter-diplomatic moves. It is unnecessary to stress further the importance of the fur trade in opening the Northwest. There were, however, other influences.

Hall J. Kelley

Hall J. Kelley, the stuttering, weak-eyed Boston school teacher whom we have already met in Chapter 18, was captivated by Oregon to the extent that he conducted a vigorous one-man crusade for the country. He had published two successful textbooks, and might have gone on to fame as an author if he had not read Biddle's edition of the Lewis and Clark *Journal* and had become an impassioned advocate for the settlement of Oregon. He knew nothing first-hand about the area, and was hardly capable of doing much personally to speed settlement of the region; yet he seems to have received tremendous vicarious joy out of contemplating a great civilizing adventure in the far-off wilds of the Northwest. No doubt he was stimulated by a nationalistic desire to see Americans claim the country and bring joint occupation to an end. Pursuing his interest with burning zeal, he goaded Congress to encourage official colonization of the Columbia Valley. He published his first propaganda pamphlet in 1830 under the title *A Geographical Sketch of that Part of North America Called Oregon.* This was only a beginning. For the next forty years he campaigned in Congress, at first advocating the colonization of Oregon, later seeking a reward for his faithful agitation.

Kelley possessed no capacity of leadership. His biggest service to Oregon was that of stimulating Nathaniel Wyeth to visit the country. Had the myopic schoolteacher been able to recognize administrative ability in another person, he would have accompanied Wyeth to the Northwest. Instead he allowed the capable Boston ice merchant to set out overland alone in 1832, while he, characteristically, followed the long way around to Oregon. He traveled westward by way of the Cumberland Road, then southward down the Ohio and Mississippi to New Orleans. He sailed to Vera Cruz and crossed Mexico by way of Mexico City and La Paz, reaching the Pacific at San Diego. Blundering on his tactless way, he alienated people as he went. Certainly he did nothing to allay Spanish suspicions when he suggested to Governor Figueroa that he be allowed to make a survey of interior California.

Going on northward, the cantankerous Yankee finally reached the Columbia River. His arrival at Fort Vancouver was hardly a triumphant one. Preceding him was a note from Governor Figueroa to Dr. John McLoughlin which said that Kelley was in close association with a band of horse thieves. The Spanish governor's information seemed to be confirmed by the fact that Kelley's company arrived with a considerable drove of horses and mules. One of his companions was the Tennessean Ewing Young, who was to become a key figure in early Oregon political history.

Once in Oregon, Kelley was unable to enjoy unlimited hospitality at Fort Vancouver or to organize a colony. Four years after leaving Boston he returned home having accomplished nothing more important than the entanglement of his own private affairs. It is hard to appraise the influence of Hall J. Kelley on the Oregon movement. His writings attracted early attention to the region, but it is doubtful that Congress did injustice to a deserving man when it refused him grants of land and money in payment for his services. His name has been intimately associated with the beginnings of the Oregon movement, but his work undoubtedly deserves no further recognition.

Ewing Young, on the other hand, was an important pioneer. Smeared with the guilt-by-association taint of horse thievery, it took him some time to clear his name. He settled on the Chehalem and quickly became an important member of the Willamette Cattle Company. Going back to California aboard Lieutenant Slacum's ship, the *Loriot*, Young, in association with P. L. Edwards, bought eight hundred head of cattle and drove them north to the Willamette. This was the beginning of a successful livestock enterprise. Young also built one of the early mills in the Northwest.

While Americans were working up an interest in lands along the Columbia, the Oregon country was under the personal domination of Dr. John McLoughlin. This Hudson's Bay Company chief factor was one of the most remarkable characters in Northwest history. Born in the Province of Quebec to an Irish father and a Scottish mother, he combined the good qualities of both nationalities. He was educated for the practice of medicine in Scotland, but upon his return to Canada he joined the Northwest Fur Company. In 1821 that company was merged with the aggressive Hudson's Bay Company, and in 1824 Dr. McLoughlin was elevated to the rank of chief factor of the Columbia post. In his new position he was able to purchase large annual stocks of furs, preserve much of the fur-bearing range, starve out competition, and discourage agricultural settlers. He located Fort Vancouver six miles up the Columbia above the mouth of the Willamette, and here he ruled as patriarch over a feudal society centered about a trading post, a farm, a mill, a mechanic's shop, and a shipyard. In this empire buried deep in the great woods of the Pacific slope he was indeed "King of Oregon."

Dr. McLoughlin, though king, was a benevolent autocrat. A handsome man with eagle-like features, he was given to tempestuous outbursts of temper of momentary duration. He exerted an almost life-and-death influence over the Indians, keeping them reasonably peaceful and always subjected to his will. When American missionaries came to work with the Indians, he gave them shelter and assistance until they could establish their own bases of operation. He did this even though he realized that they were the forerunners of settlement in Oregon.

Missionary Pioneers

Missionary campaigns in the Northwest had been stimulated by four Flathead Indians who appeared in St. Louis in 1831 seeking spiritual assistance. The facts of their visitation are vague. How they had heard of priests was not entirely clear, but certainly it might have been through Canadian trappers and traders. American trappers like Jedediah Smith were religious men, and they too might have influenced the Indians. This point, however, is of little importance. The fact that the Indians came asking for missionaries gave the preachers and editors of religious journals effective reasons for advocating support of home missions. Both pulpit and journal emphasized the call of the Northwest. New England congregations stirred themselves to meet this new challenge.

First to enter the field were the Methodists. By good fortune two young men with some experience volunteered to carry the gospel to the Columbia. They were Jason and Daniel Lee, uncle and nephew. Jason had seen active missionary service in the British provinces of eastern Canada. After considerable campaigning to raise funds it was possible to start the Lees on their way. They left New York in March, 1833, but in spite of all the excitement of their departure, the congregations had failed to provide them ample funds. On their way to Independence, the Lees preached at every stopping place in order to increase their capital resources. At Independence they were in time to join the pack train of Wyeth and Sublette on its way up the Platte. Three volunteers, Shepard, Walker, and Edwards, joined the Lees. With a small drove of horses and cattle, they set out for Oregon on April 28, 1834, and in mid-September they reached Fort Vancouver.

Dr. John McLoughlin received the missionaries with warm hospitality. He gave them material assistance as they prepared to begin construction of their mission at French Prairie in the Willamette Valley. The *May Dacre*, out from Boston with supplies for Nathaniel Wyeth, also brought materials for the missionaries. Along with livestock loaned by Dr. McLoughlin, these were removed to the site of the new mission. For the next four years Jason Lee and his colleagues labored to raise a roof over their heads, to combat disease, and to preach the Gospel to the natives. They faced many hardships, but their perseverance was a first step toward American occupation of the Oregon country. When he returned home in 1838 to solicit funds to enlarge his missionary services, Jason Lee gave important publicity to this distant frontier.

Methodist monopoly of the Oregon mission field was of short duration. When the Lees were being prepared for their labors, Presbyterian visitors had listened with interest to the discussions. The American Board of Missions of that church was somewhat more deliberate in its reactions, and it was not until 1834 that a decision was made to send missionaries on the trail of Jason and Daniel Lee. Samuel Parker of Massachusetts was the first to volunteer. Later he was joined by Dr. Marcus Whitman of Rushville, New York.

Whitman was an energetic and determined man with an abiding religious zeal. He had trained himself for the practice of medicine, but, like Dr. McLoughlin, had turned to another field. In April, 1835, Parker and Whitman were in Missouri where they joined the American Fur Company pack train which was on its way to the Green River rendezvous. At the head of this party was the French trader Fontenelle who was helpful in introducing Whitman to plains travel. At the rendezvous site, Dr. Whitman found much need for his services as a physician. Jim Bridger had carried an iron arrow imbedded in his shoulder for the last three years, and Whitman removed it. An Indian was suffering from a similar accident, and he too was relieved.

When the Nez Percés and the Flatheads gathered about the rendezvous site, Marcus Whitman got his first notion of what would be involved in missionary work in the Northwest. While Parker and the three volunteers went on to the Columbia, Whitman retraced his steps to New York and Boston, taking two Indian boys with him to give his hearers a better idea of the people with whom the missionaries would work. The Reverend H. H. Spalding and his wife agreed to go to Oregon. In a remarkably short courtship, Whitman married Narcissa Prentice who had earlier volunteered for missionary work. Between upstate New York and St. Louis, two other volunteers, William H. Gray and Miles Goodyear, were added to the party.

Hurrying on to Council Bluffs on the Missouri, the mission party sought to join Thomas Fitzpatrick's party, but in some way the plan miscarried. If Fitzpatrick had willfully passed up Dr. Whitman's party because of the presence of women, he did so without reckoning on the doctor's grim determination. The missionaries hastened on and overtook the traders at the Loup River. Fitzpatrick was not the first to be disturbed over the presence of women going westward. Back East, there was considerable discussion of the cruel folly of women attempting to reach Oregon. Narcissa Whitman was robust and equal to most of the trail hardships, but Eliza Spalding was a delicate neurotic who adapted herself poorly to the primitive life of the trail.

Equally as venturesome as taking the first women over the arduous trail to Oregon was Whitman's stated determination to make the journey all the way in his two wagons. All along the way, Whitman was discouraged from taking his wagons through to the Columbia, and at Fort Boise he was told by Thomas McKay and John McLeod that it was utterly impossible for him to continue his journey on wheels. These men were getting in practice to discourage other emigrants who came that way in wagons. Whitman was successful in getting the wagons to Fort Hall, but there he most reluctantly abandoned one and a half of them; the other half he

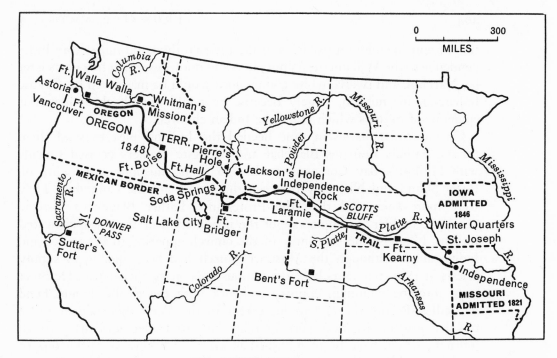

THE OREGON TRAIL

drove as a cart on to Fort Boise. At the latter place the cart was abandoned and the little party continued by pack horse to Fort Vancouver.

Once in Oregon, the Whitmans and Spaldings were kindly received at Fort Vancouver by its famous host; then they were given advice about the founding of their missions. Dr. McLoughlin requested the missionaries not to violate the Hudson's Bay Company rules, especially those setting wage scales. By December the newcomers had located mission sites at Waiilatpu and Lapwaii. The Spaldings were installed at the first, and the Whitmans at the latter. William H. Gray was sent home to seek additional help. He was successful in recruiting three married couples, one bachelor, and a wife.

For six years, Presbyterian missionaries achieved only modest success among the Indians, and even less in maintaining harmony among themselves. Dissension, especially between the Whitmans and Spaldings, marred in time what had been a courageous partnership, and the church undertook to abandon one of its stations. In order to get the Mission Board to rescind this action, Whitman set out for the East in October, 1842. He planned to reach his destination by December, but he had reckoned without knowing that hostile Indians camped across his path, or on the conditions of the late fall weather. He went southward by way of Taos and Bent's Fort, and did not reach Boston until April. By that time the publicity which the Oregon question was receiving in Congress and the press was influencing the formation of annual emigrant parties to make the two thousand miles from Independence to the Willamette. Whitman could not foresee that five years later he, Narcissa, and twelve white companions would be massacred by Cayuse Indians at his mission, largely because he could not check a disastrous epidemic of measles which killed the Indian children.

Catholic missionaries in time heeded the Indians' plea to send them priests. Fathers François Blanchet and Modeste Demers crossed Canada with Hudson's Bay Company traders to found missions at Cowlitz on Puget Sound and Nisqually between the sound and the Columbia. They were more successful than the Protestants. Father Blanchet's historic "Catholic Ladder" example caught the imagination of the unsophisticated Indians. Likewise the pageantry of the church appealed to fur trader and Indian alike. Although the Missouri church had been unable to supply priests in 1831, ten years later the famous missionary Pierre-Jean De Smet went into the mountain country to work with the Flatheads and Pend d'Oreilles. Before the end of his career in the West this diligent priest traveled greater distances perhaps than any fur trader, and his personal journals, which have been published in several editions, comprise one of the important first-hand accounts of the early penetrations of the Oregon country.

Between 1831 and 1842, missionary endeavors had accounted for much of the American activity in Oregon. The missionaries were actually the first Americans to begin the process of permanent settlement. Few fur traders had been able to compete in the Columbia Valley with the highly organized British interests. Early missions were inadequately staffed and equipped, and there was never a dependable enough economic income to insure effective work. Congregations and mission boards in the East were both slow and indifferent in supporting these home missions on the frontier. Personal tensions and conflicts marred much of the work of the various groups. Indians had responded to physical care, but they made almost no response to the white man's religion. Yet the missionaries had helped materially to open the trail to Oregon. Their pleas for assistance had attracted the attention of people who were hard-pressed in the great depression of 1837, and by 1847 the Americanization of Oregon was assured.

Congressional Attitudes

Officially the United States Government took little notice of the country, beyond participating in the treaties and agreements of joint occupation. This was true despite the fact that two major bills were placed before Congress between 1820 and 1843 which attempted to assert American ownership of Oregon. Both of these outlined plans for occupation of the country. The first bill was introduced by John Floyd of Virginia, who for eight years sought its passage. Floyd never saw Oregon, but his enthusiasm for its occupation by Americans was vigorous. After numerous tedious debates the Floyd bill was passed by the House but was defeated in 1828 in the Senate.

After John Floyd had retired to his Virginia home, a second champion of Oregon occupation appeared in Congress, this time in the Senate. Senator Lewis Fields Linn of Missouri introduced a bill proposing occupation of Oregon and the provision of the necessary safety measures to insure safe passage to the country. Like Floyd he was a persistent champion. For the next five years he kept his bill before his colleagues until they passed it in February 3, 1842, but it met defeat in the House.

An analysis of the long and tedious debate on the Oregon question in Congress would indicate that neither Floyd nor Linn met with abject defeat. Their bills, it is true, failed to pass, but both men succeeded in collecting a sizable body of information about the Northwest. They also helped to stir up a good amount of public sentiment in favor of colonizing Oregon. During debate on both bills, petitions reached Congress from groups in several states advocating construction of the necessary forts and highways to permit safe and reasonably easy passage to the new country.

John Forsythe, Secretary of War under Tyler, stimulated in part by Hall J. Kelley's writings, sent Lieutenant William A. Slacum out to Oregon in 1836 to determine the truth of charges about Indian slavery and about the domination of the country by the factor of Fort Vancouver, and to make other observations. Slacum arrived at the mouth of the Columbia River in December, 1836. He visited Fort Vancouver and Jason Lee's mission at French Prairie on the Willamette in January, and returned to his ship and departed the country on February 10th. In less than forty days he had completed a rather full tour and had reported his observations to Secretary Forsythe in an able statement. Slacum was enthusiastic about what he saw, and he no doubt had some influence in renewing the agitation for settlement of the Oregon country by Americans.

On the Road to Oregon

Up to 1841 the Oregon country had attracted only missionaries, a few fur traders, and one or two official observers. Few or no individual settlers had overcome the hardships of the long journey through the rugged plains and mountain region to reach the Columbia and Willamette valleys. In May, 1841, however, the first emigrant group was formed at Sapling Grove, Missouri. This early company formed a pattern for those which followed. It was known as the Bidwell-Bartleson party, and consisted of persons primarily interested in going to California to locate homes near the ranch of Dr. John Marsh who had emigrated earlier from Massachusetts. After considerable indecision and frustration, this company was finally organized with sixty-nine men, women, and children, under John Bartleson as captain. Fortunately they were joined by Thomas Fitzpatrick, Father De Smet and his party of missionaries.

After an adventurous journey the company reached Soda Springs on August 10, where it divided itself; precisely half the members went toward California and the other half toward Oregon. At Fort Hall the Oregon travelers abandoned their wagons and continued their journey by pack train. Although this small party of thirty-two persons had little significance in itself, it did make a dramatic beginning for the great migrations of subsequent years to Oregon.

Back of the 1841 emigration were some significant facts. Oregon had been so widely publicized that Americans everywhere looked upon it as a land of great fortune. Nationalists had kept alive the idea that if the United States Government was to extend its territorial claim beyond the Rocky Mountains it had to move quickly or not at all. Possibly one of the most important purposes of Marcus Whitman's journey back East in 1843 was to discuss Britain's growing control in the Northwest with officials in Washington. To the American frontiersmen, the promise of Oregon was bright. Beyond the great plains and the mountains lay a fresh new land of conquest which beckoned to them as had Kentucky and Tennessee to Boone, Clark, Logan, Sevier, Robertson and Henderson. This time the preponderance of population was in their favor. There had been a phenomenal increase in population in all the western states. Ohio, Indiana, Missouri, Arkansas, Kentucky and Tennessee had doubled and tripled their populations. Approximately three million people now lived in these border states, and every decade saw an important increase in numbers. Because of this fact and the fluctuations of economic conditions, the time was ripe for a deeper penetration of the frontier.

To travel the two thousand miles from Independence, Missouri, to the Willamette required enormous courage and human endurance. The trail was rough and often so vague that only an experienced guide could keep a party going in the right direction. So vast was the distance, and so difficult the terrain, that it took unusually good teams of oxen, horses, and mules to endure the constant grind over weeks and months. Wagons were seldom sturdy enough to make the entire journey without major repairs, and individuals became jaded and frustrated. Frequent stream crossings constantly threatened parties with destruction. Even known fording places could be most treacherous because of the constant rise and fall in water levels. Added to these natural physical barriers was danger from buffalo herds. Parties had to be extremely alert to avoid getting caught in the midst of a crushing stampede. Finally there were Indian bands who played havoc with the trains and the morale of travelers.

Dr. Elijah White, sub-Indian agent for Oregon, went out in 1842 with a party of eighteen wagons and 107 persons. This group was made up of tough-minded individualists who adapted themselves poorly to the organization required for efficient crossing of the country. One source of much of the party's constant bickering was the large number of dogs. Characteristic of frontiersmen, every member of the company seems to have brought his dog, and the dog in turn was as quarrelsome and noisy as his master. The animals barked, growled, fought, and ran in and out of the camp, keeping the whole party in an uproar. Almost immediately after the caravan was underway a discussion arose over the disposition of the offending dogs. Some argued that all of them would become rabid when they reached the plains; others were certain their barking and fighting would inform the Indians of the party's approach. A decision was made to kill the dogs, but when the shooting began that ancient frontier threat of "You shoot my dog and I'll shoot you" was heard, and a fair number lived to go on with the company. At Fort Laramie, Thomas Fitzpatrick was employed as a guide, and Lansford W. Hastings continued as captain. At Fort Hall the emigrants were told by the Hudson's Bay Company agent that they could not take their wagons on to Oregon, and they were abandoned. This party reached its destination in September.

White brought Marcus Whitman letters informing him of the decision of the Mission Board back in Boston to abandon one of the stations. It was this information which caused the famous missionary to leave his Walla Walla mission post in the early fall and rush back to Boston on his momentous ride. While Whitman was in the East, the Oregon fever drew a rather large number of emigrants to Independence where they prepared to begin the Oregon journey in May, 1843. This year's migration was of major importance in the history of the American population movement. Oregon had received a considerable amount of publicity in nearly all western newspapers, and in the East an unusually large amount of space was given to a discussion of Oregon. The year before there had been much anticipation of the extension of the American boundary on westward to the Pacific Coast by the Webster-Ashburton Treaty. Oregon partisans were disappointed when this agreement remained silent on the extreme western part of the northern boundary.

J. M. Shively, an immigration agent, was in Washington during the winter of 1842, and his reports had helped to increase excitement over the possibilities of American extension in Oregon. When Senator Linn again promoted his bill in the Senate, interest in the Northwest was greatly stimulated. All this, plus reactions to many private and national problems, caused a small army of prospective settlers to converge upon the rendezvous site to join the caravan of that summer. Emigrants came from all the old frontier states. Virginians, Kentuckians, Tennesseans, Hoosiers, Suckers, Missourians and Yankees were present. From the geographical backgrounds of many of these people came the story of the western movement to 1840.

Gathered around the camp fires were 120 wagons, almost 900 people and 5,000 head of cattle. The wagons were heavy canvas-covered Conestogas drawn by two to six yokes of oxen. On May 20, the party was finally organized, and the journey to Oregon was well underway by the first of June. Peter H. Burnett was elected captain and J. W. Nesmith was made orderly sergeant. To assist these officials, nine councilmen were elected to sit as a combined legislative body and supreme court. Like the wise men of Israel they were entrusted with the responsibility of settling disputes, making camp rules, and dealing with recalcitrants.

Embedded in the emotions of this large band of emigrants were all the jealousies, fears, doubts, and cussedness that give variety to human relations, and before the caravan reached the Willamette Valley, almost one year later, the council was called upon to decide many cases. After eight days' travel Captain Burnett resigned his office in despair. There were too many human complications for him to continue, and William Martin was elected in his place.

One of the most acute problems facing the emigrant band at the outset was the conflict between persons who traveled without cattle and those who drove herds. Certain necessary delays and anxieties accompanied the transportation of the cattle which did not concern those who had only their teams and wagons to manage. At the crossing of the Big Blue River in Kansas the company was divided into two parts. The faster, or "Light Column," of over sixty wagons went on ahead under the command of its own captain, while the slower one, or the "Cow Column," brought up the rear. The sixty wagons in each company were organized into units of four with a sergeant directing their arrangement and movement. At night each company's wagons were drawn into a circle and chained together to form a corral. Cattle herd and teams were turned out to grass under a watch of night herdsmen, a guard was posted about the wagon camp, and travelers went off to sleep with some feeling of security. At four o'clock in the morning reveille aroused the camp, and by seven the company had finished breakfast, wagons were repacked, and teams stood yoked and ready to start. It was important that drivers have their teams ready to move upon the order to start; otherwise they were forced to fall to the rear and eat dust all day. Positions were alternated from day to day. Wagoners who traveled out in front one day moved to the rear for the next three, whence they again advanced to the head of the line.

In 1876 Jesse Applegate, a highly literate pioneer, read a paper before the Oregon Pioneer Association in which he described in pleasant detail the routine of a day's adventure with the "Cow Column." This account has been quoted almost every time the Oregon Trail has been mentioned, and it has become one of the classic reminiscences of American pioneering. For ninety-eight days the two bands of white-topped wagons rolled slowly westward at the rate of thirteen to twenty miles a day. At Fort Hall, 1,288 miles from Independence, the emigrants had the opportunity to reconsider their situation, to re-examine their interest in the West, and to decide whether they wished to go on to Oregon or turn off to California. Also, there was a chance to repair or abandon wagons, to rest teams, and to learn about the road to Walla Walla and Boise.

For more than a thousand miles the human pageant of the Oregon migration stretched itself across the vast stage of the plains and along the Platte. Deaths occurred and bodies of emigrants were left buried beneath heaps of stones; babies were born under wagon canvas; courtships and marriages occurred along the way. Families quarreled with their neighbors over the minor irritations which have always caused dissension among people on the move. Shirkers, rascals, shavers, and prima donnas all showed their hands before the companies were far from Independence. Persons of unknown and untried qualities of leadership soon arose to positions of trust and honor which carried over to the settlements in Oregon.

The great trail was strewn for the first thousand miles with reminders of the folly of many emigrants. Reluctantly, people had left their homes in a settled society for the great unknown in the Northwest. They undertook to transport as many of the fixtures of a residual civilization as their teams could draw. Bedsteads, chests of drawers, iron stoves, boxes of books, and heaps of foodstuffs were dumped along the trail. By the time the caravans reached South Pass many families had discarded almost all their cherished belongings. Wear and tear of travel caused most families to reduce their baggage to the barest essentials of clothing and cooking utensils. Some of the emigrants even discarded the important seeds they were taking along to plant their first crops. More dramatic than the piles of freight dumped along the trail were the skeletons of animals that had died. Whitening piles of bones bore mute testimony to the animal sacrifice in the arduous task of pioneering.

Late in August the two columns of 1843 were temporarily rejoined at Fort Hall. Here the emigrants were given the standard advice by the Hudson's Bay people that it would be inadvisable to take wagons on to the

Columbia. The company agent overlooked the fact that the party was large enough to solve most of the reasonable travel problems with its own resources. There were enough men and boys to permit the organization of a sizable company of sappers and road builders to level rough places, fill up holes, clear away trees, and to locate and improve adequate approaches to stream crossings. Also, it was possible to use all the human and animal resources to effect stream crossings. The presence and advice of Marcus Whitman was a most important factor in encouraging the companies to continue their journey by wagon.

By October the wagon train arrived at the Methodist mission at The Dalles, but not before the emigrants had been victimized by the Indians who repeatedly stole and held horses and oxen for ransoms of clothing. Snow began to fall early that year, and the road between The Dalles and the Willamette Valley presented more obstacles than had the whole route back to Missouri. Supplies ran low. Many families faced starvation and would have starved had Dr. John McLoughlin not sent Hudson's Bay Company supplies to succor them. By spring, 1844, most of the emigrants were south of the Columbia in the Willamette Valley where they claimed farms and began the process of settlement. Many of the newcomers staked off claims in what later became the towns of Salem, Portland, and Oregon City.

The migration of 1843, though not the largest, was the most important of the many mass movements to the Northwest. A major settlement of Americans was made beyond the mountains, and the Oregon Trail was opened throughout its two thousand miles. No longer was there doubt of the possibility of getting through to the Willamette from Fort Hall. In the next few years, new by-passes and cutoffs were discovered which shortened the distance and lightened the burden of travel. Land was cleared, mills were built, stores were established, and supplies were quickly accumulated which erased the threat of starvation which came near defeating the settlers of 1843.

As years passed, heavy wagon wheels ground deeply into the roadway between Independence and Oregon. Hubs rubbed against crowding rock walls in the mountains and left deep channels to mark the way. Names inscribed on Independence Rock, Courthouse Rock, in South Pass and elsewhere comprised a roll call of pioneering. Between 1843 and the appearance of the transcontinental railroads, a vast number of people followed the trail to Oregon in search of new homes and prosperity.

Bringing up the rear of the big migration of 1843 was John C. Frémont and his company of "pathfinders." They traveled as far westward as Soda Springs, where they turned southward to visit the Great Salt Lake. Later this party went on to the Columbia, reaching The Dalles on November fourth. From Oregon, Frémont turned southward to California. Frémont's report of this journey became popular back in the East. Congress had ten thousand copies of it published, but Oregon pioneers who had struggled along the road ahead of his curtained and covered carriage scoffed at his "pathfinder" title.

Expansionism

By 1846, emigrants going to Oregon over the great trail left little doubt in anybody's mind that the Americans would claim the country. Soon, thousands of settlers had arrived beyond the mountains, and every year the trail from Missouri dumped a new crop onto Oregon soil. The British fur trade and the Hudson's Bay Company could not withstand this horde which came into the Northwest bringing axes, mills, wives, milkcows, and local laws. The notion was fixed in the minds of the settlers that they served a national destiny which had spurred their forbears to trudge through Cumberland Gap, to cross the Ohio, and to settle two tiers of new states. These new men of manifest destiny were able to exert some pressure in Washington if not by direct political influence, then by playing heavily upon the emotions of anxious politicians who were already inclined toward annexation of the Northwest.

In 1846 Representative Kennedy of Indiana boasted that the American multiplication table would solve the international aspects of the Oregon question. At that time five thousand Americans were settled in the region south of the Columbia, and each year's emigration season saw their ranks increased. Oregon fever, which became intense as early as 1841, continued to draw settlers westward for many years. By 1844 the issue of Oregon's northern boundary stirred ardent proponents of national expansion in the Northwest to coin one of the most effective jingoistic slogans in American history. "Fifty-four Forty or Fight!" and "Reoccupation of Oregon and annexation of Texas!" were highly euphonious campaign slogans which combined the nationalistic scream of the eagle with the wail of the panther. Democrats used these slogans to good effect in stampeding their partisans to the polls to elect James Knox Polk of Tennessee President of the United States. Henry Clay, the old jingoist of 1812, was defeated. It is doubtful if an important percentage of the electorate that screamed the famous Democratic battle cry knew specifically the location of the Oregon country. Their emotions were aroused by a distaste of British occupation of American soil and by the fact that there was a possibility of surrender of territory where the eagle had soared and the flag had waved.

Like the issues leading up to the War of 1812, the orators had an issue on which they could loose a thunderous tirade, adorned with all the expansive figures of speech they could create. The political tenor of the campaign was expansionist to the hilt, but it likewise involved a strong element of international rivalry. Britain might be a threat, especially in light of the unstable condition of Mexico. When Polk came to office on March 5, 1845, he delivered an unusually short inaugural address, but not an unimportant one. He seized the opportunity to give the tail of the British lion a sharp and painful twist in the course of declaring formal Presidential policy. After commenting on the annexation of Texas he turned to a discussion of Oregon. He declared:

> Nor will it become in a less degree my duty to assert and maintain by all constitutional means the right of the United States to the portion of our territory which lies beyond the Rocky Mountains. Our title to the country of Oregon is "clear and unquestionable," and already are our people preparing to perfect that title by occupying it with their wives and children. . . . Our people, increasing to many millions, have filled the eastern valley of the Mississippi, adventurously ascended the Missouri to its head springs, and are already engaged in establishing the blessings of self-government in valleys of which the rivers flow to the Pacific.

No stump speaker in the land had made the eagle scream more shrilly. This utterance aroused the British press, and the next twelve months witnessed a contest between American and British nationalists.

In his first annual message to Congress, President Polk reviewed at length the administration's attitude and views on the Oregon question. He traced the steps by which the Convention of 1827 had been made and admonished the legislators not to violate it, but he made clear the fact that the United States would not accept the compromise proposal which had been made by the British minister plenipotentiary Richard Pakenham. He suggested that the 49th parallel be followed from the divide of the mountains to the Columbia, and the river from that point to the sea. Twice already the United States had proposed the 49th parallel, which would extend across Vancouver Island, but the British government had rejected the compromise. Polk now made it clear that the Americans would not accept the Pakenham solution. He lashed out at the British Government and the Hudson's Bay Company, criticizing them for their trade monopoly and relations with the Indians.

Polk spoke with knowledge of the expansion of the American population south of the Columbia and of the fact that already a local self-government was functioning. Although the people in the region lacked the protection of the United States Government, he said

... they have multiplied, and their number is rapidly increasing in the territory. They have made no appeal to arms, but have peacefully fortified themselves in their new homes by adoption of republican institutions for themselves, furnishing another example of the truth that self-government is inherent in the American breast and must prevail. It is due them that they should embrace and protect our laws.

He then advised Congress that within a year it should consider ending the convention of joint occupation.

After considerable debate and diplomatic maneuvering, Britain offered to compromise on the 49th parallel all the way to the Strait of Juan de Fuca, retaining all of Vancouver Island. Polk had expressed himself as being opposed to this proposal, but fortunately he appealed to the Senate for advice prior to treaty agreement, and on June 15, 1846, the compromise treaty drafted by Secretary of State James Buchanan and the British minister Pakenham was signed. Polk remained true to the Fifty-four Forty proposition, but the Senate, after only two days' debate, resolved the Oregon question by saving a large block of territory north of the Columbia as well as a lot of political face for the administration.

Oregon Territory

Five years before the Oregon treaty was signed, the preliminary stages of organization of local government were developing. Political beginnings on the Pacific Coast varied little from those in the old Northwest Territory. When enough people arrived to create a social and political need for government, one was organized. Back of political beginnings in Oregon was a feeling that officials of the Hudson's Bay Company would oppose the Americans, and that the missionaries might attempt to monopolize the administration of local affairs. Also, there was the issue of land distribution, with some guarantees of the sanctity of land titles, and the need for regulation and protection of local trade. Early settlers, as well as those who came later, hoped that the United States Government would intervene in their behalf. Much of the discussion on this topic, however, was provoked less by recognition of the fundamental need than by the spirit of nationalism.

On February 15, 1841, Ewing Young, the companion of Hall J. Kelley on his journey northward from California to Oregon, died intestate. The week before his death an informal meeting had been held to discuss the necessity of a local government. Young's passing then created an urgent need for a probate authority. He had owned a large amount of land, a mill, and a large herd of cattle. A second meeting was held the day after Young's funeral, February 18, 1841, and a special committee was formed to draft a plan of government with Father Blanchet as chairman.

The Blanchet committee did nothing. The chairman was unsympathetic to the idea of organizing a new government, and he was influenced by Dr. McLoughlin. Two years passed without major action, and in the meantime immigrants in appreciable numbers were arriving in the American settlements. The Company lost influence almost in proportion to the arrival of the immigrant trains, and it became increasingly clear that no one could any longer delay the organization of government. The old frontier problem of protecting range livestock from "varmints" provoked two so-called "wolf meetings" in February and March, 1843. At later sessions, a scale of wolf bounties was set, and a proposed assessment of five dollars was to be levied against the settlers.

A series of meetings followed the wolf sessions, and by midsummer, 1843, the establishment of a government was assured. James O'Neal came prepared for political action, bringing in his baggage copies of the Northwest Ordinance and the Iowa *Statutes*. These documents formed the basis for the law of the Oregon country. The antislavery provision of the Northwest Ordinance was adopted. Land and marriage laws were passed, and soon the assembly was forced to consider that most ticklish of all frontier responsibilities, the levying of taxes. As the great trail emptied its annual burden of immigrants, the temporary government grew in strength. Counties came into existence with marked rapidity. The established frontier pattern of local government prevailed in Oregon long before Congress could be persuaded to cease debating the Oregon question and to supply the necessary protection for the settlers. Subsequent meetings not only reflected all the previous discussions but also the newer phases of frontier political expansion. The various legislative sessions were largely discussion meetings at which the realistic needs of the moment were analyzed and plans were made for the future. By July, 1845, settlement and political demands had advanced far enough to necessitate a sharp revision of the informal statute laws which had accumulated. At the same time a fresh plea was made to Congress for assistance.

After the treaty of 1846 was signed, Congress discussed the desirability of creating a territorial government in Oregon. A bill was introduced in the House in January, 1846, but it was immediately involved with the slavery issue. Led by John C. Calhoun of South Carolina, proslavery Congressmen demanded abrogation of the antislavery clause written into the provisional statutes of Oregon. The ensuing debate resulted in the tabling of the territorial bill. It came at a time when both slavery and pending war with Mexico were hot issues. The Northwest had to begin again the process of memorializing Congress to create a new territorial government.

When the Oregon Bill was introduced anew in June, 1848, the proslavery representatives again attacked it. In the debates which followed sectional animosities were pronounced, and the struggle became a three-cornered one with southerners opposing midwesterners and easterners. On August 2, 1848, the House passed the bill, and ten days later it was given senatorial approval. On August 13, the Oregon Territory came into existence, thus ending a long and complex campaign, first against international competitors and then against proslavery opponents. Its power broken, the Hudson's Bay Company moved its base of operation from Fort Vancouver to Vancouver Island. In the Columbia Valley, where American immigrants were multiplying as rapidly as wagon trains could deliver them from the older settlements, Manifest Destiny was asserting itself in its most tenacious manner.

Frontier society had jumped two thousand miles across country only to re-establish itself. A woods civilization from the Mississippi Valley passed over the plains country to settle in a woods environment beyond the Rocky Mountains. Grinding slowly over the arduous trail from Independence to the Willamette, settlers lost little or nothing of their old culture patterns. Their experiences differed little if any from those of pioneers who drifted down the Ohio in flatboats in the last quarter of the eighteenth century, or struggled overland through Cumberland Gap. Conditions in Oregon were ideal for planting a frontier society. Land and fauna were not radically different from those on the old frontier. Farming quickly became a comfortable way of life, and a prosperous economic society came into existence.

THE LONG ARM
OF MANIFEST DESTINY

To-night we had no shelter, but we made a large fire around the trunk of one of the huge pines; and covering the snow with small boughs, on which we spread our blankets, soon made ourselves comfortable. The night was very bright and clear, though the thermometer was only at 10°. A strong wind, which sprang up at sundown, made it intensely cold; and this was one of the bitterest nights during the journey.

Two Indians joined our party here; and one of them, an old man, immediately began to harrangue us, saying that ourselves and animals would perish in the snow; and that if we would go back, he would show us another and a better way across the mountain. He spoke in a very loud voice, and there was a singular repetition of phrases and arrangement of words, which rendered his speech striking, and not unmusical.

We had now begun to understand some words, and, with the aid of signs, easily comprehended the old man's simple ideas. "Rock upon rock—rock upon rock—snow upon snow—snow upon snow," said he; "even if you get over the snow, you will not be able to get down from the mountains." He made us the sign of precipices, and showed us how the feet of the horses would slip, and throw them off the narrow trails which led along their sides. Our Chinook, who comprehended even more readily than ourselves, and believed our situation hopeless, covered his head with his blanket, and began to weep and lament. "I wanted to see whites," said he; "I came away from my own people to see whites, and I wouldn't care to die among them; but here"—and he looked around into the cold night and gloomy forest; and, drawing his blanket over his head, began to lament.

Seated around the tree, the fire illuminating the rocks and the tall bolls of the pines around about, and the old Indian haranguing, we presented a group of very serious faces.

—JOHN C. FRÉMONT, *Report of the Exploring Expedition*
to the Rocky Mountains in the year 1842

"MOVING CAMP," FROM FRÉMONT'S *Memoirs*

CHAPTER XXI

UNLIKE Oregon, California was not the object of publicity and national concern during its early history. A remarkably small number of Americans had reached the Pacific Coast in this area; there was also a Spanish-speaking population spread over much of the region. Unlike Oregon, California was clearly a part of another country; first Spain and then Mexico. Yet the lack of legal claims to the region, as in the case of Oregon, did not reduce American anxiety over its ultimate conquest and possession.

The Spanish Frontier

Spanish history in California dates back to the second quarter of the sixteenth century and the explorations of Hernando Cortez. For approximately 170 years the Spanish, except for a coastal visit by Sir Francis Drake in 1579, were the sole explorers of California. Parties of Spanish adventurers sailed up the coast, establishing footholds at San Diego, Monterey, San Francisco and other coastal points. Subsequent expeditions

507

pushed inland across the arid desert stretches and up from that long tongue of land, Baja California. These early visitors made contacts with the Indians, and in time, missionary priests entered the area. Although there are many stories of individual endeavors, the earliest missionaries enjoyed little more success than the first explorers. It was not until the latter half of the eighteenth century that the missionaries were able to establish themselves within the region. The Jesuits led the way northward. Later the field of labor was divided among the several Catholic orders, and the pattern of missions was determined by the perseverance and ingenuity of the various groups. It took almost three quarters of a century to get the Spanish movement into California well underway.

José de Gálvez seems to have supplied the early enthusiasm and personal leadership necessary to begin a businesslike exploitation of the northern country. Until the end of the eighteenth century Spaniards struggled for the land against both Indians and nature. The history of this struggle is colored by the roles played by a small army of church and civil leaders, by periods of near starvation and by conflict with the Indians. Five missions were established in Alta California by 1773, and others were planned. These early missions suffered all the hardships and frustrations of pioneering in a country where the supply of foodstuffs was uncertain and the resistance of the natives was strong. Soon after the turn of the century the missions had succeeded in gathering about them slightly more than twenty thousand Indians, but there were as yet no more than fifteen hundred whites in the region.

The story of the missions in California would hardly be complete without specific mention of the role of the famous Franciscan, Junípero Serra. He came north from Mexico City as *presidente* of a group of five missionaries who accompanied the military expedition of Gaspar de Portolá. In the summer of 1769 this tiny band founded the Mission of San Diego, and before Father Serra died he helped to found eight more missions along the California coast. This was a romantic period in California beginnings, and the history of Father Serra himself was to become shrouded in those romantic obscurities which turn men into legends. Aside from the spiritual accomplishments of the Franciscans stated in terms of statistics above, the missionaries were to accumulate a tremendous amount of property and material wealth.

By 1820 the Spanish frontier in California began to show changes. Presidios, pueblos and ranchos appeared alongside the missions. Settlers drifted north with their families and began life all over again on the isolated Pacific Coast. The missions more or less established an economic and social pattern of life for the settlers by their management of land and

Indians. They developed a system of agriculture and domestic manufacture which aided materially in sustaining independent settlements in this Spanish outland. This early mode of life was almost purely agrarian, and there was little competition among the settlers for economic advancement. There was a rather clearly defined stratification of the social structure in which Indians and certain Mexicans fell within the laboring group, while other persons belonged to the *ranchero* class by which little or no physical labor was performed. The pastoral economy which prevailed in most instances permitted large numbers of people to escape the oppression of labor.

Arrival of the small Spanish army helped to bring about the organization of towns and outposts, and to increase the number of nonlandholding settlers. Equally as important was the sense of security offered by the army. Yet it would be easy to overemphasize either the fighting capacity or integrity of the military. In many instances, those first soldiers were almost as much a threat to peace of mind and security as the hostile Indians. A governor was appointed for Alta California in 1770, and in 1776 the *residencia* of Monterey became the home of the governors. In time this city was to become an important center of both official and social affairs. With the establishment of towns, Alta California entered a romantic period in which there was an active provincial social life. Hospitality was freely given with the limited goods available, and life went on at a pleasant pace. There was little or no contact with the outside world before 1810, and a delightful state of isolation prevailed.

Visitors who reached the California coast before the end of the first decade of the nineteenth century were mostly English, Russian, and French sailors and adventurers. In 1835 Richard H. Dana, an American, described the fandangos which he attended in the coastal villages. A great deal of flirting went on at these parties. A favorite trick was for a girl or boy to break an eggshell filled with cologne over the head of the person he or she admired. Another was for a boy to place his hat on the head of a girl who was dancing; if the girl kept the hat on, it was a sign that she would accept the boy as a companion. Cockfights drew crowds in the streets and patios. Dandies dressed up in fancy Spanish-type clothes, rode and strutted about to the delight of their womenfolk, who, not to be outdone, themselves dressed in high style. The industrious Yankee lad, Dana, thought the native Californians an idle thriftless people who would never make anything of themselves. Instead of converting their own resources into useful commodities they chose to buy goods elsewhere.

The Mexican revolution of 1821 made little difference in the general pattern of life in the northern province. Governors changed administrations with great frequency, but these political changes had little bearing on the course of everyday life. By 1844 the mission period had virtually ended. For its possession California was suspended between its own political unrest and instability and international rivalries.

The American Trade

From 1790, foreigners had appeared in California in ever-increasing numbers. They came aboard sailing vessels trading with the Orient, or they came seeking sea otter and seal skins along the coast. English, Russian, and Yankee traders competed for the coastal trade. Possibilities of riches from this trade had been advertised in China at an early period by the *Manila Galleon* which had carried rich cargoes of furs to the East. Robert Gray of Boston and other American traders had visited the Pacific Coast before 1800. After that date New England merchantmen landed on the western coast with pleas that they be allowed to restock their casks with fresh water, to tilt their vessels and scrape the hulls, to make repairs, to take on fresh stocks of food supplies, or to give the ill an opportunity to recuperate.

Otter skins, hides, and tallow lured trading vessels to California. From 1790 on, American, Russian, and British vessels were attracted to the coast by the availability of otter skins which were sold in the China trade at large profits. The otter also yielded a highly salable oil. The trade in otters, however, was seriously limited because a steady supply could not be maintained. Between 1790 and 1820, traders and trappers virtually destroyed the otter and also the seals that came to the California islands.

Almost from the beginning of the mission period there was a large supply of cowhides, tallow, pickled beef, hair, and bones. Vessels landing in the ports near the missions gathered cargoes of these commodities to be traded along the South American coast. In 1823 Hugh McCulloch and William Edward Petty Hartnell, agents for John Begg and Company of Lima, Peru, entered into a three-year contract by which they would buy hides, tallow, wheat, suet, lard and pickled beef from the missions at a scale of prices arranged in that year. Being without serious competition, these traders virtually set their own prices and expected a profitable market for a long enough period to increase the number of their trading vessels and to make fortunes. This trade, however, did not remain a noncompetitive one, and the economic history of California after 1823 was colored by the attempts of other shipmasters and traders to buy produce outside the McCullough and Hartnell contract.

Yankee shipmasters from Boston were unwilling to allow the California market to go by default. Not only could they pick up rich cargoes of hides for the boot and shoe factories of New England, but there were customers on every hand for Yankee notions. Ships that went around Cape

Horn carried everything the easterners had to sell. Richard H. Dana described the cargo of the *Pilgrim* as an assorted one:

> That is, it consisted of everything under the sun. We had spirits of all kinds (sold by the cask), teas, coffee, sugars, spices, raisins, molasses, hard-ware, crockery-ware, tin-ware, cutlery, clothing of all kinds, boots and shoes from Lynn, calicoes and cottons from Lowell, crapes, silks; also, shawls, scarfs, necklaces, jewelry, and combs for the ladies; furniture; and in fact everything that can be imagined, from Chinese fire-works to English cart-wheels of which we had a dozen pairs with their iron rims on.

Voyages and Explorers

While sea-borne Americans landed their ships along the coast, others were finding their way across desert and mountain. Those who traveled overland learned of the staggering distance to California the hard way. But it was not distance alone that helped to delay American overland penetration. There was no well-worn trail leading across the mountains to California. The adventurer who set out to visit the Pacific Coast had not only to find his way over a wide gulf of unexplored territory, but he had also to thread his way through a baffling maze of mountain passes and to cross long stretches of arid desert. On top of this, he had to be ever alert for Indians who resisted the early visitations.

Before 1850 American explorers and emigrants were poorly equipped to endure the hardships of the desert trail without suffering. Jedediah Smith penetrated the far western mountain barrier by 1826, and in 1833 Joseph Reddeford Walker traveled over different routes to reach California. James Ohio Pattie and several companions entered the region from Santa Fe. These traders left the West Coast after short visits, and, aside from their trailbreaking, had little influence on the region.

Among the first Americans to settle in California were Isaac Graham, of Kentucky, a trader and distiller, William A. Gale, John R. Cooper, Abel Stearns, Thomas O. Larkin, John Marsh, and Ewing Young. Most of these reached California before 1830, and some of them adapted themselves to the Spanish-Mexican way of life, even marrying Mexican wives. Larkin went to California in 1831 as a private trader and as consular agent for the United States. Abel Stearns, a Massachusetts Yankee, reached the West Coast by way of Mexico in 1829. He had secured Mexican citizenship in 1826, and his passage to California was without restriction. Stearns settled in Los Angeles where he engaged in the coastal trade in hides and liquor. In time he was to become one of the richest men on the coast. When the first California constitution was drafted, he was a member of the convention.

John Marsh, another Massachusetts Yankee and a graduate of Harvard, followed the fur trading frontier out to Minnesota, then to St. Louis and Santa Fe. In 1836 he arrived in Los Angeles. By the time this wandering trader had established himself on the Pacific Coast, it was clear that American frontier expansion would eventually overrun the continent. As the volume of trade increased, so did the number of American vessels stopping along the coast. Ship crews and merchants spread the news of California far and wide. John Marsh was an effective promotional agent. The letters he sent back East did much to stimulate interest in migration to the sunny climate of California.

Four years after John Marsh arrived in California, John Sutter brought his erratic wanderings to a close on the bank of the American River. He had come on a roundabout journey from Switzerland by way of New York, Saint Louis, Santa Fe, Oregon, and the Sandwich Islands. Following the established California pattern of life, Sutter soon established a ranching empire on which he came near establishing a self-contained society and economy. His ranch in time became an idyllic establishment where the free and easy way of life prevailed. In 1840 when this Swiss immigrant began to develop his grant, there were fewer than five hundred non-Mexicans in California, and a local prophet might reasonably have predicted at that moment that any considerable American invasion was still a long time off.

By 1840 there was a tremendous interest along the American frontier in new western lands, no matter how far away they might be located. American settlers approaching the treeless country of the plains were not yet conditioned to make settlement there. Excitement over Texas and Oregon had served momentarily to deflect attention away from the borderland immediately beyond the timberline. The highly-charged nationalistic campaign in Congress and elsewhere brought the Pacific Coast to the front of the public mind. Fur-trading trailbreakers had carried countless yarns of the mountains and coastal West to the frontier and to the more heavily populated Atlantic coastal region. Merchants and ships' crews spread the word about California in Boston and New York. The rich land and the romantic and easy way of life they described contrasted sharply with the workaday world of the Yankee. The climate, the agricultural and animal resources, acres of land and romance were the returned California visitor's oral stock in trade.

Most literate of all the returning voyagers was Richard Henry Dana. Because of serious eye trouble, Dana had left the classrooms of Harvard in August, 1834, to labor on the deck of the Yankee ship *Pilgrim* sailing around the Horn to California. Two years later he sailed home aboard the *Alert* after having had many adventures in the California hide and tallow trade. In 1840 he published his highly interesting book, *Two Years Before the Mast.* He had seen many things—the azure waters of the Pacific, the green coast of California, the life of the natives. He had felt a ship roll under his feet loaded with thousands of hides and hundreds of bags of tallow. He had lived in the coastal hide houses amidst the terrible odors of stinking hides. He was a commercial Ulysses coming home. His book enjoyed immediate popularity and has become one of the classic American adventure narratives. While it is difficult to say what effect such a book had in stimulating migration to California, certainly it was a factor. Far less reliable, but almost as widely read, were the various accounts of the West by Thomas Jefferson Farnham which advertised both Oregon and California.

In the beginning of that expansive decade of 1840–1850, the United States was getting its second wind. Its growth had been fast and furious, with great expansion of population and economic activities. A decade of wild megalomania, limited only by the lack of highly colored words to describe the hopes of the country, had produced the depression of 1837— a sobering jolt which had its frightening effects upon the American mind. Those individuals who had expended their personal credit beyond the point of sense and safety had been left bankrupt and hopeless. Persons just beginning their economic careers were tempted to move on to areas where an uncertain credit system and a deep-rooted competition did not prevail. On the less tangible side of the ledger was the pull of romance and adventure.

The California Trail

One of California's earliest advertising artists was the St. Louis trader, Antoine Roubidoux. This exuberant American engaged in the Taos trade at an early date, and he shuttled back and forth between the Southwest and St. Louis. He is credited with telling such wonderful stories of California's climate and fertility to a group of Missourians from Platte County that he influenced them to organize the Western Emigration Society. Capitalizing on the Oregon emigration fever which was developing, they did not find it hard to convince emigrants that life would be more pleasant on the Pacific Coast than in the flatlands of Illinois or the ague-ridden bottoms of Missouri. Viewed through that ever deceptive and rose-colored vista of distance, the American backwoodsmen could not see the realities of travel drudgery and danger. Ahead of the California-bound emigrant on the trail was conflict with Indians, the cruelty of terrain and climate, and the dirt and backwardness of life on the Coast, even though the sun did shine much of the year. Using the information supplied by Roubidoux and the letters of John Marsh, promoters of the Western Emigration Society extended its efforts widely by use of the mails and the press.

Plans were made for a party of five hundred to leave Sapling Grove, Missouri, in May, 1841, to seek lands in malaria-free California. A counter-propaganda blast by merchants and others, however, thwarted the scheme. In May, instead of a roistering band of five hundred settlers milling about the rendezvous point, only an uncertain company of sixty-four members assembled to take the trail. This company became the Bidwell-Bartleson party mentioned earlier in connection with the Oregon Trail. John Bidwell had emigrated from New York to Ohio by way of Pennsylvania. In Missouri he supported himself as a school teacher. Still a minor, he was unable to hold onto his land claim against a Missouri claim jumper. He was active in helping to organize and get underway the emigrant party that bore his name. This party was improperly equipped and organized for such an arduous journey, and the arbitrary John Bartleson was an incompetent leader. At Soda Springs thirty-two members of the party, including Mrs. Benjamin Kelsey and her young daughter, turned southwestward toward California. Hudson's Bay Company traders gave the group vague directions not to go too far south nor too far north, but to strike a middle course. They could identify no dependable landmarks that would indicate the most satisfactory route.

The Bidwell-Bartleson journey over the trail to the Pacific was a repetition of Smith's and Walker's experiences and prefaces the struggles of other emigrants. They had to abandon their wagons, and the animals which they did not lose or consume were little more than walking skeletons. So desperate did the party become for food that when one of them shot a coyote its carcass supplied a feast. As Bidwell said:

> As for myself, I was unfortunate, being among those in the rear and not aware of the feast in advance. I did not reach it in time to get any of the coyote except the lights and windpipe. Longing for fat meat and willing to eat anything but poor mule meat and seeing a little fat on the windpipe of the coyote, I threw it on the coals to warm it and greedily envoured [sic.] it.

Fortunately young Bidwell's party survived the crossing of the mountains and reached John Marsh's ranch. There are conflicting stories of Marsh's reception of the immigrants. In California he had turned doctor on the strength of his Harvard diploma and enjoyed a thriving practice. Some of the newcomers declared him a harsh bargainer with his desperate countrymen, while others called him a hospitable host. This early immigrant party left little or no visible trace of its path to California for subsequent bands to follow, yet its crossing was important as such first

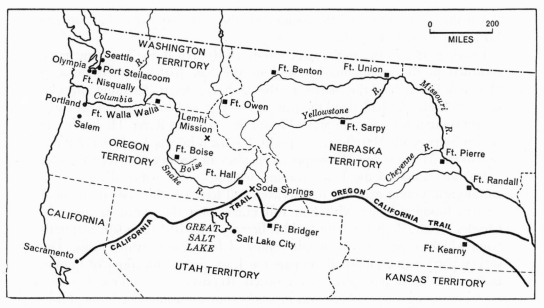

TERRITORIAL ADVANCE IN THE NORTHWEST, 1845–1860

journeys always were on the frontier. The gateway to California was partially opened, and within the next ten years the overland route west was to be established along a course of landmarks after many bitter experiences. Not only was the trail to be opened from Fort Hall to the western slope, but the southern gateway from Santa Fe and the northern one from the Columbia were to be opened. Between 1840 and 1845 there was considerable trader activity in the region, a thing which characterized American penetration of a new territory. Possibly 350 to 400 persons reached California by the overland trail in this five-year period.

One of the most dramatic early visitors was John Charles Frémont. He led his famous second exploring party, burdened with a howitzer, southward from Oregon along the rim of the Cascades and Sierra Nevada to Carson Pass, and then toward the coast and Sutter's Fort during the winter of 1844. This expedition was part of the Frémont saga of the West. He had gathered about him a company of hardy able men, among them, Charles Preuss, the highly capable German draftsman, Thomas Fitzpatrick, Kit Carson, Alexis Godey, and twenty-one other members, mostly mountain men. The journey to California was a most difficult one, and the party suffered grueling hardships due to the winter weather and the ruggedness of the mountains. Had it not contained so many experienced trailbreakers, the party might have suffered a major tragedy. In mid-January Frémont was at Truckee River where the decision was made to cross the Sierras by way of what was to become known as Carson Pass. After a wild journey down the western face of the mountains, the company arrived at Sutter's Fort early in March.

Leaving Sutter's late in the same month of its arrival, the Frémont party returned to the mountains by way of the San Joaquin, then through Walker's Pass across the Sierras to the Mohave Desert. Crossing the vast desert wastelands challenged the party's courage and endurance. Frémont's return route was by way of Santa Fe and the Arkansas River. He began the return journey on March 22, 1844. On August 6 he was back at the junction of the Missouri and Mississippi rivers after an absence of fifteen months.

Frémont enjoyed the home-coming welcome of a national hero. The enthusiastic young explorer had written full letters to his wife Jessie, and he had brought home with him full notes, plus the excellent maps of Charles Preuss. Both Frémont and his literary wife had abundant materials from which to prepare a readable report of his western wanderings. The survey party had established, on paper at least, precise locations of known landmarks. Many new places were noted. Reports of Frémont's first two explorations were published both in a generous government edition and in a large private printing. This piece of government literature enjoyed an unusually popular demand, and no doubt its pages were important in bringing about westward migration.

The years after 1841 saw various overland parties set out for Oregon and California. Some who started for the latter place changed their minds on the way and followed what they considered the safer route to Oregon. One of the most active early trail leaders was Lansford W. Hastings, who came from Ohio where he had prepared himself after a fashion to practice law. He was ambitious and enthusiastic, but in many instances most irresponsible. There seems to be more than a hint that his hopes for himself in California embraced the formation of a politically independent region in which he would play a central role. In May, 1842, Hastings left Independence, Missouri, with a party of 160 persons bound for Oregon. A year later he organized a company of emigrants in the Willamette Valley bound for California. Cattle drovers pushing northward discouraged some members of this company, but the rest went on southward, arriving on the Sacramento in July. Between this date and early 1846 Hastings was engaged in writing a book on California and in guiding parties overland from Soda Springs. His advice to emigrants was to have a substantial influence on frontiersmen getting ready to go West. Hastings' information was not always reliable. On one occasion in 1846, he advised a route for the Donner party which he had not explored.

Some of the California emigrants reached the West with a minimum amount of hardship and suffering, while others straggled to their destination more dead than alive after battling their way through the mountains. The most unfortunate emigrant band in frontier history was the Donner party which went out to California from Sangamon County, Illinois, in 1846. This company was composed of seventy-one members, including George and Jacob Donner and their families, James Frazier Reed and his family, Patrick Breen and his numerous brood, and others. The Donner party was largely a family affair. Some of the members were men in retirement seeking a more pleasant climate in which to spend their declining years. A classification of the Sangamon emigrants reveals that there were thirty-three children under the age of eighteen, twenty-six men, and twelve women.

The Donners and Reeds were fairly wealthy people, and they were able to equip themselves with good wagons and teams. Likewise they carried along a large amount of money. They left Springfield, Illinois, on April 15, and were at Independence on May 11. Traveling up the Platte River route, they reached Fort Bridger by the middle of July. Before leaving the Oregon Trail, they elected George Donner captain. At the Little Sandy camp, the party found a note from Hastings advising them to use the Hastings' Cutoff, a route which had not been explored. It led from the Great Salt Lake to the sink of the Humboldt River.

Between the Little Sandy and the Sierra Nevada range, the Donner party, already behind schedule, was delayed by one barrier after another. The leaders were not fully conscious of the importance of getting through the mountains before snowfall. They camped too long at places; they missed the trail and lost both time and mileage trying to find the right road out of the maze of mountain valleys. At the mouth of Weber Canyon, for instance, they lost eight days waiting for Lansford Hastings.

The sterile region along the Humboldt gave the party its first serious test. Short of water and grinding wearily through the sand and alkali flats, the emigrants began to experience real trouble. Violence broke out among the members; Frazier Reed killed John Snyder in a sudden explosion of anger. A second member died under suspicious circumstances. By now tragedy had become a traveling companion of the party. At the Truckee Meadows the company stopped too long to rest. By late October they had pushed on to what is now called Donner Lake. Here they met the snow and were forced to go into an emergency winter camp. Inexperienced and panicked by their plight, they allowed their animals to become lost in the snow, and they were unable to prepare the necessary shelter for their safety. Food supplies were almost exhausted, there were not enough clothes to protect bodies against the cold, and only one small log hut, built by a preceding party, was available. Poles, boughs, buffalo robes and meager clothing were used to create sheltered places. Furthermore the whole party could not be brought together. Because of poor organization the group had become so badly divided that it was impossible to be re-united.

In mid-December it was clear that unless help could be secured by some miraculous means everyone would die. Fifteen members of the party set out on a desperation march across the mountains to the settlements beyond. By sheer will power and unbelievable endurance, members of this rapidly dwindling and forlorn band reached an Indian ranch where they were able to start a small relief party back over the trail. The rescuers reached the Donner Lake group and hastened back toward the Sacramento with them. Of the twenty-one moved by this first relief mission, three died on the way. Those unfortunate members left in the mountains faced a grim situation indeed. Relief did not get to them until March 1, 1847. Food was exhausted, hands and feet were frozen, and members of the party had resorted to cannibalism. Only forty-five of the original party survived. The tragic experience of the Donners warned future emigrants that the trail to California was hard. Inexperienced emigrants courted death when they undertook the journey without the services of experienced scouts.

By the time the last pitiful victim of the Donner party had staggered into safety on the Sacramento, California was already in the grip of expansionist politics. The region had been in a state of political unrest for the preceding forty years. It was isolated from the United States and from Mexico. Means of communication with Mexico City were seriously limited. A messenger could go from Monterey by sea to Mazatlán or San Blas. Most often, however, the sea journey was delayed by a call of the ship at the Sandwich Islands. The route overland was treacherous and little used. The most direct route was by way of Sinaloa and Sonora to the Gila River over to the Colorado, and then across the desert to the coast. A third route was by way of Santa Fe over the Los Angeles–Santa Fe Trail.

Under Spanish and Mexican rule, the government of California was never stable or entirely orderly. Much internal upheaval and bickering disturbed the political scene. Such governors as Mariano Chico, José Castro, and Manuel Micheltorena did much to create doubt and fear. There was an inadequate militia on hand which did little more than arouse antagonism to the military. Equipment was almost nonexistent, and forts were badly built and equipped. More than one opportunist dreamed of separating the region from Mexico and establishing a principality in which he might rule as a sovereign.

American Expansionism

This was the situation in California between 1833 and 1848 when out-siders were becoming interested in settlement on the West Coast. The United States, France, and Britain cast covetous eyes upon the rich territory. Since 1806 the United States and Britain had been in active rivalry for the Northwest, or Oregon, coast, and since the War of 1812 Oregon had been the subject of considerable diplomatic correspondence. In a sense rivalry over California was a part of the same pattern. Those persons who agitated for the annexation of Oregon were not averse to claiming California also. A proposal was made on at least one occasion that the two territories be combined in a single republic. Of greater importance was the attitude of the Jackson administration toward California. Andrew Jackson was thoroughly alert to the force of Manifest Destiny, and he undertook unsuccessfully either to purchase the region or to promote its unification with Texas. John Tyler, the Whig expansionist, also sought to add California to the American territory, but internal conditions in both California and Mexico prevented him from doing so.

When James Knox Polk came to office after his famous campaign based on expansionism, he not only proposed the annexation of Oregon, but also the purchase of California. Taking up where Jackson and Tyler left off, his administration dispatched John Slidell on a mission to Mexico City to offer from $15,000,000 to $40,000,000 for the territory. The purpose of Slidell's mission became known, and he failed to get a hearing from either President Herrera, or his successor President Parades. Failing to establish communication with the Mexican government through diplomatic channels, Polk's administration was forced to seek other means of separating California from Mexico.

James Buchanan, Secretary of State, dispatched a message by Lieutenant Archibald H. Gillespie in 1846 to Thomas O. Larkin appointing him the President's confidential agent. Larkin was informed that if a revolution occurred in California, the United States would serve as protector. If a foreign nation attempted to colonize California then the United States would intervene. This was a bold step. It was little short of encouragement for Larkin and other pro-American leaders to foment revolution and to bring about the separation of California from its struggling parent government. This anxiety on the part of the United States was a result of feverish communications from its official observers in California, Mexico City, London, and Paris that both Britain and France looked covetously upon the West Coast. Attempts were made to plant an Irish colony in the region. The Hudson's Bay Company was active in California, even establishing a trading post in San Francisco. British shipping flourished in the California ports, and there was every reason to believe that the English government would take advantage of any opportunity that might present itself to take possession of the territory.

A series of incidents marked American progress toward annexation of California. The first of these was the abortive capture of Monterey by

Commodore Thomas Ap Catesby Jones on October 18, 1842. He had received false information in Callao, Peru, that the United States was at war with Mexico and that Britain would be given control of California. He hastened to Monterey, caught the haphazard garrison completely off guard, and captured the poorly armed fort. When he discovered his error, the Commodore was faced with an awkward situation. He had to restore the fort to Mexican control and apologize to Governor Micheltorena. No doubt it was this incident which had disrupted John Tyler's plans for acquiring California.

The second incident was the Bear Flag Revolt, which grew out of John C. Frémont's third exploring journey. After a dramatic home-coming from his second expedition, Frémont began immediately to plan another journey westward. In May, 1845, he was on his way back to California ostensibly to find a dependable and safe route to the Pacific. He led a party of sixty well-equipped men, including the famous western scouts Kit Carson and Richard Owens. A leisurely journey took the explorers across the plains, and in September Frémont was again in the mountains, but it was not until November and December that the party reached the Sierras. One of Frémont's biographers attributes his delay to the fact that possibly his primary interest was not in exploration but rather in military matters. On December 9, 1845, he stood once again before the doorway of Sutter's Fort on the American River.

During the twelve months after his second arrival in California, Captain Frémont committed at least two acts which have given him a place in California history which is highly controversial. His actions in the West were both confusing and provocative. Had his purpose been merely to explore, he needed to do little more than restock his party, buy new horses and set out either for Oregon or to return eastward over a southern trail. Arriving in California on this second visit, Frémont had rushed ahead. The company was divided, and because of a misunderstanding regarding the place of meeting there was some delay in its reunion. As a result Frémont was for some time in ignorance of the location of the division under Edward M. Kern. As he moved about California, Frémont's reappearance with armed men was questioned.

In early spring he moved through the more heavily settled areas about Santa Cruz and Monterey. This action caused Governor Castro to order him out of California. Frémont resisted by fortifying himself at a place called the Hawk's Peak. After a brief stand at this place, from which a Mexican force of two hundred men turned back without fighting, Frémont began a move that seemed indicative of an intention to leave California.

Issues came quickly to a head between the United States and Mexico. While Frémont lingered along the Sacramento, plans were being pushed to send troops under General Zachary Taylor to the Rio Grande. In the neighborhood of Klamath Lake, Frémont received word that Lieutenant A. H. Gillespie, after delivering his message to Thomas O. Larkin, had letters and messages for him. No one possibly will ever know precisely what the letters and oral messages said in their semi-code form of key words. Frémont turned back on his trail after Gillespie overtook him. He applied to Captain J. B. Montgomery of the warship *Portsmouth* for eight thousand rounds of ammunition, eight thousand percussion caps, and three hundred pounds of powder and lead, with other necessary supplies. Along the American and Sacramento rivers he gathered about him a small revolutionary army of American volunteers who had become disgruntled at Mexican mistreatment and who were afraid that they would be driven out of California as tension continued to rise.

In May, Frémont was on the Bear River not far from Sutter's Fort. As rumors built up and fear of Castro's forces grew, the Americans struck a surprise blow at the Indian villages and drove their occupants to cover. By June, Castro had a force of two hundred Mexicans on the march, and excitement was high among the Americans. The settlers concentrated about Sacramento and in the Sonoma and Napa valleys. Castro's bombastic proclamations gave credence to the American rumors and hastened the moment when they would declare themselves independent. There seems to have been little animosity towards the Americans on the part of the native Californians themselves.

On June 14, 1846, the American revolters declared the birth of the Republic of California and raised a flag carrying on its face a star, a grizzly bear and the legend "Republic of California." Purposes of the revolt and the conditions under which people would live in the new republic were set forth by William Ide four days after the declaration of independence was proclaimed. One of the first acts of the Bear Flag Revolt was the capture of two hundred of General Castro's horses which were being driven from Sonoma to the Santa Clara Valley. But before Frémont could lead this patriot army in further revolutionary exploits, news came that the United States and Mexico were at war. With this changed condition at home, the United States Navy became an active factor in California waters, and military affairs in that region fell into more fully authorized hands than Frémont's.

News that war had been declared against Mexico greatly reduced the significance of the Bear Flag Revolt. During the months in which war was impending, the United States Government had taken care to station a squadron in Mexican waters in position for a rush to California. Between May 17 and July 2, 1846, Commodore John D. Sloat moved up from Mazatlán to Monterey. For some reason he delayed taking possession of southern California for a week, and it was not until July 9 that the American flag appeared at Monterey, Sonoma, and San Francisco. A week later the slow-moving Sloat resigned, and a more energetic officer, Commodore Robert F. Stockton, took his place. Both Sloat and Stockton acted under orders from the Secretary of the Navy and the President, but these orders were vague so far as lines of authority were concerned.

In the meantime, the regular army had become involved in the California revolt. Stephen Watts Kearny had been dispatched to Santa Fe with 1,660 men upon the outbreak of the war. There was little military glory to be won in the struggle for New Mexico. Years of American trade had pretty well weakened any local opposition that might have showed itself. The military government of the region was no challenge for so hard-bitten an officer as Kearny, especially when California offered a field for possible major military operations against the enemy. On September 25, 1846, therefore, Kearny set out for California over the Gila River route with a command of three hundred men.

On the way he met Kit Carson en route to Washington with news of American victories in California and the independence of the territory. Kearny sent two hundred of his men back to Santa Fe and went on to California with the remaining hundred. Kit Carson acted as guide. The Mojave desert took its toll of Kearny's command, and when it arrived in California both men and animals were well-nigh exhausted. At San Pascual, Kearny engaged in battle, disastrously, with a much better mounted and conditioned band of native Californians. Had it not been for the timely assistance of Commodore Stockton he might have suffered complete defeat. When Kearny arrived in San Diego he found the navy in charge and was in the delicate situation, after having been rescued by the rival service, of having to raise the issue of who was in command.

For six months after the arrival of Stockton and Kearny in California, internal revolts continued, the most important of which was one that occurred about Los Angeles on January 13, 1847. The Cahuenga Capitulation ended the armed struggle in southern California; meanwhile Kearny and Stockton were engaged in a bitter dispute over personal precedence.

The conflict between Kearny and Stockton was first of all a part of the ancient rivalry between the two services; but possibly a more important cause was the vague and conflicting orders given the two officers. The dispute reached out and gathered John C. Frémont into its net. There is little doubt that Frémont was an opportunist who sought an easy chance to acquire prestige and glory for himself. Stockton had made him civil governor of California, but Kearny refused to recognize him as such. Frémont, in a fit of temper, aroused the anger of the unrelenting Kearny.

The next few months saw the "governor" involve himself financially and legally in the bitter struggle that followed. When Kearny finally received official confirmation of his orders to take command in California, the feuding between him and his subordinate Frémont had gone so far that the General determined on extreme action.

In June, 1847, Kearny and Frémont set out for the East by way of Fort Hall. At Fort Leavenworth, Frémont was placed under technical arrest and sent on to Washington. As he progressed across the country, the press began to play up the first stories of the conflict between the two men. Few conflicts within the army have received more publicity than did the Kearny-Frémont dispute. Newspapers gave a vast amount of space to both the preliminaries and the court-martial itself. Frémont was charged with insubordination, mutiny, and prejudicial conduct. After a heated trial he was found guilty of the charges, but the final decision was left up to the Polk cabinet. The cabinet was divided over the proper decision, and as a result President Polk accepted the findings of the court-martial, but remitted the penalty—a decision which caused Frémont to resign from the service. Whatever justice or injustice was done in the trial, it had enormous influence in advertising both California and Frémont to the country. Few territories enjoyed so much free publicity as did California in the winter and spring of 1847–1848.

In California, a continuous campaign was underway to bring about the organization of a territorial government. A succession of governors followed Frémont's removal until after the signing of the Treaty of Guadalupe-Hidalgo on February 2, 1848. This agreement transferred the territory of Alta, or Upper, California to the United States. The boundary line was located one marine league south of San Diego, running directly eastward to the Colorado River, and along this stream until it intersected a line leading southward to the Gila River. In return for the diplomatic transfer, the United States agreed to pay $15,000,000 for territory for which it once wished to pay $45,000,000.

Conditions in California demanded organization of a territorial government, and the subsequent discovery of gold made the need even more imperative. A convention, meeting in Monterey in Colton Hall in September, 1849, drafted a state constitution modeled largely upon those of Iowa and New York. The peculiar social and economic features of the region were taken into consideration and were given prominence in the new document. But, because of the enormous increase in population and conditions created by the gold rush, California was destined to have a remarkably short history as a Territory.

Statehood

Desire for statehood was no greater in California than in Washington. President Zachary Taylor was anxious to bring California into the Union because of the need for greater police control of the rapidly expanded gold rush population and the thorny slavery problem. Congress was all but leaderless, and its energies were being sapped by what Jefferson Davis called this most profitless of subjects. California as a state likewise would stabilize the American economic and political position on the West Coast. In the moves which the administration made to accomplish this end, the role of T. Butler King, a Georgia congressman and Presidential agent, remains somewhat mysterious. King and the ranking military officers on the West Coast lent their eloquence and prestige to the cause of statehood which might have triumphed over the territorial alternative even if the administration had not entered the picture. On June 3, 1849, Brevet Major-General Bennet H. Riley, in his capacity as acting governor under the military regime, issued a call for a constitutional convention. Though approximately half the delegates were southerners, a free-state constitution was drafted by mid-October. Ratification followed in November, state officials were elected, and William M. Gwin and John C. Frémont were named United States senators. In Washington admission of California was postponed for months while sectional debaters cleared the way for adoption of the Compromise of 1850. On August 13, and September 7, the House and Senate passed the statehood bill, and on September 9, President Millard Fillmore signed it, admitting California as the thirty-first state.

SALT LAKE CITY, 1853, FROM PIERCY'S *Route From Liverpool to Great Salt Lake Valley*

FROM NAUVOO TO DESERET

FROM NAUVOO
TO DESERET

It is over twenty years since the pioneer band of Mormons, driven off by the persecutions of their neighbors in Illinois and Missouri, and led by Brigham Young, though he was not yet the real head of the church, wandered wildly across the Plains and over the Mountains in search of a new home. Coming out of the last range of the Rocky Mountains, into this beautiful basin, no wonder they had a revelation to stop and plant their banners here. But it was then dry and unfruitful; the summer sun baked the earth; the winter's snows covered it; only by living on roots and coarse herbs and meanest of animals did they survive the first year; only by patient toil, and the introduction of irrigation over their lands, were they able to produce recompensing crops. But a fanatical zeal inspired them; necessity drove them; the will of the master spirit in Young led them; and they established themselves, and sent back for their associates, scattered through the border States of the then West. With these began, too, the overland emigration to California, inspired by the gold discoveries of 1849, and out of the latter, they drew recruits, and better, they got a market for their surplus products. Thus they gained a foothold; thus,—by gold and silver discoveries in territories beyond and around them,—have they largely gained their subsequent growth and wealth. California, Nevada, Idaho and Montana have each in turn contributed to the success of Utah. No industry, living within itself, no mere zeal of religion, no mere lust of flesh could have planted such a state, could have bred such power as centers now in the valley of Salt Lake.

—SAMUEL BOWLES, *Our New West*

526

CHAPTER XXII

BOISTEROUSNESS and vigor were not unknown characteristics of frontier social and religious behavior. Religious mysticism and idyllic communalism have also colored American social development. Just as religion played an important role in Old World and eastern seaboard history, so it did on the frontier.

Elsewhere a brief discussion of religion on the frontier has indicated the forthright approach of many of its practitioners. Backwoods ministers were loud and furious in their attempts to arouse their hearers to high pitches of emotionalism. A common expression used on the frontier to describe the vigorous preachers was that they "tackled their subjects like they were fighting bees." This was true in the 1820's and 1830's, and it continued to be true so long as there was a frontier left. It was in this era of expansionism and emotional, political and religious demonstrations that the Mormon Church had its beginning. Later, it was in a period of territorial expansion and on a rising surge of nationalism that the Mormons proved to be successful trailbreakers and exerted their greatest influence on the frontier.

The churches in America during these fermentative years of the second quarter of the nineteenth century were not entirely oblivious to the evangelical command to go into all the world and preach the Gospel, but the frontiersman's concept of his spiritual responsibilities was more closely attuned to the teachings of the Hebrew fathers. Much of the religious activity on the frontier appeared to be that of a wandering people seeking both godly and economic salvation. The principles, philosophy, and history of the Mormon Church as it was founded and moved across the frontier, except for the importance of missionary activities, were patterned more nearly after the authoritarianism of the Old Testament with emphasis upon the experiences of the Children of Israel than after those of the Christian era and the New Testament.

Joseph Smith

The Mormon prophet, Joseph Smith, fourth of ten children, was born in Sharon, Vermont, in 1805. His family was of old Puritan Colonial stock, and his father and grandfather had participated in the Colonial and Revolutionary wars; but, whatever their military records, they were poor people who casually followed various temporary callings in their attempts to earn livings. They peddled books, farmed, manufactured saltpeter and followed the sea. At times the Smiths were interested in digging for buried treasure. Some of them resorted to "dowsing," or use of a forked peach or willow branch as a divining rod to locate water and hidden treasures. Joseph used a "peep stone" concealed in the crown of his hat for unlocking the secrets of the earth. He went even further and could locate lost articles and answered questions by use of the stone. At fifteen he no longer found it necessary to use his magic stone to have visions. He stated that an angel of the Lord appeared before him and made certain intriguing revelations. When the lad was eighteen (1823) the angel Nephi, or Moroni, appeared and revealed to him the existence of a set of golden plates. But Joseph was not to be given possession of the plates for four years, despite the fact he had already uncovered them at the Hill Cumorah near Manchester, New York. In 1827 he was finally permitted to remove the plates from their subterranean hiding place and begin the task of translating them.

The script on the mysterious plates was strange and unintelligible to the lad, but the angel Moroni had provided a simple method by which it could be read. Buried with the plates was a magic sword and shield, and a pair of fabulous spectacles whose crystal lenses bore the biblical names Urim and Thummim. By girding himself in the shield, placing the sword nearby, and using the spectacles, the Yankee lad was able to translate the strange hieroglyphics inscribed on the plates. Assisting him was Oliver Cowdery, a blacksmith and school teacher who shared Joseph Smith's spiritual powers of being able to read the plates. Unfortunately in an initial effort to arrange publication for the book, the first 116 pages of the text is said to have been lost, and it was necessary to begin publication of the text with page 117. Thus translator and transcriber co-operated to produce the *Book of Mormon*. A fascinating feature of the text of the plates was a history of the American Indians which portrayed them as being descendants of the Hebrews.

The Mormon text has a strong flavor of the King James version of the Old Testament, if not its precise wording. Much of it is historical in nature, colored with some folklore and mysticism. Especially noticeable is the strong authoritarian note which seems to follow in spirit if not in word the philosophy of the Hebrew fathers. To insure a faithful translation, Smith stated that he was in frequent communication with the Angel of God. In this way he was able to clarify many controversial points which arose. By June 11, 1829, the 588 pages of the original *Book of Mormon* were finished. Its contents provoked a skeptical gentile population to loud ridicule and criticism, but the proponents of the new faith were persuasive men, and they were able from the start to win disciples. In answer to the skeptics, testimony of eleven witnesses was published verifying the existence of the golden plates, but the sources on which their testimony was based were a matter of hearsay. Many men had a hand in popularizing the new gospel. Possibly no leader was more successful in organizing this venture into a social community than Sidney Rigdon, a Pennsylvania frontiersman with a burning Calvinistic zeal. His energy, imagination, and organizational ability enabled him to preach the new gospel far and wide.

It is not the purpose of this discussion to examine further the theology of the Mormon religion, although it has been subjected to constant ridicule, defense, criticism, and analysis. This was not the first time a doctrine of specially revealed religion had been preached on the frontier. Baptist ministers had presented the idea since the middle of the eightenth century, and their rivals, the Methodists, had emphasized the personal revelations of a strong and stern personal God. Also, this was not the first religious sect to emphasize the personal appearances of angels, the ancient prophets, the Disciples, and other famous personages. In Ohio and Kentucky the Shakers stirred the derision of skeptical neighbors by their casual statements that they had received spiritual visitations. From the time of Joseph Smith's initial visions on, the historian indeed finds himself limited in his efforts to winnow fact from fancy in the material presented by faithful Latter Day Saints of Jesus Christ. Contemporary writings by both Mormons and non-Mormons are voluminous, but the great mass of this material on both sides is bogged down in prejudices and biases. Such a religious group, basing its origin and plan of administration upon a body of special revelation, could hardly expect to escape critics and humorists on one side, or to produce blind bigots on the other.

Mormonism on the Frontier

The Church of Jesus Christ of the Latter Day Saints began officially on June 6, 1830. Neither New England nor New York, however, proved to be happy places in which to nurture the new church. There was so much skepticism and derision that it could scarcely survive. This appears to have been true even though upstate New York had become in the 1830's a favorite spawning ground for unorthodox social and religious sects. The immediate necessity, and one which was to prevail for the next twenty years, was to find a more tolerant frontier community in which to organize an isolated communal settlement. Joseph Smith said that he envisioned Kirtland, Ohio, in the burned-over country, to be that place. Thus was begun in 1831 a westward movement of the Mormons which in the end was to continue on to the Great Salt Lake Basin in Utah.

The first stop westward was made by the Mormons at Kirtland, but this place proved to be little more than a temporary pause in the congregation's progress to Missouri. In that state the goal was the neighborhood of Independence, and in 1833 the faithful had crossed the Mississippi to their new home. Missouri in the 1830's could hardly be considered an isolated haven for an unorthodox religious colony. Large migrations to this area, as was pointed out earlier, brought to that state a rugged population of literal minded backwoodsmen who could hardly be considered tolerant of new and radical religious and social ideas.

Almost immediately the newcomers were involved with their neighbors. In part this involvement, no doubt, came about because of the communal aspects of Mormonism, which the average American frontiersman, with his sense of casual neighborliness, detested. The faithful further angered their neighbors because of their abolitionist sentiments and closed the door on the possibilities of staying on either in Jackson County or elsewhere in Missouri. Already there were charges of thievery, and it was next to impossible in the areas where the Mormons were in a majority to bring a law suit that got anywhere, because Mormon elders presided over the courts. From Independence, the Mormons moved to the town of Far West, and then to Nauvoo in Illinois. Moving eastward back across the Mississippi from Far West, the Saints settled at Commerce, or Nauvoo, in 1839.

In their new home they began a rather extensive program of expansion. They sought a liberal charter from the Illinois legislature, which in the end was to be their undoing. The charter contained an unrestricted militia clause which gave the Saints an unusually strong police force to employ against their detractors and enemies. Also, they were given control of a local court system which protected members from damages in suits brought by gentiles. Because of this broad protection offered by the Mormon-dominated courts, a great many persons facing trial became Mormon converts and hid behind the special jurisdiction granted by the charter. Joseph Smith and the elders had used considerable political manipulation to accomplish their objectives, and the Illinois legislators gave evidence of being more interested in securing Mormon political support than they were in passing a reasonable legislative program. From the viewpoint of the people of Illinois the Mormon charter gave its people extraordinary privileges, but even more disturbing was the fact that the sect possibly held a political balance of power, and its numbers were growing all the time.

Nauvoo

So far the Mormons had found little peace on the frontier. At the time they left Missouri they were feuding with Governor Lillburn Boggs because he had issued the order driving them from the state. In fact Joseph Smith was deemed little more than a fugitive from justice by the Missouri officials. Many persons regarded the Mormons as organized renegades who would stop at nothing to promote their own objectives. No doubt a generous amount of impudence in Mormon-gentile relations, as well as rumors and counter-rumors, kept the cauldron of local feuding on the boil.

One tangible fact was important in this constant friction. In most of the westward movement, settlers sought land on a competitive basis—even where speculators had operated; but the Mormons sought monopolistic domination of land and property. As a result, already overwrought outsiders were quick to jump to the conclusion that with the rapid expansion of the Nauvoo population, Illinois would soon be under Mormon control. Proselyting activities of the missionaries were fruitful. Immigrants from the eastern states and Europe appeared in droves, and within a remarkably short time Nauvoo promised to become one of the most important population centers in Illinois. With this rapid increase in Mormon population, the military and political potentials of the community were much greater.

With the arrival of new converts, the number of women was greatly increased. Even though there was a divergency in the ratio between men and women on the gentile frontier, there was none in the Mormon communities which received a fairly heavy influx of converts from the Old World. There the more mature population pattern of Europe rather than that of the American frontier prevailed. Women possibly were easier to convert to the new religion, and this further accounted for the disparity of the sexes. When additional women arrived in Nauvoo, gossip of the practice of polygamy became more convincing. Joseph Smith was said to have practiced polygamy in secrecy; but not until after January, 1843, and a special divine revelation on the subject, did he publicly advocate it. Such a practice among frontier people, where women were fewer than men, was abhorrent. Few issues could have done more to consolidate public opinion, or to confirm the Illinois backwoodsmen in the belief that the Mormons were essentially immoral people. There was completely lacking in the West a spirit of tolerance which would countenance such a departure from the orthodox system of monogamous marriages.

From a religious point of view there was little fundamental disagreement between gentile and Mormon. Both groups were literal in their interpretations of the Scriptures, and those denominations having strong Calvinistic backgrounds were in essential theological agreement with

Sidney Rigdon's teachings. Where they disagreed most was in the failure of the *Book of Mormon* to take into consideration the broader teachings of the New Testament.

The Mormons exerted an appreciable influence in the field of local politics. While the Saints were not numerous enough to sway an election by their own vote, they did have enough strength to hold a balance of power and possibly could have determined the outcome even of a state campaign. While their neighbors followed the lackadaisical practice of voting if it were convenient, or if they were interested in a particular contest, the Mormons, living under an authoritarian system, not only voted, but they cast their votes as a body and by prior agreement. The granting of their charter with its unusual and liberal terms was stimulated no doubt by this consciousness of the voting strength of the Mormon community. Both Democrats and Whigs sought their support, and in the Presidential elections they switched from one party to another with ease. In 1844 Joseph Smith himself became a candidate for the Presidency of the United States. After 1840 the fear of Mormon domination increased and local public opinion was being brought to the point of militant opposition. A mass meeting of gentiles in 1841 brought the issue out into the open. In this assembly a plan was projected to curb the Saints' powers by modifying their charter.

A year later when ex-Governor Lillburn Boggs of Missouri sought election to the United States Senate, he was shot and wounded by an unknown person. Because of his association with the expulsion of the Mormons from Missouri he and his friends immediately accused Joseph Smith of having instigated the act. Attempts were made to extradite the Mormon leader from Illinois to be tried in the Missouri courts. Whether or not Joseph Smith was guilty of the conspiracy, he stood convicted before the court of public opinion.

Other charges of conspiracy and wrongdoing were made against the members at Nauvoo. Epithets of immorality, treason and counterfeiting were flung at them with abandon, but none more vigorously than that of thievery. It was said that gentiles were losing property and stood little or no chance of recovering it. As pressure increased to drive the Mormons out of Illinois, any kind of story was given credence. When rioting resulted in loss of considerable property, the Mormons adopted a method for dealing with gentiles that was at least suggestive of violence, if not openly violent. When an unwelcome person appeared, a band of whittlers wielding ugly bowie knives followed him about until he left the community. Outsiders were discouraged if they attempted to extend their visits. Rumors of the bowie knives grew into stories of intimidation and threats of violence, and if the gentiles needed further confirmation of their accusations against their obnoxious neighbors, they found it in such mute threats.

From 1840 to 1846 the city of Nauvoo and its inhabitants continued to provoke bitter local animosity. If proselyting, started so effectively by Brigham Young in London in 1841, kept up, the Mormon population would exceed that of the rest of the state, and the people of Illinois ran the risk of being brought under the yoke of an incorporated theocracy in which its powerful and lustful head, Joseph Smith, would rule absolutely. Smith's advocacy of polygamy, however, brought his own community to a point of sharp dissension. It is easy to imagine the resistance that such a doctrine would engender even among the faithful who were definitely conditioned to a monogamous society. Even the Prophet's wife was most reluctant to accept her husband's recent revelation which both publicized and authorized an act which was said to have been practiced hitherto in secrecy. To pious Baptist, Methodist, Disciples of Christ, and Presbyterian neighbors such a thing was highly unacceptable, and to them the practice threatened to destroy the base of society and the home. To have more than one wife, although justified in at least one place in the Scriptures, was to them bestial and immoral.

Among the Saints a schism followed which resulted in the first and only appearance of the *Nauvoo Expositor* on June 7, 1844. As the paper's title indicated, it was an exposé publication which attacked the inner administrative circle of the church for its high-handedness and weakness. Prophet Smith and his brother Hyrum were accused of venality, of embezzlement, and of seducing women. This internal disagreement was to destroy the Nauvoo community. When Joseph Smith ordered the *Expositor* destroyed, he stirred up a mob which regarded the dissolution of the paper as a threat to the Bill of Rights. Governor Thomas Ford was forced to call out several companies of the state militia in an attempt to avert tragedy in Nauvoo. The Governor himself went to the Mormon settlements in an attempt to re-establish peace. Before the major break got underway, Joseph and Hyrum Smith surrendered themselves and were placed in the Carthage jail. The Governor then occupied himself with the task of recovering state arms from the Mormons. Before he could return to Carthage, a mob broke into the jail on June 27, 1844, and shot the Smith brothers to death. Joseph was wounded several times by bullets before he either jumped or was thrown from a window. On the ground his stunned body was propped up and further riddled by gunfire.

Brigham Young

With the death of Joseph Smith the Church of Jesus Christ of Latter Day Saints was left without an immediate head. Several of the more prominent men were absent on missionary journeys or were attending to church business. Brigham Young was in Boston; Parley P. Pratt was in New York; Sidney Rigdon was in Pittsburgh, and other leaders were scattered over the country and Europe. Rushing back to Nauvoo, the elders raised the question of who should assume the new leadership. As head of the twelve apostles, Brigham Young was able to overcome the efforts of Sidney Rigdon to succeed to the presidency of the church.

The elevation of Young to the chief administrative post of the Mormon church brought an unusual man into prominence in American life. Like Joseph Smith, he was a New Englander. By trade he was a glazier, house-painter, carpenter and farmer, but he was essentially a strong-willed leader who could govern men with an iron hand. He may not have been brilliantly imaginative, but he possessed the tireless energy and courage necessary to reorganize his people and to lead them westward to new environmental surroundings. He had the ability to make a new start with a theocratic society supported by an economy that would have destroyed a less able man. His problems were usually solved by use of common sense and shrewd judgment. Unlike the departed Smith, he did not resort to the practice of seeking revelations to meet every issue which arose. Young felt that there were enough revelations to last for a time and that his challenge lay in adjusting those that were already recorded. Death had deified Joseph Smith in the eyes of many members of the Mormon faith, but it also brought much dissension. Some authorities on the subject have observed that too much printed material of a sensational and revealing nature was in circulation for the dead Saint to be regarded as a true martyr. Possibly the antagonism of the gentile press was an even bigger factor in preventing such a thing.

It became clearly evident that the Mormons could not long survive the antagonism which existed in the surrounding counties. The Illinois governor and peace officers were all but helpless in their attempts to maintain law and order. Both Mormons and gentiles had resorted to burning, pillaging, and other crimes. Plainly the Nauvoo community either had to disband the church or move on to a new and isolated settlement. An agreement was reached late in the fall of 1845 that the Mormons would move the following spring. So great was the pressure that the exodus of the faithful was begun before the western rivers and roads were free of ice and snow. Brigham Young led the first band of two thousand across the Mississippi River in sub-zero weather to begin a long and trying journey to a spot of isolation more than halfway across the continent.

The Great Migration

The first major problem to be solved by the Mormons was that of getting as many people as possible away from Nauvoo. A second problem was that of locating way stations where they might stop temporarily. On the first leg of their movement the stations of Sugar Creek and Winter Quarters, just west of the Missouri in present day Nebraska, became famous landmarks. Thrust out of their homes, Mormon families struggled across the Mississippi with little or no provision for their comfort in the cold weather. Babies were born, people died, many suffered severe illnesses, and all survivors were brought near starvation. For Brigham Young the need to relieve the immediate suffering of his people was great, but more fundamental was the matter of deciding where to go. To follow the Oregon Trail to the Northwest would only bring more trouble. Settlers of the same set of mind as the people of Ohio, Missouri and Illinois had already gone on ahead, and to follow them would be to invite trouble. California was still beyond the political limits of this country, and Oregon was involved in the boundary dispute between the United States and Britain. But somewhere in the West was land for settlement where the Saints would be reasonably free of hostile influences. The ideal place to take the Saints was one that had neither settler nor neighbor, where the people could establish their church and communal society without outside interference. Only the wide-spreading territory of the central Far West held the answer about where such a place might be found, for the apostles had not only to avoid prospective neighbors, but they had also to take into consideration the possible attitude of the United States Government.

While the Mormons were having their troubles along the Mississippi, Parley Pratt's New York and eastern converts were confronted with similar difficulties. They were threatened with the problem of being disarmed and prevented from going West. Samuel Brannan wrote Brigham Young that through powerful political support, including Amos Kendall of Jacksonian fame, he had agreed to the organization of a land syndicate. He had agreed to turn over alternate sections of any western lands on which the Mormons might settle to the politicians sponsoring the syndicate for their personal benefit. At the time the fugitives from Nauvoo were crossing the Mississippi, Brannan and 228 immigrants sailed from New York for the Pacific Coast aboard the *Brooklyn*. Later the next year when Brigham Young's pioneer company reached the Rocky Mountains, they met Brannan coming eastward to join them. He had settled his people in California and was returning east to persuade the overland party to go on to California. Possibly one of the greatest drawbacks to the Pacific Coast, in the mind of Brigham Young, was the fear that within the foreseeable future it would come under the American flag. Brannan's immigrants remained in California, however, and were to play a part in subsequent events in that region.

It is not difficult to picture the march of the faithful westward from Sugar Creek, Iowa, in the spring of 1846. Muddy river bottoms and frozen roads, scarcity of food, disease, the usual difficulties of moving families, and the uncertainties for the future all contributed to the discouragement of the band. Young led his people slowly across Iowa to the western banks of the Missouri and established the famous way-station of Winter Quarters (Omaha, Nebraska). Here the Mormon president displayed his administrative ability more than at any time before. He seems to have governed his people with a tight if not autocratic hand. He set men to work at Winter Quarters building semipermanent structures, including a council house and a mill, which would serve immigrants still to come. Brigham Young believed labor was a sure way to keep his people from grumbling and becoming discouraged. Captain Pitt, an English convert, and his brass band accompanied this first company of immigrants, and at night their music stirred the people to mirth. Dances in which all ages participated relieved the tedium of hard conditions and constant association with the same people.

At the time the refugees from Nauvoo were on the march westward, war with Mexico became a certainty, and the Polk administration appealed to the Mormons to supply five hundred men for service. This request reached Brigham Young while he was at Winter Quarters, and he proceeded to organize a regiment of volunteers. They were promised reasonable safety and noncombatant service in California. It is likely that the President of the United States was as anxious to prevent any difficulty in the West caused by the Mormons' supporting the country's enemies as he was to have their services in the army. For the Mormons, the call for volunteers was a godsend. It gave them the soldiers' pay plus other emoluments, and assured a large part of the band safe transportation westward under the aegis of Kearny's army. The greatest drawback was the fact that a large number of ablebodied men who were needed to complete the long and difficult journey which still lay ahead of the band were taken away from the camp.

Early in the spring of 1847 plans were made to begin the trek westward in search of Zion. A call was made for volunteers, and a band of 148 persons was organized. This company left Winter Quarters with 72 wagons, a supply of grain, and enough livestock and implements to begin a farming settlement. Starting their journey on April 14, Brigham Young directed his band up the north fork of the Platte. Traveling at the rate of twenty miles a day, they arrived at South Pass in the latter week of June. Thus far on their journey the pioneers had suffered remarkably few hardships. Few or no wagon trains had moved over this territory under tighter or more efficient administration. The company had been arranged, as had become the practice on the plains, into a semimilitary organization, with various persons made responsible for carrying out orders. Brigham Young was a lieutenant general, and other ranks ran down to wagon captains. Wagons were driven forward in double file where the terrain of the country permitted such a mode of travel. At night they were drawn into a circle in such a manner as to form a corral within and a fortress without. Six days a week the band was called to prayers and work by an early bugle, and at four o'clock each afternoon the train was assembled for the night. There was little or no lack of food, but feed for the animals was dangerously short at times. On the way, there was a good amount of game, especially buffalo, and the streams yielded fish which offered a variety to the diet.

Once in the mountains, some members of the pioneer party contracted spotted, or mountain, fever which added considerably to the difficulties of the journey. Ahead of them the road grew more treacherous. At South Pass the company turned southward by way of Fort Bridger, and then over the Uinta and Wasatch ranges to the Weber valley and the Great Salt Lake. At Fort Bridger the famous mountain man Jim Bridger gave Brigham Young a most discouraging report of the Great Basin country as a place to locate an agricultural settlement. He even offered to wager on the amount of corn that could or could not be grown there.

The Great Salt Lake Country

The first pioneer party to cross the ranges and to reach the plains of the Great Salt Lake was that led by Parley Pratt. This party had gone ahead to explore and mark the way. Pratt and Lorenzo Snow first saw the great valley of the vast inland lake on July 21, and the next day they entered the valley and actually began the work of making a settlement. Behind them, Brigham Young and the rest of the party slowly made their way to the plain. Young was ill with the mountain fever, and he was confined to a bed made in Wolford Woodruff's carriage. When this vehicle was drawn up to Big Mountain lookout on July 24, Young sat up and gazed entranced at the valley. Before him stretched the land on which he and his followers were to plant the most successful theocratic community in American history. Racked with fever and worn by the journey, he turned to his companion and said, "It is enough. This is the right place. Drive on." Later this prosaic statement was shortened into the dramatic utterance, "This is the place!" It was said that Brigham Young knew in advance what the valley looked like because he had seen it in a vision.

The spreading basin was a dramatic place when seen from a high point and far off, but on closer examination the land on its floor was disappointing. There were few trees to be seen, and everywhere there were grasshoppers or crickets. Before field crops could be grown, it was necessary to supply much of the moisture by means of irrigation. This meant damming streams and feeding the soil at regular intervals from ditches. Building materials needed for constructing a fortress and houses, with the exception of clay for adobe, had to be brought from the mountains. But on July 27 Brigham Young and the elders located the site for the temple, and around it they planned a city. Fortunately the early immigrants were equipped with the necessary instruments for making scientific observations and for laying off the lots and streets of the city. Few or no cities in America were so fortunate as to be organized from such efficient plans. Streets were directed north and south or east and west, and blocks were laid off in ten-acre squares, with individual lots of an acre-and-a-quarter in area. The streets were to be 8 rods, or 172 feet wide, and the sidewalks 20 feet wide.

Almost on the halting of the first wagon the planting of crops was begun, and an elementary system of irrigation placed in operation by damming up a creek. Adobe houses were erected, brush arbors or bowers were constructed for temporary meeting places, and the groundwork was begun on the temple. A log fort was erected as protection against a possible Indian attack. The first band of Saints had themselves rebaptized and began in earnest to develop a stable society and economy. But the first years in Utah brought much hardship and privation. One of the biggest immediate problems was that of producing enough food to support the population already there, and yet have some to spare for those people yet to come from Winter Quarters.

The second phase of the removal was almost a regathering of the faithful because so many of them had scattered over the Mississippi Valley searching for employment. Late in August, Brigham Young and Elder Heber Kimball set forth overland eastward to meet the second party which had set out from Winter Quarters late in July, 1847. Profiting by experience in the first overland journey, Brigham Young had a revelation which outlined the plan of organization for the second migration. Parties of 110 wagons were placed under a captain, and efforts were made to move these forward in double columns. Pioneers were sent ahead to establish camp sites and to improve upon the route followed earlier in the year. By early fall this second party was at Salt Lake City.

Brigham Young had gone on to Winter Quarters to help organize the third immigrant party that was to set out in the spring. At this outpost the farmers had profited from their labors. Crops were good and the situation which had been so unpromising in 1846 had become a much happier one. Preparations went on during the winter, and by May, 1848, 2,417 people were ready to take the Zion trail. This third party took with it property of all sorts, including seeds and livestock for breeding which were so necessary in founding a new agrarian economy. On September 20 this company arrived in the new western settlement for a reunion with the original settlers, and to make a new beginning.

Life at the Salt Lake settlement had been strenuous the first winter. Food supplies ran short and the people faced starvation. Flour became as precious as gold, grain was exhausted as feed for livestock, meat supplies were all but consumed, and the population was forced to turn to roots and wild plants for sustenance. Housing, fortunately, was almost adequate for the mild winter. Those families which were unable to move into a cabin remained domiciled in their immigrant wagons until new dewellings could be constructed. Starvation and inadequate shelter were only some of the sufferings endured during the first winter. Wolves, mountain lions and foxes preyed upon the supplies and animals of the settlement. Swarms of desert mice flocked into the cabins and played havoc with stored supplies and human peace of mind. Efforts were made to trap and destroy these pests; at times it was said that families scarcely dared go to bed before they had driven the mice out of the houses. Walls of the cabins were heavily infested with bedbugs which dug into the logs and cracks to await darkness and the coming of their human victims. To top off these woes there were the diseases which appeared during the winter; measles especially took a heavy toll of life.

In spite of troubles and inconveniences, work went steadily ahead in the building of the mills and necessary facilities for grinding grain and preparing textiles for human use. Large fields were planted to grain in the early spring, and because of a favorable amount of rainfall, crop prospects were good. These hopes, however, were premature. While grain was heavy in head in May, there appeared swarms of crickets that all but darkened the sky. This roaring menace settled on the heads of wheat and stripped them almost instantaneously. Men, women and children battled against this voracious scourge with flail, open ditch, prayer, and fire—almost to no avail. Some of the insects settled in the great Salt Lake and were drowned, but these losses hardly dinted the ranks of those feeding on the crops. In the darkest moment of desperation, according to tradition, gulls swarmed in from islands of the lake and ate the crickets and helped save a good portion of the crop of 1848.

Before the year ended the population of the Mormon settlement was materially increased, and the hardships of the previous winter again threatened. Both housing and food were short, and the winter season grew most bitter with temperatures going below zero. It was necessary to make greater efforts to supply housing for the newly arrived immigrants and to get on with the task of building the city. City lots, streets, and common properties were being improved. Mills, mechanics' shops, common granaries and all other necessary community facilities were built. Outside, a vast acreage of ground was placed in the hands of individual claimants. A significant feature of the Mormon settlement in the Salt Lake Valley was the land held in common under the administration of the president and elders. This latter feature gave the central organization a control over the economy of the colony and at the same time made provisions for the storing in and distribution of goods from a common storehouse. As time passed, the common feature of control of the facilities continued in the construction and regulation of irrigation ditches. From the beginning of agricultural activities, irrigation was a necessity, and as farms were expanded, new irrigation lakes and ditches were constructed. Lateral ditches were the property of the individual, but the arterial streams, reservoirs and dams were held by the community. In the cases where farmers were unable to build ditches leading into their own lands because of major difficulties, group workings were instituted to overcome such handicaps. In their program of irrigation which was greatly expanded in the future years, Mormon farmers made a considerable contribution to the conquest of the arid lands of the West. This was, in fact, largely the beginning of successful reclamation of dry lands.

Government of the Mormon settlements was largely in the hands of the church officials, and their decisions reached much deeper into the individual lives of the people than did those in the gentile communities. Questions of marriage, entertainment, personal habits, tenets of faith, common economic interests, migration, military service, and social attitudes all came under the proscription of the elders. But even beyond this there was an area of common relationships which could not be regulated without some form of civil government. Here, in a community which had made departures (though not radical in all cases) from the social norms of church and society in the older eastern communities, no noticeable departure was made from the outward forms of local government. A county was established with the regular coterie of local officials. The Mormon community was not without its problems of probate, law enforcement, and protection. There were criminally inclined among the faithful, and thievery in straitened economic times was not unknown. Occasionally there were acts of violence which necessitated the presence of peace officers and trial courts. Animal depredations in Utah, as everywhere else on the frontier, required vigilant action to keep the loss of livestock at a minimum.

Added to this was the Indian problem. Mormon relationships with the Indians did not follow the usual settler pattern. The origin and history of the American Indians had been explained in the *Book of Mormon*. The primitive people were regarded as the lost tribes of Israel, and because of this there was a great deal of sentimentality displayed toward them. Attempts were made to maintain peace with the Indians, and frequently the natives visited the settlements, sometimes making themselves quite at home and becoming insufferable nuisances. One incident created a bit of concern. The Indians brought with them children whom they offered for sale, and to encourage sales they announced they would kill those that remained on their hands. Here, as elsewhere, the aborigines showed an abnormal fondness for the white man's horses and cattle and took them without leave. One of the most adept at this art was the suave Ute chief Walker, who trafficked along the Sevier. Dressed in formal English broadcloth, cambric shirt and plug hat, the chieftain made an impressive figure. But among the cattle and horse herds along the Sevier he was even more impressive, operating on an international scale which reached from the Great Salt Lake to Mexico.

Once a settlement was established in the Great Basin, the activities of the Mormons were greatly expanded. In the original settlement new housing was constructed. Mormon society was planned to include a generous amount of amusement, of worship, and of work. The doctrine of the virtue and necessity of labor went far toward the expansion of the church's economic well-being. From Salt Lake City there was movement outward into the wider areas of the West. Inevitably the rapid increase in population was to force the organization of new settlements, but farms and towns had to be organized with a view to the availability of water. In 1850 the town of Ogden was founded, and Parley P. Pratt led an exploring party southward to locate sites for new farming communities and towns. In 1851, Mormons following on the heels of the Pratt party crossed the Sierras and began a settlement in the Cajon Pass country of California. New communities or colonies were started partly by volunteers who left the parent settlement on the Great Salt Lake, but usually these volunteers were materially aided by artisans and special groups sent along by the church. At the same time the new settlers took with them the necessary supplies, seeds, and livestock for supporting themselves during the first months of settlement and for developing a new economy. Many of the Mormon volunteers in the Mexican War had gone on to California and formed the nucleus for settlements in that area. This multiplication of communities inevitably led to the creation of a territory.

Deseret

In 1848 the Treaty of Guadalupe Hidalgo had placed the Mormon settlements in the Great Basin and elsewhere within the jurisdiction of the United States, and again the Saints were subjected to the laws and restrictions of the government which they had fled two years before. Their vast land of Deseret, "the land of the honey-bee," was an empire in geographical proportions. It not only included all of the territory within the Great Basin south of Oregon, but it likewise embraced the southern part of California. Actually this region included all of present Utah and Arizona, and parts of Idaho, Wyoming, New Mexico, and California. This sprawling territory contained approximately 227,500 square miles, or 145,600,000 acres. But much of this vast acreage was barren rock-bound mountain range or sun-parched desert. Its arable lands were confined to the river basins and the proximity of potential reservoirs to permit the controlled irrigation of the soil. Here as little as twelve inches of rainfall occurred annually.

A territorial government was formed, however, a preliminary constitution adopted on March 4, 1849, and the state of Deseret was an actuality so far as the Mormons were concerned. In general political form, Deseret differed little from the orthodox pattern of other frontier governmental organizations. The important differences occurred in the mode of administration rather than in the formal plan of government. Here for the first time in state-making on the frontier was established a political hierarchy under the domination of a church. A kind of canon law was substituted for the common law, a situation which in due course of time brought on a bitter conflict between the administration of Deseret and the government in Washington.

Almon W. Babbitt was sent to Washington with the Deseret constitution to seek admission for the state. In the capital he faced immediate opposition. First, there was no clear-cut policy for the organization of the territory acquired from Mexico. The burning sectional issue of the extension of slavery then under consideration by the committee which was to formulate the Compromise of 1850 had inflamed both sides in Congress. A further aggravation was the bitter opposition to the Mormons because of their political-religious cohesiveness and because of their practice of polygamy. When Congress later adopted the Compromise, California was admitted as a state, the organization of New Mexico was anticipated, and Deseret was greatly reduced in size and became the Territory of Utah. Brigham Young was made territorial governor, and other prominent church officials were given important political offices.

The Gold Rush

The rapidly changing situation on the frontier following the Mexican War made important changes in the future of Mormon affairs; likewise the great gold rush had its influence. The migration from Winter Quarters was still in progress when gold was discovered in California. Indeed several Mormons were present when the magical metal was found in Sutter's mill race. Possibly the most dramatic figure in the first weeks of the discovery was Elder Samuel Brannan who had led the faithful from New York aboard the *Brooklyn*. His alleged shouting of "Gold! Gold! Gold from the American River!" has often been cited as the first slogan of the rush. Brannan did display a bottle of gold as evidence of its presence in California, but he did not put on the hysterical demonstration attributed to him. When news of the gold discovery reached the settlements in Utah, Brigham Young was hard pressed to maintain the organization of his people and to keep them occupied in the difficult labor of making settlement. The feverish rush to the gold fields which followed was contagious, and once a break was made in the Saints' ranks it was nearly impossible to check it. Brigham Young was stern in his warning that the faithful should remain where they were. He warned that if they chose to leave, their choice would be permanent. However, many went to the gold fields, and even the leader, Brigham Young, was touched by the fever for gold. He asked Samuel Brannan to send $40,000 worth of gold dust to Heber Kimball and him to support the Saints' work.

When the army of goldseekers began to pour across Utah from the east, the Mormons engaged in a prosperous trade with them, often securing from the travelers badly needed materials and even luxuries in exchange for fresh animals, foodstuffs and clothing. Utah was practically a half-way point, if not in precise distance, at least in travel experience and fatigue. It was here that the travelers re-ordered their supplies and equipment, traded or gave away their surplus materials and made a new start on the hard journey across the Sierra Nevada. When travelers traded with the Mormons, they were subjected to inflated prices for goods they purchased and deflated prices for those which they sold. For the Mormons there was one serious drawback—the immigrants brought with them several diseases, the most deadly of which was the Asiatic cholera. Many of the gold-mad immigrants kept journals of their experiences along the way, and there are many accounts of passing through the Utah settlements. Some of the gold rush immigrants stopped permanently in Zion and either joined the Mormon Church or established the nucleus of a future gentile population.

Border Friction

The decade 1850–1860 in Utah history was marred by friction between the United States Government and the territorial officials. No doubt the Mormon leaders were too sweeping in their unfounded criticisms of many national officials and unreasonably hard on the government representatives sent among them. Brigham Young and the other elders preached vigorous and bitter sermons in which they gave highly biased views of federal officials in both Washington and Utah. At the same time there was reason to believe that Presidents of the United States were none too tactful in selecting territorial officials to deal with the delicate situation which existed in Utah. Some of them, it was charged, seemed to believe the system of polygamy was no more than an organized system of prostitution, and the federal officials made improper approaches to the Mormon women. On the other hand, local leaders were so jealous of the outsiders that they were in no position to arrive at objective appraisals of their worth. One incident out of many will illustrate the type of friction which occurred between the territorial officials sent from Washington and the Saints. On the occasion of the dedicatory ceremony when the Utah block of stone was being prepared for shipment to be used in the Washington Monument, Judge Perry E. Brocchus, an Alabamian, delivered a gratuitous lecture against polygamy in which he urged Mormon women to lead virtuous lives. This caused much bitterness, and the tactless judge himself was charged with being lewd and an alcoholic. In time Judge Brocchus had to withdraw from office because of the opposition to him.

The most notable incident in Mormon-United States relations occurred when President James Buchanan appointed Alfred Cumming of Georgia to the territorial governorship to succeed Brigham Young in 1857. Because of the strife which had prevailed over the last seven years, Buchanan regarded conditions in Utah as being little short of insurrectionary. He believed that the rebellious Mormons had either to be brought to a state of obedience or be destroyed. Governor Cumming was sent west under the protection of the United States Army, and a detachment of infantry, artillery, and dragoons was dispatched from Fort Leavenworth to help bring order beyond the mountains. News of their approach caused great anxiety in Utah. Plans were made to destroy Salt Lake City. Dramatically, families loaded themselves into wagons with such property and foodstuffs as they could carry south, and like the ancients moving out from Gomorrah, fled the city. Behind them, they left the faithful who piled inflammable materials about the houses and awaited orders to apply the torch.

The western branch of the army was under the command of Albert Sidney Johnston. Moving westward, Johnston's command was hampered by the inevitable bungling of the quartermaster's department which had failed to make adequate provisions for an expedition in cold weather. This inefficiency, rather than Mormon resistance, threatened the expedition with defeat. The Mormons practiced sabotage against Johnston's advancing troops by stealing supplies, destroying wagons, setting grass fires, and creating other nuisances. When the army arrived in Utah, Mormon resistance had been lowered enough by the efforts of Buchanan's peace commissioners that the soldiers were allowed to pass unmolested through Salt Lake City to a camp forty-five miles away. Governor Cumming was successful in making himself acceptable to the citizens of the territory, and the need for the army soon vanished—but not until the government had spent approximately fifteen million dollars on the expedition.

The Mormons engaged in one lawless act which has remained an indelible mark against them. Again, the facts are obscured in a maze of contradictory stories and a cloud of emotionalism. The Mormon apostle Parley Pratt had become involved in a dispute with a San Francisco merchant named H. H. McClean who claimed that Pratt was trying to steal his wife. In a race to New Orleans and then northward to Arkansas, McClean was able to overtake his wife and bring the correspondent to trial in court. Feeling ran high. McClean threatened to shoot Pratt in the courtroom, and he did murder him later at Van Buren. That same year an immigrant party of 136 members, including the "Missouri Wildcats," set out from Arkansas for California, and when they reached the Mountain Meadows in southwest Utah on September 7, 1857, Indians and white men fired upon them. There followed a bloody affray in which all of the adult immigrants were killed. No doubt the immigrants had provoked a part of the attack, but there still was a nasty story of duplicity in which the Arkansas company was said to be disarmed and defenseless at the time it was murdered. A long investigation followed which led to much publicity, and suspicion of Mormon involvement in the act was further heightened. In 1876 John D. Lee, a major participant in the massacre, was executed on the spot where the original crime had occurred. Before he faced the firing squad, he published a confession which further implicated the Saints in this heartless act of reprisal. The Mountain Meadows affair was an unhappy incident, which, added to other prejudices and fears, did much to heighten public resistance to the Saints.

While the faithful were pushing overland from the Mississippi and Missouri valleys, Mormon missionaries were abroad in England and Europe seeking converts. Wherever they went they told the story of Zion. In overcrowded and socially disturbed communities of England and the continent, hundreds of people were ready to cast off the frustrations and economic uncertainties of the Old World for the joys of a far western paradise where land, space, and resources were plentiful. These converts could be kept away from the promised land just so long; then they began to lose patience and faith and wander away. In 1856 arrangements were made for their passage to America and their transport to the Missouri River, but here transportation across the plains became a serious problem. It was all but impossible to supply sufficient teams and wagons to make the journey, so the church elders devised the scheme of taking some thirteen hundred immigrants from Iowa City to Winter Quarters and on to Salt Lake City in handcart trains. Simple wooden carts of light construction were prepared, and when the European converts arrived they were started afoot on the thirteen-hundred-mile march to Zion. The first three companies went through in good condition, experiencing no more difficulties than if they had traveled by wagon. Late in August the fourth and fifth companies, known as the Martin and Willie brigades, set forth on the trail too late to reach their destination before winter closed in on the Rockies. When they reached the mountains, they ran into extremely cold weather for which they were not prepared, and before they were rescued by a party coming out to meet them, scores of deaths had occurred.

As the years went by, a stream of immigrants moved over the Mormon trail to join the faithful in their ever-expanding settlements beyond the mountains. Diligent elders working abroad continued to turn foreigners toward the promise of Zion in an unending stream. In all, almost eighty thousand souls crossed the Atlantic to seek happiness in the land where "Your bosoms burn with a desire to congregate together, and become a holy and peculiar people."

Utah Territory was created in 1850 as part of the Compromise of that year, but was not admitted to the Union as a state until 1896. Because of the issue of polygamy and the adverse public opinion created by it in the rest of the country, there was little or no possibility of securing congressional confirmation of a constitution until a monogamous society was assured. This delay, however, does not change the fundamental facts of Mormon history. For the first time a mass migration was managed so that it produced well-organized settlements almost from the beginning. Arid land which probably would have had little immediate attraction for independent settlers was brought under cultivation by shrewd management and dogged persistence. Highly practical lessons of irrigation, conservation of resources, new modes of cultivation, and an efficient and controlled domestic economy were landmarks in this major penetration of the Rocky Mountain barrier. A hardheaded but on the whole benevolent patriarchal administrative control made the people largely subservient to the will of a single shrewd and willful man. Mormon frontiersmen exhibited little or none of the individualism of their gentile neighbors. It little matters to the historian of the frontier what particular theological points of view prevailed with the Saints; the fact is that they proved successful trailbreakers and planted a tenacious community in the vital midland between the Mississippi Valley and the Pacific Coast.

THE BATTLE OF PALO ALTO FROM
G. W. KENDALL'S *War Between
the U. S. and Mexico*

AN INTERLUDE OF WAR

It has been my unalterable purpose since the commencement of
hostilities by Mexico and the declaration of the existence of war by
Congress to prosecute the war in which the country was unavoidably involved with the utmost energy, with a view to its "speedy
and successful termination" by an honorable peace.

Accordingly all the operations of our naval and military forces
have been directed with this view. While the sword has been held in
one hand and our military movements pressed forward into the
enemy's country and its coast invested by our Navy, the tender of an
honorable peace has been constantly presented to Mexico in the
other.

—JAMES KNOX POLK, *Special Message to Congress*

CHAPTER XXIII

Expansionism in 1844

THE election of 1844 was truly an expansionist jubilee, and in 1845 the
nation stood poised and ready to move on four border fronts. Oregon,
California, New Mexico, and Texas all had come clearly into focus in their
respective areas. In all four places the United States faced the necessity of
providing some form of military protection if it were to claim the territory.
British and American diplomats were still discussing northwestern boundary line issues. California was already beginning to shake off the loose
shackles of Mexican control, and New Mexico had been a focal point of
American interest for almost forty-five years. Nor did the admission of
Texas to the Union mean that all issues between that state and Mexico
were settled. There remained the whole question of the western boundary

of the state, which in a sense duplicated the issues which had accompanied the purchase of Louisiana. Texas and Mexico had made no agreement on that state's western boundary. Texas contended, of course, that the Rio Grande was the natural dividing line.

Before Texas was annexed to the Union, the military had anticipated the move. A part of the United States Army was stationed in Louisiana ready to move on to the Nueces as soon as annexation was completed. Since 1836, annexation had been delayed by Presidents who no doubt favored such a move, but who feared the criticism which might be voiced if the United States committed an overt act which would force war with Mexico. President Polk wrote in his first annual message to Congress:

> The moment the terms of annexation offered by the United States were accepted by Texas the latter became so far a part of our own country as to make it our duty to afford such protection and defense. I therefore deemed it proper, as a precautionary measure, to order a strong squadron to the coasts of Mexico and to concentrate an efficient military force on the western frontier of Texas. Our army was ordered to take position in the country between the Nueces and the Del Norte, and to repel any invasion of the Texan territory which might be attempted by the Mexican forces.

Polk's first message to Congress literally bristled with expansionism. In many respects it was as important a statement of principles as the Monroe Doctrine. In a long review of the Monroe Doctrine, Polk stated his own belief that "it should be distinctly announced to the world as our settled policy that no future European colony or dominion shall with our consent be planted or established on any part of the North American continent." This was a pointed warning to England and France that in the face of the impending Mexican crisis this country would not tolerate any attempts to colonize California and Oregon, to say nothing of the Rio Grande Valley.

The United States made a diplomatic approach to Mexico in November, 1845. President Polk appointed John Slidell of Louisiana as a diplomatic commissioner to Mexico. There can be little doubt that this mission was of peaceful intent. Slidell's main objectives were to secure an adjustment of the Texas boundary and to persuade the Mexican Government to indemnify American citizens for their loss of property. Slidell hastened to Vera Cruz, arriving there within twenty days after he received his commission. When he reached Mexico, he found the Herrera government almost ready to fall and he could not receive accreditation. Late in December, when the Paredes government came into existence, Slidell again sought accreditation and was again insulted and refused recognition. He asked for his passport and returned to the United States.

Taylor in the Rio Grande

While Slidell was seeking recognition in Mexico, the United States Army concentrated a considerable force at Corpus Christi on the Nueces River. This force was led by the rugged old border warrior, Brevet Brigadier General Zachary Taylor. This Virginia-born soldier had begun his military career on the frontier and for thirty-six years had seen service from the swamps of Louisiana, by way of Indiana, Iowa, Wisconsin, Illinois, and Florida, to Texas and Mexico. He was a frontier soldier's general, with great capacity for capturing the affections of his men, for leading them into most unattractive places, for ignoring the formalities of army dress and regulations, and finally for leading his command effectively.

Taylor was not allowed, however, to wait long in Corpus Christi before he was ordered to pull up stakes and advance to the Rio Grande. Slidell's first message reached Washington on January 12, 1846; in February, Taylor's forces were on the move to their new location on the Rio Grande opposite the Mexican town of Matamoros.

Failure of Slidell's mission and the movement of Taylor's troops forward to the Rio Grande opened one of the most dramatic and colorful incidents in frontier history. As with so many dramatic acts in history, however, the stage was poorly arranged for what was to occur. It would be hard to find another example of a nation taking so great a calculated risk of war with so little information about either the prospective enemy or the geography of the country in which the impending struggle would take place. There is good reason to believe that the War Department did not possess a single map of the southwest territory that was even remotely trustworthy. No one outside of Taylor's camp, except for a few traders, had any notion of what the army must face in the way of heat, insects, sickness, terrain, lack of transportation and supplies, and difficulties of communication.

There was a remarkable casualness about the acts of the government. Polk's messages were vigorous and heated enough, but this spirit seems not to have gone very far beyond the Houses of Congress and the editorial pages of the newspapers. No one in the War Department was wrought up enough about the impending war in Mexico to begin the necessary plans for such a conflict. On the surface at least, it was hard to tell whether Taylor at Matamoros faced a dangerous enemy, or a lackadaisical antagonist caught in the net of revolution and Mexican bombast and procrastination. Mexicans, however, had no monopoly on procrastination. Supplies for the American army went uncollected. The wagons which were later to haul Taylor's stores beyond the Rio Grande were still on the stump in Pennsylvania and elsewhere, putting out a fresh crop of spring foliage.

Clothes, foodstuffs, ammunition, and guns were still to be sought. The American people were fascinated by the romantic and sentimental spirit of expansion as long as it could be expressed oratorically rather than in such cold realities as guns, sweat, taxes, and basic planning. The game of partisan politics was more captivating than the actual and smelly labor of expansion by brawn and blood in the Southwest.

Across the Rio Grande from Taylor's camp on the north bank of that river, the activities of the Mexican Army were clearly discernible. Taylor and the Mexican General Mejía exchanged communications couched in the politest phraseology. American and Mexican scouts crossed and recrossed the river. Taylor had a first vital task to perform in opening the road to Point Isabel on the Gulf and in clearing the way for water-borne supplies to be landed and delivered to the camp. A fort was begun on the Rio Grande by the American troops, and life settled down again to a border routine, although General Mejía had declared emphatically that the appearance of the Americans on the Rio Grande was in fact an act of war.

In April General Pedro de Ampudia arrived in Matamoros and demanded that Taylor retreat beyond the Nueces, a demand which Taylor chose to disobey. In the latter part of April a third Mexican general, Mariano Arista, appeared on the scene and proceeded to order Mexican troops across the river. Some Americans were killed, and on April 26, 1846, General Taylor reported to Washington that hostilities had begun. He asked for additional supplies and troops to begin a long and arduous campaign. Even then he knew that he would have to fight south of the Rio Grande.

When Taylor's dispatch arrived in Washington both the administration and Congress were frightened into action. Congress at once approved bills for recruiting fifty thousand volunteers and an appropriation of ten million dollars. News of the opening conflict on the Rio Grande was reminiscent of the outbreak of the War of 1812. The army had not been in conflict for so many years that it suffered from the easy habits of garrison life. Except for the border forays against the Indians there had been no occasion for military activity in the nation. Most of the major officers were old and incapable of active campaigning; yet veterans of 1812 such as John E. Wool, Winfield Scott and others were active and available, and the Military Academy at West Point had provided an annual crop of second lieutenants who were pushing themselves up the promotional ladder. Many young officers were to get their baptism of fire in this border dress-rehearsal for the coming Civil War.

The decision was made to raise the first troops from the South and West. When the call for volunteers was issued men hastened to enlist, some for three months, some for six, and some for a year. In several states, volunteers appeared in such large numbers that recruiting officials were overwhelmed and were in doubt as to what they should do about accepting more than the prescribed quotas. A mountain man appeared in Lexington, Kentucky, wanting to go to the war. He did not know where it was being fought, nor did he have the slightest knowledge of the issues involved—all he wanted was a fight.

Taylor's needs on the Rio Grande were too urgent for the army to engage in a slow process of training in camps in the states where troops originated. They were hurried off to the front as soon as they were collected. The three-months troops were almost ready to leave the army by the time they reached the fighting front. Taylor was confronted with grave disciplinary and training problems. It almost seemed that he would have to stop fighting Mexicans and bring his own troops under control. More than once rival units squared off to fight out their differences.

General Taylor, as we have seen, had established his troops in Fort Brown (Texas), on the banks of the Rio Grande, a stronghold which he had had to build from the ground up. Raiding parties of Mexicans had crossed the river and had killed Colonel Truman Cross who was caught away from camp alone. A week later a reconnoitering expedition under the command of Lieutenant Theodoric Porter was caught by surprise and most of the group was slaughtered. On April 25, a considerable number of Mexican soldiers crossed the Rio Grande and were in position to begin a serious attack upon Americans. Captain Seth Thornton and his dragoons were caught in a trap and forced to surrender. This was the incident which marked the beginning of open hostilities. A week later General Taylor set out for Point Isabel with two thousand troops to protect that vital point from the horde of Mexicans who were crossing from Matamoros below Fort Texas. After strengthening the defenses of Point Isabel, Taylor's long line of troops and ponderous wagon train then turned back toward Fort Texas to meet a heavy Mexican force then blocking the road. On the evening of May 8, the Americans came within sight of the enemy near Palo Alto Pond.

The Mexican troops commanded by General Arista outnumbered the Americans at least two to one. There were, however, other significant differences between the two armies. The American troops, though inexperienced in actual warfare, were regular troops, equipped with new and accurate rifles; they were well led and were thoroughly willing fighters. The Mexican troops ranged in quality from Anastasio Torrejón's well-mounted lancers to ignorant Indian conscripts who were ready to run at the first fire. Also, the Americans had effective artillerymen like those under command of Captains James Duncan and Samuel Ringgold. The ornate Mexican cannon were fancily engraved, but were ineffective weapons. The heavy balls which they fired could be spotted across the field, and American soldiers jumped aside and allowed them to spin out their momentum without harm.

Here on the treeless plains of Palo Alto on May 8, the two armies faced each other in ranks after the fashion of continental troops. The impending fight was to be a slugging match in which commanding officers on both sides switched fronts and flanks with some degree of precision to meet the weight of the other's attacks. The American light firing was ineffective, but the artillery fire cut the charging Mexican lines to shreds. Wadding from one of the American guns set the grass on fire, and the resulting smoke obscured both lines. By sundown the battle had waned and the issue at Palo Alto was decided in favor of the Americans.

Early the next morning General Arista began the withdrawal of his troops. Though the Americans had won Palo Alto, they were to experience a second test the next day in the chaparral of the Resaca de la Palma, or Guerrero depression. On the afternoon of May 9, American troops charged the concealed enemy in a spectacular battle which cheered the hearts of Taylor's regulars. When nightfall came on the second day of fighting, the Mexicans were already rushing to the river, some of them drowning in their headlong dash for the other side. The Mexican army moved back to the south bank of the Rio Grande.

General Taylor had quick victory in his grasp, but he lacked the boats necessary to pass his troops over the river. Perhaps he lacked also organizational competence to take advantage of his situation. The Navy could not get its deep draft boats over the shoals at the mouth of the river, and there was no possibility either of building or acquiring the necessary lighter craft to transport troops across the stream. Not until May 15 did the Americans begin crossing the stream, and it took the next three days to complete the crossing. In the meantime Arista withdrew his troops and left Matamoros in American hands. Once south of the river, Taylor lacked the equipment necessary to pursue the weakened enemy and hasten the end of the conflict.

To supply General Taylor's army by overland transportation was out of the question. Before a slow-moving wagon train could cross the dry Texas country it was possible that the issues of the war would have been decided. The most direct means was by water. Steamships hauling goods to Point Isabel on the Gulf and steamboats moving them up the Rio Grande to Fort Brown were the only reasonable means of getting supplies to the army on time. Taylor's strategy for the future was to advance up the Rio Grande for almost 240 miles and then turn southward into Mexico toward Monterrey and Saltillo. Moving the American army up the Rio Grande to the village of Camargo was a most difficult undertaking. The river was winding, the current and channel were treacherous, and wet mesquite wood produced such a limited amount of steam that often the boats were unable to buck the current. Often, boats were swept into the banks and the rudders and wheels damaged.

During the latter part of July and the first weeks of August, fifteen thousand men were transported to a steaming encampment at the mouth of the San Juan. Again Taylor was vexed by the problem of disciplining the raw troops who poured into his camp. Gambling, drinking, and patronizing of brothels were commonplace activities. Health problems were staggering. Dysentery, endemic fevers, and all other contagious diseases took their toll. Insects of all sorts attacked the invaders with more relish than had the Mexican troops, and the intense heat made life all but unbearable. Yet in the face of all this, General Taylor held the army together and after a fashion whipped it into a loose-jointed fighting force. Almost as aggravating as the Mexican insects were the hero-worshipping delegations which rushed out to Mexico to honor the General for his victories at Palo Alto and Resaca de la Palma. One of these brought the very sash which had been given General Washington by General Braddock, a relic which the informal Taylor needed less even than a coal stove. These zealous patriots stayed with the General at Matamoros long enough to drink up all

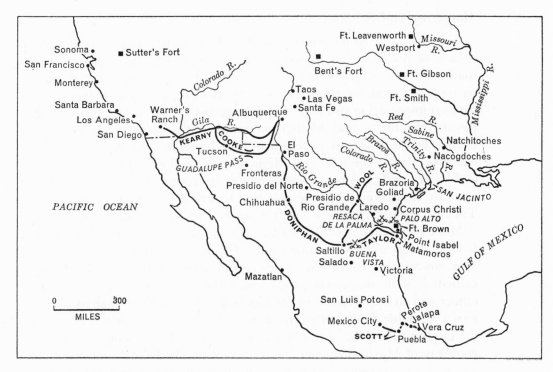

SCENE OF THE WAR WITH MEXICO

the liquor in sight, but not long enough to face the Mexican rifles. It was too hot for them at Camargo.

Meanwhile, the Mexican officials were having their own troubles. They had no stable government to maintain an integrated economic system so necessary to the support of an army. Mariano Paredes could not command the necessary political forces to stabilize the government, and it seemed dangerous for him to arm large numbers of his countrymen. His office was one to which every opportunist in Mexico might aspire, and he personally became the target of his army of rivals. Looming most prominent in Paredes' dark future was Santa Anna, of San Jacinto and Washington fame. In April a revolution broke out, and by August—the time of Taylor's arrival at Camargo—Santa Anna was back in the Mexican political saddle. The old schemer had returned to power by proclaiming loyalty to the constitution of 1824, a document which he had raped in his first rise to power. The Paredes government collapsed early in August, and political affairs were now in the control of the Santa Anna clique. Santa Anna had shipped from Havana aboard the British ship *Arab*, and had entered Vera Cruz with American blessing and knowledge on August 16, 1846. Washington had once more been taken in by this wily rascal.

Monterrey and Saltillo

The day after Santa Anna landed at Vera Cruz, Taylor held a grand review of his troops at Camargo, and the next day he began his march southward toward Monterrey and Saltillo. His fighting army numbered six thousand men. By the closest management he was able to secure mule-back transportation for the supplies necessary to move his command toward Monterrey and another encounter with the Mexican Army. The change in the Mexican government had brought back to military command Generals Ampudia and Mejía whom Taylor had met at Palo Alto and Resaca de la Palma. Ampudia moved his seven thousand troops northward to Monterrey where he prepared to strengthen the city and to block Taylor's southward march into the interior of the country.

Monterrey, capital of Nueva Leon, was a city of ten thousand people. It lay athwart a deep mountain pass. The town itself was a characteristic Mexican-Spanish collection of stone and adobe houses dominated by a cathedral, with numerous plazas and winding narrow streets. A clever officer had an opportunity to turn its buildings and their vaulted flat roofs into a veritable Gibraltar of resistance. Americans began the contest for the city on September 21, when a company of Texas Rangers attacked a company of Mexican lancers. Thus opened the battle of Monterrey which was to figure so prominently in the creation of American military heroes.

Among the officers who acquitted themselves with glory at this place were Jefferson Davis, John A. Quitman, William J. Worth, Braxton Bragg, David E. Twiggs, William O. Butler, William R. McKee, U. S. Grant, and Thomas Childs.

The maneuver by Worth to capture the gun emplacements on the heights about the city, the assaults on the outposts by Davis and Quitman, and the dashes of the Texas Rangers all made heroes. But the real drive for the capture of Monterrey took three days during which both armies pounded each other with fury. After the first assault against the outposts of the city, fighting went on from house to house, the troops cutting holes through partitions and driving on toward the main plaza. On September 24, General Ampudia proposed an end to the fighting at Monterrey, his army's withdrawal from the city, and an eight weeks' armistice. Because of the supply problem Taylor agreed to the terms, and the next day the Stars and Stripes flew over Monterrey. This battle had been a hot one in which Americans acquitted themselves well. Although Taylor's strategy became a matter of controversy, Worth's gallant maneuver that silenced the hill emplacements was both daring and ably executed.

News of victory at Monterrey touched off celebrations in the United States. General Taylor and his army stirred the American people to a most enthusiastic pitch. The Whigs, in search of a Presidential candidate, thought they saw one astride an old white army horse below the Rio Grande. All sorts of medals were struck. General Taylor was again plagued by visiting delegates who came to honor and to drink with the army, but General Taylor, taking only generous libations of river water, planned to strike the foe again. The American people believed there was no way to stop the army. In a short time it would complete its errand in Mexico to the entire satisfaction of the expansionists and everybody else. The informal frontier General who had enjoyed success on the faraway banks of the Rio Grande could look to a bright future, and from this time on the contests of the war were to have political implications.

Although the American people were celebrating, very real problems confronted the Polk administration. The political stakes in the war were high, and the Polk administration was ever conscious of the consequences of failure. At no time in American history had the difficulties of communication during a war caused so much delay, confusion and uncertainty. There was also indecision, which was a cardinal sin of the war. In addition the Mexican War was fought farther from the center of government than any previous American conflict. Congressional elections already threatened the administration's majority in both Houses. An end of war might improve this situation. Planners in the White House and the War Department were therefore anxious not only to strike the Mexican forces

deep inside their border land below the Rio Grande, but also to push the
war in other strategic places—from the north by way of Santa Fe in New
Mexico; from the east by way of Tamaulipas and Vera Cruz; and in
California on the Pacific Coast. There was little chance in July, 1846, that
a negotiated peace could be made with Mexico until late in the fall, if
then; political conditions in Mexico exposed that nation to a war of further
attrition and active invasion. Aside from the heavy loss of life and a heavy
expenditure of money, Washington had other reasons for wanting to end
the war. As in all armed conflicts, the various partisan groups were already making political capital of the responsibilities for the war, and of
the military glories and mistakes which had resulted from the conflict.
Yet, however anxious Polk and his advisors were to end the war, it was
clear by the time of the battle of Monterrey that the United States was
going to have to fight its way out of Mexico.

The decision to land forces near Vera Cruz and to besiege that city
from the rear had behind it a keen desire to bring the war to an end. Because communications were delayed between Washington and Taylor at
Monterrey, needless friction had developed between the two points. At
least one communiqué to Taylor was captured by the enemy, and Washington was uninformed of Taylor's terms to General Ampudia in accepting the surrender of Monterrey. He had committed himself to an agreement to remain north of a line from Linares to San Fernando for eight
weeks. To an uninformed President and cabinet this seemed like a willful
grant of time to the Mexicans to recoup their army and to prepare for a
second attack. Even if Taylor had been fully informed of the proposed
Tamaulipas-Vera Cruz invasion, because of the armistice he could not have
made a move southward with honor.

No doubt General Taylor deserved some criticism for the Monterrey
armistice, but it is doubtful that he could have moved even had he been
free to do so. He lacked supplies, men, and transportation facilities to conduct a campaign to overtake the Mexican army after Monterrey. Resentful
over the criticism which he was receiving, he made the mistake of writing
his friend and distant kinsman General Edmund Pendleton Gaines a long
letter which stated his position in the armistice matter. General Gaines
published this letter in the *New York Express*, and this further stirred the
embers of political resentment. Publication of the letter was an injudicious
act, and no doubt it hastened the split in the Mexican command.

Scott, Kearny, and Doniphan

President Polk was forced to make a decision on the selection of a second commander in the war. His administration had lost the congressional
elections, and General Taylor had committed himself to an unacceptable

partisan position. Yet the choice of a second commander was not easy. Polk possibly favored Senator Thomas Hart Benton of Missouri, but it was doubtful that Benton could manage an army. On the other hand General Winfield Scott had shown a startling amount of interest and activity, and it was impossible to ignore him further. On November 18, 1846, President Polk selected him to open a second front in Mexico from the Gulf by way of Vera Cruz.

While Taylor was concentrating his forces at Camargo preparatory for his drive on Monterrey, Colonel Stephen Watts Kearny, whose California exploits have been discussed in a previous chapter, advanced southwestward overland from Fort Leavenworth to Santa Fe over the famous trail to that place. He left Fort Leavenworth on June 30, 1846, with sixteen hundred men, and reached New Mexico by the middle of August, where he met with little resistance. Taking possession of New Mexico was little more than a perfunctory matter, except for difficulties with the Indians. By September 25, the campaign in that quarter had developed to the point where political control could be turned over to a civilian governor, and Kearny could go on to California.

Accompanying Colonel Kearny was one of those unusual men of the frontier who successfully combined the practice of law with a military and political career. He was Alexander William Doniphan, who, born in Kentucky, had moved in early manhood to Missouri where he distinguished himself as a trial lawyer. Doniphan had a natural capacity for leadership and a quality of courage that made him almost a legendary character. When the Mexican War began, he was instructed by Governor Edwards of Missouri to recruit the First Regiment of Missouri Mounted Volunteers. This unit was in Santa Fe when Kearny departed for California, and Doniphan was left in charge of the entire American force. The Missouri colonel made one raid out of Santa Fe against the Ute and Navaho in an effort to stop their attacks and to recover their white prisoners. In September he was ordered to move southward to Chihuahua to join General John E. Wool, but lack of maps and War Department bungling sent the Missourians wandering over a vast stretch of territory without knowing the location of Wool's command. Doniphan's march really began from the southernmost New Mexico town of Valverde, where he assembled his army of 856 men, and was joined by the army of traders with their 315 wagons for the journey to El Paso and Chihuahua.

During the next twelve months, Doniphan led his rag-tag army 3,600 miles over desolate waterless country, and then traveled with them an additional 2,000 miles by water back to New Orleans. His long marches over arid stretches of northern Mexico in search of General Wool is an American epic. At the little island of El Brazito before El Paso on

Christmas Day, 1846, his forces defeated two thousand Mexicans under the command of General Poncé. From El Paso, Doniphan's army turned southward in February on the journey to Chihuahua. On February 28 the Americans defeated General José A. Herredia's Mexican command at the battle of Sacramento Hacienda on the Arroyo Seco. Doniphan found himself in possession of Sacramento, but his position was most precarious. He had no commissary, no line of supply, no hope for reinforcements of any sort, and possibly worst of all, no knowledge of the whereabouts of other American forces. Certainly he had not found General Wool. On April 28, after receiving word of the location of Taylor's army at Saltillo, this orphaned command began its long march eastward where it ultimately united with General Wool's force.

While Doniphan was advancing toward El Paso in December, General Taylor was regrouping his forces at Monterrey. His main objective was Victoria, capital of Tamaulipas. He advanced from Monterrey to Saltillo, and there divided his forces further in his plan to take Victoria. A threat by Santa Anna from San Luis Potosí, however, caused Taylor to tighten up his lines and to concentrate his forces in the neighborhood of Saltillo. For the next few weeks the Americans engaged in a series of marches and counter-marches which at times seem to indicate a lack of decision on the part of the commander. During this period of confusion, after a letter to Taylor from Scott detailing the future plan of campaign was captured, there was grave danger that Santa Anna would capitalize on this American misfortune.

General Santa Anna's own situation in San Luis Potosí was a desperate one. The Mexican government under Valentin Gomez Farias had failed to raise the funds necessary to support the army in the field. Santa Anna's only hope of victory was to meet and defeat the Americans in a quick surprise attack. He took the offensive in January, and the result was the famous battle of Buena Vista on February 22–23. Since Taylor had warning of the approach of the Mexican army from men in advanced positions, he concentrated his forces in the mountainous pass near the Hacienda Buena Vista. The Americans had a favorable defensive terrain in the deeply eroded ridges around the ranch, and behind them they had the reasonably stable base of Saltillo. Taylor at that time commanded 4,759 troops while Santa Anna was able to field in the neighborhood of 16,000 men.

In hastening to engage Taylor in battle, Santa Anna made two major errors. He marched his men more than forty-five miles through a dry and hot region where water was available only in limited quantities. He lost almost five thousand troops by the attrition of this march, and blunted the enthusiasm of the rest of his army for battle. When he reached the frontier camp of Agua Nueva, which the Americans had abandoned so hurriedly that piles of grain and other supplies were still burning, he erred a second time in believing that Taylor was in flight before him.

On February 22, 1847, Santa Anna was before Buena Vista. He was so certain of victory that he sent his famous message to Taylor calling on him to surrender or be cut to pieces by twenty thousand Mexicans. General Taylor's actual reply to his translator was in good lusty frontier army language, but in translation it was most polite, saying, "I beg leave to say I decline acceding to your request." In midafternoon of Washington's Birthday the battle of Buena Vista got underway, and it raged until the night of February 23. This battle was costly to both armies. The Americans lost such valuable officers as Colonel Archibald Yell, the Arkansas commander, Lieutenant William McKee of Kentucky, and Colonel John J. Hardin of Illinois. Braxton Bragg and Jefferson Davis dealt out death to many hapless Mexicans who found themselves in the jaws of the bloody angle called the Buena Vista "V."

In all, 746 Americans fell casualties of Buena Vista, 267 of whom died. Five times that many Mexican casualties occurred. The dead and dying on the field of Buena Vista were only a preface to further Mexican suffering. Santa Anna's retreat to Agua Nueva and then back toward San Luis Potosí left a trail of dead and dying. Thirsty men stumbled back toward safety in the pale moonlight; many of them fell by the road and died. Wounded soldiers were dumped from litters to perish where they fell. An officer of a pursuing company of American horsemen reported three days later: ". . . the road was literally strewn with the dead and dying and with those perishing from fatigue and want of water. It was a most melancholy and touching picture, that the soldiers in uniform, who, having been spared in battle, were now yielding up their lives without a wound." Three days after the battle, Santa Anna said that he had suffered loss of almost a third of his command.

Back in San Luis Potosí, however, Santa Anna reported a victory at Buena Vista. General Miñon's cavalry had cut Taylor's line of communication with Camargo, and it was several days before a message could be sent on its way to Washington. Once again, the officials in Washington, including President Polk, were too hasty in criticizing General Taylor. Polk's embarrassment must have been great when the facts of Buena Vista finally filtered through to Washington. His blast, as recorded in his diary, was a bitter one and his enmity toward Taylor increased. Whatever the domestic political repercussions of delayed news of Buena Vista, the battle broke Mexican resistance in the north, and Taylor's army, which had fought its way from Palo Alto to the gulches of Buena Vista, was to finish out the war doing nothing more than garrison duty.

General Winfield Scott reached Mexico late in February while Taylor was involved in the fight at Buena Vista. On March 2, he sailed for Vera Cruz from Lobos Island with an army which included many of Taylor's veterans. Once in the field General Scott was also to experience the trials and tribulations which had beset General Taylor. Stores had not arrived at the rendezvous point. Surf boats so necessary for landing troops on the Vera Cruz "D Day" were not on hand. A part of the contingent which was to reinforce the fighting strength of his command was still enjoying the high life of New Orleans. When smallpox broke out among the Second Pennsylvania Regiment, this unit had to be quarantined. Nevertheless the General set forth for his objective, trusting that men and supplies would catch up with him. A stray copy of a Mexican newspaper picked up near Vera Cruz carried Santa Anna's false report of the results of the battle of Buena Vista. Thus success at Vera Cruz was imperative.

Speed was called for if the city was to be taken with ease and without unnecessary loss of life; also since the yellow fever season was approaching, it was important that the Americans get away from the coast. Commodore David Conner of the Navy was equipped to render splendid assistance both in landing men and supplies and in bombarding the fortress of San Juan d'Ulloa. On March 7, 1847, Scott began his invasion of Mexican soil. This act foreshadowed later American activities in Europe during World War II. The first troops landed were General Worth's seasoned command who had tasted victory on the heights above Monterrey. Within ten days enough troops, supplies and guns had been landed to begin a forthright siege of Vera Cruz. The Army and Navy in co-operation opened the bombardment on Mexican positions. Stormy weather interfered somewhat with the intensity of the firing, but damage done in the first five days of the siege brought a request, stimulated by the foreign consuls within the city, to state terms on which a capitulation would be acceptable. On March 29, the Mexican garrison marched out of the city and surrendered its arms. There were fewer than a hundred casualties among the Americans, and the supply of arms landed from the fleet had not suffered serious depletion. Scott had won his first major objective and was now ready to strike the Mexican army in its heartland.

From Vera Cruz the American troops began the long and arduous march to Mexico City. General Scott was faced with Taylor's old problem of finding enough pack animals and wagons to move his army. Santa Anna was on a triumphant march into central Mexico from San Luis Potosí, proclaiming his "victory" at Buena Vista. In this move he had to maneuver in front of Scott's advances, and the history of the rest of the war is the story of the fighting between the forces of the two commanders. In April, Scott's troops were strung out on the desolate sandy road between Vera Cruz and Jalapa. Santa Anna had concentrated his new army in the latter place, and within a short time met the Americans in battle in the precipitous section of Cerro Gordo. This fight occurred on April 18. Characteristic of all the battles since Palo Alto, the fight at Cerro Gordo resulted in an American victory, and Jalapa lay exposed to immediate occupation. Again Santa Anna had led an army to defeat, and it was only by good luck that he personally escaped capture. At that moment little resistance stood between Scott's forces and the capital city.

Peace Negotiations

A feeling prevailed both in General Scott's headquarters and in Washington that it would be possible to negotiate a peace with Mexico and end the war. Polk's cabinet acted on this belief, and the President chose Nicholas P. Trist to go to Mexico with the outline of a possible treaty and open discussions with the Mexican Government. Trist was another of the unusual figures who played an unorthodox role in the war. He was born in Charlottesville, Virginia, and had married the granddaughter of Thomas Jefferson. He had been a friend of Andrew Jackson and had served as consul in Havana. When Polk was elected President, Trist became chief clerk in the State Department under James Buchanan. Trist was an able man. He had excellent command of both French and Spanish, as well as a familiarity with the Latin temperament; yet his services in Mexico were less than brilliant, and at times almost comical. Failure of communications between the War and State departments, and with General Taylor, largely accounted for unhappy relations during Trist's first weeks in Mexico with General Scott. Trist was injudicious in his approach to the sensitive military commander, and, using the General's own famous technique of writing long and inept letters, he further confused matters. In fact a war of letters between the two, and to Washington, almost bogged down the military campaign. For nearly two months Trist and Scott sparred with each other. Their communications upset the administration, but before Polk's cabinet could decide on a course of action the two men, by some quirk of their perverse natures, forgot their animosities and became close friends.

Though Santa Anna suffered sore defeat at Cerro Gordo, he was not finished as a military commander. Miraculously he organized another army and threw himself across the American advance on Mexico City. At Churubusco on August 19–20, the American Army suffered its heaviest losses at the hands of the Mexicans. Nearly a thousand men were killed and wounded. To compensate for such costly fighting, three thousand prisoners were taken and four thousand Mexicans were wounded or killed. At the conclusion of this battle General Scott committed what was considered a serious blunder. On August 21 he and Trist agreed to an armistice with Santa Anna. These two had met their superior in the faithless Mexican who had several times before gulled the Americans. It is true the battle had cost Scott's command a heavy price, and many more such engagements would have exhausted the American Army, but the cost to the Mexicans had been much heavier, and they were defeated and disorganized. A quick thrust into Mexico City would have yielded that place without serious additional cost, for under pressure Santa Anna would have had almost no chance to reorganize his army. Instead, Scott wrote Santa Anna one of his famous unfortunate notes in which he called the struggle "this unnatural war between the two great republics of this continent" and suggested an armistice while peace commissioners sought to end the fighting with a satisfactory treaty.

General Scott may have been sincere in his belief that a negotiated peace was possible after Churubusco, but he was also conscious of the approaching Presidential election back home. He realized that the successful military commander who also made peace would have a great political asset in the coming contest. The armistice, however, was not the kind of material out of which a promising Presidential candidate could be made. While Mexican officials dawdled over keeping their promises to meet Trist, Santa Anna's army was being pulled back together. When peace commissioners did arrive they submitted impossible terms full of demands and conditions, and granted no concessions. When a proposed boundary settlement fell far short of Trist's instructions the peace negotiations were ended on September 6.

Scott informed Santa Anna in another unfortunate letter that the armistice would be concluded on September 7. In the meantime the Mexicans had purchased cheaply seventeen days of rest and were in a far better condition to defend their capital city. When news of the Churubusco armistice reached Washington, Polk and his cabinet debated the issue. They gave evidence of having a clearer concept of Santa Anna's motives than did Trist and Scott. On October 4, 1847, Polk issued an order for Trist's recall on the grounds that the war would be fought to a military conclusion without further danger of a disastrous armistice.

On the day the armistice ended, Scott's army was before Mexico City itself, and on September 14, after three days of heavy fighting, the city was captured, ending the major campaigning of the war. Guerillas and local resisters continued to fight for some time, but the Mexican army was defeated. The dramatic occupation of Mexico City was accomplished by many of the same troops who had fought in the initial battles on the Rio Grande.

Guadalupe Hidalgo

When the shooting war ended on September 20, 1847, United States armed forces occupied points all the way from San Francisco on the Pacific to San Blas, from Point Isabel on the Gulf to Yucatán, and from the mouth of the Rio Grande overland to San Diego, California. Only a formal ending of hostilities by diplomacy remained to consolidate American gains on these widely dispersed fronts. This, however, was not easily accomplished. After the capture of Mexico City, Trist could not treat with responsible Mexican officials until a new president and foreign minister could be selected. In November, Pedro Maria Anaya was made interim president, and the aged supreme judge Manuel de la Peña y Peña was appointed Minister of Foreign Relations, but before a meeting could be arranged with Mexican peace commissioners, Trist received Secretary Buchanan's letter recalling him. Unable to leave Mexico, he remained against orders and on February 2, 1848, he signed the Treaty of Guadalupe Hidalgo with the Mexican commissioners.

The Mexicans chose the sacred village of Hidalgo instead of the capital city in which to negotiate the agreement. Terms of this treaty were practically those prescribed in Trist's original instructions. The southern boundary of the United States was to be the Rio Grande to the junction with the southern boundary of New Mexico, thence to the Gila River and along this stream to the Colorado, and from the Colorado westward to a point on the Pacific, a league south of San Diego. In return the United States was to pay Mexico $15,000,000 in a series of stated installments, the unpaid balance to yield an annual interest at the rate of 10 per cent. Likewise the United States was to assume payment of $3,500,000 in claims of debtors against Mexico.

The biggest accomplishment of this treaty for the United States, no doubt, was peace with its neighbor to the south. To argue that it accomplished more would involve a good many of the probabilities of frontier history. Texas was already in the Union, New Mexico had been a burden rather than an asset for Mexico, and certainly California was not one of that republic's prized possessions. Moreover, all three of these territories were all but out of Mexican hands by the time the war began. Some of the critics of the treaty and of the Polk administration claimed that Trist had accepted terms which Mexico itself might have made had it been the conqueror. Conditions under which the Treaty of Guadalupe Hidalgo was made caused the Polk administration considerable embarrassment. Trist was actually guilty of insubordination if not treason, but a majority of the cabinet voted to overlook this fact and advised the President to present the treaty to the Senate for ratification. Finally it was ratified on March 10, 1848, with some modifications. In the discussion of the treaty in the Senate,

Roger S. Baldwin of Connecticut again proposed acceptance of the so-called Wilmot Proviso. It had been first proposed on August 8, 1846, when David Wilmot of Pennsylvania attempted to attach it as an amendment to the two-million-dollar appropriation bill which President Polk requested for the purpose of making peace with Mexico, and many unsuccessful attempts had been made to add it to other bills during the war.

The Wilmot Proviso

The Wilmot Proviso spelled out what many people believed to be the sectional aspects of territorial expansion as involved in the conflict with Mexico. It provided: "That as an express and fundamental condition to the acquisition of any territory from the Republic of Mexico by the United States, by virtue of any treaty which may be negotiated between them, and to the use by the Executive of the moneys herein appropriated, neither slavery nor involuntary servitude shall ever exist in any part of said territories." This proposal became an issue of debate in both the House and Senate, and between these two houses of Congress. Although it was defeated in the Senate, it remained a live issue in national politics for the next decade.

The Mexican War, in some ways, was one of the most important struggles in which the United States has engaged. The most important and immediate of its causes was friction over the annexation of Texas and the proposed boundary of that state. There was also a crude and strong expansionist factor involved which gave the war an aspect of out-and-out imperialism by conquest. Some senators had even advocated taking a deep slice of northern Mexico. Some, even including one or two factions in Mexico, talked of the United States annexing all of the Republic. On the other hand there were anti-expansionists who did not wish to go beyond the Nueces. That slavery was a factor can hardly be doubted, but it is doubtful that the struggle can be labeled a "slaveholders' war" as it has been called in some instances. It is incorrect to assume that, from a military standpoint, the war appealed only to southerners and midwesterners, and not to people in the old thirteen states. The nature of the first call for volunteers shaped the pattern of regional interest in the struggle. For the excess numbers of volunteers who poured into the recruiting centers anxious to be off to war, it was the romance of war and the expectation of tapping Mexico's gold and silver hoard that provided the attraction.

There have been few instances in American history when so many diverse personalities were involved in so many jealousies and cross-purposes as during the Polk administration and the War with Mexico. General Taylor was a rugged frontier soldier whose single ambition, up to the battle of Monterrey, appears to have been fighting Mexicans. General Winfield Scott, a man of genuine ability, had many vagaries. His personal sensitivity and spiraling ambitions combined to make him a bundle of administrative contradictions. He struggled for self-glorification in his position at the head of the army and aspired to the highest gift of the people—the Presidency. His letters survive as examples of literary ineptitude and of military maladministration. Nicholas P. Trist, himself a composer of verbose letters, antagonized his superiors and associates. James Knox Polk found himself in that most agonizing of all official positions— a President who commanded the full faith and respect of neither his friends nor his opponents. He was a one-term President, and he knew it by the time of the first congressional elections. He did have the good sense and foresight to keep a diary to which he confided his personal reactions to the storm about him, and this rich document has survived the shouting and turmoil of the stirring 1840's to reveal him as a man of common sense and sane purposes.

Many of the issues which were dragged into the open following the annexation of Texas had validity. It was hardly conceivable that in the social and political fermentation of the period, territorial expansion could take place at so rapid a pace without bringing the antislavery forces and the proslavery partisans into conflict. Clarification of title to the large block of territory covered by the Treaty of Guadalupe Hidalgo created immediate problems of political administration. This last major territorial treaty was important in frontier history because it outlined clearly the southern boundary of the nation. With the exception of the elbow of territory acquired by purchase in 1853 in the Gadsden transaction, Manifest Destiny had run one important phase of its course. After 1848 frontier expansion lost the spice of international rivalries which had prevailed since the beginning of European settlement on the continent.

GOLD, SILVER, AND MEN

Three-fourths of the houses in the town on the Bay of San Francisco are deserted. Houses are sold at the price of building lots. The effects are this week showing themselves in Monterey. Almost every house I had hired out is given up. Every blacksmith, carpenter and lawyer is leaving; brick-yards, sawmills, and ranches are left perfectly alone. A large number of the volunteers at San Francisco and Sonoma have deserted; . . . public and private vessels are losing their crews . . . Both of our newspapers are discontinued from want of workmen and the loss of their agencies; the Alcaldes have left San Francisco, and I believe Sonoma likewise; the former place has not a justice of the peace left.

—THOMAS O. LARKIN
to Secretary of State JAMES BUCHANAN

SUTTER'S FORT - NEW HELVETIA.

FROM REVERE'S *Tour of Duty in California,* 1849

CHAPTER XXIV

The Mineral Frontier

BEFORE the first eager gold-rusher crossed the Great Divide, the fur empire was definitely on the wane after having exerted its influence on national expansion. The War with Mexico and the treaty which followed had removed the border barrier in the Southwest. Settlers had already drifted into Oregon in sufficient numbers to people a territory. Immediately east of the Sierras, the Mormon movement westward was well underway.

Both the military and political exploitations of California were in an advanced stage. John C. Frémont had made his famous and highly publicized expeditions west, and the incidents of the Mexican War and subsequent political and economic activities had helped to bring California well within the common knowledge of the American people. The decade just closing had been a rousing one in which soldier, adventurer, immigrant and orator had shared the excitement to the fullest. By 1848, the pace of events had somewhat slowed down and national life might be expected to return to the normal everyday affair of making a living. There was, however, an air of expectancy about the closing of the decade. The times, with their tinge of romanticism, were ripe for the discovery of a rich

569

mineral field and a wild rush onto the far western frontier. Several trails west were blazed, the system of communication, though inefficient, was open, and the West Coast was not nearly so isolated as it was when Jedediah Smith and Joseph Reddeford Walker went to California.

As we have already seen, Spanish-speaking dons and Yankee shipowners, soldiers, traders, adventurers, and American backwoodsmen commingled with the native population of California to create a variegated social structure. The *rancho* was an attractive center of social life for the upper social class, and the sun-scorched grazing lands and fields were scenes of labor for peons and Indians. Master of one of these pleasant baronial *haciendas* was the Swiss immigrant Johann Sutter who had located his landholdings on the American River within the area of the present city of Sacramento. Here he operated his estate with a friendly and generous hand. In 1848 he began the construction of a saw mill forty-eight miles above his fort on the American River. Workmen toiling at building the mill included Mormons who had come west, either in the Mormon battalion, or with Sam Brannan aboard the *Brooklyn*.

Sutter's Mill

Sutter's sawmill operations were under the direction of James Marshall, a New Jersey carpenter who had drifted west. In order to construct the necessary tail races for the water mill, a considerable quantity of earth had to be removed. On January 24, 1848, while inspecting one of the ditches lately washed by floodwaters, Marshall discovered some flecks of bright metal which excited his curiosity. This was the beginning of a highly dramatic incident in American history. Marshall could not be sure of the true nature of his find or of its extent. Gathering up a sample, he rode the forty-eight miles to Sutter's Fort to discuss the matter with his employer. In a secret conference Sutter heard Marshall's report and saw his sample of ore. To him the news was somewhat disturbing. Sensibly, the Swiss landlord realized that this could mean the end of work at his mill. Possibly, he foresaw it even as a threat to his feudal estate. He and Marshall agreed to keep the secret, at least until the mill was finished.

Sutter and Marshall then set out to strengthen their claim to the large block of land which Sutter had secured by grant from the Mexican Alcalde Alvarado. They sent a representative to call on Colonel R. B. Mason, United States government agent in California, to secure the necessary assurance that their grant was safe. Their agent, Charles Bennett, made the fatal mistake of divulging the secret that traces of gold had been found on the American River. It would have been impossible, of course, to keep such a story suppressed for any length of time. Too many workmen were at the mill and they were finding more gold every day along the mill race and on the neighboring sandbars. An ever-widening circle of exploration revealed that the precious metal existed in many locations along the river. There was one big question in the mind of these early gold hunters: Was the stuff they were picking up really gold or was it mica or sulphuret of copper? Equipment or skill for making a dependable assay was not immediately available. There was, however, in that vicinity a Georgia gold miner, Isaac Humphries, who knew unrefined gold when he saw it. He also knew something of gold-bearing formations. Upon inspecting the ore from the American River he expressed the belief that Sutter's men had found gold.

Ho for California!

During the next six months the story of the discovery of gold in California spread first like a smouldering fire under dampened debris, and then it leaped into a wild crackling blaze. California was having a gold rush from within its boundaries. Free gold lying in pockets and drifting underground in rich veins was the catalyst which touched off a wild and greedy human scramble for quick and easily gained wealth. Stories of miners extracting fabulous amounts of gold in a week's time multiplied tenfold, and accounts of lucky prospectors uncovering rich pockets containing small fortunes were in themselves more than human frailty could endure. Farmers left their plows and herds; merchants closed their doors and slipped away. Crews in San Francisco harbor jumped ship and rushed inland to the diggings. Even ministers of the Gospel left their pulpits untended. San Francisco's population dwindled. Miners poured in by droves to the diggings, and soon new landmarks such as Bidwell's Bar, Todd's Valley, Weber Creek, Yankee Jim's Long Bar, Auburn, and countless others appeared on the scene.

Back on the coast at San Francisco, trade boomed. Merchants in the coast towns quickly disposed of their supplies of picks, shovels, knives and pans. Even their stocks of skillets, canteens and tents were soon exhausted. Red-shirted miners living as primitively as gophers in holes formed new and rowdy communities without the established law or the chastening influence of civilized institutions. This was the scene at Christmas time, 1848.

Except for some excitement in Oregon and in Hawaii, the gold fever did not spread outside California until near the close of the year. Possibly the first dependable account of what was happening in California was Colonel Mason's report to the War Department in November, 1848. Colonel Mason had brought east with him a tea caddy of dust weighing 230 ounces which assayed $3,910.10 of 894-thousandths fineness. The eastern press took up the story of the discoveries along the American River, and in a short time the Atlantic seaboard was undergoing its first stages of gold fever excitement.

The sensational news came at a time when the country was being introduced to many new and popular songs. During the 1840's Stephen Collins Foster was beginning his music-writing career, and among his first successful songs were the popular blackface or plantation ballads. In 1845 he published his famous song *Oh Susanna* with its rollicking melody that largely expressed the spirit of the times. The lyric of the song was humorous nonsense that was not intended to have meaning. The melody, however, was highly adaptable to almost any combination of words. In a short time, various adaptations of it became the music to which men rushed away to California, singing and dreaming of quick and vast riches.

All over the country gold fever infected the people. In the factories and towns of New England, the green farms of the Susquehanna, in Virginia, Kentucky, the cotton fields of the lower South, and the frontier settlements beyond the Mississippi—everywhere the news went—men made ready to be off. Many New Englanders, following the example of Nathaniel Wyeth and the Oregon immigrants, organized themselves into companies and went marching through the eastern towns dressed in the striking uniforms of their organizations and bearing knives, pistols, sabres, rifles, and gold mining equipment. Those who went overland stocked their wagons with biscuits, meat, stocks of clothing, shoes, and tools. Some overland rushers went by the Santa Fe-Gila River-Colorado-Sierra Nevada route, while others left civilization at Independence, Missouri, and went up the Kansas River by Fort Kearney to the Upper Platte; thence to South Pass; thence to Soda Springs and Fort Hall; thereafter southwestward by the Humboldt Valley, the City of Rocks, Ragtown, and Carson Pass. A southern branch of this route went by way of South Pass-Fort Bridger-Salt Lake City to the City of Rocks. All of this was at one time or another labeled the "California Trail," but it actually comprised parts of the old fur-trading routes up the Platte and to Fort Bridger, the Oregon and Mormon Trails.

Companies that started out with wagons discovered by the time they reached Fort Hall or Salt Lake City that they had undertaken a hazardous adventure. Their loads were too heavy, their livestock was jaded, and the road ahead offered a greater challenge of endurance than they could meet. Many companies abandoned their vehicles and fitted out pack trains; some clung to their wagons and loads of freight. By the end of 1849, the trails to California were strewn with discarded food, clothing, mining equipment and wagons. Many campfires were made from wagons which a few months before had begun the trek to California as bright new vehicles, the pride of their adventurous owners.

More tragic than the cast-off belongings and half-burned remains of wagon trains were the skeletons of animals and men who had dropped by the wayside, and the hastily made grave mounds and markers designating the final resting places of Argonauts who were halted short of the gold field. There were victims of accidents, of fights, and of the ordinary fatal diseases, but the greatest numbers died in an outbreak of Asiatic cholera which spread across the plains in '49. Essentially the trail to California was a trail of tears and human tragedy.

While many anxious gold rushers plodded overland, thousands of others chose what they believed to be the easier way and went forth by sea. Again, companies were organized to buy and man ships to make the journey around Cape Horn to California. Others purchased "through tickets," supposed to deliver them in the shortest time possible in the port of Chagres on the east coast of Panama whence they journeyed by boat and pack mule through the jungle to the Pacific coast port of Panama City. There they hoped to catch a coastal vessel that would take them on to San Francisco. Many of the Argonauts who went this way have left accounts of their journeys. They were victimized by the most flagrant breaches of contracts. Once in Chagres, the traveler had before him the treacherous, stifling jungle trip, but its trials for many were more pleasant than the boredom and dirt of Chagres where the only amusements were cockfighting and gambling. From New York to Chagres was 2,200 miles, and from Panama City to San Francisco was 3,500 miles—5,700 miles in all—and many a gold seeker sailed the latter leg of the trip crowded on decks of slow vessels with twice as many people as should have been aboard. Owners of shipping companies found more gold in their passengers' pockets at the start of the journey than they could dig in the hidden pockets of the American River placers.

The influx of the gold rushers created one of the most peculiar social situations in American history. Although gold had been discovered in North Carolina in the 1790's, and in Georgia in the 1830's, there had been no rush to the fields. Not even the fur trade, the trade down the Sante Fe Trail, the movement into Texas, nor the subsequent movement to Oregon created such a furious stir as the rush to California. Not only Americans rushed westward, but Europeans and orientals joined them. Before the end of 1850 the diggings had become an international social cauldron. As the flood of newcomers poured in, society in the diggings changed rapidly from that of a relatively small number of neighborly men searching for gold, and helping one another in the process, to swarms of people seeking quick fortunes. As one contemporary said, rascality became international in its complexion as scoundrels and cutthroats foregathered from everywhere.

This wild rush westward was unlike anything that had ever occurred before on the American frontier. The search for free land had attracted speculators, the trade over the trails southwestward had attracted adventurers, and the fur trade had had its share of opportunists. Most of these, however, had worked out from the outer rim of settlement and had seldom if ever made the direct jump from a settled and semimature society to a primitive state with little conditioning in between. In the California gold fields, houses were lacking, and men built tents, log huts, lean-tos and dugouts. Food supplies were limited largely to salt meat, beans and coarse bread. In the early days many of Sutter's abandoned cattle and sheep fell victims to the hungry hordes that ranged the hills. Drovers then discovered the profitable markets for their animals and appeared on the scene, to make more certain profits than those who courted fortune with pick and pan.

Seeing the Elephant

In the early days when pockets of dust were uncovered with exciting frequency, gold dust passed around with abandon. Many miners took little trouble to try to discover its true value. A pinch was a standard of measure, and the quantity of gold contained in a pinch varied with the size of the thumbs and forefingers dispensing it. Life was cut to the same generous but reckless scale. Gambling and drinking offered escape from the realities of boredom and poor living conditions. Some Argonauts had taken their wives and daughters with them, but most chose to hasten ahead without interference from their women folk. As the gold fever intensified, women of easy virtue followed the trail of fortune to the free-spending and uninhibited mining camps. In time disputes over the favors of these generous daughters of Eve were as numerous and fatal as those which arose over mine claims.

While large numbers of men and women reverted to the most primitive and lustful behavior, many individuals felt a loyalty to wives and families back home and conducted themselves according to the strict puritanical code of eastern seaboard society. Some of them even adhered to the religious practices of their homes and organized fugitive congregations with ministers and regular services. In time there were theaters with entertainers who followed the golden trail westward where the loose dust was more generously available to them than dollars were in the older states.

Rushing for gold was high adventure in which the participants courted fickle destiny. With notebook in hand and with Yankee thoroughness, New Englanders rushed westward to seek gold and to record their experiences while they did so. A century and more later, these accounts of lively expectations, enormous hardships, and final frustration, recreate at first hand this feverish phase of national expansion.

The dream of easy wealth was quickly dissipated for many. Stories of fabulous amounts of gold being picked up almost at random blinded the naive prospectors to the realities of what they might expect when they were actually on the ground—the gruelling labor and the disappointment which often came as their only reward. R. R. Taylor, a Yankee Argonaut, left his home in Williamstown, Massachusetts, in May, 1849, to get a peep at "the elephant" on the far-away Sacramento. In the course of an enormously interesting series of letters to his wife he finally admitted late in September that he was disappointed.

> As to gold digging, I am sorry to acknowledge, what everybody else here does, that I have been *humbugged*. Gold is not as plentiful as we were made to believe, & it is ten times harder work to get it than any one could have imagined. From the most diligent inquiries of old miners, & people from all parts of the mines, I am satisfied that the average proceeds will not exceed half an ounce per day for those who labor hard & faithfully. Now and then a lucky one strikes a vein & gets out several hundred dollars in a day or two, and his case is caught up by traders & speculators & published all over the union, while of the ninety & nine who are at work around him, getting five or six dollars per day, nothing is said.

Taylor then described to his wife the backbreaking work necessary to make anything. The California gold was sluiced out of the soil for the most part. Hammer mills and refiners were for the future. All sorts of crude devices such as troughs, boxes and rocker frames were tried, but none of them eased the labor nor were efficient in extracting the gold. Perhaps the most common of the hand-operated devices was the "Long Tom" which consisted of two troughs, the upper one having an iron baffle or seine in the lower half of its bottom, to feed the fine earth into the lower trough so that the gold could be caught behind a series of cleats. The sluice box was a long yard-wide trough of almost indeterminate length with cleats in the bottom to check the flow of gold dust which sank while the greater portion of earth and rock washed away. Placer mining on a big scale could be carried on only by the use of pumping machinery and the employment of large numbers of men. This required careful channeling of streams, the opening of elaborate sluiceways, and the removal of virtual mountains of earth. By the end of 1855 placer mining on the Sacramento had become mostly a corporate business; the individual miner was left to luck if he would make his way in his search for gold. The California State Mining Bureau estimated that in five years, 1848–1853, the mines yielded approximately $276,000,000, and in a decade the yield was nearly half a billion dollars.

From the long range point of view, the amount of gold which the Californians put afloat in the world of finance and commerce was not so important as the rapidity with which the West Coast was populated. Three important cities grew in the path of the gold rush: San Francisco, Sacramento and Stockton. In 1850 San Francisco was a jungle of tents and flimsy wooden shacks. Its harbor was littered with deserted ships. Its docks were crowded with goods and clumsy devices which had been brought along to extract gold from the sand. Barrooms, brothels and jerry-built stores sprang up among the prairie-dog dwellings of the predominantly male population. A fire that year leveled much of the city to the ground, but two years later an observer who had seen the city burn recorded the phenomenal rapidity by which it had been restored.

> The following morning we landed, and took a stroll about the city; but seek as we might there was nothing to remind us of the San Francisco of fifteen months before. From the ashes of the fire, another town had arisen, in some respects much better than the early one of tents and shanties, the streets more closely followed a definite plan, and there were several good buildings, with fewer tents, still, as yet a very primitive place, with a population composed mainly of men, bearded, and clothed in the roughest attire.

California grew at a breathless rate, and the gold rush hastened the need for political stability as well as the expansion of the region's economic pattern.

Socially the gold rush had brought much prosperity, a rapidly increasing population and a tremendously colorful pageant of pioneering. Its intersectional and international aspects, plus its overwhelming male composition and the free-and-easy spending of gold dust, gave society a glamour far out of proportion to the average frontier advancement. The influx of gold seekers, however, had outdistanced the normal process of frontier political organization. The territory of California was incapable in 1849 of maintaining peace and decorum in the gold camps. When the main stream of the gold rush reached the diggings, it brought with it a considerable number of knaves and scoundrels. Criminals from the eastern states and from abroad had rushed westward to escape capture and to enhance their fortunes.

Though lawlessness was a characteristic of the gold rush, and the excitement following the discovery of gold brought together a hodgepodge of the innocent and the criminal, a basic respect for the laws of human decency was far from lacking. Where the informal territorial forces proved unable to cope with the heavy police demands, groups of individuals took upon themselves the task of enforcing the law. Vigilante bands were formed, and offenders were brought into informal courts and given hasty trials. The sentences of these courts were executed with an equal haste. These early California vigilante trials were effective in carrying out the wishes of the rough disorganized society, and possibly they administered justice in many cases. There was one drawback, however. Evidence was nearly always examined in the presence of an excited mob which had already made up its collective mind as to the guilt of offenders. Likewise, decisions reached in haste and on hearsay evidence could not be re-examined in calmer moments and in the light of newer and more trustworthy information. The victim had been hanged and the case was closed. This was not the first time that rugged vigilante justice had been administered on the frontier, but it did mark the beginning of a pattern which was to prevail in the immediate future through the fast-developing West. Possibly of more importance as an elementary beginning of local government were the districts formed by miners in the gold-bearing regions. Here was a form of orderly procedure so far as property was concerned that was reminiscent of the formation of counties on the older eastern frontier.

Pike's Peak and Virginia City

Although the California gold rush fever cooled off by 1851, and gold mining entered a larger corporate phase in that region and in the mountains eastward, in no way was excitement over other mineral strikes lessened. In the decade between the discovery of gold in California and the opening of the Washoe strikes in Nevada there was at least a rush a year. Some took prospectors out into the Pacific along the California coast and northward to the Fraser River. The two big rushes, however, were those to the Pike's Peak region and to the Nevada field about Virginia City. As early as 1850 gold had been discovered near Denver, and the news of this strike caused some excitement. From that time on Colorado held interest if not genuine promise for gold seekers. It was not, however, until 1858 that the real rush was touched off in this region when the Russell-Cherokee party of miners from Georgia and California found promise of gold along Cherry Creek. Stories of the success of prospectors in the area brought on a major rush in 1859. From California on the west, and from the states on the east, an excited horde of gold seekers came to the new fields to make the fortunes which they had failed to find in California. Wagons rolling out from Kansas and Missouri bore the boastful legend "Pike's Peak or Bust!" painted on their covers. A few months later some of them dragged back with the frustrated explanation, "Busted, by God!" but the rush to Colorado was not entirely in vain. The rich Gregory lode was discovered in 1859 near Central City, and in time this new development was to pay a handsome profit. Before the rushes were over in Colorado, many new locations were found; among these was the fabulous Cripple Creek lode which yielded a vast return of both gold and silver.

While Pike's Peak rushers were swarming into the ranges about Cherry Creek, some of them even scaling the peak itself, the Comstock Lode was opened in Nevada. Of all the rich mineral strikes in the West this was possibly king of them all. The Comstock Lode yielded a rich return of gold and silver, and history was enriched by the antics of fantastic characters who participated in its discovery. Foremost among these was the hapless James Finney. Stumbling along in the dark and befuddled by drink, in 1859 "Old Virginia" as he was called, fell over a boulder and smashed his bottle of liquor. Its precious contents, except for a few drops that remained in the jagged bottom, poured out over the ground. Clamoring to his feet the old prospector downed the remaining whiskey and christened the spot Virginia Town, later changed to Virginia City, a magic name in western mining history. A close rival of Finney's was Henry T. P. Comstock. "Old Pancake," as he was called, came from a good Connecticut family which traced its lineage back to Puritan stock. Comstock had at one time been a mountain man, and in 1849 he had gone to California in the gold rush. From California he had followed the movement of prospectors to Mount Davidson where his name would be given to the famous mother lode. Yet both Old Virginia and Old Pancake lent more color than intelligent leadership to the activities about the Nevada diggings.

The Carson River gold diggings had showed promise of good, if not spectacular, returns as early as 1856, and at least two prospectors who came to Nevada believed there was more than gold to be found in the region. They were Hosea and Ethan Allen Grosch from Utica, New York, young men with more than average intelligence and training. They brought with them books, some knowledge of metallurgy, and a lively curiosity. How much precise knowledge they gained about the presence of silver in Nevada remains a moot question. Undoubtedly they knew of or suspected its presence. They operated a small assay furnace, took samples, and apparently sunk a shaft which was never uncovered. Hosea injured his foot with a pick and died of an infection. His brother, attempting to make his way to California in the winter of 1857, was caught in a bitter storm and his feet were frozen. He died from the effects of an operation in which both of his feet were amputated.

The Comstock Lode

Not until 1859 was the main Comstock or Gold Hill lead discovered. In this year Peter O'Reilly and Pat McLaughlin were working a claim in Six Mile Canyon at Gold Hill. At one point they almost gave up their search in desperation and planned to move on, but they decided to stay a few days longer. Cutting through a mass of black or blue dirt, in an effort to create a small reservoir, they discovered flecks of gold. They were uncertain as to whether or not they had really found gold, and of course had no idea what the troublesome "blue earth" was. While they were pondering the problem, H. T. P. Comstock appeared on the scene. By sheer bluff he forced the partners to grant him and Emmanuel Penrod a claim because of prior registry on 160 acres of land about the new mine. Constock's claim of ownership dated back to the death of the Grosch brothers. He contended that he had inherited their interests. Not only did he claim the land, but "Old Pancake" also claimed the right to the water for use in the sluice boxes.

While Comstock was laying claim to a share of the rich discovery of gold and silver, "Old Virginia" or James Finney had located a lead to the Ophir vein in the same area. Thus "Old Pancake" and "Old Virginia" had claims on one of the richest gold and silver lodes in America. Neither had the common sense nor vision to protect and exploit their property, and both quickly sold their interests for neglible sums. Though their ownership was brief, they both fixed their names firmly upon the region. Wherever gold mining was discussed in years to come, the Comstock Lode was a prominent topic.

The miners in Six Mile Canyon knew about the gold in the rich vein, but they were oblivious at first to the vast riches contained in the "blue earth"—the silver sulphurets. Augustus Harrison carried a sample of the blue ore to Grass Valley, California, and turned it over to Judge James Walsh. Judge Walsh in turn had the ore assayed by Melville Atwood who reported that it was silver mixed with gold and would yield a large sum per ton. When news of this assay got out, a wild rush began to buy out the claims and to begin exploitation of the rich ore. As word spread of the great strike at Washoe, another stampede was on. Old miners who had rushed from one place to another since the early days of California mining heeded the new call to Nevada. The usual flotsam of gamblers, saloon keepers, merchants, prostitutes, even lawyers seeking clients and rich fees, were all borne along by the new promise of riches. Young William Stewart who had gone to the diggings in California packed up and moved eastward to Nevada, where in a remarkably short time he had accumulated a half million dollars in fees, and was elected to the United States Senate from the newly formed State of Nevada.

During the early 1860's the Nevada mining story followed the earlier pattern of the California diggings. A veritable army of individuals floated in and out of the region. Friction with the Piute Indians brought about a short-lived war which produced both horrors and heroes. Lawlessness was put down by mobs seeking quick and decisive penalties, if not justice in the truest sense. The towns and mining camps were rowdy places. Virginia City, which Finney had so unceremoniously christened, became a landmark in mining history. Its roaring life and debaucheries were exciting even to a West already noted for social disorder.

But all of this is somewhat insignificant when compared with the great technical advances which enabled miners to extract gold and silver from chunks of quartz. Just as in California, Nevada mining quickly got beyond the stage where individuals or small groups of miners with primitive equipment could exploit the rich lode.

Possibly one of the most important men to reach Virginia City was Philip Diedesheimer, a native of Darmstadt, Germany, who had engaged in gold mining in California. His ingenuity facilitated the exploitation of the Mount Davidson vein. He developed the mining processes by which the mother lode could be followed as it dipped deeply under the great mountain mass. He introduced into western mining the art of timbering up with "square sets." It has been said that in a moment of frustration while trying to devise a scheme for timbering a mine with short timber his attention was attracted to the structure of the comb made by honeybees. On somewhat the same principle he employed short, squared lengths of mountain timber to build rectangles. These were placed under the roof of the mines. They could be extended upward as high as needed, and spread over as wide an opening as was necessary. Because of their rugged construction these rectangles were capable of bearing enormous loads of downward pressure, and at the same time dirt could be removed without danger from slate falls and cave-ins.

Inside the Consolidated Virginia mine, for example, the width of the cut ranged from fifty to a hundred and fifty feet, and the depth varied with that of the ore vein. Diedesheimer's method of mine timbering was only one of many major improvements in the process of extracting gold and silver. With the introduction of heavy hoisting machinery it was possible to tap the richest deposits of ore at great depth. The mine shafts dipped down from a thousand to sixteen hundred feet. To carry on mining activities at so great a depth called for expert engineering. Not only was it necessary to timber the shafts, but hoisting, ventilation, and heat and fire control became major problems. Heat at the lower depths was so intense that men often worked while helpers threw ice water over them.

At an approximate depth of 1,500 feet the Consolidated Virginia miners struck the fabulously rich portion of the mother lode which yielded anywhere from $90 to $625 per ton of ore. Virginia and Ophir stocks soared to unbelievably high levels almost overnight. Ophir shares jumped from $30 to $750. A fresh rush of miners returned to Virginia City, but the biggest excitement was on the stock market where speculators rather than prospectors struggled to secure possession of the wealth of the mines. The Consolidated Virginia yielded approximately a million dollars a month; yet its production was limited because of the lack of milling capacity above ground.

Before Diedesheimer and the promoters of the Ophir and Virginia interests began the tunneling which opened the great bonanza, Adolph Heinrich Sutro, a Prussian mining engineer, conceived the idea of cutting a lateral opening into the side of Mount Davidson to release the gases, provide drainage, and permit easy transportation of miners into the main shafts. He proposed a tunnel ten feet high, twelve feet wide, and, with its laterals, at least five miles long. After considerable political manipulation in Nevada and Washington he secured a charter for his company, and the privilege of cutting through the public domain. He then went to Europe where he secured the major portion of the funds necessary to carry on the construction of the tunnel. The mining companies were to pay a royalty of two dollars per ton on ore removed to finance the Sutro project. Between 1869 and 1879 the tunnel was completed. There is difference of opinion as to whether or not it was profitable since its completion almost coincided with the exhaustion of the Comstock Lode, but the tunnel introduced a new principle of mine ventilation and tunneling.

Nevada's "big bonanza" opened in 1873. That year several supposedly worked-out mining properties were consolidated into the large Virginia and Ophir Companies. In this new phase of deep scale mining, four names, Mackay, Fair, Flood and O'Brien, were most prominent in organizing and controlling the mining properties. Likewise the "Big Four" in western railroad development, Leland Stanford, Collis P. Huntington, Charles Crocker and Mark Hopkins, were casting covetous eyes upon the Nevada mining field as a possible place for profitable investment. So were an army of speculators, big and little, and Nevada mining stocks quickly became highly desirable commodities.

Within a short time after the strike at Virginia City, the new bullion fed into the country's fiscal system had a significant effect on the national economy. San Francisco took on new life, and the wealth originating in Virginia City manifested itself in feverish financial transactions in that city.

Montana and Idaho

The area of the gold rushes in the Rocky Mountain region was an ever-expanding one. From Pike's Peak or Cherry Creek, the rush went southward to the gold fields of Nevada, as we have seen, and northward to

Idaho and Montana. As early as 1852, and perhaps even earlier, gold was known to exist, in color at least, in Montana—but it was not until a decade later that the big strike came at Benetsee Creek. By June of 1862 a mild rush was in progress to this northwestern gold field. Promising discoveries were made near Bannack, and within six months a town of five hundred souls had made its appearance. Prospectors worked out in every direction searching for new leads. One of these groups went toward the Big Horn Mountains, but the Crow Indians drove them back. On their return to Bannack they stopped in camp at Alder Gulch, and a chance washing of gravel by William Fairweather and Henry Edgar revealed the existence of gold in rich quantities. Here it was that Virginia City, Montana, was founded, and like its namesake in Nevada, the new camp became a wild and reckless gold mine town where life ebbed and flowed in stormy currents.

In 1864 John Cowan, a Georgian, and a party of three companions discovered a rich vein of gold at Last Chance Gulch (Helena). So exciting was this latter strike that it drew a large population about it in a remarkably short time, and Helena became the most important town in the Montana country. Within the next five years the rich mineral belt of Montana had been expanded to include a region 150 miles in length and 100 miles in width. In all there were approximately 500 paying gulches and mine sites. Montana gold was of high quality ranging from 600 to 990 fineness. It was found both as dust and nuggets. Possibly the Montana diggings produced the greatest number of large nuggets found in the West. These varied in size from the 175-ounce lump found in a tributary of Snowshoe Gulch in 1865 to smaller ones found now and then until the 1880's.

For fifteen years the story of gold mining in Montana was that of one strike after another in the maze of gulches in the Rocky Mountain ranges. Miners with primitive tools were at first richly rewarded, but there, as everywhere else, power-driven hoists and stamping mills were necessary in order to extract much of the gold from the quartz formations. Montana produced its picturesque characters as did all of the other gold fields, but organized companies which undertook a systematic mining procedure reaped the richest harvest. The lucky strikes of the poorly equipped individual miners and prospectors were the materials from which exciting stories were written, but it was organization and machinery that actually produced the great bulk of the gold and silver. A large number of companies was organized in Montana, and considerable capital was invested in machinery and water supply. During the first twenty years, 1862–1882, gold and silver worth more than $175,000,000 was taken from the Montana gulches. In subsequent years the production of the mines was valued at $20,000,000.

The gold rush to Montana repeated the social pattern already established in California, Nevada, and Colorado. By the time the rushes reached Alder and Last Chance gulches, the lawless elements following the rich mining strikes had reached an almost professional status of cussedness. More than ever, the vigilance committee was used to keep law and order until a more stable form of local government could be organized. Robbery and murder seem to have led the list of crimes which invoked the wrath of the regulators. No time was lost in trying victims or in examining and re-examining evidence. An infuriated mob, a rope, a high limb, and a quick drop were all that were needed to send a scoundrel or a saint off to eternity without right of appeal. There were no jails, no jailers, and no one on the far western frontier had time to waste guarding prisoners. Capital offenders were hanged, and minor offenders had their ears sheared off, or they were severely whipped and run out of town. Famous victims of the noose in Montana were Henry Plummer, Buck Stinson, Jo Pizanthia, George Ives, Boone Helm, and a score of others.

Granville Stuart, the Montana pioneer, has left a graphic description of life in the early gold rush.

> These were dark days (1863) in Bannack; there was no safety for life or property only so far as each individual could, with his trusty rifle, protect his own. The respectable citizens far outnumbered the desperadoes, but having come from all corners of the earth, they were unacquainted and did not know whom to trust. On the other hand the "rough" were organized and under able leadership of that accomplished villain, Henry Plummer. At times it would seem that they had the upper hand and would run affairs to suit themselves. The law abiding citizens were beginning to get better acquainted and although the few attempts made to administer justice had failed they believed that the time would come and that at no distant day, when the community would rid themselves of this undesirable element.

What had happened in Montana occurred to a large extent in Idaho. Gold was discovered in the country along the Salmon River, and as early as 1860 there was considerable activity on Oro Fino Creek following a strike by E. D. Pierce. The expanding mineral empire in that region led to the organization of the Idaho Territory in 1863, and was to become a vital part of the state's industrial history. Elsewhere on the frontier two important gold strikes left their mark on the record of western expansion. The same year that the Great Bonanza at Virginia City, Nevada, was being developed, gold was discovered in the Black Hills of South Dakota by miners and soldiers who went there with General Custer to locate a road to Fort Laramie. A gold rush took place into the Sioux country after the

United States government was unable to persuade the Indians to vacate the treaty which gave them the Black Hills as a reservation. Custer and Deadwood became the important mining centers. Thousands of miners and camp hangers-on rushed into the country, so that by 1876 the rugged and colorful pattern of gold camp civilization was being developed all over again with specific local characters and incidents.

Cripple Creek

The last important gold and silver strike in the West was that at Cripple Creek, Colorado, in 1891–1894. Cripple Creek's history is intimately tied up with the life story of Robert Womack, a persistent prospector who followed the trail of gold from loose bits of float to the rich ledges of the western slope of the Colorado Rockies. The population of the Cripple Creek district increased from 15 in 1890 to 50,111 in 1900. Its estimated income, for sixty-three years, 1890–1953, was $412,974,848. In this Colorado mining town, America saw the last big fling of the exciting period of mineral rushes. The estimated value of gold and silver from Virginia City is $380,000,000, and from Homestake, South Dakota, $494,113,151.

The mining frontier had a rather short duration, but its appeal to all kinds of people brought a large population quickly to the frontier. Men and women rushed to the scene of mineral strikes in search of easily gained wealth, adventure, and escape from boredom of everyday life. Some went to gamble, some to practice prostitution, and not a few rushed away from their homes just ahead of the sheriff. No historian can be entirely certain how much influence the threatened panic of the late 1850's and the rising conflict between North and South may have had upon sending people away to the gold rushes. By the same token no one can be certain how important the production of gold in an increasing quantity was in the financing of the Civil War. Some have contended that western gold and silver were vital in the conduct of war. Large quantities of gold were released in financial circles, however, and its availability from native sources was doubtless contributory in fixing in the minds of the nation's creditors an attachment for gold-supported government paper.

In the western mining centers during the Civil War days an objective observer would have found it difficult to discover that a war was in progress. Miners and gold-field followers were as numerous during war as they were in peace, and they seemed to be little concerned with the national conflict. They lived beyond the reach of the battlefields. Large numbers of them had little or no access to newspapers, and they knew too little of current news to follow intelligently the fortunes of the two armies. Again no one can be certain about whether or not the administration in

Washington was not as anxious to have the western miners pouring out their monthly piles of gold dust as it was to have them manning guns in battle. Certainly deserters and draft dodgers were beyond the law in the canyons and gulches of Nevada and Montana. Not all of the draft dodgers, however, came from the North. Southerners were present in large numbers. Reflective of southern partisanship, some of the miners wished to call Virginia City, Montana, Varina in honor of Mrs. Jefferson Davis. Judge G. C. Bissell, a Unionist, refused to accept the name on legal papers, but as a compromise with southern feelings he submitted to the use of Virginia City. One gulch did bear the name "Confederate."

The movement of population into the far western frontier remains the dominant and most permanent fact of the early mining days. The details of population movement and state-making will be dealt with elsewhere, but it may be stated here that the gold and silver strikes drew into the West population enough to justify the establishment of territories almost overnight. Not only did the fact of mere numbers of immigrants justify the organization of local political bodies, but the accompanying lawlessness and confusion over property rights made the demand for organized government imperative. Frequently there was not enough time for the old processes of territory and state-making on the frontier to take the slow traditional course; it was easier to copy an established plan of government than to devise a new one. The new western state and local governments followed the orthodox pattern of the older eastern states. There were no radical experiments or departures in the new constitutions; no insistent crop of political theorists disturbed the waters of the early organizational meetings. Politicians in Washington looking to new states for support in the coming national elections and the pressure of lawlessness in the mining camps were often the prime movers in state making.

The newer mineral strikes such as those in Nevada, Idaho, Montana and Colorado were so rich that they created a greater spirit of restlessness and general disregard for both human rights and life. The stakes were high, the time for winning them short, and gambling fever increased in proportion to the general tempo—whether in the mines or at the faro table. Amid the recklessness and indifference to law and order of the mining towns and camps, few people could have felt that they were permanent settlers. The whole spirit of this phase of western expansion bore the stamp of impermanence. Nobody believed that a mother lode could last beyond the brief predictable period of time it would take to bring the ore to the surface. As in the case of the Big Bonanza, mining experts measured off its future in inches and could predict within a reasonable margin of time when it would be exhausted. Unlike many other natural resources, when the gold and silver lodes were exhausted, there was no chance of their being replenished. Their days were over, and most often the terrain where they existed was too rough and infertile to support more than a sparse grazing civilization. When mining activities ceased, a new social phenomenon appeared on the frontier in the form of ghost towns, which had to await the coming of the American tourist to be productive again. The actual financial activities of the later gold rushes took place away from the mining centers. The impersonal and detached system of corporate mining removed the policy-making of the mineral empire to the financial centers of San Francisco, Denver and New York. San Francisco especially reflected the wealth of the western mines. The denizens of its famous Nob Hill were anchored financially in the depths of the less scenic Mount Davidson, or Alder and Last Chance gulches. Social striving and bitter personal rivalries arose among the coast city businessmen in proportion to the productivity of the mines in which they were interested.

As long as the landmarks of the Comstock Lode and other rich strikes remain, however, men will not forget their day of glory, nor that army of human characters who gave rugged quality to the era. Such a rich human story as that of Sandy and Eilly Bowers, the greenhorn couple who struck it rich, will be told and freely embroidered every time a new book about Nevada mining is written. When they were married, their jocular friends gave them a million dollars in what they believed were worthless stock certificates. As it turned out the stock was literally worth a million, and in time the Bowers came into the possession of several million dollars more. They built the famous Bowers mansion near Reno, and journeyed to England with a silver tray hammered from their own stock as a gift for the Queen. In exchange they received sprigs of ivy from Windsor Castle which in time grew on the walls of their Nevada mansion. They spent more than $150,000 on their trip abroad; they bought European furnishings to equip their mansion in the best style of the day. Yet Sandy died young, and Eilly went to a pauper's grave. There were others too—such as "Old Pancake" Comstock and "Old Virginia" Finney, Senator William Stewart, Allen and Hosea Grosch, Philip Diedesheimer, Adolph Sutro, William Fairweather, Granville Stuart, and the four dukes of Nevada—Flood, Fair, O'Brien and Mackay. Even the literary men, J. Ross Browne, Bayard Taylor, Samuel Clemens, and Dan De Quille contributed their bits to this exciting personal chapter in American history. Diedesheimer's maze of scrubby pine rectangles still honeycombs the great caverns in the base of Mount Davidson, and the gaping tunnel which Adolph Sutro helped to cut into the mountainside from the Carson River is a monument to pioneer mining history. The long tradition of Deadwood and its heroes have become a part of American folklore and history.

THE TREATY OF TRAVERSE DES SIOUX, PICTURED BY FRANK B. MAYER WHO WAS PRESENT AT THE TREATY COUNCIL

STATE-MAKING ALONG THE MISSISSIPPI

STATE-MAKING
ALONG THE MISSISSIPPI

Could I present to the mind of the reader that view of this country that is now before my eyes, he would not deem my assertion unfounded. He would see the broad Mississippi, with its ten thousand islands, flowing gently and lingerringly (sic) along one entire side of this District, as if in regret at leaving so delightful a region; he would see half a dozen navigable rivers taking their sources in distant regions, and gradually accumulating their waters as they glide steadily along through this favoured region to pay their tribute to the great "Father of Waters"; he would see innumerable creeks and rivulets meandering through rich pasturages, where now the domestic ox has taken the place of the untamed bison; he would see here and there neat groves of oak, and elm, and walnut, half shading half concealing beautiful little lakes, that mirror back their waiving branches; he would see neat looking prairies of two or three miles in extent, and apparently enclosed by woods on all sides, and along the borders of which are their fields stretching far into the prairies, where their herds are luxuriating on the native grass; he would see villages springing up, as by magic, along the banks of the rivers, and even far into the interior; and he would see the swift moving steamboats, as they ply up and down the Mississippi, to supply the wants of the settlers, to take away their surplus produce, or to bring an accession to this growing population, anxious to participate in the enjoyment of nature's bounties, here so liberally dispensed.

—ALBERT LEA, *Notes on the Wisconsin Territory*

CHAPTER XXV

A NEW era of state-making which greatly enlarged the Union followed the acquisition of the Louisiana Territory. Admission of the state of Louisiana in 1812 marked the beginning of political expansion immediately beyond the Mississippi. Seven years later, Missouri's petition for statehood drove an opening wedge into the upper Louisiana Territory, creating a sectional issue which was not quieted until after 1865. In this era of expansion, a maintenance of political balance between the Southern and Northern states was attempted. Territories in the Old Northwest and the Louisiana Territory were paired with territories in the southeast and the southwest—a device which stirred up endless debate and seriously handicapped the normally complicated process of organizing new states. Not a single state was organized after 1820 which did not have to "stand and wait" while politicians debated all over again the questions involved in national expansion and its implications for slavery.

The technological changes which had occurred in agriculture and transportation greatly speeded expansion into the West after 1820. More than once, the spreading program of internal improvements encompassed an unorganized region in its prospective plans before there were enough settlers living in the region to organize a territorial government. By 1840, Manifest Destiny had become a nationalistic religion, even though the term itself was not used until after 1845. By 1850, the westward movement had reached almost flood proportions, and as the nation's map filled out with new states, even the most excessive predictions of earlier decades seemed timid indeed.

Forces which compelled the creation of new territories and states were numerous and complex. Economic conditions both individual and national, increasing prices of farm products, improved access to diverse markets, dissatisfaction with eastern urban and industrial conditions, and a marked increase in foreign immigration were all factors in increasing the flow of population in the 1830's and 40's. Availability of land, access to mineral deposits, and the constant withdrawal of the Indian frontier drew settlers across the Mississippi. The political spoils system thrived on the opportunities provided by new territorial offices. Since Washington's first administration, territorial sinecures in the form of judgeships, governorships, secretariats, peace offices, clerkships, survey posts, and revenue collectorships had constantly increased. Hundreds of these plums were given to the faithful as rewards for their good work in elections. In 1849, Robert Letcher of Kentucky, who had already enjoyed an Arkansas Territorial appointment, wrote Orlando Brown, Zachary Taylor's executive secretary, that he was anxious to accept any kind of a federal appointment from a Minnesota judgeship on up. The appointment of this army of political favorites to posts in the new territories would have influence in determining the nature and structure of future state governments.

In nearly every instance of territorial beginning beyond the Mississippi a squatter population moved onto the frontier ahead of the government surveyors. Isolated trading posts were first, and then came the squatters. Congressman Charles B. Shepard of North Carolina summed up some of the basic facts of western expansion when he observed that the trans-Mississippi region was, "a fresh and rich field [which] might be opened to those who speculate in public lands, and a batch of new offices created for such as seek executive favor." He then asked, "Who are they that . . . pray for the establishment of a new territory? Individuals who have left their own homes, and seized on the public lands . . . These men pounced on the choicest spots, cut down the timber, built houses and cultivated the soil as if it was their own property . . . without authority of law, and in defiance of government. . . ."

Only the specific local details differed in the creation of new territories and states; otherwise each story is a monotonous repetition of that of every other frontier state. Not one of the tier of states immediately west of the Mississippi differed radically from the established pattern of Missouri. Territorial experiences were repeated both to the north and south of the older states.

Arkansas

Down river along the Mississippi between Missouri and Louisiana lay the valleys of the Arkansas and Red rivers. The visits of De Soto and La Salle had brought to this area the knowledge of European explorers. Before 1763 there had been considerable activity along the Mississippi and inland into the Arkansas bottoms. Early in the eighteenth century a western trade was started at Arkansas Post. But it was not until the beginning of the nineteenth century that any major or permanent development took place in the region. As traffic increased along the Mississippi, settlers began to move into the country. Land speculators, seeking favors of both France and Spain, were active, and by the time the transfer of Louisiana was made to the United States there were enough claimants to make nuisances of themselves. It was not until the 1830's that the last of these Spanish claims were adjudicated.

When the state of Louisiana was created in 1812, the Arkansas region was left attached to the upper Louisiana or Missouri Territory. However, this region had been divided in 1804 on the 33rd parallel, and political affairs placed temporarily under the administration of Indiana Territory. By the time Missouri was ready to seek statehood, several communities of settlers were in the land to the south, with Arkansas Post as the center of activities. When Missouri defined its state boundaries, Arkansas Territory was created on March 2, 1819. Its north and south boundaries were the 36° 30' parallel, and the 33rd parallel. President James Monroe selected officials to govern the new territory. James Miller of New Hampshire was appointed governor, and Robert Crittenden of Kentucky was made territorial secretary. Charles Jouette of Michigan, Robert P. Letcher of Kentucky, and Andrew Scott of Missouri were made superior court judges. In July, 1819, the first territorial legislature was called into session and continued in force the laws of the Missouri Territory. A scale of taxation was established, and plans were made for a general election of officers in the fall. A year later the capital was ordered moved from swampy Arkansas Post to higher ground at Little Rock.

Pioneer beginnings in Arkansas were practically the same as those in Kentucky, Tennessee and Missouri. The same people who settled these states were drifting down the Mississippi or across country from Tennessee to populate the bottoms of this river-bound country. There was one significant difference between Arkansas and the older territories: Arkansas was isolated, and its eastern region was so swampy that it was almost impossible to travel overland in many places. Persons moving in behind the swamps hardly dared try to recross them. The first settlers were truly log cabin pioneers, and travelers who first visited this region after the pioneer settlement began found a primitive society indeed. Settlers isolated from intercourse with the older settlements did not present a picture either of sophistication or physical well-being. The denizens of Arkansas soon became the subject of folk stories and border humor. In time Colonel Sandy Falkner was to set to music the picturesque condition of his neighbors in his famous backwoods song *Arkansaw Traveler*.

Stories and comic songs do not, of course, describe the true situation in Arkansas. For the first sixteen years after the creation of the separate territory, settlers steadily pushed into the new country, and by the 1830's,

it contained a mixture of hunters, squatters, plantation owners, land speculators, and adventurers of all sorts. The territory's society was advancing
beyond the first primitive stages of settlement. Villages and towns appeared,
steamboats plied the three major rivers, and the agricultural system expanded quickly. Cotton culture throve in the eastern bottom lands, and
the growing of prodigious quantities of corn was entirely possible. Slavery
had gained a foothold; in much of the new country the economy of
Alabama and Mississippi plantations was being duplicated. The Ozark
Mountains saw a similar duplication of conditions in the Virginia, Carolina and Tennessee mountains.

The Arkansas population grew from 30,000 in 1830 to 97,000 in 1840.
In 1833, Ambrose H. Sevier, congressional delegate, introduced independently in Congress a bill to authorize the taking of an official census
looking to statehood. This first petition was rejected, and when news of
Sevier's action became known in Arkansas two factions quickly developed.
One group wanted statehood, while the other opposed it. Opposing statehood were plantation owners who feared for the security of slavery. This
planter group likewise foresaw a system of higher taxes which would bear
heavily upon the large landholders. In 1835 the statehood issue was revived
with considerable vigor. A series of local assemblies petitioned Governor
William S. Fulton to order a convention, which gave the call the semblance
of coming from the people. In May the people expressed informal preference as they voted in the election of local territorial officers. In October,
1835, the legislature approved the call, and in January, 1836, the convention
met in Little Rock for the purpose of drafting a constitution.

After considerable debate over the question of representation, the southern and eastern counties acquired a majority in the House and Senate.
Provisions were made to readjust this balance of representation at intervals
in the future, but the framers of the constitution had to reckon with a hot
intra-territorial sectional issue along with the need to consider the national
attitude toward slavery. Arkansas' first constitution embodied features of
the older state documents, but it most closely resembled that of Tennessee.
There was a clear indication, however, that the dominant element in the
convention feared the common people much as the early Kentucky framers
did. Provisions were made for the joint houses of the legislature to elect
most of the administrative and judicial officers. The ballot continued to be
taken by the open *viva voce* method.

When the Arkansas petition for statehood was presented in Congress,
there was a considerable amount of debate over the slavery clause in the
proposed Constitution. Something approaching a filibuster took place
in one all-day and all-night session, but the final decision overwhelmingly
favored admitting the state along with Michigan, and on June 15, 1836,

Arkansas entered the Union under the general terms of the Northwest Ordinance. This completed the tier of southern states bordering on the Mississippi, and Arkansas became an important political base of operation for future expansion into the far western frontier.

Iowa

Along Missouri's northern boundary the territory which was to become Iowa was left without political administration. Although within the next two decades after 1830 the region was to reach a full stage of settlement and expansion, agreements with the western tribes of Sauks, Fox and Sioux Indians technically closed the area to white invasion. Congress had scarcely completed its debate on Michigan and Arkansas, however, before Iowa and Wisconsin were seeking consideration for admission to statehood.

Few states on the frontier had a more complex early history than Iowa. It was successively a part of both the French and Spanish empires, but in that period a few traders comprised all its population. White men went among the Indians and established posts, intermarried with native women, and left only a faint trace of European visitation behind them. Explorers following the Mississippi and Missouri rivers inland passed through the river valleys. One of the first men to leave his name on the landscape was the French woodsman Julien Dubuque—an adventurer, trader, and lead miner, who thoroughly adapted himself to the woods environment and the Indian way of life. So did other first settlers Peter A. Sarpy, Isaac Campbell, and Moses Stilwell. One of the most interesting early immigrants was Samuel Muir, a graduate of the University of Edinburgh and a Scotchman to the core, who proved himself a tenacious frontiersman.

Politically, the Iowa Territory was first a part of the Louisiana Purchase area under the administration of the territorial governor at St. Louis, and then subsequently between 1812 and 1819 a part of the Indiana and Missouri territories. After 1819 it was an undefined part of Michigan, and then of Wisconsin Territory. Until 1833 only a small trickle of whites crossed the river to stop in the Black Hawk country. The army was under orders to turn back those who attempted to settle along the Mississippi, but a small group of adventurers went to the lead mines across from Galena, Illinois. Among the first of these were James L. and Lucius H. Langworthy who crossed the Mississippi in 1830 to open mines. In September, 1832, General Winfield Scott and Governor John Reynolds of Illinois negotiated an agreement with the Sauk and Fox Indians which resulted in the Black Hawk Purchase, a treaty that freed six million acres of land along the Mississippi between the Missouri border and Prairie du Chien for white settlement. The Indians received approximately $140,000 for their lands with promise of an annuity of $20,000. The Indians agreed to move out of the purchase strip by June 1, 1833, to make way for the appearance of white settlers. Within the next ten years a considerable population had crossed the river, and the Iowa lead mines were well developed.

Lead mining in itself was not so important historically as were the informal laws which were adopted by the mines. Since population in this region outran the establishment of any territorial government, there was need at least for the administration of justice in criminal cases. When Missouri had been formed, no one conceived of a need for a territorial law in the Iowa country. When Michigan approached statehood, Iowa was again regarded as a dark waste on the Indian frontier. To a certain extent this attitude was again revealed in the discussions which occurred in connection with the formation of Wisconsin Territory.

An incident in Iowa frontier history served graphically to emphasize the region's need for government. In 1834 Patrick O'Connor murdered George O'Keafe in a frontier brawl and defied his neighbors with the remark, "Ye have no laws in the country, and cannot try me." Despite the absence of laws, O'Connor was given an orderly jury trial, convicted, and hanged. News of this incident reached Washington and strengthened the pleas of the advocates for a new territory. Iowa's needs were identical with the earlier ones of Kentucky and Ohio. The people of the territory were too far removed from the source of government to receive efficient administrative attention. But Congress proved reluctant to grant the petition of James Doty, a member of the Territorial Council, and of his neighbors. The Iowa Territory, like that of Arkansas, was caught up in the whole complex fabric of sectional issues. Some members of Congress thought the nation was growing too large and too fast.

Squatters continued to move onto the fertile lands of Iowa and to swell the population. Government lands had not been surveyed and in the absence of a formal territorial government and a governmental survey of the land, squatters formulated their own rules for making land claims. The acts of these early settlers were in violation of the United States statutes, but these border men were both uninformed about the provisions of the federal laws and unimpressed. Besides, since 1820 Congress had showed a tendency to forgive settlers' breaches of the law. At least ten thousand squatters had made unregistered claims to Iowa lands by 1836, a year before the public surveys were begun.

In 1838, when the first public land sales were held in this area, these irregular claims were protected by the settlers' own system of common law. They had organized "claim clubs" which permitted individuals to buy the plot of ground on which they had made squatter improvements. Organized groups kept outside competitors from bidding on a settler's land, and the price was kept at a minimum of $1.25 an acre. These settler organizations had an even broader implication than their function in protecting land claims; they helped maintain law and order in the frontier community. They also prepared the way for congressional action which changed the public land laws materially. One of the first changes made in the basic land law was the general Pre-emption Act of 1841. This legislation came as a result of almost half a century of dissatisfaction and agitation for change in the system of disposing of the public lands. Distribution of the public domain had been involved from the beginning in differences of views between liberal and conservative congressmen, and between the speculator and the little homesteader. One of the basic problems of administering public lands since 1750 had been the intrusion of squatters. Frontier history is full of incidents of conflict with the illegal settlements. Between 1820 and 1834 at least four temporary relief acts were passed to legalize the claims of squatters. Land emergency legislation of the 1830's involved two major national issues: that of the conservative East versus the expanding West, and the ticklish sectional dispute between the North and the South.

The emergency pre-emption legislation was to become a political football to be kicked about between Benton, Clay and others, and between Whigs and Democrats. In August, 1841, Congress enacted into enduring legislation the Pre-emption Law—a triumph for the little homesteader. At last he had won out over the big speculator, and frontier expansion was to move forward more rapidly now that a specific land claim and all improvements made upon it could be secured to the original settler upon terms and at a price which he could pay. In 1862 Congress amplified the Pre-emption Law further in the Homestead Act by formalizing a settler's claim to 160 acres of land by dint of his own physical efforts. It was not until 1891 that the Pre-emption Law was removed from the statute books, but by that time the frontier had disappeared. No doubt the act of 1841 was a major move in democratizing the national land laws, and certainly it came at the right time to speed up settlement in Iowa and its neighboring territories.

On the organization of Michigan as a state in 1836, Iowa Territory became a part of Wisconsin. An assembly met in Burlington in November, 1837, and moved to secure the establishment of an independent district. A year later Congress approved the petition, and Iowa, including what is now Minnesota, South and North Dakota, was made a territory on June 12, 1838.

One of the first problems of the new territory was the location of a capital site. It was agreed that the state house should be placed in Johnson County on the Iowa River. This was a remote and unsettled place. No town survey had been made, and no settler had reached the spot. No road led to the site, and it was almost impossible for settler and territorial legislator alike to find the new capital. Lyman Dillard was employed to plow a guide furrow across the prairie for a hundred miles from the Mississippi to point the way to Iowa City.

Iowa's advancement to statehood is a somewhat curious story. Governor Robert Lucas, a native of Ohio, favored taking the initial steps leading to statehood as early as 1839. His suggestion did not meet with favor from the territorial assembly. Aside from the sharp partisanism which prevailed between Whigs and Democrats, people on the frontier were suspicious of the taxes necessary to support a state government. So long as Iowa remained a territory, expenses were borne by the federal government, and the pioneers felt that they were carrying too heavy a financial burden in acquiring lands and making settlement to assume the burdensome costs of government. Claims to many squatter homesteads had not yet been registered, and there was fear that the creation of an independent state government would result in serious loss to these laggard individuals. In both 1840 and 1842 the people rejected statehood proposals. The issue was again presented in 1844, and this time a Democratic majority favored the calling of a constitutional convention.

Delegates to the first Iowa convention met in October, 1844, and within twenty-six days prepared a constitution which guaranteed religious freedom, prohibited Negro suffrage, made officials elective, outlawed banks of issue, encouraged public education, and severely limited the accumulation of public debts and the scale of official salaries. Following the precedent of the Louisiana constitution, the state's boundaries were prescribed. Provisions were made for submitting the completed document to the people of the territory at the same time it reached Congress.

Submission of the Iowa petition for statehood in Washington revived anew the sectional debate. It was proposed to reduce substantially the area encompassed in the new Iowa constitution, but this suggestion was unacceptable to the western people, and the constitution of 1844 was rejected at the polls. Two years later a second constitution was drafted, which prescribed the boundaries of the first one. It was approved at the polls by a slender majority. Congress was content to let the boundaries stand, and on December 28, 1846, Iowa was admitted to the Union.

Admission of Iowa to statehood opened a period of phenomenal population expansion in the region. The western roads were filled with immigrants between 1846–1860 on their way to found new homes in the prairie country. At the time the state was admitted to the Union it contained 116,454 persons; in 1850 there were 192,214, and in 1860 this number had increased to 674,913. Southern, or border-born, people predominated, but an ever-increasing stream of New Englanders reached the state. Added to the natives were 106,081 Germans, Irish, Scandinavians, Canadians, Austrians, Holland Dutch, and French. Iowa became almost as famous a haven for the various European communal groups as Indiana and Texas. Among these were the German Amanas; the French Icarians; the Hollanders, a strong Calvinist Protestant community which settled the town of Pella; and Hungarians who came dreaming of a thriving continental city of Buda, named for their beloved Budapest. It was, however, mainly the hardy American immigrant who developed the Iowa farms that quickly made their state an important source of supply for agricultural products. Railroads reached out from Chicago and St. Louis in hot rivalry to tap the rich Iowa market; Chicago won the race. By 1860 there were rail connections with the tip of Lake Michigan and the ever-expanding railroad system of the eastern part of the country, which in time gave Iowa an efficient outlet for its products.

Iowa is a good example of the formation of a new frontier state in a period of fermentation, when Americans were most restless and sought escape from both poverty and political tensions. It was this great migration beyond the Mississippi which caused Horace Greeley to advise J. B. Grinnell to "Go west, young man, go west." The stream of immigrants who crossed the Mississippi River already had vast pioneering experience, and they quickly took advantage of fresh opportunities in this fertile area. Possibly the only variation from the established frontier pattern was the conquest of the prairies. Although the Iowa pioneers were not the first frontiersmen to approach prairie land, they were the first to begin the long adventure beyond the heavily wooded country where change in certain of their domestic and agricultural practices was required. It was here that the wide-spreading sod-house frontier began, and pioneers first mastered the problems of living beyond the forests in open country where wood and water ceased to be plentiful. Here they had to break the heavy prairie sod and to conserve the moisture in order to produce crops.

Wisconsin

The early history of Wisconsin incorporated the usual phases of American frontier development. The region was a landing place for explorers and traders from the coming of Jean Nicolet in 1634 to the end of the Black Hawk War. During these two centuries a large number of traders and adventurers tramped over the region, building trading posts, consorting with the Indians, and generating a certain romantic glamor for the history of Wisconsin. The territory was in a sense a keystone in the Indian trade, and trapping and fur-trading interests were most active in the region. Competing companies representing both American and British interests worked through the Wisconsin woods seeking big annual crops of furs. Among these were the Northwest Fur Company and John Jacob Astor's American Fur Company. There was, also, a period of military occupation from 1816 to 1832.

It was not until 1831 that an effort was made to define the territory of Wisconsin. From 1813 to the latter date the region had come under the administrative control of Michigan Territory. For a part of this time Lewis Cass was governor and William Clark was Indian superintendent. White encroachment was an aggravating problem in the Wisconsin Indian country. First traders squatted in the region, and then came the small settlers pushing the frontier movement forward in characteristic initial stages. The same vein of lead which had brought white miners to Missouri and Iowa attracted them to Wisconsin, and Indians, French and Americans exploited this resource. Henry Dodge moved up from Missouri in 1827 to make his fortune at the re-opened mines, and he gathered about him an important mining community, but this invasion of the Indian territory only led to trouble. For the next twenty years territorial and state officials were engaged in creating another set of Indian cessions. Actually the Wisconsin cessions completed the pattern of territory-making in the Old Northwest which was begun with the adoption of the Ordinance of 1787.

Once the major Indian claims were silenced, there followed a long period of white occupation of the Wisconsin country. The mining area was populated by settlers who came to work in the mines, and the rest of the eastern and southern part of the territory was populated by small land-seekers who took advantage of the modified land laws of 1804 and 1820. Wisconsin Territory was created in 1836 from the western part of Michigan Territory when that state was admitted to the Union. During the next ten years Wisconsin Territory passed through the beginning phases of county organization, the establishment of courts, the building of towns, and the planting of farming communities. The first legislative assembly was held at Belmont in 1836. The stream of immigrants, many of them German, Norwegian, Belgian, Swiss and English, swelled the population from 2,893 people in 1836 to approximately 165,000 in 1850.

Wisconsin's existence as a territory, however, displayed some interesting differences from the predominant frontier pattern as we have seen it. This was the first territory in the Northwest which drew its population overwhelmingly from the eastern part of the United States and Europe. Those cultural institutions which had developed in the older states by the slow and tedious process of trial and error were established quickly in the new territory. Towns, schools, churches, and banks came into existence almost immediately. A remarkable emphasis was placed upon the maturing of community life as quickly as possible. There was an immediate move to open roads and to build canals and railroads. This part of the Northwest enjoyed the advantages of the transportation competition which was developing about the Chicago hub of the Great Lakes system. The heavy immigration of Europeans in the 1840's swelled the population and contributed heavily to the organization of the lake cities and the expansion of the rich farming belt.

Wisconsin's advance toward statehood also differed from the usual pattern. Partisan politics of the 1840's influenced affairs in the Northwest. Although statehood was possible from 1839 on, the voters refused to undertake such a thing until the Whigs were out of power. There was a strong feeling not only against the Whig officials in Washington, but against the Presidential appointee James Doty, who was the territorial governor. He had played an active role in territorial development and had been in and out of office with the changes in the national political administrations. When James K. Polk came to office in 1845, a move was made to get Wisconsin admitted to the Union. Congress passed the enabling act in August, 1846, and by December a convention had produced a constitution. This document contained some rather generous features, such as that guaranteeing the ownership of property by women, election of judges, abolition of imprisonment for debt, and refusal to charter banks of issue. It exempted from seizure for debt a forty-acre homestead, or one thousand dollars worth of town property. The work of the 1846 convention was submitted to the voters and was defeated. A second document was produced in 1848 which was more conservative in its provisions and was accepted by a popular vote, which of itself (except for Iowa) was a novelty among the frontier states. This document was largely an adaptation of the New York and Michigan constitutions with occasional borrowings from the Northwest Ordinance. Despite the New York, New England, and European origins of most of the citizens of Wisconsin, the new constitution prohibited Negroes from voting, and it remained for a legislative act in 1849 to liberalize the franchise section in its actual application.

One of the greatest problems in organizing the state was the definition of its boundaries. There had been a long-standing dispute over the southern boundary between Illinois and the Wisconsin Territory in regard to the area at the tip of Lake Michigan. The western boundary was limited to the Mississippi and St. Croix rivers, with the establishment of an arbitrary boundary between the St. Croix and the tip of Lake Superior. When Wisconsin was admitted to statehood in 1848, the last of the land covered by the Northwest Ordinance, except for a portion of Minnesota, was organized.

Minnesota

Like its southern neighbors along the Mississippi, Minnesota had a long period of Indian and French history and was in the line of many of the earliest explorations along the upper Great Lakes chain. In one respect Minnesota's preterritorial history was different. Because of its climate and geographical conditions, and its location along the international border, it became a major fur-trading area. After the latter half of the eighteenth century Indian traders and trappers were in the region, and after 1800 a considerable trade rivalry developed between the Canadians and Americans, involving a contest for Indian favor. As a matter of fact, Drummond Island in Lake Huron was the site of British-Indian trading until after the War of 1812, and much later than this the area between Lake of the Woods and Prairie du Chien was the scene of British trade. Because of this influence Governor Lewis Cass found it difficult to come to terms with the tribes. Final removal of the British traders was as much a victory for John Jacob Astor, Ramsay Crooks, Robert Stuart, and the American Fur Company as for Governor Cass and the Michigan Territory.

In one other respect Minnesota's early history was exciting. Because a part of the national boundary before 1819 depended upon the location of the headwaters of the Mississippi, various explorers and surveyors entered the region. Beginning with Zebulon Pike's visit in 1805–1806, there followed Captain David B. Douglass with his famous colleague Henry R. Schoolcraft in 1820, Major Stephen H. Long in 1823, G. W. Featherstonhaugh in 1847, the Italian lawyer Giacomo Constantine Beltrami in 1823, George Atkin in 1835 and George Catlin in 1838. All of these visitors left diaries and journals, the most extensive and intelligent of which were Schoolcraft's, Long's, Featherstonhaugh's and Beltrami's. Their works constitute a distinguished collection of informed contemporary descriptive literature. Few of the newer states of the Union have so important a body of first-hand material about their condition prior to the pioneer invasion.

In 1817 Major Stephen H. Long located sites for military posts at the mouth of the Minnesota and St. Croix rivers. Five years later Colonel Henry Leavenworth was sent West to locate the first military post in the region at Mendota. Colonel Josiah Snelling actually carried through the task of contructing the fort near the mouth of the St. Peter's River which was to bear his name. Colonel Snelling was both efficient and ingenious. He introduced a sawmill into the heavily forested country to cut planks for the fort, and after a fashion became the father of the great northwestern lumbering industry.

At the same time that Colonel Snelling arrived at the frontier military post, there appeared Lawrence Taliaferro, a Virginian, to serve as Indian agent at St. Peter's. He brought with him several years of experience on the frontier, and for two decades he was to prove a highly successful Indian administrator. He was honest, and he was interested in the simple lives of the Indians, an unusual thing for most agents. He quickly gained the respect of both Indians and whites. The success of Indian relations, despite several incidents between the tribes, was due to Taliaferro's good sense and capable management.

Between 1819 and 1840, squatters appeared either in what was to become Minnesota Territory or along its borders. It was not until the signing of the treaty of 1837 that a part of the Minnesota Territory was opened to white settlement, but even before this there had been a migration of Scotch-Canadians from the vast Selkirk grant beyond the border. Likewise a small Swiss migration brought squatters into the region. Among the Americans who pushed up to the border at an early date were liquor sellers who came just close enough to reach their customers, but not far enough to fall into the clutches of the army and the Indian agent. Both Protestant and Catholic missionaries entered the region to work among the Indians and to serve the religious needs of the fort and the squatter settlement. Presbyterians became active at Fort Snelling, and Father Lucien Galtier established the Catholic church of St. Paul on the Mississippi in 1841, a place that was subsequently to become the state capital.

Attempts in 1847 and 1848 to get Congress to organize an independent Territory of Minnesota failed. It was not until after the creation of the state of Wisconsin that the Minnesota petitioners were successful. Minnesota Territory was created on April 9, 1849, but not until some considerable maneuvering had taken place in both the House and Senate. The Whigs wanted to hold out until Zachary Taylor came into office so that he could appoint the territorial officers, and in 1848 and early in 1849 the Minnesota bill was all but defeated. Had it not been for Stephen A. Douglas' and Henry H. Sibley's bluff at opposing the creation of the Department of Interior, a bill in which the Whigs were much interested, organization of Minnesota Territory might have been delayed indefinitely.

Stephen A. Douglas' estimate that the territory had a population of eight to ten thousand was purely a political one. By an actual count, according to a census report of July 4, 1849, there were but 3,814 civilian inhabitants. The territory, however, gained population rapidly, and its political affairs were set in order by the appointment of Alexander Ramsey of Pennsylvania as governor. Farm lands were opened, and Henry Sibley, the first Territorial Delegate, succeeded in getting two sections of public lands instead of one set aside for educational purposes. Sawmills were built, and pioneer lumbermen began to convert the great pine forest into lumber. These entrepreneurs introduced a new problem for the federal government. Timber cutters sought choice logs, and they were not at all timid about invading public lands to take timber where they found it. Although

Minnesota farmers had the same attitude toward public lands as Iowa farmers, there was not quite so much "claim club" activity. Settlers took advantage of the pre-emption law and established legal post registration claims to their lands. The Indian problem, which is treated elsewhere, proved a delicate one and delayed settlement in some areas.

Minnesota had a long territorial period before it was admitted to the Union on May 12, 1858. By the time the State was ready for admission there was an actual population of 150,092, although representatives were elected and sent along to Washington on the basis of 247,500. The question of Minnesota's admission to the Union involved a long argument which revived many of the sectional issues then before the country, including the hot one over Kansas and Nebraska. There was both an internal and a congressional struggle between Democrats and Republicans, and between Northerners and Southerners. Fear of upsetting even further the balance between slave and free states was in the picture. This issue had just been dramatized by the Dred Scott Case which involved Minnesota Territory. Also, there was a strong fear in Congress of the growing influence of foreign-born settlers in Minnesota upon the slavery dispute.

With the admission of Wisconsin and Minnesota the first trans-Mississippi River tier of states was complete. Before this was accomplished, however, the Northwestern territories showed great economic promise. They were in the direct line of the expanding transcontinental railway system, and of that part of the European migration which went on to the agrarian frontier. The Northwest quickly developed large farming and lumbering industries. Wisconsin and Minnesota were to see an expansion westward of the lumbering industries which moved from Maine to Michigan and then to the new states. Likewise this new tier of states moved the American population up to the Great Plains frontier where it stood poised, ready to move on. Louisiana, Arkansas, Missouri and Iowa served as bases for much of the activity which hastened settlers into the Southwest, and on to the Pacific Coast, and to the Rocky Mountain mineral frontier.

Within three years after the admission of Minnesota, the nation was divided by civil war. It was most fortunate for the Union that it had the grain and meat resources of the Northwest available to it and that transportation facilities to carry these products to the fighting front were expanding. The increasing manpower available in the new Mississippi Valley states contributed materially to the success of the Union Army. Many of the troops from the Northwest came directly from the virgin frontier where they had only begun the initial phases of pioneering. In the case of Minnesota there were still Indians to subdue, and much work still remained before white settlement could progress further westward into the Missouri Valley.

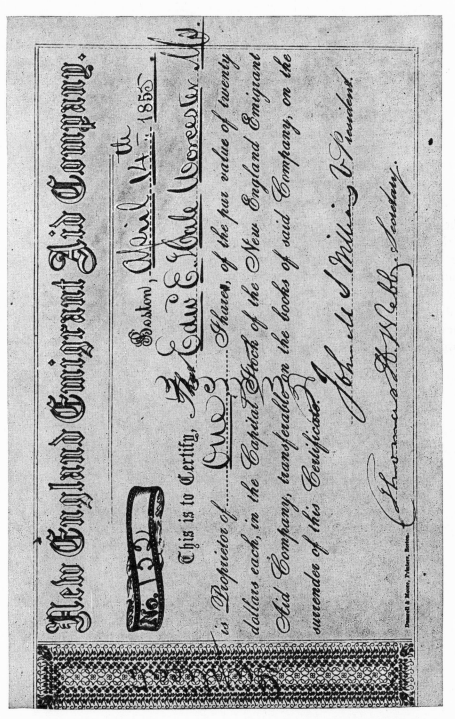

A SHARE IN THE FUTURE OF KANSAS

ON THE SNAGS OF EXPANSION

ON THE SNAGS
OF EXPANSION

The principles of the Compromise of 1850 repeal any such pledges of the Missouri Compromise line south as well as north of 36° 30'; for the principles of the Compromise bill are that Territories shall of themselves constitute their own government slave or free just as they will, and that Congress shall admit them as States just as it finds them. Under these circumstances, the practical question is, throwing theory aside, will Nebraska be settled by a slaveholding people, or by freeholders only?

—New York *Express*

CHAPTER XXVI

MID-NINETEENTH century found the Union in a state of political and social change. On February 2, 1848, the Treaty of Guadalupe Hidalgo had been signed, and this international agreement cleared away the last doubt about the ownership of the vast stretch of territory which extended from Texas to California, and from the Rio Grande to northern Utah. Territorial administrative responsibility was thereby greatly enlarged, and Americans had new frontiers opened to them without the complicating influence of any foreign overlord. An observer unfamiliar with forces then active in America might have thought that a century at least must elapse before a substantial population would be concentrated in this area.

Long before the Mexican Cession was made, Americans had penetrated both the Southwest and the Great Plains area to the north. Trappers and traders had reached Santa Fe before Zebulon Pike visited the place, and freight wagons had rolled across the sandy wastes from Independence since 1821 to transact business in the remote Mexican outpost. Doniphan's military expedition into Mexico was accompanied by Yankee traders in search of customers as far away as Chihuahua. Already military and Indian posts dotted a part of the country north and south. Since the days when the Rocky Mountain fur trade began, venturesome spirits had covered the Kansas-Nebraska-Wyoming country with trails, and after 1840 settler wagons deepened the ruts to Oregon and California across the West.

By 1850 three new territories were outlined. California, Utah, and New Mexico were being developed. All three sought status as territories, and because of the gold rush California was ready for statehood. Such rapid expansion was the essence of American progress, but congressmen found it hard to comprehend the rapidity with which the frontier had been expanded. Since the admission of Missouri in 1821, western territorial expansion had continued to provoke re-examination of the slavery issue. Now it seemed probable that slavery extension into the Southwest would

meet with insurmountable difficulties. Utah and California were not suited
to slavery, and New Mexico offered no better prospects.

The election of 1848 had brought to the White House a Whig hero of
the Mexican War. In one of the most erratic campaigns in Presidential
history, General Taylor won election. Lewis Cass, like Taylor, a product
of the frontier, had been the Democratic nominee, and ex-President Martin
Van Buren had run as a Barnburning Free-Soiler. The campaign itself was
fought in the main on the issues of the disposition of public lands, Democratic conduct of the war with Mexico, various political personalities, and
General Taylor's heroism. The Wilmot Proviso stirred anew apprehen-
sions over the slavery expansion question.

Cause for Compromise

Several major problems awaited immediate solution when General
Taylor came to office. Among these were slavery and the slave trade in
the District of Columbia, the return of fugitive slaves, the administration
of the western territories, and the growing conflict between agrarianism
and a rising industrial economy. Since the latter decade of the eighteenth
century, industrial expansion had become an increasing force in American
life. By 1850 ardent abolitionists had pushed their crusade to the point
where agitation for reform could not be further ignored. Southerners regarded the abolition campaign against slavery as involving more than the
social injustice of the institution or a lack of morals on the part of slaveholders. Economic loss of slaves through the operations of the "underground railroad" was a serious one. But perhaps more important than these
inroads upon slavery was the Wilmot Proviso, appended to the bill to
appropriate two million dollars for the negotiation of peace with Mexico,
which, if adopted, would have halted territorial expansion of the institution. In the eyes of many men of the South, the proposed legislation was
tantamount to repeal of the Missouri Compromise.

Possibly the most pronounced social and political force at work at mid-
century was the desire on the part of some slave owners to expand slavery
geographically. Restrictions of the Missouri Compromise challenged slaveholders and free-soilers alike, and the changing picture in political organization was both important and confusing. In Washington it was extremely difficult to organize the House even though Democrats controlled
the Senate. Feelings were often intense and personal. Each of the major
parties was divided into northern and southern factions, and at times the
Free-Soil party held the balance of power. The Whig party was on the
verge of disintegration, and new alignments confronted the country. With
the reshuffling of political parties there also occurred a change in leadership which brought new and aggressive personalities on to the scene.

Investors and merchants of the East looked beyond the issues of slavery to the West where profits awaited the clever trader and exploiter. Land speculators, town builders, ferry tenders, tavern keepers, and lumbermen saw an opportunity to make money. Those who foresaw the coming of the railroads were confident of profit.

Discovery of gold in California, and the phenomenal rush to the West Coast created for the administration a police problem of tremendous proportions. Clearly it was desirable to place such a responsibility in the hands of a state government. There was danger also that California might be organized into an independent republic.

President Taylor sent T. Butler King westward, therefore, to hasten California's organization as a state and to speed its petition for admission to the Union. New Mexico did not present so clear-cut a picture. The Texas boundaries had to be defined and its territorial claims reduced first. In 1850 the military governor, John Munroe, called a convention to prepare a constitution. Vast New Mexico had a sparse population of Indians, Mexicans, and Americans. It was still a trader's country. Neither rich mines nor fertile farming land beckoned settlers into the region. As for Utah, the socio-religious philosophy of its inhabitants kept the Mormon territory from being considered immediately for statehood.

For three months, July, August and September, 1950, Congress engaged in intensive debate over a closely co-ordinated compromise plan for the organization of the new western domain. Whig Senator Henry Clay assumed leadership of the moderates until they were defeated on July 31, when the Kentuckian retired to Rhode Island for a rest. Stephen A. Douglas then pushed piecemeal legislation through Congress; the new President, Millard Fillmore, signed it September 9, 18, and 20; and the Compromise of 1850 was a reality.

California was admitted under the Compromise as a free state. New Mexico and Utah territories were created, while the Texas-New Mexico boundary dispute was adjusted. The federal government agreed to pay $10,000,000 of the Texas debts. It was necessary, however, to move quickly to secure ratification of the New Mexico-Texas debt and boundary agreement. The territorial legislation involved Texas pride, which had been a factor in the adjustment of the New Mexico border. Texas debts on the other hand involved special interests far removed from the state, and, possibly, centered in the halls of Congress. Both southerners and easterners held Texas bonds, and the redemption of these bonds, made possible with federal funds, placed the bondholders in line for considerable gains. By the time the Texas bonds were redeemed, interest paid, and Indian raid damages compensated for, the federal government would expend $17,750,000.

The compromise legislation of 1850 enlarged the frontier's political perimeter. Organization of Utah and New Mexico territories and the admission of California completed the circumscription of the interior, or Great Basin, West. Time was hastening when the press of settlement would reach this area, and the frontier would eventually disappear. From the settlements along the Pacific Coast there was a backlash of the westward movement which also fed settlers into the interior West.

The slavery issue was to make itself felt in the immediate period of expansion even though much of the slavery legislation in the Compromise had little or no direct bearing upon the West. Almost before congressmen revived from the intensive debates in 1850, a second and even more troubled issue appeared in Congress. The great Nebraska territory immediately west of Missouri and Iowa became the subject of arduous political maneuvering. This territory presented a somewhat more complex problem in western expansion than most other parts of the frontier. Not only did it contain a considerable residual Indian population, but various Indian tribes which had been removed from east of the Mississippi were located along its eastern border. Possibly the most influential nation of Indians was the highly civilized Wyandot which had been removed from Ohio and Michigan in 1842. These and others, on resettling in the plains West, had been assured of permanent residence by the government. Immigrants moving across the plains had to pass through this loose cordon of Indian nations, and then through the more formidable barrier of the original plains and mountain tribes who were capable of rugged and hostile resistance. Despite the presence of these two groups of Indians, there were large areas of unoccupied lands. From the 1820's on, the amount of traffic across the Nebraska country and along the Kansas and Platte rivers had steadily increased. Oregon and Mormon migration followed the fur traders up the Platte. In 1849, gold rushers pushed across country toward California. All of these invasions tended to excite the Indians.

Railroads and Sectional Rivalries

In 1844 Stephen A. Douglas, serving his first term in Congress, had been impressed by the recommendation of Secretary of War William Wilkins that Nebraska be organized, and that military posts be placed along the way to Oregon. Douglas actively supported this idea up until 1848, when he seems temporarily to have lost enthusiasm for this aspect of the western question. He knew the uncertainty of the Indian situation and favored extension of military posts. His principal motive, however, was the promotion of a transcontinental railroad west from Chicago. Asa Whitney's memorial to Congress in 1844 coincided with Secretary Wilkins' report, and Douglas became a convert at once. The thing which possibly agitated Douglas most about Whitney's proposed railroad was the suggestion that it should have some unspecified beginning on Lake Michigan and then go through South Pass to the mouth of the Columbia. He responded to this proposal with an eight-page pamphlet in which he maintained that Chicago was the logical terminus in the East, and San Francisco in the West. Chicago in 1844 was by no means the assured railway center of the Great Lakes area; not until the city gained a connection with the Atlantic seaboard was it assured of its position as a transportation hub.

The fifteen years following 1845 were to witness many arguments over railway lines, and the granting of public lands as government support for railroads gained attention in state and national legislatures. The location of the proposed transcontinental line became deeply involved in sectional rivalries. New Orleans, Vicksburg, Memphis, St. Louis and Chicago all hoped to be the eastern terminus. A belief seems to have prevailed that only one road would ever be built to the Pacific, and the city which became the eastern terminus would have continuing prosperity. Douglas advocated a northern route through South Pass so strongly in the 1849 St. Louis railway convention that he set off a heated debate and resigned the presidency of the convention. The cession at Guadalupe Hidalgo, the beginning of the gold rush, and the organization of New Mexico Territory in 1850 made a transcontinental railway along a southern route a much greater possibility than ever before. In Jefferson Davis, active in national politics and later to become Secretary of War, the partisans of a southern route and terminus had a strong and aggressive friend.

The addition of the Gadsden Purchase to the public domain in 1853 further favored such a construction. Completion of the Gadsden Purchase was followed by extensive surveys which sought the location of the southern railway route to the Pacific. Much of the land over which the proposed railroad would have to pass was of a rugged nature. Despite the fact that there was an extensive delay in the construction of this southern railway to California, the surveys revealed extensive geographical knowledge of this part of the Southwest.

While southerners battled to secure location of the Pacific railroad in their section, northern promoters were equally as active. Congressman Shepherd Leffler of Iowa introduced a bill in Congress in 1848 to charter a railroad from Davenport to Council Bluffs. At the same time Willard P. Hall and David R. Atchison of Missouri sponsored companion bills in the national House and Senate for a road from Hannibal to St. Joseph. Both Iowa and Missouri were anxious to develop western railway connections, envisioning tons of farm produce to sell, and the Pacific Coast as a good market. People of the older states were forced into the position of agitating the organization of the Nebraska territory in order to assure a politically organized area through which the road might be built.

Kansas-Nebraska

It was clear to the more intelligent Indian leaders in the Nebraska country that the activity of white immigrants and agitation for a western railroad would lead to an inevitable invasion of their lands, treaty or not. Between 1848 and 1851 the western territorial question remained quiet, but late in 1851 Hall proposed organizing the Platte Territory. A year later Atchison urged that the same area be made into Nebraska Territory. Bills to create this political division were introduced simultaneously in the House and Senate by J. G. Miller of Missouri and A. C. Dodge of Iowa.

Introduction of the Nebraska Bill stirred anew many of the old sectional issues. Despite the Missouri Compromise the proposed creation of the new territory raised questions about possible slave expansion. The bill was highly favored in both Missouri and Iowa, and in Missouri a hot political dispute developed between former Senator Thomas Hart Benton and the aggressive incumbent Atchison. Benton had been denied re-election to the Senate in 1850, partly because of Atchison's opposition. During the next four years the two men engaged in a political feud which ended with both of them losing their seats in the Senate. Robust, hotheaded, direct in his approaches, profane in his language, Atchison sided with the strong proslavery and States' rights southern senators. Benton had long favored the West in his career as senator. He had promoted the idea of a western railway, opposed the Compromise of 1850, and detested the Calhoun point of view as endangering the safety of the Union.

Alert to discussions in Congress and elsewhere concerning the western territory, Wyandot Indian leaders called an intertribal meeting for July, 1853. Steps had been taken to establish a provisional government for Nebraska Territory, with William Walker as governor and Thomas Johnson as congressional delegate. Later, Johnson was to find himself involved in a dispute with Hadley D. Johnson of western Iowa, who also claimed the delegate position. Almost from the beginning the Indians were drawn into the Benton-Atchison feud, but their main concern was over the protection of their valuable land about the mouth of the Kansas River.

While political issues were agitating the Nebraska Indians, their white neighbors in Iowa and Missouri wished to see the new territory created. Local conventions in both states urged its formation. The major points of the numerous resolutions were the extinguishment of Indian titles, location of a transcontinental railroad over a central route, and eventual removal of the western Indian barrier. The Iowa and Missouri conventions viewed the slavery question with a degree of concern, some delegates advocating local and popular decision of the issue when it arose.

On December 14, 1853, Senator Dodge introduced the Nebraska Bill which was immediately referred to the Committee on Territories, of which Stephen A. Douglas was chairman. Eight days later Representative Miller introduced a companion measure in the House. Senator Douglas' committee reported the Nebraska Bill on January 4, 1854. The original report did not provide for the repeal of the Missouri Compromise, nor did it specify that the territorial legislature might abolish slavery within the area. Instead there was a strong implication that slavery would be restricted in Nebraska Territory. The Douglas committee, sensing the strong feeling of proslavery congressmen, restored what was said to have been an oversight in the original draft. This guarantee that the same terms would prevail in Nebraska as in the 1850 territories was, however, too vague to please the southerners. Archibald Dixon, a slaveholding Kentucky Whig, threatened to offer an amendment repealing the Missouri Compromise outright.

After considerable discussion between Douglas and Dixon, a group of Democrats including Jefferson Davis took the Nebraska issue to the White House. They arrived on Sunday evening to confer with Franklin Pierce, who had steadfastly refused to transact business on the Sabbath. In this case the emergency seemed more demanding than the President's piety, and he joined his callers in analyzing the Nebraska issue. From this conference emerged two fundamental changes in the Dodge-Douglas Bill. There were to be two territories, Kansas and Nebraska, and a section was inserted into the Bill categorically repealing the Missouri Compromise. Douglas induced Pierce to write out in longhand the terms of the conference so there could be no future reversal of executive commitments. When he returned to the Senate on Monday with his revised bill, the Illinois senator was assured of administration support in its future passage.

Between January 23 and May 22, 1854, Congress was hotly aroused over the sectional issue. Salmon P. Chase of Ohio and William H. Seward of New York, with the help of the free-soilers, led the attack on the measure. Douglas, Atchison and the proslavery partisans engaged in a debate that bordered on violence. The final Senate vote stood 37 to 14 in favor, but in the House the margin was closer, 113 to 100. Although the bill has been interpreted as an attempt to placate southern slaveholders, there is nothing in either territorial law to indicate that this was true. Apparently no one in Congress seemed to believe Kansas would become a slave state while Nebraska by common consent would remain free. The division was stimulated by the desires of Missourians and Iowans to equalize the distribution of settlers so that each state would have a thickly populated region along its western borders. This was especially true of the Iowans who feared that newcomers in the larger Nebraska Territory would prefer the rich Kansas and Neosho valleys; the plains would then be left without settlers and towns, hence more exposed to Indian attacks. No doubt such a situation would also reduce the possibility of a transcontinental railway there. As far as the spread of slavery was concerned, geography was a more potent deterrent than was statutory law.

It was reasonable to suppose that in 1854 migration to Kansas and Nebraska would have followed the normal and established frontier pattern. Every fact favored this conclusion. Both territories were too far removed from the free-soil East and the slaveholding South to permit a convenient migration. Despite the early success of slavery on the southern "cotton frontier," the institution was not adaptable generally to pioneering. Settling in Kansas and Nebraska was a rugged venture. Climatic and seasonal conditions differed from those prevailing in most of the East and South. Even hardy woodland pioneers had to make radical adjustments in the grasslands. They needed to adjust themselves psychologically and economically to the empty space of the plains country which lacked adequate wood and water.

Some consideration of the age in which the Kansas movement began is necessary in order to understand conditions which so deeply colored this period of frontier expansion. Technology was catching up with the frontier. Saw mills had become almost as necessary to pioneering at this point in the nineteenth century as the axe was in earlier years. The steamboat offered a more efficient form of transportation; it helped largely to solve the staggering problem of moving thousands of tons of heavy freight. Steam locomotives offered an even more diversified form of transportation. Building railroads across country necessitated a peaceful situation where unguarded track and trains could be operated. In the plains West, this meant the establishment of army posts and settlements. Just as important was production of freight along the railroads. National industrialism thrust out its tentacles to the frontier in search of customers and materials. It was against this background of realistic economics that slavery had to compete, as well as against political theories and sectional emotions.

There seems to be no substantial historical reason for believing that slavery could ever have prospered in Kansas. To begin with, the immediate prospects for settlers poised to move westward were small landholders who had pushed the log cabin frontier westward from the valleys of Pennsylvania and Virginia. Obviously these people were nonslaveholders. Field crops that could be grown in Kansas were not adaptable to the use of slave labor. Numerically there was, of course, a short labor supply on the frontier, but the promises of immigration were good. Thousands of foreigners, politically and economically troubled in these mid-century years, sought new homes in America. Americans themselves were on the move. Texas, Utah, Oregon, and California had drawn streams of people westward.

Kansas-Nebraska debates in Congress and press comments were largely academic at first. By the time the act was signed by Franklin Pierce, however, the Kansas-Nebraska issue had become a national fixation. So profoundly was public opinion aroused that significant numbers of people regarded repeal of the Missouri Compromise as a revocation of a part of the Constitution. Douglas, Pierce, and others were hanged and burned in effigy in New England towns, and the "Little Giant" was branded another Benedict Arnold.

In the South itself, editorials and popular feelings were as oddly restrained as feelings in the East were aroused. There was nevertheless considerable uneasiness over the fact that Congress had seen fit to deal with slavery, a prerogative which proslavery men thought rested with the people and their local legislatures. The South was anxious to bolster its waning national political influence, but it was difficult to achieve this by spreading slavery to an inhospitable borderland. Many leaders of the Kansas movement selfishly sought to recoup political fortunes, to grab generous slices of public lands, to push the Indians back, and possibly to insure location of a transcontinental railroad westward from St. Louis.

Wounds of the Benton-Atchison feud were still tender, and Atchison and his confederate B. F. Stringfellow agitated western Missourians in the struggle to rescue Kansas for the slaveholders. In discussing the Kansas commotion, one or two preliminary facts should be considered. The people who in 1853 and 1854 wished to enter Kansas from Iowa and Missouri were essentially boomers, as were many of the early Iowa settlers. As preemptors, laying claims to public lands generally, they had promoted the idea of occupation of the new western lands and extinguishment of Indian titles. Likewise they were frontiersmen who had developed a strong dislike for outside interference. It was a simple matter for demagogues to generate heat by suggesting that outsiders proposed to invade the frontier and to change the normal course of events. In this way the stage was set for the eastern invasion which followed.

Where slavery extension was in dispute, the question was not so much actual movement of slaves into the western territory as it was the creation of a barrier of safety west of Missouri. In the states of the Ohio and Mississippi valleys, operation of the underground railroad caused heavy economic losses. Tennessee and Kentucky, for instance, had a six-hundred-mile band of freedom along their borders, and loss of slaves became so heavy that delegations went to Columbus, Ohio, to formulate an agreement to check underground railway activities. In 1852 Harriet Beecher Stowe glorified the underground railroad in her fabulously popular novel *Uncle Tom's Cabin*. For these reasons Missouri slaveholders feared a border of freedom to the west.

Eli Thayer and Emigrant Aid

Easterners under the leadership of Eli Thayer, a free-soiler of Worcester, Massachusetts, organized the Massachusetts Emigrant Aid Society, April 26, 1854, and on February 16, 1855, the title was changed to the New England Emigrant Aid Company. Thayer was more of a social organizer than a reformer. He appears not to have been so disturbed by slavery as some of his fellow New Englanders. Thayer's interest was in promoting education and in relieving social problems. His company was a common stock organization which had for its primary purpose procuring public lands in the West and enabling settlers to reach the lands. Thayer, though a public-spirited citizen, was fundamentally a banker. He sought to make the Emigrant Aid Company yield a profit. It was to advance funds to Kansas emigrants to establish farms, mills, towns, and businesses. For two years Thayer boomed the idea in New England and New York, gaining influential newspaper support including that of Horace Greeley and his *New York Tribune*. For the next three years, however, the company's history was fraught with numerous economic and emotional problems.

In Kansas and Nebraska there was intense activity among land-grabbers and settlers. As Iowans feared, the greatest activity occurred in the Kansas, Marais des Cygnes, and Osage valleys. Publicity of western legislation gave Kansas lands a vast amount of advertising, which was reflected in the sudden demand for steamboat and stagecoach lines from St. Louis to Kansas City. In the excitement over this new land rush the fact was ignored that significant areas of eastern Kansas and Nebraska territories were Indian lands and not open to white settlement. The Indian agent at Fort Leavenworth warned, with little effect, that the Delaware and Wyandot lands were closed to settlers.

By late 1854 rumors and counter-rumors were afloat. News of the organization of the New England Emigrant Aid Company had enabled Missouri demagogues to arouse tremendous feeling against the hordes of abolitionists who were said to be on their way to Kansas to halt slavery expansion. The opposition appears not to have been so much against the free-soil attitude toward slavery as it was against the action of the East in dumping poverty-stricken victims of the abolitionists' own slums and factories into the West. Newspaper editors used the most derogatory terms in referring to settlers from the East. No doubt frontier pride was injured by this implication, and this partly explains the unhappy responses to the invasion of Kansas. At this stage no easterners had arrived in Kansas. The unseen monster was fiercer when imagined than when it appeared in the form of timid and inexperienced eastern settlers. Meetings were held on June 3 and 5, 1854, in Westport and Independence to organize vigilance committees to resist the easterners. Other meetings followed and other resistance groups were formed, thus setting the sage for the storm which broke over Kansas.

Settlement began along the Kansas River. Towns, farms and mills were established. By the time the first settlers arrived, a newspaper, the *Kansas Weekly Herald*, had begun publication. Except for agitation over slavery extension by the various leagues and societies, early settlement of eastern Kansas differed little from that on the rest of the frontier. On hand were the usual exploiters, adventurers, and pre-emptors who sought to make a quick dash into the territory to gain early advantages and who were not concerned with the issues of slavery one way or another. Then there were the cabin settlers who were constantly pushing on to the frontier.

New England settlers in the Kansas Territory underwent an experience different from that of most border people. Easterners usually came by rail through Buffalo, Cleveland, Chicago or Indianapolis, and St. Louis, and then by boat to Kansas City. From Kansas City they traveled to the settlements in ox wagons. A characteristic journey was that of Miriam Davis Colt's family who went to Kansas in the spring of 1856 as members of the Vegetarian Company from Potsdam, New York. This company headed for the Neosho Valley under the leadership of Henry S. Chubb. On May 1, the Colt party arrived in Kansas City, after having their vegetarian convictions sorely tested by the sumptuous display of meats on board the boat from St. Louis. In the streets of Kansas City Mrs. Colt saw Santa Fe wagons ready to depart for the Southwest. Of the city she wrote, "Large droves of cattle are driven into town to be sold to emigrants, who, like us, are going into the territory; our husbands are all out today buying oxen, provisions and cooking utensils for our ox wagon journey into the territory."

A day later the vegetarians left Kansas City. "We hitherto travelled by steampower," wrote Mrs. Colt. "Now we are going to try the virtue there is in ox power—'slow and steady win the race.' All ready! women with bonnets on, and children walk along up the hill out of this 'Great City—' wait under a tree—what a beautiful country is spread out before us! Will our Kansas scenery equal this?

"Here come the ox wagons with their white tops; we shall look like a band of Mormons bound for Salt Lake City—"

Rolling uphill from Kansas City many of the vegetarians were moving on toward heartbreak and failure. Only by the most nightmarish dream could the New England mother have foreseen what was in store for her.

Laboring to build a home, and failure of the company to send mechanics and build mills made life hard. Border raiding and anxieties added to settler woes. Ague and fevers were fatal to Mrs. Colt's husband and son, and to some of her neighbors. A year later the author and her daughter were back in Lyme, Connecticut. Watson and Lizza Stewart wrote her from Neosho, Kansas, on May 13, 1857, giving a graphic picture of the frustration and failure of the Vegetarian Company. "Mr. Adams," said the Stewarts, "went shortly after you left to Maysville, Arkansas; we had a letter from them in the winter; their health had improved. The Broadbents both died shortly after old Mr. Colt. Mr. Hobbs went back to Kansas City with the intention of going home. Buxton is still in the neighborhood. Blackburn went to Tennessee, home to his family." Even manager Chubb was forced to leave.

In Washington, President Pierce was obligated to choose territorial officials following the passage of the Kansas-Nebraska Act. For the frontier governorship he chose Andrew Reeder, whose only real qualification was that of being a safe popular sovereignty Democrat who had supported the President. Samuel D. LeCompte of Maryland was appointed chief justice; Rush Elmore of Alabama and S. W. Johnston of Ohio were made associate justices. Daniel Woodson was selected territorial secretary. These were political appointments made by a weak President who lacked adequate understanding of western problems. Reeder was methodical but lackadaisical in his work. He took until October to reach Kansas, and then delayed establishing the territorial government until he and his fellow officials made an inspection tour. Unfortunately he weakened his position in the West by speculating in lands, an excuse used later by President Pierce to dismiss him from office. Judge LeCompte lacked nearly all the qualifications of a competent jurist, and the other officials were as poorly prepared for their delicate tasks.

Governor Reeder took a political census to determine the population of the territory. On November 29, 1854, the first election was called to select congressional delegates. This unfortunate election ended the young dream of an unobstructed popular sovereignty. Proslavery "Social Bands" and "Blue Lodges" were organized to insure a political victory in Kansas. Swarms of Missouri voters entered Kansas temporarily to vote and then withdrew. John W. Whitfield, a proslavery partisan, was elected territorial delegate to Congress.

Immediately after the November election there was a demand for the assembling of a territorial legislature. Approximately eighty-five hundred people had migrated to Kansas, but extra-territorial voters greatly increased the proportional number of votes cast at the polls. The last day of March, 1855, was election day for state representatives. Again proslavery borderers from Missouri entered the territory to insure a victory for this group. Voting was highly irregular and openly fraudulent. Because of local protests, Governor Reeder disqualified the results of six districts which registered heavy Missouri majorities. This act, moral and just though it was, initiated a pattern which prevailed in Kansas until the period of the Civil War. Reeder's act stirred the Missourians to anger. William Phillips of Leavenworth, who had signed one of the protest petitions, was seized by a mob which shaved one side of his head, tarred and feathered him, and then sold him at auction for a cent and a half.

Bleeding Kansas

However reasonable an administrative plan might have seemed in Washington, it was not applicable in Kansas for several reasons. Officials like Reeder were both administratively inexperienced and morally unable to forego profits from land speculation. They represented the Democratic administration in Washington, but political regularity was lacking on the border, and it was not possible for a governor to organize a party. Border ruffians acknowledged allegiance to men like Atchison, Stringfellow and LeCompte—not to a party. Certainly they were not subject to political discipline from Washington. Wealth beckoned, and it seemed easiest to gain it by an avoidance of national political leadership.

Governor Reeder returned to Washington to confer with President Pierce. He wished to withdraw, but the President refused to accept his resignation, threatening him, moreover, with dismissal for speculating in lands if he did not return to Kansas. Back in Kansas the Governor faced a willful proslavery legislature. He called a meeting of the territorial government at Pawnee up the Kansas River, but immediately found himself at odds with legislators over the location of the temporary capital. The assembly moved to the Shawnee Manual Labor School near Westport. There it adopted the Missouri Civil and Criminal Codes, and petitioned Pierce to remove the territorial governor from office. Before this petition reached Washington, however, the President had acted, appointing Wilson Shannon to succeed Reeder.

At this point Kansas found itself with two willful political groups on hand trying to organize separate territorial governments. The free-soilers met at Topeka in a constitutional convention from October to November, and on December 15, 1856, ratified a free-soil constitution. Ex-Governor Reeder was chosen congressional delegate, and Charles Robinson was elected free-soil governor. At the same time the proslavery partisans met in convention at Leavenworth. Adoption of the Topeka Constitution, and the Lawrence Convention to select state officers, marked the beginning of the bloody Kansas War. Yet, troubled as the local Kansas situation was in 1856, the most aggravating fact was the unrealistic leadership in Washington. President Pierce and his cabinet had only a foggy notion of the western border, and had they been well informed, it is doubtful that they could have risen above the level of uncertain partisan politics to make and execute positive decisions. A preview of the impending violence was the so-called Wakarusa War of December, 1855, in which border ruffians and free-soil defenders of Lawrence made bloodless demonstrations against each other. Bloodshed was averted by Governor Shannon's plea for both sides to withdraw.

The free-soil legislature met at Topeka in March, 1856, selected Andrew Reeder and James Lane to be United States Senators, and petitioned Congress to admit the state. Congress in the meantime sent an investigating committee to the territory to determine what was happening. Before the congressmen arrived, free-soil and proslavery border ruffians were girding for a struggle. Kansas aid societies in the East were actively gathering money and Sharps rifles to sustain free-state settlers. Missourians were crying through the land for southern assistance to save Kansas. Investigating committee and ruffians arrived almost together in Lawrence. Sheriff Jones entered the town to arrest men who had helped a prisoner named Bronson to escape jail almost five months before. So tense had resistance to the Sheriff become that Governor Shannon requested troops be sent to the free-soil town of Lawrence to maintain order. Jones was shot while sitting in his tent, and a pretense was made for some time that he was dead. Judge LeCompte in an intemperate charge directed the federal grand jury to regard the free-soil officials as guilty of treason. By May excitement was at a high pitch, and free-soilers were either on the run or were under bail.

News of the Kansas outrages stirred anew the anger of partisans in the East and South. Eastern supporters sent cases of improved Sharps rifles to Kansas to be sold for twenty-five dollars apiece. Most of these were intercepted en route through Missouri. Colonel Jefferson Buford of Eufaula, Alabama, hastened west with southern volunteers bearing guns and Bibles. Not to be outdone by the Bible-packing southerners, Henry Ward Beecher offered both Bibles and Sharps rifles as contributions of his congregation. In time the term "Beecher's Bibles" came to be a symbol for the rowdiness and hypocrisy of the Kansas War.

While political leaders in Kansas and Washington maneuvered for position on territorial problems, the Missouri army was active in the territory. An appeal was made to southerners for aid. Adventurers of all sorts crossed the border to be on hand if trouble started. On May 20, a posse of eight hundred men surrounded the free-soil town of Lawrence, and the convalescent Sheriff Jones came out of hiding and demanded that Samuel C. Pomeroy and the people of the town surrender their arms. Pomeroy gave up two small cannon, but ignored the demand for small arms on grounds that they belonged to private citizens. In the meantime Atchison and Stringfellow had led the armed ruffians into Lawrence, where Atchison worked emotions even higher with a speech delivered from atop a cannon. The mob destroyed the newspapers and public buildings, and gutted the hotel with cannon shot and fire. News of the sacking of Lawrence spread across the nation. So impassioned did the antislavery senators become, that Charles Sumner in his speech, "The Crime Against Kansas," denounced Stephen A. Douglas and Andrew Butler of South Carolina for championing human wrongs. It was this intemperate outburst which caused Butler's nephew, Preston Brooks, to cane Sumner on the Senate floor.

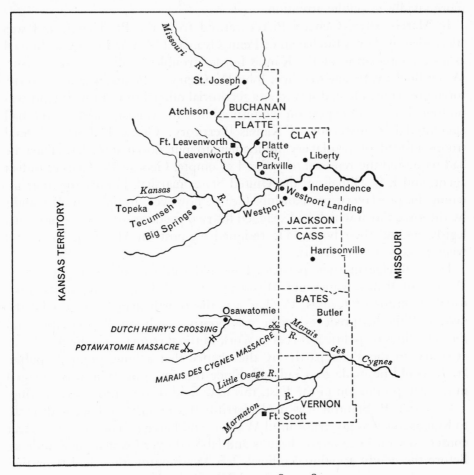

THE KANSAS BORDER, 1854–1859

Another result of the Lawrence debacle was the notorious John Brown raid at Dutch Henry's Crossing of Potawatomie Creek. The leader of this murderous assault was a Connecticut Yankee who came of a family in which insanity was a notable characteristic. "Old Osawatomie" was a fecund man, siring twenty children by two wives. He was, despite his numerous family, a ne'er-do-well moving westward across the frontier until he joined his five sons in Kansas. John Brown was obsessed with the idea of freeing the slaves, and at one time he maintained an underground railway station in Pennsylvania. On the night of May 24, 1856, this old man, four of his sons, a son-in-law, and two neighbors armed with guns and short swords set out to visit the Lord's vengeance upon five innocent victims along Potawatomie Creek. These unfortunates were not proslavery men, nor had they participated in the border troubles. News of the John Brown raid became a national horror story which brought bleeding Kansas more vividly to public attention.

In March, 1857, General Pierce retired from the Presidency and was succeeded by James Buchanan of Pennsylvania. The new President showed as little appreciation of the Kansas border troubles as did his predecessor. When Buchanan came to office, John W. Geary of Pennsylvania was territorial governor. He had served as a territorial official in California, and was presumed to be an expert on western affairs. In August, 1856, Pierce had appointed him governor of Kansas Territory. Geary had used federal troops instead of proslavery militiamen to put down disorder. Then he had requested the removal of Judge LeCompte, George W. Clarke, Indian agent, and I. B. Donalson, the United States marshal, because of their intemperate proslavery partisanship. Geary, however, found himself caught by the same thorn which had snagged his two predecessors—the proslavery legislators and their bosses. He resigned his post on March 4, 1857, and went home to Pennsylvania.

James Buchanan then persuaded his old cabinet colleague, Robert J. Walker of Pennsylvania and Mississippi, to accept appointment as territorial governor of Kansas. Walker was the fourth man to undertake the task, and like his predecessors he was poorly conditioned to comprehend the actualities of political forces at work in the territory. No doubt he was attracted to the West partly by the chance that a huge grant of public lands would be made to a railroad. Since the new governor was engaged in railway promotion in the East, this new field of operation was inviting.

Frederick P. Stanton was made territorial secretary and went directly to Kansas to act as governor until Walker could arrive. The governor-elect conferred with Democratic leaders and labored over his inaugural address. Before the newly appointed officials left Washington they had their first unfortunate meeting with two local Kansas leaders—General John Calhoun, surveyor general, and L. A. McClean, land clerk. As has been said already, the Democratic party as an administrative force did not exist in Kansas. Walker and Stanton began their administration in a rivalry with the local proslavery leaders.

At Lecompton, in an atmosphere of raw frontier society and politics, Walker suffered a snubbing if not outright insult by Calhoun and McClean. The cardinal point of difference between them was the issue of popular sovereignty, with Walker contending that the prospective state constitution should be submitted to the people for approval before it was sent on for congressional approval. The Governor's immediate task was dissolution of the free-state legislature and the establishment of political harmony. But Walker's contention that the issue of slavery would be voted upon as it might be treated in the state constitution or as a separate issue only antagonized the proslavery leaders. The summer of 1857 was an anxious one politically as the country went to the polls to select congressmen. Walker and his Kansas policy were important issues in the election, especially in the South.

A constitutional convention met at Lecompton in September, 1857, but it was unable to settle down to work before the election for a congressional delegate and legislators brought about a recess. When results of the election were known, it was found that a flagrant fraud had been perpetrated in two precincts. Governor Walker declared no returns from the precincts in question, and immediately found himself involved in a legal battle that was reminiscent of Governor Reeder's troubles. When the Lecompton convention was again in session, proslavery leaders were safely in control. Calhoun assumed leadership of the convention, and in November that body produced a document which guaranteed protection to slave property already in the territory, permitted immigrants to bring additional slaves to the state, forbade legislative emancipation except for compensation, and excluded free Negroes.

Adoption of the Lecompton Constitution precipitated a political impasse in Washington among Walker, Douglas, and Buchanan, and between northern and southern Democrats. Calhoun's handiwork in Lecompton hastened the division and disruption of the Democratic party, and moved the Union itself closer to dissolution. An unrestricted election in Kansas no doubt would have resulted in a free-soil victory. The Lecompton Constitution was rejected when proslavery men refused to vote, but Buchanan submitted the document to Congress, where it was ratified in the Senate but defeated in the House. Nevertheless the free-state forces gained control in Kansas in 1857 and 1858.

Slavery was abolished in Kansas in January, 1860. A year later the state was admitted to the Union. The complex and bitter territorial struggle had a major bearing on almost every aspect of national politics after 1853. Some of its most notable landmarks were the failure of the Democratic party to remain a unified body, the rise of the national Republican party, and the significant Lincoln-Douglas debates. Besides the broader political implications, creation of the new state paved the way for rapid organization of the remaining frontier area. The succeeding decades saw an expansion of population, construction of transcontinental railroads, and the permanent breaching of the Indian barrier. Once the cause of the major emotional and sectional issues was removed, Kansas and Nebraska once again became a part of the vast plains frontier which absorbed the energies of thousands of westward-moving pioneers.

A DRIVE OF LONGHORNS INTO DODGE CITY, 1878. FROM *Frank Leslie's Illustrated Newspaper*

THE CATTLE TRAIL FRONTIER

THE CATTLE TRAIL FRONTIER

Few occupations are more cheerful, lively and pleasant than that of cowboy on a fine day or night; but when the storm comes, then is his manhood and often his skill and bravery put to test. When the night is inky dark and the lurid lightning flashes its zig-zag course athwart the heavens, and the coarse thunder jars the earth, the winds moan afresh and lively over the prairie, the electric balls dance from tip to tip of the cattle's horns—then the position of the cowboy on duty is trying far more than romantic.

—JOSEPH G. McCOY, *Historic Sketches of the Cattle Trade*

CHAPTER XXVII

ONE of the most colorful reminders of the expanding American frontier
to survive into our own time is the cowboy, his history and folklore.
Even foreigners who know almost nothing factually about the United
States have a smattering of knowledge of the old cattle business with its
cowboys, Indians, cattle towns and long trail herds. Historically, cattle-
grazing was not unique to Texas and the rest of the plains country. Research to date in the background of the frontier grazing industry has been
so sketchy and defective that knowledge of it is far too inadequate. Only
within the last few years a new and revealing chapter on this subject has
been published in Frank L. Owsley's *Plain Folk of the Old South*.

Cattle grazing was an old and established frontier practice long before
the American settlers approached Texas. Dating from the settlement of
the Virginia and Pennsylvania valleys, frontiersmen herded cattle into the
backwoods and later drove them eastward to market. This earlier cattle
trade was most undramatic. There were few or no men on horseback, and
no straggling herds stirred up long trails of dust in cross-country drives.

Grazing Frontier

Man and cows advanced westward across the American frontier to new
grazing lands without fanfare. They kept to the outer fringes of civilization, and drovers were well down on the social scale, even in rude and
unsophisticated frontier society. They donned no flamboyant clothes distinctive of their trade, their horses carried no fancily adorned saddles, but
these men were handy with the rifle and they created a certain amount
of common law applicable to the range as they went. Like their descendants
on the plains they encroached upon the public domain almost at will and
were forced to change their mode of life when settlers with land warrants,
deeds and plow tools appeared.

From Kentucky westward, cattlemen of the Ohio and upper Mississippi valleys encountered the buffalo. Trails and grasslands about the great salt licks east of the river bear testimony of the periodic migrations of these heavily plodding beasts. Once this area below the Ohio fell within the settlement line, the buffalo retreated westward, and in subsequent years the great animals concentrated upon the western plains. At the beginning of the nineteenth century there were possibly forty million buffalo grazing back and forth in the grasslands of the West, but this number declined almost to the point of extinction by the end of the century. The buffalo had the peculiar habit of grazing in separate herds of bulls and cows except in the breeding seasons. Males segregated themselves into vast droves while females and calves went their own way. Wherever the buffalo was found, there was water nearby and reasonably good grazing lands. Both hunter and cattleman could follow in his tracks with assurance of meat, hides and grass.

Between 1840 and 1880 the buffalo was virtually destroyed. Hunters who sought a monetary return from their shooting cut out tongues, hump steaks, and occasionally stripped off hides to make robes, but thousands of carcasses rotted where they fell. Possibly there has never been more shameless butchery of animal life on this continent than that which brought destruction of the buffalo. Roaming the plains without benefit of protective covering, these clumsy animals were well-nigh defenseless. An unarmed man was helpless before a charging bull or a stampeding herd, but mounted and armed he could do serious damage to these stolid galloping creatures. After the Civil War, the arms companies equipped plainsmen with improved heavy-calibre guns which were most effective in wiping out the herds.

As railroads were extended onto the plains, track-laying crews as well as professional hunters slaughtered thousands of buffaloes. So-called sportsmen rode the trains and fired their newly developed buffalo guns into herds from car windows, leaving trails of dead and wounded animals behind them. In fact, the building of the Union Pacific Railroad across the plains divided the great herd into two parts. The northern one grazed as far as Canada, while the southern one ranged between the Platte and Arkansas rivers.

Unfortunately for his future existence, the buffalo's bones, hide and meat were of commercial value. As soon as the railways supplied ready transportation, grisly commercial hunters flocked to the plains to earn meager wages gathering hides, meat, bones and tallow until the last of the big herds was gone. These gangs of buffalo skinners were held in low esteem by other plainsmen. Cattlemen and cowboys looked upon them as being in a class with skunks and coyotes. They were often denied other human company, and sometimes were driven away from saloons and brothels because of their loathsomeness. Nevertheless these hunters were proficient in their trade. A man named Tom Nixon was said to have killed 120 buffalo from a single stand in forty minutes' time, and in thirty-five days he killed 2,173 animals. The buffalo helped along its own slaughter. Although the buffalo was frightened by the sight of man, it was not frightened by the report of a gun. When a concealed hunter dropped one buffalo, others, smelling blood, rushed around the fallen animal, and the entire drove could be wiped out. General Phil Sheridan understood the vital role of the buffalo in the life of the plains Indians, and because of this he encouraged its destruction. "Instead of stopping the hunters," he said, "you ought to give each hunter a medal of bronze with a dead buffalo on one side and [a] discouraged Indian on the other. . . . Send them powder and lead, if you will, but for the sake of peace, let them kill, skin, and sell until the buffalo are exterminated. Then your prairies can be covered with cattle and the cowboy, who follows the hunter as a second forerunner of an advanced civilization." It is an irony of frontier history that Phil Sheridan's philosophy was so well memorialized, not in bronze but in nickel. On one side of our coin is a buffalo, and on the other a Plains Indian.

The "second forerunner of civilization" was not long in making his appearance in all the plains country. Lowing herds and armies of cowboys soon ranged the plains where once the buffalo had grazed on the stout grama, blue-stem and buffalo grasses. Coming from the East were the stocky English and western European types of cattle which had undergone several generations of adaptation to American environment and breeding refinements. Up from the Southwest came the Spanish type, rangy in build, heavily horned, and rugged in stamina. They differed radically from their eastern European and English cousins. By original breeding and environmental conditioning on the dry plains, they were of a lean, spare build with hard constitutions, capable of making adjustments to rather severe conditions. They were usually crowned with heavy protective horns. Actually there were four distinct types of cattle in the Southwest: the wild, mealy-nosed brown cow, marked with a light stripe down its back and wide spreading blue horns; the vari-colored, long horned Texan type; the small-boned Spanish cow; and the curly-haired, or chino, breed with heavy body and sturdy legs. These generally were the animals that composed the trail herds on which was founded the range cattle industry.

Cattle droving in the Southwest had its beginning as an industry in the decade of the 1830's when the old drovers of the East crossed the Mississippi and moved on westward with the Texas migration. In Texas several important new factors entered droving history. New types of range cattle were present, distances were great, the country was open, water was scarce, and potential markets for such a large volume of cattle were restricted. It was out of the question to consider the eastern seaboard market; so this left only New Orleans and the West Indies, neither of which supported sufficient buyers to purchase the large herds of the Texas plains.

While the Mexican War was being fought, the early Texas cattlemen found a ready market for much of their beef, and some historians cite this as the beginning of the range cattle trade. By 1861, and the outbreak of the Civil War, a promising cattle industry in the Southwest had made a good beginning. Already trail herds had moved northward to Ohio and other northern markets. Edward Piper took a thousand cattle to Ohio from Texas in 1846, and in 1859 John C. Dawson drove a herd to the Colorado gold fields. The wild cattle and the grasslands of southwestern Texas were attracting an increasing number of cattlemen. Four years of Civil War created a demand for both meat and leather, but at the same time disrupted delivery of cattle to market. Some herds were driven across the Mississippi River to the Confederacy, but occupation of that stream by Yankee gunboats interrupted this trade. Some herds of wild cattle were assembled and driven northward to the virgin ranges of Kansas and Nebraska and were then started in search of buyers. But sales of beef cattle from 1861 to the end of the Civil War scarcely touched the great herds that roamed the plains without molestation. For four years wild cattle multiplied and fattened in Texas. A shortage of men and the distance to the northern and northeastern markets defeated the idea of immediately driving herds in that direction. By 1865 it was estimated that there were 3,111,475 head of cattle in Texas. No one, of course, knew how many cows there were among the wild and untended herds, and the precise figures given in the various sources of information can be little more than statistical whimsicalities.

Trail Herds

The end of the Civil War brought both a supply of drovers and a sharp increase in the demand for meat. Cities of the East and Middle West had grown in size; increased industrialization during the war had developed a cash market for meat; and military and Indian purchasing continued good for a considerable time. Steers which could be bought on the Texas range for as little as three or four dollars could be sold at prices ranging from twenty-five to fifty dollars. Transportation costs ran around four dollars a head in the early drives. Moving cattle from range to market, however, had its serious drawbacks after 1865. The transcontinental railway systems were still in the organizational stage. Only the Union Pacific was actually started across the plains; consequently the early trail herds had to be driven into Missouri and Illinois with St. Louis and Chicago as final destinations. To reach railheads which connected with these cities involved a drive of eight hundred to twelve hundred miles across dry country, through Indian territory, and over the farming lands of western Missouri. It was a tossup whether Indians or farmers were more hostile. The first drives of 1866 moved up from the Nueces and Colorado river valleys of Texas by way of Fort Worth to the Denison crossing of the Red River, then to Fort Smith, Arkansas, and then northward to Sedalia, Missouri, and a connection with the Missouri Pacific Railroad.

The early drovers ran into serious trouble controlling their herds when they reached the timbered lands of the western Ozarks. Farmers objected strenuously to cattle running over their cultivated fields, and owners of eastern cattle were afraid that Texas fever would be transmitted to their own herds. In the Indian territories, cattlemen either braved the hostility of the tribes or had to pay stiff bounties for the privilege of driving across their lands. By 1867 Missouri and Kansas had passed quarantine laws which made it difficult to market southwestern cattle in the settled areas of those states. As a result of these barriers, the cattle trails were forced to take more westerly routes in order to reach market points which lay beyond the immediate settlement lines. Nevertheless the cattlemen, like fur traders, carried on a business which in this early form was doomed. Railroads and settlers were attracted perforce to its main centers of activity.

Between 1866 and 1886, however, trailing cattle up from Texas became a prosperous and picturesque business. Possibly no other group of pioneers beguiled the imagination of the American people more than did the plains cattlemen. Successful drovers had to possess much knowledge and common sense to succeed. First of all, they had to know something of geography cut out on a vast pattern. Like early mariners on an endless sea they had to be able to find their way with few or no scientific instruments. Not only had they to know "the lay of the land," but they had to be able to find waterholes, safe stream crossings, and grass. Early cattlemen learned that herds of approximately 2,500 were the most manageable, and that smaller herds were not so profitable. To herd 2,500 cattle required the services of eight to twelve cowboys, or one puncher to approximately every 200 head. To mount these men necessitated a *remuda*, or horse herd, of 80 to 125 saddle horses. The *remuda* was watched over by a horse wrangler who kept his animals abreast of the movement of the chuck wagon. The chuck wagon on the earlier drives was drawn by steers; later, mule teams were used. It was driven by the cook, who moved on somewhat more rapidly than the grazing herd in order to establish camps and to have food ready for the men. Some outfits carried with them night herders or "hawks" so that the day riders could get uninterrupted sleep; this, however, was an idyllic situation which seldom materialized. Cowboys were most often called upon to stand night watches of two or three hours each, and if cattle were nervous and restless, watches might last all night.

Cowboys

Aristocrats of the cattle trail were the cowboys. Immediately following the Civil War it was not difficult to get young men to become cowboys. Many southerners who came home from the war to find their country devastated went on to the West to make a new start. From the beginning, herding cattle had its aura of romance and glamor; likewise it enforced a process of natural selection among men which was characteristic of the older frontiers. The chosen ones had to possess a high degree of courage and dependability; the weaker ones quickly demonstrated their incapacity. On the trail, beleaguered cattlemen often faced situations where they had only one chance to make a decision and to act, or they imperiled the lives of everybody about them. If cowboys turned yellow or faithless, then herds were lost and their companions were injured and killed. Weaklings seldom got started because of a rugged and crude process of initiation which weeded out the misfits. Every newcomer was a challenge to the whimsical natures of the established company, and he was subjected to much hazing until he could prove himself. By joking and pranking, men tested the natures of their companions and could judge how well they would behave under pressure.

Although the cowboy was not new in the annals of American life, the drama of their lives on the plains was. To the Southwest, Mexican *vaqueros* had herded cattle in the plains country for at least two centuries; they set the pattern for the subsequent American invasion. Many of the colorful trappings adopted by the American cowboys came from the *vaqueros* of old Mexico, and in turn from Spain. Fancy saddles, bridles, chaps, spurs, and lariats were among articles of Spanish design and origin. Terminology which described both the cattle trade and its equipment possessed a rich Latin piquancy. Among these were *cincha* (cinch), *caballerango* (wrangler), *chaparejos* (chaps), *la reata* (lariat), and *caballo* (cayuse). Before the end of the nineteenth century Pecos Bill, the orphaned cowboy, had taken his place alongside Paul Bunyan, Mike Fink and other American folk heroes. Men like Andy Adams, Bat Masterson, James Butler Hickok, J. G. McCoy, Teddy Blue Abbott, and scores of others were well-known flesh and blood characters and legends as well. Life on the plains was fraught with the realities of frontier life. The plainsman was possibly little different from the old grazers and drovers in basic temperament and outlook on life. But once beyond the timber belt and out onto the plains, a country lad astride a tough cow pony, clothed in chaps, crowned with a sombrero, and armed with a Colt revolver became a sort of hero even in his own eyes. He was the West's man on horseback who regarded walking as one of God's sternest curses upon depraved common men. Cowboys rode the range in open country where they and their herds could be seen. Distances were great, and physical and emotional endurance were important. Possibly an argument could be made that the openness and vastness of the country contributed a new perspective to these men who had been conditioned to wooded country.

The dress of the cowboys often attracted attention; however, the great majority wore the orthodox denim jeans of the backcountry store trade. The spreading Mexican sombrero or the wide-brimmed black wool hat of the cotton belt South and Southwest crowned a majority of the range riders. High-heeled, sharp-toed boots were designed for safety's sake. The heels kept the rider's feet from slipping through the stirrups and supplied a scotch by which the cowboy braced himself in quick turns and stops of the horse. Sharp toes enabled horsemen to thrust their feet into stirrups with certainty and speed. Chaps kept brush from tearing trousers and scratching legs and, in the sultry weather of the plains, prevented chafing of the thighs. Both the vest and the bandanna had high utilitarian value. The former was a carryall in which tobacco, watches, pencils, paper, matches and other supplies were packed. The bandanna was both a neck shade and a dust filter. Topping off this picturesque dress was the cartridge belt and holsters which swung from the hips. The revolver was a necessary tool of the cattle trade. It sometimes served as an instrument with which to stop the charge of a maddened steer or to kill a rattlesnake; sometimes as a noisemaker to turn back frightened and stampeding herds; sometimes for self-defense against rustlers and Indians. Some cowboys often forgot the lethal natures of their weapons and fired them carelessly in public places, or shot at people just for the fun of seeing them run for cover. Teddy Blue Abbott describes his initiation into the roistering fraternity of the railhead towns in his delightful book, *We Pointed Them North*. He "winged" the town marshal as a starter. It would be easy to overstate the place of the revolver in the cowboy's life. Many of them seldom if ever carried guns.

Everyday work was hard and grimy and without glamor. Herding wild cattle was always hazardous. A rampant bull or a cow with a young calf could show a lot of fight, and wild cattle milling about could gore and trample a man to death if he had no immediate means of protection. Indians, rattlesnakes, wolves and coyotes also could make life precarious for the unarmed man. Riding range was a lonesome business. Sometimes cowboys would be gone from ranch houses and human associations for extended periods. In nearly every case the range rider had to adapt himself to coarse food of his own cooking, to sleeping on the ground and to many other hardships. His daily work consisted of driving cattle back on to home ranges, branding calves, running off strays, rounding up and counting grazing herds, and keeping a lookout for Indians and rustlers. Before the advent of barbed wire much of the range rider's time was spent in line riding, that is, serving the purpose of fencing, riding over sections of the border of grazing areas to keep the home herd in bounds and invaders out.

Trail driving differed from ranch labor in many respects; it meant equally as strenuous work. Trail herds were often organized from several bands of range cattle. Generally a trail herd was assembled from among the better and more mature cattle of several ranches. Once the requisite number of head were formed into a herd, they were trail-branded so they could be identified if they stampeded on the drive. For the first two weeks after the herd was started north, the drovers had to keep a keen lookout to see that it did not stampede; during these first days of a drive the cattle were most fractious. Stampedes played havoc with both the size of herds and the peace of mind of the herders. Almost any unusual thing could start trail cattle on the rampage—electric storms with sudden flashes of lightning and rolling peals of thunder, driving gusts of wind and rain, and any unusual noises in the night. The snort of a cowboy's horse in the dark might make a sleeping herd jump up and go scurrying off in all directions. Worst of all were the planned stampedes by Indians and rustlers who frightened cattle away with the hope of capturing them. Night herders sang continually so that drowsing steers would not be startled by their presence.

Heading off a stampeding herd and turning it back onto the trail was an experience that few cowpunchers forgot. Sometimes it took days to reorganize herds, and in doing so cowboys and horses were worked to exhaustion. Occasionally cattle became mixed with herds of buffalo, and their separation was a superhuman task. Crossing cattle over sand-bound rivers imperiled both animals and men. If the water were deep, many head drowned and quicksand pulled others down to destruction; but most tedious of all, the herd was temporarily divided so that danger was doubled. But none of the perils of the trail surpassed the long dry drives in which cattle were sometimes kept from water so long that they were both maddened and blinded. Drovers preferred to add scores of miles to their journeys by going over roundabout trails rather than cover the long and treacherous waterless stretches.

Little wonder then, that when dusty and worn cowboys reached the railheads and disposed of their cattle they spent money freely and enjoyed relaxation wherever they could find it. The arrival of every trail herd at its destination was an act of triumph on the part of a dozen or so men. They celebrated their achievement by partaking freely of the town's generous supplies of liquor, gambling and women. Sometimes they gambled away their wages in a night's time, and it was not unusual for some of them to spend time in local calabooses. There have never been greater practical jokers in America than cowboys. They teased tenderfeet, stuffed strangers with weird stories, held kangaroo courts, put carbon bisulphite (hokey pokey) on dozing horses, and engaged in mock gun battles in which obnoxious braggarts were forced to show their feathers and run. They were also masters at bragging and telling humorous stories. Measured by the staid standards of the sober settler, the cowboy was a sinful person— a drunkard, a speed-maddened fiend astride a horse, a seducer of women, a gunman, and a menace to peace and decency. Actually the cowboy's mode of life was diametrically opposite that of the settler with his plodding institutions and reliance upon law and order.

Railheads

The early Texas drive of 1866 had resulted in frustration for the cattle-men. Unless they could find a market for their stock removed both from woods and settlers, they were finished almost at the start. No one realized this more than the three McCoy brothers who bought Texas cattle for the midwestern and eastern markets. Joseph G. McCoy set out to solve the problem of a stable market center for the Texas ranchers. He first sought land for pens and sidings in Junction City on the Kansas-Pacific; and when he was forced to look elsewhere, he met with the officials of the Kansas-Pacific in St. Louis to get their assistance in locating and equipping a cattle market. These short-sighted men were unwilling to take a chance, and once again McCoy was forced to go elsewhere. He called on the haughty president of the Missouri-Pacific and was summarily dismissed with in-sulting rudeness, an act which McCoy believed kept St. Louis from becom-ing the great packing center of the United States.

Upon being turned down by the two most important railroads, McCoy made successful proposals to the struggling Hannibal and St. Joseph road which connected the Missouri River by way of Quincy with Chicago. He then visited central Kansas to select a suitable place to establish a trailhead. Solomon City and Salina refused to tolerate the idea of stock yards. Finally McCoy selected Abilene, a struggling, dirty prairie village of a dozen huts that had neither life nor civic consciousness enough to protest against the smell, dust and iniquity of the Texas cattle trade. Before Abilene, located later on the Kansas-Pacific, could be converted into a cattle town, it was necessary to construct pens and sidings, a public facility which the citizens of the town could hardly be expected to support. When the Abilene market became a certainty, McCoy dispatched W. W. Sugg, an experienced trail herder, out to the plains to spread the news. Within a short distance of the new town there were several herds wandering around with no place to go. Sugg's news was cheering, but there was question as to whether or not it might be a rustler's trick to catch unwary cattlemen. The first herd driven into Abilene had been brought up from Texas by a ranchman named Thompson and sold to Smith, McCord and Company. A second consignment was driven to Abilene by Wheeler, Wilson and Hicks. On September 5, 1867, the first train of twenty cars of cattle departed for Chicago, and before the year ended a thousand carloads had been sent away to the Great Lakes market.

Not all was smooth sailing for the cattlemen. Many eastern buyers had well-developed prejudices against western stock and even refused to pay cost on shipments. Railway cars were ill-adapted to deliver their live cargo in good condition. It took considerable organization and boosting to establish the western cattle trade on a profitable basis. Before this first railhead town had more than settled down to steady operation, both the railroad and the cattle industry shifted farther west, but already Abilene had become a magic name in pioneer range cattle history.

Railhead cowtowns, in many respects, portrayed raw American frontier character in its most reckless and uninhibited condition. Beginning with Abilene in 1867, other towns sprang up as railways were built westward. Among these were Newton, Big Bend, Ellsworth, Hays, Wichita, Dodge City, Cheyenne and Ogallala. None of these places had extended histories as permanent railheads, but all of them were important. As western railroads were extended across the plains, and as hordes of settlers followed in their wake, the cattle trails were pushed ever westward. Possibly the most famous of all the cowtowns was Dodge City, consisting largely of cattle pens, rail sidings, saloons, hotels, dance halls, houses of prostitution and gambling dens. Located almost astride the hundredth meridian, it began as a station on the old Santa Fe Trail and later became a frontier military outpost and buffalo hunters' outfitting station. In 1872 the Santa Fe Railroad reached Dodge City. This new frontier railhead drew the cattle trails far enough west to avoid the settlements, so that there was little or no immediate danger of becoming entangled with a settler's wheat field or his barbed wire entanglements at this end of the railroad.

Dodge City itself was relatively free of those refining social influences of civilization that made a little boisterous relaxation an abomination in the sight of God. People who flocked there were not particularly noted for inhibitions or puritanical introspection. The most famous reflection of the character of Dodge City was its cemetery landmark, Boot Hill. Between

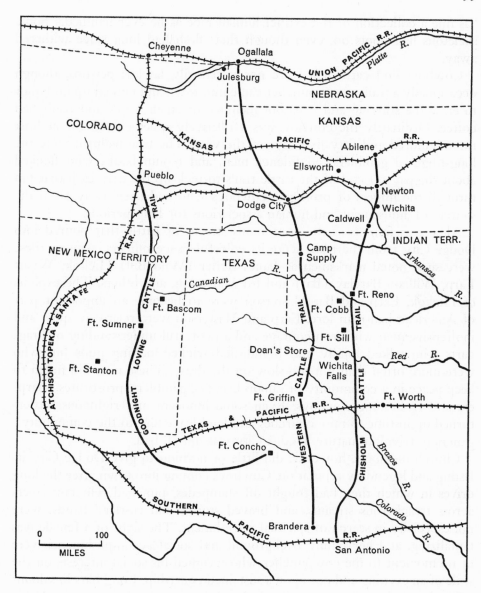

CATTLE TRAILS AND COWTOWNS

1872 and 1878 sixty-four victims of "lead poisoning" were taken up to the brow of the hill to lie in peace until the awakening of civilization in town disturbed them to make way for a schoolhouse. Boot Hill and its victims reflected the roistering, lawlessness, and uncertainties which existed around the early cowtowns. In 1879 when some of the hastily-made graves were opened, Coroner John W. Straughn described the skeletons as being "as fine a collection of the extinct human race as he ever handled." Some skeletons had boots on, even though their flesh had long since withered away.

Cowboys and cattlemen were not necessarily lawless persons, though occasionally a trail-weary puncher came into town and tanked up on liquor to erase the stinging and nauseous memory of alkali water and panboiled coffee. Ordinarily the cowboy was a relatively quiet citizen for at least three hundred and fifty-five days of the year. The true badmen were the long-fingered gamblers, confidence men, and mountebanks who flocked about the pay-off end of the cattle trails to pick up the easy cash that ran through the fingers of profligate cowboys who had been away from the sources of amusement and human associations for long periods.

Almost as famous as the continuous stream of cattle that poured into Dodge City from the trails were its colorful peace officers. Among these were such noted marksmen as James Butler (Wild Bill) Hickok, Wyatt Earp, William Barclay (Bat) and Ed Masterson, and others. The exploits of Hickok, Earp and Bat Masterson were to become an important part of American bad-man lore. Earp and Masterson were relatively quiet and inoffensive men with iron courage and a masterful understanding of brag-garts who talked loudly and brandished wicked-looking guns but who were more often than not too slow on the draw. These men did much to keep peace in a community of saloon keepers, gamblers, prostitutes, sharp-ers and frolicsome cowboys. Even some innocent and righteous settlers turned up in time to raise churches and lend leavening to the community's generally frivolous nature. Dodge City was not all bad.

Church members, however, did little or nothing to give Dodge City its lasting and legendary reputation. Cowboys coming into town after the long drives in which they had fought off stampedes, punched reluctant steers across treacherous streams, and braved storms and rustlers' bands, were not especially in search of spiritual refreshment. The sight of a female was tantalizing, and her family background and social accomplishments were of no moment to the cowpuncher who weighed his social interests on the scale of an evening and not upon a sustained courtship. Long bars in saloons offered abundant cheer to men whose pockets carried easy money. What the flush cowhand did not lay down on the bar for drinks all around, he used to feed the tiger at faro or roll away on the crap tables. Thus it was only a momentary interlude between the time the boys from Texas galloped into town feeling they could buy the place until they rode away with nothing but a headache and a horse to keep them company going home. Playful visitors to the cowtowns sometimes celebrated their de-partures by shooting up the place. Occasionally an exuberant cowhand galloped his pony into a saloon, popped out street lights, and even yielded to the temptation offered by glass windows. Tolerant businessmen were not especially fond of these jocular escapades, but they liked the easy cash the boys brought to town, so what was the loss of a little glass in comparison with the profits the boys left behind?

New railroad towns sprang up like mushrooms on the plains. Construction gangs warmed up the places for the cattlemen, and the latter increased the momentum. These towns often moved well ahead of organized municipal government, and they lacked cores of established settlers immediately to effect law and order. All of them were full of easy money, and this kind of money has never in the history of frontier expansion developed much social consciousness.

According to the Washington, D. C., *Evening Star* in 1878, "Dodge City is a wicked little town, indeed its character is so clearly and egregiously bad that one might conclude, were the evidence in these later times positive of its possibility, that it was marked for special providential punishment. Here those nomads in regions remote from restraints of moral, civil, social and law-enforcing life, the Texas cattle drovers, from the very tendencies of their situation the embodiment of waywardness and wantoness, end the journey with their herds, and here they loiter and dissipate for months, and share the boughten dalliance of fallen women. Truly the more demonstrative portion of humanity at Dodge City gives now no hopeful sign of moral improvement, no bright prospect of human exaltation. . . ."

On the Range

Because of the colorful reputation of places like Dodge City, the cowboy and cattlemen of trail herding days figure in a considerable body of literature. Novelists of all degrees of art and validity have created a company of swaggering cowpunchers stamping in and out of swinging doors, armed with Colts .44 and .45. In literature, at least, they were all dead shots—quick to take exception to slighting remarks, and even quicker to avenge insults. Some of the old-timers themselves have left colorful first-hand accounts of their experiences. Joseph G. McCoy published his memoirs under the title *Historic Sketches of the Cattle Trade*. Charley Siringo's *A Texas Cowboy, or Fifteen Years on the Hurricane Deck of a Spanish Pony* was a butcher boy favorite for years. Phillip Ashton Rollins' *The Cowboy* is a valid personal source book. Teddy Blue Abbott's memoirs published under the title of *We Pointed Them North* is one of the best of the personal stories. Con Price's two books, *Trails I Rode* and *Memoire of Old Montana* are flavorful documents. In song and verse the heroic deeds and the hardships of the range riders have been immortalized.

In fact, the average cowpuncher was a country boy who occasionally went to town. He was young, not always a good shot, meagerly educated, a good horseman but by no means in every case a bronco buster. He did not always go armed. Carrying a gun weighing two and a quarter pounds slung from the hip was tiresome, to say the least. Stories of triggers being filed so as to permit hairbreadth action, or taking the triggers off altogether and "fanning" a pistol by sweeping the hammer back with the left hand have made fine reading, but hardly represent a general fact. Few workaday cowboys indeed ever mastered this reckless art. Had he lived to view the slick, gaily-bedecked sports of movie and television who sing so nostalgically of range, saddle, and herd, he would have turned away in derision.

Breaking wild horses was not what the average cowboy considered a pleasant pastime. There was grave danger of being thrown and injured, if not killed. Even when a bronco buster kept his seat, the bucking animal was liable to cause a rupture. Six years was about as long as most rough riders could hope to keep in shape physically to take so much jarring and twisting. The wild horse of the plains was hard to break, and it took skillful handling to make a saddle horse out of him. Many of them never surrendered completely to training. A short period of rest and running idle on the range, a spell of cold weather, a sore back, or an accidental gouging with a spur rowel put them on enough of a wire-edge to require a second breaking. This periodic gentling was called taking the "top" off a horse. Some cowboys were much better at this than others. What most of them wanted was a string of four or five dependable horses with one particular favorite. The type and temperament of the horse depended largely upon the job the rider was doing. If he were trailing a herd, then a horse with straight plunging speed, good stamina and peaceful temperament was most desirable. In roundups riders preferred an agile cutting horse that could dart in and out of a herd of cattle and hold steady when a steer was roped. There was often a close affinity between cowboys and their horses. Some of them grieved when their favorite mounts died, and buried them and marked their graves with sentimental inscriptions. As for the cowboys themselves, they were in a sweaty, picturesque business; in fact, as Bart Smith said, they were "merely folks, just plain, everyday, bow-legged humans."

Cattle herding in the period from 1866 to 1886 consisted largely of three activities—range herding, roundups, and trail driving. In the beginning a cattle range might take in all the lands along a river, or within a certain natural boundary of plains country. Ownership of the land had little or nothing to do either with its use or with the common law governing it. From Virginia to Texas, frontier cattlemen made free use of the public domain as a grazing ground, looking upon it as a kind of heavenly largesse which was theirs for the taking. Ownership of cattle was established by claim of original herds and by brand and earmarks. This latter form of title was neither new nor unique in the West. Almost every county courthouse in the old frontier grazing areas contained its brand books. Brands and marks consisted of figures, symbols and letters burned on shoulders, flanks and hips of the cattle. Ears were cropped and slit to give a double guarantee of ownership. The best brands were those which were easily distinguishable, and which could not be successfully altered by rustlers and thieves. On the loosely tended ranges attempts were made to brand calves according to their mothers' marks. Large numbers of strays and motherless calves presented difficulty. The unbranded calf without motherly attachment was a maverick and might become the property of anyone who ran it down and put his brand on it.

The great roundups of the cattle country were immensely exciting events. All the cattle from a given range were driven to a central point for sorting and branding. Neighboring ranchmen and their outfits gathered at central points, selected captains of the roundups, chose herding grounds and then set out to bring in the cattle. Once the cattle were driven into the chosen grounds, the man on whose range a roundup occurred was given the first choice or cut of the cattle. Then the remaining animals were sorted out and claimed by other owners. There was much hard riding and joking, with kangaroo courts doing big business, and generous amounts of food being consumed. The company abided carefully by range-made laws, and captains were serious leaders who performed their duties with great care. The roundup was the plains' version of the logrolling and house-raising of the eastern wooded frontier.

Trail driving to railheads and northern grass lands had a remarkably short history—approximately from 1866 to 1886—yet it played an important role both in national economy and in frontier expansion. News that there was money in cattle attracted scores of speculators to the West. Many of these sought wealth by the investment of small amounts of capital. With one good drive a cattleman could accumulate a comfortable nest egg of wealth. A drover could buy Texas range cattle for five to fifteen dollars a head and drive a herd of twenty-five hundred north at an approximate cost of a dollar a mile. In the northern market these same cattle sold from twenty-five to fifty dollars, leaving a substantial profit. Many dreamers trailed paper herds northward at enormous imagined profits, but when they tried the actual operation they discovered that they had overlooked the realities of the situation.

Cattle driven from the range were headed to two markets. One was that of the eastern states and Europe; the other, the feeder market of the northern plains states of Iowa and Illinois. Farmers of the older states and ranchers on the northern plains purchased lean range cattle and fed them grain or ran them on grass to condition them for the beef market. The stocker and feeder trade was especially popular with the northern ranchers. Winter grazing in Wyoming and Montana promised a good return on investments.

Before the days of trail herding ended, at least a dozen trails reached up from the south to the shifting market centers north of Texas. This series of trails fanned out all the way from Baxter Springs on the eastern Kansas border to Albuquerque in the west. One of the best known, but possibly not the most important, was the Chisholm Trail which began near San Antonio and extended northward to Abilene, Kansas. A second trail began in Texas and extended northward by way of Doan's Store to Dodge City and Ogallala, and a third, the Goodnight-Loving Trail, started near Fort Belknap in Texas and ran westward to Albuquerque.

By 1886 the first phase of range cattle history was drawing to a close. Several new developments were blocking the trails and preparing the way for the confinement of grazing activities to set ranges and pastures. Farmer-settlers were beginning to advance rapidly from the lagging frontier of the eastern border, planting wheat on the old buffalo range and building highways, villages and towns where the trail herds had grazed. Schools, churches and courthouses crowded town squares and main streets where saloons and brothels had flourished. Even Abilene, Newton, Big Bend, Dodge City and Ogallala succumbed to the influences of civilization. Trail herds no longer came to them in booming clouds of dust; instead reapers felled waving fields of golden grain into rows of bundled shocks. In the enclosed pastures the chunky short-horned steers had forced the hardy old longhorn to surrender. It was meat and not trail stamina and color that the newer generation of beef eaters in America and Europe were demanding. The old days of *laissez-faire* ranching and herding were all but memories. Cattle ranching as an organized and confined industry had expanded over the entire plains area from Texas westward to Arizona and New Mexico, and from central Kansas to Colorado and northward to Wyoming, Montana, Nebraska, and the Dakotas. Sharp competition had developed for grazing lands. The more cattlemen moved into the country, the more important it became to acquire possession of large blocks of range. A ranchman could homestead 160 acres in his own name, and he could get each one of his employees to make an entry for a quarter section. Sometimes these co-operative homesteaders located their claims so as to box in blocks of public lands, making them well-nigh useless to outside homesteaders and purchasers. Finally, a ranchman could purchase public lands outright, but however he acquired a claim to land, he became as much a part of the established order of the new civilization as the settlers at the plow handles and the store counters.

Barbed Wire and Quarantine

American technology was to play a role in bringing quick change to the plains country. Cattle driving after the Civil War hardly lasted a decade before it was threatened with extinction. Not only was it being forced against the western mountain wall by settlers, hostile legislation aimed at preventing the passage of Texas cattle and the extension of transcontinental railroads, but barbed wire threatened to block the trails and break up the range. Fencing was as old as North American settlement itself, but early pastures and, more especially, fields were barricaded behind rail, rock and brush barriers. At least one Presidential candidate made rail-splitting a high and sentimental calling which smoothed his way to the White House. Once beyond the eastern timberline, agricultural settlement slowed down. It was impossible to grow field crops and livestock at the same time without fences, and fencing of the traditional type was out of the question. Not even mud fences were practical, even though the descriptive American idiom "ugly as a mud fence," was in common usage. Use of wire for fencing was known in the *ante bellum* period, but these early strands lacked barbs to repel livestock.

Yankee ingenuity was challenged. It had solved problems of plow and reaper, and fencing was no more complicated. Joseph Farwell Glidden, a New Hampshire immigrant living in De Kalb County, Illinois, introduced his version of barbed wire in 1873. A year later his neighbor Jacob Haish sought a patent for his new type of wire. Excitement over barbed wire fencing in the West attracted the attention of the "plain" wire manufacturers, Washburne and Moen of Worcester, Massachusetts, and in 1876 this company secured the Glidden patents for barbed wire, perfected the Putnam winding machine, and began producing fencing on a big scale. By 1883 the Washburne and Moen factory at De Kalb was fabricating enough barbed wire daily to build six hundred miles of fence.

The significance of barbed wire on the frontier lay obviously not in manufacturing statistics, but out on the plains where cattle trails were being closed and patterns of range law and custom were being revised. Free grazing lands were rapidly disappearing, and use of the public domain was becoming more difficult. Ranches were being enclosed behind fences. The XIT owners in Texas built 781 miles of fence to enclose their boundaries. So radical a change was this new phase of exploitation of the plains that friction between settlers and ranchers and between big and little cattlemen was inevitable. The plains cattle trails could hardly be blocked without vigorous resistance from the cattlemen. The cattle associations sought to restrict the use of wire fencing to the area east of the hundredth parallel. There was dissatisfaction among cattlemen with the advance of

the fences, and night riders resorted to fence cutting. Cowboys representing both little and big grazers engaged in this activity. Sometimes it was the
little drover resisting the encroachment of the big ranchers, and sometimes it was the big trail herder resisting the farmer. In the end both farmer
and rancher were to profit by fencing; the farmer could protect his crops,
and the rancher was able to gain possession of vast acreage of grasslands and
water resources. Use of barbed wire numbered the days of the famous
old Texas longhorns and ushered in an improved type of cattle by making
controlled breeding and protection of cattle health possible. Railroads
gained additional patronage in the longer hauls to market, and the westward-moving farmer's frontier again thrust forward with its fields and
homesteads safely protected behind their barricades of wire.

While the wire manufacturers were closing the old western trails with
their products, a second invention was helping to sustain the settler on the
arid lands of the region. The windmill pumping away at bored wells substituted the water trough for the water hole. This partially self-controlled
machine, using the natural force of the plains breezes, made it possible to
move both humans and cattle around with a great deal more freedom than
had been possible when all was dependent on natural supplies of water. No
longer did herds of cattle have to be kept within six or seven miles of
streams and water holes, nor did settlers have to halt at unfavorable places
because of the more urgent need for water.

Before the plains were completely brought under private ownership and
blocked by thousands of miles of wire fencing, an effort was made to keep
the trail open between the plains of Texas and the great pasture lands of
the northern range. In 1884 Joseph Nimmo, a Treasury Department
statistician, gave the United States Congress an accounting of the range
cattle industry. In eighteen years, 1866 to 1884, 5,201,132 head of cattle
had come up the trails from Texas. That state still remained the breeding
ground, and its ranches supplied grazing stock for the vast territory from
New Mexico to North Dakota. Until the very end of the long drives, Texas
cattlemen were beset by the troubles and prejudices aroused by the prev-
alence of Texas fever. The Kansas legislature passed a troublous quarantine
law, and the issue was before Congress in the form of a request for the
maintenance of a great national cattle trail from Bandera, Texas, to Ogallala, Nebraska, and on northward to the Canadian border. Texas fever was
at that time a mystery. Cattle driven north from that state did not themselves have fever, cattle driven slowly did not seem to transmit it, and it
did not prevail north of the Platte River. By 1885 cattlemen had built up a
large body of speculation about causes of the fever. Some believed it was
a baccillus spread by the faeces of range cattle. Some were sure it was
breathed into the air, and some thought cattle rubbed its germs off onto the

grass. The four months from June to September were the most infectious ones. In all the speculation no one seems to have guessed that it was the Texas tick that spread the disease and that prevention of it was relatively simple.

The proposed national cattle trail cut a considerable slice out of the national domain. From the southern border of Colorado to the Canadian line was a distance of 690 miles. The trail was to average three miles in width and was to include 1,324,800 acres. Although this acreage was large, it seemed rather modest when compared with 49,402,227 acres granted to states and railroads for support of internal improvements.

By 1886 the trend of the cattle industry was away from trail herding and toward ranching and railroad shipments. This trend had actually begun six years earlier when cattle prices were good. Railroads conducted an advertising campaign to attract settlers out along their various lines. Newspapers in the older sections of the country carried large numbers of advertisements and letters to the editors praising the West. Some of the letters perhaps were written over fictitious signatures, but they were convincing nevertheless.

Company Ranching

That the West was a land of prosperity was proved by the cheering meat prices of the early 1880's. Texas steers in 1882 were bringing $6.80 per hundred pounds. Grass was relatively free, and all a speculator had to do was to organize a herd of cattle and strike out for the northern markets. The Evans-Jackson Company was formed in 1877, but the big boom did not come until after 1882. Almost at once several cattle companies were organized in Texas, Montana, Wyoming, Nebraska, Colorado, Kansas and New Mexico. Scotchmen, Englishmen and Europeans competed with Americans for grass lands and water rights. Promoters talked European and Scotch bankers into backing them. Even wealthy individuals entrusted their capital to the western adventurers. Large stock companies like the Swan Land and Cattle Company, the Wyoming Ranch Company, the XIT Ranch of Texas, and the Powder River Company all came into existence. Eastern Colorado and Wyoming soon took on the atmosphere of landed estates in England or the eastern United States. Cattle towns had clubs and associations which catered to an aristocracy of cattlemen. Stockholders here and abroad counted hopefully upon their dividends and profits. Some of the companies paid dividends out of their capital stock, and within a short time were in bankruptcy.

The most fabulous of the big cattle companies was the famous XIT organization of the Texas panhandle. It involved three million acres of land, politics in Chicago and Austin, and capital investment in both the United States and England. In 1881 the old capitol of Texas was destroyed by fire, and the so-called capitol lands of that state were traded to contractors to construct a new one. These contractors were Colonel Amos C. Babcock, Abner Taylor, and John V. and Charles B. Farwell. None of them knew anything about ranching, nor had they seen the two-hundred mile stretch of dry land along the New Mexico border for which they had traded. Building the new Texas Statehouse required several years and more than three million dollars, but organizing and stocking the XIT Ranch was an even bigger undertaking. From 1882 to 1915 this vast cattle empire was to have its influence on western ranching and cattle trading. A fifteen-million-dollar syndicate was organized, and thousands of investors put their savings into this gigantic venture. Hundreds of miles of fences were built, and approximately nine counties were organized on its lands, but its vastness was largely its undoing. Administration of so vast a cattle empire was more than the Capitol Lands Company could manage, and in 1915 the last of its affairs were liquidated, but not before the XIT brand had become a symbol of the expansiveness of the cow country.

This latter phase of the cattle industry belongs to American economic history rather than to that of the frontier. The cowboy in the long trail drives, the mad rush westward of the railroad builders, the advent of the improved cattle car, and the use of the refrigerated car helped to destroy the old free range, but not the cattle industry. The trail herder became the private range rider, and the cattleman became a residual citizen getting himself elected to territorial governorships, legislatures, and even to Congress.

The early cattle days were not to pass, however, without having a profound influence upon frontier history. Cattlemen's associations were effective in the creation of a considerable body of common law. The operation of pools, roundups, and trail herds by common agreement helped to shape a western pattern of law and order ahead of the organization of adequate law enforcement agencies. Even criminality was kept at a reasonably controllable level by the formation of vigilante committees and the activities of marshals and constables. Respect for brands and private ownership of cattle was in itself one of the major accomplishments of a common law of expediency in a frontier condition of isolation. No pioneers marched off the scene more heroically than did the old-time cattlemen and their trail outfits of cowpunchers and their *remudas* of high-spirited horses. They left behind them one of the most romantic legends of man on horseback in all civilization's history. Long ago the fiddler in the Lady Gay Theater in Dodge City laid down his fiddle and the bow. Dirty Face Charley, Eat-Em-Up Jake, Frosty, Shot Gun Collins, Hurricane Bill and Shoot-His-

Eyes-Out-Jack slapped their last silver dollar down on the bar of the Long Branch Saloon, ordered drinks for everybody and then rode off into oblivion. Even Bat Masterson of the cool nerve, quick hand, and iron courage died in bed after a peaceful career as a New York newspaper man. These last frontiersmen, however, were not to depart unsung. Poets and composers have told of their deeds of pushing back the frontier in a thousand poems and ballads.

> *"Yes, thing's a heap sight diff'rent now!*
> *Tain't like in them ol' days*
> *When cowmen trailed their herds north*
> *'N forty diff'rent ways*
> *We ship 'em on the railroad now,*
> *Load out on the big S. P."*
> *Says the relic of Texas cowman*
> *As he takes a drink with me.*

Following the Woolies

While cattlemen drove their herds up from the Texas plains, a second band of drovers pushed their wooly charges inland from California and Oregon. Sheepherding was an ancient calling in North America. Sheepmen competed with cattlemen for grass and water on the western plains almost from the coming of the white man. In history, man's oldest crime against man was the row over sheepherding and farming which ended so disastrously for Cain and Abel. Sheep, though individually docile animals, are voracious, and, grazing in flocks, they strip grasslands bare as they go.

On the older eastern frontier, sheep raising was one of the necessary adjuncts to farming and family life. Almost every frontier family had its flock which supplied wool for clothing and meat for the table. There was such a craze for improving the breeds of American sheep in the early part of the nineteenth century that fabulous prices were paid for imported breeding stock. Wherever American farmers migrated along the frontier, they took sheep with them as necessary domestic animals.

Along the southeastern and California frontier sheepherding had an ancient beginning. Early Catholic missionaries introduced flocks to the mission lands. Missionaries in the Southwest, as everywhere else in the world they have gone, had first to stabilize the economic conditions of the people whom they would convert. Sheepherding and weaving were ideally suited to mission economy and to the capabilities of primitive peoples. The padres brought Spanish sheep into California, Arizona and New Mexico, and soon herds of thousands were grazing in these areas. The later *ranchero* period in California was famous for its herds. Even the failures of many of the missions did not destroy the flocks.

When gold was discovered in California in 1848, sheepherding was given a new impetus. As gold seekers poured into California, the shepherds of New Mexico followed on their heels with their droves of sheep to supply meat to the diggings. Among these early drovers were Kit Carson and "Uncle Dick" Wooton. Kit Carson drove a flock of thirteen thousand sheep from Taos to the California gold camps and sold them for a good profit. Many other herders found there was more money in driving mutton to the gold rush market than there was in taking a chance with a pan and a rocker. At the same time the western military detachments under Phil Sheridan's command offered a market for mutton which helped to encourage a revival of the sheep industry. North of New Mexico, the Mormons in Utah engaged in sheep raising for domestic purposes, and that area became famous for its flocks.

Possibly the most interesting early experiment in sheep raising was that of George Wilkins Kendall of New Orleans. A New Hampshire Yankee, Kendall had drifted South in the early 1830's to embark upon a newspaper career. He had gone first to Mobile and then to New Orleans, where, in 1837, he founded the New Orleans *Picayune*. Four years later he went with General Mirabeau Lamar's expedition to Santa Fe where he was captured by the Mexicans and thrown in jail. In 1830 he purchased a flock of sheep and began an extensive grazing business in the neighborhood of Boerne and Fredericksburg, Texas. For the next seventeen years this famous newspaper man engaged in sheep raising as a serious business. In these years he enjoyed much success and suffered many reverses. He imported pure bred rams from Europe and developed range sheep that produced a profitable wool clip. His grade rams were distributed throughout Texas and helped to improve the breed of many flocks. He combatted disease and vermin with the dipping vat. Kendall experienced all of the normal troubles of sheep raising plus those that were politically inspired by the Civil War, Reconstruction and cattle competition. When he died he left no monetary fortune, but his breeding and grazing experiences were of marked value to the sheep industry in general.

After the Civil War the sheep drives, like cattle driving, became economically and socially important. The early trails led eastward from California to Colorado, Nebraska, Wyoming, Montana and the Dakotas. For the most part the early flocks were ewes being driven to the grazing and breeding grounds beyond the mountains. After 1880 both ewes and wethers were driven overland; later, wethers alone made up most of the trail herds. Major G. C. Kimball trailed a herd eastward from California to the Missouri Valley in 1866. Sheep were purchased for $2.50 a head in California and were sold for a nice profit across the mountains. On the long drives they more than yielded the expenses of their transportation with their growth of wool.

Trailing sheep was unlike cattle herding in many ways; yet they had many things in common. It was necessary to drive long distances over the Sierra Nevada and Rocky Mountain trails. On the trail, sheep were able to travel day after day without developing foot trouble, whereas cattle and horses going over the same ground might become lame. They would eat both grass and weeds, but would drink only fresh running water. They ignored still or stagnant water, but submitted to long, dry drives more readily than cattle.

Sheep were moved in large flocks, sometimes numbering four to ten thousand head. To move such large numbers, the sheep had to be divided into several droves and to be driven in close co-ordination with each other. Four or five men were required to handle the large flocks, one in front, one on each flank, and one or two trailing behind. Usually these men were on foot, with dogs to keep the flock organized and going in the right direction. The cook kept up with the flock and also served as freight man, commissary keeper, and wagon driver. The distance covered each day varied with the availability of grass and water. Following a regular time habit, sheep arose from the bed ground early in the morning and moved out to graze. They traveled ahead until almost noon and then went to shade and water if these were available. If no shade was available, they flocked together, hiding their heads under one another's flanks. A well-ordered day in which the sheep went off in the right direction required a minimum of exertion on the part of the shepherds; otherwise the herdsmen were run to exhaustion. Possibly the dry drives with sheep were just as hazardous as drives with cattle. When sheep reached water after one of these long drives, they often refused to drink, and the flockmasters' ingenuity was sorely taxed to get them to do so.

There were more threats of disaster to a flock of sheep than to cattle. They were subject to several diseases, they had to be dipped, they would stampede if frightened and run off in all directions, or they would bunch up in fright into tight huddles and smother to death. Herdsmen had to be on constant guard against wolves, coyotes and eagles, and in settled areas they had to guard against dogs. The sheep is a defenseless animal, and his meek surrender to his enemies is frustrating. When ewes were trailed, lambs were born along the way, but these were killed at once and the mothers driven on with the flock. On the breeding grounds, lambing presented endless difficulty. Getting mothers to accept their young was laborious, and getting a ewe to accept a lamb other than her own required ingenuity. If a ewe lost her own lambs, shepherds sometimes skinned the lambs and tied their pelts to orphans and induced bereaved mothers to adopt them.

Millions of head of sheep were moved into the northern plains before 1900. Cache La Poudre and the Arkansas River country were favorite grazing grounds. Sheep were driven to Wyoming, Nevada, Colorado, Nebraska, Kansas, the Dakotas, Idaho and Utah from Oregon, California, New Mexico and Texas. Californians had supplied flocks to the early trails, but subsequently Oregon breeding grounds stocked the trails eastward across Idaho to Wyoming, Montana and the Dakotas.

Like two vast streams flowing in counter directions, the sheep and cattle trails crossed. Even when they ran parallel, they were nearly always at cross purposes. There was a strong belief that cattle would not eat grass after sheep had grazed over it. Cattlemen claimed that sheep had small sacs of oil in their feet that gave the grass an offensive odor. Actually, sheep clipped grass closer to the ground than cattle, sometimes lifting it out by the roots. They muddied waterholes and created other troubles, but their worst fault was that they aroused the jealous natures of cattlemen. Since time immemorial shepherds and mutton have been under a cloud of suspicion. Cowboys on horseback looked with disdain upon the shepherds on foot. In many cases the latter were Mexicans or Europeans who spoke English with a broken accent or not at all and thus added to the friction between the two groups. Many cattlemen believed without reason that they had a more legitimate claim to public grazing lands. Sheepmen were nearly always the more timid in the encounters between the two groups. Usually they were defenseless, for sheepherders were nearly always afoot and were greatly outnumbered by cowboys. But most important, perhaps, was the fact that the herders' charges were helpless docile creatures and could be run to death, smothered in crowded, frightened flocks, and clubbed and dynamited to death without too much difficulty. It was true that cattle could be stampeded, but escapes from such ventures were fraught with danger. Some of the famous outbreaks between cattlemen and shepherds were the Tonto Basin War in Arizona in 1887, the Holbrook War, the Big Horn Basin (Montana) Feud, and the Blue Mountain (Colorado) War.

Despite predatory raids, wars with cattlemen, blizzards and disease, the sheep frontier not only survived but flourished. Sheepherding broke some new trails and helped to popularize those already known. The millions of sheep brought on to the plains grazing lands offered a diversified base for animal husbandry in that region, and in a remarkably short time a sufficient population had moved into this vast country to establish ranches and to produce stockpiles of wool and meat for a rapidly growing consumer's market. Expansion of railroads broke up the long sheep trails. Double-decked railway cars helped to avoid the nightmare of dry drives, animal attacks upon flocks, and range wars.

Both cattle and sheep were to figure as prominently in closing the frontier as they had in opening it. The two industries had spread across the plains under the same burning sun and bright stars in a rapacious conquest of the endless sea of grass. Not even the tenacious settler-plowman fully supplanted either. Though the lamb and the steer were not allowed to lie down in entire peace by their human masters for years to come, they at least shared the honors of having helped to extend the railroads, people the plains, build the great cities of Chicago, Kansas City, Omaha, St. Paul, Dallas, and Fort Worth, and to subdue the vast frontier which they had helped to make both colorful and memorable.

A DESERT AND
MOUNTAIN EMPIRE

We claim that any body, or community of American citizens, which
from any cause or under any circumstance, is cut off from, or from
isolation is so situated, as not to be under any active and protecting
branch of the central government, have a right, if on American soil,
to frame a government, and enact such laws and regulations as may
be necessary for their own safety, protection, and happiness, always
with the condition precedent, that they shall, at the earliest moment
when the central government shall extend an effective organization,
and laws over them, give it their unqualified support and obedience.

—WILLIAM N. BYERS,
The Rocky Mountain News, January 4, 1860

MAIN STREET IN HELENA, MONTANA—1869

CHAPTER XXVIII

The Great American Desert

IN the year 1840 there was a vast mountain and basin empire west of the 103rd meridian, east of the Sierra Nevadas, north of the Gila River and south of the 49th parallel, which appeared on the American political map as a blank space. Within the next decade, the Oregon Treaty of 1846 was to establish the northern boundary, and the Treaty of Guadalupe-Hidalgo was to establish the southern limits, with nature itself defining the Western ocean and western mountain demarcations. This area represented a certain amount of kinship within itself because of its mountainous nature, its desert stretches with high basins interlocked by rocky mountain rims, the penetration of deeply eroded stream beds, its rich grazing lands, and because of the existence within the bowels of the earth of rich mineral resources. Most of the parts of this region also had a common background in human history. Indians of varying tribal and ethnic groups occupied the

651

region in varying degrees of density; Spanish and French explorers had made hurried visits to much of the country; American adventurers since the closing decades of the eighteenth century had penetrated its fastness; and, after the Lewis and Clark, and Pike expeditions, trappers and traders had wandered along the stream courses in search of furs.

In 1817 Colonel Stephen H. Long of the United States Topographic Engineers began a series of explorations of the trans-Mississippi West for the War Department which were to extend two years later to the Rocky Mountains. In July, 1820, he was in the Rockies in the Colorado area around the headwaters of the Arkansas. His explorations in this part of the West were cursory and most incomplete; yet his report was to have a far-reaching influence on American expansion for the next thirty years because it created one of the great frontier myths. Edwin James prepared the famous two-volume "Long Report" for publication in the Ohio River village of Smithland, Kentucky. Its style is good, and its descriptive matter graphic. Two brief paragraphs sum up the attitudes of the explorers toward the mountain and basin West.

> In regard to this extensive section of country [wrote James over Long's signature] I do not hesitate in giving the opinion, that it is almost wholly uninhabitable by a people depending on agriculture for their subsistence. Although tracts of fertile land considerably extensive are occasionally to be met with, yet the scarcity of wood and water, almost uniformly prevalent, will prove an insuperable obstacle in the way of settling the country. This objection rests not only against the section immediately under consideration, but applies with equal propriety to a much larger portion of the country. Agreeably to the best intelligence that can be had, concerning the country both northward and southward of the section, and especially to inferences deducible from the account given by Lewis and Clark of the country situated between the Missouri and the Rocky Mountains above the river Platte, the vast region commencing near the sources of the Sabine, Trinity, Brassos, and Colorado, and extending northwardly to the forty-ninth degree of north latitude, by which the United States' territory is limited in that direction, is throughout of a similar character. The whole of this region seems peculiarly adapted as a range for buffaloes, wild goats, and other wild game; incalculable multitudes of which find ample pasturage and subsistence upon it.
>
> This region, however, viewed as a frontier, may prove of infinite importance to the United States, inasmuch as it is calculated to serve as a barrier to prevent too great an extension of our population westward, and secure us against the machination or incursion of an enemy that might otherwise be disposed to annoy us in this part of our frontier.

At the time Long and James made their report, the great American frontier push was consolidating its gains in the trans-Appalachian and the immediate Mississippi Valley region. In 1840 the frontier movement was just becoming poised for invasion of the great western country beyond the immediate Mississippi tier of territories. Behind this movement was an expanding national economic and industrial system, a socially and politically disturbed Europe, and a marked expansion of the American pioneering population. Already the call of Texas, the romance of the Santa Fe trade, and the saga of the Rocky Mountain fur trade were powerful on the frontier. These motives, coupled with the availability of cheap lands, set a veritable flood of adventurers and settlers moving into the great mountain and basin West and Northwest. The Mormon, Oregon, and gold rush movements have been reviewed previously. Within the decade 1840–1850 enough settlers had pushed their way over the long and arduous road to Oregon to establish a territory, but before this was accomplished the seeds for yet another northwestern political unit were already planted in the soil north of the Columbia River.

The Northwest

When Americans arrived in the Columbia Valley they were encouraged to stay south of the river by the officials of the Hudson's Bay Company, but it was poor psychology to suggest that the area north of the river was undesirable for Americans. Company officials tried to confine the pioneers to the southern area in the hope that the boundary between the United States and Canada could be established on the Columbia. If there were American settlers beyond that stream, their pretentions would be considerably weakened. One of the first American settlers to enter the trans-Columbia country was Michael T. Simmons, an illiterate but determined pioneer who had migrated to Oregon from Shepherdsville, Kentucky. His first venture was to the mouth of the Cowlitz River, and in 1845 he moved his family to the site of Tumwater on Puget Sound. Within a decade Americans had settled in several places along the Cowlitz and Chehalis rivers, on Whidbey Island, and along the Washington Inlet or Puget Sound.

Beyond the Columbia, frontiersmen reproduced a familiar American pioneering pattern, building rude homes that did little more than shelter them from the elements, clearing fields, establishing mills, blazing trails, establishing trading posts, and opening ports on the sound. The initial needs of shelter and food were easily served. Timber of extraordinary quality grew in abundance almost every place a settler needed to build, and the sea and the fertile lands produced food in great abundance. Trade in timber, agricultural products, minerals and sea foods was quickly expanded on the basis of the old Puget Sound commerce which had its beginnings in the last decade of the eighteenth century. In 1852 Seattle was located on the eastern shore of the Sound; in a short time it was to become a focal center of territorial development. Olympia, Steilacoom, Walla Walla, and Port Townsend were older and established centers of regional activity. The open savanna of Whidbey Island attracted agricultural settlers who shuddered at the prospects of removing heavy timber from the river bottom lands to the east.

Before the American settlers had been in the Washington or Columbia area three years, need for organized government was manifest. Settlers beyond the Columbia almost lived up to that proud boast of a frontiersman: "Just think that within two weeks of arrival of a few dozen Americans in a wilderness, they set to work to elect a delegate to the United States Congress, and ask to be set apart as a new territory! But we are of a fast race and in a fast age and must plod along." Claim jumping, grazing trespasses, and domestic complications all prompted some form of local governmental organization. The Puget Sound Agricultural Association or Company, a subsidiary of the Hudson's Bay Company, provoked a strong reaction when it drove its cattle onto private claims to graze. Antagonisms toward the British only added to the current resentment against the high-handed acts of the Company. The assembled settlers resolved against the Company, and gave it a week to drive its herds off pioneer holdings. The terms of the Northwest boundary agreement of 1846 fresh in their minds, Americans asserted their sovereign position in the new country with the vehemence of the American eagle.

In accord with the long-established pioneering process, the country north of the Columbia was divided in 1845 into the counties of Lewis and Vancouver. Within six years political activities increased as the population expanded. Local problems had a strong bearing upon popular opinion, and the time had come when a far-seeing politician might broach the subject of independent territorial status. There was nothing like a Fourth of July celebration by frontiersmen in a politically obscure condition to stir up potent territorial sentiments. A shrewd orator had a ready-made audience on which to urge his patriotic ideas. In 1851 lawyer J. B. Chapman introduced this theme into his patriotic address at Olympia. Immediate steps were taken to seek separation from Oregon Territory largely on the grounds of distance and lack of facilities for transportation and communication between the two parts of the vast area. The convention meeting at Cowlitz requested that a separate territory be established as Columbia Territory and that funds be made available to construct certain key roads. In Washington, D. C., Congress made a favorable response to Governor Joseph Lane's presentation of the issue, and on March 2, 1853, President Millard Fillmore signed the bill which created Washington (rather than

Columbia) Territory. The new territory was located north of the Columbia River, south of the 49th parallel, and west of the summit of the Bitter Root Range.

One of the first requirements in Washington Territory was for roads which would connect the various towns and ports. It was particularly desirable to construct a road across the Cascades north to the Columbia which would tap the great immigration artery, the Oregon Trail. Not only were the territorial leaders interested in development of transportation routes, but also the administration in Washington and eastern railway promoters. President Franklin Pierce appointed the handsome West Point-trained Isaac Ingalls Stevens of Andover, Massachusetts, as territorial governor. At the same time Secretary of War Jefferson Davis gave him the responsibility of heading the Northern Pacific railway survey. He secured the assistance of several young military officers, including George B. McClellan, to assist him in the explorations westward. In his first years in office the young governor devoted a great deal of attention to finding passes through which a railroad might cross the eastern mountain range, an activity which involved him in an argument with Colonel McClellan.

In Search of a Mountain Gateway

General Stevens was, in fact, in search of a pass from east to west, and of a desirable route thereafter to the coast. In 1853 he reported:

> I can speak advisedly of the beautiful St. Mary's Valley just west of the Rocky Mountains and stretching across the whole breadth of the territory; of the plain fifty miles wide bordering the south bank of the Spokane River; of the valley extending from the Spokane River to Colville; of the Coeur d'Alene Prairie of six hundred square miles; the Walla Walla Valley. The Nez Percés country is said to be rich as well as the country bordering on the Yakima River.

The alert governor was all but overwhelmed, and his statement of regional potentialities was as sweeping as a view from atop a Cascade peak.

Governor Stevens had several immediately pressing administrative problems which absorbed his time and energies. One of these was trying to make peace with the rebellious Indian population. He was not always adept at treating with Indians, and his failure to make a lasting peace subjected the territory to long and bitter Indian uprisings. On top of this, Stevens and General John Wool engaged in an argument over military aid that was almost as devitalizing as the Indian wars. When Stevens proclaimed martial law in Pierce and Thurston counties on the grounds that certain people had not been molested by the Indians because they were aiding and abetting the enemy, and thereupon denied the writ of *habeas corpus,* he involved himself with the courts. This led to the arrest of a territorial judge and the issuance of a court warrant for the governor's arrest for contempt. The United States Marshal, however, lacked courage to serve it. The state of martial law was of brief duration.

In 1852 gold was discovered near Fort Colville, and there was a mild rush to the area. Eight years later, after the gold rush to British Columbia, the search for gold in Washington was revived with some small strikes at Colville, at the mouth of the Pend Oreille River, and on the Wenatchee.

In 1859 when Oregon was admitted to the Union as a state its eastern boundary was sharply curtailed, and the vast area now forming Idaho and western Montana was added on to Washington, where it remained until the creation of Idaho Territory in 1863. The Northwest Pacific territory had to await the passage of three decades, a revolution in national politics, and the development of a northwestern railway empire before it changed its political status.

Land of Gold and Silver

East of California in the great basin beyond the Sierras, a tremendous territory stretched northward from the Gila River to the Blue Mountains along the Oregon boundary. It was enclosed in a rock-rimmed wall of the Rockies, Sierras and Wasatch Mountains. A good part of this region was an enormous basin. Inside it were two fascinating natural phenomena, the great Salt Lake and the Humboldt River with its mysterious sink. The Great Basin was itself an irregular region which ranged from 1,150 feet to nearly 10,000 feet above sea level. Here was a subarid area which in some respects had a fair water supply, but it was rigidly confined to certain places. Human existence in the basin was controlled by extreme conditions, most of which were created by lack of moisture.

Here was land which offered pioneers an unusual challenge. It was not the first area Americans had approached where such conditions prevailed. The Great Basin country had been known since the 16th century when Tabor and Cardenas visited it from Cibola or Zuñi. After that time there were periodic invasions by white men. It was not until the first quarter of the nineteenth century, however, that there were visits which promised eventual settlement. British fur traders from the Northwest in the employ of the Hudson's Bay Company came as far south as the Ogden River. Almost at the same time American mountain men visited the same region. In 1824 Jim Bridger explored the Salt Lake area and then trapped in the surrounding country. Between that date and the arrival of the Mormons in the basin, there were many other visitors. Explorers and immigrant parties which sought to reach California across the Sierras came this way.

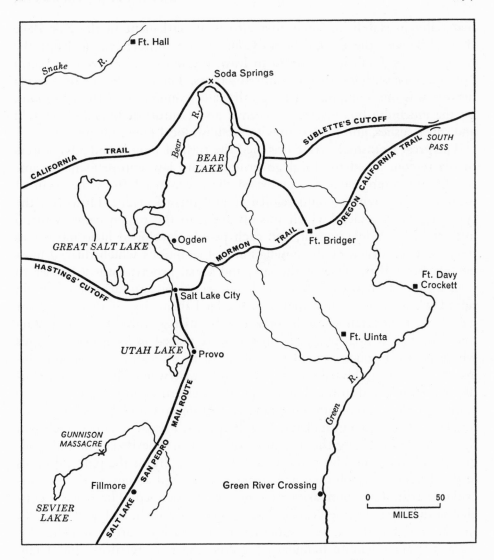

ROCKY MOUNTAIN CROSSROADS, 1840–1860

Among them were Jedediah Strong Smith, and the Walker, Bartleson, Bidwell, Hastings, Frémont and Donner parties.

For a decade after the Mormons arrived in Utah in 1847 small islands of settlement appeared in many parts of the basin territory. The first settlement in Nevada was begun in Carson Valley by Californians. News of the Treaty of Guadalupe-Hidalgo stimulated the organization of the greater territory of Deseret, of which the future Nevada was a part. The Mormons had hardly unpacked their baggage and learned the conditions of the country before the onrushing horde of gold seekers was upon them, aiding materially in stabilizing their first efforts at settlement in the Salt Lake Basin. Likewise the United States Congress was influenced to define the boundaries of Utah in 1850 and to leave the unorganized western Sierra Nevada slope with less than a hundred settlers. The next decade of Nevada history was one complicated by rivalry and conflict with the Mormons, by the indefinite boundaries between it and California, by fabulous gold and silver rushes, and by attempts to establish local government.

The great Comstock strike hastened the rush of miners and adventurers to the region. Need for local government and law enforcement became urgent. As mining activities increased there was need for some form of local authority which could regularize and record claims. However, the type of human society which was attracted to the region came with no interest in local government, and such people developed little interest as time went on. Much of the population had ambitions which thrived most happily beyond the pale of the law, and social progress was a barrier to their welfare. Others came to get rich and were ready to turn the mountain sides back to nature when they had dredged them dry of their hoard of wealth. In 1854 Utah made the orthodox frontier gesture by creating Carson County. Essential political controls were placed in local official hands where political policies could be molded to fit immediate needs and philosophies. Then followed six years of conflict between Mormon and gentiles which resulted in the desertion of the western county by Utah.

In 1859 a local convention submitted a petition to Congress seeking territorial status, and two years later, March 2, 1861, President James Buchanan signed the bill creating the Territory of Nevada. The President and Congress had little or no idea about either the geography or the political needs of the Territory which they had created. It covered a huge and as yet unexplored area. The boundaries were not clearly defined. There was a conflict on the west of some years' standing with California, and after the gold and silver strike this issue became more vital to both areas. On the east there was an indefinite boundary between the new territory and Utah. The next decades were to see surveyors tramping the steep ridges attempting to establish boundaries, and there were constant visitations between Sacramento, Carson City, and Salt Lake City which attempted to establish geographical and jurisdictional lines.

Nevada was possibly one of the least of the federal administration's worries. The Union itself was coming apart at the seams, and President Lincoln's interest was directed toward what was happening in Montgomery and at Fort Sumter. Neither he nor Congress had time or patience to struggle with the problems of a thinly populated subarid western mountain territory. One of William H. Seward's most ardent supporters had been a New York police commissioner, James Warren Nye, and Lincoln obliged his Secretary of State by appointing his friend territorial governor. To even things with the West he obliged his Attorney General, Edward G. Bates of St. Louis, by appointing the plodding Orion Clemens territorial secretary.

Carson City and New York were about as unlike as any two places could be. Governor Nye had three shining qualifications for office: a jovial sense of humor, infinite patience, and an extraordinarily good appetite for California wine. Orion Clemens expected something else in Carson City. He and his private secretary, his younger brother Sam, packed their trunks with dress suits and top hats, and set off with $300 in borrowed funds to buy stagecoach tickets across the plains. At the stage office they were shocked to find that they could take only 25 pounds of baggage. They reduced their holdings therefore to a Webster's *Dictionary*, the *Iowa Statutes*, a supply of tobacco, writing materials, and a few official necessities, chief of which was a formidable State Department instruction book. Possibly the most enduring result of this safari to the governmental halls of faraway Carson City was the American classic *Roughing It*, written by the imaginative private secretary.

Governor Nye arrived ahead of the Clemens brothers. He had brought with him, as Mark Twain observed, "a worthy French lady by the name of Bridget O'Flanigan, a camp follower of his Excellency the Governor. She had known him in his prosperity as commander-in-chief of the Metropolitan Police of New York, and she would not desert him in his adversity as Governor of Nevada." Besides the imperious Bridget there were fourteen masculine "voluntary camp followers of the Governor, who had joined his retinue by their own election at New York and San Francisco and came along, feeling that in the scuffle for little territorial crumbs of offices they could not make their condition more precarious than it was, and might reasonably make it better." This free-loading "Irish Brigade" which had no notion of the obligations of a rendered board bill was almost as great an administrative problem as were the Nevada boundaries. The Governor sent his band of admirers out on one of Nevada's great outdoor pastimes, a surveying expedition. He headed them eastward, and in the beginning of their survey they came home every night bearing tarantulas which they had captured while searching out the line. The nightly contention between them and landlady Murphy kept Carson City in an uproar. Governor Nye expressed the hope they would blunder into Utah and Brigham Young would have them hanged.

As has been said, neither the President nor Congress was concerned about Nevada. At a time when the nation's financial system was being strained to finance the Civil War, there were only limited funds for territorial use. An appropriation of $20,000 in deflated greenbacks was made to support a territorial government on top of one of the richest gold and silver lodes on this continent. Both the appropriation of greenbacks and the book of bureaucratic instructions proved inadequate to cope with realistic conditions. There was no statehouse and little local interest in providing one. Luckily Orion Clemens found a building in which the government could be housed, and there the territorial legislature was organized. One of the governmental frills was the employment of the Reverend F. A. White as a dollar-and-a-half-a-day chaplain, an expenditure which council president J. L. Van Bokklen believed to be nonessential.

Mark Twain observed, "That was a fine collection of sovereigns, that first Nevada legislature. They levied taxes to the amount of thirty or forty thousand dollars and ordered expenditures to the extent of about a million. Yet they had their little periodic explosions of economy like other bodies of the kind." The chief concern of the body seems to have been toll roads. Overland freighting was becoming an important industry, and everyone was conscious of the enormous amount of freight which would have to be hauled across the mountains. Also, a certain amount of military activity increased the excitement for profits to be made from roads. "When they adjourned," said Mark Twain, "it was estimated that every citizen owned about three franchises, and it was believed that unless Congress gave the Territory another degree of longitude there would not be room enough to accommodate the toll roads. The ends of them were hanging over the line everywhere like a fringe." Toll road fortunes promised to equal those of the gold and silver barons.

The code of laws adopted by the legislature was a combination of those of New York and California, despite the fact that the conscientious secretary had lugged along the *Statutes of Iowa*. Nine counties were created, even though some of these had only a few transitory freight station-keepers for population. Some of the statutes regulating pioneer Nevada morals seemed to be brave attempts to create enough restrictions to make sinning attractive. Three judicial districts were created by gubernatorial proclamation, and the Nevada Territory became a functional reality.

Between 1861 and 1864 Nevada underwent significant economic expansion, as explained previously in the chapter on the mineral frontier. Gold and silver from Nevada mines gave the nation a supply of those precious metals in its moment of greatest need. In fact the mineral resources of the Territory gave it a position of economic and political importance far in excess of its actual social maturity. As early as 1863 a movement was begun to organize a state government. A constitutional convention was called to meet in September, 1863. The first attempt to create a fundamental document was defeated because of a peculiarity in providing for the election of constitutional officers at the same time the voters ratified the document itself. A second convention met on July 4, 1864, and a new constitution was framed which was substantially the same as the first. This one was ratified by a fair majority.

In Washington the administration's political situation was critical. There were two vital issues in which it was concerned, aside from ending the war: the re-election of Lincoln and congressional approval of the Thirteenth Amendment. So anxious was President Lincoln to muster all possible support, including Nevada's three votes, that he instructed territorial officials to transmit the constitution to Washington by wire, in what is still one of the longest telegraph messages on record. On October 31, 1864, the President by administrative proclamation declared Nevada a state.

Colorado

East of the Mormon territory of Utah was the Pike's Peak and Arkansas River country. Its background history has been covered in our accounts of Pike's expedition and the activities of the mountain men, the Mormons, and the Oregon and California emigrants. All of them passed through or near the area. Jim Bridger, Kit Carson, the Sublette brothers, George Bent, and Céran de St. Vrain were associated with the early history of Colorado. Bent and St. Vrain had established their famous fort on the Arkansas, which became a landmark in the early period of exploration and trade.

The heated Kansas-Nebraska issue involved the plains territory as far west as the Rocky Mountain foothills. But it was the backlash of the gold rush, the Panic of 1857, and the famous Pike's Peak excitement of 1858 which, stirred up by the Russell party's prospectings, brought Colorado into frontier focus. Rich strikes at such places as Jackson, Gregory and Gold Hill in 1859 brought miners stampeding west through Kansas and east from California. Politically the Colorado gold rush was to be of more than passing interest. In a short time this Territory was to undergo the same experience as its western neighbor Nevada. Approximately 50,-000 persons reached Colorado in the gold rush, and possibly half of them remained in the territory. There was developed early a body of mining rules and regulations derived from local conditions and the experiences of other mineral communities in the West. This collection of rules and regulations constituted a significant body of common laws growing out of a series of specialized needs and experiences.

The mineral rush of 1858 and 1859 brought not only miners who sought fortunes, but also many families because of the easier access to the region from the east. The presence of women and children created an immediate demand for an established political body and laws. One of the first organized political communities was the Jefferson Territory, which

Hiram J. Graham, its representative in Washington, undertook unsuccessfully through Alexander H. Stephens, to have organized by Congress an as independent territory.

W. N. Byers of the *Rocky Mountain News* had boasted: "Here we go, a regular triple-headed government machine; south of 40 deg., we hang on to the skirts of Kansas; north of 40 deg., to those of Nebraska; straddling the line, we just elected a Delegate to the United States Congress from the 'Territory of Jefferson'; ere long we will have in full blast a provisional government of Rocky Mountain growth and manufacture."

The Colorado, or Jefferson Territory, bill was reported out of committee but was tabled. Colorado representatives, like those from Nevada, found Washington officials too deeply involved in the threat of war to give an objective hearing to the subject of territorial expansion. The sectional cross currents which had arisen since 1850 were active and thwarted any further attempts to enlarge the political union. In the Colorado mining camps there were developed enough local rules of government to permit a fairly peaceful procedure, but a feeling grew among the westerners that the central government had no interest in the region. This no doubt had been one of the motivating forces behind the organization of the Jefferson Territory. For more than two years, November, 1858, to February, 1861, the Colorado Territory functioned largely under the administration of the Jefferson organization. At length, organization of the Colorado Territory was authorized by Congress, and on February 28, 1861, the bill was signed as one of the final acts of the Buchanan administration. A month later William Gilpin, a Pennsylvania Quaker, was appointed territorial governor. He did not come, however, to the position as inexperienced as were many of the other territorial governors. Gilpin had served under Doniphan in his famous Mexican expedition and had achieved the rank of lieutenant colonel. In 1860 he published a book, *The Central Gold Region,* in which he optimistically viewed the Valley of the Mississippi and its western tributaries as the future heartland of America. As territorial governor, the ambitious Gilpin, unlike Orion Clemens of Nevada, ignored the bureaucratic rule book and ran the federal government into debt with his military activities. His first acts as Governor were to create legislative and judicial districts, and after a few skirmishes among rival towns, Denver was chosen the territorial capital.

For a decade and a half, Colorado history was colored by nearly all the typical incidents of western history. Its rowdy gold camps reflected the primitive conditions of western mineral communities. Rich strikes and colossal disappointments affected the history of the region. A wild, carefree and boisterous society co-existed with considerable sobriety and social propriety. Few of the mining territories had so strong and promising an agricultural society as that developed by Colorado in the early years. There were organized early the important towns of Boulder, Golden, Black Hawk, Colorado City, and Pueblo as supply and mining centers. Denver, at the mouth of Cherry Creek, embodied in its consolidation the mining villages of Fountain City, El Dorado, El Paso, Arapahoe, Aurari, Montana, and St. Charles. Freighting and stagecoach lines contributed materially in boosting the population. Sectional forces, with considerable southern sentiment prevailing, created an appreciable amount of tension. But none of these was so important as the Indian conflicts.

Since the coming of the first trappers to the region, there was conflict of varying degrees of intensity with the Indians. The old frontier story was to be repeated in this Rocky Mountain stronghold. The country was Indian property until the discovery of gold, and then the rush of miners ignored any rights the Indians might have possessed. The Civil War created its own peculiar strains, and on November 29, 1864, the Sand Creek Massacre brought the Colorado Indian situation into national perspective. Racial tensions in the region increased to the breaking point. From that time until the last of the western Indian conflicts, Colorado was acutely aware of the bitter struggle with the red man, if not actively involved.

Colorado reached its first stage of political maturity before the war ended. A faction of territorial representatives petitioned Congress to enact an enabling law to permit the framing of a Constitution and the admission of the new state. This was done in 1864 on the basis of an exaggerated representation of territorial population. There was local opposition, however, to the admission of the territory. The population was small, and the state's agricultural and industrial systems, except for the mines, were under-developed. People believed that they could save themselves money by retaining the territorial government. It was the old frontier fight all over again between the penurious territorial settler who favored letting Congress bear the cost of territorial government, and the politically ambitious local citizens who sought opportunities to hold national and state offices, and to secure the right to enact local legislation free of federal oversight.

The first call for a constitutional convention was defeated, but in 1865 a rump convention met and drafted a document which it submitted to Congress without popular approval. Congress accepted the constitution even with its restrictions on the Negro and mulatto vote, but Andrew Johnson vetoed the act. For the next decade the Colorado statemakers attempted unsuccessfully to secure acceptance of their Constitution with its vote restrictions for Negroes. In 1875 there was agreement about the future structure of the Colorado government and electorate, and the state was admitted to the Union in July, 1876. One interesting innovation was proposed in the voting provisions. A strong plea was made to the convention that women be given the right to vote by striking out the word "male" in the franchise section. This provoked considerable discussion. Delegates were under pressure from local woman suffrage advocates as well as those of the national movement. Women were extended the privilege of voting in school elections, but the delegates deftly sidestepped the bigger issue by deferring decision to the voters in an early election. Admission of Colorado, except for the complicated situation in Utah, completed the first contiguous political band of states across the continent.

By the time Colorado was admitted, certain fundamental national changes had occurred. Reconstruction was at a virtual end. The western rail system was being expanded over several transcontinental routes. Colorado itself was recovering from the blow of not being able to secure the routing of the Union Pacific Railroad through Denver and Berthoud Pass. By 1870, the Denver and Pacific connected the capital city with Cheyenne, and the transcontinental road, the Colorado and Pacific, and the Kansas-Pacific were either in operation or in process of construction. Running south from Denver, and into the hot "Royal Gorge war" with the Santa Fe for a connection with El Paso, was General William J. Palmer's famous Denver and Rio Grande, chartered in 1870. Also at the time Colorado was entering statehood, western shippers were beginning to support a series of moves which within a single decade, after the *Munn* vs. *Illinois* decision in 1876 led to the passage of the Interstate Commerce Act, 1887, saw the enactment of basic regulatory legislation in many of the states.

Nebraska, Arizona, Idaho

While Colorado statesmen wrestled with the problems of creating a state, their neighbors beyond the Platte in Nebraska were doing somewhat the same thing. Nebraska was on the great continental highway, the Overland Trail, and the river passage west, and was soon to secure the important eastern terminus of the first transcontinental railroad, but it had not gained enough population to sustain adequately a state government. The long and heated territorial controversy of the 1850's was focused largely upon Kansas; it was to that area that the great body of settlers migrated. The Civil War checked population expansion, and in 1866 Nebraska was still largely virgin country except for the Iowa fringe. That year Congress passed an enabling act, but a called convention decided that the expenses of maintaining a state government would be too great and failed to produce a constitution. The territorial legislature in 1868 offered a constitution of its own making, and Nebraska was admitted to the Union on the eve of the completion of the Union Pacific Railroad.

South of Nevada the sprawling desert country of Arizona was organized into a territory in 1863, but Arizona was not to achieve statehood for a half century. Congress authorized the organization in 1863 of Idaho Territory out of the rugged Rocky Mountain spine which extended as far south as the northern boundary of Utah. This territory was in the heart of the region in which the great mountain fur trade was centered. Geographically it was rugged mountain country rising in elevation up to 13,500 feet. South Pass served as its eastern gateway, and the gorge of the Snake River as its western outlet. Settlers on their way to Oregon passed famous landmarks in Idaho—Fort Henry, Fort Hall, and Boise. Creation of this new territory sheared off the eastern area of Washington and consolidated into one political unit a vast area of 326,373 square miles.

Idaho's territorial history closely paralleled that of other mineral-mountain regions. Its early population was concentrated about the gold strike centers in what is now Idaho and Montana. Mixed populations of miners and Indians created problems for territorial administrators. The acts of miners and their camp followers brought about extralegal police control, or vigilantism. As Thomas Donaldson of *Public Domain* fame said, "a vigilante, or vigilance committee, is a terrific power in a new country." A rapidly shifting population, a lack of established social institutions, a virtual absence of social responsibility, and a generous sprinkling of robbers, cheats, and murderous fugitives made some form of policing imperative. Idaho Territory was widely publicized because of the effectiveness of its vigilance committees.

Idaho Territory had its trials with the Nez Percés Indians in 1877, which were climaxed by the famous pursuit and capture of Chief Joseph and his people. During the long territorial period, Idaho saw a procession of inexperienced political faithfuls come and go as governors and lesser officials. One of the most fabulous of all the territorial governors was Caleb Lyon of Lyonsdale, New York. This "carpetbagger" was a glib and educated scamp who took life as he found it. Like Governor Nye of Nevada, he was a friend of William H. Seward. Lincoln appointed him the second territorial governor of Idaho in 1864, and reappointed him after he had left the territory with $50,000 of public funds. His second administration was distinguished by a diligent search for a diamond mine in the mountain, by flagrant lawlessness, and further rifling of the territorial treasury. When Governor Lyon died in 1875, his estate placed on sale a remarkable collection of books and art objects, much of it associated with the Washington Family. It must be remembered that Governor Lyon "saved" the contents of Arlington at the outbreak of the Civil War. Possibly there was no place on the frontier where the evils of this type of political appointment were more clearly revealed than in Idaho.

Before Lee and Grant met at Appomattox, Congress lessened the strain on Idaho by creating Montana Territory in 1864, and three years later Wyoming was organized. Except for specific details of territorial history there was little fundamental difference among these new territories in the mineral, mountain, Indian and grazing land areas. All of them had a shortage of population, limited transportation facilities, a boisterous society, isolated pioneer settlements, and a lack of financial resources from stable tax systems to maintain state governments. Successful statehood in most of these territories had to await the coming of the railroads and an increase in population to stabilize economic expansion and to convert the vast landed area into settled communities.

PROMONTORY POINT, UTAH—MAY 10, 1869

LINKING THE CONTINENT WITH HIGHWAY AND RAIL

LINKING THE CONTINENT
WITH HIGHWAY AND RAIL

"Here he comes!"

Every neck is stretched further, and every eye strained wider. Away across the endless dead level of the prairie a black speck appears against the sky, and it is plain that it moves. Well, I should think so! In a second or two it becomes a horse and rider, rising and falling, rising and falling—sweeping toward us nearer and nearer —growing more and more distinct, more and more sharply defined —nearer and still nearer, and the flutter of hoofs comes faintly to ear—another instant a whoop and a hurrah from our upper deck, a wave of the rider's hand, but no reply, and man and horse burst past our excited faces, and go winging away like a belated fragment of a storm!

So sudden is it all, and so like a flash of unreal fancy, that but for the flake of white foam left quivering perishing on a mailsack after the vision had flashed by and disappeared, we might have doubted whether we had seen an actual horse and man at all, maybe.

—MARK TWAIN, *Roughing It*

CHAPTER XXIX

Once frontier settlers crossed the Mississippi they were confronted with vast stretches of territory which, for the most part, lacked established trails and roads. The trail northward from Mexico to Santa Fe had been opened by Spanish traders and missionaries coming up from south of the Rio Grande. From the Rio Grande to Natchitoches, Louisiana, the same travelers had blazed the way toward the Mississippi. Fur traders moving westward opened trails up the Missouri and across the plains to the Rockies, and through the mountains to Oregon and California. At the same time general traders in search of the southwestern market opened the northern end of the Santa Fe Trail from the Missouri to New Mexico. In the 1840's, immigrants to Oregon, Utah, and California opened new roads along the old trails, but despite all this travel there was still no satisfactory route from east to west when the great gold rush occurred in 1849.

The West was bound by the same kind of isolating forces which had prevailed east of the Mississippi. Distance, lack of freight concentration, sparsity of settlement, and an absence of local capital handicapped the development of both highways and railways. There were other deterrent factors which were peculiar to the West. These were the vast stretches of uninhabited and politically unorganized country, the Indian menace, and the bitter rivalries among the sections in Congress. Later, the Civil War would interfere with the opening of roads through the West. It was virtually impossible to build railroads over so long a stretch of territory without substantial government subsidy, a thing which had to await the departure of the southerners from Congress.

The government did subsidize early western transportation after a fashion. When the western army was not engaged in maneuvers against the Indians, it was occupied in making surveys and in opening roads and trails. A network of roads and trails was planned, and some of them were put into use by the army. The army's interest was not an entirely detached one because it had to transport supplies over vast distances where there were no roads or trails. These military roads were later to facilitate western travel.

By Sea and By Land

Tremendous territorial changes as we have seen occurred in the decade and a half, 1840–1855. Beginning with the annexation of Texas in 1845, there had followed in quick succession the Treaty of Guadalupe Hidalgo, and finally the Gadsden Purchase of 1853. Carrying the mail from the East to the new West was a staggering problem, for the nation was, in effect, now in two widely separated parts. Enormous funds were involved, and the selection of the most efficient routes was essential. One of the first suggested solutions for the mail delivery problem was to send it to California by ship. Water routes to California and the West Coast, however, were long and involved. From New York around Cape Horn to San Francisco was a distance of 15,348 miles, and by the Isthmus of Panama the distance was 6,077 miles; while the overland distance was only 3,265 miles. In 1845 Postmaster General Cave Johnson undertook to secure a bid on a ship contract to carry the mails, but A. G. Sloo was the sole bidder, and he proposed only to carry the mail from New York by way of Havana to New Orleans, and then from New Orleans to Havana and Chagres on the east Panamanian coast. Sloo's bid was unacceptable.

Again in 1847 the question of the West Coast mail came before Congress. An act was passed authorizing the construction of four first-class steamships to be put in the mail service, and contracts were to be offered for five other ships in an east-coastal service to deliver the mail to Chagres. It was not until 1848, and after the Post Office Department had encountered complications in awarding temporary contracts to Sloo and Harris to deliver the mail from New Orleans to Oregon, that three mail steamers— *California*, *Panama*, and *Oregon*—were commissioned. Despite all efforts to establish a mail line to California by sea, the service never became efficient. The effort to shorten the distance by way of Panama, however, raised the question of both a railway and a canal to the Pacific.

Between 1848 and 1859 several western mail contracts were awarded, but none of them proved satisfactory. Expansion of the population in Oregon, the discovery of gold in California, and the organization and admission of that state to the Union increased the government's responsibility to establish a transcontinental mail service. The army made route surveys and maintained a limited system of communication among its several posts. Speed of delivery was important, but it was difficult to achieve this with ship, stagecoach, and freight wagons. The old Red River and Southern Emigrants Trail by way of El Paso and the Cooke road across

New Mexico offered one route; the old trail by the Platte River to Salt Lake City, and thence across the Sierras to California offered another.

Overland Mail

Western mail contracts with private individuals were numerous, and it is at times difficult to tell who was delivering which mail. Constant efforts were made, however, to speed up and increase the number of lines serving the West, although up to 1856 there was no clear-cut policy concerning the delivery of mail in the West. One of the most serious problems involved was that of establishing new trails and roads across unsettled stretches of country. In March, 1857, Congress came to grips with the postal needs of the country and authorized the establishment of an overland mail from some suitable place on the Mississippi to San Francisco. This bill provided for a monthly, weekly, or semiweekly mail service as the postmaster general might choose. The route was to be selected on the basis of the broadest possible service, and the mail was to be carried in stagecoaches and wagons. On September 16, 1857, the famous Overland Contract to carry the mail over the southern route was signed between the Post Office Department and John Butterfield and Associates. The route would run from St. Louis to Memphis, then to Little Rock, then by Preston, Texas, to El Paso and on to Fort Yuma and California.

Adoption of the southern route opened a hot controversy among partisans favorable to northern and central routes. Up to 1860 the contest between southern congressmen and the central route partisans was a bitter one. Some southerners favored the New Orleans, San Antonio, El Paso route while others argued for both Memphis and St. Louis as starting places. Central route partisans agitated for that later followed by the Pony Express, with St. Joseph, Missouri, and Placerville, California as terminals. Leaders of the westerners were Senator W. H. Gwin, and Governor Milton S. Latham of California, and Joseph Lane of Oregon. The Butterfield interests were able to get Fort Smith made the converging point instead of Little Rock, and St. Louis was finally made the eastern terminus. Organizing the Overland Mail was a major task. It took a year to locate roads and ferries, to establish stations, distribute equipment and supplies, and to train personnel. Innumerable pieces of equipment and animals were needed to keep the mail going over the 2,812 miles of road. Stocky horses and freight mules were purchased to draw the coaches and wagons. Team changes were to be made every twelve or fifteen miles. Concord type coaches, and light stages or "celerity" wagons were built to haul passengers and mail. Coaches seated nine persons inside and several top riders outside. Mail was carried in the boot and in the box under the driver's seat. These

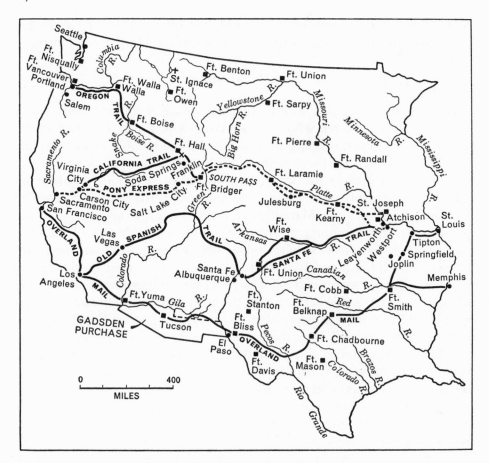

TRANS-MISSISSIPPI ROADS AND TRAILS

were to all intents the first western coaches to figure in the romantic chronicles of the West—the ones that tossed along over the rough roads like boats on choppy waves and sometimes came sailing into stations ahead of Indians and robbers.

Mark Twain wrote of his stagecoach trip West in his lively book *Roughing It:*

> Our coach was a great swaying stage, of the most sumptuous description —an imposing cradle on wheels. It was drawn by six handsome horses, and by the side of the driver sat the "conductor," the legitimate captain of the craft; for it was his business to take charge and care of the mails, baggage, express matter, and passengers. We three were the only passengers this trip. We sat on the back seat, inside. About all the rest of the coach was full of mail bags—for we had three days' delayed mails with us. Almost touching our knees, a perpendicular wall of mail matter rose up to the roof. There was a great pile of it strapped on top of the

stage, and both the fore and hind boots were full. We had twenty-seven hundred pounds of it aboard, the driver said—"a little for Brigham, and Carson, and 'Frisco, but the heft of it for the Injuns, which is powerful troublesome 'thout they get plenty of truck to read." But as he just then got up a fearful convulsion of his countenance which was suggestive of a wink being swallowed by an earthquake, we guessed that his remark was intended to be facetious, and to mean that we would unload the most of our mail matter somewhere on the Plains and leave it to the Indians, or whosoever wanted it.

We changed horses every ten miles, all day long, and fairly flew over the hard level road. We jumped out and stretched our legs every time the coach stopped, and so the night found us still vivacious and unfatigued.

The Overland Mail was operated at great cost. When Joseph Holt became Secretary of War, he undertook to reduce the costs of mail contracts, but a cleverly designed agreement checked him. A long argument ensued, and after April, 1860, John Butterfield gave up the management of the company that bore his name. In 1861 the line was shifted to the central route and continued in existence until 1866. After that it ran under the Wells-Fargo management until 1869.

Pony Express

The Overland Mail was efficient but there was still a lack of speed. As early as 1855 an attempt had been made to use horseback riders to hasten the mail between the two parts of the country. This proposal again was brought to the fore as rivalry increased between the Butterfield Overland interest and the freight trucking firm of Russell, Majors and Waddell. The latter company wished to acquire a cross-country mail contract over the central route. In 1859 when it seemed certain that the route by Salt Lake City would be selected, William H. Russell proposed the organization of the fast Pony Express. In January, 1860, when the decision was made to organize the Pony Express, his company went to great expense to select horses, men, station sites, and to distribute supplies along the route. Alexander Majors was largely a reformer at heart. He asked his riders to pledge they would not drink, swear or fight while they were in the employ of the Pony Express. When each rider signed the pledge he was given a leatherbound Bible. What was possibly more important than Majors' pledge was the selection of riders for their daring and durability. Riding the Pony Express was high adventure, and possibly the devil-may-care riders were caught up more by the thrill and challenge than by any prosaic sense of duty.

On April 3, 1860, amidst dramatic celebrations, riders were started from San Francisco, and St. Joseph, Missouri, to carry the first fast mail in each direction. Riding hard between stations, carriers stopped only long enough at most places to grab the *mochila*, or mail pouch, mount a fresh horse and dash off on another section of the route. From St. Joseph to Sacramento was 2,000 miles, and seventy-five riders covered the distance in ten-and-a-half days. Arrival of riders at each terminal was again occasion for celebrating. Twelve-day communication between the two coasts was then possible.

From April 3, 1860, to October 24, 1861, the Pony Express carried much of the transcontinental letter mail. Completion of the telegraph line across the continent, however, brought fast mail service to an end, but the Pony Express was effective in getting the mail from coast to coast in the shortest possible time and was no doubt a contributory factor in keeping California unionist in sentiment. The news of Lincoln's election, the text of his first inaugural address, and the onset of secession and war, were brought westward by its riders. During the nineteen months the Pony Express was in operation it produced some astonishing horsemanship. On a few occasions riders continued in the saddle for 200 to 350 miles without rest. The routine distance for each rider, however, was from fifty to eighty miles. Some riders were killed by Indians. Occasionally a horse dropped dead and the rider had to pick up his *mochila* and continue on foot. Snow, rain, mud, heat, and cold took their toll. A few of the famous riders were "Pony Bob" Haslam, Johnny Frey, Gus Cliff, Don Rising, Jack Keetley, Alex Carlisle, and Henry Wallace. "Wild Bill" Hickok was a station keeper. Charges for mail ranged from $5.00 an ounce down to $1.00 per half ounce, plus ten cents U. S. Postage. An average of 350 letters were carried per trip.

Financially the Pony Express was a failure, but few commercial failures in American history have produced such a durable and romantic history as the Pony Express. Russell, Majors, and Waddell spent approximately $700,000 on the service and collected $500,000. Possibly the heaviest loss was by the transfer of the Butterfield contract to the central route in 1861.

Butterfield and Holliday

One of the most urgent needs of the expanding West Coast was a regular transportation system that would supply a dependable daily flow of mail. At the same time there was a demand for stagecoach and freight services. Almost inevitably the mail line west had to be shortened from the long and wandering Butterfield southern route. While debates over routes and services and contracts dragged on, the nation faced the serious threat of secession. When the southern states withdrew from the Union in 1861, controversy over the central and southern routes ended. On February 27, 1861, the Butterfield Company was given the million-dollar mail contract, and its operations were moved northward. Immediately a consolidation of lines followed which resulted in a better delivery of western mails. Butterfield absorbed the Central Overland Company of California and the Pike's Peak Express Company services.

The new mail line was to operate for eight years before the railway mail car displaced the stagecoach and the locomotive turned the horse out to grass. Indian troubles and robbers were as much a threat over the northern route as they had been over the older one. Rain, snow, mud, and dust delayed the service. As population expanded and more settlements appeared, a network of connecting stage lines developed which necessitated a constant revision of mail routes and contracts. In 1864 Ben Holladay was the successful bidder for the four-year mail contract between the Missouri River and Salt Lake City. William B. Dinsmore of the Overland Mail secured the contract from Salt Lake City across the Sierra Mountains to California. Holladay's entry into the mail and coaching field was the beginning of strong competition for mail and stage revenue. Holladay, a Kentuckian, had gone West with the old Santa Fe trade. Later he bought government military surplus goods following the Mexican War and hauled them overland to Utah. By 1864 he had become a wealthy man and had moved to New York and Washington to be near the source of government, to watch after his interests, and to live the good life of the eastern cities. Holliday's line was equipped with thousand-dollar coaches which hauled twelve passengers and were drawn by carefully matched four- and six-horse teams, a spectacular part of the western pageantry. Holliday specialized in speed, comfort, and security. Consolidations gave him a good share of the western passenger trade and mail service, a patronage he enjoyed until the railroads took away his clientele. Mark Twain told the story of the young American traveling in the Holy Land who was shown Mount Moab and was told that it took Moses forty years to lead the children 300 miles. He replied, "Ben Holladay would have fetched them through in thirty-six hours!"

While mail coach companies opened routes westward and developed the trans-Mississippi postal service, freight and express lines were transporting heavier goods across the continent. Between 1820 and 1869, the West beyond the 100th meridian became a land of grinding wagon wheels. Horse, mule, and ox teams dragged creaking covered wagons over the thousands of miles of plains, desert and mountain roads. Goods were shipped overland to western consumers at fabulous freight costs. Among the important freighters were Russell, Majors, and Waddell. These three partners had organized their company in 1855 as a military transport outfit. They had hauled supplies to Fort Kearney, to the army in Utah in 1857, and then to the boom gold rush around Pike's Peak. At one time they employed four to six thousand men, and owned 3,500 freight wagons, 1,000 mules, and 40,000 oxen.

A company was organized in 1852 by Henry Wells and William G. Fargo to operate a western express as an associate of the American Express Company. Unlike the big western freighting firms, Wells-Fargo carried mail, express, and gold and silver bullion. Expansion of mining activities in the West brought it fame and fortune. Its offices, coaches, and freight wagons became transporters of frontier wealth, and were frequently victimized by bandit raids.

Rails West

With the appearance of the transcontinental railroads, the express and freight companies went the way of the contract mail stages; yet they had done a good job. With the help of the army, they had opened many of the better routes to the Pacific. They had developed the primary pattern of western commerce and travel, and after a mighty struggle had established communication with nearly all parts of the Union. Human energy and daring had been expended in prodigious quantities, for operation of western freight and passenger lines demanded almost foolhardy courage. As settlers followed in their footsteps, the increase of population rang the knell of the old western transportation system.

The age of the railroad was upon the West before the end of 1862. While railway promoters east of the Mississippi kept up a roar of promotional oratory and many of the older states were being checkered with expanding railway lines, ambitious dreamers were looking toward the Far West. One of the first promoters of the transcontinental railway idea was the ambitious Connecticut Yankee, Asa Whitney. He had engaged successfully in the 1840's as a New York merchant in the rich China trade. While in the Orient he conceived the idea of a railroad through South Pass and across the Sierras to the Pacific Coast. Between 1844 and 1851 he conducted a vigorous campaign before the public, in Congress, and abroad, in an effort to secure financial support. Whitney proposed to begin his road on the shores of Lake Michigan and build on to the Pacific at San Francisco. During the summer of 1854 he traveled, with a small company of companions, over 800 miles of the proposed route, familiarizing himself with the physical problems which railroad builders would encounter. His pamphlet, *A Project for a Railroad to the Pacific* (1849), has become a classic in western American railway history. The year it was published Stephen

A. Douglas and a group of southern railway promoters were struggling with Congress over subsidizing the Illinois Central system and several of the southern roads. At the same time, railroads in the East were being extended toward the Mississippi, and some promoters were becoming captivated with the idea of building on beyond the river.

Eastern railroad builders faced all sorts of problems, but probably none of them was so important as lack of capital. Local and national credit sources were tapped for financial support, as well as the international money markets. Nearly all the eastern roads were built through settled communities, or connected settled areas. There was a reasonable hope that passengers and freight were awaiting the completion of the older roads. A transcontinental road, however, could not hope to have access to paying quantities of freight along the way for a long time to come, nor could it tap freight concentrations except at either end of the line. To await the coming of settlers would have meant delaying the building of railroads to the Pacific indefinitely. Such undertakings involved the expenditure of an enormous amount of capital, but private sources were not willing to make such heavy investments. Government subsidies of land and money were necessary to speed up the connections between the East and West.

Preliminary surveys for a western railroad line were made, and much discussion of the subject appeared in the various journals between 1853 and 1862. The building of lines had actually begun westward from the Mississippi in one or two instances. Eastern lines had been built as far as Vicksburg, New Orleans, Memphis, and Chicago. Some time prior to 1854, Edwin F. Johnson prepared an elaborate paper survey of the route, and he estimated the cost to build a railroad from Chicago to the Pacific Coast, a distance of 1,960 miles, at $100,000,000. Southerners argued for a southern road to run west from one of the lower river cities. In 1854 the great Southern Convention met in Charleston, South Carolina, and a major topic of discussion was the building of a transcontinental railroad. A proposal was made that Virginia charter a Pacific railroad, and that each of fourteen southern states contribute $2,000,000 to finance its building. A long report was made which recited many conjectures but gave few concrete facts. More attention was given to the location of the eastern terminus than to the long arid route across west Texas and New Mexico and Arizona. The states, of course, were not able to help finance the ambitious projects already building within their own borders; thus the resolution of the Charleston Commercial Convention did nothing more than illustrate the nature of the sectional struggle which handicapped any planning of a transcontinental railroad that would require public aid.

It was impossible to secure the passage of legislation through Congress that would achieve more than a preliminary survey of an acceptable route westward. The chartering of a railroad was all but out of the question, and it was not until after 1861 that the subject could be revived with any assurance of success. Outbreak of the Civil War made it most difficult to secure capital, labor and materials for railways beyond the immediate areas of conflict, yet some western roads, like the Minnesota and Pacific, and the Pacific of Missouri continued slowly to extend their lines.

Union Pacific

On July 1, 1862, President Lincoln approved the charter of the Union Pacific Railroad Company to build westward from the 100th meridian to the Wasatch Range, and on toward the eastern border of California. This road was to connect with points on the Missouri River by a series of feeder lines. At the same time the Central Pacific of California was authorized to build eastward from the coast to the Nevada border. The two roads were to receive five alternate sections of public lands (mineral rights excepted) per mile on each side of the track for ten miles back from the right of way. The Union Pacific was to be capitalized at $100,000,000, and its builders were to receive a thirty-year loan of $16,000 per mile across the plains, $48,000 for 150 miles west of the east base of the Rockies, and $32,000 in United States bonds for the stretch of line between the Rockies and the Sierras. The government was to retain 25 per cent of the bonds until the road was finished. There were to be 162 commissioners to solicit stock subscriptions, and fifteen directors, two of whom were to be appointed by the President of the United States.

Ground was broken for the Union Pacific at Omaha, Nebraska, on December 2, 1863, but company finances were low, officials had over-bought materials and rolling stock, and the project all but came to a halt at its beginning. In 1864 the company's charter was amended so that it was permitted to sell 1,000,000 shares at $100 each instead of the original plan to sell 100,000 shares at $1,000 each. The land grant was increased to twenty sections per mile, ten alternate sections on each side of the track, with mineral rights to iron and coal included. As an added attraction to investors, the Union Pacific could issue first mortgage bonds to the amount of government subsidy. The company under the new act was to receive land and money subsidy upon the completion of each twenty miles of track, and two-thirds of the subsidy was made collectable as the grade was prepared for track-laying. Construction of the road was started again in 1865, and in a short time 247 miles of track were placed in operation.

Financial and construction management of the Union Pacific was involved in the complex and corrupt activities of a holding company, the Crédit Mobilier. This construction agency succeeded the Pennsylvania

Fiscal Agency in 1864, and it in turn became a combine of high officials in the Union Pacific Railroad Company and Congress who not only built the railroad, but also stripped it of most of its financial support, bringing the railroad company almost to bankruptcy. In all, approximately $23,-000,000 in land and income bonds and stocks went into private pockets. Important figures in the omnibus fiscal organization were Congressman Oakes Ames of Massachusetts and his brother Oliver. For the next five years, the Union Pacific was to become so deeply and mysteriously involved in irregularities of fiscal management, that even yet it is impossible to ascertain all the precise facts of the road's early history. It is an established fact that large profits were made by the contractors. Some Congressmen reaped benefits from the Crédit Mobilier through the Ames practice of distributing stock at greatly reduced prices in an attempt to prevent a congressional investigation. Nevertheless the Ameses, James Brooks of New York, James A. Garfield of Ohio, Vice President Schuyler Colfax, and James W. Patterson were subjected to public investigation, and Oakes Ames and James Brooks were censured.

Construction of the Union Pacific was one of the most rugged undertakings in American economic history. All materials had to be shipped phenomenally long distances by rail and steamboat and then hauled by wagon to the end of the road. General Grenville Dodge became chief engineer for the road in 1866. Before going to the Union Pacific, he had seen western military service and knew something about the terrain over which the road would run. One of the barriers which loomed before the engineers was the Laramie Mountain range in Wyoming. By accident the survey party was caught by surprise in an Indian raid, and in escaping their attackers they discovered Evans' Pass, which simplified extension of the road.

The Indian menace was highly irritating. Workmen had to learn to use pick, shovel, and gun with equal efficiency. Indian fighting was often as much a part of the construction process as making grades and building bridges. Bad roads, lack of water, epidemics, and extremely cold weather all delayed the work gangs. Workmen were divided into parties to work at the various tasks of road building. Ahead of the construction crews were surveyors who were still engaged in locating the line while it was in the process of construction. Graders worked ahead of the bridge builders, and track layers and freight haulers brought up the rear. Building across the plains was a fairly simple matter, and track was laid at a rapid pace. During 1867–1868, 450 miles of track were constructed; at the peak of the construction race, gangs laid as much as seven miles of rail a day.

Construction of the road was hurried and often flimsy. Bridges either had to be rebuilt or ballasted almost at once, grades were narrow and improperly made, and track settled dangerously, sometimes sliding completely out of place. Government inspectors insisted that the track should be built on the level, and the company was forced to make cuts through the gently rolling ridges, which wasted millions of dollars creating snow traps that halted winter operation of trains.

At times during the mad race with the Central Pacific, 10,000 laborers and as many draft animals were employed in grading and track laying. Railhead camps were comparable to rowdy mining camps and cattle towns. When construction crews went into winter quarters, flimsy shacks arose out of the plains to house gamblers, saloon keepers, prostitutes, and sharpers of all sorts. Although money was neither so easily earned nor so plentiful as in the gold fields, it was spent freely on the sordid diversions of the boisterous camps. In the spring when construction gangs again pushed the railhead westward, the winter camp, or "hell on wheels," moved on, leaving what had been a scene of rowdiness and debauchery a silent, deserted, and trash-littered void on the prairie. Most famous of these camps were at North Platte, Julesburg, Cheyenne, and Laramie.

Building eastward from the Pacific, engineers and gangs of imported Orientals hustled the Central Pacific eastward toward Utah. This road was largely a result of the agitation of Theodore De Hone Judah. An engineer with wide railway-building experience, Judah went to California in 1854 to help build the Sacramento Valley Railroad. When he had completed this task, he began a series of preliminary surveys in search of a railway route across the mountains. In 1859 he was an active figure in the California Railroad Convention, and a year later he was able to interest Leland Stanford, Mark Hopkins, Charles Crocker, and Collis P. Huntington in building a railway across the Sierra Nevadas. These four men, known as the "Big Four," were a remarkable quartet of promoters. All of them were shrewd Yankees who had either followed the gold rush westward in 1849 or had reached California in the early '50's. They had gone into business and were rapidly becoming wealthy when they became interested in building the Central Pacific Road.

The "Big Four" raised among them $200,000 in capital which Stanford and Judah took East to be used in their work with Congress. On June 28, 1861, California chartered the Central Pacific Railroad Company, and in 1862 Huntington secured a federal subsidy comparable to that granted the Union Pacific. During the next five years the four California partners were successful in putting pressure on town and county governments to contribute heavily to the financing of the Central Pacific in order to secure its location through their boundaries. Leland Stanford was elected governor of California in 1861 and as a powerful political figure was able to manipulate political favors for the company.

On January 3, 1862, the Central Pacific Company broke ground for its first track, and the wild race eastward began. Under the watchful eye of Charles Crocker, track was put down at a staggering pace. By the end of the Civil War, 3,000 Irishmen and 10,000 Chinese were clearing right of way and establishing grades; track was being laid across rough mountain terrain at the rate of three miles a day. In six years the Central Pacific crews completed work which was estimated to take ten years to build. Public and private investors subsidized the Central Pacific to the extent of $79,-000,000 in stocks, bonds, and cash. In 1866 Congress authorized the Central Pacific to continue building on past the original Nevada western line until it met the Union Pacific. This set off a mad construction race. Each company sought to claim as much public subsidy as possible. Not only did they seek greater shares of government land and funds, but the rich Mormon trade as well. Before the race was ended, the two companies had graded 300 miles parallel to each other. Their crews were caught up in the rivalry, and at times their conflicts were almost as serious as those between whites and Indians. Not until Congress arbitrated the race, and designated Promontory Point in Utah as the junction point, was the rivalry checked.

On May 10, 1869, the tracks of the rival companies were joined in an elaborate ceremony. The nation was alerted to observe the linking of its two coasts. A large number of people were present at Promontory Point to see the laying of a polished California laurel cross-tie bearing a silver plate indicating the historic spot. A Union Pacific official drove a silver spike, and Leland Stanford drove a gold spike, and the taps of the hammer were sent out to the waiting nation by telegraph. People paraded through villages, town orators proclaimed the nation's glory, and everywhere Americans were happy to know that the two oceans were at last connected by rail.

The meeting of the Union and Central Pacific lines in Utah actually did little more for a time than symbolize the completion of preliminary roads to the coast. There still remained the enormous tasks of rebuilding, regrading, and relocating much of the two roads. Numerous readjustments had to be made in operation plans. Moving trains were not guarantees of safety against the Indian menace. Settlements were slow in forming along the right of way, and the Union Pacific was dogged with scandals growing out of the activities of the Crédit Mobilier. Hardly had the first kinks been ironed out of operation before the paralyzing panic of 1873 struck. But in time the two roads were to justify the dreams of Whitney, Judah, and General Dodge.

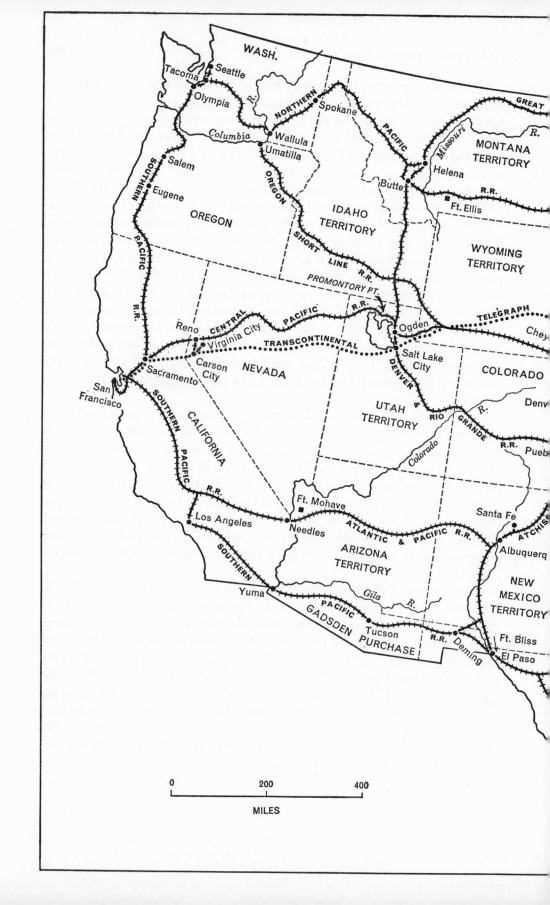

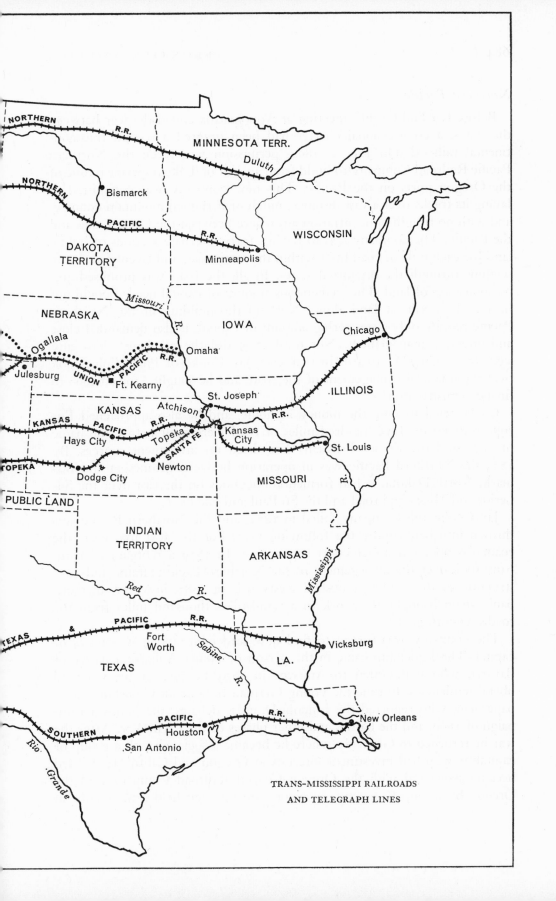

TRANS-MISSISSIPPI RAILROADS
AND TELEGRAPH LINES

Northern Pacific

Before Lee and Grant's meeting at Appomattox ended the war between the states, a congressional charter had been granted a second transcontinental railroad. On July 2, 1864, permission was given the Northern Pacific Railroad Company to build from a point on Lake Superior to one of the Oregon ports on the Pacific. This new company was committed to laying its tracks over a vast distance, much of it rugged mountain country, and with no freight concentration anywhere between the Great Lakes and the Pacific. The company was to receive forty alternate sections of public land for each mile of road built within the territories, and twenty alternate sections through the organized states. In all, the road was promised 40,-000,000 acres of land. The tremendous amount of capital needed could not be raised by sale of land alone. Nor did the building of the Northern Pacific require only a staggering amount of capital; it also demanded close and effective management. Not until 1869 did the company show any signs of building westward. In that year Jay Cooke of Philadelphia took over the financial management of the road, and he sought $100,000,000 to finance construction.

Cooke tried to raise the money at home, and he also approached European investors. Five hundred miles of road were built before the panic of 1873 and the Franco-Prussian War dried up investment sources. By 1873 the Northern Pacific was in operation between Minnesota and Bismark, North Dakota. It had formed connections on the east over the Superior and Mississippi road and the St. Paul and Pacific.

Jay Cooke and Company failed in 1873, and the Northern Pacific was thrown into bankruptcy the following year. For the next five years the road was operated under court supervision. In 1879 a reorganized company took over the management of the Northern Pacific affairs, and construction of the road was pushed westward. In 1882, however, financial panic again brought the work to a standstill a thousand miles from the road's western goal.

The company was forced to find new leadership and new sources of capital. The leadership came in the person of Henry Villard, a native of Bavaria, who immigrated to America in 1853 because of his youthful liberal tendencies. In time the young German became an important newspaperman, who reported the Lincoln-Douglas debates, the political campaign of 1860, and the battles and other phases of the Civil War. After the war he returned to Germany where he became associated with a group of capitalists who had investment interests in Oregon and California. Villard became associated with the Oregon Central Railroad Company and the Oregon Steamship Company, two companies which held a monopoly in the northwestern transportation field. He hoped to extend this control of transportation by buying Northern Pacific stock. To do this he organized the famous "Blind Pool" in which he persuaded New York investors to subscribe $8,000,000 for carrying out an unannounced purpose. By 1881 the "Blind Pool" group had acquired a controlling interest in the Northern Pacific and Villard became the road's president. His administration was an important one for the company, but for Villard personally it was frustrating. He fell short of his dream during the lean years of the early '80's when an insufficient amount of capital was available to place the road in efficient operation.

The Northern Pacific made connection with the Oregon Railway in 1883. Four years later the main line was extended to Seattle. Like the Union Pacific, the northern road had a colorful history of construction, aside from its numerous financial crises. Building across the Rockies was an enormous struggle against terrain and climate. The vast territory which the road crossed necessitated a sprawling system which was difficult to operate. And before the Northern Pacific could secure an operational monopoly of the northern overland trade and extend its interest on to the Orient, construction of another northern transcontinental road was underway.

Big Jim Hill

In 1878 James Jerome Hill began the reorganization of the rusting St. Paul and Pacific Railroad. This company had been organized and given a land grant in the expansive postwar years, but the enthusiasm of its backers was short-lived. The company was overcapitalized, and the track that was laid was exceedingly poor. The stifling panic of 1873 forced the company into bankruptcy, and it was not until 1878 that it was reorganized and construction was again begun.

"Jim" Hill was born in Ontario. As a youth he had followed the fur trade westward. He had varied experiences in the Northwest, some of them in the field of steamboat transportation. He was a good-natured, friendly, and observant person. His enthusiasm was high, and he was thorough in his work. Before he ventured into the reorganization of the St. Paul and Pacific Railroad Company, he gathered together a vast amount of information not only about that road, but about railroad operation in general. His information was vital to him, and also to the Scotch Canadians, Norman Kittson, Donald Smith, and George Stephens whom he wished to associate with himself in securing control of the St. Paul and Pacific. This group of men raised the capital for the venture which resulted in the organization of the Great Northern Railroad Company in 1890.

One of the first moves of the new company in 1878 had been to build the road northward toward Winnipeg and a junction with the Canadian railway system. A second line was started westward across the Dakotas and Montana. By 1887 the Hill line had reached Great Falls, Montana Territory. Six years later it had been extended to Seattle. This company escaped the financial hazards of the time and continued operation and building. The road made annual dividend payments, and because of close management avoided many of the mistakes which defeated other companies. One of its successful policies was dictated by Hill's attitude toward locating track. He himself attended to the details of selecting the route, keeping in mind the factor of a low-cost roadbed. He spent weeks seeking the best passes across the western mountain ranges. At the same time, territory was selected immediately adjacent which could be developed into freight-paying country. The directors were careful not to over-capitalize their company. Every monetary expenditure had to yield a profit. Long barren stretches of territory which had threatened other roads with failure were turned into settlements by a vigorous campaign to attract immigrants to the Northwest. Once the Great Northern Railroad was built, President Hill gave much attention to improving farming methods in the Northwest. He spent much of his energy speaking to farmer groups, in the promotion of livestock breeding and encouraging the production of larger farm crops.

By 1900 James J. Hill had become one of the outstanding railway men of America. To his biographers he was a hero of Bunyanesque proportions. His energy, vibrant personality, and imagination were impressive. Not only did he envision the rusting and bankrupt St. Paul and Pacific expanding into a prosperous transcontinental system, he also saw the vast tier of territory between Lake Superior and the Puget Sound developing into freight-producing and profitable land. Beyond that even, he shared Henry Villard's dream of thrusting his road's trade tentacles outward to capture a share of the oriental trade. Jim Hill was one of the strongest personalities to be associated with the building of the American railroads and the development of their territories. To Hill's critics he was hard-headed, opinionated, and determined. At least one of them regarded him as the Northwest's worst enemy. His efforts to develop small farms resulted eventually in poverty, heartbreak and panic for the people, and destruction for the land. Yet Hill was possibly more intimately associated with both his business enterprise and the people whom it served than any of the great financial barons of his period.

Southern Routes

While promoters were pushing three railroads westward to the Pacific Coast across the central and northern belt of the continent, promoters to the south were planning and building the Southern Pacific from New Orleans to Los Angeles and San Francisco. The route of this westward connection was one of the earliest discussed in plans to reach the West Coast by rail. In 1853 the Pierce Administration made the $10,000,000 Gadsden Purchase from Mexico to insure an all-United States Railway route across the Southwest to California. This important elbow of land east of the Rio Grande and south of the Gila rivers contained 42,535 square miles, enough to form one of the larger middle-sized states. Sectional bickering and lack of practical planning and capital prevented the chartering and building of the southern road before 1860. It was not until the end of the Civil War that the Southern Pacific Railroad Company was chartered, and by this time it was the fruit of the ambitions and planning of the "Big Four," Stanford, Hopkins, Crocker, and Huntington. The first western branch of what became the Southern Pacific was designed to give the Central Pacific a connection to the southern and eastern part of California. In 1877 the road was directed inland by way of Needles and Yuma to a connection with the Southern Pacific roads of Arizona and New Mexico.

The western end of the Southern Pacific was involved in an intricate monopoly of interests. For the sake of a favorable public opinion, the central and southern roads maintained separate management. The Southern failed to secure a government grant of lands and was forced to build its line entirely with private capital. Crossing the Yuma Indian Reservation created some embarrassment in which both the Secretary of War and resident army officers did considerable vacillating under pressure. Despite a lack of permission to cross the reservation, the Southern Pacific officials pushed the building of their line forward in a wild race with the Texas Pacific before official permission was granted in 1877. An operational agreement was formed with the Texas Pacific to operate over its lines eastward from El Paso. By 1883 the Southern Pacific had consolidated the Galveston, Harrisburg and San Antonio, and several short lines to reach New Orleans over its own tracks. With the completion of this system, the southern part of the United States had rail connections from New Orleans to the Pacific; in fact New Orleans had connections with Seattle by way of the Southern Pacific and the independent San Francisco and Northern Pacific. The Southern Pacific lines were welded into a highly unified system after 1884 by the Huntington empire.

The southern transcontinental trade, however, was not to be monopolized by the Southern Pacific. Already building into the Southwest were the Atchison, Topeka and Santa Fe, and the Denver and Rio Grande. The first of these was chartered in 1859, and again in 1863, as a connecting line between Kansas and the Southwest. It was the hope of Cyrus H. Holliday, a native of Pennsylvania, that such a connection could be formed. He promoted the road to give Kansas an outlet to the Gulf and with Mexico by which wheat and cattle could be hauled to market. After a long and frustrating fight to build the road, ground was first broken on October 30, 1868, in Topeka.

For the next twelve years track was laid southward. Geography forced the railroad to miss the town of Santa Fe, but it went on to Albuquerque and a connection with the Southern Pacific at Deming, New Mexico, on March 8, 1881. The main branch was connected a month later with El Paso; at the same time the Sonora Railway was being built north from Guaymas, Mexico, on the Gulf to Benson, New Mexico. A year after the Santa Fe reached Deming, the Sonora route was completed.

By consolidating short lines and taking over the Atlantic and Pacific tracks (a land grant road chartered in July, 1866, to be built from Springfield, Missouri, to Needles, California), the Santa Fe reached the Pacific on November 9, 1885, after a settlement with the Southern Pacific over the use of its line from Needles to the coast. Three years later, by more new construction and by consolidation of short routes, the road was extended to Chicago. The system had become by this time one of the most extensive in the United States, operating 9,300 miles of track. It not only connected Lake Michigan with the Gulf, and with the Pacific, but it also owned a complex system of local feeder lines.

The Santa Fe did not reach the Pacific without a series of dramatic western railway "wars." The first of these began in 1878 in a headlong race with General William J. Palmer's Denver and Rio Grande, which had been chartered in 1870 to capture the southern Colorado and New Mexico trade, for the use of Raton Pass. The Santa Fe caught its rival napping and gained possession of the strategic mountain defile. In its second rivalry with the Denver road the General was more alert, and only after a wild horse race with a work train did the Santa Fe engineers reach the Royal Gorge of the Arkansas River first. The Santa Fe lost its claim, however, in the courts. By 1872 the Denver and Rio Grande had built southwestward to the Laban coalfields, but neither it nor the Santa Fe had thought of building on through the narrow river pass from Pueblo, Colorado, to the sterile country around Leadville. But when the mineral resources of that area were developed, there was a mad scramble to reach the gold and silver mines by rail. This scramble for the use of the gorge was one of the most colorful conflicts between two railroads in the rather colorful period of western railroad building. This so-called "Royal Gorge War" was fought out in the cañon and the courtroom, including the United States Supreme Court.

By 1890 the American continent was spanned by five transcontinental roads, and several other lines reached the coast by a series of favorable connections. Just as important was the network of local lines which helped to develop the wide stretches of intervening territory. Towns and farming communities were connected with the main lines.

The building of the western railroads involved many complex problems of railway expansion. They were constructed at a time when industrial America was in its most expansive years. Financier, politician, contractor, and railway operator lived by the code of those lusty years from 1865 to 1900. The stakes were high, and the morals were often low. Profits awaited the company that got there first. Success often hinged on how well government and local subsidies could be used to attract enough private capital for so much grading, bridging, and trackage. Yet regardless of the business and political morals of the age, the engineering accomplishments were genuine.

The Farmers and the Railroads

As important as the actual building of the railroads was the development of the vast western farming country. Mountains of farm produce and great herds of cattle appeared at the way stations for shipment to both domestic and world markets. The American frontier was now caught up in a new phase of development. Old isolative barriers were lowered, and frontiersmen who had looked only to the land were now confronted with the even greater and more confusing problems of production and distribution.

Neither frontier farmer nor railway magnate had thought much past the basic problems of building railroads and gaining connections with the outside. When thousands of new farmsteads were brought quickly into existence and millions of new settlers appeared on the plains and along the mountain and Pacific slopes, they erased the frontier and produced the farm problem. The farmer who labored to the point of exhaustion to produce crops was not happy when he saw the railroads wipe out his profits in freight rates. The railroads themselves were caught up in a net of competition, heavy overhead expenses, and an uncontrolled system of individualistic operation. The geography and the great distances of western territory were conducive to the long and short haul abuses. At certain points there was murderous competition for freight, while at others the shipper was at the mercy of the public carrier. When farm prices fell, farmers and legislators became sufficiently aroused to force the adoption of both local and national regulatory legislation. A full-scale revolt would grow out of the headlong period of uncontrolled expansion following the Civil War. This era of dissatisfaction would see a change in both economic attitudes and political alignments.

The West found in the railroads a quick means to transport its products to market; eastern manufacturers and merchants found in them an efficient means of transporting their goods to the farmer customers. The development of a new system of distribution and the expansion of credit was to make an almost revolutionary difference in the expansion of the frontier. The panics which threatened the western farmer after 1885 could no longer be alleviated by an escape to the great area of free lands. Railroads and vast immigration had pretty well destroyed that economic factor in American life. Relief could be had only through government and political channels. Public regulation alone, for example, could control the transportation colossus.

The railroads of the West were thrown into sharp competition for settlers, freight and passengers. Throughout the last quarter of the nineteenth century the rural press of the eastern part of the United States carried lengthy advertisements describing the advantages of the lands available along the various western roads. Prospective emigrants were led to believe that the various railway territories offered eternal security and prosperity. An even more fascinating publicity device was the appearance of letters in small weekly papers, purporting to come from some former neighbor, which described how good life was in certain areas of the West. Thousands of legitimate letters, of course, were written back to homefolks by persons who had left the states east of the Mississippi River. Collectively these last give a very realistic picture of what happened to the rear guard pioneers who followed the railways to cheap lands and to fresh economic opportunity on the receding frontier. As yet, historians have made little or no use of these sources. In summary, the expansion of the western railway system hastened the backsweep of the frontier from the West Coast and brought about the fusion of the two population movements which converged on the open lands of the plains and the eastern foothills of the Rocky Mountains. It also hastened economic expansion of the United States into the world market.

SPOTTED TAIL'S DELEGATION IN WASHINGTON, 1877

THE INDIANS' LAST STAND

THE INDIANS' LAST STAND

"I am tired of fighting. Our chiefs are killed. Looking Glass is dead. Tu-hul-hil-sote is dead. The old men are all dead. He who led on the young men, Alikut, is dead. It is cold and we have no blankets. The little children are freezing to death. My people, some of them, have run away to the hills, and have no blankets, no food; no one knows where they are—perhaps freezing to death. I want to have time to look for my children and see how many of them I can find. Maybe I shall find them among the dead. Hear me, my chiefs. I am tired; my heart is sick and sad. From where the sun stands I will fight no more forever."

—CHIEF JOSEPH *of the Nez Percé*

CHAPTER XXX

THE year 1849 divides Indian history into two rather distinct chronological periods during the nineteenth century. By the congressional act of 1849, administration of Indian affairs was shifted from the War Department to the Department of Interior. The change-over was accompanied by the usual amount of bureaucratic lagging, which resulted in a disturbing hiatus in the management of ticklish Indian matters. Yet, even if the transfer of administration had been expeditious, it could not have altered the long history of border conflict west of the Mississippi. This had its beginnings with the first settlement of the Louisiana Territory. As has been said before, Lewis and Clark opened the earlier phase of the trans-Mississippi rivalry between the two races; they were engaged in Indian diplomacy during much of the time they were traveling to the far Northwest. They were highly successful in dealing with the tribes, as the fortunes of their journey proved, but they did not have to combat evils of white origin which made subsequent Indian relations in that general area so tedious.

The nature of the frictions which marred Indian history east of the river differed from those in the West, and the difference was largely of environmental origin. Rivalry for land and game was basically the same in both areas, and unscrupulous, irresponsible traders and rapacious settlers put self-interest above national welfare in both places. An influx of eastern tribes, however, created new pressures in the eastern plains area. Rapid advance of the settlement line, the killing off of the buffalo herds, the building of the transcontinental railroads, the mineral rushes, the American Civil War, interdepartmental rivalries in the government, corrupt and indifferent Indian officials, and rivalries between the two houses of Congress over terms of Indian treaties all contributed to border conflict.

Search for a Basic Policy

Indian history is filled with noble statements from responsible government officials. None of them is more short-sighted and unrealistic than the one James Monroe submitted to Congress on January 27, 1825, regarding the proposed removal of the southern tribes. Most of this message pertained to the immediate problem in the southern states, but in summarizing his remarks Monroe observed that among the many advantages which the government offered the Indians was that of a stable political society for the future. Blissfully he wrote:

> By the establishment of such a government over these tribes with their consent we become in reality their benefactors. The relation of the conflicting interests which has heretofore existed between them and our frontier settlements will cease. There will be no more wars between them and the United States. Adopting such a government, their movement will be in harmony with us, and its good effect be felt throughout the whole extent of our territory to the Pacific. It may be fairly presumed that, through the agency of such a government, the condition of all tribes inhabiting that vast region may be essentially improved; that permanence of peace may be preserved with them, and our commerce much extended.

Monroe's final phrase, "and our commerce much extended," was a reality, for already it was causing sharp conflict. While the President in Washington was writing his generous sentiments, mountain men on their way up the turgid Missouri had already tasted the wrath of the western Indians. Colonel Henry Leavenworth and his Fort Atkinson troops had battled the Arikaras, and on up stream the Mandans and Crows lay in wait to take toll of the white traders.

A decade later Congress passed the famous Indian Intercourse Act of 1834 which, in the minds of many representatives, must have promised a permanent settlement of Indian problems. On the face of it the new law guaranteed the Indians once again a free and uninterrupted possession of their western lands. Ostensibly the law was designed to encourage Indian removals and to forestall possible public criticism. Traders were to be controlled by rigid government license, and settlers were to be excluded from the territory. Two factors were then important: Congress had placed mistaken confidence in the licensing system, and settler pressure was momentarily low enough not to cause any serious difficulty. Within a quarter of a century the picture was changed. The Indian domain was again threatened, and the Intercourse Act was being honored more in its breach than by its observance. Administrative failures in the management of Indian affairs and the use of military resistance had had important bearing upon Indian relations. Granting of government licenses involved favoritism, corruption, and flagrant violation of the law. Once the settlement line advanced, the need to protect white humanity became a fact loaded with political emotion, and this condition forced the use of the military despite the law.

The Indian lacked political influence, the settler had it, and this affected important policy decisions.

Before the change-over of administration of Indian affairs in 1849, the southwestern frontier was greatly expanded by terms of the Treaty of Guadalupe Hidalgo. This diplomatic agreement between the United States and Mexico greatly extended the official American frontier by adding the territory of the present states of Utah, New Mexico, Arizona, Nevada, and parts of California, Wyoming, and Colorado. The new administration of Indian affairs found its difficulties compounded. Not only was its geographical responsibility doubled, but rapid social and political changes added to its woes.

Trader and trapper trails and camp sites became inroads and settlements. Within three decades after the mountain fur trade reached its peak, western Indians saw themselves becoming hemmed in from both coasts, with ominous penetrations slicing into the interior of their lands. Between 1820 and 1850 the Texas frontier was virtually freed of Indians. A highly publicized border war resulted in their final removal to the Oklahoma country. Beyond the mountains, the California tribes were swamped by the kaleidoscopic changes caused by the gold rush. The tribes along the eastern frontier from Missouri to Iowa saw doom in the rapid expanse of white settlements. As new political territories were created, new frictions occurred, and border history repeated itself.

Neither James Monroe's expressed desire for permanence in the new Indian territory nor the later restrictions prescribed in the act of 1834 stemmed the tide of white settlement. Like a sagging island in the path of an angry flood, the Indian country only waited the inevitable passage of time to be submerged. The vast plains and mountain regions had appeared to be an inexhaustible area of free lands; now it was shrinking yearly. White men cut roads through the area, set up stage coach stations and telegraph lines; even before 1860, surveyors were spying out routes for proposed transcontinental railroads. Many travelers who crossed this wild western and southwestern country were in fact observers who unconsciously spotted likely lands for settlements, routes for roads, and resources for future exploitation. By the outbreak of the Civil War, travel literature which described the great plains and western mountain country had expanded into a considerable volume. Some population figures will illustrate this rising flood of settlers. In the decade 1850 to 1860, Texas' population rose from 212,000 to 604,000; New Mexico Territory experienced a growth from less than 62,000 to 93,000; Utah increased from 11,000 to 40,000, and California leaped upward from fewer than 93,000 to more than 380,000.

Minnesota Problems

One of the best examples of both population growth and its oppressive effects upon the Indian frontier was Minnesota Territory. Congress created this Territory in April, 1849, and almost immediately there was a phenomenal increase in the white population. At the beginning of territorial history the fringe of white settlement had scarcely penetrated the interior. The military and trading post at Fort Snelling dated back to 1819 when it had been established as an explorer's base of operations. St. Paul, Stillwater, and Mendota were founded as farmer-lumbering centers. The white population in 1849 was made up largely of those whites who were left out of the new state of Wisconsin when its western boundary was fixed at the St. Croix River. At least nine-tenths of Minnesota Territory was still in the possession of the Sioux and their linguistic cousins the Winnebagoes, along with a sprinkling of Fox, Sauks and Menominees. Because of the rapid influx of the white settlers, territorial officials found it necessary to reach an agreement with the Indians regarding their relocation, and the release of large blocks of lands. Before the treaties could be made, however, the territorial government was confronted by difficulties bred of rivalries among various special-interest groups. British and American traders and trappers competed for furs in the region, and at the time the new territory was created, both Hudson's Bay traders and American law violaters were engaged in a prosperous trade in liquor with the Indians. This commodity contributed to keeping the tribes in an unpredictable state of mind. Settlers moving up to the Indian barrier were reluctant to enter Indian lands because of the certain dangers which lurked there. All along the settlement frontier, tension mounted and promised to turn into a severe border war.

In April, 1850, Henry M. Rice entered into a contract with the Commissioner of Indian Affairs, Orlando Brown, to remove the Winnebagoes to a reservation in northern Minnesota for $70.00 per head. This contract became a burning issue in both local and national politics, but it was allowed to stand, and Rice collected almost $25,000 for his services. Disposition of the Sioux problem was more complicated than that of the less numerous Winnebagoes.

For the Indians themselves, Minnesota was no longer a happy hunting ground. Game was being killed off, and the white invasion into the interior tended to force several Indian groups into competition among themselves. Local traders were anxious because of their Indian debts. No longer were there rich pickings in the land, and there was grave danger that a change in government policy would enable the Indians to escape altogether the debts which they had contracted in more promising days. Possibly some traders saw a treaty as a way to pull themselves out of what otherwise promised to be a disastrous situation. The Indian trade in this part of the Northwest exhibited all the bad social and financial features that would plague southern cotton tenant farmers in the twentieth century. Goods were sold on credit at exorbitantly increased prices, and in this way honest customers helped bear the burden of dishonest ones. Interest rates were staggering, and the mode of settlement was seldom a clear-cut one by which the unsophisticated debtor could understand what was happening to him. Such groups as the American Fur Company put on pressure, and internal politics in the territory offered little relief from the chaos that prevailed.

Luke Lea, Indian Commissioner, and Alexander Ramsey, first territorial governor, assumed the task of negotiating treaties with the Sioux and Chippewas. Important Sioux agreements were made at Traverse des Sioux and at Mendota. In the first agreement the Indians promised to surrender claims to their ancestral lands and move onto a reservation to be located ten miles along each bank of the Mississippi to Lake Traverse and the Yellow Medicine River. They were to receive $1,665,000 to be paid in fifty annual instalments, and more than $250,000 was to be held in a special cultural fund. Signing of this treaty was accompanied by a most unhappy incident. Traders who sought to secure their debts led the chiefs aside from the official treaty table to sign a second agreement authorizing payment of their debts to the traders from government funds that were to be held in escrow. The signing of the latter agreement was done in such a way that it was made to appear as part of the original process. This extralegal authorization, known as the "Traders' Paper," lacked enforceable authority. Immediately, the Indians protested that they were uninformed as to the contents of the trader document. White agents, however, contended that the Indians knew they were authorizing payment, even though the "Trader Paper" was not read to them. Certainly this was not a promising beginning of reservation history for the upper Sioux. The second, or Mendota Treaty, was practically the same as that of Traverse des Sioux.

Following the making of the Indian treaties there was a period of conflict among Minnesota political leaders. Both Alexander Ramsey and Henry Sibley became involved in charges and countercharges which led to a senatorial investigation. The delay in government payments and general administrative failures were disquieting to the Indians, and the next decade was marked by restlessness, bloodshed and other border troubles.

On August 17, 1862, Indian dissatisfaction came to a dramatic head. At Acton, in Meeker County, a party of braves fell upon a group of settlers and wiped them out. The next day they attacked New Ulm. This outbreak led to others along the Minnesota River, and within a week more than 700 settlers were killed. Governor Ramsey ordered troops to the scene of trouble from Fort Snelling. Henry Sibley who commanded the troops had a long background experience as a frontier trader. For several years he had been in the employ of the American Fur Company, and later he traded successfully along the Minnesota frontier. When he took the field at the head of the Minnesota militia, it was not without a great deal of understanding of his enemy the Sioux.

For two months following the Acton massacre, Sibley and his army tracked down the Indians who were under the leadership of Chief Little Crow. Sibley had almost no cavalry, and his task was thereby made more difficult. He was forced into bloody encounters without achieving the desired results, and his men were seriously handicapped by use of the defective Austrian rifles which were issued to them in the trying times of the Civil War. Because it was necessary to depend on infantry, the army often moved too slowly to keep up with the Indians' maneuvers. Nevertheless the Minnesota war was ended early in October, but not before the advanced settlement line had been drawn back, and the borderland left almost deserted. In Little Crow's war the Minnesota frontier had been thrown into almost the same kind of panic as had prevailed in Illinois during Black Hawk's War thirty years before.

When the Indians gave up the fight and began coming in to surrender at Fort Snelling, Sibley found that he had more than 1,500 prisoners on his hands. Local opinion was embittered, and there was an outcry that those who were guilty of inciting the war should be severely punished. There was not much public concern over guilt or innocence in selecting victims to be punished. General John Pope, in command of military forces in the Minnesota area, favored executing nearly 300 of the prisoners, and some Minnesotans were in a hurry to carry out his recommendations. President Lincoln, however, intervened, and possibly stayed much heedless action. Bishop Henry B. Whipple, the first Episcopal bishop of Minnesota, took a strong stand against such harsh treatment of the Indians. He had had considerable experience in Indian affairs, and was a sharp critic of the dilatory methods employed by the government. Despite the infuriated opinion of his neighbors, Bishop Whipple reviewed the failures of the government, revealed the crafty practices of the traders, and cited the crowding into Indian lands of white settlers. He published his views in the St. Paul *Pioneer* and the St. Paul *Press*, and in doing so no doubt lessened, if he did not check, the fury of the moment. Fearing delay and even presidential pardon for the prisoners, a mob undertook to seize the Indian captives and execute them without trial or care as to selection of victims. Bishop Whipple's plea and this mob action aroused public opinion the country over. Justice took a speedy toll, despite the conditions of overwrought opinion, and the day after Christmas, 1862, thirty-two Sioux prisoners were hanged at Mankato.

The Mankato executions did not end the Minnesota Indian problem. A demand now was made to drive the Sioux out of the Territory altogether. Henry Sibley was made a brigadier general with instructions to pursue and chastise the Indians who were now scattered over a wide area of the plains country and up the Mississippi River. In his big push up the Minnesota, Sibley commanded an army of 3,000 men. Late in July, 1862, he broke the Indians in the battles of Big Mound and Stony Lake. Engaging approximately 2,500 warriors in the last battle, Sibley scattered the tribes before him. Near Missouri Coteau, Little Crow was killed, and the whites took his scalp, skull and wristbones as gruesome relics. For another year small raiding bands harassed the settlers' peace of mind, but the day of Indian influence in Minnesota was ended.

Problems in the Plains and Mountains

While General Sibley was battling the Minnesota Indians, outbreaks occurred elsewhere on the frontier. Forcing the eastern Sioux to seek haven in the Missouri Valley had a highly disturbing effect upon the natives of the middle plains and mountain areas. The eastern refugees brought with them stories of the white man's war, and of their flight from their homelands. News of the Minnesota war spread panic in all the white frontier settlements and to the border posts north of the 38th parallel. In western Missouri, Kansas, Dakota and Iowa there was much uneasiness. Officials in Washington were besieged with telegrams and other pleas for help. In the popular mind the whole settlers' advance was on the verge of being drowned in blood.

Officers and soldiers who had been trained along the frontier were now fighting in northern Virginia, or pushing southward through Tennessee and Mississippi. Many of the officers who could be spared to patrol the Indian border were at best second- or third-rate men, and many of their soldiers were recruited along the border. Commanding officers such as Major General S. R. Curtis, Brigadier General Robert B. Mitchell, Brigadier General James Craig and Lieutenant Colonel J. M. Chivington, were either naive and incapable or were unfriendly toward the Indians. Their soldiers were largely men who looked upon Indians as animals and wished to destroy them in any way they could. This was especially true of men who were recruited in Colorado and in the mining areas of Montana. The border military posts were drab places where men suffered intense boredom at times. They had little or no recreation or diversion, and they resorted to heavy use of liquor and sometimes to malicious mischief for entertainment. There is some evidence that they took shots at innocent Indians for pastime.

From the Indian's point of view, his situation on the plains and in the mountains was becoming more precarious every year. Buffalo herds were being reduced at a highly perceptible rate. Already a string of wires across the Indian country carried the white man's telegraphic messages westward. The great stage route divided the plains country into halves, and freight and stage stations were tangible points of white expansion and settlement. In 1863 long trails of white covered wagons moved forward up the newly made Bozeman Trail from Julesburg on the South Platte, moved over the headwaters of the Platte, across the Tongue and the Rosebud and on beyond the Big Horn to the Yellowstone and Virginia City in the Montana goldfields. The opening of this trail was properly regarded as a serious invasion of Indian lands, for it pierced the heart of the Sioux hunting preserve. The next decade was to see many attacks made upon its posts and way stations before the last one was abandoned. In many respects it was one of the greatest irritants to the Indians in this part of the West.

The great wagon road up the Platte and westward to Denver fed its continual stream of canvas-topped prairie schooners onto the plains. Not only did they bring rich stores of goods, but many of them dropped off land speculators and settlers' families who came to stay. Oglalas, Brulés, Miniconjous, Hunkpapas, and other Sioux groups as well as Cheyennes and Arapahoes watched this white activity with something approaching panic. Between the Arkansas and the Platte their lands were slipping away; they were being hemmed in, and they were unwilling to acknowledge the paper agreement of 1860 in which some of their chiefs had cleared the way for the coming of this white horde.

Sand Creek

Along the roads and about the white stations, the Cheyennes were finding post raiding a profitable thing. Colonel J. M. Chivington, once a Methodist minister and an Indian missionary, had moved to hold the Cheyennes at bay. Rumor ran strong that a Confederate contingent was pulling northward from New Mexico and other southern points. The rebels, however, failed to appear, but the Cheyenne problem loomed large in the mind of Indian-hater Chivington. Along the Platte the white posts were being attacked, and the Indians found it easy to capture men, animals, and goods. By 1864 they had disrupted a long stretch of the overland stage line and had forced a redirection of the United States mail to California.

As winter came on in 1864, two chiefs—Black Kettle and White Antelope—both of whom had called upon the Great White Father in Washington and had some appreciation of the white man's might, led their friendly Cheyenne and Arapahoe followers into winter camp on Sand Creek almost under the shadow of Fort Lyon in Colorado. On November 29, 1864, Colonel Chivington attacked this encampment of 200 war-riors and 500 women and children and slaughtered large numbers of them in what seemed to be cold blood. Estimates of the number of Indians killed range from 150 to 500. Conditions under which the raid was con-ducted seem to establish that it was a heartless and unnecessary attack. Naturally controversy surrounded an incident where the aggressors would emphasize the faithlessness and treacherous nature of their victims, yet the evidence seems to be all but conclusive that Black Kettle and White Antelope's people were of peaceful intent. White Antelope was killed. Black Kettle, after seeing his wife shot, escaped only to be driven from his place of leadership and even from his tribe.

Sand Creek stands historically as a bloody monument to lack of judg-ment, calmness, and humanity on the part of Curtis and Chivington. Their act hastened the passage of the war pipe from one Indian winter camp to another. Sioux, Brulés, Arapahoes, Oglalas, and southern Cheyennes were aroused to avenge this bloody assault outside Fort Lyons. Their first retaliatory blow came in January, 1865, against the isolated frontier post and stage station at Julesburg. Eighteen soldiers and civilians were killed, and the other residents were driven into the stockade while screaming warriors ran away a rich haul of horses and cattle and grabbed the stock of the stage company's warehouses and store. During the rest of the year Indian raiding between the Arkansas and the Platte seriously threatened settler and soldier alike. The price the combined tribes exacted for Chiving-ton's brutality at Sand Creek was indeed a heavy one. Likewise the Sand Creek affair was to have its repercussions to the east on the Kansas frontier.

Civil War

Although the Colorado massacre was not specifically a part of the Civil War, it did have some connections with it. The War itself had varying effects upon the Indian question in the West. For those Indians who looked to the government for annuities, there were frequent delays and some-times even failures to deliver them. Financing the Civil War was a major undertaking, and the Indians were asked to be patient and await the com-ing of peace. Likewise there was a withdrawal of troops from the western posts, and many tribes which faced interference from the military before 1861 were now freed to continue their traditional wandering. Where frontier posts were maintained, they were often staffed with officers and men of limited training and experience. Among the civilized tribes some Indians fought in the Union Army, but more supported the South. When war broke out, the Oklahoma Indians were under the administrative control of the southern superintendency. When the Confederacy was formed in 1861, General Albert Pike became Confederate Indian commissioner. He sought to win the support of the tribes by making a swing through the Indian country in which he signed treaties with the Chickasaws, Choctaws, Seminoles, and Creeks. Under the leadership of Chief John Ross the Cherokees at first held off making an alliance with the South, but they did follow the examples of their neighbors at last and cast their lot with the Confederacy.

There was some friction among the Indians themselves between the pro-Southern and pro-Union groups. The Unionists became semipolitical refugees who were dependent upon the Union military posts for protection and support. On at least two occasions these refugees returned to their homelands from Kansas and assisted in attempts to win support for the North. Cherokee troops took part in the battle of Pea Ridge in Arkansas, and Colonel Stand Watie became a distinguished officer in the Confederate service. John Ross, however, continued to support the Union. After 1863 and the fall of Vicksburg, the Indians ceased to be of much importance in the war. One block of the Cherokees even repudiated their alliance with the Confederacy in the Cowskin Prairie meeting of that year. At most it can be said only that the Indians who participated in the war inherited the white man's political troubles and gained neither advantage nor glory for themselves. Union expeditions twice entered the Indian Territory. The first invasion occurred in 1862 when Colonel William Weer and William A. Phillips captured Talluquah and moved on to occupy the famous old frontier post at Fort Gibson.

Children of the Plains

Farther west, the plains Indians had little or no notion of the white conflict east of the Mississippi. They heard rumors of the Civil War, but it is doubtful that they had any really intelligent concept of its meaning, nor did they fully appreciate the ultimate strength of the United States Government. Three things stood out in their minds. First, the annuity payments were slow in reaching them; second, the Sioux and Santees from Minnesota and the Cheyennes and Arapahoes who had suffered from Chivington's murderous attack made out a strong case against the dependability of the government; third, the various raids on white posts and along the roads yielded rich returns in animals and goods; and, finally, competition was growing oppressive for possession of the rapidly shrinking island of land available to the two races.

At the end of the war, many Union officers and troops were shifted from the battlefields of the East to the frontier posts in the West. In the first postwar years the military leadership was not skillful enough to cope with the crafty tactics of the combined Indian foes. Hardly had the Grand Review ended in Washington, before Indian chieftains on the upper Platte were organizing an all-out drive against the invaders. Pitted against such fumbling military leaders as Major General S. R. Curtis and Brigadier Alfred Sully were the clever chiefs Red Cloud, Man-Afraid-of-His-Horses, High Backbone, Little Wolf, and others. A large combination of Indians organized to thwart the white army. There were Cheyennes, Oglalas, Sans Arcs, Miniconjous, Sioux, Brulés, and Hunkpapas. Possibly the most outstanding leader in this group was Red Cloud, chief of the Oglalas and Teton Sioux. It was he who had strode out of the Laramie Council in 1865 in a rage when the United States Government sought rights to open the Bozeman Trail, and it was his effective campaigning that forced the closing of that trail in 1868. He combined in his character the traits of a gentleman, the temper of a wild man, the suspicions of an Indian, and the loves of a natural man of the plains.

Before he gave up warring against the white man, Red Cloud had led his Indian army in several effective raids, the two most important of which were Fetterman's Defeat in December, 1866, and the Wagon Box Fight of the next year. The Sioux war in the Powder River country was provoked by the Indian determination to close the Bozeman Trail, and by the highly unrealistic attitude taken by officials in Washington. There was a prevailing belief that peace could be negotiated with the Sioux and their allies and that costly campaigning could be avoided. A peace commission with General Curtis at its head was sent out early in the fall of 1865 with a steamboat load of presents to make terms with the Indians on the headwaters of the Missouri and Platte. In October of that year a treaty was made, but it was made only with the friendly Indians along the river and not with the hostile group which remained away from the council ground and its heap of presents. General Curtis and his associate Newton Edwards apparently remained oblivious of true conditions in the Little Missouri and Powder River country.

This tricky peace in October, 1865, was to be near fatal for large numbers of people. Travelers on their way over the Bozeman Trail to the Montana gold fields were lulled into a false sense of security. Both military and political officials had a dangerously superficial notion of the state of affairs in the West, and they blundered most stupidly in sending troops up the Platte. In the spring of 1866, E. B. Taylor of the Indian Office, in Washington went out to Fort Laramie with Colonel H. E. Maynadier in an attempt to bring the hostile Sioux to peace terms, but because of the proposal to keep open the road piercing the heart of the Powder River country, the hostile chiefs would not sign. Again the realities of the situation were obscured by a failure to report on the true conditions.

While Taylor and Maynadier were attempting to secure peace, Colonel Henry B. Carrington appeared on the upper Platte with a large command of infantry and a wagon train. Because of the sense of false security existing along the line, Colonel Carrington, an administrative officer, had been sent out to build two military posts to protect the road across the Sioux country. He was to establish Fort Phil Kearny on the Piney Fork and Fort C. F. Smith on the Big Horn. There is every indication that Colonel Carrington ignored the signs of war which appeared about him. He was an efficient army quartermaster rather than a field officer. For a long period beforehand, the Indians had planned blows to be made against the two offending outposts, and on December 21, 1866, the blow fell near Fort Phil Kearny.

The Sioux under the leadership of Crazy Horse, Red Cloud, and High Backbone and others executed a perfect trap for Captain William Fetterman and the hundred men who had gone out with him to protect a train of wood gatherers. A decoy led Fetterman and his men between Lodge Trail Ridge and Reno Head to a level valley, and there the main body of warriors surrounded and killed the entire company. The bodies of Fetterman's men were found huddled within a plot forty feet square.

Fetterman's defeat came as a sharp and bloody warning that the whole Indian question was to be re-opened and belied the optimism of blundering and uninformed peacemakers. The following year was one of constant raiding. The failures of Indian commissioner and soldier to relieve the tense situation which prevailed in the Platte, Powder and Missouri River triangle were most disturbing. Red Cloud and his fellow chiefs, leading their federation of many tribal groups, challenged the United States Army to put forth its maximum efforts. No one knew how many troops it would take to remove the red menace from this part of the frontier.

Less than a year after Fetterman's defeat, the occupants of Fort Phil Kearny again experienced an Indian onslaught. This time a company under the command of Captain J. N. Powell were standing guard over a band of woodcutters when the Indians once more attempted to trap the white troops by their famous decoy trick. The attempt to draw the troops into a trap failed largely because the over-anxious braves refused to wait until the precise moment to attack. Captain Powell removed the boxes from his wagons and arranged them as a temporary fortress. The whites had an advantage in another way. They were equipped with the new-type breech-loading, pin-firing rifles, and they were able to stand off their attackers with a deadly fire. The Wagon Box Fight was of major importance. Captain Powell's infantrymen had proved the new rifles an effective weapon against the Indians, and the incident jolted the government officials into the realization that they would have to embark upon a full-dress war if they hoped to defeat the Sioux. It was also clearly demonstrated that Red Cloud was leading a real army and not a small band of Indians as some had supposed to be the case. Colonel Carrington was recalled from the Phil Kearny command in favor of a more vigorous and experienced field officer. A vigorous policy of defeating the Indians and then resettling them on a reservation was obviously the only chance for peace in the Sioux country, for the Indians had no intention of surrendering by treaty their claims to their rich territory.

Not only was there armed conflict in the upper plains country with the Sioux, but there was also a sharp difference of opinion between the civilian peacemakers and the army about the proper methods by which the belligerents could be brought to terms. In Washington two basic questions dominated administrative discussions. The first of these was the proposal to concentrate the western Indians on reservations; the second was the argument which had gone on since 1849 about transferring the management of Indian affairs back to the army.

In view of the intensity of Indian resistance, the peacemakers proposed to meet the demands of the tribes by withdrawing all troops from the Indian hunting grounds. In 1867 a peace commission composed of N. G. Taylor, General J. B. Sanborn, and General W. S. Harney, with the assistance of such persons as Father DeSmet, Reverend S. D. Hinman and others, set out to secure signatures to a new treaty. This commission, however, had the same experience as had others in the past. The peaceful Indians were ready to sign, but the really important chiefs refused to meet the commissioners. Although the army was clamorously ready to force the Indians to come to terms, any increased activity on the part of the military promised to bring about an extended Sioux war. No one appears to have known fully what would be involved in an all-out war against Red Cloud and his allies. Making a true peace with the Sioux seemed a virtual impossibility. The conditions under which the Indians were willing to make peace involved the white man getting out of their hunting grounds and destroying the roads and fortresses which he had built there.

President Grant's Indian Policy

When General Grant was elevated to the Presidency, he advocated a policy of peaceful settlement, which, of course, meant that the army would be less in evidence, and that the Indian agencies would become more responsible. The President had inherited an enormous number of major problems of reconstruction and readjustment everywhere in the nation, but few of these more urgently demanded solution than those pertaining to Indian affairs. An important part of Grant's plan for making peace with the western tribes was to have the American churches supply agents and participate actively in the administration of Indian affairs. He was aware that there had been a strong current of humanitarianism running in favor of the Indians for the last forty years.

Characteristic of social thinking in this postwar period, was the fixed belief that a principal cause of failure of Indian administration was dishonesty of the agents. If honest and Christian men could only be found for agents, then an important source of Indian troubles would be removed. The prevailing belief was that honesty was not one of the government's possessions. Without doubt there was a crying need for honesty in Indian management, but an intelligent concept of the nature of the Indian problem was also lacking. No one had been given formal training in the operation of agencies and reservations. Few administrators had sufficient sociological and psychological experience to meet the task, first of concentrating a free and nomadic people within a defined geographical area, and then converting them from a hunting to a localized agrarian way of life. There was such implicit faith in the white man's domesticated scheme of frontier livelihood that well-meaning but ignorant administrators thought it inconceivable that the Indians could not adopt it without extensive and time-consuming conditioning.

By bringing the American churches into the plan for administering Indian affairs, the Grant administration embarked upon a vexing social experiment which was a departure from both constitutional and political tradition in this country. Primarily, it was believed that the churches were reservoirs of integrity and that they could do what the government had failed to do—find honest Indian agents. While it may be true that the churches had access to honest and well-meaning men, they could not solve the bigger problems of training, the loneliness and dangers of isolated Indian agencies, the great economic problems of Indian and government, and the changing of Indian mores and customs. Churches were basically interested in saving men's souls, and those of their members who were willing to become missionaries were seldom if ever skilled in the art of business and personnel management. Those who had such abilities preferred to stay nearer home where the joys of salvation and economic well-being were more comfortably blended.

In this land of religious freedom there was no such thing as an established American Church. There were scores of denominations which immediately began bickering over the assignments of posts. President Grant and the Indian Bureau got a lesson in religious rivalries and in the complexities of American church organization and attitudes. Differences of views among Protestants, Catholics and Jews tended to become magnified once they approached the Indian problem under governmental direction, and much confusion resulted. Among the Protestant denominations heat was generated over purely competitive matters. Some of the churches had foreign mission programs and were unable to stir their constituents to further financial effort or to interest them in the Indians of the West. Others feared a change of government policy with the departure from office of President Grant and were reluctant to commit themselves too heavily by participating in the peace policy. Denominations contended over the number and location of agencies assigned to them. In spite of all the drawbacks and loss of time, it must be said that the scheme of church participation in Indian affairs had a reasonable and extensive test and that it was largely a failure. The fault, however, lay not with the churches, but rather in a lack of understanding of the whole broad problem of Indian resettlement and governmental relationships with a people who as late as 1870 were regarded as belonging to separate nations and social groups though they inhabited lands within the territorial limits of the United States.

In the midst of the Sioux crisis the government resorted to the old device of inviting important Indian chiefs to Washington to visit the Great White Father and those of his assistants who had charge of Indian matters. Red Cloud, Spotted Tail, Red Dog, Brave Bear, Little Bear, Swift Bear and others were taken from the western country to Washington to visit President Grant and to see all the sights of civilization. It was an open question whether the greater curiosities were the Washington ladies with their décolleté gowns standing in the reception line trying to appear gay before the unsophisticated children of the plains, or the simple Indians with their feathers and mixture of plains and city clothing. The social managers of the Sioux learned a lot about Indian jealousies and stubbornness and were frequently at their wits' end to smooth over the little incidents that occurred at every turn. One mandatory amenity was that the chiefs have their pictures taken. It is doubtful if the procession of Indian chiefs to Washington ever brought a wilder delegation than Red Cloud's, but through it all the great Sioux chief kept his head and his perspective. His price for peace was withdrawal of soldier and settler from his people's hunting grounds and the abandonment of forts Phil Kearny, C. F. Smith and the Bozeman Trail.

From Washington, Red Cloud was virtually kidnapped and taken on to New York where he was presented to an audience that was highly favorable to his cause. When the great chieftain and his traveling companions returned West, they carried with them rich government presents and some concept of the white man's power. In the fall of 1868 the groundwork for peace was laid, and Red Cloud and his fellow chiefs, Man-Afraid-of-His-Horses, Red Dog and American Horse came to terms with the peace commissioners, F. R. Brunot and Robert Campbell. A large quantity of goods was distributed, and between October 5th and 7th the agreement was signed. This treaty removed the Indians from the path of the Union Pacific Railroad in Kansas and Nebraska. A Sioux reservation was to be created in present-day South Dakota west of the Missouri River, and for four years the Indians were to be fed and trained for domesticated life. Finally it was agreed that the offending forts would be removed and the Powder River-Big Horn-Rosebud-Tongue River area would become unceded Indian territory and would be closed to white entry.

One important question was left unresolved in the negotiations of 1868 and that was the location of the Sioux trading agency. Lack of opportunities to trade had hurt the Sioux and their allies. They had accumulated large stores of buffalo skins and other commodities, but they had been unable to dispose of them. Dispute over the trading agency centered about its location and the particular traders who would be permitted to deal with the Indians. Though the great Sioux war was averted, Red Cloud was far from being defeated. He was both proud and haughty, and peace for the future depended upon grants from the government. Actual peace in the Sioux country was still somewhat remote. The agreement of 1868 was by no means conclusive, and the stage was set for the crisis which led to the Custer holocaust eight years later.

Between the signing of the treaty of 1868 and the year 1876, Indian affairs in the Powder River country were colored by many incidents. Soldiers continued to patrol the frontier and to trail hostile bands. The Spotted Tail, Red Cloud and Standing Pine agencies were organized and relocated a time or two and made some headway toward drawing the Indians in from the plains and mountains and establishing them on reservations. In Washington, Congress itself had changed its policies. After two-and-a-half centuries, the whites on the North American continent were abandoning the ancient and defective treaty device. A clause inserted in the Indian appropriation bill adopted into law on March 3, 1871, required that the government no longer recognize Indian nations and tribes as powers with which treaties could be made. This action finally resolved the ancient dispute between the House of Representatives and the Senate about the Senate's making treaties which required appropriations by the House to validate them.

The Sioux

The Indian agency in the Sioux country was faced with a multitude of practical problems. Securing the services of good agents was almost beyond hope in the prevailing social and political situation. The congressional crisis over the large Indian appropriation bill of $2,312,240.12 in the Fortieth Congress resulted in failure of the House to adopt the bill. This meant that the government could not deliver on its agreement made in the treaty of 1868. There was conflict between the Indian Bureau officials and the military forces. Jealousies between soldiers and civil officials were many. Rumors of mismanagement, coddling, supplying with arms, and other agency shortcomings were used against the civil officials. The Indian population on the reservations rose and fell with the seasons. In spring, summer and fall the Indians went off to their hunting grounds, and in the winter they hustled back to the agencies. This was true of both friendly and hostile Indians; in fact, it was most difficult to tell just who was friendly or hostile in cold weather. The Indians themselves were hard to satisfy. They took the attitude on occasion that the agents were their servants and treated them with great inconsideration and discourtesy. They complained about the slowness with which presents were handed out, demanded special concessions and otherwise made themselves aggravating. There were, however, many among the Indian leaders who could read the handwriting in the sands—the buffalo were disappearing from the plains, the iron rails of the transcontinental railroads were cutting the country in half, and the force of white expansion was yearly becoming more irresistible. The roving bands of Sioux and Cheyennes could still give a good account of themselves, but their days of wild freedom were rapidly drawing to a close.

Since the Civil War the Sioux country had been troubled by periodic outbreaks, but the treaty of 1868 with its territorial definitions had somewhat appeased the Indians. There was some temporary promise at least that their hunting grounds would be left undisturbed. In 1874, however, this hope faded when General George Custer set out from Fort Abraham Lincoln on the Missouri to locate a route to Fort Laramie. On the way, gold was discovered in the Black Hills by members of his company, and within a year there was a wild rush of miners and gold-camp hangers-on into this Sioux heartland. General Custer's great scouting expedition had amounted only to a glorified prospecting journey.

During the decade following the Civil War, the United States army had been redistributed, and, reminiscent of the ante-bellum period, the border service had again claimed the most attention. The blundering and inexperienced officers who had formerly been in command of the western posts were replaced by men battle-seasoned in the Civil War. Chivington, Mitchell, Curtis and others were replaced by General Phil Sheridan, General Nelson A. Miles, General George Crook, General Alfred Terry, General O. O. Howard, Colonel George A. Custer, Major M. A. Reno, and many others.

Six years of the peace policy had brought little peace. Red Cloud and Spotted Tail with many of their fellow chiefs and warriors had come into the agencies which bore their names and had given up, but this had not ended Sioux resistance. Crazy Horse and Sitting Bull were still at large with bands of warriors which fluctuated with the seasons from 1,500 to 4,000 strong. At least seven tribal circles could be counted at the main camping site, which meant that the old allies—Cheyennes, Hunkpapas, Oglalas, Brulés, Sans Arcs, and Miniconjous with a scattering of Yanktonnais and Santees—were still banded together to hold their hunting grounds. They were led by such men as Sitting Bull, Crazy Horse, Black Moon, Big Road, Gall, and others. Sitting Bull, a Hunkpapa chief, was head of the war council and a medicine man rather than a fighter. He engaged in the big Sun Dance just prior to the victory of 1876 and danced until he sank into a state of unconsciousness. When he revived, he had received a vision that foretold the future. He saw white soldiers falling into the Indian camp upside down.

While Sitting Bull swooned in the great Sun Dance, white soldiers were on their way to fall into his camp as he predicted. On May 17, 1875, General Alfred Terry led his command of 600 cavalrymen and 400 infantrymen westward from Fort Abraham Lincoln on the Missouri opposite Bismark, North Dakota, to the Sioux country about the head streams of the Powder River. The central unit of this expedition was the Seventh Regiment of cavalry. Organization of this regiment was authorized on July 28, 1866, and it had been since commanded by Colonel George Armstrong Custer. Custer was a colorful officer of long and able service in the battlefield. He had graduated from West Point at the foot of a class of thirty-one. At the outbreak of the Civil War he proved himself a good officer at the first battle of Bull Run, and it was he who in the end blocked Lee's progress before Appomattox. When the war ended, Custer had attained the honorary rank of major general, but in active service he was reduced to rank of captain. After extensive border service he rose again to a colonelcy. Custer had been called to testify in the famous Belknap scandal about graft in the War Department, and his testimony had given great offense to General Grant. Because of this he narrowly missed being denied the privilege of returning to his command of the Seventh Cavalry as it set out for the Powder River country.

Movement of troops in this area was a part of the government's changed policy toward the hostile Indians who had refused to sell their lands in the Black Hills and come into the agencies and give up warring against the whites. Without doubt the military had chafed under the peace policy regime. It was obvious that there was a marked discrepancy between the number of Indians that could actually be counted in the agency reservations and the amount of supplies issued as reported by the agents. For instance, at the Red Cloud agency only 4,600 Indians could be counted, but twice this number had been reported by the agent. The military were convinced that the peace policy was a failure and that the only language the Sioux and their allies could understand was that of bullets. Yet they had to stand by and see the agencies supply the enemy with food, clothing, arms and ammunition. During the winters hundreds of Indians came in from the plains and mountains to accept governmental hospitality, but when spring broke, they returned to their hunting grounds with new equipment and arms to lead their wandering wild life.

Back in Washington there was constant confusion over the management of Indian affairs. The issue of transferring control of recalcitrant tribes back to the army was a bitter one. President Grant's peace policy seemed pretty tepid to the robust border warriors, who could see peace only in piles of Indian corpses. This bureaucratic infighting came to a head in the winter of 1875–1876 when the army found a satisfactory excuse to order the hostile Indians into their assigned agencies by January 31, 1876, or be driven in by troops.

Runners were sent to all of the winter camps with the War Department instructions, but no results were accomplished. Instead, the orders seem rather to have unified the hostile bands. Before the spring thaw began, General George Crook left Fort Fetterman with ten cavalry and two infantry companies to strike the hostile tribes while they were still in winter camps. He marched his command through the rugged winter weather with light stores, hoping to capture well-filled Indian camps and to feed his men off the country. In the middle of March the expedition came on fresh signs of Indians, and on March 17, Colonel J. J. Reynolds led an attack on what was said to be Crazy Horse's camp near the mouth of the Little Powder River. He caught the Indians early in the morning by complete surprise, ran them away from their lodges, and destroyed the supplies which he was supposed to take, for he was forced to retreat from the captured camp because of the strong show of Indian force. Destruction of the Little Powder encampment denied the Sioux a large stock of powder and lead which had just arrived from the agencies, and also they lost their winter food supply and a large portion of their extensive horse herd. Reynold's failure to save the Indian supplies left Crook without food and a safe base of operation, and he was obliged to return to Fort Fetterman. Behind him he left Crazy Horse and Sitting Bull satisfied that they had defeated the white army.

In June when the army again took to the field, there was at least a rough overall plan of strategy. Crook was to come up from Fort Fetterman with his troops, while Terry and Custer pushed toward the Powder River from the east. The two forces were to converge and act as support to each other. Once in the field the first task of the army was that of locating the Indians' encampment. The terrain of the country was rugged, communication was almost impossible, and it was most difficult to find an Indian camp; consequently, the early army activities amounted to little more than scouting advances.

Terry's command was in a sense engaged in scouting the countryside in search of information. His officer personnel was a rare study in conflicting personalities and intense jealousies. Both Captain Frederick Benteen and Major Marcus A. Reno disliked Colonel Custer. Reno was given the task of scouting for Indian trails along the Powder and Tongue Rivers, trails which he found about June 20th and reported to General Terry the next day. Terry then formulated his plan to send Colonel John Gibbon with his four hundred infantrymen along the Big Horn in a flanking move. Custer was to lead the entire Seventh Cavalry up the Rosebud until he came on the trail reported by Reno. He was to ascertain the direction it led, and if it went up the Little Big Horn, he was to swing south to the headwaters of the Tongue and then advance northward so as to meet Gibbon's approaching forces.

Custer took with him the crack scout George Herendeen who was to keep General Terry, then with Gibbon, informed of Custer's movement. In the controversy which has prevailed since June 25, 1876, it has been charged that Terry's orders lacked positiveness and that Custer was left free to follow his judgment. No one can say what Custer had in mind when he began his march to the Little Big Horn. It is known that he force-marched his men, and if he seriously intended to follow Terry's instructions, he threw the timing off. Also, Custer—along with Terry, Crook and all the rest who had opposed the Sioux—had no idea how strong an army of warriors he would meet. Even had he known, it is doubtful that he would have exercised the necessary caution demanded because of his low esteem for the Indians' will to stand and fight.

Further on the debit side of the ledger, no one had anything like a correct notion of how well armed were Sitting Bull's warriors. They did not know precisely where the Sioux camp was or if it existed anywhere near the Little Big Horn Valley. When Terry sent Gibbon and Custer forward, he no doubt hoped to surround the Indians rather than assault them in a bold frontal attack. Custer's strategy was quite the opposite of Terry's.

About 9 A.M. on June 24 he found signs which indicated that the Indians were in the valley of the Little Big Horn. He moved up rapidly to be in a position to make a predawn attack, but when his scouts finally determined the proximity of the camp from the divide above Reno's Fork of the Little Big Horn, Custer's troops were still fifteen miles away. It was now impossible to make a surprise attack. Custer knew that his presence had been discovered when soldiers returning down the trail found an Indian inspecting the contents of a pack which had been dropped. Also, they had seen lookouts observing them.

From the Crow's Nest lookout on the divide overlooking the valley the scouts saw a high swirl of dust off in the distance which misled Custer into believing the Sioux were running away. Possibly he doubted that there actually was a camp in the near vicinity and believed he could take chances.

At noon of the 25th he divided his forces into three parts. One command he sent off under Benteen to scout to the left as far as two or three succeeding distant ridges; the second he sent forward under the command of Major Reno, and the third he led up the right bank of the creek himself. As Reno advanced on the Indian village, he faced a dust screen which obscured the massed warriors behind it. When he charged the Indian line, it offered heavy resistance, and within minutes his men were forced either to retreat or suffer annihilation. Reno was able to withdraw those of his men who remained and cross the Little Big Horn to the high barren ground where he was forced to remain for the next twenty-four hours.

In the meantime Custer had pushed ahead to the slope of the ridge above the camp. There he ran head-on into the full Sioux charge. No one can ever say precisely what took place. Custer and his entire command of 225 men were killed. The only living thing known to escape was Captain Keogh's badly wounded horse Comanche. An argument has persisted as to the fate of Lieutenant H. M. Harrington. His body was never found, and no one knows what happened to him.

Two days later when Lieutenant James H. Bradley, at the head of Gibbon's scouts, found the stripped bodies of his comrades on the field, Custer's face bore an expression of peace, and there was no sign of mutilation on his body. Reno and Benteen's men were saved by the appearance of Terry and Gibbon's forces. Benteen had returned from his scouting mission and by his courage had rallied the hysterical Reno's men to the defense. No doubt he saved them from Custer's fate. The Sioux were again victorious, but in many ways their victory was a Pyrrhic one. Never again were they able to offer such rugged resistance.

Almost before the dust settled on the Little Big Horn battlefield, arguments began about where the blame lay. Both Reno and Benteen were accused of failure to support Custer, and Terry was criticized for not making his orders specific. Those who attacked Custer accused him of driving his command ahead without waiting for Gibbon and Terry to come up, and without sufficiently scouting the Indian position. He was charged with violating orders, disregarding the safety of his men, and of seeking selfish glory in a fight that would wipe away the ill will in Washington against him. As always following disastrous frontier attacks, charges and counter-charges were hurled. This was not the first time that Custer had played the role of scapegoat. In 1867 he was accused of causing the failure of Hancock's Indian campaign.

Custer's disaster will ever remain a foggy issue because dead men bear no testimony about their thoughts and intended actions. The Indians themselves followed their leaders in a wild and individualistic defense, and they were never able to piece together a thoroughly adequate story. When the battle was over, they returned to their hunting grounds for the rest of the summer. They broke up into smaller groups, and in the following winter most of them showed up at the agencies. Sitting Bull and a band of followers fled to Canada, but in 1881 he came in and surrendered and spent the rest of his life on a reservation hating white men.

The Nez Percé

While white soldiers and Sioux braves struggled for possession of the lands between the Missouri and Platte and along the headstreams, the Nez Percé of the Wallowa Valley in Oregon and Idaho between the Blue and Bitter Root Mountains had troubles of their own. Land-hungry settlers had eyed this territory since the 1850's. Beginning with 1855 these Indians had agreed to treaties with the whites in which they transferred large blocks of lands to the United States Government. The Nez Percé were highly intelligent Indians who led a semi-nomadic life in their mountain valley paradise along the Snake River. One main source of their livelihood, like that of the Sioux, was the great northern buffalo herd which they had access to through the mountain passes. The Idaho gold rush around Lewiston in 1860 brought them their first major trouble from white invaders. As gold seekers poured in, it was necessary to negotiate a second treaty in which Nez Percé lands were further reduced. At the head of the tribes was the able Chief Joseph. Like his father before him, he refused to acknowledge the terms of the treaty of 1863 largely because it proposed to confine his people to the Lapwai Reservation in Idaho.

Between 1863 and 1875 numerous negotiations with the Nez Percé sought to reduce their homelands. The state government of Oregon was insistent that the federal government remove the Indians. In 1876 a special commission, of which Zachariah Chandler, Secretary of Interior, was a member, visited Chief Joseph for the purpose of talking him onto a reservation. Again in 1877 General O. O. Howard, a master of Indian diplomacy, visited the Nez Percé chief insisting that he accept annuities and generous portions of white man's culture in exchange for the tribal lands. Joseph and his followers would agree to no proposition that would disrupt their established mode of life.

Relations between the Nez Percé and their white neighbors were tense. Joseph's young men were aroused, and in an unfortunate moment started a fight. First they settled personal scores, but soon troops appeared and the Indians were forced into a running battle. Against his will Chief Joseph was drawn into the conflict and was forced to flee with his people across the rugged mountain country. Burdened with his women and children, the crafty Indian leader took his followers more than 1,300 miles and fought the troops under Howard, Terry, Gibbon and Miles nearly all the way. He slipped through the mountain passes and eluded his pursuers with unbelievable skill. Once he was caught by surprise in the battle of Big Hole River in Montana, but he held his forces together and defeated Gibbon. At Camas Meadows he cut the bells off a lead mare and ran the horse herd through the soldiers' night camp to repay for the Big Hole surprise.

Joseph worked his way toward Canada, but the odds were too great. He was cornered at Sanke Creek on Bear Paw Mountain in Montana by General Miles. In one of the most eloquent of Indian speeches, he informed General Miles that his people were cold, hungry and wounded and could go no farther. He called the roll of those of his compatriots who had fallen, and then promised not to fight again. In his flight he had brought the restored Seventh Cavalry into the field and had raced the one-armed General Howard 1,321 miles in 75 days. The other officers had covered a tremendous amount of ground and had endured many hardships. When General Miles accepted Chief Joseph's surrender, he found that this master strategist had entrenched his warriors and had used his pitiful army to its best advantage. From Bear Paw Mountain the Nez Percé were started on a long and unhappy journey which took them to the Indian Territory and then back to reservations in Idaho and Washington. Chief Joseph and 150 followers were sent to Coleville Reservation in Washington where the old chief died in 1904.

A War of Attrition

To the southwest the Indian problem was as complex and troublous as on the northern plains. Since the Santa Fe Trail was opened and trade and travel began in this region, the Indians had offered a threat to personal safety. Actually the problem of peace was much greater than the mere numbers of Indians would indicate. There were not over 70,000 in New Mexico, Arizona and Nevada, and these were distributed among the four or five major groups of Apaches, Pimas, Navajo, and Pueblos. The Apaches were, in the minds of the whites, devils who were as highly adapted to the plains and desert as horned frogs. They were good fighters, adept at getting around in the arid country, and they lived by a code of pillage and murder when opportunities presented themselves. During the Civil War they got out of hand, and between 1865 and 1887 they caused the United States Army to expend a vastly disproportionate amount of energy in bringing them to peaceful confinement on reservations.

During the seventeen years that the army was running down Apaches in the Southwest an illustrious parade of Civil War field officers saw service in the region. Among these were O. O. Howard, George Crook, E. O. C. Ord, J. M. Schofield, Irvin McDowell, and Nelson A. Miles. With these were several thousand subordinate officers and men. Because the Apaches committed countless atrocities in their hit-and-run tactics and because trailing them was akin to trying to catch a phantom, the whites in the region lived in a constant state of terror. There was a popular clamor to exterminate the Indians wherever they were found, regardless of any protestations of friendship which they might make. For both the army and Indian agent, the big task was that of getting the nomadic Apaches to exchange their ancient mode of life for a more restricted one on a reservation.

As a part of this program Vincent Colyer, Secretary of the Board of Indian Commissioners, General O. O. Howard and General George Crook traveled thousands of miles in efforts to secure the surrender and peaceful removal of the offending Apaches. General Howard, more than any other officer, ventured far afield in efforts to get the Indians to desert the warpath. One of his greatest exploits was that of tracking down Chief Cochise in the Chiricahua mountains. After a fascinating visit with the famous old raider he was able to persuade him to give up and go to a reservation. It was difficult to make peace with the Apaches because they were afraid of white men and they knew something of the intensely bitter local opinion which favored execution of every defenseless Indian.

By 1873 most of the southwestern Indians had found their way onto a reservation, but a contingent of Apaches remained free to cause constant

trouble. Leader of these was the old bandit Geronimo. He and his followers raided back and forth over the Mexican border causing panic in both
countries. They murdered and pillaged wherever they went. In March,
1877, agent John P. Clum of the San Carlos Reservation succeeded in
arresting Geronimo and was holding him for trial when criticism of Clum
caused him to resign. Geronimo was allowed to go free by the succeeding
agent H. L. Hart, and for the next nine years he was a veritable terror
in the Southwest. Before his second capture Geronimo cost the government thousands of dollars and had occupied the attention of an astonishingly large number of troops. But in August, 1886, he, like Chief Joseph,
was cornered by General Miles and was forced to surrender. This time
he and his warriors were sent off under heavy guard to Fort Pickens,
Florida. In 1894 they were removed to Fort Sill, Oklahoma. Geronimo
became a much sought-after public figure. He was with Pawnee Bill's Wild
West Show, he visited the St. Louis, Buffalo and Omaha expositions, and
on March 5, 1905, he was prominently displayed in the Roosevelt inaugural parade. General Franklin J. Bell called him, in 1907, "a worthless,
thriftless old vagabond, apparently without either pride or self-respect."
Geronimo's greatest triumph was posthumous. In the Second World War
his name was adopted as a jumping shout by the paratroopers.

Adopting the White Man's Culture

Back of the Indian upheaval all across the frontier was the onrush of
settlers and the competition for land. The government was forced by degrees to develop a policy that would promote both peace and the humane
and economic welfare of the tribes. For the Indians to continue free and
with full access to the vast areas of western lands was out of the question,
no matter what emotional objections were raised. Nevertheless, the United
States Government permitted bloodshed and waste of energy to take place
for lack of any efficient and imaginative policy that actually attempted to
solve the Indian problem. Indian commissioners were caught between
points of view of two extreme groups: the extremely sentimental and good,
but inexperienced people, and the corrupt and selfish who sought gain by
any means. Almost every evil that could be thought up by crafty exploiters was allowed to prevail at some time before sufficient reform was made.
The agency system was never entirely satisfactory. Its failures ranged
from personal bickering among little officials to maladministration. Some
posts were efficiently managed and did achieve marked success, but they
were in a minority. Grant's peace policy on the whole was ineffective,
doing little more than involve an already ticklish problem in an unnecessary
dispute among the churches and between the civilian Indian management

and the military. As Loring Benson Priest has said in his competent book, *Uncle Sam's Stepchildren*, "The so-called Peace Policy of these years was more a product of confusion regarding the proper course to pursue than of an intelligent effort to solve Indian problems."

Public opinion, though often aroused, was seldom intelligently informed about the true situation on the frontier. The treaty device was a failure, and attempts to maintain reservations and concentrations of Indians was often just as unsuccessful. One of the most influential persons to call public attention to the western Indian problem was Helen Hunt Jackson. In 1881 she published her summary volume, *A Century of Dishonor*, the fruit of her research into Indian relations and treaties which she carried on in the New York Astor Library. This documentary book was prepared from a distinctly partisan point of view. It was the *Uncle Tom's Cabin* of the Indians' cause. Three years after the appearance of her first book Mrs. Jackson published a novel, *Ramona*, in which she dealt with the life of the California mission Indians.

Mrs. Jackson's partisan writings gave her friends the kind of material they needed to awaken public sentiment. Coupled with this was the intelligent work of Carl Schurz, Secretary of the Interior under Rutherford B. Hayes. Schurz was an effective official despite bitter criticism of him. In 1883 the Indian Rights Association, composed largely of Boston crusaders, brought the Indian problem to the public in the Mohonk Conference of Friends of the Indians. President Cleveland was aware of these movements, and in 1887 his administration supported the Dawes Allotment Act. Back of the passage of this legislation was an influential ground swell of public demand for reform. The allotment idea was an old one dating back to the 1820's when John C. Calhoun had favored such a plan. Several proposals had been introduced subsequently in Congress but had failed of adoption. Some Indians were brought under a special application of the Homestead Law, but this applied to only limited special cases.

Thus far the government had failed to inaugurate a satisfactory program by which Indian and white man could live together in a common civilization. The device of the Indian treaty was a notorious failure, and certainly the early policy of Indian removal had only delayed the moment when some final and permanent decision would have to be made between the white man and his red neighbors. Military attempts at solving the problem contained only one answer, and that was annihilation. The more humane peace policy had had some virtue in recognizing that the Indian problem was sociological in nature.

The Dawes Act itself was the work of Henry Lauren Dawes, Senator from Massachusetts. Dawes, like Carl Schurz, was an energetic humanitarian. In Congress he had promoted a high tariff, he had offered a plan to complete the Washington Monument, he had written legislation to establish the Fish Commission, and had supported the scheme to gather daily weather information. Dawes was Chairman of the House Committee to investigate the corrupt Sanborn Contracts and the Indian Affairs Committee. In 1886 he introduced his Allotment Act, which was the most important piece of legislation which had been proposed to turn the Indian from his old wandering and tribal way of life toward that of a homesteading settler. Provisions were made to break up the tribes and to grant individual Indians parcels of land in their own names. Heads of households were to receive 160 acres, single persons over eighteen years were to have 80, orphan children got 80, and minor children were to have 40 acres each. The President was given strong discretionary powers, and lands granted were to be held under the guardianship of the government for twenty-five years before they were surrendered to the holder in fee simple. This legislation passed Congress and was signed by President Cleveland on February 8, 1887.

Indians coming under the Allotment Act were subjected to the laws of the states and territories in which they resided. This meant that they could appeal to the law for protection, but at the same time the law could be applied against them. They were now politically responsible to the white man's state instead of being bound by their ancient tribal laws in so far as their behavior and economic welfare were concerned. With this privilege came citizenship for all native-born Indians who had "adopted the habits of civilized life." This latter provision was to have its unhappy results. Indians unprepared for a settled white political society fell prey to grasping opportunists who sought support for their political ambitions and profits from liquor sales. Possibly an even larger problem confronted the commissioners who undertook to administer the Dawes Act. It was well-nigh impossible to take wandering Indians and make frontier farmers of them overnight. To do this at all required a great deal more technical assistance than Congress was willing to employ. Minors and helpless persons were difficult to manage because of the leasing practices which prevailed. This was true of all Indian lands that were subject to lease by grazers and mining company interests. One subtle failure in the basic intent of the law was the philosophy that possession of a home would tend to make the individual a responsible and interested citizen. As Francis E. Leupp, an Indian Commissioner, said in his book, *The Indian and His Problem*, ownership of a home in American civilization had always been a goal rather than a point of beginning. But the Indians under the Allotment Act received both a home and subsistence without having to labor for either. The government innocently created a state of idleness which added to the woes of absorbing the Indian wards into white civilization.

Education was one of the most serious problems which the government faced. During the latter part of the nineteenth century the white public school system was still in an experimental stage. Purposes of Indian education were still too vague to project a clear-cut scheme. In order to educate the Indians who came under the provision of the Dawes Act, schools had to start at the foot of a primitive social ladder, and teachers had to learn as they taught. In addition, the government Indian schools had all the faults of a political bureau. Personnel was allowed little or no discretion nor was there much place for individual initiative. Teachers under civil service appointments were not always the most imaginative persons to be found, and many of them got their jobs through some form of political favoritism.

Mission schools were closed, and the government assumed responsibility for preparing its wards for their final freedom at the end of twenty-five years. One of the most interesting extra-governmental educational experiments was that of the Indian School at Carlisle, Pennsylvania. This institution was founded in 1879 by Captain R. H. Pratt who sought to train his pupils vocationally in the practical ways of white civilization. As one means of doing this he sent his students into white homes for a year, to live with families and to learn by doing the things necessary in a settled way of life. This "outing" system had many advantages and produced good results. Generally, the educational need of the Indian was radically different from that of his white neighbors. His teachers not only had the problem of showing him how to live in his new type of life, but they had constantly to battle against the mores of an ancient Indian civilization which had strong ancestral ties with the minds and hearts of the people. The Indian youth who were sent away to school were likely to experience much unhappiness on their return. Any radical departure from the old ways was immediately called an act of unfaithfulness to racial traditions. This was one of the handicaps which confronted graduates of the Carlisle school.

The break with Indian customs and traditions was not made without its ragged edges. During the five years following the passage of the Dawes Act there was a strange emotional upheaval among the northern Sioux which was caused by a messiah and Ghost Dance craze. Since the middle of the century, prophets such as Smohalla of the Nez Percé and Tavibo of the Ute had preached the return of the Indians to their old ways and the final defeat of the whites. Wovoka (Jack Wilson), a Piute, preached the messiah doctrine among the northern plains Indians. With it were introduced the Ghost Dance, the wearing of the ghost shirt and the singing of ghost songs which had the effect of stirring up the idle Indians into a near messianic craze. At the agency of the Standing Rock Reservation on Grand River in the Dakota Badlands, Sitting Bull, still an unrelenting enemy of the white man, became an important apostle of the messiah movement. On December 15, 1890, when Indian police attempted to arrest him, he was killed. When troops were called in to help put down the riot, hundreds of Sioux fled the reservations. One band under the leadership of Chief Big Foot was pursued by a detachment of the Seventh Cavalry which had good reason to remember Sitting Bull. On December 29, 1890, while the Indians were being disarmed, a fight was begun which resulted in the slaughter of 200 Indians and 29 white soldiers. This historic battle of Wounded Knee was the last major armed conflict between the whites and Indians. After that date Indian relations were of a purely political nature, with the decisions being made through the office of the Indian Commissioner and in the halls of Congress.

Within a remarkably short time there was a clamor for revision of the Dawes Act. Its weaknesses were so obvious that in order to protect the Indian wards of the government, additional legislation was mandatory. The proposed revision offered by Congressman Charles H. Burke of South Dakota was enacted into law on May 8, 1906. This revisionary act postponed the granting of citizenship until land patents were given in fee simple. That is, the Indian was not to become a citizen until the government felt he had demonstrated that he could take care of his economic responsibilities. There was a tightening up on the sale of liquor to Indians, and in some other respects the naive wards of the government were protected against white exploitation. Citizenship now was extended to the Indian only upon the discretion of the government; thus he was prevented from exercising a privilege which he could not even define. One of the most serious criticisms of the Dawes Act was that, although the government realized that the Indian lacked sufficient knowledge and experience to operate a 160 acre farm and gave him twenty-five years under its watchful care to get prepared, the Congress nevertheless thrust the right of franchise upon him immediately. Subsequent legislation in 1924 restored full citizenship to all Indians, but ten years later the Wheeler-Howard Act attempted to restore a degree of tribal organization and control to those Indians who still remained in groups socially cohesive enough to participate in such a form of government.

The process of forcing the Indian to adopt the white man's culture was long drawn out. Its history was full of both bloodshed and social injustice, but whatever the moral and humane attitudes might be toward the process by which this occurred, it was one of the inevitabilities of frontier expansion. Competition between the Indian and the white man is one of the most important themes of the westward movement, and it assumes varied forms. Social crusaders have ever been able to work up recurring emotions on the subject. Western story writers have used the Indian as a salable piece of property; so have moving pictures and television. It is not at all strange to hear an Englishman speaking critically of the American Indian policy, or to see children, influenced by the popular writings of Karl May, playing Indians, soldiers and cowboys in a Viennese tenement district, or to observe East Indians crowding into a Calcutta movie house to see a picture that is centered about the warring activities of Crazy Horse and Red Cloud. Sitting Bull and George Armstrong Custer go marching on; the first as a magic man with a strong appeal to the messianically inclined, the latter as the center of a hot and insoluble argument over military behavior which will retain life and vigor so long as there are soldiers. Library shelves receive yearly their heavy toll of new volumes about the Indians, Custer, and the United States Indian policy—so the Great Spirit still flourishes.

CHICAGO AND NORTHWESTERN RAILROAD
POSTER

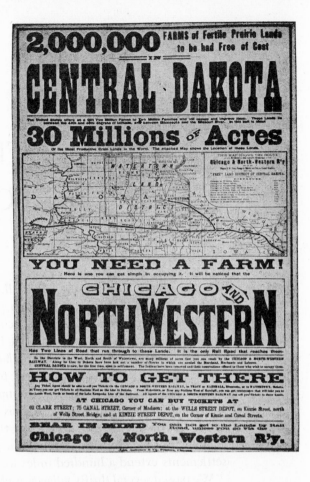

SOD HOUSE, NEBRASKA, 1888

THE LAST SOCIAL BARRIER

THE LAST
SOCIAL BARRIER

We passed into Nemeha and Marshall, with many farms along the timbered creeks, but few on the high prairies. Here, seventy miles from the railway, though with the locomotive approaching by two lines, unimproved lands were held at two to five dollars per acre, and farms at eight to twenty-five dollars. Settlers have grown rich supplying emigrants, and freighters to Colorado and Utah. At Marysville, a large flouring mill, running night and day, supplies an extensive region. Until lately, Kansas farmers shipped their wheat to St. Louis, and bought flour from the same city; but with age comes wisdom. Marysville was long the outpost of civilization; now settlements extend a hundred miles westward.

We passed several thrifty villages, each with its weekly newspaper; and many excellent farms. Besides our road a threshing machine, run by eight horses and twelve men, was taking out of straw four hundred bushels of wheat a day. Horse-rakes, mowers, planters, and quadruple "stirring plows" begin to abound. Machinery is increasing fourfold the efficiency of labor. This riding around the country on the spring seat of a mower or a planter is little like the old farming of New England! The great unsupplied need is the steam plow, but that will surely come.

—ALBERT D. RICHARDSON, *Beyond the Mississippi*

CHAPTER XXXI

JAMES BRYCE visited the last great frontier on his tours of America in the 1880's. He viewed the region against a background of the rest of America, and tried to define the forces which had driven American expansion across the continent. "All the passionate eagerness," he wrote, "all the strenuous effort of the Westerns is directed towards the material development of the greatest quantity of ore, to scatter cattle on a thousand hills, to turn the flower-spangled prairies of the Northwest into wheat fields, to cover the sunny slopes of the Southwest with vines and olives; this is the end and aim of their lives, this is their daily and nightly thought."

The Congress of the United States had long been conscious of the "daily and nightly" thought identified by Lord Bryce. Since the day when expansion began in Ohio, legislators and politicians were conscious of the importance of land laws. On February 28, 1862, Congress passed its last major land act. Two years before, Grow's Homestead Law had passed Congress after a long and complex argument over the issue, but President James Buchanan had vetoed it. In 1860, Republicans made the issue a major plank in their platform, and their candidate Abraham Lincoln was highly favorable to homestead legislation. Once the southern Democrats had withdrawn from Congress, following the election of that year, it was possible to re-enact the law and to get a sympathetic reception for it at the White House. On May 20, 1862, Lincoln signed a new bill which ended in part the struggle of three-quarters of a century to secure privileges for the poor settler.

After January 1, 1863, the frontiersman was to enjoy terms of land acquisition which he had sought in fact as early as 1787. Heads of families, or persons, twenty-one years of age, who were citizens of the United States, and who had not borne arms against the government were permitted to enter a claim for a quarter-section of 160 acres for actual settlement and cultivation. At the end of five years, if the claimant had met the terms of the law he was to receive a certificate of ownership, provided he had paid a fee—$34 along the West Coast, and $26.00 elsewhere. A claimant might shorten the period of waiting by paying $1.25 per acre. Homestead lands were not to be held liable for debt. Enactment of the Homestead Law did not, however, annul the Pre-emption Law, and conflicts between the two were in time to create confusion in the land system.

By the outbreak of the Civil War the settlement line extended to California, Utah, Colorado, and Oregon on the west, and to western Iowa, Minnesota, Missouri, Kansas and Texas on the east. Between those two lines lay the vast High, or Great, Plains area which included the Dakotas, Montana, Wyoming, Nebraska, Kansas, Colorado, Oklahoma, western Texas, New Mexico, and Arizona. Up to 1865 most settlers had passed up this region in preference for better wooded and watered areas. By 1865, however, settlers were approaching the plains. Although settlement on the high, arid and semihumid plains did not make any fundamental changes in the social process of pioneering, it did produce some fascinating agricultural innovations.

The influx of settlers who poured on to the plains after 1865 for the most part developed an agrarian society. They were not the original settlers of the region. Preceding them were the Indian traders, and those who had established the stage, freight stations and army posts. Though there were vast stretches of unsettled country, it was not unknown and unexplored territory. Immigration to this part of the frontier resulted partly from internal expansion of population, partly from the shifting of population following the Civil War, partly from the absorption of more desirable lands in the border states farther east, and, after 1870, the rise of European immigration. An interesting aspect of the population approach to the plains country is the fact that a good portion of the settlers first passed through the prairie areas of the Mississippi Valley. Illinois, for instance, lost 320,000 in population in the decade 1870 to 1880. The Ohio and Mississippi tier of states, except Arkansas and Minnesota, showed a loss of population. At the same time some of the plains areas were experiencing rapid gains. This loss in older states, and gain in the newer areas continued until 1900.

The plains country was not uniform in its nature. As in the eastern Mississippi Valley, there were sectional variations. The northern plains differed from those of the Southwest. There were pronounced variations in the availability of water and moisture. Actually, however, the social differences were not marked. There were, of course, different areas of Indian culture, and in the Southwest the Spanish influence had been strong. This was to color the American advance. For the most part, the pattern of social and economic pioneering that we have already studied prevailed all across the region.

Within three years after the passage of the Homestead Act, a flood of settlers moved into the great public land areas of the West. Many Union veterans went directly on to the frontier to begin life anew. In camp and battlefield bivouac, the West had beckoned to soldiers; they made plans to seek free lands in pairs or in companies as soon as the war ended. It was Daniel Freeman, a soldier home on furlough, who was allowed to register the first homestead claim on January 1, 1863. His claim was located near Beatrice, Nebraska, and the registry book was opened just long enough on the New Year's holiday to allow him the opportunity to make his entry before he returned to the army. After 1866, Confederate veterans were permitted to claim homesteads in the West. Many of them returned home to find economic and social chaos, and it seemed easier to go West and make a new start than to stay at home and endure the period of readjustment. As soon as claim offices were opened, prospective settlers flocked to Kansas, Nebraska, the Dakotas, Wyoming, and Montana.

The Homestead Law was not a satisfactory piece of legislation. It was characteristic of legislation which results from public pressure. Possibly no one before 1840 gave much serious consideration to the area involved, for the Great Plains were regarded as a desert where settlement would be long delayed, if in fact it ever occurred. Provisions of the act were devised largely from landholding experience on the 98th meridian. A quarter-section of land was ample to support a family in Illinois, Iowa, or Missouri, but it was probably inadequate on most of the plains. Some of this western land required eight to thirty acres to graze a steer, while other parts grew an abundance of grass. Where field crops were to be grown, farmers had to think in terms of larger acreage than in regions with more abundant rainfall. Some idea of the inadequacy of the law is suggested by the fact that out of the 86,936 entries made for Kansas lands between 1862 and 1882 involving 11,746,949.80 acres, only 34,055 entries were registered for 4,660,734.83 acres. In Nebraska there were 64,328 original entries for 8,183,076.25 acres, and 29,140 final entries were registered for 3,566,447.29 acres.

Beyond its basic inadequacies, the Homestead Law threatened dangerous disaster to the plains. Where the native sod was broken, wind erosion drifted top soils into piles of dust and sand. The native grasses were destroyed, and the soil was exposed to the merciless winds and dehydrating sun. In 1873, Congress in a partial effort to correct its former mistake passed the Timber Culture Act. This law provided for the encouragement of timber culture on the High Plains where nature had decreed otherwise. A settler was required to plant and maintain forty acres of trees not more than twelve feet apart for ten years; if he did so he would be given the quarter-sections on which the trees were planted. Settlers already holding a homestead grant could shorten the time of final entry to three years by planting an acre of trees on their claims. A belief prevailed that the climate of the plains could be modified by the growing of trees. Even precipitation could be increased by the presence of forests.

After the passage of the new law, it was possible for a settler to establish claim to 480 acres of land under the combined terms of the Pre-emption Law, the Homestead Law, and the Timber Culture Act. By locating his claims strategically he might even gain control of a couple of sections. The three quarter sections might be located around the outer edges of sections so as to make the interior units undesirable for another settler. On March 3, 1877, Congress enlarged the possibilities for a claimant to acquire an additional section of land by passing the Desert Land Act. This provided that if an individual would irrigate his lands within three years after filing a claim he could purchase it for $800.

These laws often served to open the West to wholesale exploitation by unscrupulous claimants. Not even Congress could make trees grow in places where nature had failed to accomplish the task. For the chiseler, these laws offered just the right pretext to lay claims to large blocks of the public domain. All kinds of subterfuges were used to secure possession of land claims. In order to enlarge holdings under the Homestead Act, a man and a woman might build a house astride a section line and claim lands on either side. At the same time they withheld legal marriage until their claims were proved. Families might locate a house on a section corner so a family of grown children could lay claim to a full section of land. Cattle companies placed their hirelings about on desirable lands to establish flimsy claims, and then they consolidated their ill-gotten tracts into large holdings. In some cases legitimate claimants were driven off the lands by threats of violence. Rich mineral lands fell into the hands of shrewd exploiters by methods little short of public robbery. When W. A. J. Sparks became Land Commissioner in 1885, he instituted several reforms and suspended entries which he believed were fraudulent. It was not until 1891, however, that the Pre-emption, Timber Culture, and Desert Land laws were repealed. By that time the frontier had technically ceased to exist.

Lone easterners came west after 1862 to locate claims and to develop them enough to provide a home; then they sent for either their sweethearts or families to join them. It generally required from one to four years to settle a western plains homestead. Moving beyond the 98th meridian, pioneers had to adjust themselves to new environmental conditions. Beyond that line settlers left the woods and a plentiful water supply. The land ranged from arid to subhumid. Nature had cleared the fields, leaving little enough wood behind for man's use. Cottonwoods, willows, hackberry, and stands of scrubby cedar grew along the streams and occasionally on the ridges. Almost every basic practice of American pioneering had to be revised once the settlement line reached the plains country.

Most early houses on the plains were either "dug-outs" or "sod houses." Dug-outs were cut into hillsides and banks. They were lighted and ventilated with improvised doors and windows. Sod houses were constructed from clumps of sod cut from the land with a special sodbusting plow. Long strips of turf twelve to fifteen inches wide were sliced loose from the ground following a rain. These long ribbons were then cut into blocks fifteen inches long and were laid into walls somewhat after the fashion of bonded brick. Crude frames were erected to hold windows and doors, and the sod was pressed firmly around them. Walls varied in height from four to ten feet. Tree forks were placed at the peaks of gable ends and in the middle to support ridge combs and the weight of roofs. Rails or poles were laid from the walls to the peaks and heavy grass or cornstalk mats were then put down to catch the leakage of dirt which filtered down from the sod roof.

Dug-outs of necessity were small, dark, and dirty. They had the virtue of being dry most of the time, they were easy to build, and were cool in hot weather, and reasonably snug in winter. On the other hand they were dusty, leaky, and were all but impossible to ventilate. Dirt was forever dropping to the floor. Animals, snakes, and birds burrowed into the walls and roofs. Occasionally a rattlesnake worked his way inside to cause panic, and sometimes tragedy. Cattle roaming about the plains would stumble onto a dug-out roof and fall through, or a traveler driving in the dark would land his team and wagon atop a caving roof before he saw it. Yet, for the minimum expenditure of less than $5.00, an industrious man could purchase the necessary materials to build his plains burrow. One further virtue of the dug-out was the fact that it was below storm level and there was little danger of disaster from this source. Many settler families survived their first plains winter cooped up in a dug-out. As the "Lane County Bachelor" lamented:

> My name is Frank Bolar, 'nole bachelor I am,
> I'm keepin' ole bach on an elegant plan.
> You'll find me out West in the County of Lane
> Starving to death on a government claim;
> My house it is built of the national soil,
> The walls are erected according to Hoyle,
> The roof has no pitch but is level and plain
> And I always get wet when it happens to rain.
> But hurrah for Lane County, the land of the free,
> The home of the grasshopper, bedbug, and flea,

I'll sing loud her praises and boast of her fame
While starving to death on my government claim.

Sod houses corresponded somewhat to the more commodious log houses of the earlier frontier. They were more spacious and versatile structures. In fact, they could be made almost as large as the builder chose, and they could be erected at almost any desirable spot so long as a suitable supply of sod was available nearby. Some degree of specialization of domestic functions was possible for families living in these structures. Being above ground the sod house afforded more light and ventilation than did the dug-out; at the same time rain and wind storms caused greater damage. Seldom, however, was fire a hazard. There was no way to keep a sod house from shedding dirt or leaking. Often it was necessary to prepare meals under a sheet or an opened umbrella. Hunks of wet sod fell into cooking food or beds, and not infrequently walls and roofs became water-logged and fell down.

Howard Ruede, a Pennsylvania immigrant to Kansas in 1877, described a sod house for his eastern family.

> This was another hot day, and we had heavy work too, laying up sod. Snyder broke a lot for us this a.m. and we began laying up the wall. It is 20 inches thick. These "Kansas brick" are from 2 to 4 inches thick, 12 inches wide and 20 long, and the joints between them we fill with ground. Just before sunset we got the ridgepole into position on crotches, so that the room will be about 7 feet high. We expect to get the roof in and have the place in condition to live in by the end of the week. The sod is heavy and when you take 3 or 4 bricks on a litter or hand barrow, and carry it 50 to 150 feet, I tell you it is no easy work.

The same author described the interior of a fairly elaborate sod house.

> At first these sod houses are unplastered, and this thought perfectly allright, but such a house is somewhat cold in the winter as the crevices between the sods admit some cold air; so some of the houses are plastered with a kind of "native lime!" made of sand and a very sticky native clay. This plaster is very good unless it happens to get wet. In a few of the houses this plaster is whitewashed, and this helps the looks very much. Some sod houses are mighty comfortable places to go into in cold weather, and it don't take much fire to keep them warm.

Much of the plains frontier environment inflicted genuine hardships upon families. Many a wife went west to join her husband and discovered that she and her children would have to live like animals under the ground in a dug-out, or in a crumbling soddy. Tears flowed in emotional torrents from women who yearned for the comforts and security of society in a wooded country. Some easterners were driven almost to the point of distraction by the constant blowing of the wind. There was seldom the stillness on the plains which prevailed in heavily wooded country. Day and night the wind swept across the plains in dust-ladened gales. This continuous blowing was physically and psychologically frustrating. At no place on the frontier did the pioneer move so far away from the conveniences and associations of a settled society, or from the materials with which he could make himself comfortable, as he did on the High Plains.

Not until railroads were built across the plains and lumber could be imported from the timber-growing regions was it possible to substitute wooden frame houses for those made of sod. In the beginning even churches and courthouses were built of sod. Even then many settlers were unable to afford the cost of new houses. Towns grew along the rail lines, and rows of frame stores and houses reared their heads. Churches, courthouses, hotels and other public buildings lined main streets. Northern and southern woods sent endless train loads of lumber to the High Plains to dot that country with its characteristic frame houses. In time long train loads of eastern and western coal supplied fuel where an uncertain supply of native materials were both limited and unsatisfactory.

Vast areas of the western plains were without timber. So long as settlement remained along the streams, wood of a sort was available, but once people moved away from the valleys they left the timber line behind them. In some areas during the early rush of settlers, government and railroad lands were denuded of trees. In fact settlers considered that the railroads had all but stolen the land from the government; therefore they thought little of lifting timber from the public domain. Long cold winters in most of the plains country necessitated the maintenance of fires for extended periods. People traveled long distances in search of wood, and they used every sort of substitute. Cow and buffalo chips were gathered from the grazing lands. Large weeds, sunflower, and cornstalks were cut into fuel. Experiments were made with grass and grass-burning stoves. Corn and corn cobs were used in place of wood. Coal was too expensive for the poor homesteader to buy, and most often he was too far removed from the railroad to permit him to procure it even if he had the money. The mere act of keeping a fire going on wintry days and nights was almost a full time job for a man. Frequently houses were heavily smoked and begrimed by the fire. Some of the substitutes for wood, such as grass bats, created a smoke that often threatened members of households with suffocation.

Water was almost as scarce as wood on the arid and subhumid plains. Not only was it difficult to obtain water for ordinary domestic purposes, but the land often lacked the necessary moisture to produce crops. Orthodox crops and orthodox methods of cultivation were not sufficient for agricultural success west of the 98th meridian. There were recurring drouths in the Ohio and Mississippi valleys, but these were seldom of an extended duration. Almost never were settlers left without water. On the plains, however, it was obtainable in many instances only after the expenditure of a vast amount of labor. Wells were bored or punched in the ground to a depth sufficient to tap the natural water table. It was then hauled to the surface by the use of a long slender bucket, or by a pump. After 1870, windmills came into common use to operate pumps. This was a slow but relatively effortless method of obtaining water. Because the wind blew constantly, the mills could be kept at work.

Occasionally settlers lacked access to well-drilling rigs, or they lacked money with which to pay for a well, and they dug them by hand. These wells, however, were not always successful. Often it was necessary to dig to great depths. Walls caved in, or there was not enough timber available to build curbings. So long as rains replenished the water table, wells could be dug in certain areas with success. In extended dry seasons, however, when the table dropped, they went dry and families were left without water. Punched wells often reached deep enough into the ground to keep below the drop of the water table which constantly sought a level with the sea.

Many settlers were forced to desert their homesteads for lack of water. For those who had known the well water and seasonable conditions of the eastern river valleys, a new type of agriculture became necessary. Dry farming became imperative. No one knew in the early years of plains settlement the art of farming subhumid soil.

The scientific process known as dry farming has expanded since the 1850's as a result of vast experimentation. Actually it is one of the oldest agricultural practices in the history of civilization, but not on the North American continent. From the beginning of recorded history, man has struggled with aridity in extracting a living from the soil. Ancient Asiatics learned many of the secrets of tilling dry soils. For thousands of years men, like the East Indians of the Punjab and those living near the Rajasltan Desert, or along the Malabar Coast, have battled drouth year after year. Millions of sleepy camels and bullocks have tramped around deeply padded circles dragging levers of creaking Persian well wheels in efforts to lift enough water from the ground to produce meager crops. Moses and Aaron battled aridity in their long wanderings with the children of Israel. Countless generations of nomadic Arabs have drifted over the boundless middle-eastern deserts. Man long ago learned to adapt his activities and agricultural practices to conditions of the seasons.

In keeping with ancient traditions, American frontiersmen approached a new mode of life on the plains. They were forced to use all their ingenuity to survive. In certain restricted areas enough natural stream resources existed to permit irrigation. There was not enough available water, however, in all the West to irrigate the region's arid lands. Even if water had been available, capital was lacking with which to finance the construction of facilities for getting water to the land. The next best answer was the "new" agricultural practice of dry farming. Almost 700,000,000 acres of land lay within the area where dry farming had to be practiced in order to utilize available moisture. For dry farming to be feasible it was necessary to have an annual rainfall of more than ten inches. The principle of this kind of cultivation was to plow a depth of seven to ten inches just before the winter rains and snows fell. Then it was necessary to keep the top soil stirred so a fine dust mulch would form and maintain a capillary action that drew moisture up to root systems of plants. This process of cultivation necessitated a constant stirring of the soil, and in some cases crops were planted on a bi-annual system of rotation.

Another element of dry farming was the selection of hardy types of plants which would endure the drouths of the plains and still produce. The old staple varieties of American field crops were not so well suited to the needs of the plains. Corn, for instance, required considerable moisture to produce good yields, and so did the domestic varieties of small grains. Through experimentation, farmers turned to the cultivation of drouth-resistant small grains such as kaffir corn, feterita, and types of hard spring and winter wheats which did most of their growing while there was the most moisture in the soil. Wheat was the most successful of the commercially profitable dry farm field crops.

Soil types, climatic conditions, and availability of moisture governed the practice of wheat farming. In much of the more northern area wheat was sown in March and April and was harvested in late July and early August. Experimentation was necessary from the beginning of farming on the Great Plains. Types of dry land crops were imported from other parts of the world to the West. Plant breeding and experimentation with cultivation practices began early. Some notion of the expansion of wheat farming alone can be gained from the following production figures. In 1866 there were 15,424,000 acres planted to wheat which yielded 152,000,000 bushels. Twenty years later there were 36,806,000 acres producing 457,218,000 bushels.

Peculiar environmental conditions of the plains area worked an unusual hardship on the American frontiersmen. The social pattern beyond the ninety-eighth meridian, however, varied little if any from that which had prevailed along the Ohio, Wabash, Illinois, and Wisconsin rivers. Common workings enabled neighbors to accomplish tasks which otherwise could not have been performed so efficiently or pleasantly. There was no need for logrollings, but house-raisings, common plowings, and harvesting demanded an increased amount of labor.

In many areas, breaking the virgin plains sod with its shallow but heavily matted root system was a burdensome task which required additional teams and manpower. Common plowings were organized in which neighbors contributed their labors along with that of their teams. Late summer harvests again brought neighbors together in common workings. Sweating crews cut the grain and then threshed it. At first, harvesting machinery was dragged across grain fields by horse and ox teams. Later steam tractors pulled reapers and binders and turned threshers. Before 1872 it was necessary for men to bind by hand the bundles of wheat deposited by reapers. After that date the bundles were delivered, bound and ready for shocking or delivery to the threshers. The first bindings were wire, but this caused so much difficulty for the threshers that it was replaced by strong grass bindings in 1878.

As the grain belt of the plains expanded, threshing became a bigger chore than neighbors alone could perform. In time seasonal threshing crews moved across the great wheat belt with their machines from farm to farm. An army of seasonal harvest hands came from everywhere. On the northern plains men came from the great northern woods to work summers during the slack lumbering season. In the fall these lumberjacks went back to the pineries. Farther south, "hoboes," college lads, romantics in search of the West, and adventurous workers wandered across the country. Some of these followed the threshing season from the time it opened in the ripening fields of the southern plains to the late-maturing crops of the Dakotas. Farmers furnished food, water, and, occasionally, blankets. It was impossible to shelter so many men, and most of them dropped down on straw stacks and slept on the spot where they worked. The farmer paid for this threshing service at a bushel rate. Not until highly improved mechanical header combines were introduced in the 1880's was this practice changed. The harvest seasons for the plains families brought a momentary period of change and excitement.

In between harvest seasons life moved on at a monotonous pace. Families were often so badly isolated that they literally hungered for human associations. Women and children especially longed for opportunities to see other people. Not infrequently families would drive astonishing distances to attend country dances, box suppers, church meetings, or to shop at crossroads stores, or to visit in towns. Plains settlers, like those in the Ohio and Indiana backwoods, held square dances in unbelievably small shacks and sod houses. Often barefooted dancers raised such clouds of dust from earthen floors that it was necessary to sprinkle the floor to prevent suffocation. Few dances went off without a good bit of drinking, a little fighting, and a generous amount of boasting and swearing. Candy pullings and play parties also served to make plains life more pleasant.

Music for dances and parties was the product of boisterous maestros who drank their way to the bottom of generous bottles, and sawed through three to five fiddle strings in an evening. Their repertoires were limited to the old folk tunes such as "Old Dan Tucker," "Old Joe Clark," "Arkansas Traveler," "Fisher's Hornpipe," and to a score of other well-worn favorites. Off to one side tipsy callers droned their endless rigmaroles that sent sets swirling forward and backward, stepping through intricate formations, turning, bowing, and "sasshaying" as though they were electronically controlled by the caller. One call instructed couples to:

> *How will you swap, and how will you trade*
> *This pretty girl for that old maid?*
>
> *Rope the cow, and kill the calf,*
> *Swing your partner around and a half.*
>
> *Wave the ocean, wave the sea,*
> *Wave that pretty girl back to me.*

Preachers reached the plains with the first settlers. Baptist preachers were themselves settlers, and Methodist circuit riders kept up with the creaking homesteaders' wagons. Presbyterian, Episcopal, and Congregational ministers went West either to accept charges, or as missionaries. Regular church services were held first in cabins and sod houses. Occasionally ambitious women established Sunday schools and maintained combination educational and religious programs either to supplant the infrequent religious services or to take their place altogether. Periodic "bush arbor" or outdoor revivals brought people together for both spiritual and social gatherings. The social aspects of these meetings at times possibly outweighed the spiritual ones. Permanent churches made their appearances and religious services became more regular. Preachers offered vast comfort to the people in their moments of misfortune and grief. Often they were almost as much in demand as were doctors and midwives. In many places on the frontier, ministers were subjected to indignities. In the lusty young towns where saloons and brothels held sway, they were regarded either as objects of ridicule or as competitors.

Drinking, gambling, fighting and lawbreaking in general marred social life in many communities. Much of the free and easy characteristic of plains border life grew out of the peculiar nature of the country. Men turned to vices as forms of amusement to break the monotony of living in isolation. They sometimes flaunted their boisterous behavior in the faces of more religiously inhibited neighbors in a sort of brazen easement of their guilty consciences. It was some of this brassy type of behavior which gave a certain amount of flavor to the "wide open" West. Not infrequently a homesteader was a temporary settler who expected to stay in a community only long enough to "prove a claim" and then move on. At the beginning the plains population had a predominance of men, and this accounts for the rugged society which first existed on this part of the frontier.

Conditions often forced settlers to resort to the practice of vigilantism in certain frontier areas. Victims of these informal law-enforcement bodies were thieves, gamblers, dissolute moral offenders, and bands of robbers. Conflict between settler and cattlemen provoked local "wars" which sometimes saw hooded companies of farmers confront their common enemy, the free-grazing trail herders, with shot guns and ropes. Rustlers brought out the regulators in force. Claim jumpers were sure to provoke the wrath of neighboring homesteaders, and often a brazen "jumper" would be sent on his way after he had infringed, legally perhaps, upon the claim of an original settler. On top of the more spectacular provocations for law enforcement were the petty breaches which landed individuals in court. Many of these were conflicts between the code of the saloon and gambling halls and the mores of a more refined society.

Western towns sprang up on the plains as population moved westward. The frontier town was in fact a bubble of the eternal optimism of the American promoter. Speculators and promoters hoped to locate a town, secure the state capital or county seat, and sell off cheap land at premium prices. One of the major sports of the period, 1865–1900, was that of trying to guess right in locating a town. Crossroads, sites of blacksmith shops, railhead camps, ends of cattle trails, stagecoach stations, country stores, and railway stops all gave promise of growing into metropolises. Many promoters undertook to force the law of town location by promoting sites on the plains that had few or no justifiable reasons for becoming population centers. Railway agents worked hard at locating towns for various selfish reasons. Politicians often took a hand at town building. Such a case was the clever manipulations of Alexander McKenzie, boss of the Dakotas. He secured the passage of legislation through the Dakota general assembly to move the capital from Yankton to some undesignated spot. He outmaneuvered the grasping territorial governor Nehemiah Ordway. McKenzie, who represented the Northern Pacific Railroad Company, wished to have the capital moved to Bismark on its main line. A meeting of the capital committee took place as prescribed by law, in Yankton, but it was held in a railway car that was hauled in and out of the town before the enraged citizens knew what was happening. Railroad manipulators figured prominently in the location and fortunes of many towns along their lines.

Town organizers and immigration agents had purposes other than financially speculative ones. Sometimes they wanted to develop the social and cultural institutions of an older society. A community had to have a population, which included pupils for schools and churches, and church congregations. A successful town possessed a mill, a boarding house, a post office, a blacksmith shop, a doctor's office, a bank, a weekly newspaper, churches, a school, and a railway station. At the same time it was a market center for a large farming and grazing community. The location of the courthouse in a struggling hamlet was almost certain assurance of the development of the necessary institutions which aided social growth.

The average plains town was a rather unattractive place from an aesthetic standpoint. It stood stark and naked on a treeless knoll, as raw and unadorned as a picked chicken. Its gray wood buildings lined a dusty main street, and it possessed little of architectural taste and beauty. Occasionally rickety boardwalks paralleled the street. Hitching racks ranged along the streets in front of store doors, and heaps of horse manure gave the towns something more than a nostalgic odor. In some of these frontier towns, saloons and gambling houses outnumbered stores. Saloons were social centers where gamblers, prostitutes, and promoters of all sorts of rackets made themselves at home. Such institutions were more common in cattle, mining, and rail camp towns than they were in the purely agrarian villages. Churches were built alongside saloons and soon had a chastening effects upon their rowdy neighbors. Hotels and boarding houses accomodated travelers and temporarily homeless persons. Most western country hotels were small, dirty and crowded. Visitors not infrequently had to sleep with total strangers. Even husbands and wives sometimes shared beds with other couples. Next to the saloon, the livery stables were centers of greatest activity. They not only sheltered teams and rigs for transients, but they also had outfits for rent. They were places where strangers could find information; they were often scenes of fights and brawls. In a land where horses and vehicles were of such great importance, the livery stable was visited by almost everybody who reached the towns.

Just as ministers helped to sober the tone of social life so did country editors. Almost before stakes were driven at the corners of town lots, itinerant editors and publishers were on the scene to establish papers with bundles of Chicago and Minneapolis readyprint and clumsy hand-operated Washington presses. Almost every county seat had its newspapers. Editors recorded weekly chapters of local history, and when they were men of unusual courage they criticized both public sinning and civic indifference. Lack of local pride provoked many an editor to stirring protests. Filthy conditions of streets and public wells drew imaginative criticisms. Not all of the editor's copy, however, contained blasts at the shortcoming of their neighbors or told of local calamities. There were human notes recording marriages, births, deaths, social events, arrival of new families, local humor, and historical items. Nothing was too insignificant to get into print in the little four-page journals. As for the two pages of readyprint, there was a great variety of material which described life in Ceylon, the eating habits of the English Queen, how pencils were made, and which recorded count-less stories of people being buried alive. Too, there were always the be-whiskered "doctors" who offered cure-all patent medicines for every hypochondriac that ever reached the western sod.

Editors had plenty of local calamities to record. Nature fought back with a vengeance at settlers who broke the virginal silence of the plains. Those who rushed westward with hopes of claiming their share of the national domain not only had to combat aridity, and a lack of timber, but also the fierce insect scourges, dry winds, dust storms, blizzards, and prairie fires. During the years 1874–1877 the great grasshopper invasion ate almost every green thing before it in a wide strip across Kansas. The swarm of insects in 1874 first appeared as a dark cloud rising and falling in erratic swells, displaying a silvery hue as it swirled in the sun, just above the land-scape. At first settlers thought it was a rain cloud, and then they discovered the grasshoppers dropping down upon their crops. Settling to the ground in clicking hordes they gave a slight impression of a vast hail storm. Within a day's time almost every green thing was consumed. Onions and turnips were eaten down into the ground. Harness was gnawed to pieces. Tool handles were nibbled so badly that they were hardly usable again. Even the boards on houses were eaten bare of their softer weather-beaten surfaces. Streams and wells were contaminated by the insects that dropped into them or by the excrement of the vast swarms. Professor John Ise has described most graphically the struggle of his father and mother to rescue a part of their corn crop from the grasshoppers. His father cut the corn while his mother dragged it into shocks, but on the second day the hoppers had devoured the remaining crop and there was nothing left to harvest.

Combatting the insect invasion caused settlers to waste energy and to suffer tremendous heartbreak and disappointment. Both state and federal governments attempted to grant relief to sufferers of the plague and to find means to destroy the insects. Experiments were undertaken to destroy both eggs and young grasshoppers before they had a chance to swarm over the land. After 1877 the ravenous swarms ceased to appear, although the grass-hopper menace in a more limited way continued. The use of poison, and development of a more complete knowledge of the life cycle of the pests helped to bring them under control.

While grasshopper swarms stripped fields and grazing lands of crops and grass, dry, hot winds blew over the land withering plant life before them. Early drouths prevented seeds from sprouting, and those that came later in the season destroyed growing crops. Many a plains farmer felt the hot winds blow in his face day after day and saw his fields and pastures parched to a crisp. Water resources failed, and livestock either perished or became so weakened that it was all but worthless. Settlers left the country in droves, going east to keep from starving, sometimes driving cattle and hogs before them to pay the expenses of their retreats from failure.

Behind the searing drouths came the suffocating dust storms of summer, and the death-dealing blizzards of winter. Thunder storms of summer sometimes developed into wild blows which reached tornado proportions. In the open country the flashes of electrical storms, and the rolling dark clouds could be seen for miles away. The surging of the clouds and the long rolls of thunder created a sort of majestic horror. Dust storms boiled up in the same way. Often it seemed the whole earth was being lifted heavenward, and as the storm thundered on it deposited drifts of dust and sand against every barricade in its path. Winter blizzards swept much of the plains country with blinding ice and snow storms. A traveler caught in a plains blizzard was in real danger. He not only had the problem of withstanding the cold and exposure of the storm, but he had to think of the dangerous psychological confusion which would occur. He was in grave danger of losing his sense of direction and identification so that he might travel in circles or fail to identify familiar landmarks.

The growth of prairie grass and intense drouth of the region heightened the danger of fire. A careless traveler allowed his campfire to get out of hand, gun wadding sometimes fell afire into a clump of grass, or a tongue of lightning started fires. Huge rolls of flames leaped into billowing waves of destruction. Clouds of ominous black smoke darkened the sky, and falling ash and cinders indicated destruction on a scale dreamed of only by Dante. Albert D. Richardson described prairie fires which he saw in Kansas in 1858. He wrote:

> During night rides in winter I often saw prairie fires blazing along the horizon. Though never dangerous to men or animals, as depicted in our school geographies [in this case the geographies were more nearly correct] they are always startling and grand. The sky is pierced with tall pyramids of flame, or covered with writhing, leaping, lurid serpents as transformed into a broad ocean lit-up by a blazing sunset. Now a whole avalanche of fire slides off into the prairie, and then opening its great, devouring jaws closes in upon the deadened grass.

When these disasters swept over the land, they left death and poverty in their paths. Many settlers turned back, but many more remained and brought the country under their conquest. Those who survived were tempered in the furnace of hardship and discouragement. Though a peaceful, simple folk at heart, these settlers had to fight greedy men and corporations, the elements, and their own psychological frustrations. There were many whose lives could be substituted for Marie Sandoz's stout-hearted Old Jules, or Hamlin Garland's parents, or for John Ise's courageous Henry and Rosie. These were all simple-living frontiersmen who extracted a living from the soil in the most arduous way. They endured the final hardships of American pioneering and established an American civilization in a region where extraordinary perseverance and courage were required.

At few times in the history of civilization was man so passionately materialistic as in the conquest of the Great Plains. Expansion of the railway system across the continent, the development of an expanded domestic economy, and the frantic reaching out for world markets created a rising demand for western products. Following his visits to the West in the 1880's, Lord Bryce observed that,

> To have an immense production of exchangeable commodities, to force from nature the most she can be made to yield, and to send it east and west by the cheapest routes to the nearest markets, making one's city a center of trade, and raising the price of its real estate—this, which might not have seemed a glorious consumation of Isaiah or Plato, is preached by western newspapers as a kind of religion. It is not really, or at least it is not wholly sordid. These people are intoxicated by the majestic scale of the nature in which their lot is cast, enormous mineral deposits, boundless prairies, forests which, even squandered—wickedly squandered—as they now are, will supply the United States for centuries; a soil which, with the rudest cultivation, yields the most abundant crops, a populous continent for their market. They see all around them railways being built, telegraph wires laid, steamboat lines across the Pacific projected, cities springing up in the solitudes, and settlers making the wilderness to blossom like a rose. Their imagination revels in these sights and sounds of progress, and they gild their own struggles for fortune with the belief that they are the missionaries of civilization and the instrument of Providence in the greatest work the world has even seen.

In the frontiersman's rush to settle the continent he brought under exploitation a territory which might well have taken a less energetic society centuries to accomplish. The American could not withstand the challenge of so large a block of public lands. Individual and corporation sought to get their share of the public domain. Both helped to create economic and social problems which radically changed concepts of the function of government. At the same time the national government was forced to reach a high state of maturity in a remarkably short interval of time.

WAITING FOR THE NOON SIGNAL—GUTHRIE, OKLAHOMA

ROUNDING OUT A CONTINENT

ROUNDING OUT
A CONTINENT

If they spoke truly—as no doubt they did—there was in their words a further evidence of the predominance of material efforts and interests over all others, even over those political instincts which are deemed so essential a part of the American character. The arrangements of his government lie in the dim background of the picture which fills the Western eye. In the foreground he sees ploughs and sawmills, ore-crushers and railway locomotives. These so absorb his thoughts as to leave little time for constitutions and legislation; and when constitutions and legislation are thought of, it is as means for better securing the benefits of the earth and of trade to the producer, and preventing the greedy corporation from intercepting their fruits.

—JAMES BRYCE, *American Commonwealth*

CHAPTER XXXII

Frontier on the Wane

BY 1870 the stage was set for the absorption of the territorial frontier into organized states. All the vast frontier region, with the exception of the Indian country of Oklahoma, had been organized into territories, and in most of them people looked forward to statehood. Free land was rapidly disappearing as populations increased and as the stream of European immigration poured into the country. Idaho, Montana, Colorado, Nevada, and Washington were all gaining. Railroad expansion opened new immigrant trails, expanded the American agricultural system and emphasized the establishment of productive communities all along their lines. James J. Hill and the Great Northern System made a fetish of population expansion. Hill's dream was an idyllic railway territory across the vast Northwest with a family on every quarter section of land, and every quarter section in full agricultural production. As statistical tables of grain and livestock shot upward after 1870, railroads counted their dividends.

Bales of promotional literature were distributed at home and abroad tempting people to seek their fortunes in the Northwest. In 1878 John Wesley Powell made his famous *Report on the Lands of the Arid Region of the United States* which was hardly a promotional tract but, by its controversial nature, certainly called attention to the northwestern territories. Internally, the southern cotton system was beginning to fail. Cotton prices were turning downward to a ruinuously low point following the inflationary period of the war. Southerners, discouraged with conditions during and immediately following Reconstruction, followed in the footsteps of those who had gone into the Far West in the 1850's. They found friends and sympathetic neighbors in those immigrants who had rushed to the gold and silver fields of Nevada, Colorado, Montana, Idaho and to the Black Hills of Dakota.

As described previously, the age of the railway baron was in full bloom by the 1880's, and transcontinental railroads were a vital part of national political expansion. Behind every issue in the West after 1865 was the shadow of the railroad. Not only did great systems of rails spread out across the land, but vigorous and hard-fisted personalities grew up with roads. Behind most of the lines were men, like J. Gould, Huntingdon, Stanford, Crocker, Hill, Harriman, Palmer and others whose personal views were almost as powerful in shaping the course of history in the territories of their roads as were environmental conditions. On top of this, vast mineral and cattle empires were organized which had their distinctive bearings on the course of western history after the war.

In Washington a cloak and dagger system of national politics controlled the fate of territories and the organization of new states. Generally speaking it was more desirable for the Republican party to operate from within the established framework of states rather than to increase the number of states. Too, there were a certain number of political plums which could be shared in the form of territorial governorships and other offices. While it is true that most of the new territories promised Republican support in coming elections, Republican Presidents and congressmen might have been reluctant to see new states organized. But by no means can all the fault be laid at the door of the Republicans. Democratically controlled congresses were even more reluctant to see the opposition party gain control of a larger block of national support in the delegations which would be admitted from new states.

In other areas there were important forces at work. There still prevailed in the West the old frontier element which had pushed American civilization across the continent and was now concentrating on the mountain, basin and plains territories. The process of pioneering was still going on with the same momentum which had been built up in Ohio, Kentucky and Missouri. Bearded men armed with rifles and blacksnake whips still hauled families and meager worldly goods from one block of free land to another in search of the idyllic garden of the American frontier. From log cabin to sod house, to framed isolated cottages they continued to live a primitive form of life. They enjoyed the same simple forms of amusements, practiced the same vices, committed the same crimes, listened to the same political speeches, and reacted with the same emotions which had motivated the famous Donelson party in Tennessee, or sent the Boone and Henderson parties hustling into Kentucky, or brought the Marietta settlers drifting down the Ohio aboard flatboats.

Agricultural Unrest

The long white covered-wagon trains which crossed the Blue and Cascade mountains, drifted down the Santa Fe Trail, or wound their way across the Dakota, Montana, and Wyoming plains, were but continuations of those that had gone before. Each succeeding generation of frontiersmen were but legatees of the Robertsons, Seviers, Boones and Kentons. Except for specific geographical conditions and vast changes in basic scenery, there was after all little or no difference in the human element of pioneering. But there was a vast difference in the overhead mechanics of national expansion. Technological advances after the Civil War greatly facilitated the pioneering process. Railway expansion, steamboat improvements, revolutionary changes in the field of farm implements, vastly improved firearms coming out of the Civil War, and the general restlessness created by the war itself added new and quickening elements to frontier expansion. Development of new markets abroad for American products and the expansion of the industrial process were vital factors in filling out the political continent. Finally, the growing unrest among the farmers of the country was to bear heavily upon the final phases of pioneering. Failure of debtors to meet their obligations, rising tax rates, high interests, ruinous freight rates, the high price of agricultural implements, and the falling prices of farm products after 1875 brought about conditions reminiscent at least of those which had prevailed in the panic of 1819. There was, however, a fundamental difference; the modern problem was much larger in pattern and more intense in its influence. Possibilities of running away from one's social and economic mistakes were becoming limited so far as a free land frontier was concerned. Likewise possibilities of individual adjustments to oppressive conditions had disappeared.

Farming in the United States after 1865 had changed radically in its basic meaning in local and domestic economy. Inflation caused by the war had sent prices of farm products up to unprecedented levels, and farming became as nearly profitable for all farmers as it had ever been in the history of the country. It was in the initial stages of the postwar era that the transcontinental railway systems began functioning, and their desperate need for freight caused them to place heavy emphasis upon immigrants to move into their territories and upon settled farmers and ranchers to produce increasing quantities of farm products. At the same time when roads themselves were competing with each other for freight, certain abuses were practiced in an unregulated industry which tended to exploit shippers in noncompetitive areas. Soon abuses such as "long" and "short" haul rates, rebates, and other types of technical discriminations became a part of the thinking of western shippers. Roads were accused of concealed rates, overcapitalization, stock watering and preferential treatment.

Along with the high freight and interest rates was the matter of prices. Now that American farm products were competing with those of other countries in a world market, domestic prices were often governed by the world surplus supply of grains and meat. Just as important as the prices

paid for farm products were the emotional reactions of the farmers themselves. When a farmer bought clothing, farm machinery or paid his taxes,
he was left in an angry frame of mind toward his unseen oppressors.

Back of the economic disturbance of the farmers in the period from
1870 to 1900 was a fundamental fact. Americans had always been an
agrarian people. Farming was basic to their way of life, and the greater
part of the frontier advance was agricultural in nature. Land was the very
lodestone of the movement. From it came the fortunes and misfortunes of
the people. In most of the frontier advance, however, farming was a
frantic matter of the moment; a stable way of farm life had to await the
future. In 1866 Oliver Hudson Kelley brought this fact into focus in the
report of his journey into the South. The next forty years saw the organization of granges, the Farmer's Alliance and other bodies which
dealt with the social, economic and political aspects of the agrarian crusade.

The West was vitally concerned with this phase of national unrest.
Its farmers had multiplied in staggering numbers. A vast new acreage of
land had been put to plow, and mountainous storehouses of grain and meat
were being piled on a sagging market each year. Silver mines of the region
supplied an increasing amount of bullion; at the same time the greenback
evil placed the man who had to enter a glutted market each year with
further economic woes. Out of the West came a group of agrarian crusaders who by picturesque speech, unbridled anger, a generous streak of
idealism, and a tincture of demagoguery, gave the farmers' unrest wide
publicity. Among the western leaders were Mrs. Mary Lease of Kansas,
James B. Weaver of Iowa, "Bloody Bridles" David H. Waite of Colorado,
and "Sockless" Jerry Simpson of Kansas. In some considerable measure the
sins of wasteful exploitation of frontier resources were catching up with
the American settler. On the other hand, the rapid advance of the frontier
after 1865 left a vast amount of social and economic immaturity in its
path. James Bryce described this restless surging against the free land
barrier:

> This constant reaching forward to and grasping at the future does not
> so much express itself in words, for they are not a loquacious people, as
> in the air of ceaseless haste and stress which pervades the West. They
> remind you of the crowd which Vathek found in the hall of Eblis, each
> darting hither and thither with swift steps and unquiet mien, driven to
> and fro by a fire in the heart. Time seems too short for what they have to
> do, and result always to come short of their desire. One feels as if caught
> and whirled along in a foaming stream, chafing against its banks, such
> is the passion of these men to accomplish in their own life-times what
> in the past it took centuries to effect.

Extensive governmental oversight of corporations became a necessity after 1870. This was to be true at both the federal and state levels, but an established fact well known to both constitutional convention delegate and corporation was that a state legislature was much more amenable to pressure than was Congress. Despite the fact the state legislator lived politically closer to the people than the national representatives, their inclination to corporate vassalage was much greater.

A new frontier was developing before the old one disappeared. The tide of emigration was beginning by the 1870's to reverse itself. Young men and women who had sought fortunes in the backwoods now began to turn to the cities. The frontier advance itself had created numerous urban communities in which possibilities of fortune and excitement were much greater than slaving away on a drouth-strickened government claim. Industrial cities in the older parts of the country beckoned to youths who formerly might have gone west. The new frontier of finance, technology, and management were in time to produce frontiersmen as highly glorified as the great scouts and trailbreakers of an earlier period. Incorporated industry, transportation and even farming, not only produced a new frontier of endeavor, but also made planned efforts to see that promising talents achieved even greater results.

These were the new stage properties which were being moved onto the national stage, even before the old play was finished. Indian fighters fired their last guns in the smothering fumes of locomotives. Individual miners with flowing beards and gaunt cheeks leading pack-worn burros from one bit of outcropping to the next were only antiquated ornaments on the landscape. Powerful machines which moved mountains and crushed rocks in their great jaws were now the real actors. The sweaty frontier plowman being jerked and tossed behind a clumsy ox-drawn sodbuster was pushed aside by the smoking tractor leviathan. Brick factories fired with imported coal, and northern and western sawmills dug the people out of the ground like boring machines destroying prairie dog burrows. Centers of economic interest shifted to San Francisco, Denver, Omaha, St. Louis, Chicago and the financial nerve center of New York. The prices of the main western products, wheat and cattle, were now governed to an important extent by the fluctuations of world conditions and the greater international market. The local banker was only a handmaiden to the bigger financial world. The local gambler became part of a bigger city ring, and the local prostitute in all her tawdriness either had to join the grand circuits, moving from hotel to hotel in the cities, or turn respectable and marry a hard working country boy and spend the rest of her life living down her past.

Delegates to state constitutional conventions after 1870 were called upon to consider new facts in establishing state government. It was no longer enough to produce the most recently-drafted state constitution, make a few local adaptations, permit the writing-in of a few pet ideas of leading delegates, accept a lengthy statement of rights which usually showed definite signs of descent from the Second Pennsylvania Constitution, and rush the document off to an anxious congress for creation of the new state. Now there were new and insistent pressure groups knocking at the convention doors. Women everywhere were demanding their rights. Suffragettes were driving home the embarrassing point, after the adoption of the Fourteenth Amendment, that they should be given the same political privileges as Negroes. Local sisterhoods rushed into the fray with the weight of the national woman's movement behind them. After the decision of Munn *vs.* Illinois, farmers and other shippers demanded regulation of public carriers. In fact the whole issue of the corporation monster had to be considered. Long clauses now had to be written and fought through conventions regulating the money powers, whether they were railroads or manufacturing and mining industries. The organized granger or farmer movements were enormously influential in shaping public opinion and political attitudes on the frontier.

Historians of the frontier have tended to ignore the influence of the weekly newspapers in determining the course of political events. The rural editors lived close to the soil, and they had a realistic notion of the problems which confronted farmers in the field of low prices and rising freight rates. Though most of the editors were politically conservative and were often swayed by forces which controlled the awarding of favors, collectively they helped to form an aroused public opinion. The issue of broadening the suffrage base was ready-made for them, and their resistance was high.

Old frontier constitutional issues had centered around such academic questions of ages and qualifications of officials, the base of the electorate, the composition of the courts, and the place of localities in the larger structure of state government. Occasionally a radical wing of a convention was able to drive through an innovation, but orthodoxy was the rule. The radicals dissipated their energies in letters to the press and by writing pamphlets. But the last quarter of the nineteenth century was a different age. Radicals of a new sort were appearing on the scene. There was grave danger that orthodox forces could not hold out against them much longer. Southern states, bound down by the forces of reconstruction, were now undoing the handiwork of the radical conventions. Even states which had not experienced the bitterness of Reconstruction were reappraising their constitutions as safeguards against stormier days of changing political philosophies. As a result, the new state constitutions were long and ponderous documents which contained numerous ambiguities and obscurities. Attempts were made to regulate institutions and persons for all time to come. Never in American history have constitutional delegates assumed themselves to be wiser men of destiny than in this period. As a result much of their work in this age of economic change was obsolete almost before the last voter had scratched his ballot approving its ratification.

Possibly no writers of constitutions ever had so little faith in representative government as did those of the last two decades of the nineteenth century. A fear of the people had been demonstrated in the eighteenth century documents, but modern delegates had come to know the power of railroad lobbyists and special interest pressure groups. They were even afraid of the farmers, and they spelled out in the constitutions their restrictions on taxes, state debts, railroads, corporations, and public resources. Amendment clauses were carefully designed so as to prevent runaway changes of constitutions. Collectively the new state constitutions all over the nation comprised a bulwark of conservatism and finality of action that has handicapped the states in making governmental progress.

It was in this age that the so-called "omnibus states" came into being. As stated previously, the territories of Washington, Idaho, Wyoming, Montana and Dakota had been created in 1853 and during the Civil War years. These territories were isolated, and their populations were not stabilized really until the coming of the Northern Pacific and Great Northern railroads. In the mining areas, population had drifted in and out with the rise and decline of mining prospects. The war itself had its effects on the growth of the territories, but the greatest drawback was the lack of adequate transportation facilities to transport population into the region and to carry farm and industrial products out of it. To a certain extent, as has been said, the territorial offices were political plums which Lincoln had passed out to his own personal friends or to the friends of his cabinet members.

When radical forces gained control of the national government after 1865, they found the territorial offices fruitful places in which to exploit the resources of the frontier. Political favorites were put into office with indifferent results for the territories themselves. The great national scandals such as the Credit Mobilier, the Indian supply contracts and the public land grabs all had their bearings on conditions in the territories, as did the earlier conflict between the President and Congress during the Johnson administration. In 1876 Oregon became deeply involved in the Hayes-Tilden disputed election when two sets of returns were sent to Washington in what was proved to be a questionable political maneuver to reverse the decision of the voters at the polls to favor Samuel J. Tilden.

In the area of public opinion, the American people regarded the northern plains of the West and the Northwest as lawless areas where Indian
wars prevailed and where robbers and thieves of every description operated
with a free hand. Thousands of inches of readyprint published by country
newspapers everywhere gave publicity to the sensational aspects of this
phase of territorial civilization. Activities of the vigilantes even found
their way into the nation's most popular literary resource, the famous dime
novels. These books from the houses of Beadle, Adams and Monroe gave
lurid pictures of life in the West. Heroes grew tall while multitudes of
villains stretched rope before snarling vigilantes. The road agent became,
in the popular mind, a distinguished citizen in the wild mountain and plain
stretches; and the possibilities of statehood for the territories was a thing
of the unpredictable future.

Of far more fundamental importance to the territories was the political
situation in Washington. After 1876 the Democrats either had control of
the House or exercised enough influence in the Senate to block the organization of new states. Possibly the Republicans might have exerted enough
pressure to have admitted the territories as states with the expectancy of
gaining electoral votes. There was a definite trend toward Republican
regularity with the expansion of the homestead movement, but the final
decision was not with the Republicans despite the fact Republican Presidents sat in the White House from 1861 to 1885. In the period, 1880–1882,
when a Republican majority in congress might have permitted the admission of Dakota Territory, the state could not be organized ahead of the
arrival of a Democratic majority in Congress in 1882.

With the Democrats in power after 1885 there was still a delay in organizing the new states. In only one of the territories could they be sure of
acquiring a safe Democratic majority and that was in New Mexico. Its admission involved several significant exceptions to the congressional prescriptions for the admission of new states. In the western and northwestern territories, however, Congress faced a problem which it could not
ignore. Since 1876 there had been a sharp rise in population. Every territory had well over the necessary 60,000 population which had been accepted in the past. In 1890 Washington had 349,390; Idaho, 84,385; Montana, 132,159; Wyoming, 60,705; North Dakota, 182,719; and South
Dakota, 328,308. All of these states experienced a sharp rise in population
in the decade, 1880–1890. Some of this was due to foreign immigration.
North Dakota had 44.58 per cent foreign born; South Dakota, 27.60; Montana, 32.61; Wyoming, 24.57; Washington, 24.76; and Idaho, 20.69.

After the election of 1888 the Democrats had the choice of admitting
the new states and possibly gaining some favor from them in the future
or of permitting the Republicans to do so. As a result an enabling act was

passed and signed on February 22, 1889, permitting Washington, Montana, North and South Dakota to frame constitutions and to seek admission to the Union. Idaho was not included in the congressional action, but it proceeded under its own authority to prepare a constitution. Montana was the first of the "omnibus states" to be admitted. It became a member of the Union on November 8, 1889, and was followed in quick succession by North and South Dakota, Washington, Idaho and Wyoming. Within the space of eight months six new states were added to the Union, and many of the old western problems which had prevailed under territorial management were now erased. The admission of these territories to the Union did not necessarily halt the pioneering process, but much of the color and social chaos was taken out of it.

Congress had seen fit in passing the enabling acts to require the states to abolish racial discrimination in the field of civil rights, to insure a public school system, to promote religious toleration, to renounce claims on public lands and to establish a republican form of government. Even more important was the political philosophy written into state constitutions. These documents showed a remarkable kinship in their contents and organization. They all dealt in some detail with local problems such as mining laws, grazing problems, water rights and the regulation of corporations. Possibly the most distinct liberal innovation among the six documents was the provision that women were given full right to vote in all elections in Wyoming.

Fear of debt, taxes and corporations was amply demonstrated, and as a result much material which might be clearly classified as statutory found its way into the constitutions. Aroused founding fathers of the 1880's and 1890's tried hard to be specific in their efforts to protect themselves and their progeny against the tyrannies of the present and the follies of future generations. Possibly this pattern was largely set for them by the unusually long enabling acts which instructed all the territories except Idaho to proceed with state organization. Congress itself had developed a fear that territorial irresponsibility would produce constitutions that would leave loopholes either for exploitative corporations to drain off the substance of the nation or for radicals to destroy democracy at the fountainheads of state constitutions.

Indian Territory

While emigrants and miners drifted westward across Kansas to Colorado and Utah or followed the trail across the mountains to Oregon, Washington and Idaho territories, Kansas settlers had their eyes on the open lands in the Indian Territory. There were approximately 75,000 Indians in an area of 68,000 square miles. Obviously the land was not being absorbed by the tribes. Too, there were two prevailing local attitudes toward the Indians in 1875. First, some of the tribes or nations had supported the South in the Civil War; second, the Kiowas, Comanches, Arapahoes and Cheyennes were on the war path in 1870–1875 and stirred anew the old border hatreds.

Aside from the emotional attitudes which prevailed along the border in the 1870's, there were two important new economic activities which were to have a major bearing on frontier expansion. Cattlemen were driving their herds north after the war; three major trails, Chisholm, Shawnee, and Western, went directly across the Indian country. Four famous cattle trail and military landmarks were either in the Indian country or just on its border. These were Doan's Store at the Red River crossing, Forts Reno and Gibson and Baxter Springs. When the herds first started across the prairies of the Indian Territory their owners were either forced to pay in beef for the privilege of going on or suffer losses from stampedes and attacks upon their cowboys. In time a working arrangement was agreed upon by which the cattle drovers could cross the country and even lease parts of the territory for extended grazing privileges. One of the most notable instances of such a leasehold was that of the Cherokee Strip Livestock Association, which in 1882 leased 6,500,000 acres of highly desirable virgin prairie lands from the Cherokee National Council. In return they paid the Indians $140,000 in fees. Conditions surrounding this agreement were of a suspicious nature, and charges were made both within and without the Indian nation that there were bribes. In time other cattlemen acquired grazing rights in the territory, and in combination they became a powerful pressure group which influenced the course of future events in this part of the West.

In 1866 the United States entered into a new series of treaties with the Creek, Choctaw, Chickasaw, Seminole, and Cherokee nations. Back of these treaties was the whole confused condition caused in the Indian Territory by the Civil War. Internecine dissension and fighting had left all the Five Civilized Tribes in difficulty. In some instances the ravages of the war had been relatively as great as in the path of Sherman's Army in Georgia and South Carolina. Houses and farms were left in ruin. Dissension rent the political organizations, and the issue of loyalty of the leaders were all factors in current Indian affairs.

At the same time the people of Kansas were repeating the unhappy chapter of Georgia history in the 1830's. The Kansas Indians were being squeezed out, and the United States Government was forced to find a place for them to go. Railroad promoters looked to the west. At least three lines—the Missouri, Kansas, and Texas Pacific—the Atchison, Topeka and Santa Fe—and the Atlantic and Pacific, as projected—proposed to cross the territory. This was added pressure which gave excuse to make political attacks on the territorial Indians. A hireling, no doubt, of the railroad interest was Elias Cornelius Boudinot. He was part Cherokee, the son of the famous Elias Boudinot who had been killed in 1839 because of his act in signing the treaty of removal in 1835. Young Boudinot had been given a fair education, he possessed special talents, one of which was musical, and he was an impressive man among backwoodsmen because of his intellectual abilities. He became active in supporting the Confederate cause. He served as secretary of the secession convention in Arkansas and became a congressional representative in the Confederate Congress at Richmond. Actually his associations with the Cherokees in the Indian Territory were tenuous at best. Boudinot was pitted against the aging John Ross for control of Cherokee affairs in Washington. He was a forthright opportunist who raised superficial issues and dragged up Cherokee supporters from as far away as California to support his cause. Financially, Boudinot found that agitating the Indian issue as a paid railroad lobbyist was profitable.

In March, 1865, the Senate passed the Harlan Bill which proposed a complete reorganization of Indian policy for the Territory. This measure suggested the creation of a territorial government, distribution of lands in severalty, and the admission of white settlers to the region. This was a radical departure from the philosophy which had been developed upon Indian removal from the South. Before the Harlan Bill could pass the House, however, the treaties of 1866 with the civilized tribes and their neighbors were signed, and reasons for enacting the bill were removed. These latter agreements provided for the freeing of slaves held by Indians and made economic provisions for them in the territory. Provisions were also made for the granting of railway right-of-ways across tribal lands, surrender of the Choctaw-Chickasaw "Leased District," the purchase of 2,169,000 acres of Seminole lands for fifteen cents an acre and the resale to the Seminoles of 200,000 acres at fifty cents an acre. The Creeks were to surrender 3,250,560 acres at thirty cents per acre. In addition to these agreements, room was to be made for the removal of the Kansas Indians to the Territory, and for the removal of future tribes who found themselves in the path of white expansion. Essentially the treaties of 1866 established the Indian Territory of Oklahoma. These negotiations were made in the opening years of Reconstruction when governmental energies were being turned in another direction, and it is fair to observe that the Indian Office did little to distinguish the government in either fair or intelligent administration. Pressure groups of all sorts were now ready to pounce upon the large blocks of freed lands, and again the government failed to develop a clear-cut policy beforehand.

Here in the Indian Territory was what really amounted to one of the last big blocks of free lands on the frontier. It lay in the heart of the fertile plains country, and the very nature of the region invited cattlemen and settlers to its borders. Its rolling prairies of tall buffalo and blue stem grass, its waving fields of wild flowers, wooded valleys, and pleasant streams indeed gave it the characteristics of a bountiful garden. As more land-hungry settlers crowded up to the Arkansas, Texas, and Kansas borders, the more seductive the giant meadow became. Adding to the natural allurements of the country were the pressures, subtle and otherwise, which merchants and railroad promoters put on the prospective settlers. For border town merchants, the equipping of settlers was profitable business, and the more settlers that appeared in the towns, the more business flourished. Railway promoters sought farmers, town dwellers, and freight producers. No more horrible spectre ever faced railway builders than vast stretches of unsettled country. On the other hand, cattlemen applied just an opposite type of pressure. Settlers with women, children, milk cows, wire fences, and plows were anathema.

Boomers

Seekers after free land in Kansas found a leader in David L. Payne. Payne was born of frontier parents in Fairmount, Indiana. He had received a rudimentary education in backwoods schools, but, characteristic of his age, his dreams for the future directed his ambitions westward. Relatives had gone to Kansas, and newspapers told of the Mormon disturbances. In 1857 David and his brother Jack went West to join Albert Sidney Johnston's "Mormon" army, but when they arrived in Kansas, the army was gone. The young Hoosier acquired a claim to a homestead and gave promise of settling down as a Kansas farmer. The times were too exciting, however, for a thrill-seeking lad, and during the next ten years of his life David Payne served in the Union Army on the frontier and with the Army of the Potomac, and then participated in the Indian campaigns in the 1860's and 70's. At one time he served under the command of George Armstrong Custer. In several of the postwar years when not in military service Captain Payne went from one job to another, with no success in any of them.

In many respects this border soldier was a true legatee of John Sevier, George Rogers Clark, and Daniel Boone. Apparently he had little desire for personal glory. His restless and thriftless nature kept him from being either a successful farmer or a dependable businessman. His sense of money was preadolescent, and his capacity for faithfully transacting business was of the same degree of immaturity. Among his virtues was his absolute fearlessness. He also possessed that indefinable quality which drew men to him. He was self-sacrificing and uncomplaining even in the face of the meanest hardships. Even when he failed to fulfill his financial responsibilities, he seems to have retained the confidence and regard of his friends. In physical appearance Payne was of a rugged build, he was dreamy-eyed, and in many respects boyishly handsome.

Drifting from one homestead to another, and from one job to another, Payne wound up in Washington with a small political sinecure as assistant doorkeeper in the House of Representatives. While in this job he became acquainted with Elias Boudinot who no doubt influenced him in his thinking about the free lands south of the Kansas border. Payne lost his political job and drifted back to Kansas in the late fall of 1879. During that winter he organized Payne's Oklahoma Colony and the Oklahoma Town Company. Dues in the first organization were two dollars, and in the latter, twenty-five. Possibly Payne collected as much as $100,000 by the time of his death in 1884, but he died penniless.

"Booming" was an old frontier art even before David Payne was born. It had occurred along the frontier in protest against the Proclamation in 1763, in the old Northwest, in West Florida, in Texas, California, Iowa, Minnesota, Kansas, and Washington. Possibly the most recent act of booming had been that of the drifter C. C. Carpenter and the 15,000 miners who had invaded the Sioux Territory in the Black Hills of South Dakota and Wyoming in 1875–1876. Carpenter was an astonishing character who wore long curls draped over a velvet jacket, a fancy vest, and a tall beaver hat. In April, 1879, he and his wife appeared in Kansas and undertook to raise funds from border merchants to support a boomer movement into the Indian Territory. A considerable number of settlers gathered in Coffeyville and other border towns to begin a land rush. In the meantime President Rutherford B. Hayes and Secretary of the Interior Carl Schurz established military forces along the border under the command of General John Pope of Bull Run fame. Carpenter was frightened away, taking with him the local merchants' cash and the stranded settlers' hopes.

This was the situation as David Payne found it in the winter of 1879. In the spring of 1880 he and the Oklahoma boomers began a long series of invasions of the Indian lands which brought repeated arrests and removals by the army. The boomer leader contended that he and his followers were not encroaching upon Indian lands, that under the terms of the treaties of 1866 the ceded areas were now a part of the public domain and subject to claim under the terms of the Homestead Act. Possibly Payne conscientiously believed that the President would relent and open the territory to settlement. From a legalistic point of view the boomers were subject only to removal and frustration of their efforts to establish claims because there was no penalty attached to the invasions. Laws protecting Indian lands were most defective, and legally, at least, the government was defenseless against the invaders.

David Payne was a persistent man who organized repeated invasion parties. His orations were persuasive, and even when he was under the influence of alcohol, his followers still had great faith in what he said. He no doubt enjoyed considerable support from the merchants in the border towns who thrived on the increased business which each wave of settlers brought. The railroads were likewise effective in giving him both moral support and material aid. Payne alternated between a state of bankruptcy with court judgments hanging over his head and a state of solvency in which settler enlistment funds permitted him rather free action. He invested all of his personal resources in the movement so that court judgments against him only wasted the time of judges.

In four years Payne kept the trails well-worn between the Kansas border and the north bank of the Canadian River. He and his immigrant bands covered the landscape with claim stakes. Behind them they left numerous dug wells and piles of ashes of cabins and camp sites as reminders they had invaded the country. The army used Negro soldiers largely to combat this stubborn band of invaders. In a short time the settlers and "yellow legs," as the soldiers were called, became well-acquainted. One of the biggest complaints the soldiers had against the boomers was the fact that they chose the worst weather of the year to make their invasions, and the barracks were filled with men who suffered frostbite and other damages of the trail. Often the soldiers and settlers played an extended hide-and-seek game by riding for miles side by side along the Kansas border, the soldiers waiting for the boomers to invade the territory below the line. Payne was equally as well-known in the federal courts at Wichita, Kansas, and Fort Smith, Arkansas, under the "dead-letter" territorial trespass law which Congress had refused to revise. Only civil action could be brought against Payne and the boomers. Only once did the army and court frighten the invasion leader, and that was the occasion when he was charged with introducing whisky into the territory in the Rock Falls invasion of 1884. Violation of the liquor statute carried the penalty of a jail sentence.

Payne possessed many qualities of leadership, but in a final analysis his personal weaknesses and instabilities possibly overbalanced his virtues. He drank excessively, was wholly irresponsible where money was involved, and was everlastingly optimistic and impulsive on occasions when he should have been informed and judicious. On the other hand he was persistent and dedicated in promoting his cause. Even in the face of terrific hardship, exposure and intense physical pain, he continued his crusade. He thrived on the stimulus of the acclaim of his followers and he was highly subject to self-intoxication by his own orations. His detractors seemed to have made little headway against him, though he was often subjected to the bitterest criticisms and accusations. By 1884 there was a slight ray of promise that the rugged boomer leader would win. He had won a significant court decision in a charge of conspiracy when Judge C. G. Foster in the federal court at Fort Smith dismissed the charges against him.

Four years of boomer activities had created a tremendous interest in the Territory. The newspaper press was active in giving widespread publicity to the movement. In fact, public opinion in border areas had become so actively aroused that the lower house of Congress refused to support an effective trespass law that would make invasion of the Territory a criminal act. In 1884 Senator Preston B. Plumb of Kansas introduced a bill in the Senate to open Indian territory to homestead entry. Senator George C. Vest of Missouri offered a substitute bill to purchase the lands free of restrictions to be opened to white settlement. Secretary of the Interior Henry M. Teller favored purchase of the surplus lands in his report to the President, and in January, 1885, Colonel Edward Hatch expressed the opinion he could not hold the boomers back. There were even signs that the administration in Washington might even relent. But Payne's booming days were over, his soul was on the verge of invading other lands. At breakfast on November 27, he turned to his common-law wife Anna Haines with a startled expression on his face and slumped forward in death.

When the oratorical tongue of David Payne was stilled, and no longer was he present to ride beside the long invasion trains in his characteristically slumped position in the saddle, W. L. Couch, a trusted lieutenant, assumed leadership. The army of boomers was growing, and in January, 1885, Couch led his first train of settlers to Stillwater Creek. Here he just barely missed a serious brush between his people and the "yellow legs" under the command of Colonel Edward Hatch. A month after the removal of Couch's party, Grover Cleveland took the oath of office as President, and a change was instituted in governmental policy in Oklahoma. Couch made a second invasion to the Canadian River, but generally speaking he and his people were fairly quiet until 1889.

Cattlemen had been unrelenting enemies of the settlers. Cowboys had even appeared at times when the soldiers arrived to drive the settlers back over the Kansas border. Their derision in these trying moments had not been acts of public good will. Too, the settlers were convinced that cowboys had informed the soldiers of their whereabouts. In the summer of 1885 a Senatorial committee arrived in Kansas to investigate the situation of the Indian Territory. Its chairman was Senator H. L. Dawes, who had become a crusader in the field of Indian legislation. Couch aired the grievances of the boomers before this committee, including the feeling of discrimination which had been aroused by the cattlemen's leases. These leases, he was convinced, enjoyed official sanction and protection. The old question of bribery by the cattle interests was revived, and it was pointed out that hundreds of miles of wire fencing enclosed great stretches of the prairies in the Cherokee Outlet. There were ranch houses, stables, sheds, loading pens, and other necessary permanent structures for the operation of a grazing industry. Hundreds of thousands of ranch cattle grazed in the Cherokee lands and elsewhere in the territory. As a result of these hearings and recommendations from the army, President Cleveland ordered the removal of the herds. This resulted in the destruction of the fences, ranch buildings, and the removal of the cattle, many of which were placed on an already glutted beef market to further reduce prices.

General Nelson A. Miles, in command of the Missouri District, recommended that changes be made in the Indian Territory. It had outlived its usefulness. Either it had to be absorbed into the American social and political system or be destroyed by the press of population crowding in about it. This recommendation was in fact a sad commentary on the lingering heedlessness of the Jackson administration. Indian removal had been heartless and unplanned beyond the mere physical displacement of the tribes. Government officials were offering the "wastelands" beyond the Mississippi to the tribes in perpetuity. Even President Jackson set the pattern in his uninformed oratorical flourishes which he sent Congress, and that body had responded with the Indian Intercourse Act of 1834. Now the day of reckoning had arrived. The Dawes Act embodied the principle of holding lands in severalty, but the Five Civilized Tribes, and the Osage, Sac, Fox and Miamis were excepted. It was necessary to negotiate individually with these Indians to establish the principle of severalty. By making rather large monetary payments for surplus lands reclaimed by the government, a new series of agreements were signed. On March 2, 1889, President Cleveland signed the law which opened the Oklahoma Territory to homestead rights. Senator Dawes attached a rider to the act which promised that if a "sooner" should enter the territory ahead of the official time of entry he would be required to forfeit his ill-gotten claim.

When Benjamin Harrison came to office he proclaimed the entry time as noon, April 22, 1889. At this hour settlers might enter the Territory to locate and register official claims. Almost two regiments of soldiers were moved into Oklahoma to keep the "sooners" out and to attempt to insure a fair race for the lands. Excitement mounted. Legitimate settlers mingled with adventurers who came for the thrill of the race. All around the borders of the Territory people crowded up to the line waiting for the entry signal. Some came in wagons, carriages, mounted on horseback, and afoot. The Santa Fe Railroad ran five settler trains into the region. Stagecoach lines made special runs to haul settlers. When the noon signal was sounded there was a wild rush. Wagoners turned their vehicles over, some were stuck in the quicksands of the streams, and others were in collision accidents. Many of those who went by rail did not wait for the trains to stop but jumped off, taking chances that they would not be injured in the falls.

Efforts to keep the "sooners" out had not been altogether successful. Some had entered the territory ahead of time and had remained hidden until the official moment to make entry arrived. Some were even found plowing their lands when the legitimate homesteaders arrived. One group of claimants made the start from railway construction camps in the territory. Among these were W. L. Couch and Anna Haines, both of whom lost their claims because of illegal entry. Reminiscent of Daniel Boone and Simon Kenton on the old trans-Appalachian frontier, these last free land pioneer leaders entered the garden, but they were unable to pluck the fruit.

There were 12,000 tracts of quarter section homesteads, and an estimated 100,000 prospective claimants with 20,000 people present for the rush. Oklahoma City, Kingfisher, Guthrie and other towns came into existence almost overnight. The peculiar condition prevailed that Congress had not made legislative provision for the claiming of town lots. Town areas were restricted to 320 acres, and this caused the organization of many villages which clustered about an original core. On May 2, 1890, the Oklahoma Territory was created, and an organized government was begun in the territory which already had a population of more than 60,000 souls. George W. Steele of Indiana was appointed governor by President Harrison.

The Oklahoma landrush symbolized a significant fact in frontier history. The supply of free lands of a prime and desirable quality of any considerable quantity was all but exhausted. There were to be other smaller land rushes, but none of them equalled the so-called "Harrison's Hoss Race." In a century and a half, American frontiersmen had overrun the continent. When the census report of 1890 was published, the superintendent reviewed a hundred years of national expansion, giving detailed attention to the population aspect of American growth. He located the spread of population across the frontier by decades and analyzed the environmental and topographic influences which shaped the patterns of settlement. Centers of population in a hundred years had advanced from Maryland to a cornfield near the village of Westport, Indiana.

Factors such as improved transportation, a growing national industrial system, an expanding international trade and a rising tide of foreign immigration all played important parts in changing the social and political patterns of the country. So far as the frontier was concerned the most important fact was that only four territories, Utah, Arizona, New Mexico, and Oklahoma, remained outside the Union of states, and political reasons largely kept them without the pale. The nation had most of its frontier experience behind it. The dream of an inexhaustible supply of free land was ended, a dream that had been phenomenally brief. Then national energies and interests were to be devoted to domestic integration of its human and natural resources and to the great field of international challenges. But sentimentally and spiritually the pioneering experiences on a vast continent left their marks, however difficult their fundamental meanings and contributions are to define and evaluate.

The Frontier in Transition

The free land frontier was considered to be closed technically in 1890. This fact was determined in the area of abstract statistical reporting rather than in a visible close of the frontier. Obviously the spiritual frontier in fact remained open. There was still some free land left, and there was still a huge challenge of exploitation of territory. There are no precise standards by which the historian can determine the exact meaning of the westward movement in conditioning the American spirit and mind, nor the influence the movement had upon the adaptations of the civilizing institutions of the country. It is possibly enough to say that the distinguishable influences of the westward movement were powerful and that the patterns of human behavior were stamped heavily upon the face of American social and economic development.

The technical closure of the frontier in 1890 coincided with three or four major events in American history, among which were the growth of heavy industry, the revolt of the farmers, rise of the influence of the United States in the community of nations and the rise of the American cities. Railway expansion afforded a ready solution to the basic problems of movement of heavy freight across the continent. The heyday of the steamboat was ended, and rail centers rather than the river towns became major centers of trade. Already machines were replacing an appreciable portion of manpower on the farm. The tractor and automatic harvesting machines gave the individual farmer enormous powers of exploitation. An individual farmer found himself in possession of tremendous facilities for disturbing the ancient balances between land, forests and grass, and for creating hazardous conditions in the realm of the conservation of resources. At the same time, man in a sense entered a new and scientific frontier in which he resorted to use of new farming methods, chemical fertilizers, and the adaptation of new and improved plant types. A plain dirt farmer was in time to multiply tenfold his contributions to the maintenance of a rising national and world population. In moments of crisis the American farmer supplied the necessary amount of economic security to tide the nation through its difficulties.

Politically, both farmer and the several special sectional interests made an impact on the course of national decisions. Farmers in revolt spurred legislative reforms at state and national levels, and they effected changes in both major political parties. Regulatory legislation was brought about by changing conditions in most of the agrarian parts of the country. The drabness and monotony of rural life forced enactment of legislation which promised variety and a freshening of interests. Paradoxically, a spirit of isolation was to express itself most clearly in an age when the industrial and political nation was reaching beyond its borders for solutions to many of its domestic problems. As the United States advanced toward a position of world leadership, it had to reckon with political reactions in many of its sections.

Expansion of the national population, the rise of industry and the growth of American cities checked, if they did not halt, the frontier movement. Youths who in other years would have escaped social and economic competition in older settled communities by moving westward then turned their steps toward the expanding cities. Wage-paying factories, packing houses and offices opened new opportunities to rural and farm youths. Cities such as Chicago, St. Louis, Dallas, Omaha, Denver, San Francisco, Seattle and Portland in time drew millions of agrarian migrants to their factories and service industries. Later the great automobile manufacturing centers on the Great Lakes were fed by burgeoning streams of rural workers. The bright lights, the sidewalks, places of amusement, and the relative assurance of steady pay checks drew people away from the hard regimen of the land.

In the latter half of the twentieth century there are still discernible underlying influences of frontier origin in national society, politics, and economics. In large measure American folk nostalgia is frontier based. Much of the national literature and historical writings treat western themes, and scholars continue to search for basic facts and sources and to apply fresh interpretations to the pioneering era of American history. So long as the memory of the great pioneer experience remains bright, or historians probe searchingly into the past, the westward movement will remain an important element of our history.

The end is not yet in sight when politics born of sectional interests no longer figure in the making of major national decisions. For instance, joint issues of administering public lands and resources are almost as deeply involved in the latter half of this century as they were a hundred years ago. The fight to preserve the Grand Canyon was intense, but friends of the wilderness won temporary stay of spoliation of this beauty spot, and the President of the United States joined in the public debate to preserve blocks of virgin forests. In other areas the federal government is engaged in acquiring hundreds of thousands of acres of land either to enlarge the public domain or to convert it to public use. Across the sweep of the earliest trans-Appalachian frontier, national parks, forests, and watersheds are slowly reverting to virginal states. The accumulation of vast reservoirs of water, the development of wilderness recreation areas, and reforestation of millions of acres of private and public submarginal lands partially reverse the course of the westward movement. Modern conservation policies attempt in limited fashion to correct mistakes of earlier policies and misuses. Development of the Tennessee Valley Authority with its multiplicity of purposes combines restoration of the land with modern utilization of the resources. It has stirred endless political and economic debate, and so has the increase of public control of segments of the flood plains of the Missouri, Colorado, Columbia, and lesser streams.

Pressures of selfish origins were exerted in the dispersal of the national domain in the eighteenth and nineteenth centuries. These are still active forces. Over the years conservation policies have provoked charges of creeping socialism, and public reclamation of land and resources has brought charges that the delicate balance between private enterprise and government ownership has been upset. Even more fundamental, the politics of conservation has been concerned more directly with both national security and economic well-being of the American people. Conservation ideas promoted by John Wesley Powell, W. J. McGee, Gifford Pinchot, and Hugh H. Bennett have in time brought reappraisal of the American's occupation and exploitation of his vast domain. Intelligent management of the continent's natural resources, argued these pioneers, involved the nation's destiny as deeply as did the original conquest and exploitation of the continent. Historically, failure to acknowledge this doctrine has produced a crisis of broader implication than have some of the sectional political conflicts.

With the formal announcement that the frontier was closed, however little meaning such a statement had, there arose questions of how well Americans had dealt with the great issues raised in pioneering. How well did they manage Indian matters, the dispersal of public lands, the conquest of distance and space, the compromises of international questions, of sectional issues, and the formation of new states? What rewards did the individual American reap from the frontier? In seeking answers to the latter question there is raised the bigger one of how successful were the pioneers in finding peace, perfectibility as a national people, and fortune in the "garden"? How successful were they as individuals in the westward movement? To what extent did they create distinct national and regional cultures and personalities? Finally, what contribution did they make to the realization of national aims and objectives stated so often in public documents, and implied so clearly in areas of the ethics of culture, manifest destiny, nationalism, and the essential attainment of freedom by men?

The larger concept of the frontier as a possible "garden" of human redemption was based upon a false premise anyway. There were too many chastening and corrupting influences in the way. First, the heavy physical task of combating hardships of the land, of nature, of enduring toil and sweat, of establishing a primitive home, organizing an elemental economy, and establishing basic political institutions challenged men. Pioneers, no matter how isolated, were driven under the lash of progress whether it was enlarging a tiny clearing into a field, adding a shed to a cabin, inventing a more efficient farm implement, or building roads, canals, and railroads. As a corrupting influence, few people in the history of civilization were exposed to such temptations of greed and avarice as were those who approached the great landed and mineral frontiers on this continent.

The intervals of societal evolution in many large islands of the frontier were phenomenally brief. Productivity of highly fertile soils reduced greatly the lapse of time between the first human penetration of the virginal forest or prairie Eden and the rise of towns and cities. It also hastened the appearance of many rural-farm problems. However much promotional palaver there may have been about promises of the land, the personal stories contained in diaries, forlorn letters, and contemporary observations of travelers, which now repose in hundreds of libraries and family archives, document the laboriousness and frustrations of pioneering.

The realities of the frontier were even more dramatically revealed in the continuing debates which have occurred since 1763 concerning the maturing of public land policies. Rivalries between speculators and corporate land claimants and settlers in search of modest homesteads stirred almost endless discussions of the virtues of yeoman homesteaders versus feudal land barons who sought to enrich themselves from sales of western lands. Those who stoutly argued the settler's cause revealed rather clear concepts of the dynamics of the westward movement as primarily a social and political phenomenon. The very fabric of American society itself would be patterned by the relationships of people to the land.

From Thomas Jefferson down to the outcries of contemporary conservationists, the crusade to prevent creation of a corporate feudalism by favoritism in land grants has continued. Jefferson actively opposed the speculative land companies of the eighteenth century. Fundamental in his view was fear of transplanting Old World feudalism in America. In subsequent years congressional debates reflected this same fear. This was especially true when pressure groups sought of Congress vast grants of mineral, timber, canal, and railway subsidy lands. Debates preceding the major legislative acts relating to dispersal of the public domain produced revealing discussions of national policy. These debates nearly always centered about the question of creating a stifling monopoly of land owner-ship which in time would be predominantly influential in the courses of local and national legislation.

If the garden failed to flourish for many reasons, some of which have already been discussed, it was sullied most seriously in the area of public integrity. At all levels, from shiftless unwashed squatter moving a jump ahead of organized settler to preemptioners who claimed land and then disposed of it outside the intent of the law, and to corporate claimants who operated at times barely within the secondary spectrum of color of title and law, there was trickery and chicanery. At no time in the history of the westward movement were people oblivious to fraudulent acts. Among the law and policy makers themselves there was infidelity to political trusts. Few if any areas of national concern have been so thoroughly marred by a lack of integrity by so many people as the administration of public lands.

That Americans overcame many errors of land administration and escaped feudalism at the same time is a marvel of frontier history. The germ was ever present for disaster. In some areas land barons exerted enormous political and economic powers. Omnivorous lumbermen robbed virgin stands of timber and moved on leaving behind ghastly scars of waste and pillage. As horrible as this butchery was, it may have been fortunate from a long-range political viewpoint that it happened in this way. Lumbermen were empire builders, but their empires crumbled as rapidly as they exhausted the forests, and few lumbermen remained behind to reclaim the lands and to establish lasting controls over their impoverished baronies. Holders of mineral lands lingered longer, and many of them have exerted an almost feudal control over their areas. They, like lumbermen, have also exhausted their resources and left barren wastes which are almost beyond restitution.

How well the yeoman homesteader himself thrived in the expansion of the western frontier is constantly being appraised by changing standards. He too laid waste to the resources of forest and soil by careless practices of cultivation and grazing. With the introduction of the simplest improved mechanical devices, the frontier Eden was subjected to radical change, if not destruction. Increased production of farm crops created constantly rising pressures. Production and marketing demanded degrees of effi-ciency in land use, application of machines, and management policies seldom adaptable to small family homesteads. This fact was revealed be-fore the Civil War and became more pronounced in each succeeding decade. As American industrial and farm products reached world markets in increasing volume, farming rapidly became a capital enterprise. Whatever other facts figured in the post-Civil War agrarian crisis, changing demands for larger blocks of farm capitalization was of basic importance. It was in these years that vast areas of the frontier were brought into production, and this fact was back of much agrarian unrest.

In other areas of American life the impact of the westward movement exerted itself. The rise of rich urban centers in close proximity to new lands, mineral beds, and timber stands created a fresh driving force in American life. The transporting and fabricating of raw materials into finished products drew on the rural farm population for laborers. The West itself became a profitable market for goods as it produced more supplies for national and world trade. Rise of the cities, and especially those across the frontier, represented more than making good an early nineteenth-century boast that America would surpass the Old World in culture and industry; it was a realization of the bright promises of the land itself. Inland cities were spawns of the westward movement. They bore the imprint of the land and its resources upon their organizations and personalities.

If there ever was a "garden" in fact in frontier America, it existed only in remote places. Doubtless it existed nowhere really except in the minds of romantic frontiersmen and in the pages of promotional land brochures. Constantly the twin cancers of change and impermanence destroyed man-made monuments as fast as they were erected. The idyll of the moment was disrupted by promises of the future. Progress itself was the impelling ethic of the westward movement, and perpetual change reflected progress. Visitors to America commented that nothing remained the same; houses, public buildings, institutions, towns, roads and streets were constantly being demolished, moved, or rebuilt. There were left almost no landmarks of the past like those in Europe. Restless Americans were ever in pursuit of the future and its promise of fortune.

Despite the impermanence of the faces of American civilization, the fact that the federal political system had been spread across the continent was a fact of permanent historical importance. New states were created with almost monotonous repetition with basic constitutional provisions and restraints, under which they were operated with fair degrees of efficiency no matter in which section of the continent they were located. It was this fact rather than innovation and theoretical originality and political experimentation which distinguished the application of federal policies to the expanding frontier. The Nation itself faced and resolved crises born of the westward movement with remarkable success; others it has not yet solved.

An equal challenge—creating an American personality—lingered on in amalgamating a diffuse population. It is remarkable that people of such diverse national cultures, who arrived in America at such broadly spaced intervals, ultimately came to accept concepts of common American political and social aims. It is just as remarkable that widely differing religious views were reconciled without open conflict. The frontier itself produced new religious organizations and doctrines, but disputes never got beyond argumentative and splintering stages.

That Americans solved the problems born of distance and space in so short a time was a monument to both an implicit faith in progress and to national ingenuity. No part of the societal evolution took place so rapidly or with greater impact than did the development of communication and transportation facilities. Though the Nation muddled through almost a century and a half of public-land problems without ever solving them, it never blurred seriously the image of the yeoman American as the key figure in the national population. By congressional acts, court decisions, and compromises many of the conflicts between public and private ownership have been resolved, occasionally with the federal government correcting mismanagement errors of the past.

The major contribution of the westward movement as a meaningful present-day fact may well lie in the willingness of diverse social and economic interests in the Nation to accept compromises and readjustment of issues which often have roots well back into the past when the earliest population flow across the continent began. Thomas Jefferson and men of like views would feel some sense of victory in the modern attitudes toward parts of the public domain, even though forest and prairie are being constantly gnawed to pieces by the machines of progress.

Whether or not a rising urban-industrial America and a constantly shrinking rural-farm population result in the virtual obliteration of most of the social and political landmarks of the westward movement is a matter which only the passage of time can reveal. So far in the interpretation and application of his fundamental beliefs in human rights, the American has not been fully free of a struggle with his conscience and prejudices. Even though there is a sharp rise in urban centers, and urban problems have obscured many of those which once troubled rural Americans, the cities are in fact collections of people, and those people have brought up from the past certain personality traits, traditional economic and political views, and social mores which remain a part of the great pioneering traditions. The history of the city and of a complex industrial age including the American economy is still firmly based on the exploitation of the continent itself in the formative years of the westward movement. The atomic age finds space in the path of the frontier in which to create and test its New World sources of energy, and perhaps to bring about a monstrous societal revolution in the span of years instead of decades.

As American historians in this modern age of the Republic come to re-appraise some of the older concepts of the frontier and its influence on the shaping of the national mind and society, they will no doubt revise sharply many ideas which seemed so solidly fixed in the first quarter of this century. They will review and revise long-held theses about the impact of land and environment on people as a long-enduring fact in national life. No part of the philosophical development of individual Americans will require more penetrative reviewing than their attitudes toward the rapid changes in the way of American life brought about by rapid expansion of the urban and technological age, and the internationalizing of national viewpoints. Viewed over the long period of population movement in the West, the historian has good reason to question many of the older concepts, that the frontier experience left an abiding legacy of a liberal social and political tradition. The ultra conservative reactions in many parts of the West in the latter half of this century seem to indicate a reversal of old ideas and concepts, or the opening of another age in which Americans choose to ignore many of the historic forces of the founding years.

BIBLIOGRAPHY

APPENDIX

CHAPTER 1

The American Frontier—A Perspective

Preparation of a bibliography in American frontier history is a difficult undertaking. This subject includes a central interest in the writing of general American history. Since 1920, historians have produced a large volume of materials which fall into three distinct classes: material which deals with the frontier movement in its broader aspects, treatments of specific regions, and material which is purely local in character. This last category has accounted for ever-growing collections of local books, pamphlets and articles which recount the pioneering experiences of people in various communities across the continent. There are extensive collections of frontier materials in many special libraries and in all of the state historical society holdings. Local sources sometimes record the most satisfactory stories of the frontier.

The subject as a whole has been treated in various comprehensive books. Unlike the history of the United States itself, that of the frontier has a fairly definite concluding date, and its extensiveness is due to extended research rather than an extending chronological period.

In 1893, Frederick Jackson Turner read his famous essay on "The Significance of the Frontier in American History," which was later published as a chapter in his provocative book, *The Frontier in American History*. This essay and the book were to express the so-called Turner thesis, and to open the vistas of frontier history to modern historical scholarship. Some of the more notable fruits of the Turner work are: Dixon Ryan Fox, ed., *Sources of Culture in the Middle West, Background versus Frontier*, N. Y., 1934. This book contains essays by Benjamin F. Wright, Jr., Avery O. Craven, John D. Hicks, and Marcus L. Hansen. A collection of points of view toward the frontier versus background issue is contained in George R. Taylor, ed., *The Turner Thesis Concerning the Role of the Frontier in American History*, Boston, 1949. This volume contains essays by Turner, F. L. Paxson, Benjamin F. Wright, Jr., Fred A. Shannon, Louis M. Hacker, George W. Pierson, Carlton J. Hayes and Avery O. Craven. It presents the various arguments supporting and attacking the Turner thesis. Several of the general histories of the frontier movement contain essays on the subject of the influences of this phase of American history. Stanley Elkins and Eric McKitric have examined the Turner interpretation of the frontier in "A Meaning for Turner's Frontier, Democracy in the Old Northwest," *Political Science Quarterly*, pp. 321–353, vol. LXIX, September, 1954, and "The Southwest Frontier and New England," *ibid.*, pp. 565–602, December, 1954.

Three background works which contain provocative viewpoints of frontier expansion are Henry Nash Smith, *Virgin Land*, Cambridge, 1950, and Marcus L. Hansen, *The Atlantic Migration*, Cambridge, 1941. Walker D. Wyman and Clifton B. Kroeber, ed., *The Frontier in Perspective*, Madison, Wis., 1957.

There is an enormous source of frontier materials in the state historical society publications. There is at least one journal published in all of the states, and in some cases there are several. For instance, The Filson Club of Louisville has published since 1928 a quarterly devoted to frontier history, and other regional journals have done the same thing. The major journal is the *Mississippi Valley Historical Review*, 1914–1964 (*Journal of American History*, 1964–   ). The Mississippi Valley Historical Association published an annual volume of proceedings from 1907–1924 which contains a number of important essays. This is true of the *Journal of Southern History*, 1935– . Brief articles in the historical journals have often contained as much meaning as some books dealing with the frontier. In a selected bibliography of this type it is impossible to list any appreciable number of these articles, or to include more than a slender list of books.

GENERAL WORKS

BILLINGTON, RAY A. and HEDGES, JAMES BLAINE, *Westward Expansion, A History of the American Frontier*, New York, 1949.
BRANCH, DOUGLAS, *Westward*, New York, 1930.
CHANNING, EDWARD, *A History of the United States*, 6 vols., New York, 1905–1925.
HAFEN, LEROY, and RISTER, CARL COKE, *Western America*, New York, 1950.
McMASTER, JOHN BACH, *A History of the People of the United States*, 8 vols., New York, 1883–1913.
PAXSON, FREDERIC L., *The Last American Frontier*, New York, 1924.
———, *History of the American Frontier*, Boston, 1924.
RIEGEL, ROBERT E., and ROBERT ATHEARN, *America Moves West*, New York, 1966.
TURNER, FREDERICK JACKSON, *The Frontier in American History*, New York, 1920.

SPECIAL GUIDES

ADAMS, JAMES TRUSLOW, and COLEMAN, R. V., eds., *Atlas of American History*, New York, 1943.
ADAMS, JAMES TRUSLOW, ed., *Dictionary of American History*, 5 vols., New York, 1942.
GRIFFEN, GRACE GARDNER, et al., *Writings on American History*, Washington, D.C., 1902.
HANDLIN, OSCAR, et al., *Harvard Guide to American History*, Cambridge, 1954.
JOHNSON, ALLEN, and MALONE, DUMAS, eds., *Dictionary of American Biography*, 22 vols., New York, 1928–1958.
KRAUSE, MICHAEL, *The Writing of American History*, Norman, 1953.
TURNER, FREDERICK JACKSON, and MERK, FREDERICK, *References on the History of the West*, Cambridge, 1922.
VAIL, R. W. G., eds. *Voices of the Old Frontier*, Philadelphia, 1949.
WINTHER, OSCAR O., *The Trans-Mississippi West: A Guide to Its Periodical Literature, 1811–1938*. Bloomington, 1942.

CHAPTER 11

The Allegheny Frontier

British rivalries in the Ohio and Mississippi valleys grew to important proportions. Here was developed a major fur and Indian trade in which the two nations struggled desperately to gain and to hold. This was also a period when the great gateway to the lands beyond the mountains were being opened. Trader, land speculator and surveyor all visited the West.

CONTEMPORARY WORKS

DARLINGTON, W. M., ed., *Christopher Gist's Journals*, Pittsburgh, 1893.
JOHNSTON, J. STODDART, *First Explorations of Kentucky*, Louisville, 1898.
POWNALL, THOMAS, *A Topographical Description of the Dominions of the United States of America*, ed. Lois Mulkearn, Pittsburgh, 1949.

GENERAL WORKS

ABERNETHY, THOMAS PERKINS, *Western Lands and the American Revolution*, New York, 1937.

ALDEN, HENRY GEORGE, *New Governments West of the Alleghanies before 1780*, Madison, 1897.

ALVORD, CLARENCE, *The Mississippi Valley in British Politics*, 2 vols., Cleveland, 1917.

—— and BIDGOOD, LEE, *The First Explorations of the Trans-Alleghany Region by the Virginians, 1650-1674*, Cleveland, 1912.

BAILEY, KENNETH, *The Ohio Company of Virginia and the Westward Movement, 1748-1792*, Glendale, 1939.

BOND, BEVERLY, *Foundations in Ohio* (*History of Ohio*), Columbus, 1941.

BROWN, RALPH H., *Historical Geography of the United States*, New York, 1948.

BYARS, W. V., *B. and M. Gratz, Merchants in Phi'adelphia*, Jefferson City, Mo., 1916.

CARUSO, JOHN ANTHONY, *The Mississippi Valley Frontier: The Age of French Exploration and Settlement.* Indianapolis, 1966.

CRANE, VERNER W., *The Southern Frontier, 1670-1732*, Durham, 1928.

FERNOW, BERTHOLD, *The Ohio Valley in Colonial Days*, Albany, N.Y., 1890.

FREEMAN, DOUGLAS SOUTHALL, *George Washington, a Biography*, vols. I, II, New York, 1948.

GIPSON, LAWRENCE H., *The British Empire before the American Revolution*, vols. III–VII. New York, 1936–1965.

GRIFFIS, W. E., *Sir William Johnson and the Six Nations*, New York, 1891.

HANNA, CHARLES A., *The Wilderness Trail*, 2 vols., New York, 1911.

HULBERT, A. B., *Braddock's Road and Three Relative Papers*, Cleveland, 1917.

——, *Washington's Road*, Cleveland, 1903.

LEACH, DOUGLAS EDWARD, *The Northern Colonial Frontier, 1607-1763*, New York, 1966.

PARKMAN, FRANCIS, *A Half Century of Conflict*, 2 vols., Boston, 1907.

ROOT, W. T., *The Relations of Pennsylvania with the British Government, 1696-1765*, Philadelphia, 1912.

STONE, W. L., Jr., *Life and Times of Sir William Johnston*, 2 vols., Albany, 1865.

THWAITES, REUBEN GOLD, *France in America, 1497-1763*, New York, 1905.

VOLWILER, ALBERT T., *George Croghan and the Westward Movement, 1742-1782*, Cleveland, 1926.

WINSOR, JUSTIN, *The Mississippi Basin*, New York, 1895.

CHAPTER III

The Frontier at War

The French and Indian War in North America was one of major decisions for the future of the continent. The struggle was not only for possession of the continent and its rich trade, but also for its cultural growth in the future. Involved in this struggle was the Indian problem, expansion of the American population and the settlement of several major international issues. This was the first of the American participations in what was in fact a world war.

CONTEMPORARY WORKS

McDONALD, WILLIAM, *Documentary Source Book of American History, 1606-1926*, New York, 1924.

"Papers of the Albany Convention," *Pennsylvania Archives*, Second Series, VI, pp. 193–210.

STOBO, ROBERT, *Memoirs of Major Robert Stobo*, Pittsburgh, 1854.

WILLIAMS, SAMUEL COLE, ed., *Lieut. Henry Timberlake's Memoirs, 1756-1765*, Marietta, Ga., 1948.

GENERAL WORKS

ALDEN, JOHN R., *John Stuart and the Southern Colonial Frontier*, Ann Arbor, 1944.
ANDREWS, CHARLES M., *Colonial Background of the American Revolution*, New Haven, 1924.
BAKER-CAROTHERS, HAYES, *Virginia and the French and Indian War*, Chicago, 1928.
BECKER, CARL, *Eve of the American Revolution*, New Haven, 1911.
BEER, G. L., *British Colonial Policy, 1754-1765*, New York, 1907.
FLICK, A. C., ed., *History of the State of New York*, vol. II, New York, 1933.
FREEMAN, DOUGLAS SOUTHALL, *George Washington, a Biography*, vols. I, II, New York, 1948.
GIPSON, LAWRENCE H., *The British Empire Before the American Revolution*, vols. III–VII, New York, 1936-1965.
HALSEY, F. W., *The Old New York Frontier*, New York, 1901.
HULBERT, ARCHER B., *The Old Glade* (Forbe's) *Road*, vol. V, Cleveland, 1903.
KERCHEVAL, SAMUEL, *A History of the Valley of Virginia*, Woodstock, Va., 1902.
KOONTZ, LOUIS, *The Virginia Frontier, 1754-1763*, Baltimore, 1925.
OSGOOD, HERBERT L., *The American Colonies in the Eighteenth Century*, vol. IV, New York, 1924.
PARKMAN, FRANCIS, *Montcalm and Wolfe*, 2 vols., Boston, 1901.
SIPE, C. H., *The Indian Wars of Pennsylvania*, Harrisburg, 1931.
THWAITES, REUBEN GOLD, *France in America*, New York, 1905.
WRONG, GEORGE M., *New France*, New Haven, 1921.

CHAPTER IV

A Colonial Interlude

The colonial period of frontier expansion was one in which political eruptions occurred with increasing frequency. Most important, however, was the fact that settlers were moving onto the frontier, and the pressure of the westward movement was beginning to assert itself. This was a formative period in frontier history.

CONTEMPORARY WORKS

ALBACH, JAMES, *Annals of the West*, Pittsburgh, 1857.
BAILEY, KENNETH P., *The Ohio Company Papers*, Agata, Calif., 1947.
BURNABY, ANDREW, *Burnaby's Travels Through North America*, New York, 1904.
DODDRIDGE, JOSEPH, *Notes on the Settlement and Indian Wars of the Western Parts of Virginia and Pennsylvania from 1763-1783*, Albany, 1876.
JEFFERSON, THOMAS, *Notes on the State of Virginia*, Richmond, 1856.
POWNALL, THOMAS, *A Topographical Description of the Dominions of the United States of America*, ed. Lois Mulkearn, Pittsburgh, 1949.
PECKHAM, HOWARD, *George Croghan's Journal of His Trip to Detroit in 1767*, Ann Arbor, 1939.
THWAITES, REUBEN G. and KELLOGG, LOUISE P., eds., *Documentary History of Dunmore's War, 1774*, Madison, 1905.

GENERAL WORKS

ABERNETHY, THOMAS PERKINS, *Western Lands and the American Revolution*, New York, 1937.
——, *Three Virginia Frontiers*, Baton Rouge, 1940.

BODLEY, TEMPLE, *Our First Great West*, Louisville, 1938.

COLLINS, LEWIS, *History of Kentucky*, 2 vols., Covington, 1874.

CORT, CYRUS, *Colonel Henry Bouquet and His Campaigns of 1763 and 1764*, Lancaster, Pa., 1883.

FAUST, A. B., *The German Element in the United States*, 2 vols., New York, 1927.

HART, F. H., *The Valley of Virginia in the American Revolution*, Chapel Hill, 1942.

KENT, DONALD, and STEVENS, S. K., eds., *Wilderness Chronicles of Northwestern Pennsylvania*, Harrisburg, 1941.

KOONTZ, LOUIS, *The Virginia Frontier, 1754–1763*, Baltimore, 1925.

MARKS, M. A. M., *England and America, 1763–1783*, 2 vols., New York, 1907.

MASON, KATHERINE HARROD, *James Harrod of Kentucky*, Baton Rouge, 1951.

PARKMAN, FRANCIS, *The Conspiracy of Pontiac*, 2 vols., Boston, 1901.

PECKHAM, HOWARD, *Pontiac and the Indian Uprising*, Princeton, 1947.

RAMSEY, J. G. M., *The Annals of Tennessee*, Charleston, 1853.

ROOSEVELT, THEODORE, *The Winning of the West*, 2 vols., New York, 1905.

SIPE, C. H., *The Indian Wars of Pennsylvania*, Harrisburg, 1931.

TALBERT, CHARLES G., *Benjamin Logan, Kentucky Frontiersman*, Lexington, 1962.

TURNER, FREDERICK JACKSON, *The Frontier in American History*, New York, 1920.

CHAPTER V

The Revolutionary Frontier

During the American Revolution there was almost as much expansion as during the years immediately following. Settlers streamed across the mountains and through Cumberland Gap to plant American civilization in the region below the Ohio. At the same time frontiersmen under the leadership of Clark, Boone, Sevier and others were turning back Indian and British attacks. This period has stimulated the production of an enormous amount of material.

CONTEMPORARY WORK

JAMES, JAMES A., ed., *George Rogers Clark Papers*, Springfield, 1912–1926.

GENERAL WORKS

ABERNETHY, THOMAS PERKINS, *Western Lands and the American Revolution*, New York, 1937.

ALDEN, JOHN R., *John Stuart and the Southern Colonial Frontier*, Ann Arbor, 1944.

——, *The Revolutionary South—History of the South*, vol. III, Baton Rouge, 1957.

AMBLER, CHARLES H., *West Virginia, the Mountain State*, New York, 1940.

BAKELESS, JOHN, *Background to Glory*, New York, 1957.

——, *Daniel Boone, Wilderness Scout*, New York, 1939.

BALDWIN, LELAND, *Pittsburgh, the Story of a City*, Pittsburgh, 1938.

BARNHART, JOHN D., *Henry Hamilton and George Rogers Clark*, Crawfordsville, Indiana, 1951.

BEAN, R. B., *The Peopling of Virginia*, Boston, 1938.

BOND, BEVERLY, *The Foundations of Ohio*, Columbus, 1941.

BROWN, R. E., *Historical Geography of the United States*, New York, 1948.

BROWN, JOHN P., *Old Frontiers*, Kingsport, Tenn., 1938.

CATLING, GEORGE B., *The Story of Detroit*, Detroit, 1923.

CHANNING, EDWARD, *A History of the United States*, vol. III, New York, 1920.

CLARK, THOMAS D., *A History of Kentucky*, Lexington, 1960.

CONNELLEY, W. E., and COULTER, E. MERTON, *A History of Kentucky,* 2 vols., New York, 1922.

COTTERILL, ROBERT S., *History of Pioneer Kentucky,* Cincinnati, 1917.

DARLING, A. B., *Our Rising Empire, 1763–1803,* New Haven, 1940.

DOWNES, RANDOLPH C., *Council Fires on the Upper Ohio,* Pittsburgh, 1940.

DRAPER, LYMAN C., *King's Mountain and Its Heroes,* New York, 1929.

DRIVER, CARL, *John Sevier,* Chapel Hill, 1932.

ECKENRODE, H. J., *The Revolution in Virginia,* New York, 1916.

FLICK, ALEXANDER C., ed., *History of the State of New York,* vols. II and III, New York, 1933.

GREENE, F. V., *The Revolutionary War and the Military Policy of the United States,* New York, 1911.

HAMER, PHILLIP M., ed., *Tennesee, A History, 1673–1932,* 4 vols., New York, 1932.

HARRELL, I. S., *Loyalism in Virginia,* Durham, 1926.

HART, F. H., *The Valley of Virginia in the American Revolution,* Chapel Hill, 1942.

HENDERSON, ARCHIBALD, *The Conquest of the Old Southwest,* New York, 1920.

JAMES, JAMES A., *The Life of George Rogers Clark,* Chicago, 1928.

KENTON, EDNA, *Simon Kenton,* New York, 1930.

KOONTZ, LOUIS K., *Robert Dinwiddie, His Career in American Colonial Government and Westward Expansion,* Glendale, 1941.

LESTER, WILLIAM S., *The Transylvania Colony,* Spencer, Indiana, 1935.

OSGOOD, HERBERT L., *The American Colonies in the Eighteenth Century,* 4 vols., New York, 1924.

RAMSEY, J. G. M., *The Annals of Tennessee,* Charleston, 1853.

RANCK, GEORGE, *Boonesborough,* Louisville, 1901.

ROOSEVELT, THEODORE, *The Winning of the West,* 6 vols., New York, 1905.

SUMMERS, G. P., *History of Southwest Virginia, 1746–1786,* Richmond, 1903.

THWAITES, REUBEN G., *Daniel Boone,* New York, 1902.

—— and KELLOGG, LOUISE P., *The Revolution on the Upper Ohio,* Madison, Wis., 1908.

VAN TYNE, C. H., *The War of Independence, American Phase,* Boston, 1929.

WHITE, KATHERINE K., *The King's Mountain Men,* Dayton, Va., 1924.

WILLIAMS, SAMUEL C., *Tennessee During the Revolutionary War,* Nashville, 1944.

WRONG, GEORGE M., *Washington and His Comrades in Arms,* New Haven, 1921.

CHAPTER VI

The Frontier on the Ohio and Mississippi

Settlers moved westward in great numbers between 1775–1790. Many of them pushed into the Tennessee country, while others came down the Ohio to begin settlement along that stream. As these emigrants pushed into the region they helped to create several major problems, two of which were disposition of the public domain and relations with the Indians. Both in the Southwest and in Ohio the latter problem was a difficult one. The success of the legal profession from the beginning on the frontier attested the nature of the land problems.

CONTEMPORARY WORK

CUTLER, JULIA P., *William Parker Cutler, Life, Journals, and Correspondence of Rev. Manasseh Cutler,* 2 vols., Cincinnati, 1888.

GENERAL WORKS

ABERNETHY, THOMAS PERKINS, *Western Lands and The American Revolution,* New York, 1937.

BROWN, JOHN P., *Old Frontiers*, Kingsport, Tenn., 1938.
CHANNING, EDWARD, *A History of the United States*, vol. IV, New York, 1920.
COTTERILL, ROBERT S., *The Old South*, Glendale, 1939.
DARLING, A. B., *Our Rising Empire, 1763–1803*, New Haven, 1940.
DONALDSON, THOMAS, *The Public Domain*, Washington, 1884.
DOWNES, R. C., *Council Fires on the Upper Ohio*, Pittsburgh, 1940.
HASSLER, EDGAR W., *Old Westmoreland*, Pittsburgh, 1900.
HAYWOOD, JOHN, *The Civil and Political History of the State of Tennessee*, Nashville, 1891.
HENDERSON, ARCHIBALD, *Conquest of the Old Southwest*, New York, 1920.
HIBBARD, B. H., *A History of the Public Land Policies*, New York, 1924.
HINSDALE, B. A., *The Old Northwest*, New York, 1891.
JENSEN, MERRILL, *The Articles of Confederation*, Madison, 1940.
McLAUGHLIN, A. C., *The Confederation and the Constitution, 1783–1789*, New York, 1905.
PETERS, W. E., *Ohio Lands and Their Subdivision*, Athens, Ohio, 1930.
PHILBRICK, FRANCIS S., *The Laws of Illinois Territory, 1809–1818*, vol. V, Springfield, 1950.
POOLE, W. F., *The Ordinance of 1787, and Dr. Manasseh Cutler as an Agent in Its Formation*, Cambridge, 1876.
RAMSEY, J. G. M., *The Annals of Tennessee*, Charleston, 1853.
ROBBINS, ROY M., *Our Landed Heritage*, Princeton, 1942.
SCOTT, JOHN A., *Fort Stanwix and Oriskany*, Rome, N.Y., 1927.
TREAT, PAYSON J., *The National Land System, 1785–1820*, New York, 1910.

CHAPTER VII

Widening the Arc of Settlement

This period in frontier expansion involved many cross currents, not only of national expansion, but also of international complications. Literature in this field deals with the domestic affairs of the frontier, and with the diplomatic aspects of American history.

CONTEMPORARY WORKS

CARTER, C. E., comp. and ed., *The Territorial Papers of the United States*, vol. II, Washington, 1934.
McDONALD, WILLIAM, ed., *Documentary Source Book of American History, 1606–1926*, New York, 1926.
TURNER, FREDERICK JACKSON, ed., *Correspondence of the French to the United States, 1791–1797*, Annual Report, Am. Hist. Ass'n., vol. II, Washington, 1934.

GENERAL WORKS

ABERNETHY, THOMAS PERKINS, *From Frontier to Plantation in Tennessee*, Chapel Hill, 1932.
ARNOW, HARRIETTE, *Seedtime on the Cumberland*, New York, 1960.
ARNOW, HARRIETTE, *Flowering of the Cumberland*, New York, 1963.
BAILEY, THOMAS A., *A Diplomatic History of the American People*, New York, 1955.
BEMIS, SAMUEL FLAGG, *Jay's Treaty*, New York, 1923.
BOND, BEVERLY, *The Foundation of Ohio*, Columbus, 1941.
———, *Civilization of the Old Northwest*, New York, 1934.
BOYD, THOMAS, *Mad Anthony Wayne*, New York, 1929.
BURNET, JACOB, *Notes on the Settlement of the Northwestern Territory*, Cincinnati, 1847.
CARUSO, JOHN ANTHONY, *The Great Lakes Frontier: An Epic of the Old Northwest*, Indianapolis, 1961.

CAUGHEY, JOHN W., *McGillivray of the Creeks*, Norman, 1938.

CHANNING, EDWARD, *A History of the United States*, vol. IV, New York, 1920.

CONNELLEY, W. E. and COULTER, E. M., *History of Kentucky*, 2 vols., New York, 1922.

COTTERILL, ROBERT S., *The Old South*, Glendale, 1939.

DARLING, A. B., *Our Rising Empire, 1763–1803*, New Haven, 1940.

DOWNES, R. C., *Council Fires on the Upper Ohio*, Pittsburgh, 1940.

FOREMAN, GRANT, *Indians and Pioneers*, New Haven, 1930.

FORTIER, ALCÉE, *A History of Louisiana*, vol. II, New York, 1904.

GIBBS, GEORGE, *Memoirs of the Administrations of Washington and Adams*, New York, 1846.

GREEN, T. M., *The Spanish Conspiracy*, Cincinnati, 1891.

HINSDALE, B. A., *The Old Northwest*, Boston, 1899.

JENSEN, MERRILL, *The New Nation*, New York, 1950.

KELLOGG, LOUISE P., *The British Regime in Wisconsin and the Northwest*, Madison, 1935.

KNAPP, H. S., *History of the Maumee Valley*, Toledo, 1872.

MCELROY, ROBERT M., *Kentucky in the Nation's History*, New York, 1909.

OGG, FREDERICK A., *The Old Northwest*, New Haven, 1920.

PRESTON, JOHN H., *A Gentleman Rebel, Mad Anthony Wayne*, New York, 1934.

RIDELL, W. R., *John Graves Simcoe*, Toronto, 1926.

ROOSEVELT, THEODORE, *The Winning of the West*, vol. IV, New York, 1896.

SCHACHNER, NATHAN, *Thomas Jefferson*, 2 vols., New York, 1951.

SLOCUM, CHARLES E., *The Ohio Country between the Years 1785 and 1815*, New York, 1910.

SPEARS, JOHN R., and CLARK, A. H., *A History of the Mississippi Valley from Its Discovery to the End of Foreign Domination*, New York, 1903.

STILLÉ, C. J., *Major General Anthony Wayne and the Pennsylvania Line in the Continental Army*, Philadelphia, 1893.

WHITAKER, A. P., *Spanish-American Frontiers and The Mississippi Question*, New York, 1934.

WILDES, H. E., *Anthony Wayne*, New York, 1941.

CHAPTER VIII

Formative Political Years

These were important years in the political expansion of the American system of government. Kentucky was the first state created on the trans-Appalachian frontier. There is a considerable body of materials on this subject of political expansion, much of which is local in character.

CONTEMPORARY WORK

ELLIOTT, JONATHAN, *The Debates in the Several States on the Adoption of the Federal Constitution*, Philadelphia, 1891.

GENERAL WORKS

ABERNETHY, THOMAS PERKINS, *Three Virginia Frontiers*, Baton Rouge, 1940.

BALDWIN, LELAND D., *Whisky Rebels*, Pittsburgh, 1939.

BARNHART, JOHN D., *Valley of Democracy*, Bloomington, 1954.

BEARD, CHARLES A., *Economic Origins of Jeffersonian Democracy*, New York, 1915.

BEVERIDGE, ALBERT J., *The Life of John Marshall*, 4 vols., New York, 1916–1919.

BROWN, JOHN MASON, *Political Beginnings of Kentucky*, Louisville, 1889.

BURNET, JACOB, *Notes on the Early Settlement of the Northwest Territory*, New York, 1847.

CLARK, THOMAS D., *A History of Kentucky*, New York, 1937.
CONNELLEY, W. E. and COULTER, E. M., *A History of Kentucky*, 5 vols., New York, 1922.
DOWNES, R. C., *Frontier Ohio, 1788–1803*, Columbus, 1935.
FERGUSON, R. J., *Early Western Pennsylvania Politics*, Pittsburgh, 1938.
GREEN, T. M., *The Spanish Conspiracy*, Cincinnati, 1891.
HAY, T. R. and WERNER, M. R., *The Admirable Trumpeter*, New York, 1941.
HAYWOOD, JOHN, *The Civil and Political History of the State of Tennessee*, Nashville, 1891.
HIBBARD, BENJAMIN H., *A History of the Public Land Policies*, New York, 1924.
LINK, E. P., *Democratic-Republican Societies, 1790–1800*, New York, 1942.
MARSHALL, HUMPHREY, *The History of Kentucky*, 2 vols., Frankfort, 1824.
McLAUGHLIN, A. C., *A Constitutional History of the United States*, New York, 1935.
MILLER, WILLIAM, "The Democratic Societies and the Whisky Insurrection," *Pa. Magazine of Hist. and Biog.*, vol. 62, 1938, pp. 234–349.
PHILBRICK, FRANCIS S., *The Rise of the New West, 1754–1830*, New York, 1965.
RAMSEY, J. G. M., *The Annals of Tennessee*, Charleston, 1853.
SCHACHNER, NATHAN, *Thomas Jefferson*, 2 vols., New York, 1951.
SHREVE, R. O., *The Finished Scoundrel*, Indianapolis, 1933.
SPEED, THOMAS, *The Political Club, Danville, Kentucky, 1786–1790*, Louisville, 1894.
THORPE, FRANCIS N., *The Constitutional History of the United States*, 2 vols., Chicago, 1901.
TREAT, PAYSON J., *The National Land System,1785–1820*, New York, 1910.
UTTER, WILLIAM T., *The Frontier State, 1805–1825* (History of Ohio), Columbus, 1935.
WARFIELD, ETHELBERT D., *The Kentucky Resolutions*, New York, 1887.
WHITE, LEONARD D., *The Federalists*, New York, 1948.
WILLIAMS, SAMUEL C., *History of the Lost State of Franklin*, New York, 1933.

CHAPTER IX

A Pioneer Way of Life

Pioneer life has been a recurring subject of interest. Contemporaries recorded their experiences, and historians in great numbers have kept alive the memories of struggles of human beings in the raw frontier backwoods. All the western state histories concern themselves with this phase of local background. There are many works of a broad sectional, and even national, nature which emphasize the social aspects of national growth.

CONTEMPORARY WORKS

The American Pioneer, 2 vols., Cincinnati, 1842.
COBBETT, WILLIAM, *A Year's Residence in the United States of America*, London, 1828.
DODDRIDGE, JOSEPH, *Notes on the Settlement and Indian Wars, of the Western Part of Virginia and Pennsylvania*, Wellsburgh, Va., 1824.
FEARON, HENRY BRADSHAW, *Sketches of America, A Narrative of a Journey of Five Thousand Miles through the Eastern and Western States of America*, London, 1819.
FINLEY, J. B., *Sketches of Western Methodism*, Cincinnati, 1854.
FLINT, TIMOTHY, *Recollections of the Last Ten Years*, Boston, 1826.
GADDIS, MAXWELL P., *Footprints of an Itinerate*, Cincinnati, 1855.
IMLAY, GILBERT, *A Topographical Description of the Western Territory of North America*, London, 1792.
PECK, JOHN M., *A New Guide for Emigrants to the West*, Boston, 1837.
Second Census, United States Bureau of the Census, Washington, D.C., 1901.
TINLING, MARION and DAVIES, GODFREY, *The Western Country in 1793*, San Marino, 1948.

TIPPLE, EZRA S., *The Heart of Asbury's Journal*, New York, 1904.
TOCQUEVILLE, ALEXIS DE, *Democracy in America*, Cincinnati, 1851.
TOULMIN, HARRY, *A Description of Kentucky*, ed. Thomas D. Clark, Lexington, 1945.

GENERAL WORKS

ABERNETHY, THOMAS PERKINS, *From Frontier to Plantation in Tennessee*, Chapel Hill, 1932.
AMBLER, CHARLES H., *West Virginia, Mountain State*, New York, 1940.
ATWATER, CALEB, *The General Character, Present and Future Prospects of the People of Ohio*, Columbus, 1827.
BALDWIN, LELAND D., *Pittsburgh, The Story of a City*, Pittsburgh, 1937.
BISHOP, J. L., *A History of American Manufacture from 1608–1860*, 3 vols., Philadelphia, 1861–1868.
BULEY, R. C., *The Old Northwest*, 2 vols., Bloomington, 1951.
BUTLER, *History of Kentucky*, Louisville, 1834.
CALHOUN, ARTHUR W., *Social History of the American Family*, 3 vols., Cleveland, 1917–1919.
CASSEDAY, BENJAMIN R., *History of Louisville*, Louisville, 1852.
CLARK, THOMAS D., *The Rampaging Frontier*, Indianapolis, 1939.
CLARK, VICTOR S., *History of Manufactures in the United States*, vol. 1, New York, 1929.
CLEVELAND, CATHERINE, *The Great Revival in the West*, Chicago, 1916.
COTTERILL, ROBERT S., *History of Pioneer Kentucky*, Cincinnati, 1917.
CROUSE, D. E., *The Ohio Gateway*, New York, 1938.
DICK, EVERETT, *The Dixie Frontier*, New York, 1948.
DOWNES, R. C., *Frontier Ohio, 1788–1803*, Columbus, 1935.
DRAKE, DANIEL, *Pioneer Life in Kentucky*, New York, 1948.
GEWEHR, WESLEY, *The Great Awakening in Virginia, 1740–1790*, Durham, 1930.
HAYWOOD, JOHN, *The Civil and Political History of the State of Tennessee*, Nashville, 1891.
HILDRETH, SAMUEL P., *Pioneer History*, Cincinnati, 1848.
———, *Original Contributions to the American Pioneer*, Dayton, 1844.
HOWE, HENRY, *Historic Collections of Ohio*, vol. 1, Cincinnati, 1854.
HOWELLS, WILLIAM C., *Recollections of Life in Ohio from 1813–1840*, Cincinnati, 1895.
HULBERT, ARCHER BUTLER, *The Ohio River, A Course of Empire*, New York, 1906.
KERCHEVAL, SAMUEL, *A History of the Valley of Virginia*, Strasburg, 1925.
KINCAID, ROBERT L., *The Wilderness Road*, Indianapolis, 1947.
MCMASTER, JOHN B., *A History of the People of the United States*, vols. II–III, New York, 1883–1913.
MARSHALL, HUMPHREY, *History of Kentucky*, 2 vols., Frankfort, 1824.
MONETTE, JOHN W., *History of the Discovery and Settlement of the Valley of the Mississippi*, 2 vols., New York, 1846.
OGG, F. A., *The Old Northwest*, New Haven, 1919.
PICKARD, MADGE E. and BULEY, R. C., *The Midwest Pioneer, His Ills, Cures and Doctors*, Crawfordsville, Ind., 1945.
ROGERS, JAMES R., *The Cane Ridge Meeting House*, Cincinnati, 1910.
SKINNER, CONSTANCE L., *Pioneers of the Old Southwest*, New Haven, 1921.
SWEET, WILLIAM WARREN, *Story of Religion in America*, New York, 1939.
WRIGHT, J. E. and CORBETT, D. S., *Pioneer Life in Western Pennsylvania*, Pittsburgh, 1940.

CHAPTER X

Louisiana

The decade, 1800–1810, covered an exciting period of American history. It was during this era that expansionistic forces were active everywhere. Rampant orators were begging for an extension of national boundaries. Frontier farmers were drifting to market with ever increasing piles of farm produce, and diplomatic relations between the United States and Spain were in such an uncertain state that the southern market was likely to be closed at any time. Frontiersmen expressed a determination to break this deadlock and to acquire possession even if it became necessary to resort to arms. Election of Thomas Jefferson to the presidency brought relief from the Louisiana complications, but the Burr episode created further confusion.

CONTEMPORARY WORKS

BAKELESS, JOHN, *Lewis and Clark, Partners in Discovery*, New York, 1954.
BIDDLE, NICHOLAS, *History of the Expedition under the Command of Captain Lewis and Clark*, Philadelphia, 1814.
COUES, ELLIOTT, ed., *History of the Expedition under the Command of Lewis and Clark*, 4 vols., New York, 1893.
———, ed., *The Expedition of Zebulon Montgomery Pike, to Headwaters of the Mississippi River*, 3 vols., New York, 1895.
———, ed., *An Account of the Expeditions to the Sources of the Mississippi*, 4 vols., New York, 1895.
DE VOTO, BERNARD, ed., *The Journals of Lewis and Clark*, Boston, 1953.
DILLON, RICHARD, *Meriwether Lewis, A Biography*, New York, 1965.
SAFFORD, W. H., ed., *The Blennerhassett Papers*, Cincinnati, 1861.
THWAITES, REUBEN GOLD, ed., *Original Journals of the Lewis and Clark Expedition*, 8 vols., New York, 1904–1905.
WILKINSON, JAMES, *Memoirs of My Own Times*, 3 vols., Philadelphia, 1816.

GENERAL WORKS

ABERNETHY, THOMAS PERKINS, *The Burr Conspiracy*, New York, 1954.
BAILEY, THOMAS A., *A Diplomatic History of the American People*, New York, 1955.
BEMIS, SAMUEL F., *Diplomatic History of the United States*, New York, 1955.
CHANNING, EDWARD, *A History of the United States*, vol. IV, New York, 1920.
COX, I. J., *West Florida Controversy*, Baltimore, 1918.
CRESSON, W. P., *James Monroe*, Chapel Hill, 1946.
FULLER, HURBERT BRUCE, *The Purchase of Florida*, Cleveland, 1906.
GAYARRÉ, CHARLES E., *History of Louisiana*, 4 vols., New Orleans, 1903.
GRIFFIN, C. C., *The United States and the Disruption of the Spanish Empire*, New York, 1937.
HAY, T. R., and WERNER, M. R., *The Admirable Trumpeter*, New York, 1941.
HOLLON, W. EUGENE, *Lost Pathfinder*, Norman, 1949.
LYON, E. W., *The Man Who Sold Louisiana*, Norman, 1942.
McCALEB, W. F., *The Aaron Burr Conspiracy*, New York, 1936.
McMASTER, J. B., *A History of the American People*, vol. III, New York, 1883–1913.
OSGOOD, ERNEST S., ed., *The Field Notes of Captain William Clark, 1803–1805*, New Haven, 1964.
QUAIFE, MILO M., *The Journals of Captain Merriwether Lewis and Sergeant John Ordway, Kept on the Expedition of Western Exploration, 1803–1806*, Madison, 1965.
SCHACHNER, NATHAN, *Thomas Jefferson*, 2 vols., New York, 1951.
———, *Aaron Burr, A Biography*, New York, 1937.
WHITAKER, ARTHUR P., *Spanish-American Frontier and The Mississippi Question*, New York, 1934.
———, *The Spanish-American Frontier, 1783–1795*, New York, 1927.

CHAPTER XI

A War of Expansion

Expansionists looked to the West for elbow room, and at the same time they stirred up an intense nationalistic feeling because of British activities in the region. The war as a military achievement was largely lacking in brilliance, but not so with the exploits of individual heroes. Few struggles, unless it be the Mexican War, have produced so many heroes in so short a time in proportion to the number of men engaged. This explains why there is such a disproportionate number of biographies dealing with the struggle.

GENERAL WORKS

ADAMS, HENRY, *History of the United States, 1809-1813, During the First Administration of James Madison*, vol. II, New York, 1890.

BABCOCK, KENDRIC C., *The Rise of the American Nationality*, New York, 1906.

BAILEY, THOMAS A., *A Diplomatic History of the American People*, New York, 1955.

BEIRNE, FRANCIS F., *The War of 1812*, New York, 1949.

BEMIS, SAMUEL FLAGG, *Diplomatic History of the United States*, New York, 1955.

BRANT, IRVING, *James Madison: The Virginia Revolutionist*, vol. I, and *James Madison: The Nationalist*, vol. 2, Indianapolis, 1956.

CLEAVES, FREEMAN, *Old Tippecanoe*, New York, 1939.

CONNELLEY, W. E., and COULTER, E. MERTON, *History of Kentucky*, 5 vols., New York, 1922.

CRESSON, W. P., *James Monroe*, Chapel Hill, 1946.

DEWEERD, H. A., ed., *The War of 1812 by Henry Adams*, Washington, 1944.

DILLON, J. B., *History of Indiana*, Indianapolis, 1859.

EATON, WILLIAM CLEMENT, *Henry Clay and the Art of American Politics*, Boston, 1957.

GOEBEL, DOROTHY BURNE, *William Henry Harrison*, Indianapolis, 1926.

JAMES, MARQUIS, *Andrew Jackson, the Border Captain*, Indianapolis, 1933.

———, *The Raven, a Biography of Sam Houston*, Indianapolis, 1929.

LUCAS, C. P., *The Canadian War of 1812*, Oxford, 1906.

MAYO, BERNARD, *Henry Clay, Spokesman of the New West*, New York, 1937.

McAFEE, R. B., *History of the Late War in the Western Country*, Lexington, 1816.

McELROY, ROBERT M., *Kentucky in the Nation's History*, New York, 1909.

MEYER, L. W., *Life and Times of Col. Richard M. Johnson*, New York, 1932.

PARKS, JOSEPH, *Felix Grundy*, Baton Rouge, 1940.

PRATT, JULIUS, *Expansionists of 1812*, New York, 1926.

ROOSEVELT, THEODORE, *The Naval War of 1812*, New York, 1882.

ROSSITER, JOHN, *The War of 1812-15*, New York, 1882.

ROWLAND, ERON OPHA, *Andrew Jackson's Campaign Against the British*, New York, 1926.

SILVER, JAMES, *Edmund Pendleton Gaines, Frontier General*, Baton Rouge, 1949.

TUCKER, GLENN, *Poltroons and Patriots, A Popular Account of the War of 1812*, Indianapolis, 1954.

———, *Tecumseh, Vision of Glory*, Indianapolis, 1956.

UTTER, WILLIAM T., *The Frontier State, 1803-1825 (History of Ohio)*, Columbus, 1942.

VAN DEUSEN, GLYNDON, *The Life of Henry Clay*, Boston, 1937.

WILTSE, CHARLES M., *John C. Calhoun, Nationalist*, Indianapolis, 1944.

YOUNG, BENNETT H., *The Battle of the Thames*, Louisville, 1903.

CHAPTER XII

Peopling the Greater Frontier

The frontier expansion in the first quarter of the nineteenth century brought thousands of people westward. Their appearance in the Ohio Valley is one of the great folk stories of American history. Literally hundreds of persons observed and recorded some of the details of this movement. A considerable body of contemporary literature has to do with pioneering.

CONTEMPORARY WORKS

ALBACH, JAMES R., *Annals of the West*, Pittsburgh, 1857.
ATWATER, CALEB, *The General Character, Present and Future Prospects of the People of Ohio*, Columbus, 1827.
BAIRD, ROBERT, *View of the Valley of the Mississippi*, Philadelphia, 1832.
BROWN, SAMUEL R., *The Western Gazetteer; or Emigrant's Directory*, Auburn, N. Y., 1817.
CARLETON, ROBERT, *The New Purchase*, 2 vols., Philadelphia, 1843.
DRAKE, DANIEL, *Natural and Statistical View or Picture of Cincinnati and the Miami Country*, Cincinnati, 1815.
GRIFFITH, D., *Two Years Residence in the New Settlement of Ohio*, London, 1835.
HALL, JAMES, *Statistics of the West at the Close of the Year 1836*, Cincinnati, 1836.
——, *Sketches of History, Life and Manners in the West*, 2 vols., Philadelphia, 1835.
HOWELLS, WILLIAM COOPER, *Recollections of Life in Ohio from 1813–1840*, Cincinnati, 1895.
JENKINS, WARREN, *The Ohio Gazetteer and Traveler's Guide*, Columbus, 1839.
PECK, JOHN M., *A New Guide for the Emigrants to the West*, Boston, 1837.

GENERAL WORKS

BULEY, R. C., *The Old Northwest*, 2 vols., Bloomington, 1951.
DeBOW, JAMES D. B., *Industrial Resources*, 3 vols., New Orleans, 1853.
DICK, EVERETT, *The Dixie Frontier*, New York, 1948.
DILLON, JOHN B., *History of the Early Settlements of the Northwestern Territory*, Indianapolis, 1854.
DUNBAR, SEYMOUR, *A History of Travel in America*, 4 vols., Indianapolis, 1915.
FLINT, TIMOTHY, *The History and Geography of the Mississippi Valley*, 2 vols., Cincinnati, 1828.
HIBBARD, B. H., *A History of the Public Land Policies*, New York, 1924.
GATES, PAUL W., *Frontier Landlords and Pioneer Tenants*, Ithaca, 1945.
HOWE, HENRY, *Historical Collections of the Great West*, 2 vols., Cincinnati, 1854.
HULBERT, ARCHER BUTLER, *The Ohio River, a Course of Empire*, New York, 1906.
KNAPP, HORACE S., *History of the Maumee Valley*, Toledo, 1872.
KILBOURN, JOHN, *The Ohio Gazetteer, Topographic Dictionary*, Columbus, 1831.
McCONNELL, JOHN L., *Western Characters; or, Types of Border Life*, Redfield, Conn., 1835.
McMASTER, JOHN BACH, *A History of the People of the United States*, vol. III, New York, 1883–1913.
MONETTE, JOHN, *History of the Discovery and Settlement of the Valley of the Mississippi*, 2 vols., New York, 1846.
OWSLEY, FRANK L., *Plain Folk of the Old South*, Baton Rouge, 1949.
PHILLIPS, ULRICH B., *Life and Labor in the Old South*, Boston, 1929.
TREAT, PAYSON J., *The National Land System, 1785–1820*, New York, 1910.

TURNER, FREDERICK J., *Rise of the New West, 1819–1829*, New York, 1906.
TUTTLE, CHARLES R., *History of the Border Wars of Two Centuries*, Chicago, 1874.

CHAPTER XIII

Enlarging the Political Perimeter

The period of frontier history following the War of 1812 was an important one. Many acts of that period led to events of national importance. The great panic of 1819, the Missouri Compromise, and the admission of new western states to the Union had a marked effect upon national political developments.

CONTEMPORARY WORK

FLINT, TIMOTHY, *Recollections of the Last Ten Years*, Boston, 1826.

GENERAL WORKS

BOLLES, ALBERT S., *The Financial History of the United States*, New York, 1894.
BULEY, R. C., *The Old Northwest, the Pioneer Period, 1815–1840*, 2 vols., Bloomington, 1951.
COLTON, CALVIN, *The Life and Times of Henry Clay*, 2 vols., New York, 1846.
COMAN, KATHERINE, *The Industrial History of the United States*, New York, 1912.
DEWEY, D. R., *Financial History of the United States*, New York, 1936.
EATON, W. CLEMENT, *Henry Clay and the Art of American Politics*, Boston, 1957.
ESAREY, LOGAN, *History of Indiana*, Indianapolis, 1915.
HAMMOND, M. B., *The Cotton Industry*, Ithaca, New York, 1897.
LYNCH, WILLIAM O., *Fifty Years of Party Warfare*, Indianapolis, 1931.
MCMASTER, JOHN BACH, *History of the People of the United States*, vol. V, New York, 1906.
MOORE, GLOVER, *The Missouri Compromise*, Lexington, Ky., 1954.
PEASE, T. C., *The Frontier State, 1818–1848* (History of Illinois), Springfield, 1918.
REZNECK, SAMUEL, "The Depression of 1819–1822, a Social History," *American Historical Review*, vol. XXXIX, Oct. 1933, pp. 28–47.
ROBBINS, ROY M., *Our Landed Heritage*, Princeton, 1942.
SUMNER, W. G., *A History of American Currency*, New York, 1874.
SYDNOR, CHARLES S., *The Development of Southern Sectionalism, 1819–1848* (History of the South), Baton Rouge, 1948.
VAN DEUSEN, GLYNDON V., *The Life of Henry Clay*, Boston, 1937.
VIOLETTE, EUGENE M., *A History of Missouri*, New York, 1918.
WEISENBURGER, FRANCIS P., *The Passing of the Frontier, 1825–1850* (History of Ohio), vol. III, Columbus, 1941.
WILTSE, C. M., *John C. Calhoun, Nationalist*, Indianapolis, 1944.

CHAPTER XIV

Breaking the Bonds of Isolation

One of the most pronounced characteristics of the frontier was isolation. Often when settlers moved beyond the mountains they went to stay. The transportation of produce to market was all but impossible for those frontiersmen who moved any distance away from the navigable streams. It took almost a quarter of a century to get the trails, rivers, and roads into a satisfactory state of operation. The story of breaking down isolative forces involves overland and river travel, plus the later innovation of railroads.

CONTEMPORARY WORKS

FLINT, TIMOTHY, *A Condensed Geography and History of the Western States of the Mississippi Valley*, 2 vols., Cincinnati, 1828.
SCHULTZ, CHRISTIAN, *Travels on an Inland Voyage*, 2 vols., New York, 1810.

GENERAL WORKS

AMBLER, CHARLES H., *A History of Transportation in the Ohio Valley*, Glendale, 1932.
BLACK, ROBERT C., *The Railroads of the Confederacy*, Chapel Hill, 1952.
BLAIR, WALTER, and MEINE, FRANKLIN J., *Mike Fink, King of the Mississippi Keelboatmen*, New York, 1933.
BOGART, ERNEST L., *Internal Improvements and State Debt in Ohio*, New York, 1924.
CLARK, THOMAS D., *Beginning of the L. & N.*, Louisville, 1933.
——, *A Pioneer Southern Railroad, New Orleans to Cairo*, Chapel Hill, 1936.
COLEMAN, J. WINSTON, *Stagecoach Days in the Bluegrass*, Louisville, 1935.
CORLISS, CARLTON J., *Main Line of Mid-America*, New York, 1950.
DUNBAR, SEYMOUR, *A History of Travel in America*, 4 vols., Indianapolis, 1915.
HULBERT, ARCHER BUTLER, *Historic Highways of America*, 12 vols., Cleveland, 1902.
HUNGERFORD, E. L., *The Story of the Baltimore and Ohio Railroad*, 2 vols., New York, 1928.
——, *Men of Erie*, New York, 1949.
HUNTER, LOUIS T., *Steamboats on the Western Rivers*, Cambridge, 1949.
KINCAID, ROBERT L., *The Wilderness Road*, Indianapolis, 1947.
PEASE, T. C., *The Frontier State, 1818–1848 (History of Illinois)*, Springfield, 1918.
PETERSEN, WILLIAM J., *Steamboating on the Upper Mississippi*, Iowa City, 1937.
MEYER, BALTHASAR, *History of Transportation in the United States before 1860*, Washington, 1917.
PHILLIPS, ULRICH B., *History of Transportation in the Eastern Cotton Belt*, New York, 1908.
POOR, H. V., *History of Railroads and Canals in the United States*, New York, 1860.
SEAWRIGHT, THOMAS B., *The Old Pike*, Uniontown, Pa., 1894.
SHAW, RONALD E., *Erie Water: A History of the Erie Canal, 1792–1854*, Lexington, 1966.
STEVENS, F. W., *The Beginnings of the New York Central Railroad*, New York, 1926.
TRUETT, RANDLE, *Trade and Travel Around the Southern Appalachians before 1830*, Chapel Hill, 1935.
TURNER, FREDERICK J., *Rise of the New West, 1819–1829*, New York, 1906.
UTTER, WILLIAM T., *The Frontier State, 1803–1825 (History of Ohio)*, Columbus, 1942.
WEISENBURGER, FRANCIS P., *The Passing of the Frontier, 1825–1850 (History of Ohio)*, Columbus, 1941.

CHAPTER XV

Frontier Arts and Sciences

This subject covers a large area of frontier activities. It is difficult to list materials which apply specifically to all the subjects which might come under this heading. Every phase of the frontier cultural and intellectual development has now been described in several works. The student is fortunate in this area by having so many contemporary sources from which to view frontier life first-hand.

CONTEMPORARY WORKS

ARESE, FRANCESCO, *A Trip to the Prairies*, New York, 1934.
BAIRD, ROBERT, *A View of the Valley of the Mississippi*, Philadelphia, 1834.
BALDWIN, JOSEPH G., *The Flush Times of Alabama and Mississippi*, New York, 1853.
BÖDMER, CHARLES, Atlas volume, Thwaites, *Early Western Travels*, Cleveland, 1905.
BRADBURY, JOHN, *Travels in the Interior of America, 1809–1811*, Liverpool, 1817.
CATLIN, GEORGE, *Letters and Notes on the Manners, Customs, and Condition of the North American Indians*, 2 vols., London, 1842.
FARNHAM, T. J., *Travels in the Great Western Prairies*, 2 vols., London, 1843.
FLINT, TIMOTHY, *Recollections of the Last Ten Years*, Boston, 1826.
GADDIS, M. P., *Footprints of an Itinerant*, Cincinnati, 1855.
HALL, BASIL, *Forty Etchings*, Edinburgh, 1829.
HAMILTON, THOMAS, *Men and Manners in America*, 2 vols., Philadelphia, 1833.
HOFFMAN, CHARLES FENNO, *A Winter in the Far West*, 2 vols., New York, 1835.
LITTELL, WILLIAM, *Festoons of Fancy*, Lexington, Ky., 1940.
LUDLOW, N. M., *Dramatic Life as I Found It*, St. Louis, 1880.
MARTINEAU, HARRIETT, *Society in America*, 3 vols., London, 1837.
SMITH, SOL., *Theatrical Management*, New York, 1868.
THWAITES, REUBEN G., ed., Maximilian, Prinz zu Wied, *Travels in the Interior of North America*, vols., XII–XIV, Cleveland, 1905.
TOCQUEVILLE, ALEXIS DE, *Democracy in America*, Cincinnati, 1838.
TROLLOPE, FRANCES, *Domestic Manners of the Americans*, London, 1832.

GENERAL WORKS

BLAIR, WALTER, *Horse Sense in American Humor*, Chicago, 1942.
———, *Native American Humor, 1800–1900*, New York, 1937.
BULEY, R. C., *The Old Northwest, Pioneer Period, 1815–1840*, Bloomington, 1951.
CLARK, THOMAS D., *The Rampaging Frontier*, Indianapolis, 1939.
CUBBERLEY, ELLWOOD, *Readings in Public Education in the United States*, Boston, 1934.
DEVOTO, BERNARD, *Across the Wide Missouri*, Boston, 1947.
DEXTER, EDWIN G., *History of Education in the United States*, New York, 1906.
DUNBAR, SEYMOUR, *History of Travel in America*, 4 vols., Indianapolis, 1915.
ESAREY, LOGAN, *History of Indiana*, Indianapolis, 1915.
FLINT, TIMOTHY, *A Condensed Geography and History of the Western States of the Mississippi Valley*, 2 vols., Cincinnati, 1828.
HAYES, C. W., *The State Geological Surveys of the United States*, Washington, 1911.
HAZARD, LUCY, *The Frontier in American Literature*, New York, 1927.
HOOLE, W. STANLEY, *Alias Simon Suggs*, Tuscaloosa, Ala., 1952.
HUDSON, ARTHUR P., *Humor of the Old Deep South*, New York, 1936.
JOHNSON, CHARLES A., *The Frontier Camp Meeting, Religion's Harvest Time*, Dallas, 1955.
KENNEDY, M. F. and HARLOW, A. F., *Schoolmaster of Yesteryear*, New York, 1940.
KIRKPATRICK, J. E., *Timothy Flint, Pioneer, Missionary, Author, Editor, 1780–1840*, Cleveland, 1911.
LEOPOLD, R. W., *Robert Dale Owen, A Biography*, Cambridge, 1940.
Life in America, (Catalog of a special exhibition of genre paintings, Metropolitan Museum of Art) New York, 1939.
MEINE, FRANKLIN J., *Tall Tales of the Southwest*, New York, 1930.
MONETTE, JOHN, *History of the Discovery and Settlement of the Valley of the Mississippi*, 2 vols., New York, 1846.

Moore, Arthur K., *The Frontier Mind*, Lexington, 1957.
Newcomb, Rexford, *Architecture in Old Kentucky*, Urbana, 1953.
Noble, Stuart G., *A History of American Education*, New York, 1938.
Osborne, James I., and Gronert, Theodore G., *Wabash College, the First Hundred Years*, Crawfordsville, Indiana, 1932.
Rusk, Ralph L., *The Literature of the Middle Western Frontier*, 2 vols., New York, 1925.
Sonne, Henry Niels, *Liberal Kentucky, 1780–1828*, New York, 1939.
Strickland, W. P., ed., *Autobiography of Reverend James B. Finley*, Cincinnati, 1855.
Sweet, William Warren, *Revivalism in America*, New York, 1944.
Taft, Robert, *Artists and Illustrators of the Old West; 1850–1900*, New York, 1953.
Townsend, John Wilson, *Kentucky in American Letters*, Cedar Rapids, 1913.
Vail, H. H., *A History of the McGuffey Readers*, Cleveland, 1911.
Venable, W. H., *Beginnings of Literary Culture in the Ohio Valley*, Cincinnati, 1891.
Watterson, Henry, *Oddities of Southern Life and Character*, Boston, 1883.
Weisenburger, Francis P., *The Passing of the Frontier (History of Ohio)*, Columbus, 1941.
Wish, Harvey, *Society and Thought in America*, vol. I, New York, 1950.
Wright, Louis, *Culture on the Moving Frontier*, Bloomington, 1955.

CHAPTER XVI

Beyond the Sabine

Texas with its colorful history has existed under various flags. Like California it has a rich Spanish background, a rugged period of territorial and republic history, and as a state of the Union it has not lost its position as one of the most complex of the frontier communities. Its historians have reflected the great pride of the people, and books about Texas are possibly as numerous as they are varied in quality and subject matter.

BIBLIOGRAPHICAL

Streeter, Thomas W., *Bibliography of Texas*, 2 vols., Cambridge, 1955.

CONTEMPORARY WORKS

Barker, Eugene C., ed., *The Austin Papers, Annual Report*, American Historical Association, 2 vols., Washington, 1919.
Garrison, G. P., ed., *Texan Diplomatic Correspondence, Annual Report*, American Historical Association, 3 vols., Washington, 1907–1908.
Pratt, Willis, *Galveston Island, or a Few Months off the Coast of Texas*, Austin, 1954.
Quaife, Milo M., ed., *The Diary of James K. Polk during His Presidency*, 4 vols., Chicago, 1910.

GENERAL WORKS

Bancroft, H. H., *The North Mexican States and Texas*, San Francisco, 1883–1889.
Barker, Eugene C., *The Life of Stephen F. Austin*, Nashville, 1925.
Beals, Carleton, *Stephen F. Austin, Father of Texas, 1793–1863*, New York, 1953.
Binkley, W. C., *The Texas Revolution*, Baton Rouge, 1952.
Bolton, Herbert E., *Texas in Middle Eighteenth Century*, Berkeley, 1915.
———, *Spanish Explorations in the Southwest, 1524–1706*, New York, 1916.

CALLCOTT, W. H., *Santa Anna, the Story of an Enigma Who Once Was Mexico*, Norman, 1936.

CASTEÑEDA, C. E., *The Mexican Side of the Texas Revolution*, Dallas, 1928.

CHITWOOD, O. P., *John Tyler*, New York, 1939.

CREEL, GEORGE, *Sam Houston, Colossus in Buckskin*, New York, 1928.

HOGAN, WILLIAM R., *The Texas Republic, A Social and Economic History*, Norman, 1946.

JAMES, MARQUIS, *The Raven, a Biography of Sam Houston*, Indianapolis, 1929.

JOHNSON, F. W., *A History of Texas and Texans*, 5 vols., Chicago, 1914.

LOWRIE, SAMUEL H., *Culture Conflict in Texas, 1821–1835*, New York, 1932.

McGRATH, Sister Paul of the Cross, *Political Nativism in Texas, 1825–1860*, Washington, 1930.

RICHARDSON, R. N., *Texas the Lone Star State*, New York, 1943.

SMITH, J. H., *The Annexation of Texas*, New York, 1941.

SCHMITZ, JOSEPH W., *Texas Statecraft, 1836–1845*, San Antonio, 1941.

STEPHENSON, NATHANIEL W., *Texas and the Mexican War*, New Haven, 1921.

WORTHAM, L. J., *A History of Texas from Wilderness to Commonwealth*, Fort Worth, 1924.

YOACUM, HENDERSON, *History of Texas, 1658–1846*, Austin, 1935.

CHAPTER XVII

The Road to Santa Fe

Santa Fe was a faraway end of the trail to the Southwest. Like all of the other frontier advance posts, it was first visited by traders who went from the older American frontier to this distant mountain settlement of the Spanish Empire. Some of the same traders who visited the mountain fur grounds beyond South Pass and up the Missouri River drifted down the ranges to Santa Fe. The real significance of this Spanish outpost, however, lay in the field of commerce. The rich trade which grew up between the western states and this place opened a line of communication not only with Santa Fe, but with California and Mexico.

CONTEMPORARY WORKS

BECKNELL, WILLIAM, "The Missouri-Santa Fe Trade," Missouri Historical Society *Collections*, Vol. 2, July, 1906, pp. 55-67.

DRUMM, STELLA, ed., *Down the Santa Fe Trail and into Mexico, the Diary of Susan Shelby Magoffin, 1846–1847*, New Haven, 1926.

FULTON, MAURICE G., ed., *Diary and Letters of Josiah Gregg*, 2 vols., Norman, 1944.

GREGG, JOSIAH, *Commerce of the Prairies, or the Journal of a Santa Fe Trader*, 2 vols., New York, 1845.

MOOREHEAD, MAX L., ed., *Josiah Gregg, Commerce of the Prairies*, Norman, 1954.

WEBB, JAMES JOSIAH, *Adventures in the Santa Fe Trade, 1844–1847*, ed. Ralph P. Bieber, Glendale, 1931.

GENERAL WORKS

DUFFUS, R. L., *The Santa Fe Trail*, New York, 1930.

GARRARD, LEWIS H., *Wah-To-Yah and the Taos Trail*, Norman, 1955.

INMAN, HENRY, *The Old Santa Fe Trail, 1844–1847*, Glendale, 1931.

PRUCHA, FRANCIS PAUL, *A Guide to the Military Posts of the United States, 1789–1895*, Madison, 1964.

RISTER, CARL COKE, *Southern Plainsmen*, Norman, 1938.

WATERS, L. L., *Steel Rails to Santa Fe*, Lawrence, Kansas, 1950.

YOUNG, OTIS E., *The First Military Escort on the Santa Fe Trail, 1829*, Glendale, 1952.

CHAPTER XVIII

Men Against the Mountains

The fur trader was a trailbreaker extraordinary. Most often it was he who came first in contact with the Indians, or who saw the country beyond the mountains. Fur trading has been a part of all the American frontiers from the coming of the first Europeans down to the middle of the nineteenth century.

CONTEMPORARY WORKS

COUES, ELLIOTT, ed., *Forty Years a Fur Trader on the Upper Missouri, the Personal Narrative of Charles Larpenteur, 1833–1872*, 2 vols., New York, 1898.

DEVOTO, BERNARD, *Across the Wide Missouri*, Cambridge, 1947.

FLINT, TIMOTHY, ed., *The Personal Narrative of James O. Pattie of Kentucky*, new introduction and footnotes by Milo M. Quaife, Chicago, 1930.

HARRIS, BURTON, *John Colter, His Years in the Rockies*, New York, 1952.

NUTE, GRACE LEE, ed., *Calendar of the American Fur Company's Papers. Annual Report*, American Historical Association, vols. II and III, Washington, 1945.

——, *The Voyageur*, New York, 1931.

SMITH, OLSON J., *Men Against the Mountains: Jedediah Smith and the Southwest Expedition of 1826–1829*, New York, 1865.

THWAITES, REUBEN G., ed., *Nuttall's Journal of Travels into the Arkansas Territory*, Early Western Travels, XVIII, Cleveland, 1905.

——, *Wyeth's Oregon, or a Short History of a Long Journey, Ibid.*, vol. XXI, Cleveland, 1905.

——, *Townshend's Narrative of a Journey Across the Rocky Mountains, Ibid.*, Cleveland, 1905.

——, *Journal of a Voyage up the Missouri, performed in 1811 by H. M. Brackenridge, Ibid.*, vol. VI, Cleveland, 1904.

——, Maximilian, Prinz zu Wied, *Travels in the Interior of North America, Ibid.*, vols. XXII–XXIV, Cleveland, 1905.

TOWNSHEND, J. K., *Sporting Excursion in the Rocky Mountains*, 2 vols., London, 1840.

GENERAL WORKS

ALTER, CECIL, *James Bridger*, Columbus, Ohio, 1951.

BANCROFT, H. H., *History of the Northwest Coast, 1800–1846*, vol. II, San Francisco, 1890.

BILLINGTON, RAY A., *The Far Western Frontier, 1830–1860*, New York, 1956.

CHITTENDEN, H. M., *The American Fur Trade*, 3 vols., New York, 1935.

CLELAND, ROBERT GLASS, *This Reckless Breed of Men*, New York, 1950.

COYNER, D. H., *The Lost Trappers, a Collection of Interesting Scenes and Events*, Cincinnati, 1858.

DALE, H. C., *The Ashley-Smith Explorations*, Glendale, 1941.

GHENT, W. J., *The Road to Oregon*, New York, 1934.

HAFEN, LEROY, ed., *The Mountain Men and the Fur Trade of the Far West*, vol. I, Glendale, 1965.

HAFEN, LEROY, and GHENT, W. J., *Broken Hand*, Denver, 1931.

HAWGOOD, JOHN A., *America's Western Frontiers, The Exploration and Settlement of the Trans-Mississippi West*, New York, 1967.

IRVING, WASHINGTON, *Adventures of Captain Bonneville*, London, 1837.

LAUT, AGNES, *The Fur Trade of America*, New York, 1921.

———, *The Conquest of the Great Northwest*, 2 vols., New York, 1908.

LAVENDER, DAVID, *Bent's Fort*, New York, 1955.

MERK, FREDERICK J., *Fur Trade and Empire*, Cambridge, 1931.

MORGAN, DALE L., *Jedediah Smith and the Opening of the West*, Indianapolis, 1953.

NICHOLS, ROGER L., *General Henry Atkinson: A Western Military Career*, Norman, 1965.

PHILLIPS, PAUL CHRISLER, and JOHN W. SMURR, *The Fur Trade*, 2 vols., Norman, Oklahoma, 1961.

SAUM, LEWIS O., *The Fur Trader and the Indian*, Seattle, 1965.

SKARSTEN, M. O., *George Drouillard, Hunter and Interpreter, 1807–1810* (Western Frontier Series, XI), Glendale, Cal., 1964.

SMITH, A. D. H., *John Jacob Astor Landlord of New York*, 2 vols., Philadelphia, 1929.

VANDIVER, C. A., *The Fur Trade and Early Western Exploration*, Cleveland, 1929.

VICTOR, FRANCES, *The River of the West*, Hartford, 1870.

CHAPTER XIX

Across the Settler's Path

The North American Indian has not lacked historians to tell his story, and the historians have found publishers. A sizable library of American history pertains to the place of the Indian in our history. Writers from travelers to social reformers have devoted their attention to the subject. Even artists have left vivid records of the way of life of their subjects.

OFFICIAL DOCUMENTARY SOURCE

RICHARDSON, J. D., *A Compilation of the Messages and Papers of the Presidents*, II, Washington, 1896.

CONTEMPORARY WORKS

CATLIN, GEORGE, *Letters and Notes on the Manners, Customs, and Conditions of the North American Indians*, 2 vols., London, 1842.

FORD, THOMAS, *A History of Illinois*, Chicago, 1854.

GENERAL WORKS

ALFORD, THOMAS WILDCAT, *Civilization as Told to Florence Drake by Thomas Wildcat Alford*, Norman, 1836.

BRITT, ALBERT, *Great Indian Chiefs*, New York, 1938.

CLARKE, DWIGHT L., *Stephen Watts Kearny, Soldier of the West*, Norman, 1961.

COLE, CYRENUS, *I Am a Man, the Indian Blackhawk*, Iowa City, 1938.

———, *A History of the People of Iowa*, Cedar Rapids, 1921.

COULTER, E. M., *Georgia, A Short History*, Chapel Hill, 1947.

DALE, E. E., and LITTON, GASTON, *Cherokee Cavaliers*, Norman, 1939.

DANGERFIELD, GEORGE, *The Era of Good Feelings*, New York, 1952.

EATON, WILLIAM CLEMENT, *A History of the Old South*, New York, 1966.

ELLSWORTH, RICHARD DAY, *Flagellant on Horseback*, Philadelphia, 1950.

FOREMAN, GRANT, *The Five Civilized Tribes*, Norman, 1934.
———, *Indian Removal*, Norman, 1932.
———, *The Last Trek of the Indians*, Chicago, 1946.
———, *A History of Oklahoma*, Norman, 1942.
GITTINGER, ROY, *The Formation of the State of Oklahoma*, Norman, 1939.
HANNA, A. J. and KATHERINE, *Florida's Golden Sands*, Indianapolis, 1950.
KIMMINS, GREER JAMES, *Colonel Jack Hayes*, New York, 1952.
LUMPKIN, WILSON, *The Removal of the Cherokee Indians from Georgia*, 2 vols., New York, 1907.
MACLEOD, WILLIAM C., *The American Indian Frontier*, New York, 1928.
MANEYPENNY, GEORGE, *Our Indian Wards*, Cincinnati, 1880.
MOORE, A. B., *A History of Alabama*, Tuscaloosa, 1934.
PEASE, THEODORE C., *The Frontier State, 1818–1848 (History of Illinois)*, Springfield, 1918.
RODDIS, LOUIS H., *The Indian Wars of Minnesota*, Cedar Rapids, 1956.
SUNDERMAN, J. F., ed., *Journey into Wilderness*, Gainesville, 1953.
TURNER, KATHERINE C., *Red Men Calling on the Great White Father*, Norman, 1951.
TUTTLE, CHARLES R., *History of the Border Wars of Two Centuries*, Chicago, 1874.
WARDELL, MORRIS L., *A Political History of the Cherokee Nation, 1838–1907*, Norman, 1938.
WEBB, WALTER P., *The Texas Rangers*, New York, 1935.
WHITNEY, ORSON F., *History of Utah*, vol. I, Salt Lake City, 1892.
WISSLER, CLARK, *Indians of the United States*, New York, 1941.

CHAPTER XX

The Frontier in Oregon

Oregon, like California, has excited the imagination of the American people. From the beginning of white activities in the region historians have recorded its history. Opening the fur trade, the Oregon Trail and the development of two states in the extreme Northwest were exciting facts in American expansion. Oregon does not lack local histories, and fortunately some of the works pertaining to the territory have a broader perspective than the confines of a single state. The history of the Oregon Trail is of epic proportions, and scarcely a work on the trans-Mississippi West fails to discuss this phase of pioneering.

DOCUMENTARY SOURCE

RICHARDSON, J. D., *A Compilation of the Messages and Papers of the Presidents*, IV, Washington, 1897.

CONTEMPORARY WORKS

APPLEGATE, JESSE, *A Day with the Cow Column*, ed. Joseph Schafer, Chicago, 1934.
FRÉMONT, J. C., *Report of the Exploring Expedition to the Rocky Mountains in the year 1842, and to Oregon and North California in the years 1843–1844*, Washington, 1845.
PARKER, SAMUEL, *A Journey Beyond the Rocky Mountains in 1835, 1836 and 1837*, Edinburgh, 1841.
QUAIFE, MILO M., ed., *The Diary of James K. Polk during His Presidency*, 4 vols., Chicago, 1910.
ROSS, ALEXANDER, *Adventures of the First Settlers on the Oregon and Columbia Rivers*, in Thwaites, R. G., *Early Western Travels*, VII, Cleveland, 1904.

SPAULDING, K. A., ed., *On the Oregon Trail, Robert Stuart's Journey of Discovery, 1812–1813,* Norman, 1953.
YOUNG, F. G., ed., *Sources of Oregon History,* Eugene, 1899.

GENERAL WORKS

ANONYMOUS, *The Oregon Trail, American Guide Series,* New York, 1939.
BAILEY, THOMAS A., *Diplomatic History of the American People,* New York, 1955.
BANCROFT, HUBERT H., *History of Oregon,* 2 vols., San Francisco, 1888.
———, *The Pacific Northwest,* 2 vols., San Francisco, 1884.
BARROWS, WILLIAM, *Oregon: the Struggle for Possession,* Boston, 1883.
BELL, JAMES CHRISTY, *Opening a Highway to the Pacific, 1838–1846,* New York, 1921.
BILLINGTON, R. A., *The Far Western Frontier, 1830–1860,* New York, 1956.
BROOKS, JUANITA, ed., *On the Mormon Frontier: The Diary of Hosea Stout, 1844–1861,* Salt Lake City, 1964.
CAREY, CHARLES H., *A General History of Oregon,* 2 vols., Portland, 1836.
CAUGHEY, JOHN W., *History of the Pacific Coast,* New York, 1938.
DRURY, C. M., *Henry H. Spaulding,* Caldwell, 1936.
———, *Marcus Whitman, M.D., Pioneer and Martyr,* Caldwell, 1937.
FULLER, G. W., *A History of the Pacific Northwest,* New York, 1931.
GASTON, JOSEPH, *The Centennial History of Oregon, 1811–1912,* 4 vols., Chicago, 1912.
GHENT, W. J., *The Road to Oregon,* New York, 1929.
GOODWIN, CARDINAL, *Trans-Mississippi West,* New York, 1922.
GREENHOW, ROBERT, *The History of Oregon and California and the Other Territories of the North-West Coast of North America,* Boston, 1845.
HAFEN, LEROY and ANN W., *To the Rockies and Oregon, 1839–1842,* 3 vols., Glendale, 1955.
HOLMAN, FREDERICK V., *Dr. John McLoughlin, the Father of Oregon,* Cleveland, 1907.
McCORMAC, E. I., *James K. Polk, A Political Biography,* Berkeley, 1922.
MARSHALL, P. W. I., *Acquisition of Oregon,* 2 vols., Seattle, 1911.
MERK, FREDERICK, *Albert Gallatin and the Oregon Problem,* Cambridge, 1950.
PARKMAN, FRANCIS, *The Oregon Trail,* New York, 1911.
POWELL, F. W., *Hall J. Kelley on Oregon,* Princeton, 1932.
SCHAFER, JOSEPH, *A History of the Pacific Northwest,* New York, 1921.
SCOTT, H. W., *History of the Oregon Country,* 6 vols., Cambridge, 1924.
SELLERS, CHARLES, *James K. Polk, Jacksonian, 1795–1843,* Princeton, 1957.
SPALDING, ELIZA WARREN, *Memoirs of the West,* Portland, 1916.

CHAPTER XXI

The Long Arm of Manifest Destiny

The Pacific Coast has made a romantic appeal to the American people since the first sailors from the East visited that coast. At the same time it has been a most vital part of American expansion. Fortunately historians of mature qualifications have been available to interpret the history of California and that of its neighbors. Hubert H. Bancroft's seven volumes alone make available to the modern reader a staggering amount of detailed information.

CONTEMPORARY WORKS

BRYANT, EDWIN, *What I Saw in California, being the Journal of a Tour, in the years 1846, 1847,* New York, 1848.

Dana, Richard H., *Two Years Before the Mast*, Boston, 1840.

Farnham, T. J., *Life, Adventures, and Travels in California*, New York, 1849.

Frémont, John C., *Report of the Exploring Expedition to the Rocky Mountains in the Year 1842, and to Oregon and California in the Years 1843–1844*, Washington, 1845.

Stewart, George R., ed., *The Opening of the California Trail*, Berkeley, 1953.

GENERAL WORKS

Bailey, Thomas A., *Diplomatic History of the American People*, New York, 1955.

Bancroft, Hubert H., *History of California*, 4 vols., San Francisco, 1889–1890.

Bartlett, Richard A., *Great Surveys of the American West*, Norman, 1962.

Bolton, Herbert E., *The Spanish Borderlands*, New Haven, 1921.

Caughey, John W., *California*, New York, 1935.

———, *History of the Pacific Coast*, New York, 1938.

Chapman, C. E., *A History of California, the Spanish Period*, New York, 1939.

Cleland, Robert Glass, *From Wilderness to Empire, A History of California, 1542–1900*, New York, 1944.

———, *Pathfinders*, Los Angeles, 1929.

DeVoto, Bernard, *The Year of Decision, 1846*, Boston, 1943.

Hunt, R. D., and Sanchez, N. V., *A Short History of California, 1542–1900*, New York, 1944.

Lummis, Charles F., *The Spanish Pioneers and the California Missions*, Chicago, 1929.

Marshall, T. M., *A History of the Western Boundary of the Louisiana Purchase, 1819–1841* (Univ. of California, Publications in History), II, Berkeley, 1914.

Morgan, Dale, ed., *Overland in 1846: Diaries and Letters of the California-Oregon Trail*, 2 vols., Georgetown, California, 1963.

Nevins, Allan, *Frémont, the West's Greatest Adventurer*, 2 vols., New York, 1928.

Richman, I. B., *California under Spain and Mexico, 1535–1847*, New York, 1911.

CHAPTER XXII

From Nauvoo to Deseret

The literature treating Mormon history falls into three categories: the books which are highly partisan in favor of the movement, those which attack it, and the histories of Utah and the Great Salt Lake Region. There are, of course, those books which deal with the religious aspects of the Mormon Church. The list given here is representative only of the vast amount of general historical materials available on this subject. In the last three decades historians have published a considerable number of studies which represent extensive research in the settlement of Utah and the Mormon movement.

CONTEMPORARY WORKS

Alter, J. C., *Utah, the Storied Domain*, 3 vols., Chicago, 1932.

Beadle, J. H., *Life in Utah*, Philadelphia, 1870.

Bryant, Edwin, *What I Saw in California, being the Journal of a Tour, in the Years 1846, 1847*, New York, 1849.

GENERAL WORKS

Bancroft, Hubert Howe, *History of Utah, 1540–1887*, San Francisco, 1890.

Cleland, Robert Glass, and Brooks, Juanita, *A Mormon Chronicle; The Diaries of Jason D. Lee, 1848–1876*, 2 vols., San Marino, 1955.

Coman, Katherine, *Economic Beginnings of the Far West*, 2 vols., New York, 1912.
Evans, John Henry, *Joseph Smith, An American Prophet*, New York, 1933.
Fisher, Vardis, *Children of God*, New York, 1939.
Flanders, Robert Bruce, *Nauvoo, Kingdom on the Mississippi*, Urbana, 1965.
Ghent, W. J., *The Road to Oregon*, New York, 1929.
Hammond, O. G., ed., *The Utah Expedition, 1857–1858*, Concord, N. H., 1928.
Larson, G. O., *Prelude to the Kingdom*, Francestown, N. H., 1947.
Linn, W. A., *The Story of the Mormons*, New York, 1902.
Ludlow, F. H., *The Heart of the Continent*, New York, 1870.
McClellan, R. G., *The Golden State*, Chicago, 1872.
McClintock, J. H., *Mormon Settlement in Arizona*, Phoenix, 1921.
Morgan, Dale, *The Great Salt Lake*, Indianapolis, 1947.
Pease, Theodore C., *The Frontier State, 1818–1848* (*History of Illinois*), Springfield, 1918.
Werner, M. R., *Brigham Young*, New York, 1925.
Whitney, Orson F., *History of Utah*, 4 vols., Salt Lake City, 1892–1904.
Widstoe, Leah D., *The Life Story of Brigham Young*, New York, 1931.
Young, L. E., *The Founding of Utah*, New York, 1923.

CHAPTER XXIII

An Interlude of War

The annexation of Texas was only a beginning for the United States of the southwestern struggle. Like all frontier wars this one produced its personal crosscurrents, and soldier-heroes rushed home to receive the literary plaudits of their admirers and to produce a few plaudits themselves. On the other hand scholars have written some solid studies in this field.

CONTEMPORARY WORKS

Blackwood, Emma Jerome, *To Mexico with Scott*, Cambridge, 1917.
Doubleday, R. V. T., ed., *Journals of the Late Brevet Major Phillip Norbourne Barbour*, New York, 1936.
Myers, William S., ed., *The Mexican War Diary of General George B. McClellan*, Princeton, 1917.

GENERAL WORKS

Bailey, Thomas A., *A Diplomatic History of the American People*, New York, 1950.
Bill, A. H., *Rehearsal for Conflict*, New York, 1947.
Callcott, Wilfred H., *Santa Anna, the Story of an Enigma Who Once Was Mexico*, Norman, 1936.
DeVoto, Bernard, *The Year of Decision, 1846*, Boston, 1943.
Dyer, Brainerd, *Zachary Taylor*, Baton Rouge, 1946.
Fuller, J. D. P., *The Movement for the Annexation of all Mexico, 1846–1848*, Baltimore, 1936.
Garber, Paul N., *Gadsden Treaty*, Philadelphia, 1923.
Hamilton, Holman, *Zachary Taylor, Soldier of the Republic*, Indianapolis, 1941.
Henry, Robert Selph, *The Story of the Mexican War*, Norman, 1936.
Mansfield, Edward D., *The Mexican War*, New York, 1849.
Reeves, J. S., *American Diplomacy under Tyler and Polk*, New York, 1907.
Rippy, J. F., *The United States and Mexico*, New York, 1931.
Rives, George L., *The United States and Mexico, 1821–1848*, 2 vols., Baltimore, 1913.
Smith, Justin H., *The War with Mexico*, 2 vols., New York, 1919.

CHAPTER XXIV

Gold, Silver, and Men

The California gold rush of 1849 touched off a series of mineral strikes which in a remarkably short time was to speed up the westward movement. Not only did westerners rush to the gold fields, but they were soon joined by easterners and Europeans in large numbers. The gold rush caught people in just the proper frame of mind to send thousands of them over the sea lanes and western trails. Every man who reached the gold fields seemed to feel obligated to record his memoirs, and today unpublished journals are still being brought to light. A sizable collection of colorful books pertain to this era in American history.

CONTEMPORARY WORKS

BOWLES, SAMUEL, *Our New West*, Chicago, 1869.
CAUGHEY, JOHN, ed., *Rushing for Gold*, Berkeley, 1949.
CLARK, THOMAS D., ed., *Gold Rush Diary: Being the Journal of Elisha Douglas Perkins on the Overland Trail in the Spring and Summer of 1849*, Lexington, 1967.
CLEMENS, SAMUEL L., *Roughing It*, Hartford, 1872.
COLTON, WALTER, *Three Years in California*, New York, 1850.
COUES, ELLIOTT, ed., *The Journal of Jacob Fowler*, New York, 1898.
DELANO, ALONZO, *Across the Plains Among the Diggings*, New York, 1936.
DEQUILLE, DAN, *The Big Bonanza*, New York, 1947.
———, *A History of the Comstock Mines* (orig. ed.), Virginia City, 1889.
DIMSDALE, THOMAS J., *The Vigilantes of Montana*, Helena, 1929.
DRURY, ELLA BISHOP, ed., *An Editor on the Comstock Lode*, New York, 1936.
GREEVER, WILLIAM S., *The Bonanza West: The Story of the Western Mining Rushes, 1848–1900*, Norman, 1963.
HELPER, HINTON ROWAN, *The Land of Gold*, Baltimore, 1855.
Idaho and Montana, New Gold Regions. The Emigrant's Guide, Chicago, 1865.
MCILHANY, E. W., *Recollections of a '49er*, Kansas City, 1908.
MORGAN, DALE, ed., *The Overland Diary of James A. Pritchard from Kentucky to California in 1849*, Denver, 1959.
PHILLIPS, PAUL C., ed., *Forty Years on the Frontier*, Cleveland, 1925.
WHITE, KATHERINE A., *A Yankee Trader in the Gold Rush*, Boston, 1930.

GENERAL WORKS

BANCROFT, H. H., *History of California*, vol. VI, San Francisco, 1888.
BIRNEY, HOFFMAN, *Vigilantes*, Philadelphia, 1929.
CLELAND, ROBERT GLASS, *A History of California*, New York, 1922.
———, *From Wilderness to Empire*, New York, 1944.
COLLINS, CARVEL E., *Sam Ward in the Gold Rush*, Stanford, 1949.
COY, OWEN C., *Gold Days*, San Francisco, 1929.
HAFEN, LEROY, *Overland Routes to the Gold Fields*, Glendale, 1942.
HOWE, O. T., *Argonauts of '49*, Cambridge, 1923.
HUNT, ROCKWELL D. and SÁNCHEZ, NELLIE VAN DE GRIF, *A Short History of California, 1542–1900*, New York, 1929.
JACKSON, JOSEPH H., *Gold Rush Album*, New York, 1949.
KEMBLE, JOHN H., *The Panama Route, 1848–1869*, Berkeley, 1943.

LANGFORD, NATHANIEL P., *Vigilante Days and Ways*, Boston, 1890.

LEWIS, OSCAR, *Sea Routes to the Gold Fields*, New York, 1949.

——, *Silver Kings, the Lives and Times of Mackey, Fair, Flood, and O'Brien, Lords of the Nevada Comstock Lode*, New York, 1947.

LYMAN, G. D., *The Saga of the Comstock Lode*, New York, 1934.

MICHELSON, MIRIAM, *The Wonderlode of Silver and Gold*, Boston, 1934.

PAUL, RODMAN, *California Gold! the Beginning of Mining in the Far West*, Cambridge, 1947.

——, *Mining Frontiers of the Far West, 1848–1880*, New York, 1963.

READ, GEORGIA WILLIS, and RUTH GAINES, eds., *Gold Rush: The Journals, Drawings, and other Papers of J. Goldsborough Bruff, Captain, Washington City and California Mining Association, April 2, 1849–July 20, 1851*, 2 vols., New York, 1944.

SHINN, C. H., *Mining Camps—a Study in American Frontier Government*, New York, 1948.

SPRAGUE, MARSHALL, *Money Mountain*, Boston, 1953.

WEBSTER, KIMBALL, *The Goldseekers of '49*, Manchester, N. H., 1917.

CHAPTER XXV

State-making Along the Mississippi

The history of state-making along the Mississippi follows rather closely the orthodox pattern which had been established elsewhere in westward expansion. Materials relating to this subject are largely of a local nature.

CONTEMPORARY WORK

SHAMBAUGH, B. F., ed., *Notes on the Wisconsin Territory by Albert Lea*, Iowa City, 1937.

GENERAL WORKS

CAMPBELL, H. C., *Wisconsin in Three Centuries, 1634–1905*, 4 vols., New York, 1906.

COLE, CYRENUS, *A History of the People of Iowa*, Cedar Rapids, 1921.

——, *Iowa Through the Years*, Iowa City, 1940.

EASTON, A. B., *History of the St. Croix Valley*, 2 vols., Chicago, 1909.

GUE, B. F., *History of Iowa from the Earliest Times*, 4 vols., New York, 1903.

McBRIDE, THOMAS H., *In Cabins and Sod Houses*, Iowa City, 1923.

PETERSON, WILLIAM J., "Iowa in Louisiana and Michigan," *Palimpsest*, Feb. and March, 1934, pp. 33–35.

RANEY, WILLIAM F., *Wisconsin a Story of Progress*, New York, 1940.

RICHMAN, IRVING BERDINE, *Ioway to Iowa*, Iowa City, 1931.

SALTER, WILLIAM, *Iowa, the First Free State in the Louisiana Purchase*, Chicago, 1905.

SHAMBAUGH, B. F., *History of the Constitutions of Iowa*, Des Moines, 1902.

THOMAS, DAVID Y., *Arkansas and Its People*, New York, 1930.

WATTS, WILLIAM, *A History of Minnesota*, 4 vols., New York, 1903.

CHAPTER XXVI

On the Snags of Expansion

This chapter deals with one of the Nation's most difficult periods of sectional controversy. Every history of the United States down to 1865 deals with the

Compromise of 1850, the Kansas-Nebraska issue, and national politics in some way. Obviously there are differing points of view and, sometimes, radically different interpretations of facts. Among the major works which treat specifically of this period some deal with the issues of expansion while others discuss the more local problems of the subject.

CONTEMPORARY WORKS

COLT, MIRIAM DAVIS, *Went to Kansas*, Watertown, Maine, 1862.
HALE, EDWARD E., *Kansas and Nebraska*, Boston, 1854.
ROBINSON, SARA T. L., *Kansas: Its Interior and Exterior Life*, Boston, 1856.

GENERAL WORKS

CONNELLEY, W. E., *History of Kansas*, 5 vols., Chicago, 1928.
CORDLEY, RICHARD, *Pioneer Days in Kansas*, New York, 1903.
CRAVEN, AVERY O., *The Growth of Southern Nationalism, 1848–1861*, Baton Rouge, 1953.
CURTIS, G. T., *Life of James Buchanan*, 2 vols., New York, 1883.
EATON, WILLIAM CLEMENT, *A History of the Old South*, New York, 1966.
HAMILTON, HOLMAN, *Zachary Taylor, Soldier of the Republic*, Indianapolis, 1951.
HODDER, FRANK H., "The Railroad Background of the Kansas-Nebraska Act," *Mississippi Valley Historical Review*, XII, June, 1925, pp. 3–22.
———, "Genesis of the Kansas-Nebraska Act," *Wisconsin Historical Proceedings*, 1912, p. 69.
JOHNSON, ALLEN, "Genesis of Popular Sovereignty," *Iowa Journal of History and Politics*, vol. III, 1905, p. 3.
McMASTER, JOHN BACH, *A History of the People of the United States*, vol. VIII, New York, 1913.
MACY, J., *Political Parties in the United States, 1846–1861*, New York, 1900.
MALIN, J. C., *John Brown and the Legend of Fifty-Six*, New York, 1942.
———, "Pro-Slavery Background of the Kansas Struggle," *Mississippi Valley Historical Review*, vol. X, 1923, p. 285.
———, *The Nebraska Question, 1852–1854*, Lawrence, 1954.
MILTON, GEORGE FORT, *The Eve of Conflict, Stephen A. Douglas and the Needless War*, New York, 1934.
MONAGHAN, JAY, *Civil War on the Western Border, 1854–1865*, Boston, 1955.
NEVINS, ALLAN, *Ordeal of the Union*, 2 vols., New York, 1947.
NICHOLAS, ALICE, *Bleeding Kansas*, New York, 1954.
NICHOLS, ROY F., *The Disruption of American Democracy*, New York, 1948.
———, *The Democratic Machine*, New York, 1923.
ORMAN, RAY P., *The Repeal of the Missouri Compromise, Its Origin and Authorship*, Cleveland, 1909.
PHILLIPS, ULRICH B., *The Life of Robert Toombs*, New York, 1913.
RHODES, JAMES FORD, *History of the United States from the Compromise of 1850*, vols. I and II, New York, 1893.
VILLARD, O. G., *John Brown*, New York, 1943.
WILDER, D. W., *The Annals of Kansas*, Topeka, 1886.

CHAPTER XXVII

The Cattle Trail Frontier

This has been one of the most popular subjects in frontier history. A large number of books, official reports, and articles in periodicals describe the cattle and sheep industry. Cowboys, cattlemen, travelers and westerners in general have left rich personal records of their lives with the lowing herds.

PERSONAL MEMOIRS

ABBOTT, EDWARD C. and SMITH, HELENA H., *We Pointed Them North*, New York, 1939.
CLAY, JOHN, *My Life on the Range*, Chicago, 1924.
NIMMO, JOSEPH, JR., *Range and Cattle Traffic*, Washington, 1885.
O'REILLY, HARRINGTON, *Fifty Years on the Trail*, New York, 1889.
PRICE, CON, *Trails I Rode*, Hollywood, 1947.
———, *Memories of Old Montana*, Pasadena, 1945.
SHAW, JAMES C., *North from Texas*, edited by Herbert Brayer, Evanston, 1952.

GENERAL WORKS

ADAMS, ANDY, *The Log of a Cowboy*, New York, 1931.
ATHEARN, ROBERT, *Westward the Briton*, New York, 1953.
BANKS, ELEANOR, *Wandersong*, Caldwell, 1950.
BRANCH, E. D., *The Cowboy and His Interpreters*, New York, 1926.
BRIGGS, HAROLD E., *Frontiers of the Northwest, A History of the Upper Missouri Valley*, New York, 1940.
BROWN, DEE, and SCHMITT, MARTIN, *Trail Driving Days*, New York, 1952.
CLAWSON, MARION, *The Western Range Livestock Industry*, New York, 1950.
CONRAD, HOWARD LOUIS, *Uncle Dick Wootten*, Chicago, 1890.
CRAIG, JOHN R., *Ranching with Lords and Commons*, Toronto, 1903.
DALE, E. E., *The Range Cattle Industry*, Norman, 1930.
DICK, EVERETT, *Vanguards of the Frontier*, New York, 1941.
DOBIE, J. FRANK, ed., *A Texas Cowboy*, New York, 1950.
DUVAL, JOHN C., *Early Times in Texas*, Austin, 1892.
ELLIS, EDWARD S., *The Great Cattle Trail*, Philadelphia, 1894.
FRANTZ, JOE B., and CHOATE, J. E., JR., *The American Cowboy: The Myth and the Reality*, Norman, 1955.
GANN, WALTER, *Tread of the Longhorns*, San Antonio, 1949.
GARD, WAYNE, *The Great Buffalo Hunt*, New York, 1960.
GILFILLAN, ARCHER B., *Sheep*, Boston, 1929.
HALEY, J. EVETTS, *George W. Littlefield, Texan*, Norman, 1943.
———, *Charles Goodnight Cowman and Plainsman*, New York, 1936.
———, *Jeff Milton, A Good Man with a Gun*, Norman, 1948.
———, *Life on the Texas Range*, Austin, 1952.
HOWE, CHARLES WILLIS, *Timberleg of the Diamond Tail*, San Antonio, 1950.
JACKSON, W. H., and LONG, S. A., *The Texas Stock Directory or Book of Marks and Brands*, San Antonio, 1865.
LOMAX, JOHN A., *Songs of the Cattle Trail and Cow Camp*, New York, 1950.
McCOY, JOSEPH G., *Historical Sketches of the Cattle Trade*, Kansas City, 1874.
MERCER, A. S., *The Banditti of the Plains, or the Cattleman's Invasion of Wyoming in 1892*, Norman, 1954.
OSGOOD, ERNEST S., *The Day of the Cattleman*, Minneapolis, 1929.
PELZER, LOUIS, *The Cattleman's Frontier, A Record of the Trans-Mississippi Cattle Industry*, Glendale, 1936.
RAINES, WILLIAM M., and BARNES, WILL C., *Cattle*, New York, 1930.
RISTER, CARL COKE, and RICHARDSON, R. N., *The Greater Southwest*, Glendale, 1934.
———, *The Southwestern Frontier*, Cleveland, 1928.
ROLLINS, PHILIP ASHTON, *The Cowboy*, New York, 1922.
SANDOZ, MARI, *The Buffalo Hunters*, New York, 1955.

THOMPSON, ALBERT W., *They Were Open Range Days*, Denver, 1946.
TOWNE, CHARLES WAYLAND, and WENTWORTH, EDWARD N., *Shepherd's Empire*, Norman, 1945.
WATERS, L., *Steel Trails to Santa Fe*, Lawrence, Kansas, 1950.
WEBB, WALTER PRESCOTT, *The Great Plains*, Boston, 1931.
WENTWORTH, EDWARD N., *America's Sheep Trails, History-Personalities*, Ames, Iowa, 1948.
WILSON, RUFUS ROCKWELL, *Out of the West*, New York, 1936.
WRIGHT, ROBERT M., *Dodge City the Cowboy Capital*, Wichita, 1913.

CHAPTER XXVIII

A Desert and A Mountain Empire

The western territories have been the subject of numerous histories, personal journals, and articles in historical society publications. The histories have been of three kinds: the voluminous publications of Hubert Howe Bancroft, the ponderous vanity books which are one-third history and nearly two-thirds worthless material, and, finally, the more modern works which contain highly competent interpretations of the area.

The color and excitement of this part of the American frontier movement was to attract all sorts of people and to produce many varied personalities. Many of the people who visited the region felt impelled to write of their experiences at the time they were in the West, while others wrote memoirs in later years.

CONTEMPORARY WORKS

BOWLES, SAMUEL, *Our New West*, Hartford, 1869.
CLEMENS, SAMUEL L., *Roughing It*, Hartford, 1872.
DONALDSON, THOMAS, *Idaho of Yesterday*, Caldwell, 1941.
QUAIFE, MILO M., ed., *The Narratives of the Adventures of Zenas Leonard*, Chicago, 1934.
RICHARDSON, A. D., *Beyond the Mississippi*, Hartford, 1867.
RICHARDSON, J. D., *Compilation of Messages and Papers of the Presidents*, vols. III–VI, 1789–1897, Washington, 1897.
STUART, GRANVILLE, *Forty Years on the Frontier*, ed. P. C. Phillips, Cleveland, 1925.
THORPE, FRANCIS NEWTON, *The Federal and State Constitutions*, vols. 2, 4–7, Washington, 1909.

GENERAL WORKS

ANONYMOUS, *An Illustrated History of The State of Idaho*, Chicago, 1899.
BANCROFT, HUBERT H., *History of Washington, Idaho, and Montana, 1845–1889*, San Francisco, 1890.
——, *History of Nevada, Colorado, and Wyoming, 1540–1888*, San Francisco, 1890.
BARTO, H. E., and BULLARD, CATHERINE, *History of the State of Washington*, Boston, 1947.
BROSNAN, C. J., *History of the State of Idaho*, New York, 1935.
CAREY, C. H., *A General History of Oregon*, 2 vols., Portland, 1935.
CAUGHEY, JOHN, *History of the Pacific Coast*, New York, 1938.
FRITZ, P. S., *Colorado, the Centennial State*, New York, 1941.
FULLER, GEORGE W., *A History of the Pacific Northwest*, New York, 1931.
HAFEN, LEROY, *Colorado, the Story of a Western Commonwealth*, Denver, 1933.
HAWLEY, J. H., *History of Idaho, The Gem of the Mountains*, 4 vols., Chicago, 1920.
HOLLON, W. EUGENE, *The Great American Desert, Then and Now*, New York, 1966.

Humphrey, Seth K., *Following the Prairie Frontier*, Minneapolis, 1931.

Lavender, David S., *Bent's Fort*, New York, 1954.

Mack, Effie Mona, *Nevada, A History of the State from the Earliest Times Through the Civil War*, Glendale, 1936.

——, *Mark Twain in Nevada*, New York, 1947.

Schafer, Joseph, *A History of the Pacific Northwest*, New York, 1918.

Smiley, Jerome C., *Semi-Centennial History of the State of Colorado*, 2 vols., Chicago, 1913.

Stout, Tom, *Montana, Its Story and Biography*, 3 vols., Chicago, 1890.

Villard, Henry, *The Past and Present of Pike's Peak Gold Regions*, Princeton, 1932.

Winther, Oscar O., *The Great Northwest*, New York, 1950.

CHAPTER XXIX

Linking the Continent with Highway and Rail

Written history of western transportation is of a varied nature and quality. To begin with there is a rather marked diversity of subject matter, and writings have ranged from superficial travel accounts to mature studies based upon the records of the various agencies of transportation.

CONTEMPORARY WORK

Clemens, Samuel L., *Roughing It*, Hartford, 1872.

GENERAL WORKS

Banning, William, and Banning, Hugh George, *Six Horses*, New York, 1930.

Beebe, Lucius, and Charles Clegg, *U. S. West, the Saga of Wells-Fargo*, N. Y., 1949.

Bender, Averman B., *The March of Empire*, Lawrence, Kansas, 1952.

Brown, Margaret L., "Asa Whitney and His Pacific Railroad Publicity Campaign," *Mississippi Valley Historical Review*, vol. XX, September, 1933, pp. 209–224.

Chapman, Arthur, *The Pony Express*, New York, 1932.

Connelley, William E., *Wild Bill and His Era*, New York, 1933.

Frederick, J. V., *Ben Holladay the Stagecoach King*, Glendale, 1940.

Hafen, Leroy, *The Overland Mail, 1849–1869*, Cleveland, 1926.

Haney, Lewis, *A Congressional History of Railways in the United States to 1850*, Madison, Wis., 1908.

Harlow, Alvin F., *Old Post Bags*, New York, 1928.

Hungerford, E. L., *Wells Fargo*, New York, 1947.

Jackson, W. Turrentine, *Wagon Roads West*, Berkeley, 1952.

Josephson, Matthew, *The Robber Barons, The Great American Capitalists, 1881–1901*, New York, 1934.

Lewis, Oscar, *The Big Four*, New York, 1938.

Loomis, Nelson H., "Asa Whitney; Father of the Pacific Railroads," *Proceedings of the Mississippi Valley Historical Association*, vol. 6, 1913, pp. 166–175.

Marshall, James, *Santa Fe*, New York, 1945.

Moody, John, *The Railroad Builders*, New Haven, 1919.

Ormsby, Waterman L., *The Butterfield Overland Mail*, San Marino, 1962.

Overton, Richard C., *Burlington West*, Cambridge, 1941.

Pyle, Joseph G., *The Life of James J. Hill*, 2 vols., New York, 1917.

Riegel, Robert E., *The Story of Western Railroads*, New York, 1926.

RIPLEY, WILLIAM Z., *Railroads, Finance and Organization*, New York, 1920.
STARR, JOHN W., JR., *One Hundred Years of American Railroading*, New York, 1928.
THOMPSON, R. L., *Wiring a Continent*, Princeton, 1947.
TROTTMAN, NELSON, *History of the Union Pacific*, New York, 1923.
WATERS, L. L., *Steel Trails to Santa Fe*, Lawrence, Kansas, 1950.
WINTHER, OSCAR O., *The Transportation Frontier: Trans-Mississippi West, 1865–1890*, New York, 1964.

CHAPTER XXX

The Indians' Last Stand

The white man may have discriminated against the Indians in the woods, but they have more than made it up to them on the printing presses. Books relating to Indian history are numerous indeed, and they range from sentimental discussions of the noble red man to soldier reminiscences of warfare on the plains. For people who left few written records of their own, it is somewhat of a literary phenomenon that so many aspects of Indian life have received the attention of historians, sociologists, soldiers and economists.

CONTEMPORARY WORKS

CUSTER, G. A., *Life on the Plains*, New York, 1874.
SHERIDAN, PHILIP H., *Personal Memoirs*, 2 vols., London, 1888.
SHERMAN, WILLIAM T., *Memoirs*, 2 vols., New York, 1886.

GENERAL WORKS

BENDER, AVERMAN B., *The March of Empire*, Lawrence, Kansas, 1952.
BERTHONG, DONALD J., *The Southern Cheyennes*, Norman, 1963.
BOURKE, JOHN G., *On the Border with Crook*, Columbus, 1950.
BRANCH, E. D., *Hunting of the Buffalo*, New York, 1929.
BRININSTOOL, E. A., *Troopers with Custer*, Harrisburg, 1952.
CAREY, CHARLES H., *A General History of Oregon Prior to 1861*, 2 vols., Portland, 1935–1936.
DALE, E. E., *The Indians of the Southwest*, Norman, 1949.
DICK, EVERETT, *Vanguards of the Frontier*, New York, 1941.
GOODWIN, GRENVILLE, *The Social Organization of the Western Apache*, Chicago, 1942.
GRAHAM, W. A., *The Story of the Little Big Horn*, New York, 1926.
GREER, JAMES K., *Colonel Jack Hayes*, New York, 1952.
HAINES, FRANCIS, *The Nez Percés: Tribesmen of the Columbia Plateau*, Norman, 1955.
HALEY, J. EVETTS, *Jeff Milton, a Good Man with a Gun*, Norman, 1948.
HANKS, LUCIEN and JANE R., *Tribe Under Trust*, Toronto, 1950.
HOWARD, O. O., *My Life and Experiences Among Our Hostile Indians*, Hartford, 1907.
HYDE, GEORGE E., *Red Cloud's Folk*, Norman, 1937.
———, *A Sioux Chronicle*, Norman, 1956.
JACKSON, HELEN HUNT, *A Century of Dishonor*, Boston, 1885.
KING, CHARLES, *Campaigning with Crook*, New York, 1880.
LEUPP, FRANCIS, *The Indian and His Problem*, New York, 1910.
LOCKWOOD, FRANK C., *The Apache Indians*, New York, 1938.
MACLEOD, W. C., *The American Indian Frontier*, New York, 1928.
MANEYPENNY, G. W., *Our Indian Wards*, Cincinnati, 1880.

MARCY, R. B., *Thirty Years of Army Life on the Border*, New York, 1866.
MAZZANOVICH, ANTON, *Trailing Geronimo*, Hollywood, 1931.
OLSON, JAMES C., *Red Cloud and the Sioux Problem*, Lincoln, Nebraska, 1965.
POMEROY, EARL, *The Pacific Slope: A History of California, Oregon, Washington, Idaho, and Nevada*, New York, 1965.
PRIEST, LORING B., *Uncle Sam's Stepchildren*, New York, 1942.
RISTER, CARL COKE, *The Southwestern Frontier*, Cleveland, 1928.
SANDOZ, MARI, *Crazy Horse*, New York, 1942.
SEYMOUR, FLORA W., *Indian Agents of the Old Frontier*, New York, 1941.
SCHMITT, MARTIN F., *General George Crook: His Autobiography*, Norman, 1960.
———, ed., *General George Crook: His Autobiography*, Norman, 1946.
———, and BROWN, DEE, *Fighting Indians of the West*, New York, 1948.
TATUM, LAWRIE, *Our Red Brothers and the Peace Policy of President Ulysses S. Grant*, Philadelphia, 1899.
TURNER, KATHERINE C., *Red Men Calling on the Great White Father*, Norman, 1951.
WEBB, WALTER PRESCOTT, *The Great Plains*, New York, 1931.
WISSLER, CLARK, *North American Indians of the Plains*, New York, 1934.
WINTHER, OSCAR O., *The Great Northwest, a History*, New York, 1950.

CHAPTER XXXI

The Last Social Barrier

The Homestead Act of 1862 sent an army of home seekers westward following the Civil War. This army of new settlers speeded up the pioneering process and transferred to the West patterns of an older frontier culture. Under the influence of new environmental conditions they developed a distinct local history of their own.

CONTEMPORARY WORKS

DONALDSON, THOMAS, *The Public Domain*, Washington, 1884.
ISE, JOHN, ed., *Sod House Days*, New York, 1937.
KELLEY, O. H., *Origin and Progress of the Order of the Patrons of Husbandry*, Philadelphia, 1875.
RICHARDSON, ALBERT D., *Beyond the Mississippi*, New York, 1867.

GENERAL WORKS

ATHERTON, LEWIS, *Main Street on the Middle Border*, Bloomington, 1954.
BOTKIN, B. A., *A Treasury of American Folklore*, New York, 1944.
BRYCE, JAMES, *The American Commonwealth*, 2 vols., New York, 1893.
BUCK, SOLON JUSTUS, *The Agrarian Crusade*, New Haven, 1920.
DARRAH, WILLIAM CULP, *Powell of the Colorado*, Princeton, 1951.
DICK, EVERETT, *The Sod House Frontier*, New York, 1937.
EVERETT, E. E., "American Agriculture—the First 300 Years," *Farmers in a Changing World, Agriculture Yearbook*, Washington, 1940.
FITE, GILBERT, *The Farmer's Frontier, 1865–1900*, New York, 1966.
GATES, PAUL W., *Fifty Million Acres; Conflicts over Kansas Land Policy*, Ithaca, 1954.
HUMPHREY, SETH K., *Following the Prairie Frontier*, Minneapolis, 1931.
HUTCHINSON, W. T., *Cyrus Hall McCormick*, 2 vols., New York, 1935.
ISE, JOHN, *Sod and Stubble*, New York, 1936.
KAEMPFFERT, W. B., *A Popular History of American Invention*, 2 vols., New York, 1924.

NELSON, BRUCE O., *Land of the Dakotahs*, Minneapolis, 1946.
QUAINTANCE, H. W., *The Influence of Farm Machinery*, Madison, 1904.
RISTER, CARL COKE, *Southwestern Frontier*, Cleveland, 1928.
———, *Southern Plainsmen*, Norman, 1938.
ROBBINS, ROY, *Our Landed Heritage*, Princeton, 1942.
RUTTER, WILLIAM P., *Wheat Growing in Canada, the United States and the Argentine*, London, 1911.
SANDOZ, MARI, *Old Jules*, Boston, 1935.
SHANNON, FREDERICK A., *The Farmer's Last Frontier*, New York, 1945.
SMITH, HENRY NASH, *Virgin Land*, Cambridge, 1950.
STEPHENSON, GEORGE M., *The Political History of the Public Lands from 1840–1862*, Boston, 1917.
WEBB, WALTER PRESCOTT, *The Great Plains*, Boston, 1931.
WITTKE, CARL, *We Who Built America*, New York, 1939.
WYMAN, WALKER D., *Nothing but Prairie and Sky*, Norman, 1954.

CHAPTER XXXII

Rounding Out a Continent

Much of the material given in the bibliography for Chapter XXVIII applies with equal pertinency in this chapter, and for that reason most of it is not repeated.

CONTEMPORARY WORKS

DIMSDALE, T. J., *Vigilantes of Montana*, Helena, 1915.
JACKSON, HELEN HUNT, *A Century of Dishonor*, New York, 1885.
LANGFORD, N. P., *Vigilante Days and Ways*, Boston, 1890.
McCOY, JOSEPH G., *Historic Sketches of the Cattle Trade*, Kansas City, 1874.
RICHARDSON, J. D., *Compilation of the Messages and Papers of the Presidents*, vols. III–VI, Washington, 1897.
THORPE, FRANCIS N., *The Federal and State Constitutions*, vols. 2, 4–7, Washington, 1909.

GENERAL WORKS

ATHEARN, ROBERT, *Westward the Briton*, New York, 1935.
BINING, A. C., *The Rise of American Economic Life*, New York, 1943.
BOGART, E. L., and KEMMERER, DONALD, *Economic History of the American People*, New York, 1947.
BRILL, CHARLES J., *Conquest of the Southern Plains*, Oklahoma City, 1938.
BRYCE, JAMES, *The American Commonwealth*, 2 vols., New York, 1893.
BUCK, SOLON J., *The Agrarian Crusade*, New Haven, 1921.
CLINE, GLORIA GRIFFIN, *Exploring the Great Basin*, Norman, 1963.
DALE, E. E., *The Indians of the Southwest*, Norman, 1949.
———, and WARDELL, MORRIS, *History of Oklahoma*, New York, 1948.
FOREMAN, GRANT, *A History of Oklahoma*, Norman, 1942.
GITTINGER, ROY, *The Formation of the State of Oklahoma*, Norman, 1939.
HARGREAVES, MARY WILMA, *Dry Farming in the Northern Great Plains, 1900–1925*, Cambridge, 1957.
HICKS, JOHN D., *The Populist Revolt*, Minneapolis, 1931.
HOWARD, JOSEPH, *Montana, High, Wide, and Handsome*, New Haven, 1943.
HYDE, GEORGE, *Red Cloud's Folk, A History of the Ogallala Sioux Indians*, Norman, 1937.

JOSEPHSON, MATTHEW, *The Robber Barons, the Great American Capitalists, 1881–1901*, New York, 1934.

KRAENZEL, CARL F., *The Great Plains in Transition*, Norman, 1955.

LAMAR, H. R., *Dakota Territory, 1861–1889, A Study in Frontier Politics*, New Haven, 1956.

LaMOORE, EDNA, *Dakota*, Caldwell, 1913.

LEUPP, FRANCIS, *The Indian and His Problem*, New York, 1910.

LEWIS, OSCAR, *The Big Four*, New York, 1938.

LIMFORD, VELMA, *Wyoming, Frontier State*, Denver, 1947.

LOUNSBURY, C. A., *Early History of North Dakota*, Washington, 1919.

McCONNELL, J. W., *Early History of Idaho*, Caldwell, 1913.

NELSON, BRUCE O., *Land of the Dakotahs*, Minneapolis, 1945.

OSGOOD, ERNEST S., *The Day of the Cattleman*, Minneapolis, 1929.

PAXSON, FREDERICK L., *The Last American Frontier*, New York, 1910.

PELZER, LOUIS, *The Cattlemen's Frontier*, Glendale, 1936.

PYLE, J. G., *The Life of James J. Hill*, 2 vols., New York, 1917.

RIEGEL, ROBERT, *The Story of the Western Railroads*, New York, 1926.

RISTER, CARL C., *Land Hunger: David L. Payne and the Oklahoma Boomers*, Norman, 1942.

SCHELL, HERBERT S., *South Dakota, Its Beginnings and Growth*, New York, 1942.

——, *History of South Dakota*, Lincoln, Nebraska, 1961.

THOMAS, BENJAMIN, *Abraham Lincoln*, New York, 1952.

PRESIDENTIAL TERMS
1789–1969

GEORGE WASHINGTON, 1789–1797

JOHN ADAMS, 1797–1801

THOMAS JEFFERSON, 1801–1809

JAMES MADISON, 1809–1817

JAMES MONROE, 1817–1825

JOHN QUINCY ADAMS, 1825–1829

ANDREW JACKSON, 1829–1837

MARTIN VAN BUREN, 1837–1841

WILLIAM HENRY HARRISON, 1841

JOHN TYLER, 1841–1845

JAMES KNOX POLK, 1845–1849

ZACHARY TAYLOR, 1849–1850

MILLARD FILLMORE, 1850–1853

FRANKLIN PIERCE, 1853–1857

JAMES BUCHANAN, 1857–1861

ABRAHAM LINCOLN, 1861–1865

ANDREW JOHNSON, 1865–1869

ULYSSES S. GRANT, 1869–1877

RUTHERFORD B. HAYES, 1877–1881

JAMES A. GARFIELD, 1881

CHESTER A. ARTHUR, 1881–1885

GROVER CLEVELAND, 1885–1889

BENJAMIN HARRISON, 1889–1893

GROVER CLEVELAND, 1893–1897

WILLIAM MC KINLEY, 1897–1901

THEODORE ROOSEVELT, 1901–1909

WILLIAM HOWARD TAFT, 1909–1913

WOODROW WILSON, 1913–1921

WARREN G. HARDING, 1921–1923

CALVIN COOLIDGE, 1923–1929

HERBERT CLARK HOOVER, 1929–1933

FRANKLIN DELANO ROOSEVELT, 1933–1945

HARRY S. TRUMAN, 1945–1953

DWIGHT D. EISENHOWER, 1953–1961

JOHN F. KENNEDY, 1961–1963

LYNDON B. JOHNSON, 1963–1969

CHRONOLOGICAL TABLE
OF UNITED STATES HISTORY

A partial table of major events in American history is given here so that the reader of *Frontier America* may refer to events happening in the rest of the country while the frontier was being settled.

1689. Colonial population: New England, 80,000; the middle colonies 40,000; southern colonies 85,000.

1733. Molasses Act

1744–1748. King George's War

1754. Meeting of the Albany Congress

1757. First exhibition of colonial paintings

1763. Grenville Ministry came to office in Great Britain

1765. Stamp Act passed in England. Stamp Act Congress in October in New York

1774. First Continental Congress

1775. April 19, Battle of Lexington

1775. July 3, Washington took command of army at Cambridge

1776. July 4, Declaration of Independence

1776. December 26, battle of Trenton, and January 3, 1777, battle of Princeton

1781. October 19, Surrender of Cornwallis at Yorktown

1784. Debt of states and nation combined equaled approximately $61,000,000

1786–1787. Shay's Rebellion in Massachusetts

1784–1787. Mount Vernon, Annapolis, and Philadelphia conventions

1788. New Hampshire, the ninth state to ratify the United States Constitution

1790. Alexander Hamilton reported to Congress on credit and the National Bank

1791–1792. Hamilton reported to Congress on manufactures

1793. Citizen Edmund Genêt reached the United States to seek this country's aid for the French revolutionists

1798. The X. Y. Z. affair reported to Congress

1798. Naval War with France

1798. Alien and Sedition Acts adopted by Congress

1800. Population of the United States was 5,308,000

1803. Marbury *vs.* Madison

1806–1810. British, European and American blockades
    a. 1806. Nonintercourse Act

  b. 1806–1807. Berlin and Milan decrees
  c. 1807. Orders in Council
  d. 1807. Embargo Act
  e. 1810. Macon's Bill No. 2

1811. Appearance of the Steamboat *New Orleans*

1815. Hartford Convention

1819. Dartmouth *vs.* Woodward and McCullough *vs.* Maryland

1824. Tariff increased duties on enlarged list of items

1828. "Tariff of Abominations"

1830. Webster-Hayne Debate

1831. The Nat Turner Rebellion

1832. New England Antislavery Society organized

1833. Enactment of the Force Bill

1834. Clay's party became the National Whig party

1836. Jackson issued the Specie Circular

1836. Martin Van Buren elected President of the United States

1837. The *Caroline* incident on the Niagara River.

1846. New Hampshire Legislature passed first child labor law

1847. Cyrus Hall McCormick of Virginia established harvester plant in Chicago

1849. Elizabeth Blackwell first graduate woman medical doctor

1851. William Kelly introduced the Bessemer process of decarbonizing iron

1851. The fast sailing ship *Flying Cloud* sailed from New York to San Francisco in 89 days

1856. Preston Brooks attacked Charles Sumner with a walking cane

1857. Dred Scott Decision handed down by the United States Supreme Court

1858. Lincoln-Douglas Debates

1859. John Brown's Raid on Harper's Ferry

1860. Famous presidential year. Lincoln elected. South Carolina called secession convention. Crittenden Compromise

1861. March, April, Fort Sumter fired upon. First Battle of Bull Run

1863. Battles of Vicksburg, Gettysburg, and Chickamauga

1865. April 9, Civil War ended with surrender of General Lee's army

1865. April 14, Abraham Lincoln assassinated

1865. May 29, Andrew Johnson issued Amnesty Proclamation

1866. June, Fourteenth Amendment approved by Congress and sent to the states for ratification

1867. October, United States took possession of Alaska.

1868. Armour Packing Company as adjunct of Milwaukee and Chicago grain business

1868. U. S. Grant elected President of the United States

1869. Illinois Legislature passed laws regulating railways

1866–1877. Reconstruction governments replaced in southern states

1870. Standard Oil Company organized

1871. Tweed Ring broken in New York

1873. The great financial panic; United States Supreme Court handed down decisions in the Slaughterhouse cases

1875. At least a dozen plants in United States producing relatively cheap steel

1876. Belknap scandal exposed; telephone introduced to public; disputed presidential election in which Rutherford B. Hayes was declared to be elected President of the United States; celebration of Republic's centennial

1878. February 28, Bland-Allison Silver Purchase Act passed by Congress; the great railway strike occurred that year

1878. John F. Appleby invented twine binder and placed it in production

1880. Whisky sales in the United States amounted to $193,000,000; 1880–1890, improved farm lands increased by 129,724,445 acres

1886. American Federation of Labor organized

1882. John L. Sullivan won heavyweight title from Paddy Ryan

1883. Pendleton Civil Service Act passed. United States Treasury surplus $145,000,000

1884. Grover Cleveland, Democrat, elected President of the United States

1886. May 4, Hay Market Riot in Chicago

1889. First meeting of Pan American Congress

1890. Sherman Silver Purchase Act

1892. Homestead Strike in Pennsylvania

1893. Queen Liliuokalani deposed by Americans in Hawaii

1894. The Pullman Strike in Chicago

1895. March 8, United States *Alliance* fired on in Cuban waters

1896. William McKinley, Republican, elected President of the United States

1897. Dingley Tariff Act passed by Congress

1898. Public demands for war with Spain; February 15, *Maine* sunk; April 25, war formally declared on Spain

1899. September 6, "Open Door" policy in China announced

1890–1910. Decades of tremendous business consolidations; United States Steel Corporation became the first billion dollar business. 1902–1916, period of political and social reform

1901. Theodore Roosevelt, Republican, became President of the United States

1904. Theodore Roosevelt announced the corollary to the Monroe Doctrine

1906. Congress passed the Hepburn Railway Regulation Act; United States *Nashville* ordered to "prevent landing of any armed forces with hostile intent whether government or insurgent"

1906. Pure Food and Drug Acts passed by Congress

1907. Theodore Roosevelt appointed the national forestry commission

POPULATION OF THE 50 STATES, 1790–1960 *

(IN THOUSANDS)

	1790	1800	1820	1840	1860	1870	1880	1890	1900	1910	1920	1930	1940	1950	1960
Continental U. S.	3,929	5,308	9,638	[1]17,069	31,443	[2]39,818	50,156	[3]62,948	75,995	91,972	105,711	122,775	131,669	150,697	179,323
Regions:															
Northeast	1,968	2,636	4,360	6,761	10,594	12,299	14,507	17,407	21,047	25,869	29,662	34,427	35,977	39,478	44,678
North Central		51	859	3,352	9,097	12,981	17,364	22,410	26,333	29,889	34,020	38,594	40,143	44,461	51,619
South	1,961	2,622	4,419	6,951	11,133	12,288	16,517	20,028	24,524	29,389	33,126	37,858	41,666	47,197	54,973
West					619	991	1,768	3,102	4,091	6,826	8,903	11,896	13,883	19,562	28,053
New England	1,009	1,233	1,660	2,235	3,135	3,488	4,011	4,701	5,592	6,553	7,401	8,166	8,437	9,314	10,509
Maine	97	152	298	502	628	627	649	661	694	742	768	797	847	914	969
New Hampshire	142	184	244	285	326	318	347	377	412	431	443	465	492	533	607
Vermont	85	154	236	292	315	331	332	332	344	356	352	360	359	378	390
Massachusetts	379	423	523	738	1,231	1,457	1,783	2,239	2,805	3,366	3,852	4,250	4,317	4,691	5,149
Rhode Island	69	69	83	109	175	217	277	346	429	543	604	687	713	792	859
Connecticut	238	251	275	310	460	537	623	746	908	1,115	1,381	1,607	1,709	2,007	2,535
Middle Atlantic	959	1,403	2,700	4,526	7,459	8,811	10,497	12,706	15,455	19,316	22,261	26,261	27,539	30,164	34,168
New York	340	589	1,373	2,429	3,881	4,383	5,083	6,003	7,269	9,114	10,385	12,588	13,479	14,830	16,782
New Jersey	184	211	278	373	672	906	1,131	1,445	1,884	2,537	3,156	4,041	4,160	4,835	6,067
Pennsylvania	434	602	1,049	1,724	2,906	3,522	4,283	5,258	6,302	7,665	8,720	9,631	9,900	10,498	11,319
East North Central		51	793	2,925	6,927	9,125	11,207	13,478	15,986	18,251	21,476	25,297	26,626	30,399	36,225
Ohio		[4]45	581	1,519	2,340	2,665	3,198	3,672	4,158	4,767	5,759	6,647	6,908	7,947	9,706
Indiana		[5]6	147	686	1,350	1,681	1,978	2,192	2,516	2,701	2,930	3,239	3,428	3,934	4,662
Illinois			55	476	1,712	2,540	3,078	3,826	4,822	5,639	6,485	7,631	7,897	8,712	10,081
Michigan			[6]9	212	749	1,184	1,637	2,094	2,421	2,810	3,668	4,842	5,256	6,372	7,823
Wisconsin				[7]31	776	1,055	1,315	1,693	2,069	2,334	2,632	2,939	3,138	3,435	3,952
West North Central			67	427	2,170	3,857	6,157	8,932	10,347	11,638	12,544	13,297	13,517	14,061	15,394
Minnesota					172	440	781	1,310	1,751	2,076	2,387	2,564	2,792	2,982	3,414
Iowa				[8]43	675	1,194	1,625	1,912	2,232	2,225	2,404	2,471	2,538	2,621	2,758
Missouri			67	384	1,182	1,721	2,168	2,679	3,107	3,293	3,404	3,629	3,785	3,955	4,320
North Dakota					[9]5	2	37	191	319	577	647	681	642	620	632
South Dakota						12	98	349	402	584	637	693	643	653	681
Nebraska					29	123	452	1,063	1,066	1,192	1,296	1,378	1,316	1,326	1,411
Kansas					107	364	996	1,428	1,470	1,691	1,769	1,881	1,801	1,905	2,179
South Atlantic	1,852	2,286	3,061	3,925	5,365	5,854	7,597	8,858	10,443	12,195	13,990	15,794	17,823	21,182	25,972
Delaware	59	64	73	78	112	125	147	168	185	202	223	238	267	318	446
Maryland	320	342	407	470	687	781	935	1,042	1,188	1,295	1,450	1,632	1,821	2,343	3,101

Dis. of Columbia		8	23	34	75	132	178	230	279	331	438	487	663	802	764
Virginia	692	808	938	1,025	1,220	1,225	1,513	1,656	1,854	2,062	2,309	2,422	2,678	3,319	3,967
West Virginia	56	79	137	225	377	442	618	763	959	1,221	1,464	1,729	1,902	2,006	1,860
North Carolina	394	478	639	753	993	1,071	1,400	1,618	1,894	2,206	2,559	3,170	3,572	4,062	4,556
South Carolina	249	346	503	594	704	706	996	1,151	1,340	1,515	1,684	1,739	1,900	2,117	2,383
Georgia	83	163	341	691	1,057	1,184	1,542	1,837	2,216	2,609	2,896	2,909	3,124	3,445	3,943
Florida				54	140	188	269	391	529	753	968	1,468	1,897	2,771	4,952
East South Central	**109**	**335**	**1,190**	**2,575**	**4,021**	**4,404**	**5,585**	**6,429**	**7,548**	**8,410**	**8,893**	**9,887**	**10,778**	**11,477**	**12,050**
Kentucky	74	221	564	780	1,156	1,321	1,649	1,859	2,147	2,290	2,417	2,615	2,846	2,945	3,038
Tennessee	36	106	423	829	1,110	1,259	1,542	1,768	2,021	2,185	2,338	2,617	2,916	3,292	3,567
Alabama		[10] 1	128	591	964	997	1,263	1,513	1,829	2,138	2,348	2,646	2,833	3,062	3,267
Mississippi		[11] 8	75	376	791	828	1,132	1,290	1,551	1,797	1,791	2,010	2,184	2,179	2,178
West South Central			**168**	**450**	**1,748**	**2,030**	**3,334**	**4,741**	**6,532**	**8,785**	**10,242**	**12,177**	**13,065**	**14,538**	**16,951**
Arkansas			14	98	435	484	803	1,128	1,312	1,574	1,752	1,854	1,949	1,910	1,786
Louisiana			153	352	708	727	940	1,119	1,382	1,656	1,799	2,102	2,364	2,684	3,257
Oklahoma								259	790	1,657	2,028	2,396	2,336	2,233	2,328
Texas					604	819	1,592	2,236	3,049	3,897	4,663	5,825	6,415	7,711	9,580
Mountain					**175**	**315**	**653**	**1,214**	**1,675**	**2,634**	**3,336**	**3,702**	**4,150**	**5,075**	**6,855**
Montana						21	39	143	243	376	549	538	559	591	675
Idaho						15	33	89	162	326	432	445	525	589	667
Wyoming						9	21	63	93	146	194	226	251	291	330
Colorado					34	40	194	413	540	799	940	1,036	1,123	1,325	1,754
New Mexico					[12] 94	92	120	160	195	327	360	423	532	681	951
Arizona						10	40	88	123	204	334	436	499	750	1,302
Utah					[13] 40	87	144	211	277	373	449	508	550	689	891
Nevada					[14] 7	42	62	47	42	82	77	91	110	160	285
Pacific					**444**	**675**	**1,115**	**1,888**	**2,417**	**4,449**	**5,878**	**8,622**	**10,229**	**15,115**	**21,198**
Washington					12	24	75	357	518	1,142	1,357	1,563	1,736	2,379	2,853
Oregon					52	91	175	318	414	673	783	954	1,090	1,521	1,769
California					380	560	865	1,213	1,485	2,378	3,427	5,677	6,907	10,586	15,717
Alaska							33	32	64	64	55	59	73	129	226
Hawaii								90	154	192	256	368	423	500	633

[1] Includes 6,100 persons on public ships in service of the United States, not credited to any region, division, or State. [2] Revised; unrevised figure is 38,558,371. Census of Southern States considered incomplete but there has been no revision of State figures, hence State and region figures do not add to total shown here. [3] Includes 325,464 persons in Indian Territory and Indian reservations, specially enumerated. [4] Territory Northwest of River Ohio. [5] 1800 includes 3,124 persons in those portions of Indiana Territory which were taken to form Michigan and Illinois Territories in 1805 and 1809, respectively, and that portion which was separated in 1816. [6] Michigan Territory as then constituted; boundaries changed in 1816, 1818, 1834, and 1836. [7] Includes that part of Minnesota northeast of Mississippi River. [8] Includes that part of Minnesota lying west of Mississippi River and a line drawn from its source northwards to Canadian boundary. [9] Dakota Territory. [10] Those parts of Mississippi Territory now in present State.

[11] Those parts of present State included in Mississippi Territory as then constituted. [12] Includes area taken to form part of Arizona Territory in 1863

[13] Utah Territory exclusive of that part of present State of Colorado taken to form Colorado Territory in 1861. [14] Nevada Territory as organized in 1861.

* Adapted from the *Statistical Abstract of the United States, 1920, 1966:* Washington, D. C.

PICTURE SOURCES

COURTESY NEW YORK PUBLIC LIBRARY
    GENERAL

Page

  1 From P. Campbell, *Travels through . . . North America* (1793).

 25 From William Smith, *An historical account of the expedition against the Ohio Indians, in the year 1764, under the command of Henry Bouquet, Esq. . . . .* (Philadelphia, 1765).

103 From Herring and Longacre, *National Portrait Gallery of Distinguished Americans,* 1835, Vol. 2.

199 From A. Welby, *A Visit to North America,* London, 1821.

337 From W. H. Brown, *The History of the First Locomotives in America,* 1871. Parsons Collection.

548 From G. W. Kendall, *The War Between the United States and Mexico.* Stuart Collection.

569 From Joseph Warren Revere, *A Tour of Duty in California,* 1849.

RESERVE ROOM

 81 From the front page of the *Pennsylvania Journal and Weekly Advertiser,* March 21, 1765.

232 From Edwin James, *Account of an Expedition from Pittsburgh to the Rocky Mountains,* Philadelphia, 1822.

525 From F. Piercy, *Route from Liverpool to Great Salt Lake Valley* (edited by James Linforth) 1855.

AMERICAN HISTORY ROOM

319 From Frances Trollope, *Domestic Manners of the Americans.*

397 From Thomas Jefferson Green, *Journal of the Texian Expedition Against Mier,* 1845.

507 From John C. Frémont, *Memoirs of My Life.*

OTHER SOURCES

 III By Alfred Jacob Miller. Courtesy, The Thomas Gilcrease Institute of American History and Art, Tulsa, Oklahoma.

 54 Engraving by Laurie & Whittle, London, 1797. Courtesy, Sigmund Samuel Canadiana Gallery, The Royal Ontario Museum, Toronto.

131 By Allen Gaylord. Courtesy, Western Reserve Historical Society, Cleveland, Ohio.

154 Courtesy, Chicago Historical Society.

179 Courtesy, The New-York Historical Society, New York City.

259 Courtesy, Irving S. Olds Collection, New York.

289 By John Booth. Courtesy, Michigan Historical Commission.

367 Courtesy, Lexington Public Library, Kentucky.

421 U. S. Senate, *Executive Document No. 41,* 30th Congress, 1st session. Courtesy, Library of Congress.

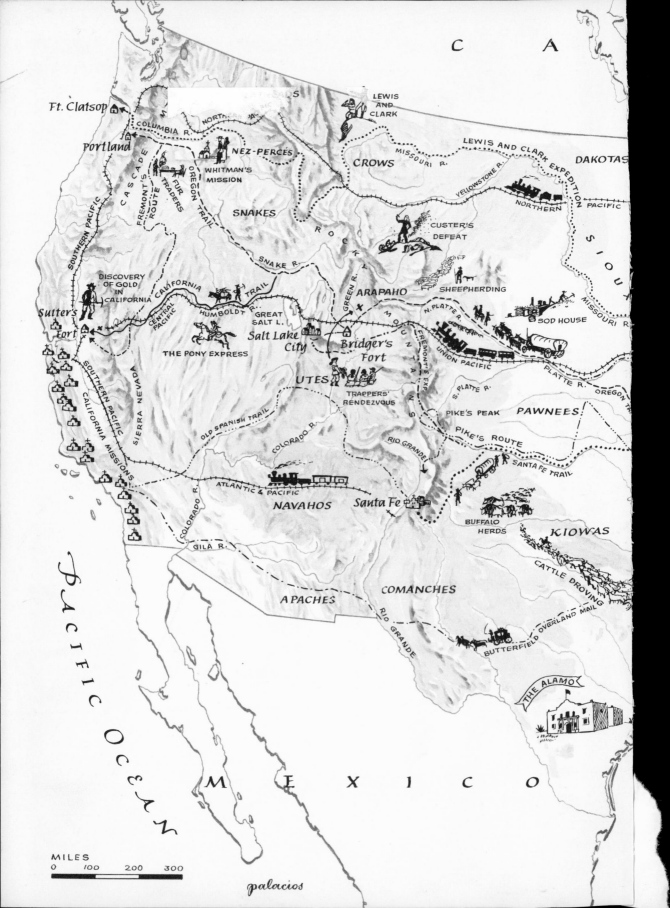

C A

LEWIS AND CLARK

Ft. Clatsop

COLUMBIA R.
NORTHERN

Portland

NEZ-PERCES

WHITMAN'S MISSION

FUR TRADERS

OREGON TRAIL

CASCADE

FREMONT'S ROUTE

SNAKES

SNAKE R.

CROWS

MISSOURI R.

LEWIS AND CLARK EXPEDITION

DAKOTAS

YELLOWSTONE R.

NORTHERN PACIFIC

CUSTER'S DEFEAT

SIOUX

SHEEPHERDING

MISSOURI R.

ARAPAHO

GREEN R.

SOD HOUSE

DISCOVERY OF GOLD IN CALIFORNIA

CALIFORNIA TRAIL

HUMBOLDT R.

GREAT SALT L.

N. PLATTE R.

Sutter's Fort

SOUTHERN PACIFIC

CENTRAL PACIFIC

THE PONY EXPRESS

Salt Lake City

Bridger's Fort

UNION PACIFIC

S. PLATTE R.

PLATTE R.

OREGON TR.

SIERRA NEVADA

UTES

TRAPPERS' RENDEZVOUS

FREMONT'S EXP.

PIKE'S PEAK

PAWNEES

CALIFORNIA MISSIONS

OLD SPANISH TRAIL

COLORADO R.

RIO GRANDE

PIKE'S ROUTE

SANTA FE TRAIL

ATLANTIC & PACIFIC

COLORADO R.

NAVAHOS

Santa Fe

BUFFALO HERDS

KIOWAS

GILA R.

CATTLE DROVING

APACHES

COMANCHES

RIO GRANDE

BUTTERFIELD OVERLAND MAIL

PACIFIC OCEAN

THE ALAMO

M E X I C O

MILES
0   100   200   300

palacios